The Dyck/Neubert Road

Why Study Management?	*To promote:* • Skills to become a manager • Improved working relationships with bosses • Understanding of the role managers play in society • Self-understanding
What is Management?	*Four management functions:* • *Planning:* identifying organizational resources, goals, and strategies • *Organizing:* designing systems and structures to facilitate meeting those goals • *Leading:* influencing others to meet goals • *Controlling:* ensuring that members' actions match the organization's standard values
Defining Effective Management	• *Mainstream:* High emphasis on materialism and individualism • *Multistream:* Emphasis on multiple forms of well-being for multiple stakeholders

Comparing Mainstream and Multistream management (as opposite ends of continuum):

	MAINSTREAM MANAGEMENT ⟷	MULTISTREAM MANAGEMENT
Planning via	quantifiable goals, top-down analysis	practical wisdom, participation
Organizing via	standardization, specialization	courage, experimentation
Leading via	instrumental motivation, output	relational self-control, dignification
Controlling via	vigilance, information systems	justice/fairness, sensitization

Why study two approaches to management?

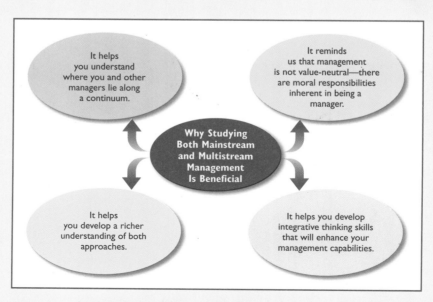

MANAGEMENT

Current Practices and New Directions

MANAGEMENT

Current Practices and New Directions

Bruno Dyck
UNIVERSITY OF MANITOBA

Mitchell J. Neubert
BAYLOR UNIVERSITY

HOUGHTON MIFFLIN HARCOURT PUBLISHING COMPANY
BOSTON   NEW YORK

This book is dedicated to my family, and also to my students and many others from whom I have learned the importance of being responsible stewards of the opportunities we are privileged to have.
—Bruno

This book is dedicated to my loving family who patiently endured my many evenings of "writing," and who inspire me to be the best person I can be.
—Mitch

Executive Publishers: George Hoffman, Melissa Acuña
Sponsoring Editors: Lise Johnson, Kathleen McMahon, Joe Sabatino
Marketing Team: Nicole Hamm, Kimberly Kanakes, Clint Kernan
Discipline Product Manager: Damaris Curran
Development Editors: Julia Perez Chase, Elsa Peterson
Senior Project Editor: Nancy Blodget
Senior Media Producer: Nancy Hiney
Content Manager: Rachel Wimberly
Art and Design Manager: Jill Haber
Cover Design Manager: Anne S. Katzeff
Senior Photo Editor: Jennifer Meyer Dare
Composition Buyer: Chuck Dutton
New Title Project Manager: Patricia O'Neill
Editorial Assistants: Katilyn Crowley, Matthew DiGangi
Marketing Assistant: Lauren Foye
Editorial Assistant: Jill Clark

Cover image credit: © Warren Morgan / CORBIS

Printed in the U.S.A.

Library of Congress Control Number: 2008927704

Instructor's edition:
ISBN 13: 978-0-324-78671-2
ISBN 10: 0-324-78671-9

For orders, use student text ISBNs:
ISBN 13: 978-0-618-83204-0
ISBN 10: 0-618-83204-1

1 2 3 4 5 6 7 8 9 – CRK – 12 11 10 09 08

Brief Contents

Contents

PART TWO

The Environment and Context of Management

PART FOUR	Organizing

PART FIVE	# Leading

PART SIX

Controlling

18

"[The Dyck/Neubert text] is far and away the best management textbook that I have ever come across in my 12 years as a business professor."
—George Alexakis, *Florida Gulf Coast University*

"The major strength of this text is the Mainstream and Multistream discussions; no other text does it this way, to my knowledge. The traditional materials, theories, studies, etc. covered in most traditional management texts are included here . . . ."
—James Hess, *Ivy Tech Community College*

"I think students will love this text . . . wonderfully rich and interesting examples. I believe this text is truly unique. It offers the same basic 'core' technical knowledge found in other management texts but distinguishes itself in directly addressing the values associated with different styles of management . . . . I am anxious to adopt it."
—Jill Bradley, *California State University, Fresno*

"This new book is written in a more personal voice. When I read the chapters of this new book, it seems the authors are having a conversation with me. Quite enjoyable and engaging . . . . I am eager for it to be published."
—Carolyn J. Fausnaugh, *Florida Institute of Technology*

"I appreciate the value-centered approach to management that emphasizes concern for profit along with responsibility to others. It is important to convey the message that profit and social concern are not mutually exclusive values."
—Melodie Toby, *Kean University*

"One major strength is the thoroughness and completeness of the coverage of the topics in the text. Another strength is the concrete, real-world examples that the authors use to illustrate various concepts throughout the text."
—Travis Hayes, *Chattanooga State Technical Community College*

"It is a unique book, bringing in a fresh approach to Management thought, and incorporating a traditional approach, contemporary views, and practical applications."
—Peter Antoniou, *California State University, San Marcos*

About the Authors

BRUNO DYCK Growing up the son of an immigrant entrepreneur, Bruno has always been interested in how organizations are managed and how they can help make the world a better place. He studied management as an undergraduate student in Manitoba and Virginia, and earned a Ph.D. in Business from the University of Alberta in 1991. As an organizational theorist, he has focused his research on organizational learning and change, on issues like distributive justice and sustainable development, and especially on how people's beliefs and values influence what they do. His work has been published in leading scholarly journals, such as *Administrative Science Quarterly, Academy of Management Review, Business Ethics Quarterly, Case Research Journal, Journal of Applied Behavioral Science, Journal of Business Venturing, Journal of Developmental Entrepreneurship, Nonprofit and Voluntary Sector Quarterly,* and *Journal of Management Studies* (Best Paper award winner). He has also done consulting work for a variety of businesses and other organizations, and he spent a year doing voluntary service work overseas.

Bruno is now a Professor in the I. H. Asper School of Business at the University of Manitoba, where he has won research and teaching awards. His students have encouraged him to write this book, a book that shows how management is never value-neutral, and that enables readers to think about how their character as persons can influence the kind of manager they want to become.

He is married to Heather, and they have three children (Sara, Paul, and Jonathan), the oldest of whom is headed to university this coming year. Bruno comments, "I wanted to write a book that my kids would *enjoy*, and that is relevant to readers and the careers that they will have. Hopefully we've achieved that goal."

MITCHELL NEUBERT Mitch grew up in suburban Minneapolis, completed his undergraduate degree at the University of Minnesota, and, after stints with a global manufacturing company and a nonprofit organization, earned his Ph.D. in Business Administration at the University of Iowa, with emphases in human resource management and organizational behavior.

Mitch now serves at Baylor University, where he holds the H. R. Gibson Professorship in Management Development within the Hankamer School of Business. He promotes virtue-based ethics and leadership in his classes and in the community.

Mitch describes his research as somewhat eclectic and practical in its orientation. His research related to teams and personality made its way into journals such as *Journal of Applied Psychology, Human Relations, Journal of Business and Psychology,* and *Personnel Psychology*. He has also published research in *Personnel Psychology* and *Journal of Applied Behavior Psychology,* exploring issues of commitment, particularly as they relate to organizational change. His research on leadership has been published in journals such as *Leadership Quarterly, Business Horizons,* and *Journal of Business Venturing*. Recently, his interest in leadership has been focused on ethical leadership and servant leadership, the latter of which is evident in a recent *Journal of Applied Psychology* article.

When not teaching or writing, Mitch takes time to consult with and learn from current and future business leaders through his association with Leadership Trek Corporation (www.LTrek.com), and to serve as a board member for the Better Business Bureau of Central Texas, the Academy of Leadership Development and Civic Engagement, and the Servant Leadership Institute of Central Texas. Regarding his personal life, he comments, "I am blessed to be married to my understanding and encouraging wife, Alison, and to be a dad to our four wonderful kids, Jacob, Emily, Rachel, and Bethany."

Preface

OUR APPROACH

Our textbook is unique because it presents, in each chapter, two parallel approaches to management, with a focus on helping readers think about how management is linked with important issues that they will be facing in their careers (e.g., ecological sustainability, teamwork, globalization, corporate social responsibility), and on enabling them to consider how their personal values can inform what sort of manager they want to become. Much of the content is similar to what is found in other management textbooks, but other content will be, we hope, refreshingly novel in discussing management practices that are guided by a contrasting set of underlying values. We present both approaches in a compelling manner and encourage readers to arrive at their own conclusions regarding which management practices to adopt.

The first approach described in each chapter, which we call **_Main_stream management,** is based on the **_ma_**terialist-**_in_**dividualist assumption that effective management is about maximizing productivity, profitability, competitiveness, and other "bottom-line" values. Scholars have long recognized the merits of Mainstream management theory and practice (e.g., it has fostered an unprecedented creation of financial wealth and productivity) but have also noted its shortcomings (e.g., erosion of meaningful work, environmental degradation). We followed a rigorous process to ensure that our book includes all the core material found in other leading Mainstream management textbooks.

While there are obviously important positive aspects to Mainstream management, there is growing agreement that it should not be the only approach presented to students. Accordingly, in each chapter of our book we develop and present what we call **_Multi_stream management** theory and practice, which seeks to achieve a balance among **_multi_**ple forms of well-being (e.g., material, physical, social, ecological, spiritual, intellectual, aesthetic) for **_multi_**ple stakeholders (e.g., owners, employees, suppliers, customers, competitors, neighbors, future generations). A Multistream approach is being increasingly advocated by management professors and becoming more evident among vanguard practitioners. This is evident, for example, in the growing interest in areas like corporate social responsibility, stakeholder theory, servant leadership, stewardship, social entrepreneurship, and positive organization studies. It is also consistent with recent trends in social values and student interests. For example, a recent survey[1] found that 93 percent of Americans believe that there is too much emphasis on working and making money, and not enough emphasis on family and community. More than half of those surveyed have voluntarily chosen _not_ to maximize their material wealth, opting instead to facilitate other forms of

---

[1]Roberts, S. (2004). "Survey Confirms that Americans Are Overworked, Overspent, and Rethinking the American Dream." Found April 10, 2008, at http://www.newdream.org/newsletter/survey.php. Poll results are from a census-balanced and nationally representative poll of 1269 American adults 18 years of age and older conducted by Widmeyer Communications of Washington, D.C.

well-being. And this trend is evident not only among Americans. A recent review of various studies suggests that people around the globe are becoming less materialistic and more interested in nurturing community.

By presenting both the Mainstream and Multistream approaches, we encourage students to think critically about management from more than one perspective, help them to consider how their own personal moral point of view can be expressed in their managerial careers, and provide them with ideas about how to achieve success financially as well as in terms of ecological sustainability, social justice, and other values. In particular, students are encouraged to think about where they lie along a Mainstream–Multistream continuum, as shown below:

MAINSTREAM ⟷ **MULTISTREAM**

MANAGEMENT **MANAGEMENT**

Classroom experience with teaching these two approaches to management has been positive. For example, whereas virtually no students complain about needing to learn two types, many do complain about learning *only* two approaches to management! As one student put it, "Teaching that there are different types of management is very important. This fosters a sense of growth, because students can start to look beyond even Multistream versus Mainstream and start to form their own ideas of what it means to them to be a manager." Students expressed a wish for similar perspectives in other management courses they took: "I think it is important to address the 'Multistream' element in *all* of our courses." Moreover, rather than compromise their ability to master Mainstream material, in-class testing suggests that concurrently learning Multistream management helped students to understand Mainstream management better. Perhaps this should not come as a surprise; deeper understanding is often possible when more options are examined. Consider, for example, the research finding that speaking a second language helps people to master the first, and that experience in a variety of organizational settings helps people to understand their "home" setting better.

Of course, our goal is not to suggest that managers should or will follow one approach to management instead of the other. Rather, just like our understanding of concepts like "personality" may be enriched by understanding introversion versus extroversion and recognizing that people lie somewhere along a continuum between the two, so also the goal of our textbook is to provide a framework that allows readers to think critically about different approaches to management, and to enable them to develop a style that is suitable for them. Consistent with this goal, most chapters have a self-assessment exercise that allows readers to determine where their style places them along the Mainstream–Multistream continuum. By juxtaposing the Mainstream and Multistream approaches to management, we prompt readers to recognize that no approach to management is value-neutral. They are also given tools to help them reflect upon and discern how their own values will inform the way that they think about and practice management.

Even though we recognize that virtually all managers lie somewhere along a Mainstream–Multistream continuum, in our book we still use examples of specific managers and theories to illustrate either Mainstream or Multistream management. Of course, as with almost any example in a textbook, this is an oversimplification. The examples we use in this book are meant to illustrate certain aspects of Mainstream or Multistream management, but definitely not to label specific managers, organizations, or theories as being wholly Mainstream or wholly Multistream. Indeed, as we have already indicated, most everyone lies somewhere along a continuum between the two. But readers' understanding of management and of their own managerial approach benefits from being able to see the endpoints along a continuum. This dual approach provides a much richer understanding of management than is possible by a monolithic approach.

In sum, this book is designed to help the reader—just as it has helped its authors—to think about management theory and practice and its underlying assumptions and values. While it may not always be comfortable or popular to weigh and balance different approaches in management, our hope with this book is to foster more civil conversations among people from a range of perspectives. Moreover, because we believe the two positions at the ends of the continuum both have merit, and because we have attempted to represent those merits fairly, the conversations that we hope will occur among readers of this text are likely to generate novel "third options" that will be valuable for management theory and practice as well as for society.

ORGANIZATION OF THE BOOK

As instructors, we are well aware of the challenges of adopting a new textbook. With those challenges in mind, we have designed this book from the ground up to be *adopter-friendly*. For example, we carefully analyzed the chapter arrangement and content of six leading management textbooks to ensure that our book included all the core content that was common to at least four of them. Thus, like other management texts, our book is organized according to the familiar four main functions of management: planning, leading, organizing, and controlling. Chapters devoted to these topics comprise Chapters 7 through 18 of the book. Before we examine these four functions, we first provide an introductory chapter, which outlines the fundamentals of management, and a chapter on the history of management. After this introductory section, we further equip students with chapters on the environment, the international context of management, ethics, and entrepreneurship.

Rather than present the innovative Multistream viewpoint in a separate section of the book, or in boxed features throughout the chapters, we have integrated it throughout the narrative of each chapter, generally focusing on it in the latter part of each chapter after the more traditional Mainstream core material has been discussed. For example, in the entrepreneurship chapter we first describe the four basic steps of (Mainstream) entrepreneurship, and then describe four steps of (Multistream) social entrepreneurship. By following a framework pegged to the main functions of management, we hope to make it as easy as possible for instructors to set up course outlines and to adapt their existing lecture materials to this new text.

FEATURES

In addition to presenting both Mainstream and Multistream approaches to management, our book contains many features that provide readers an interesting, positive experience in their introductory management course. Our overarching desire was for a book that was timely, thoughtful, thought-provoking, and fun to read (e.g., the closing case in Chapter 2 describes the role of managers in how the meaning of chocolate has changed through history). Students have commented that they have found the writing style in our textbook to be more engaging than that found in other textbooks: One student said, "I felt like you were writing to me." We have tried hard to develop a reader-friendly writing style. As the lead author put it, "I wanted to write a book that was interesting and accessible enough to be used in my daughter's high school classroom, but deep and thoughtful enough that it would appeal to my graduate students." Our chapters are grounded in the scholarly literature and highlighted by relevant and instructive examples and thoughtful questions. Our book also contains more comprehensive endnotes than other textbooks, for readers who want to get more background information on specific topics.

"ROAD MAPS" AT THE START OF EACH CHAPTER   Because of feedback from students, we start each chapter with a "road map" of the chapter rather than simply listing learning goals. The road map provides the same essential information as learning goals, but in a form that students have found to be more useful. Each road map is designed to: (a) help readers anticipate where the chapter is heading; (b) provide readers with a quick reference point as they navigate the chapter; and (c) provide an overarching look at the chapter for review after reading it (e.g., see the road map in Chapter 8, which clearly contrasts and compares the four-step goal-setting process from a Mainstream and a Multistream perspective, highlighting, for example, SMART goals with SMART2 goals).

INSPIRING CASES, PRACTITIONER EXAMPLES, AND "MANAGEMENT IN PRACTICE" FEATURES   Students have told us that, unlike others textbooks in other courses, in this textbook they actually read the opening and closing cases. We believe that this is because the cases have been crafted to provide an overview of the main processes described in each chapter, and because we have chosen managers and organizations that readers find inspiring. Because the book highlights both Mainstream and Multistream management, the reader will be introduced to a wide range of thought-provoking practitioners. We include stories of Mainstream managers (e.g., Jack Welch of GE, opening case, Chapter 1) who can inspire students to go out and maximize a corporation's profits, but we also include interesting stories of Multistream managers (e.g., Dennis Bakke of AES, opening case, Chapter 15) who have effectively managed businesses where the pursuit of profit does not trump other goals. Mainstream and Multistream examples are drawn from small and large organizations, for-profit and not-for-profit organizations (including NGOs), family-owned and publicly traded companies, top management and middle management, and national and international companies. For example, students will read about

- Ralph and Cheryl Broetje, Multistream owners/managers of one of the largest privately owned apple orchards in the United States, who donate 75 percent of their profit to charity. They are leaders in environmentally friendly agricultural practices. Noticing that many of their migrant workers lacked adequate housing, they invested $6 million to build such homes (see opening case, Chapter 3).
- Mohammed Yunus, a Nobel Prize–winning pioneer in the micro-financing movement, who started a bank—by loaning $27 of his own money to 42 entrepreneurs—that has since changed the lives of millions of businesspeople (see opening case, Chapter 6).
- The strategy used by Microsoft (Bill Gates) and how it contrasts and compares with the strategy used by Linux (e.g., Linus Torvalds) (see closing case, Chapter 9).
- The experience of Diane Davidson, as an incoming manager at W. L. Gore, in adapting to the unique team-based culture of an organization that encourages collaboration and innovation (see opening case, Chapter 16).

"WHAT DO YOU THINK?" FEATURES   Throughout each chapter there are "What Do You Think?" boxes that deliberately raise issues that require thoughtful responses. The questions are designed to facilitate reflection and class discussion.

Instructors and students will soon recognize that although there may not be one "right" answer to a question, a "good" answer demands thoughtful reflection and mastery of the material. Working through these questions will not only help readers to learn and "own" the material, it will also help them to develop a better understanding of themselves and of others. For example, the What Do You Think? feature on page 146 asks students whether philanthropy is ethical (because it helps charities) or unethical (because it spends money that belongs to shareholders).

CLASS-TESTED END-OF-CHAPTER "HANDS-ON EXERCISES" The textbook features many end-of-chapter Hands-On Exercises, many of which were designed to permit students to place themselves along the Mainstream–Multistream continuum. The questions have been class-tested, and scales have been developed based on statistical properties (e.g., they load as factors), and results from previous students are provided in the Instructors' Resource Manual. For example, based on anonymous end-of-term survey data, students indicated that they considered their own management style to be "in the middle" between Mainstream and Multistream (3.05 on a 5-point Likert scale, where 1=Mainstream and 5=Multistream), but indicated that in the future they would prefer to move in the direction of Multistream (3.52 on the Likert scale). (See Chapter 18.)

OTHER PEDAGOGICAL FEATURES In addition to these distinct features, the book has all the same features that instructors and students have become accustomed to in other top-selling texts. For example, the book has a glindex (a combined glossary and index), opening and closing cases, end-of-chapter questions, and so on. The Instructor Support Package includes, among other items, an Instructor Website, an Online Instructors' Resource Manual, PowerPoint Slides, Classroom Response System (clicker) questions, a Testing CD (electronic Test Bank files), a DVD program, an online course management system, BlackBoard/WebCT course cartridges, and an Interactive eBook. The Student Support Package includes a Student Website with many helpful study aids available to students. Some of these items include downloadable audio summaries and quizzes, interactive tests, and many other useful self-study tools.

Perhaps the most outstanding feature of the book is that it is very practical, thanks in large part to the many examples of practicing managers, and also because it captures the best sense of Kurt Lewin's adage that "nothing is as practical as a good theory." Students also find the book engaging simply because it explicitly talks about how managers address important issues of the day, such as ecological sustainability, international issues, and social justice (e.g., see opening case, Chapter 4). The book compels readers to think about how they will put their own values into practice in the organizations that they will manage or belong to. By demonstrating that management is not value-neutral, and by contrasting and comparing how differing sets of values influence management theory and practice, readers are invited and enabled to think about what kinds of managers they aspire to become. As Socrates put it, "An unexamined life is not worth living."

ACKNOWLEDGMENTS

We want to acknowledge that this book was developed in a community of colleagues and students. This includes literally hundreds of reviews from colleagues on chapters, and feedback from hundreds of students on two earlier drafts of the textbook. It also includes many hallway talks, e-mails, talks at conferences, and discussions with friends and acquaintances. As a result, we want to acknowledge that there are many people whose names could be mentioned here but are not. This includes colleagues, family members, and friends, whose ongoing encouragement and support have inspired and sustained us.

That said, Bruno would like to acknowledge some of these people. First, he thanks the many undergraduate students who over the years provided encouragement to write this book, to the MBA students who felt validated by and wanted to learn more about Multistream management, and to the doctoral students who provided helpful encouragement and feedback (especially Rob Kleysen and Kent Walker). He also thanks family and friends who asked for early drafts of the chapters so that they could read them (especially Trevor De Ryck), and his colleagues who provided counsel and understanding about the textbook writing process (especially Fred Starke, but also John Godard and Norm Frohlich). He is also thankful for colleagues who contributed to the research that informs this book, and to the many acquaintances at conferences who willingly told him about what they would like to see in a textbook and who listened and affirmed how the book was taking shape. And thanks also to colleagues who invited Bruno to their campuses to talk about and help him develop ideas during the formative stages of the book (Harold Harder at Trinity Western University, Kenman Wong at Seattle Pacific University, and Paul Stevens at Regent College), to the Loewen Foundation for providing financial support to the project in its early stages, and for the research assistance of Darcy Fudge, Jeremy Epp, Nathan Gerbrandt, Paula Sturrey, and Sara Jane Friesen. Finally, Bruno is especially thankful to his family (Heather, Sara, Paul, and Jonathan) for their feedback and patience when he talked to them (too much) about Mainstream and Multistream approaches.

Mitch would like to thank Bruno for inviting him to be a partner in this exhilarating project. It has been a challenging and enriching experience. He would also like to thank his colleagues at Baylor University whose open and sincere engagement in the "deeper issues" fosters a continual development of the "life of the mind." Also, to his former colleagues at Bowling Green State University whose diversity of thought and practice expanded his perspective on creating positive change, he expresses his appreciation. Mitch extends a special thanks to Diana Wong, a friend and colleague, for being an unfailing source of encouragement and help, and to Rick Martinez, for challenging him to live an integrated life. Mitch also greatly appreciates the undergraduate and master's students who have joined with him in wrestling with the application of virtue in business leadership. Last, but not least, Mitch thanks those he holds dearest—his immediate family and parents—for their enduring support and love.

This book has also benefited from amazing professionals at Houghton Mifflin Harcourt. In particular, we appreciate the wise counsel and ongoing championing we received from Lisé Johnson, our signing acquisitions editor (and from Kathleen McMahon, who brought that work to fruition). We also appreciate Julia Perez Chase for her tireless prodding, scheduling, and recruiting of reviewers, and for overseeing all the other work that goes into writing a book from scratch (and Elsa Peterson and Suzanna Smith for ably taking over when Julia went on maternity leave). Thanks also to many of the others for their important contributions to the production of this book: Nancy Blodget for coordinating the production, Jill Hobbs and Susan Myers for copyediting the manuscript, Julie Low for her excellent work as photo researcher, Karen Lindsey for developing the figures, Maria Sas for rendering the figures, Andy Fisher and Nicole Hamm for their marketing expertise, and many others at Houghton Mifflin Harcourt.

Program Contributors

George Alexakis (Florida Gulf Coast University)

Forrest Aven (University of Houston—Downtown)

Jill Bradley (California State University, Fresno)

Charlie T. Cook, Jr. (University of West Alabama)

James P. Hess (Ivy Tech Community College)

Adilia James (Urbana-Champaign, Illinois)

Rick Martinez (Charleston Southern University)

John Overby (University of Tennessee, Martin)

Diana J. Wong (Eastern Michigan University)

Reviewers/Advisory Board Members

Bruce Bloom (DeVry University)

Jill Bradley (California State University, Fresno)

Kenneth G. Brown (University of Iowa)

Carl Case (St. Bonaventure University)

Bruce H. Charnov (Hofstra University)

Kay Devine (Athabasca University)

Richard E. Dulski (Medaille College)

Teri Elkins (University of Houston)

Carolyn J. Fausnaugh (Florida Institute of Technology)

Michael Frandsen (Albion College)

Edward Fritz (Nassau Community College)

J. Michael Geringer (California Polytechnic University, San Luis Obispo)

Jackie Gilbert (Middle Tennessee State University)

Carol Gottuso (Metropolitan Community College)

J. W. Haddad (Seneca College of Applied Arts and Technology)

Jon Harbaugh (Southern Oregon University)

Travis Hayes (Chattanooga State Technical Community College)

Samuel Hazen (Tarleton State University)

Stephen Horner (Arkansas State University)

Carol Jensen (Northeast Iowa Community College)

Marvin Karlins (University of South Florida)

Lianlian Lin (California State Polytechnic University, Pomona)

Harold S. Lowe (Wilmington University)

Ivan Lowe (Winthrop University)

Brian Maruffi (Fordham University)

James Mazza (Middlesex Community College)

Daniel W. McAllister (University of Nevada, Las Vegas)

Thomas McKaig (University of Guelph)

David Meyer (University of Akron)

Thomas Moliterno (University of South Carolina)

Peter Moutsatson (Central Michigan University)

Mark Nagel (Normandale Community College)

Allison Pearson (Mississippi State University)

Ingrid Peters-Fransen (Canadian Mennonite University)

Michael Pitts (Virginia Commonwealth University)

Stephan Schuster (California State University, Northridge)

Mansour Sharifzadeh (California State Polytechnic University, Pomona)

John Daniel Sherman (University of Alabama, Huntsville)

James Smith (Rocky Mountain College)

Warren Stone (University of Arkansas, Little Rock)

Barry Van Hook (Arizona State University)

Susan L. Verhulst (Des Moines Area Community College)

Kenneth Wendeln (Indiana University)

Fred Whitman (University of Mary Washington)

Focus Group Members

Verl Anderson (Dixie State College)

Jeffrey Anstine (North Central College)

Peter H. Antoniou (California State University, San Marcos)

Kathleen Barnes (East Stroudsburg University)

Stephanie Bibb (Chicago State University)

Joseph Bucci (Bryn Mawr College)

Diane Caggiano (Fitchburg State College)

Elizabeth Cameron (Alma College)

Russell Casey (Clayton State University)

Wade Chumney (Belmont University)

Janet Ciccarelli (Herkimer County Community College)

Terry Coalter (Northwest Missouri State University)

Richard Custin (University of San Diego)

Alexander Czachura (Purdue University, Calumet)

Helen Davis (Jefferson Community and Technical College)

Christine Day (Eastern Michigan University)

Ron DiBattista (Johnson & Wales University)

Lon Doty (San Jose State University)

Bruce Fischer (Elmhurst College)

Mahmoud Gaballa (Mansfield University)

Kelly Gredone (Bucks County Community College)

Jason Harris-Boundy (San Francisco State University)

Nathan Himelstein (Essex County College)

Gordon Holbein (University of Kentucky)

Zhenhu Jin (Valparaiso University)

Claire Kent (Mary Baldwin College)

Casey Kleindienst (California State University, Fullerton)

Nada Kobeissi (Long Island University)

Tony Mifsud (Catawba Valley Community College)

Marcia Miller (George Mason University)

Diane Minger (Cedar Valley College)

Daryle Nagano (California State University, Fullerton)

Lynn Patten (Clark Atlanta University)

Dyan Pease (Sacramento City College)

Jeff Podoshen (Temple University)

Machelle Schroeder (University Of Wisconsin, Platteville)

Kelli Schutte (William Jewell College)

Lee Sellers (Eastern Oregon University)

Thomas Sgritta (University of North Carolina, Charlotte)

Marc Siegall (California State University, Chico)

Thomas Sigerstad (Frostburg State University)

Gerald Smith (University of Northern Iowa)

Katrina Stark (University of Great Falls)

Robert Tanner (DeVry University)

Melodie Toby (Kean University)

Tom Tudor (University of Arkansas, Little Rock)

Gloria Walker (Florida Community College)

Mark Wasserman (Texas State University)

Liesl Wesson (Texas A&M University)

David White (Missouri State University)

IN-TEXT FEATURES

Whole-Systems Change at Brio Technology[1]

Brio Technology was in free fall when Craig Brennan took on the role of CEO. Brennan quickly realized that the crisis at the database software company required an altogether different response than the "command and control" approach that he had experienced in other technology companies.

Brennan put in a call to Kathy Dannemiller to help him take a whole-systems view in approaching the problem. Dannemiller's approach to change was formed in the trenches at Ford Motor Company in the early 1980s, when the company sought to transform its culture from a "command and control" model to a more participative style. Brennan and Dannemiller partnered to implement a change initiative at Brio that would bring about "one brain and one heart" among all its employees. Brennan was convinced that the only way Brio could be turned around was through a collective vision of the future that was understood and accepted throughout the whole system. Leaders, including Brennan himself, would need to throw out old leadership rules and adopt a new set of rules.

Old rule: Leaders know all and act as the final authority in important decisions.

New rule: Leaders call people together to uncover and connect the wisdom of the people.

Old rule: Leaders control information, people, . . . everything.

New rule: Leaders ask questions and encourage conversations across the system.

Old rule: Leaders drive performance and punish failure.

New rule: Leaders inspire performance and celebrate success.

A critical component of leading in this new way is to engage the whole system in addressing problems and creating solutions. The "whole-scale change" approach created by Dannemiller is a large-group intervention intended to get the organizational members representing the whole system into one room to discuss common dissatisfactions, a vision of what is possible based on common yearnings, and a set of action steps to move toward the future. Typically, the large-group event lasts three days.

The first step was to get widespread recognition of the need for change. This occurred during the first day at Brio's three-day event, when 400 employees across different levels were brought together and placed in mixed groups to share their stories of what was working, what was not working, and what each person wanted to see change in the future. This activity was supplemented by brief presentations from other stakeholders such as Brio partners and customers.

Once the need for change was evident, the next step was to get members talking about what the change might look like and to overcome their desire to hold on to the status quo. To stimulate thinking about the future, Brennan presented a draft strategic plan and asked the members who were seated randomly at different tables to discuss and react to the proposal. The first day concluded with a revised draft of a picture of the future built upon the suggestions of those in attendance.

On the second day, the focus was to get people involved in thinking about and designing specific changes. It started with a presentation of results from day 1, which was handled by a cross-sectional group of employees who served as the event planning team. The Brio event team members sorted through reams of flipchart paper and notes to summarize the firm's current state and strategic vision.

Members were then given time to work together to put flesh on the bare bones of the strategic vision by proposing and discussing potential action steps for specific goals. This creative process was summarized and presented during the morning of the third day, where for the first time participants were organized by functional areas. That final morning was used to translate ideas into concrete action steps that the group committed to implementing in the next few weeks and months.

Feedback from this event indicated that the participants—many of whom had entered the event with skepticism from a previous change that was poorly implemented—had committed to the new collective vision for Brio. The action steps from this initial planning event and the subsequent changes in the structure and focus of Brio's operations resulted in a substantial reduction of costs and the introduction of several products that helped

Case Studies Each chapter opens with an interesting story of a manager. The managers come from a variety of backgrounds, including large corporations and smaller businesses. The managers exemplify both Mainstream and Multistream practices, and show real-life successes and failures that will intrigue students.

...sal of fortune at Brio. The changes at Brio, ...rmulated and implemented in a distinct ...ns approach, did not easily translate into tan-... A competitive environment marked by a re-... spending on products at the heart of Brio's ...ved the transformation, but the process re-...o approaching profitability for the first time

...ely, after much positive change, Brio was ... its competitor Hyperion. Was the change ...erhaps not, if the goal of the change was

to return to profitability and rebuff buyout offers. Nevertheless, the positive changes at Brio enabled it to stay in business and increased the company's value as an acquisition target. Alternatively, consider what might have happened if the organization's free fall had not been reversed. In the end, positive change within an organization contributes to—but does not guarantee—growth or survival in complex and dynamic competitive markets where innovations, customer preferences, and competitive forces change on a day-to-day basis.

...DUCTION TO ORGANIZATIONAL CHANGE

Organizational change is any substantive modification to some aspect of an organization. It may consist of a change in technology (e.g., the process used to transform inputs into outputs), structures (e.g., where the organization falls on the mechanistic–organic or closed–open continuum), people (e.g., training and skills), or mission or values (e.g., philosophy and culture). Change is an organizational reality, and managing change is an integral part of every manager's job. "The handwriting on the wall is clear: The world is changing, and those companies that fail to change . . . find themselves out of business."[2] Managers must understand when change is needed and be able to guide their organization through it.

The change process can be described as following four steps:[3]

1. Recognize the need for change
2. Unfreeze
3. Change
4. Refreeze

Although the basic four-step change process can be seen in all types of change, the way these steps unfold and need to be managed may be influenced by the type of change. As shown in Figure 13.1, there are at least three ways to differentiate between types of change:

- Scope
- Intentionality
- Source

First, the scope of the change can be either transformational or incremental.[4] **Transformational change** occurs when an organization changes its strategic direction or reengineers its culture or operations in response to dramatic changes such as a technological

Organizational change is any substantive modification to some aspect of an organization.

Transformational change occurs when an organization changes its strategic direction.

Road Maps Each chapter provides a road map, which is designed to: (a) help readers to anticipate where the chapter is heading; (b) provide readers with a quick reference point to look at as they navigate the chapter; and (c) provide an overarching look at the chapter for reviewing after reading it.

ROAD MAP

FOUR STEPS OF THE PLANNING PROCESS	MAINSTREAM APPROACH 	MULTISTREAM APPROACH
1. Set mission/vision	*Managers:* Establish the purpose and aspirations of the organization	*Managers and other stakeholders:* Recognize their shared purpose and aspirations for the organization
2. Set strategic goals/plans	Seek to achieve competitive advantage	Seek to achieve mutual advantages
3. Set operational goals/plans	*Set SMART goals:* Specific, Measurable, Achievable, Results-based, and Time-specific	*Set SMART2 goals:* Significant, Meaningful, Agreed-upon, Relevant, and Timely
4. Implement and monitor goals/plans	Make plans that cover both new and ongoing goals. Ensure that goals and plans are achieved and implemented	Make plans that cover both new and ongoing goals. Continually learn from and improve upon goals and plans during implementation

⊕ MANAGEMENT IN PRACTICE

Managing a Matrix Organization

Perhaps the largest and most well-documented example of a matrix organization is ABB, which was created by the merger of the Swedish firm Asea and the Swiss firm Brown Boveri, and managed by Percy Barnevik for its first decade after the merger. Barnevik's challenge was to create a streamlined entrepreneurial organization with as few hierarchical layers as possible, starting with what was essentially a group of 1300 companies with more than 200,000 employees in 150 countries. To do so, he introduced what came to be a highly regarded and very complex matrix structure, which divided ABB into 35 business areas, more than 100 country organizations, and 5000 profit centers (i.e., managers of each of these 5000 divisions were expected to show a profit). The manager of a profit center would report to both a country manager and business area managers.[15]

Management In Practice Boxes These inserts show it like it is, connecting real-world anecdotes with the principles of management.

◢ DIGGING DEEPER

Perspectives on Earth's Carrying Capacity[57]

For much of our history, humankind has not been very concerned about the effects of our decisions on the natural environment. This lack of attention was understandable when the population of humankind was relatively small and our ability to affect the natural environment was relatively limited. For example, it was not until 1830 that the human population reached 1 billion people. But our population has been *doubling* roughly every 65 years since then, and it is expected to reach 8 billion around 2025 (although the rate of growth seems to be slowing). Also, we now have technology capable of extracting, transporting, and processing natural resources on a scale and in quantities unheard of in the past, which is also increasing humankind's effects on the environment.

Some researchers have argued that at some point the natural environment will not be able to sustain these growing demands.[58] One proponent of this view, Dr. David Suzuki, uses a metaphor to point out the danger of our growing demands on the natural environment.[59] Imagine that the planet is like a test tube full of food for bacteria, and that humankind is represented by bacteria. Now imagine that one bacterial cell is introduced into the test tube, and assume that the bacterium grows at some steady rate and *doubles* in size over a specific period of time—for example, every minute. Thus, in one minute there are two bacterial cells, in two minutes there are four cells, in three minutes there are eight cells, and so on. Of course, this steady growth means that at some point the test tube will be completely full of bacteria and there will be no food left. Let's say that this event occurs in exactly one hour. Under this assumption, at 55 minutes, the test tube is only about 3 percent full of bacteria, but at 59 minutes the test tube is 50 percent full of bacteria. At 55 minutes, concerns about potential problems may fall on deaf ears; at 59 minutes, the problem would be acknowledged but nearly irreversible. Dr. Suzuki believes that humankind is long past its own "55 minutes" point. He notes that even if science and technology quadruple humankind's resources so that we now have the equivalent of four test tubes, this will in effect result in only two extra "minutes" before those test tubes are also used up.

In contrast, Dr. Thomas DeGregori points to technological progress as one reason to question the dire predictions of consumption outstripping the supply of natural resources.[60] In addition to suggesting that there are problematic assumptions associated with others' population growth rate models, he argues that technological innovations such as bioengineered foods have reduced the need for pesticides, increased crop yields, and generally improved human well-being and life expectancy. Dr. DeGregori also asserts that without the use of modern agricultural technologies, people in poor countries would inordinately suffer the ill effects of pests, naturally occurring diseases, and poor crop yields. He offers evidence to suggest that the well-being of people and the planet are well served by technologies that increase yields and reduce diseases, which in turn reduces the need for cultivated land and thereby reduces soil erosion and facilitates biodiversity.

What are the strengths and weaknesses of each argument? Which argument seems more convincing? What might your conclusions mean for management practice?

Digging Deeper Boxes provide students with application of text material to their own lives.

WHAT DO YOU THINK?

Are Executives Worth Their Wages?

Forbes magazine recently reported that executives from the top 500 U.S. companies earned on average $10.9 million.[37] In one year, the CEO of Capital One Financial, Richard D. Fairbank, took home $249.3 million in total pay, almost entirely from exercised stock options.[38]

Huge payouts to CEOs occur in other countries, but there is a much higher wage differential between those at the top and bottom of the pay scale in the United States. In the United States, one report asserts that CEOs of large corporations are paid $364 for every $1 paid to the average worker (a ratio of 364:1). By comparison, the ratio in the United States is approximately 15 times the same ratio in European firms, where the ratio averages close to 25:1.[39]

Theorists have attempted to explain the substantial pay disparity in the United States by arguing that it is the product of excessive management power in setting compensation, whereas others argue that the disparity is explained by free-market forces and the unique competitive environment of the United States. Some supporters of executive pay even argue that the pay is based on performance, but research evidence indicates otherwise.[40]

Do executives deserve their pay? Why do you think there are differences between the pay of U.S. and European executives? (You may wish to refer to Table 4.1 in Chapter 4 when considering these questions.)

What Do You Think? Boxes ask students to form an opinion based on different scenarios. An excellent feature for jump-starting class discussion and critical thinking.

Chapter Summary At the end of each chapter a bulleted list of main points is reiterated for student reinforcement and for quick reference. This concise list summarizes the chapter's overarching message.

SUMMARY

Managers spend three-fourths of their time communicating with others.
From a Mainstream perspective, the four-step communication process proceeds as follows:

1. Managers craft messages that are consistent with improving task-related organizational performance.
2. Managers encode and transmit messages based on an attempt to reduce noise, with a bias toward choosing large-scale and written communication media and channels.
3. Receivers decode messages individually, tuning out distraction so as to maximize the amount of task-related knowledge being acquired.
4. Receivers provide feedback to the sender to confirm that the message was understand as intended.

From a Multistream perspective, the four-step communication process proceeds as follows:

1. Members craft messages that are consistent with a wide variety of perspectives about how to enhance collective well-being.
2. Members encode and transmit messages based on an attempt to embrace diversity, with a bias toward choosing small-scale, face-to-face communication media and channels.
3. Receivers decode messages collectively, paying attention to the meaning of messages for their coworkers so as to enhance relational understanding in the organization.
4. Members seek feedback, and use feedforward information previously received from others, to identify messages to be sent.

HANDS-ON ACTIVITIES

How Much Emphasis People Place on Various Forms of Well-Being

Many different forms of well-being exist, and a manager has only a limited amount of time and energy to pay attention to each form. As a consequence, managers may decide to place primary emphasis on some forms of well-being, place secondary emphasis on other forms, and neglect other forms of well-being altogether.

This activity asks which forms of well-being you think are most important for yourself, and asks you to consider which forms might be most important for others. You will be asked to allocate a total of 100 points among each of nine forms of well-being, thereby indicating the relative emphasis you place on each.

For example, in one column, you might assign 75 points to "aesthetic" well-being, 10 points each to "emo-tional" and "social" well-being, 5 points to "material" well-being, and 0 points to the rest (total = 100). In another column, you might assign 30 points each to "ecological" and "material" well-being, 17 points to "aesthetic" well-being, 8 points each to "intellectual" and "spiritual" well-being, 6 points to "individual" well-being, and 1 point to "physical" well-being (total = 100). You can assign 100 points for each column in any way you want, but the total points assigned to each column should equal 100.

Each of the four columns in the chart below should be answered from a different perspective. Reflect on the differences in the four columns. Compare your results with the results of your classmates, and discuss interesting similarities and differences.

Hands-On Activities Students give their opinion by rating or grading how a manager should act.

Column A: How much emphasis do you think an **effective manager** would place on each form of well-being?
Column B: How much emphasis do **you** place on each form of well-being?
Column C: How much emphasis do you think **your parents** place on each form of well-being?
Column D: How much emphasis do you think **people living 500 years ago** placed on each form of well-being?

A	B	C	D	Form of Well-Being
				Aesthetic: beauty, art, poetry
				Ecological: natural environment, minimal pollution
				Emotional: satisfaction, positive feelings, hope, joy
				Individual: personal convenience, looking after own interests
				Intellectual: ideas, clear rationale, theory, concepts
				Material: finances, productivity, tangible goods, efficiency
				Physical: health, safety, security
				Social: community-mindedness, justice, helping others
				Spiritual: meaning, interconnectedness, transcendent purpose
				Total (the total for each column should equal 100)

Questions for Reflection and Discussion

These questions, whether assigned by instructors or initiated by a student, allow students to process the chapter information more deeply and put specific concepts into practice. The questions allow for reinforcement and application.

Closing Case

At the end of each chapter, a closing case that is distinct from the opening case is provided before the end-of-chapter questions. The closing case provides a look into different industries' advances and changes, and asks students to answer pointed questions from a manager's perspective.

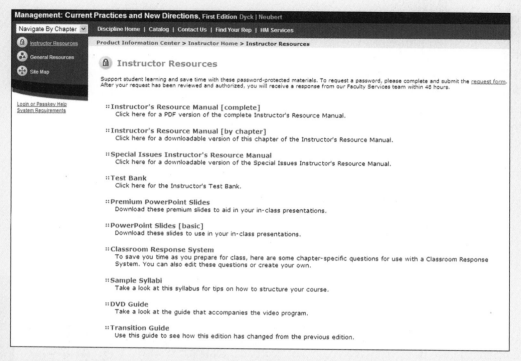

Management: Current Practices and New Directions, First Edition Dyck | Neubert

Navigate By Chapter

🔒 Instructor Resources
🔒 General Resources
✛ Site Map

Discipline Home | Catalog | Contact Us | Find Your Rep | HM Services

Product Information Center > Instructor Home > Instructor Resources

Login or Passkey Help
System Requirements

🔒 **Instructor Resources**

Support student learning and save time with these password-protected materials. To request a password, please complete and submit the request form. After your request has been reviewed and authorized, you will receive a response from our Faculty Services team within 48 hours.

:: **Instructor's Resource Manual [complete]**
Click here for a PDF version of the complete Instructor's Resource Manual.

:: **Instructor's Resource Manual [by chapter]**
Click here for a downloadable version of this chapter of the Instructor's Resource Manual.

:: **Special Issues Instructor's Resource Manual**
Click here for a downloadable version of the Special Issues Instructor's Resource Manual.

:: **Test Bank**
Click here for the Instructor's Test Bank.

:: **Premium PowerPoint Slides**
Download these premium slides to aid in your in-class presentations.

:: **PowerPoint Slides [basic]**
Download these slides to use in your in-class presentations.

:: **Classroom Response System**
To save you time as you prepare for class, here are some chapter-specific questions for use with a Classroom Response System. You can also edit these questions or create your own.

:: **Sample Syllabi**
Take a look at this syllabus for tips on how to structure your course.

:: **DVD Guide**
Take a look at the guide that accompanies the video program.

:: **Transition Guide**
Use this guide to see how this edition has changed from the previous edition.

Instructor Website

Instructor Resources include the Instructor's Resource Manual, Powerpoint Slides, Classroom Response System questions, and Lecture Outlines. The website also includes access to the student assets of Ace Tests, Quizzes, Audio Podcast summaries and quizzes, Flashcards, Glossary, Chapter outlines, Exercises, Crossword Puzzles and other games, and AP News Feeds.

Instructor's Resource Manual Located on the password-protected Instructor Web Site, this resource contains downloadable files of the chapter objectives, opening case discussion starters, a lecture outline, instructional tips, suggested answers to discussion/essay questions, closing case interpretation/solutions, and more.

Testing CD The computerized version of the Test Bank allows instructors to select, edit, and add questions, or generate randomly selected questions to produce a test master for easy duplication. Online Testing and Gradebook functions allow instructors to administer tests via their local area network or the World Wide Web, set up classes, record grades from tests or assignments, analyze grades, and produce/compile class and individual statistics.

Powerpoint Slides (Lecture and Premium) Powerpoint slides on the instructor website provide an effective presentation tool for lectures. The Lecture powerpoint program provides an outline of each chapter with key figures and tables from the main text. The Premium powerpoint program includes all of the lecture slides as well as additional slides that contain unique content that supplements text material. Premium slides are noted with a yellow checkmark.

Challenging Ethical Norms

• Whistleblowers
– Organizational insiders who identify unethical behavior and display the courage to report it, even though it may personally cost them money, their jobs, and possibly their reputations.

© Digital Vision at Getty Images®

Question 18

A stakeholder of an organization can include its owners, employees, customers, suppliers, and the surrounding community.
1/a. True
2/b. False

Answer 18

A stakeholder of an organization can include its owners, employees, customers, suppliers, and the surrounding community.
1/a. True *Correct Answer*
2/b. False

Classroom Response System Using state-of-the-art wireless technology and text-specific content, a Classroom Response System (CRS) provides a convenient and inexpensive way to gauge student comprehension, deliver quizzes or exams, and provide "on-the-spot" assessment. Ideal for any classroom, a CRS is a customizable handheld response system that will complement any teaching style. Various answering modes, question types, and display options mean that a CRS is as functional as you want it to be. As a testing platform, as an assessment tool, or simply as a way to increase interactivity in the classroom, a CRS provides the technology you need to transform lecture into a dynamic learning environment. Content available on the Instructor Web Site includes true-false and multiple-choice questions customized for reviewing key content in the student text. Instructors can also edit these questions or create their own.

Blackboard and WebCT Cartridges Include course material, course information, course documents, chapter outlines, detailed lecture outlines, chapter objectives, chapter summaries, PowerPoint slides, Classroom Response System questions (clicker questions), Discussion Boards, all questions from the textbook with suggested answers, downloadable Microsoft Word files for every chapter or the entire PDF version of the Instructor's Resource Manual, Test Bank content, and much more.

Eduspace Powered by Blackboard is a course management system that includes chapter outlines, detailed lecture outlines, chapter objectives, chapter summaries, PowerPoint slides, Classroom Response System questions (clicker questions), Discussion Boards, all questions from the textbook with suggested answers, links to content on the websites, downloadable Microsoft Word files for every chapter or the entire PDF version of the Instructor's Resource Manual, Test Bank content, and much more.

DVD To illustrate important concepts from the text, real-world video examples from leading organizations are provided. Segment lengths vary, but are built to design ample time for classroom discussion. The DVD Guide provides suggested uses, teaching objectives, an overview, and issues for discussion with each video segment.

STUDENT RESOURCES

Student Website

Includes the Ace Tests, Audio Chapter Reviews (MP3), Flashcards, Glossary, Chapter outlines, Exercises, Crossword Puzzles and other games, and AP News Feeds.

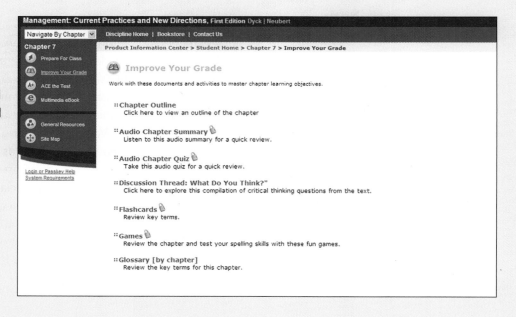

eBooks (Downloadable and Multimedia) The eBooks offer a convenient cost-effective choice for students. Flexible tools such as annotating, highlighting, and keyword searching make these texts ideal for use in distance learning programs.

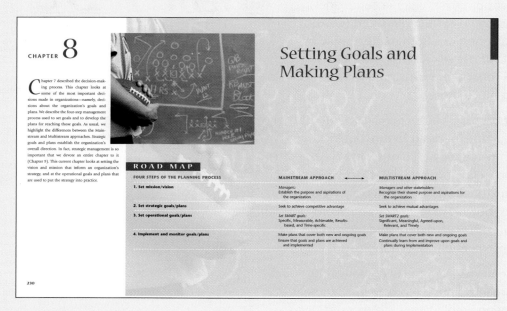

MANAGEMENT

Current Practices and New Directions

CHAPTER 1

Before embarking on any long journey, it is always a good idea to have a road map to help you see where you're headed and remember where you've been. Each chapter in this book begins with a "road map" specific to that chapter. Each road map is designed to help you anticipate where the chapter is heading, to provide a quick reference point when you are navigating in the chapter in case you may be getting lost, and to provide an overarching look at the chapter for review after reading it. Just as when you are using a road map on a long car trip, you may have some idea of the "destinations" based on previous experience or stories you've heard, but each place on the map becomes more meaningful once you've actually visited it yourself. We sincerely hope that you will enjoy your journey learning about management and that our maps can help you on your way!

ROAD MAP

Why Study Management?

What is Management?

Defining Effective Management

Comparing Mainstream and Multistream management (as opposite ends of continuum)
Planning via
Organizing via
Leading via
Controlling via

Why study two approaches to management?

Introduction to Management

To promote	• Skills to become a manager • Improved working relationships with bosses • Understanding of the role managers play in society • Self-understanding
Four management functions	• *Planning:* identifying organizational resources, goals, and strategies • *Organizing:* designing systems and structures to facilitate meeting those goals • *Leading:* influencing others to meet goals • *Controlling:* ensuring that members' actions match the organization's standard values

MAINSTREAM MANAGEMENT ⟷	MULTISTREAM MANAGEMENT
High emphasis on materialism and individualism	Emphasis on multiple forms of well-being for multiple stakeholders

MAINSTREAM MANAGEMENT ⟷	MULTISTREAM MANAGEMENT
quantifiable goals, top-down analysis standardization, specialization instrumental motivation, output vigilance, information systems	practical wisdom, participation courage, experimentation relational self-control, dignification justice/fairness, sensitization

• Nurtures self-understanding
• Develops deeper understanding of management
• Enhances critical thinking skills
• Reduces bias

What Do We Admire in a Manager?[1]

Jack Welch, the former chief executive officer (CEO) of General Electric (GE), was voted the "most respected CEO" four times by *Industry Week*, named the "manager of the century" by *Fortune*, and identified as the "gold standard against which other CEOs are measured" by *BusinessWeek*. Welch illustrates the dramatic difference that a manager can make in an organization. Under his leadership, GE experienced 22 consecutive years of dividend increases, a near perfect record of ever-higher profits, and a remarkable 4000 percent increase in share price. With Welch at the helm, GE became the first corporation to be valued at more than $200 billion, one of the most profitable firms in the world, and "the model U.S. corporation."[2] Clearly, Welch deserves to be an icon of management for others to learn from.

Management textbooks draw attention to how Welch performed each of the four basic functions of management: planning, organizing, leading, and controlling. First and foremost, Welch was seen as a brilliant strategic planner and decision maker. He was especially known for his decision rule that GE exit industries in which its divisions were not in the number 1 or 2 position. This decision rule, in turn, helped to set the tone for the decisions and goals that other GE managers set for their subordinates.[3]

Second, Welch was known for his innovations in organizing, especially for introducing "Work-Outs" throughout GE. Work-Outs were part of Welch's intention to achieve "boundary-less behavior" that "ends all barriers of rank, function, geography and bureaucracy in an endless pursuit of the best idea."[4] Work-Outs are akin to "town hall" meetings, where employees give advice to their managers on how to cut costs and improve quality.

Third, Welch was seen as an influential leader. In particular, he was famous for his handwritten notes praising or prodding employees throughout the company: "The biggest job I have is to let people know how I feel about 'em," he once said. "You gotta tell them you love 'em and you gotta kick 'em in the [butt] when they're not doing their job. And you got to be able to hug 'em and kick 'em in the [butt] frequently."[5]

Finally, Welch was known for establishing innovative systems that facilitate the control of people and information at GE. He established a culture of innovation where employees continually share best practices and transfer knowledge among organizational units.[6] He is also known for controlling people via GE's emphasis on "Six Sigma," which is "a disciplined methodology to relentlessly pursue higher quality and lower costs."[7]

All of this is pretty impressive. Nevertheless, Jack Welch also provides an instructive example of shortcomings associated with conventional management theory and practice. For example, he earned the moniker "Neutron Jack" because of his penchant for closing divisions—moves that left tens of thousands of people unemployed. Often the people he fired and the divisions he closed were profitable but just weren't number 1 or 2 in their industries. The price of winning was high for GE employees. Little wonder that Welch's practices contributed to feelings of fear and job insecurity at the company, and that his handwritten notes to employees were so effective.

In this climate some GE employees were motivated to act illegally and unethically, perhaps in an effort to remain number 1 or 2 in their industry. Moreover, GE under Welch had a less-than-glowing record in terms of the environment (improperly disposed industrial wastes), workplace safety (excessive radiation in the workplace), and illegal behavior (fraud in military contract procurement).[8] As a consequence, some socially responsible investment money management firms avoided investing in GE. These social and emotional costs associated with Jack Welch's type of "effective" management are rarely mentioned in textbooks.

WHY STUDY MANAGEMENT?

This book is all about management; it is written for people who are studying what it means to be a manager. Most people have at least some idea of what managers do because we live in a time when organizations dominate our lives. We generally think of a manager as "the boss" who is "in charge." A manager has status, power, and influence. A manager gets to tell others what to do, and he or she usually earns more money than other workers. Managers also have a chance to make a difference in the lives of others.

Studying management is valuable for at least four reasons (summarized in Figure 1.1). First, it will increase your opportunities to be offered a job as a manager. Managers must develop strong **technical skills** (expertise in a particular area such as marketing, accounting, finance, or human resources) and strong **human skills** (abilities in getting along with people, leadership, helping others to be motivated, communication, and conflict resolution). But technical and human skills by themselves are insufficient to get promoted into management. Rather, it is strong **conceptual skills** that distinguish people who get promoted—that is, the ability to think about complex and broad organizational issues. And that is a focus of this book: to introduce and develop a solid conceptual framework of what management is all about. The book will also help you to develop human skills and some technical skills in areas such as strategic management.

Second, studying management is valuable because the better you understand the work of your own boss, the more likely you will be to get along with that person. This "greasing of the wheels" will make your work experience less stressful and more enjoyable and should also help make the organization run more smoothly.

Technical skills refer to expertise in a particular field, such as marketing, accounting, computer software development, or international trade agreements.

Human skills refer to the ability to work well with other people and groups, and include skills in leadership, motivation, interpersonal communication, and conflict management.

Conceptual skills refer to the ability to think about complex and broad organizational issues. These skills enable managers to understand how the individual parts of the organization fit together to serve the organization as a whole, and how the organization fits into its larger environment.

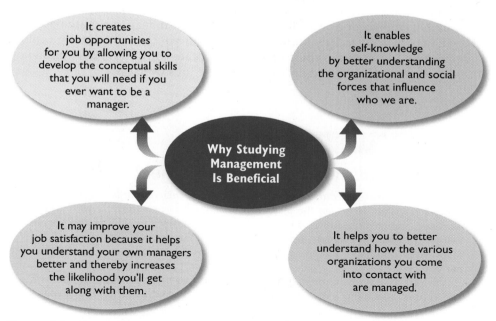

Figure 1.1   Four reasons to study management

Third, the study of management is important because management is needed in all types of organizations. Large businesses need managers, but so do small start-up firms, nonprofit organizations, government agencies, and nongovernmental organizations. You can apply the management knowledge and skills described in this book whether you are running a multinational corporation or a neighborhood sports team. Managerial skills are valuable at every level in organizations, including:

- **First-line supervisors,** who manage the work of those organizational members who are involved in the actual production or creation of an organization's products or services
- **Middle managers,** who manage the work of first-line supervisors and others
- **Top managers,** who have organization-wide managerial responsibilities, such as chief executive officers (CEOs), vice-presidents, and board chairs

Of course, the nature of managerial work changes depending on the level and type of organization. What a manager does may change depending on the size of the organization, the kind of technology it uses, the nature of its external environment, its local culture, and so on. Studying management is valuable even for managers who remain in one managerial position for their entire careers, because they must learn to adapt how they manage to match the changes that occur as their organizations and industries evolve. The basic conceptual knowledge provided in this book is relevant whether you end up working in a small or large organization, in a for-profit or nonprofit organization, in a local or international organization, or in a traditional or virtual organization.

Fourth, the study of management is important because it enables self-understanding. By understanding management, we get a better sense of the values and forces that shape us as persons and as societies. According to prominent management philosopher and scholar Peter Drucker, management "deals with people, their values, and their personal development . . . management is deeply involved in moral concerns."[9] Thus one goal of this book is to help you develop a rich understanding of how different approaches to management are based on different sets of values. This knowledge will help you to thoughtfully explore contemporary issues such as personal and corporate corruption, environmental degradation, downsizing, and decisions to move jobs overseas.

First-line supervisors manage the work of organizational members who are involved in the actual production or creation of an organization's products or services.

Middle managers manage the work of first-line managers and others.

Top managers (e.g., CEOs, vice-presidents, and board chairs) have organization-wide managerial responsibilities.

? WHAT DO YOU THINK?

Do You *Really* Want to Be a Manager?

Many people are attracted to the status, power, and financial rewards associated with being a manager. However, the lifestyle of managers can be stressful, with a high workload and an unrelenting sense of obligation and responsibility to the people being managed. For example, research suggests that senior managers in the United States work long hours and enjoy an average of only 12.2 vacation days or holidays per year.[10]

Why are you studying management? What do you think are some of the pros and cons of becoming a manager? Is this a profession and a lifestyle that appeals to you?

WHAT IS MANAGEMENT?

Despite the fact that managers are commonplace in our society, many people would not be able to provide a clear definition of what "management" is. And without knowing the hallmarks of management, it is difficult to aspire to become a successful manager, to be a good follower, or to understand the role of management in our society.

The most common definition of management has two components. **Management** is (1) the process of planning, organizing, leading, and controlling human and other organizational resources with the aim of (2) the effective achievement of organizational goals. The first part of the definition identifies the four main functions of management, and the second part identifies the purpose of management. We will look at each component in turn.

> **Management** is the process of planning, organizing, leading, and controlling human and other organizational resources in order to effectively achieve organizational goals.

The Four Functions of Management

Planning, organizing, leading, and controlling are the four main functions of management. These functions were first identified by Henri Fayol[11] almost a century ago, and they are commonly used as the organizing framework for management courses and textbooks. The same four management functions are also evident in the basic definition of an **organization:** a goal-directed (planning), deliberately structured (organizing) group of people working together (leading) to achieve results (controlling).

> **Organization** is a goal-directed, deliberately structured group of people working together to achieve results.

Although these four functions of management continue to serve as the *conceptual* framework most often used to describe management, a famous study by Henry Mintzberg helps to understand what managers *actually do*.[12] Mintzberg literally followed managers around for weeks on end and took careful notes on what they did every minute of each day. Rather than the orderly and thoughtful picture that might be implied by Fayol's four functions, Mintzberg found that managers' workdays are fragmented (the average time a manager spends on any activity is less than 9 minutes), have a lot of variety, and move at a relentless pace. For example, whereas Fayol's approach might imply that managers spend a lot of their time at their desks, Mintzberg found that deskwork actually accounts for only 22 percent of managers' time.

> In Greek theater, a single actor could play multiple roles by putting on different masks. In similar fashion, managers must learn to play multiple roles to perform the four functions of management.

Mintzberg's study also suggested that managers play a variety of "roles" in the "drama" that is the "improv theater" of organizational life. In particular, he found that managers play three overarching roles (and ten subroles):[13]

- Interpersonal roles: leader, liaison, and figurehead

- Decisional roles: resource allocator, negotiator, entrepreneur, and crisis handler

- Informational roles: monitor, disseminator, and spokesperson[14]

Of course, there is some overlap between Mintzberg's roles and Fayol's four functions. We will now briefly describe the four functions and examine how each of Mintzberg's subroles can be associated with a specific function.[15]

Planning means identifying an organization's goals and strategies and allocating the appropriate organizational resources required to achieve them.

PLANNING. **Planning** means identifying an organization's goals and strategies, as well as the appropriate organizational resources required to achieve those goals and implement those strategies. The planning function draws attention to managers' hierarchical authority. It is managers who call meetings and set the agendas regarding what will be discussed at those meetings. It is managers who represent their department's goals and strategies to the rest of the organization and who are often involved in planning the exchange of resources with key suppliers and customers. It is managers who coordinate the collection and analysis of data and who are ultimately held responsible for their organization's decisions, goals, and strategies.

Mintzberg's study suggested that planning might involve either developing strategic organizational change or merely fine-tuning the status quo. For example, Mintzberg's *entrepreneur* subrole involves proactively and voluntarily initiating, designing, or encouraging change and innovation. The manager may delegate parts of the implementation process to others but will supervise the overall process and keep the authority to make final decisions. The *negotiator* subrole often involves making incremental changes to ongoing plans and resources. In this role, a manager represents the organization in major negotiations affecting the manager's area of responsibility (e.g., negotiating a union contract, negotiating the fee that a consulting company will be paid, negotiating the price to be paid for a new acquisition). The public face of planning is often seen in the *spokesperson* subrole, where the manager transmits information and decisions up and across the hierarchy, and/or to the general public.

We will cover planning in Chapter 7 (decision-making processes), Chapter 8 (setting goals and making plans), and Chapter 9 (organizational strategy).

Organizing means ensuring that tasks have been assigned and a structure of organizational relationships created to facilitate meeting organizational goals.

ORGANIZING. **Organizing** means ensuring that tasks have been assigned and a structure of organizational relationships created that facilitates meeting organizational goals. Organizing has to do with the structures and systems that managers establish and maintain. This includes the authority structure of the organization, the types of departments that are established, the technology that the organization uses, the physical layout of a factory or office space, budgets, human resource policies, and so on. When senior managers are asked about the most challenging part of their job, they often talk about implementing changes to organizational structures and systems.

Mintzberg's managerial roles view organizing as the allocation of organizational resources. The *resource allocator* subrole is defined very broadly and involves the distribution of all types of resources (e.g., time, funds, equipment, human resources). Managers create the organizational structure that members work within, such as what sort of departments an organization has and how budgeting processes are used to allocate financial resources.

We will discuss organizational structure in Chapter 10 (the four fundamentals of organizing), Chapter 11 (different ways that organizations can be structured and designed), Chapter 12 (how human resources are structured), and Chapter 13 (the dynamics of organizational change).

Leading means relating with others so that their work efforts result in the achievement of organizational goals.

LEADING. **Leading** means relating to others so that their work efforts lead to the achievement of organizational goals. Leading is often the first function that comes to mind when people think about management, because it is the most obvious and visible "face" of management for most subordinates. Managers must have the interpersonal skills necessary to ensure that members of the organization are motivated, to communicate with members, to encourage them, to resolve interpersonal conflict, and so on. Often groups will have informal leaders who may be more skilled than the formal manager at some aspects of leading.

DILBERT: © Scott Adams/Dist. by United Feature Syndicate, Inc.

Mintzberg found that managers spent approximately 75 percent of their time interacting with people. The *leader* subrole is the most important of the three interpersonal subroles; it includes virtually all forms of communicating with subordinates, including motivating and coaching. Most of the focus of the leader role is on face-to-face interactions, which includes activities such as staffing, training, and motivating. The *liaison* subrole includes building and maintaining a good network of information contacts beyond the boundaries of a manager's specific work unit. It is evident in activities such as meeting with bosses and other managers at the same level within the organization, and dealing with competitors, suppliers, and customers. In the *disseminator* subrole, managers transmit information that was gathered either internally or externally to members of their own organizational unit. This includes sending memos, scheduling and attending weekly staff meetings, retelling the myths and anecdotes that represent an organization's culture, and relaying information from top management.[16]

We will cover leadership in Chapter 14 (how members are motivated), Chapter 15 (how managers can lead organizational members), Chapter 16 (how managers can help to build and facilitate the work of groups and teams), and Chapter 17 (how managers communicate with others).

CONTROLLING. **Controlling** means ensuring that the actions of organizational members are consistent with the organization's values and standards. Controls can be very visible, such as a time clock to ensure members do not overstay their lunch hour, but the most effective controls are often less visible. These include professional norms, organizational culture, and the informal understanding employees have of "the way we do things around here" that characterize organizations. This "invisible" activity of management is important because it determines the organization's "identity," shapes the identities of individual members within the organization, and provides members with "meaning" in their jobs. For example, in some hospitals, cleaning staff may see themselves as doing menial or degrading work, whereas in other facilities, cleaning staff may see themselves as part of an overall team where each member does his or her part to care for those who are ill.[17]

Mintzberg's roles draw attention to the fact that controlling includes both correcting things that are going wrong and supporting things that are going well. In the *monitor* subrole, a manager seeks internal and external information about issues that can affect the organization. This subrole is evident in activities like talking to members, taking observational tours in the organization, and asking questions. Monitoring also includes reading newspapers and attending conferences to keep abreast of trends in the field, reading performance data, and reading minutes from meetings.

> **Controlling** involves ensuring that the actions of organizational members are consistent with the organization's values and standards.

MANAGEMENT IN PRACTICE

Evidence of the Four Basic Management Functions in Your Management Class

Imagine that your introductory management class is an organization and that your instructor is the manager. How are the four functions of management evident in this class?

In terms of *planning*, the goals for the course have likely been approved by a group of instructors, and the course is designed to fit into students' overall programs of study. The strategy for delivering the course has also been planned, whether it is by correspondence, by distance education, or via the traditional in-class attendance method.

In terms of *organizing*, the instructor has prepared a course outline, assigned chapters to read, provided a series of projects and exams for students to complete according to deadlines, and so on. The instructor tries to ensure that students have adequate resources available to complete assignments, such as library materials and time (e.g., instructors recognize that students have responsibilities and time commitments beyond

the introductory management course). Where appropriate, instructors may organize students into study groups.

In terms of *leading*, the instructor strives to deliver course material in an engaging and motivating manner. The instructor may also interact with students outside of class individually or in small groups during office hours, or while working on small-group activities and projects.

In terms of *controlling*, the instructor monitors whether students are keeping up with learning objectives by administering quizzes, assignments, and exams. Students use these same checkpoints to monitor their own performance. Input from an end-of-term course evaluation can help the instructor improve the course the next time he or she teaches it. Students' behavior may also be controlled by external factors to which the instructor draws their attention, such as suggesting that higher grades may translate into better job offers when they graduate.

The *crisis handler* subrole requires taking corrective action when things are not going as planned. Often it includes coping with unexpected difficulties (e.g., fire damage in a factory, loss of a major customer, and the breakdown of an important machine). The *figurehead* subrole highlights the important symbolic role that managers play for their organizational units. Organizational members pay special attention to their managers' behavior, taking cues from them regarding work, company values, and even their personal dress codes. The figurehead subrole is evident when a manager hands out a plaque for performance at an organizational banquet, is present at the ribbon-cutting ceremony for a new plant, or is interviewed by the media to announce a new organizational initiative.[18]

Controlling will be addressed in Chapters 5 and 18. Chapter 5 examines the values that managers hold and are evident to others, and how those values influence management style and decision making. Chapter 18 looks at how behavior in organizations is controlled based on structures and systems that are consistent with organizational values.

As we shall see later in this book, these four management functions, taken together, provide a helpful framework for understanding management theory and practice. Indeed, like most other "Introduction to Management" textbooks, this book is divided into sections and chapters based on these four classic "functions."

Defining "Effective" Management[19]

The second part of the definition of management focuses on ensuring that the four management functions are performed *effectively*. Considerations of effective performance may vary in part depending on the type of organization at hand. For a community-run soup kitchen, performing effectively may mean providing people with nourishing food in a way that enhances their dignity. For a business, it may mean maximizing profitability. For a government agency, it may mean serving the public in a timely fashion.

Effectiveness means choosing the "right" overarching organizational goals to pursue. But what is "right"? The idea of effectiveness draws attention to the fact that a manager—like anyone who makes decisions that affect other people—has *moral* obligations. Unfortunately, it is often not clear how to evaluate the rightness of the goals an organization is pursuing. Is profit maximization a legitimate effectiveness goal? Is it the only one? Is there more to being an effective manager than simply maximizing profits? Are firms being effective when they provide products to customers at the lowest possible cost but relocate production to low-wage foreign countries with poor working conditions so as to achieve that goal? Has a marketing manager in a cigarette firm been effective and made the "right" decision by successfully targeting young women to purchase cigarettes? Was Jack Welch effective when he increased shareholder value by closing or selling off entire profitable divisions because they were not among the top two performers in their industries and, in the process, putting tens of thousands of people out of work? Was Aaron Feuerstein effective when he risked bankruptcy to pay his workers even though they were not working because his factory burned down? (See the opening case in Chapter 5.)

Often the moral question of "What is effective?" is rephrased into a question that looks at visible results: "What is *efficient*?" **Efficiency** refers to the level of output that is achieved with a given level of inputs. Put another way, efficiency means maximizing **outputs** (the goods, services, and other resources that an organization puts into the environment) while minimizing **inputs** (the human, material, and information resources that an organization takes from the environment). However, the criteria used to determine efficiency are often problematic, and there is a failure to ask *for whom* something is efficient. A down-to-earth example comes from the field of agriculture. It seems efficient to grow and harvest thousands of acres of wheat using sophisticated farm technology (e.g., the latest machinery and fertilizers), but research suggests that these modern agricultural techniques actually use two to eight times more kilocalories of energy to produce one kilocalorie of food energy than is required in countries that rely on more traditional, labor-intensive technology.[20] Which form of farming is truly more efficient?

In sum, it is important to understand the difference between effectiveness and efficiency. Effectiveness means doing the right things, while efficiency means doing things right. In other words, effectiveness deals with the issue of *which* goals an organization should pursue, whereas efficiency focuses on *how* to achieve those goals with the minimum expenditure of resources. Although the two are certainly distinct, notions of effectiveness and efficiency are related in the practice of management. For example, if maximizing profits is deemed effective, then in many cases it may be efficient to pollute the environment within legal limits. By contrast, if criteria for effectiveness include the natural environment or the quality of life for future generations, then pollution becomes less efficient and less effective. Likewise, overseas "sweatshops" may be efficient if effectiveness focuses on reducing costs and increasing profits, but not if effectiveness has concern for treating people humanely.

Effectiveness means choosing the "right" overarching organizational goals to pursue and draws attention to the fact that a manager—like anyone who makes decisions that affect other people—has *moral* obligations.

Efficiency refers to increasing the level of output that is achieved with a given level of inputs.

Outputs are the goods, services, and other resources that an organization puts into the environment.

Inputs are the human, material, and information resources that an organization takes in from the environment.

WHAT DO YOU THINK?

What Is the Meaning of *Effectiveness* in the Classroom?

Consider the example of your management class once again. Are students *members* of the class, or are they simply paying *customers* who purchase knowledge via their tuition? Or are students *products* that are moving along an assembly line, where professors fill each student's head with enough knowledge to satisfy the people who are paying the tuition bills (e.g., students, taxpayers, parents, and scholarship providers)? Or are students *apprentices* and instructors *mentors* (a common assumption in doctoral programs)?

What we see as "effective" management of the class will depend on which metaphor we use. What might happen to the more difficult (and perhaps more important) parts of a course if a professor treats students as customers, given the adage that "The customer is always right"? This interpretation might lead to a watering down of education. Is the class more "effective" when the focus is on what the instructor-as-mentor believes to be the most important course content, or when the focus is on what the student-as-customer finds the most entertaining or the easiest? Alternatively, with the student-as-product metaphor, there is an incentive to turn the class into an efficient assembly line with large class sizes and very little in-class interaction with the instructor. Indeed, why offer any in-class instruction at all? If truth can be written down in a textbook, then perhaps it would be far more efficient for universities to offer only correspondence courses.

Perhaps the most costly approach is the student-as-apprentice notion, yet it seems to have stood the test of time. Imagine simply reading textbooks versus reading them *and* having the opportunity to talk with your instructor and classmates about what it means to be a manager. The fact that so many resources have been invested in universities and their infrastructures suggests that society continues to value the student-as-apprentice approach.

What do you think? Is the face-to-face student-as-apprentice education the most effective way to teach, or will it be replaced as technology paves the way for an increasingly "virtual" world and online education?

Students may be viewed as class members, customers, products, or apprentices. Similar metaphors apply to people being managed in other organizations: hired hands, subordinates, human resources, staff, workers, members, and so on. Each term has certain assumptions built into it. Which terms do you like the best and least?

Figure 1.2   Two basic approaches to define effective management

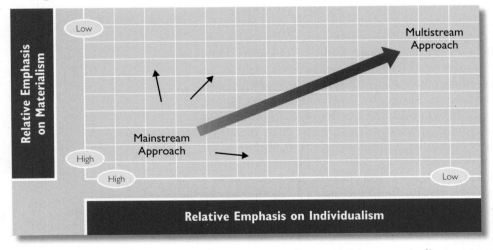

The century-old work of the great German sociologist Max Weber—whose influence on our understanding of behavior in organizations has been profound[21]—provides a conceptual framework that helps us to think more carefully about what constitutes effective management. Weber points to two different sets of criteria for determining what is "effective" management, which we will call the *Mainstream* and *Multistream* effectiveness criteria. Figure 1.2 provides a visual framework to help understand the two approaches, and the arrows indicate recent movement within some management theory and practice from a Mainstream toward a more Multistream approach.[22]

Mainstream management
is characterized by its primary emphasis on materialist–individualist well-being.

MAINSTREAM MANAGEMENT. <u>Mainstream management</u> is characterized by its emphasis on <u>ma</u>terialism and <u>in</u>dividualism. From a materialist–individualist perspective, *effective* management is primarily about maximizing productivity, profitability, and competitiveness. The Mainstream approach is evident in catchphrases like "Keep your eye on the bottom line," "Winning is everything," and "Time is money." Because financial well-being is a primary emphasis, this approach tends to place relatively less emphasis on other forms of well-being, such as physical, social, spiritual, aesthetic, ecological, and intellectual well-being.[23] These other forms of well-being are sometimes seen as a means of achieving financial well-being (e.g., job satisfaction is effective because it improves workers' productivity).

The Mainstream approach is based on the idea that if everyone works in his or her own self-interests, then organizational needs will be served.[24] The logic behind this view is captured in the popularized interpretation of Adam Smith's metaphor of the "invisible hand," which suggests that the good of the community is assured when all individuals are permitted to pursue their own self-interested goals.[25] Moreover, emphasis is placed on financial well-being, because people can choose to use their financial resources to pursue a variety of other forms of well-being (e.g., to purchase a nice house, to go on vacation to visit relatives, or to donate money to charity).

Research suggests that a materialist–individualist orientation can be learned, and that business students tend to become more materialist–individualist as they proceed through their program of studies.[26]

Weber argues that the Mainstream approach has made major contributions to our unprecedented productivity and the creation of financial wealth. Even so, he suggests that it ultimately renders a disservice to humankind. In what has become one of the most famous metaphors in all the social sciences, Weber argues that this materialist–individualist approach leaves humankind captured in an "iron cage" (see Chapter 2). He goes on to suggest that the way for managers to escape the iron cage is to embrace theory and practice that places less emphasis on materialism and individualism.

 WHAT DO YOU THINK?

Does Money Buy Happiness?

There is a common belief that although money may not actually buy happiness, it certainly can't hurt. One study found that a $631,000 salary raise "buys" about the same amount of happiness as increasing your physical health from "very poor" to "excellent," and that a $179,000 raise buys as much happiness as increasing the amount of time you spend time with friends and family from less than once a month to "most days."[27] In contrast, some research suggests that money and materialism may result in a *decline* in life satisfaction and personal well-being.[28] Research shows that a materialist–individualist emphasis is associated with lower satisfaction in life, poorer interpersonal relationships, and increased mental disorders.

Other research suggests that money can indeed buy happiness, *but only if you give it away.* A series of studies show that people are happier if they spend money on gifts or charities than on themselves, that workers who received a profit-sharing bonus were happier if they gave some of the bonus to others instead of keeping it all for themselves, and that students who were given $5 to $20 and told to spend it on others were happier at the end of the day than students who were instructed to spend it on themselves.[29]

Think of someone who is truly happy and content. What would that person say about the relationship between overall well-being and money? Do you agree or disagree with the idea that money can buy happiness?

Multistream management
is characterized by its emphasis on multiple forms of well-being for multiple stakeholders.

Stakeholder is any group or person within or outside an organization who is directly affected by the organization and has a stake in its performance.

MULTISTREAM MANAGEMENT.   **Multistream management** is characterized by its emphasis on **multi**ple forms of well-being for **multi**ple stakeholders. A **stakeholder** is any group or person within or outside an organization that is directly affected by the organization and has a stake in its performance. Stakeholders include owners, members, suppliers, competitors, customers, neighbors, and so on. In the Multistream approach, effective management is all about working with stakeholders toward creating a balance among multiple forms of well-being. This approach does not ignore the importance of financial well-being or the interests of shareholders. However, compared to the Mainstream approach, the Multistream approach places greater emphasis on a wider variety of forms of well-being. Multistream management may hamper the *maximization* of individual wealth and organizational growth, but it fosters notions such as community, work that is inherently more meaningful, ecological sustainability, social justice, and so on.

Multistream management theory and practice rests on several conceptual and philosophical bases.[30] For example, it is consistent with Adam Smith's earlier—and less famous—work, *The Theory of Moral Sentiments.*[31] When he says that everyone should be "perfectly free to pursue his [or her] own interest," for Smith this freedom must take into account virtues such as benevolence, practical wisdom (prudence), justice, and self-control.[32] Put differently, Smith's "invisible hand" is "effective" only if it is attached to a "virtuous arm."

Building on this idea, the Mainstream approach is also based on Aristotle's virtue theory,[33] a highly regarded perspective that has stood the test of time. From an Aristotelian perspective, the purpose of management is not to maximize productivity, efficiency, and profitability, nor is it to maximize self-interest. Rather, the purpose of human action is to maximize people's *happiness,* which Aristotle called the "supreme good." Happiness is achieved by practicing virtues *in community.*[34] From a virtue theory approach, Multistream management is primarily about modeling and facilitating members' practice of the four cardinal virtues—practical wisdom, self-control, courage, and justice—which are related to the four functions of management (see Table 1.1).[35] In short, Multistream management seeks to nurture community and happiness by modeling and enabling the practice of virtues in financially viable organizations.

Interest in, and examples of, Multistream management are becoming ever more prevalent.[36] Many practitioners often act in ways that place higher priority on improving the multidimensional well-being of humankind rather than merely maximizing the financial wealth of their organizations. In the same vein, management scholars are doing research that challenges the Mainstream approach, and management students

DIGGING DEEPER

What Does *Effectiveness* Mean to Millennial Students?[37]

Research suggests that the inclination toward a more Multistream approach to management may be especially prevalent among so-called **Millennial** students (those born in the period 1982–2001). Compared to the generation that preceded them (Generation Y), Millennial students are less selfish, more likely to believe in their collective power, more inclined to promote social justice and responsibility, and more concerned about the natural environment (e.g., they believe, by a ten-to-one majority, that they will do more than their parents' generation to protect the environment over the next 25 years).

Millennial students want conceptual tools that allow them to make up their own minds about what is "right," and are

capable of parallel thinking that allows them to supplement Mainstream management theory with a Multistream complement. This suggests that although most management course outlines promise that students will learn Mainstream management theory and practice, many Millennial students may actually be more interested in Multistream management theory and practice because it will help them address environmental problems, alleviate poverty, nurture work–life balance, and so on.

Which of the characteristics associated with the Millennial generation ring true based on your own observations? Which are the most surprising? What are the implications for the study and practice of management?

---

are increasingly interested in thinking outside the materialist–individualist box. Consistent with these arguments and needs, each chapter in this book presents theory and examples of effective management from *both* a Mainstream approach and a Multistream approach.

Millennial students were born in the period 1982–2001.

COMPARING MAINSTREAM MANAGEMENT AND MULTISTREAM MANAGEMENT

The Mainstream and Multistream "Ideal-Types" as Extremes Along a Continuum

When we recognize that there are at least two approaches to identifying what effectiveness means—a Mainstream approach and a Multistream approach—it draws our attention to the fact that there are at least two different approaches to performing each of the four functions of management (planning, organizing, leading, and controlling). A Mainstream manager will perform these functions differently than a Multistream manager. This book will describe, contrast, and compare these two approaches to management. However, before we begin to do so, it is important to discuss two points.

First, the Mainstream and Multistream approaches to management are what Weber calls **ideal-types**. This term does not mean that they are necessarily the "best" or "ideal" way of managing, but rather that they are theoretical extremes intended to help us think about what management means and orient our thinking and practices. Just as for other ideal-types with which you may be familiar—for example, introverts versus extroverts—we would not expect to find many managers who are always a perfect example of a Mainstream manager or a Multistream manager. As a consequence, even though this textbook will provide many examples of managers who *illustrate* a Mainstream or Multistream approach, we suspect that those very same managers sometimes utilize the opposite approach. For example, even Jack Welch, who was used to illustrate the Mainstream ideal-type in the

Ideal-type describes a "pure" model or approach at a theoretical extreme that helps to orient people's thinking and practices.

Comparing Mainstream and Multistream Management Definitions

	Mainstream Approach ← →	Multistream Approach
Management	The process of planning, organizing, leading, and controlling human and other organizational resources with the aim of achieving organizational goals *efficiently* and, therefore, effectively	The process of planning, organizing, leading, and controlling human and other organizational resources with the aim of achieving organizational goals *virtuously* and, therefore, effectively
Key ideas	*Maximize productivity via self-interest*	*Nurture community via virtue*
Planning	*Setting* an organization's goals and strategies and deciding on the appropriate organizational resources required to enable achieving them	*Working together* to identify an organization's goals and strategies as well as the appropriate organizational resources required to enable achieving them
Key ideas	*Measurable goals, top-down linear analysis*	*Practical wisdom, participation*
Organizing	*Assigning* tasks and *arranging* resources to meet organizational goals	*Ensuring* that tasks are assigned and adequate resources are arranged to facilitate meeting organizational goals
Key ideas	*Standardization, specialization, centralization*	*Courage, experimentation*
Leading	*Motivating* others so that their work efforts serve to meet organizational goals	*Working alongside* others so that *together* everyone's work efforts serve to meet agreed-upon organizational goals
Key ideas	*Instrumental motivation, output*	*Relational self-control, dignification*
Controlling	*Monitoring* organization members' performance, comparing it to standards, and taking corrective action to improve performance as necessary	*Ensuring* that actions of organizational members are *just* and consistent with the organization's underpinning values
Key ideas	*Vigilance, information systems, value chains*	*Justice/fairness, sensitization, value loops*

opening case, does not always act in ways that are not in his own self-interest or that are solely intended to maximize GE's profits.

This understanding leads to the second point: *These two approaches to management represent the opposite ends of a continuum, and most managers can be located somewhere along that continuum.* Indeed, many of the Hands-On Activities at the ends of the chapters in this book provide self-evaluation exercises to help you identify where you are located along the continuum and to encourage you to reflect on where you want be in the future. Understanding this Mainstream–Multistream continuum, rather than studying just one approach to management, will make it easier for you to understand the nature of management—just as it is easier, for example, to understand the nature of personality by studying *both* introversion and extroversion.

This section briefly discusses some of the key ideas and practices associated with Mainstream and Multistream management. As shown in Table 1.1, we will highlight some of the key similarities and differences regarding how the two approaches look at each of the four functions of management.

Two Approaches to Planning

MAINSTREAM.   From a Mainstream perspective, planning is all about managers setting goals, making plans, and designing strategies to achieve these goals. Thus managers analyze data and make decisions that maximize organizational efficiency, productivity, profitability, and competitiveness. Which goals and strategies are selected are the result of decisions that are influenced by the materialist–individualist perspective. Such goals are often expressed in quantifiable and material terms such as market share, profit growth, return on investment, share prices, dividends, and

MANAGEMENT IN PRACTICE

Wal-Mart Versus Costco: Is Wall Street Ready for Multistream Strategies?[38]

Does Wall Street favor businesses that follow a Mainstream strategy, or a Multistream strategy? Consider Wal-Mart, an example of a firm with a Mainstream strategic approach. Even though Wal-Mart has taken a public relations pounding for paying low wages and providing health insurance for fewer than half of its 1.4 million U.S. workers,[39] it remains a favorite among Wall Street investors who believe that shareholders are best served when managers do all they can to hold down costs, including labor costs.

In contrast, Wall Street hasn't been as impressed with the more Multistream strategy adopted by archrival Costco. Even when Costco handily beat Wall Street expectations and posted a 25 percent profit gain on top of a 14 percent sales increase, the market responded by driving Costco's stock price *down* by 4 percent. Why would the market respond in this way?

It turns out that Wall Street doesn't like the fact that Costco pays its workers considerably more than Wal-Mart does.[40] Investors have also noted, with some derision, that shareholders are placed behind customers, employees, and suppliers on Costco's list of stakeholders. Ian Gordon, analyst for Sanford C. Bernstein & Company, argues that Costco treats its employees *too* well: "Whatever goes to employees comes out of the pockets of shareholders." According to Deutsche Bank analyst Bill Dreher, "At Costco, it's better to be an employee or a customer than a shareholder."

Why does Costco pay such relatively high wages? "Paying your employees well," says Costco CEO James D. Sinegal, "is

the right thing to do." He thinks it is "wrong" for competitors to pay rock-bottom wages: "It doesn't keep employees happy. . . . When employees are happy, they are your very best ambassadors." He is concerned by the fact that retail workers are increasingly unable to afford the merchandise sold in their own stores, which he feels is not a sustainable situation in the long term: "You wind up with a greater and greater shift of wealth into the hands of the few."

Beyond being the right thing to do, Sinegal argues that paying livable wages is also good business. Costco promotes from within, and the company wants to have a highly talented pool of workers from which to draw management candidates. Costco has one of the most loyal and productive workforces in retailing. Its employee turnover rate after the first year of employment is one-third of other retailers' rates (Wal-Mart estimates that it costs $2500 to test, interview, and train a new hire).[41] Costco also has significantly greater sales per square foot, and it has lower labor and overhead costs (9.8 percent of revenue, versus Wal-Mart's 17 percent).

So what about the skeptics on Wall Street? Sinegal says, "If we take care of the business and keep our eye on the goal line, the stock price will take care of itself. You just can't get too focused on worrying about what's going to happen in the next quarter. You have to worry about where the business is headed long-term."

cost savings. Mainstream planning lays the foundation for the other three management functions.

MULTISTREAM.   The Multistream approach to planning emphasizes how managers work alongside others to set goals and design strategies. Multistream managers also use measurable goals, but they do not avoid goals that are difficult to measure, such as goals related to environmental sustainability, human dignity, and happiness. Multistream managers use **practical wisdom** to achieve multiple forms of well-being for multiple stakeholders.[42] Instead of having an individual *or* a community focus, Multistream managers view *persons* as being embedded in a *community,* and they understand that the differences between the two are more superficial than real. Such managers strive to ensure that decisions reflect the needs of multiple stakeholders.[43] They deliberately include others in setting goals and making decisions, often resulting in better-informed strategies and more motivated members.

Practical wisdom (prudence) is a virtue that fosters the capacity for deliberation and action to obtain what is good for the community, especially by asking insightful questions, evaluating real-world management situations, and applying relevant knowledge.

Two Approaches to Organizing

MAINSTREAM.   Organizing follows from planning because it involves arranging human and other organizational resources in such a way as to achieve planned goals and strategies. Mainstream managers use rational analytic skills to develop structures and systems and to assign jobs within them. From this perspective, all organizational resources—including human resources—are seen as a *means* to accomplish desired *ends* (e.g., goals, objectives). Basic organizing issues include concepts such as centralization (how much authority people at different organizational levels have), specialization (dividing large, complex tasks into a series of simpler tasks), and standardization (achieving coordination across organizational members). These concepts will be explored in greater detail in Chapters 10 and 11.

MULTISTREAM. Multistream management de-emphasizes the hierarchical approach to organizing that is evident in Mainstream management. This difference is evident both in the means by which organizing takes place (many stakeholders participate in the Multistream process) and in the result of how resources are organized (e.g., there is relatively more emphasis on team-based structures). Multistream organizing supports a spirit of experimentation, which is evident when members support one another when implementing changes to improve the organization. This atmosphere encourages members to have the courage required to challenge current structures and systems that may be serving the needs of the powerful but not the powerless. The virtue of **courage** refers to implementing initiatives that have potential to improve overall happiness *even if the initiative might threaten one's own status.* Courageous organizing implies the hope that structures and systems can be improved so that resources are allocated in such a way that all stakeholders are treated with more dignity and justice. Courageous managers are able to envision and nurture a sense of wholeness and integrity in an increasingly fragmented organizational context.[44]

> **Courage** is a virtue that involves acting in hopes of correcting unjust structures, and is evident when someone promotes change initiatives that have the potential to improve overall happiness *even if this might threaten one's own status.*

For example, Multistream managers would try to reverse the growing disparities between the rich and the poor, between nations, within nations, and within organizations (see Figure 1.3).[45] Whereas the average CEO in 2005 earned more than 800 times as much as a minimum wage earner (up from 50 times in 1965), Multistream managers like those at Reell Precision Manufacturing have developed policies that deliberately limit executive pay to roughly seven to ten times that of the lowest-paid employee.[46] Similarly, Costco's CEO James Sinegal says, "I figured that if I was making

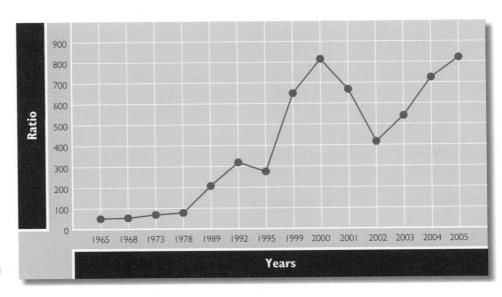

Figure 1.3   Ratio of CEO wages to minimum wage, 1965–2005[47]

Source: Lawrence Mishel, Economic Policy Institute, Washington, D.C. www.epi.org (analysis of Mercer Survey data). Reprinted with permission.

DIGGING DEEPER

Instrumental and Relational Leadership Skills

People need human skills to interact with others. Sometimes called "social skills" or "interpersonal skills," these skills are taught in schools, learned in the family, and developed in the everyday course of interacting with others. Researchers point to two basic types of social skills: instrumental and relational. Mainstream management training focuses on developing instrumental interpersonal skills, which are designed to get people to do productive things for you. Unfortunately, these skills do "not lead to success in friendships and other relationships. **Instrumental skills** are mainly about getting what you need and about fitting in. Scientists refer to them as 'instrumental' because, when we employ them, we tend to use people like instruments to get our needs met."[48]

Multistream managers, in contrast, seek to nurture a workplace that facilitates building meaningful relationships. Life is too short to spend most of it working in organizations where noninstrumental relationships are seen as inefficient or are a poor use of time. "**Relationship skills** have a very different purpose. They are used to create and deepen connections between people, share excitement and joy, and participate in joint creative efforts."[49] Relationship skills are similar to the emotional intelligence competencies of empathizing with others, managing one's own emotions to improve communication, and establishing trusting and mutually satisfying relationships.[50]

A growing number of medical schools have recognized the importance of going beyond merely teaching instrumental skills, and are now requiring medical students to take courses in the humanities that, it is hoped, will improve their ability to see their patients as people.[51] Dr. David Muller, the chairman of medical education at Mount Sinai School of Medicine, describes the merits of an art-appreciation course for medical students: "To make a better doctor means to me—and I can't speak for everyone—one who sees the person and not just the patient . . . not just an organ system that is screwed up."

Similarly, becoming a better Multistream manager means seeing the person, and not simply the customer, supplier, subordinate, or boss. The challenge facing such managers is to facilitate meaningful connections and creativity between people without resulting in confusion and chaos, and to meet the instrumental needs of the organization without undermining deeper relationship aspirations.

In which courses do you learn how to develop meaningful relationships with other people, instead of merely learning how to get other people to serve your instrumental purposes? Should more such courses be offered in our schools?

---

something like 12 times more than the typical person working on the floor, that was a fair salary" (Sinegal's salary is around $350,000 per year).[52]

Two Approaches to Leading

MAINSTREAM.   In order to motivate others so that their work efforts help to achieve organizational goals, Mainstream managers use systems and interpersonal skills. The key is for managers to use the leadership style or motivational technique that is most appropriate for maximizing individual productivity. For example, Mainstream managers often rely on extrinsic rewards, such as pay or promotions, to motivate employees to work harder. From a Mainstream perspective, managers who exhibit a strong desire to lead and achieve, and who demonstrate confidence that they can deliver results, are identified as *leaders*.

MULTISTREAM.   Multistream leadership nurtures workplaces where the emphasis on financial and productivity goals is balanced by an emphasis on healthy social relationships. Self-control is necessary for fostering other corporate virtues such as caring, gentleness, and compassion.[53] **Self-control,** sometimes called "temperance," relates to a person's emotional regulation and ability to overcome impulsive actions and greed. Managers require self-control to use, but not abuse, their leadership power. Multistream managers strive to treat others with dignity, even if this approach may not maximize organizational profits. Rather than seeing their task primarily as motivating subordinates to meet instrumental goals, Multistream

Instrumental skills are human skills used to get other people to meet your own interests or the interests of the organization.

Relationship skills are used to deepen connections between people and to participate in collaborative creative efforts.

Self-control (temperance) is a virtue that helps individuals overcome impulsive actions, self-serving use of their power, and greediness.

managers facilitate members' motivation with intrinsically meaningful work and other noble goals. From a Multistream perspective, managers take on the role of a servant leader focusing on the development of others and work together to meet mutually accepted organizational goals.

Two Approaches to Controlling

MAINSTREAM.   For Mainstream managers, controlling is all about ensuring that organizational members do what they are supposed to be doing, and that their performance meets expectations. Because it is impossible to control everything that goes on inside an organization, managers have developed tools such as value chains and information systems to aid them in this endeavor. A **value chain** is a sequence of activities needed to convert an organization's inputs (such as raw materials) into outputs (such as products). Value chains enable managers to identify the most critical steps in how the organization transforms input into outputs. Management **information systems** help to identify, collect, organize, and disseminate information (see Chapter 18).

Organizational control may be achieved in any of three basic ways.[54]

Value chain refers to the sequence of activities needed to convert an organization's inputs (e.g., raw materials, new employees) into outputs (e.g., products and services).

Information systems help to identify, collect, organize, and disseminate information.

Bureaucratic control is evident when rules, regulations, policies, and standard operating procedures are used to control the behavior of organizational members.

Market control is evident when competition is used to control the behavior of organizational members.

Clan control is evident when shared values, norms, and expectations are used to control the behavior of organizational members.

- Managers may use **bureaucratic control** to monitor how well standards are being met. Bureaucratic control is evident when rules, regulations, policies, and standard operating procedures are used to control the behavior of organizational members. For example, managers may introduce a time clock to monitor when members arrive and depart from work, or they may monitor how many items a grocery clerk scans in one hour.

- Managers may use **market control** when they implement structures that directly reward employees for performance, such as piece-rate systems or profit-sharing plans. Market control is evident when competition among organization members is used to control their behavior.

- **Clan control** is evident when shared values, norms, and expectations are used to control the behavior of organizational members. Managers use clan control when they establish organizational cultures and implement employee selection and training processes to ensure that members will share organizational values and be intrinsically motivated to do their jobs. For example, managers may celebrate or recognize certain high-performing employees to signal expectations for acceptable behavior.

Justice is a virtue that justifies organizations, holds them together, and ensures that everyone connected with an organization is treated fairly.

MULTISTREAM.   For Multistream managers, control goes beyond simply ensuring that organizational directives are followed, and instead focuses on overseeing the values, and particularly the sense of justice, that guides organizational behavior. Aristotle's idea of **justice**—a sense of "fairness" that ensures everyone connected with an organization gets his or her due—can be seen as a basic virtue that justifies organizations and holds them together. A drive for social justice and a special sense of compassion for people who are ill served by the status quo are hallmarks of management based on Aristotle's virtue theory. Multistream managers differ from their Mainstream counterparts in terms of the kinds of opportunities they seek *to act justly*. The impetus for Multistream action often comes from being sensitive to and recognizing unaddressed needs or opportunities. This may include ways to improve organizational efficiency, new market opportunities for organizational products or services, and identification of opportunities to improve social justice or ecological sustainability.

WHY STUDY TWO APPROACHES TO MANAGEMENT?

There are many different ways to study management. Whereas some people believe that students can be trained to learn the "one best way" to manage, others suggest that management education is most valuable when students learn at least two different approaches to management.[55] As summarized in Figure 1.4, studying two different approaches to management offers at least four distinct advantages:

- It nurtures self-understanding.
- It improves understanding of management.
- It develops critical thinking skills.
- It reduces bias.

First, studying both approaches allows students to think about where they, and where other managers, are located along the Mainstream–Multistream continuum. Moreover, this allows students not only to consider what their *current* management approach is, but also to give thought to what kind of managers they would like to become (or to work for) in the *future*. For example, on average, students who have learned about both the Mainstream and Multistream approaches tend to place themselves near the middle along the Mainstream–Multistream continuum. However, when asked which approach they would like to use in the future, students typically move toward the Multistream end. Similarly, students tend to want to work in a more Multistream organization in the future than they do at present.[56]

Second, understanding one ideal-type helps students to better understand a second ideal-type. For example, we develop a richer understanding of extraversion when we contrast and compare it to introversion. Similarly, we gain a deeper understanding of Mainstream management if we contrast and compare it with Multistream management, and vice versa. This emphasis on having two ideal-types to

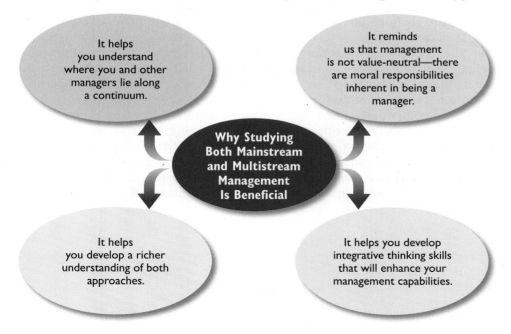

Figure 1.4   Benefits of studying two approaches to management

As symbolized in the principle of yin and yang, sometimes to understand a phenomenon it is helpful to examine two complementary opposites that serve to define the concept. Just as a single coin has two sides, so too looking at two "sides" of management promises to enhance our understanding of its essence.

contrast and compare may be particularly helpful when students are learning a new subject. Just as it is easier to learn about *personality* if you learn about *both* introversion and extraversion, so too it is easier to learn about *management* if you learn about *both* Mainstream and Multistream approaches.

Third, learning two approaches to management helps students to develop their abilities to resist simple answers and to explore and integrate opposing ideas or viewpoints, both of which are hallmarks of outstanding managers.[57] In practice, managing is never as easy as it seems in a book, nor are the issues that managers face usually as straightforward as they might appear at first glance. Management is complex and filled with challenges, as managers seek to balance a variety of ideas and values. Thinking about two approaches to management helps you develop critical and integrative thinking skills. Moreover, learning more than one approach is particularly relevant because managers will be expected to change their approach during the course of their career, as they work in different contexts and with different people.

Fourth, studying two approaches to management helps to reduce bias because it serves as an ongoing reminder that managers' actions and practices are not value-neutral. This draws attention to the fact that it is impossible to develop management theory that is *not* based on some values. Thus both the Mainstream and the Multistream ideal-types are value-laden (i.e., each is based on a different set of values). Studying only one approach often acts as a self-fulfilling prophecy, such that students forget that the particular approach is based on specific values and increasingly adopt those values.[58] In contrast, learning two approaches enables and compels you to think about what your own moral point of view is and to ponder how it can be expressed in the workplace. This is particularly relevant, given that you will likely spend a significant portion of your life at work. Studying two approaches to management will help you to think about what kind of manager *you* want to become in the future. Where do you lie on the Mainstream–Multistream continuum, and to which ideal-type would you like to move closer as your career unfolds? You may feel drawn to either a Mainstream or a Multistream perspective, but you may also want to develop your own distinct approach to management.

In sum, we hope that our book helps readers to examine more closely their own ideals and aspirations related to management, echoing Socrates' observation that "the unexamined life is not worth living." When we fail to think about what we believe in and who we want to become, we are left vulnerable to wrongly believing that how we manage has nothing to do with our nature as moral persons. If we do not spell out our values, and if by default we unthinkingly accept a status quo moral point of view, then we deny our fundamental nature as moral persons and render a disservice to those around us. Similarly, if we impose our moral point of view on others (even if we do so unintentionally), then we deny *their* fundamental nature as moral persons and, therefore, render a disservice to the institution of management. We hope this book will help readers to explicitly examine, articulate, and consider how their values influence their thinking about management.

OVERVIEW OF THE REMAINDER OF THE BOOK

Figure 1.5 provides an overview of how this book will unfold. At the bottom of the figure is the context within which management takes place.

Before we describe each of the four management functions in greater detail, we explore the larger context of management in the next five chapters. First, we describe some of the history that has led to contemporary management theory and practice, and we consider how research into each of the four management functions has evolved over time (Chapter 2). We follow this with a discussion of the environment of management, including its sociocultural, ecological, political–legal, and economic–technological dimensions (Chapters 3 and 4). Chapter 5 looks at ethics, and Chapter 6 delves into entrepreneurship, the activity that creates the organizations.

Chapters 7 through 18 look at each of the four management functions in turn. The three chapters on planning focus on decision-making processes (Chapter 7), setting goals and making plans (Chapter 8), and organizational strategy (Chapter 9). They are followed by four chapters on structuring, including the four fundamentals of organizing (Chapter 10), different ways that organizations can be designed (Chapter 11), ways to structure human resources (Chapter 12), and the dynamics of organizational change (Chapter 13). Then come four chapters that look at leading, focusing on motivation (Chapter 14), leadership (Chapter 15), groups and teams (Chapter 16), and communication (Chapter 17). The final chapter examines the issue of control in organizations (Chapter 18).

Figure 1.5   Overview of flow of book

An Example of Multistream Management at Work

The chapter-opening case describes how the four management functions are evident in Jack Welch, a leading example of a manager who uses the Mainstream approach. The Multistream approach is exemplified by the management style of Robert Greenleaf, who is credited with coining the term "servant leadership." Greenleaf deliberately used what he called a "four-step disentangling process" while working as a senior manager at AT&T. Each of his four steps can be seen to illustrate a Multistream approach to one of the four functions of management. Here is an example of how he used this four-step process to get more women hired at AT&T.

First, Greenleaf noticed an injustice: Women were underrepresented in the AT&T workforce. Things were not as they should be (*controlling*). However, rather than blame individuals for causing the problem, Greenleaf realized that the problem was attributable to the traditional culture and values at AT&T. Indeed, he realized that he himself was part of a shared culture that did not treat women justly.

Second, rather than calling a meeting and demanding that his subordinates correct the problem, Greenleaf consciously exhibited self-control and adopted an inclusive and dignifying approach to discussing the issue with the managers responsible for making hiring decisions (*leading*).[59] When Greenleaf met with managers, for example, he deliberately started the conversation by talking about shared experiences and friendships at AT&T, and noting how well they had worked together in the past.

Third, Greenleaf exhibited practical wisdom by asking the other managers to help "disentangle" the problematic behavior from the traditions with which it was associated. Greenleaf did not use his hierarchical authority to generate or to impose solutions. Rather, he invited the managers who reported to him to discuss the traditions and structures that gave rise to the problem and, on this basis, to develop new ways to address the problem (*planning*). In this case, managers suggested that few women were hired because the job demanded regularly lifting 50-pound rolls of wire, which were too heavy for most women.

Finally, Greenleaf exhibited and facilitated courage when he actively supported any managers who were willing to experimentally implement changes to the structures and systems at AT&T (*organizing*). Managers who wished to experiment with using 25-pound rolls in the workplace were invited to do so, and in the end more women were hired (the men were also happier to have lighter rolls).

QUESTIONS FOR DISCUSSION

Robert Greenleaf and Jack Welch illustrate two different approaches to management. For whom would you prefer to work? Which person would you like to be your role model? Which person would you like to be at the helm of a firm in which you've invested? Explain your answers.

SUMMARY

The study of management is important for several reasons:

- It provides skills that make it more likely you will have opportunities to become a manager.
- It improves the working relationships you will have with your own bosses.
- It allows you to better understand how organizations operate.
- It facilitates a better understanding of who you are and what your life ambitions are.

The definition of management has two parts.

1. The four management functions:

- *Planning* involves deciding on an organization's goals and strategies.
- *Organizing* means ensuring that tasks have been assigned and a structure of organizational relationships created that facilitates the meeting of organizational goals.
- *Leading* means relating to others so that their work efforts help achieve organizational goals.
- *Controlling* means ensuring that the actions of organizational members are consistent with the organization's underpinning values and standards.

2. The criteria used to describe effective management:

- For *Mainstream* management, effectiveness comes from maximizing <u>m</u>aterialist–<u>in</u>dividualist outcomes (e.g., productivity, competitiveness, profitability).
- For *Multistream* management, effectiveness comes from finding a balance among <u>multi</u>ple forms of well-being (e.g., material, individual, social, ecological, intellectual, physical, and spiritual) for <u>multi</u>ple stakeholders (e.g., owners, members, customers, suppliers, competitors, and neighbors).

There are two types of management: Mainstream and Multistream.

1. For Mainstream managers, the four functions are being performed effectively when organizational efficiency, productivity, and competitiveness are maximized. The Mainstream approach tends to emphasize:

- Planning via measurable goals and rationally designed strategies
- Organizing via standardization, specialization, and centralization
- Leading via motivating others to achieve organizational goals
- Controlling via vigilant monitoring of organizational performance

2. For Multistream managers, the four functions are being performed effectively when virtues are practiced in the community and happiness is achieved. The Multistream approach tends to emphasize:

- Planning via practical wisdom, participation, and higher-order goals
- Organizing via courage and experimentation
- Leading via relational self-control and treating members with dignity
- Controlling via fairness and being sensitive to suboptimal conditions

All management theory and practice is value-laden. The two ideal-types presented in this book are designed to help readers think about and practice their own moral point of view of management.

QUESTIONS FOR REFLECTION AND DISCUSSION

1. Think for a moment about a current or past manager for whom you have worked. Would you characterize that person as a Mainstream or Multistream manager? Which factors did you take into account when classifying the manager?

2. What do *you* think constitutes "effective" management? Why?

3. Mainstream management has been the dominant approach in the industrialized world for more than a century, but Max Weber argued that it is not sustainable over the long term. Do you agree with Weber? Explain.

4. Identify the four functions of management. Describe how each function differs from a Mainstream approach versus a Multistream approach.

This exercise is designed to see how your understanding of effective management compares to that of other students. The questions ask how important you think different forms of well-being are to being an effective manager.

Rate each statement using the five-point scale provided. Your instructor will have information on how other students have answered these questions.

TO BE AN EFFECTIVE MANAGER, I SHOULD . . .	Strongly Disagree	Disagree	Neutral	Agree	Strongly Agree
1. Maximize organizational efficiency (e.g., minimize inputs while maximizing output).	1	2	3	4	5
2. Maximize organizational profitability.	1	2	3	4	5
3. Focus on maximizing productivity, efficiency, and profitability.	1	2	3	4	5
4. Maximize organizational productivity.	1	2	3	4	5
5. Genuinely care for the people around me.	1	2	3	4	5
6. Be a kind-hearted person.	1	2	3	4	5
7. Be a loyal and faithful person.	1	2	3	4	5
8. Be someone who generously "goes the extra mile" for those around me.	1	2	3	4	5
9. Look after my own self-interests first.	1	2	3	4	5
10. Expect the people around me to be looking after their self-interests first.	1	2	3	4	5
11. Look after the self-interests of shareholders.	1	2	3	4	5
12. Recognize that everyone is motivated to maximize their own self-interests.	1	2	3	4	5

ENDNOTES

1. Morris, B. (2006, July 24). The new rules. *Fortune,* 70–87; Hegele, C., & Kieser, A. (2001). Control the construction of your legend or someone else will: An analysis of texts on Jack Welch. *Journal of Management Inquiry,* 10(4), 298–309; Schwartz, N. D. (2007, July 22). Is G.E. too big for its own good? *New York Times.* Accessed February 7, 2008, at http://www.nytimes.com/2007/07/22/business/yourmoney/22ge.html?_r=1&scp=1&sq=&st=nyt&oref=slogin. O'Boyle, T. F. (1998). *At any cost: Jack Welch, General Electric, and the pursuit of profit.* New York: Alfred A. Knopf.
2. Robbins, S. P., & Coulter, M. (2003). *Management* (7th ed., p. 471). Upper Saddle River, NJ: Prentice Hall.
3. Griffin, R. W. (2002) *Management* (7th ed., p. 197). Boston, MA: Houghton Mifflin; Jones, G. R., & George, J. M. (2003). *Contemporary management* (3rd ed., p. 340). New York: McGraw-Hill.
4. Daft, R. L. (2003). *Management* (6th ed., p. 667). Mason, OH: Thomson South-Western.
5. Daft (2003), p. 560.
6. Robbins & Coulter (2003), p. 355.
7. Daft (2003), p. 667.
8. O'Boyle, T. F. (1998). *At any cost: Jack Welch, General Electric, and the pursuit of profit.* New York: Alfred A. Knopf. See also Litz, R. (2003). Book review essay: Looking at both sides—Jack Welch in review. *Academy of Management Review,* 28, 670–673.
9. Drucker, P. F. (2001). *The essential Drucker* (pp. 12–13). New York: HarperCollins.
10. One study found that in the United States, senior managers work an average of 44 hours per week. In Germany, senior managers work on average 38.6 hours per week and enjoy 29.7 holidays per year; in France, they work an average of 35.6 hours per work and take 32.3 holidays per year. Bloom, N., Dorgan, S., Dowdy, J., Van Reenen, J., & Rippin, T. (2005). *Management practices across firms and nations.* Working paper, Centre for Economic Performance, London School of Economics.
11. Fayol, H. (1916 [original in French]). *General and industrial management.* Dunod: Paris. Fayol actually identified a fifth function—coordination—but most scholars today believe the first four capture the functions of management.

12. Mintzberg, H. (1973). *The nature of managerial work*. New York: Harper & Row.

13. According to Mintzberg (1973, p. 54), a "role" is defined as an organized set of behaviors belonging to an identifiable office or position. Individual personality may affect *how* a role is performed, but not *that* it is performed.

14. The relative emphasis on the different roles changes across an organization's hierarchy, with the "leader" role being more important at lower levels, and top managers placing greater emphasis on the disseminator, figurehead, negotiator, liaison, and spokesperson roles (Robbins & Coulter, 2003, p. 9).

15. This discussion draws from a study that analyzes the videotapes of actual managers and uses the Fayolian functions and Mintzbergian roles to categorize each activity: Dyck, B., & Kleysen, R. (2001). Aristotle's virtues and management thought: An empirical exploration of an integrative pedagogy. *Business Ethics Quarterly*, 11(4), 561–574. Of course, our description here is somewhat of a simplification. For example, the spokesperson subrole is critical in both planning and leading, and the figurehead subrole is an important aspect of both controlling and organizing.

16. Part of this role includes taking inputs from other parts of the organization and disseminating information on overall organizational values to subordinates who use it as a guide in decision making. For Mintzberg, the dissemination of values occurs in terms of specific statements on specific issues, not in terms of lofty global principles (Mintzberg, 1973, p. 97).

17. Wrzesniewski, A., & Dutton, J. E. (2001). Crafting a job: Revisioning employees as active crafters of their work. *Academy of Management Review, 26*, 179–201.

18. The figurehead role can sometimes be seen as part of the leading function. We present it under the controlling function to draw attention to the importance of symbols in the controlling function.

19. This section draws on three papers. The Weberian "ideal-types" framework—and an extended discussion of the Multistream (also known as "radical") ideal-type—is presented in Dyck, B., & Schroeder, D. (2005). Management, theology and moral points of view: Towards an alternative to the conventional materialist–individualist ideal-type of management. *Journal of Management Studies, 42*(4), 705–735. The Mainstream and Multistream ideal-types are contrasted and compared in Dyck, B., & Weber, M. (2005). Conventional and radical moral agents: An exploratory look at Weber's moral-points-of-view and virtues. *Organization Studies, 27*(3), 429–450. We also draw on Dyck and Kleysen (2001).

20. Research also suggests that organic agriculture is about twice as efficient as conventional agriculture. Hoeppner, J. W., Entz, M. H., McConkey, B., Zentner, B., & Nagy, C., (2005). Energy use and efficiency in two Canadian organic and conventional crop production systems. *Renewable Agriculture and Food Systems, 19*, 1–8. Dyck, B. (1997). Build in sustainable development and they will come: A vegetable field of dreams. *British Food Journal, 99*(9), 325–335.

21. Indeed, it has been suggested that Weber's influence on organization studies may be unrivaled: Greenwood, R., & Lawrence, T. B. (2005). The Iron Cage in the information age: The legacy and relevance of Max Weber for organization studies [editorial]. *Organization Studies, 26*, 493–499.

22. Additional background material for this Weberian conceptual framework and description of the movement in the literature are provided in greater detail in Chapter 2.

23. Proponents of the Mainstream approach may downplay nonmaterial forms of well-being for a variety of reasons, including (1) a belief that the value of nonmaterial forms of well-being are more subjective, whereas the value of material wealth is objective, and (2) a belief that material wealth provides the means to acquire these other (perhaps more subjective) forms of wealth. For more discussion, see MacIntyre, A. (1984 [1981]). *After virtue: A study of moral theory* (2nd ed., pp. 25–25). Notre Dame, IN: University of Notre Dame Press.

24. Weber's argument has reverberated in the literature often over the past century; for a review, see Dyck and Schroeder (2005). In a recent example, Ferraro, Pfeffer, and Sutton underscore how materialist-individualist assumptions have served as a self-fulfilling prophecy. They suggest that economics (financial materialism) has "won the battle for theoretical hegemony in academia and society as a whole" (p. 10) and that its most fundamental idea is self-interest (individualism): Ferraro, F., Pfeffer, J., & Sutton, R. I. (2005). Economic language and assumptions: How theories can become self-fulfilling. *Academy of Management Review, 30*(1), 8–24.

25. We will return to this point in Chapter 2.

26. See studies cited in Ferraro, F., Pfeffer, J., & Sutton, R. I. (2005). Economic language and assumptions: How theories can become self-fulfilling. *Academy of Management Review, 30*(1), 8–24. See also Krishnan, V. R. (2003). Do business schools change students' values along desirable lines? A longitudinal study. In A. F. Libertella & S. M. Natale (Eds.), *Business education and training: A value-laden process* (Vol. 8, pp. 26–39). Lanham, MD: University Press of America.

27. Powdthavee, N. (2007 [in press]). Putting a price tag on friends, relatives, and neighbours: Using surveys of life satisfaction to value social relationships. *Journal of Socio-Economics*; and Harris, M. (2007, June 18). How much is a good friend worth to you? *Winnipeg Free Press*, p. A2.

28. See articles reviewed in Dyck and Schroeder (2005), as well as Kasser, T. (2003). *The high price of materialism*. Cambridge, MA: Bradford Book, MIT Press. A materialist–individualist lifestyle may contribute to lower satisfaction with life [Burroughs, J. E., & Rindfleisch, A. (2002). Materialism and well-being: A conflicting values perspective. *Journal of Consumer Research, 29*, 348–370], poorer interpersonal relationships [Richins, M. L., & Dawson, S. (1992). A consumer values orientation for materialism and its measurement: Scale development and validation. *Journal of Consumer Research, 19*, 303–316], and an increase in mental disorders [Cohen, P., & Cohen, J. (1996). *Life values and adolescent mental health*. Mahway, NJ: Erlbaum]. An important exception is for the very poorest among us, for whom materialism is positively correlated with well-being and life satisfaction.

29. Tierney, J. (2008, March 20). Yes, money can buy happiness . . . *New York Times*. Accessed March 24, 2008, at http://tierneylab.blogs.nytimes.com/2008/03/20/yes-money-can-buy-happiness/. See also Dunn, E. W., L. B. Aknin, and M. I. Norton (2008, March 21). Spending Money on Others Promotes Happiness. *Science, 319*(5870), 1687–1688.

30. For example, perspectives such as corporate social responsibility and sustainable management offer a counterpoint to the Mainstream approach's focus on maximizing the self-interests of shareholders.

31. Smith, A. (1982 [1759]). *The theory of moral sentiments* (D. D. Raphael & A. L. Macfie, Eds.; Glasgow ed.). Indianapolis, IN: Liberty Press.

32. "The man who acts according to the rules of perfect prudence, of strict justice, and of proper benevolence, may be said to be

perfectly virtuous. But the most perfect knowledge of those rules will not alone enable him to act in this manner: his own passions are very apt to mislead him; sometimes to drive him and sometimes to seduce him to violate all the rules which he himself, in all his sober and cool hours, approves of. The most perfect knowledge, if it is not supported by the most perfect self-command, will not always enable him to do his duty (Smith, 1982, p. 237)."

33. E. F. Schumacher, in his cleverly subtitled book *Small Is Beautiful: A Study of Economics as if People Mattered* (1973, London: Blond & Briggs), argues that there are many classic moral points of view that could be used to underpin an alternative to the Mainstream approach. In particular, he suggests that "there is perhaps no body of teaching which is more relevant and appropriate to the modern predicament than the marvelously subtle and realistic doctrines of the Four Cardinal Virtues—*prudential* [practical wisdom], *justitia* [justice], *fortitudo* [courage], and *temperentia* [self-control] (pp. 248–249). This section draws heavily from Dyck and Kleysen (2001), who use Aristotle's discussion of "community" as a springboard to apply these concepts to contemporary organizations, even though the modern notions of organization and management would have been unfathomable to Aristotle. Of course, the challenge that others have raised [e.g., Hartman, Edwin M. (1998). The role of character in business ethics. *Business Ethics Quarterly*, 8, 547–559; MacIntyre (1984 [1981]); and Mintz, S. M. (1996). Aristotelian virtue and business ethics education. *Journal of Business Ethics*, 15, 827–838], and that informs this textbook is to make virtues observable in management practice and a relevant guiding framework for management theory. Dyck and Kleysen (2001) were surprised to find that, on average, students were able to classify a greater percentage of videotapes of managers' workdays using Aristotle's virtues than either Mintzberg's roles or Fayol's functions.

34. Aristotle. (1962). *Nichomachean ethics* (trans. M. Oswald). New York: MacMillan.

35. Just as Fayol's original functions have been adapted and reformulated over time to fit and reflect contemporary concerns, so too we have adapted Aristotle's four cardinal virtues for our discussion. Toward this end, we found the work of Solomon particularly helpful: Solomon, R. C. (1992). *Ethics and excellence: Cooperation and integrity in business*. Oxford, UK: Oxford University Press. Thus our description of wisdom, justice, courage, and self-control takes into account contextual and embedded quality of virtues as relevant for present-day managers.

36. This trend is evident in survey data [e.g., New American Dream. (2004). More of what matters survey report. www.newdream .org], popular media and books [e.g., extensive coverage of Aaron Feuerstein and Malden Mills; books such as Batstone, D. (2003). *Saving the corporate soul—and (who knows?) maybe your own: Eight principles for creating and preserving wealth and well-being for you and your company without selling out*. San Francisco: Jossey-Bass]; scholarly research and pedagogical journals [e.g., Ferraro et al. (2005); Ghoshal, S. (2005). Bad management theories are destroying good management practices. *Academy of Management Learning and Education*, 4(1), 75–91; Kanter, R. M. (2005). What theories do audiences want? Exploring the demand side. *Academy of Management Learning and Education*, 4(1), 93–95; Mintzberg, H. (2005). How inspiring. How sad. Comment on Sumantra Ghoshal's paper. *Academy of Management Learning and Education*, 4, 108; and Pfeffer, J. (2005). Why do bad management theories persist? A comment on Ghoshal.

Academy of Management Learning and Education, 4(1), 96–100]; and growing interests in a variety of theoretical perspectives including stakeholder theory, corporate social responsibility, ecological concerns, work–life balance, and so on.

37. Daniels, D., Norman, C. S., & Stewart, I. (2004). A profile of the millennial generation: Implications for teaching and learning in the business classroom. *Journal of the Academy of Business Education*, 5(Fall), 50–62; Howe, N., & Straus, W. (2000). *Millennials rising*. New York: Vintage Books. http://www.millennialsrising .com/aboutbook.shtml; Olian, J. (2007). The Millennials and us. *eNEWSLINE*, 6(7), AACSB International. Accessed July 17, 2007, at http://www.aacsb.edu/publications/enewsline/Vol-6/Issue-7/ ChairsExchange.asp?nav=n; and Rivedal, K. (2005, June 20). The changing face of college graduates. *Wisconsin State Journal*.

38. Barbaro, M., & Abelson, R. (2007, November 13). A health plan for Wal-Mart: Less stinginess. *New York Times*. Accessed February 7, 2008, at http://www.nytimes.com/2007/11/13/business/ 13walmart.html?scp=1&sq=&st=nyt; Cascio, W. F. (2006). Decency means more than "always low price": A comparison of Costco to Wal-Mart's Sam's Club. *Academy of Management Perspectives*, 20(3), 26–37; At Costco, "good jobs and good wages." (2004, May 31). *BusinessWeek* online. Accessed February 7, 2008, at http://www.businessweek.com/magazine/content/04_22/ b3885011_mz001.htm; Holmes, S., & Zellner, W. (2004, April 12). The Costco way. *BusinessWeek* online. Accessed February 7, 2008, at http://www.businessweek.com/magazine/content/04_ 15/b3878084_mz021.htm.

39. Public pressure has resulted in Wal-Mart improving its healthcare plan, but its insurance still pales when compared to that offered by Costco.

40. When Wal-Mart's average hourly wage for full-time employees was $9.64, Costco's average hourly wage was $15.97; the average hourly wage at Sam's Club, a more direct competitor to Costco, was $11.52.

41. Costco's employee turnover rate is about 17 percent, compared to 44 percent for Wal-Mart. Moreover, Costco has the lowest "inventory shrinkage" (i.e., employee theft) rate in the industry at 0.2 percent of sales (the industry average is 1.7 percent). Costco employees are also known for their innovative ideas to increase company revenues faster than labor costs. For example, Costco has been especially adept at finding new ways to repackage goods and to cater to small-shop owners. Costco was the first wholesale club to offer fresh meat, pharmacies, and in-store photo labs.

42. Practical wisdom is the opposite of an attitude to life that is small and calculating, and "[that] refuses to see and value anything that fails to promise an immediate utilitarian advantage" (Schumacher, 1973, p. 249).

43. When Mintz (1996, p. 829) notes that wisdom is an "intellectual" virtue and is considered to be "the consequence of teaching and for that reason requires experience and time to be cultivated," he draws particular attention to the responsibility of scholars and leaders who shape how we think about and understand management.

44. To nurture oneself as an intimate part of a community, for example, courage implies resisting the ongoing pressures for impression management, job-hopping, and self-aggrandizement in today's organizations, all of which may potentially undermine other virtues necessary for community, such as honesty, loyalty, and trust.

45. According to one study (Batstone, 2003), in 1980 the pay of the average CEO of a large company was 42 times greater than that of

nonsupervisory workers. In 1995, it was 160 times greater, and in 2000 it was 458 times greater.

46. Benefiel, M. (2005). *Soul at work* (p. 21). New York: Seabury Books.

47. Mishel, L. (2006). CEO pay-to-minimum wage ratio soars. Economic Prosperity Institute: Research for Broadly Shared Prosperity. Accessed August 21, 2007, at http://www.epinet.org/content .cfm/webfeatures_snapshots_20060627.

48. Taken from Gutstein, S. E., & Sheely, R. K. (2002). Friendships are relationships. In *Relationship development intervention with young children* (pp. 17–22). London: Jessica Kingsley Publishers. (Emphasis added here.)

49. Taken from Gutstein and Sheely (2002). (Emphasis added here.)

50. Goleman, D., Boyatzis, D., & McKee, A. (2002). *Primal leadership: Realizing the power of emotional intelligence.* Cambridge, MA: HBR Press.

51. Kennedy, R. (2006, April 17). At some medical schools, humanities join the curriculum. *New York Times.* Accessed February 7, 2008, at http://www.nytimes.com/2006/04/17/arts/design/17sina .html?ex51146024000&en56412dcc4b97ef90c&ei55070&emc5eta1.

52. As cofounder of the company, Sinegal also owns a lot of Costco's stock and is worth about $150 million on paper. See Cascio, W. F. (2006). Decency means more than "always low price": A comparison of Costco to Wal-Mart's Sam's Club. *Academy of Management Perspectives,* 20 (3/August), 26–37.

53. Solomon (1992).

54. Bradach, J. L., & Eccles, R. G. (1989). Price authority, and trust: From ideal types to plural forms. *Annual Review of Sociology,* 15, 97–118; Ouchi, W. (1980). Markets, bureaucracies, and clans. *Administrative Science Quarterly,* 25, 129–141; and Powell, W. W. (1990). Neither market nor hierarchy: Network forms of organization. *Research in Organizational Behavior,* 12, 295–336.

55. Giacalone, R. A., & Thompson, K. R. (2006). Business ethics and social responsibility education: Shifting the worldview. *Academy of Management Learning and Education,* 5(3), 266–277. See also Ghoshal, S. (2005). Bad management theories are destroying good management practices. *Academy of Management Learning and Education,* 4, 75–91; and Bennis, W. (2000). *Managing the dream: Reflections on leadership and change.* New York: Perseus.

56. This is based on two studies described in Dyck, B., Walker, K., Starke, F., & Uggerslev, K. (In press). What happens when management students are taught to question the materialist–individualist status quo? Three exploratory studies. *Working paper,* University of Manitoba. See also Dyck et al. (2006).

57. Martin, R. (2007). How successful managers think. *Harvard Business Review,* 85(6), 60–67.

58. Research suggests that business students become increasingly materialist–individualist over their program of studies, thanks to the self-fulfilling prophecies that underlie the Mainstream paradigm they are taught. For a review, see Ferraro, Pfeffer, & Sutton (2005) [recipient of the Academy of Management Review's "Best Paper of the Year"]. See also Krishnan, V. R. (2003). Do business schools change students' values along desirable lines? A longitudinal study. In A. F. Libertella & S. M. Natale (Eds.), *Business education and training: A value-laden process* (Vol. 8, pp. 26–39). Lanham, MD: University Press of America.

59. He specifically talked about adopting a "friendly manner" at this stage, thereby reflecting the nature of the kinds of interpersonal relationships he sought to nurture in the workplace.

CHAPTER 2

In this chapter, we will describe some of the key formative ideas and people who have helped to develop the management theory and practice that we take for granted today. We must travel back in time several centuries to understand where today's emphasis on materialism and individualism came from, to identify pioneers who developed methods for managing large-scale organizations, and to understand how our views of organizations have changed over time. Once we have made this journey, we will be ready to focus on important contributions to the management literature that have been made over the past century. We conclude the chapter with a look at where management theory and practice may be heading in your future.

ROAD MAP

	Background for Contemporary Management Theory and Practice	**HALLMARKS OF CONTEMPORARY**	
		Organizing	**Leading**
Era	*Reformation/ Industrial Revolution*	*Classical*	*Human*
Years	*After 1530*	*1910–1930*	*1930–1950*
Key ideas associated with each era (and names of exemplary contributors)	Unprecedented emphasis on materialism and individualism (Weber) Industrial Revolution: pioneers of modern large-scale management (Wedgwood) Increasing prevalence and size of corporations	"One best way" Micro approach: scientific management (Taylor) Time-and-motion studies (F. Gilbreth) Macro approach: bureaucracy (Weber) Basic organizing principles (Fayol)	Interpersonal aspects of management Leader as facilitator (Follet) Job stress (L. Gilbreth) Informal structure (Barnard) "Hawthorne effect"/SFP (Mayo & Roethlisberger) Theory X/Y (McGregor)

A Short History of Management Theory and Practice

MANAGEMENT THEORY AND PRACTICE

Planning	Controlling	Future of Management Theory and Practice
Calculating	*Values and beliefs*	*Reconsidering/call for Multistream approach*
1950–1970	*1970–1990*	*1990–present*
Management science; operations research/management; strategic management	Social construction of reality (Berger & Luckmann)	Corporate social responsibility; stakeholder theory; servant leadership; positive psychology; social entrepreneurship
Systems theory (Katz & Kahn)	Institutionalization (Selznick, Zucker)	Mainstream emphasis on maximizing materialist–individualist goals (e.g., profitability, productivity, competitiveness) gets in the way of other forms of well-being (e.g., social, ecological, spiritual, physical, aesthetic)
Bounded rationality (Simons)	"Natural" facts of daily life are really "moral" (Garfinkel)	
Mechanistic versus organic structures (Burns & Stalker)	Organizational culture (Schein)	
Contingency theory and strategic choice (Child)		

Josiah Wedgwood and the Rise of Mainstream Management[1]

To understand origins of contemporary management, it is helpful to go back at least as far as the Industrial Revolution, which started around 1760 in Great Britain—a colonial superpower at the time—and eventually spread to other countries by the 1800s. The Industrial Revolution was facilitated by the interplay among sociocultural factors, economic/technological factors, political/legal factors, and, of course, new management techniques.

The story of how Josiah Wedgwood's company came to dominate the pottery industry provides insight into the origins of the distinctive features of modern-day management and can help us understand why his way of managing spread to many other organizations. Wedgwood was a British entrepreneur whose managerial genius over a period of 40 years starting in 1759 helped to transform a geographic region that had been an economic backwater—around Manchester, England—into one of the leading growth areas of the Industrial Revolution.

Sociocultural Factors

Whereas today it is taken for granted that factory work takes place in a regimented setting (e.g., show up for work on time, work according to standard rules), such was not the case for the core of Wedgwood's workforce. Many of Wedgwood's employees had grown up as self-sufficient serfs or peasants who had been forced off the land that they had been farming for generations when the common lands on feudal manors were fenced in to raise sheep. They were accustomed to working in short spurts (usually Tuesday through Friday) and then using the rest of the time for feasting, drinking, gambling, and sheer idleness. These employees were accustomed to flexible working hours and to taking time off for "St. Monday" and for every fair and wake. By today's standards, it was a simple and hard life with little material wealth, with an average life expectancy of approximately 40 years.

The emergence of new religious teachings helps to explain in part why people would be willing to change

their lifestyle and begin to work regimented hours. In Wedgwood's case, the legitimization of a materialist–individualist view came by way of John Wesley, who began preaching in the region in 1760. While most of his competitors greeted Wesley with a mixture of hostility and indifference, Wedgwood provided support and encouragement for the preacher, and within a year Wesley had a large congregation. Wesley "convinced the poor that they had their proper worth before God. He also convinced them that to be 'saved' they must live more sober and respectable lives."[2] In short, the message was that everyone was called by God to their job, that God wanted people to work hard in their jobs, and that doing so would lead to salvation and material blessings.

Economic/Technological Factors

Such a gospel was good news to people like Wedgwood, because it blessed the pursuit of wealth, and because it helped to create a disciplined and motivated workforce. It also legitimized an economy that valued material "luxuries" (such as fine pottery for drinking tea). When Josiah Wedgwood started his small pottery operation in 1759, part of his motivation was to exploit the opportunity that was being created by the growing demand for earthenware associated with the general rise in the British standard of living and the growth of tea and coffee drinking in England (a middle-class custom) in particular.[3] This demand had already inspired the formation of many small pottery firms. Wedgwood recognized that to capture a significant share of this growing market, he needed to produce better and less expensive pottery than his competitors. At the time, those firms were also small organizations characterized by a simple division of labor and a master–worker hierarchy. Wedgwood knew that he needed to offer a truly excellent product, so he carried out 7000 experiments to develop a form of pottery—which he called "Queen's Ware"—that could be made cheaply and quickly but was still attractive enough to be used even by royalty.

Political/Legal Factors

Wedgwood was able to persuade government officials to pay for transportation infrastructure improvements that were key to his gaining an edge over his smaller competitors. When Wedgwood started his firm, the transportation infrastructure in his region was dismal, and losses from transporting finished goods on packhorses over muddy roads frequently amounted to 30 percent of an order. Wedgwood joined with other potters in his area to lobby first for a new turnpike to get transport goods to Liverpool (completed in 1763), and then for a canal to reduce the cost of acquiring raw materials and enable the shipping of pottery by barge to larger cities (approved by 1766). Wedgwood purchased land beside the waterway and erected his new factory there.[4]

Wedgwood also benefited from other governmental regulations, such as those governing whom he could hire and how the economic gains of his company were distributed. For example, by 1790, approximately 25 percent of Wedgwood's staff were children, many of them girls who were paid about the same amount as apprentices had earned 100 years earlier.[5] The lion's share of the economic benefits of his firm went to Wedgwood. When he died in 1795, he left £500,000 to his estate—more than $64 million in today's U.S. dollars.[6]

Management Techniques

Imagine a time when division of labor was a novelty, when disciplined work hours were unusual, and when ideas about standardization were considered revolutionary. What is commonplace today was industrial espionage two centuries ago, when Wedgwood's competitors learned how to bureaucratize the making of pottery by luring his employees away and persuading them to spill Wedgwood's secrets.

Wedgwood devised an intricate system of rewards and punishments for his workers. For example, bringing alcohol onto the premises resulted in withholding of 10 percent of the worker's weekly pay. He also promoted his best employees to higher-paid positions to encourage obedient and competent performance, and he made deliberate efforts to ensure that employees who were punctual received verbal praise and commendation. Within ten years, these inducements helped Wedgwood to transform what he had described as "drunken, idle workmen" into "a very good set of hands"[7] who believed that Wedgwood was a "kind and good employer."[8] His employees worked much harder and longer than his competitors' employees, typically ten hours per day, six days per week, with only two holidays each year. Long gone was the practice of working three days per week and partying for four, and his workers lost much variety, liberty, and opportunities for social enjoyment as a result of Wedgwood's system.

Wedgwood's management techniques completely revolutionized the pottery industry, and they served as a model for his competitors to mimic. Those who ignored the new way of working did so at their peril—at the risk of bankruptcy. Traditional small-scale firms simply could not compete with Wedgwood's organization, which featured hard-working employees who consistently produced high-quality outputs. By 1790, Wedgwood had 220 employees and was producing about the same volume of goods as his 150 smaller competitors combined.

Introduction to Management History

The idea of *studying* management is barely a century old, yet today management is an undeniably popular course in colleges and universities. Management has become an unavoidable feature of modern life. However, we often forget that our modern-day understanding of management is relatively new, and that it is a subjective, socially constructed concept.[9] Put differently, the idea of "management" was invented and is constantly being reinvented by people who, like us, live in a specific social context. For example, as we saw in Chapter 1, management can

The meaning of the Liberty Bell has changed along with the societal transformations it has been used to symbolically support. Initially, it was used to symbolize Americans' freedom from British rule. Later, the Liberty Bell was used to symbolize the freedom of African Americans from slavery. More recently, it was used as a symbol in women's fight to gain equal rights with men.

be seen as performing the four management functions—planning, organizing, leading, and controlling—so as (1) to maximize productivity, profitability, and competitiveness (Mainstream approach) *or* (2) to achieve a balance among multiple forms of well-being for multiple stakeholders (Multistream approach).

To illustrate the importance of studying the history of management and to see how it is a socially constructed concept, we can look at how other socially constructed ideas have changed over time. For example, consider what it means to be a woman or a man, and how that understanding has changed over time. Not so long ago women were treated as "objects" owned by men. Three generations ago, American women did not even have the right to vote. Similarly, the wage gap between men and women is narrowing: Since 1970, women's pay as a percentage of men's pay has increased from approximately 60 percent to approximately 80 percent in the United States.[10] Clearly, the meaning of gender is changing, and it will continue to do so in the future. Other examples include changing social attitudes toward the use of language and sexual innuendo on daytime television, and changing views on violence in entertainment and children's video games. In the same way, the social construction of what it means to be a manager has also changed over the years.

Keep in mind that every way of seeing management is also a way of *not* seeing management. For example, if management textbooks do not provide an in-depth treatment of the ecological environment in their chapters on "managing the environment," then students may see ecological concerns as an unimportant aspect of the environment for managers. Similarly, when we expect *managers* to make the most important decisions in an organization, then there are fewer opportunities for non-managers to make important decisions. And if we see management as being primarily about maximizing materialist–individualist well-being, then other forms of well-being become secondary and subservient to that perspective.

We will begin our brief tour of the history of management theory by reviewing some of the important antecedent conditions that influenced the development of management theory and practice. We will then provide a brief overview of the development of management thought over the past century.

As the chapter-opening case suggests, many historical events have shaped how management has been studied since the early twentieth century. We will highlight two that are of particular importance: (1) the origins of our emphasis on maximizing materialism and individualism, which form the basis of Mainstream management, and (2) the increasing prevalence and size of organizations.

THE EMPHASIS ON INDIVIDUALISM AND MATERIALISM

Max Weber (1864–1920), who was perhaps the most influential scholar in the field of management and organizational theory,[11] suggests that what we now call Mainstream management can be characterized by its emphasis on materialism and individualism.[12] To understand how this materialist–individualist emphasis is not simply a rational or objective expression of the way things are, it is helpful to briefly review how it came to be. Ours is the first time in the history of humankind that an economic system has been based on the principle of economic *gain*. Prior to the 1400s and the end of feudalism in Western Europe, all known economic systems were based on one or more of the following three principles:

- **Reciprocity**—neighborliness, trading with one another
- **Redistribution**—ensuring that everyone has enough
- **Householding**—being a good steward of resources for the sake of the family or larger community[13]

According to Weber, the present-day secular emphasis on materialism and individualism can be traced back to religious teachings associated with the European reformation that started about 500 years ago. A central feature of these teachings was that God *calls* individuals to their specific work, and that God is interested in how *individuals* perform their day-to-day jobs. According to Weber, this soon was interpreted to mean that individuals' eternal salvation would be evident in how well they lived out their calling in their everyday jobs. The emphasis on *individual* works stood in contrast to the previously held view that forgiveness and salvation came via the larger *church* (e.g., via holy sacraments and confession to a priest).[14] Further legitimacy for individualism came from the publication and popular interpretation of Adam Smith's (1776) *Wealth of Nations*. As Smith imaginatively put it, an "invisible hand" would guide apparently chaotic individualism toward collective good. In short, over time individualism was transformed from being "unheard of in most ancient societies" into a secular virtue of the highest order.[15]

Materialism, the second defining feature of a Mainstream view, also arose from the emphasis on calling. As one famous reformation preacher said, "Religion must necessarily produce both industry and frugality [via individuals living out their calling], and these cannot help but produce riches."[16] This link between eternal salvation and earthly material wealth provided unprecedented legitimacy to the pursuit of profit.[17] Prior to the legitimation of materialism, the accumulation of wealth had been seen as a vice—that is, an unwillingness to share resources.

Weber argues that this materialist–individualist worldview has become the dominant and a wholly secularized societal view that people now take for granted (i.e., it no longer needs to be based on religious values). Moreover, in one of the most well-known sociological metaphors, he argues that we have been captured in an "iron cage" because we care too much about material goods:

> *The care for external goods* should only lie on the shoulders of the "saint like a light cloak, which can be thrown aside at any moment." But fate has decreed that the cloak should become an *iron cage*. . . . material goods have gained an increasing and finally inexorable power over the lives of men [sic] as at no previous period in history.[18]

Reciprocity refers to an economic system organized around the principles of neighborliness and trading with one another.

Redistribution refers to an economic system organized around the principle that everyone should have enough.

Householding is an economic system organized around the principle of being a good steward of resources for the sake of the family or larger community.

Self-help books on wealth and success continue to be best-sellers.

For Weber, the **iron cage** is an "irresistible force" that compels us all to live and work in a world where materialist–individualist goals are treated as more important than other forms of well-being, where maximizing financial self-interests overwhelms other considerations, and where this view is seen as a natural fact of life. According to Weber, in our pursuit of self-interested financial wealth we have lost the essence of our humanity: "Specialists without spirit, sensualists without heart; this nullity imagines that it has attained a level of civilization never before achieved."[19] Weber challenges us to embrace a more balanced approach to management, where materialist–individualist goals are not seen as primary.

Iron cage is Max Weber's metaphor for the force that causes people to live and work in a world where materialist–individualist goals trump other forms of well-being, where maximizing financial self-interests overwhelms other considerations, and where this is seen as a natural fact of life.

 WHAT DO YOU THINK?

Are We Still Enslaved in the Iron Cage?

Max Weber believed that the materialist–individualist worldview had achieved its highest form of development in the United States, where the pursuit of wealth had become associated with the everydayness of life, and it could be characterized as a "sport" with well-defined winners and losers. Is that perception still accurate today? What are the "games" being played in our world today?

How do we decide who are the "winners" and who are the "losers" in our society? Are our judgments based on how "compassionate" someone is, or how "generous," or how "humble"? Or are our perceptions based on how much money and power someone has, and how well dressed he or she is? What influences our attitudes toward life priorities, body image, and the environment?

The media certainly have a lot of power in shaping what we think is important and worth striving for in our lives. Consider the fact that by the time he or she graduates from high school, the average U.S. teenager will have seen 350,000 commercials. Every day you receive 3000 messages to buy something, via television advertisements, newspapers, magazines, T-shirts, shopping bags, radio ads, movies, sponsorships, and so on. The average adult sees 21,000 commercials per year. Corporations spend more money on trying to get us to buy their stuff than is spent on all of secondary education in the United States.[20] That's a lot of money and effort being invested into telling us what is important—that is, telling us what we need to do to become winners.

Have our lives really become dominated by the primacy of materialism and individualism, where our sense of well-being depends on our material wealth? Or are we placing increasingly greater emphasis on other forms of well-being (e.g., social, physical, and ecological wellness)? Has the iron cage tightened in the past century, or are we becoming increasingly liberated from commercialization, consumerism, and self-interested wealth maximization?

THE INCREASING DOMINANCE AND SIZE OF CORPORATIONS

Until a few centuries ago, there were very few large organizations like the type that are so common today. One exception was the Roman Catholic Church—currently numbering about 1.2 billion people—which has been the largest organization in the world for centuries. Historically, other significant organizations included guilds,[21] various nation-states and city-states, and occasional empires. Until recently, most work took place in very small businesses (often called cottage industries because work was literally done in cottages). Many family firms existed, in which the owner was the manager and was personally related to most of the workers. Because organizations were small, workers knew how their work fit into the whole, and a strong sense of community and interdependence was evident in the workplace.[22]

Over time, this emphasis on working in small-scale organizations started to change, facilitated in part by a variety of social, technological, and legal changes (see the chapter-opening case about Josiah Wedgwood and the Industrial Revolution). Adam Smith's description of a "pin factory," published in 1776, provides what is perhaps the single best example to help us understand the shift that occurred when people moved toward working in factories and away from working in households. Smith demonstrated the merits of specialization and a "division of labor" by describing how four workers, each performing a specialized task, could produce 48,000 pins per day instead of the 12 pins per day that each would produce working independently and doing all the tasks. By "rationalizing" work in factories, productivity could be dramatically increased. Smith's analysis was compelling, and it reflected how the Industrial Revolution was changing both the sites where people worked (in factories) and the type of work they did (highly specialized and repetitive).

A brief history of corporations is in order at this point.[23] Modern management would not be possible without changes to the social and legal meanings attached to an organization. Traditionally, most "businesses" were seen as an extension of a household. However, profound changes took place when organizations were given a life of their own and were allowed to act as legal citizens. The privileges associated with incorporation were granted because organizations were supposed to enhance the common good, and their corporate charter was to be taken away if they failed to act in the common good. This responsibility to act for the common good extended far beyond merely maximizing the financial investments of owners and shareholders.

Before the advent of the corporation, any debts that businesspeople incurred were passed on from one generation to the next. As a result, people might find themselves forced to pay for their grandparents' failed business or else risk being thrown into prison.[24] This situation changed with the arrival of **limited liability**, which simply means that the organization's owners are not personally responsible for financial costs that exceed the amount they invested in the organization. In other words, owners of a corporation can limit the amount of money that they are liable to pay if things go bad. For example, if you invested $10,000 in a pizza company, and the company went bankrupt while owing $100,000 to different suppliers, the most you could lose as the business owner would be $10,000.

The history of modern corporations and the idea of limited liability can be traced back approximately 500 years, to the time when European states established corporate charters to fund the exploration of the New World. Ships that sailed from England or Spain to trade for spices in the East Indies took big risks during these journeys: They could be hit by deadly storms, attacked by pirates, or lose their

Limited liability refers to the concept (and resulting legislation) that an organization's owners are not liable for financial costs greater than the amount they have invested in the organization.

Figure 2.1 *Fortune 500* companies are getting bigger and bigger

In a span of 11 years at the end of the twentieth century, the profits of the top 500 corporations in the United States more than doubled from $167 billion to $451 billion, and these firms' share of the total profits of the private sector increased from 52 percent to 58 percent. This growth can be seen as a measure of success, or possibly a measure of increased influence.

precious cargo at sea. To make it feasible for businesspeople to engage in the important economic work of international trade and discovery, the corporate form was established, whereby shareholders were limited to liabilities no greater than their investments. As a result, Europeans became more willing to engage in the risky and expensive commercial projects of their day. This strategy followed them to North America, where corporations were given charters expressly for the building of canals, turnpikes, and other public infrastructures.

For several centuries, it was difficult to get a charter to start a corporation, except for those very special large-scale projects that were clearly in the public interest and could not be completed otherwise. Even in the United States, only several hundred corporations existed at the beginning of the nineteenth century. Citizens were wary that corporations, whether domestic or foreign, for-profit or not-for-profit, might threaten their newly won democratic freedoms. Indeed, "citizens openly and presciently expressed concern that corporations with specific rights granted under the charters would nevertheless become so powerful that they could take over newspapers, public opinion, elections, and the judiciary. . . . Some states even required public votes to *continue* certain charters."[25]

Over time, however, corporations lobbied the government, gained more power, and became more prevalent. For example, U.S. business was transformed with the reinterpretation of the Fourteenth Amendment—originally introduced to protect the rights of former slaves—to provide the power of a "natural person" to corporations.[26] It has been argued that corporations have turned the Bill of Rights upside down:

> The first Amendment, guaranteeing the right of every citizen to engage in free speech, was established to encourage, promote, and preserve democratic institutions. . . . By invoking the First Amendment privilege to protect their "speech," corporations achieve precisely what the Bill of Rights was intended to prevent: domination of public thought and discourse. Although corporations profess that they are legitimately exercising their democratic rights in their attempt to influence the government, their argument presupposes that all parties from the single voter to the multinational company have an equal voice in the political debates surrounding important issues.[27]

The influence of corporations on government policy and social thought continues to grow, through advertising and lobbying and think tanks (see Chapter 3). For good or for bad, we have come a long way from the idea of "limited liability" designed to protect corporations from risks similar to those faced by European explorers or builders of public infrastructure projects that enhance the common good. Indeed, as Figure 2.1 shows, corporations have come to dominate much of the private sector.[28]

FIVE ERAS OF MANAGEMENT THOUGHT

The formal study of management is about a century old. As depicted in Figure 2.2, the history of management theory has evolved in five phases.[29] Each of the first four phases corresponds roughly to one of Fayol's four functions of management (which were introduced in Chapter 1). The fifth phase, which we are currently in, is one that questions the Mainstream answer to the meaning of "effective" management. Of course, within each phase, helpful research has been done in all four management functions. Even so, there are identifiable changes over time in terms of the relative emphasis being placed on the various aspects of management. In the sections that follow, we describe the essential features of each of these phases.

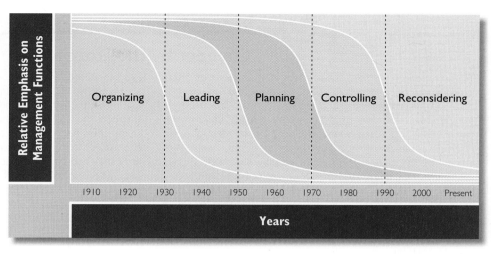

Figure 2.2   **Simplified overview of relative emphases in management research**

In the early years, emphasis was placed on developing the best way to structure and design organizational work (organizing, 1910–1930). This emphasis on organizing continues to this day, but some unexpected research findings in the 1930s triggered a shift in relative emphasis to leading (1930–1950). Later, the focus shifted to planning (1950–1970), triggered by research that was initially conducted in an effort to increase production during World War II, when many able-bodied workers were serving in the military. The social unrest and countercultural movements of the 1960s inspired new interest in controlling (1970–1990). Finally, as a result of increasing recognition of the need for nurturing community and environmentally friendly sustainable development, today's reconsidering phase is characterized by a growing challenge to the materialist–individualist management paradigm.

An Emphasis on Organizing: The "Classical" Era (1910 to 1930)

The "classical" era can be subdivided into two separate schools of thought. The first has a "micro" focus (looking at how to design specific jobs), whereas the second has a "macro" focus (looking at how the various jobs fit together in an organization). The micro approach, called **scientific management,** focuses on defining and maximizing the productivity of *individual jobs.* The macro approach, called **bureaucracy,** focuses on the structure and functions of management so as to maximize productivity of the *overall organization.*

Scientific Management refers to the rational study of tasks and people in order to design and maximize the productivity of *individual jobs.*

Bureaucracy refers to a rational way of organizing based on formal rules, a clear division of labor, and legitimate authority for managers.

THE MICRO APPROACH.   Frederick W. Taylor (1856–1915) is often called "the father of scientific management." His philosophy has been captured in this statement: "In the past, man [sic] has been first. In the future, the system must be first."[30] Taylor's most famous study helped increase the shoveling productivity at the Bethlehem Steel plant in Pennsylvania. At the time, workers brought their own shovels to the plant. Taylor carried out studies to determine the best-sized shovel for the different weights of materials being shoveled. In one study, after management provided optimally designed shovels for workers, the average output per worker increased almost 280 percent, from 12.5 tons per day to 47.5 tons per day. At the same time, workers' pay was increased about 60 percent from $1.15 per day to $1.85 per day. This was seen as a "win-win" situation, and Taylor's ideas and methods quickly spread throughout industry.[31]

MANAGEMENT IN PRACTICE

Cheaper by the Dozen

To their credit, the pioneers of scientific management often lovingly practiced at home what they preached in factories. For example, when Frank and Lillian Gilbreth were on their honeymoon, they were discussing how many children to have. Frank suggested a dozen would be an ideal and efficient number, because many things were cheaper if purchased by the dozen. The couple actually did have 12 children, and they often used management science techniques in managing their own household. For example, Frank would make movies of his children washing dishes so that he could analyze the work and subdivide it into its basic steps to al-low his children to complete the task more efficiently. Process and work charts were installed in the bathroom, which the Gilbreth children had to initial in the morning after they had brushed their teeth, taken a bath, combed their hair, and made their bed. In the evening, the children had to weigh themselves and plot the figure on a graph, and initial charts after they had done their homework, washed their hands and face, and brushed their teeth. Gilbreth also provided record players in the bathrooms to play foreign-language lessons, so that his children could learn new languages as they went about their daily business.[32]

Gantt Chart is a bar graph that managers use to schedule and allocate resources for a production job. It identifies various stages of work that need to be completed, sets deadlines for each stage, and monitors the process.

Time and motion studies use stopwatches and ergonomic principles to design jobs to maximize productivity.

Other researchers also made important contributors to the scientific management approach. Henry Gantt (1861–1919), for example, developed the **Gantt chart**—a bar graph that managers could use to schedule and allocate resources for a production job.[33] The Gantt chart is still used today to plan project timelines. It identifies various stages of work that need to be completed, sets deadlines for each stage, and monitors the process. In this way, it helps managers determine in advance when (and which) workers will be needed in the production process.

Another important contributor to this approach was Frank B. Gilbreth (1868–1924),[34] who worked independently from Taylor to develop **time and motion studies.** Gilbreth is known for his emphasis on efficiency and his quest to find the "one best way" to organize work. In his work with bricklayers, for example, his analysis streamlined the bricklaying process from 18 different motions to 5 motions, which resulted in a productivity increase of more than 200 percent. Gilbreth's pioneering work in time and motion studies inspired such innovations as foot levers for garbage cans, aided in the design of ergonomic products and practices, and improved modern surgery techniques.

THE MACRO APPROACH.   Max Weber's description of the "bureaucratic organization" helps to understand the organizing function from a more macro perspective. Weber noticed that organizations were becoming more formally rational and efficient. The old ways of organizing, which involved (among other things) an emphasis on providing jobs for relatives and friends, were being replaced by a more professional way of organizing, which focused on employees' competence. In this new bureaucratic way of organizing, managers depended less on their personality or interpersonal relationships to get work done, and more on their positional authority and their ability to design and implement rules and procedures that would result in efficient and productive structures and systems. Weber's rich theory and conceptual frameworks continue to serve as the foundations of contemporary management and organizational theory.

Henry Ford provides perhaps the most famous example of putting the classical approach to organizing into practice. Together with his engineers, Ford pioneered the development of mass production of automobiles. By 1920, seven years after he started the assembly line at the Model T plant in Highland Park, Michigan (near Detroit), the cost of a car had been reduced by two-thirds. Efficiency was enhanced by innovations such as conveyor belts that moved cars to workers located along a production line. Each worker did one job, such as bolting the door to the frame or attaching the handle to the door. Each job was highly specialized and repetitive.[35]

Another scholar who made important contributions in the classical era was Henri Fayol (1841–1925). In addition to identifying the four functions of management described in Chapter 1—planning, organizing, leading, and controlling—Fayol developed several principles of management. For example, the notion of **unity of command** states that each employee reports to only one superior, the idea of **unity of direction** states that managers and employees should be guided by a single plan of action, and the **scalar chain** principle states that organizations should have a chain of authority extending from the top to the bottom of its hierarchy that includes every employee.

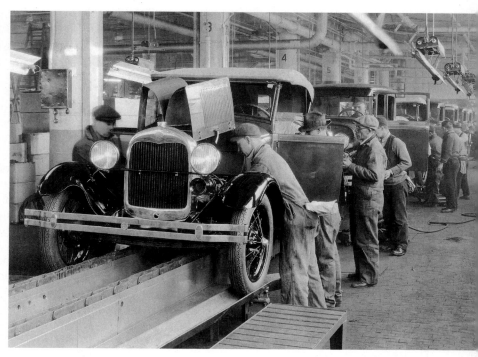

Assembly line workers at a Ford factory, 1927.

An Emphasis on Leading: The "Human" Era (1930 to 1950)

If Frederick Taylor is the "father" of the classical organizing era, then Mary Parker Follett (1868–1933) is the "mother" of the leading era. Follett's emphasis on the human (rather than the technical) side of management was in stark contrast to the scientific management school. This perspective is evident in her advice: "Don't hug your blueprints."[36] Follett argued that authority should not always go to the person who formally holds the position of manager, but rather that power is fluid and should flow to the worker whose knowledge and experience makes that person best able to serve the organization at any given time.

Follett studied how managers actually did their jobs by observing them in their workplaces. In arguing that managers should *facilitate* the work of subordinates rather than *control* employees, Follett diverged from the organization-as-machine ideas of the classical school. She viewed organizations as "communities" where managers and workers should work in harmony, without one dominating the other, and where each person had the freedom to discuss and resolve differences and conflicts. Follett's behavioral approach was far ahead of its time, as she drew from sociology and psychology to help managers see the benefits of recognizing people as a collection of beliefs and emotions rather than as machines.

Lillian Gilbreth (1878–1972), whose husband was Frank Gilbreth (the scientific management researcher), also focused on the human side of management.[37] She made substantial contributions to the field of human resources management. In particular, Gilbreth studied ways to reduce job stress, championed the idea that workers should have standard workdays, and influenced the U.S. Congress to

Unity of command is a principle of management that states that each organizational employee reports to only one superior.

Unity of direction is a principle of management that states that managers and employees should be guided by a single plan of action.

Scalar chain is a management principle that says organizations should have a chain of authority that extends from the top to the bottom of its hierarchy that includes every employee.

Lillian M. Gilbreth

USA   40c

Lillian Gilbreth was the first woman to earn a Ph.D. in industrial psychology, and later became a professor at Purdue University.

Hawthorne effect indicates that workers' performance will improve if workers are given positive attention by managers.

establish child-labor laws and develop rules to protect workers from unsafe working conditions. Interestingly, the work of practitioners and female researchers such as Mary Follett and Lillian Gilbreth did not get much attention from most management scholars until a series of studies was conducted by their male counterparts.

Another early proponent of the view that people were important in organizations was Chester Barnard (1886–1961), an executive with AT&T and president of New Jersey Bell Telephone. Barnard drew attention to the importance of leadership and the informal organization, pointing out that all organizations have social groups and cliques that form alongside its formal structures. In his view, organizations were not machines, and they could not be managed effectively in the impersonal way implied by scientific management theory. Another of Barnard's contributions was his notion that employees have a "zone of indifference," which refers to those activities that they will not rebel against doing. For example, students may accept it when professors assign certain pages of the textbook to be read (because this task lies within their "zone of indifference"), but they may well rebel against being asked to read the same pages aloud in a singing voice.

THE HAWTHORNE EFFECT.   A key contribution to the shift in emphasis from organizing to leading was made by Elton Mayo and Fritz Roethlisberger, who worked on a research project originally sponsored by General Electric.[38] The company wanted to sell more light bulbs by demonstrating to potential business customers that factory workers' productivity would increase with improved lighting. The research conducted in one particular research location, a Western Electric Company plant in Hawthorne, Illinois, provided unexpected results.

Ironically, the research design took the form of a classic laboratory study associated with scientific management. Five independent assembly lines in the Hawthorne plant were divided into two groups: (1) a *control* group, which consisted of three assembly lines where the amount of lighting stayed constant, and (2) an *experimental* group, which was a separate room with two assembly lines where the amount of lighting was systematically varied. Researchers walked around and monitored workers in both the control and the experimental groups. As expected, productivity increased in the experimental group when lighting was increased. However, productivity also increased in the control group. Indeed, productivity increased in both groups regardless of whether the amount of lighting in the experimental group went up or down. Productivity finally decreased for the experimental group when lighting was dimmed to the level of moonlight or twilight. Not surprisingly, General Electric withdrew its sponsorship of the study![39]

After further studies were conducted in an attempt to account for these unexpected results, researchers basically concluded that *workers' productivity will increase whenever managers treat them with respect.* The results—labeled the **Hawthorne effect**—suggested that relationships are important in understanding behavior in organizations.[40] To modern ears, these findings may sound obvious, but at the time they served as a turning point in the evolution of management thought from the classical era to the human era. Of course, this is not to suggest that organizing was no longer important, but rather that relative emphasis had shifted to leading.

THE HUMAN RELATIONS MOVE-MENT. The results of the Hawthorne studies led to the **human relations movement,** which focused on managerial actions that would increase employee satisfaction in an effort to improve productivity. Human relations has been colorfully described as the "happy cow" approach to management: Just as contented cows give more milk, so satisfied workers will be more productive. This movement can be differentiated from the scientific management approach by its emphasis on managers' use of social skills to motivate employees and by its attempts to design jobs that are more humane and less fatiguing.

Productivity in the Hawthorne plant increased when workers were given positive attention.

Human relations movement focuses on managerial actions that will increase employee satisfaction in order to improve productivity.

One of the best-known early contributions to the human relations perspective was made by Douglas McGregor (1906–1964), who identified what he called Theory X and Theory Y assumptions made by managers.[41] Theory X managers assume that people are inherently lazy, dislike work, will avoid working hard unless forced to do so, and prefer to be directed rather than accepting responsibility for getting their work done. As a consequence, Theory X managers design structures and systems intended to ensure that people will work hard. Such measures may include introducing control systems, setting the pace with assembly lines, implementing piece-rate pay systems, and threatening to lay off workers who fail to work hard enough.

McGregor argued that Theory X assumptions reflected the "classical" approach to management. He argued that managers should adopt Theory Y assumptions because they are a more realistic (and better) approach to management practice. Under Theory Y, workers are not merely seen as a set of hired "hands" and managers as the "brains" of an organization. Instead, managers allow workers to use their full selves. Theory Y managers assume that work is as natural as play, that people are inherently motivated to work, and that people will feel unfulfilled if they do not have the opportunity to work and thereby make a contribution to society. Theory Y also assumes that workers prefer to have as much control as possible over their own work, and that people will gladly take responsibility for their work providing that adequate structures and systems are in place to facilitate this. Thus, from a Theory Y perspective, the challenge of management is to provide the support necessary to allow people to excel at their work. This may be accomplished by allowing employees to set their own pace for their work, providing opportunities to work in teams, implementing profit-sharing plans, investing in ongoing training and development for

DIGGING DEEPER

From the "Hawthorne Effect" to Self-Fulfilling Prophecies

Mayo and Roethlisberger were initially puzzled about why workers' productivity was improving. They had not anticipated that workers would perceive themselves to be "special" simply because of the attention they were receiving from scientists in white lab coats. The workers who participated in the study did not want to disappoint these scientists.

More recently, researchers have identified a "self-fulfilling prophecy" that is different from the Hawthorne effect, yet works in a similar way. Whereas the Hawthorne effect suggests that people are more productive when *they* believe that managers have high expectations of them, the self-fulfilling prophecy has found that people perform better when *their managers* have high expectations of them.

A well-known early study of the self-fulfilling prophecy took place in an elementary school setting.[42] At the beginning of the school year, teachers were given class lists that divided students into three groups. Teachers were told that based on psychological testing done the previous year, approximately one-third of the students were expected to excel in the coming year, another third were expected to perform poorly, and the expected outcomes for the final third were uncertain. (No

such tests had been conducted, and students were assigned to the three categories randomly.) By the end of the school year, those students whom teachers expected to do well outperformed those who were expected to perform poorly.

A more recent study was performed among adults. Researchers examined an 11-week training program of 29 platoons in the Israeli Defense Forces. Managers of 10 randomly chosen platoons were told that based on pretesting, their trainees had an "appreciably higher command potential than usual." Consistent with the self-fulfilling prophecy idea, members of the 10 chosen platoons outperformed the trainees in the remaining 19 platoons in four areas (theoretical knowledge, practical skills, physical fitness, and target shooting), even though only two of these four areas were directly related to the training that they had received![43]

Can you think of instances where the Hawthorne effect has been evident in your workplace or school? How about self-fulfilling prophecies? Can you think of both positive and negative examples? Design an experiment to test an interesting hypothesis about the Hawthorne effect or self-fulfilling prophecies in the workplace.

---

workers, and providing a sense of long-term commitment to workers. McGregor argued that this Theory Y approach would maximize productivity.

An Emphasis on Planning: The "Calculating" Era (1950 to 1970)

During World War II, industry and government recognized two needs: a need to improve industrial productivity to aid the war effort, and a need to develop new techniques to manage the war effort. The British, for example, assembled mathematicians and physicists into teams that analyzed the compositions, routes, probable location, and speed of Nazi submarines. These teams developed an approach, later called **systems analysis,** that was used to analyze complex problems that could not be solved by intuition, straightforward mathematics, or simple experience. The lessons learned from these military activities were later adapted and applied to managing civilian organizations. For example, lessons learned about deploying troops, submarines, and other equipment during the war were applied by managers at General Electric to decide where to deploy employees, where to locate plants, and how to design warehouses.

These war-related efforts laid the groundwork for what has become research on planning and strategic decision making. Three different subfields have emerged to aid in managerial planning and decision making:

Systems analysis is an approach used to analyze complex problems that cannot be solved by intuition, straightforward mathematics, or simple experience.

Management science is a subfield of management that aids in planning and decision making by providing sophisticated quantitative techniques to help managers make optimal use of organizational resources.

- **Management science** aids in managerial planning by providing sophisticated quantitative techniques for decision making.

- **Systems theory** highlights managers' unique responsibilities and vantage points in overseeing the entire organization.
- **Contingency theory**—which suggests that there is an ideal fit between organizational structures and systems, technology, and the larger environment—highlights the need for managers to weigh many different concerns in making plans.

MANAGEMENT SCIENCE.   Management science applies mathematics, statistics, and other quantitative techniques to management planning, decision making, and problem solving. It is sometimes seen as having two subfields: **operations research,** which emphasizes mathematical model building,[44] and **operations management,** which uses quantitative techniques to help managers make decisions that allow organizations to produce goods and services more efficiently. It includes the use of the following techniques:

- Break-even analysis—determines the sales volume and prices required to earn a profit, decide which product lines to keep and which to drop, set prices for products and services
- Forecasting—projections that help managers plan ways of meeting production targets, whether and when to expand production facilities
- Inventory modeling—helps managers decide on the timing and quantity for ordering supplies to maintain an optimal inventory, how much end-product inventory to keep on hand
- Linear programming—suggests how to allocate scarce resources among competing uses
- Simulations—mathematical models that permit testing the outcomes associated with making different decisions

SYSTEMS THEORY.   The systems theory approach draws attention to the complexity of managing organizations and, in particular, of the need for managers to look beyond their organizational boundaries. Leading contributors to this approach include James D. Thompson[45] as well as Daniel Katz and Robert L. Kahn.[46] In systems language terms, rather than look at an organization as a closed system, managers should adopt an open systems perspective. The **closed system** view looks at managing activities as though the organization were a self-contained and self-sufficient unit; thus the focus is on activities within an organization's boundaries. For example, a manager who views her pizza restaurant as a closed system will focus on the activities happening within the walls of the restaurant (e.g., friendly customer service, cleanliness in the kitchen, and adequate staff training). In contrast, the **open systems** view emphasizes the organization's place within the larger environment. A manager with an open systems perspective will be more aware of where to recruit staff, how to advertise for specific target markets, which suppliers to choose, and so on. Thus managers who adopt an open systems perspective highlight their organization's place in the larger environment and recognize their dependence on that environment. In other words, the organization requires access to *inputs* (e.g., raw materials, labor) and a market (e.g., customers) for its *outputs.*

Managers who adopt an open systems view are more likely to achieve **synergy,** which occurs when two or more systems are more successful working together than they are working independently. By contrast, managers who adopt a closed system

---

Systems theory is a subfield of management that aids in planning and decision making by highlighting managers' unique responsibilities and vantage points in overseeing the entire organization.

Contingency theory is a subfield of management theory that suggests that there is a fit between organizational structures and systems, technology, and the larger environment.

Operations research is a subfield of management science that emphasizes mathematical model building.

Operations management is a form of applied management science that uses quantitative techniques to help managers make decisions that allow organizations to produce goods and services more efficiently.

Closed system is a perspective on organizations that looks at managing activities as though the organization were a self-contained and self-sufficient unit.

Open systems is a perspective that emphasizes an organization's place in the larger environment and its dependence on access to *inputs* (e.g., raw materials, labor) and a market (e.g., customers) for its *outputs.*

Synergy occurs when two or more systems are more successful working together than they are working independently.

Entropy is the natural tendency for a system to fail because it is unable to acquire the inputs and energy it requires to survive.

view are likely to experience **entropy,** the natural tendency for a closed system to fail because over time it is unable to acquire the inputs and energy it requires to survive.

Today, aspects of systems theory are also evident in subfields such as *management information systems* and *total quality management* (which are discussed in Chapter 18).

CONTINGENCY THEORY. Advances in understanding of quantitative methods and open systems helped to refine the planning and decision-making processes that are central to managers' jobs. However, both perspectives still perpetuated the view that managers could find the "one best way" to manage and to make decisions. Herbert Simon—who won a Nobel Prize for his insightful research—disagreed with this view, arguing that even the best management decision-making process is limited by a lack of complete information and limited cognitive ability when processing information.[47] Simon called this constraint **bounded rationality.**

Bounded rationality recognizes that the management decision-making process is limited by a lack of complete information and limited cognitive ability when processing information.

Other scholars developed the contingency view further, by stating that there was no one best way to do things and that the best management decision depends on the particular situation. For example, consider the question of whether an organization should adopt a **mechanistic structure** (one characterized by many written rules and procedures and by concentration of authority at the top of the organizational hierarchy) or an **organic structure** (one characterized by less rigid rules and decentralized authority). The contingency answer—developed by Tom Burns and G. M. Stalker—was that organizations should adopt a mechanistic structure if they operate in relatively stable environments, but should adopt an organic structure if they operate in less stable environments.[48] This issue is discussed further in Chapter 11.

Mechanistic structure is an organizational structure characterized by a relatively high level of standardization, specialization, centralization, and functional departmentalization.

Organic structure is an organizational structure characterized by a relatively low level of standardization, specialization, and centralization, and by a divisional departmentalization.

An influential model of contingency theory, and one that links it to strategic management (see Chapter 9), has been developed by John Child.[49] His idea of **strategic choice theory** suggests that based on their values and beliefs, managers (or, more generally, what Child calls the **dominant coalition**) make three key strategic decisions (see Figure 2.3):

Strategic choice theory describes how managers, influenced by their values, make three key interrelated decisions regarding an organization's performance standards, domain, and organizational design.

1. Managers must decide what constitutes "effective" organizational performance. From a Mainstream approach, this means maximizing productivity and efficiency and return to shareholders, but Child's discussion recognizes that Multistream performance standards are also often chosen. (See Chapter 8.)

2. Managers must choose their organization's "domain." This is determined by answering questions like these: In which **industry** will the organization operate (e.g., will it provide automobiles, health care, or income tax services?)? Where will it find inputs and a market for its outputs? Put differently, what is the larger "open system" that the organization will be nested in? (See Chapters 3, 4, and 9.)

Dominant coalition refers to the subgroup of an organization's members (usually managers) that makes its strategic decisions.

3. Managers must make decisions about the organization's internal structures and systems. Will the organization be mechanistic or organic? What sorts of subsystems and departments will it have? How will activities across departments be integrated? (See Chapters 10 and 11.)

Industry refers to a subset of organizations that can be grouped together because they are active in the same branch of the economy or society (e.g., the automobile industry, the fast-food industry, the education sector, and the social services sector).

An Emphasis on Controlling: The "Values and Beliefs" Era (1970 to 1990)

The 1960s were a time of phenomenal technological and large-scale organizational accomplishment, exemplified by space travel and astronauts walking on the moon. At the same time, the 1960s were a time of "flower power" and questioning of the

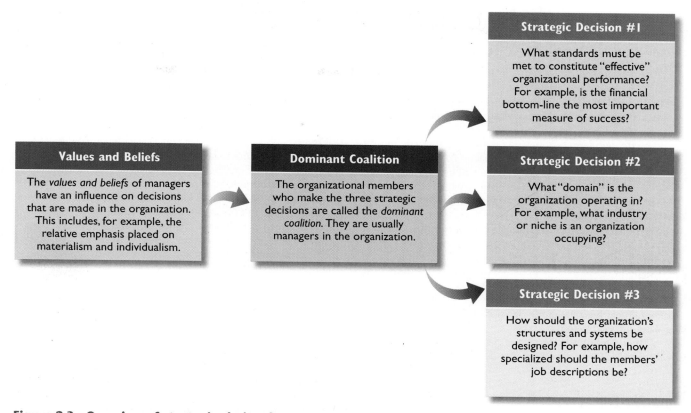

Figure 2.3   Overview of strategic choice theory
Source: Adapted from discussion in Child, J. (1972). Organizational structure, environment, and performance: The role of strategic choice. *Sociology,* 6, 1–22; and Dyck, B. (1994). Build in sustainable development, and they will come: A vegetable field of dreams. *Journal of Organizational Change Management,* 7(4), 47–63.

status quo. Within the study of management, this prompted an era marked by heightened interest in the role of values and beliefs within organizations. These values and beliefs play an important role in the controlling function.

INSTITUTIONALIZATION.   Recall that more than a century ago, Weber was already arguing that a materialist–individualist view had become so ingrained in social structures and systems that change was difficult. Put differently, we are controlled by social or cultural **scripts** that we have learned in the course of our lives, and that are difficult to change. Sometimes scripts may have been rational in the era in which they were developed, but they may still continue to be followed in future situations where they are dysfunctional. For example, one goal of management education and a textbook like this one is to teach students scripts that they may apply in organizations. Ideally, students are not only *trained* to learn scripts, but also *educated* to evaluate the meaning of scripts and acquire the tools needed to write the future scripts that will be required in their careers.[50]

Philip Selznick described how scripts may become dysfunctional over time when he studied management practices at the Tennessee Valley Authority (TVA).[51] Many of the standard operating procedures (organizational scripts) at the TVA had been rational when they were initially developed, but they were no longer deemed rational by the time Selznick began studying the organization. Selznick called this

Scripts are learned frameworks that provide direction for people by helping them to interpret and respond to what is happening around them.

MANAGEMENT IN PRACTICE

Strategic Choice Theory and Mainstream Agribusiness[52]

The various aspects of the strategic choice model can be highlighted by looking at agribusiness and comparing it to traditional agriculture. First, in terms of *values and beliefs,* agribusiness is characterized by its materialist–individualist emphasis. Food costs are reduced by using high-tech farming techniques and by treating farm outputs as commodities that are bought and sold in an impersonal marketplace. These modern-day values and beliefs differ from the values and beliefs that guided farming during most of human history, when farmers grew food that was bought and sold to their friends and neighbors at a local farmer's market.

Second, these differing values have, in turn, influenced who acts as the *dominant coalition.* Large companies have a great deal of power in Mainstream agribusiness. For example, farmers depend on six multinational corporations to supply most of their inputs, and five multinational corporations to purchase most of their farm outputs. By contrast, in traditional agriculture, farmers typically made decisions based on the needs of their family and friends.

The first of the three *strategic choices* focuses on *criteria of effectiveness.* The performance standards, or goals, of agribusiness are to maximize profitability, to maximize yield (productivity), and to produce crops that look good and are easily transported. The nutritional value of most fruits has actually decreased in the past decades, as some genetic engineers and farmers have responded by developing new products that ca-

ter to the market's emphasis on the appearance and durability of food at the expense of its nutritional value. This differs from effectiveness criteria that emphasize providing healthy food grown in a way that is sustainable for the land, for farmers, and for consumers.

The second strategic choice concerns *domain*. The domain of agribusiness is international in scope, and it is characterized by three types of distancing. First, there is greater distance between where the food is grown and where it is consumed (e.g., the average forkful of food in the United States has traveled more than 1000 miles).[53] Second, there is a greater distance between people and their knowledge of how food is grown. Third, there is a greater distance between the food that is grown and the food that is consumed (e.g., consider all the processing that goes into Oreo cookies). This is vastly different from the time when virtually everything people ate had been grown within 100 miles of where they lived.

The final strategic choice concerns *organization design*. Agribusiness is necessarily regimented, conducted on a large scale, and follows a mechanistic model. Because harvesting is done by large machinery, there is a need for uniform ripening, which creates the need for monoculture in seeds, which leaves crops vulnerable to single pests, which leads to the need for chemical pesticides. This model differs from labor-intensive practices, where one year's harvest provides seeds for the following season.

Institutionalization means that certain practices or rules are seen as valuable in and of themselves, even though they may no longer be rational for the organization.

Social construction of reality occurs when something is *perceived* as an *objective* reality and people allow it to shape their subsequent thinking and action, even though its meaning has been created by humans and must be constantly re-created by humans in order to exist (e.g., the meaning given to a $100 bill).

phenomenon **institutionalization,** which means that certain practices or rules have become "valued" in and of themselves, even though they may no longer be useful for the organization.[54] Institutionalization occurs when members of an organization find themselves being controlled by norms that often are not rational, by peer pressure, and by simple inertia. Institutionalized practices can act like self-fulfilling prophecies as they shape and control people's behavior. Institutionalized social norms can control people's actions by setting up predefined patterns of behavior, and these patterns may in turn channel behavior in one direction instead of the many different directions that would theoretically be possible.[55]

CONTROL AND THE SOCIAL CONSTRUCTION OF REALITY. The main idea behind the **social construction of reality** is the notion that what we experience as "real" has actually been socially constructed.[56] For example, we ascribe meaning to money that is not inherent in a physical $100 bill, we attach more value to the job of CEO than to the job of day-care worker, and we come to accept advertisements that teach us that happiness is a by-product of buying the latest stuff. Even things that we think are objectively "real" have meaning that is socially created and re-created.

DIGGING DEEPER

The Institutionalization of the QWERTY Keyboard[57]

A well-known example of institutionalization comes from the world of typewriters and keyboards. Chances are that the keyboard you work on has its keys configured in the QWERTY system (named after the row of letters starting on the upper-left side of the keyboard). When you first learned how to type, you were probably annoyed at the seemingly random configuration of keys, and gave little thought as to why this particular pattern had been chosen.

The QWERTY system was developed by a man named Christopher Lathan Sholes, who patented the typewriter in 1868. He and his associates chose the QWERTY arrangement for the keys in part to *slow down* the speed of typists, because in those days typewriters had mechanical moving arms for each letter that were prone to jamming if the typing speed was too fast. In 1873, Sholes sold his patent to E. Remington & Sons, which made further mechanical improvements to the typewriter and brought it into commercial production. At the time, a number of other keyboard configurations were on the market as well.

A big step toward adoption of the QWERTY keyboard as the industry standard came in a typing contest held in Cincinnati in 1888, where Frank McGurrin (who used a QWERTY keyboard) won a decisive victory over Louis Taub (who used an alternative keyboard). McGurrin's victory had more to do with the fact that he was one of the first "touch typists" (whereas Taub used the "hunt-and-peck" method). Because McGurrin happened to be using the QWERTY keyboard, however, Remington was able to argue that its keyboard led to greater productivity.

The advent of electronic typewriters and computers meant that keyboards could be designed to optimize typing speed without regard for "jamming" keys. Nevertheless, the QWERTY configuration remains the industry standard: It seems to have become infused with value even though it may not be the most technically rational configuration for the task of keyboarding.

One example of a configuration of keys purported to be better than QWERTY—called the Dvorak Simplified Keyboard—was invented in 1936 by August Dvorak, a professor at the University of Washington. Dvorak claimed that his keyboard provided advantages of greater speed, reduced fatigue, and easier learning. During World War II, the U.S. Navy did experiments showing that the cost of converting typists to the Dvorak keyboard would be repaid, thanks to increased typing speed, within ten days from the start of retraining. Even so, Dvorak's keyboard never gained widespread acceptance.

Your current word-processing software probably has the Dvorak Simplified Keyboard built into it. All you need to do is click onto it and do some retraining, and for the rest of your life you will have the benefits of a configuration of keys that was not anti-engineered to slow you down. But you probably won't do that. Instead, you'll continue to use the QWERTY keyboard. Why? Because that keyboard configuration has been institutionalized.[58]

For example, one study showed how something as "real" as a computed tomography (CT) scanner could have different meanings and social consequences in two different hospital settings. In one of the hospitals, introducing the CT scanner resulted in greater equality between radiologists and technologists; in the other hospital, introducing the CT scanner simply reinforced radiologists' higher status compared to the technologists'.[59] This example illustrates how even "objective" technology, such as a CT scanner, should be treated as a *social* rather than a *physical* object. Put differently, the meaning of introducing a CT scanner is *not* objective, it is *socially constructed*.

Harold Garfinkel[60] designed a series of experiments that demonstrated how most of our behavior is based on routines and taken-for-granted norms that lie far beneath the level of our consciousness. These often invisible scripts, in turn, form the basis for the relatively few visible decisions that we make consciously and rationally. Garfinkel's experiments showed how quickly others get annoyed when someone refuses to accept a commonly accepted script. Somewhat paradoxically, the experiments also demonstrated how quickly change can occur when someone deliberately chooses to adopt a new script. As an example of this second finding, in one experiment students were instructed to engage someone in conversation and to

DIGGING DEEPER

Institutionalization at the Office

Lynn Zucker designed an intriguing laboratory experiment that shows how the influence of norms—even nonrational norms—is especially powerful in organizational settings.[61] Her experiment is based on a physiological phenomenon of the human eye called *Sherif's autokinetic effect*, which simply means that a stationary point of light in a darkened room will appear to "shake" (e.g., imagine looking at an LED clock across the room at night). Based on the findings with a control group in her laboratory study, the stationary beam of light is perceived to move an average of 4 inches.[62]

In Zucker's first experimental manipulation, two people—a "confederate" (hired by Zucker) and a "subject"—entered a room where there was already a Light Operator. The Light Operator explained that the experiment had to do with people's perception of moving light. Each person would be asked to state how far they thought the light had appeared to move. The lights in the room were dimmed, and the point of light turned on. The confederate, who was given the first opportunity to state how far the light appeared to move, had been instructed to say about 12 inches. When the subject was asked how far the light appeared to move, rather than say 4 inches (i.e., the average amount of movement perceived by people not in an experimental manipulation), the subject might say

10 inches. After this round, the confederate was asked to leave the room, and a second subject joined the first. The same instructions were given, but this time the first subject said that the light moved 9 inches, and the second subject said that it moved 7 inches. The experiment continued, with one subject leaving the room and a new one entering, until the "right" answer of 4 inches was reached.

Zucker repeated the experiment two more times, with slight variations in the instructions given to subjects. In one variation, the Light Operator asked the subjects to act as though they were members of the same *organization*. In another variation, subjects were told to act as though they were members of the same *office*. Even these very subtle changes in instructions had significant results in terms of how subjects acted. As it turns out, it took the longest for the right answer to be arrived at in the office setting, and the second longest in the organizational setting.

These results suggest that organizational and office practices are especially likely to become institutionalized, even if these are not "rational" or accurate from an objective point of view. The way we behave in organizations can be very difficult to change, even if the need for change is as obvious as a light in a room.

assume that the other person was trying to mislead them. Many students found that once they started acting in the role, they actually came to feel it to be true.

Garfinkel's work has two important lessons for managers. First, much of what we accept as objective or "natural facts of life" are really socially constructed (or what Garfinkel calls "moral facts of life"), and we would do well to look at the implicit values that underpin our thinking and behavior. Second, once we believe and act upon socially constructed facts of life as being true, then they *become* true for ourselves and for others around us.

Everyone's actions help to socially construct the world around us. For example, teachers in our schools provide the scripts and concepts that shape how students interpret the world.[63] In our society, managers have a special influence in constructing the meaning of the social world inhabited by others. Specifically, they help to create self-fulfilling prophecies that shape the lives of others. This power creates additional responsibilities for managers.

Once the importance of values in shaping people's behavior in organizations had been discovered, it created a huge interest among Mainstream scholars to see whether managers could manage an organization's values so as to improve organizational productivity and profitability. By the 1980s, organizational culture had become a leading topic of study among management scholars. Leading academics such as Jeffrey Pfeffer and Edgar Schein were publishing books and articles that talked about the important "symbolic" role of management and explained how the essence of leadership was to create the "meaning" that guides, inspires, and motivates organizational members.[64]

The Call for Multistream Management: The Reconsidering Era (1990 to Present)

There has been a growing discontentment with the Mainstream status quo since about 1990. This interest in Multistream management may be attributed to multiple factors, and it has been expressed in multiple ways. A common theme, however, is that managers are increasingly being looked upon to help resolve many of the major problems facing the planet and humankind:

- *Ecological sustainability.* As we will see in our discussion of the environment in Chapter 3, a growing body of scientific evidence suggests that our current lifestyle is causing significant problems for the natural environment and linking Mainstream values to environmental degradation.[65] Consensus is building that managers, consumers, and investors simply must take greater account of their impact on the environment. There is little comfort in achieving great financial wealth if future generations will suffer massive cleanup costs.[66]

- *Social justice.* Research suggests that the gap between the rich and the poor is growing, both within organizations and within countries, as well as across countries.[67] Participating in systems and structures where the rich benefit from the poor is morally questionable, and an increasing number of people are recognizing that management practices that increase the divisions between rich and poor are problematic. Even people from relatively wealthy countries are challenging systems that they see as unjust, despite the fact that those systems serve their own financial self-interests.[68]

- *Physical well-being.* Organizational activities can produce a great deal of pollution. The alarming increase in the rates of asthma, cancer, depression, attention-deficit disorder, stress, and other ailments may be a by-product of the various forms of pollution associated with the status quo. A growing body of scholarly research indicates that the conventional obsession with materialism—that is, maximizing productivity and profitability—results in significant physical and emotional costs, such as decreased overall well-being and happiness.[69] An increasing segment of society is looking for new ways of managing organizations that are more sensitive to people's physical well-being.

- *Aesthetic costs.* Some commentators suggest that the Wal-Marts and McDonald's of the world are doing little to give us a sense of beauty or pride in our communities.[70] Moreover, many of the jobs that such companies create, and the jobs that we send overseas, have little redeeming aesthetic value or meaning. What do we lose when we value our art and architecture primarily in terms of their financial costs and benefits? What is lost if literature and music are seen as commodities and "industries" to maximize profit, rather than as expressions of artistic purity and goodness? Of course, there is a paradox here, in that financial wealth also enables the development of the arts and aesthetical dimensions of a society.

- *Spiritual interest.* Since the 1990s, there has been increased interest in spirituality and religion. Indeed, books dealing with spirituality now account for the fastest-growing segment of the publishing industry, and there is a growing interest in spirituality in the workplace.[71] Almost by definition, a focus on the material realm is opposed to a focus on spirituality. Similarly, the self-interested nature of individualism counters the teachings of many religions.

WHAT DO YOU THINK?

Spirituality and Management

Should ideas about spirituality be part of the study of management? It seems likely that religious and spiritual worldviews have helped to shape management theory and practice, given that more than 80 percent of the people in the world espouse and hold such worldviews.[72] The growing interest in this area is reflected in the creation (2000) of the "Management, Spirituality, and Religion" interest group in the Academy of Management (the world's largest and most prestigious scholarly association of management). Since the 1990s, interest in spirituality has increased significantly, and today it is not unusual to find meditation rooms, chapels, prayer circles, and Bible studies in the workplace.

Four of every five professors in the United States (81 percent) describe themselves as spiritual persons. Three of every five business professors also think that the spiritual dimension of faculty members' lives has a place in their jobs as academics, and one of three business professors thinks that colleges should be concerned with facilitating students' spiritual development. We also know that four of every five students have an interest in spirituality (80 percent), and that almost half (48 percent) of all incoming college students believe that it is "very important" or "essential" that their college encourages their personal expression of spirituality. Even so, most students report that professors never encouraged such discussion (62 percent), nor have professors raised questions about the meaning and purpose of life (56 percent).[73]

Should an introductory course in management deal with issues such as the meaning and purpose of life, and how these are related to management? Should there be a discussion of the place of spirituality in management? Why or why not? What are the pros and cons of doing so?

Research suggests that people around the world are becoming increasingly Multistream in their orientations. People are more interested in the quality of life and a sense of community and social equity, compared with material and economic rewards, prosperity, and control.[74] For example, 93 percent of Americans believe that people are too focused on working and making money and not focused enough on family and community. More than half have voluntarily opted not to maximize their material wealth so as to facilitate other forms of well-being.[75]

This shift toward a Multistream view is also evident in management theory and practice. For example, the Academy of Management now includes special groups on "Social Issues in Management" and "Our Natural Environment." As is reflected in this book, a growing body of literature is addressing concerns related to Multistream management: servant leadership, corporate social responsibility, stewardship, social entrepreneurship, positive scholarship, and stakeholder theory. Stakeholder theory research, for example, notes that shareholders are not the only groups with a stake in organizational behavior: Employees, neighborhoods, customers, suppliers, and future generations are also stakeholders in what managers do. By the turn of the millennium, stakeholding had become one of the most cited and familiar terms in academic management literature.[76] Along the same lines, there has been unprecedented growth in the area of research known as *corporate social responsibility* (see Chapter 5). For example, a large portion of U.S. investments are now devoted to ethical funds (see Chapter 3).

Of course, research and interest in Mainstream management are far from dead. The majority of management research is still concerned with maximizing the productivity, profitability, and competitiveness of organizations. Researchers even defend the merits of stakeholder theory and corporate social responsibility

Fair Trade is a system of international trade that is based on dialogue, transparency, and respect, and that is beneficial for producers in poorer countries, consumers in richer countries, and the Earth.

Cooperative is an organization that is owned and democratically run directly by its members.

by demonstrating how they can be used to help managers to meet traditional materialist–individualist criteria of success.[77] At the same time, more tools—such as balanced scorecard and triple-bottom-line accounting—are being developed to provide alternative measures of success. These tools will be examined at appropriate places in the remainder of the book.

Management and a Short History of Chocolate[78]

Chocolate may be our favorite flavor (preferred by 52 percent of Americans, with vanilla and berry flavors tied for second at 12 percent), but most people know little about how the chocolate industry has developed over time or how current chocolate companies are managed (it is one of the most secretive of industries). Consider the various roles that managers have played to help shape and socially (re)construct the meaning of chocolate over time.

Chocolate as Idol

The first people to make use of cocoa were the Mayans, who lived in the Yucatan Peninsula as long ago as A.D. 600. The Mayans worshipped the cocoa bean as an idol, and cocoa was also closely linked to the Mayan merchant god, Ek Chuah.[79]

Chocolate as Money

The Mayans, and later the Aztecs, used cocoa beans as currency. In fact, in some parts of Central America, cocoa beans were used as currency as recently as the 1800s. Early explorers of the Americas found that with 100 cocoa beans you could buy a slave, and with 10 cocoa beans you could buy a rabbit. When the Spanish explorer Don Cortes was introduced to a chocolate drink by the Aztec emperor Montezuma, Cortes wasn't particularly impressed—but he did like the idea that money could grow on cocoa trees! Realizing the product's value as currency, he established a cocoa plantation to cultivate cash (this gives new meaning to the idea of a chocolate mint!).[80]

Chocolate as Medicine

The Mayans used cocoa for the treatment of coughs, fever, and discomfort during pregnancy. The Aztecs thought that wisdom and power came from eating the fruit of the cocoa tree. In Europe, some of the earliest cocoa makers were apothecaries (early chemists) who were interested in the supposed medicinal properties of cocoa. In seventeenth-century Holland, cocoa was recommended by doctors as a cure for almost every ailment. More recent research points to the health benefits of eating dark chocolate—for example, as a means of preventing cancer, heart disease, and stroke.

Chocolate for Everyone

Chocolate became an item for the masses thanks to the efforts of businesspeople and inventors such as C. J. Van Houten, a Dutch chocolate master whose invention of the cocoa press helped to make it more affordable. Many leading businesspeople in the chocolate industry were Quakers, whose motivation for getting into the business included a desire to persuade the poor to give up alcohol in favor of the healthier chocolate drink.[81]

One such Quaker was John Cadbury, who started Cadbury Limited in 1831. An important turning point for the company occurred in 1866, when it introduced a process for pressing the cocoa butter from the cocoa bean. By 1879 the firm had grown so successful that George Cadbury built what came to be known as the "factory in a garden" on a parklike property in Bournville, England.[82] Much as Wedgwood became famous for his management innovations (see the chapter-opening case), so Cadbury's Bournville factory set a standard for other companies in non-Mainstream industrial relations. For example, Cadbury was the first firm to introduce the Saturday half-day holiday (5$\frac{1}{2}$-day workweek), promote the idea of workers continuing their education while working, offer medical and dental departments, and provide workers with a kitchen where they could heat up their dinners (a forerunner to staff dining rooms).

Wanting to offer wage earners affordable housing in pleasant surroundings, in 1895 George Cadbury purchased another 120 acres near the Bournville plant and began to establish a community consistent with the then popular Garden City movement. In 1903, the estate had grown to include 330 acres of land and 313 cottages, and George Cadbury decided to turn it into a charitable trust for future generations to enjoy. He handed over the land and houses to the Bournville Village Trust with the proviso that revenues should be devoted to the extension of the estate and the promotion of housing reform. Today, the Bournville Estate covers 1000 acres and has 7600 dwellings.

Chocolate as Big Business

Once chocolate had become a mass-consumption item, it was only a matter of time before it turned into big business. In the United States, chocolate sales now exceed $15 billion per year. Globally, about 60 percent of all chocolate is consumed in the United States and the European Union. With sales of $10 billion per year, Mars Inc. has become the largest confectionary company in the world.

The modern chocolate industry is known for its intense competitiveness and secretiveness. For example, Mars' candy-making machinery is designed and run by its own engineers. Akin to the world depicted in *Charlie and the Chocolate Factory*, few outsiders ever see the inside of a Mars chocolate manufacturing facility. If there is need for an outside worker to fix a problem in the plant, the outsider is blindfolded, escorted to the problem area where their expertise is required, unblindfolded in order to perform the work, and then reblindfolded and escorted out.

As the industry has grown, it has become dominated by a few very large firms via processes of globalization and concentration. For example, 75 percent or more of the global retail market in chocolate confectionary is dominated by three firms: Cadbury, Mars, and Nestlé. In the United States, 75 percent of the candy rack is owned by Hershey's and Mars.

Unfortunately, the farmers who grow the 3.5 million tons of cocoa beans produced every year are not particularly well served by an industry structure where so much power is concentrated in the hands of a few major players.[83] Over the past decades, the price of cocoa (corrected for inflation) has experienced an almost continuously declining trend (e.g., in the 2003–2004 cocoa year, real prices were less than half of what they were in 1970–1971).[84] Today, cocoa ingredients represent less than 10 percent of the price of a chocolate bar, whereas noncocoa ingredients account for 15 percent, chocolate companies' costs and profits account for more than 50 percent, and more than 25 percent goes to the shops that sell the chocolates.[85]

Chocolate as Social Justice and Ecological Sustainability

Recognizing some of the problems facing especially small producers in an economic system where large-scale companies are trying to maximize their profits, "fair trade" companies such as the Day Chocolate Company have been started with the intention of mixing both social and business goals. **Fair Trade** is a system of international trade that is based on dialogue, transparency, and respect, and that is beneficial for producers in poorer countries, consumers in richer countries, and the Earth.[86] A key to Day's success, for example, is the fact that cocoa farmers in Africa own one-third of the shares in the company, have a direct say in how the company is run, and receive a share of its profits. Consider that there are approximately 2 million cocoa farmers in Ghana, each of whom earns about $350 per year. Encouraged by the Fair Trade movement, farmers have set up cooperatives[87] to sell their cocoa beans. A **cooperative** is an organization that is owned and run democratically by its members—in this case, directly by the cocoa farmers. Fair Trade chocolate companies such as Day promise to pay a fair price to farmers to ensure that they can make a living wage and give back to their communities (e.g., a floor of $1600 per ton, plus an extra $150 per ton to spend on community projects as decided on by the farmers, such as building new drinking wells and toilets). Fair Trade chocolate represents about 2 percent of the global market.

There is also a growing demand for organic chocolate, whose sales are expected to grow 30 percent per year (compared to an overall growth rate for chocolate of 4 percent per year). Organizations such as Equal Exchange have pioneered a Fair Trade program that ensures that the farmers who grow the organic chocolate also receive a fair price for their beans.

Since the 1990s, the chocolate industry has been working on expanding sustainable cocoa farming efforts. The World Cocoa Foundation, which was formed in 2000, has helped to increase farm incomes by teaching cocoa farmers how to reduce crop losses and costs and how to diversify the crops grown for family income. It also helps farmers to organize themselves into cooperatives to sell their cocoa. Farm families participating in such programs have seen their income rise by as much as 55 percent (Cameroon) or 24 percent (Ivory Coast).

QUESTIONS FOR DISCUSSION

1. The socially constructed meaning of chocolate has changed over the centuries. Describe how managers may have had an effect on these changes. Can you think of ways that these changes have, in turn, influenced the way that the four management functions are put into practice?

2. Both Wedgwood and Cadbury were innovators in the field of management. How were they similar, and how were they different?

3. With which forms of well-being has the chocolate industry been concerned? Contrast and compare the forms of well-being that are the concern of Mainstream versus Multistream managers.

SUMMARY

The meaning of management is constantly being socially (re)constructed over time.

Within the history of humankind, our current notions of management are relatively unique, and have been influenced by two things in particular:

- A growing emphasis on materialism and individualism that coincided with the Industrial Revolution
- The increasing number and size of corporations

The development of management and organization theory can be divided roughly into five eras:

- The organizing era (1910 to 1930) saw the development of basic concepts such as division of labor, bureaucracy, time and motion studies, and the unity of command.
- The leading era (1930 to 1950) drew attention to the importance of recognizing the informal organization, treating people with dignity and respect, and developing teams and groups.
- The planning era (1950 to 1970) pointed out the importance of open systems and managing organizational inputs and outputs, and thereby laid the foundation for future work in strategic management.
- The controlling era (1970 to 1990) highlighted how managers influence organizational members' behavior by setting organizations' basic values, core standards, and culture.
- The reconsidering era (1990 to present) reflects the general societal shift away from the materialist–individualist worldview and toward Multistream management theory and practice.

QUESTIONS FOR REFLECTION AND DISCUSSION

1. Identify several specific actions that Josiah Wedgwood took in developing his company, and indicate how those actions were consistent with (or in contrast to) ideas or schools of thought that were discussed in this chapter.

2. Make a list of the pros and cons associated with a materialist–individualist perspective, and contrast and compare your list with your classmates' views.

3. Describe the key ideas or insights in this chapter that provided you with a better understanding of contemporary management theory and practice.

4. Do you agree with the argument that our understanding of management has been socially constructed? Do you think that it should be socially reconstructed differently? Explain.

5. Is there "one best way" to manage still waiting to be discovered? Explain.

6. As you reflect on how our thinking about management theory and practice got to the place where it is today, which of the people and ideas presented in this chapter have had the greatest influence on the present situation (either positive or negative)?

7. Think about the future and how you would like it to look in 30 years, when the next generation of management students is taking this course. Which sorts of key events and examples would you like future students to be reading about that will have taken place during your career? More importantly, what will your contribution be to socially constructing the reality that you desire for the future?

8. What sort of workplace would you like your manager to construct for you? What sort of organizational "reality" will you socially construct for others when you are a manager? Is it a social reality that emphasizes Mainstream views like meeting financial targets and quarterly financial statements?

HANDS-ON ACTIVITIES

How Much Emphasis People Place on Various Forms of Well-Being

Many different forms of well-being exist, and a manager has only a limited amount of time and energy to pay attention to each form. As a consequence, managers may decide to place primary emphasis on some forms of well-being, place secondary emphasis on other forms, and neglect other forms of well-being altogether.

This activity asks which forms of well-being you think are most important for yourself, and asks you to consider which forms might be most important for others. You will be asked to allocate a total of 100 points among each of nine forms of well-being, thereby indicating the relative emphasis you place on each.

For example, in one column, you might assign 75 points to "aesthetic" well-being, 10 points each to "emotional" and "social" well-being, 5 points to "material" well-being, and 0 points to the rest (total = 100). In another column, you might assign 30 points each to "ecological" and "material" well-being, 17 points to "aesthetic" well-being, 8 points each to "intellectual" and "spiritual" well-being, 6 points to "individual" well-being, and 1 point to "physical" well-being (total = 100). You can assign 100 points for each column in any way you want, but the total points assigned to each column should equal 100.

Each of the four columns in the chart below should be answered from a different perspective. Reflect on the differences in the four columns. Compare your results with the results of your classmates, and discuss interesting similarities and differences.

Column A: How much emphasis do you think an **effective manager** would place on each form of well-being?
Column B: How much emphasis do **you** place on each form of well-being?
Column C: How much emphasis do you think **your parents** place on each form of well-being?
Column D: How much emphasis do you think **people living 500 years ago** placed on each form of well-being?

A	B	C	D	Form of Well-Being
				Aesthetic: beauty, art, poetry
				Ecological: natural environment, minimal pollution
				Emotional: satisfaction, positive feelings, hope, joy
				Individual: personal convenience, looking after own interests
				Intellectual: ideas, clear rationale, theory, concepts
				Material: finances, productivity, tangible goods, efficiency
				Physical: health, safety, security
				Social: community-mindedness, justice, helping others
				Spiritual: meaning, interconnectedness, transcendent purpose
				Total (the total for each column should equal 100)

ENDNOTES

1. Jacob, M. C. (2004). Industrial Revolution. In *World Book Encyclopedia*; Langton, J. (1984). The ecological theory of bureaucracy: The case of Josiah Wedgwood and the British pottery industry. *Administrative Science Quarterly, 29*(3), 330–354; Perrow, C. (1985). Comment on Langton's "Ecological theory of bureaucracy." *Administrative Science Quarterly, 30*, 278–283; and Langton, J. (1985). Reply to Perrow. *Administrative Science Quarterly, 30*(2), 284–288.

2. Archer, S. M. (1973). *Josiah Wedgwood and the potteries* (p. 53). London: Longman. Cited in Langton, J. (1984). The ecological theory of bureaucracy: The case of Josiah Wedgwood and the British pottery industry. *Administrative Science Quarterly, 29*(3), 330–354.

3. Perrow points out that although historians are quick to describe peasants as lazy and ignorant for their penchant for taking long weekends, historians seldom describe the idleness and foolishness of drinking nonnutritious tea as laziness and ignorance. Perrow, C. (1985). Comment on Langton's "Ecological theory of bureaucracy." *Administrative Science Quarterly, 30*, 278–283. See also Langton, J. (1985). Reply to Perrow. *Administrative Science Quarterly, 30*(2), 284–288.

4. Perrow (1985) notes that the costs of building the turnpike and canal that Wedgwood lobbied for were not reflected in his business costs or prices, and that this in fact gave him a decided advantage over competitors that were located elsewhere. What if for-profit businesses that provide nonessential products or services were required to pay the true costs of the infrastructure provided by the government (including cleanup costs associated with pollution due to production or transportation)? In this case, would the change have increased the transportation costs so much that smaller potteries, which were located closer to their customers, would have been able to outcompete large bureaucracies that shipped inputs and outputs over great distances?

5. Of course, the laws of the land are influenced by who is in government and by how they gained and are able to retain their power. At the time of Wedgwood, to vote in an election, you had to be male and to pay a certain amount of taxes. Despite this structural bias, which favored landowners, for a time Parliament had levied a small tax on those wealthy landlords who drove farmers off their land. As discussed in Chapter 3, the "varieties of capitalism" literature points to the different outcomes that result when differing laws and institutions are created by government. For example, what if laws had been passed that allowed workers to organize so as to increase their portion of the firms' economic benefits? What if laws had been passed that prevented the highest-paid managers from increasing their pay beyond a certain point? For example, what if the highest-paid person in a firm—including the owner—could receive no more than, say, ten times the amount of pay of the lowest-paid person?

6. This was calculated by using the retail price index to estimate that £500,000 in 1795 would equal more than £35 million in 2004, and with the knowledge that the exchange rate in 2005 was $1.83 for every £1.00. Calculated using information found December 29, 2006, at http://eh.net/hmit/.

7. Cited in Langton, 1984, p. 347.

8. Archer, 1973, p. 42 (cited in Langton, 1984, p. 348).

9. The idea of the social construction of reality is described later in this chapter. For now, it is sufficient to note that an institution such as management, no matter how objective it might appear to be, is produced and sustained by human activity. It is a paradox that humans are capable of producing an idea like "management" that they then experience as something other than a human. To paraphrase Berger and Luckmann, "Management is a human product that is perceived as an objective reality and that shapes subsequent thinking about management": Berger, P. L., & Luckmann, T. (1966). *The social construction of reality: A treatise on the sociology of knowledge* (p. 61). Garden City, NY: Anchor Books.

10. The figure in Canada is 71 percent, virtually unchanged from the figure in the previous decade. Although a growing number of women are attending university (57 percent of university students are women, compared to 37 percent some 20 years earlier), the percentage of senior managers who are women *declined* between 1996 and 2004. See Greenaway, N. (2006, March 8). Most working women in pink ghetto: Report. *Winnipeg Free Press*, pp. A1, A5.

11. Greenwood and Lawrence suggest that Weber's influence on organization studies may be unrivaled; see Greenwood, R., & Lawrence, T. B. (2005). The Iron Cage in the information age: The legacy and relevance of Max Weber for organization studies [editorial]. *Organization Studies, 26*, 493–499. Some of Weber's most influential works include the following: Weber, M. (1958 [1904–1905]). *The Protestant ethic and the spirit of capitalism* (trans. T. Parsons). New York: Scribner's; Weber, M. (1947). *The theory of social and economic organizations* (ed. T. Parsons, trans. A. M. Henderson & T. Parsons). New York: Free Press; Weber, M. (1946). *From Max Weber: Essays in sociology* (ed. H. H. Gerth & C. W. Mills). New York: Oxford University Press; Weber, M. (1978). *Economy and society* (ed. G. Roth & C. Wittich). Berkeley: University of California Press; Weber, M. (1927). *General economic history* (trans. F. H. Knight). London: Allen & Unwin. Weber remains one of the most frequently cited authors in scholarly management journals. See Lounsbury, M., & Carberry, E. J. (2005). From king to court jester? Weber's fall from grace in organizational theory. *Organization Studies, 26*(4), 501–525.

12. Weber's basic argument and description of how a materialist–individualist emphasis underpins contemporary management and organization theory remains widely accepted (Golembiewski, 1989; Herman, 1997; Hershberger, 1958; Jackall, 1988; Langton, 1985; Nash, 1994; Naughton & Bausch, 1994; Novak, 1996; Pattison, 1997; Pfeffer, 1982; Redekop, Ainlay, & Siemens, 1995), and Weber is still considered to be a leading management moral philosopher (Clegg, 1996). Weber's conclusion that this materialist–individualist point of view leaves us imprisoned in an "iron cage" has also been very widely noted; his metaphor has been cited as among the most well known in the social sciences. A fuller description of how Weber's writings suggest that Mainstream management theory and practice are characterized by their materialist–individualist emphasis can be found in Dyck and Schroeder (2005; see also Dyck & Weber, 2006).
Dyck, B., & Schroeder, D. (2005). Management, theology and moral points of view: Towards an alternative to the conventional materialist–individualist ideal-type of management. *Journal of Management Studies, 42*(4), 705–735; Dyck, B., & Weber, M. (2006). Conventional and radical moral agents: An exploratory look at Weber's moral-points-of-view and virtues. *Organization Studies, 27*(3), 429–450; Golembiewski, R. T. (1989). *Men, management, and morality: Toward a new organizational ethic*. New York: McGraw-Hill; Herman, S. W. (1997). *Durable goods: A covenantal ethic for management and employees*. Notre Dame, IN: University of

Notre Dame Press; Hershberger, G. F. (1958). *The way of the cross in human relations*. Scottdale, PA: Herald Press; Jackall, R. (1988). *Moral mazes: The world of corporate managers*. Oxford, UK: Oxford University; Nash, L. L. (1994). *Believers in business*. Nashville, TN: Thomas Nelson; Naughton, M. J., & Bausch, T. A. (1994). The integrity of a Catholic management education. *California Management Review*, 38(4), 119–140; Novak, M. (1996). *Business as a calling: Work and the examined life*. New York: Free Press; Pattison, S. (1997). *The faith of the managers: When management becomes religion*. London: Cassell; Pfeffer, J. (1982). *Organizations and organization theory*. Marshfield, MA: Pitman; Redekop, C., Ainlay, S. C., & Siemens, R. (1995). *Mennonite entrepreneurs*. Baltimore, MD: John Hopkins University Press; Clegg, S. (1996). The moral philosophy of management: Book review. *Academy of Management Review*, 21, 867–871.

13. Biggart, N. W., & Delbridge, R. (2004). Systems of exchange. *Academy of Management Review*, 29(1), 28–49. They cite Polanyi, K. (1957). *The great transformation*. Boston: Beacon.

14. Of course, this is an oversimplification of Weber's argument, and there is some debate whether aspects of Weber's argument are even historically accurate. For Weber, the materialist–individualist view was consistent with what he called the "Protestant ethic," which went against the traditional teachings of the Catholic Church. Indeed, Weber viewed *individualism* as a defining characteristic of the Protestant ethic moral point of view and "the absolutely decisive difference" from Catholicism (see Weber, 1958, pp. 80–81, 104, 105, 160). Some scholars suggest that there may not be as much difference between Catholics and the Protestant ethic as Weber suggests [see, for example, Novak, M. (1982). *The spirit of democratic capitalism*. New York: Touchstone]. In any case, contemporary scholars agree that Weber was "correct in singling out the doctrine of vocation as the source of Puritan *individualism* in the economic realm . . . One could hardly have placed a more radically individualistic doctrine at the center of one's economic ethic. . . . The conventional interpretation of the ethic also accurately reflects the Puritan emphasis on *material* success" [emphasis added; p. 1575 in Frey, D. E. (1998). Individualist economic values and self-interest: The problem in the Puritan ethic. *Journal of Business Ethics*, 17, 1573–1580].

15. Solomon, R. C., & Hanson, K. R. (1983). *Above the bottom line: An introduction to business ethics* (p. 37). New York: Harcourt Brace Jovanich.

16. Weber (1958, p. 175) is quoting John Wesley, whose theology was clearly not as simplistic as suggested by this quote. Similarly, as discussed in Chapter 1, Smith's "invisible hand" is an oversimplification and a misrepresentation of his larger argument.

17. Solomon & Hanson, 1983.

18. Weber, 1958, p. 181; emphasis added here.

19. Weber, 1958, p. 182.

20. Hawken, P. (1993). *The ecology of commerce: A declaration of sustainability* (p. 131). New York: HarperBusiness.

21. A guild is basically a group of people who share a common interest. Guilds were popular in the Middle Ages, but became less important by 1600. Merchant guilds (for traders) and craft guilds (for bakers, goldsmiths, tailors, and other craftworkers) were the most important, but guilds could also be charitable, religious, and social in nature. See Rosenthal, J. T. (2004). Guild. In *World Book Encyclopedia*.

22. Community was also fostered by the fact that back then people were often more vulnerable to the whims of weather and disease, so there was a greater dependence on other people. It is still true today that poor people tend to share more generously than the relatively well-to-do. When you have personally experienced what it means to be in need, when you have depended on your neighbors, or when you have known the satisfaction of banding together so that everyone's needs are met, then you have had opportunities to experience and build community.

23. Content and quotations in this discussion are from Hawken (1993, pp. 105–106).

24. An unintended outcome associated with this loss of a transgenerational, long-term view is that it may make corporations more prone to ecological abuse.

25. Hawken, 1993, p. 106.

26. "It is interesting to note that the death penalty of individuals [i.e., truly 'natural persons'] is less controversial than the mere suggestion that a few corporations [i.e., pseudo 'natural persons'] may have forfeited their right to exist" (Hawken, 1993, p. 122).

27. Hawken, 1993, p. 106.

28. During that time, the top 500 firms' share of private-sector employment hovered around 21 percent, but their share of the private-sector payroll dropped from 26.3 percent to 23.9 percent. See White, L. J. (2002). Trends in aggregate concentration in the United States. *Journal of Economic Perspectives*, 16(4), 137–160.

29. It is difficult to try to condense more than a century's worth of research into one chapter. We offer the five stylized "eras" described here to try to make this history more reader-friendly, but be aware that history is much more complex and nuanced than represented in this relatively simple framework.

30. Cited on page 42 in Daft, R. L. (2003). *Management*. Mason, OH: Southwestern. Taylor's concern for maximizing materialism is evident in Taylor, F. W. (1911). *Principles of scientific management*. New York: Harper; there, Taylor states, "The principal object of management should be to secure maximum prosperity for the employer, coupled with maximum prosperity for the employee" [cited on page 93 in Schermerhorn, J. R. (2002). *Management* (7th ed.). New York: John Wiley & Sons]. See also Taylor, F. W. (1903). *Shop management*. New York: Harper; Wrege, C., & Stoka, A. M. (1978). Cooke creates a classic: The story behind F. W. Taylor's *Principles of Scientific Management*. *Academy of Management Review*, October, 736–749; and Kanigel, R. (1997). *The one best way: Frederick Winslow Taylor and the enigma of efficiency*. New York: Viking.

31. Although this was a "win-win" situation, it is noteworthy that the firm's proportion of the winnings was greater than the workers' share.

32. Gilbreth, F. B., Jr., & Carey, E. G. (1948/1963). *Cheaper by the dozen*. New York: Thomas Y. Crowell.

33. Gantt, H. L. (1921). *Industrial leadership*. Easton, MD: Hive.

34. Gilbreth, F. B. (1911). *Motion study*. New York: Van Nostrand; Gilbreth, F. B. (1912). *Primer of scientific management*. NewYork: Van Nostrand Reinhold; and Gilbreth, F. B., & Gilbreth, L. M. (1916). *Fatigue study*. New York: Sturgis & Walton.

35. Jones, G. R., & George, J. M. (2003). *Contemporary management* (3rd ed., pp. 39, 40). New York: McGraw-Hill Irwin. See the interestingly titled Ford, H. (1926). Multistream manufacture. In *Encyclopedia Britannica* (13th ed.). New York: Encyclopedia Company.

36. Cited in Daft (2003, p. 45). See also Follett, M. P. (1918). *The new state: Group organization: The solution of popular government*. London: Longmans, Green; Follett, M. P. (1924). *Creative experience*. London: Longmans, Green; Metcalf, H. C., & Urwick, L. (Eds.). (1940). *Dynamic administration: The collected papers of Mary Parker Follett*. New York: Harper & Row; Parker, L. D. (1984). Control in organizational life: The contribution of Mary Parker Follett.

Academy of Management Review, 9, 736–745; Graham, P. (1995). *M. P. Follett—prophet of management: A celebration of writings from the 1920s.* Boston: Harvard Business School Press; and Follett, M. P. (1995). *Prophet of management.* Boston: Harvard Business School Press. We also draw on descriptions of Follet's contributions found in Jones and George (2003, p. 55) and Schermerhorn (2002, p. 95).

37. Even though Lillian Gilbreth was more interested in the human side of work, textbooks typically place her with her husband Frank in the "classical" era, sometimes describing her as "the first lady of management" (Daft, 2003, p. 42). For more information on Lillian Gilbreth, see Wren, D. (1994). *The evolution of management thought.* New York: Wiley.

38. Roethlisberger, F. J., Dickson, W. J., & Wright, H. A. (1939). *Management and the worker.* Cambridge, MA: Harvard University Press; Mayo, E. (1933). *The human problems of an industrial civilization.* New York: MacMillan; and Mayo, E. (1945). *The social problems of an industrial civilization.* Boston: Harvard Business School. Note that there is some debate about the correct interpretation of some of the results of their research: Adair, J. G. (1984). The Hawthorne effect: A reconsideration of a methodological artifact. *Journal of Applied Psychology,* 69(2), 334–345; Diaper, G. (1990). The Hawthorne effect: A fresh examination. *Education Studies,* 16(3), 261–268; Carey, A. (1967). The Hawthorne studies: A radical criticism. *American Sociological Review, 32,* 403–416; Jones, S. R. (1992). Was there a Hawthorne effect? *American Sociological Review,* November, 451–468; and O'Connor, E. S. (1999). The politics of management thought: A case study of the Harvard Business School and the human relations school. *Academy of Management Review,* 24, 117–131.

39. Although this example may seem humorous, large corporations may have a great say in the "reality" that is being socially constructed.

40. Actually, the term "Hawthorne effect" was not coined by the original researchers, but rather by French [French, J. R. P. (1953). Experiments in field settings. In L. Festinger & D. Katz (Eds.), *Research methods in the behavioral sciences* (pp. 98–135). New York: Holt, Rinehart and Winston], who used it to describe "marked increases in production which were related only to the special position and social treatment they [workers] received" (cited in Jones, 1992, p. 452). The idea that the Hawthorne effect shows that it is giving "attention to employees, not working conditions per se, that has the dominant impact on productivity" (Peters & Waterman, 1982, pp. 5–6; cited in Jones, 1992, p. 454) has been perpetuated in the popular management literature. However, scholars today use the term to refer to "the problem in field experiments that subjects' knowledge that they are in an experiment modifies their behavior" (Adair, 1984) and, indeed, question whether the original data even demonstrate a Hawthorne effect (e.g., Adair, 1984; Jones, 1992).

41. McGregor, D. (1960). *The human side of enterprise.* New York: McGraw-Hill. See also Heil, G., Bennis, W., & Stephens, D.C. (2000). *Douglas McGregor revisited: Managing the human side of the enterprise.* New York: John Wiley & Sons.

42. Rosenthal, R., & Jacobson, L. (1968). *Pygmalion in the classroom.* New York: Rinehart and Winston.

43. Eden, D., & Shani, A. B. (1982). Pygmalion goes to boot camp: Expectancy, leadership, and trainee performance. *Journal of Applied Psychology,* 67(2), 194–199.

44. Called *operational* research teams in Great Britain and *operations* research teams in the United States (Daft, 2003, p. 50).

45. Thompson, J. D. (1967). *Organizations in action.* New York: McGraw-Hill.

46. Katz, D., & Kahn, R. L. (1966). *The social psychology of organizations.* New York: Wiley.

47. Simon, H. A. (1947). *Administrative behavior.* New York: MacMillan; Simon, H. A. (1957). *Models of man.* New York: Wiley; March, J. G., & Simon, H. A. (1958). *Organizations.* New York: Wiley; Simon, H. A. (1960). *The new science of management decision.* New York: Harper & Row; and Simon, H. A. (1987). Making management decisions: The role of intuition and emotion. *Academy of Management Executive,* February, 57–63.

48. Burns, T., & Stalker, G. M. (1966). *The management of innovation* (2nd ed.). London: Tavistock.

49. Child, J. (1972). Organizational structure, environment, and performance: The role of strategic choice. *Sociology, 6,* 1–22.

50. Godard, J. (1992). Education vs. training in business schools: The case of industrial relations. *Canadian Journal of Administrative Sciences, 9,* 238–252.

51. Selznick, P. (1949). *TVA and the grassroots.* Berkeley: University of California Press; and Selznick, P. (1957). *Leadership and administration.* New York: Harper & Row.

52. Dyck, B. (1994a). Build in sustainable development, and they will come: A vegetable field of dreams. *Journal of Organizational Change Management,* 7(4), 47–63; and Dyck, B. (1994b). From airy-fairy ideals to concrete realities: The case of shared farming. *Leadership Quarterly,* 5(3/4), 227–246.

53. Kneen, B. (1989). *From land to mouth: Understanding the food system.* Toronto, CA: NC Press Limited. Food issues will be discussed further in subsequent chapters.

54. Selznick (1949) defines *institutionalization* as occurring when something is "infused with value beyond the technical requirements of the task at hand." Many of today's social structures and systems may have been rational when they were introduced, but over time they have become institutionalized and are difficult to change even if they are no longer rational.

55. Berger & Luckmann, 1966, p. 52.

56. Berger & Luckmann, 1966.

57. Liebowitz, S. J., & Margolis, S. E. (1990). The fable of the keys. *Journal of Law and Economics,* 33; and Liebowitz, S. J., & Margolis, S. E. (1996). Typing errors. *Reasononline.* Accessed at http://reason.com/9606/Fe.QWERTY.shtml.

58. It seems that this story itself has become institutionalized as an example of institutionalization. The story persists even though Liebowitz and Margolis argue that specific elements of it are based on weak or faulty evidence. [See Liebowitz, S. J., & Margolis, S. E. (1990). The fable of the keys. *Journal of Law and Economics,* 33; and Liebowitz, S. J., & Margolis, S. E. (1996). Typing errors. *Reasononline,* accessed at http://reason.com/9606/Fe.QWERTY.shtml.] For example, they point to methodological problems in Dvorak's original experiments and to the fact that there may have been some conflict of interest in the U.S. Navy study because the study was apparently done by Dvorak himself. At the time, Dvorak was the Navy's top expert in time and motion studies. The Navy study claims that a group of typists who received training on a Dvorak keyboard increased their productivity by 75 percent, compared to an increase of 27 percent for typists who received further training on the QWERTY keyboard. In their critique of this study, Liebowitz and Margolis suggest that the advantage may have been more like 40 percent to 20 percent. They cite subsequent studies in the 1950s through the 1970s that suggest that retraining on

the Dvorak keyboard is actually inferior to retraining on the QWERTY keyboard. There are two lessons here. First, the use of the story itself has become an example of institutionalization. Second, by focusing on whether the Dvorak keyboard is superior to the QWERTY keyboard, we lose sight of the fact that the QWERTY keyboard has become so institutionalized that we still lack a new-and-improved configuration of keys to replace a century-old configuration that had been initially developed in part to slow down typing speeds.

59. Barley, S. R. (1986). Technology as an occasion for structuring: Evidence from observations of CT scanners and the social order of radiology departments. *Administrative Science Quarterly*, 31, 78–108.

60. Garfinkel, H. (1964). Studies of the routine grounds of everyday activities. *Social Problems*, 11(3), 225–250.

61. Zucker, L. G. (1977). The role of institutionalization in cultural persistence. *American Sociological Review*, 42, 726–743.

62. These numbers are not exact.

63. "Universities and professional training institutions are important centers for the development of organizational norms among professional managers and their staff" [page 152 in DiMaggio, P. F., & Powell, W. W. (1983). The iron cage revisited: Institutional isomorphism and collective rationality in organizational fields. *American Sociological Review*, 48, 147–160].

64. See, for example, Pfeffer, J. (1977). The ambiguity of leadership. *Academy of Management Review*, 2(1), 104–112; and Schein, E. H. (1985). *Organizational culture and leadership*. San Francisco: Jossey-Bass.

65. For example, see McCarty, J. A., & Shrum, L. J. (2001). The influence of individualism, collectivism, and locus of control on environmental beliefs and behavior. *Journal of Public Policy and Marketing*, 20(1), 93–104.

66. A number of management journals have devoted "special issues" to the natural environment beginning in the 1990s.

67. This point will be discussed in more detail in Chapter 4.

68. Even so, evidence suggests that many people continue to see this gap as legitimate, perhaps because these views have become institutionalized. See Blount, S., Jost, J. T., Pfeffer, J., & Hunyady, G. (2003, August). *Fair-market ideology: Its cognitive–motivational underpinnings*. Stanford GSB Research Paper No. 1816. Available at SSRN: http://ssrn.com/abstract=441005.

69. For an excellent summary, see Kasser, T. (2003). *The high price of materialism*. Cambridge, MA: MIT Press, Bradford Book.

70. For example, some communities have decided for aesthetic reasons to limit the size of McDonald's "golden arches" [see, for example, Kripalani, J. (2004, August 14). Rules on poles, signs keep city's aesthetic look. *Miami Herald*, p. 44WW. People oppose Wal-Mart because of its aesthetics—"even its champions don't claim it's pretty" [Dicker, J. (2005, November 6). All the rage: Wal-Mart as the great divider. *Boston Globe*. http://www.boston.com/business/articles/2005/11/06/all_the_rage?mode=PF on June 14/06].

71. An early proponent has been Judi Neal, who maintains a Spirituality-at-Work website.

72. Kriger, M., & Seng, Y. (2005). Leadership with inner meaning: A contingency theory of leadership based on the worldviews of five religions. *Leadership Quarterly*, 16, 771–806.

73. These data were taken from two studies—"The Spiritual Life of College Students: A National Study of College Students' Search for Meaning and Purpose" and "Spirituality and the Professoriate: A National Study of Faculty Beliefs, Attitudes, and Behaviors"—both done by the Higher Education Research Institute, University Graduate School of Education and Information Studies, University of California, Los Angeles. See also anecdotal evidence in Finder, A. (2007, May 2). Matters of faith find a new prominence on campus. *New York Times*. Accessed February 8, 2008, at http://www.nytimes.com/2007/05/02/education/02spirituality.html?_r=1&scp=1&sq=&st=nyt&oref=slogin

74. The ratio between those holding primarily materialist values and those holding these emerging nonmaterialist values changed from 4:1 in 1970 to 4:3 by 1990; see Giacolone, R. A. (2004). A transcendent business education for the 21st century. *Academy of Management Learning and Education*, 3(4), 415–420.

75. New American Dream Survey. (September, 2004). www.newdream.org.

76. Stoney, C., & Winstanley, D. (2001). Stakeholding: Confusion or utopia? Mapping the conceptual terrain. *Journal of Management Studies*, 38(5), 603–626.

77. Margolis, J., & Walsh, J. P. (2003). Misery loves company: Rethinking social initiatives by business. *Administrative Science Quarterly*, 48, 268–305.

78. Brenner, J. G. (1999) *The emperors of chocolate: Inside the secret world of Hershey and Mars*. New York: Random House. Cadbury company website, http://www.cadbury.co.uk; Doherty, B. (2005). New thinking in international trade? A case study of the Day Chocolate Company. *Sustainable Development*, 13(3), 166–176; Lehman, G. (2007, September 7). *Socially responsible chocolate: Cadbury Brothers in England's Victorian era*. Annual Howard Raid Chair Lecture, Faculty Colloquium, Bluffton University, Bluffton, OH; *The history of chocolate*. (2006, June 16), http://www.middleboro.k12.ma.us/Middleboro/CHOC/chocolate.htm; www.divinechoclate.com; www.papapaa.org/ks3/legal.htm; *Chocolate industry expands sustainable farming efforts*, Susan.smith@worldcocoa.org; Moran, M. (2005, June 1). Confections 2005: State of the industry. *Gourmet Retailer*, accessed June 17, 2006, at http://www.gourmetretailer.com/gourmetretailer/magazine/article_display.jsp?vnu_content_id=1000946002); and International Cocoa Association website, http://www.icco.org.

79. The word "chocolate" comes from the Mayan word *xocolatl*, which means "bitter water"; the Mexican Indian word for chocolate comes from the terms *choco* (foam) and *atl* (water). For most of its history, chocolate was consumed as a beverage. The bitter beverage was made from roasted cocoa beans, water, and spices. The cocoa bean also played an important role in the religious lives of the Aztecs, an ancient people who ruled a mighty empire in Mexico during the 1400s and 1500s. They believed that Quetzalcoatl, their creator and god of agriculture, had traveled to Earth on a beam of the morning star and carried the cocoa tree from paradise. Like the Mayans, the Aztecs drank the chocolate, but added ingredients such as honey and vanilla to make it tastier than the Mayans' recipe.

80. Cortes brought cocoa beans to Spain, where they were hidden in Spanish monasteries. They became the secret ingredient in a fashionable drink that only the wealthy and Spanish nobility could afford. The sources of this ingredient remained secret for almost a century. Spain lost its monopoly on European chocolate in the early 1600s, when plantations began to sprout up in other parts of Europe, where chocolate grew in popularity among the well-to-do.

81. In those days, chocolate was sold in drinking houses. A Quaker named Joseph Fry made the first chocolate bar in Great Britain in 1847. Quakers, also known as the Society of Friends, are a

nonconformist and pacifist group that emerged in the seventeenth century in protest against the formalism of the established Church of England. Their strong beliefs and ideals motivated Quakers to pursue projects that fostered justice, equality, and social reform and that alleviated poverty and deprivation.

82. George Cadbury was clearly interested in facilitating different forms of employee well-being outside of the factory, asking, "Why should an industrial area be squalid and depressing?"

83. Cocoa is produced in 47 different countries, mostly within 10 degrees of the equator, where temperatures range between 70°F and 90°F and annual rainfall is 60 to 100 inches. The largest producer of cocoa is Cote d'Ivoire (1,250,000 tonnes per year), and the second largest is Ghana (370,000 tonnes per year).

84. Cocoa prices are also related to the laws of supply and demand. For example, in the 2003–2004 growing year, some 3.5 million tons of cocoa beans were produced worldwide. Because this supply was more than was needed, the price dropped by almost 25 percent (*ICCO Annual Report, 2003/2004*). Between 1998 and 2000, the price of cocoa beans declined by almost one-half (from $1236 per tonne to $672 per tonne). In many cases, the control that large firms have over small farmers dates back to colonialism, when rich European powers used their colonies overseas to provide cheap raw materials. Even after many of the colonies gained their political independence, little changed for small farmers overseas. They had no bargaining power over the large companies that controlled the chocolate trade, so prices continued to fall. In addition, the situation was often made worse by corruption or mismanagement within the newly independent governments. Moreover, rich nations also use restrictions such as tariff barriers to tax some imports differently than others. For example, importing cocoa beans into Europe is much less expensive than importing coca butter into the same region, and even less expensive than importing chocolate. This tariff system serves to penalize low-income countries if they try to add value to raw materials such as cocoa beans.

85. These figures are for sales of chocolate bars in the United Kingdom, and do not include taxes paid when purchasing the bar.

86. This definition of Fair Trade is adapted from the TransFair USA and TransFair Canada websites, accessed June 20, 2006, at http://www.transfairusa.org/content/about/overview.php, and http://www.transfair.ca/en/fairtrade/, respectively.

87. The Kuapa Kokoo is a cooperative in Ghana with approximately 45,000 members.

CHAPTER **3**

I n this and all subsequent chapters, the road map provides an overview of how we will first describe the Mainstream approach to the chapter material, and then contrast and compare it with the Multistream approach. Think about the different routes that you might drive to travel from your home to your job or school. The routes may cover the same territory, but each has a different "feel" to it. Sometimes you may wish to travel on the main highway, and other times on a more scenic route. In this chapter, we will see how differences in the Mainstream and Multistream approaches influence how the task and macro environments are perceived and managed.

ROAD MAP

TASK ENVIRONMENT

View of Key Stakeholders

Customers

Members

Owners

Other organizations (suppliers, competitors)

MACRO ENVIRONMENT

View of Key Dimensions

Sociocultural

Natural

Political–legal

Economic–technological

The Task and Macro Environments of Management

MAINSTREAM MANAGEMENT	**MULTISTREAM MANAGEMENT**
Serving customers permits maximizing an organization's financial viability.	An organization's financial viability permits serving customers.
Members should be as productive as possible.	Members should be engaged and productive.
Managers maximize the owners' financial well-being.	Managers serve owners' multiple forms of well-being.
Managers try to gain relative power over other organizations.	Managers nurture mutually beneficial relationships among organizations.
Managers nurture and satisfy materialist–individualist values and norms.	Managers nurture overall well-being values and norms.
Managers find inexpensive inputs and inexpensive places to dispose of waste.	A proactive approach is used for sustainable development.
Managers lobby for managerial rights and financial self-interests.	Managers lobby for stakeholder rights and interests.
Acquisitive economics focuses on the short term, promotes financial self-interests, and is money-based.	*Sustenance economics* focuses on the long term, promotes community interests, and is overall well-being-based.

Managing as Appleseeds[1]

Since starting their First Fruits apple orchard in Washington in 1980, Ralph and Cheryl Broetje have been very sensitive to managing the environmental aspects of their organization. Today First Fruits is the largest privately owned contiguous apple orchard in the United States, covering more than 4300 acres in a virtually frost-free microclimate stretching for nearly 10 miles along the Snake River. Ralph has been recognized as the Apple Grower of the Year.[2]

When the Broetjes first planted 800 acres of apples on the banks of the Snake River in southeastern Washington, they were surrounded by fields of alfalfa, hay, and wheat and a lot of sage bush. Irrigation was a key to their orchard's success, and they realized that the dams then being built on the Lower Snake River would supply the water needed to develop the potential of the nutrient-rich but arid land next to the new reservoirs.[3]

Ralph Broetje developed long-term working relationships with leading horticulturalists in the field and read extensively. He also paid close attention to consumer preferences and trends for apples, which is especially important because apple trees do not produce fruit until three years after being planted. Broetje needed to plant varieties of apples that would be in demand in the future—not the ones that had been successful in the past. For

First Fruit employees sort apples.

example, Broetje began to plant Granny Smith apples well before they had become common in the marketplace.

Today the Broetjes recognize that consumers are becoming increasingly concerned about the health and safety of their food. Their orchard is the first in the United States to receive certification from the independent Safe Quality Food agency,[4] which is the highest level of certification that can be achieved in this field. The Broetjes are also on the cutting edge when it comes to organic farming. Their daughter Sara Broetje Dahle oversees the organic program. The company has a 550-acre organic orchard and, in terms of pest control, is only one chemical away from being organic in its main orchard thanks to its use of mating disruption and other tactics to attack "bad" pests.[5]

The Broetjes are also leaders in technologies for handling the apples once they have been harvested. First Fruits was one of the first apple growers to implement centralized computer-controlled atmosphere rooms. Its system permits workers to control the temperature of each room to within one-tenth of one degree, and it provides control over the nitrogen, oxygen, carbon dioxide, and other gases in the atmosphere in each room to within 0.1 percent. This close monitoring ensures that customers receive the freshest product available year-round.

Although consumers, technology, and ecological issues are important, the Broetjes believe that the real key to building a successful organization is the people who work there. Apple orchards are very labor-intensive operations, and First Fruits employs approximately 2000 workers during the peak harvest season. Rather than provide only seasonal apple-picking jobs for migrant workers, the Broetjes deliberately enlarged the firm to develop year-round jobs for employees. First Fruits now employs some 1000 permanent workers who store, sort, and package apples. This emphasis on year-round work also prompted the Broetjes to open a daycare center to help meet the child-care needs of their packing plant employees, 80 percent of whom are women. And when the Broetjes became aware of the housing shortage and the poor living conditions employees were experiencing, Ralph convinced the planning committee in his county to approve the construction of a $6 million community at considerable financial risk for First Fruits. This town, which the residents named Vista Hermosa ("Beautiful View"), includes 121 single-family homes, 28 apartment units, a chapel, an elementary school, and a convenience store. The rents are kept below the average in the area to ensure affordable housing for families.

First Fruits is committed to caring for its employees and for others in need around the world. The Broetjes talk about being blessed by having the opportunity to help their workers afford decent housing. Their management style, and particularly their human resources management, can be summarized by the idea of "servant leadership" and looking out for the effect that their business has "on the least privileged in society." As Cheryl Broetje notes:

> When we started our business, we had nothing but a dream and the commitment to work it out. It was with the help of others who gave us every opportunity to learn, to participate, that we learned to fly. We needed an empowering team around us. When we finally became financially successful, it would have been easy to continue stockpiling money (as opposed to true wealth) around us. However, the spiritual values that we are also committed to would not let us. For us, it was impossible to separate business goals from spiritual values which promote the equality and connectedness of all people, using their unique gifts and skills to serve one another while together serving the common good.[6]

This emphasis on community values represents the primary reason for First Fruits' organizational success. Each year the company donates nearly 75 percent of its profits to local, domestic, and international projects. Consider the example of the cherry orchards, where 100 percent of all profits are donated to charity (the amount ranges from $200,000 to almost $1 million per year). A council of 20 elected employees makes the decisions as to where these donations are sent. Little wonder that First Fruits' employees are highly motivated, that its orchards are among the most productive in the industry, and that price-competitive retailers such as Wal-Mart and Costco are among its most important customers.

"Sure, we have to make money or we'd have to shut the doors," Cheryl Broetje explains. "But profit isn't our main motive. It becomes the by-product of treating people with dignity, respect, and mutuality, and as equals in every sense of the word. We all have a role to play in creating a community of people who care for a business that then cares for them. We believe that if we ever stopped doing that, we would implode."[7]

INTRODUCTION TO THE ENVIRONMENTS OF MANAGEMENT

Chapters 3 and 4 describe the three environments that managers work within: task, macro, and international. This chapter explores the task environment and the macro environment. The international environment is discussed in Chapter 4.

To investigate the environments faced by managers, we will move in concentric circles, starting with the **task environment,** which has the greatest immediate influence on managers (see Figure 3.1). This environment contains four key groups of stakeholders that managers need to pay attention to: customers, members, owners, and other organizations (e.g., suppliers and competitors). We then move to a regional or national level of analysis. This **macro environment** contains four dimensions: sociocultural, natural, political–legal, and economic–technological environments.

We will look at the task and macro environments first from a Mainstream perspective, and then from a Multistream perspective. Often the actions of Mainstream and Multistream managers may be very similar, even though their motivation is quite different. For example, by definition Multistream managers are willing to offer environmentally friendly products and services even if this practice does not maximize their profits, whereas Mainstream managers will offer environmentally friendly products and services if they see it as a market opportunity to maximize their profits and to gain a positive reputation with customers.[8]

> **Task environment** contains four key groups of stakeholders that managers need to pay attention to: customers, members, owners, and other organizations (e.g., suppliers and competitors).
>
> **Macro environment** contains four dimensions that managers must deal with at the regional or national level: sociocultural, natural, political–legal, and economic–technological environments.

THE MAINSTREAM VIEW OF KEY STAKEHOLDERS IN THE TASK ENVIRONMENT

No organization exists within a vacuum. Managers have key stakeholders to whom they must pay attention. Recall from Chapter 1 that a *stakeholder* is any group within or outside the organization that is directly affected by the organization and has a stake in its performance. In a sense, stakeholders can be seen as the "faces" of various aspects

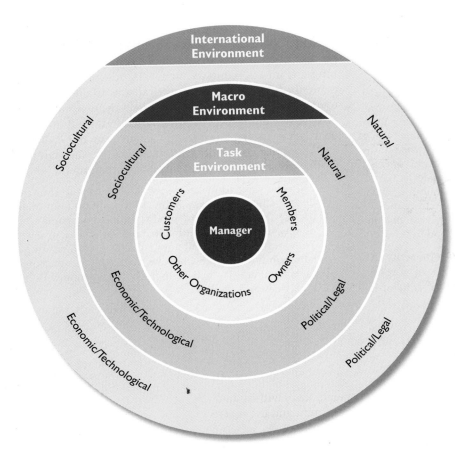

Figure 3.1   Three basic levels of the environment for managers

of an organization's environment. Stakeholders have many different expectations, but with a few exceptions, they all want the organization to remain sustainable and viable.[9] For example:

- Customers want products and services that meet their needs and wants.
- Members want rewarding and meaningful work and interactions on the job.
- Owners want to receive an appropriate reward for their investment.
- Other organizations such as suppliers want predictable orders with on-time payment, and competitors expect fair and legal actions.

Managers also have expectations from each of these stakeholders. Mainstream managers, for example, want paying customers, productive members, supportive owners, and influence over other organizations. Figure 3.2 summarizes these expectations and relationships. As indicated by the two-way arrows in the figure, managers are both influenced by and attempt to influence each stakeholder.

Customers

Customers are the stakeholders who consume an organization's product and service outputs.

INFLUENCE OF CUSTOMERS ON MANAGERS.   Paying customers are the lifeblood of business organizations because they provide the money needed to pay salaries to members, purchase inputs from suppliers, and provide dividends to shareholders. In nonbusiness organizations, other terms are used instead of "customers"—for example, soup kitchens have *patrons*, hospitals have *patients*, schools have *students*, and so on. In each case, the **customer** is the stakeholder who is the focal point of an organization's product and service outputs. An organization cannot last long without customers. The importance of customers is reflected in the familiar maxim, "The customer is always right." From a Mainstream perspective, customer service is especially important because better service leads to greater loyalty (repeat business), which in turn leads to higher profits.

INFLUENCE OF MANAGERS ON CUSTOMERS.   Business managers try to develop a stable or growing customer base. This can be accomplished in a variety of ways, including advertising and marketing, providing excellent products and services at reasonable prices, designing products and services to meet the needs of customers, and outperforming competitors. Creating a demand for the organization's products and services is a key way to maximize the bottom line. For example, Steve Jobs of Apple Computers is known for his uncanny ability to conceive of and design products that become highly valued by customers. As Bill Gates, CEO of Microsoft, put it: "I'd give a lot to have Steve's taste, his intuitive taste, both for people and products."[10]

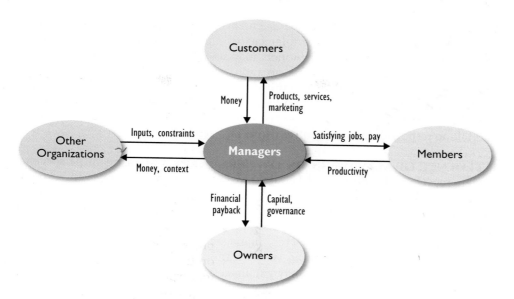

Figure 3.2   Mainstream aspects of relationships with key stakeholders in the task environment

Members

INFLUENCE OF MEMBERS ON MANAGERS.   For most managers, the nearest and most highly visible stakeholders are the other **members** of their organization, particularly their own subordinates. In most cases, members are paid employees (e.g., staff in a hospital, sales clerks in a grocery store, social workers in a welfare agency). In other cases, members may be volunteers (e.g., parents in a neighborhood sports league, worshippers in a local mosque, supporters of Greenpeace). Members do the everyday work of the organization. Organizations are often described as "smooth-running machines" when each member, as a "cog in the wheel," works for the whole organization to be as productive as possible. From a Mainstream perspective, a primary goal of managers is to maximize members' productivity in the workplace. If members are productive, then mangers will be evaluated as doing a good job. Managers who adapt their style to the strengths and weaknesses of members will be more successful.

Members are employees and volunteers who work for or belong to an organization.

INFLUENCE OF MANAGERS ON MEMBERS.   Managers commonly try to maximize members' efforts by appealing to their self-interests, such as linking their on-the-job productivity to their pay or future promotions. Naturally, members will be motivated to work harder if they are rewarded for their efforts. Pay is a primary area of concern for employees, along with benefits such as affordable health insurance, paid sick leave, and secure pension and retirement benefits. Their relationships with their managers have an influence on members' motivation, self-confidence, identity, and job satisfaction. In some situations, productivity may be maximized by empowering members, providing them with opportunities to work in teams and groups, and linking their rewards to effective team performance (e.g., via profit-sharing plans, team bonuses).

Owners

INFLUENCE OF OWNERS ON MANAGERS.   **Owners** make the basic decisions as to what an organization is and does. In other words, they are responsible for its creation and governance. In corporations, shareholders elect the board of

Owners are stakeholders who make the basic decisions as to what an organization is and does, and are responsible for the creation and overarching governance of the organization.

directors, who (together with top management) decide how and in which industry the organization will compete. Similar factors are also important in nonbusiness organizations. For example, parishioners may set up and oversee a local church, a volunteer community group may set up and oversee a community club, or a group of parents may set up and oversee a private school. Managers in both business and nonbusiness organizations must look out for owners' interests by following proper accounting procedures, providing reports about the organization's performance, and taking responsibility for their decisions and actions.

INFLUENCE OF MANAGERS ON OWNERS.   From a Mainstream perspective, owners represent the primary stakeholder group that managers serve. In corporations, other stakeholders' interests are subordinate to shareholders' financial interests. The Mainstream management approach is to focus on the material interests of the owners—for example, by maximizing profits, earnings per share, share value, and dividends. For a community club, managers may try to keep costs down for participants while fielding winning sports teams. Because owners depend on the judgment and information provided by managers, managers have a lot of influence about what owners know and thus which kinds of decisions owners will make.

Other Organizations

INFLUENCE OF OTHER ORGANIZATIONS ON MANAGERS.   Suppliers and competitors set constraints on what managers can do. For example, a manager cannot purchase specific products or services if there are no suppliers in the marketplace. Also, managers must consider competitors' prices and product lines when establishing their own organizations' prices and product lines.

INFLUENCE OF MANAGERS ON OTHER ORGANIZATIONS.   Suppliers expect payment from their customers, and competitors expect fair practices in a shared marketplace. From a Mainstream perspective, the goal of management is to gain as much control as possible over suppliers and secure advantages over competitors. For example, thanks to its huge purchasing power, Wal-Mart can demand lower prices from suppliers than its competitors can.[11] In turn, Wal-Mart can charge lower prices to its customers than its competitors can. From a Mainstream perspective, the idea is to defeat competitors. Indeed, Wal-Mart has been accused of entering a geographic trading area and driving the smaller local competitors out of business.[12]

Mainstream managers may also be sensitive to concerns of organizations other than suppliers and competitors, especially when it enhances the bottom line. For example, managers may try to improve their organization's financial performance by enhancing its reputation. A company might invest in philanthropic causes such as supporting museums, symphonies, and not-for-profit foundations. A company could also take a visible role in improving public health and education.

THE MAINSTREAM VIEW OF THE FOUR DIMENSIONS IN THE MACRO ENVIRONMENT

In addition to the specific task environment that confronts them, managers must also understand the larger macro environment that surrounds them. The macro environment includes four key components: sociocultural, natural, political–legal,

Figure 3.3   Mainstream aspects of relationships with key dimensions of macro environment

and economic–technological. As depicted by the two-way arrows in Figure 3.3, managers can both influence and be influenced by each of these four dimensions.

Sociocultural Environment

INFLUENCE OF THE SOCIOCULTURAL ENVIRONMENT ON MANAGERS.   The **sociocultural environment** refers to the norms, customs, and values of the general population and its demographic subgroups. This environment influences the needs and wants of customers, the expectations of members and owners, and the attitudes of competitors and suppliers. As a result, managers must monitor trends in demographics, health care, education, and other social institutions, among other areas. For example:

- The September 11, 2001, terrorist attacks continue to have repercussions that influence social views and ideas of appropriate behavior. In general, people are feeling less secure, government policies and regulations have been tightened with regard to cross-border travel, and greater interest has arisen in international security and peacemaking.

- Managers should expect increasing diversity among the people with whom they work, as immigration and birth patterns are expected to lead to a greater variety in ethnic and religious backgrounds. For example, by 2070, no single ethnic group is expected to account for more than 50 percent of the U.S. population. In other words, *every* ethnic group will be a minority. The number of nontraditional families, such as single-father households, is also increasing in the United States.[13]

- Because of a generational shift, baby boomers (i.e., people born in 1946 to 1964) are no longer the dominant economic group in some markets, but are becoming dominant consumers in other markets such as leisure and health care. This is particularly true for affluent boomers (i.e., those making more than $75,000 annually), who account for 67 percent of the total wealth in the United

Sociocultural environment refers to the norms, customs, and values of a general population and its demographic subgroups.

States.[14] In health care, for example, baby boomers are spending more money and demanding greater participation in the decision-making process both for themselves and for their aging parents.[15] By contrast, in other markets the most important demographic group are Web-savvy young people who share information and ideas globally, and whose tastes and tendencies drive demand for electronics, entertainment, food, and fashion.[16]

Mainstream managers adapt to trends in the sociocultural environment so that they can maximize the material gains for their organizations. They want to be the first to recognize new opportunities in the marketplace, because doing so permits them to gain market share relative to their competitors. For example, "big box" retailers such as Home Depot were among the first in the home improvement industry to recognize the fact that compared to the previous generation of homeowners, the baby-boom generation is (1) less interested in and has less time to complete "do-it-yourself" home improvement projects, but (2) still wants user-friendly, one-stop-shopping and hands-on involvement in choosing the products (e.g., carpet, wall coverings, plumbing fixtures) that they then hire tradespeople to install. Unlike the traditional corner hardware stores, which served as a meeting place catering to do-it-yourselfers, the most successful retailers in the present sociocultural environment focus on selling décor products to consumers, and hard-core products (e.g., nuts-and-bolts items, tools, electrical wiring, lumber) to the tradespeople who actually install the products.[17]

INFLUENCE OF MANAGERS ON THE SOCIOCULTURAL ENVIRONMENT. One way that managers can shape public opinion and sociocultural values is by supporting think tanks that promote their organizational interests.[18] A **think tank** is an organization that conducts research to inform and influence areas such as social and public policy, technology, and defense. Think tanks can provide a valuable service to both organizations and society as a whole, but sometimes they appear to favor the business interests. One particularly infamous example was described in a *New York Times* article that reported that Microsoft had bankrolled a California think tank (Independent Institute) to run full-page newspaper ads supporting Microsoft's claim of innocence in the face of federal antitrust charges. The ads presented an ostensibly unbiased and scholarly view in the form of a letter signed by 240 academic "experts" who thought that the government had gone too far in its case against Microsoft. The *Times* article noted that Microsoft had paid for the ads and was, in fact, the single largest donor to the Independent Institute.[19]

Another way that managers try to shape the sociocultural environment is via the media. Most people agree that the media—including television, radio, billboards, newspapers, magazines, and the Internet—play a significant role in shaping social values. However, people give less thought about the role of *managers* in determining the content of the media, and in particular in promoting materialist–individualist values.[20] Consider the fact that 75 percent of the advertising you see is paid for by the world's 100 largest corporations.[21] Which sociocultural values and messages do you think these large corporations will promote? Dr. David Walsh identifies four key values that dominate the mass media:

1. Happiness is found in having things (materialism).
2. Get all you can for yourself (individualism).
3. Get it all as quickly as you can (short time horizon).
4. Win at all costs (competitiveness).[22]

Think tank is an organization that conducts research to inform and influence areas like social and public policy, technology, and defense.

Natural environment is a component of the macro environment that includes all living and nonliving things that have not been created by human technology or human activity.

Ecological footprint refers to how many of Earth's natural resources, measured in acres, are required to sustain human consumption and to absorb the resulting waste.

DIGGING DEEPER

Media and the Sociocultural Environment

Research suggests that mass media both reflect and influence societal values. One study examined how various articles in the print media reported on an important issue of the day—namely, the causes of global warming.[23] In particular, the researchers looked at whether published articles reported (1) only the human factors that cause global warming (e.g., use of fossil fuels), (2) only the nonhuman factors (e.g., methane gas due to animal manure[24]), or (3) a "balanced" view that included both human and nonhuman factors.

The researchers found that of articles published in two top scholarly journals (*Nature* and *Science*), 85 percent focused exclusively on human factors, none reported only nonhuman factors, and 15 percent referred to both human and nonhuman factors. In contrast, for articles in two leading U.S. newspapers (*New York Times* and *Washington Post*), 41 percent focused exclusively on human factors, 15 percent reported only nonhuman factors, and 44 percent referred to both human and nonhuman factors.[25]

Why are U.S. newspaper articles four times more likely than scholarly articles to report on nonhuman causes of global warming? The authors speculate that one reason is because one major component of the U.S. economy is the fossil fuel industry, which newspaper publishers do not wish to offend.

A different explanation may be that the newspapers in general may be more likely to provide "balanced" reporting than scientific journals. The study offered data to test this latter explanation, and examined the content of newspaper articles from countries that are less dependent on the fossil fuel industry (*New Zealand Herald* and Finland's *Helsingen Sanomat*). The researchers found that 90 percent of these articles focused exclusively on human factors, 2 percent reported only nonhuman factors, and 8 percent referred to both human and nonhuman factors. In short, these newspaper articles were more consistent with how global warming is written about in scientific journals. This finding lends support to the idea that economic interests may well influence what is reported in the media.

Natural Environment

INFLUENCE OF THE NATURAL ENVIRONMENT ON MANAGERS. The **natural environment** is composed of all living and nonliving things that have not been created by human technology or human activity.[26] Managers depend on the natural environment to draw organizational inputs (e.g., raw material, natural resources, minerals, water, air) and to dispose of organizational outputs (e.g., products, waste). Natural resources can serve as inputs (e.g., farmland to grow food, mines for getting minerals) and can also help to get rid of organizational waste (e.g., forest land to convert carbon dioxide into oxygen).

The concept of one's **ecological footprint**—which is the amount of Earth's natural resources required to sustain a particular lifestyle—is becoming a popular way for managers to think about how many natural resources their organizations use. Researchers can estimate how many "acres" of natural resources are used by a person or an organization or a nation. Using equivalency measures based on acres of existing cropland, forestland, pastureland, built space, marine and inland fisheries, open ocean, and so on, researchers have estimated the bio-capacity of our planet. Based on these measures, Earth has an average of about 39 acres of resources available per person. However, the ecological footprint of the average person in the world is currently about 54 acres, which means we are using 15 more acres of resources per person than our planet can sustain in the long term. For example, humankind is drawing more fish from our marine and

Figure 3.4 Ecological footprints
The ecological footprint of the average person in various countries differs widely. The bio-capacity of Western Europe is about 42 acres per person, and the bio-capacity of the United States is approximately 50 acres per person. This means that the average Western European uses about 108 acres and the average American uses about 219 acres from other parts of the world. To calculate your personal ecological footprint, go to http://www.myfootprint.org/ or zerofootprint.net/, which also provides information about what steps different organizations and cities are taking to reduce their ecological footprints.[27]

U.S.
269 acres

Canada
205 acres

UK
159 acres

Japan
131 acres

Germany
129 acres

China
31 acres

India
12 acres

inland fisheries than are being reproduced, and we are putting more pollution into the atmosphere than the Earth can manage. Compared to the world average, the ecological footprint rises to an average of 150 acres in Western Europe and 269 acres in the United States (see Figure 3.4 on the preceding page).[28]

INFLUENCE OF MANAGERS ON THE NATURAL ENVIRONMENT.   It is important for managers to become involved in reducing the ecological footprint, because organizations use far more natural resources than individual households do.[29] A growing social awareness of ecological problems (e.g., global warming, nonsustainable ecological footprints) has prompted managers to become increasingly sensitive to the natural environment. Many leading organizations have announced "green" initiatives, such as Wal-Mart promising to be "packaging neutral" by 2025, GE's "ecomagination" program that supports environmentally friendly products, and DuPont's "2015 Sustainability Goals" to derive $6 billion in new revenues from operations that reduce harmful emissions or create energy efficiency.[30]

As shown in Figure 3.5, the approach that managers take to the natural environment varies along a continuum. Because their explicit emphasis on multiple forms of well-being is sensitive to the natural environment, Multistream managers would tend to be farther to the right on the continuum than are Mainstream managers.

The *obstructionist stance* is the least sensitive to the natural environment. Managers taking this approach do as little as possible to address environmental problems. Instead, their focus is on narrowly defined economic priorities, and they resist any social demands lying outside the organization's perceived financial self-interests. This may sometimes lead to illegal activity and doing whatever it takes to prevent knowledge of such behavior from reaching other organizational stakeholders and society at large. This kind of behavior is exemplified by the practice of illegally dumping toxic waste in low-income countries in an effort to avoid paying the high costs associated with proper cleanup available in high-income countries.[31]

With a *defensive strategy* (or *legal approach*), managers do only as much as is legally required. Managers adopting this approach exhibit little environmental sensitivity and may even try to use the law to their own advantage. They will insist that their employees behave legally, but they put the interests of shareholders first at the expense of other stakeholders and the environment. For example, Willamette Industries of Portland, Oregon, agreed to install $7.4 million worth of pollution control equipment in its 13 factories to comply with Environmental Protection Agency requirements—but the move came only after Willamette was fined $11.2 million for violating emissions standards.[32]

With the *market approach*, managers show concern for environmental concerns in response to demands or opportunities in the marketplace. Such managers respond to customers, and if customers are willing to pay for environmentally friendly products and services, then managers will provide them. For example, every time an oil crisis occurs, automobile manufacturers increase their emphasis on fuel-efficient cars. When the crisis passes and the market appears ready for bigger and less fuel-efficient cars, however, managers are quick to invest their marketing and production dollars in less environmentally friendly cars and sport-utility

Figure 3.5 Five options to manage the natural environment

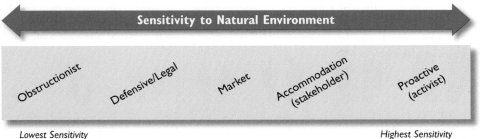

vehicles (SUVs). In short, the market gets what it wants. Recently, customers have shown increased interest in buying "green" products. For example, initially people purchased the Toyota Prius because they liked its innovative technology, but more recent owners of the car are likely to be influenced by concern for global warming.[33] In 2007, 35 million Americans regularly bought products that claimed to be "Earth-friendly."[34] While market-driven, ecologically friendly initiatives by Mainstream managers may have positive implications for the natural environment, some environmental activists fear that

Numerous organizations sell "carbon offsets" to pay for the damage that people's lifestyles contribute to global warming. For example, if you drive 12,000 miles per year in a midsized car that gets 30 miles per gallon, you can neutralize the amount of carbon dioxide emitted by your car by purchasing about $20 worth of "carbon offsets." These carbon offsets may be achieved by using windmill-generated electricity or planting trees.[36]

these efforts are sometimes "greenwashing" (i.e., doing little more than public relations)[35] and that managers will revert to less environmentally friendly ways when they feel that such a move will increase profits.

The *accommodation* or *stakeholder approach* goes beyond the market approach and responds to the environmental concerns of various stakeholder groups, including customers, the local community, business partners, and special-interest groups. With this approach, managers acknowledge the need to be socially responsible and desire to make ecological choices that are reasonable in the eyes of society. They may agree to participate in specific programs when solicitors convince them that these programs are worthy of support. For example, in response to demands by various stakeholders, Compaq Computer Corporation (which is now part of Hewlett-Packard) developed corporate programs to recycle and reduce waste and energy consumption.[37]

Managers exhibit a *proactive approach* when they take the initiative and actively seek out opportunities to enhance the natural environment. They go out of their way to learn about the needs of different stakeholder groups, and they are willing to use organizational resources to promote the interests of the community and the environment. For example, 284 university presidents from some of the most prestigious U.S. schools pledged to make their campuses "carbon neutral": "We're saying that sustainability is no longer an elective," said Cornell president David Skorton.[38]

Another example comes from 3M.[39] In 1975, Joseph Ling, head of 3M's environmental department, developed a program called Pollution Prevention Pays, which was the first integrated, intracompany approach to designing out pollution from manufacturing processes. His plan created incentives for technical staff to modify product manufacturing methods to prevent hazardous and toxic wastes and to reduce costs. More than 6000 separate initiatives were undertaken in the first 30 years of the program to change processes, redesign equipment, and recover waste. The program allowed 3M to eliminate 2.5 billion pounds of pollutants and produced savings of more than $1 billion (counting only the first year of each initiative).[40]

WHAT DO YOU THINK?

Is Modern Agriculture Good for the Natural Environment?

The majority of the world's people are farmers. However, in countries like the United States and Canada, less than 5 percent of people farm, thanks to the output of large-scale farms and the use of high-tech farming techniques.[41] This distancing from farming comes with some costs, as people are less aware of the natural world that sustains us. For example, today most Americans are not able to identify ten local plants, yet they can identity more than 1000 corporate logos![42]

Modern agricultural practices used by large-scale farms in predominantly high-income countries have many benefits. Examples include higher yields, improved control of pests and fungi that damage crops and can threaten human health, and less dependence on fertilizer from animal manure.[43] However, modern agriculture also has some downsides. For example, modern high-technology agricultural practices are two to eight times *less* energy-efficient than more labor-intensive agricultural practices in low-tech countries.[44] A lot of energy is required to fuel tractors, mine and produce fertilizers and pesticides, build farm machinery, and so on. The use of pesticides can also have negative effects on humans and other animals.[45] Finally, there is the issue of the energy used to ship food around the world, which is one reason a growing number of people are subscribing to a "100-mile diet"—that is, trying to eat food grown and produced within 100 miles of where they live.[46]

Even though farmers in low-income countries are more energy efficient in growing food, they find it difficult to compete partly because of large agricultural subsidies in high-income countries (see Chapter 4), and because the big organizations that dominate the global food system prefer to deal with large-scale farmers. Even when a giant like Wal-Mart announced its major initiative to sell organic food at not more than 10 percent more than the cost of conventional foods, reaction was mixed. Environmentalists welcomed the reduction of nonorganic fertilizers and pesticides, but noted that other environmental costs associated with large-scale agriculture and long-distance food remain.

What are the pros and cons of modern agriculture? Is it a good idea to treat farms just like any other business? When it comes to rating the merits of agricultural practices, what are the key inputs and outputs that we measure, and that we fail to measure? What are the pros and cons of bringing organic foods into the mainstream?

Political–legal environment includes both the prevailing philosophy and objectives of the various levels of government, as well as existing laws and regulations.

Documentational capitalism is characterized by an emphasis on detailed contracts, public financial reports, and management independence and rights.

Relational capitalism is characterized by an emphasis on relational contracts, the long-term reputations of organizations, and interdependence and rights of stakeholders.

Political–Legal Environment

INFLUENCE OF THE POLITICAL–LEGAL ENVIRONMENT ON MANAGERS. The **political–legal environment** includes both the prevailing philosophy and objectives of the various levels of government, as well as their ongoing laws and regulations. For example, it includes legislation dealing with workplace health and safety, consumer protection, pollution, international trade, and antitrust laws.

To illustrate how the political–legal environment influences management practice, consider two basic varieties of capitalism.[47] **Documentational capitalism**—which is prevalent in English-speaking countries such as the United States, Canada, the United Kingdom, and Australia—is characterized by an emphasis on detailed contracts, public financial reports, management independence and rights, stringent antitrust legislation, rewarding a labor force that is mobile and has transferable skills, short-term maximization of financial performance, and the use of stock options to motivate managers. In contrast, **relational capitalism**—which tends to be

TABLE 3.1

Characteristics Associated with Documentational Capitalism Versus Relational Capitalism

Measure	Documentational Capitalism	Relational Capitalism
Purchasing power*	Higher growth rate	Higher purchasing power
Job opportunities	Greater job mobility (more going from one organization to another)	Lower unemployment
Innovation	More radical innovations	More incremental fine-tuning
Income equality	More chance to get very rich	Greater income equality
Managerial freedom	Greater freedom for managers to hire and fire employees	Greater employee protection

*Purchasing power is based on GDP per capita and the GDP growth rate. GDP refers to gross domestic product, which is the total financial value of goods and services produced in a country. The per capita GDP is determined by dividing GDP by a country's populations and looking at purchasing power parity.

Source: Based on Hall, P. A., & Soskice, D. (2001). An introduction to varieties of capitalism. In P. A. Hall & D. W. Soskice (Eds.), *Varieties of capitalism: The institutional foundations of comparative advantage* (pp. 1–68). Oxford, UK: Oxford University Press.

found in countries such as Japan, Germany, France, Finland, and Italy—is characterized by an emphasis on relational contracts (e.g., fewer details, greater trust), the long-term reputation and financial performance of organizations, employee rights, the needs of many different stakeholder groups, and investment in developing the skills of employees. Some characteristics associated with each type of capitalism are summarized in Table 3.1. In general terms, documentational capitalism creates an environment that is more consistent with Mainstream management, whereas relational capitalism creates an environment that is more conducive to Multistream management.

Managers in documentational capitalism tend to enjoy more freedom to make decisions and act quickly. There is also greater emphasis on developing radical innovations, and more generous financial rewards for managers who are able to maximize their organization's profits. By comparison, managers in relational capitalism generally look at the longer term. There is less job hopping from one organization to another, and greater emphasis on developing strong relationships with managers in other organizations instead of developing strong contracts.

INFLUENCE OF MANAGERS ON THE POLITICAL–LEGAL ENVIRONMENT.
Managers invest considerable resources in managing the political–legal environment. For example, organizations make financial donations directly to political parties in the hope of influencing their decisions, and lobbyists are hired by businesses to influence decisions that are in their clients' best interests (they also try to convince politicians that those interests will benefit the public). *The Hill,* a newspaper about and for the U.S. Congress, reports that total lobbying expenditures exceeded $2 billion in 2005.[48] For example, Rupert Murdoch, who commands a multimedia organization valued at nearly $68 billion, pays outside lobbyists approximately $1 million per year. This lobbying has helped Murdoch in matters such as convincing legislators to raise limits so that he could own local television stations that reach more than 39 percent of Americans.[49] Corporations such as FedEx, R. J. Reynolds, and BellSouth are among organizations that view providing politicians with seats on corporate jets as a way to discuss complex issues facing their business.[50]

Economic–Technological Environment

Economic environment refers to how financial resources are used and distributed within a specific region or country.

Technology is the combination of equipment (e.g., computers, machinery, tools) and skills (e.g., techniques, knowledge, processes) by which the acquisition, design, production, and distribution of goods and services can be managed.

The **economic environment** refers to how financial resources are used and distributed in a specific country or region. **Technology** refers to the combination of equipment (e.g., computers, machinery, tools) and skills (e.g., techniques, knowledge, processes) by which the acquisition, design, production, and distribution of goods and services are managed.

INFLUENCE OF THE ECONOMIC ENVIRONMENT ON MANAGERS.   The economic environment includes factors such as the following:

- Unemployment rates (the ease of hiring workers)
- Interest rates (the ease of getting working capital)
- Inflation rates (the stability of prices and costs)
- Disposable income (the overall amount of money that consumers have available for spending)

Mainstream managers focus on those factors that influence their organizations' short-term financial interests. Of course, economic conditions are important for all managers, not just those in business. For example, during economic downturns, managers of social welfare agencies often face greater demand for their services but have fewer financial resources available to meet that demand.

INFLUENCE OF MANAGERS ON THE ECONOMIC ENVIRONMENT.   The goal of Mainstream managers is to earn as much money as possible for their organizations' shareholders, and to do it as quickly as possible. Mainstream management tends to build on an understanding of economics described at least 2000 years ago by Aristotle, who developed the idea of **acquisitive economics** to refer to the management of property and wealth in such a way that the short-term monetary value for owners is maximized.[51] Modern economic theory has refined this basic notion and explicitly adds the assumption that economic actors are self-interested and are prone to lie, steal, cheat, and give out bad information in a calculated effort to mislead or confuse partners in an exchange.[52]

Acquisitive economics refers to managing property and wealth in such a way as to maximize the short-term monetary value for owners.

Mainstream theory and practice has advanced a fairly refined set of techniques with which to manage according to acquisitive economics. The Mainstream approach to economics adopts a materialist–individualist perspective, where it is assumed that all individuals will pursue their material self-interest. When managers learn to expect this behavior from others, it helps them to understand how the world works. Moreover, in light of the idea of self-fulfilling prophecies (see Chapter 2), the more that management students are taught acquisitive economics theory, the more likely it is that their actions will reflect its goals. For example, economics professors are more likely to make decisions based on acquisitive economics (e.g., they give less money to charity than other professors), and students who take courses in microeconomics are more likely to believe that self-interested behavior is appropriate and normal.[53]

INFLUENCE OF THE TECHNOLOGICAL ENVIRONMENT ON MANAGERS. Technology determines the choices available to managers regarding how inputs are transformed into outputs in their organization. Mainstream managers try to keep abreast of changing technologies, and they choose those that will maximize productivity and profitability (see Figure 3.6).

Just as the Industrial Revolution was facilitated by technologies such as the steam engine and new management practices, so the computer represents perhaps the best example of how technology has affected modern management. Ever since it began appearing on desktops, and now on laptops and personal digital assistants (such as BlackBerries), computerized technology has become increasingly important in organizations. This technology has facilitated easier access to communication (cell phones, faxes, e-mail) and the processing of information (see Chapter 18). It has even led to new ways of doing business, as evidenced by dot-coms and e-businesses (e.g., Amazon.com). As we will see in later chapters, computers influence how managers *plan* (e.g., more information to make decisions), *lead* (e.g., communication channels), *organize* (e.g., coordination of members around the world through virtual organizations), and *control* (e.g., the ability to monitor others).

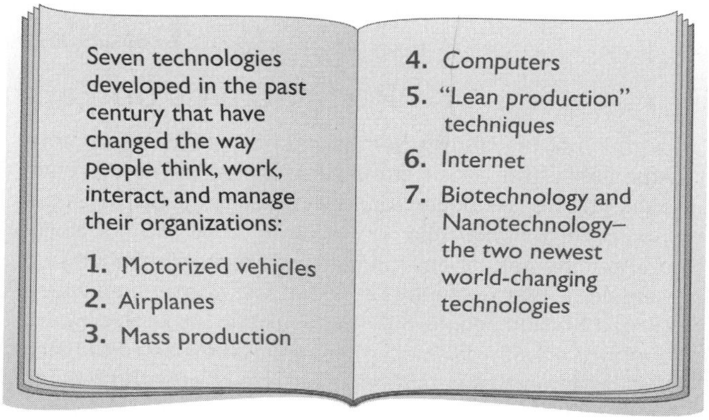

Seven technologies developed in the past century that have changed the way people think, work, interact, and manage their organizations:

1. Motorized vehicles
2. Airplanes
3. Mass production
4. Computers
5. "Lean production" techniques
6. Internet
7. Biotechnology and Nanotechnology— the two newest world-changing technologies

Figure 3.6   Top seven technologies

Source: Lipsey, R. G., Carlow, K. I., & Bekar, C. T. (2005). *Economic transformations: General purpose technologies and long-term economic growth.* Oxford, UK: Oxford University Press. Cited in Scoffield, H. (2006, June 3). The man who wrote the book. *The Globe and Mail,* p. B6.

INFLUENCE OF MANAGERS ON THE TECHNOLOGICAL ENVIRONMENT. For Mainstream managers, an important goal in managing technology is to stay ahead of the competition. The focus is on developing or finding those new technologies that allow better customer service, state-of-the-art products, and increased efficiency. One increasingly popular way that managers influence which kind of technology is being developed is by forming strategic alliances with university researchers.[54] Such combining of public and private funding for research promises to provide a win-win-win proposition:

- Taxpayers win because they pay less for scientific research at public institutions (and it is presumably done more efficiently, given the belief that private industry is more efficient than publicly run organizations).

- Private organizations win because they get research work done for them at bargain-basement prices (often the researchers' salaries and facilities have been paid for by tax dollars).

- The paying customers win because they get access to state-of-the-art products and services.

Technology is also seen as helping to solve significant problems. For example, the development of pesticides, high-yield varieties of grain, and improved agricultural management techniques have substantially increased agricultural productivity during the past decades.[55] Similarly, there is great hope that new technologies will help solve problems such as disease, pollution, and global warming. For example, high-tech solutions being discussed to fight global warming include shooting dust into the upper atmosphere to scatter sunlight away from the Earth; reflecting sunlight away from Earth by sending into space a fleet of 55,000 mirrors (each with an area of 100 square kilometers, which is larger than the island of Manhattan); and pumping liquid carbon dioxide deep into the ocean.[56]

THE MULTISTREAM VIEW OF KEY STAKEHOLDERS IN THE TASK ENVIRONMENT

Multistream managers face the same key stakeholders in the task environment, and the same dimensions of the macro environment, as do Mainstream managers. However, as noted in the road map at the beginning of this chapter, Multistream

Perspectives on Earth's Carrying Capacity[57]

For much of our history, humankind has not been very concerned about the effects of our decisions on the natural environment. This lack of attention was understandable when the population of humankind was relatively small and our ability to affect the natural environment was relatively limited. For example, it was not until 1830 that the human population reached 1 billion people. But our population has been *doubling* roughly every 65 years since then, and it is expected to reach 8 billion around 2025 (although the rate of growth seems to be slowing). Also, we now have technology capable of extracting, transporting, and processing natural resources on a scale and in quantities unheard of in the past, which is also increasing humankind's effects on the environment.

Some researchers have argued that at some point the natural environment will not be able to sustain these growing demands.[58] One proponent of this view, Dr. David Suzuki, uses a metaphor to point out the danger of our growing demands on the natural environment.[59] Imagine that the planet is like a test tube full of food for bacteria, and that humankind is represented by bacteria. Now imagine that one bacterial cell is introduced into the test tube, and assume that the bacterium grows at some steady rate and *doubles* in size over a specific period of time—for example, every minute. Thus, in one minute there are two bacterial cells, in two minutes there are four cells, in three minutes there are eight cells, and so on. Of course, this steady growth means that at some point the test tube will be completely full of bacteria and there will be no food left. Let's say that this event occurs in exactly one hour. Under this assumption, at 55 minutes, the test tube is only about 3 percent

full of bacteria, but at 59 minutes the test tube is 50 percent full of bacteria. At 55 minutes, concerns about potential problems may fall on deaf ears; at 59 minutes, the problem would be acknowledged but nearly irreversible. Dr. Suzuki believes that humankind is long past its own "55 minutes" point. He notes that even if science and technology quadruple humankind's resources so that we now have the equivalent of four test tubes, this will in effect result in only two extra "minutes" before those test tubes are also used up.

In contrast, Dr. Thomas DeGregori points to technological progress as one reason to question the dire predictions of consumption outstripping the supply of natural resources.[60] In addition to suggesting that there are problematic assumptions associated with others' population growth rate models, he argues that technological innovations such as bioengineered foods have reduced the need for pesticides, increased crop yields, and generally improved human well-being and life expectancy. Dr. DeGregori also asserts that without the use of modern agricultural technologies, people in poor countries would inordinately suffer the ill effects of pests, naturally occurring diseases, and poor crop yields. He offers evidence to suggest that the well-being of people and the planet are well served by technologies that increase yields and reduce diseases, which in turn reduces the need for cultivated land and thereby reduces soil erosion and facilitates biodiversity.

What are the strengths and weaknesses of each argument? Which argument seems more convincing? What might your conclusions mean for management practice?

managers approach these considerations in a qualitatively different manner. For example, Multistream managers adopt a greater service and relationship-building orientation to their stakeholders, as illustrated in Figure 3.7. Rather than see stakeholders as factors that must be managed to maximize the organization's financial well-being, Multistream managers strive to work together with stakeholders in order to enhance multiple forms of well-being for multiple stakeholders.

Customers

INFLUENCE OF CUSTOMERS ON MANAGERS.   Both Mainstream and Multistream managers recognize that customers provide financial resources that organizations require to be financially viable. Multistream managers are more likely to also emphasize that serving customers provides a sense of purpose for members. For example, Jim Smucker, manager of the Bird-in-Hand Family Inn in Pennsylvania, was discussing with his staff a monthly financial report that showed less-than-stellar performance. There had been a blizzard in the region. When many customers had to spend an extra night as a result of the poor travel conditions, they were invited to stay another night at a greatly reduced rate. Smucker was very pleased when a staff member said that it had, in fact, been a great month, because the organization had met its overarching mission of truly providing hospitable service to customers.

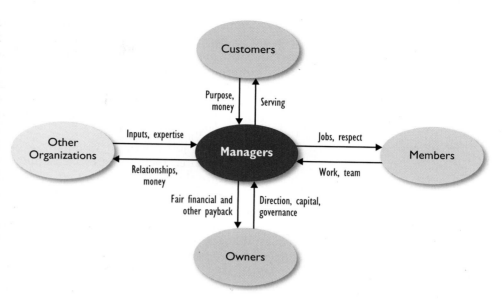

Figure 3.7 Multistream aspects of relationships with key stakeholders in the task environment

This example shows that although both approaches to management emphasize customer service, the motivation for doing so differs. In Multistream management, customer service is an *end* in and of itself, not merely a *means* to maximize profits. For Multistream managers, work is more than simply an instrumental means to getting a paycheck—it is an opportunity to help and serve others. Multistream managers get satisfaction from serving customers, just as friends get satisfaction from helping one another, and just as parents get satisfaction by giving their best to their children.

INFLUENCE OF MANAGERS ON CUSTOMERS. Managers who see customer service as an end in itself treat their customers fairly and honestly. In return, customers often make a special effort to buy products and services only from companies with reputations for ethical conduct and social responsibility, even if their prices are not the lowest. Multistream organizations are of special interest to the growing number of customers who are learning to appreciate products and services that are not promoting materialist–individualist values. For example, many customers were initially attracted to the Seikatsu Club in Japan because it offered less expensive groceries; over time, however, they became loyal to the Seikatsu Club because it is environmentally friendly and socially responsible.[61]

Members

INFLUENCE OF MEMBERS ON MANAGERS. Members perform the everyday work of the organization, and they also participate as key stakeholders in the decisions and direction of the organization. Rather than being cogs in the overall organizational machinery, a Multistream metaphor sees them as members of an overall organizational body. Each member is important and makes a unique contribution. Each member also performs best when he or she participates as a member of a larger team. Managers are sensitive to their members and, therefore, are influenced by them.

INFLUENCE OF MANAGERS ON MEMBERS. Multistream managers, like Cheryl and Ralph Broetje in the chapter-opening case, treat other organizational members fairly and respect their dignity and basic human needs. This approach helps members to see themselves as part of the larger organizational body. Multistream managers look for ways to facilitate a sense of interdependence, so that members can make positive contributions both to the organization and to the larger community to which they belong. Multistream managers recognize that members need to have a living wage, but also understand that members are motivated by the pursuit of transcendent goals that defy quantification.[62] Many people are willing to take a cut in pay to work in organizations where managers treat them with dignity.

Consider two job offers. In Company 1, which offers an annual salary of $60,000, newly hired members are given opportunities to participate in decision making, to voice their preferences about project assignments, and to suggest improvements to company policies. In Company 2, which offers an annual salary of $75,000, newly hired members are given few opportunities to participate in decision making, are assigned projects by senior managers, and are not permitted to request changes. Senior managers make decisions about training, job objectives, and career advancement. Which job would you take?

When MBA students evaluated these two job offers, they were three times as likely to accept the job in Company 1 (73 percent) as to take the job in Company 2 (27 percent). This finding suggests that a significant number of people are willing to work at 20 percent less pay in organizations that offer participative (rather than individualistic) decision-making processes.[63] Interestingly, when evaluating jobs in a group, most chose Company 2 (63 percent) over Company 1 (37 percent), possibly due to social norms that suggest that maximizing personal financial gain is the most important criterion.

In sum, members value jobs where they are treated with respect and dignity. People are willing to lower their financial well-being in order to increase other forms of well-being. Yet, because society often uses salary as an important indicator of a "good" job, many people give in to peer pressure and accept jobs that look best according to Mainstream criteria of success.

Owners

INFLUENCE OF OWNERS ON MANAGERS.   There is a growing tendency for people to make investment decisions based on criteria that go beyond financial performance. For example, in the United States, nearly one in ten dollars under professional management is invested using some sort of criteria related to social and environmental responsibility. The amount devoted to such **socially responsible investing (SRI)** has been overall doubling about every 5 years, with SRI mutual funds doubling every 2.5 years.[64]

Socially responsible investing (SRI) is using criteria of social or environmental principles to make investment decisions.

There are basically three types of SRI:

- *Positive screening* refers to investing in certain companies because they do good things (e.g., they have good environmental practices, safe products, and good employee–employer relations), while *negative screening* means not investing in certain companies because they do harmful things (e.g., they produce cigarettes, liquor, or military hardware).

- *Shareholder advocacy* involves investing in certain companies specifically to encourage socially responsible change (e.g., via bringing proactive ecological resolutions to annual meetings).

- *Community investing* provides financial resources to communities and needs that are underserved by traditional financial services.

When owners base their investment decisions on SRI criteria, they are giving directions about which sorts of activities they want managers to undertake, and indicating which sorts of nonfinancial rewards they want their investments to provide.

INFLUENCE OF MANAGERS ON OWNERS.   Multistream managers are more likely to foster, and to be attuned to, owners' nonfinancial agendas for organizations. Multistream managers recognize that owners deserve a fair financial return on their investment, and they know that this consideration must be balanced with also treating other stakeholders fairly. For example, Multistream managers recognize and promote how owners' well-being may be served by earning adequate financial rewards *as well as* by providing employment for marginalized people in society, minimizing environmental costs of organizational initiatives and products, considering the social costs of opening new factories overseas, and so on. Owners are likely to become more interested in a greater variety of forms of well-being when they are provided with relevant organizational information about them by managers. Community-minded owners will find such managers especially attractive.

WHAT DO YOU THINK?

How Would You Make Investment Decisions About Which Company to Own?

Assume you can make a choice about which one of two companies to invest in. Company A makes computer role-play games based on cooperative play and sharing, and Company B makes computer role-play games based on violence and competitive behavior. Based on their histories and projected futures, you have every reason to believe that the financial return on both companies will be about the same.

Which company would you choose to invest in, and why? Which company should the manager of a large pension fund invest in, and why?

Now suppose you subsequently learn that the company in which you chose to invest is likely to have a 2 percent decrease in profits in the foreseeable future, and at the same time the company in which you chose not to invest is expected to have a 2 percent increase in profits. Will this information change your investment decision? What if instead of 2 percent, the expected increase and decrease were 10 percent or 25 percent? Would this information change your decision? Why or why not?

Other Organizations

INFLUENCE OF OTHER ORGANIZATIONS ON MANAGERS.   Managers depend on other organizations for supplies and expertise. Rather than focus exclusively on expertise and inputs that serve to maximize organizational financial well-being, Multistream managers look for ways to improve other forms of well-being as well. They are likely to be more sensitive to, and proactive in, dealing with concerns for a wider range of organizations and stakeholders. For example, two or three times each year the management team of Tomasso Corporation—a very successful food-processing plant in Montreal, Canada—serves food in a soup kitchen. After the meal, they sit with the people they have served and get to know them.[65] Other workers from the plant who wish to may join the managers; they go during work hours and are paid for their time. In this way, managers at Tomasso deliberately allow themselves to be influenced by the soup kitchen staff and its patrons.

INFLUENCE OF MANAGERS ON OTHER ORGANIZATIONS.   Multistream managers are inclined to respect and cooperate with suppliers and competitors in an effort to establish sustainable long-term relationships. Compared to Mainstream managers, Multistream managers are more likely to become involved in joint ventures (where two organizations share the risk and gain for developing a new technology).[66] Instead of trying to maximize control over a supplier, Multistream managers seek to benefit from inviting suppliers' expertise.[67] In essence, they tend to foster a sense of community among organizations in their network.

Consider the Multistream management practices evident in this story about Latex International, an organization based in Connecticut that was, at the time, the only firm in North America to produce premium latex cores for mattresses.[68] Thanks to the work and attitudes of its cofounders, Latex International had the reputation of treating people well. This helps to explain why, when its 10-acre factory burned down, many people were willing to help out. For example, when Jim Smith, the CEO of the Webster Bank, found out about the fire, he phoned Alan Schwartz, president of Glenn Equities. Glenn Equities owned the building across the street from the burned-down factory, and Schwartz had been planning to move some of his organization into that building. However, upon hearing about the fire, Schwartz delayed the move "just as a neighborly favor" so that Latex International could open temporary offices there starting the next day. Help also came from managers at several overseas competitors in this relatively small industry, who agreed to supply Latex Industries with badly needed latex foam. As Stephen Russo, who was CEO of Latex Industries when the fire occurred, explained, "In the small community of companies, we all help each other out, even though we compete. Everybody was very understanding and sympathetic."

Within a year after the fire, a new state-of-the-art factory had been built, and soon the company was thriving, thanks in part to a 25 percent growth rate in the industry. Its new CEO, Michael K. Lorelli, has changed his title to Chief Passionate Officer and continues to manage the firm in Multistream ways: "We are having so much fun doing what we're doing." For example, members are paid to sleep on the job, so long as they fill out a form to evaluate the mattress after their hour-long snooze in the firm's nap room.

THE MULTISTREAM VIEW OF THE FOUR DIMENSIONS IN THE MACRO ENVIRONMENT

The four dimensions of the macro environment are the same for both Mainstream and Multistream managers, but the dimensions are managed somewhat differently (see Figure 3.8). Because they are explicitly interested in forms of well-being that go beyond simple financial well-being, Multistream managers have a broader agenda when it comes to how they manage the macro environment.

Sociocultural Environment

INFLUENCE OF THE SOCIOCULTURAL ENVIRONMENT ON MANAGERS. Compared to Mainstream managers, Multistream managers are more likely to follow trends that facilitate participation and community building in the workplace. Multistream managers seek to enhance team building and develop links to external organizations and groups, even when these activities are not related to increased profits. They are also more likely to offer on-the-job daycare centers and flexible work time. Although the trend to offer similar programs may also be followed by Mainstream managers if they believe that this will maximize productivity, a Multistream approach places greater emphasis on fostering social well-being and sustainable development.

Instead of focusing on customer *wants*, Multistream managers are more likely to be sensitive to customer *needs*, especially those needs that are not being met by existing organizations. For example, we all need food, but we may choose food that tastes good instead of food that is nutritious. In light of this tendency, Hannaford Brothers, a grocery store chain with more than 150 supermarkets in five states, rates the nutritional value of each of the 27,000 products on its shelves on a scale of zero to three "Guiding Stars" (more than three of four products receive zero stars, the lowest nutritional rating). With this system, managers are reflecting and enhancing the growing interest in healthier eating. They hope that their system will be used by other grocers as well.[69]

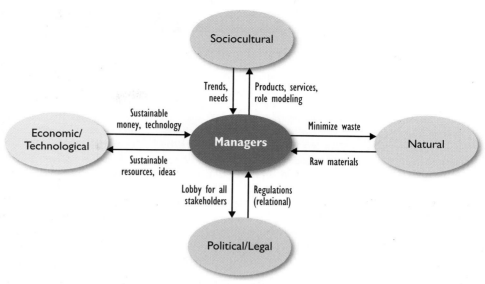

Figure 3.8 Multistream aspects of relationships with key dimensions of the macro environment

INFLUENCE OF MANAGERS ON THE SOCIOCULTURAL ENVIRONMENT. Multistream managers deliberately provide opportunities for their members to engage the larger society in ways that go beyond meeting simply materialist–individualist goals. For example, managers at Tom's of Maine—which specializes in natural personal care products—encourage employees to spend as much as 5 percent of their paid work time volunteering in their communities.[70]

Multistream managers have been known to facilitate positive changes in the sociocultural environment. Consider businessman John Woolman, who is credited with almost single-handedly getting rid of slavery among the Quakers during the eighteenth century. His efforts helped to eventually change the sociocultural view of slavery throughout the United States. Woolman had ample opportunities to grow his business to a large size, but he consciously opted not to follow this course. His reluctance was not because he feared being tempted by an affluent materialist–individualist lifestyle: "I had, in a good degree, learned to be content with a plain way of living." Rather, he had two reasons for not wanting his business to grow too large:

- To grow the business would have meant paying greater attention to serving customers' *wants* rather than their *needs*, and Woolman did not want to participate in the vanity of materialist consumerism.

- Woolman did not want to be encumbered by a larger business, a consideration that was ultimately the deciding factor for him. Keeping his firm at a manageable size "set him free to engage in a remarkable traveling ministry that was to be a major force in causing Quakers to rid themselves of slavery even before America had gained independence from the British Empire."[71]

Multistream managers believe that societal well-being encompasses much more than just financial success. One U.S. study used 16 measures to rate social health

MANAGEMENT IN PRACTICE

Profits and Freedom of the Press

Because the mass media play a significant role in shaping social views,[72] people are right to emphasize the freedom of the press. Unfortunately, we often forget that the goal of managers in many media outlets is to maximize their profits. Advertising is an important component of their profitability, accounting for nearly 75 percent of the total revenues received by newspapers, magazines, and broadcasters.

If a primary goal of managers in media outlets such as television networks is to attract advertisers, and if advertisers want to promote materialist–individualist values, then what kind of shows will get produced? Are programs likely to point out how consumerism contributes to environmental problems? Or will advertisers support shows that depict happy people having fun doing things that are expensive,

and "reality shows" that depict people competing against one another to get more money? Why is it that managers at Adbusters, an organization that produces television ads pointing out the dysfunctional aspects of materialism, are often not allowed to purchase time on television stations to show their ads?[73]

Can we envision a different sociocultural environment, one where the norms and messages are less materialistic, less individualistic, less short-term oriented, and less competitive? What can managers do to promote a message that happiness is found via healthy relationships (not from having stuff), sharing (rather than accumulating and hoarding), having a longer time horizon (versus immediate gratification), and valuing cooperation more than competition?

over a period of 30 years. Despite continuous growth in the country's GDP over that time, Americans' social health has actually declined quite drastically, as problems such as child poverty, lack of health insurance, and youth suicide rate have all worsened. People's sociocultural views about of the role of management might be very different if a national "Social Health Index" would receive as much attention in the daily news as the Dow Jones Industrial Average.[74]

Natural Environment

INFLUENCE OF THE NATURAL ENVIRONMENT ON MANAGERS. Because we often take our natural environment for granted, we ignore it and know surprisingly little about it. We often forget that with every breath we take, we interact with our environment. We forget that the food we eat is affected by how we treat our natural environment. We forget to marvel at ecosystems, photosynthesis, flowers, and sunsets. We forget that the natural environment provides the living context for everyday organizational activity.

Compared to Mainstream management, the Multistream approach is more likely to be sensitive to the environmental implications of an organization's use of inputs and production of outputs. As we will see in Chapter 9, Multistream organizational strategies seek to produce less waste than their competitors, and to find ways to take existing waste in the environment and transform it into useful goods and services. Multistream managers would be eager to belong to the zero-emission industrial parks that are being designed by industrial engineers. In these parks, tenants form an industrial ecosystem where the nontoxic and useful "wastes" of one organization become inputs for another organization.[75] A similar example comes from Gunter Pauli, who helped Belgian-based Ecover produce cleaning products from natural soaps and renewable raw materials operating in a near-zero-emissions factory.[76]

INFLUENCE OF MANAGERS ON THE NATURAL ENVIRONMENT. As discussed earlier in this chapter, Multistream managers tend to occupy the *proactive* end of the "sensitivity to the environment" continuum shown in Figure 3.4. In particular, they are interested in **sustainable development**—that is, "development that meets the needs of the present without compromising the ability of future generations to meet their own needs."[77]

As an example, consider the energy industry.[78] What if profits and growth were tied to *reducing* consumption rather than increasing it? This is the idea behind *negawatts*, which starts with the observation that creating "new" energy (e.g., by building a new power plant) costs about five times as much as finding "saved" energy (e.g., by becoming more energy efficient). Instead of spending $5 for one kilowatt of new electricity, we could instead pay someone $1 to reduce their current use of electricity by one kilowatt. Energy companies could pay people to install energy-efficient windows in their homes because that "saved energy" would be cheaper than developing an equal amount of "new energy." In effect, energy-efficient services and products (e.g., better insulation, more fuel-efficient cars or appliances) would become the "new" oil wells of the future. For example, it has been estimated that Americans have the technology to reduce their energy consumption by 80 percent.[79] Obviously, such changes would require a change in the kinds of organizations and jobs being created, and might alter which industries are the most profitable.

One way to conserve energy and better respect the environment is to adopt an "intelligent product design" system for commerce. This view suggests that managers should think of their organizations as offering one of two types of outputs: (1) consumables or (2) products that offer an ongoing service to customers.[80]

The first category, consumables, includes products that are often used only once and then become some sort of "waste" that is wholly *biodegradable* and capable of becoming inputs for another organism. Most foods fall into this category, but other products could also be manufactured to fit within it. For example, rather than tanning shoe leather with chromium and toxic dyestuffs—which technically makes shoes a toxic waste—footwear could be made in a more environmentally friendly way. If it were made a priority, engineers could surely design environmentally friendlier products. For example, by 1941 Henry Ford had already designed a prototype automobile that had a body made of soybean plastic, was powered by ethanol fuel, and ran on tires made from goldenrod. Ford believed that oil prices would rise after World War II, and that the United States would soon be "growing" its cars.[81]

The second category of organizational output includes durables that provide a service. Cars provide transportation, refrigerators provide cold beverages, and televisions provide entertainment. Under the intelligent product system, rather than buying the product itself, consumers would purchase a transferable license to use the product. This product could not be thrown out, but instead would have to be returned to the manufacturer at some point. At present, most of these products are not recycled at all, but rather "down-cycled" (reduced to scrap, or melted down to yield glass, aluminum, and plastic). In an intelligent product system, products or services would be designed for complete and easy disassembly for reuse, remanufacture, or reclaiming (see the discussion of "value loops" in Chapter 18). Manufacturers would view both the materials and the methods of production in an entirely new way, because they would always have to imagine how they would reuse and reclaim the product upon its return.

The realization of this concept calls for entirely novel principles of design that mimic what nature tells us: The *waste* of one organism equals the *food* for a different organism. Instead of thinking of the value of the product just as it goes out the door, the manufacturer would have to consider its value when it comes back in the door. This plan favors those companies and designs that employ materials and components in ways that they can be most efficiently rearranged, changed, reused, or reclaimed.

Sustainable development
refers to development that meets the needs of the present without compromising the ability of future generations to meet their own needs.

Figure 3.9 Graduation Pledge of Social and Environmental Responsibility

Sources: Graduation Pledge Alliance. (no date). Accessed June 11, 2007, at http://www.graduationpledge.org. Reprinted with permission; Beyond the green corporation. (2007, January 29). *BusinessWeek*. Accessed March 10, 2008, at http://www.businessweek.com/magazine/content/07_05/b4019001.htm.

This "cradle-to-cradle" (instead of "cradle-to-grave") thinking is evident in the leasing of photocopiers (pioneered by Agfa Gevaert N.V.) and when air-conditioning companies such as Carrier Corporation sell "coolth" to its customers while retaining ownership of the actual air conditioner.[82]

As a final example of how managers can influence the environment, students at more than 100 universities and colleges are using the "Graduation Pledge of Social and Environmental Responsibility" at some level (see Figure 3.9). It is up to students to define for themselves what exactly it means to be environmentally and socially responsible. People who have signed the pledge have turned down some jobs with which they did not feel comfortable, and have worked to introduce responsible social and environmental changes in organizations where they do work (e.g., promoted recycling, removed racist language from company documents, convinced their employer to refuse a chemical weapons-related contract).

Political–Legal Environment

INFLUENCE OF THE POLITICAL–LEGAL ENVIRONMENT ON MANAGERS. The actions of Multistream managers, like those of Mainstream managers, are influenced by the kind of government and rules and regulations they face. We have already discussed how Multistream managers might prefer relational capitalism, where the emphasis is on building trust and relationships with people rather than on developing comprehensive contracts.

INFLUENCE OF MANAGERS ON THE POLITICAL–LEGAL ENVIRONMENT. Multistream managers lobby the government for ways to enhance the well-being of multiple stakeholders. Consider the case of union–management relationships. Rather than lobby for legislation that strengthens management rights vis-à-vis the rights of unions, Multistream managers may support initiatives that support healthier relationships between unions and management.[83] The Multistream approach does not assume that the relationship between management and unions must always be antagonistic. In Germany, for example, legislation (influenced by the sociocultural environment) leads to a three-way joint relationship between business, government, and workers. In this scenario, managers from all three stakeholder groups sit at the table and focus on what is in everyone's mutual interests.

Multistream managers are less likely to lobby government for regulations that help their industry's short-term bottom line but threaten its longer-term viability and overall well-being. For example, Sweden's largest refiner and retailer of gasoline, OK Petroleum, joined with 24 other companies to lobby the government to *increase* carbon taxes.[84] Managers at OK Petroleum had begun to think about their company as a clean energy company. After formulating low-carbon gasoline, OK wanted to increase the financial incentives for other companies to also clean up their energy. Similarly, U.S. firms that have developed totally recyclable or compostable carpets could hasten the move toward an environmentally friendlier industry by lobbying to impose fines on manufacturers whose carpets end up in landfills.

Economic and Technological Environment

THE ECONOMIC ENVIRONMENT. Both Mainstream and Multistream managers share the view that part of their job is to find the proper place for their organizations within the economy, but they have different views of economics. Just as the Mainstream approach dates back to Aristotle's notion of acquisitive economics, so the Multistream approach can be traced back to his idea of sustenance economics. **Sustenance economics** refers to the management of property and wealth in such a way as to increase the long-term, overall well-being for owners, members, and other stakeholders. Sustenance economics emphasizes community-oriented values, long-term multigenerational concerns, and stewardship. It speaks to issues of quality of life that cannot be meaningfully expressed or reduced to quantifiable measures such as financial wealth, income, or goods consumed.[85]

Cow pie technology: When Microgy opened its "manure-to-gas digester" plant in Texas, it could take the manure from 10,000 cows and turn it into natural gas, which will eventually meet the electrical needs of 10,000 homes. The company holds the exclusive North American license to an anaerobic digestions technology developed in Europe over the past 20 years.[87]

When Cheryl and Ralph Broetje wanted to expand the apple-sorting and packaging capacity at First Fruits, they had two options. From an acquisitive economics perspective, the most cost-effective choice was to simply add a second shift to work in their current facility. But because they followed a sustenance economics perspective, the couple decided to build a new facility when they recognized that adding a second shift would take parents away from their children in the evenings and, therefore, disrupt the family life of their workers.

From a Multistream perspective, acquisitive economics is a simply a *means* to help manage sustenance economics. Multistream managers agree with Aristotle's observation that it is dysfunctional for acquisitive economics to become an *end* in and of itself.[86] Dysfunctions occur when managers are driven to maximize profits, when finances are seen to be the bottom-line consideration for the organization, and when concerns for the wealth of shareholders trump all other concerns and stakeholders.

Sustenance economics refers to managing property and wealth in such a way as to increase the long-term overall well-being for owners, members, and other stakeholders.

From a Mainstream acquisitive economics perspective, the first five years of the new millennium may be seen as an economic success in the United States, as corporate profits hit a record level of $1.35 trillion in 2005, up 65 percent since 2001. However, that success was accompanied by considerable sustenance economic costs, especially when we consider how long-term debt increased around the same time. U.S. *household* indebtedness grew by 60 percent in the first five years of the new millennium to $4.5 trillion (approximately $15,000 for every man, woman, and child). Similarly, since 1999, the U.S. *national* debt grew from $5.7 trillion to $9 trillion (another $10,000 of new debt for every man, woman, and child). In addition, the U.S. government would need a cash infusion of another $43 trillion to meet all of its future *obligations* under Medicare and Social Security (another $150,000 per person).[88]

And these figures don't even begin to look at the financial cleanup and healthcare costs associated with environmental degradation. In short, maintaining a focus on short-term acquisitive economics may carry significant long-term sustenance economic costs.

THE TECHNOLOGICAL ENVIRONMENT. Like their views of the economic environment, Multistream and Mainstream managers' views of technology differ. Multistream managers are concerned that focusing research efforts on developing technologies that promise to maximize profits may unintentionally demean work or ignore technologies that improve our quality of life. Consider this fact: The two top-selling drugs in the world, both designed to lower cholesterol, target middle-class consumers.[89] Mainstream pharmaceutical companies tend to focus on developing products like these medications—which are targeted at consumers who are able to help maximize profits—rather than on other products that might be important in dealing with the medical concerns facing the majority of the world's population, who cannot afford medicine.

A similar situation is evident in the agricultural sector, where an increasing portion of the research is being funded by private companies that want to maximize their profits. In the process, conflicts of interest are created. For example, when a university professor's research pointed out the problems with aerial spraying of pesticides, his manager asked him not to publish the results because they might negatively affect the university's ability to attract additional private funding in the future. All managers must keep the organization's financial viability in mind when they adopt or develop new technologies, but if they become too obsessed with profits, technologies that serve needs other than profit may get overlooked.

Like Mainstream managers, Multistream managers are always seeking new technologies, but their interests go beyond merely maximizing profitability. For example, the Multistream approach favors environmentally friendly technology, new computer software and information systems that facilitate team building and sharing information among team members, technologies that allow for financial rewards to be meaningfully tied to team performance rather than individual performance, office space design and technologies that allow for cross-fertilization of ideas among different functional areas, and so on.

As suggested by the example of the QWERTY keyboard in Chapter 2, it can be difficult to change technologies that have become institutionalized. Nevertheless, if managers persevere, they can achieve positive results. When DesignTex (a division of Steelcase—the largest manufacturer of office furniture in the United States) wanted to create environmentally friendly upholstery, the firm approached 60 different chemical companies to work with it. All declined. Finally, Ciba-Geigy agreed to join DesignTex's project team, which examined 8000 different chemicals used in the industry. In the end, team members developed a line of fabrics that used only 38 chemicals and that was so safe it could literally be eaten (it could also be used as mulch in the garden). Regulators who came to the factory to measure the levels of pollution at first thought that their instruments were broken, because the water coming out of the factory was as clean as the water coming in.[90]

A Look at the U.S. Automobile Industry

The U.S. automobile industry provides an instructive example of how the four dimensions of the macro environment are interrelated.

Sociocultural Environment

The automobile has long been an important part of American culture, and it can be seen as a prominent symbol of its materialist–individualist character. In terms of materialism, the automobile has been called "the epitome of possessions."[91] After the first automobiles hit the road and were driven by the social elite, they became a symbol of social status and a way to flaunt wealth. Over the years, cars have also been linked to increased individualism, personal freedom and mobility, stress (because of their expense), and weakening of the traditional family unit. As automobiles became more commonplace, they permitted a decentralization of cities, facilitating the rapid development of suburbs, regional shopping centers, and increased tourism in national parks.

Owning and driving a car is a deeply entrenched social norm in the United States, which has more vehicles on the road than there are registered voters or drivers (about 72 automobiles for every 100 men, women, and children).[92] Eighty-eight percent of all U.S. workers (118 million people) use a motor vehicle as their primary means of transportation to work. The average home-to-work distance is 11.8 miles, and the average shopping trip is 5.6 miles (one way).[93] Approximately half of all Americans live within five miles of their workplace, yet less than 10 percent use transit, a bike, or walk to work.[94] In contrast, in Europe 40 to 50 percent of all trips are made by cycling or walking, and about 10 percent are by transit.[95]

Natural Environment

The effects of the automobile on the natural environment are significant. Today when people think of the impact of automobiles on the environment, they usually focus on its negative effects, such as the link between exhaust fumes and global warming, and the fact that much of the pollution of the Earth's ozone layer is attributable by automobiles. Ironically, when cars first replaced horses, they were seen as a solution to a pollution problem (during the late 1800s it was estimated that horses in New York City created daily about 1 million pounds of manure).[96] Today U.S. vehicles use 44 million gallons of gas in total each day,[97] and they generate more than 8 billion pounds of carbon dioxide every day. That's over 25 pounds every day for every person in the United States.[98] The United States, with 4 percent of the world's population, uses about half of the world's gasoline, and its automobiles use nearly 40 percent of all oil consumed in the United States.[99]

The effects of automobiles on the natural environment, of course, go beyond the air pollution that they create. By some estimates, one third of the environmental damage created by automobiles occurs during their production (e.g., mining for metals, using oil to make plastics). One study estimates that manufacturing one car produces 29 tons of waste and 1207 million cubic yards of polluted air.[100]

Political–Legal Environment

Ralph Nader points out that in 1946 Americans recorded 23.4 billion trips via public transportation, more than twice as many as today despite today's larger population.[101] He attributes part of this decline in public transit to the efforts of the "Highway Lobby," consisting of managers in the auto, oil, tire, and cement industries who recognized that public transit would limit the demand for vehicles, tires, and roads. These lobbyists engaged in a variety of political activities designed to decrease the use of public transit, including exerting their influence over financial institutions, lobbying the government (e.g., to build more roads), and in some occasions even resorting to illegal activities.

Legislation influences numerous automobile-related issues, including fuel efficiency. In the decade prior to the 1973–1974 energy crisis, gasoline consumption in the United States had risen by about 50 percent. The energy crisis prompted Congress to require cars to become more fuel efficient and to achieve an average of 27.5 miles per gallon by 1985, essentially doubling the 1976 average. Between 1976 and 1991, total fuel consumption increased by only 5 percent, a rate that was quite a bit lower than the 50 percent increase seen during the previous decade. However, this trend toward lower fuel consumption began to reverse in 1988, when U.S. legislators relaxed the constraints on automakers.[102] Even companies such as Toyota, which is now famous for its Prius hybrid car, joined the U.S. auto manufacturers in lobbying Congress for laxer fuel standards.[103] The decrease in fuel efficiency since 1988 is roughly equivalent to the total U.S. oil imports from the Persian Gulf.[104]

Legislation can also have an effect on the types of vehicles that are bought and sold, such as when tax cuts provide incentives to purchase different kinds of vehicles.[105]

Economic–Technological Environment

The automobile industry is especially important to the U.S. economy, where the annual total vehicle sales of about 17 million vehicles is greater than the combined automobile sales in the next four leading countries.[106] The automotive industry accounts for more than 13 million jobs in the United States, or about 10 percent of all U.S. jobs.[107] The automotive industry accounts for almost 15 percent of all advertising in the United States,[108] which amounts to an average of about $1000 in advertising for each new car sold.[109]

The automobile is also a focal point of economic life for individual households. In the United States, the direct costs of owning a car (e.g., purchase price, gas, maintenance, insurance) represent about 25 percent of the average owner's net income. Another 10 percent or more of the owner's net income may be devoted to additional indirect costs (e.g., road construction, pollution/health costs, costs for parking, subsidies for oil companies).[110] This prompts the question: Would you be willing to give up car ownership to reduce your workweek by 25 percent? One study suggests that if you take the to- tal distance the average American travels by car and divide it by the time spent on the car (e.g., working to pay for it, driving and maintaining it), the average speed is about 5 miles per hour. The high environmental and financial costs associated with car ownership make "car sharing"[111] and bicycling increasingly attractive alternatives, and the future may hold more velomobiles than SUVs.[112]

QUESTIONS FOR DISCUSSION

1. Identify the pros and cons of becoming less reliant on automobiles.

2. What are the task and macro environmental factors that support continuation of the status quo in the U.S. automobile sector? Which factors favor change?

3. What changes do you foresee in the next 20 years in the automobile sector? What are the implications for your career? Which sorts of organizations will flourish where you might want to find employment?

Velomobiles are three-wheeled recumbent bikes with an aerodynamic "shell" that permits year-round travel and lowers wind resistance by one-third. In an hour, an average rider can travel about 20 miles. The world speed record is over 80 miles per hour. Velomobiles with small electric motors are also available.

SUMMARY

A. All managers

All managers must pay attention to the key stakeholders in their task environment. This means managers should:

- Ensure that they are in tune with customer needs and wants to serve those stakeholders adequately;
- Attract and retain an adequately qualified workforce;
- Ensure that owners' needs are met; and
- Develop and maintain relationships with suppliers, competitors, and neighbors.

All managers must also attend to the key dimensions of their macro environment, which means managers should:

- Monitor sociocultural trends and changes in demographics, health care, education, and other social institutions;
- Consider how sensitive they will be with respect to the natural environment;
- Keep informed of developments in the political–legal environment; and
- Pay close attention to economic opportunities and threats and remain technologically up-to-date.

B. Mainstream managers

Mainstream managers realize that their organization's financial goals are enhanced by attending to stakeholders in the task environment as follows:

- Offering customer service and profitably exploiting consumer wants;
- Maximizing workers' productivity;
- Maximizing financial returns to owners; and
- Gaining power over suppliers and competitors.

In addition, Mainstream managers must attend to the macro environment by:

- Nurturing a materialist–individualist sociocultural environment;
- Acquiring raw materials and disposing of waste as cheaply as possible;
- Lobbying for managerial rights and marketplace rules in their favor; and
- Adopting a short-term and exploitive approach to economics and technology.

C. Multistream managers

Multistream managers realize that overall organizational well-being is enhanced by attending to stakeholders in the task environment as follows:

- Offering customer service and identifying unmet consumer needs;
- Engaging workers via meaningful work and productivity;
- Serving owners' multiple forms of well-being; and
- Fostering healthy relationships among organizations.

In addition, Multistream managers must attend to the macro environment as follows:

- Nurturing social justice and well-being;
- Practicing sustainable use of natural and human resources;
- Lobbying for sustainable and environmentally friendly markets; and
- Adopting a long-term and needs-based approach to economics and technology.

QUESTIONS FOR REFLECTION AND DISCUSSION

1. What are the three levels of the environments that managers need to attend to?

2. Identify the four stakeholders in a manager's task environment. Which do you think would be the most challenging to manage? Which is the easiest? Do you think your answers would have been different if you were a student 40 years ago? Explain your answers.

3. Identify the four dimensions of a manager's macro environment. Which do you think is the most important to manage? Which is the least important? Do you think students would have different answers 40 years from now? Explain your answers.

4. How might a Mainstream manager and a Multistream manager respond differently to the following provocative observations made by Paul Hawken, a leading thinker on the ecology of commerce?

   Natural and Economic–Technological Environments: "Gasoline is cheap in the United States because its price does not reflect the cost of smog, acid rain, and other subsequent effects on health and the environment. Likewise, American food is the cheapest in the world, but the price does not reflect the fact that we have depleted the soil, reducing average topsoil from a depth of twenty-one to six inches over the past hundred years, contaminated our groundwater . . . and poisoned wildlife through the use of pesticides."[113]

   Natural, Political–Legal, and Economic–Technological Environments: "When wind power first started as a serious source of alternative energy in California in the 1970s, it benefited from both federal and state tax credits, earning the somewhat derisive moniker of 'tax farms' instead of wind farms. And indeed, some windmills were put up that had little to recommend them other than their write-offs. But companies like U.S. Windpower persisted, and today, without the benefit of any tax credits, they are generating power at rates competitive with those of nuclear power. If, at the outset, they had been competing on a price basis without the tax credits, they would have failed because their competitors not only do not integrate the full costs of nuclear waste into their prices, but also have been subsidized by billions of taxpayer dollars given to the Departments of Defense and Energy since World War II."[114]

5. Consider the following opinion:

   The negative aspects of Mainstream management (e.g., pollution, reduced quality of life, global warming) have been blown all out of proportion. Sure, there are problems in the world, but the doomsday predictions that are being made by people who don't like the current system are just scare tactics. All sorts of doomsday predictions have been made by various people in the past, and none of those predictions ever came true. The fact is that most people are naturally materialistic and individualistic, and you can't change that. Mainstream management theory and practice simply reflects innate human characteristics—it doesn't cause them.

   Do you agree or disagree with this opinion? Defend your answer.

6. Imagine that you've been hired as a consultant to provide feedback to managers at First Fruits apple orchards about their key strengths and weaknesses in how they manage their task and macro environments. Prepare a short report, basing your analysis on the information provided in this chapter and in the chapter-opening case.

HANDS-ON ACTIVITIES

What Is Your Management Style Along the Mainstream–Multistream Continuum?

For each of the statements below, circle the number on the continuum that reflects your view.

A. Task Environment

TO BE AN EFFECTIVE MANAGER, I SHOULD . . .

Get other organizational members to be as productive as possible.	1 2 3 4 5 6 7	Help other organizational members to be engaged in their work.
Maximize owners' financial well-being.	1 2 3 4 5 6 7	Serve owners' multiple forms of well-being.

Gain relative power over other organizations (e.g., suppliers, competitors).	1 2 3 4 5 6 7	Develop mutually beneficial relationships with other organizations.
Nurture and satisfy materialist–individualist values and norms.	1 2 3 4 5 6 7	Nurture and satisfy overall well-being values and norms.

B. Macro Environment

TO BE AN EFFECTIVE MANAGER, I SHOULD . . .

Search the natural environment for inexpensive inputs and places to dispose of waste.	1 2 3 4 5 6 7	Search for ways to operate more sustainably in the natural environment.
Encourage legislators to promote managerial rights and financial interests.	1 2 3 4 5 6 7	Encourage legislators to promote stakeholder rights and interests.
Seek economic gain that maximizes owners' financial self-interests in the short term.	1 2 3 4 5 6 7	Seek economic gain that serves multiple forms of well-being for a variety of stakeholders.
Measure the ethicality of an action based on its consequences.	1 2 3 4 5 6 7	Measure the ethicality of an action based on its motivation.

ENDNOTES

1. Personal visit to site and discussion with Roger Bairstow, Thursday, July 21, 2005; company website: http://www.firstfruits.com/; Sparks, B. (2003, August). Apple grower of the year: Ralph Broetje. *American Fruit Grower*; Roberge, E. (2003, Summer). First Fruits—Broetje Orchards. *Washington Business Magazine*; Top apple/pear and stone fruit growers. (2004, November/December). *American Fruit Grower*; Broetje, C. (no date). Servant leadership blossoms at Broetje orchards. Accessed June 2006 at http://www.greenleaf.org/leadership/read-about-it/articles/Servant-Leadership-Blossoms-at-Broetje-Orchard.htm.

2. Sparks, B. (2003, August). Apple grower of the year: Ralph Broetje. *American Fruit Grower*.

3. Roberge, E. (2003, Summer). First Fruits—Broetje Orchards. *Washington Business Magazine*.

4. Safe Quality Food (SQF) was developed by the Australian produce industry and is based in Switzerland. It certifies more than 3300 businesses in 16 countries.

5. Top apple/pear and stone fruit growers. (2004, November/December). *American Fruit Grower*.

6. Broetje, C. (no date). Servant leadership blossoms at Broetje orchards. Accessed June 2006 at http://www.greenleaf.org/leadership/read-about-it/articles/Servant-Leadership-Blossoms-at-Broetje-Orchard.htm.

7. http://www.firstfruits.com/.

8. For example, the Mainstream idea of "green consumerism" is an oxymoron from a Multistream perspective; see the quote from P. Hawken in Williams, A. (2007, July 1). Buying into the green movement. *New York Times*. Accessed February 14, 2008, at http://www.nytimes.com/2007/07/01/fashion/01green.html?_r=1&scp=1&sq=&st=nyt&oref=slogin.

9. Exceptions may include organizations that cause problems (e.g., many stakeholders would want to get rid of organized crime) and organizations that are trying to eradicate a problem. For example, it would be nice if we had a cure for cancer and no longer needed organizations to find the cure. What would happen if the American Cancer Society found a cure for cancer? Would the organization go out of existence? Maybe not. Remember the example of the March of Dimes, which had as its mission the eradication of polio; once the Salk vaccine was developed, the organization adopted a new mission.

10. Comment made during a joint session at the 2007 "D: All Things Digital Conference." Evans, J. (2007, May 31). Video from Steve Jobs and Bill Gates meet-up: A mutual admiration and respect between two tech titans. Accessed June 12, 2007, at http://www.macworld.co.uk/mac/news/index.cfm?newsid=18169&pagtype=allchandate.

11. When large organizations are unable to find satisfactory suppliers, they may start a new company or purchase an existing supplier. This practice, which is called backward integration, is discussed further in Chapter 9.

12. Wal-Mart is aware of this accusation, and is trying to make amends. Gunther, M. (2006). The green machine. *Fortune*, 154(3), 42.

13. Daft, 2003, p. 78. Daft, Richard L. (2003). *Management—6th Edition*. Mason, OH: Thomson South-Western.

14. Arora, R., & Saad, L. (2005, June 9). Marketing to older affluents. *Gallup Management Journal Online*, pp. 24–29.

15. Noble, S. M., Schewe, C. D., & Kuhr, M. (2004). Preferences in health care service and treatment: A generational perspective. *Journal of Business Research*, 57(9), 1033–1041.

16. Hamm, S. (2007, July 2). Children of the web. *BusinessWeek*, pp. 50–58.

17. Gaudes, A. J. (2005). A longitudinal study of incumbent retailers and the arrival of large-format competitors in the home improvement industry: A look at the effectiveness of incumbent product specialization, customer specialization, and adaptation

on firm performance. Doctoral dissertation, I. H. Asper School of Business, University of Manitoba, Manitoba, Canada.

18. Burton, B. (2005). Battle tanks: How think tanks shape the public agenda. *PR Watch*, 12(4). Center for Media and Democracy. Accessed August 24, 2006, at http://www.prwatch.org/prwissues/2005Q4/battletanks.

19. Callahan, D. (1999, November). The think tank as flack: How Microsoft and other corporations use conservative policy groups. *Washington Monthly*. Accessed August 24, 2006, at http://www.washingtonmonthly.com/features/1999/9911.callahan.think.html.

20. Ghoshal, S. (2005). Bad management theories are destroying good management practices. *Academy of Management Learning & Education*, 4(1), 75–91; and Ferraro, F., Pfeffer, J., & Sutton, R. I. (2005). Economic language and assumptions: How theories can become self-fulfilling. *Academy of Management Review*, 30(1), 8–24.

21. Page 131 in Hawken, P. (1993). *The ecology of commerce: A declaration of sustainability.* New York: HarperBusiness.

22. Walsh, D. (1994). *Selling out America's children: How America puts profits before values and what parents can do.* Minneapolis, MN: Fairview Press. Taken from Batstone, D. (2005, July 20). Mass media are sucking out your kids' brains. SojoMail. Found February 14, 2008, at http://www.sojo.net/index.cfm?action=sojomail.display&issue=050720. Batstone presents two additional key values that Walsh identifies: (5) Violence is entertaining; and (6) always seek pleasure and avoid boredom. See also Shrum, L. J., Burroughs, J. E., & Rindfleisch, A. (2005, December). Television's cultivation of material values. *Journal of Consumer Research*, 32(3), 473–479. They argue that television plays a significant role in glamorizing affluence and cultivating viewers to become materialists.

23. The study examined newspaper articles published in the year 2000. Dispensa, J. M., & Brulle, R. J. (2003). Media's social construction of environmental issues: Focus on global warming—a comparative study. *International Journal of Sociology and Social Policy*, 23(10), 4–105. Since then, support for the importance of human contribution to global warming seems to have increased: Kanter, J., & Revkin, A. C. (2007, January 30). World scientists near consensus on warming. *New York Times*. Accessed February 14, 2008, at http://www.nytimes.com/2007/01/30/world/30climate.html?scp=1&sq=&st=nyt; and Kluger, J. (2007, April 9). Global warming: What now?" *Time* (Canadian edition), pp. 46ff.

24. This outcome can also be linked to humans, as it is estimated that the international meat industry generates about 18 percent of the world's greenhouse gases. Vegetarians save about 1.4 tons of carbon annually (Kluger, 2007).

25. The results in the two newspapers were similar to each other, but the reporting in the *New York Times* (which is considered to lean more to the right) was somewhat more similar to the scholarly journals than the reporting in the *Washington Post* (which is considered to be a more liberal newspaper): 43 percent of *NYT* and 38 percent of *WP* articles focused exclusively on human factors; 16 percent of *NYT* and 15 percent of *WP* articles reported only nonhuman factors; and 41 percent of *NYT* and 47 percent of *WP* articles referred to both human and nonhuman factors.

26. The U.S. Environmental Protection Agency and the European Environment Agency provide a similar definition: "The complex of atmospheric, geological and biological characteristics found in an area in the absence of artifacts or influences of a well developed technological, human culture" (accessed August 2, 2006, at http://oaspub.epa.gov/trs/trs_proc_qry.navigate_term?p_term_id=4910&p_term_cd=TERM.

27. Venetoulis, J., & Talberth, J. (2005). *Ecological footprint of nations.* Oakland, CA: Redefining Progress. www.RedefiningProgress.org.

28. These scores are taken from the following source: Venetoulis, J., & Talberth, J. (2005). *Ecological footprint of nations.* Oakland, CA: Redefining Progress. www.RedefiningProgress.org. As readers familiar with this literature will recognize, these are Ecological Footprint 2.0 data, which try to address some of the concerns raised by others on the original ecological footprint research [Rees, W., & Wackernagel, M. (1996). *Our ecological footprint.* Gabriola Island, BC: New Society Publishers; van den Bergh, J. C. M., & Verbruggen, H. (1999). Spatial sustainability, trade and indicators: An evaluation of the ecological footprint. *Ecological Economics*, 29(1), 61–72]. For example, unlike the original index, Ecological Footprint 2.0 attempts to measure use of cropland, built space, and marine and inland fisheries.

29. For example, even if everyone recycled everything that enters and leaves their homes, this would recycle less than 5 percent of the resources that we are using (Hawken, 1993).

30. Deutsch, C. H. (2007, May 12). Incredible shrinking packages. *New York Times*. Accessed February 6, 2008, at http://www.nytimes.com/2007/05/12/business/12package.html?scp=1&sq=&st=nyt; and Mitchell, D. (2006, October 14). Going, going, trying to go green. *New York Times*. Accessed February 6, 2008, at http://www.nytimes.com/2006/10/14/business/14online.html?scp=1&sq=&st=nyt.

31. This is what is alleged to have happened in the Ivory Coast with the Probo Koala, a Greek-owned tanker that flew a Panamanian flag and was leased by the London branch of a Swiss trading corporation that had its fiscal headquarters in the Netherlands. See Polgreen, L., & Simons, M. (2006, October 2). Global sludge ends in tragedy for Ivory Coast. *New York Times*. http://www.nytimes.com/2006/10/02/world/africa/02ivory.html?scp=1&sq=&st=nyt.

32. http://www.epa.gov/compliance/resources/cases/civil/caa/willamette.html. Accessed April 3, 2008.

33. Maynard, M. (2007, July 4). Say "hybrid" and many people will hear "Prius." *New York Times*. Accessed February 14, 2008, at http://www.nytimes.com/2007/07/04/business/04hybrid.html?scp=1&sq=prius+hybrid&st=nyt.

34. Williams, A. (2007, July 1). Buying into the green movement. *New York Times*. Accessed February 14, 2008, at http://www.nytimes.com/2007/07/01/fashion/01green.html?scp=1&sq=&st=nyt.

35. Deutsch, 2007; Mitchell, 2006.

36. http://www.ecobusinesslinks.com/carbon_offset_wind_credits_carbon_reduction.htm.

37. Another term for this is "social obligation": These organizations are simply following their legal obligations of pollution prevention and environmental protection. For more on Compaq, see http://h18000.www1.hp.com/corporate/ehss/2001rpt/wastemin.html, and http://h18000.www1.hp.com/corporate/ehss/97–98rpt/conservation.html (accessed August 24, 2006).

38. Underwood, A. (2007, August 20–27). The green campus: How to teach respect for the environment? The three R's: Reduce your carbon footprint, reuse and recycle. *Newsweek*. Accessed September 18, 2007, at http://www.msnbc.msn.com/id/20216979/site/newsweek/page/0/.

39. Hawken, 1993, pp. 60–61.

40. 3P celebrates 30 years. (no date). Accessed June 18, 2007, at http://solutions.3m.com/wps/portal/3M/en_US/global/

sustainability/s/governance-systems/management-systems/30-years-3p.

41. Many people would rather be a manager than a laborer or a farm worker. Yet who has an intrinsically richer life? When the great Russian novelist Leo Tolstoy inherited his family estate, complete with hundreds of serfs whom he observed carefully, he decided that they knew more about the meaning of life and work, and of how to endure suffering. Of aristocratic managers like himself, he wrote: "We think the feeling experienced by people of our day and our class are very important and varied; but in reality almost all the feelings of people in our class amount to but three very insignificant and simple feelings—the feeling of pride, the feeling of sexual desire, and the feeling of weariness of life" [from Tolstoy's *What is art*; cited on page 124 in Yancey, P. (2001). *Soul survivor*. New York: Doubleday].

42. See Hawken, 1993, p. 214. See also http://www.worldwatch.org/node/755 (accessed April 3, 2008); and Fiedler, D. (2003). Quantifying our children's necessity for nature. *Conservation Biology*, 17(2), 643–644. A review of Kahn, P. H., Jr., & Kellert, S. R. (2002). *Children and nature: Psychological, sociocultural, and evolutionary investigation*. Cambridge, MA: MIT Press.

43. DeGregori, T. R. (1996, October 1). Can organic agriculture feed the world? *American Council on Science and Health*. www.acsh.org/healthissues/newsID.717/healthissue_detail.asp.

44. Research suggests that organic agriculture is about twice as energy efficient as conventional agriculture. Hoeppner, J. W., Entz, M. H., McConkey, B., Zentner, B., & Nagy, C., (2005). Energy use and efficiency in two Canadian organic and conventional crop production systems. *Renewable Agriculture and Food Systems*, 19, 1–8. Bayliss-Smith, T. P. (1982). *The ecology of agricultural systems*. Cambridge, UK: Cambridge University Press. See also Kneen, B. (1989). *From land to mouth: Understanding the food system*. Toronto, ON: NC Press. This book is available for free to download at http://www.ramshorn.ca/Books.html.

45. Pollan, M. (2006, June 4). The way we live now: Mass Natural. *New York Times*. http://www.nytimes.com/2006/06/04/magazine/04wwln_lede.html?pagewanted=1&ei=5088&en=07310c42ac1a390c&ex=1307073600.

46. For more information, see the home page for "100 Mile Diet: Local Eating for Global Change" at http://100milediet.org/ (accessed June 12, 2007).

47. In the "varieties of capitalism" literature, what we here call documentational capitalism is often called "liberal market economics," and what we call relational capitalism is called "coordinated market economics." Our discussion draws from the following excellent review of the literature: Hall, P. A., & Soskice, D. (2001). An introduction to varieties of capitalism. In P. A. Hall & D. W. Soskice (Eds.), *Varieties of capitalism: The institutional foundations of comparative advantage* (pp. 1–68). Oxford, UK: Oxford University Press.

48. Snyder, J. (2006, August 23). Business and lobbying: Growth on K Street slows; Patton Boggs retains top slot. *The Hill*. Accessed August 25, 2006, at http://www.hillnews.com/thehill/export/TheHill/Business/081606.html.

49. Becker, J. (2007, June 25). Murdoch, Ruler of a Vast Empire, Reaches Out for Even More. *New York Times*. Accessed February 14, 2008, at http://www.nytimes.com/2007/06/25/business/media/25murdoch.html?scp=1&sq=&st=nyt.

50. Dunham, R. S. (2006, May 22). Loopholes a jet can fly through. *BusinessWeek*, 3985, 34–36.

51. Aristotle's Greek word for what we call acquisitive economics is *chrematistics*. See Hawken, 1993; Stahel, A. W. (2006). Complexity, oikonomia and political economy. *Ecological Complexity*, 3(4), 369–381; and Wilson, D. J. (2005). The growth syndrome: Economic destitution. *Future Times*, 4, 3–5.

52. This idea of "self-interest with guile" is associated with Oliver Williamson's transaction cost theory and the opportunistic self-interest with agency theory, two of the leading schools of economic thought in management. See pages 112 and 118 in Barney, J. B., & Hesterly, W. (1999). Organizational economics: Understanding the relationship between organizations and economic analysis. In S. R. Clegg & C. Hardy (Eds.), *Studying organization: Theory and method* (pp. 109–141). London: Sage.

53. A number of other similar findings are reviewed in Ferraro et al., 2005.

54. More and more research, especially in private "think tanks" but also in public institutions, is being funded by private enterprise. See Burton, B. (2005), and Robitaille, J. P., & Gingras, Y. (1999, May). The level of funding for university research in Canada and the United States: A comparative study. *Research File*, 3(1).

55. This movement is the "green revolution," which some call "counterfeit green" because agricultural chemicals have become the most important source of water pollution and land management techniques have resulted in soil erosion that is greater than occurred during the Dust Bowl years of the 1930s. For more on this topic, see Dyck, B. (1994). Build in sustainable development: A vegetable field of dreams. *Journal of Organizational Change Management*, 7(4), 47–63.

56. Critics point out that these solutions may create greater problems, provide a false sense of security for solving current problems, and distract people from becoming less dependent on fossil fuels. For further examples and discussion, see McIlroy, A. (2006, June 3). Going to global extremes to fight global warming. *Globe and Mail*, pp. A1, A8.

57. The ideas in this feature draw heavily from Suzuki, D. (1989). The challenge of the 21st century. In M. R. Byers & C. Nichols (Eds.), *The Empire Club of Canada speeches 1988–1989* (pp. 154–167). Toronto, Canada: Empire Club Foundation. Accessed July 20, 2006, at http://empireclubfoundation.com/details.asp?SpeechID=468&FT=yes. See also the following sources: Suzuki speaks. (2004, October 16). Accessed July 20, 2006, at http://www.cbc.ca/cgi-bin/newsworld/viewer.cgi?FILE=NL20041016.html&TEMPLATE=newsreal_archive.ssi&SC=NL; and U.S. Census Bureau. http://www.census.gov/ipc/www/world.html.

58. *Limits to Growth*, a book that raised this issue in the 1970s, even predicted the tipping point to be at the turn of the twenty-first century: Meadows, D. H., Meadows, D. L., Randers, J., & Behrens, W. W., III. (1972). *The limits to growth*. New York: Universe Books.

59. Suzuki, D. (1989). The challenge of the 21st century. In M. R. Byers & C. Nichols (Eds.), *The Empire Club of Canada speeches 1988–1989* (pp. 154–167). Toronto, ON: Empire Club Foundation. Accessed July 20, 2006, at http://empireclubfoundation.com/details.asp?SpeechID=468&FT=yes.

60. DeGregori, T. R. (2002). *Bountiful harvest: Technology, food safety, and the environment*. Washington, DC: Cato Institute.

61. Dyck, 1994.

62. Giacolone, R. A. (2004). A transcendent business education for the 21st century. *Academy of Management Learning and Education*, 3(4), 415–420.

63. The original research was done in the early 1990s. If there has since been a decreasing emphasis on materialist–individualist values, then today an even greater proportion of people might choose the lower-paying job. The original experiment is described in the following source: Bazerman, M. H., Schroth, H., Pradhan, P., Diekmann, K., & Tenbrunsel, A. (1994). The inconsistent role of comparison others and procedural justice in reactions to hypothetical job descriptions: Implications for job acceptance decisions. *Organizational Behavior and Human Decision Processes*, 60, 326–352. Subsequent research suggests that people may want to accept a Multistream job, but choose to accept a more Mainstream job because they have been socialized to feel that they should do so (especially in light of self-fulfilling theories, such as argued in Ferraro et al., 2005). See Bazerman, M. H., Tenbrunsel, A. E., & Wade-Benzoni, K. (1998). Negotiating with yourself and losing: Making decisions with competing internal preferences. *Academy of Management Review*, 23(2), 225–241.

64. In the United States, socially responsible investing (SRI) grew from $639 billion in 1995 to $2,290 billion in 2005, and mutual funds (the fastest-growing segment of SRI) increased from $12 billion in 1995 to $179 billion in 2005. Information in this paragraph was drawn from the following source: *2005 report on socially responsible investing trends in the United States: 10-year review*. (2006). Social Investment Forum, Social Research Program.

65. Glen, B. (2006, February 13). His work is a precious place. *Western Catholic Reporter*. Found February 14, 2008, at http://www.wcr.ab.ca/news/2006/0213/business021306.shtml.

66. This is different from collusion. Whereas collusion seeks to gouge the consumer to maximize short-term self-interested financial gain, cooperation can strengthen the sustainable enterprise for all. See the discussion of sustenance economics later in this chapter.

67. Minato, T. (1994). *Strategic alliances between small and large businesses*. Paper presented International Federation of Scholarly Associations of Management (IFSAM) conference, Tokyo, Japan, September 8, 1994.

68. This description is taken from Kalra, R. (2005, November 13). Back from the ashes. *Hartford Courant*, pp. D1, D3.

69. Martin, A. (2006, November 6). The package may say healthy, but this grocer begs to differ. *New York Times*. Accessed February 19, 2008, at http://www.nytimes.com/2006/11/06/business/06grocery.html?_r=1&scp=1&sq=&st=nyt&oref=slogin.

70. Tom's of Maine a national "workplace model of excellence." (2003, May 9). Accessed September 18, 2007, at http://www.tomsofmaine.com/about/press/2003_05_09_hmhb.asp.

71. Foster, R. J. (1981). *Freedom of simplicity*. New York: HarperCollins.

72. Dispensa & Brulle, 2003.

73. Adbusters has battled for a decade for the right to show its ads on national television networks in Canada, and it expects those legal battles to continue. Al Hudak, the Canadian Television Network's (CTV's) group director of national sales, told Adbusters that "all hell would break loose" if CTV ran a particular Adbusters' ad that highlighted that 52 percent of the calories in a Big Mac come from fat: "We're in business to make money and . . . to sell our customers' products." See Kennedy, J. (2005, April 14–20). Adbusters' fat chance: Networks tell alt mag to take anti-corporate ads and shove 'em. *Now On-Line Edition*, 24(33). Accessed October 30, 2007, at http://www.nowtoronto.com/issues/2005-04-14/news_story.php.

74. The study from the Fordham University Institute for Innovation and Social Policy was published in 1999 under the name "The Social Health of the Nation: How America Is Really Doing" (Oxford University Press). Cited in Stille, A. (2002, April 27). With the index of leading economic indicators, a social report card. *New York Times*, p. B11. Note that other similar scales, such as the Genuine Progress Indicator (which is to GDP what net profit is to gross profit), come up with similar findings (see http://www.rprogress.org/projects/gpi/).

75. Hawken et al., 1999, p. 16.

76. Butler, S. (1996, June). Gunter Pauli's radical eco-factories completely eliminate pollution. *Fastcompany.com*. Accessed June 18, 2007, at http://www.fastcompany.com/magazine/03/gunterp.html; and Infusing "intelligence" into the globalized economy key theme at annual gathering of environment. (2007, February 1). United Nations Environment Program, Environment for Development, news release from Nairobi. Accessed June 18, 2007, at inistershttp://www.unep.org/Documents.Multilingual/Default.asp?DocumentID=499&ArticleID=5504&l=en.

77. Based on the definition developed in 1987 by the World Commission on Environment and Development (the Brundtland Commission).

78. Hawken, 1993, pp. 142, 192.

79. Hawken, 1993.

80. A third type, called "unsaleables," would be phased out over time. The discussion in this section draws from Hawken, 1993, pp. 67–68: "intelligent product system" [based on the work of Dr. Michael Braungart and Justus Englefried of the Environmental Protection Encouragement Agency (EPEA) in Hamburg, Germany].

81. Hawken, 1993, pp. 67–68.

82. Hawken et al., 1999, p. 71.

83. The increasing complexity of global competition suggests that U.S. managers may want to explore new ways to partner with labor: Rousseau, D. M., & Batt, R. (2007). Global competition's perfect storm: Why business and labor cannot solve their problems alone. *Academy of Management Perspectives*, 21(2), 16–23.

84. Examples in this paragraph are taken from Hawken et al., 1999, p. 318.

85. The word Aristotle used for sustenance economics is *oikonomia* (Hawken, 1993; Stahel, 2006; Wilson, 2005).

86. For example, see Hawken, 1993.

87. Smith, J. B. (no date). Company's new manure-to-gas plant promises relief for Texas' dairy industry. Accessed August 20, 2007, at http://www.environmentalpower.com/companies/microgy/technology.php4.

88. The financial data in this paragraph come from Maich, S. (2006, April 17). The worst president in 100 years? *Maclean's*, pp. 28–33.

89. Herper, M. (2004, March 16). *The world's best-selling drugs*. Forbes.com. Accessed March 10, 2008, at http://www.forbes.com/2004/03/16/cx_mh_0316bestselling.html.

90. Note that trimmings from regular textile mills have been defined as hazardous waste by European government regulators. This example is found in Hawken et al., 1999, p. 72; these authors cite McDonough, W., & Braungart, M. (1998). The NEXT Industrial Revolution. *Atlantic Monthly*, 282(4). Accessed February 14, 2008, at http://www.theatlantic.com/doc/199810/environment.

91. Many of the ideas in this paragraph, and this quote—which is attributed to the sociologist and philosopher Henri Lefebvre—are drawn from http://en.wikipedia.org/wiki/Car_culture (accessed June 9, 2006).

92. There are approximately 217 million vehicles on the road in the United States [McAlinden, S. P., Hill, K., & Swiecki, B.

(2003). *Economic contribution of the automotive industry to the U.S. economy—an update: A study prepared for the Alliance of Automobile Manufacturers.* Economics and Business Group, Center for Automotive Research, Ann Arbor, MI], and the total population is about 300 million. There is about one vehicle for every person of legal driving age (accessed June 9, 2006, at http://bicycleuniverse.info/transpo/almanac.html#sources).

93. McAlinden et al., 2003.

94. In 1990, approximately 54 percent of Americans lived within 5 miles of work, and only 3 percent cycled to work and fewer walked (Hawken et al., 1999, p. 44).

95. Hawken et al., 1999, p. 46.

96. Melosi, M. V. (2004). The automobile and the environment in American history. *Automobile in American Life and Society.* Accessed August 24, 2006, at http://www.autolife.umd.umich.edu/Environment/E_Overview/E_Overview8.htm.

97. McAlinden et al., 2003.

98. *Global warming basics.* (no date.) Natural Resources Defense Council. Accessed June 9, 2006, at http://www.nrdc.org/globalWarming/f101.asp.

99. World Resources Institute. (1998). *1998–99 world resources: A guide to the global environment.* New York: Oxford University Press.

100. See Whitelog, J. (no date). *Dirty from cradle to grave.* Accessed June 13, 2007, at http://afo.sandelman.ca/cc1.html.

101. Nader, R. (2002, August 31). The Highway Lobby. *CounterPunch.* Accessed June 9, 2006, at http://www.counterpunch.org/nader0831.html.

102. By 2003, the average fuel economy had dropped below 25 miles per gallon (*Time,* "Why America Is Running Out of Gas," July 13, 2003). Apparently, raising the average fuel efficiency for cars in the United States by 2.7 miles per gallon would equal all U.S oil imports from the Persian Gulf (*Newsweek,* April 15, 2002, cited in http://bicycleuniverse.info/transpo/almanac.html#sources; accessed June 9, 2006).

103. Kluger, 2007.

104. *Newsweek,* April 15, 2002, cited in http://bicycleuniverse.info/transpo/almanac.html#sources. Accessed June 9, 2006).

105. For example, sales of SUVs in the United States (which produce 40 percent more global warming pollution than the average car) were enhanced when President George W. Bush introduced a tax cut in 2003 that permitted small businesses to immediately deduct up to $100,000 of the cost of any newly purchased light truck weighing more than 6000 pounds (including SUVs). In 2004, the allowable deduction for these vehicles was reduced from $100,000 to $25,000. See the following source: *The consumer's truth: Myths and facts about American consumers and fuel economy.* (no date). Accessed June 9, 2006, at www.citizen.org/documents/Consumer_Choice_Fact_Sheet.pdf.

106. Based on 2002 figures, when U.S. sales amounted to 16.8 million vehicles, followed by sales in Japan (5.8 million vehicles), Germany (3.5 million vehicles), China (2.9 million vehicles), and Great Britain (2.9 million vehicles) (McAlinden et al., 2003). The United States is also the largest vehicle producer in the world (12.3 million vehicles in 2002).

107. This figure includes direct manufacturing jobs (approximately 1 million jobs), suppliers (e.g., approximately 15 percent of the steel industry, or 15,000 jobs), and related services (e.g., more than 900,000 jobs at gas stations, almost 300,000 jobs in highway and street construction, and nearly 150,000 jobs each in tire sales, car washes, and car rental agencies).

108. In 2004, this was more than $20 billion of the $135 billion total industry (*Advertising Age,* June 27, 2005; see also McAlinden et al., 2003).

109. $20,518 million in advertising (2004 data, *Advertising Age,* June 27, 2005) divided by 16.8 million vehicles (2002 data) = $1221 per vehicle.

110. According to http://www.uwlax.edu/parking/costofdriving.htm (accessed June 9, 2006), if you include both direct and indirect costs, the cost of driving is about $1.20 per mile. The average vehicle is driven 13,000 miles per year and incurs approximately $11,250 in annual direct driver's expenses and an additional $4300 in annual societal costs. The median household income in the United States in 2002 was $42,900 (*Income in the United States:* 2002, U.S. Department of Commerce, Donald L. Evans, Secretary). According to U.S. Department of Transportation Federal Highway Administration's *Highway Statistics 2000,* total construction, improvements, and repair of roadways costs amounted to $65 billion in 2002, with about two-thirds of that amount being covered by fuel taxes and user fees, and the remaining $23 billion being paid by taxpayers through state and local sources. Approximately 64 percent of the $30.9 billion spent for maintenance and operation of roadways came from fuel taxes and user fees; the remaining $11 billion was financed by taxpayers.

111. "Car-sharing" is a new "technology" that helps to minimize some of the environmental and financial costs of car owners while retaining its key benefits. Today there are more than 600 cities in the world where you can car-share, which essentially means that you own a "share" of a car with others (the car may be parked in a nearby lot or driveway). With organizations such as Zipcar in Boston, you can "book" your car for times when you really need it (e.g., when public transit is awkward or unavailable) and the rest of the time you can use more environmentally friendly technologies (e.g., walking, cycling, or mass transit).

112. See the North American Velomobile website at www.velomobiles.net. The "Stormy Weather" velomobile is being manufactured by Lightfootcyles (http://www.lightfootcycles.com/velo_proj.htm) (photo found June 12, 2007). For a superb study of the history and social construction of the velomobile, see Van De Walle, F. (2004). *The velomobile as a vehicle for more sustainable transportation: Reshaping the social construction of cycling technology.* Masters of science thesis, Kungliga Tekniska Hoegskolan, Royal Institute of Technology, Department for Infrastructure, Stockholm, Sweden. Other alternative technologies being developed rely on ultra-light materials, hybrid–electric propulsion, hydrogen fuel cells, and hypercars (Hawken et al., 1999).

113. Hawken, 1993, p. 76.

114. Hawken, 1993, pp. 88–89.

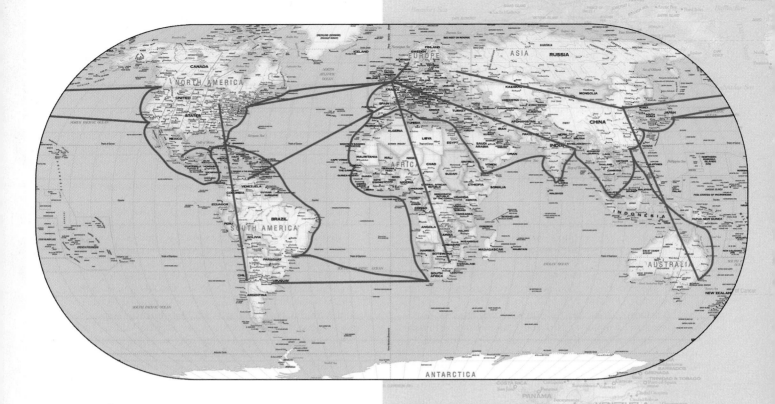

This chapter provides a quick glimpse at a complex subject—the whole world! Our itinerary covers some of the most important and interesting places. As shown in the road map, our journey includes a look at different approaches to internationalization, as well as trips to each of the four dimensions of the international environment. We will first visit these destinations from a Mainstream perspective, and then again from a Multistream perspective. Put your seat in the upright position, fasten your seat belt, and enjoy the trip!

Map courtesy of The Seeger Map
Co., Inc.

ROAD MAP

Levels of Internationalization

Importing/exporting

Licensing/franchising
Strategic alliances and joint ventures

Foreign subsidiaries

Key Dimensions of the International Environment

1. *Sociocultural*
   Cross-cultural differences (especially Hofstede's dimensions)
2. *Natural*
   Source of inputs and place to deposit unsalable outputs
3. *Political/legal*
   Tariffs/quotas/subsidies
   General trade agreements
4. *Economic/technological*
   Ease of moving jobs/resources, knowledge, and money

CHAPTER 4

The International Environment

MAINSTREAM APPROACH	←→	MULTISTREAM APPROACH

MAINSTREAM APPROACH	MULTISTREAM APPROACH
Easy access to low-cost inputs (imports) and new markets (exports)	Improve wages (imports) and serve new markets (exports)
Moderate access and control	Provide service to new markets
Access to new markets and new partners' knowledge/resources	Build mutually beneficial networks
Full control of operations/profit	Model responsible management
Ethnocentrism ("My way is best") versus polycentrism ("The local way is best")	Egali-centrism ("Our way is best")
Seek lowest-cost raw materials and places to dispose of waste	Sustainable development
Provide rules/regulatory framework: • Protect national industries • Promote free trade (e.g., WTO)	Reduce barriers: • Nurture emerging economies • Fair Trade
Lower input/process costs Enhance efficiency Seek highest rate of return	Serve greatest needs Distribute/learn latest information • Support needy (microfinance)

Everyday Marvels[1]

International business has become so commonplace that we no longer marvel at it. But imagine that you belong to the San people living in Africa's Kalahari Desert, and that you have never had contact with the outside world prior to receiving an empty Coke bottle thrown from a small airplane passing overhead. This is what happened in the movie *The Gods Must Be Crazy*, which was an international sensation when it first came out. At first, the San people think that the bottle is a gift from the gods and find it useful for all sorts of tasks in everyday village life (e.g., they use it as a rolling pin and as a musical instrument). However, when they begin to fight among themselves over who gets to use the foreign bottle, they decide to respectfully return it to the gods.

Now think about the foreign things you take for granted every day. For example, consider how many people and industries around the world are involved in producing the common cola can. The bauxite used to make a can is mined in Australia and then trucked to a chemical reduction mill, where it is processed into aluminum oxide. If you live in the United Kingdom, the aluminum oxide is then loaded onto giant ore carriers and shipped to Sweden or Norway, where hydroelectric dams provide inexpensive electricity for a smelting process that turns the aluminum oxide into aluminum metal ingots. These ingots are then shipped to rolling mills in Sweden or Germany, where the ingots are heated and transformed into ten-ton coils that are only one-eighth of an inch thick. They are then sent to a cold rolling mill in the same or another country, where they are rolled to a thickness of one-eightieth of an inch. The aluminum is then ready for fabrication, and the sheets are sent to the United Kingdom. There, they are punched, formed into cans, washed and dried, painted twice, lacquered, flanged, and sprayed with a protective coating inside.

A French ad for the movie *The Gods Must Be Crazy*.

The cola inside the can has a similarly international lineage. It consists of water, carbon dioxide, flavored syrup (with sugar harvested from beets grown in France), phosphorus (from open-pit mines in Idaho), and caffeine (perhaps a by-product of making decaffeinated coffee from beans grown in South America). When filled with this multisourced cola, the cans are shipped to retailers in cardboard boxes made from forest pulp that may originate in British Columbia, Sweden, or Siberia.

It is truly amazing that all this effort and activity—literally spanning the globe—can be managed efficiently to provide a can of soda pop. It requires the coordination of various natural resources (from bauxite to sugar to forests), technology to process and transport materials (from ships to hydroelectricity to painting), and the ability to make payments and convert from one currency into another. All that effort just to satisfy our appetite for soda pop!

In Chapter 2, we discussed how the growth in popularity of drinking tea contributed to the conditions that enabled Wedgwood's pottery company to flourish. In this case, we have looked at another popular beverage—Americans use 100 billion soda pop cans each year—to illustrate how globalization has transformed the marketplace.

But the story does not stop there. There are hidden aspects of the soda pop story that are not so positive. For example, the second biggest use of U.S. corn is for syrup to make soda pop. To increase yields, U.S. farmers often use Atrazine, a pesticide now banned in parts of Europe because of its unwanted characteristics.[2] There are also widespread concerns about the obesity trend linked to consumption of a diet high in sugary drinks. Another concern is the use of water for the production of soda pop: It takes nine liters of clean water to make one liter of Coke. This water consumption is especially problematic in regions where drinking water is scarce. For example, in Kerala, India, the government ordered the closure of the local Coca-Cola plant after it drilled more wells than permitted, illegally installed high-powered pumps (the water table fell from 45 to 150 meters below the surface, and caused 260 other wells to run dry), and polluted the local water supply[3]

and soil (local villagers were given "free fertilizer" from the factory's toxic waste that was rich in cadmium and lead, both known carcinogens).[4]

In short, there is much more to a can of cola than meets the eye. The tiny can is a symbol of the amazing accomplishments of international business, but it also points to less positive aspects.

\

This chapter builds on the discussion of environments presented in Chapter 3, and extends this discussion into the international arena. We compare and contrast Mainstream and Multistream management by first looking at why the international environment is increasingly important to managers, and then describing several ways that organizations can internationalize. This prepares us to discuss some international aspects of the same four dimensions of the macro environment that were introduced in the previous chapter.

MAINSTREAM MANAGEMENT AND THE INTERNATIONAL ENVIRONMENT

From a Mainstream perspective, the international environment is important because it provides managers with access to less expensive organizational inputs, lower production costs, and a larger market for outputs. Mainstream wisdom suggests that managers who ignore the international environment risk failure. Even though it wasn't until the 1960s that multinational corporations became commonplace, they are now a dominant fixture on the organizational landscape. Although no official definition exists, a **multinational company (MNC)** is often defined as an organization that receives more than 25 percent of its total sales revenue from outside its home country. This description includes both large corporations such as General Electric and small businesses such as Botanical PaperWorks, a Canadian company that makes handmade stationery that it sells online to markets outside Canada. According to the World Bank, MNCs hold about one-third of the world's productive assets, and they conduct approximately 70 percent of world trade. Today there are nearly 50,000 MNCs worldwide, considerably more than the 7000 that the United Nations had counted in the mid-1970s.[5] The combined sales of the world's largest 200 MNCs is equivalent to roughly one-quarter of the $60 trillion world gross product, yet these organizations employ less than 1 percent of the world's workforce.[6] Today, more than half of the world's 100 largest economic entities are MNCs instead of countries—more than double the proportion in 1990.[7]

To the extent that globalization is profitable for businesses,[8] it is also profitable for the people who can afford to invest in them and for the managers who lead them. **Globalization** refers to the changes in the four dimensions of the external environment that have resulted in increased interdependence and integration among people and organizations around the world.[9] According to a Mainstream approach, increasing global trade promises to improve the economic condition for everyone in the world, as captured in the motto: "A rising tide lifts all the boats."[10] The reason is relatively simple. Just as specialization helps to improve productivity *within* organizations (recall Adam Smith's example of the pin factory from Chapter 2), so also there are

Multinational company (MNC) is an organization that receives more than 25 percent of its total sales revenue from outside its home country.

Globalization refers to changes in the four dimensions of the external environment (i.e., socio-cultural, natural, political–legal, and economic–technological factors) that result in increased interdependence and integration among people and organizations around the world.

Figure 4.1 Ways to internationalize an organization

Exporting occurs when an organization produces goods and services in its home country and sells them in another country.

Importing is bringing in finished products from a foreign country for resale domestically.

Global outsourcing is importing from another country one or more subcomponents of an organization's products or services.

Countertrade occurs when products or services from one country are traded (rather than bought and sold for currency) for products or services from another country.

Licensing occurs when an organization in one country sells specific resources—for example, patent or trademark rights and technical expertise—to an organization in another country.

Franchising occurs when a franchisor sells to a franchisee (for a lump-sum payment and a share of the franchisee's profits) a complete package required to set up an organization, including but not limited to its trademark and trade name, its products and services, its ingredients, its technology and machinery, and its management and standard operating systems.

Strategic alliance (international) is when managers from different organizations in at least two countries pool their organizations' resources and "know-how" in order to share the risks and rewards for developing a new market or product.

mutual advantages *among nations* when each develops and focuses on different strengths. For example, the weather in some countries is conducive to growing bananas; the weather in other countries is conducive to growing wheat or rice. Some countries have expertise in growing flowers; other countries are good at making watches or cameras or computer components. Instead of every country having its own car companies, it is more efficient for fewer car companies to manufacture cars for use around the world. The argument is that everybody wins when people in one country can trade the goods and services that they are adept at producing for goods and services from other countries. This creates a web of interdependence and integration across nations.

How to Internationalize an Organization

Managers have several options for internationalizing their organizations:

- Exporting and importing
- Licensing and franchising
- Strategic alliances and joint ventures
- Foreign subsidiaries

Figure 4.1 shows how these options can range from relatively simple arrangements that require small investments and can be easily reversed to complex arrangements that require long-term commitments and substantial sums of money. These methods are not mutually exclusive. Managers can and do choose to use several at the same time.

EXPORTING AND IMPORTING.   Perhaps the simplest ways for a domestic firm to internationalize are (1) to export its products or services or (2) to import products or components from another country. In either case, overseas investment is minimal and the decision can be reversed relatively quickly and inexpensively. When **exporting,** an organization manufactures products in its home country and transports them to other countries for sale there (e.g., American companies export computers, Japanese companies export cameras, Swiss companies export watches). An exporting strategy can be implemented by simply advertising on the Internet. **Importing** occurs when a finished product is brought in from another country for resale domestically (e.g., Canadian-made ice-hockey skates and French wine are imported into the United States). The value of goods and services being exported from the United States increased from about $1 trillion in 1995 to $1.75 trillion in 2005, during which time the value of imports increased even more rapidly—from approximately $1.1 trillion in 1995 to $2.5 trillion in 2005.[11]

Variations of exporting and importing include global outsourcing and countertrade. **Global outsourcing** occurs when one or more subcomponents for an organization's products or services are imported from another country. Global outsourcing is evident when kitchen chair parts produced in China are assembled in the United States, and when software for U.S. computer video games is created in India.

Countertrade, which accounts for 25 to 30 percent of world trade, occurs when products or services from one country are traded (rather than being bought and sold for currency) for products or services from another country.[12] This sort of trade is especially important when dealing with less economically developed countries, where currency fluctuations may make barter a better choice than buying or selling with currency. For example, many deals involving Russia employ some form of counter-trade. At one time, concerts in Poland by the rock band ABBA were traded for Polish coal.[13]

LICENSING AND FRANCHISING.   Managers can use licensing and franchising to help their organization to grow, both within their home country and internationally. Licensing and franchising require greater investments than exporting, but they also provide managers with more control and the opportunity to offer a more complete product line.

With **licensing,** an organization in one country sells specific resources—for example, patent or trademark rights and technical expertise—to an organization in another country. The licensee usually pays the licensor royalties based on sales. For example, Heineken, which has been called the world's first truly global brand of beer, usually enters a new market by exporting its product so as to establish a presence and get a sense of the market. If the market looks attractive enough, then Heineken licenses its brands to a local brewer.[14]

Franchising is a special variation of licensing, wherein the franchisor in one country sells to the franchisee in another country (for a lump-sum payment and a share of the franchisee's profits) a complete package required to set up an organization, including its trademark and trade name, its products and services, its ingredients, its technology and machinery, its management and standard operating systems, and so on. For example, McDonald's, KFC, and Burger King franchises are found in almost every large city in the world. Franchising can be risky—all of the company's secrets are entrusted to the franchisee, and the reputation of the worldwide franchise name can suffer with weak franchisees—but the benefits often outweigh the risks.

STRATEGIC ALLIANCES AND JOINT VENTURES.   A higher level of involvement occurs when an organization becomes directly involved in managing productive assets in another country. In a **strategic alliance,** managers from organizations in at least two countries agree to pool some of their organizations' resources and "know-how" and share the risks and rewards for developing a new market or product. For example, General Motors has a minority ownership in several Asian auto manufacturers, including Daewoo and Suzuki. A **joint venture** is a specific variation of a strategic alliance, in which the partnering organizations agree to form a separate, independent, jointly owned organization. For example, the British company Alcatel and Shanghai Bell have a joint venture to make telephone switching equipment. In such situations, both organizations invest expertise and resources, and both stand to gain from a successful partnership.

FOREIGN SUBSIDIARIES.   Rather than merely outsourcing or importing components or products from abroad, an organization can gain greater control and profits

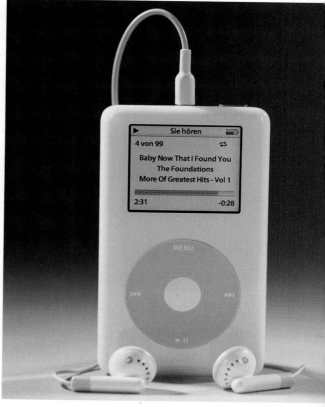

Apple outsources the manufacture of its iPods to a number of Asian organizations, and the final assembly of the iPod's 451 parts represents less than 2 percent of its total selling price. The iPod's most expensive components are its hard drive (which accounts for 25 percent of the device's selling price and is manufactured by the Japanese company Toshiba, although Toshiba makes most of its hard drives in the Philippines and China), its display module (7 percent), and its video/multimedia and controller chips (less than 5 percent; supplied by U.S. companies Broadcom and PortalPlayer, although most Broadcom chips are manufactured in Taiwan). The largest portion of the selling price—more than 25 percent—goes to Apple for creating and promoting the iPod. Another 25 percent pays for the distribution and retail costs.[15]

Joint venture is a variation of a strategic alliance, where the partnering organizations agree to form a separate, independent, jointly owned organization.

by purchasing the factories where these components or products are made. For example, some Japanese businesses have moved their manufacturing operations to Thailand, where labor costs are lower. Such direct investment requires intimate knowledge of the foreign country's environment, and it typically involves making a longer-term commitment and requires greater initial expenses and risks. When an organization purchases another organization overseas, it becomes a wholly owned foreign affiliate. When an organization builds a new plant overseas, it is called a **greenfield venture.**

Some countries create special geographic regions in an effort to attract foreign investment. The *maquiladora* regions in Mexico, for example, have been somewhat of a model for other countries. *Maquiladora* refers to assembly plants and factories in special regions in Mexico along the U.S. border where international corporations can take advantage of low wages and enjoy low duties and tariffs when their products are exported to the United States. In fact, U.S. firms own many of the Mexican *maquiladora* factories. This approach offers foreign firms access to low wages and few trade restrictions, and provides people in the host country with much-needed jobs, often at higher wages than they could get elsewhere in the country. Today, more than 100 countries have established these kinds of special export processing zones (up from 25 countries in 1975).[16]

In sum, managers can internationalize in many different ways. Regardless of which options they choose, however, they must be aware of four important dimensions of the international environment.

The Four Dimensions of the International Environment

The four dimensions of the international management environment are the same as the four dimensions of the macro environment that were presented in Chapter 3. As depicted in Figure 4.2, from a Mainstream view these dimensions fit together to form an integrated whole. For example, starting with the sociocultural dimension, internationalization is thought to enhance the opportunity to lower costs and increase revenues for all. The international natural environment provides greater opportunities to find less expensive raw materials and places to dispose of unsalable outputs (e.g., pollution). This, in turn, influences the types of political institutions that are developed to regulate international trade. The markets should enable goods and services to flow freely across borders, unimpeded by national constraints. This, in turn, influences the economic–technological dimension, where emphasis is on the free flow of money, knowledge, jobs, and goods and services. As we discuss each dimension, we will refer to Table 4.1, which provides some basic data on these dimensions for more than 50 countries.[17]

THE SOCIOCULTURAL ENVIRONMENT. Mainstream managers typically choose between two basic approaches to managing in the international sociocultural environment: (1) polycentrism and (2) ethnocentrism. **Polycentrism** is evident when there is an assumption that managers in a host country know the best way to manage an organization in their country. Managers with a polycentric orientation believe that the best way to maximize their firms' profits is to adapt to the practices found in foreign countries.[18] For example, because of the emphasis in China on establishing interpersonal relationships among business partners, starting a new trade relationship with managers in China may require many more visits than starting a new trade relationship with managers in the United Kingdom.

Greenfield venture occurs when an organization builds a new plant where none existed before.

Maquilidora refers to assembly plants and factories in special regions in Mexico located along the U.S.–Mexico border where international corporations can take advantage of low wages and enjoy low tariffs when their products are exported to the United States.

Polycentrism is evident when there is an assumption that managers in a host country know the best way to manage an organization in the host country.

Ethnocentrism is evident when managers enter a foreign country with the belief that their own home country offers the best way to manage in a foreign country. An ethnocentric approach may be especially likely when managers believe that their home country is more developed or more advanced than the foreign country in which they are working. Ethnocentrism has potential dangers. For example, many of the initial assumptions for managing Disney's theme park near Paris (such as the alcohol sales restrictions found in the U.S. parks) were changed after it opened so as to account for differences in cultures.

Contemporary ideas about international management have been shaped by important events in the past. As we learned in Chapter 2, an important event in the development of organizational forms came when Europeans began to explore the world. Such exploration was a very risky business, and it demanded the creation of a corporate organizational form so that the risk would not land in the lap of any individual businessperson. Our contemporary understanding of international management has also been influenced by colonialism when, for example, European nations enhanced their financial self-interests by ruling over weaker or dependent nations. There seemed to be an attitude that the rest of the world was there to be explored and conquered. These sorts of values and outlooks may also be evident when today's managers are motivated to go overseas to exploit opportunities that are in their own economic self-interests.

Christopher Columbus—a manager who made *plans* to sail overseas, gathered and *organized* the necessary resources to fulfill his plans, *led* the expedition, and exercised *control* over the resources entrusted to him—remains one of the most famous European explorers who "discovered" and began to foster trade with a new world. Like many modern-day international managers, Columbus went overseas seeking adventure and fortune. He found both in the Americas. In his 1492 journal, Columbus described the First Nations people he met as "well built and handsome." He wrote that they greeted him with "parrots, balls of cotton and many other things," and that "They willingly traded everything they owned." Columbus was impressed by the economic opportunity the people in this new land represented: "They are so naive and so free with their possessions that no one who has not witnessed them would believe

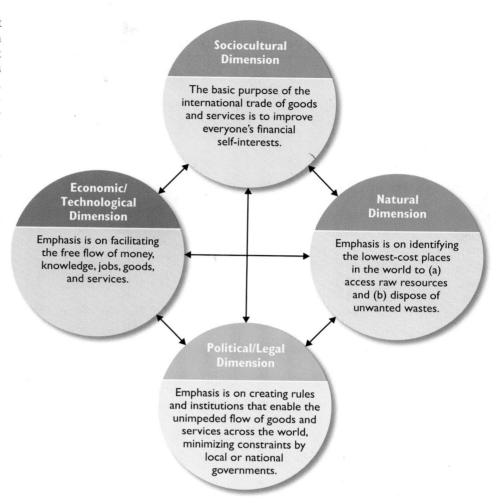

Figure 4.2 Mainstream view of relationships between the four dimensions of the international environment

Ethnocentrism is evident when managers enter a foreign country with the belief that their own home country offers the best way to manage.

TABLE 4.1

Data on Sociocultural, Natural, Political, and Economic Environments of Selected Countries

	A: Individualism	B: Materialism	C: Time orientation	D: Deference to authority	E: Uncertainty avoidance	F: Life satisfaction	G: Life expectancy	H: Ecological footprint	I: Population	J: GDP per capita	K: Internationalization	L: GDP per capita/ ecological footprint	M: Satisfaction/ ecological footprint
Argentina	46	56		49	86	6.8	74.5	57	39.9	$13,100	0.13	$230	0.12
Australia	90	61	31	36	51	7.3	80.3	195	20.3	31,900	0.34	163	0.04
Austria	55	79		11	70	7.8	79.0	126	8.2	32,700	0.90	259	0.06
Belgium	75	54		65	94	7.3	78.9	170	10.4	31,400	1.64	184	0.04
Brazil	38	49	65	69	76	6.3	70.5	35	188.1	8,400	0.12	241	0.18
Canada	80	52	23	39	48	7.6	80.0	205	33.1	34,000	0.61	166	0.04
Chile	23	28		63	86	6.5	77.9	48	16.1	11,300	0.37	236	0.14
China	15	55	114	80	40	6.3	71.6	31	131.4	6,800	0.15	220	0.20
Colombia	13	64		67	80	7.2	72.4	27	43.6	7,900	0.11	288	0.26
Costa Rica	15	21		35	86	7.5	78.2	35	4.1	11,100	0.37	314	0.21
Czech Republic	60	45		35	60	6.4	75.6	117	10.2	19,500	0.78	167	0.05
Denmark	74	16		18	23	8.2	77.2	153	5.5	34,600	0.65	227	0.05
Ecuador	8	63		78	67	5.6	74.3	34	12.5	4,300	0.33	128	0.17
El Salvador	19	40		66	94	6.6	70.9	19	6.8	4,700	0.32	250	0.35
Finland	63	26		33	59	7.7	78.5	110	5.2	30,900	0.77	281	0.07
France	71	43		68	86	6.6	79.5	163	60.9	29,900	0.50	184	0.04
Germany	67	66	31	35	65	7.2	78.7	129	82.4	30,400	0.73	236	0.06
Greece	35	57		60	112	6.3	78.3	168	10.7	22,200	0.28	132	0.04
Guatemala	6	37		95	101	7.0	67.3	19	12.3	4,700	0.20	249	0.37
Hong Kong	25	57	96	68	29	6.6	81.6		6.9	32,900	2.55		
Hungary	55	79	50	45	83	5.7	72.7	86	10	16,300	0.78	189	0.07
India	48	56	61	77	40	5.4	63.3	12	1095.4	3,300	0.05	276	0.45
Indonesia	14	46		78	48	6.6	66.8	20	245.5	3,600	0.16	181	0.33
Iran	41	43		58	59	6.0	70.4	63	68.7	8,300	0.17	132	0.10
Ireland	70	68		28	35	7.6	77.7	162	4.1	41,000	1.00	254	0.05
Israel	54	47		13	81	6.7	79.7		6.4	24,600	0.53		
Italy	76	70		50	75	6.9	80.1	103	58.1	29,200	0.45	285	0.07
Jamaica	39	68		45	13	7.0	70.8	64	2.8	4,400	0.46	69	0.11
Japan	46	95	80	54	92	6.2	82.0	131	127.5	31,500	0.25	240	0.05
Malaysia	26	50		104	36	7.4	73.2	88	24.4	12,100	0.90	138	0.08
Mexico	30	69		81	82	6.9	75.1	57	107.4	10,000	0.41	175	0.12
Netherlands	80	14	44	38	53	7.5	78.4	120	16.5	30,500	1.37	254	0.06
New Zealand	79	58	30	22	49	7.4	79.1	171	4.1	25,200	0.45	148	0.04
Norway	69	8		31	50	7.4	79.4	230	4.6	42,300	0.87	184	0.03
Pakistan	14	50		55	70	4.3	63.0	12	165.8	2,400	0.09	207	0.37
Panama	11	44		95	86	7.2	74.8	55	3.2	7,200	0.70	131	0.13
Peru	16	42		64	87	5.6	70.0	18	28.3	5,900	0.17	336	0.32
Philippines	32	64	19	94	44	6.4	70.4	21	89.5	5,100	0.18	240	0.30

TABLE 4.1

Data on Sociocultural, Natural, Political, and Economic Environments of Selected Countries—cont'd

	A: Individualism	B: Materialism	C: Time orientation	D: Deference to authority	E: Uncertainty avoidance	F: Life satisfaction	G: Life expectancy	H: Ecological footprint	I: Population	J: GDP per capita	K: Internationalization	L: GDP per capita/ecological footprint	M: Satisfaction/ecological footprint
Poland	60	65	37	55	78	5.9	74.3	85	38.5	13,300	0.37	157	0.07
Portugal	27	31		63	104	6.1	77.2	122	10.6	19,300	0.48	159	0.05
Singapore	20	48	48	74	8	6.9	78.7		4.5	28,100	3.11		
South Africa	65	63		49	49	5.7	48.4	100	44.2	12,000	0.20	120	0.06
South Korea	18	39	75	60	85	5.8	77.0	98	48.8	20,400	0.55	208	0.06
Spain	51	42		57	86	7.0	79.5	125	40.4	25,500	0.45	204	0.06
Sweden	71	5	33	31	29	7.7	80.2	165	9	29,800	0.86	181	0.05
Switzerland	68	70		34	58	8.2	80.5		7.5	32,300	1.17		
Taiwan	17	45	87	58	69	6.6	76.1		23	27,600	0.58		
Thailand	20	34	56	64	64	6.5	70.0	147	64.6	8,300	0.40	56	0.04
Turkey	37	45		66	85	5.3	68.7	40	70.4	8,200	0.30	204	0.13
United Kingdom	89	66	25	35	35	7.1	78.4	155	60.6	30,300	0.47	196	0.05
United States	91	62	29	40	46	7.4	77.4	269	298.4	41,800	0.21	155	0.03
Uruguay	36	38		61	100	6.3	75.4	56	3.4	9,600	0.22	172	0.11
Venezuela	12	73		81	76	7.4	72.9	72	25.7	6,100	0.49	86	0.10
Overall Average	**45**	**50**	**49**	**55**	**65**	**6.7**	**74.8**	**98**	**88.7**	**19,211**	**0.58**	**198**	**0.12**
Mainstream[19]	77	66	29	38	52	7.2	75.2	139	72.0	31,113	0.57	176	0.04
Multistream[20]	17	34	66	64	86	6.5	73.0	55	25.9	9,486	0.34	236	0.21

Key to columns:

A: Individualism. The higher the number, the greater the emphasis on individualism.[21]
B: Materialism. The higher the number, the greater the emphasis on materialism.[22]
C: Time orientation. The higher the number, the more the country focuses on the long term.[23]
D: Deference to authority. The higher the number, the more likely people are to defer to the authority of managers.[24]
E: Uncertainty avoidance. The higher the number, the less comfortable people are with uncertainty and change.[25]
F: Life satisfaction. The higher the number, the more satisfied people are with their lives.[26]
G: Life expectancy. This number indicates the average age that people in each country are expected to attain.[27]
H: Ecological footprint. These figures indicate how many acres of biological productive space are required to support the consumption of an average person in each country.[28]
I: Population. This figure, in millions, shows the total population of each country.[29]
J: GDP per capita. This figure, in U.S. dollars, shows the gross domestic product (i.e., the value of good and services, factoring in purchasing power parity) produced on average by a person in each country.[30]
K: Internationalization. This figure measures how active a country is in international trade: The higher the number, the greater the proportion of country's imports and exports are compared to its GDP.[31]
L: GDP per capita/ecological footprint. This is an efficiency measure of how many U.S. dollars of GDP per capita are associated with each acre of the natural environment that is utilized to support the consumption of an average person in each country (L = J ÷ H).
M: Satisfaction/ecological footprint. This is an efficiency measure of the amount of life satisfaction an average person gets from each acre of the natural environment that is utilized to sustain his or her consumption (M = F ÷ H).[32]

it."[33] Columbus carefully observed the sociocultural ways of the "New World," and was able to use that knowledge to achieve his employer's economic goals.

Just as Columbus took note of differences and opportunities in the Americas, so today's international managers must likewise be sensitive to social and cultural

National culture includes the shared values, beliefs, knowledge, and general patterns of behavior that characterize its citizens.

Self-reference criterion is evident when a person uses the assumptions and terms of his or her own culture to try to understand and relate to people from other cultures.

differences if they are to meet their organizational objectives. **National culture** includes the shared values, beliefs, knowledge, and general patterns of behavior that characterize a country's citizens. People's beliefs about what is good, right, desirable, or beautiful are influenced by the national cultures where they grow up. People exhibit a **self-reference criterion** when they use the terms and assumptions of their own culture in order to understand and relate to people from other cultures.

 WHAT DO YOU THINK?

When in Doubt, Whose Customs Should You Follow?

The meaning of a specific action may be different in different cultures. For example, what might be a familiar hand gesture to say "okay" in many countries (forming a circle with your thumb and index finger) is an obscene gesture in Germany and Brazil. The same gesture may mean something else in a different country—for example, in Japan it means "money."

Similarly, consider how the difference between a "bribe" versus a "tip" is socially constructed. In some countries, people find it acceptable to give a poorly paid restaurant worker extra money for assigning a nice table or for fast service (this payment is called a "tip," an acronym for "to insure [sic] promptness"). In other countries, people find it acceptable to give a poorly paid government worker a "tip" for fast service in processing paperwork. By contrast, in other countries, giving a tip to a government worker is seen as an unethical bribe, and tipping restaurant workers is seen as odd and unnecessary.

When European explorers came to America, they experienced some major cultural misunderstandings. For example, the values of the aboriginal Ojibwa people are such that their understanding of land ownership is very unlike Europeans' concept. For the Ojibwa, the land was something that people could use, and something that they were stewards over for future generations. When the Europeans asked to make trades for prop-erty and land treaties, the Ojibwa saw the deals as requests to *share* the use of the lands. They did not see these agreements as giving up their ownership of the lands because in their culture, that sort of ownership had never existed in the first place. For them, it would be presumptuous to think that a person could own a piece of land, because land was sacred and defied ownership (e.g., just like you could not "own" a god).[34]

Things can get even more complicated when a power imbalance exists between visitors and the people living in a foreign country. For example, superior weaponry and military capabilities were factors in colonialism, when explorers and settlers in America established a rule of law based on their European traditions. Today economic power is also evident, for example, when international managers represent corporations that are larger economic entities than many of the countries in which they do business.

How should cross-cultural misunderstandings and differences be managed when going overseas? Should the people with the most power be able to set the tone? Or should everyone follow the traditions of the people who are already there (i.e., "When in Rome, do as the Romans do")? What if traditional practices in the overseas country violate basic human rights?[35]

Unlike Columbus, modern managers have more information beforehand about the international cultures where they will work. The most influential research look-ing at cross-cultural differences and their implications for management was done by Geert Hofstede, who gathered data between 1967 and 1973 from more than 100,000 IBM employees working in 64 different countries.[36] As shown in Figure 4.3,

Hofstede identified five dimensions of national culture:

- Individualism
- Materialism
- Time orientation
- Deference to authority
- Uncertainty avoidance[37]

Even though Hofstede's research is still widely used, it is worth noting that we would expect at least some changes to have occurred since he first collected his data. For example, consider the cultural and economic changes over the past few decades in countries such as China and South Korea. Also, keep in mind that just as there tend to be differences *between* countries, so too there is a lot of variation *within* countries (i.e., not everyone from the same country shares the same cultural values).

Individualism	Collectivism
Emphasis on individual self-interests	Emphasis on interests of group
Materialism	**Quality of Life**
Possessions and money	Relationships and social well-being
Short-Term Orientation	**Long-Term Orientation**
Emphasis on immediate gratification even with long-term cost	Emphasis on deferred gratification even with short-term cost
Deference to Authority	**Challenge to Authority**
Authority of manager seen as appropriate and preferred	Authority of manager challenged
Avoidance of Uncertainty	**Comfortable with Uncertainty**
Conformist, value stability	Adaptable, open to change

Figure 4.3 Overview of Hofstede's five dimensions of national culture

Individualism. Some cultures place a high emphasis on **individualism,** where people tend to act in their own self-interest. In these societies, individuality and individual rights are paramount. Managers in these cultures should expect members to be motivated by opportunities to achieve personal gain and to look out for themselves. For example, in countries with high levels of individualism, using piece-rate systems may be a very effective way to increase workers' productivity. In such countries, it is not unusual to base promotions and salary on workers' *individual* performance rather than, for example, on the length of time they have worked in an organization.

Other cultures value **collectivism,** where the interests of the group take precedence, people look out for one another, and there is higher loyalty to the group. These societies emphasize extended families and collectives where everyone takes responsibility for the overall well-being of one another. Managers in these cultures should expect to help out members in need, and to be helped out themselves when they are in need. For example, in Japan, everyone in an office might stay at work until a colleague who must work overtime is finished, and promotions may be based on seniority rather than on individual performance.

Materialism. Cultures that emphasize **materialism** place a high value on things such as getting better jobs, material possessions, money, and assertiveness.[38] Managers in such cultures should expect members to be motivated by extrinsic rewards—for example, higher salaries, bonuses, and opportunities to be number 1.

By contrast, cultures where greater emphasis is placed on overall **quality of life** tend to value relationships, the welfare of others, and the intrinsic satisfaction that comes from performing meaningful work. In such cultures, people may be more interested in the aesthetic and spiritual realms and be less motivated by financial rewards and status symbols.[39] Managers in such countries should expect and allow

Individualism emphasizes the interests of the individual over the interests of the group, and suggests that people should act in their own self-interest.

Collectivism emphasizes the interests of groups over the self-interests of individuals, and that people look out for one another and demonstrate high loyalty to the group.

Materialism places a high value on material possessions, financial well-being, and productivity.

Quality of life refers to placing a high value on relationships, the welfare of others, and social well-being.

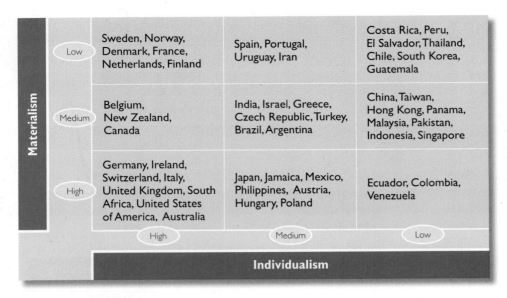

		High	Medium	Low
Materialism	Low	Sweden, Norway, Denmark, France, Netherlands, Finland	Spain, Portugal, Uruguay, Iran	Costa Rica, Peru, El Salvador, Thailand, Chile, South Korea, Guatemala
	Medium	Belgium, New Zealand, Canada	India, Israel, Greece, Czech Republic, Turkey, Brazil, Argentina	China, Taiwan, Hong Kong, Panama, Malaysia, Pakistan, Indonesia, Singapore
	High	Germany, Ireland, Switzerland, Italy, United Kingdom, South Africa, United States of America, Australia	Japan, Jamaica, Mexico, Philippines, Austria, Hungary, Poland	Ecuador, Colombia, Venezuela

Individualism

Figure 4.4 Relative emphasis of countries on Hofstede's materialism/ individualism scores

time for members to develop personal relationships, camaraderie in the workplace, and interpersonal cooperation.

Figure 4.4 shows where countries rank in terms of their relative emphases on materialism and individualism (low, medium, or high).[40] As might be expected, countries that rate high in both materialism and individualism—such as the United States, the United Kingdom, Germany, Australia, and Ireland—are precisely the ones where Mainstream management theory and practice have been most thoroughly developed. Conversely, we would expect to see management practices more aligned with a Multistream view in countries such as Costa Rica and Peru. Consistent with this expectation, Costa Rican managers are five times more likely to prefer a management style where they consult with and invite members to participate in decision making than a style based on the use of managerial authority as a means of persuasion.[41] Perhaps not surprisingly, given its culture, Costa Rica is seen as a world leader in using eco-tourism (which promotes natural attractions while minimizing visitors' ecological impact) as a strategy for economic growth[42] and is a leader among developing countries in environmental programs[43] (to the point where one study has suggested that its forest stock is "suboptimally large").[44] More generally, in a study that compared 178 countries according to how well people were able to live long, happy lives with minimal impact on the natural environment, Costa Rica ranked in the top three.[45]

How a country rates in terms of materialism and individualism may also help to predict its relative emphasis on Hofstede's three remaining cultural dimensions. This is evident in comparing columns A (individualism) and B (materialism) with columns C (time orientation), D (deference to authority), and E (uncertainty avoidance) in Table 4.1. In particular, countries that emphasize materialism and individualism tend to have a relatively short-term orientation, are more likely to challenge authority, and are more open to tolerate ambiguity and change. The "Digging Deeper" feature describes the data for two countries that exemplify Mainstream (United States) and Multistream (Costa Rica) cultures.

Time orientation differentiates between cultures that have a short-term versus a long-term orientation.

Time Orientation.   The concept of **time orientation** differentiates between cultures that have a short-term view versus a long-term perspective. *Short-term orientation cultures* (such as Pakistan, the Philippines, the United Kingdom, and the United States) emphasize living for the present. Managers should expect members of such cultures to prefer immediate rewards over delayed gratification. There may also be a tendency to cut corners that won't get noticed until much later. Such countries may provide greater opportunities for organizations that offer quick fixes such as "fast food" and "instant credit." Managers in these countries might also expect to experience an increased desire and capacity for making changes quickly.

Comparing a Mainstream and a Multistream Culture

The United States is a prime example of a Mainstream culture. Indeed, its emphasis on individualism (91) is greater than that found for any other country in Hofstede's study, although its materialism score (66) is one of the lower "high materialism" scores. By contrast, Costa Rica is a clear example of a Multistream culture: No other country in Hofstede's study had a lower overall score in terms of Hofstede's individualism and materialism data.[46]

Table 4.1 shows that compared to Costa Rica, the United States places greater emphasis on the short term versus the long term. As this would suggest, managers in the United States more highly value things such as quarterly reports, and the country has a much more fully developed stock market than is found in Costa Rica. Likewise, it follows that Costa Rica would assign greater value to the use of long-term resources, such as ecological resources, consistent with its reputation as a world leader in eco-tourism and the long-term management of its forest reserves.

Hofstede's data indicate that the authority of managers is more likely to be challenged in the United States, for a variety of reasons. For example, workers in the United States may often be wary of their managers' motives, perhaps because they assume that the managers are focusing on their own self-interests (as is consistent with a high individualism score). In contrast, in Costa Rica there is an assumption that all people share common goals that transcend their self-interests, that people work together in organizations toward these common goals, and that it would be socially undesirable for any one person to put his or her own self-interests ahead of that of other team members.[47]

People in the United States generally have a higher tolerance for uncertainty than do people in Costa Rica. This may be because members of U.S. culture—again, consistent with their high emphasis on individualism—value the contributions of innovative organizational members and expect that taking risks is an essential characteristic of successful organizations. This expectation and openness to uncertainty provide a space

for individuals to develop, express, and pursue creative new ideas. For their part, Costa Ricans expect members of an organization to cooperate with one another and work as a team, and they may have less tolerance for actions by individuals that upset this balance. This preference for certainty results in incremental changes and fine-tuning of "proven" ways of doing things.

Instructive differences and similarities between the two countries can also be observed by examining some of the other scales shown in Table 4.1. For example, as might be expected, thanks to the cultural emphasis in the U.S. on individual initiative, productivity, and innovation, the per capita GDP in the United States ($41,800) is almost four times greater than the per capita GDP in Costa Rica ($11,100). There are also important differences in terms of the ecological footprints of the two countries. Whereas it takes approximately 269 acres to sustain the consumption of the average American, it takes only 35 acres for the average Costa Rican.[48]

Perhaps the most striking finding in the comparison between the two countries is that in terms of overall life satisfaction, the scores for the United States (7.4) and Costa Rica (7.5) are virtually identical. The same holds true for life expectancy scores, with life expectancy for the United States being 77.4 years and that for Costa Rica being 78.2 years (the highest life expectancy in the Western Hemisphere). From a Mainstream perspective, it may come as a surprise that the average Costa Rican, who consumes 13 percent of the resources and whose GDP is 27 percent that of his or her U.S. counterpart, lives a life that is just as satisfying as that of an American.

These differences are reflected in the efficiency measures in Table 4.1, which show that Costa Ricans make much more efficient use of Earth's resources, reaping ten times more satisfaction and twice as much GDP from each acre of natural resources. Although the cultural orientation of the U.S. has contributed to its ascent to be one of the wealthiest and most productive nations, this progress has come with costs that Costa Rica has so far avoided in its development.

By comparison, *long-term orientation cultures* (such as China and Japan) have a greater concern for the future, are more likely to persevere patiently in the face of short-term setbacks, and are more likely to save up for purchases than to buy on credit. Managers in such countries should provide members with a long-term organizational vision and make decisions that respect the future. For example, some Native American cultures try to keep in mind how their decisions will affect people living seven generations in the future. Hofstede's data suggest that long-term orientation is associated with less individualistic cultures.

Deference to Authority. The relative emphasis placed on power differences in a culture is called **deference to authority.** In cultures with a high level of deference to

Deference to authority recognizes that it is legitimate and desirable to give formal power to managers.

authority, it is considered entirely appropriate that power is distributed unevenly throughout society. Managers in these cultures (for example, in Mexico, the Philippines, and China) are expected to make decisions, and lower-level employees will hesitate to voice disagreement with those decisions. In addition, subordinates will react negatively when they are asked to do work or are held responsible for tasks that are traditionally part of managers' jobs. In some cases, high deference to authority is found in countries with totalitarian governments and distinct social class systems.

In cultures characterized by low deference to authority, power differences across different positions are less readily evident. In these cultures, it is considered appropriate to challenge a manager's directive. Everyone may be involved in decision making—not just the manager. Thus, in countries such as Israel (which had the lowest score of all the countries listed in Table 4.1 on this criterion), managers may have relatively little authority over other members, especially on matters where the latter have greater knowledge and experience. In Israeli *kibbutzim*, for example, leadership is often rotated on a cyclical basis so that everyone gets a turn at various jobs in the organization.

Uncertainty Avoidance. Cultures with high uncertainty avoidance scores prefer predictable rules and regulations over ambiguity and risk. When managing in countries that have high uncertainty avoidance, such as Greece and Japan, managers should expect members to respond well to stable and predictable structures and systems, to have a heightened appreciation for conformity, and to become anxious when routines are disrupted. People in these cultures prefer to make only small improvements to the "tried-and-true" traditions that have served society well in the past.

By comparison, managers in cultures characterized by low uncertainty avoidance, such as Singapore and Denmark, are more likely to value risk taking and innovativeness.[49] Managers in such cultures should expect members to be relatively adaptable and willing to try new things. Organizations in countries with low uncertainty avoidance are likely to reinforce risk taking by recognizing and rewarding members who take reasonable risks that result in benefits for the organization. Furthermore, a culture with low uncertainty avoidance is likely to encourage investments in novel research and development.

THE NATURAL ENVIRONMENT. Mainstream management has historically tended to view the natural environment as a collection of physical resources that organizations require as inputs to create products and services, and as a place to dispose of unwanted outputs (e.g., pollution). Factors such as supply and demand help to determine the price of natural resources: High demand and low supplies result in high prices. Managers shop around the globe to find the lowest cost for the natural resources they require.

Thanks to increasing concern related to issues such as pollution and global warming, managers are beginning to recognize the value of resources that were previously taken for granted. For example, clean air is now seen as a valuable resource that can be managed and exploited. From an acquisitive economics point of view, it is irrational for a country to be overforested or to have air that is "underpolluted."[50] From this perspective, it makes sense for managers in high-polluting industries to relocate their "dirty" operations to underpolluted countries, or to countries where environmental regulations are relatively weak. Some research suggests that as high-income countries increase their environmental standards, managers of high-polluting organizations tend to relocate their operations, thereby creating jobs in lower-income countries.[51]

THE POLITICAL–LEGAL ENVIRONMENT.   The political–legal environment covers a broad range of issues. In this section we will highlight three aspects of this environment:

- National laws and regulations
- General trade agreements
- Other institutions

National Regulations.   Different countries have different laws and regulations governing minimum wages, unionization, consumer protection, information and labeling, workplace safety, and so on. Managers must be aware of these constraints when entering new countries. We cannot discuss all of these subjects here, but we will explore how governments regulate international trade using tariffs, quotas, and subsidies.

A government may impose **tariffs**—taxes on goods or services entering its country—to protect domestic companies from international competitors. For example, people in the United States pay about three times the world price for sugar because the U.S. sugar lobby has persuaded Congress to implement special tariffs and import quotas to protect its industry. These tariffs can have a negative effect on businesses such as Heartland-By-Products, whose costs for importing a sugar–molasses mixture from Canada increased by 7000 percent when sugar lobbyists convinced the U.S. Customs Service to reverse its 1995 decision that had exempted this product from the sugar restrictions.[52]

Tariffs are taxes on goods or services entering a country.

Quotas place restrictions on the quantity of specific goods or services that can be imported (or exported). One reason that Honda has opened automobile manufacturing plants in the United States is because it has been allowed to export only 425,000 autos each year to the United States.[53]

Quotas are restrictions on the quantity of certain goods or services that can be imported or exported from a country.

Government **subsidies** are direct or indirect payments to domestic businesses that help them compete with foreign companies. For example, many high-income economies provide subsidies to ensure that their domestic agricultural products can compete on price in global markets. Worldwide food production by farmers accounts for approximately $1.2 trillion in revenues, and farmers receive about $200 billion in subsidies, which suggests that on average, 17 percent of farm income consists of some form of subsidy.[54] However, these subsidies are not spread evenly throughout the world: The United States accounts for one-third of all farm subsidies, and the **European Union (EU)** accounts for another third.[55] Such subsidies give farmers in high-income countries an advantage when they are competing with farmers from other countries, even if the agricultural produce grown in the latter countries is less costly and more energy efficient. The Mexican government estimates that since the passage of the **North American Free Trade Agreement (NAFTA),** the availability of subsidized corn from the United States has forced nearly 2 million agricultural workers off the land. However, NAFTA has helped to reduce corn prices by 70 percent and to increase exports of other vegetables from Mexico.[56] As another example, the EU pays subsidies to encourage sugar cultivation in unlikely places such as Sweden and Finland. This practice has contributed to a surplus of sugar on the world market, reducing prices and contributing to poverty-level income for sugar producers in tropical low-income countries. Similarly, when the U.S. government provides subsidies to cotton growers, it lowers world cotton prices, thereby hurting Brazilian and African cotton producers (although the subsidies may benefit consumers) and going against international trade rules.[57]

Subsidies are direct or indirect payments made by a government to domestic firms, which help them to compete better with goods and services produced in other countries.

European Union (EU) is a political and economic community consisting of 27 European countries that are committed to making trade among members easier by lowering tariffs and reducing other impediments to trade.

North American Free Trade Agreement (NAFTA) reduces tariff and nontariff barriers between the United States, Mexico, and Canada.

It may be no coincidence that the U.S. food system is awash in added fats (derived mainly from soy) and sugars (derived from corn): They are two of the five main crops subsidized in the United States (the other three are wheat, cotton, and rice). Because the U.S. farm bill provides little to support farmers growing fresh produce, between 1985 and 2000 the real price of fruits and vegetables increased almost 40 percent while the price of soft drinks (think liquid corn) decreased by more than 20 percent.[59]

World Trade Organization (WTO) facilitates trade among its more than 150 member countries by urging countries to lower tariffs and to work toward free trade and open markets.

Free trade is international trade that is not subject to national constraints such as tariffs, quotas, and subsidies.

Association of South-East Asian Nations (ASEAN) is a group of ten nations in South-East Asia that are committed to reducing barriers to trade among members.

General Trade Agreements. General trade agreements serve as important mechanisms to manage trade between different countries. The **World Trade Organization (WTO),** for example, strives to make it easier for goods to flow among its member countries, by urging them to lower tariffs and work toward free trade and open markets. **Free trade** is international trade that is free from national constraints such as tariffs, quotas, and subsidies. Created in 1995, the WTO has more than 150 member countries. It replaced the General Agreement on Tariffs and Trade (GATT), which had been created by 23 countries in 1947.

In addition to the WTO, a series of regional free trade agreements have been forged among different countries. NAFTA, which was signed in 1994, eliminated numerous tariff and nontariff barriers between the United States, Mexico, and Canada. This agreement covers markets with more than 400 million consumers and in excess of $600 billion in annual economic activity (more than double the amount of pre-NAFTA trade). It allows firms in the United States and Canada access to relatively low-cost Mexican labor, which increases profits for investors and lowers costs for consumers. Approximately 40 percent of Mexico's manufacturing takes place in foreign-owned *maquiladora* plants located near the U.S.–Mexico border. Recently, there has been talk of extending NAFTA farther south, down to the southernmost tip of Chile, perhaps linking up with smaller trading blocs in the region.[58]

The EU is much more than a general trade agreement; it is a group of approximately 30 European countries committed to making trade among members easier by lowering tariffs and other impediments to trade. The EU comprises some 500 million consumers, and it has a common currency (the euro) to facilitate trade among member nations that is now part of the everyday life of more than 300 million Europeans (some countries, such as the United Kingdom, have been reluctant to adopt the euro).[60] There is wide disparity in the degree to which members' economies have developed, with EU members ranging from longtime economic leaders, such as Germany and France, to newer members emerging from the breakup of the former Soviet Union.

Finally, the **Association of South-East Asian Nations (ASEAN),** with a total trade of more than $1 trillion, includes ten nations in one of the fastest-growing economic regions in the world.

Other Institutions. Almost 200 countries in the global community own the **World Bank,** an organization that provides financial and technical assistance to reduce poverty in low-income countries.[61] The World Bank provides interest-free credit, low-interest loans, and grants to low-income countries for purposes such as advancing health care, education, and infrastructure initiatives. Often these financial services have been linked to Structural Adjustment Programmes, which are designed to ensure that low-income countries have balanced budgets and play according to the rules of the free market. For example, Structural Adjustment Programmes discourage the use of subsidies and tariffs (because these are perceived to hinder competition).

THE ECONOMIC–TECHNOLOGICAL ENVIRONMENT.[62]   International managers monitor the economies of countries where their organizations are active. As part of this ongoing assessment, they consider issues such as the rate of inflation, the stability of the economy, the currency exchange rate, interest rates, and the tax system. Managers also need to be aware of the technological capabilities of different countries, including their physical infrastructure (e.g., roads, airports, telephone lines) and the technological knowledge, educational level, and skills of their workforce (e.g., managerial talent, engineers). The economic–technological environment in many countries must be supplemented with outside supports if it is to be able to meet the expectations of international managers. For example, when McDonald's opened its first franchise in Moscow, the company needed to provide machinery and tools to suppliers, including teaching Russian farmers how to grow potatoes, and teaching food processors how to cut french fries that met McDonald's standards.

Three aspects of the economic–technological environment are of particular interest to international managers.[63] Globalization as we know it would not be possible without advances in the past 50 years that have

- Improved our ability to transport jobs, people, and goods around the world;
- Increased the rate at which knowledge is being created and disseminated; and
- Enabled money to be transferred with just a few clicks on the keyboard.

Flow of Jobs.   A central characteristic of Mainstream globalization is the unending movement of jobs, goods, and services.[64] Thanks to highly developed international transportation systems, coupled with the ability to communicate instantly around the world by telephone and computer, factories can be located wherever labor costs are the lowest. Indeed, in many ways this development is the genius of Mainstream globalization: It provides financial incentives for multinational corporations to create jobs in economically depressed regions of the world. This transformation is evident, for example, in the international movement of the garment industry to China, Thailand, Vietnam, and Indonesia. Similarly, some estimate that 3.3 million service-sector jobs will have left the United States by 2015 as a result of this ability to locate jobs where the costs are lowest.[65]

Flow of Know-How.   The ability to transfer knowledge and documents 24 hours a day, seven days a week, has created the opportunity to develop international teams of workers who can work on a project around the clock. In this way, service-sector "smart jobs" can be located anywhere in the world, including being exported to countries where labor is less expensive. For example, exported services account for a majority of the computer software industry in India, the number 1 location for outsourcing. Infosys Technologies—with 75,000 employees and more than $3 billion in annual sales—is the largest firm in India to benefit from computer jobs being outsourced from the United States. Recently, Infosys has begun outsourcing its outsourcing by opening offices in Mexico, the Czech Republic, Thailand, and China. As a result, a company in the United States may outsource work to an Indian firm located 7000 miles away, which in turn supplies its customer with work that is actually performed by Mexican workers located 150 miles south of the U.S.–Mexico border.[66]

World Bank provides financial and technical assistance in an attempt to reduce poverty in developing countries.

International Monetary Fund (IMF) is an international financial institution that was established to: (1) promote orderly and stable international monetary exchange; (2) foster international economic growth and high levels of employment; and (3) provide temporary financial assistance to countries to help ease balance of payment problems.

Flow of Money.   The combination of technological improvements and eased flow of money has also been an important element of Mainstream globalization.[67] This flow of money is facilitated by the **International Monetary Fund (IMF),** an organization with approximately 200 member countries that was established for the following purposes:

- To promote orderly and stable international monetary exchange
- To foster international economic growth and high levels of employment
- To provide temporary financial assistance to countries to help ease their balance of payments

To meet these goals, the IMF monitors international commerce and provides financial and technical assistance as appropriate.[68] The work of the IMF allows capital to move to those locations where it receives the highest return, and seeks to minimize national boundaries and governments from constraining economic investment.

MULTISTREAM MANAGEMENT AND THE INTERNATIONAL ENVIRONMENT

Mark Kwadwo is a six-year-old boy who was leased by his parents to a fisherman for $20 per year. Child trafficking is a problem in many parts of the world, with more than 1 million children being sold into servitude every year. For example, a 2002 study showed that nearly 12,000 trafficked children work in the cocoa fields of the Ivory Coast. When parents earn less than $1 per day, they may think their children are better off learning a trade than starving at home.[69]

Multistream managers are well aware of the financial and competitive reasons to internationalize, but they are also driven by a desire to go beyond financial concerns and to help find solutions for larger problems. For example, more than 1 billion people on the planet live on less than $1 per day, and almost 3 billion live on less than $2 per day. The 50 least economically developed countries account for more than 10 percent of the world's population, but only 0.6 percent of the world's gross domestic product (GDP).[70] More than 1 billion people do not have access to clean water, and more than 2 billion lack adequate sanitation facilities.[71] Add to this environmental problems such as global warming, which often have a greater negative effect on people in low-income countries.[72]

Multistream managers are attuned to leading-edge practices that offer solutions to these sorts of problems. This may mean providing technologies to improve access to clean drinking water, creating opportunities for poorly paid people around the world to increase their earnings, and opting for environmentally friendly technologies in their organizations. For example, businesses may work with non-government organizations such as Global Water to develop safe water.[73] **Non-government organization (NGO)** refers to a nonprofit organization whose primary mission is to model and advocate for social, cultural, legal, or environmental change.

Multistream managers are inspired by people like Edna Ruth Byler, who is cred-

ited with starting the Fair Trade movement that seeks to help people in low-income countries. The organization she founded, the award-winning Ten Thousand Villages,[74] started in 1946 after Byler had visited a sewing class in Puerto Rico run by U.S. volunteers who were looking for ways to improve the lives of their students, many of whom lived in poverty. Byler took home pieces of embroidery to sell to friends and neighbors. Encouraged by those sales, she expanded her operation by importing hand-carved Haitian woodenware and cross-stitch needlework from Palestinian refugees to add to her inventory. Today Ten Thousand Villages is the largest Fair Trade retailer in the world, and includes thousands of people working in more than 70 stores and 180 outlets across North America. This NGO works with artisans from more than 35 different countries, and over 100,000 of the poorest people in the world depend on it for their next meal.[75]

Shopper at Ten Thousand Villages store in Philadelphia, Pennsylvania.

How to Internationalize an Organization

The approaches for internationalizing used by Multistream managers are basically the same as those used by Mainstream managers—ranging from relatively simple exporting and importing operations to wholly owned subsidiaries—but with two important differences. First, compared to their Mainstream counterparts, Multistream managers are more likely to talk about international "partnerships" and "networks," thereby reflecting their inclination to consider a wider variety of stakeholders and issues. Second, Multistream managers are more likely to consider the implications of their actions on the financial and overall situation of people overseas.

EXPORTING AND IMPORTING.   The simplest way for Multistream managers to internationalize is to import and export, as is demonstrated in the story of Ten Thousand Villages. Another example comes from Starbucks Coffee, North America's largest purchaser of Fair Trade coffee, which it sells in more than 20 countries around the world.[76] Starbucks pays more for its coffee because of this practice, which it sees as part of its larger effort to be socially responsible in its relationships with coffee farmers and communities. Because Multistream managers don't choose items to import (or to export) based solely on financial considerations, they are likely to build relationships with suppliers and buyers that transcend financial aspects. As these relationships grow and evolve, managers learn more about larger social and business networks and find new opportunities to engage in Multistream activities. For example, many of the new

Non-government organization (NGO) refers to a nonprofit organization whose primary mission is to model and advocate for social, cultural, legal, or environmental change.

products that Ten Thousand Villages imports are discovered because of the networks to which it belongs in low-income countries.

LICENSING AND FRANCHISING.   Although the Multistream approach tends to favor locally owned and operated organizations, many firms that are known for Multistream management practices have expanded through franchising. For example, Ben & Jerry's Ice Cream has franchises in 20 different countries, and The Body Shop is active in more than 50 countries. Licensing that permits the labeling of goods or services as Fair Trade or as organic is especially relevant to Multistream management.[77]

STRATEGIC ALLIANCES AND JOINT VENTURES.   Multistream strategic alliances and joint ventures may look like their Mainstream counterparts, but they are often set up with different criteria for effectiveness. For example, Mennonite Economic Development Associates (MEDA)[78] is a pioneer in the **micro-financing movement,** which sets up financial institutions that provide loans and other banking services to micro-entrepreneurs who have no access to financial services in conventional banks. When MEDA joined forces with existing financial institutions in Bolivia to set up a new micro-financing organization in that country, it did so with the intent of giving complete ownership of the new organization to its local Bolivian partners once staff had been trained and the organization had become well established. This relationship was designed to ensure that there were enough revenues to adequately cover MEDA's costs, but not to maximize MEDA's profits.

> **Micro-financing movement** develops financial institutions that provide small loans and other banking services to micro-entrepreneurs and other poor people.

Another example involves the Day Chocolate Company. When it was established in 1998, managers wanted to build a new kind of Fair Trade business partnership. One-third of its shares are owned by a cooperative organization called Kuapa Kokoo (whose name means "Good cocoa farmer," and whose membership is 45,000 farmers in 1000 villages in Ghana), 52 percent of the shares are owned by Twin Trading (a Fair Trade NGO), and 14 percent of the shares are owned by The Body Shop International. The Body Shop uses Kuapa Kokoo's cocoa butter in more than 20 of its products as part of its Community Trade Programme. This ownership by the farmers is crucial to the success of Day Chocolate, and is held up as an example for other international Multistream organizations to follow.[79]

FOREIGN SUBSIDIARIES.   Mainstream managers are interested in opening foreign subsidiaries in low-income countries if they can obtain benefits such as access to low-cost natural resources and new consumers; incentives such as tax breaks, subsidies, or tariff protection from the overseas country; and the ability to transfer their profits to their home country. Unfortunately, these considerations may all work against the sustenance economic interests of the host country, for any of the following reasons:

- The host country may receive less for its natural resources than the going rate elsewhere.
- Its domestic organizations may become unviable because of the size or tax incentives offered to the incoming foreign organization.
- Tax breaks to businesses reduce tax revenue, making it difficult for the host government to provide adequate educational and healthcare services for its population.[80]

Multistream managers recognize that foreign subsidiaries—including those found in foreign investment zones such as *maquiladora* factories in Mexico—may do

⊙ **MANAGEMENT IN PRACTICE**

Putting a Face on International Business

According to Art DeFehr, a Multistream CEO of Palliser Furniture, one of the largest furniture manufacturers in Canada, globalization limits opportunities to put a "face" on the people who produce our goods. Because the faces of those workers are so far away, decisions are made based on dollars and cents, regardless of the effect it has on working conditions.

This consideration is one reason why Palliser still manufactures the majority of its products in Canada, and why when it opened a plant in Mexico, it opted not to open the factory in the *maquiladora* region and not to manage expenses by moving its operations to wherever the costs were lowest. Mainstream approaches might have made acquisitive economics sense, but they did not seem to improve the quality of life for Mexican workers. So, instead of setting up its factory in the *maquiladora* region, Palliser deliberately chose to locate in a city farther from the U.S.–Mexico border. Moreover, rather than *rent* buildings and thereby keep its options open for finding cheaper facilities, Palliser chose to *purchase* land and build a factory. The purpose of these decisions was to develop a long-term relationship with the Mexican workers.

These decisions were consistent with DeFehr's desire to lessen the likelihood that managers would be tempted to treat workers as disposable parts that could be abandoned when cheaper workers became available elsewhere. When decision makers are no longer able to look into the eyes of the people working on the shop floor, workers become faceless "its"[81] and "commodities" whose work is bought and sold based on price alone. Although financial costs may be incurred with a Multistream approach, DeFehr thinks it is a much better option than treating workers simply as means to meet organizational ends.

more harm than good. For example, the government-mandated minimum wage for *maquiladora* workers has remained unchanged at $4.20 per day for more than a decade. Since 1985, the purchasing power of Mexican workers has decreased by 75 percent, and it now takes more than 5 hours of work to pay for one gallon of milk. Workers' rights have also been eroding under NAFTA. The World Bank recommended that Mexico do away with most of its Federal Labor Law, thereby eliminating workers' rights such as mandatory severance pay and the 40-hour work week. While this change may help managers to improve the profitability of their *maquiladora* firms, it would also serve to worsen working conditions. Consumers may benefit from lower prices, but those higher profits and lower prices come with other costs. For example, during the first seven years after the adoption of NAFTA, the U.S. Department of Labor certified more than half a million U.S. workers for extended unemployment benefits because their jobs had moved to Mexico.[82]

The Four Dimensions of the International Environment

For Multistream managers, the interplay between the four dimensions of the international environment occurs as depicted in Figure 4.5. Multistream managers begin with the assumption that the purpose of international trade is to improve the condition of humankind. They are especially attracted to opportunities to become more ecologically sustainable, to develop institutions and rules that serve the neediest people in the world, and to seek flows of technology, jobs, and money that improve overall well-being.

THE SOCIOCULTURAL ENVIRONMENT.   When it comes to international sociocultural differences, Multistream managers try to practice an egali-centric approach, which recognizes that a key opportunity of international management is the ability to learn from one another.[83] **Egali-centrism** is characterized by two-way, give-and-take communication that fosters mutual understanding and community. Multistream

Egali-centrism is evident when people from different cultures work together in a manner characterized by two-way, give-and-take communication that fosters deeper mutual understanding, community, and new insights.

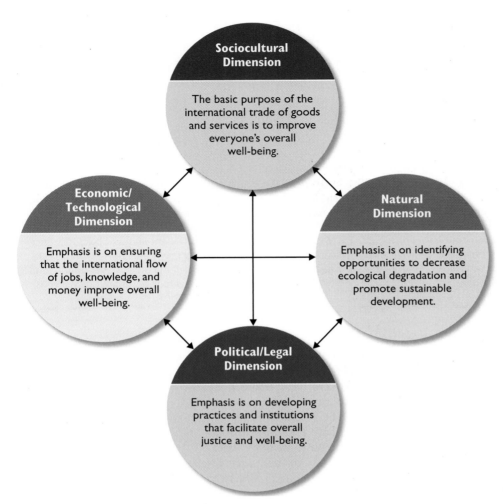

Figure 4.5 Multistream view of relationships between the four dimensions of the international environment

managers do not try to impose a "one size fits all" management style in foreign countries (ethnocentrism), nor do they simply assume that the "local managers know best" (polycentrism). Rather, Multistream managers recognize that international management works best when people from different cultures interact with and learn from one another, resulting in knowledge and practices that neither could imagine on their own. Egali-centrism is more a means of developing new practices than it is a process of picking and choosing the "best of" practices from around the world. An egali-centric approach tries to overcome shortcomings related to the self-reference criterion by deliberately seeking to learn from people in other countries.

THE NATURAL ENVIRONMENT. From a Multistream view, the influence of internationalization on the natural environment has a paradox: In the short term, it may hasten ecological degradation. At the same time, however, the more that people become aware of what is happening around the world, the sooner they realize the need for sustainable development.

On the one hand, internationalization may delay the realization that consumerist lifestyles are not sustainable. Globalization makes it easier for people in high-income countries to maintain their current standard of living, because they can access the resources they want from abroad. When the effects of ecological damage are located in distant lands far from everyday observance, it is not surprising that people are not aware of the environmental costs of industrialization.[84] Our *global* average ecological footprint of 55 acres per person is already 40 percent greater than the 39 acres carrying capacity that Earth can sustain (i.e., we are depleting our stock of nonrenewable resources).[85] People may sincerely wish that everyone around the world could enjoy a Western standard of living, while failing to acknowledge research that suggests that the Western standard of living is ecologically unsustainable and does not necessarily provide a greater sense of well-being than moderately consumptive lifestyles.

On the other hand, people are often motivated to take greater care of the natural environment precisely because of their international experience, which prompts them to confront firsthand the stress that human activity has put on the environment. For example, the prime innovator behind Canada's Shared Farming movement spent several years in Africa working for an NGO in agricultural development before deciding that the solution to global agricultural problems was for everyone everywhere to take more local ownership of their everyday food needs.[86] This emphasis on bio-regions and regional autonomy is a characteristic of the Multistream view.[87]

In any case, there is increasing interest in taking care of the natural environment. Some of the world's largest and most influential organizations are getting involved, sometimes simply because managers think it will help their firms' financial bottom line. For example, Wal-Mart has undertaken initiatives to become more energy efficient and to introduce organic products, General Electric is developing LED lighting (which is more energy efficient), and Kimberly-Clark is providing compressed toilet paper. However, the road ahead is still long. Some observers suggest that even if every organization on the planet were to adopt the best environmental practices of the leading firms—such as The Body Shop, Patagonia, or 3M—the world would still be not practicing sustainable development.[88]

Setting up a system of "green taxes" would be consistent with a Multistream approach.[89] This idea is a relatively simple one: increase taxes on practices that degrade the environment (e.g., energy sources that pollute the environment) and reduce taxes on practices that you want to encourage (e.g., reduce payroll taxes to help increase employment). These green taxes could be phased in over a period of 15 or more years to allow for a smooth transition. Green taxes would be used to pay for health-related and cleanup costs associated with pollution, thereby ensuring that people pay for the damage they cause when they engage in environmentally unfriendly activities. Many people already voluntarily pay for "carbon offsets" to account for their use of fossil fuels; green taxes would ensure that all parties pay for the ecological damage that their actions cause.

Some critics argue that governments that promote green taxes undermine the international competitiveness of their domestic businesses. Proponents counter that green taxes could stimulate the development of environmentally friendly technologies that will be in demand in the future. Coming down on the latter side, countries such as Denmark, Sweden, the Netherlands, the United Kingdom, and Germany have all begun to implement green taxes.

THE POLITICAL–LEGAL ENVIRONMENT. The Multistream view recognizes that internationalization may help a country to improve its GDP, and that there are clearly positive aspects to this growth. However, focusing solely on GDP as a measure of success is unwise. GDP was never designed to be an indicator of overall well-being. As Simon Kueznets, an economist and central figure in the development of the GDP, reminded the U.S. Congress, "The welfare of a nation can scarcely be inferred from a measurement of national income."[90] According to one study of 63 countries, "postmaterialism" is a better predictor of life satisfaction than GDP;[91] In other words, governments should remember that money does not buy happiness. **Postmaterialism** is evident when people decrease their emphasis on material well-being and increase their emphasis on values such as the free expression of ideas, improved democratization, and the fostering of humane societies.[92]

National Regulations. Whereas Mainstream managers would support tariffs, quotas, and subsidies if they served the financial interests of the organization, Multistream managers might support these mechanisms for very different reasons. Unlike the present situation, where tariffs, quotas, and subsidies are more generously provided in high-income countries than in low-income countries, a Multistream approach would be more likely to favor subsidies for countries that are developing

Postmaterialism is evident when people decrease their emphasis on material well-being, and increase their emphasis on values like the free expression of ideas, improved democratization, and the development of societies that are more humane.

their economies. Indeed, many of today's largest economies initially tried to nurture their domestic enterprises with national tariffs and quotas. However, instead of encouraging today's low-income countries to protect and nurture their emerging economies, institutions such as the World Trade Organization and World Bank often require that they lower protectionist walls and thereby learn how to compete in the international marketplace. (The World Bank's position is consistent with economists who argue that protectionist tendencies in North America in the 1700s and 1800s actually inhibited economic growth in this region.)

Consider how existing subsidies in agriculture can have negative implications for farmers in developing countries (and for the natural environment). Recall from Chapter 3 that, although modern technologically advanced agricultural practices are very productive, traditional practices are two to eight times more energy efficient. This difference should give food grown in developing countries a decided advantage in the free market. Unfortunately for these energy-efficient farmers and for the planet's ecological environment, the market is not free because farmers in high-income countries receive many subsidies. Indeed, the unwillingness of high-income countries to reduce their barriers (e.g., tariffs and subsidies) to agricultural exports from developing countries was one of the main reasons for an impasse after years of WTO negotiations to liberalize world trade.[93]

General Trade Agreements.   Critics point out that international trade agreements may undermine national sovereignty, citing instances where a government has been prevented from making changes that would improve ecological or social conditions.[94] For example, when Denmark tried to introduce an environmentally friendly law requiring that all beverages be sold in returnable containers, it was struck down by the European Community (the EU's predecessor) because it inhibited the free movement of goods.[95] In a similar example, when Taiwan wanted to introduce laws that would reduce cigarette smoking (e.g., restrict public smoking areas, prohibit tobacco ads, educate people to convince them to give up smoking), the U.S. trade representative threatened Taiwan with trade sanctions.[96]

Multistream managers also have reservations about current international trade arrangements because they are seen as benefiting the rich at the expense of the poor.[97] While it is true that a Mainstream approach to managing the economic environment has been associated with impressive growth in the global economy,[98] it is not clear that this has been a win-win proposition. The disparities between rich and poor have been increasing, both within and across countries, and the economically wealthy have benefited more from globalization than the poor.[99] Worldwide, as much as 95 percent of the economic benefits of globalization go to the richest 5 percent of the world.[100] While the proportion of the world's population that is malnourished or living for less than $1 per day has declined, the absolute numbers are still very large. The number of people living with incomes of less than $1 per day, for example, decreased from 1.25 billion people in 1990 (24 percent of the world's population) to "only" 985 million people in 2004 (18 percent of the world).[101] The number of malnourished people declined from 950 million people in 1980 (22 percent of the world's population) to 800 million in 2006 (12 percent of the world). In 2006 there were also more than 1 billion obese people in the world.[102] There are also widening gaps between the world's richest and poorest nations (e.g., regions of sub-Saharan Africa and rural South Asia and China).[103]

As an alternative to free trade, Multistream managers support Fair Trade. The mission of the International Federation of Alternative Trade (IFAT) is "to improve the livelihoods and well-being of disadvantaged producers by linking and promoting Fair Trade Organizations, and speaking out for greater justice in world trade."[104] IFAT members come from 300 Fair Trade Organizations in 70 countries. The key principles of Fair Trade include paying a *fair* price (versus the *lowest* price the market will withstand), gender equity (women are notoriously underpaid in many parts of the world), healthy working conditions (no sweatshops or child labor), mutual respect between producer and consumers, and environmentally friendly practices. Fair Trade retail organizations—such as Ten Thousand Villages and Pura Vida Coffee—are doing well, and approximately two-thirds of Fair Trade goods are sold in a traditional retail setting (e.g., Starbucks, Wal-Mart).[105] The sale of Fair Trade products in the EU, which accounts for about two-thirds of worldwide sales, grew by 20 percent in the first five years of this millennium. In the United Kingdom alone, for example, 3 million Fair Trade hot drinks are consumed every day.[106]

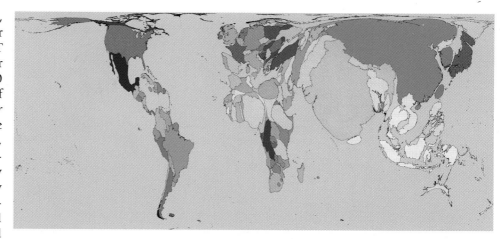

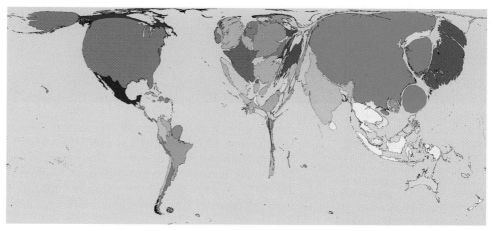

Have you ever wondered what a map of the world would look like if the size of countries were drawn proportionate to their total populations? This is depicted in the top map, which shows that China and India have the world's largest populations. The lower map shows the size of each country proportionate to expected total national wealth in the year 2015. Note the relative decrease in the size of Africa, and the increase in Europe and North America. To see these maps and others like them, go to worldmapper.org.

Other Institutions. Multistream management is interested in some of the work of institutions such as the United Nations (UN). The UN has the following goals:

- To cooperate in solving international economic, social, cultural, and humanitarian problems and in promoting respect for human rights and fundamental freedoms
- To maintain international peace and security
- To develop friendly relations among nations and serve as a place for harmonizing the actions of nations in attaining these ends[107]

In June 2000, the UN launched its Global Compact, an initiative with the aim of making the process of globalization more inclusive. A wide variety of organizations (including businesses, governments, labor, and civil society) have voluntarily joined the Global Compact. This initiative's dual mission is (1) to create networks where participants internalize values that pay particular attention to the world's poorest people, and (2) to facilitate cooperation and collective problem solving between different groups of stakeholders. Many firms have found that their

It is estimated that every day tens of thousands of people around the world die from diseases directly related to drinking polluted water. Businesses that work with NGOs like Global Water help to provide safe water supplies in rural villages in Central and South America. Earth Water, a water-bottling company based in Edmonton, Canada, donates 100 percent of its net profits to the United Nations and has in return received exclusive rights to use UN logos for marketing purposes.[111]

participation in the Compact has unintentionally resulted in revenue enhancements or cost savings. For example, the Tata Group (India's largest private-sector business group, with about 100 companies in various sectors operating in 40 countries) and Gerling (a leading insurance company from Germany) have identified improvements in customer relations, staff commitment, and satisfaction.[108]

The growing importance of voluntary networks such as Fair Trade and the Global Compact are part of a larger international "civil society" movement that is trying to address shortcomings associated with Mainstream internationalization. The past decades have seen an unprecedented growth in NGOs as the civil society movement grows, especially in Southern Hemisphere countries. For example, the 1990s witnessed a 94 percent increase in NGO memberships in Southern Hemisphere countries (190,363 to 369,811), and a 54 percent increase in memberships in Northern Hemisphere countries (75,016 to 117,377).[109] Such organizations are promoting fundamental changes in the way trade agreements and tax systems are designed.[110]

THE ECONOMIC–TECHNOLOGICAL ENVIRONMENT. Internationalization has been facilitated by the ability to move jobs, knowledge, and money around the world. The opportunities associated with these three characteristics are different from a Multistream perspective than from a Mainstream view.

Flow of Jobs. Having jobs move to places where they are most needed sounds like a win-win proposition. Consumers and shareholders "win" because labor costs are lowered, and unemployed people "win" because they get jobs. Unfortunately, because of the relative power advantage that large organizations enjoy over unemployed people in poor countries, poor people have little negotiating power.

Multistream management seeks creative ways to offer jobs that treat people with dignity and respect. This is evident in earlier examples in this chapter, such as the Ghanaian cocoa farmers who own 33 percent of the Day Chocolate Company and Palliser Furniture's decision to open its Mexican operations away from the *maquiladoras*. It is also evident in how AES became one of the world's largest energy companies, with operations in more than 30 countries and global revenues exceeding $8 billion, under the leadership of Multistream CEO Dennis Bakke. Bakke describes AES's goal as the creation of meaningful jobs—what he calls "joy at work"—for all of its 40,000 employees around the world. Moreover, if AES acquires a business that is overstaffed, it sets up a generous and voluntary severance program rather than simply lay off employees. In Panama, AES created a loan fund for employees who took the

DIGGING DEEPER

Technology and Genetically Modified Food[112]

There has been much debate recently regarding genetically modified foods and the right to patent seeds. The four major genetically modified crops in the world are corn, canola, soybeans, and cotton. The United States grows about two-thirds of the world's genetically modified crops, Argentina about one-quarter of these crops, and Canada and China about 5 percent each. More than 90 percent of all genetically modified crops produced around the world are grown from the seeds of Monsanto Corporation, which owns patent rights to the seed.

Genetic modification allows scientists to move genes from one species to another. For example, by splicing a gene from a soil bacterium that is toxic to insects into corn's genetic make-up, scientists can make corn that is resistant to insect pests, thereby reducing the use of pesticides (although critics argue that the corn itself has been transformed into a pesticide). Other crops are genetically modified to be resistant to specific herbicides, so that spraying a field with the herbicide will kill the weeds but not the crop.

Some scientists are concerned that long-term testing on how consuming these genetically modified foods will affect ecological or human health is lacking. In the European Union, all foods that contain genetically modified ingredients must be labeled as such, and some countries have banned certain crops. In 2003, Zambia refused to accept genetically modified food aid from the United States because of health and environmental concerns.

There is concern that genetically modified foods may be good for some Mainstream businesses and farmers, but harmful to others. For example, when winds blow genetically modified seeds onto neighboring fields, it causes troubles for organic farmers. In Saskatchewan, Canada, organic farmers sued Monsanto, claiming that modified canola contaminated their fields so much that they could no longer grow organic canola. Also, because Monsanto requires farmers to sign contracts that make it illegal to save and plant its patented seeds in subsequent years, the high-tech seeds are of little use to the 1 billion farmers in low-income countries who depend on seeds that they save from the previous planting season.

How should we manage technologies such as genetically modified agriculture? Are they value neutral? Would they be evaluated and used differently from a Mainstream perspective than from a Multistream perspective?

severance package. Within a year, 71 new businesses had been started by these former employees, most of whom had taken advantage of the AES loan fund.[113]

Flow of Know-How. Conventional wisdom suggests that internationalization can facilitate the flow of technical and managerial knowledge around the world,[114] but others have argued that there is little transfer of know-how from multinational corporations to the developing countries where they operate.[115] Transfer of know-how may be limited when a Mainstream ethnocentric or polycentric orientation is not very conducive to mutual learning.[116]

Although technological improvements may appear to be value neutral, in reality they are often driven by a Mainstream agenda.[117] Most of the world's research and development (R&D) capacity is in high-income countries and serves acquisitive economics. This has important implications for the lives of people in low-income countries in terms of the kinds of technology being developed, especially in areas such as health care and agriculture.[118]

Multistream managers want to develop technology and transfer know-how that also benefits others. An instructive example comes from the pharmaceutical company Merck. A scientist there—who had previously worked with the World Health Organization (WHO) in Africa—helped to develop a product called Mectizan. Mectizan can prevent river blindness, which is prevalent among the poorest people in the world. Recognizing that these people could not afford the medicine (even if it cost only pennies per year), Merck proposed that governments in Africa, Europe, and the United States purchase Mectizan (at a low price) and then supply it for free to people who were infected with river blindness. None of the governments agreed, so Merck decided that it would supply the medicine for free to anyone in the world who needed it. The company also began to work together with other organizations (such as the World Bank and the WHO) that were better able to distribute the medicine in remote areas where it was needed. Merck is committed to reaching 50 million people per year with Mectizan, and hopes that by doing so it can help to eradicate river blindness in 10 to 15 years. The company's managers believe that actions such as these help make their firm more attractive to the world's best scientists, because they know that discoveries at Merck may reach sick people regardless of their economic status.[119]

Flow of Money. Although the intent of allowing money to flow freely across nations was to make everyone better off, this has often not been the outcome.[120] In fact, critics suggest that the easier flow of money has had several unintended outcomes. The vast majority of money being traded and a lot of the profits being generated do not contribute to productivity in any real sense. Today as much as $2 trillion travels around the world every day, about 60 times more than the value of "real" goods and services that are traded in world markets.[121]

Consider the "game" played by derivatives dealers, who bet on others' *expectations* about prices of shares, bonds, or currencies in the future. The nominal value of contracts in derivatives doubled every two years from 1989 to 1995, when it reached $41 trillion worldwide. Ninety-seven percent of these transactions are simply bets: "I bet that in a year's time the Dow Jones Average will be 250 points higher than now. Otherwise, I'll pay" *x* amount of money.[122] This practice is an example of acquisitive economics, not sustenance economics. It results in a situation where objective economic relationships are less significant than the subjective *expectation* of what others will do. In the past, such an orientation has contributed to international monetary crises in Mexico, Thailand, and South Korea: These countries experienced rapid devaluation of their currencies even though objective economic conditions, based on the services and goods being produced, did not change.[123] In 2008, a world leader in derivatives, a French bank named Société Générale, lost over $7 billion due to the surreptitious transactions of one of its traders, Jérôme Kerviel.[124]

The ease of transferring money has also resulted in growing influence for tax havens, where corporations and others (including organized crime) can hide their funds and avoid paying taxes. The Cayman Islands is a leading tax haven, where 14,000 residents share 14 square kilometers and 500 banks. Other tax havens include Gibraltar, Cyprus, Liechtenstein, and Luxemburg.[125] According to IMF statistics, more than $2 trillion is managed in the various offshore mini-states, far beyond the reach of the countries where the money was made. These tax havens weaken the ability of nations to provide a healthy social infrastructure (e.g., education, health care) by diverting funds away from the government.[126] Stopping this tax avoidance would be an easy matter, but it would fly in the face of the free movement of capital.

A variety of Multistream options are being promoted to reform the flow of money in the economic–technological environment, such that it becomes better aligned with sustenance economics. Perhaps the most notable "reformer" is Nobel Prize winner James Tobin, who proposed a simple 1 percent tax on all foreign currency transactions to solve some of the difficulties with the deregulated flow of capital. This 1 percent tax would ensure that financial transfers are based more on "real" changes in production and market opportunities than on gambling based on the acquisitive economics of investors. For example, gone would be the day when traders purchased $100 million of French francs only to sell them 15 minutes later for a profit of $10,000 when their value increased by 0.01 percent (because the profit from such a transaction would be insufficient to pay the Tobin tax—in this case, $1 million). The Tobin tax would also give national governments greater freedom to change interest rates in their jurisdictions. There is widespread agreement that the Tobin tax is theoretically brilliant. Unfortunately, it is not likely to be implemented because it goes against the dominant ideology of the free movement of capital.[127]

The growing interest in micro-financing represents another Multistream example of how to manage the international flow of money. Rather than have money flow to the point of highest financial return, the idea is to have money flow to the place where it is has the greatest potential to improve the welfare of humankind. Micro-financing involves providing financial services to the very poor, especially to poor micro-entrepreneurs. Providing a loan of $100 can make a world of difference to an entrepreneur whose annual income is $300, but providing such a loan has traditionally not been of much interest to Mainstream financial institutions, whose managers correctly note that administering such a small loan program may be more expensive than making a multimillion-dollar loan to a large corporation.

Today, the largest organization that focuses on micro-financing is the Grameen Bank in Bangladesh, which has made small loans totalling over $1.2 billion. The bank was started by Mohammed Yunus, a Bangladeshi with a Ph.D. from the United States. He became frustrated when Mainstream economic theory failed to help him address the poverty all around him (see the opening case in Chapter 6 for more details).[128]

Reflections from a White American Woman Working in a Garment Factory in the Philippines[129]

When we look at statistics and financial information about globalization and international management, we often lose sight of real "on-the-job" work experiences. To get a sense of what is involved in some of the jobs that have been created via globalization and what sort of standard of living they provide, researchers sometimes use a method called "participant observation." The following study by Patricia Wagner took place in the Philippines in the early 1990s; it describes conditions that are certainly not the worst, but not the best either.

The demand for a living wage means something to me now that it did not before, because I just finished working in a factory in the working-class district of Manila. It was just about the scariest thing I have ever done: walking around the factory district, knocking on the gates, talking to security guards, asking for work. I looked ridiculous: a white person asking for factory work. But I kept applying and asking and taking I.Q. tests and sewing tests, realizing along the way that this is how new immigrants to America feel when they apply. I stood in line with everyone else, waited in the hot sun, cowered under the glare of supervisors, and got a lot of stares. [Finally, Wagner is hired.]

. . . The very nice Taiwanese technical assistant in the sampling section where I work demands perfection. We are creating the samples that will go to the buyers. At first I am stimulated by the challenge to create something new. They are patient with my early mistakes and help me rip out piece after piece. But then it strikes me—they are demanding perfection, but they pay slave wages. If they expect artistry, they should pay for it. Daisy has sewn for fifteen years, and she started at this factory three months ago at 89 pesos a day [less than 50 cents per hour]. After 15 years experience! . . .

The nice Taiwanese supervisor comes in two hours later than we do, but works hard, usually till 7 P.M., including Sundays. But she is compensated for her efforts; the workers are not. She works in air-conditioned surroundings and goes home to cooked meals and clean clothes. The thousand workers share three broken toilets and stifling heat. What right do these "nice" people [managers] have to demand perfection, speed, and promptness from these women? It is their money that gives them power.

. . . What is mandatory is what the management wants or what the market demands, even if it is not "required" or legal. And so, we work 6 to 6, Monday to Friday, 6 to 3 on Saturday and 6 to 2 on Sunday, then back to regular hours Monday. [That's 77 hours per week at work!]

Many of the workers in my section had moved together from the Greenfields garment factory that closed down when a KMU-affiliated union was organized. I heard the same story again and again. As soon as workers try to negotiate for fair wages and conditions, the companies shut down.

. . . [The factory workers] earn three to four dollars a day for 12 hours work. They leave their homes before sunrise and arrive home after dark. They barely see their children, or their husbands, who are also working overtime. They work every day of the week; no time for strolls in the park and for concert halls. The poor women sit, and with tired hands, create beautiful clothes for the relatively rich. The clothes are tagged before they leave the factory door. The black satin is $48, the silk is $89 . . .

. . . I talked with Julie, a woman who . . . talked about working with the fine quality cotton cloth, sewing the slit between the front and the back on T-shirts with the long-backed style. She had crossed her feet while removing some stitches—taking that opportunity away from her foot pedal to stretch her ankle—and was reprimanded by her supervisor. She was also yelled at when she laughed or spoke to those sitting with her. And she was required to work seven nights a week unless she had a special excuse.

After her first week, Julie was exhausted. As she told me her stories, her throat caught with anger and fatigue. She broke down in sobs. I sat beside this woman, holding a pillow to her face to catch the tears, a woman I had never known to weep, and thought, "I want to remember this moment for the rest of my life." This woman who makes. . . clothes that are supposed to make you feel free and causal—who weeps from the pain of work, who is not even allowed to cross her ankles.

QUESTIONS FOR DISCUSSION

1. How unusual do you think the jobs like this are?
2. Where do you hear about them?
3. Given the competitive pressures of the international marketplace, is there anything managers can do to avoid such situations?

SUMMARY

From a Mainstream perspective:
Internationalization helps managers lower their costs of inputs and production and reach larger markets.
Managers can choose among four basic levels of internationalization:

- Importing/exporting, which provides relatively easy ways to lower costs or to expand one's market
- Licensing and franchising, which provide access to new markets with greater control and a more complete product or service
- Strategic alliances and joint ventures, which demand establishing a close working relationship with an organization in another country
- Foreign subsidiaries, which provide complete control of international operations and its profits and losses

Managers must pay attention to four key dimensions of the international environment:

- The sociocultural dimension, which refers to adapting to differences in a culture's materialism, individualism, time orientation, deference to authority, and uncertainty tolerance
- The natural dimension, which refers to finding less expensive places to source inputs, to add value to goods, and to deposit waste
- The political–legal dimension, which refers to getting incentives from a host country (e.g., tax breaks) and freeing trade internationally (e.g., trade agreements)
- The economic–technological dimension, which refers to taking advantage of the international flow of jobs (e.g., find countries with the lowest input/processing costs), knowledge (e.g., locate in three international time zones to work 24/7), and money (e.g., move capital to where it can receive the highest return)

From a Multistream perspective:
Managers internationalize for financial reasons *and* because it provides new opportunities to better address human needs. Managers can choose among four basic levels of internationalization:

- Importing/exporting, which provides opportunities to access new markets and to improve wages and living conditions overseas
- Licensing and franchising, which provide access to new overseas markets to serve and in which to share know-how
- Strategic alliances and joint ventures, which provide opportunities to establish mutually beneficial relationships with people in foreign organizations
- Foreign subsidiaries, which provide opportunities to model a style of management that seeks to enhance overall well-being

Managers must pay attention to four key dimensions of the international environment:

- The sociocultural dimension, which is best managed via egali-centrism and attempting to build relationships where teaching and learning flow two ways
- The natural dimension, which provides opportunities to improve sustainable development internationally
- The political–legal dimension, which refers to appropriate policies from a host country that protect its domestic organizations (e.g., subsidies, tariffs) and socially just international trade (e.g., Fair Trade)
- The economic–technological dimension, which refers to taking advantage of the international flow of jobs (e.g., find countries with greatest needs), knowledge (e.g., develop/distribute information to improve human welfare), and money (e.g., support needy, Tobin tax, micro-financing)

QUESTIONS FOR REFLECTION AND DISCUSSION

1. Identify what you think are the three most important aspects of each of the four dimensions of the international environment. Where and how do international managers acquire the information they need to do their job?

2. Assume that someone you know wants to be an international manager. After reading this chapter, what advice would you give that person as he or she prepares for a career?

3. Describe the four main levels of internationalization. Be sure to list key pros and cons for each level.

4. Almost 1 billion people go to bed malnourished every night. Each day 30,000 children die of hunger and related causes. Do people in high-income countries have a moral obligation to use their skills and training to improve the lives of people in low-income countries? Explain your answer.

5. The overarching goal of internationalizing from a Mainstream perspective is quite clear: to improve the financial bottom line. Low-income countries with high unemployment are desperate for international jobs, know-how, and money, which creates many

opportunities for managers from high-income countries to maximize their profits. This leads to a thorny question for managers: "Where do you draw the line?" If you can lower your costs by outsourcing to an organization that uses child labor, is that acceptable? What if you know that if the children did not have factory jobs, then they would be likely to get involved in child prostitution? What if workers are required to spend 60 hours per week earning low wages in difficult working conditions, with rarely a chance to see their children or spouses? If workers were to unionize in an effort to improve their situation, would you transfer the work to a nonunionized plant to keep costs as low as possible (especially if you know that your competition will do so)? Answers to these questions depend, at least in part, on your approach to management and your moral point of view (see Chapter 5). Where do *you* draw the line?

6. Reread the opening case, and assume that Coca-Cola has hired you to try to reopen its plant in Kerala, In-

dia. Based on what you have learned in this chapter, develop a plan and spell out the key steps you would follow.

7. This chapter on international management has covered a lot of territory. Which topics in this chapter would you like to study in greater depth? What surprised you the most? What did you find the least interesting?

8. Geert Hofstede found that there is a strong relationship (correlation = 0.67) between a country's deference-to-authority score and its gross national product (GNP) per capita. In particular, he found that countries with the highest GNP per capita were more likely to challenge authority. Provide several plausible explanations for this relationship. For example, do you think that challenging authority leads to economic success, or does economic success lead to challenging authority? Be prepared to defend your views.

HANDS-ON ACTIVITIES

What Are Your Views on the Natural Environment?

The following five statements are taken from a "New Ecological Paradigm" scale that researchers have developed to measure people's attitudes toward the natural environment, and in particular whether humans have a substan-

tial adverse effects on the natural environment.[130] Rate the following statements, and compare your views with those of your classmates.

	STRONGLY DISAGREE	DISAGREE	NEUTRAL	AGREE	STRONGLY AGREE
1. The "ecological crisis" facing humankind has been greatly exaggerated.	1	2	3	4	5
2. The Earth is like a spaceship with limited room and resources.	1	2	3	4	5
3. If things continue on their present course, we will soon experience a major ecological catastrophe.	1	2	3	4	5
4. The balance of nature is strong enough to cope with the impacts of modern industrial nations.	1	2	3	4	5
5. Humans are severely abusing the environment.	1	2	3	4	5

To calculate your total score, add the following:

____ (response to statement 1, subtracted from 6 to reverse-code your response)

+ ____ (response to statement 2)

+ ____ (response to statement 3)

+ ____ (response to statement 4, subtracted from 6 to reverse-code your response)

+ ____ (response to statement 5)

_____

= _____ Total: New Environmental Paradigm score

ENDNOTES

1. Hawken, P., Lovins, A., & Lovins, L. H. (1999). *Natural capitalism: Creating the next Industrial Revolution.* Boston: Little, Brown, who draw on Womack, J. P., & Jones, D. T. (1996). *Lean thinking: Banish waste and create wealth in your corporation.* New York: Simon and Schuster; Ryan, J. C., & Durning, A. T. (1997). *From stuff: The secret lives of everyday things.* Seattle, WA: Northwest Environment Watch; Shiva, V. (D. Hounam, trans.). (2005). India: Soft drinks, hard cases. *Environment and Times, 4,* 8–9.

2. Pollan, M. (2006, June 4). The way we live now: Mass Natural. *New York Times.* http://www.nytimes.com/2006/06/04/magazine/04wwln_lede.html?pagewanted=1&ei=5088&en=07310c42ac1a390c&ex=1307073600.

3. For example, dirty wastewater had been pumped into dry boreholes, which contaminated the aquifers and caused the local drinking water to be declared unfit for consumption by the district medical officer.

4. "When Coca-Cola refused to account for its practices, the *panchayat* [village council] withdrew its operating licence. It has been alleged that the company responded by offering the council's president, Anil Krishnan, and 330m rupee bribe ($6.8m), which he refused" [page 8 in Shiva, V. (D. Hounam, trans.). (2005). India: Soft drinks, hard cases. *Environment and Times, 4,* 8–9].

5. Clarke, T., Dopp, S., et al. (2005). *Challenging McWorld* (2nd ed.). Ottawa, Canada: Canadian Centre for Policy Alternatives.

6. Based on WorldWatch Institute. (2006, July 12). *Vital signs 2006–2007: Economic gains mask underlying crisis;* and Clarke et al., 2005.

7. Waddock, S. (2006). *Leadership integrity in a fractured knowledge world.* Academy of Management Learning & Education, 6(4).

8. The profits of the top 200 corporations grew by 224 percent between 1983 and 1997, according to the Institute for Public Studies in Washington, D.C. Cited in Clarke et al., 2005.

9. For a helpful discussion of globalization, see the literature review in Bruning, E. R., & Fudge, D. K. (2004). *International marketing education and the globalization debate: A content analysis of North American textbooks.* Quebec City, Quebec: ASAC Proceedings.

10. This quote has been attributed to U.S. president John F. Kennedy, who used it in a speech in Frankfurt, Germany, in June 1963. On July 18, 1984, the Reverend Jesse Jackson spoke to the Democratic National Convention and said, "Rising tides don't lift all boats, particularly those stuck at the bottom." Cited in http://www.phrases.org.uk/bulletin_board/42/messages/1052.html. Accessed September 21, 2007. Research lends support to both views. For example, some research suggests that globalization leads to greater income inequality, whereas other studies contend that it may help the poorest people: Atkinson, A. B. (2003). Income inequality in OECD countries: Data and explanations. *CESifo Economic Studies,* 49(4), 479–513; Milanovic, B. (2005). Can we discern the effect of globalization on income distribution? Evidence from household surveys. *World Bank Economic Review,* 19(1), 21–44.

11. Data from Bureau of Economic Analysis, U.S. Department of Commerce. (2006, June 16). *U.S. international transactions: First quarter 2006.* Accessed August 22, 2006, at http://www.bea.gov/bea/newsrel/transnewsrelease.htm.

12. Hellriegel, D., Jackson, S. E., & Slocum, J. W. (2002). *Management: A competency-based approach* (9th ed., p. 110). Cincinnati, OH: Thomson South-Western.

13. Hellriegel et al., 2002, p. 110.

14. Daft, R. L. (2003). *Management* (6th ed., p. 123). Mason, OH: Thomson South-Western.

15. Varian, H. R. (2007, June 28). "An iPod has global value: Ask the (many) countries that make it." *New York Times.* Accessed March 13, 2008, at http://www.nytimes.com/2007/06/28/business/worldbusiness/28scene.html?_r=1&scp=1&sq=&st=nyt&oref=slogin.

16. Horowitz, M. (2004). *Attitudes towards wage fairness in the maquiladora zone: Social identities, reference groups, and the sale of labor power.* Ph.D. dissertation, University of Kansas. Lawrence, KS.

17. These specific countries were chosen because they were in a study by Geert Hofstede, which is one of the most cited studies of cross-cultural differences for management. For more information see http://www.geert-hofstede.com/; and Hofstede, G. (2003) *Culture's consequences: Comparing values, behaviors, institutions, and organizations across nations* (2nd ed.). CA: Sage. See also Thousand Oaks Hofstede, G. (1980). *Culture's consequences: International differences in work-related values.* Beverly Hills, CA: Sage.

18. This discussion draws from and builds upon ideas found in Roesen, R. (2004). How to overcome ethnocentrism: Approaches to a culture of recognition by history in the twenty-first century. *History and Theory,* 43(4), 118–129; and Michailova, S., & Nielsen, B. B. (2006). MNCs and knowledge management: A typology and key features. *Journal of Knowledge Management,* 10(1), 44–54.

19. These are the average scores of the eight countries that had relatively high individualism and materialism scores (see description in Figure 4.4).

20. These are the average scores of the seven countries that had relatively low individualism and materialism scores (see description in Figure 4.4).

21. This is based on the data collected by Hofstede.

22. This is based on the data collected by Hofstede.

23. Data taken from Hofstede website (August 28, 2006).

24. Data taken from Hofstede website.

25. Data taken from Hofstede website. Note that the time orientation data were collected later, and are available for only a subset of countries of the countries for which Hofstede collected the original data.

26. The scores are developed from a variety of sources, but the basic underlying question is this: "If you consider your life overall, how satisfied would you say you are nowadays?" Responses are based on a scale of zero (not at all satisfied) to ten (extremely satisfied). The data in Table 4.1 are taken from Marks, N., Abdallah, S., Simms, A., & Thompson, S. (2006). *The unhappy planet: An index of human well-being and environmental impact.* London, UK: New Economics Foundation (Economics as if People and the Planet Mattered). www.happyplanetindex.org. This publication draws on a variety of sources, but most heavily on Veenhoven, R. (2005). Average happiness in 91 nations 1995–2005. *World Database of Happiness* (see Veenhoven, R., States of Nations, World Database of Happiness, Erasmus University, Rotterdam, Netherlands. www.worlddatabaseofhappiness.eur.nl/statnat).

27. Taken from Marks et al., 2006.

28. These scores are taken from Venetoulis, J., & Talberth, J. (2005). *Ecological footprint of nations.* Oakland, CA: Redefining Progress. www.RedefiningProgress.org. As readers familiar with this literature will recognize, these are Ecological Footprint 2.0 data,

which try to address some of the concerns raised by others on the original ecological footprint research [Rees, W., & Wackernagel, M. (1996). *Our ecological footprint*. Gabriola Island, BC: New Society Publishers; van den Bergh, J. C. M., & Verbruggen, H. (1999). Spatial sustainability, trade and indicators: An evaluation of the ecological footprint. *Ecological Economics, 29*(1), 61–72]. For example, unlike the original index, Ecological Footprint 2.0 attempts to measure use of cropland, built space, and marine and inland fisheries.

29. From U.S. Central Intelligence Agency. (2006). *The world factbook*. Accessed August 23, 2006, at https://www.cia.gov/library/publications/the-world-factbook/.

30. From the U.S. Central Intelligence Agency's *The World Factbook*. Purchasing power parity takes into account what a similar item, such as a Big Mac hamburger at McDonald's, costs in each country.

31. The formula used was Internationalization = (Imports + Exports) ÷ GDP. Figures were taken from the U.S. Central Intelligence Agency's *The World Factbook*. The same formula is used to measure globalization and the degree of economic openness of different countries by the following authors: Hass, M. K., Waheeduzzaman, M., & Rahman, A. (2003). Defense expenditure and economic growth in the SAARC countries. *Journal of Social, Political, and Economic Studies, 28*(3), 275–293.

32. This is adapted from Marks et al. (2006), who use a more complicated and refined approach to develop what they call a "Happy Planet Index."

33. Quotes taken from Beach, M. (1990, June 10). Indians discover Columbus '92 not to their liking. *Sunday News* (Lancaster, PA), p. B1.

34. Based on a presentation by R. Miller, March 29, 1993; interview with R. Shuttleworth.

35. For a copy of the Universal Declaration of Human Rights, go to http://www.un.org/Overview/rights.html.

36. Of course, other international data sets have become available since Hofstede collected his data, including the World Values Survey and the data collected by the following authors: Javidan, M., Dorfman, P. W., de Luque, M. S., & House, R. J. (2006). In the eyes of the beholder: Cross cultural lessons in leadership from Project GLOBE. *Academy of Management Perspectives, 20*(1), 67–90.

37. Hofstede's work has been frequently cited, and some of his five dimensions have been relabeled. For example, what we call "materialism," others have labeled as "quantity versus quality of life" [Robbins, S. P., & Coulter, M. (2003). *Management* (7th ed.). Upper Saddle River, NJ: Prentice-Hall; "achievement versus nurturing orientation" [Jones, G. R., & George, J. M. (2003). *Contemporary management* (3rd ed.). New York: McGraw-Hill Irwin]; and "aggressive versus passive goal behavior" [Griffin, R. W. (2002). *Management* (7th ed.). Boston: Houghton Mifflin].

38. Although we follow others in emphasizing how this dimension may be related to materialism [e.g., see Deresky, H. (1997). *International management: Managing across borders and cultures* (p. 75). Reading, MA: Addison Wesley Longman], no items in Hofstede's Values Survey Model 1994 Questionnaire directly measure materialism per se (available online at http://www.geert-hofstede.com/). A similar observation holds for the postmaterialism scale associated with the World Values Survey [see MacIntosh, R. (1998). Global attitude measurement: An assessment of the World Values Survey postmaterialism scale. *American Sociological Review, 63*(3), 452–464]. This is an issue for future research.

39. Deresky, 1997.

40. For categorizing individualism scores, "low" means that Hofstede's score was from 6 through 26 (number of countries, N, = 18); "medium" scores were from 27 through 60 (N = 18); and "high" scores were from 63 through 91 (N = 17). For categorizing materialism scores, "low" means that Hofstede's score was from 5 through 43 (N = 17); "medium" scores were from 44 through 58 (N = 18); and "high" scores were from 61 through 95 (N = 18).

41. A study of female managers in Costa Rica asked them to choose their preferred style among four types of managers. Approximately 15 percent chose either the authoritarian style (managers make decisions and expect subordinates to implement them) or the persuasive style (managers make decisions and explain them to subordinates before implemented). Approximately 85 percent chose either the consultative style (managers consult with subordinates before making decisions) or the participative style (managers present issues to subordinates and allow them to make decisions): Osland, J. S., Synder, M. M., & Hunter, L. (1998). A comparative study of managerial styles among female executives in Nicaragua and Costa Rica. *International Studies of Management and Organization, 28*(2), 54–73.

42. Costa Rica's approach is being copied by other countries: Higgins, M. (2006, January 22). If it worked for Costa Rica . . . ." *New York Times*, p. 5.10.

43. Zbinden, S., & Lee, D. R. (2005). Paying for environmental services: An analysis of participation in Costa Rica's PSA program. *World Development (Oxford), 33*(2), 255.

44. The study's authors point out that Costa Rica could make more optimal financial use of its forests if it received financial compensation for the forests' carbon-fixing value: Bulte, E. H., Joenje, M., & Jansen, H. G. P. (2000). Is there too much or too little natural forest in the Atlantic Zone of Costa Rica? *Canadian Journal of Forest Research, 30*(3), 495–506.

45. Marks et al., 2006.

46. Costa Rica ranked the fifth lowest in individualism (21) and seventh lowest in materialism (15). Moreover, Costa Rica is an appropriate comparison country for the United States because like the United States but unlike some other Multistream countries, Costa Rica has enjoyed a relatively stable political situation, democratic institutions, and a free press. Of course, the two countries are different in size, in terms of both geography and population.

47. Under this scenario, managers are more likely to be motivated and to be trusted to work in the interests of the larger group. This is consistent with research suggesting that Costa Rican managers practice participative management and consult with others (rather than use their authority to influence others and to impose their decisions on others). It is also consistent with research showing that formalization is a barrier to trust in individualistic countries, but not in collectivistic countries: Huang, X., & Van de Vliert, E. (2006). Job formalization and cultural individualism as barriers to trust in management. *International Journal of Cross Cultural Management, 6*(2), 221–242.

48. Costa Rica is living well beneath its ecological "means" given that the biological capacity of its natural environment is about 47 acres per capita. Meanwhile, the biological capacity of the United States' natural environment is slightly larger, at 50 acres per capita. Given that the biological capacity of the entire planet is approximately 39 acres per capita, Costa Rica may serve as a better model for global development than the United States.

49. Shane, S. (1995). Uncertainty avoidance and the preference for innovation championing roles. *Journal of international business studies,*

26(10), 46–68. Although research supports the link between uncertainty acceptance and innovation, when managers present a very careful plan of the future that reduces uncertainty and legitimizes innovative behavior, then people who tend to avoid uncertainty may, in fact, welcome change.

50. According to a widely publicized memo written by Lawrence Summers, then chief economist of the World Bank: "Underpopulated countries in Africa are vastly underpolluted, the air quality is probably vastly inefficiently low [in pollutants] compared to Los Angeles or Mexico City." Quoted in Hawken, P. (1993). *The ecology of commerce: A declaration of sustainability* (p. 174). New York: HarperBusiness.

51. Wilson, J. S., Otsuki, T., & Sewadeh, M. (2002). *Dirty exports and environmental regulation.* Development Research Group (DECRG), World Bank. Accessed June 18, 2007, at http://72.14.205.104/search?q=cache:YNmyhVbBmFsJ:www-wds.worldbank.org/external/default/WDSContentServer/IW3P/IB/2002/04/12/000094946_02040304241091/additional/110510322_20041117161524.pdf+dirty+products+as+a+percent+of+total+exports&hl=en&ct=clnk&cd=1&client=safari. See also Low, P., & Yeats, A. (1992). Do "dirty" industries migrate? In P. Low (Ed.), *International trade and the environment.* Washington, DC: World Bank.

52. Hellriegel, D., Jackson, S. E., & Slocum, J. H., Jr. (2002). *Management: A competency-based approach* (9th ed., p. 117). Cincinnati, OH: Thomson South-Western.

53. Griffin, 2002, p. 147.

54. Arnold, B. (under supervision of R. Hitchner, J. Kile, & D. Moore). (2005). *Policies that distort world agricultural trade: Prevalence and magnitude.* Congress of the United States, Congressional Budget Office. These numbers are somewhat simplified, because there are many ways to measure subsidies that go beyond the scope of this book.

55. For example, the total domestic support provided as a percentage of agricultural output value was 140 percent for Iceland, 37 percent each for the United States and the European Union, 13 percent for Canada, and 2 percent for New Zealand.

56. Pollan, M. (2007, April 22). You are what you grow. *New York Times.* Accessed March 13, 2008, at http://www.nytimes.com/2007/04/22/magazine/22wwlnlede.t.html?scp=1&sq=&st=nyt; and Becker, E. (2003, August 27). U.S. corn subsidies said to damage Mexico. *New York Times.* Accessed June 25, 2007, at http://www.mindfully.org/WTO/2003/US-Corn-Subsidies27aug03.htm, and February 19, 2008, at http://query.nytimes.com/gst/fullpage.html?res=9902E3DB1039F934A1575BC0A9659C8B63&scp=1&sq=&st=nyt. Within a decade of opening its borders to U.S. corn via NAFTA in 1994, approximately one-third of the corn used in Mexico was imported from the United States and the price of corn in Mexico had dropped 70 percent. That change may be good for consumers but has reduced the income of 15 million Mexicans who depend on growing corn for their livelihood. U.S. corn farmers receive about $10 billion per year in agricultural subsidies. See also http://ipsnews.net/print.asp?idnews=21623.

57. WTO strikes down U.S. cotton subsidy appeal. (2005, March 4). *Globe and Mail,* p. B10; Kilman, S., & Thurow, R. (2005, August 5). To soothe anger over subsidies, U.S. cotton tries wooing Africa. *Wall Street Journal,* pp. A1, A6.

58. Such as MERCOSUR, CARICOM, and the Andean Pact.

59. Pollan, M. (2007, April 22). "You are what you grow." *New York Times.* Accessed March 13, 2008, at http://www.nytimes.com/2007/04/22/magazine/22wwlnlede.t.html?scp=1&sq=&st=nyt.

60. June 25, 2007, at http://ec.europa.eu/economy_finance/euro/our_currency_en.htm.

61. The World Bank includes two institutions: (1) the International Bank for Reconstruction and Development (IBRD), which focuses on middle-income and developing countries that have been deemed credit worthy; and (2) the International Development Association (IDA), which focuses on the poorest countries in the world. Much of the information in this paragraph is taken from http://web.worldbank.org.

62. Much of the content in this section is drawn from Dyck, B., Bruning, E. R., & Buckland, J. (2003). A critical view of conventional globalization: Making an argument for a new paradigm for the new millennium. Halifax, Nova Scotia: ASAC Proceedings.

63. Thurow, L. (1996). *The future of capitalism: How today's economic forces shape tomorrow's world* (pp. 115–116). New York: Penguin.

64. Rifkin, J. (1995). *The end of work.* New York: F. P. Putnam's Sons.

65. Kirby, C. (2003, June 2). Techies see jobs go overseas. *San Francisco Chronicle.* Accessed November 1, 2007, at http://www.sfgate.com/cgi-bin/article.cgi?f=/c/a/2003/06/02/BU270141.DTL.

66. Giridharadas, A. (2007, September 26). India tries outsourcing its outsourcing. *International Herald Tribune.* Accessed November 1, 2007, at http://yaleglobal.yale.edu/display.article?id=9724.

67. Soros, G. (1998). *The crisis of global capitalism* (pp. 101–134). New York: Public Affairs.

68. http://www.imf.org.

69. Lafraniere, S. (2006, October 29). Africa's world of forced labor, in a 6-year-old's eyes. *New York Times.* Accessed September 21, 2007, at http://www.nytimes.com/2006/10/29/world/africa/29ghana.html?_r=1&th=&oref=slogin&emc=th&pagewanted=print.

70. Accessed August 1, 2006, at http://www.unctad.org/Templates/Page.asp?intItemID=3713&lang=1.

71. Waddock, 2006.

72. Rees, W. E. (2002). Globalization and sustainability: Conflict or convergence? *Bulletin of Science, Technology and Society, 22*(4), 249–268. See also the UN report "Poor first to feel global warming's effects," described April 6, 2007, on America's Public Media: Marketplace website. Accessed September 21, 2007, at http://marketplace.publicradio.org/shows/2007/04/06/PM200704062.html.

73. Accessed August 23, 2006, at http://www.globalwater.org/index.htm and http://www.clearly.ca/. Of course, companies that sell bottled water also have their critics, including those who suggest that water should be a public resource available to everyone.

74. This name was inspired by a Mahatma Gandhi quote, which captures the idea that Multistream managers look beyond the interests of organizations and people in large cities, to pause and ensure that the people living in small villages "get sufficient to eat and clothe themselves with." The organization had been called "SELFHELP Crafts of the World" prior to 1996. The information in this paragraph was accessed August 2, 2006, at http://www.tenthousandvillages.ca/. See also the following article: Ten Thousand Villages wins Green Business Award. (2006, January 9). *Canadian Mennonite, 30*(1), 19.

75. These figures are from a speech by former Ten Thousand Villages CEO P. Leatherman at the Ten Thousand Villages 60th Anniversary, Vancouver, BC, June 6, 2006.

76. Information taken from the Starbucks website: Starbucks, fair trade, and coffee social responsibility. Accessed August 23, 2006, at http://72.14.207.104/search?q=cache:iGeOwZgrX9MJ:www

.starbucks.com/aboutus/StarbucksAndFairTrade.pdf+starbucks +and+fair+trade&hl=en&ct=clnk&cd=3&client=safari.

77. Or as approved by some other Multistream-oriented organizations, such as fish approved by the Marine Stewardship Council.

78. MEDA's involvement in Bolivia is described in the following article: Dyck, B. (2002). Organizational learning, microfinance, and replication: The case of MEDA in Bolivia. *Journal of Developmental Entrepreneurship, 7*(4), 361–382.

79. For an excellent overview and analysis of the Day Company, see the following article: Doherty, B., & Tranchell, S. (2005). New thinking in international trade? A case study of the Day Chocolate Company. *Sustainable Development, 13,* 166–176.

80. Many of the ideas in this paragraph are drawn from the following source: Todaro, M. P., & Smith, S. C. (2006). *Economic development* (9th ed.). Boston: Pearson/Addison Wesley.

81. Buber, M. (1958). *I and thou.* New York: Scribner.

82. Bacon, D. (2004, December). Up for grabs: It was sold on a promise of boosting employment, increasing wages and bringing job security. But a decade later, the effects of the North American Free Trade Agreement have been nothing short of disastrous. *New Internationalist, 374,* 14.

83. This discussion of ethnocentrism, polycentrism, and egalicentrism draws from and builds upon ideas found in Roesen (2004) and Michailova and Nielsen (2006).

84. The consumption of the average American requires using the natural resources of more than 200 acres of the natural environment from other parts of the world. The human costs associated with overburdening and degrading the environment are disproportionately borne by people in poor countries, who tend to be the most directly dependent on their local ecosystem for their livelihood (Rees, 2002).

85. Rees, 2002. Every *day* the world-wide economy burns up 27 years worth of the earth's stored energy (Hawken, 1993, pp. 21–22).

86. Dyck, B. (1994). From airy-fairy ideals to concrete realities: The case of Shared Farming. *Leadership Quarterly, 5*(3/4), 227–246.

87. Rees, 2002.

88. Hawken, 1993, p. xiii.

89. Ideas in the paragraph are taken from the following sources: Klok, J., Larsen, A., Dahl, A., & Hansen, K. (2006). Ecological tax reform in Denmark: History and social acceptability. *Energy Policy, 34,* 905–916; Hawken, 1993; Hawken et al., 1999; and Martin & Schumann, 1997, p. 160.

90. Quoted in Marks et al., 2006, p. 9.

91. See Marks et al., 2006, p. 32. Even after controlling for GDP per capita, 68 percent of the variance in a country's mean life satisfaction score was accounted for by its location on a materialist–postmaterialist scale developed by the World Values Survey. The simple correlation was $r = 0.875$ before controlling for GDP per capita. The partial correlation controlling for the logarithm of GDP per capita is $r = 0.823$.

92. Definition adapted from MacIntosh, 1998.

93. This was in the Doha Round: Troubled trade talks. *BBCNews.* Accessed August 11, 2006, at http://news.bbc.co.uk/2/hi/ business/5209996.stm.

94. Stiglitz, J. (2002). *Globalization and its discontents* (pp. 10–22). New York: W. W. Norton & Company.

95. Hawken, 1993, p. 100.

96. Hawken, 1993, pp. 99–100.

97. Rees, 2002; also drawing on Smith, J. W. (2000). *Economic democracy: The political struggle for the 21st century.* Armonk, NY: M. E. Sharpe. See also Stiglitz, 2002, Chapter 2.

98. The size of the global economy has tripled in the past 20 years, whereas the overall population has grown by only 30 percent (Rees, 2002).

99. For example, between 1960 and 1980, the wealthiest 1 percent of the U.S. population increased its wealth 150 times faster than the bottom 99 percent (Hawken, 1993, p. 136). Put in different terms, whereas in 1970 the richest 10 percent of the world owned 19 times more than the poorest 10 percent, by 1997 the ratio had increased to 27:1 (Rees, 2002).

100. Even the World Bank, a champion of Mainstream globalization and market reforms, could not find convincing evidence regarding benefits of market reforms for reducing poverty (Stiglitz, 2002, p. 5).

101. Approximately 40 percent of the world's population— 2.6 billion people—lives on less than $2 per day: News release. (2007, April 15). *Poverty drops below 1 billion, says World Bank.* Accessed September 21, 2007, at http://web.worldbank.org/WBSITE/EXTERNAL/NEWS/ 0,,contentMDK:21299914~pagePK:64257043~piPK:437376 ~theSitePK:4607,00.html.

102. According to a report by Professor Barry Popkin, reported by *BBC News* in August 2006: Overweight *"top world's hungry."* Accessed September 21, 2007, at http://news.bbc.co.uk/1/hi/ health/4793455.stm.

103. A 2001 study examined major economic and social indicators for all countries where data were available, comparing the effects of globalization for the period of 1980–2000 to the effects observed in the previous 20 years (1960–1980). The indicators included growth of income per person; life expectancy; mortality among infants, children, and adults; literacy; and education. In terms of economic growth and most other indicators, the 1980–2000 years have clearly shown a decline in progress compared to the 1960–1980 period (the decline was least pronounced for the wealthiest countries, and most pronounced for the poorest countries, where the economic growth rate was negative): Weisbrot, M., Baker, D., Kraev, E., & Chen, J. (2001). *The Scorecard on Globalization 1980–2000: Twenty years of diminished progress.* Washington, DC: Center for Economic and Policy Research. www.cepr.net/globalization/ scorecard_on_globalization.htm.

104. From the IFAT website. Accessed August 2, 2006, at www.ifat.org.

105. Mui, Y. Q. (2006, June 12). For Wal-Mart, fair trade may be more than a hill of beans. *Washington Post,* p. A01.

106. *European Parliament supports Fair Trade.* (2006, July 6). International Fair Trade Association. http://www.ifat.org/current/ EPsupportsFT.shtml.

107. http://www.un.org/aboutun/basicfacts/unorg.htm.

108. Kell, G. (2003). The Global Compact: Origins, operations, progress, challenges. *Journal of Corporate Citizenship,* 11, 35–49.

109. Anheier, H., Glasius, M., & Kaldor, M. (2001). *Global civil society* (p. 290). Oxford, UK: Oxford University Press.

110. Many of these organizations have a clear international focus, defying the stereotype of grass-roots movements being narrowly focused on local issues: Batliwala, S. (2002). Grassroots movements as transnational actors: Implications for global civil

society. *Voluntas: International Journal of Voluntary and Nonprofit Organizations, 13*(4), 393–409.

111. Information and photo found at http://www.globalwater.org/index.htm. Accessed June 20, 2007. Information about Earth Water found in Lillebuen, S. (2007, February 12). Water-bottling company donates net profits to UN. *Winnipeg Free Press*, p. A6.

112. Pages 98 and 99 in Clarke, T., Dopp, S., et al. (2005). *Challenging McWorld* (2nd ed.). Ottawa, Canada: Canadian Centre for Policy Alternatives.

113. See the opening case in Chapter 15 for more on AES. Also see Bakke, D. W. (2005). *Joy at work: A revolutionary approach to fun on the job* (p. 186). Seattle, WA: PVG.

114. Gamble, J. (2006). Multinational retailers in China: Proliferating "McJobs" or developing skills? *Journal of Management Studies, 43*(7), 1463–1490.

115. Todaro & Smith, 2006, p. 712.

116. Dyck, B., Buckland, H., & Wiens, D. (2000). Community development as organizational learning: The importance of agent-participant reciprocity. *Canadian Journal of Developmental Studies, 21*, 605–620.

117. See Stiglitz, 2002, p. 12; and Friedman, T. L. (2000). *The Lexus and the olive tree* (p. 9). New York: Anchor Books.

118. See especially Mander, J., & Goldsmith, E. (1996). *The case against the global economy and for a turn toward the local* (Chapter 11, pp. 244–258). San Francisco: Sierra Club Books; and Pardey, P. G., Roseboom, J., & Craig, B. J., (1999). Agricultural R&D investments and impacts. In J. Alston, M. Pardey, & V. H. Smith (Eds.), *Paying for agricultural productivity* (pp. 47, 50). Baltimore, MD: Johns Hopkins University Press.

119. Vagelos, P. R. (2001). Social benefits of a successful biomedical research company: Merck. *Proceedings of the American Philosophical Society, 145*(4), 575–578.

120. Martin & Schumann, 1997.

121. Clarke et al., 2005, p. 128.

122. These crippling and sometimes life-changing currency devaluations were more the result of decisions made by money managers in large international organizations than the result of objective factors (Martin & Schumann, 1997, p. 52; Soros, 1998, pp. 141–146).

123. For more on how the actions of the International Monetary Fund can have unintended negative outcomes, see Martin & Schumann (1997) and Stiglitz (2002).

124. Schwartz, N. D., & Bennhold, K. (2008, February 5). A trader's secrets, a bank's missteps. *The New York Times.* Accessed February 19, 2008, at http://www.nytimes.com/2008/02/05/business/worldbusiness/05bank.html?scp=1&sq=&st=nyt.

125. Martin & Schumann, 1997, p. 63.

126. Andrews, E. L. (2007, May 3). I.R.S. curtails many audits in tax havens. *New York Times.* Accessed February 19, 2008, at http://www.nytimes.com/2007/05/03/business/03tax.html?scp=1&sq=&st=nyt.

127. Martin & Schumann, 1997, p. 83.

128. For more on the Grameen bank, see the opening case in Chapter 6 and Dyck (2002).

129. Taken from Wagner, Patricia (1991). "Pagsunog–Kilay," Mennonite Central Committee WOMEN'S CONCERNS REPORT, No. 98 (Sept–Oct): pp. 4–6. Wagner, born and raised in the U.S., worked for Mennonite Central Committee, Roman Catholic, and non–governmental democracy-building groups in the Philippines between 1980 and 1993. She currently serves as a United Methodist pastor in Ohio as well as in an interfaith prison ministry. Reprinted with permission of Mennonite Central Committee U.S.

130. This short version of the NEP scale is taken from the following source: Stern, P. C., Dietz, T., Abel, T., Guagnano, A., & Kalof, L. (1999). A value–belief–norm theory of support for social movements: The case of environmentalism. *Research in Human Ecology, 6*(2), 81–97. (The additive scale has an alpha reliability = .073.)

aking ethical decisions and engaging in actions may appear to be rather straightforward—as simple as following the directions on a map. In reality, however, ethical management can be very complex. Just as a person on a journey can get lost when the weather turns bad or when the map doesn't match the terrain, so too managers can become confused in organizations when they receive confusing signals from powerful people or when a strong organizational culture acts like a fog, making clear thinking difficult. Furthermore, just as it is more challenging to navigate a forest once you are in the midst of it, so it is difficult to maintain your ethical bearings in the midst of an organization. This chapter is intended to help you find and maintain your moral or ethical compass as you travel through organizations. It describes the various sources from which managers learn their ethics, the unique moral point of view for each manager, the four-step process by which managers make ethical decisions, and the ways in which managers' ethics are evident in the four management functions.

ROAD MAP

FOUR ASPECTS OF MANAGEMENT ETHICS TO CONSIDER

1. Sources of Management Ethics

2. Moral Points of View
- *Overarching goals*

- *General rationale*

3. The Process of Making Ethical Decisions
- *Recognize ethical issues*
- *Gather information and develop alternatives*
- *Evaluate information and make ethical choice*
- *Implement the ethical decision*

4. Ethical Influences on the Four Management Functic
- *Planning*
- *Organizing*
- *Leading*
- *Control*

Ethics

MAINSTREAM APPROACH ⟷	MULTISTREAM APPROACH
Formal/informal Public/private	Formal/informal Public/private
Consequentialism Maximize productivity, efficiency, profits, and competitiveness. Social well-being comes from rewarding individuals (i.e., increasing material wealth).	*Virtue theory* Provide meaningful work, operate sustainably, be attentive to internal and external stakeholders, and facilitate servant leadership. Social well-being comes from practicing and fostering virtuous character in the community.
Threats and opportunities related to the owner's wealth. Emphasis on facts, checking policies. Choose what maximizes profit within legal bounds. Courageously challenge norms.	Threats and opportunities related to overall well-being. Listen to others, ask for help. Collaboratively choose what maximizes overall well-being. Courageously try new things.
Exercise organization-specific responsibility. Focus on deterrence and adherence. Transactional leadership. Emphasize compliance codes.	Exercise corporate social responsibility. Focus on promoting positive organizational behavior. Servant leadership. Emphasize community codes.

A Fire, Profits, and People[1]

Aaron Feuerstein, owner and CEO of Malden Mills Industries in Lawrence, Massachusetts, is an example of a manager whose ethics correspond to a Multistream moral point of view. When most of the Malden Mills factory burned to the ground in December 1995, the then 70-year-old Feuerstein could have taken the $300 million insurance money and enjoyed retirement. Or, he could have followed the lead of others in his industry and used the money to rebuild the factory in the South, where labor costs were lower than in the Northeast.

Instead, Feuerstein remained loyal to his economically depressed community: He rebuilt the factory on the same site, even though the insurance covered only three-fourths of the reconstruction costs. He also voluntarily kept all 3000 employees on the payroll during the long reconstruction process. Clearly Feuerstein, who found guidance in Jewish moral law and tradition, placed a high value on community: "I simply felt an obligation to the entire community that relies on our presence here in Lawrence; it would have been unconscionable to put 3000 people out on the streets."[2] His willingness to use his financial resources to nurture community in a counter-Mainstream way attracted a lot of media attention: "I got a lot of publicity. And I don't think it speaks well for our times. . . . At the time in America of our greatest prosperity, the god of money has taken over to an extreme."[3]

Feuerstein's actions generated a lot of good will. When the factory reopened, customers sought out his

Aaron Feuerstein outside Malden Mills in Lawrence, Massachusetts.

product. Suppliers, buyers, and employees all went the extra mile to support the company through tough times after the new factory began operations. Even so, a series of warm winters and cheaper overseas goods conspired to reduce the sales of the firm's fleece products, and its furniture upholstery customers, who turned to other supplies after the fire, never returned.[4] Despite its state-of-the-art mill and popular Polartec products, these unforeseen market challenges forced Malden Mills to operate under bankruptcy between 2001 and 2003. Although the company emerged from bankruptcy, Feuerstein left the company's board in 2004 (he still owned about 5 percent of the company). By 2006, its annual revenue was around $160 million, including $25 million in revenues garnered from producing high-tech clothing for the U.S. military. Ultimately, heavy debts forced the firm to declare bankruptcy again, and it sold its assets to Chrysalis Capital Partners. In 2007, the company reemerged as Polartec LLC.[5]

It would be nice to conclude such an uplifting story on a positive note, but that is not the case. Like hundreds of other Northeastern textile operations, Malden Mills struggled to compete with foreign companies that offered far lower wages and that were less concerned about environmental issues. Even so, given the quality of the product it produces and with the assistance of military contracts, Malden Mills has a fighting chance to survive as Polartec.

WHY STUDY ETHICS?

The past decade has seen a surge of interest in managerial ethics. Many business schools, for example, have begun to make courses in business ethics compulsory for all students. The emphasis on ethics can be related to at least three factors:

- The world is changing rapidly.
- Unethical decisions by managers are receiving more attention.
- Managers are moral agents.

Factors such as globalization and technological complexity have changed the world of management. For example, while it is clear in some countries that bribing government officials is unethical, in other countries it is considered a normal part of doing business and an expected part of an official's salary (akin to giving a tip to restaurant workers). Examples of technological change are evident in areas such as stem-cell research, genetically modified foods, and bioengineering: Is it ethical to "play God" and make clones? Issues like these are relatively new to society, so managers have little experience with them, and no clear consensus has emerged among moral philosophers regarding how these issues should be ethically resolved. Moreover, society is continually changing. For example, as more people become less materialistic and less individualistic,[6] they want managers who can lead organizations and social institutions in a way that is consistent with these values. Managers need ethical training to meet their constantly evolving responsibilities in society.

Another factor contributing to the focus on workplace ethics relates to the increasing awareness of unethical decisions made by managers. Well-known examples include the greed and corruption demonstrated by managers at Enron and WorldCom. Abusive behavior by people in authority is also evident in other settings, including religious organizations, government, and educational institutions. Managers need better ethical training on how to deal with the temptations and pressures associated with their responsibilities. The need for such training is clear: Research conducted at the Center for Creative Leadership indicates that unethical behavior—specifically, dishonesty—can destroy an individual manager's career.[7]

Perhaps the most important reason to study ethics is because all managers are moral agents. Management guru Peter Drucker argues that "management is deeply involved in moral concerns."[8] Managers act as moral beings whenever they make choices about what is "effective" management, or what is "good" and what is "bad." As we will discuss, the ethics that managers choose and the structures and systems that they implement can profoundly influence stakeholders. To refuse to acknowledge the ethical component of management is to deny a manager's identity as a moral agent.

What is ethics? **Ethics** is a set of principles or moral standards that differentiate right from wrong. **Management ethics** can be defined as the study of moral standards and the ways in which they influence managers' actions. The study of management ethics tries to help managers to make decisions and take actions that are good and right in the context of organizations. As depicted in Figure 5.1, this chapter focuses on four components of management ethics:

- The sources from which managers may get their moral standards
- The moral points of view that managers follow
- The process that managers use to make ethical decisions
- The influence of ethics on how managers practice the four management functions (which serves as an example to others in the workplace who are sources of influence themselves)

Ethics is a set of principles or moral standards that differentiate right from wrong.

Management ethics is the study of moral standards and how they influence managers' actions.

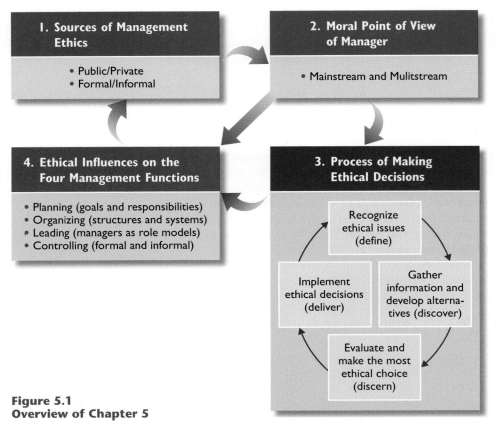

Figure 5.1
Overview of Chapter 5

As shown in Figure 5.1, a manager's sources of ethics will influence his or her moral point of view, which in turn influences the manager's decision-making process. Either directly or indirectly, this process then influences management practices related to the four management functions.

SOURCES OF MANAGEMENT ETHICS

There are many different sources from which managers get their moral standards and principles. Table 5.1 identifies four basic types of sources. As observed along the vertical dimension of the table, a person's ethics can be influenced by formal sources (e.g., ethical principles presented in a Business Ethics course or in religious teachings) and by informal sources (e.g., observations and learning of ethical principles from family, friends, coworkers, and society at large). Similarly, as noted along the horizontal dimension of Table 5.1, ethics may be drawn from the private sphere (e.g., family, friends, personal philosophies, and religious convictions) and from a more public sphere (e.g., work experience, ethics training seminars at work, and media and advertising).

Informal/Public Sources of Ethics

A manager's moral development can be influenced by personal experiences in organizations and the ethical challenges faced in those environments. Research has shown that employees who have been exposed to unethical behavior in the workplace

TABLE 5.1

The Four Types of Sources of Ethics

	Public	Private
Informal	Coworkers, managers Social norms, media	Family Friends
Formal	Education Ethics training	Personal philosophies Family maxims Religious teachings

show more tolerance for similar behavior.[9] Peers and managers are especially important as public sources of ethical standards due to the example they set with their behavior and the influence they have on the ethical climate of the workplace.[10] **Ethical climate** refers to the informal shared perceptions of what are appropriate practices and procedures.[11]

Ethics and morals also are often associated with the idea of custom—that is, what is customary in society.[12] In this sense, what is perceived as ethical is influenced by accepted standards in the organization or broader society about what is right or wrong. For many people, however, ideas about what is right or wrong are universal and timeless, and go beyond the informal etiquette or norms of a culture or context. For example, Norm Frohlich and Joe Oppenheimer used ingenious laboratory experiments to uncover universal norms about what is the fairest way to distribute resources.[13] When groups are asked to develop a fair distribution rule, and members do not know the nature of the tasks that will be rewarded, they favor paying people in a way that first makes sure everyone has his or her basic needs met, and only then paying people according to their contributions.

Informal/Private Sources of Ethics

The examples set by the behavior of immediate family members may be the most influential source of ethics. Much of a person's ethical and moral development occurs at an early age and is influenced by family.[14] Children learn about what is right and wrong by observing their parents and other family members. Your childhood home has a great influence on your attitudes toward and values related to money, politics, goals, relationships, and so on. Friends and peer pressure exert increasing influence as children grow up, especially through the high school years, but friendship usually has a less significant effect overall compared to the influence of family.[15] A person's spouse and own children also can be important influences shaping an individual's ethics.

Taken together, informal private and public sources of morals include family, friendship circles, peer groups, societal expectations, and unspoken universal human norms. Whereas the informal sources of ethics and morals can be quite strong in comparison to formal sources, they are often less easy to identify because they are generally not written down or codified.

Formal/Public Sources of Ethics

Formal education can have an important influence on the development of students' values and ethics. What is taught in class contributes to ethical beliefs about issues such as cheating, competition, and respecting others and the natural environment. More generally, students can learn to value competition or cooperation depending on what is recognized and rewarded in school. As mentioned in Chapter 1, research suggests that economics and business students tend to become more materialist–individualist during their time in college.[16] Perhaps in response to criticisms of the actions of business leaders, ethics courses are now being required as part of the graduation criteria for an increasing number of management students, and many organizations now offer in-house ethics training.[17] Nevertheless, *knowing about* ethics is not the same as *being* ethical. In other words, passing a class on ethics does not make a person ethical.

Some of our understanding and perception of what is ethical also comes from laws and those in authority in government. For example, the Sarbanes–Oxley Act, which was passed by the U.S. Congress in response to the Enron and WorldCom

Ethical climate is the informal shared perceptions of what are appropriate practices and procedures.

Liam Neeson, front and center, as Oscar Schindler, in the movie *Schindler's List*.

accounting failures, requires extensive documentation of internal controls and heightens accountability for those who violate specified standards and the executives who are responsible for oversight of compliance procedures.[18] Although behaving legally is not the same as behaving ethically, the law generally serves as a minimum standard for ethics. Nonetheless, there are times when to be ethical or do what is right may be illegal. For example, the movie *Schindler's List* portrays the true story of German businessman Oskar Schindler, who defied the Nazi regime's mandated discrimination by employing Jewish people in his factories and saving many of them from concentration camps.[19] Conflicts between law and ethics are also possible when the law enforces outdated and misinformed social policies, such as denying voting rights to women and minorities.

Formal/Private Sources of Ethics

Relatively less public and more explicit sources of ethics and morals may be based on "maxims" that you have heard from family and others (e.g., "Take time to smell the flowers" or "Time is money") or principles you have internalized from secular or sacred writings or religious education.[20] These principles can be easily recalled and recited. Of course, exposure to these maxims or principles does not ensure they will be followed, but given that these principles originate from a legitimate or recognized authority (such as a parent, expert, or God), they often carry great weight.

Part of maturing as a person is the process of thinking about and developing your own principles or moral point of view to guide your life. Kohlberg suggests that people's moral development can be at one of three basic levels, as shown in Figure 5.2:[21]

Pre-conventional is the lowest level of moral development, in which ethical judgments are influenced by rewards and punishments.

Conventional is the second level of moral development, in which ethical judgments are influenced by social norms or external standards.

Post-conventional is the highest level of moral development, in which ethical judgments are influenced by transcendent universal principles.

- The first and lowest level of moral development is described as **pre-conventional.** For a manager at this level, what is right and wrong is determined by what is rewarded and punished. In other words, his or her ethics is determined by self-interest: "What is in it for me?"

- The next level of moral development is described as **conventional.** For a manager at this level, what is right and wrong is determined by social norms or external standards. In other words, his or her ethics is determined by others: "What is everyone else doing?"

- The final level of moral development is **post-conventional.** For a person at this level, what is right and wrong is determined by transcendent universal principles established through conscience and reason: "What are timeless truths?" Philosopher Immanuel Kant's categorical imperatives—such as never stealing or deceiving others—are examples of universal principles or duties that he argued could be arrived at by reason.[22]

Not everyone is at the same stage of moral development, nor does everyone proceed through all of the stages described by Kohlberg. Put differently, what one manager sees as ethical behavior, another manager may see as unethical, and vice versa. After the long-term effects of an action or decision have been weighed, the

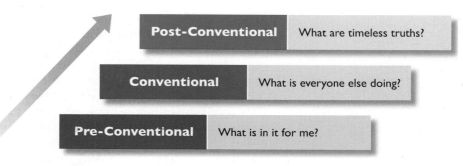

ethicality of that action or decision is usually more apparent,[23] but in the meantime different managers will have different moral points of view of management, which can make it difficult to argue that one choice is "more ethical" than another. Nonetheless, gaining a deeper understanding of others' ethical perspectives, promoting ethical discussions, and seeking the moral "high ground" are worthwhile pursuits.

Figure 5.2 Increasing levels of moral development

? WHAT DO YOU THINK?

Does Religion Matter in Management Ethics?

Mark Krieger and Yvonne Seng note that 72 percent of the world's population are members and practitioners of the belief and value systems of the Buddhist, Christian, Hindu, Islamic, and Jewish religions.[24] They suggest that religion influences a manager's ethical norms and inner leading, which in turn influence the manager's values and behavior, which influences how the workplace is organized and managed, which ultimately influences employee satisfaction and organizational profits.

Certainly, most of us would agree that religious beliefs can influence how a person acts in the workplace, but research findings confirming these assertions have been spotty. Ethical theorists have argued that it is one thing for someone to claim that he or she is a member of a certain religious group, but quite another for that religious affiliation to affect the individual's actions in the workplace.[25] In other words, the importance of a person's religious values is what predicts behavior, not the person's specific religious affiliation.

In one study, researchers tested this hypothesis in a sample of 1200 employees. Across a set of 16 scenarios, employees with high or moderate commitment to a religion were more likely to rate questionable or unscrupulous behavior as unethical than those who indicated low or no commitment to a religion.[26]

How does the importance of one's religion—or lack of religious belief—influence behavior? Why do you think there are differences between the ethics of people who belong to the *same* religion? Do you think the study of management ethics should include studying religious ethics?

MAINSTREAM MANAGEMENT ETHICS

A **moral point of view** refers to any particular framework of values, among many possible value frameworks, used to develop internally consistent and logically justified principles and standards of right and wrong. It acts as a sort of lens that influences how managers view the process of making ethical decisions and how they act ethically in the workplace. We will describe the moral point of view that is associated with

Moral point of view is any particular framework of values, among many possible value frameworks, used to develop internally consistent and logically justified principles and standards of right and wrong.

Mainstream management, and consider how it compares and contrasts with the different moral point of view associated with Multistream management.[27]

Obviously, a textbook like this one cannot possibly represent all the different moral points of view of management that exist. Nevertheless, once readers develop an understanding of how a moral point of view influences what ethical management looks like, then they will be well equipped to think about ethical management from their own moral point of view, whatever it is. In short, our purpose here is not to convince readers that one moral point of view is more ethical than others. Instead, the goal is to examine the assumptions and implications associated with different moral points of view, especially for Mainstream and for Multistream management.

To illustrate, consider how one of the most widely known ethical principles in the world—the so-called Golden Rule—can be agreed upon by two managers but interpreted very differently. A variation of the moral principle "Treat other people as you would like to be treated" is found in various forms across a very wide range of religious and philosophical traditions (see Table 5.2). It is certainly a good principle, but we must remember that people have different expectations of how they themselves would like to be treated. For example, some managers expect the marketplace to be a rough-and-tumble world—a more cynical variation of the Golden Rule says, "The person who has the gold makes the rules"—where everyone looks after his or her own self-interests and tries to maximize profits. In contrast, other managers may have a more collaborative vision of the marketplace, seeing it as a venue where people gather to engage in fair exchanges of goods and services. Because these two sets of managers have different expectations about how they expect to be treated, they will treat others differently.

In sum, managers' ethics are influenced by a wide variety of factors. Even if managers agree on basic ethical principles—such as the Golden Rule—their interpretation of the meaning of those principles may vary greatly depending on their moral point of view. Thus a key to the study of managerial ethics, and the goal of the rest of this chapter, is to think about how a manager's moral point of view influences behavior.

The Mainstream Moral Point of View

A managerial moral point of view can be seen as having three components:

- Its overarching goals
- A general rationale to explain why the overarching goals are worthy of pursuit
- A description of key practices that are seen as virtuous or effective[28]

TABLE 5.2

Variations of the Golden Rule

Buddhism: "Hurt not others in ways that you yourself would find hurtful." (Udana Varga 5:18)

Christianity: "Do to others as you would have them do to you." (Luke 6:31)

Confucianism: "Try your best to treat others as you would wish to be treated yourself. And you will find that this is the shortest way to benevolence." (Mencius VII.A.4)

Hinduism: "This is the sum of all true righteousness . . . Treat others, as thou wouldst thyself be treated . . ." (Mahabharaia 5:1517)

Islam: "No one of you is a believer until he desires for his brother that which he desires for himself." (Sunnah)

Judaism: "Thou shalt love thy neighbor as thyself." (Leviticus 19:18)

Taoism: "Regard your neighbor's gain as your gain . . ." (Tai Shang Kan Yin P'ien)

Source: Adapted from Deckop, J. R., Cirka, C. C., & Andersson, L. M. (2003). Doing unto others: The reciprocity of helping behavior in organizations. *Journal of Business Ethics*, 47(2), 101–113.

The three components of the materialist–individualist moral point of view associated with Mainstream management have been described as follows:[29]

- Its overarching goals are to maximize productivity, efficiency, profitability, and competitiveness.
- The general rationale is grounded in a variation of consequentialist utilitarianism, and asserts that encouraging and rewarding increases in individual material wealth is the best "generic" way to improve overall societal well-being.
- In practice, effective management focuses the four functions of management on promoting measurable improvements in productivity or profits.

In terms of moral philosophy, the Mainstream moral point of view draws from **consequentialist theory,** which considers the consequences of an action in determining what is ethical. In simple terms, this approach suggests that an action that results in beneficial outcomes (e.g., financial or social) is deemed ethical, whereas an action that results in harmful outcomes (e.g., costs) is deemed unethical.

Perhaps the best-known consequentialist theory is utilitarianism. Espoused by the nineteenth-century philosophers Jeremy Bentham and John Stuart Mill, **utilitarianism** holds that ethical managers strive to produce "the greatest good for the greatest number." Utilitarianism is usually seen as a results-oriented moral point of view that assesses decisions in terms of their consequences. In other words, the "utility" of an option is the option's benefits minus its costs. Under this approach, to be ethical a manager is expected to consider the effect of each alternative on all parties and select the one that benefits the greatest number of people.

Another consequentialist approach is **egoism.** With this approach, the utility of the option depends on the consequences for the individual decision maker. Simply stated, this approach amounts to deciding which option "benefits me the most."

Over time, a variation of consequentialism has developed that represents a Mainstream moral point of view toward ethics. Basically, this variation depends on two assumptions. The first assumption comes from determining *what* is "the greatest good." How does one measure "good"? Different people will value different consequences. Mainstream consequentialism solves this problem by essentially assuming that the best "generic" measure of good is wealth or money. Because different people will have different preferences for basic human needs (e.g., food, clothing, shelter) and because money can be used to buy each of these resources, then the best way to maximize the greatest good is by creating individual financial wealth, which people can then use according to their own preferences of what constitutes a "good life." As an example of this approach, Koch Industries, a diverse group of companies operating across a range of industries from energy to paper products, prides itself on the good it does by having efficient companies that generate sustainable profits.[30] One of Koch's key beliefs is that "the greatest value creation is one based on economic freedom, individual responsibility, and the rule of law."[31] Koch has leveraged this approach to become the largest private company in the United States.[32]

The second assumption comes from determining *how* to maximize wealth. From a Mainstream perspective, the answer is to embrace and encourage individualism (much more so than was originally suggested by utilitarianism theory). This shift to individualism is exemplified by popular interpretation of Adam Smith's (1776) idea of the "invisible hand," which suggested that collective good and the wealth of nations could be maximized by individualism (see Chapter 2).[33] The greatest good would be achieved by rewarding people for investing their resources into economic activity. In modern-day language, the greatest good for the greatest

Consequentialist theory considers the consequences of an action in determining what is ethical.

Utilitarianism is a moral philosophy that holds that ethical managers strive to produce "the greatest good for the greatest number."

Egoism is a moral philosophy that focuses on the consequences for the individual decision maker; it is based on the idea of what "benefits me the most."

number is achieved when an organization's profits are maximized on behalf of shareholders. Nobel Prize laureate Milton Friedman is the best-known advocate of this Mainstream perspective, which suggests that what is ethical for an organization is the course of action that is most profitable, within legal bounds, for its shareholders. In short, maximizing the financial return for an organization's owners expands the economy, which in turn maximizes the "good" for the larger community.

In summary, the moral point of view associated with Mainstream management is a variation of consequentialism, which suggests that the *greatest good* is *financial wealth*. Moreover, this view places particular emphasis on the financial interests of organizational owners. As a result, from a Mainstream perspective, to be an ethical manager requires producing the greatest wealth for the owners and shareholders. When applied to business, managers tend to judge the ethicality or morality of a decision based on its effect on performance measures such as productivity, efficiency, and profitability. Following such a view, for example, a Mainstream manager such as Jack Welch might conclude that laying off 20 percent of a plant's workforce is a moral and ethical action because it serves the best financial interests of the shareholders.

 WHAT DO YOU THINK?

Is Philanthropy Always Ethical?

At first thought, it seems very ethical for managers to donate money from an organization to charity. From this perspective, the general public might conclude that managers are becoming less ethical when it learns that corporate giving as a percentage of profits in the United States decreased by 50 percent over the 15 years ending in 2002.[34] In reality, although giving money to charity may seem to be a good idea generally, there are also questions about whether philanthropy is always ethical.

From a Mainstream consequentialist perspective, it is unethical for managers to donate corporate profits to charities, unless these donations can be seen to improve the corporation's bottom line. One approach that is consistent with this perspective is giving to charity to boost the organization's reputation. For example, Philip Morris gave $75 million to charity and then spent another $100 million to advertise its generosity.[35]

Another approach is suggested by strategy experts Michael Porter and Mark Kramer, who argue that social spending can indirectly benefit the bottom line in an organization.[36] For example, organizations that contribute to "The Kalamazoo Promise,"[37] a scholarship program for graduates of Kalamazoo, Michigan, public schools, get a return on their giving because the program enhances the education of their potential workforce. Furthermore, because this program is attractive to current and future employees, it can improve recruiting and retention rates for employees of the donor organizations. Finally, the prospect of more educated employees living and working in Kalamazoo is likely to spur community development that contributes to improved support services and more business partners for participating organizations.

While there may be some debate about the ethicality of managers donating *corporate* profits, consequentialists agree that it is ethical for investors to give their *own* money to charity. Even so, it has been suggested that sometimes such philanthropy may be little more than a tool to improve the donor's public image and influence over government. For example, in the early 1900s, John D. Rockefeller, Sr., pledged $50 million to start a foundation to promote well-being in the United States and beyond; his critics assumed that Rockefeller was trying to use his wealth to manipulate public opinion at a time when the U.S. Congress was breaking up his Standard Oil Company monopoly.[38] Some also questioned the business practices that contributed to his estimated annual income of $100 million, when the average U.S. family was earning only $500 per year.[39]

Is philanthropy more ethical if it does not benefit the financial interests of the giver? Is philanthropy more ethical if comes from profits that were generated in a socially responsible manner? Put differently, do the "ends" (i.e., giving money to charity) justify the "means" (i.e., whether the money was generated in a socially responsible manner)?

The Mainstream Process of Making Ethical Decisions

Figure 5.1 provides an overview of the discussion presented in this section. We have seen how different sources of management ethics contribute to different moral points of view. We have also described the consequentialist moral point of view associated with the Mainstream approach. This moral point of view, in combination with other characteristics of the organizational context and the manager's personality, has an effect on each phase of the process of making ethical decisions.[40] The process of ethical decision making encompasses four steps:

1. Recognizing ethical issues (**define**)
2. Gathering information and developing alternatives (**discover**)
3. Wrestling with ethical choices (**discern**)
4. Implementing ethical intentions (**deliver**)

This process influences how managers put into practice the four management functions: planning, leading, organizing, and controlling.

RECOGNIZE ETHICAL ISSUES. Managers' moral points of view act as a lens that determines what they see (and what they do not see) as ethical issues, and how they respond to those issues. For example, stealing office supplies or not putting in an honest day's work is wrong, as is accepting bribes, sexually harassing employees, and falsifying accounting reports. These actions can both cost an organization quite a bit of money (either in operating expenses or legal fines) and damage the organization's reputation. Managers see these activities as ethical issues because they undermine the overarching goals of the Mainstream moral point of view—to maximize productivity, efficiency, profits, and competitiveness. From this moral point of view, overpaying employees, donating money to charity, and voluntarily reducing the pollution generated by the organization also may be seen as ethical issues because these actions can, perhaps, reduce profits. For example, donating money to charity is not necessarily unethical, but the point is that the money belongs to the firm's owners, who should be allowed to choose whether to give it to charity and which charity should receive it.

Ethical definition is identifying a situation or behavior as having ethical implications.

Ethical discovery is the process of gathering information and developing alternatives.

Ethical discernment is evaluating various alternatives to choose the best course of action.

Ethical delivery is demonstrating courage to implement an ethical choice even if it is contrary to the prevailing norms and may have some negative consequences.

"We're supposed to attend a conference on business-casual ethics."

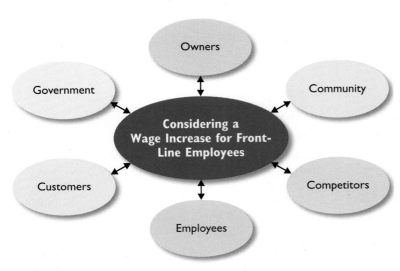

Figure 5.3   A possible stake-holder map for Home Depot

Once general awareness of an ethical issue has been raised, managers need to define more precisely the ethical issue. For example, is it an issue for all employees, or just for some? An important part of this step is to define the key stakeholders. The issue does not exist in a vacuum; it exists in the context of a system with other stakeholders. Managers might ask themselves this question: "Who will be influenced by my choice?" The answer will almost always include the organization's owners, and it may include managers, coworkers, other employees or departments, customers, suppliers, government, community members, and even the environment.

To avoid overlooking the many stakeholders involved in an ethical decision, managers can draw out a stakeholder map—a visual representation of who might be influenced by the decision. Figure 5.3 shows a possible stakeholder map for Home Depot. Although a Mainstream view considers the manager's priority to be the interests of the firm's owners, sometimes the concerns of other stakeholders need to be addressed because of their impact on profitability. For example, as illustrated in Figure 5.3, a decision to increase the starting wage for employees at a local Home Depot store may satisfy employees, benefit the community, and attract employees from competitors—but it might also anger critical customers, such as contractors who pay similarly skilled workers less money. If these customers move their business to a competitor, their reaction will decrease profits for the owners of Home Depot stock.

GATHER INFORMATION AND DEVELOP ALTERNATIVES.   Individuals' moral points of view influence not only their awareness of what makes something an ethical issue, but also how they collect data and what sorts of alternatives are generated. Some managers are quick to make ethical judgments based on the information readily at hand, whereas other managers are inclined to collect more information to minimize their likelihood of making ethical mistakes. In general, gathering more information tends to make for better decisions. Part of the information-gathering process may entail an examination of existing codes of ethics or policies. It is also helpful to collect background information on how the issue came to be and what its possible causes are. Although many issues are unique, other people may have wrestled with a similar issue: Did they resolve it satisfactorily, or did the issue blow up in their faces? A key stakeholder might also have critical information or a different perspective. This raises a new question: Who should provide input? Not only is input likely to contribute to making a better choice, but it also increases perceptions of fairness in the eyes of those who might be influenced by the decision. Mainstream managers may seek the input of a variety of stakeholders, but are likely to be primarily interested in hearing the views of their owners regarding the issue under consideration.

Research shows that the best decisions are made by comparing alternatives or options. On the face of it, each ethical issue probably has at least two options. For example, even a decision such as being asked to tell a lie has two options: to lie or to not lie. Managers ask themselves, "What are my current options?" and "What are some creative options?" With a bit more consideration, additional options usually

MANAGEMENT IN PRACTICE

How Do Managers Actually Make Ethical Decisions?

Researchers in one study wanted to determine the relative importance of various factors in how managers actually made ethical decisions. They questioned managers a year after they had graduated from the Harvard MBA program.[41] These former students had all taken a course on business ethics, and many now worked in organizations that had an explicit code of ethics, offered ethics training, and had top management teams who communicated the importance of ethics. Even with all this support, the young managers participating in the study stated that their most important external source for determining the ethicality of the decisions was their family: "Can I comfortably tell my parents what I did?" They also looked inside themselves, invoking what might be called the Sleep Test: "If I do this, can I fall asleep at night? When I look at myself in the mirror in the morning, will I see the kind of person I want to be?"

In addition, the researchers identified four rules of thumb that managers had learned on the job to help them make ethical decisions:

1. Performance is what really counts, so make your numbers.
2. Be loyal and demonstrate that you are a team player.
3. Don't break the law.
4. Don't *over*-invest in ethical behavior.

Perhaps the most discouraging finding emerged in the responses that managers gave when asked if fear of being punished motivated them to do the *right* thing: They indicated that the fear of punishment motivated them to do the *wrong* thing! The research also pointed out that ethics are indeed a slippery slope; once a manager starts acting unethically, his or her behavior will worsen.

In another study in which researchers interviewed managers about how they handle ethical decisions, the main conclusion indicated that ethical decision making is often fraught with pressures from powerful people in the organization. The conclusion was that in the minds of many managers, "What is right is what the guy above you wants you to do."[42]

become evident. Sometimes we can be so absorbed in a situation that we need to ask others to identify possible options; their input can give us a neutral or fresh perspective on the issue at hand.

EVALUATE OPTIONS AND CHOOSE WISELY. In this step, the options are weighed against one another, and the manager's moral point of view influences which alternative is chosen. Some decisions are relatively easy to make, but often managers feel as if they need to choose among the "lesser of two evils," such as when two or more stakeholders are likely to be harmed by the decision. For example, a manufacturing plant may be producing waste at a level that is harmful to the environment but is within legal and industry standards. The decision to voluntarily implement additional pollution control measures may be complicated by the fact that these measures will increase the cost of doing business. The higher costs might result in higher prices for customers, reduced profits for owners, or layoffs of workers. How managers weigh the interests of various stakeholders is influenced by their moral point of view.

IMPLEMENT THE ETHICAL DECISION. Managers implement their ethical decisions by performing the four management functions. Implementing ethical decisions in some cases is relatively straightforward given their consistency with the norms of society, the organization, or leaders. In other cases, what is ethical to a manager is contrary to the prevailing norms and may have negative consequences. To move forward in such cases requires courageously challenging ethical norms. Courage is the middle ground between fearful inaction and fearless rashness.[43] Courage may be called for when a manager realizes that an action that results in short-term gain for a firm and its owners will result in long-term pain.

An example of courageously challenging ethical norms can be seen in the actions of Enron's Sherron Watkins. She identified questionable accounting practices within Enron and, despite being told she did not have the support of her superiors, continued her investigation. Initially, Watkins reported the claims anonymously in a memo to Chairman and CEO Ken Lay, but she later discussed the issue with Lay directly.[44] Nonetheless, based on the advice of external legal counsel, Lay decided nothing was illegal or worth correcting. Watkins put herself on the line, despite the potential negative consequences for herself, in hopes of correcting the problems and benefiting the company and its shareholders.

Following through on difficult decisions can be facilitated by support from others. Certainly, support internally, in the form of powerful coworkers or leaders, is ideal but not always available or known. For example, Sherron Watkins had an ally in Vince Kaminski, an executive in risk management at Enron, but it appears that she was unaware of Kaminski's potential support and his independent actions to stem the tide of unethical behavior at Enron.[45]

Whistleblowers are organizational insiders who identify unethical behavior and have the courage to report it, even though doing so may personally cost them promotions, their jobs, and possibly their reputations. As an internal auditor for WorldCom, Cynthia Cooper exposed $3.8 billion in fraudulent accounting practices, which led to a bankruptcy that cost shareholders more than $175 billion.[46] Watkins and Cooper were applauded for their behavior, but often whistleblowers are not rewarded for their efforts; indeed, many are punished or fired. From a Mainstream moral point of view, whistleblowing may be encouraged if it exposes actions that put profit or the financial viability of the organization at risk. Complicating matters for some managers are situations where questionable behavior appears to be good for the organization's financial bottom line, and is not likely to be discovered or perceived as having negative long-term effects. Under these circumstances, some people may rationalize that fraud, misinformation, or manipulation is acceptable.

> **Whistleblowers** are organizational insiders who identify unethical behavior and display the courage to report it.

Mainstream Ethical Influences on the Four Management Functions

A manager's moral point of view can be expressed in each of the four functions of management. Managers make goal setting and resource allocation decisions within the company (planning), implement structures and systems that facilitate and measure progress toward those goals (organizing), act as role models (leading), and create and monitor an organization's formal and informal control systems (controlling). In each of these four functions of management, the manager communicates—either directly or indirectly—his or her ethics and values.

PLANNING: GOALS AND RESPONSIBILITIES. The goals and responsibilities entrusted to people are powerful influences on behavior. They are a crucial aspect of how Mainstream managers try to create an ethical workplace. Mainstream managers know that although goals can have a positive effect in directing people's efforts toward important organizational outcomes, they

Sherron Watkins testified before Congress regarding the accounting practices and leadership behaviors that led to the financial collapse of Enron Corporation.

also have a dark side sometimes. The drive to meet goals can detract from ethical behavior or even encourage unethical behavior that harms the organization and other stakeholders.[47] Ed Rust, CEO and chairman of State Farm Insurance, remarked:

> Business leaders urge their subordinates to do "whatever it takes" to meet the goals. Even when strong ethics are present at the top, the "whatever it takes" message can get distorted as it cascades down through the ranks. "Whatever it takes" can be interpreted literally as an order without conditions, without limitations. That at the very least, it means one should push the boundaries of the law and internal standards to reach a goal and, if necessary, even quietly cross those boundaries so we can "make the numbers." And, as we've seen time and again, more than a few people, when pushed, are willing to modify, to rationalize their thinking and their actions so they can be seen as successful in difficult and challenging circumstances, as willing to do "whatever it takes" to get the job done.[48]

Managers have numerous goals, but two are especially important from a Mainstream moral point of view:

- Managers are ethically obligated to primarily serve the interests of the organization's owners.
- Consistent with the utilitarianism perspective, Mainstream managers should maximize organizational profits because this is assumed to be the best way to maximize the greatest good for the greatest number in society.

With these two goals in place, it follows that actions that undermine profit maximization may be unethical, even if they promote other valuable causes. This idea is consistent with Milton Friedman's basic argument that business managers should focus on their organization-specific responsibilities, and leave broader issues such as social justice and ecological sustainability to others (e.g., governments, charitable organizations). Indeed, in a fast-paced globalized marketplace, maintaining financial viability is challenging enough on its own without adding social and ecological responsibilities. Proponents of this perspective would argue that organizational profits rightfully belong to the organization's owners, to dispose of as they wish, and that managers do not have the right to use that money for any other cause, no matter how worthy. Besides, corporate managers are already too powerful—adding social and ecological issues to their role would simply make them even more powerful. Moreover, there is concern that many corporate managers may lack the expertise to make appropriate judgments as to which social and ecological initiatives should be supported.

ORGANIZING: STRUCTURES AND SYSTEMS. Structures and systems can reinforce ethical or unethical behavior. For example, the official values espoused in formal organizational codes may be ignored if the reward systems reinforce something else.[49] Enron is a well-known example of an organization whose corporate statements espoused the value of ethics, but whose systems contributed to performance pressures that encouraged unethical behavior. The firm's human resources management system had a practice of ranking employees and then "yanking" or firing the lowest-ranking employees.[50] Ironically, the lucrative rewards for performance and innovation were keys to Enron's early success and growth, before excesses in pursuit of these goals contributed to the ethical failures that ultimately destroyed the company. Managers need to be attentive to precisely which behaviors their organization's reward systems reinforce. Sometimes the unintended consequences of a seemingly reasonable reward system can undermine the ethical behavior of employees.

The Mainstream approach to ethics often focuses on creating systems that identify and punish unethical behavior. This **deterrent approach** is based on the assumption that misconduct often comes from rational calculations about the likelihood of getting caught and the severity of the punishments compared to the potential "benefits" of misconduct.[51] The deterrent approach increases awareness of what is unethical and provides fair warning of the consequences for those who are caught in such behavior.

Management can also signal the importance of ethics by creating formal positions within the organizational hierarchy that are devoted to ethics. For example, Wal-Mart has created the position of "director of global ethics," perhaps in response to a wave of bad publicity that highlighted discrimination lawsuits filed against the firm, questionable approaches to employee benefits, and padding of expense accounts by top executives.[52] Although this measure may be perceived as a defensive response, it may also be a proactive attempt to formally support ethics and direct resources toward reducing ethical violations. To be effective, such positions must be more than a window dressing; a position such as a director of ethics or an ethics officer must have access to and the support of top management.

Another systematic way that managers can shape the ethical behavior of the organization's members is by providing ethics training. Ethics training seeks to help employees understand specific ethical aspects of decision making and incorporate the organization's ethical standards into their daily behavior. Approximately 25 percent of U.S. businesses provide ethics training on a regular basis, and another 20 percent provide it on an "as needed" basis.[53] One study noted that programs containing four specific elements—standards, training, advice lines, and reporting systems—were linked with a 78 percent greater likelihood that employees would report unethical conduct.[54]

Despite their increasing popularity, ethical training seminars, workshops, and programs are not without their critics. Many suggest that they have little effect because people establish their individual value systems when they are very young. Others argue that teaching ethical problem solving and reviewing real-world models of both ethical and unethical behavior can make a difference.[55] Following this line of thought, many organizations offer ethics training that emphasizes problem-solving skills and explains the organization's standards of conduct. A few training programs even include instruction on the Federal Sentencing Guidelines related to corporate misconduct.[56]

LEADING: IMPLICIT AND EXPLICIT ACTION. Ethical leadership has been defined as "the demonstration of normatively appropriate conduct through personal actions and interpersonal relationships."[57] That is, ethical leadership is more than talk; it is the walk of leaders. The ethical behavior of managers—especially top management—has a great influence on the behavior of other members of the same organization, because managers act as role models for the rest of the organization. Peter Holt, CEO of Holt Companies, manages by a clear set of ethical values.[58] Holt visits each of the firm's locations twice a year to meet with employees, answer questions, and talk about the importance of each employee upholding the organization's core values every day in every action. Within both large and small organizations, employees are acutely aware of their bosses' ethical strengths and lapses. For example, if managers act according to a Mainstream

---

Deterrent approach is based on the assumption that misconduct is related to rational calculations pertaining to the severity of the associated punishments compared to the potential "benefits" of misconduct.

utilitarian moral point of view, and if they talk about and act as though maximizing shareholder wealth is the primary goal of the organization, then members will act and begin to think the same way. Conversely, if managers bend the rules to suit their own self-interests, it can be expected that other members will begin to act in a similar fashion. This is consistent with the research on self-fulfilling prophecy described in Chapter 2: Subordinates fulfill the expectations that their managers have for them.

Research shows that leaders who are perceived to be ethical use reward systems to hold people accountable for ethical behavior.[59] At Holt Companies, the organization's evaluation and reward systems are explicitly tied to how well managers and employees live the values in their everyday actions. Consistently rewarding ethical behavior, disciplining unethical conduct at all levels, and setting realistic performance goals for others are crucial components of ethical leadership. In other words, from a Mainstream perspective, ethics is viewed as a transaction whereby leaders reward ethical behavior and punish unethical behavior.

CONTROLLING: FORMAL AND INFORMAL. Managers' moral points of view also are evident in how they control the ethical behavior of organizational members. A commonly implemented measure for exerting control is an organization's code of ethics. A **code of ethics** is a formal written statement of an organization's primary values and the ethical rules it expects its employees to abide by. More than 90 percent of corporations have a formal code of ethics, one-half have value statements, and about one-third have credos.[60] A code of ethics is designed to serve as a guideline for how to behave in situations where ethical dilemmas are likely to arise. It may also give instructions that detail how employees are to treat suppliers, customers, competitors, and other constituents. The code of ethics should also state the values and behavior that will *not* be tolerated, and the ensuing punishment for such actions.

Of course, an organization's formal code of ethics may or may not be aligned with how its members actually act. Codes of ethics by no means ensure universal ethical conduct, but they do formally state the ethical expectations of top managers. Ultimately, the value of any formal code of ethics rests on how it is used by organizational managers and members.

In addition to formal means of control such as codes of ethics, organizational control is also achieved informally. This may be most evident in **organizational culture,** which is the set of informal shared values, norms, standards, and expectations that influence the ways in which individuals, teams, and groups interact with one another and work toward company goals.[61] Put differently, an organization's culture is its set of unwritten codes of conduct. This culture is a powerful influence on the ethical conduct of its members.[62] It specifies which beliefs and behaviors are "really" encouraged and which are not tolerated. For most of us, doing something we know is wrong becomes easier when "everyone else is doing it." In particular, the behavior and moral point of view of managers is a strong influence in setting and maintaining the "ethical tone" of the organization's culture.[63]

Organizational culture has been cited as a critical factor in numerous ethical failures. For example, a performance culture that discouraged dissension and dismissed ethical considerations in favor of meeting schedules and controlling costs is said to have contributed to the National Aeronautics and Space Administration's (NASA) *Columbia* and *Challenger* space shuttle disasters.[64]

Code of ethics is a formal written statement of an organization's primary values and the ethical rules it expects its members to abide by.

Organizational culture is the set of informal shared values, norms, standards for behavior, and expectations that influence the ways in which individuals, teams, and groups interact with one another and cooperate to achieve company goals.

MULTISTREAM MANAGEMENT ETHICS

The Multistream Moral Point of View

Just as a materialist–individualist moral point of view influences Mainstream ethical decisions, so too a Multistream moral point of view forms a basis for making ethical decisions and putting them into practice. The three components of a Multistream moral point of view have been described as follows:[65]

- Its overarching goals are to provide meaningful work, operate sustainably, be attentive to internal and external stakeholders, and facilitate servant leadership.
- The general rationale is grounded in virtue theory, and asserts that practicing and fostering virtuous character is the best "generic" way to improve overall societal well-being.
- In practice, effective management focuses the four management functions on promoting overall well-being in community.

Virtue theory is a moral philosophy closely associated with the Multistream approach to management.[66] **Virtue theory** focuses on character and the ways in which people practice and facilitate the practice of virtues in community, thereby facilitating happiness, which Aristotle called the "supreme good."[67] **Virtues** are good ways of acting that are noble or have value *regardless* of the end result or consequences. Recall from Chapter 1 that from a virtue theory perspective, the purpose of management is not to maximize productivity, efficiency, and profitability, nor is it to maximize self-interest. Rather, the purpose of management is to maximize peoples' *happiness* or *well-being* by practicing virtues in community or in organizations.

Virtue theory, as applied to organizations, focuses on the character of managers and organizational members.[68] A focus on character offers guidance and constraints, but avoids *legalistic* rules. In this sense, a manager may do one thing in one situation and a different thing in another situation, yet both actions may be an expression of the same virtue, without being a rule. A virtue approach turns its attention to answerable questions such as "Is this consistent with who I am or aspire to be" rather than the often unanswerable question of "What is the right thing to do?"[69] Rather than focus on the impossible task of trying to design a perfect management and social structure (all structures are prone to abuse, although some structures are less oppressive than others), the goal is to freely facilitate virtue and thereby happiness within any social structure.

Although a Multistream moral point of view can be characterized by many virtues, the following four key virtues are typically found in the context of organizations:

- Service
- Human development

Virtue theory is a moral philosophy that focuses on character and how people practice and facilitate the practice of virtues in community, and thereby facilitate happiness.

Virtues are good ways of acting that are noble or have value regardless of the end result or consequences.

Plato and Aristotle (right) are at the center of a larger mural entitled *School of Athens*, which was painted by artist Raphael. The larger painting is an imagined gathering of famous Greek philosophers.

Two Additional Moral Points of View

This chapter has briefly described two moral philosophies: (1) an approach to consequentialism, which places a high emphasis on both materialism and individualism, and (2) a variation of virtue theory, which places a relatively low emphasis on both materialism and individualism.

But what about managers with a relatively *low-materialist, high-individualist* emphasis? The moral point of view of such managers may be best described by a specific version of the **moral-rights view,** which stems from the teachings of John Locke and Thomas Jefferson. This view asserts that managers should strive to maintain and protect the fundamental rights and privileges of individuals. From this perspective, an ethical decision is one that protects individual rights to privacy, free speech, life and safety, and due process. It would include, for example, protecting the free speech rights of employees who report legal violations by their employers. This emphasis on the protection of the rights of stakeholders trumps both the utilitarian emphasis on productivity and efficiency and the virtue theory emphasis on character.

Some employment policies, such as employment at will (where a manager can fire a person without due cause), have been argued to be contrary to the moral-rights view, but critics of this perspective counter that expanding and legislating the list of what is considered a "moral right" may, in fact, limit other individual rights. For example, if legislation or policy prohibits employment at will, it restricts the freedom of employees in a market system to choose less job security in ex-change for more pay—a choice that many young professionals may favor.[70]

Similarly, managers who have a relatively *high-materialist, low-individualist* perspective may be guided by yet another moral point of view. The **justice approach** involves evaluating decisions and behaviors with regard to how benefits and harms are distributed among individuals and groups. The emphasis here is on ensuring that *all* members are given their due; owners and managers of the organization enjoy no special privilege or priority. A justice approach highlights the need for people to be treated consistently and with dignity, so that even members with little formal power are treated fairly. For some, distributing resources fairly and impartially across the organization may mean that everyone receives the *same* amount (equality). For others, distributing resources fairly takes *need* into account. Still others believe that fair distribution is related to a person's relative *contributions* or inputs.[71]

Together with the Mainstream perspective (relatively high in materialist and individualist values) and the Multistream perspective (relatively low in materialistic and individualistic values), the moral-rights and justice perspectives provide four of potentially many moral points of view. Considering other points of view helps us understand other people and may serve to improve our own perspective. Perhaps other moral points of view, if not serving as the primary foundation for a manager's ethics, may at least be secondary considerations that supplement or constrain a manager's dominant moral point of view.[72]

- Nurturing community
- Balance

First, a service ethic suggests that managers should see themselves as serving others, thereby facilitating others to get their work done. From this perspective, the organization exists to serve its employees, rather than the employees existing to serve the organization.[73]

Second, Multistream managers view work as a means for people to express themselves and to grow. The focus is not merely on achieving rational efficiency, but also on assigning tasks and designing jobs so that people develop capabilities and are given opportunities to express something of who they are and what they are passionate about doing. That is, Multistream managers consider the growth and development of organizational members as a worthwhile end in and of itself.[74]

Third, with regard to nurturing community, Multistream managers actively listen to and seek ways to satisfy the interests of all stakeholders. They nurture community by providing opportunities for different stakeholders to hear one another's concerns. In this way, stakeholders grow to understand one another better and are more likely to treat one another with dignity and respect. Aaron Feuerstein modeled this concern for the community in the opening case.

Moral-rights view is a moral philosophy concerned with maintaining and protecting the fundamental rights and privileges of individuals.

Justice approach is a moral philosophy concerned with how benefits and harms are distributed among individuals and groups.

Sustaincentrism is a perspective promoting balance between the human and ecological concerns in organizational endeavors.

Finally, Multistream managers value balance. More specifically, they promote **sustaincentrism.** In other words, they seek to achieve a *balance* between human and ecological concerns, avoiding the extremes of disregard for the environment and putting the environment over human needs. This perspective recognizes the interconnectedness and complexity of the relationship between humankind and the environment.[75]

The Multistream Process of Making Ethical Decisions

RECOGNIZE ETHICAL ISSUES.   As we have discussed, the kinds of ethical issues a manager becomes aware of are, in part, determined by his or her unique moral point of view.[76] Because Multistream management is sensitive to a wider variety of forms of well-being and virtue, managers may consider a broader range of ethical issues. Examples include ecological sustainability and social justice issues (some of which may overlap with the concerns of owners and other stakeholders). Furthermore, Multistream managers will be sensitive to issues of employee development, treating everyone with dignity, and empowering people.

Of course, the Multistream moral point of view can be more complicated because it requires managers to be aware of multiple forms of well-being for multiple stakeholders. Consider the Hobby Lobby retail store. A Mainstream manager at a competing craft store is likely to set store hours with an eye toward profitability. At Hobby Lobby, stores are closed on Sundays, in recognition that Sundays hold religious and family significance for many of the firm's employees.

This is not to say that a Mainstream moral point of view does not consider the needs of organizational members or is not aware of social justice or ecological sustainability concerns. It can, but only insofar as these considerations remain *secondary* initiatives that support the *primary* purpose of enhancing shareholder wealth. For this reason, many proponents of the Mainstream point of view try to justify corporate social responsibility by arguing that it *enhances* an organization's financial performance.[77] As such, Mainstream managers may be sensitive to environmental concerns to the extent that this effort *maximizes* financial returns, but in the same manner they are likely to turn a "blind eye" to these concerns if there is no clear link between such initiatives and profit maximization.[78] In contrast, Multistream managers consider such issues, regardless of whether they maximize profits.

To illustrate how a Multistream moral point of view heightens the awareness of managers to certain issues, consider Tom Briggens, who had worked his way to the top of the hierarchy in a large national organization. The climb was intense, and the politics and jockeying for position with other managers was, at times, quite rough-and-tumble. After a successful career at the top, Briggens became deliberately downwardly mobile. In the past

decade, he has worked as a manager in various inner-city organizations trying to facilitate economic development among the urban poor. He has a highly honed set of political and negotiating skills that he can use to promote his cause, but he tempers his use of those skills with an awareness that there are many other worthy causes and stakeholders:

> Part of that is, for example, [my awareness about] what sort of presence I bring to a meeting. When I go into a room and interact with people, how does it feel to them? Do I bring out a healing influence, or do I would bring more of an influence that creates mistrust or a feeling of inadequacy? How the folks feel about the encounter is a really important issue to me. I try to really work at the kind of experience I'm having with personal interactions. What that means to me is not bringing a competitive spirit into a room, trying not to bring an aggressive spirit into a room, trying not to bring too assertive a spirit into a room. The difficulty is that a lot of where I live my life is a pretty competitive environment. There's a difference in simply being a doormat (and letting people walk all over you) and bringing this more shalom[79] type of mood into your dealings. And I have not found a good way to resolve that tension. I find that I'm frequently tempted to become competitive, to let my point of view dominate or prevail, and to try to bring power toward myself or towards the organization that I represent at the expense of somebody else. Because that's what they're doing, they are trying to bring power toward them, they are trying to have their point of view win out, et cetera. I find it very hard to not be a doormat, but also not play the game in a way lots of others play it.[80]

This quote from Briggens illustrates the ethical tensions that occur when managers are aware of multiple forms of well-being, rather than have a singular focus on the financial well-being of their employers.

GATHER INFORMATION AND DEVELOP ALTERNATIVES. Like their Mainstream counterparts, Multistream managers facilitate ethical decision making by gathering information. However, the process has different emphases in terms of the kinds and sources of information that Multistream managers gather. In particular, Multistream management invites participation from a wider spectrum of stakeholders. This approach is more receptive to stakeholders' personal experiences and needs, rather than just paying attention to codified information and documents.

For example, Janet Mungabe, a Multistream human resources manager, was having a meeting with an employee who had drug addiction problems. Mungabe knew the policies, but deliberately took time to listen to her employee.

> So I looked at the man and I asked: "How does this make you feel?" And here's this really big tough guy, who had spent a number of years in prison, and who was one of our [troublemakers], and I suspected he was one of the guys who had brought drugs into the plant and I just hadn't been able to prove it yet. So he wasn't, at the moment, one of my favorite people. And he looked at me, and tears started coming out of his eyes, and he said: "It reminded me of being a little kid." The man broke down and started telling me about his abuse as a child. And here I am sitting, listening to this, thinking: "God, I almost missed it."
>
> Three months later, he was in a drug rehabilitation program and coming to terms with his abuse. For him to have a manager say that they had also been abused and addicted opens doors for people to see that there are opportunities to escape their situations. And I listened to him. He was vulnerable and I allowed myself to become vulnerable. . . . And you know what, I can give you examples like that for almost every day. Can you imagine how that blesses me!? Can you imagine how rich I am? It's unbelievable![81]

Because of her Multistream moral point of view, Mungabe took the time to listen to and learn from the drug addicts in her firm, even though this activity would likely not improve her employer's profits. Her approach enabled her to think about alternatives that might never get noted in policy manuals. Of course, Mungabe's approach might not be advisable in every situation, particularly if even one relapse would put others' safety at risk. No doubt other Mainstream managers would also try to help drug addicts, but perhaps in different ways, because spending time with employees to address their personal problems might be seen as an inefficient (and thus unethical) use of the owners' time and money.

EVALUATE OPTIONS AND CHOOSE WISELY.   When practical, Multistream managers welcome the input from stakeholders affected by a decision, and invite those stakeholders to participate in making the decision. If stakeholders are involved in gathering information and developing alternatives, then they have the information and capacity to participate in evaluating options and making wise choices. Multistream managers follow this path not only because it often improves the quality of the decision, but because they also see it as the right thing to do, even if the decision turns out to be a poor one. For example, William Pollard, former CEO and chairman of ServiceMaster, believes it to be immoral to exclude employees from decision making that affects them.[82]

In other cases, participation of other stakeholders in making decisions may be indirect, as illustrated in the chapter-opening case, where the perspectives of multiple stakeholders were weighed heavily by the manager in the decision-making process. Surely Aaron Feuerstein considered all his options in light of the comments he heard at the community coffee shop or when interacting with his employees. From a Mainstream perspective, his alternatives would be quickly narrowed down to either relocating to places with less expensive labor costs or taking the insurance money and enjoying an early retirement. Instead, Feuerstein considered a broader array of options, and he ultimately chose an option with more risk and a lower probability of financial return for himself. Even though his firm eventually went bankrupt (for a variety of reasons), it was still the right thing for him to have done. For Feuerstein, failing to act on his moral point of view would have been far riskier than acting on what he believed to be right. For example, what if Feuerstein had listened to conventional wisdom, and the company failed anyway? Or, what if he followed conventional wisdom and made a ton of money with offshore workers, while his former employees in Lawrence suffered?

This discussion is not meant to suggest that Multistream ethical decisions are easy or do not require compromise. It can be time-consuming and difficult to take into account the competing needs of various stakeholders. Compromise is still necessary, but it may be a different kind of compromise than that which characterizes the Mainstream approach. Rather than grudgingly giving up something to get an agreement, stakeholders often are happy to compromise when they understand the needs and interests of others. Furthermore, involving stakeholders may lead to the development of new options that satisfy even more stakeholders.

IMPLEMENT THE ETHICAL DECISION.   It can require courage to act according to a Multistream moral point of view, especially if the actions are novel or may threaten the firm's financial viability. Implementing decisions that consider the interests of a broad set of stakeholders—some powerful and others not—is a road less traveled. This sentiment is captured in a story told by Tom Briggens:

> I remember an aboriginal elder once in this community had been asked to start a meeting with the prayer. His prayer was: "God, we ask you not for an easy life, but for a good life." And I was really struck by the distinction between a "good life" and an "easy life."

And I think often, when we say that we want a nice life, we mean an easy life. Sure, there's a little more tension when you are accountable to a team rather than to only a manager, but I think that there is a whole mix of relationships happening there that makes life richer, even if it makes it a little more complicated.

Of course, not all initiatives from a Multistream moral point of view have negative effects on an organization's financial performance. Indeed, implementing such initiatives can be associated with improved financial performance. This benefit may emerge thanks to lower costs from becoming more energy efficient or enjoying the fruits of a more loyal and motivated workforce as a result of empowering others. The CEO of a large organization describes why he implemented initiatives to improve the quality of work life for people in his organization, and what happened after he did:

> While I recognized . . . that by improving people's quality of work life there would be pay-offs to the company, in productivity, efficiency, etc., I also knew that wasn't the ultimate issue for me, that wasn't why I was interested in quality of work life. I was interested in it for that reason, but I was also interested in it because I believed in it in terms of this issue of human dignity. . . . We had fabulous results. For four years we had unprecedented performance.[83]

Because the Multistream moral point of view places so much emphasis on listening to a variety of stakeholders when making ethical decisions, managers who follow this approach are often more open to adapting to the new circumstances once the decision has been implemented. If a decision is not having the desired effect, everyone knows about it and will be more amenable to revising the solution so as to achieve the desired outcomes. In this way, Multistream decisions are more experimental, such that change readily emerges from their ongoing evaluation by a community of stakeholders.

Multistream Ethical Influences on the Four Management Functions

PLANNING: GOALS AND RESPONSIBILITIES. Like their Mainstream counterparts, Multistream managers use goals to direct attention and increase effort toward important outcomes. Nonetheless, the type and scope of these goals are likely to differ in comparison with those outlined by Mainstream managers. Multistream goals tend to be balanced in terms of the amount of attention paid to the financial and other needs of multiple stakeholder groups.[84] In contrast, the Mainstream focus of goals is primarily on profit for shareholders.

Kenneth Goodpaster describes an excessive and narrow focus on one primary goal as evidence of **teleopathy,** a disease (*pathy*) that entails an addiction to the unbalanced pursuit of a single purpose or goal (*teleo*).[85] Like persons with other addictions, those who have teleopathy are fixated on the pursuit of satisfying their goal, are prone to rationalizing its supreme worth in relation to other goals, and, ultimately, are likely to detach themselves from their normal ethical inclinations. In other words, they pursue a goal at all costs with little regard for other goals and seem to have no conscience. A person with teleopathy may be laudably described as being loyal, driven, dedicated, and enthusiastic, but selecting or promoting a person with such traits in excess can amount to "a deal with the devil" whereby one achieves the goal but loses one's soul.[86]

Table 5.3 contrasts and compares some of the differences in assumptions between the Mainstream and Multistream moral points of view. The Mainstream view is more consistent with the classical view that emphasizes the **organization-specific responsibility (OSR)** of managers to ensure that plans serve the financial interests and goals

Teleopathy is an addiction to the unbalanced pursuit of a single purpose or goal.

Organization-specific responsibility (OSR) is the managers' obligation to ensure that plans serve the financial interests and goals of the organization's owner(s).

TABLE 5.3

Assumptions About Social Responsibilities

	Mainstream View (OSR)	Multistream View (CSR)
1. Management is ethically obligated to . . .	the organization's owners.	*all* organizational stakeholders.
2. The general public wants organizations . . .	that maximize profits.	that take care of economic and social goals.
3. Managers who pursue CSR actions . . .	tend to weaken financial performance.	enhance financial viability in the long term.
4. The costs of CSR are . . .	too high (let someone else pay).	lower than long-run non-CSR costs.
5. Caring for the natural environment . . .	dilutes the purpose of organizations.	enhances organizations' long-term sustainability.
6. Businesses . . .	know how to make money but lack CSR skills.	have resources needed by the public and charities.
7. Social justice is the responsibility of . . .	the government and, ultimately, the consumer.	government, management, and consumers.
8. The power of organizations in society . . .	is too great already (and CSR would add to it).	obligates them to become more responsible.
9. Managers who pursue CSR initiatives . . .	exercise power without accountability.	reduce the need for government regulation.

Corporate social responsibility (CSR) refers to managers' obligation to act in ways that protect and improve the welfare of society over and above the owners' (e.g., stockholders) self-interests.

of the organization's owners. The Multistream view is consistent with the growing interest in **corporate social responsibility (CSR),** which refers to managers' obligation to act in ways that protect and improve the welfare of society *over and above* the owners' financial self-interests. Multistream managers recognize their OSR responsibilities, but they do not always act to *maximize* financial well-being. Rather, they explicitly acknowledge that while financial sustainability is clearly a necessary obligation, they also should actively work toward meeting their obligations to other stakeholders, including the natural environment and future generations. Multistream managers believe that because organizations create many of the problems that need to be addressed, such as air and water pollution and resource depletion, those same organizations should be heavily involved in solving these problems.

Managers can assess their organization's performance in relation to community needs, employment practices, diversity practices, and general philanthropy. Ultimately, assessing all of these areas serves to help an organization form a picture of its approach to OSR/CSR. A formal method of achieving this understanding is through a **social audit,** a systematic analysis of the effects that an organization is having on its stakeholders and society as a whole. Four primary areas are often covered in a social audit:

Social audit is a systematic analysis of the effect that an organization is having on its stakeholders and society as a whole.

1. Assessing an organization's economic responsibility: Is it profitable?
2. Is it meeting all its legal responsibilities?
3. Are its ethical responsibilities being met?
4. Is the organization contributing to the broader community?

Social audits are helpful because they spell out and underscore the emphasis put on following an organization's ethical standards. An example of a company that devotes a great deal of energy to its social audits is Ben & Jerry's Homemade Inc. Favorable or otherwise, its managers publish the results of a formal social audit each year in the firm's annual report. On one occasion, the audit revealed that the company had been using a misleading label and consequently wrote this error up in its annual report, along with a promise to both correct the error and strive to avoid similar errors in the future.[87]

ORGANIZING: STRUCTURES AND SYSTEMS.   A Multistream approach to ethics focuses more on promoting positive behavior than on preventing unethical behavior and punishments. A focus on deterrence can draw attention to opportunities for unethical behavior. For example, what are you tempted to do when a sign says "Do not touch" or a package label states "Do not open"? In one unfortunate attempt to improve ethics through training students to understand how accounting practices could be manipulated, tests showed that the students indicated they were *more* likely to act unethically as a result of learning how easy and common it is to manipulate the financial records.[88] Sometimes surveillance systems and threats of punishment also can have the effect of turning employees against the company because they do not feel they are trusted, or it can focus employees' decision making on how likely they are to get caught and not on whether the behavior is ethical.[89]

A critical difference between Multistream and Mainstream ethics training relates to the emphasis of the training. Whereas Mainstream training places greater emphasis on unethical behaviors to avoid and rules that should not be broken, Multistream training places greater emphasis on the positive behaviors and values that should guide behavior in the organization. This orientation not only increases the likelihood of members acting positively, but also reduces the likelihood of employees behaving in a negative or unethical manner. In other words, the focus of the training becomes a self-fulfilling prophecy, whereby what you focus attention on and expect in others influences how people act.[90]

In contrast to the Mainstream focus on deterrence, the Multistream approach concentrates on aligning structure and systems to promote the right types of behavior. In the classic article "The Folly of Rewarding A, While Hoping for B," Steven Kerr points out several examples of how organizational executives hope for things such as managers' acting with a concern for the environment, but then reward quarterly earnings; similarly, executives may hope for safe, quality products, but reward shipping even with defects.[91] Multistream managers can institute rewards for meeting safety milestones, refusing to send out defective products, using environmentally friendly materials, going beyond one's job responsibilities to help a coworker, or even whistleblowing. For example, in healthcare environments, managers who encourage a "safety climate" by valuing, modeling, and rewarding safe behavior in the workplace can promote ethical behavior as well as positive outcomes such as increased patient satisfaction.[92]

LEADING: IMPLICIT AND EXPLICIT ACTION.   Mainstream managers typically behave in a manner that emphasizes the importance of the bottom line as their main concern. Multistream managers, in contrast, model a servant leadership style that promotes other forms of well-being as coequal with financial well-being. James Autry, former president of Meredith Corporation, argues that leadership is about caring for people, not controlling them; letting go, not holding on; and being present, not being the boss.[93] A **servant leader** is active, purposeful, and self-controlled in working toward others' growth, gain, and esteem.[94] Research suggests that when a leader emphasizes employee development, organizational members are less likely to engage in deviant or unethical behavior.[95] Sometimes servant leadership may be wrongly perceived as passive or weak. In fact, the opposite is true. Servant leaders model not only humility but also a powerful yet controlled will to do what is best for the organization and

Servant leader is one who is active, purposeful, and self-controlled in working toward others' growth, gain, and esteem.

The Code of Values at The Dwyer Group[96]

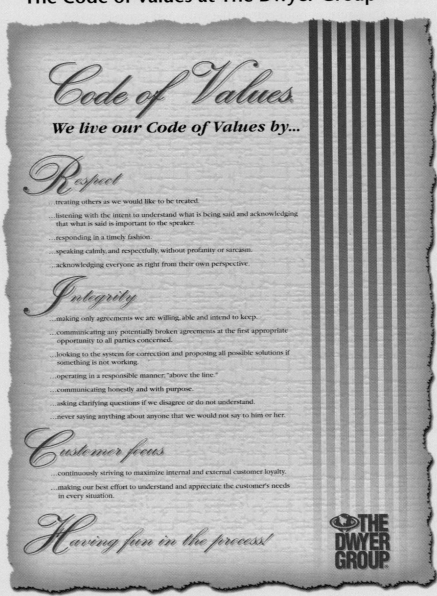

Reprinted by permission of The Dwyer Group.

others.[97] Servant leadership is noteworthy because it has been shown to contribute to the positive behavior of being creative and helping others.[98]

Leadership behavior sends a strong yet often implicit message about the values of the leader. Sometimes leaders are more explicit in promoting their perspective. Consider the leadership approach of King Jigme Singye Wangchuck, the fourth-generation ruling monarch of Bhutan. Drawing from a Buddhist view of economics,[99] King Wangchuck instituted a measure of Bhutan's well-being using a gross national happiness index instead of the standard gross national product metric.[100] Thanks to the King's far-sighted sustenance economics vision, which embraces long-term socio-economic and ecological benefits instead of short-term economic gains, Bhutan has acquired an international reputation as an eco-friendly nation and a global hotspot for biodiversity. In 1998, King Wangchuck also took the initiative to democratize how the country was governed (essentially permitting himself to be voted out of the job).

CONTROLLING: FORMAL AND INFORMAL. Both Mainstream and Multistream managers recognize that a code of ethics can provide clarity around expected behavior. However, a Multistream code of ethics tends to differ from a Mainstream code in both *content* and the *process* by which it is created. The content of a Multistream code of conduct is more likely to include expectations for its stakeholders. For example, the German shoe company Adidas-Salomon achieved a number 1 ranking among its competitors in its social responsibility orientation by requiring suppliers to comply with certain standards outlined as part of the company's code of ethics.[101] In comparison to a Mainstream code of ethics, a Multistream code also is likely to be more balanced in describing both positive behaviors to promote and negative behaviors to avoid. The code of values of service franchiser The Dwyer Group states such positive behaviors.

The Multistream *process* by which codes of conduct are created is usually more inclusive than a Mainstream approach. Instead of top managers or human resources professionals developing and handing down the code from on high, the Multistream approach favors having organizational members at all levels participate in the code's creation. A high-involvement approach amounts to ethical community building in which members create and own a set of agreed-upon standards and aspirations.[102] It may also mean that the code is treated more as a work in process rather than a hard-and-fast policy.

Another way to formalize positive behavior is to include it in the organization's calendar. For example, to recognize the value of corporate citizenship, Dutch staffing firm Vitae sponsors a citizenship day, when employees are encouraged to use their skills for charitable causes.[103] Setting aside time for employees to dedicate to ethical activity such as corporate citizenship projects can be expensive, but it formally announces to the organization's stakeholders that doing good is part of its organizational identity.

As with Mainstream management, not all controls are formal in the Multistream approach. Multistream managers also rely upon—perhaps even more so—the powerful influence of organizational culture to influence ethics. During his 12 years as CEO of Medtronics, Bill George helped to create an organizational culture that reinforced integrity in all actions, commitment to satisfying customers and developing employees, and responsible leadership.[104] A strong ethical culture guides behavior beyond what is listed in the code of conduct or policy manual. Creating and maintaining an ethical culture involves top managers communicating a consistent message in all of the organization's activities, such as which goals its members should pursue (planning), what is rewarded and receives support (organizing), what is modeled (leading), and what is reinforced in the organization's policies and procedures (controlling). It also involves managers throughout the organization providing support for organizational members to behave in ways that are consistent with their shared values. When their immediate managers provide organizational support, members are encouraged to care about the welfare of the organization, which in turn results in members who engage in less deviant behavior and are more likely to go beyond the bounds of their normal job to benefit the organization and its stakeholders.[105] The end-of-chapter case describes the influence of values on an organization and its members.

The Rise and Fall of Arthur Andersen

The Arthur Andersen accounting firm was built upon a stringent set of values that industry insiders often recognized as setting the standard for ethics in accounting. A story that was typical of those told about Arthur Andersen recounted the tale of a young auditor, Mike Gagel, working his way through pallet after pallet of bricks in the vast storage yard of a client in the Midwest.[106] After several times through, his count still registered as being 100,000 bricks short of what the organization indicated were in the inventory. The client rejected Gagel's findings and angrily complained to Andersen authorities about the rookie's insistence that there was an error in its books. Andersen partners stood firmly behind Gagel's claims, and further investigation revealed that the plant manager was secretly selling bricks at night, off the books.

This is a typical example of the vigilance that shaped the reputation of Arthur Andersen. So how did a firm that once stood for such vigilance and integrity end up closing its doors amidst a cloud of scandal? A short history of the company is instructive.[107]

Arthur Andersen and partner Clarence Delany founded Andersen, Delany, and Company in 1913. Originating as a small auditing firm, the organization soon added tax and consulting services to its client services. Delany left the company in 1918, allowing Andersen to shape the firm that now bore only his name. Over the next 30 years, Andersen reinforced a core set of values embodied in his "Think straight, talk straight" motto (controlling). Decades after his death, partners would reminisce about how Andersen did the right thing even when it cost him clients or money. One such story told of a major client arriving at Andersen's home and demanding changes in the audit; Andersen is said to have replied, "There is not enough money in the city of Chicago to induce me to change the report."[108]

Andersen hired graduates straight out of college and immersed them in both formal and informal systems of training in his way of doing accounting. Until his death in 1947, he maintained a strong hold on the culture of the firm, insisting that it stay relatively small to maintain its spirit of unity and voice. Under Andersen and his successor, Leonard Spacek, the firm assumed a dominant position in the industry in promoting fair and unbiased accounting methods and rigorously training its partners to adhere to these standards (leading).

After Andersen's death, a battle for control of the firm ensued that resulted in a reformulation of the partnership. Under the new arrangement, each partner had one vote in all matters and all partners shared in the profits and losses of the firm, with Leonard Spacek as the managing or lead partner (organizing). While attempting to maintain the "Think straight, talk straight" motto, the company expanded domestically and internationally, and moved toward a more decentralized structure of decision making at local offices. Under the leadership of Harvey Kapnick, the firm reorganized into three divisions: Accounting and Auditing, Tax, and Consulting (called Administrative Services). The firm shared profits among the three divisions. A later reorganization combined the Accounting and Auditing division with the Tax division. This set the stage for divisiveness. Although the Consulting division originally lost money, in the 1980s its members' aggressive sales tactics increased its revenues to a point where the division's partners began to complain about inequity in the shared-profit model and challenged the core culture of Andersen. It was a battle for power and profit.

Although subsequent restructuring continued to distance Consulting from the original Auditing/Tax foundation of Andersen, the Auditing/Tax division engaged in increasingly more consulting, reflecting both the appeal of consulting to new accounting graduates and the attractive profit margins generated in that business area (planning). In the 1990s, Auditing/Tax competed for profits and people not only with other accounting firms, but more importantly with the Andersen Consulting partners. This competition contributed to the end of the association between the two entities in 2000, with Auditing/Tax proceeding under the name of Andersen, and Consulting adopting a new name of Accenture. Nonetheless, the seeds sown by the damage to Andersen's core culture and its predominant focus on profit and sales opportunities came to fruition in the Enron disaster.

In 2000, Andersen and its partners had become addicted to the rush of profits from fees paid by large clients, of which Enron was the largest. That year Enron paid Andersen more than $52 million in fees, an amount that was expected to double in the following year. It seems implausible to blame the demise of Andersen on a single person or a small group of rogue employees, nor is it reasonable to argue that the shredding of Enron documents that led to a federal indictment for Andersen was an isolated incident. The Andersen organization that lost all of its clients and was dissolved after the indictment was on tenuous footing without a clear ethical foundation. Andersen had strayed from its renowned values, turned away from its core founding identity, and embraced an unrestricted pursuit of profit and financial growth.

Questions for Discussion

1. What do you think was the main reason that Andersen turned away from its core founding identity? How could this change have been avoided?

2. Do you have any suggestions for how Andersen could have attracted high-quality graduates without offering the high salaries associated with consulting work?

SUMMARY

Managers face increasing instances where they are called to make ethical decisions, thanks to the internationalization of organizations, the introduction of morally ambiguous technologies, heightened performance expectations, and the shift away from materialist–individualist values.

Managers learn ethics from a variety of sources (private and public, formal and informal) that they combine over time into a coherent moral point of view. Managers' moral points of view influence how they make ethical decisions and how they put the four management functions into practice.

Mainstream managers have a moral point of view that recognizes overarching goals as being to maximize productivity, efficiency, profitability, and competitiveness. Its rationale is grounded in a variation of consequentialist utilitarianism, which suggests that material wealth is the best "generic" way to improve overall societal well-being, and that the best way to grow material wealth is to create structures that encourage and reward individuals who seek it. Managers with a Mainstream moral point of view make ethical decisions in the following general manner:

1. Recognize as ethical issues that threaten or promote owners' wealth
2. Gather information and develop alternatives that are consistent with facts and policies
3. Evaluate information and make ethical choices that maximize profit within legal bounds
4. Implement ethical decisions, which may require courageously challenging norms

Multistream managers have a moral point of view that has as its overarching goals the following considerations: provide meaningful work, operate sustainably, be attentive to internal and external stakeholders, and facilitate servant leadership. The general rationale is grounded in virtue theory, which argues that practicing and fostering virtuous character is the best "generic" way to improve overall societal well-being. Managers with a Multistream moral point of view make ethical decisions in the following general manner:

1. Recognize as ethical issues that threaten or promote overall well-being
2. Gather information and develop alternatives that are consistent with listening to others
3. Evaluate information and make ethical choices that nurture overall well-being
4. Implement ethical decisions, which often take the form of courageous experiments

The moral point of view of managers will be evident in how they plan, organize, lead, and control:

- Mainstream management focuses on organization-specific responsibilities, whereas Multistream management focuses on corporate social responsibilities.

- Mainstream management emphasizes deterrence of negative behavior in its structures and systems, whereas Multistream management emphasizes promotion of positive behavior.

- Mainstream management utilizes a transactional form of leadership to evoke ethical behavior, whereas Multistream management models servant leadership.

- Mainstream management stresses compliance with formal and informal codes and rules of behavior, whereas Multistream management stresses commitment to growth and empowerment.

QUESTIONS FOR REFLECTION AND DISCUSSION

1. To whom or what do you attribute your moral point of view and ethics? In other words, which sources have most strongly influenced your moral or ethical development?

2. What are the three levels of moral development described in this chapter? Think of three examples of ethical decisions you have made. How well do these levels describe the questions that you asked in making your decisions?

3. A moral point of view is said to have three key components: (1) overarching goals, (2) a rationale, and (3) supporting virtues or practices. Briefly describe these three components of the moral points of view associated with both Mainstream and Multistream management.

4. Many years ago, Socrates argued that "the unexamined life is not worth living." Failing to articulate your own moral point of view leaves you vulnerable to wrongly believing that how you manage has nothing to do with your nature as a moral person.[109] Think about and describe your own moral point of view of management. What are your overarching goals? What is the rationale for your approach? What are the key practices or virtues associated with your moral point of view?

5. How might managers who fail to examine their own moral point of view render a disservice to their subordinates? How do managers consciously and unconsciously impose their moral point of view on others?

6. How might maintaining and living out your moral point of view differ in a smaller organization compared to a large one?

7. Most professions (e.g., medicine, law, engineering, nursing) have a code of ethics. What might be included in the code of ethics of a professional management association? How are your suggestions influenced by your own moral point of view?

HANDS-ON ACTIVITIES

Ethics Reporter

Take on the role of a reporter for your local newspaper. Your task is to write an article that includes input from interviews with "people in the trenches." Conduct three to five interviews with people who have experience working in organizations. Attempt to interview men and women of various ages with different experiences and backgrounds. Ask them the following five questions and a few of your own. Write up your conclusions and impressions in a one-page news story.

1. From where do you get your ethics (sense of what is right or wrong)?

2. How much ethics training have you received on the job?

3. How often are you faced with situations that have ethical implications?

4. How do you make ethical decisions?

5. What parts of your job are most influenced by your ethics?

ENDNOTES

1. Batstone, D. (2003). *Saving the corporate soul and (who knows?) maybe your own.* San Francisco: Jossey-Bass; The mensch of Malden Mills. (2003, July 3). CBSNews.com, *60 Minutes*; Browning, L. (2001). Management; Fire Could Not Stop A Mill, but Debts May. *New York Times*, November 28, 2001; Kerber, R. (2007). Malden Mills files for second Chapter 11. *The Boston Globe* (January 11); Clark, E. (2007). Malden Exits Bankruptcy as Polartec.

Women's Wear Daily, 193(59), 10; and http://www.hoovers.com/malden-mills/—ID__46974—/free-co-factsheet.xhtml.

2. Page 133 in Batstone, D. (2003). *Saving the corporate soul and (who knows?) maybe your own.* San Francisco: Jossey-Bass, 2003; The mensch of Malden Mills. (2003, July 3). CBSNews.com, *60 Minutes*.

3. Quoted in "The Mensch of Malden Mills," 2003.

4. Browning, L. (2001). Management; Fire Could Not Stop A Mill, but Debts May. *New York Times*, November 28, 2001.

5. Kerber, R. (2007, January 11). Malden Mills files for second Chapter 11. *Boston Globe*. http://www.hoovers.com/malden-mills/—ID__46974—/free-co-factsheet.xhtml.

6. New American Dream Survey. (2004, September). www.newdream.org; Giacalone, R. A. (2004). A transcendent business education for the 21st century. *Academy of Management Learning and Education*, 3, 415–420; and Etzioni, A. (2001). *The monochrome society*. Princeton, NJ: Princeton University Press.

7. McCall, M. W., & Lombardo., M. M. (1983). *Off the track: Why and how successful executives get derailed*. (Technical Report No. 21). Greensboro, NC: Center for Creative Leadership.

8. Drucker, P. F. (2001). *The essential Drucker* (pp. 12–13). New York: HarperCollins.

9. Weeks, B., Longenecker, J., McKinney, J., & Moore, C. (2005). The role of mere exposure effect on ethical tolerance: A two-study approach. *Journal of Business Ethics*, 58(4), 281–294.

10. Keith, N. K., Pettijohn, C. E., & Burnett, M. S. (2003). An empirical evaluation of the effect of peer and managerial ethical behaviors and the ethical predispositions of prospective advertising employees. *Journal of Business Ethics*, 48(3), 251–265; and Appelbaum, S. H., Deguire, K. J., & Lay, M. (2005). The relationship of ethical climate to deviant workplace behaviour. *Corporate Governance*, 5(4), 43–55.

11 . Grojean, M. W., Resick, C. J., Dickson, M. W., & Smith, B. (2004). Leaders, values, and organizational climate: Examining leadership strategies for establishing an organizational climate regarding ethics. *Journal of Business Ethics*, 55, 223–241.

12. Pojman, L. (1995). *Ethics: Discovering right and wrong*. Belmont, CA: Wadsworth.

13. Frohlich, N., & Oppenheimer, J. A. (1992). *Choosing justice: An experimental approach to ethical theory*. Berkeley, CA: University of California Press.

14. Farnsworth, J. R., & Kleiner, B. H. (2003). Trends in ethics education at U.S. colleges and universities. *Management Review Research News*, 26(2–4), 130–140.

15. According to Walker (2006), Sanford found that college students were quick to abandon their own previous beliefs and adopt the opinions and values of their fellow students. Sanford, N. (1964). Freshman personality. A stage in human development. In N. Sanford (Ed.), *College and character* (pp. 86–90). New York: John Wiley and Sons. Walker, K. R. (2006). *Examining ethics from a moral point of view framework: A longitudinal analysis*. Master's of Science thesis, Faculty of Management, University of Manitoba.

16. Ferraro, F., Pfeffer, J., & Sutton, R. I. (2005). Economic language and assumptions: How theories can become self-fulfilling. *Academy of Management Review*, 30, 8–24; and Krishnan, V. R. (2003). Do business schools change students' values along desirable lines? A longitudinal study. In A. F. Libertella & S. M. Natale (Eds.), *Business education and training: A value-laden process* (Vol. 8, pp. 26–39). Lanham, MD: University Press of America. However, students often do not recognize that their ethics are changing, or that becoming more materialist–individualist is a moral concern: By propagating ideologically inspired amoral theories, business schools have actively freed their students from any sense of moral responsibility (Ghoshal, 2005, p. 76). Bad management theories are destroying good management practices. *Academy of Management Learning and Education*, 4(1), 75–91.

17. Even so, the effect of formal ethics education may be minimal and short-lived. McCabe, D. L., Dukerich, J. M., & Dutton, J. E. (1994). The effects of professional education on values and the resolution of ethical dilemmas: Business school vs. law school students. *Journal of Business Ethics*, 13(9), 693–700.

18. http://www.sec.gov/about/laws.shtml#sox2002

19. *Schindler's list*. (1993). Universal Pictures. http://www.schindlerslist.com.

20. For an example of how religious beliefs can support a Mainstream and a Multistream moral point of view, see Dyck, B., & Schroeder, D. (2005). Management, theology and moral points of view: Towards an alternative to the conventional materialist–individualist ideal-type of management. *Journal of Management Studies*, 42(4),705–735. For a review of the literature on how religious beliefs influence managerial ethics, see Weaver, G. R., & Agle, B. R. (2002). Religiosity and ethical behavior in organizations: A symbolic interactionist perspective. *Academy of Management Review*, 27(1), 77–97. For a study of how religious faith provides grounding for a set of managers who hold a Multistream moral point of view, see Dyck, B. (2002). A grounded, faith-based moral point of view of management. In T. Rose (Ed.), *Proceedings of organizational theory division* (Vol. 23, pp. 12–23). Winnipeg, MB: Administrative Sciences Association of Canada.

21. Kohlberg, L. (1969). Stage and sequence: The cognitive development approach to socialization. In D. A. Goslin (Ed.), *Handbook of socialization theory and research* (pp. 347–380). Chicago: Rand McNally.

22. Pojman, L. (1995). *Ethics: Discovering right and wrong*. Belmont, CA: Wadsworth.

23. MacIntyre, A. (1981). *After virtue: A study in moral theory*. Notre Dame, IN: University of Notre Dame Press.

24. Krieger, M., & Seng, Y. (2005). Leadership with inner meaning: A contingency theory of leadership based on the worldviews of five religions. *Leadership Quarterly*, 16, 771–806.

25. Weaver, G. R., & Agle, B. R. (2002). Religiosity and ethical behavior in organizations: A symbolic interactionist perspective. *Academy of Management Review*, 27(1), 77–97.

26. Longenecker, J. G., McKinney, J. A., & Moore, C. W. (2004). Religious intensity, evangelical Christianity, and business ethics: An empirical study. *Journal of Business Ethics*, 55, 373–386.

27. Dyck & Schroeder, 2005.

28. Our approach follows Dyck & Schroeder, 2005. Our intent here is not to engage in the ongoing debate among philosophers as to precisely what constitutes a moral point of view. The three-part framework we use serves our purposes and is in keeping with arguments presented by the following leading moral philosophers: Frankena, W. K. (1973 [1963]). *Ethics*. Englewood Cliffs, NJ: Prentice-Hall; and MacIntyre, A. (1981). *After virtue: A study in moral theory*. Notre Dame, IN: University of Notre Dame Press.

29. Dyck & Schroeder, 2005.

30. For more information about Koch see its website at http://www.kochind.com.

31. http://www.kochind.com/about/living_values.asp.

32. http://www.forbes.com/lists/2006/21/biz_06privates_Koch-Industries_VMZQ.html.

33. For more on this issue, see Frey, D. E. (1998). Individualist economic values and self-interest: The problem in the Puritan ethic. *Journal of Business Ethics*, 17, 1573–1580; and Solomon, R. C., & Hanson, K. R. (1983). *Above the bottom line: An introduction to business ethics*. New York: Harcourt Brace Jovanovich.

34. Porter, M. E., & Kramer, M. R. (2002, December). The competitive advantage of corporate philanthropy. *Harvard Business Review*, 57–68.

35. Porter & Kramer, 2002.

36. Porter & Kramer, 2002.

37. Prichard, J. (2005, December 17). Promise of free college tuition changing lives in Kalamazoo. *Detroit News*.

38. Ryan, L. V., & Scott, W. G. (1995). Ethics and organizational reflection: The Rockefeller Foundation and postwar "moral deficits," 1942–1954. *Academy of Management Review*, 20(2), 438–461.

39. Hill, A. (2002, July 31). Rethinking Rockefeller and the rest. *Financial Times*, p. 10.

40. See Rest, J. R. (1986). *Moral development: Advances in research and theory*. New York: Praeger; Trevino, L. K. (1986). Ethical decision making in organizations: A person–situation interactionist model. *Academy of Management Review*, 11(3), 601–617; and Weaver, G. R., & Agle, B. R. (2002). Religiosity and ethical behavior in organizations: A symbolic interactionist perspective. *Academy of Management Review*, 27(1), 77–97.

41. Badaracco, J. L., Jr., & Webb, A. (1995). Business ethics: A view from the trenches. *California Management Review*, 37, 2, 8–28.

42. Jackall, R. (1988). *Moral mazes: The world of corporate managers* (p. 109). New York: Oxford University Press.

43. Bragues, G. (2006). Seek the good life, not money: The Aristotelian approach to business ethics. *Journal of Business Ethics*, 67, 341–357.

44. Eichenwald, K. (2005). *Conspiracy of fools: A true story*. New York: Broadway Books.

45. Eichenwald, 2005.

46. Kadlec, D. (2002, July 8). WorldCon. *Time*. http://www.time.com/time/magazine/article/0,9171,1002807,00.html.

47. Schweitzer, M., Ordonez, L., & Douma, B. (2004). Goal setting as a motivator of unethical behavior. *Academy of Management Journal*, 47, 422–432.

48. Abridged text of keynote address by Edward B. Rust, Jr., chairman and CEO of State Farm, at the international conference of the Association to Advance Collegiate Schools of Business in San Francisco, CA, April 22, 2005.

49. Badaracco & Webb, 1995.

50. Salter, M. S. (2004). *Innovation corrupted: The rise and fall of Enron*. Boston: Harvard Business School Publishing.

51. Gibbs, J. P. (1975). *Crime, punishment, and deterrence*. Amsterdam: Elsevier.

52. Boyle, M. (2006, March 7). Wal-Mart: Desperately seeking ethics. *Fortune*. http://money.cnn.com/2006/03/07/news/pluggedin_fortune/.

53. Walker (2006).

54. Walker (2006).

55. Alsop, R. (2006). Business ethics education in business schools: A commentary. *Journal of Management Education*, 30, 11–14.

56. Palmer, D. E., & Zakhem, A. (2001). Bridging the gap between theory and practice: Using the 1991 Federal Sentencing Guidelines as a paradigm for ethics training, *Journal of Business Ethics*, 29, 77–84.

57. Brown, M. E., Trevino, L. K., & Harrison, D. A. (2005). Ethical leadership: A social learning perspective for construct development and testing. *Organizational Behavior and Human Decision Processes*, 97, 117–134.

58. http://www.holtcat.com/company_values.asp.

59. Trevino, L. K., Brown, M., & Pincus, L. (2003). A qualitative investigation of perceived executive ethical leadership: Perceptions from inside and outside the executive suite. *Human Relations*, 56(1), 5–37.

60. Murphy (1995). Cited in B. Dyck, F. Starke, H. Harder, & T. Hecht. (2005). Do the structures of religious organizations reflect their statements of faith? An exploratory study. *Review of Religious Research*, 47(1), 51–69.

61. Schein, E. (1985). *Organizational culture and leadership*. San Francisco: Jossey-Bass.

62. Trevino, L. K., Butterfield, K. D., & McCabe, D. L. (1998). The ethical context of organizations: Influences on employee attitudes and behaviors. *Business Ethics Quarterly*, 8(3), 447–476.

63. Schminke, M., Ambrose, M. L., & Neubaum, D. O. (2005). The effect of leader moral development on ethical climate and employee attitudes. *Organizational Behavior and Human Decision Processes*, 97, 135–151. Grojean, M. W., Resick, C. J., Dickson, M. W., & Smith, D. B. (2004). Leaders, values, and organizational climate: Examining leadership strategies for establishing an organizational climate regarding ethics. *Journal of Business Ethics*, 55(3), 223–241.

64. Goodpaster, K. (2007). *Conscience and culture*. Malden, MA: Blackwell.

65. Adapted from Dyck & Schroeder, 2005.

66. Dyck & Schroeder, 2005.

67. Aristotle. (1962). *Nichomachean ethics* (trans. M. Oswald). New York: Macmillan.

68. Weaver, G. R. (2006). Virtue in organizations: Moral identity as a foundation for moral agency. *Organizational Studies*, 27(3), 341–368.

69. These questions are found on p. 832 of Mintz, S. M. (1996). Aristotelian virtue and business ethics education. *Journal of Business Ethics*, 15, 827–838; who is citing Pincoffs, E. L. (1986). *Quandaries and virtues*. Lawrence: University Press of Kansas.

70. Maitland, I. (1989). Rights in the workplace: A Nozickian argument. *Journal of Business Ethics*, 8(12), 951–954.

71. Leventhal, G. S. (1976). The distribution of rewards and resources in groups and organizations. In L. Berkowitz & W. Walster (Eds.), *Advances in experimental social psychology* (Vol. 9, pp. 91–131). New York: Academic Press.

72. Whetstone, J. T. (2001). How virtue fits within business ethics. *Journal of Business Ethics*, 33, 101–114.

73. Quinn, R. E. (1988). *Beyond rational management*. San Francisco: Jossey-Bass.

74. Giampetro-Meyer, A., Brown, T., Browne, M. N., & Kubasek, N. (1998). Do we really want more leaders in business? *Journal of Business Ethics*, 17, 1727–1736; and Graham, J. W. (1991). Servant-leadership in organizations: Inspirational and moral. *Leadership Quarterly*, 2(2), 105–119.

75. Pamela Johnson provides a concise summary of various perspectives on this issue: Johnson, P. (1996). Development of an ecological conscience: Is ecocentrism a prerequisite? *Academy of Management Review*, 21(3), 607–611.

76. How you view a specific situation or potential action is also influenced by the places you have experienced (e.g., lived in the city or country, traveled internationally), the ethical challenges you have faced (e.g., previous ethical dilemmas, work experiences), and the people who have played critical roles in your moral development (e.g., parents, teachers, peers, coworkers).

77. For an excellent summary of this argument, see Margolis, J., & Walsh, J. P. (2003). Misery loves company: Rethinking social

initiatives by business. *Administrative Science Quarterly, 48,* 268–305.

78. See Dyck, B. (1994). Build in sustainable development, and they will come: A vegetable field of dreams. *Journal of Organizational Change Management, 7*(4), 47–63.

79. "Shalom" is a Hebrew word that describes a deep sense of peace and socio-ecological well-being.

80. Quote taken from Dyck (2002). The names of people drawn from this article have been disguised, but the situations are accurate.

81. Quoted in Dyck, 2002.

82. Pollard, W. (2003, Spring). Leading in turbulent times. *Baylor Business Review.* http://www.baylor.edu/bbr/index.php?id=4168.

83. Quoted in Dyck, 2002.

84. This will be discussed further in Chapter 8. For a description of the call for goals that transcend financial profit maximization, see Giacalone (2004).

85. Goodpaster, 2007.

86. Spreier, S., Fontaine, M., & Malloy, R. (2006, June). Leadership run amok: The destructive potential of overachievers. *Harvard Business Review,* 72–82.

87. Cohen, B., & Greenfield, J. (1997). *Ben & Jerry's double dip: How to run a values led business and make money too.* New York: Fireside.

88. Citation from Teaching Ethics Conference presentation (2006). Boulder, CO.

89. Tenbrunsel, A. E., & Messick, D. M. (1999). Sanctioning systems, decision frames, and cooperation. *Administrative Science Quarterly, 44*(4), 684–707.

90. Gardner, W. L., & Schermerhorn, J. R., Jr. (2004). Unleashing individual potential performance gains through positive organizational behavior and authentic leadership. *Organizational Dynamics, 33*(3), 270–281.

91. Kerr, S. (1995). The folly of rewarding A, while hoping for B. *Academy of Management Executive, 9,* 7–14.

92. Hofmann, D. A., & Mark, B. (2006). An investigation of the relationship between safety climate and medical errors as well as other nurse and patient outcomes. *Personnel Psychology, 59*(4), 847–869.

93. Autry, J. (2001). *The servant leader: How to build a creative team, develop great morale, and improve bottom line performance.* Roseville, CA: Prima.

94. Whetstone, J. T. (2001). How virtue fits within business ethics. *Journal of Business Ethics, 33,* 101–114.

95. Colbert, A. E., Mount, M. K., Harter, J. K., Witt, L. A., & Barrick, M. R. (2004). Interactive effects of personality and perceptions of the work situation on workplace deviance. *Journal of Applied Psychology, 89*(4), 599–609.

96. The Dwyer Group's values are found at http://www.dwyergroup.com/values.asp. For a more detailed explanation and specific examples, see Dwyer-Owens, D. (2005).

97. Molyneaux, D. (2003). "Blessed are the meek, for they shall inherit the earth": An aspiration applicable to business? *Journal of Business Ethics, 48,* 347–363.

98. Neubert, M. J., Kacmar, M., Carlson, D., Roberts, J., & Chonko, L. (2007, August). *Regulatory focus as a mediator of leadership influence on employee outcomes.* Academy of Management Meetings, Philadelphia, PA.

99. See Schumacher, E. F. (1973). *Small is beautiful: A study of economics as if people mattered.* London: Blond & Briggs. For more on how Buddhist ethics are related to virtue ethics, see Keown, D. (1992). *The nature of Buddhist ethics.* New York: Palgrave; and Velez de Cea, A. (2005). The criteria of goodness in the Pali Nikayas and the nature of Buddhist ethics. *Journal of Buddhist Ethics, 11,* 123–142. Accessed December 23, 2006, at http://jbe.gold.ac.uk/11/current11.html.

100. Based on Lhundup, S. (2002). The genesis of environmental ethics and sustaining its heritage in the kingdom of Bhutan. *Georgetown International Environmental Law Review, 14*(4), 693–737; Schumacher (1973); and Tideman, S. (2004, August). Gross national happiness: The true measure of success? *Global Village News and Resources,* 89.

101. Corporate social responsibility ranking. (2006, February 23). http://www.theglobeandmail.com/servlet/story/RTGAM .20060223.rmcsr0224/BNStory/specialComment/ ?pageRequested=2.

102. McCabe, D. L., Butterfield, K. D., & Trevino, L. K. (2006). Academic dishonesty in graduate business programs: Prevalence, causes, and proposed action. *Academy of Management Learning and Education, 5*(3), 294–305.

103. Great Places to Work Institute Europe. (2006). *100 best workplaces in Europe: 2006 report.*

104. Gardner & Schermerhorn, 2004.

105. Rhoades, L., & Eisenberger, R. (2002). Perceived organizational support: A review of the literature. *Journal of Applied Psychology, 8,* 698–714.

106. McRoberts, F. (2002, September 1). The fall of Andersen: Greed tarnished golden reputation. *Chicago Tribune.* http://www .chicagotribune.com/business/showcase/chi-0209010315sep01 .story?coll=chi%2Dsite%2Dnav.

107. Squires, S., Smith, C., McDougal, L., & Yeack, W. (2003). *Inside Arthur Andersen: Shifting values, unexpected consequences.* Upper Saddle River, NJ: Prentice Hall.

108. Arthur Andersen & Company. (1974). *The first sixty years: 1913–1973.*

109. Naughton, M, J., & Bausch, T. A. (1994). The integrity of a Catholic management education. *California Management Review, 38*(4), 119–140; and Weber, M. (1958). *The Protestant ethic and the spirit of capitalism.* New York: Scribner.

CHAPTER 6

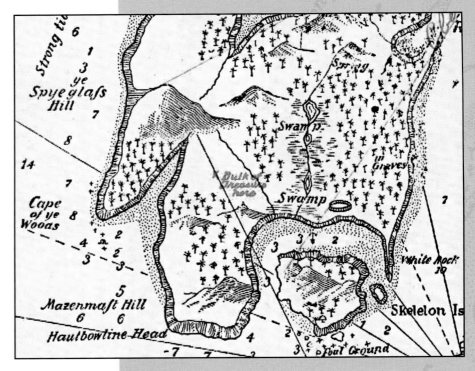

Entrepreneurs who start new organizations follow four steps: (1) They identify an opportunity, (2) they show entrepreneurial initiative, (3) they develop plans for the new venture, and (4) they mobilize resources. This chapter describes these steps in depth. It lies at the crossroads between the first section of the textbook, which introduced management and explored the environment in which it operates, and the remaining 12 chapters, which look at the four functions of management: planning (Chapters 7–9), organizing (Chapters 10–13), leading (Chapters 14–17) and controlling (Chapter 18).

ROAD MAP

FOUR STEPS OF THE ENTREPRENEURIAL PROCESS

1. Identify opportunity

2. Show entrepreneurial initiative
- Personality traits
  - Need for accomplishment
  - Sense of confidence
- Life-path circumstances

3. Develop plans for the new venture

4. Mobilize resources

Treasure map from John Louis Stevenson's novel *Treasure Island*.

Entrepreneurship

MAINSTREAM APPROACH	⟷	MULTISTREAM APPROACH
Offer a product or service that meets a need that people are willing to pay for		Offer a product or service that meets or eliminates a need that people have
• Need for achievement • Self-confidence • Transition, push, pull		• Need to help others • Confidence in community • Transition, push, pull
Have plans in place prior to start-up; highlight financial costs and benefits		Focus on flexible ongoing learning; highlight financial, social, and ecological costs and benefits
Attract financial resources and get started		Establish community support and get started

A Nobel Peace Prize–Winning Entrepreneur[1]

Can you imagine the Nobel Peace Prize being awarded to an entrepreneur and manager of a bank? That's exactly what happened in 2006, when the prize was awarded to Mohammad Yunus and the Grameen Bank. Yunus's story provides insight into entrepreneurship at its very best, and we want readers to hear it in his own words. The story starts in 1974, when an estimated 1.5 million people in Bangladesh died in a famine.[2] We have divided Yunus's description of how the Grameen Bank was started into the four steps of the entrepreneurial process.[3]

Step 1: Identify Opportunity

I was teaching economics at that time, at the University, and I felt terrible. Here I was, teaching the elegant theories of economics in the classroom with all the enthusiasm of a brand-new Ph.D. from the United States. You feel as if you know everything. You have the solutions. But you walk out of the classroom and see skeletons all around you, people waiting to die. . . .

I wanted to find out, is there anything I can do as a human being to delay it, to stop it, even for one single person? I would go around and sit down with people in the village, talking . . . I learned many things along the way, and tried to involve myself in whatever capacity I could to resolve those kinds of problems.

One particular incident took me in a new direction. I met a woman who was making bamboo stools. After a long discussion I found out that she made only two pennies U.S. each day, and I couldn't believe anybody could work so hard and make such beautiful bamboo stools and make such a tiny amount of profit. So I tried to under-

stand. She explained to me that she didn't have the money to buy the bamboo to make the stools, so she had to borrow from the trader—and the trader imposed the condition that she had to sell the product to him alone, at a price that he decided . . . she was virtually in bonded labor to this person. And how much did the bamboo cost? She said, "Oh, about 20 cents." . . .

Step 2: Entrepreneurial Initiative

I debated whether I should give her 20 cents, but then I came up with another idea—let me make a list of people who needed that kind of money. I took a student of mine and we went around the village for several days and came up with a list of 42 such people. When I added up the total amount they needed, I got the biggest shock of my life: it added up to 27 dollars! . . .

I took the money out of my pocket and gave it to my student. I said: "You take this money and give it to those 42 people that we met and tell them this is a loan, that they can pay me back whenever they are able to. In the meantime, they can sell their product wherever they can get a good price."

Step 3: Develop a Plan

Ninety-five percent of the more than 6 million microentrepreneurs who borrow from the Grameen Bank are women.

After receiving the money, they were excited. And seeing that excitement made me think: "What do I do now?" I thought of the bank branch which was located on the campus of the University. I went to the manager and suggested that he lend money to the poor people that I had met in the village. . . . He said, "You are crazy. It's impossible. How could we lend money to poor people? They are not creditworthy. . . . They cannot offer collateral, and such a tiny amount is not worth lending." He suggested that I see the high officials in the banking hierarchy in Bangladesh.

I took his advice and went to the people who matter in the banking sector. Everybody told me the same thing. Finally, after several days of running around I offered myself as a guarantor. I'll guarantee the loan, I'll sign whatever they wanted me to sign, but they can give the money, and I'll give it to the people that I want to.

So that was the beginning. They warned me repeatedly that the poor people who receive the money will never pay back. I said, "I'll take a chance." And the surprising thing was, they repaid me every penny—there was not a single penny missing. I got very excited and came to the manager and said, "Look, they paid back, so there's no problem." But he said, "Oh, no, they're just fooling you. Soon they will take more money and never pay you back." So I gave them more money, and they paid back. I told this to him, but he said, "Well, maybe you can do it in one village, but if you do it in two villages it won't work." So I hurriedly did it in two villages—and it worked.

So it became a kind of struggle between me and the bank manager and his colleagues in the highest positions. They kept saying that a larger number—five villages probably—will show it. So I did it in five villages, and it only showed that everybody paid back. Still they didn't give up. They said, "Ten villages." I did it in ten villages. "Twenty villages." "Fifty villages" [and so on] . . . I come up with the results they cannot deny because it's their money I'm giving, but they will not accept it because they are trained to believe that poor people are not reliable. Luckily, I was not trained that way so I could believe whatever I am seeing, as it revealed itself. But their minds, their eyes were blinded by the knowledge they had.

Finally I had the thought: Why am I trying to convince them? I am totally convinced that poor people can take money and pay back. Why don't we set up a separate bank? That excited me, and I wrote down the proposal and went to the government to get the permission to set up the bank. It took me two years to convince the government. . . .

Step 4: Mobilize Resources

On October 2, 1983, we became a bank. A formal bank, independent . . . now that we had our own bank and we could expand as we wished. And we did expand.

We reached the first billion dollars in [1994], and we celebrated it. A bank that started its journey with 27 dollars, giving loans to 42 people, coming all the way to the billion dollars in loans, is a cause for celebration we thought. And we felt good. Nobody had believed in us, everybody said, Well, you can give tiny amounts to tiny people—so what? You cannot expand, you cannot reach out to the poor people. So coming all the way to the billion dollars in loans to so many borrowers was quite an excitement.

At the time of receiving the 2006 Nobel Peace Prize, Grameen Bank had 6.6 million borrowers (more than 95 percent of whom are women[4]) and 18,795 employees in 2225 branches[5] working in 71,371 villages. Since its inception, the bank has disbursed more than $5.7 billion to help people escape poverty. Its loan recovery rate is 98.85 percent, and Grameen Bank has made a profit almost every year of its operations. The compellingly simple idea of providing credit to the world's poorest micro-entrepreneurs to enable them to grow their businesses has proven to be enormously effective. Yunus is known for saying that our grandchildren will need to go to a museum to see poverty. He notes that 58 percent of the poor who had borrowed from Grameen Bank are now out of poverty, and that 2005 had been declared the "Year of Microcredit" when more than 100 million people worldwide were involved with micro-credit programs (including some in high-income economies, such as the United States): "At the rate we're heading, we'll halve total poverty by 2015. We'll create a poverty museum in 2030."

Introduction to Entrepreneurship

Whereas the remaining chapters in this book will focus on managing organizations that are already operating, this chapter will look at the initial creation of organizations, which is called the study of entrepreneurship. **Entrepreneurship** refers to conceiving an opportunity to offer new or improved goods or services, showing the initiative to pursue that opportunity, making plans, and mobilizing the resources necessary to convert the opportunity into reality. It often leads to the creation of a new organizational start-up, and almost every organization we know today (e.g., Liz Claiborne, Microsoft, Fed-Ex, or the pizza joint down your street) had an entrepreneurial

Entrepreneurship refers to conceiving an opportunity to offer new or improved goods or services, showing the initiative to pursue that opportunity, making plans, and mobilizing the resources necessary to convert the opportunity into reality.

beginning. Sometimes entrepreneurship can be found within *existing* organizations, a phenomenon that is often referred to as *intrapreneurship*. Intrapreneurship is evident, for example, when managers in organizations like 3M and Google expect employees to allocate as much as 20 percent of their time to dreaming up new innovations that will eventually become the organization's future products and services.

The term "entrepreneurship" is sometimes used interchangeably with "small business management" and "family business management." This is understandable, because these ideas often overlap. For example, many entrepreneurs manage small businesses, and many small business managers are entrepreneurs. Nevertheless, some entrepreneurs manage large businesses (e.g., Microsoft and the Grameen Bank are quite large), and some small business managers are not entrepreneurs (e.g., someone who manages a local hardware store in much the same way as it was managed by his or her entrepreneurial parent from whom the current owner inherited the store is not an entrepreneur). Similarly, some family firms are small businesses run by entrepreneurs, but many *Fortune* 500 companies are family owned or family controlled (e.g., the Mars family owns the world's largest chocolate company).

Note also that entrepreneurship may be just as active in the not-for-profit sector as it is in the for-profit sector. For example, entrepreneurship is evident when enthusiasts start a new "ultimate Frisbee" league via their local community center, or when a new charitable organization is started.

Thus, as defined here, entrepreneurship simply entails the pursuit of new or innovative opportunities, regardless of organization type or size.

This chapter will describe the entrepreneurial process as having four basic steps (see Figure 6.1):

1. Opportunity identification
2. Entrepreneurial initiative
3. Development of a plan
4. Mobilization of the resources required to pursue the opportunity

Entrepreneurs started the nonprofit Digger Foundation in 1998 to develop an affordable technology for the removal of landmines. The D-2 in the photo increases the amount of land that one worker can de-mine in one day from approximately 15–20 square meters to 120 square meters. It costs about $1000 to remove a landmine, but as little as $3 to place it in the ground in the first place. De-mining machines reduce the risk for the de-miners and reduce the cost of removing the mines.[6]

We will first describe how these four steps unfold from a Mainstream perspective, and then contrast that view with a look at how the four steps unfold from a Multistream perspective.

THE FOUR STEPS OF MAINSTREAM ENTREPRENEURSHIP

Step 1: Identify Opportunity

Entrepreneurial opportunities may emerge from unmet needs or from changes in the task, macro, or international environments. **Entrepreneurs** are people who conceive opportunities to offer new or improved goods or services (or even new markets or ways of doing things), exhibit initiative to pursue those opportunities, and make plans and mobilize the resources necessary to convert their concepts into reality.

Entrepreneurs may look at the world differently from the rest of us. This difference in perspective is illustrated by Harvard psychologist Ellen Langer's visits to classrooms where she shows students a picture of a person in a wheelchair. In one class she asks, "Can this person drive a car?" and usually students answer "no" and give plenty of reasons why not. In another class Langer asks, "How can this person drive a car?" and students often come up with many creative ideas for how a person who uses a wheelchair could drive a car. The orientation evident in the second class is more consistent with the way entrepreneurs, by their very nature, look at the world.[7]

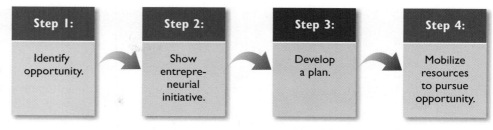

Figure 6.1 The four steps of the entrepreneurial process

In short, entrepreneurs are more likely to have an orientation that looks at possibilities of how something can be done, rather than think of reasons why it can't be done. Mainstream entrepreneurs are constantly looking for better and more financially rewarding ways to meet needs. They are looking for places where they can outperform existing competitors, either by lowering costs or providing unique added value. They look for opportunities to invest resources that will yield a higher financial return than they currently get. As the French economist Jean Baptiste Say put it at the turn of the nineteenth century: "The entrepreneur shifts resources out of an area of lower and into an area of higher productivity and greater yield."[8] In other words, the Mainstream entrepreneur maximizes the financial return of wealth within acquisitive economics.[9]

Because of their capacity to see opportunities where others see problems, entrepreneurs make very important contributions to society. Most notably, entrepreneurship plays an important role in keeping the economy going in areas such as job creation and innovation.[10] For example, in the United States, small businesses (defined as firms with fewer than 500 employees) create nearly three-fourths of all new jobs and are responsible for approximately 55 percent of the innovations in the U.S. marketplace, including 95 percent of the radical innovations.[11]

Another positive spin-off may be the quality of jobs being created. Insofar as entrepreneurship is associated with the creation of smaller organizations, entrepreneurs may be creating jobs that are particularly satisfying. One study found that 43 percent of people are "extremely satisfied" when working in companies with fewer than 50 employees. This proportion decreases to 31 percent in firms with 50 to 999 employees, and it decreases again to 28 percent in firms with more than 1000 employees. Small firms may not be able to compete with large companies in terms of pay and benefits, but they may offer employees opportunities to develop and use a wider variety of skills, and to see clearly how their work relates to the organization's mission and outcomes.[12] A study of 323 small businesses showed that companies where managers provided more autonomy for employees and created a supportive environment outperformed (as measured in terms of revenues and profit) those companies where managers were more controlling and used individual monetary rewards to motivate people.[13]

Sometimes, the best entrepreneurial ideas come from people who have little or no experience in an industry, and so are able to bring a fresh perspective to it. For example, entrepreneur Larry Mauws knew little about building cars when he first started his company—Westward Industries—to build parking patrol vehicles (see the opening case in Chapter 18). More often, however, the best entrepreneurial ideas

Entrepreneurs are people who conceive opportunities to offer new or improved goods or services (or even new markets or ways of doing things), exhibit initiative to pursue those opportunities, make plans, and mobilize the resources necessary to convert the concepts into reality.

Sometimes a new invention enjoys greater success if its creator does not seek to control it. For example, Tim Berners-Lee invented the World Wide Web, which continues to transform the world's economy, and he launched the world's first website in August 1991. The invention could have made Berners-Lee very wealthy, but he explains why he decided to leave the World Wide Web in the public domain rather than patenting it: "It was simply that had the technology been proprietary, and in my total control, it would probably not have taken off."[16]

occur when people build on experience and expertise developed by working in a particular industry or sector. This relationship is illustrated by the entrepreneurs who started PayPal and the dozens of people who left the company after it was purchased by eBay for $1.5 billion in 2002. Since then, PayPal alumni have been involved in starting up YouTube, Room9 Entertainment, Slide, and LinkedIn. The shared experience of working together at PayPal seems to have increased the likelihood and success of future start-ups created by its former employees.[14]

The Internet has had a positive effect on entrepreneurs in many sectors of the economy by opening up previously unimaginable opportunities for small organizations to compete on the international stage. Whereas international business was once primarily the domain of large organizations, many smaller firms are now finding opportunities to expand into foreign markets. For example, an eBay lark started off the entrepreneurs who gave birth to Canada's $500 million Internet pharmacy industry. A year after purchasing a pharmacy in the small town of Minnedosa, Manitoba—and on the verge of bankruptcy with virtually no customers—a bored Andrew Strempler listed a box of nonprescription Nicorette gum on eBay that sold instantly. Within a couple of months, Andrew and his wife Catherine, and their friends Mark and Chantelle Rzepka, were running full-page ads in the *New York Times* listing their low-priced prescription drugs. Within five years after that seminal event, their firm Mediplan was sold to CanadDrugs.com for approximately $20 million.[15]

Step 2: Show Entrepreneurial Initiative

Of course, simply identifying an opportunity does not automatically make someone an entrepreneur. Many people love the idea of having a great cup of coffee in a nice coffee shop, but Howard Schultz actually did something about it when he started Starbucks.[17] Research suggests that, on average, some 6 percent of Americans are actively trying to start their own businesses.[18]

We know that personality traits and life-path circumstances have an effect on whether people show entrepreneurial initiative (see Figure 6.2). The two *personality traits* that are most often associated with Mainstream entrepreneurs are (1) a high need for achievement[19] and (2) a high level of self-confidence.[20]

First, people with a high need for achievement learn to set achievable yet challenging goals. They look for feedback on performance as a way to evaluate their achievement. Mainstream entrepreneurs are especially likely to set financial goals.

Second, Mainstream entrepreneurs must have enough self-confidence to carry out the necessary tasks involved in running their business. Entrepreneurship is not for the timid. Entrepreneurs must trust their own abilities to fulfill the unmet needs that they have identified. This self-confidence runs deep, as many successful entrepreneurs have failed several times before they finally attain success, as illustrated by the families of the entrepreneurs who founded Hershey and Mars. For example, the founder of Hershey Chocolate, Milton S. Hershey, grew up in a household where his father had unsuccessfully tried 17 different new ventures (none of which earned him a living). Listening to the advice of his father also contributed to Milton's first venture going bankrupt.[21]

In addition to a high need for achievement and self-confidence, entrepreneurs tend to have a high level of energy, be more action oriented, have greater tolerance for ambiguity and uncertainty, desire independence, and have an internal locus of control (belief that success is due to their own actions, rather than being dependent on others' actions).

Life-path circumstances also affect the likelihood that someone will start a new organization. People are more likely to act on their entrepreneurial urgings if they are

- In the midst of a transition,
- Being pushed away from the status quo, or
- Being pulled into an entrepreneurial venture.

Figure 6.2 Factors that influence the likelihood of exhibiting entrepreneurial initiative

First, people are more likely to start a new organization if they have just gone through a planned or unexpected transition in their lives. Such an event might include completing an education or training program, finishing a major project, having a mid-life crisis, or having recently been divorced, fired, or moved. For example, the people who left PayPal when it was purchased by eBay were in a period of transition, looking for the next project to work on.

Second, people are more likely to start a new organization if their current job is dissatisfying or if they have little hope of finding satisfying employment. This group includes intrapreneurs who believe that their good ideas are being stifled[22] or who face dead-end jobs in their current workplace. Silicon Valley is filled with stories of engineers and executives who left a company to start a new one. For example, Fairchild Semiconductor was started by eight engineers who left Shockley Semiconductor; subsequently, two of those engineers (Robert Noyce and Gordon Moore) left Fairchild to start Intel,[23] and two others (William Hewlett and David Packard) left Fairchild to form Hewlett-Packard. Entrepreneurship is especially important for persons who have been marginalized in the larger society, such as minorities and women who face glass ceilings.[24] In the United States, between 1997 and 2002, the number of Asian-owned firms increased by 24 percent, Hispanic-owned businesses by 31 percent, and African American–owned firms by 45 percent, whereas the number of businesses started by the rest of the population increased by only 10 percent.[25]

Third, people are more likely to become entrepreneurs if they have positive pull influences, such as availability of financial resources and active encouragement from mentors, friends, and family members. One pull factor is membership in a *group* of people who want you to join them in a new venture. Indeed, countering the myth of the "lone entrepreneur," a start-up is more likely to find success if the new venture is led by a group of entrepreneurs,[26] as is illustrated by firms such as YouTube and Intel. Approximately one-fifth of existing organizations in a variety of industries started when a group of people left a common parent organization.

Many new ventures have been started by frustrated intrapreneurs who exited an existing organization. As it turns out, research shows that there is a predictable process—similar to the four-step entrepreneurial process—that leads a group of intrapreneurs to leave their parent organization and form a new one.[27]

Step 1: The process starts when a subgroup of members in an existing organization are exposed to a trigger event that allows them to *identify an opportunity* for a new good or service. Members seldom act on this new idea until doing so has been legitimated. Usually this legitimization comes from a statement by a senior manager, who says that the organization encourages members to develop initiatives based on new ideas.

Step 2: Once such a legitimizing event has occurred, the intrapreneurs actively begin to *initiate changes*. These changes are tolerated for a while by managers, but eventually the intrapreneurs push their agenda so hard that other members become alarmed and begin to actively resist the change. The lines have now been drawn, and polarization develops between the intrapreneurial group that wants to implement more changes and other members who want to protect the status quo.

Step 3: At this stage, the intrapreneurs recognize that their *plans* for change are being opposed. As members on each side continue to mobilize organizational resources on their behalf, the conflict comes to a head. The intrapreneurial group members are told in no uncertain terms that their new initiatives are not welcome.

Step 4: The now entrepreneurs exit the parent organization en masse and *mobilize resources* to create a new start-up. Members who remain in the parent organization are left feeling wounded by the talent drain, and it can take several years for the organization to regroup and move forward. By contrast, members of the new venture are energized to work hard and establish new routines.

 WHAT DO YOU THINK?

Why Are Some People More Likely to Show Entrepreneurial Initiative?[28]

Research suggests that there are differences among groups in terms of how much entrepreneurial initiative their members show. For example, in the United States, men are significantly more likely than women to be actively engaged in starting a new firm (8 percent of men versus 4.5 percent of women). Also, African Americans (9.5 percent) are more likely than either Hispanic Americans (7.1 percent) or Caucasian Americans (5.7 percent) to engage in entrepreneurship. The level of schooling also makes a difference, especially for African American and Hispanic American men. African American men with graduate school experience are twice as likely to be involved in a start-up as Caucasian American men.

Which factors do you think account for these differences across genders and ethnic backgrounds? Do you think there are significant differences in entrepreneurial spirit across other demographic factors such as age or socioeconomic status? If so, why?

Step 3: Develop a Plan for the New Venture

Even though they tend to be action oriented, before they start a new venture entrepreneurs need to do some research to see if their idea is feasible. In particular, before starting a new venture, entrepreneurs develop a plan. This plan provides a clear direction by laying out the strategy necessary to reach the objectives. Perhaps not surprisingly, preparing plans has been identified as the most important feature of entrepreneurship education.[29]

Preparing a plan for a new venture prior to start-up provides several benefits.

- It ensures that entrepreneurs think through the different aspects of the new venture before starting up. Unfortunately, once a new venture is under way, the ongoing pressures of running the organization often leave little time for reflection.[30]

- Preparing a plan ahead of time forces entrepreneurs to set up standards or milestones against which to measure performance at a time when they are able to think more clearly and are not overwhelmed by intense day-to-day management issues. For example, an entrepreneur may decide a new organization should have at least $100,000 in revenue within the first year or a positive cash flow within three years. If these milestones are not met, then the entrepreneur (and investors) can walk away from the venture before investing any more resources into it.

- Perhaps the most important reason to write a well-developed plan is to win the support of other stakeholders, whether they are financers, employees, suppliers, or customers. The creation of such a plan improves both the likelihood of success and the potential for securing outside funding.

There are different ways to set up a plan, but the checklist in Table 6.1 provides a practical start.

1. SUMMARY. The summary—which should not be longer than three pages—gives a brief description of the product or service that will be provided, identifies the market where the organization will operate, indicates the resources already in place and those that are still required, and offers an appraisal of the organization's expected financial performance. The summary must be written in a compelling way so that it captures the reader's attention. Write the summary *after* the other parts have been written.

TABLE 6.1

The Five Parts of a Mainstream Plan for a New Venture

1. Summary: Identify the opportunity and highlight how it enhances the financial well-being of investors.

2. Concept of the new venture: Specify the unmet need in the economic context of customers and other organizations, and describe how the new venture's goods or services will meet that need.

3. Management team: Highlight the strengths and roles of team members.

4. Operations: Specify all of the resources required, along with their expected financial costs.

5. Timeline, projected performance, and contingency plans: Focus on expected financial performance over time.

Sources: Allen, K. R. (2006). *Launching new ventures: An entrepreneurial approach* (4th ed). Boston: Houghton Mifflin; Kuratko, D. F., & Welsch, H. P. (2004). *Strategic entrepreneurial growth* (pp. 253–254). Mason Ohio: Thomson South-Western; Lasher, W. R. (2005). *The perfect business plan made simple.* New York: Broadway Books; and Daft (1991). Daft, Richard L. (2003). *Management* (6th ed). Mason, Ohio: Thomson South-Western.

2. CONCEPT OF THE NEW VENTURE.   The second part of the plan contains two basic components. The first component describes customers and other organizations in the new venture's task environment (see Chapter 3). The second component describes the new venture's product or service.

Regarding the task environment, the plan should identify the unmet need that the new venture will address—for example, the need for more daycare services in a community, for a video game to play the latest extreme sport, or for a better Internet search engine. This section of the plan should provide relevant background information, and describe how the new venture will fit with the products and services offered by existing organizations. This description might include demographic information, such as the number of children aged five and younger in a neighborhood who do not have access to daycare services, or the age and gender of a "typical" extreme sport video gamer. It could also include relevant trends and historical information (e.g., the shift toward online video games or motion-sensitive game controllers) and organizations that offer similar resources (e.g., key competing daycare services or video game producers). Once you have identified the attributes of key customers and other relevant organizations, you should evaluate the strengths and weaknesses of your new venture relative to the opportunities and threats you have identified. This analysis, in turn, will allow you to develop and describe an appropriate strategy that your new venture will pursue. This section should also include advertising plans, sales projections, and an idea on what position or share of the market you hope to secure. It should be based on current data to convince readers that you know your stuff and assure them that your proposal is based on solid information.

Regarding the product or service that you propose to offer, you need to provide a detailed description of the product or service, show how it differs from what is already available, and demonstrate how it meets the unmet need that you have identified. For example, does the daycare center you intend to open have a more convenient location, lower price, or higher-quality service? Does your video game work on a variety of consoles, offer state-of-the-art graphics, or is it unusually user-friendly? Your description should incorporate the research and testing that have already been completed, and identify what still needs to be done. For example, have you developed a prototype and tested it on potential customers? In addition, you should describe access to resources that will help to complete and refine the design of the product or service to be offered (e.g., experts in the design of daycare centers or the design of video games).

Sometimes the development of the basic concept can happen very quickly. For example, at a restaurant during the twenty-ninth birthday party for Max Levchin, one of PayPal's cofounders, a conversation began on how difficult it can be to find a good dentist. That topic got two former PayPal engineers at the party (Jeremy Stoppleman and Russel Simmons) talking about creating a website where people could review professional services available in their neighborhoods. The conversation continued on the walk back to their offices after lunch, at which time they pulled Max Levchin aside and pitched the basic concept of the new venture. Levchin liked the idea, and the next day he agreed to back the project with $1 million—and so Yelp was born.[31]

3. MANAGEMENT TEAM.   This section of the start-up plan is intended to convince readers that you have the management capability to make your new organization work. Studies suggest that venture capitalists place great emphasis on the characteristics of the entrepreneurs leading a new start-up, and particularly on their ability to work as a cohesive team.[32]

Your plan should provide a clear description of the management team's experience and expertise to manage this venture. Include the résumés of all key people in the management of your venture. Also, specify which member will do which work (e.g., who will manage finance and accounting, who will be responsible for human resources management, and so on). Identify any gaps and explain how you will access advisors and consultants to fill those gaps. For example, note whether you have someone with years of industry experience and success who is willing to help on an as-needed basis. Clearly, entrepreneurs who belong to an informal network (like the PayPal alumni) have access to very valuable sources of counsel and financing.

In addition, this section of the plan should provide information on your basic

The three entrepreneurs who started YouTube all left PayPal in 2005 when it was purchased by eBay for $1.5 billion. YouTube was purchased by Google for $1.65 billion in 2006. Two of YouTube's founders, Chad Hurley (left) and Steven Chen, are shown in this photo.

management philosophy (e.g., will you promote from within, offer flexible work hours, or focus on low-cost overseas service providers?). It should also describe the legal structure of the venture (e.g., is it a sole proprietorship, partnership, corporation, or worker-owned cooperative?). In addition, you should provide information about how much time and energy key people will invest in this venture and how they will be compensated. For example, which members are willing to put in 60 hours per week, and which members have other jobs and commitments? Which members are paid a salary, who shares in the profits, and who owns shares in the organization?

For example, Jawed Karim, one of the three entrepreneurs who cofounded the video site YouTube, never took a salary, benefits, or even a formal title in the company. He simply assumed the role of an informal advisor to the other two cofounders, Chad Hurley and Steven Chen. All three had left PayPal by 2005, after they had hit the jackpot when the firm was purchased by eBay for $1.5 billion. They would often meet late at night to brainstorm at Max's Opera Café, close to Stanford University. Karim initially pitched the basic idea of video sharing, but ultimately decided to go back to study at the university; Hurley and Chen subsequently turned the idea into what became YouTube. When YouTube was sold to Google for $1.65 billion in 2006, Karim (then 27 years old) was one of its largest individual shareholders (although he owned fewer shares than Hurley and Chen).[33]

4. OPERATIONS.   This section of the start-up plan describes the resources required to operate your new venture. A key resource is suppliers. For example, if you are starting a new daycare center, then your plan may describe how a key supplier of your human resources is a local community college that trains credentialed daycare professionals. You should indicate how many people graduate from this program in a typical year, how much demand there is for their services, what the going wage rate is, and so on. If you are a software developer, you will look for recruits from other organizations or from educational programs. You need to identify what sorts of people you need with what sorts of skill sets and how much it will cost to

DIGGING DEEPER

How the Internet Helps to Overcome Liabilities of Newness[34]

Many new ventures fail because of what researchers call "liabilities of newness." This term refers to those unique characteristics of new organizations that make them especially vulnerable to failure. We will describe four liabilities of newness, and indicate how entrepreneurs can use the Internet to minimize their negative effects.

The first liability of newness comes from the need to *assemble all of the different skills and systems* required to operate an organization. For example, an organization may need marketing skills, a payroll department, human resources policies, and so on. Thanks to the Internet, it is becoming easier for entrepreneurs to outsource (i.e., purchase) some of these services and systems online. **Outsourcing** involves using contracts to transfer some of an organization's recurring internal activities and decision-making rights to outsiders.[35] This practice allows entrepreneurs to focus their energy on their unique value-added product or service, rather than on all the general activities that are part of any organization. Sometimes managers of new firms overcome this liability of newness by aligning themselves with larger organizations that have complementary skills and systems. For example, Peanutpress.com—a company founded in 1998 that provides contemporary books and newspapers for reading on handheld computers—gained an important advantage over larger competitors (e.g., Microsoft, Adobe Systems, and Barnes and Noble) because it designed its service for use on Palm Connected Organizers, which at the time had 80 percent of the handheld computer market.

The second liability of newness relates to the lack of an organizational history that might otherwise help establish *trust and legitimacy* with key stakeholders (e.g., suppliers, customers, investors). The Internet can provide a substitute for this kind of trust, thanks to its capacity for dissemination of information regarding the reliability of a new venture. Organizations can quickly develop a reputation on the Internet based on the rating systems on auction sites and customer testimonials that are common on online communities. For example, Peanutpress.com quickly became known as a trustworthy vendor via newsgroups and Web-based forums devoted to Palm products and systems.

A third liability of newness is due to a new organization's lack of *social capital*. The Internet can help entrepreneurs belong to active networks that help them stay on top of market and technological information. For instance, Peanutpress.com became a member of important networks and gained valuable social capital (e.g., access to different book publishers) via the Internet, which facilitated the creation and management of interorganizational linkages.

The final liability of newness is the lack of *economic ties*. Having a home page on the Internet provides access to a wide range of potential capital providers. Many entrepreneurs report that their organization's website (especially the investor relations section) plays an important role in attracting investors. Similarly, the Internet makes it easier for entrepreneurs to disseminate their business plans to venture capitalists (e.g., vfinance.com, venturecaptial.org) and providers of alternative sources of debt financing.

Outsourcing is using contracts to transfer some of an organization's recurring internal activities and decision-making rights to outsiders.

hire them. Your plan should provide key job descriptions as well as an organizational chart that describes who reports to whom.

Other key resources for most organizations are physical buildings and location. For example, what are potential sites for the daycare center, do those sites have enough parking, are they conveniently located for parents to pick up and drop off their children, and are they close to parks and libraries? What are the zoning regulations, property taxes, and insurance costs? What sorts of equipment and supplies do you need—crayons, floor mats, indoor/outdoor climbing structures, and so on? Similar questions apply to starting up a software development company, except that important resources might include proximity to other computer professionals, powerful computer equipment, and office furniture. The plan should also specify how much floor space is required and indicate whether future growth can be accommodated at the proposed site.

For some organizations, the distribution network is a key resource. Even if you produce the best video game in the world, sales may suffer if you do not have an adequate distribution network. For example, if you have a new consumer item to sell, you need shelf space on stores like Wal-Mart. The Internet has helped some new ventures meet the challenges of distribution.

5. TIMELINE, PROJECTED PERFORMANCE, AND CONTINGENCY PLANS.
The final section of the start-up plan describes how resources will be mobilized over time, presents expected financial performance over time, and identifies contingency plans that will be put in place in case events do not unfold as planned. In terms of the timeline, the plans should present a timetable or chart to indicate when each phase of the venture will be completed. For example, for a new day-care organization, the timeline should indicate when a location will be selected, when equipment will be installed, when and what kind of advertising will be done, and when different staff members will be recruited and hired. For a video game producer, the timeline would include how long each phase of the development would take (e.g., prototype, product testing, marketing campaign) and identify the human and computer resources required to complete each stage. For any start-up, the timeline included in the initial plan should run at least five years into the future.

The new venture start-up plan should also contain financial projections for the first five years, including analysis of expected expenses and revenues. These projections should be relatively detailed at first (e.g., provide quarterly cash-flow projections in the first year) but then become more general over time. The plan should include budgets and financial statements that describe the specific times and amounts when financing will be required over a period of three years. Often plans identify specific "milestones" that are designed to help the entrepreneurs and investors know whether they should pull out. For example, if a new daycare center needs 40 children to be viable, and it has only 20 children after two years of operation, then it may be prudent to close the business. A milestone schedule for a software development firm might be to have a working prototype developed within three years; if that is not accomplished, then the firm should close its doors. An important part of the financial planning for the organization is to identify its sources of financing (e.g., bank loans, venture capitalists' investments, entrepreneurs' personal savings) and specify when specific amounts of money will be needed.

Finally, the plan for the new venture should describe how critical risks will be managed if circumstances change. Competitors might engage in price cutting; unexpected delays in development or cost overruns could occur; difficulties might arise in acquiring timely inputs from suppliers. For example, a new daycare center might unexpectedly have a competitor open nearby three months later, or its staff might be accused of inappropriate behavior. Contingency planning helps managers to think beforehand how to handle these situations (see Chapter 8).

Step 4: Mobilize Resources

With a detailed plan for the new venture in place, the entrepreneur is now prepared to acquire and mobilize the necessary resources. This phase involves arranging the required financing, establishing relationships with suppliers and other stakeholders, and creating and implementing the organizational structure and systems.

For most new Mainstream ventures, adequate financing is the key resource that needs to be mobilized. Unless the entrepreneurs are self-financed, they will need either debt or equity financing. **Debt financing** occurs when entrepreneurs *borrow* money from family and friends, a bank, or another financial institution that must be paid back at some future date. Oftentimes collateral—such as personal assets or

Debt financing occurs when entrepreneurs *borrow* from a bank, family members, friends, or a financial institution money that must be paid back at some future date.

DIGGING DEEPER

Entrepreneurs Who Don't Start from Scratch

In the United States, the most common form of business entrepreneurship involves an entrepreneur starting a new venture from scratch. Starting from scratch allows for the most freedom in decision making, avoids problems caused by previous owners, and provides an exciting environment for growth and development. At the same time, it does have some disadvantages, as described in the "liabilities of newness" Digging Deeper feature (on page 182).

A popular alternative to starting from scratch is for an entrepreneur to purchase the rights to *open a franchise* in a new location, which increases the likelihood for success significantly.[36] As described in Chapter 4, *franchising* occurs when a franchisor sells to a franchisee (for a lump-sum payment and a share of the franchisee's profits) a complete package required to set up an organization, including but not limited to its trademark and trade name, its products and services, its ingredients, its technology and machinery, and its management and standard operating systems. A disadvantage of buying a franchise is that the entrepreneur must pay a high initial fee for these rights, must pay an ongoing share of profits to the franchisor, and may see the image of the franchise suffer through no fault of the franchisee. For example, franchise owners of McDonald's restaurants all suffer when movies and books draw attention to undesirable qualities of the McDonald's food. At the same time, the franchise owners benefit for similar reasons because McDonald's has an Active Issues Management program, where staff work to analyze public relations issues and identify effective strategies for handling them.[37]

Sometimes an entrepreneur may opt to *purchase an existing organization* rather than start from scratch or purchase a franchise. It may be especially rewarding to purchase an existing business that is underperforming and needs an injection of creativity and energy. That is what happened when Dan Brady, his brother, and his father bought out existing franchises of Mail Boxes Etc. (now "The UPS Store") in the Philadelphia area. Rather than build a new venture from scratch, these entrepreneurs decided to rejuvenate an existing organization. As Brady put it, "If you buy a tired preexisting location with an existing customer base and cash flow, and infuse it with operational smarts and great execution, the rate at which you can grow positive cash flow and your odds of success go way up as compared to starting the whole thing from scratch."[38]

Equity financing occurs when investors in a new venture receive shares of stock and become part owners of the organization.

Venture capitalist is a company or individual that invests money in an organization in exchange for a share of ownership and profits.

business assets—is required to guarantee a loan. **Equity financing** occurs when investors in a new venture receive shares and become part owners of the organization; this type of financing usually comes from venture capitalists. A **venture capitalist** is a company or individual that invests money in an organization in exchange for a share of its ownership and profits. Venture capitalists often become quite heavily involved in the operations of a business, sometimes even requiring that they approve any major decisions regarding the organization.

Sometimes governments also provide resources specifically geared to support entrepreneurial activity. This support may include educational programs for potential entrepreneurs, including subsidies to local community colleges and universities. It can also involve "incubators" designed to help particular types of entrepreneurs get started. For example, incubators may provide subsidized office space, support services, and management advice to entrepreneurs. Governments may also provide subsidies or incentives to start particular types of organizations. For example, "wind farms" that generate electricity by harnessing the power of the wind were initially subsidized but are now self-sustaining.

Social entrepreneurship refers to the conceiving of an opportunity to provide social value (not just private financial value), relentlessly pursuing that opportunity while being accountable to relevant stakeholders, continuously learning from and improving upon plans, and mobilizing the resources necessary to sustainably convert that opportunity into reality.

THE FOUR STEPS OF MULTISTREAM ENTREPRENEURSHIP

The idea of Multistream entrepreneurship is evident in the growing interest in social entrepreneurship,[39] responsible entrepreneurship,[40] sustainable entrepreneurship, and ecopreneurship.[41] For example, **social entrepreneurship** can be defined as conceiving an opportunity to provide social value (not just private financial value), relentlessly pursuing that opportunity while being accountable to relevant stakeholders, continuously learning from and improving upon plans, and mobilizing present and future resources necessary to sustainably convert the opportunity into reality.[42] In short, whereas the goal of Mainstream entrepreneurship focuses on maximizing the *financial* wealth of the entrepreneurs and other investors, the goal of Multistream entrepreneurship focuses on providing *multiple* forms of well-being for the entrepreneur, other investors, and other stakeholders.

Like Mainstream entrepreneurship, Multistream entrepreneurship can be evident in a wide variety of organizations, including the for-profit and not-for-profit sector, in small and large organizations, and in family-run or publicly traded organizations. The study of Multistream entrepreneurship is relatively new, but its practice has been evident for years in well-known companies such as Ben and Jerry's, Patagonia, AES, ServiceMaster, Timberland, and many others. As Sir Edmund Hillary—who is remembered more for climbing Mount Everest than for his four decades of social entrepreneurship that helped establish more than 30 schools, 12 medical clinics, and 2 hospitals for impoverished Nepalese people— said, "My most worthwhile things have been the building of schools and medical clinics. That has given me more satisfaction than a footprint on a mountain."[43]

The basic four-step entrepreneurial process is the same for Mainstream and Multistream entrepreneurs, but the focus of that process will be different because of their differing views on the importance of materialism and individualism.

Step 1: Identify Opportunity

Both Mainstream and Multistream entrepreneurs think about how new products or services can meet people's needs. However, Multistream entrepreneurs differ from their Mainstream counterparts in two ways.

First, whereas Mainstream entrepreneurs focus on identifying needs that can provide financial payoffs, Multistream entrepreneurs look at needs that can enhance a variety of forms of well-being (e.g., financial, social, ecological, physical). For example, Multistream entrepreneurs may seek to reduce environmental degradation in a financially sustainable way.[45] This is evident in the triple-bottom-line approach, where Multistream entrepreneurs try to enhance financial, social, *and* ecological well-being simultaneously. The triple bottom line is depicted in Figure 6.3, which shows three overlapping circles, where one circle is concerned with financial interests, a second circle with ecological issues, and the third circle with social justice issues. In the center of the figure is a section where all three circles overlap. This "sweet spot" is what triple-bottom-line Multistream entrepreneurs aim for. Of course, Multistream entrepreneurs may also look at quadruple-bottom-line or quintuple-bottom-line opportunities, and pursue opportunities related to a variety of forms of well-being.

Multistream entrepreneurs seek opportunities to improve a variety of forms of well-being. In addition to achieving sustainable financial returns, they look for opportunities to improve employment opportunities for the marginalized of society or to model new ways of taking care of the environment. In short, the Multistream approach represents a different way of entrepreneurial "seeing" than the Mainstream

Sean Blagsveldt was working for Microsoft Research in Bangalore, India, when he identified a great opportunity to help the under-employed poor in that country, like house painter Manohar Lakshmipathi (pictured above). Bangalore has many laborers who are desperate for work, and yet many well-to-do people complained about the shortage of maids and cooks. Blagsveldt quit Microsoft and cofounded Babajob.com, a social-networking site that connects Bangalore's yuppies, via a chain of personal connections, with its independent laborers who earn $2 to $3 per day.[44]

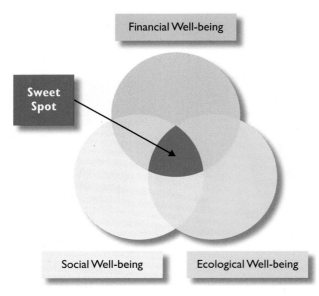

Figure 6.3 in the triple-bottom-line approach has labels: Financial Well-being (top), Social Well-being (bottom left), Ecological Well-being (bottom right), and Sweet Spot (left).

Figure 6.3   The sweet spot in the triple-bottom-line approach

approach. Mohammed Yunus spearheaded the Grameen Bank because he saw this venture as a way to help poor entrepreneurs in Bangladesh—not because he wanted to maximize financial returns for himself and other investors. At the time, Mainstream managers had difficulty in seeing the same opportunity because their minds and eyes had been "blinded" by their training and knowledge. Now many years later, thanks to the success of organizations such as Grameen Bank, big banks have become involved in micro-credit, because their managers increasingly recognize its merits for acquisitive economics instead of only sustenance economics. As one-time McKinsey & Company consultant Vikram Akula notes, the "magic" of micro-financing is that it can work even if banks are "driven only by greed."[46]

A second difference between Multistream and Mainstream entrepreneurs is that whereas Mainstream entrepreneurs often seek to *create* needs or demand for their products or services, success for Multistream entrepreneurs sometimes comes when they *eliminate* needs or demand for their products or services. In short, Multistream organizations often try to work themselves out of a job. For example, the entrepreneurs who founded the Digger Foundation and its volunteers who design machinery to remove landmines would be thrilled if all landmines were eliminated and there were no need for their equipment. Similarly, Yunus is looking forward to eliminating poverty, thereby eliminating the need to provide loans to impoverished people. Others may be seeking to eliminate social injustice, illness, pollution, or other societal problems.

 WHAT DO YOU THINK?

Is There a Difference Between "Green" and "Clean"?

Venture capitalists are excited by the prospects of saving the planet by transforming the $1 trillion energy market in the United States. They have begun pouring billions of dollars into environmentally friendly, energy-related start-ups such as SunPower, Lilliputian Systems, and Nanosolar. Innovations that are energy efficient and ecologically friendly are considered to be "clean tech," as distinguished from "green" projects that are considered to place a greater emphasis on the environment than on profits.[47]

Zhang Yin, who is from China, started a company in the 1990s with her husband to collect paper for recycling in the United States and then ship it to China. This "green" venture has certainly been very profitable, enabling Zhang Yin to become one of the wealthiest self-made women in the world. The demand for paper products increased so quickly that the Nine Dragons paper-making company she formed in China in 1995 had grown to 5300 employees and $1 billion in annual revenues within a decade, with profits reaching $175 million in 2006. While recycling paper may seem "green," some aspects of Nine Dragons' operations do not seem to be "clean." For example, a key to the firm's international competitiveness is that Nine Dragons burns cheap coal rather than cleaner but more expensive natural gas.[48]

Does a new business have to be "green" to be "clean," and vice versa? Do you think there will be differences in how Mainstream versus Multistream entrepreneurs manage "green" and "clean" aspects of new ventures?

Step 2: Show Entrepreneurial Initiative

Many people identify opportunities but lack the initiative to do something about it. For example, many people have ideas on how to help poor people, but an entrepreneur like Mohammad Yunus actually acted on his.

There are both similarities and differences between the personality traits associated with Mainstream and Multistream entrepreneurs. Both have a high need to accomplish something, but for Mainstream entrepreneurs the focus is on achieving tangible and quantifiable financial goals, whereas Multistream entrepreneurs are more likely to want to accomplish something that may defy measurement but is significant and timeless (e.g., pursuit of happiness as described by Aristotle). For example, Yunus was driven to help improve the lives of poor people in Bangladesh.

Similarly, both Mainstream and Multistream entrepreneurs have a sense of confidence in their ventures, but for Mainstream entrepreneurs that confidence is grounded in themselves, whereas for Multistream entrepreneurs it is grounded in a community. Multistream managers recognize that they cannot make a venture happen on their own—the support and cooperation of other stakeholders are required. For example, Yunus worked together with clients, university students, and other bankers as he developed the Grameen Bank. Because Multistream entrepreneurs are more likely to seek other stakeholders' advice and involve them in developing a new venture, they can be confident of their support.

Similar life-path circumstances are also evident when both Multistream and Mainstream entrepreneurs start up organizations: transition, push, and pull. Once again, however, the nature of these influences is often qualitatively different. For Multistream entrepreneurs, *transitions* often result from recognizing and wanting to escape the materialist–individualist character of the status quo. At a general societal level, this kind of transition is illustrated in the growing voluntary simplicity movement. As part of this trend, many previously well-paid professionals have voluntarily become "downwardly mobile" in an effort to escape jobs and lifestyles associated with acquisitive economics.[49]

For example, Tom Chappell left corporate America in 1968 to "move back to the land" and eat and live healthier. When he and his wife Kate were unable to find natural personal care products, they cofounded Tom's of Maine in 1970 with a $5000 loan from a friend. The company grew, but when Chappell saw that its founding values were being challenged by its MBA-trained managers, he became the first sitting CEO to enroll in the Harvard Divinity School. His goal was to rediscover the mission for both himself and his company—that is, to simultaneously be financially successful and socially and environmentally responsible. By 2006, the company had become the leading natural care brand in the United States, and Tom and Kate decided that they could best meet the growing demand for their products by partnering with a larger company. They were very careful to choose a partner they thought would honor their firm's values, and thus chose to become part of the Colgate-Palmolive Company.[51]

Examples of people who are *pushed* to become Multistream entrepreneurs include intrapreneurs or whistleblowers whose efforts were not welcome in their former organizations.[52] In a similar vein, some religious organizations and denominations began

Remember Tom Williams? He's the entrepreneur who started his own computer game company when he was 13, and became famous at 14 when he became perhaps the youngest person ever hired to work for Apple, Inc., in Silicon Valley. Although he earned "an absurd amount of money" and achieved great success there (e.g., Williams was a pioneer in online music), by the time he was in his mid-twenties he realized that meaning was missing from his life. Eventually Williams left Apple to start GiveMeaning.com, a place where people could post project-specific appeals and where donors could have a hassle-free and tax-efficient way to make contributions. In short, Tom Williams is an entrepreneur who makes it easier for people to show initiative when they see opportunities to help others.[50]

Natural Cycle, a cooperative bicycle courier service, has been growing exponentially since it was started by David Geisel and two others. Not only are bicycles 100 times more energy efficient than cars, but they can often deliver within-city letters and packages more quickly and at lower costs than regular couriers.[55]

when a group of members became frustrated with the practices of a parent religious organization and left in order to start something new.[53]

Finally, people may experience *positive pulls* to become Multistream entrepreneurs from friends or others who are encouraging and offer support for a new organization. The story of social entrepreneur George Willdridge provides an example where all three life-path circumstances are evident. Willdridge had become a very successful managing director of an import/export firm when, as part of his job to entertain wealthy Asian customers who enjoyed high-stakes gambling, he became addicted to gambling himself. Soon he had no job (transition), no money, and huge debts, and he contemplated suicide every day for six weeks. Willdridge knew that the status quo behavior associated with his gambling addiction needed to be changed (push). He became a social entrepreneur when the Salvation Army asked him to set up the Oasis Centre for Problem Gamblers in Auckland, New Zealand (pull). For Willdridge, the depths of despair associated with his gambling addiction became a life-changing moment, when he came to realize that "quality of life does not stem from wealth. Once you have enough, it makes no difference."[54]

Step 3: Develop a Plan for the New Venture

From a Multistream perspective, Mainstream theory places too much emphasis on developing a detailed plan for a new venture.[56] For example, one study found that only 28 percent of a sample of *Inc.* 500 firms had completed a prototypical business plan, and other research has shown no relationship between having a new venture plan and future profitability.[57] Critics of developing detailed plans for new ventures argue that planning may be irrelevant and constraining, limiting the likelihood of ongoing experimentation as the organization grows. These critics point out that the planning process focuses on **explicit knowledge,** whereas much of what entrepreneurs do is based on tacit knowledge that is learned by experience. **Tacit knowledge** is difficult to codify or articulate, and this very characteristic makes it a source of strategic advantage for entrepreneurs. In particular, it can be harmful for managers to stick with rigid plans that no longer apply to the situation.[58]

Managers at the World Bank, for example, encourage flexible planning to foster intrapreneurship. In one case, a team had been given the planned goal to increase milk *production* for rural farmers in Africa. When team members visited the field, they found out that the real problem was *spoilage* of milk as it traveled from producer to consumers. Their flexibility allowed them to change their focus to the problem they had learned about as a result of their in-person investigation. As the team leader put it, "I now realize how much of the overall success of the effort depends on people discovering for themselves what goals to set and what to do to

Explicit knowledge is information that can be articulated or codified, such as that found in an organization's standard operating procedures, blueprints, mission statements, and so on.

Tacit knowledge is information or an ability that people hold that is difficult to articulate and/or codify.

achieve them."[59] Whereas an emphasis on planning reinforces *convergent* thinking (where managers seek to find a single precise answer), a Multistream approach encourages *divergent* thinking (where managers discover multiple alternative solutions based on the same information).[60]

These observations are not meant to suggest that all planning is unimportant, or that you should not try to put into words the tacit knowledge that leads to entrepreneurial success. They do, however, point out that making detailed plans prior to start-up may have unintended negative outcomes, and following them in a linear sequential manner may be harmful. Rather, according to a Multistream approach, plans should be made in the specific content areas when appropriate, with emphasis on creating feedback paths and flexibility at each critical stage of development and remaining open to change. Although the various parts of the plan are related, it is best to work on each part when the time is right. Such a Multistream approach allows for continual feedback and reevaluation.[61]

Another significant difference between Mainstream and Multistream entrepreneurship is that whereas Mainstream entrepreneurs *use the plan to convince stakeholders to support the organization*, Multistream entrepreneurs *use stakeholders to write a convincing plan*. This difference in perspective is what makes writing a Multistream plan a process of continual revisions.

Consider what happened when managers of Kowalski's, a Minnesota grocery chain, purchased four store locations in 2002, including an existing grocery store in a lower- to middle-class neighborhood that did not fit the grocer's typical upscale demographic. Rather than sell this property, managers decided that they had an obligation to provide the neighborhood with a viable grocery store (which the former tenant had failed to do). Founders Mary Anne and Jim Kowalski shared their vision for their newly acquired store at a community meeting in the neighborhood. They promised to provide a clean, safe store and vowed not to sell lottery tickets or cigarettes. They then invited residents of the neighborhood to name the store and to spend all of its profits. In return, the couple asked the neighborhood residents to shop at the store. The residents shocked the Kowalskis by stating that they would rather have a prosperous store in the neighborhood than to take any profits, and they felt that keeping the Kowalski's name would attract more businesses into the community. As expected, the store has made a valuable contribution to the neighborhood, including an increased sense of community spirit and increased property values. Even though the store did not turn a profit in its first few years, the Kowalskis viewed it as a success because of the sense of community it has fostered. As Mary Anne Kowalski notes, this entrepreneurial endeavor shows the importance of neighborliness and citizenship: Business can't do it on its own.[62]

Probably the most striking difference between a Multistream new-venture plan and a Mainstream start-up plan is that the Multistream plan includes an ongoing reference to multiple forms of well-being (e.g., the triple-bottom-line approach). For Mainstream entrepreneurs, the focus of the plan is on the financial aspects of the new organization, with the goal being to demonstrate that the new venture will be financially viable and offer greater-than-average returns. It would be unusual for such plans to refer to ecological or social justice implications, unless these considerations would explicitly enhance the financial bottom line. In contrast, for Multistream entrepreneurs, the organizational plan may focus on the social or ecological aspects of the organization just as much as on its financial viability. For example, any plan that Yunus would write about the Grameen Bank would include mention of how the bank would help poor people to escape poverty, provide women with greater opportunities to meet their needs and those of their children, and develop a sense of community.

Comparing Mainstream and Multistream Plans for New Ventures

Five Parts of Plan	Mainstream Approach	Multistream Approach
1. Summary	Identify the opportunity and highlight how it enhances the financial well-being of investors	Identify and describe opportunities that enhance a variety of forms of well-being for investors and other stakeholders
2. Concept of the new venture	Specify the unmet need in the *economic* context of customers and other organizations, and describe how the new venture's goods or services will meet that need	Specify the unmet need in the *overall* context of customers and other organizations, and describe how the new venture's goods or services will meet that need
3. Management team	Highlight the strengths and roles of team members	Highlight the strengths and roles of team members *and* external stakeholders
4. Operations	Specify all the resources required, along with their expected financial costs	Specify all the resources required, along with their expected financial, social, and environmental costs
5. Timeline, projected performance, and contingency plans	Focus on expected financial performance over time	Focus on financial, social, and ecological performance over time

The structure of a Multistream plan for a new venture is the same as for a Mainstream plan. However, as highlighted in Table 6.2, some of the content is different.

1. SUMMARY.   The summary in a plan utilizing a Multistream approach is similar to that for a plan utilizing the Mainstream approach, except that the Multistream approach highlights not only how the new venture can enhance financial well-being, but also how it may enhance other forms of well-being. For example, the Grameen Bank was started not because Yunus saw an opportunity to make a profit by meeting an unmet need among poor people, but because he saw how micro-credit could help poor people to escape poverty and enhance village life in Bangladesh.

2. CONCEPT OF THE NEW VENTURE.   This section is also similar to the corresponding section in a Mainstream plan. However, rather than concentrate only on issues related to acquisitive economics, the Multistream approach also describes strengths, weaknesses, opportunities, and threats in light of ecological or social concerns and sustenance economics. For example, a new daycare center may be promoted as operating in a community with many single parents who cannot afford existing daycares, or a new video game may be touted for its health benefits when players control their screen by pedaling on exercise bikes (CycleScore, which is being developed by MIT students, matches this description)[63] or because the game promotes nonviolent behavior. Similarly, the description of the product or service itself will draw attention to its multiple benefits, perhaps including a reduced ecological footprint compared to competitors.

3. MANAGEMENT TEAM.   Compared to a Mainstream plan, a Multistream plan is likely to place greater emphasis on the involvement of key external stakeholders in the design and ongoing operation of the organization. This involvement of external stakeholders was evident in the description of Kowalski's new grocery outlet, when the store's owners invited residents in the neighborhood to name the store and spend its profits. As another example, an inner-city Multistream daycare center may highlight the input of representatives from local schools and social welfare agencies, and

emphasize their ongoing presence on the daycare center's
board. A video game producer
may draw attention to the role
of educators and even social
anthropologists who help to
design a game that is both compelling and socially constructive. These stakeholders are important not only in giving shape
to the organization, but also in
ensuring its ongoing development. Similarly, the management philosophy will be evident in the organization's
structures and systems, which,
for example, will pay more attention to empowerment at all
levels of the organization.[64]

Founded by sisters Erica and Sara Ku-
bersky, MooShoes sells stylish and affordable animal-free footwear, bags,
wallets, and other items. "MooShoes
insists that one cannot have fashion
without compassion."[65]

4. OPERATIONS. Perhaps
the most distinct feature of a
Multistream approach is its concern for the ecological footprint of the new venture.
A Multistream start-up plan is much more likely to cover issues such as the energy
efficiency of the physical plant and equipment, a description of how waste will be
minimized and recycled, and so on. This is illustrated by the Multistream organization called Bioplaneta started by Hector Marcelli to promote Fair Trade, organic
agriculture, and sustainable development. Bioplaneta helps Mexican entrepreneurs
develop plans for new ventures that protect natural resources and minimize ecological impact (sometimes called ecopreneurship).[66]

A Multistream plan is also more likely to describe how suppliers are chosen
based on their perceived corporate social responsibility and to look at how hiring
practices affect social justice. For example, a daycare center operating in the inner
city may be more inclined to hire local people and provide training for them.

Greyston Bakery was started more than 20 years ago with the goal of hiring
chronically unemployed New Yorkers and training them how to work in a bakery.
Its business profits are used to help fund daycare centers, counseling services, and
health clinics. The bakery does not hire people to bake cookies, but rather bakes
cookies to hire people. It employs approximately 65 people, many of whom are
previous drug addicts and people straight from prison. About half of the people it
hires drop out, but many of the others have moved on to other full-time jobs with
good benefits. Greyston Bakery was founded by Bernie Glassman, a Jewish aero-
space engineer who became a Buddhist priest with an interest in social entrepreneurship: "I wanted to show that people [who] are homeless, if they're given the
chance and the right training, could not only work in our labor force but can produce the high niche items of our society. They could produce items that only the
French chefs could create . . . We had a tremendous amount of obstacles [in the
beginning]. Almost, we almost went broke a few times."[67]

Multistream entrepreneurs also try to make sure that their distribution network is
environmentally friendly and socially responsible. Some ideas demand the creation of
a brand-new distribution network. For example, car manufacturers that are working to

Customers at Denise Cerreta's One World Café in Salt Lake City range from homeless people to well-to-do professionals. Everyone gets a high-quality meal and pays what he or she can afford or thinks is fair. Cerreta receives many requests from other entrepreneurs who wish to open a similar café, so the café formed a nonprofit organization to help others replicate the original venture (www .oneworldeverybodyeats.com). For example, Cerreta spent a month helping Libby and Brad Birky open their SAME (So All May Eat) Café in Denver: "Our philosophy is that everyone, regardless of economic status, deserves the chance to eat healthy, organic food while being treated with dignity." Guests who cannot afford to pay are encouraged to help out by sweeping, washing dishes, or weeding the organic garden, while guests who can afford it are encouraged to leave a little extra.[68]

introduce hydrogen-powered, environmentally friendly automobiles recognize that to sell cars they need to have a network of hydrogen stations for refueling. Building such a distribution network is a challenge, because there must be enough customers who own cars that use hydrogen as fuel for the hydrogen stations to be financially viable.

5. TIMELINE, FINANCIAL PROJECTIONS, AND CONTINGENCY PLANS. Compared to a Mainstream plan, a Multistream plan is more likely to supplement financial concerns and measures with social and ecological measures. For example, success measures at Greyston Bakery may include satisfied customers, financial viability, job opportunities for people on the margins of society, and a small ecological footprint. Multistream plans will seek to enhance overall well-being in the long term, which may in turn influence things like decisions about overseas expansion. Contingency plans will include social and ecological contingencies.

Step 4: Mobilize Resources

Both Mainstream and Multistream entrepreneurs need to mobilize financial resources to get their organizations started. As the opening case illustrates, Mainstream financial institutions may prefer providing financing to Mainstream entrepreneurs, and as a result, Multistream entrepreneurs need to become more creative in gaining access to financial resources.

In any case, Multistream entrepreneurs are more likely to recognize the importance of nonfinancial resources, and especially the fact that good relationships with stakeholders can reduce the need for financial resources. Multistream entrepreneurs develop social networks to develop their credibility. While doing so, they invite stakeholders to give shape to, identify with, and create opportunities to support the values and basic concept of the new venture. For example, ever since its earliest days Celestial Seasonings, the leading herbal tea company in the United States, has done extensive product testing with consumers.[69] This same emphasis on developing relationships with stakeholders is also evident in the examples set by entrepreneurs like Yunus and the Kowalskis.

Multistream entrepreneurs are also more mindful of how they mobilize the physical resources required for their new venture. What is the effect of operations on the ecological footprint? Again, these concerns are addressed by working together with stakeholders who are concerned about the ecological environment. For example, every year thousands of "bioneers" gather for a three-day conference in San Rafael, California (another 10,000 participants are beamed in by satellite). Attendees include entrepreneurs like Jay Harman, who demonstrated an energy-saving technology for pumps and fans, and John Maus, a contractor looking for the latest information on green building.[70]

Because Multistream entrepreneurs are more sensitive to using resources responsibly, and because they are more likely to welcome input from key stakeholders, their venture should be more sustainable over the long term and enjoy wider support in the larger community. This support can also come from financial institutions. For example, as discussed in Chapter 3, there is increasing interest in socially responsible investing—such portfolios now account for approximately $2 trillion in investments.[71] Specialist networks can help sustainable organizations find venture capital; examples include Cleantech Venture Network, Investor's Circle, and World Resources Institute's New Ventures.[72] Organizations like Ashoka look for social entrepreneurs to invest in whom no one else will.[73] In short, because of their attention to nonfinancial resources and benefits, Multistream ventures will be more attractive to certain investors, and particularly to investors who look for more than simply maximizing their financial return. At the Grameen Bank, for example, entrepreneurs are more likely to get a loan the *poorer* they are and the *less* financial collateral they have.

Googling Google[74]

By almost any measure, Google Inc. represents an amazing entrepreneurial success story. Within the span of eight years, it went from a student research project in a university dorm room (1996) to a company valued at almost $30 billion. Its initial public offering (IPO) raised $1.6 billion, a new record for a technology IPO. The company is known for its motto of "Do no evil," for bringing unbiased information to people speaking many languages around the world, for giving small businesses affordable access to advertising,[75] for creating a fun work environment, and even for being a leader in ecological responsibility.[76] Here are some excerpts from the story of Google's formative years.

Larry Page and Sergey Brin, the cofounders of Google, met in 1995 when they were graduate students at Stanford University. At the time, Brin was 23 years old and had been assigned to show the 24-year-old Page around campus. The pair argued with each other about almost everything, but their divergent points of view came together in January 1996, when they began working on one of the biggest challenges in computing—namely, retrieving relevant information from a huge data set. Their unique approach was based on the ability to analyze the "back links" that pointed to a given website. The mission of Google continues to be "to organize the world's information and make it universally accessible

and useful." For Page and Brin, a better search engine was everything—profit was peripheral.

After a couple of years' work, Page and Brin had developed their ideas and built a beta version of their better mousetrap. They had never intended to start a new venture, but rather wanted to license their search technology to an existing organization. However, when managers at potential partner organizations failed to see the value of their technology, the pair took a break from their university studies to start their own new venture. An early attempt at finding an investor involved demonstrating a prototype to Andy Bechtelsheim, a cofounder of Sun Microsystems and a legend in Silicon Valley for his ability as an engineer and his nose for talent. Brin recalls that fateful day in 1998: "We met him very early one morning on the porch of a Stanford faculty member's home in Palo Alto. We gave him a quick demo. He had to run off somewhere, so he said, 'Instead of us discussing all the details, why don't I just write you a check?' It was made out to Google Inc. and was for $100,000."

Page and Brin knew they couldn't deposit the check until they actually completed the legal work to create "Google Inc." By September 1998, they had accumulated an initial investment of almost $1 million from family, friends, and acquaintances, and Google opened its first off-campus office in a friend's garage in Menlo Park,

California. At the time Google had a staff of three, and the beta version of Google.com was answering nearly 10,000 search queries per day.

By February 1999, the beta version was answering 500,000 queries per day, and Google's staff of eight employees had relocated to an office in Palo Alto. Google's first commercial search customer was Red Hat, partly because of Google's commitment to run its servers on the Linux open-source operating system.

Page and Brin were aware that their $1 million wouldn't last long, so they went looking for support from leading venture capitalists in Silicon Valley. Specifically, they sought the support of John Doerr of Kleiner Perkins, who was arguably the most influential venture capitalist in the Valley, and Mike Moritz of Sequoia Capital, who had backed Yahoo!. Both Doerr and Moritz were as impressed as Bechtelsheim had been—they were not concerned by the lack of a detailed business plan—but both wanted to do the deal *alone*. Page and Brin insisted they wanted *both* Doerr and Moritz as backers, something that had never happened before. Doerr and Moritz agreed to invest jointly only after Page and Brin threatened to look for investment capital elsewhere. On June 7, 1999, Google secured $25 million from the two influential venture capital firms, and both Doerr and Moritz joined Google's board of directors (who met around a ping-pong table). Soon, traffic on Google surpassed 3 million searches per day, and on September 21, 1999, the "beta" label came off the website. By the end of 2000, Google was handling more than 100 million search queries every day.

To generate revenue, in 2000 Google started experimenting with getting advertisers. Both Page and Brin were strongly opposed to pop-up and banner ads and preferred a minimalist approach, with text-based ads appearing on the right side of the screen. In 2001, they introduced AdWords, where advertisers bid for keywords to get the best placement possible, for which they paid only if the user clicked on their ads. In 2003, Google added AdSense, essentially allowing other Web operators (e.g., the *New York Times*) to use a system like AdWords on their screens. In 2001, Google barely turned a profit with $87 million in revenues; by 2003, however, its revenues were $1.5 billion and its profits totaled $340 million.

Meanwhile, Google's unique organizational culture flourished as the company kept growing. The desks of its 60 or so employees were doors laid across a pair of sawhorses, and office chairs were often large rubber exercise balls. Google hired a company chef who prepared many health-conscious recipes. Twice a week, employees used the parking lot to play roller hockey. This informal culture fostered collegiality and facilitated the exchange of ideas. In Google's entrepreneurial culture, there is minimal corporate hierarchy and staff often wear several hats.

Not surprisingly, given these unconventional management practices, Doerr and Moritz insisted that Page and Brin hire a professional manager to become CEO of the firm. At first Page and Brin resisted, but they soon saw the merits of having a professional manager after Doerr arranged meetings with a variety of leading industry executives in Silicon Valley. Eric Schmidt, previous CEO of Novell, became Google's CEO in 2001: "We're not just three random guys. We're all computer scientists with the same interests and backgrounds. The first time we met, we argued for an hour and a half over pretty much everything—and it was a really good argument."

However, outside observers continued to note the apparent lack of well-defined organizational structures and systems at Google. For example, when asked how decisions were made at Google, Schmidt spent 45 minutes trying to come up with an answer. He noted that they had found a new way of doing business, breaking all the rules—a triumvirate of equals with no hierarchy.[77]

Page and Brin were not eager about offering Google for public sale. The main reason that any firm goes public is to raise cash, but Google already had enough. They also knew that previous IPOs had created "forces of greed and envy that wreaked havoc on promising start-ups." But Doerr and Moritz were eager to cash in on their investment, and the employees who had been working hard for years were also eager for the payday that would come with an IPO. Page and Brin relented, but insisted the IPO be set up to make it clear that managers at Google would not feel compelled to play the short-term financial games based on acquisitive economics required by Wall Street. Take a look at your textbook website for excerpts from a "Letter from the Founders" written prior to Google's IPO in 2004. It was entitled "An Owner's Manual" for Google's shareholders.[78]

QUESTIONS FOR DISCUSSION

1. Can you identify the four steps of the entrepreneurship process in the formation of Google? Which step was the most important for this firm? Which seemed least important? Explain your answers.

2. Imagine that you had been hired by Page and Brin in 1999 to write a start-up plan for the new venture to attract the attention of venture capitalists. What would you put in that plan?

3. What are the secrets to the entrepreneurial success of Page and Brin? Which aspects of their approach are crucial to the success of Google, and which threaten Google's long-term stability? Where would you place them along the Mainstream–Multistream continuum? Why?

4. Do you agree with the people who argue that shareholders will permit Google's managers to use unconventional management practices only as long as the organization is growing and making a lot of money? These critics argue that by making Google public, entrepreneurs like Page, Brin, and Schmidt essentially crossed a point of no return, with the company having "sold its soul" to stockholders and the idea of "good versus evil no longer a practical consideration."[79] According to this view, when a significant downturn occurs, as inevitably happens with all organizations, shareholders will demand a more Mainstream management approach. What do you think?

5. Note the similarity between Mohammad Yunus and the duo of Larry Page and Sergey Brin: None initially wanted to start his own new venture, but each felt compelled to do so when managers in established organizations failed to see the merit of their innovations. What other similarities do you see in the opening and closing cases in this chapter? What are the implications for aspiring entrepreneurs? For other managers?

SUMMARY

Both Mainstream and Multistream entrepreneurs follow a similar four-step entrepreneurial process, but there are differences in how the process unfolds. In the Mainstream approach, entrepreneurs:

1. **Identify opportunities** to offer a product or service that meets a need that people are willing to pay for.

2. **Show entrepreneurial initiative** resulting from a combination of the entrepreneur's personality traits (predisposition to see financial opportunities, need for achievement, and self-confidence) coupled with his or her life-path circumstances (transition, push, pull).

3. **Develop a plan** for the new venture with an emphasis on financial costs and benefits.

4. **Mobilize resources,** especially attracting the required start-up financing.

In the Multistream approach, entrepreneurs:

1. **Identify opportunities** to offer a product or service that meets or eliminates needs that people have.

2. **Show entrepreneurial initiative** resulting from a combination of the entrepreneurs' personality traits (predisposition to see opportunities that enhance multiple forms of well-being, need to help, and confidence in the community) coupled with their life-path circumstances (transition, push, pull).

3. **Develop a plan** for the new venture with an emphasis on financial, social, and ecological costs and benefits.

4. **Mobilize resources,** especially attracting the support from other stakeholders.

QUESTIONS FOR REFLECTION AND DISCUSSION

1. Identify and describe the four steps of the entrepreneurial process. What are the differences between the Mainstream and Multistream approaches in each step?

2. Identify and describe the five parts of the plan for a new venture. How is each part related to the entrepreneurial process?

3. What are the pros and cons of developing a detailed plan for a new venture prior to start-up?

4. What are the benefits of entrepreneurship for society?

5. How often do you talk with your friends or family about ideas for starting a new venture? How are you different from the entrepreneurs in this chapter, who also had good ideas and put them into practice? How are you similar? Which do you think is more important for entrepreneurial initiative: personality traits or life-path circumstances? Explain your answer.

HANDS-ON ACTIVITIES

Each of the following questions contains two opposing or contrasting statements. Rate yourself on a scale from 1 to 7 to place yourself on the continuum between the two statements.

HOW LIKELY ARE YOU TO BECOME AN ENTREPRENEUR?*

I generate work for myself and for others.	1 2 3 4 5 6 7	I complete assignments very well and look to my boss for the next one.
I have been fired more than once.	1 2 3 4 5 6 7	I always get along with my boss.
I learn from my mistakes.	1 2 3 4 5 6 7	I'm devastated by mistakes.
I'm always talking about my work with my friends.	1 2 3 4 5 6 7	I keep my job and my personal life separate.
I'm good at multitasking.	1 2 3 4 5 6 7	I'm at my best when I can finish one project before proceeding to the next.

*These items were developed based on a self-test found in Lasher, W. R. (2005). *The perfect business plan made simple* (pp. 179, 183). New York: Broadway Books.

The lower your score, the more likely you are to become an entrepreneur.

WHERE ARE YOU ALONG THE MAINSTREAM–MULTISTREAM CONTINUUM?

I have a high need to achieve defined goals.	1 2 3 4 5 6 7	I have a high need to help others.
I have confidence in myself.	1 2 3 4 5 6 7	I have confidence in the community that I belong to.
I tend to focus on the financial costs and benefits of a business opportunity.	1 2 3 4 5 6 7	I tend to focus on the social and ecological costs and benefits of a business opportunity.
Financial resources are key to a successful organizational start-up.	1 2 3 4 5 6 7	Community support is key to a successful organizational start-up.

The higher your score, the more you lean toward Multistream entrepreneurship; the lower your score, the more you lean toward Mainstream entrepreneurship.

ENDNOTES

1. Grameen Bank home page; Dyck, B. (2001) Micro-financing and international development: The MEDA approach. Presented at *CIBER*, San Diego, March 28–31, 2001; Jolis, A. (1996, May 5). The good banker. *The Independent (Sunday Supplement)*. Accessed November 8, 2006, at http://www.grameen-info.org/agrameen/ profile.php3?profile=2; Tharoor, I. (2006, October 13). Paving the way out of poverty: Bangladeshi economist Muhammad Yunus was awarded the 2006 Nobel Peace Prize not for giving to the poor, but for helping them to help themselves. *Time*. Accessed November 8, 2006, at http://www.time.com/time/world/ article/0,8599,1546100,00.html; Yunus, M. (1996, November/ December). Fighting poverty from the bottom up: An address by Muhammad Yunus. *TIMELINE*. Accessed November 8, 2006, at http://www.grameen-info.org/mcredit/timeline.html; Twenty great Asians. *Asiaweek*; The lender: Muhammad Yunus. Accessed November 8, 2006, at http://www.grameen-info.org/agrameen/ profile.php3?profile=3.

2. Jolis, A. (1996, May 5). The good banker. *The Independent (Sunday Supplement)*. Accessed November 8, 2006, at http://www .grameen-info.org/agrameen/profile.php3?profile=2.

3. The quotes in the four phases are from Yunus, M. (1996, November/December). Fighting poverty from the bottom up: An address by Muhammad Yunus. *TIMELINE*. Accessed November 8, 2006, at http://www.grameen-info.org/mcredit/timeline.html.

4. According to Yunus: "When we started, we looked at all the other banks in Bangladesh and found that only 1 percent of their membership were women. We aimed for 50/50 in the beginning. The main challenge for a poor woman was overcoming the fear in her which was holding her up. We found that compared to men who spent money more freely, women benefited their families much more. Women wanted to save and invest and create assets, unlike men who wanted to enjoy right away. Women are more self-sacrificing, they want to see their children better fed, better dressed, and, as a result, the conditions of the entire community improved" [Tharoor, I. (2006, October 13). Paving the way out of poverty: Bangladeshi economist Muhammad Yunus was awarded the 2006 Nobel Peace Prize not for giving to the poor, but for helping them to help themselves. *Time*. Accessed November 8, 2006, at http://www.time.com/time/ world/article/0,8599,1546100,00.html].

5. According to Yunus: "Each branch is self-contained, its own Grameen Bank, made up of a community of borrowers and local staff who all know each other. We have a total staff of 20,000, and lend $800 million a year to 6.6 million members nationwide. The Bank is very close to its community; there is a relationship of trust and the system as a whole [that] encourages repayment. There is no attempt on anyone's part to outsmart anyone. After all, everyone wants to keep the door open to opportunity and we present that opportunity" (Tharoor, 2006).

6. Koop, P.J. (2006). Engineering answers to landmine problem. *Peace Projections*, 22(1), 1–2; http://www.digger.ch/foundation/ history/?lang=; Email from N. Kunz, February 28, 2008.

7. This example is taken from pages 3 and 4 in Dees, J. G., Emerson, J., & Economy, P. (2001). *Enterprising nonprofits: A tool kit for social entrepreneurs*. New York: John Wiley and Sons.

8. Dees et al., 2001, p. 3.

9. In some cases, especially when an entrepreneur's financial goals have already been more than adequately met, the goal of entrepreneurship may be to seek status or fame rather than to achieve financial success. For example, sometimes owners of professional sports teams expect to lose money in their business venture, but enjoy the high profile that comes with owning a team.

10. Reynolds, P. D., Carter, N. M., Gartner, W. B., & Greene, P. G. (2004). The prevalence of nascent entrepreneurs in the United States: Evidence from the panel study of entrepreneurial dynamics. *Small Business Economics, 23*, 263–284.

11. See page 175 in Daft, Richard L. (2003). *Management* (6th ed.). Mason, OH: Thomson South-Western; and Hellriegel, D., Jackson, S. E., & Slocum, J. W. (2002). *Management: A competency-based approach* (9th ed.). Cincinnati, OH: Thomson South-Western.

12. Hellriegel et al., 2002, p. 136. See also page 236 in Schermerhorn, J. R. (2002). *Management* (7th ed.). New York: John Wiley and Sons.

13. Davermann, M. (2006). HR = higher revenues? *Fortune Small Business, 16*(6), 80–81.

14. Helft, M. (2006a, October 16). It pays to have pals in Silicon Valley. *New York Times*. Accessed February 19, 2008, at http://www.nytimes.com/2006/10/17/technology/17paypal .html?scp=1&sq=&st=nyt.

15. Redekop, B. (2006, December 29). Online pioneers sell business. *Winnipeg Free Press*, pp. A1, A3.

16. Avery, S. (2004, June 15). Idea finally spins gold for Web's inventor: Tim Berners-Lee will receive $1.7 million for concept that changed the world. *The Globe and Mail*, p. B9.

17. Allen, K. R. (2006). *Launching new ventures: An entrepreneurial approach* (4th ed.). Boston: Houghton Mifflin.

18. The exact figure is 6.2 out of every 100 adults (older than age 18) in the United States (Reynolds et al., 2004).

19. Collins, C. J., Hanges, P. J., & Locke, E. A. (2004). The relationship of achievement motivation to entrepreneurial behavior: A meta-analysis. *Human Performance, 17*(1), 95–117.

20. Although management textbooks often talk about entrepreneurs' self-confidence, the scholarly research typically focuses on self-esteem. For example, see Robinson, P. B., Huefner, J. C., & Hunt, H. K. (1991). Entrepreneurial research on student subjects does not generalize to real world entrepreneurs. *Journal of Small Business Management, 29*, 42–50.

21. Brenner, J. G. (1999). *The emperors of chocolate: Inside the secret world of Hershey and Mars*. New York: Broadway Books.

22. Some organizations foster *intrapreneurship*, which basically provides opportunities for entrepreneurs to work within an existing organization. An intrapreneur is a person who, within a larger organization, behaves like an entrepreneur. Intrapreneurs see an opportunity that has potential for the organization and are given the freedom to act on it. Because intrapreneurship may require nontraditional methods for development and growth of the idea, *skunkworks*—teams that are intentionally separated from normal organizational constraints and given the freedom to create and develop new products—may be used to support intrapreneurs.

23. Helft, 2006a.

24. For example, see Jalbert, S. E. (2000). *Women entrepreneurs in the global economy*. Centre for International Private Enterprise. Accessed December 30, 2006, at http://www.cipe.org/pdf/ programs/women/jalbert.pdf.

25. Perman, S. (2006, June 6). The entrepreneurial melting pot. *Business Week Online.* Accessed February 19, 2008, at http://www.businessweek.com/smallbiz/content/jun2006/sb20060606_980521.htm.

26. Dyck, B., & Starke, F. A. (1999). The formation of breakaway organizations: Observations and a process model. *Administrative Science Quarterly, 44,* 792–822.

27. Based on Dyck & Starke, 1999.

28. Reynolds, P. D., Carter, N. M., Gartner, W. B., & Greene, P. G. (2004). The prevalence of nascent entrepreneurs in the United States: Evidence from the panel study of entrepreneurial dynamics. *Small Business Economics, 23,* 263–284.

29. Honig, B. (2004). Entrepreneurship education: Toward a model of contingency-based business planning. *Academy of Management Learning and Education, 3*(3), 258–273.

30. *Sunday not rest day for Welsh entrepreneurs.* (2006, July 24). Accessed December 30, 2006, at http://www.itwales.com/799355.htm.

31. Helft, M. (2006, October 12). With YouTube, grad student hits jackpot again. *New York Times.* Accessed February 19, 2008, at http://www.nytimes.com/2006/10/12/technology/12tube.html?scp=1&sq=&st=nyt.

32. Franke, N., Gruber, M., Harhoff, D., & Henkel, J. (2008, in press). Venture capitalists' evaluation of start-up teams: Trade-offs, knock-out criteria, and the impact of VC experience. *Entrepreneurship Theory and Practice, 32* (in press).

33. Helft, 2006. As with other examples in this textbook, being included in this part of the chapter does not necessarily mean that entrepreneurs are Mainstream.

34. Most of the information in this feature comes from Morse, E. A., Fowler, S. W., & Lawrence, T. B. (2007). The impact of virtual embeddedness on new venture survival: Overcoming the liabilities of newness. *Entrepreneurship Theory and Practice, 31*(2), 139–159. See also Stinchcombe, A. L., (1965). Social structure and organizations. In J. G. March (Ed.), *Handbook of organizations* (pp. 142–193). Chicago: Rand McNally; and Zahra, S. A. (2005). Theory of international new ventures: A decade of research. *Journal of International Business Studies, 36,* 20–28.

35. Travica, B. (2005). Virtual organization and electronic commerce. *Data Base for Advances in Information Systems, 36*(3), 45–68.

36. Fein cites data from the U.S. Chamber of Commerce suggesting that 97 percent of franchises are still in business five years after starting, and that 62 percent of nonfranchised businesses close within the first six years of opening: Fein, K. (2007, July 17). In five years—97% success rate or 62% failure rate. *EzineArticles.* Accessed August 18, 2007, at http://ezinearticles.com/?In-Five-Years—97%25-Success-Rate—Or—62%25-Failure-Rate&id=649310.

37. For example, the Active Issues Management program had anticipated the public concern over obesity that followed in the wake of the best-selling book *Fast Food Nation,* but senior McDonald's executives didn't think it would affect the company and refused to allocate the required resources to deal with it: Savitz, A. W., & Weber, K. (2006). *The triple bottom line: How today's best-run companies are achieving economic, social and environmental success—and how you can too.* San Francisco: Jossey-Bass. See also Schlosser, E. (2001). *Fast food nation: The dark side of the all-American meal.* Boston: Houghton-Mifflin.

38. Cited in *Choosing a business? Why not skip the startup phase?* (2006). Accessed April 14, 2008, at http://www.startupnation.com/pages/articles/AT_Choosing-Business-Skip-Startup.asp.

39. For example, the magazine *Fast Company* selects and reviews "25 entrepreneurs who are changing the world." Also, several journals have devoted special issues to social entrepreneurship—for example, *Journal of World Business, New Business Venturing, International Journal of Entrepreneurship Education,* and *Entrepreneurship and Regional Development.* In addition, some special business plan competitions focus on social entrepreneurship [Crocket, C. (2006). *The impending obsolescence of "social entrepreneurship."* Working paper presented at CCCU Network Scholars Meeting, SPU, Washington, DC]. See also Dees et al., 2001.

40. Hall, C. (2001). *The responsible entrepreneur: How to make money and make a difference.* Franklin Lakes, NJ: Career Press. Reviewed by Cosgrove, J. M., & Williams, P. M. (2004). Book Review: *The Responsible Entrepreneur: How to Make Money and Make a Difference* (Book). *Academy of Management Learning and Education, 3*(3), 330–331.

41. Schaper, M. (Ed.). (2005). *Making ecopreneurship: Developing sustainable entrepreneurship.* Aldershot, Hampshire, UK: Ashgate.

42. There is some debate about how to define "social entrepreneurship." This definition builds on the ideas in this chapter and draws from the following sources: Dees, J. G. (1998). *The meaning of "social entrepreneurship."* Working paper, Kauffman Center for Entrepreneurial Leadership. Accessed October 10, 2007, at http://72.14.205.104/search?q=cache:myjQGSKKjAcJ:www.fntc.info/files/documents/The%2520meaning%2520of%2520Social%2520Entreneurship.pdf+definition%22social+entrepreneurship%22&hl=en&ct=clnk&cd=5&client=safari); definition found on website of The Schwab Foundation for Social Entrepreneurship. Accessed October 10, 2007, at http://www.schwabfound.org/definition.htm); Chell, E. (2007). Social enterprise and entrepreneurship: Towards a convergent theory of entrepreneurial process. *International Small Business Journal, 25*(1), 5–26.

43. Cited on page 48 in Roberts, D., & Woods, C. (2005, Autumn). Changing the world on a shoestring: The concept of social entrepreneurship. *Business Review* (University of Auckland), 45–51.

44. See Giridharadas, A. (2007, October 30). In India, poverty inspires technology workers to altruism. *New York Times.* Accessed February 19, 2008, at http://www.nytimes.com/2007/10/30/technology/30poor.html?scp=1&sq=&st=nyt.

45. Thomas, D. J., & McMullen, J. (2007). Toward a theory of sustainable entrepreneurship: Reducing environmental degradation through entrepreneurial action. *Journal of Business Venturing, 22*(1), 50–76.

46. Quotes taken from Bellman, E. (2006, May 15). Entrepreneur gets big banks to back very small loans. *Wall Street Journal,* pp. A1, A12.

47. Richtel, M. (2007, March 14). Start-up fervor shifts to energy in Silicon Valley. *New York Times.* Accessed February 19, 2008, at http://www.nytimes.com/2007/03/14/technology/14valley.html?scp=1&sq=&st=nyt.

48. Barboza, D. (2007, January 16). Blazing a paper trail in China: A self-made billionaire wrote her ticket on recycled cardboard. *New York Times.* Accessed February 19, 2008, at http://query.nytimes.com/gst/fullpage.html?res=9C03E5DA1030F935A25752C0A9619C8B63&scp=1&sq=&st=nyt.

49. The voluntary simplicity movement is characterized by people who start up organizations such as used-book stores, bicycle repair shops, organic coffee shops, and other ventures that are inherently slower paced and more environmentally friendly: Elgin, D. (1993). *Voluntary simplicity: Toward a way of life that is outwardly simple, inwardly rich* (rev. ed.). New York: Quill.

50. Spaner, D. (2007, March 11). Family ties bring meaning to his life. *The Province* (Vancouver, BC), p. B.10; and Williams,

T. (2007, August 30). *The $5 philanthropist: Thoughts on social networks, philanthropy, markets.* www.givemeaning.com.

51. Taken from the Tom's of Maine company website http://www.tomsofmaine.com/. For more on Chappell's story, see Chappell, T. (1993). *The soul of a business: Managing for profit and the common good.* New York: Bantam Press.

52. These individuals are identified as "frustrated corporate social entrepreneurs" in the following article: Hemingway, C. A. (2005). Personal values as a catalyst for corporate social entrepreneurship. *Journal of Business Ethics, 60,* 233–249.

53. For example, see Dyck & Starke, 1999.

54. Willdridge is irritated by being called an *entrepreneur,* because for him this label implies that the Oasis Centre was created by one person, which it clearly was not. Example and quote taken from Roberts & Woods, 2005.

55. See Thiessen, J. (2005, April 22). Bicycle courier service flexes its muscle power. *Winnipeg Free Press,* p. A13.

56. Honig, 2004. See also Gumpert, D. E. (2002). *Burn your business-plan: What investors really want from entrepreneurs.* Needham, MA: Lauson.

57. Honig, 2004, p. 259.

58. Honig, 2004.

59. Honig, 2004, p. 268. Also see page 112 in Matta, N., & Ashkenas, R. (2003). Why good projects fail anyway. *Harvard Business Review, 8,* 109–113.

60. Honig, 2004.

61. Honig, 2004. Note that many of the ideas that we apply to Multistream management draw from what Honig calls a "contingency model" approach.

62. Taken from Pennington, A. Y. (2004, October). A world of difference. *Entrepreneur Magazine.* Accessed November 16, 2006, at http://www.entrepreneur.com/article/printthis/72618.html.

63. Bray, H. (2004, May 5). MIT students make computer "biking" a "fun exercise." *Boston Globe.* Accessed November 14, 2006, at http://www.boston.com/news/globe/living/articles/2004/05/05/mit_students_make_computer_biking_a_fun_exercise/.

64. The organizational form chosen by Mainstream managers may also differ from that selected by Multistream managers. Indeed, as society moves toward Multistream thinking, legislative changes may be required to facilitate Multistream management practices. For example, the law in the Netherlands needed to be changed to give Multistream managers the legal right to empower their workers beyond the parameters associated with Mainstream management practices.

65. http://www.mooshoes.com/about.html; Vegetarian footwear. (2006, July 24). *Maclean's,* p. 63; *Going green: Environmentally-friendly fashion hits runways.* (2007, March 20). Interview on WNBC-TV, 5:20 p.m. ET (found on MooShoes webpage).

66. Kruks-Wisner, G. (2005). Promoting sustainability, building networks: A green entrepreneur in Mexico. In M. Schaper (Ed.), *Making ecopreneurship: Developing sustainable entrepreneurship* (pp. 225–238). Aldershot, Hampshire, UK: Ashgate.

67. Quoted in a report by correspondent Simon, B. (2004, January 9). Greyston Bakery: Let 'em eat cake. *CBS News,* Accessed November 16, 2006, at http://www.cbsnews.com/stories/2004/01/09/60minutes/main592382.shtml.

68. Owens-Liston, P. (2006, December 26). Where "Check please" is your call. *Time: Arts and Entertainment.* Accessed February 19, 2008, at http://www.time.com/time/arts/article/0,8599,1572805,00.html?cnn=yes.

69. The importance of developing strong relationships with stakeholders is underscored in Dees et al., 2001.

70. Taken from Brown, P. L. (2006, October 26). At this gathering, the only alternative is to be alternative. *New York Times.* Accessed February 19, 2008, at http://www.nytimes.com/2006/10/24/science/24conference.html?scp=1&sq=&st=nyt.

71. Savitz & Weber, 2006, p. 58.

72. O'Rourke, A. F. (2005). Venture capital as a tool for sustainable entrepreneurship. In M. Schaper (Ed.), *Making ecopreneurship: Developing sustainable entrepreneurship* (pp. 122–128). Aldershot, Hampshire, UK: Ashgate.

73. Roberts & Woods, 2005. Ashoka works in more than 40 countries with more than 1400 social entrepreneurs and has provided the equivalent of about $40 million in financing.

74. Google website, www. google.com (accessed November 17, 2006); Heilmann, J. (no date). *Journey to the (revolutionary, evil-hating, cash-crazy, and possibly self-destructive) center of Google.* Accessed November 15, 2006, at http://:men.style.con/gq/features/full?id5content_422; Richtel, M. (2006, October 17). Search power takes a stand for sun power. *New York Times.* Accessed February 20, 2008, at http://www.nytimes.com/2006/10/17/technology/17solar.html?_r=1&scp=1&sq=&st=nyt&oref=slogin; Sloan, A. (2004, August 24). IPO's success doesn't justify Google's price. *Washington Post,* p. E03). Accessed November 17, 2006, at http://www.washingtonpost.com/wp-dyn/articles/A27391-2004Aug23.html; Williams, A. (2006, October 15). Planet Google wants you. *New York Times.* Accessed February 20, 2008, at http://www.nytimes.com/2006/10/15/fashion/15google.html?sq=&st=nyt&adxnnl=1&scp=1&adxnnlx=1203527833-jI6GzaPI8vDDF7Dx9IuITg .

75. For example, in February 2002 Google's self-service advertising system, AdWords, was overhauled to utilize a cost-per-click (CPC) pricing model that made search advertising as cost-effective for small businesses as for large corporations.

76. For example, in 2006 Google started to build a large solar electricity system designed to provide approximately 30 percent of the electricity used at its million-square-foot office complex in Mountain View, California. The initiative is designed to pay for itself within five to ten years, be environmentally and socially responsible, and help attract smart, high-level engineers who want to work for an organization that is trying to diminish its ecological footprint. Nicholas Parker, chairman of the Cleantech Venture Network, anticipated that Google's name and influence would encourage the continued growth of the solar energy industry.

77. Schmidt said: "We developed the equivalent of what's known in basketball as a run-and-shoot offense: Larry and Sergey's only goal is to run to the other end of the court as fast as possible, so they're always ahead of everyone else, strategically, technologically, culturally. I'm the not-running-ahead person. I stay back and get the rebounds." Taken from Heilmann, J. (no date). *Journey to the (revolutionary, evil-hating, cash-crazy, and possibly self-destructive) center of Google.* Accessed November 15, 2006, at http://:men.style.con/gq/features/full?id=content_422.

78. The idea for writing such a letter was inspired by Warren Buffett's "An Owner's Manual" to Berkshire Hathaway shareholders and his essays in his firm's annual reports. A copy of this letter from Larry Page and Sergey Brin can also be found online at http://investor.google.com/ipo_letter.html.

79. Quoting John Perry Barlow, a founder of the Electronic Frontier Foundation in San Francisco, and a fellow at the Berkman Center for Internet and Society of Harvard Law School. Found in Williams, A. (2006, October 15). Planet Google wants you. *New York Times.* Accessed February 19, 2008, at http://www.nytimes.com/2006/10/15/fashion/15google.html?scp=1&sq=&st=nyt.

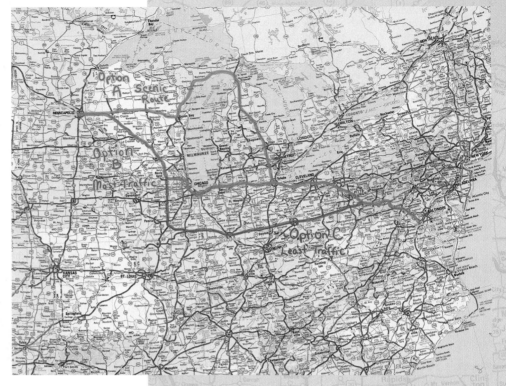

CHAPTER 7

The next three stops on our journey include the three chapters that look at the planning function of management. After looking at the decision-making process (this chapter) and goals and plans (Chapter 8), we will be ready to visit one of the most important chapters in the book, which examines organizational strategy (Chapter 9). The decision-making process described in Chapter 7 is important because managers must make decisions when carrying out each of the four functions of management. Decisions must be made about all of the following issues: which goals, plans, and strategies to pursue (planning); which sorts of organizational structures and systems to design and implement (organizing); how to motivate and communicate with others (leading); and which values and meaning will provide guidance to organizational members (controlling). Of course, as highlighted by the road map, just as Mainstream and Multistream managers perform each of these four functions differently, so they also take a different approach to the four-step decision-making process.

Map © AAA, used by permission.

ROAD MAP

FOUR-STEP DECISION-MAKING PROCESS

1. Identify the need for a decision (problems/opportunities)

2. Develop alternative responses
- Do nothing
- Make a programmed decision
- Make a nonprogrammed decision

3. Choose the appropriate alternative
- Goal consensus
- Available know-how

4. Implement the choice
- Overcome resistance
- Get feedback

The Decision-Making Process

MAINSTREAM APPROACH	⟷	MULTISTREAM APPROACH
Managers identify problems or opportunities to improve the bottom line		Managers and stakeholders identify problems or opportunities to improve various forms of well-being
Ensure that financial benefits outweigh financial costs		Ensure that overall well-being is enhanced
Seek conformity		Celebrate diversity
Avoid uncertainty (emphasize explicit knowledge)		Balance tacit knowledge and explicit knowledge
Selective participation		Ongoing participation
Bias to staying the course		Bias to experimentatio

A Classic Example of Decision Making Gone Awry[1]

It is the early 1970s and Ford Motor Company is working hard to develop its $2000 Pinto, which the company hopes will compete effectively against the low-priced Volkswagen Beetle. To lower costs, the Pinto engineers locate the gas tank behind the rear axle, just in front of the rear bumper (which makes the fuel tank vulnerable to being ruptured in an accident).

Now imagine that it is a few years later and you are Ford's "Field Recall Coordinator." You have just received data showing that its design makes the Pinto prone to explosions when the car is rear-ended.

You immediately recognize that a decision needs to be made, and you gather data and develop two options. The first option is to recall all 12.5 million Pintos on the road and install an $11 baffle plate between the fuel tank and the axle housing. The estimated cost of this option is $137.5 million. The second option is to not recall the vehicles, but instead pay the damages that arise from lawsuits. Using data provided by the U.S. National Highway Safety Transportation Administration, you estimate that the total cost will be $49.5 million ($200,000 for each of the 180 anticipated burn deaths, $67,000 for each of the 180 anticipated burn injuries, and $700 for each of the 2100 anticipated burned vehicles).

The numbers send a clear message, and so senior managers at Ford choose the second option, which will cost Ford $88 million less than the first option. After the decision is implemented, the public finds out, and many people are outraged. For example, in February 1978, a California jury is so offended by Ford's cost–benefit analysis that it awards an accident victim $125 million in punitive damages (this amount is lowered to $3.5 million by the judge).[2] Some observers view this incident as the beginning of a long decline for U.S. automobile manufacturers.

Unfortunately, this case is based on a true story. How is it that managers' so-called rational decision-making processes can result in a decision that so many people find morally offensive? People often have two reactions to this story. First, they hope that similar decisions are rare in the real world. Second, they tend to blame the individual manager(s) who would dare to make such a decision, failing to understand that in a similar context, they would likely be tempted to do the same.

To understand this better, consider what happened to Dennis Gioia, a manager who worked as Ford's Recall Coordinator in the years when the problems with the Pinto were first noticed. Prior to joining Ford, when he was still an MBA student, Gioia was often critical of the conduct of business:

> To me, the typical stance of business seemed to be one of disdain for, rather than responsibility toward, the society of which they were prominent members. I wanted something to change. Accordingly, I cultivated my social awareness; I held my principles high; I espoused my intention to help a troubled world; and I wore my hair long.

His MBA classmates were dumbstruck when he accepted a job offer from Ford:

> I countered that it [working at Ford] was an ideal strategy, arguing that I would have a greater chance of influencing social change in businesses if I worked behind the scenes on the inside, rather than as a strident voice on the outside. It was clear to me that somebody needed to prod these staid companies into socially responsible action. I certainly planned to do my part. Besides, I liked cars.

Gioia was definitely not a typical Mainstream manager, and he was probably the last person in his graduating class whom anyone expected to drop the ball on the Pinto case.[3]

So, what happened? Well, for starters, Gioia describes how he became resocialized at Ford while competing for attention with other MBAs who had recently joined Ford: "The psychic rewards of working and succeeding in a major corporation proved unexpectedly seductive." Soon the basic routines of the organization—the "scripts" that managers learned and followed—and the often unspoken organizational culture and norms upon which they were based became second nature to Gioia. His job was intense, and involved overseeing approximately 100 active recall campaigns. Routines were important aids in managing the caseload and in making rational decisions. The Pinto problems had been one of the files on his desk. Although he was no longer the Recall Coordinator in 1978, had Gioia acted earlier and voted to order a recall, perhaps the future damage could have been avoided. No one individual was responsible for ordering a recall; rather, officers in the Recall office had a vote on whether to recommend a recall to managers at higher levels within Ford.

In his early days on the job, Gioia took very seriously the fact that his job literally involved life-and-death decisions:

> That soon faded, however, and of necessity the consideration of people's lives became a fairly removed, dispassionate process. To do the job "well" there was little room for emotion. Allowing it to surface was potentially paralyzing and prevented rational analysis about which cases to recommend for recall. On moral grounds I knew that I could recommend most of the vehicles on my safety tracking list for recall (and risk the label of a "bleeding heart"). On practical grounds, I recognized that people implicitly accept risk in cars.[4]

The routines, or programmed decisions, that he inherited in his position seemed practical and rational. They provided Gioia with ways of behaving and making decisions, and he lacked well-developed scripts to enact his countercultural values.

> In retrospect, I know that in the context of the times my actions were legal (they were all well within the framework of the law); they were probably also ethical according to most prevailing definitions (they were in accord with accepted professional standards and codes of conduct); the major concern for me was whether they were moral (in the sense of adhering to some higher standards of inner conscience about the "right" actions to take).[5]

In short, scripts and routines can have a great effect on how decisions are made. Decisions that are "rational" according to a Mainstream perspective may seem immoral from a Multistream perspective, and vice versa. For example, from a materialist–individualist moral point of view, recalling the Pintos might have been considered unethical because of the extra costs of $88 million that would be imposed on shareholders.

INTRODUCTION TO DECISION MAKING

All people make multiple decisions every day, in both their their personal and their professional lives. A **decision** is a choice that is made among a number of available alternatives. Fig. 7.1 provides an overview of the four-step decision-making process.

The first step of this process is to identify the *need* for a decision. A decision is deemed necessary if expectations are not being adequately met, or if there is an opportunity to meet them better. These expectations are often based on organizational norms, values, and past practices.

The focus in the second step is to *develop alternatives* for meeting the need. When developing alternatives, it is sometimes important to consider new and untried ways to meet the need.

The third step is to *choose* which alternative to implement. Two important factors in choosing are the amount of knowledge available and the level of goal consensus among organizational members.

The fourth step involves *implementing* the chosen alternative. After implementation, the four-phase cycle starts over again at the first step, as the outcome is monitored to see if it has solved the problem or perhaps unintentionally created a new problem.

Decision is a choice that is made from a number of available alternatives.

Figure 7.1 The four-step decision-making model

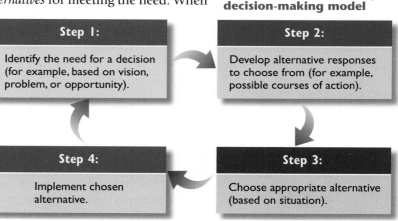

Step 1: Identify the need for a decision (for example, based on vision, problem, or opportunity).

Step 2: Develop alternative responses to choose from (for example, possible courses of action).

Step 3: Choose appropriate alternative (based on situation).

Step 4: Implement chosen alternative.

Jamie Foxx won an Oscar for his multi-faceted portrayal of musician Ray Charles, illustrating how scripts can involve learning attitudes, physical behaviors, and even how people see the world.

Scripts are learned frameworks that provide direction for people by helping them to interpret and respond to what is happening around them.

This chapter discusses each of these four steps from both a Mainstream and a Multistream perspective.

THE MAINSTREAM APPROACH TO THE FOUR-STEP DECISION-MAKING PROCESS

Step 1: Identify the Need for a Decision

In Step 1, the manager recognizes a problem or an opportunity. At any one time, a manager may face many problems and opportunities. There is always room to improve internal practices and procedures, for example, and there are always opportunities to expand the offerings of products or services. As a result, managers must "screen" situations to determine which ones require a decision now, and which can be delayed or even ignored. For example, a decision is more likely to be seen as necessary if the viability of the organization is at stake, or if previous events that were similar had always prompted a decision to be made.

Managers use scripts when they make decisions. Just as movie scripts help actors to know what to do and say in specific scenes, managers' scripts help them to identify which situations require decisions and often prescribe what those decisions should be. More generally, **scripts** can be seen as learned guidelines or procedures that help people interpret and respond to what is happening around them.[6]

People learn scripts for a variety of settings, from knowing what to do and say when meeting new people to driving a car. Drivers read road signs, follow routines to determine whether it is safe to change lanes, and adjust their speed for weather and traffic. Results can be disastrous if drivers have limited experience in recognizing potential dangers, or are distracted from their scripts by a billboard, an accident, or their cell phones.

Just as drivers use their learned scripts, so managers use learned scripts to recognize (or fail to recognize) whether a situation requires a decision. Managers learn to pay attention to key financial reports, productivity reports, consumer trends, and so on. As we learned in the chapter-opening Pinto case, decision scripts not only help managers recognize the need for a decision, but also provide guidance on how to respond to the situation.

Step 1 in the decision-making process triggers two basic types of decisions:

• Programmed decisions
• Nonprogrammed decisions

An important part of identifying the need for a decision is to understand the *underlying* issues. Consider how you might react if your doctor made a quick diagnosis of your backache symptoms based on a speedy exam and a few questions. Would you have much confidence in the diagnosis? In contrast, how would you feel if the doctor gave you a thorough exam and took the time to ask you several detailed questions about your symptoms and the possible causes? *It is important to understand and address the underlying problem instead of just focusing on the symptoms.* If someone arrives late for work, the manager should find out whether his or her child is sick, or whether the person is fearful of a conflict with a coworker, or whether the employee is simply irresponsible. Likewise, the manager should identify the causes underlying a recent surge in sales: Is it due to an improved product, a new advertising campaign, or a general economic upturn? The more time and resources managers devote to thoroughly understanding the problem or opportunity, the better chance they have to make a good decision.[7]

A complicating factor in identifying the need to make a decision is that a stimulus can be interpreted in different ways, depending on the scripts that are being used by managers. A classic example is how managers from different tobacco companies used different scripts to respond to the Surgeon General's announcement in 1950 that smoking may cause cancer.[8] Managers in some tobacco companies interpreted this announcement as a need for a programmed decision (specifically, a decision to fine-tune current operations). Other managers perceived it as a need for a nonprogrammed decision (a decision to develop new products and markets). We will see how these differences play out in our description of the next three steps in the decision-making process.

Step 2: Develop Alternative Responses

When the need for a decision has been identified, managers can develop three basic kinds of alternative responses:

1. Do nothing.
2. Follow a routine response.
3. Develop a nonprogrammed response.

The first alternative—"do nothing"— requires no effort to develop, which is a welcome feature when managers do not have much time or many resources to invest. Doing nothing is the appropriate response for all those situations where doing something else is not worth the effort. For example, should someone who is "caught" chatting about the football game at the water cooler be reprimanded? Doing nothing is also appropriate when the cost of the effort exceeds the benefits. For example, should an individual photocopier be provided for each staff member to avoid "downtime" waiting for a departmentally shared photocopier?

The second alternative is to follow a routine response, such as simply adhering to standard operating procedures. This response is consistent with **programmed decisions**—or routine decisions—where standard alternatives are chosen in response to recurring organizational problems or opportunities. For example, an organization may have routines for reordering office supplies, responding to employees who arrive late for work, or dealing with irate customers who do not receive their orders on time. Over time, "decision rules" and policies are typically developed to handle situations that recur frequently. For example, when an employee arrives late for work, the manager usually has several programmed alternative responses from which to choose:

Programmed decisions involve choosing a standard alternative in response to recurring organizational problems or opportunities.

1. Excuse the employee if he or she provides an acceptable explanation
2. Reduce the employee's pay
3. Provide the employee with a professional development course on time management
4. Fire the employee if the person has a long history of tardiness and has been warned that dismissal is the next step

These programmed decisions are "shortcuts" that help managers avoid going through the entire in-depth four-step decision-making process. As described in the opening case, Dennis Gioia inherited such programmed decision "scripts" when he worked as the Recall Coordinator at Ford. Of course, these scripts need to be reviewed occasionally to ensure that they have not become obsolete. For example, old human resources policies are not likely to work well for employees who have flexible work schedules or those who work from home.

Managers must guard against the temptation to limit themselves to programmed decision making when the situation actually calls for developing nonprogrammed alternatives. For example, for many years Motorola was the market leader in the analog cell phone market. Because managers were so successful and proud of their technology, they greatly underestimated the potential of digital technology, which ultimately allowed other companies to take away a healthy chunk of Motorola's market share.[9]

The third option is for managers to develop nonprogrammed alternatives. This is consistent with **nonprogrammed decisions,** which refers to developing and choosing new alternatives in situations where programmed alternatives have not yet been developed or are not appropriate. Not surprisingly, nonprogrammed decision making requires more time to develop alternatives and complete the decision-making process. This is especially true when the issue requires a strategic decision such as responding to a new competitor, changes in legal regulations, or an opportunity for a major expansion. As highlighted in Figure 7.2, the amount of time and resources invested in developing nonprogrammed alternatives is influenced by three considerations:

- The perceived *importance* of the decision. For example, the selection of the location of a new headquarters or the decision to launch a new product will be given more time than the choice of which brand of photocopier paper to purchase.
- The *newness* of the situation. The greater the newness of the issue, the greater the amount of time that will be spent on the decision.
- The *urgency* of decision making. In a crisis situation, managers will have less time to develop alternatives.

To prepare for urgent decision-making situations, managers can develop alternative responses ahead of time to possible crisis scenarios (e.g., a fire in the plant, a major lawsuit, a crash in the stock market, or the sudden death of the CEO). Then, if such an event occurs, managers will have thoughtfully developed alternatives from which to choose.

The quality of the nonprogrammed alternatives depends on the amount of time and resources a manager invests in developing them. For example, the best alternatives are often based on input from a variety of sources, including members of the organization, customers, and suppliers. Generating alternatives may be enhanced by consulting experts, brainstorming, or using a variety of group-oriented creativity techniques, which are discussed in subsequent chapters (e.g., the Delphi method).

As indicated at the end of the discussion of Step 1 of the decision-making process, managers from the leading tobacco companies recognized that there was a need for a

> **Nonprogrammed decisions** involve developing and choosing among new alternatives in situations where programmed alternatives have not yet been developed or are not appropriate.

Figure 7.2   Considerations that influence how much time managers invest in developing alternatives

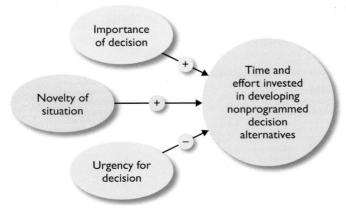

decision as a result of the Surgeon General's announcement linking smoking to cancer, although some managers thought the need was for a programmed decision and others saw it as needing a nonprogrammed decision. The managers' next step was to develop possible alternative responses. The first alternative would be to simply ignore the announcement and to continue business as usual (i.e., the do-nothing alternative). In this case we might not expect this to be the only alternative developed by managers, although it might happen in situations such as when managers are blinded by their past successes. The second alternative would be to fine-tune existing operations (i.e., to make a programmed decision). Managers promoting this alternative would focus on ensuring that current customers remain loyal to their brand, and adjust their operations to reduce production costs in expectation of lower sales revenue. The third alternative would be to consider more radical (nonprogrammed) alternatives, such as inventing "healthier" cigarettes, developing new and different ways to attract new smokers, or diversifying into products not related to tobacco.

Step 3: Choose the Appropriate Alternative

The third step—choosing the best alternative—lies at the heart of the decision-making process. *How* this choice is made depends on two key factors:

- Goal consensus
- Available knowledge

As shown in Figure 7.3, these two factors can be used to create a chart that defines five basic methods that managers may utilize to choose an alternative. We will first explain the meaning of the two basic dimensions shown in Figure 7.3, and then discuss each of the five basic approaches to choosing an alternative.

GOAL CONSENSUS. **Goal consensus** refers to the level of agreement among members about which goals the organization should pursue.[10] Mainstream managers prefer high goal consensus with widespread agreement throughout the organization as to what the key goals are. Low goal consensus means that considerable debate exists regarding what the organization's goals should be. For example, the Boy Scouts have a problem of goal consensus when some people in the organization argue for a continuation of the Scouts' traditional emphasis on camping and woods lore, while others argue that the organization should move away from this emphasis because most boys attending Scouts programs live in the inner city.

Even among managers who agree that maximizing shareholder financial well-being is the ultimate goal, there may be debate about precisely which subgoals will help achieve the ultimate goal. For example, after several decades of running computer simulations of student-led organizations in the magazine publishing industry,

> **Goal consensus** is the level of agreement among members about which goals the organization should pursue.

Figure 7.3 Five basic methods for choosing an option

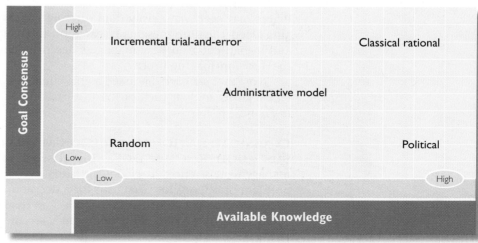

Roger Hall[11] found that different groups choose different subgoals to reach their ultimate goal of maximizing shareholder wealth. In these simulations, groups may choose to maximize any of several subgoals: sales revenue, or advertising revenue, or the subscription base, or the "quality" of the magazine, and so on. According to Hall, "There is a lot of variety among management teams in what they choose as goals. In some cases, agreement comes easily. In other situations, it is a matter of lengthy debate."

AVAILABLE KNOWLEDGE.   Even if there is widespread agreement on *which* goals to pursue, there may be a lack of information about *how* to achieve the goals. For example, imagine that managers of a magazine company agree to pursue the goal of maximizing the number of readers. Even with this consensus, significant debate may arise about how this goal can be achieved: Should the company offer special prices to subscribers, expand the number of newsstands that offer the magazine, decrease the advertising content in the publication, hire a new editor, or invest in higher-quality printing? In many cases, managers have historical data to help them make a decision, but more-recent changes in the environment may sometimes make such data less useful.

> **Uncertainty** is evident when decision makers do not know what outcomes to expect from choosing a particular alternative.

Managers choose goals and develop organizational knowledge in an effort to reduce the risk and uncertainty that come with decisions.[12] **Uncertainty** is evident when decision makers do not know what outcomes to expect from choosing a particular alternative. For example, based on past experience, airline managers may be quite certain that 90 percent of customers who have been "bumped" off an overbooked flight will be satisfied if they are given a voucher for a free *domestic* flight. They may also be quite certain that the percentage of bumped customers who are satisfied would increase to 95 percent if the travel voucher was for a free *international* flight. However, managers may be uncertain about the percentage of customers who would be satisfied with a voucher for the chance to win free flying lessons.

> **Risk** is the likelihood that an alternative chosen by decision makers will result in a negative outcome.

Whereas certainty has more to do with the knowledge available for a particular decision, risk has more to do with the outcomes in the context of the overarching goals for the organization. **Risk** is the likelihood that an alternative chosen by decision makers will result in a negative outcome related to a larger goal. For example, in the case of the bumped airline customers, based on the larger goal of optimizing customer *satisfaction* rates, offering vouchers for international flights may seem less risky than offering vouchers for domestic flights. By contrast, based on the larger goal of reducing *financial* costs, offering vouchers for international flights may seem *more* risky than offering vouchers for domestic flights. The Digging Deeper feature presents research on the relationship between risk and goals, and in particular on how managers describe the goals of an organization during the decision-making process.

Now that we have discussed a goal consensus and available knowledge, we can take a closer look at each of the five basic decision-making approaches identified in Figure 7.3.

CLASSICAL RATIONAL DECISION-MAKING METHOD: HIGH CONSENSUS, HIGH KNOWLEDGE.   The classical rational method—which includes management science—is evident in situations where goal consensus is high, the problem or opportunity that calls for a decision is clearly understood, and there is adequate time and information to collect all required information for each alternative. Thanks to the capacity of computers, recent years have seen a renewed interest in the classical rational method of decision making. The list of tools developed for

DIGGING DEEPER

The Effect of Framing on Decision Making

Consider a situation where the outcome is certain, but where changing how you describe the goal influences the decision that people make in the face of risk. Researchers have found patterns in how the framing of information affects decision making.[13] **Framing** refers to the presentation of ideas and alternatives in a way that influences the choices people make.

As an example, suppose that a manufacturing firm with 60 employees is having severe financial problems, and that the CEO has developed two alternatives. As it turns out, the alternative people will choose depends on whether the goal of the two alternatives is presented in terms of (A) securing gains versus (B) avoiding losses.[14]

Scenario A: A desire to secure gains is the implicit overarching goal if the CEO presents the two alternatives as follows:

- Alternative 1 will result in saving 20 jobs.
- Alternative 2 has a one-third probability that all 60 jobs will be saved and a two-thirds probability that no jobs will be saved.

Scenario B: A desire to avoid loss is the implicit overarching goal if the CEO presents the same two alternatives as follows:

- Alternative 1 will result in losing 40 jobs.
- Alternative 2 has a one-third probability that no jobs will be lost, and a two-thirds probability that all 60 jobs will be lost.

Note that the two "Alternative 1" options are actually equal to each other. There are 60 jobs in question, so saving 20 jobs is the same thing as losing 40 jobs. Also note that there is no uncertainty about the outcome of Alternative 1.

The two "Alternative 2" options are also mathematically equal because the expected values are equal. That is, the expected value of saving 20 jobs is the same as the expected value of losing 40 jobs. However, Alternative 2 introduces the idea of probability: It is not certain or guaranteed that exactly 20 jobs will be saved and exactly 40 jobs will be lost.

Research shows that when the overarching goal of a decision focuses on securing gains—as in Scenario A—then 75 percent of people become risk averse and choose Alternative 1. Conversely, when the overarching goal focuses on avoiding losses—as in Scenario B—then 75 percent of people become more risk seeking and choose Alternative 2. People tend to accept more risk when avoiding losses than they do when securing gains.

For another example of the effect of framing, consider the negotiation of a new labor contract. Suppose that the union is not willing to settle for a pay rate of less than $12 per hour, and that company management won't offer more than $10 per hour. Now suppose that each side has the opportunity to settle for $11 per hour. If managers frame this figure as a "loss" of $1 per hour from their initial positions, then they will be more willing to take the risk of rejecting the compromise and stick to their original positions. By contrast, if managers see it as "gaining" a concession of $1 per hour, then they would be more likely to accept the offer.[15]

---

managers includes decision trees, break-even analysis, inventory and supply chain management models, and so on. However, despite the ready availability of so many tools, full-fledged rational decision-making techniques are evident in only a minority of managerial decisions.[16] It is rare to find situations where managers have complete information at their disposal. Moreover, as illustrated in the opening case, poor decisions may be made even in situations where managers think that they have all the information they require to make a rational decision.

POLITICAL DECISION-MAKING METHOD: LOW CONSENSUS, HIGH KNOWLEDGE. The political method—which includes bargaining, compromise, and coalition formation—is evident in situations where there is much debate about which goal to pursue, even though a lot of knowledge is available. Debate can be intense, even when the consensus is that the overarching goal is to maximize the financial interests of shareholders. For example, marketing managers might argue that the organization should try to maximize sales revenue, manufacturing managers might argue that the focus should be on production costs, and research and development (R&D) managers might argue for developing the most technologically advanced product on the market. Often these competing goals are mutually exclusive,

Framing refers to presenting ideas and alternatives in a way that has an influence on the choices that people make.

or the organization lacks the resources to pursue them all at the same time. This can lead to a politicized decision-making process, where managers do things like:

* Trade "favors" with each other in their own long-term self-interests
* Withhold information that will weaken their own position
* Form coalitions and build alliance networks
* Blame others for failure

When employees perceive managers to be acting politically, anxiety increases, job satisfaction decreases, and managers are judged as being ineffective.[17] In political decision making, it appears that casualties are high. Moreover, sometimes managers become so obsessed with managing the day-to-day political battles that they engage in actions that are detrimental to the overall organization.

For example, Christian Streiff resigned after just three months as CEO of Airbus owing to a political conflict between the decisions he was making and the goals of the firm's corporate parent, the European Aeronautic Defense and Space Company. Streiff's bold ideas, such as moving production of the A380 aircraft from Germany to France—both of which are influential nations in the project—collided with the political interests in Germany. Meanwhile, Airbus experienced costly delays in the production of its A380 aircraft, which created an opportunity that could be exploited by its archrival, Boeing.[18]

INCREMENTAL TRIAL-AND-ERROR DECISION-MAKING METHOD: HIGH CONSENSUS, LOW KNOWLEDGE. The incremental trial-and-error method—which may include some forms of intuition—is evident in situations where there is high agreement on goals, but a low level of technical knowledge. For example, managers may want to increase unit sales of their key product through advertising, but they may not agree on whether to use television, radio, computer, or print media for this purpose, because they have little knowledge about the relative effect of these different media on their product. In this case, managers often opt for an incremental approach. For example, they may try to fine-tune existing strategies, make small changes, or pilot-test a decision with a small group of employees or customers. **Continuous improvement** refers to the process of making many small, incremental improvements on an ongoing basis to how things are done in an organization. Mainstream managers use continuous improvement to constantly improve efficiency and productivity in organizations. Called *kaizen* in Japanese, continuous improvement has been a pillar of the success for companies such as Toyota, where it helps members be open to new ideas and to build high-quality automobiles.

Managers often rely on their intuition to make decisions.[19] **Intuition** refers to making decisions based on tacit knowledge, which can be based on experience, insight, hunches, or "gut feelings" (see Figure 7.4). As discussed in Chapter 6, *tacit knowledge* refers to abilities or pieces of information that people hold that are difficult to articulate or codify. Tacit knowledge is evident in the ability to ride a bicycle, a skill that is difficult to put into words and must be "learned by doing." Experienced managers and experts often have tacit knowledge. For example, their tacit knowledge helps experts to distinguish between authentic and counterfeit works of art.[20]

Examples of intuitive decision making are especially striking when they go against the rational analysis of the information at hand. For example, prior to Ray Kroc's purchase of McDonald's, his accountant advised against the deal, but Kroc had a "gut feeling" that this investment would turn out to be a winner.[21] In another example, a

Continuous improvement refers to making many small, incremental improvements on an ongoing basis to how things are done in an organization.

Intuition refers to making decisions based on tacit knowledge, which can be based on experience, insight, hunches, or "gut feelings."

researcher asked managers to guess 10-digit computer-random-generated numbers, and found that successful businesspeople were significantly better at guessing the numbers than those with average ability in the business world.[22]

RANDOM DECISION-MAKING METHOD: LOW CONSENSUS, LOW KNOWLEDGE. The random method—which also includes chaotic, mimetic, and inspiration decision making—is evident in situations where there is no agreement on goals, and no knowledge about how to reach goals. In these cases, managers rely on luck or inspiration rather than on reasoned decisions. This decision-making method is generally not considered to be a "good" quadrant in the model, but perhaps it is more likely to yield "breakthrough" decision making than the other quadrants. At best, managers may look to copy decisions made in other organizations. However, the chaos associated with a lack of goal consensus and a lack of knowledge makes it difficult even to mimic other organizations. During such times, people may look for *inspiration*—literally, spiritual insight from within.

 WHAT DO YOU THINK?

Is Seeking Spiritual Inspiration Rational?

Research from around the world suggests that the more uncertainty and risk a decision holds for managers, the more likely those managers are to turn to spiritual or to metaphysical sources for help. Here *metaphysical* refers to sources of information that are above or beyond physical knowledge or data that are tangible or explicit.

For example, spiritual disciplines such as prayer and guidance are often used by managers who are facing uncertainty and risky decisions.[23] For example, Genny Nelson, cofounder of Sisters of the Road Café in Portland, Oregon, describes how her daily prayer time grounds her and gives her insight regarding the challenges she is facing.[24] Another study noted that 96 million Japanese claim to be Shintoist, and that many Japanese managers seek advice from Ebisu, the Shinto god of business. The same study found that two-thirds of managers in Singapore use *feng shui*—a discipline that helps make decisions based on spiritual forces and the patterns of *yin*. According to the study, Chinese managers in Singapore are more likely to use such spiritual or metaphysical aids when making important nonprogrammed decisions, but seldom resort to them when making everyday programmed decisions. Nearly one-third of these managers feel uneasy about this practice: "I feel shameful to tell my former finance professor that I rely more on god's advice than discounted cash flow analysis when evaluating investment projects." [25]

Why are people more likely to appeal to spiritual forces in times of great uncertainty or risk? Is this true for yourself? Is it rational? Given that this practice is not unusual among managers, would it be appropriate for a management school to offer a course in how to use spiritual sources to make decisions? Or is the purpose of management education exactly the opposite—that is, to introduce rationality into decision making so that people do not need to rely on spiritual sources?

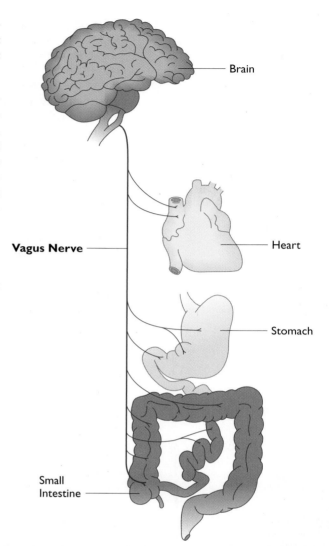

Figure 7.4   Intuition's physiological basis

Listen to your gut: The wrapping of organs evident in a person's gut may give that part of the body characteristics of a "lower-order brain," as it is physiologically similar to the brain in the human head. The gut contains every class of nerve-transmitting chemical that has been found in the brain, and almost all of the nerve fibers in the vagus nerve transmit messages from the gut to the brain, although everything that runs up the vagus nerve doesn't reach consciousness.

Source: Arehart-Treichel, J. (2001). The gut is said to have a mind of its own. *Psychiatric News*, 36(14), 16 (American Psychiatric Association). The article quotes Michael Gershon, Ph.D., chair of anatomy and cell biology at Columbia University College of Physicians and Surgeons. Accessed October 5, 2006, at http://pn.psychiatryonline.org/cgi/content/full/36/14/16.

**ADMINISTRATIVE MODEL: MEDIUM CONSENSUS, MEDIUM KNOW-
LEDGE.**   Because managers usually have *some* knowledge and at least *partial* goal
consensus, most decision making employs a combination of the four methods discussed so far. The administrative model describes how decisions are *actually* made,
rather prescribing how they *should* be made. Recall from Chapter 2 Herbert Simon's
argument that even the best management decision-making process is constrained by
a lack of complete information and by limited cognitive abilities to process information.[26] Simon called this *bounded rationality*. As a result of incomplete information and a lack of complete goal consensus, managers tend to satisfice when they
make decisions. **Satisficing** is evident when managers do not even attempt to develop an *optimal* response, but rather collect information and develop alternatives
until they are able to choose one that provides an *adequate* response.

Many reasons may explain why managers lack complete information and goal
consensus. Human beings have limited cognitive processing capacities, limited
amounts of information to work with, and limited resources and time to collect
data and make decisions. Even with the widespread use of computers to analyze and
process data, the world is simply too complex to analyze all possibilities and outcomes. Thus it is impossible for managers to know precisely how subordinates,
suppliers, customers, and competitors will respond to a particular decision. Finally,
managers lack the resources—especially time—required to fully process the existing
information.

In addition to "objective" factors that limit the possibility for a decision to be
completely rational, "subjective" factors contribute to bounded rationality. For example, just as first impressions are important in personal encounters (such as a job
interview), so they are important in how we respond to potential solutions to problems. When collecting information to resolve a problem, decision makers tend to use
the earliest-received pieces of information as "anchor" points around which they add
subsequent information. In terms of how people process information, this early information assumes a more prominent position than it truly warrants. Similarly, information that is experienced firsthand often
outweighs much richer information that is
presented in reports prepared by others.
For example, when the city of Columbus,
Ohio, wanted to celebrate the 500-year anniversary of Christopher Columbus's first
voyage to America, the idea to host an international flower show was proposed and
strongly backed by an influential local
businessperson with a personal interest in
flower shows. This proposal quickly became the only alternative that was developed and pursued. Unfortunately, the
prospect of attending a flower show did
not attract as many tourists as hoped, and
the "non-event" lost $30 million.[27]

There is a related tendency for our
judgment to become clouded by current
practices and past decisions. We are more
likely to "see" what we expect to see,
which has been shaped by what we have
seen before. Likewise, managers may as-

Satisficing is evident when managers accept an *adequate* response
to a problem or opportunity, rather
than make the effort to develop an
optimal response.

International flower show hosted in
Columbus, Ohio.

sign little or no value to information that goes against their existing practices. As we saw in the opening case, Dennis Gioia used a preexisting script to assess the situations he was facing in making recall decisions. Similarly, as we saw in the opening case in Chapter 6, many bank managers used scripts that left no room for loaning small amounts to micro-entrepreneurs. To consider choices that represent new directions may be seen as undermining the earlier decisions that led to current practices.

Let us now consider which alternatives were chosen by managers of the leading tobacco companies after the Surgeon General's warning in 1950 that smoking may lead to cancer. Recall that they had three basic alternatives from which to choose: (1) do nothing; (2) try to secure the firm's current position by playing it safe and fine-tuning current operations; or (3) attempt to avoid losses by taking risks and trying new ideas. As it turns out, managers in each of the four leading firms made different choices, based in part on their goal consensus and perceived available knowledge.

Which alternative would *you* have chosen? Would you be at a loss about what to do, unsure what your goals should be and feeling as if there was a lack of information regarding what might happen next? With this lack of information and goal consensus, your decision making might be random and chaotic. If so, then you might be most like the managers at Ligget & Myers, who did not follow any clear, consistent strategy in the years following the Surgeon General's announcement. The company floundered, often seeming to make random decisions that resulted in general chaos. It was eventually bought by Philip Morris in 1999.

Alternatively, would you have seen the Surgeon General's announcement as "the beginning of the end" for the tobacco industry? Would you assume that existing smokers would slowly stop, and that fewer and fewer people would start smoking, given tobacco's link to cancer? Would you think that the best way for your company to secure its profitability would be to focus on retaining its current customers and on reducing production costs? If this describes your response, then you would be most likely to adopt a rational approach, building upon your current knowledge and goals. This was the alternative pursued by managers at American Brands—one of the two companies with the highest market share in 1950. They essentially decided to fine-tune the firm's existing operations. It seemed reasonable to assume that fewer people would take up smoking, so the managers worked hard to hold on to the customers that they already had. American Brands also sought to minimize its costs by reducing its investment in new-product development and by designing highly efficient production practices.

Perhaps the Surgeon's General announcement would have motivated you to conclude that your firm needed to be more pro-active. You might start looking for new customers and products to make up for the expected losses associated with the announcement. In fact, you might rethink your whole approach to business—from the kinds of cigarettes your firm produces to the customers you target and the advertising you use. This alternative would mean experimenting with different goals and building on emerging knowledge. If this describes your response, then you would be most like the managers at Philip Morris, which at the time had the *smallest* market share of the four industry leaders. Rather than see the market as declining, managers at Philip Morris produced and marketed new, "healthier" cigarettes. Philip Morris was the first company to introduce "low-tar" cigarettes, which accounted for 70 percent of industry-wide sales within 16 years. By comparison, low-tar cigarettes accounted for only 30 percent of the sales of American Brands, and it took Ligget & Myers more than 20 years to successfully launch a filter cigarette. Philip Morris was also the first to advertise cigarettes on the radio (previously most of the advertising had been in the print media), the first to introduce innovative packaging, and the first to target female smokers.

Finally, the Surgeon General's announcement might have prompted you to consider a wait-and-see response, where you actively monitor and collect knowledge and information from what others in the industry are doing, learning what works and what does not work. This more incremental approach is like the choice made at R. J. Reynolds (RJR), which was the co-industry leader (with American Brands) at the time. RJR established two spheres of operations. In the first sphere, for its established brand-name products it followed a similar approach to American Brands, focusing on customer loyalty and efficiency. In the second sphere, it sought to copy the successful product innovations from companies such as Philip Morris; RJR enjoyed a 94 percent success rate in launching new products during the 25 years after the Surgeon General's announcement. For example, within one year of copying the other firms' filter and low-tar cigarettes, RJR products were number one in both niches.

Step 4: Implement the Choice

Obviously, some decisions will require more effort to implement than others. A nonprogrammed decision, such as the acquisition of another company, will be more difficult to implement than choosing carpet for the reception area of an office building. The most difficult decisions to implement are the ones that challenge an organization's basic ways of operating. Even a technically brilliant decision along these lines will fail if it is not implemented in such a way that members will embrace it. A key challenge for managers in Step 4, therefore, is to overcome resistance to implementation.

One way that managers can increase the likelihood that decisions are implemented (Step 4) is to involve members in earlier steps of the decision-making process. From a Mainstream perspective, this practice can be costly and is not necessary for *most* decisions, but it may be cost-effective in *particular* situations. Researchers have developed a model to identify situations where implementation is improved by involving more members of the organization in the decision-making process (see Table 7.1).[28] This model, which seeks to make timely decisions with minimal cost, contains variables evident in the four-step decision-making process. Related to Step 1 in the decision-making process, the first question in the model looks at the significance of the problem for the organization (e.g., Is it routine?). Related to Step 2, the model looks at whether the members have the competence to analyze the problem and develop alternatives. Related to Step 3, the model looks at whether there are (1) adequate knowledge available (including both the manager's and other members' expertise) and (2) general goal consensus among members (e.g., Do members have commitment to and support for the goals related to solving the problem?). Related to Step 4, the model looks at whether members will be committed to implementing the decision.

The model recommends five levels of employee involvement, ranging from low to high participation, depending on the situation (shown along the right side of Table 7.1). In the highest level of participation (recommended for 7 percent of situations described in the model), managers are recommended to *delegate* decisions. Here managers do not play a direct role in the decision-making process except to provide encouragement, distribute resources, and set prescribed limits within which group members are permitted to identify and diagnose the problem (Step 1), develop alternatives (Step 2), and choose which alternative to implement (Step 3). In another

TABLE 7.1

How Various Aspects of the Four-Step Decision-Making Process Influence the Level of Participation That Managers Are Recommended to Use

Step 1	Step 2	Step 3		Step 3		Step 4		
		Available Knowledge		Goal Consensus		Importance of Members' Commitment to Implement the Decision	Proportion of All Possible Situations in the Model	What Type of Decision-Making Method Managers Are Recommended to Use Based on the Model
Decision Significance/ Need	Members' Competence to Develop Alternatives/ Solve Problem	Leader's Expertise	Members' Expertise	Members' Support	Members' Commitment			
Low	Any	Any	Any	Any	Any	Low	25%	Manager **decides alone** (total = 56%)
Low	Any	Any	Any	Any	High	High	13%	
High	Any	High	Any	Any	Any	Low	13%	
High	Any	High	Any	Any	High	High	6%	
High	Any	Low	Any	Low	Any	Low	6%	Manager decides after **consulting with individual members** (total = 16%)
High	Any	Low	Low	High	Any	Low	3%	
High	Any	Low	High	Low	High	High	3%	
High	Low	Low	High	High	Any	Low	2%	
High	Any	Low	Low	High	High	High	2%	
High	Low	Low	High	High	High	High	1%	
High	Any	High	Any	Low	Low	High	3%	Manager decides after **consulting with group members** (total = 11%)
High	Any	Low	Low	Low	Low	High	3%	
High	Any	Low	High	High	Low	High	2%	
High	Any	High	Low	High	Low	High	2%	
High	Low	High	High	High	Low	High	1%	
High	Low	Low	High	High	Low	High	1%	
Low	Low	Any	Any	Any	Low	High	6%	Manager **facilitates** group decision making (total = 9%)
High	High	Low	High	High		Low	2%	
High	High	Low	High	High	High	High	1%	
High	High	Low	Any	High	Low	High	1%	
Low	High	Any	Any	Any	Low	High	6%	Manager **delegates** to group members (total = 7%)
High	High	High	High	High	Low	High	1%	

LOW ↑
PARTICIPATIVENESS
HIGH ↓

Source: Building on Vroom, V. H. (2003). Educating managers for decision making and leadership. *Management Decision*, 41(10), 968–978.

9 percent of the situations described in the model, managers are recommended to use a *facilitative* approach, where a manager presents to a group the problem and the boundaries within which it is to be solved, respects each group member's ideas without regard to the member's hierarchical position, and tries to get everyone to agree on a decision. In the remaining conditions (representing more than 80 percent of the situations in the model), managers are recommended to make the

"I have not failed. I have just found ten thousand ways that won't work." This famous quote is from Thomas Edison, the famous inventor shown here working in his lab in 1929.[31]

decisions either alone (56 percent), after consulting with others individually (16 percent), or after consulting with others in the group (11 percent).[29]

Regardless of the level of participation, once the attempt has been made to implement a decision, the decision-making process goes back to Step 1. Managers monitor whether their decision has resolved the problem or has caused some unanticipated additional problems, or created some unexpected opportunities. Research suggests that about half of all decisions fail.[30] The key is to learn from these mistakes and then apply that knowledge to the future decision-making processes. Perhaps something was learned about how to develop better alternatives in Step 2 or how to make a more informed decision in Step 3. For example, in the early 1990s, managers at R. J. Reynolds wanted to increase the firm's market share in the United States (Step 1), developed some alternatives (Step 2), and eventually chose to offer lower-priced cigarette brands (Step 3). What RJR managers apparently did not anticipate was that Philip Morris would respond by cutting its own prices and moving into Eastern Europe, where RJR had been establishing a market position (feedback in Step 4). The ensuing price war hurt the profitability of both companies (triggering a need for a new Step 1). RJR managers developed alternatives to respond to the decreasing profits (Step 2) and chose to neglect the company's efforts in Eastern Europe so as to protect its U.S. market share (Step 3).[32] The next time managers at RJR want to increase their firm's market share in the United States, they would be less likely to do so by offering lower-priced cigarette brands—a lesson learned from the tussle with Philip Morris.

Escalation of commitment occurs when a manager perseveres with the implementation of a poor decision despite evidence that it is not working.

Information distortion refers to the tendency to overlook or downplay feedback that makes a decision look bad, and instead focus on feedback that makes the decision look good.

Many poor decisions persist for longer than they should because managers are reluctant to admit that they made a mistake. This leads to **escalation of commitment,** which occurs when a manager perseveres with the implementation of a poor decision despite evidence that it is not working. As shown in Figure 7.5, escalation of commitment can occur for a variety of reasons, but they also have basically the same origin: Managers want to avoid admitting that they made a poor decision. This often occurs in tandem with **information distortion,** which refers to the tendency to overlook or downplay feedback that makes a decision look bad, and instead to focus on feedback that makes the decision look good. For example, Jill Barad, former CEO of Mattel, remained committed to her $3.5 billion acquisition of the Learning Company despite its poor performance. Her persistence was explained in part by her having fostered an organizational culture that made it difficult to deliver bad news.[33]

Escalation of commitment can also be caused by the high regard given to persistence, as expressed in the saying, "When the going gets tough, the tough get going."

This message is reinforced by stories about managers who refused to admit failure despite early negative feedback and were subsequently treated as heroes when their decision turned out to have been right. For example, an engineer named Chuck House at Hewlett-Packard received a "Medal of Defiance" because even though Dave Packard himself had told him to quit working on a particular project, House persisted with using organizational resources to develop a highly successful new product.[34] In this case, not listening to the boss garnered a medal of defiance; in many other cases, however, it will be "rewarded" with a certificate of a different sort (a "pink slip," indicating termination of employment).

Escalation of commitment can also occur when managers make a decision using the same process as they had used for a successful decision that they made earlier. For example, when he was CEO of Quaker, William Smithburg relied on his taste buds to make his highly criticized decision to acquire Gatorade for $22 million; ultimately, the venture became a $3 billion success with innovative advertising. However, when Smithburg again relied on his taste buds to acquire Snapple for $1.8 billion, the result almost brought Quaker down. Quaker sold Snapple two years later for $300 million, a huge loss.[35]

Finally, escalation of commitment can occur because of **administrative inertia,** which describes what happens when existing structures and systems persist simply because they are already in place. For example, if a decision was previously made to create a new department and hire five people, then at a later date managers will likely be reluctant to remove the department and fire the five people. Similarly, if millions of dollars have been spent on a merger that is proving to be a poor decision, managers will have a difficult time "un-merging." This tendency to shy away from acknowledging poor decisions is also reflected in the business press, which publishes more stories about business mergers and acquisitions than stories about companies selling off businesses, even though one study showed that 61 percent of the largest mergers and acquisitions over a two-year period actually destroyed shareholder wealth, and only 17 percent created positive returns.[37]

What can management do to reduce the likelihood that escalation of commitment will occur? One tactic is to view the results of previous decisions simply as important information, rather than as a legacy that must be continued. Managers need to ask themselves what they have learned during the decision-making process that will inform future decisions. In addition, managers must be bold enough to take what they have learned and undo poor decisions. Recognizing a previous faulty decision is often easier for new managers than for the managers who made the poor decision. For example, new managers are 100 times more likely to sell a business unit acquired in a poor decision than are the managers who made the decision in the first place.[38]

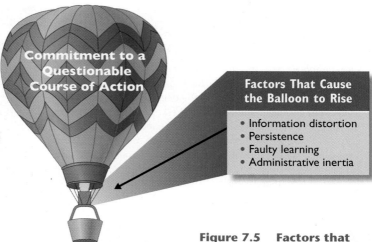

Factors That Cause the Balloon to Rise

• Information distortion
• Persistence
• Faulty learning
• Administrative inertia

Figure 7.5 Factors that contribute to escalation of commitment

Administrative inertia describes what happens when existing structures and systems persist simply because they are already in place.

The idea of "throwing good money after bad" is sometimes called "the Concorde fallacy." The Concorde was a passenger jet that could fly faster than the speed of sound. The governments of the United Kingdom and France continued to fund it even after it was apparent that it would never be profitable.[36]

DIGGING DEEPER

Culture and the Decision-Making Process

Organizational and societal values and scripts influence how managers make decisions. For an example of societal scripts, consider the differences between the decision-making processes in Western countries and Japan. In Western cultures, formal rationality and individualism are highly valued. These values are consistent with a more centralized approach to decision making where *managers* (1) identify problems, (2) generate solutions, (3) rationally evaluate and choose the best solution, and (4) implement the solution by telling others what to do.

In contrast, Japanese managers are more likely to follow the *ringi* decision-making process, which is based on the values such as *wa*, a virtue that places the group above individuals and thereby fosters a cooperative ethic that values maintaining interpersonal peace and harmony.[39] In Japan, trying to "get ahead" of others may disrupt harmony. The four-step *ringi* decision-making process involves group consensus and collective responsibility: (1) The need for a decision can be informally presented by any member of the organization; (2) once it has been discussed informally, it is written in a memo and formally circulated; (3) further discussion takes place as the memo is circulated and approved by each member; and (4) the final decision is formally recorded and "stamped" as approved by members. Compared to the Mainstream approach, the *ringi* process

may take longer and seem less efficient, but once it is completed, implementation of the decision is basically assured.[40]

This example illustrates how the basic "scripts" in the four-step decision-making process vary across countries. Decision-making scripts may also vary across organizations. As illustrated in the chapter-opening case, the script used in an organization can have a profound influence on its members. Gioia joined Ford with a desire to challenge Mainstream management norms, but soon he was managing according to the decision-making scripts in place at Ford. Research suggests that it takes less than a month for newcomers to adopt the attitudes and decision-making scripts of the organization where they are hired.[41] Put differently, within a month of joining an organization, you are likely to adopt its decision-making scripts, whether they are Mainstream or Multistream.

One way to break away from the scripts or thought patterns that an organization or culture might reinforce is to be mindful of the values that influence decision making.[42] To be "mindful" means to be aware of and attentive to values in each of the four steps of the decision-making process. This mindfulness is enhanced when you are able to contrast and compare two different approaches to the four-step decision-making process, as described in this chapter.

In closing out this discussion, consider how implementation of the decisions in the tobacco industry in turn triggered subsequent decision-making processes. Philip Morris, the company that chose to develop new products and new markets, achieved an 8.4 percent compounded average growth rate in earnings per share in the 25 years after the Surgeon General's announcement. Subsequently, the firm diversified by purchasing Kraft Foods, Miller Brewing, and General Foods. In each of the acquired companies, managers adapted and implemented Philip Morris's decision-making style and marketing-oriented outlook.

The other tobacco firms also did well. American Brands, whose managers chose the fine-tuning alternative, posted a 5.6 percent compounded average growth rate in earnings per share in the 25 years following the Surgeon General's announcement. R. J. Reynolds, where managers had chosen a two-pronged approach that tried to achieve the successes of both the Philip Morris and American Brands approaches, enjoyed the highest overall performance with an annual growth rate of 9.2 percent. Even at Ligget & Myers, where managers floundered in a chaotic variation of a do-nothing approach, growth was still 0.8 percent.

Lawsuits represent another form of public feedback related to decisions made by managers of tobacco companies after the Surgeon General's warning. The awards in these suits can be on the order of $100 billion or more. Perhaps most interesting for our present analysis are the suits that have to do with the so-called light or low-tar cigarettes, which managers at tobacco firms apparently knew were not as "healthy" an alternative to regular cigarettes as they would have had consumers believe. One response has been to introduce legislation that bans the use of the terms "light" and "low tar" on cigarettes.[43]

THE MULTISTREAM APPROACH TO THE FOUR-STEP DECISION-MAKING PROCESS

The values underlying the Multistream approach to decision making place more emphasis on participation and less emphasis on materialism than the values associated with the Mainstream approach. As we present the Multistream four-step decision-making process, we will pay special attention to aspects that distinguish it from the Mainstream process.

Step 1: Identify the Need for a Decision

The first step of the Multistream decision-making process differs from the Mainstream decision-making process in two ways: (1) It goes beyond simply maximizing material gain, and (2) it is more likely to be prompted by stakeholders other than only managers. Therefore, a comparatively wide set of concerns can trigger the decision-making process for Multistream managers. We will look at each factor in turn.

First, the Multistream decision-making process starts when an opportunity to make an improvement on any of a wide variety of forms of well-being is recognized. For example, AT&T manager Robert Greenleaf noticed that the recruitment and promotion decision-making "scripts" at his organization had resulted in women being underrepresented in its workforce, and also that African American employees were being promoted at a slower rate. In doing so, he recognized the need for decisions that—because they were not expected to improve organizational productivity—likely would not have been recognized and acted upon within a typical Mainstream point of view.[44] Put differently, because the Multistream approach is concerned with more diverse kinds of well-being, it increases the likelihood that managers will be sensitive to needs for decisions that may have little to do with materialist–individualist matters. At that time AT&T did not have explicit standards for measuring such issues of equal opportunity. Instead, Greenleaf identified the need for a decision based on standards that were outside the operating norms and scripts of his organization. Moreover, in identifying the need for decisions on these matters, and guiding the decision-making process accordingly, these forms of social well-being were improved at AT&T. The new practices soon became part of the taken-for-granted scripts used by many managers in the workplace.[45]

Second, the Multistream decision-making process can be triggered not only by managers (as in the example of Robert Greenleaf), but also by other stakeholders. While other stakeholders can similarly trigger the Mainstream decision-making process (recall how the Surgeon General's announcement set off the decision-making process at the tobacco companies), recognition of the role of other stakeholders— particularly of less powerful stakeholders—is by its nature more commonplace in Multistream management. Indeed, Multistream managers are well known for adopting a "listening" posture, trying to be sensitive to the needs of other stakeholders, and putting those needs on the decision-making agenda.[46] This posture is illustrated by managers who listen to the need for environmentally friendlier practices and social justice.

For example, in light of exploitive working conditions in low-income countries, managers in a growing number of organizations have voluntarily chosen to

A group of artists have formed the "The Invisible Dignity Project" to draw attention to the need for humankind to take action against the modern-day slave trade. It is estimated that 4 million people are trafficked every year for forced labor purposes. An estimated 27 million people are currently enslaved worldwide, and human trafficking is the third highest source of revenue in organized crime (worth about $10 billion a year).[48]

adopt an international standard of social accountability—SA8000—where adherents agree to pay wages that are adequate to cover basic needs (and not just the legislated minimums), agree not to employ children younger than 15 years of age, and agree not to use forced labor. Some large retailers have committed themselves to choose suppliers that follow the same standards, even if they are not the lowest-price option. For example, the large European retailer C&A stopped dealing with 19 of its suppliers when managers discovered the suppliers had not been following the company's code of conduct.[47]

Step 2: Develop Alternative Responses

Multistream managers have the same three basic options for developing alternatives that Mainstream managers have, but with two qualitative differences.

First, Multistream managers have a comparatively larger range of alternatives to develop because they are not limited to issues of maximizing the owners' financial well-being. Consider again the example of the Surgeon General's announcement linking smoking to cancer. From a Mainstream perspective, it makes sense that managers in tobacco firms developed and chose alternatives that would protect or enhance the financial well-being of the firms' shareholders. However, from a Multistream perspective, it seems very odd to assume that managers would try to maintain or increase the sale of products that they know will harm customers. Obviously shareholders' concerns should be taken into account, but developing ways to attract new smokers (the alternative pursued by Philip Morris) or ensuring the long-term loyalty of existing smokers (the alternative pursued by American Brands) does not seem to address the most important problems evident in the Surgeon General's announcement.

To address these larger needs for a decision, managers could have met with doctors, customers, shareholders, and suppliers to see if there were any mutually beneficial ways of responding to the Surgeon General's announcement. For example, they could have tried to develop new technologies to truly make cigarettes less unhealthy, rather than simply marketing "light" cigarettes that may have little advantage in terms of health.[49] Or, by applying the logic behind the idea of *negawatts* described in Chapter 3, perhaps cigarette companies could be paid to *reduce* the number of smokers. Just as it is cheaper to "save" a barrel of oil by helping people to reduce their consumption than it is to find a "new" barrel of oil, so too it might be possible that the money "saved" by getting one person to stop smoking would be greater than the profit that comes from selling a new person a cigarette. (Research estimates that the total "social cost" of a pack of cigarettes is about $2.50.[50])

Because Multistream managers consider alternatives that are not limited to simply maximizing the financial returns of shareholders, they are open to opportunities that are financially viable, but perhaps less profitable than other alternatives. Examples of such alternative initiatives are Fair Trade products or businesses (e.g., the Day

Chocolate Company), increased diversity in management (e.g., AT&T), cooperatives that promote car sharing (e.g., CarSharing.net), and health-conscious organizations that help people to stop smoking (e.g., Nicorette Gum made by Pharmacia AB of Sweden). In sum, there are many problems and opportunities facing the world today, especially from a Multistream perspective. The challenge from a Multistream perspective is to develop creative alternative responses that enhance sustenance economics.

Second, just as in Step 1 of the decision-making process, a Multistream approach is more likely to involve not only managers but other stakeholders as well in developing alternatives. For example, rather than give explicit product specifications to their suppliers, Japanese car manufacturers such as Toyota and Nissan have drawn on the expertise of *suppliers* and asked them to help identify the appropriate specifications for automobile components. Similarly, Ricardo Semler, the Multistream CEO of Semco (see the opening case in Chapter 10), sometimes provides *customers* with a complete report of the costs associated with a product or service Semco is selling, and welcomes the customer's input in setting a fair price.[51]

This discussion is not meant to suggest that Mainstream managers *never* invite other stakeholders to participate in this step of the decision-making process. But, as is evident in models like the one in Table 7.1, the level of other-stakeholder participation in the Mainstream approach seldom goes beyond involving group members. Even then, participation is recommended only in special circumstances (mainly when it is needed to prevent resistance to implementation of the decision). In contrast, the Multistream approach invites participation of organizational members as a matter of principle, and it is not unusual to include external stakeholders in this step.[52]

Step 3: Choose an Appropriate Alternative

We have discussed how two key dimensions are important in this step: goal consensus and available knowledge. Again, there are differences between the Mainstream and Multistream views. By way of general introduction, Multistream managers do not assume that the "high goal consensus/high knowledge available" quadrant is automatically the ideal to strive for.

GOAL CONSENSUS. The Multistream approach emphasizes multiple goals, multiple forms of well-being, and multiple criteria to evaluate decisions. In short, Multistream managers *expect* to encounter a variety of goals. In contrast, Mainstream managers place greater emphasis on "the bottom line"—the financial well-being of shareholders—which helps to simplify the decision-making process.

Multistream managers do not expect goal consensus and do not feel threatened by a lack of it. Instead, they recognize that an organization is a complex place, and that different people will emphasize different forms of well-being at different times. The key is to respect those differences, which in turn fosters mutual respect and open-minded communication among stakeholders. When members, including managers, are aware of and sensitive to the competing goals among an organization's stakeholders, they are more likely to respect them and to make choices that enhance the mutual benefit of everyone. Most people have observed this kind of community of mutual respect, and many have had a chance to experience it, whether in the context of a workplace, a caring family, a sports team without selfish teammates, or in friendship circles where people look out for one another.

Reell Precision Manufacturing is known for its culture of mutual respect and participative decision making. These aspects of its culture are captured in the phrase in its Direction Statement that invites members "to treat the concern of others

MANAGEMENT IN PRACTICE

Moving from a Mainstream to a Multistream Company

Cari Hunter was a manager at a Big Six accounting firm before she joined Protegra as Director of Finance. Protegra, a fast-growing firm that provides software and consulting services, is managed according to Multistream principles by CEO Wadood Ibrahim. Hunter notes that the decision-making process is very different at Protegra than it had been at the accounting firm. In her previous job, *she* identified the decisions that needed to be made, *she* developed the alternatives and assigned staff to collect the data to analyze the pros and cons, and *she* made the decisions about what to do. Hunter enjoyed the power of decision making—but she didn't like the fact that staff often expected her to solve their problems, and that she often felt pulled in many directions.

In Hunter's current job, things are much different. First, the decisions are much broader in scope. Not only do decisions need to be made about items such as invoicing and bill pay-ment, but decisions must also be made about how to promote ecological, physical, and social well-being in the workplace. This scope of decision making could be overwhelming, except for the fact that Hunter does not need to consider all the alternatives and make all the decisions on her own. At Protegra, decisions are much more likely to be discussed among colleagues and made participatively. Does this approach take away from Hunter's enjoyment of having the power to make decisions? Not at all! She loves being part of the give-and-take that comes from making decisions participatively: It gives her the opportunity to mentor and to learn from others. She enjoys being part of a team that has diverse points of view, which is quite different from feeling pulled in many directions.

In which kind of organization would you rather be a manager? One where you have the power and make the decisions? Or one where you foster participative decision making? Why?

(co-worker, customer, suppliers) equally with our own concerns." Like all companies, Reell has experienced its ups and downs, and it has faced difficult decisions. One year it became apparent that because of a situation with a key customer, Reell's revenues would not keep up with its expenses. Instead of laying people off, everyone at the company agreed to take a 10 percent pay cut (with the three founding owners/managers taking an even greater cut in pay).[53] Examples like Reell and First Fruits Orchards (see the Chapter 3 opening case) provide a window into the sense of community that Multistream managers encourage in the workplace.

Perhaps the ultimate "goal consensus" within Multistream organizations occurs when members share the goal of respecting one another's differing views. In organizations that adopt this perspective, such as Reell and First Fruits Orchards, it seems entirely "natural" to make decisions that balance materialist–individualist well-being with social, ecological, and/or physical well-being. In these organizations, decision making is often not the typical rational process that can be captured by some explicit set of rigid rules. Instead, it is more of an organic process, during which people receive genuine satisfaction from helping others. Respecting one another's differences facilitates learning, overall well-being, and community.

Of course, sometimes these differing views can challenge the core of the identity of an organization and its founding managers. This occurred when some members of Reell Precision Manufacturing felt excluded by the phrase in its Direction Statement that "Reell is committed to following the will of God." Rather than shy away from this dissenting view, an ad hoc group was created to look at the problematic statement and develop alternatives. Ultimately, members chose an alternative that was a better reflection of what Reell was *actually* doing in terms of welcoming diversity in its hiring and promotion practices. The revised statement contained the phrase, "We are challenged to work and make decisions consistent with God's purpose for creation according to our individual understanding."[54]

ORGANIZATIONAL KNOWLEDGE. Because Mainstream managers have a materialist perspective, they are more likely to emphasize explicit knowledge rather than tacit knowledge. As defined in Chapter 6, *explicit knowledge* is information that can be codified in an organization's standard operating procedures, blueprints, mission statements, and so on. From a Mainstream perspective, reliance on intuition or inspiration has sometimes been seen as a weakness, something that managers might have to use only when explicit knowledge is not available. (However, there is increasing awareness that an organization's tacit knowledge may be a key resource for achieving competitive advantage—see Chapter 9).

Multistream managers pay attention to *both* explicit and tacit knowledge. A Multistream approach goes beyond written guidelines, and is more likely to take into account holistic concerns that are often more difficult to quantify, such as the meaning of neighborliness, social justice, and environmental sustainability. For example, Reell did not have an explicit policy specifying what to do in case of economic downturn, but rather fostered a strong sense that all members should be treated with dignity and respect. As a result, when Reell faced economic hardship due to problems with its major customer, a series of discussions and meetings were held to consider the needs of all coworkers. This process resulted in members agreeing to take cuts in pay or in hours worked, and no one was laid off.

As it turns out, researchers are discovering that despite the Mainstream bias toward rational decision making, decisions are often made using factors that are difficult to quantify. For example, people often make decisions in light of difficult-to-define outcomes that they hope to achieve.[55] Such outcomes can include hard-to-measure ideas such as "happiness" or "treating the concerns of others as equal to our own concerns." A Multistream approach acknowledges and encourages these considerations in decision making.[56]

Multistream managers embrace tacit knowledge because they do not want to rely solely on explicit knowledge.[57] As noted previously, decisions based on tacit knowledge are intuitive. Trusting intuition is not a rejection of logic and data, but rather a recognition that our reactions to and understanding of issues are often so complex that they cannot be easily made explicit or codified. For example, after watching 15-minute videos of conversations between married couples, researcher John Gottman can predict with 90 percent accuracy which couples will eventually get divorced. How does he do it? Through a rigorous research process, his intuitive judgments were shown to be linked to his (and others') ability to notice and assess critical emotions—such as contempt—that destroy relationships.[58]

Step 4: Implement the Choice

The final step of the decision-making process focuses attention on two key considerations:

- Ways to manage resistance
- Feedback during implementation

The Mainstream approach tries to overcome resistance by the selective use of participation, and it has a bias toward looking for feedback that supports the decision. The Multistream approach differs from these assumptions on both accounts.

First, regarding resistance, the Multistream approach is both less likely to meet resistance and more likely to respect it. It is less likely to meet resistance because of its emphasis on participation. This participation is evident in all four stages of the decision-making process: It has an effect on the kinds of decision that are considered (Step 1), the kinds of alternatives that are developed (Step 2), and the

In some situations, an open-ended invitation to participate or not participate in implementing a decision is not advisable. A humorous example from politics comes from the satirical Rhinoceros Party of Canada. In one national election campaign, Rhinoceros Party candidates said that they wanted to adopt the system of driving used in the United Kingdom, where vehicles are driven on the left side of the road. To make the transition gradual so that people could become accustomed to left-side driving, they proposed that the system be phased in over a period of five years, with large trucks first, then buses, then cars, and finally bicycles. Its candidates never won an election, but did place second in several cases.[59]

alternatives that are chosen (Step 3); it also decreases the likelihood of resistance during implementation (Step 4).

Research suggests that managers are much more likely to engage in participative decision making when they are trying to develop their members, rather than trying to save time and costs. For example, with regards to models like the one presented in Table 7.1, when managers want to focus on *developing* employees rather than on *minimizing* time and costs, then the recommended number of occasions where decisons should be delegated more than doubles (increasing from 7 percent of cases to 19 percent).

Of course, it is naive to assume that participation will always lead to unanimity; there will often be people who would rather not implement a particular decision. Whenever possible, however, Multistream managers are likely to make implementation invitational. If practical, those members who oppose implementing a decision are free not to implement it. For example, the unit manager of a hospital's Neonatal Intensive Care Unit noted that nurses often wanted to change their work shifts in order to accommodate events in their personal lives, so the unit manager began to offer them the opportunity to self-schedule their shifts. Nurses were still required to work the same number of weekend and night shifts, but had greater flexibility as to when. Nurses could choose not to participate in the self-scheduling plan and to have their shifts scheduled in the regular manner.

Second, regarding feedback, Multistream managers' tendency to see decisions as "experiments" makes them more likely to look for feedback that will help them *improve* their decisions rather than *defend* their decisions. Because of this, a Multistream approach reduces the likelihood of escalation of commitment, information distortion, inappropriate persistence, and administrative inertia. In addition, it increases the likelihood that managers will learn from poor decisions.

When Robert Greenleaf noticed that African American employees were underrepresented at the higher managerial levels at AT&T (Step 1), he met with a group of managers and invited them to talk about different alternatives to address the situation (Step 2). The group developed various alternatives, including recruiting more African American employees for management training programs and providing African American specialists with job experiences that would better prepare them for managerial positions (Step 3). Managers were invited to implement both, one, or neither of these options. Those who did implement the alternatives did so with a spirit of experimentation and a desire to learn from and improve upon practices based on feedback. Over time, an increasing number of people implemented these decisions (put differently, managers began to adopt the new "scripts" that were being developed). During a nine-year period, these activities together helped to increase the proportion of African American managers at AT&T almost tenfold (Step 4).[60]

How Decisions Can Lead to a $7 Billion Loss[61]

The 144-year-old French bank Société Générale was known as a world leader in derivatives when it lost more than $7 billion in January 2008. How can an organization with a reputation of making good investment decisions suddenly lose so much money? There may be a variety of factors at play, but the story centers on decisions made by Jérôme Kerviel, a 31-year-old bank employee accused of circumventing bank controls and rules in his trades.

An early signal that something was amiss occurred on November 7, 2007, when compliance officers at Société Générale received an e-mail from Eurex, one of Europe's biggest exchanges, stating that Kerviel, over a period of seven months, had been engaged in several transactions that had raised red flags. Société Générale receives about 15 to 20 such queries from exchanges like Eurex each year. The compliance officer at Société Générale looked into the problems, and Kerviel's supervisor indicated that there was no anomaly. Société Générale responded with a memo to Eurex describing how the increase in volatility in the European and American markets explained the need for Kerviel's after-hours trading. Eurex sent a follow-up e-mail on November 26, 2007, asking for more information. Société Générale provided more details on December 10, 2007, and the issue seemed settled. Kerviel reported that by the end of December his trades had resulted in a profit of about $2 billion for the bank and he had been rewarded with a $400,000 bonus for 2007.

Unfortunately, a few weeks later when Kerviel set off the next alarm, it was too late. Kerviel had exposed the bank to over $70 billion in risk—more than the bank's market value. After his trades were unwound, the result was $7 billion in trading losses within a week.

So, how could this happen? Various explanations have been offered. First, Société Générale had a culture that rewarded risk and encouraged its employees to engage in "proprietary trading," which means using the bank's money to make bets on the market. As a result, to get bigger rewards, managers would be tempted to take larger risks, and in a complex industry, a bank's internal controls cannot always keep up with the clever actions of its members. In Kerviel's case, thanks to his earlier job experience in the bank's back office, he knew what time its reconciliation for each day's trades took place, and he was able to use this information to delete his unauthorized transactions and then reenter them.

Another explanation notes that specific challenges in maintaining self-control may be inherent in a trader's job. Research in neuroeconomics indicates that the brain images of drug addicts about to take another hit are identical to the brain images of traders who are making money and are about to make another trade. Put differently, making money is similar to a chemical addiction.

For his part, Kerviel accepted a share of the responsibility for his decisions, but he refused to become the scapegoat, insisting that his managers had been aware of his unusually large trades and had received warnings about his activities nine months earlier.

QUESTIONS FOR DISCUSSION

1. What step or steps in the decision-making process are problematic in this case?

2. Explain how ideas from "framing" theory might help to explain what happened at Société Générale.

3. Explain how ideas from escalation of commitment might help to explain what happened.

4. In light of your analysis, what advice about decision making would you give to Société Générale?

SUMMARY

Both Mainstream and Multistream managers follow the same basic four-step decision-making process, but there are differences in how the process unfolds.

In the Mainstream approach:

1. Managers identify problems and opportunities for the organization to meet or surpass its financial goals.

2. Managers develop alternative ways to respond to those problems or opportunities, with an eye toward ensuring that the financial benefits of an alternative outweigh its financial costs.

3. Managers choose one of the alternatives, using an appropriate method based on how much goal consensus and knowledge are available for each alternative.

4. Managers implement the chosen alternative, using a participative approach if necessary to overcome resistance.

In the Multistream approach:

1. Managers and other stakeholders identify problems and opportunities for the organization that will improve a variety of forms of well-being.

2. Managers and other stakeholders develop alternative ways to respond to those problems or opportunities, with an eye toward ensuring that overall well-being is enhanced.

3. Managers and other stakeholders choose one of the alternatives that have been developed, appreciating the healthy tension among various goals, and drawing on both explicit and tacit knowledge.

4. Managers and other stakeholders implement the chosen alternative, using an experimental approach that nurtures continuous learning.

QUESTIONS FOR REFLECTION AND DISCUSSION

1. Identify and briefly describe each of the four steps in the decision-making process.

2. Which of the four steps do you think is the most challenging for managers? Why do you think so?

3. Which of the decision-making methods in Figure 7.3 would you find most helpful? Why?

4. How important is politics in organizations? Explain how politics influences management decision making. What is the best way to deal with politics?

5. What advice do you have for the "Multistream" students in your class who, like Dennis Gioia in the chapter-opening case, aspire to become managers who will foster a greater sense of social responsibility in organizations?

6. Explain how you decided which school to attend or which major to choose. Did your decision-making process follow the four-step process described in the chapter? Which steps were most important? Why?

7. Managers at cigarette companies faced a crisis in 1950 when the Surgeon General announced that smoking could cause cancer. There are similar announcements and crises facing managers today whose companies make products linked to cancer and other health problems, global warming, and so on. Based on this chapter, what advice would you have for a manager facing such a situation?

HANDS-ON ACTIVITIES

Where Are You Along the Mainstream–Multistream Continuum?

Circle the number that best corresponds to your views.

TO BE AN EFFECTIVE MANAGER, I SHOULD . . .

Identify problems and opportunities for the organization *that will meet or surpass its financial goals*	1 2 3 4 5 6 7	Identify problems and opportunities for the organization *that will improve both financial and other forms of well-being*
Develop alternative ways to respond to organizational problems or opportunities, ensuring *that the financial benefits of an alternative outweigh its financial costs*	1 2 3 4 5 6 7	Develop alternative ways to respond to organizational problems or opportunities, ensuring *that overall well-being is enhanced*
Make choices among various alternatives by using an appropriate method *based on how much goal consensus and knowledge there is available for each alternative*	1 2 3 4 5 6 7	Make choices among various alternatives that have been developed, *appreciating the healthy tension among various goals, and drawing on both explicit and tacit knowledge*
Implement decisions using *a participative approach only when necessary to overcome resistance*	1 2 3 4 5 6 7	Implement decisions *using an experimental approach that nurtures continuous learning*

ENDNOTES

1. All quotes in this case are taken from Dennis A. Gioia (1992). Pinto fires and personal ethics: A script analysis of missed opportunities. *Journal of Business Ethics*, 11, 379–389. With kind permission from Springer Science and Business Media. See also Nutt, P. C. (2002). *Why decisions fail: Avoiding blunders and traps that lead to debacles.* San Francisco: Berret-Kohler; Birsch, D., & Fielder, J. H. (Eds.). (1994) *The Ford Pinto case: A study in applied ethics, business, and technology.* New York: State University of New York Press.

2. Needless to say these financial numbers served to change the decision calculus, and in 1978 Ford upgraded the integrity of Pinto's fuel system. It stopped producing the Pinto in 1980.

3. Gioia served as Ford's Recall Coordinator from 1973 to 1975. When he started in 1973, he inherited the oversight of approximately 100 active recall campaigns, and had additional files of incoming safety problems, one of which included reports of Pintos "lighting up." The decision described in the opening paragraphs, to pay damages instead of issuing a recall, was made after Gioia had left the position. Important stories in the public media on Pinto problems were published in 1976 and 1977. After three teenage girls died in a Pinto fire, a grand jury took the unprecedented step of indicting Ford on charges of reckless homicide. See Gioia, D. A. (1992). Pinto fires and personal ethics: A script analysis of missed opportunities. *Journal of Business Ethics*, 11, 379–389.

4. Gioia, 1992, p. 382.

5. Gioia, 1992, p. 384.

6. Dyck, B. (1991). *Prescription, description and inscription: A script theoretic leadership model.* Presented in the Organization and Management Theory Interest Group, Administrative Sciences Association of Canada, Niagara Falls, Ontario.

7. Dawes, R. (1988). *Rational choice in an uncertain world.* Orlando, FL: Harcourt Brace Jovanovich.

8. See Miles, R. H., in collaboration with Cameron, K. S. (1982). *Coffin nails and corporate strategies.* Englewood Cliffs, NJ: Prentice-Hall.

9. Shimizi, K., & Hitt, M. (2004). Strategic flexibility: Organizational preparedness to reverse ineffective decision. *Academy of Management Executive*, 18(4), 44–59.

10. In Chapter 8, we will look more closely at how goals are set. For now, we concentrate on whether there is goal consensus.

11. He collected these data while a professor at the University of Manitoba. His simulation is based on the following article: Hall, R. I. (1976). A system pathology of an organization: The rise and fall of the old *Saturday Evening Post. Administrative Science Quarterly*, 21(2), 185–211.

12. Our definitions are not entirely consistent with the classic distinction between risk and uncertainty associated with the economist Frank Knight: Knight, F. H. (1921). *Risk, uncertainty, and profit.* Boston: Hart, Schaffner & Marx/Houghton Mifflin.

13. The work of Daniel Kahneman and Amos Tversky suggests that how the facts are presented, or framed, has an effect on the kinds of decisions people make [e.g., see Kahneman, D., & Tversky, A. (1979). Prospect theory: An analysis of decision under risk. *Econometrica*, 47, 263–291]. Daniel Kahneman won (half) the 2002 Nobel Prize in economic sciences "for having integrated insights from psychological research into economic science, especially concerning human judgment and decision-making under uncertainty" (taken from cite accessed October 13, 2006, at http://nobelprize.org/nobel_prizes/economics/laureates/2002/).

14. This example is adapted from and builds on the discussion described in Bazerman, M. (1998). *Judgment in managerial decision making* (4th ed.). New York: John Wiley & Sons.

15. From Bazerman, 1998, p. 131.

16. Bazerman, 1998; Miller, C. C., & Ireland, R. D. (2005). Intuition in strategic decision making: Friend or foe in the fast-paced 21st century? *Academy of Management Executive*, 19(1), 19–30.

17. Kacmar, K. M., Bozeman, D. P., Carlson, D. S., & Anthony, W. P. (1999). An examination of the perceptions of organizational politics model: Replication and extension. *Human Relations*, 52(3), 383–416.

18. Landler, M., & Clark, N. (2006, October 10). Airbus chief of 3 months resigns post. *New York Times*. Accessed on February 20, 2008, at http://www.nytimes.com/2006/10/10/business/worldbusiness/10airbus.html?scp=1&sq=&st=nyt.

19. Burke, L. A., & Miller, M. K. (1999). Taking the mystery out of intuitive decision-making. *Academy of Management Executive*, 13(4), 91–99. See also Sadler-Smith, E., & Shefy, E. (2004). The intuitive executive: Understanding and applying "gut feel" in decision-making. *Academy of Management Executive*, 18(4), 76–91.

20. Gladwell, M. (2005). *Blink*. New York: Little, Brown.

21. Miller & Ireland, 2005.

22. Dean, E. D., Mihalasky, J., Ostrander, S., & Schroeder, L. (1974). *Executive ESP*. Englewood Cliffs, NJ: Prentice-Hall.

23. Nutt, P. C. (2002). *Why decisions fail: Avoiding blunders and traps that lead to debacles*. San Francisco: Berret-Kohler; Delbecq, A., Liebert, E., Mostyn, J., Nutt, P. C., & Walter, G. (2004). *Discernment and strategic decision making: Reflections for a spirituality of organizational leadership*. Accessed September 23, 2006, at lsb.scu/ISOL/discernment.pdf.

24. Benefiel, M. (2005). *Soul at work: Spiritual leadership in organization*. New York: Seabury Books.

25. Information in this paragraph was drawn from Tsang, E. W. K. (2004). Superstition and decision-making: Contradiction or complement? *Academy of Management Executive*, 18(4), 92–104.

26. Simon, H. A. (1947). *Administrative behavior*. New York: Macmillan; Simon, H. A. (1957). *Models of man*. New York: Wiley; March, J. G., & Simon, H. A. (1958). *Organizations*. New York: Wiley; Simon, H. A. (1960). *The new science of management decision*. New York: Harper & Row; Simon, H. A. (1987, February). Making management decisions: The role of intuition and emotion. *Academy of Management Executive*, 57–63.

27. Nutt, 2002.

28. See Vroom, V. H. (2000). Leadership and the decision-making process. *Organizational Dynamics*, 28(4), 82–94. See also Vroom, V. H., & Yetton, P. W. (1973). *Leadership and decision-making*. Pittsburgh, PA: University of Pittsburgh Press. Note that we have adapted the items in their model to fit the four-step decision-making process described here.

29. These percentages are calculated based on the fact that the model has a combined total of 128 possible ways to rate each of the seven questions as "high" or "low" (that is, $2^7 = 128$). As highlighted elsewhere in this chapter (on page 224), in a different variation of the model, which focuses on *developing* employees rather than on *minimizing* time and costs, (a) 19 percent of the decisions are recommended to be *delegated*; (b) 9 percent are to be *facilitated*; and (c) in more than 70 percent of the situations in the model, managers are recommended to make the decisions, either alone (38 percent) or after consulting with others in groups (35 percent). See Vroom, V. H. (2003).

30. Educating managers for decision making and leadership. *Management Decision*, 41(10), 968–978.

30. Moreover, almost all failures are due to actions of the decision maker, not inherent in the situation itself. Nutt, P. C. (2004). Expanding the search for alternatives during strategic decision-making. *Academy of Management Executive*, 18(4), 13–28.

31. Tugend, A. (2007, November 24). The many errors in thinking about mistakes. *New York Times*. Accessed Febraury 20, 2008, at http://www.nytimes.com/2007/11/24/business/24shortcuts.html?_r=2&scp=1&sq=&st=nyt&oref=slogin&oref=slogin.

32. Ketchen, D. J., Snow, C. C., & Street, V. L. (2004). Improving firm performance by matching strategic decision-making processes to competitive dynamics. *Academy of Management Executive*, 18(4), 29–43.

33. Shimizi & Hitt, 2004.

34. Simurda, S. J. (1996, November/December). There's a word for it: Intrapreneurism. *Worldbusiness*. Accessed October 6, 2006, at http://www.umass.edu/journal/faculty/steve/bizarticles/innovation.html; Guarnaccia, S. (1998). The truth is, the truth hurts. *Fast Company*, 14, 93. Accessed October 6, 2006, at http://www.fastcompany.com/online/14/one.html.

35. Taken from Nutt, 2004.

36. For more on the Concorde saga, see the following article: Cater, C. R., Kaufmann, L., & Michel, A. (2007). Behavioral supply management: A taxonomy of judgment and decision-making biases. *International Journal of Physical Distribution and Logistics Management*, 37(8), 631–669.

37. Shimizu & Hitt, 2004.

38. Shimizu & Hitt, 2004.

39. Glisby, M., & Holden, N. (2003). Contextual constraints in knowledge management theory: The cultural embeddedness of Nonaka's knowledge-creating company. *Knowledge and Process Management*, 10(1), 29–36.

40. Note that our description of Multistream decision making in this chapter also has some overlap with the ideas in the four-phase model of organizational learning, especially as described by the Japanese scholar Ikijuro Nonaka. See Nonaka, I. (1994). A dynamic theory of organizational knowledge creation. *Organization Science*, 5(1), 14–37. See also Deresky, H. (no date). Decision-making in Japanese companies.

41. Barney, J. B. (2004). An interview with William Ouchi. *Academy of Management Executive*, 18(4), 108–116.

42. Mindfulness is a state of awareness and attentiveness that promotes intentional self-regulation. See Ryan, R. M., & Deci, E. R., (2001). Self-determination theory and the facilitation of intrinsic motivation, social development, and well-being. *American Psychologist*, 52, 141–166.

43. Johnston, D. C., & Warner, M. (2006, September 26). Tobacco makers lose key ruling on latest suits. *New York Times*. Accessed September 26, 2006, at http://www.nytimes.com/2006/09/26/business/26tobacco.html?pagewanted=1&_r=1&th&adxnnl=0&emc=th&adxnnlx=1159279217-s01aKalpZ7X6wlVPAxfKRA.

44. The ongoing example of Robert Greenleaf in this chapter builds on material found in Nielsen, R. P. (1998). Quaker foundations for Greenleaf's servant-leadership and "friendly disentangling" method. In Spears, L. C. (Ed.), *Insights on leadership* (pp. 126–144). New York: John Wiley & Sons. Greenleaf joined AT&T in 1929 as a laborer's assistant and retired in 1964 after having served as corporate human resources vice president and as director of management development and research.

45. Similarly, John Woolman was motivated by larger issues of social justice when he invested time and money into abolishing slavery. The Multistream decision-making process is not merely concerned with self-interested material matters—it is based on a holistic framework that recognizes the need to make decisions that foster a wider variety of forms of well-being. Moreover, because the Multistream approach emphasizes stakeholders who are external to the focal organization, it is distinct even from a participative Mainstream approach.

46. Dyck, B., & Weber, M. (2006). Conventional and radical moral agents: An exploratory look at Weber's moral-points-of-view and virtues. *Organization Studies, 27*(3), 429–450.

47. Biggart, N. W., & Delbridge, R. (2004). Systems of exchange. *Academy of Management Review, 29*(1), 28–49.

48. This watercolor by Ray Dirks is entitled "Mama Kadi and her daughters" and was taken from the "Invisible Dignity Project" website, accessed February 20, 2008, at http://www.invisible-dignity.org/about.aspx. Information was also drawn from *Present Day Slavery: The Report of the Washington State Task Force Against Trafficking of Persons* (June, 2004, Office of Crime Victims Advocacy), accessed February 21, 2008, at http://72.14.205.104/search?q=cache:Y42z1-rxE8cJ:www.cted.wa.gov/_cted-documents/ID_29_Publications.pdf+slavery+present+day&hl=en&ct=clnk&cd=1&client=safari. This figure of 4 million slaves per year comes from: *United Nations. Integration of the Human Rights of Women and the Gender Perspective: Report of the Special Rapporteur on Violence Against Women, Its Causes and Consequences, Economic and Social Council*, U.N. Doc E/CN.4/2000/68, February 29, 2000.

49. According to a report by Judge Gladys Kessler of the Federal District Court for the District of Columbia, the tobacco industry has engaged in a 40-year conspiracy to defraud smokers about the health dangers of tobacco, including deceptions about lights and low-tar cigarettes. However, according to William S. Ohlemeyer, associate general counsel of Altria, whose Philip Morris division makes half of all cigarettes sold in the United States, it is the government—not tobacco companies—that promoted the idea that lights were a safer alternative cigarette (Johnston & Warner, 2006).

50. These costs are based on older data; they may well be higher today. A 1985 report by the Office of Technology Assessment (OTA) of the U.S. Congress estimated the cost to be about $2.17 per pack of cigarettes sold. In its 1993 report, OTA pegged the cost at about $2.59. These cost estimates include both societal costs (e.g., health care) and personal costs to the smoker (e.g., lost earnings caused by illness and earlier death). McCormick, R. E., Tollison, T., & Wagner, R. E. (1997). Smoking, insurance, and social costs. *Regulation: The CATA review of business & government, 20*(3). Accessed November 8, 2007, at http://www.cato.org/pubs/regulation/reg20n3c.html.

51. Semler, R. (2004). *The seven-day weekend: Changing the way work works.* New York: Penguin/Portfolio.

52. Thompson, G., & Driver, C. (2005). Stakeholder champions: How to internationalize the corporate social responsibility agenda. *Business Ethics, 14*(1), 56–66. Retrieved November 5, 2007, from ABI/INFORM Global database (document ID: 868723941).

53. Moreover, the practice at Reell is that the pay of executive managers does not exceed roughly seven to ten times that of Reell's lowest-paid employee (Benefiel, 2005).

54. Benefiel, 2005.

55. Lee Roy Beach's image theory describes decisions as being made not "by the numbers," but in comparison with ideal states or images of self or outcomes. Beach, L. (1990). *Image theory: Decision making in personal and organizational contexts.* New York: Wiley.

56. Giacalone, R. A. (2004). A transcendent business education for the 21st century. *Academy of Management Learning and Education, 3*(4), 415–420.

57. The Mainstream tendency to favor explicit over tacit knowledge may be linked to Western culture. For example, Richard Pascale notes that just as Americans find sumo wrestling to be a curious and odd form of entertainment that provides a window into Japanese culture, so also many Japanese managers find it odd how much emphasis Americans place on trying to codify their strategic management. For the Japanese, strategic management is much more about learning unexpected things "as you go" rather than rationally planning everything out ahead of time. See Pascale, R. T. (1984). Perspectives on strategy: The real story behind Honda's success. *California Management Review, 26*, 47–72.

58. Malcolm Gladwell (2005) describes the process of evaluating options quickly with limited information as "thin-slicing."

59. Rhinoceros Party of Canada. (2005, September 29). Accessed November 8, 2007, at http://www.bbc.co.uk/dna/h2g2/A5287845.

60. The increase in the proportion of African American managers at AT&T increased from about 0.5 percent to 4.5 percent. This voluntary improvement—achieved in a time when there were no orders from top management to increase the number of African American employees being promoted, no timetables, no quotas, no performance reviews tied to promoting African American managers, and so on—was especially impressive in contrast to the subsequent increase achieved at AT&T with much acrimony and struggle via the legislated Civil Rights Act (Nielsen, 1998).

61. Samuel, H., & Allen, N. (2008). Jérôme Kerviel: Bank knew what I was doing. *Telegraph.* Accessed March 24, 2008, at http://www.telegraph.co.uk/core/Content/displayPrintable.jhtml;jsessionid=DOJ53RYKPX15DQFIQMFSFFWAVCBQ0IV0?xml=/money/2008/01/29/bcnkerviel129.xml&site=1&page=0; Clark, N. (2008, Feb 6). French trader says he won't be made a scapegoat. *New York Times.* Accessed March 24, 2008, at http://www.nytimes.com/2008/02/06/business/worldbusiness/06bank.html?scp=1&sq=&st=nyt; Anderson, J. (2008, February 7). Craving the High That Risky Trading Can Bring. *New York Times.* Accessed March 24, 2008, at http://www.nytimes.com/2008/02/07/business/worldbusiness/07trader.html?scp=1&sq=&st=nyt and; Schwartz, N.D., & Bennhold, K. (2008, Febuary 5). A trader's secrets, a bank's missteps. *New York Times.* Accessed March 24, 2008, at http://www.nytimes.com/2008/02/05/business/worldbusiness/05bank.html?scp=2&sq=&st=nyt.

CHAPTER 8

*C*hapter 7 described the decision-making process. This chapter looks at some of the most important decisions made in organizations—namely, decisions about the organization's goals and plans. We describe the four-step management process used to set goals and to develop the plans for reaching those goals. As usual, we highlight the differences between the Mainstream and Multistream approaches. *Strategic* goals and plans establish the organization's overall direction. In fact, strategic management is so important that we devote an entire chapter to it (Chapter 9). This current chapter looks at setting the vision and mission that inform an organization's strategy, and at the operational goals and plans that are used to put the strategy into practice.

ROAD MAP

FOUR STEPS OF THE PLANNING PROCESS

1. Set mission/vision

2. Set strategic goals/plans

3. Set operational goals/plans

4. Implement and monitor goals/plans

Setting Goals and Making Plans

MAINSTREAM APPROACH	**MULTISTREAM APPROACH**
Managers: Establish the purpose and aspirations of the organization	*Managers and other stakeholders:* Recognize their shared purpose and aspirations for the organization
Seek to achieve competitive advantage	Seek to achieve mutual advantages
Set SMART goals: Specific, Measurable, Achievable, Results-based, and Time-specific	*Set SMART2 goals:* Significant, Meaningful, Agreed-upon, Relevant, and Timely
Make plans that cover both new and ongoing goals	Make plans that cover both new and ongoing goals
Ensure that goals and plans are achieved and implemented	Continually learn from and improve upon goals and plans during implementation

A Vegetable Field of Dreams[1]

Wiens Family Farm is owned and operated by two Multistream managers—Dan and Wilma Wiens. Dan and Wilma helped to found the idea of Shared Farming, which belongs to the larger Community Shared Agriculture movement, and they have helped to inspire the start-up of many organizations like it across the Midwest. Consider how planning and goal setting take place at Wiens Family Farm.

First, the mission of Wiens Family Farm is to provide fresh, organically grown vegetables on a weekly basis to sharers. Sharers are city people who purchase in spring a "share" of the farm's harvest. This mission was not conceived by Wilma and Dan Wiens on their own. Rather, it initially grew out of a community of people who had gathered at the invitation of Dan Wiens, who wanted to explore alternative ways of practicing agriculture on his five-acre vegetable farm. Wiens invited people from various walks of life to a series of meetings to discuss some of their ideas about how agriculture could be practiced. It was only after several meetings that the mission and vision for Shared Farming were born. Its vision is to provide a viable, environmentally friendly, community-enhancing way of doing agriculture that can be duplicated by others.

Second, with a mission and a vision in hand, the process of developing strategic goals and plans could begin. Two early challenges were (1) to develop a market for this new form of agriculture and (2) to develop a distribution system to get the vegetables from the farm to sharers. The goal of 200 sharers was surpassed on the same day a local newspaper first described the project. Soon people were placed on waiting lists to participate as sharers. The Wiens' support group also helped develop plans for distributing the vegetables. The strategy would be to provide each sharer with a "blue box" full of vegetables, which would be delivered once a week at several centrally located neighborhood "depots" where sharers could pick up their produce and drop off their compost materials for use on the farm. Some sharers offered their garages, driveways, or parking lots as depots. The farm itself also serves as a depot. Sharers are always welcome to volunteer to work on the farm, and many do. In autumn, sharers are invited to a pot-luck celebration on the farm, where favorite recipes are exchanged.

Third, sharers became involved in setting operational goals and action plans, particularly the details of the farm that affected them personally, such as the quantity of vegetables to plant. Most notably, sharers became involved in setting the price of a share. In the first year, the share price had been set by the farmers, but soon they wanted to give the responsibility to sharers. Said Dan Wiens, "These are our friends, and we're sure they will treat us fairly." Dan and Wilma Wiens called a meeting, to which they brought a list of the different expenses involved in running the farm, and then asked sharers to set the price for a share. Sharers decided that a 40 percent increase in share price was in order.

Dan and Wilma Wiens with two of their children.

Finally, the sharers' views and opinions on the ongoing running of the farm are regularly sought and valued. This feedback informs future goals and plans, so the shape of Wiens Family Farm changes every year. In recent years, three young people have been living on the farm doing much of the work. Dan and Wilma have also helped start numerous similar farms. One farm is run by Salvadorian refugees, and provides both employment and varieties of vegetables that cannot be found at regular grocery stores. The Wiens family has also helped to find land for a group of underemployed inner-city people to use for growing vegetables. Finally, although Dan and Wilma are not Catholics, a nun recently moved onto the farm, creating a mini spiritual-retreat center.

The four-step process of setting goals and making plans at Wiens Family Farm is clearly an ongoing process and includes a variety of stakeholders. As a result, many of the farm's goals and plans have been different than Dan and Wilma could have anticipated, and the farm has remained viable and relevant for stakeholders.

INTRODUCTION TO GOALS AND PLANS

Setting goals and making plans are the two basic components of the planning function. **Goals** refer to the desired results or objectives that members in an organization are pursuing. The idea of goals is central to understanding management. Goals also provide guidelines for arranging resources (organizing), help to direct and motivate employees (leading), and provide criteria against which to evaluate performance (controlling). Given that goals are such an important part of management, it should come as no surprise that goal-setting theory has been rated as the most important among 73 different theories for understanding organizational behavior.[2]

Plans describe the steps and actions that are required to achieve goals. For example, the goal of a local community club may be to nurture relationships within a neighborhood while promoting physical fitness. The managers of the community club may plan to meet this goal by offering sports programs for children and youth, bingo nights for older adults, or coaching clinics for parents. Managers in two different organizations may have similar goals, but their ability to meet the goals will depend on whether they have made appropriate plans and have adequate resources at their disposal.

The four basic steps of the goal-setting and planning process are shown in Figure 8.1. All four steps are evident in the opening case.[3]

The first step, which is of particular relevance to top-level managers, involves setting an organization's overarching mission and vision. This long-term "big picture" establishes the main purpose of the organization.

The second step, which is relevant for both top- and mid-level managers, involves setting strategic goals and plans. These usually have to do with the nature and kinds of relationships that are developed with stakeholders. For example, the goals might focus on the number of customers or clients, the kinds of relationships with suppliers or distributors, or the competitive position in an industry. General Electric's goal of being number one or two in market share is an example of a strategic goal. These plans and goals often have a three- to five-year timeline.

The third step, which is relevant to mid- and lower-level managers, is to take the strategic goals and plans and put them into practice in everyday operations. In this step, the big picture (Step 1) and the strategic goals and plans (Step 2) are broken down into parts so that members in the organization will know what their departmental or personal goals and plans are. The goals and plans in this third step often extend for one year or less.

The fourth (and final) step is to implement and monitor the goals and plans. In this step, the organization ensures that the planning process works as it is supposed to.

It is helpful to talk about two basic "types" of organizational goals and plans:

- Ongoing
- Change oriented

Ongoing goals and plans guide the continuing activities that are consistent with the basic purpose of the organization. As described in this chapter, an

Goals are the desired results or objectives that members in an organization are pursuing.

Plans describe the steps and actions that are required to achieve goals.

Ongoing goals and plans guide the organization's continuing activities that are consistent with the basic purpose of the organization.

Figure 8.1 Overview of the four steps of the planning process

Step	Managerial Level of Particular Relevance	Time Frame/Duration
1. Set mission/vision	Top	Very long term: 5–10+ years
2. Set strategic goals/plans	Top/middle	3–5 years
3. Set operations goals/plans	Middle/lower	Annually/quarterly
4. Monitor	Everyone	Ongoing/monthly/quarterly/annually

organization's ongoing goals and plans are reflected in its mission statement, its standing plans, and its standard operating procedures. These goals and plans often correspond to the "programmed" decision-making process described in Chapter 7.

Change-oriented goals and plans describe new initiatives and changes to be made in an organization's practices.

Change-oriented goals and plans refer to new initiatives and changes to be made in an organization's practices. The changes may be *incremental*, such as increasing sales by the inflation rate plus 3 percent in the coming year, or *transformational*, such as privatizing a public hospital. An organization's change-oriented goals and plans are evident in its vision statement, in its ad hoc plans, and in its new operating procedures. Change-oriented goals and plans often correspond to the "nonprogrammed" decision-making process described in Chapter 7.

THE MAINSTREAM APPROACH TO GOALS AND PLANS

The focus in Mainstream planning is on setting goals and making plans to enhance the organization's financial well-being. From a Mainstream perspective, the four-step process is typically managed in a top-down manner, so that *managers* decide which goals should be pursued and which plans should be followed.

Step 1: Develop the Organization's Overarching Mission and Vision

Mission statement identifies the fundamental purpose of an organization as well as what an organization does, whom it serves, and how it differs from similar organizations.

At the top of the organization's hierarchy of goals is its mission statement. A **mission statement** identifies the fundamental purpose of the organization, and it often describes what the organization does, whom it serves, and how it differs from similar organizations. A mission statement can provide social legitimacy and a sense of identity for the members of the organization. One study suggests that as many as 90 percent of companies have a mission statement.[4]

Here is a sample of mission statements from a variety of organizations:

University of Central Arkansas: "to maintain the highest academic quality and to ensure that its programs remain current and responsive to the diverse needs of those it serves. A partnership of excellence among students, faculty, and staff in benefit to the global community, the University is committed to the intellectual, social, and personal development of its students; the advancement of knowledge through excellence in teaching and research; and service to the community. As a leader in 21st-century higher education, the University of Central Arkansas is dedicated to intellectual vitality, diversity, and integrity."[5]

International Committee of the Red Cross (ICRC): "an impartial, neutral and independent organization whose exclusively humanitarian mission is to protect the lives and dignity of victims of war and internal violence and to provide them with assistance."[6]

Dell Inc.: "to be the most successful computer company in the world at delivering the best customer experience in markets we serve."[7]

Nine different ideas are commonly mentioned in mission statements:

1. Products/services
2. Customers
3. Organizational self-concept
4. Survival/growth/profitability
5. Employees
6. Markets

7. Philosophy
8. Technology
9. Public image

For good reasons, very few mission statements contain all nine items. Instead, the content of an organization's mission statement is greatly influenced by mission statements of other organizations in its industry. For example, one study found that more than 60 percent of banking organizations mention "employees" in their mission statement (e.g., "We value our employees"), but "employees" are mentioned in less than 25 percent of computer hardware firms' mission statements. Similarly, about half of the mission statements of banks mention the philosophy of the firm (e.g., "We believe in quality"), but philosophy is mentioned in less than one-fourth of the mission statements of computer software or hardware organizations.[8]

Some firms deliberately try to set themselves apart from other members of their industry. For example, Southwest Airlines was the first airline to see itself primarily as a service provider; in fact, its mission statement doesn't even mention air travel!

> **Southwest Airlines:** "The mission of Southwest Airlines is dedication to the highest quality of customer service delivered with a sense of warmth, friendliness, individual pride, and company spirit. To our employees: We are committed to provide a stable work environment with equal opportunity for learning and personal growth. Creativity and innovation are encouraged for improving the effectiveness of Southwest Airlines. Above all, employees will be provided the same concern, respect, and caring attitude within the organization that they are expected to share externally with every Southwest customer."[9]

Mission statements can cause problems, especially if organizational members take them too literally. For example, at the time of the infamous Exxon *Valdez* oil-tanker spill (1989), the mission statement of Exxon was this: "To provide our shareholders with a superior return on investment." This mission statement has since been rewritten to avoid confusion about how employees are expected to balance their obligations to a variety of stakeholders.[10]

The organization's ongoing mission statement is often accompanied by a change-oriented **vision statement,** which describes what an organization is striving to become and, in this way, provides guidance to organizational members. Typically, the vision statement describes goals that an organization hopes to achieve five or more years into the future. For example, the *mission* of a university may be to teach students, engage in research, and provide service to the community; the *vision* of the university may be to become a world leader in medical research, to maximize diversity in the classroom, or to foster a sense of global citizenship. A tourist destination may have the *mission* to provide local employment and be friendly to tourists, and the *vision* of becoming the honeymoon capital of the world.

From a Mainstream approach, vision statements focus on things that will contribute to the future competitiveness and financial success of an organization. Research suggests that managers should develop vision statements that have a future orientation and are inspiring, challenging, brief, clear, and stable.[11] As with mission statements, the content of a vision statement may be influenced by the industry to which an organization belongs. For example, one study showed that the growth of entrepreneurial firms is associated with vision statements that express a need for power (for example, "We will be number one in our industry"), whereas in government service agencies performance is related to vision statements that recognize the need for members to have strong interpersonal relationships (e.g., "We will provide excellent working conditions and service").[12]

Vision statement describes what an organization is striving to become.

Organizations can use their logos to give expression to aspects of their mission and vision. For example, the arrow in Amazon's logo suggests that it offers everything from A to Z, and that it'll put a smile on your face.[15]

Although we have described the conceptual difference between a mission statement and a vision statement, these differences are often not so clear in actual mission and vision statements. For example, researchers note that an organization's vision statement can include elements of its mission, such as its guiding philosophy, purpose, and core beliefs.[13] A lot of overlap occurs between the two, and sometimes the two can even be interchangeable. *The important thing is that managers develop an understanding of their organization's overarching purpose* and *its long-term aspirations.* Often organizations do not even have a formal mission or vision statement, but instead have similar statements that function in the same way. For example, a fitting mission statement associated with Apple Computer comes from its cofounder, Steven Jobs: "To make a contribution to the world by making tools for the mind that advance humankind." Jobs' early vision statement for the firm had been "An Apple on every desk."[14]

Step 2: Develop Strategic Goals and Plans

Once the mission and vision statements have established the overall direction for an organization, managers must set strategic goals and plans. Strategic goals and plans typically encompass all of an organization's activities, and they often have a three- to five-year time horizon. For example, a university may strive to become a world leader in medical research (vision) by pursuing any or all of the following strategic goals and plans: hiring Nobel Prize winners, investing in world-class medical equipment and laboratories, publishing prestigious journals, and so on. The specific strategic goals and plans that are considered will be determined by a number of factors, including the current strengths and weaknesses of the university, and the opportunities and threats in the organization's environments. The basic question is how managers can position the organization in the eyes of stakeholders so as to achieve advantages over its competitors. This process is discussed in much greater depth in Chapter 9.

Step 3: Develop Operational Goals and Plans

Just as an organization's overall mission and vision (Step 1) inform its strategic goals and plans, so the strategic goals and plans set by top managers (Step 2) guide the operational goals and plans (Step 3).

Operational goals refer to outcomes to be achieved by an organizational department, work group, or individual member.

OPERATIONAL GOALS. **Operational goals** refer to outcomes to be achieved by an organizational department, work group, or individual member. Operational goals, which are typically set by mid- and lower-level managers and supervisors, spell out the practical implications of strategic goals. The time horizon of these goals is typically less than one year. People are usually able to focus on three to seven

◎ MANAGEMENT IN PRACTICE

Dedication to Its Mission Is Key to Wal-Mart's Success

Wal-Mart provides a great example of how commitment to a simple mission can yield financial success. The essence of this mission is printed on every Wal-Mart bag: "Always low prices. *Always.*" In 1962, when Sam Walton opened the first Wal-Mart, he "somehow knew in his gut" the power in this mantra. Analysts argue that Wal-Mart's brilliant, obsessive focus on this core mission—delivering low prices—has created what has become "the largest and most powerful company in history."[16] As an indicator of its influence, consider that Wal-Mart generates more than $300 billion in annual sales, and the firm is the largest employer in the world with 1.8 million employees. Also, consider how within ten years of starting to sell groceries—between 1990 and 2000—Wal-Mart had become the leading food retailer in the United States and now sells more groceries than any other company in the world (more than Safeway and Kroger combined).

Today, 90 percent of all Americans live within 15 miles of a Wal-Mart store.[17]

Almost all of the actions of Wal-Mart managers, whether good or bad, can be explained by looking at the mission statement on its shopping bag. To lower costs, Wal-Mart has been an industry leader in reducing product packaging (good for the ecological environment), but in other areas the desire to minimize costs has led managers to ignore environmental concerns. Wal-Mart's grocery prices are 15 percent lower than competitors' prices, partly because the company pays lower wages and offers fewer health benefits than key competitors. Wal-Mart managers also keep prices low by using the power that comes from Wal-Mart's size to get low prices from suppliers. For example, before its merger with Gillette, 17 percent of Procter & Gamble sales came from Wal-Mart, more than P&G's next nine largest customers combined.[18]

---

operational goals at a time, depending on how complex the goals are and how much time is available to reach the goal.[19]

Mainstream goal-setting research has found that performance is maximized when goals have certain characteristics. Companies such as Microsoft use the acronym SMART to draw attention to the characteristics that such a goal should have (see Figure 8.2). A quick look at these characteristics may make them seem like common sense and easy to implement. In reality, however, managers need to ensure that they are implemented properly. For example, after an audit was done on SMART goals at Microsoft, managers discovered that nearly 25 percent of members' goals were not specific, and that more than half of the goals were not "measurable." This characteristic caused goals to be more activity focused than result focused, and made it difficult to determine whether the goals were actually achieved.[20]

Let's explore the characteristics of SMART goals. First, SMART goals are *specific*. According to goal-setting guru Gary Latham, having a specific goal clarifies expectations and improves performance.[21] For example, rather than simply trying to increase sales revenues, managers at Microsoft could set the following specific goal: increase the sales of Microsoft Office software to small business owners in the United Kingdom by 30 percent in the next fiscal year. The more specific the goal is, the more likely it is to be accomplished.

Second, SMART goals are *measurable*. Managers must be able to monitor how well goals are being met. This may mean using existing data (for example, total sales revenues for Microsoft Office software in the United Kingdom) or setting up systems to collect the required data (for example, determining the sizes of businesses that purchase the Office software). Managers at Microsoft knew they had a problem when an internal audit showed that only 40 percent of

Figure 8.2   The five characteristics of Mainstream goals

Specific	The goal is precise as to what is to be accomplished.
Measurable	The goal to be accomplished can be assessed objectively.
Achievable	The goal is within reach, yet also challenging.
Results-based	The goal has clear, demonstrable outcomes (not just activities).
Time-specific	The goal has a clear time by which it is to be accomplished.

members' goals had a reasonable way to measure whether the goal had been achieved.[22] Measuring goals provides feedback so that people can evaluate whether their behavior is helping to meet the goal or whether their actions should change. For example, one manager planned a contest where the sales representative with the highest sales would win a two-week vacation for two people to Hawaii. At the end of the contest, the manager discovered that there were no accurate measures to determine the winner.

Third, SMART goals are *achievable*. This is not to say that goals should be easy. In fact, research is clear that goals should be challenging, yet achievable. People perform better if they are given challenging goals rather than easy goals or are told to "do your best." For example, a "C" student who sets the goal of reaching a C+ is likely to succeed (a little bit challenging and readily achievable), but a "C" student who sets the goal of reaching a B is also likely to succeed (more challenging, yet still attainable). However, a "C" student who sets the goal of getting an A+ may quit halfway through a course, upon realizing that the quest for an A+ is too challenging and not attainable. Gary Latham uses the example of independent loggers working in the southern United States, where pulpwood crew supervisors used goal-setting theory to give workers specific high-production goals and provided tally meters so that the loggers could count the number of trees that they cut down. Productivity soared, as the goals instilled a sense of purpose, challenge, and meaning into what had previously been perceived as tedious and physically tiring work.[23]

At General Electric, Jack Welch extended the idea of achievable goals by introducing the **stretch goal**—a goal so difficult that people do not know how to reach it. Welch illustrated stretch goals with the example of "Bullet Trains" in Japan, which whiz along at 200 miles per hour—a feat that could not have been achieved simply by making incremental changes to the status quo. Rather, it required outside-the-box thinking that included the building of a new train track. Stretch goals go beyond normal incremental changes to dramatically improve productivity, efficiency, and profitability.[24]

Fourth, SMART goals are *results based*. Goals should focus on specific *outcomes*, not on *activities*. Results-based goal setting is effective because it focuses attention on goal-relevant behavior. From a Mainstream perspective, it is important that members are rewarded for achieving the desired results. To do so, managers must ensure that financial reward systems are in place and that they measure the desired performance. Safeguards must be put in place to ensure that members don't "cheat" to achieve their rewards. For example, members may be tempted to reduce quality so as to meet quantity goals, or they may ignore long-term maintenance needs so as to meet short-term production goals.[25] Given this fact of life, when supervisors assign more than one goal, they must be sure to tell subordinates which goals and which results have the highest priority.[26]

Finally, SMART goals are *time specific*. Having a deadline provides a sense of urgency for members to reach their goals, and it also helps managers to reconsider goals on a regular basis. Returning to our example of Microsoft Office software, it makes a big difference whether the goal to achieve a 30 percent

Stretch goal is a goal so difficult that people must think "outside the box" in order to achieve it.

DILBERT: © Scott Adams/Dist. by United Feature Syndicate, Inc.[27]

increase in sales is set at six months or at six years. Once the time allotted to achieve a specific goal has passed, it provides managers with information that they can then use to set the goals for the next round.

✓ A. Describe exactly what steps and actions are necessary to meet your goal(s).

✓ B. Identify what resources (material, financial, time) are necessary to perform the activities.

✓ C. Ensure that the required resources are available (this means getting resources you don't already have).

✓ D. Identify in what order and when each action needs to be performed.

✓ E. Put your plan into action.

Figure 8.3 Checklist for making a plan

Although we have used the term "goals" throughout this section, other words can be used to describe operational goals. For example, at Microsoft the word "commitments" is preferred to "goals." The "commitment" terminology came directly from leaders who believed that it would make members more accountable and more likely to meet the goals. "Standards" is another term that is similar to "goals." For example, when managers set the goals that subordinates are expected to meet, these may be called **performance standards.** Just as students know exactly how many points they need to earn their desired grade in a course, so too salespeople know exactly how many sales they need to get a bonus.

Performance standards are goals that subordinates are expected to meet.

OPERATIONAL PLANS.   Once SMART goals have been set, they serve as the basis for operational plans. **Operational plans** are the steps and actions that will help to meet short-term goals (usually around a year). Figure 8.3 provides a helpful checklist for making a plan.

Operational plans are the steps and actions that will help to meet short-term goals (usually with a timeline of a year or less).

At Microsoft, about five to seven operational SMART goals are set for each member. A multiple-step operational plan is then developed to describe how each goal will be achieved. These plans include identifying key dependencies and resources required to achieve the goal, as well as key milestones that describe what must be accomplished by when. There is also emphasis on defining the measures that will be used to determine whether and when goals have been accomplished.[28] For example, if the goal is to achieve a 30 percent increase in sales of Microsoft Office software to small businesses, then a plan may be to (1) determine current sales in this target market, (2) run focus groups that look at which marketing campaigns might attract this type of customer, (3) develop an advertising campaign and budget the costs, and (4) implement the plan and measure the results.

Managers need to answer two overarching questions in forming plans:

- What activities and resources are necessary?
- What constraints and contingencies apply?

First, managers need to identify which specific *activities* need to be performed to accomplish a goal. This process includes putting the activities in the required sequential order, estimating how much time is required to complete each activity, and identifying other resources that will be required to complete each activity. For example, if you work in an ice cream shop and your goal is to introduce a new flavor of ice cream, you must do the following: (1) experiment with different combinations of ingredients (requires access to a kitchen), (2) do taste tests with customers (requires access to a sample of people willing to try new flavors), (3) think of a name for your new flavor, (4) standardize the recipe, (5) acquire ingredients (requires access to suppliers), and (6) make the product in appropriate quantities (requires production facilities).

Once the activities and required resources have been specified, the next step is to identify potential constraints and contingencies. This includes taking into account members' existing commitments and their potential difficulties in acquiring the necessary external resources. In the ice cream example, key constraints might be difficulty in finding consumers willing to do taste tests or difficulty in finding suppliers for new and exotic ingredients. Time constraints might arise because you are also responsible for the ongoing management of the organization's marketing department.

Once these pieces of the puzzle have been developed, they must be put together in a way that allows the goal to be accomplished. The plan specifies *which* activities need to be accomplished to meet a goal, *when* they will be accomplished (in light of existing commitments and constraints), and *how* the required resources will be acquired. In the ice cream example, you might make a commitment to work on the project for several months on Friday afternoons (when many customers visit the store and are available for taste tests, and when few other meetings are scheduled) and make arrangements with suppliers ahead of time to ensure that the various ingredients being used in the taste tests will be available. Once the product development and testing have been completed and a new flavor has been successfully developed, then the production and sales of the new ice cream will be conducted according to ongoing procedures and policies.

Standing plans provide guidance for activities that are performed repeatedly.

Standard operating procedures outline specific steps that must be taken when performing certain tasks.

Contingency plans set out in advance how managers will respond to possible future events that could disrupt the organization's existing plans.

Crises are events that have a major effect on the ability of organizational members to carry out their daily tasks (e.g., a natural disaster, an economic recession).

Policies provide guidelines for making decisions and taking action in various situations.

Rules and regulations are prescribed patterns of behavior that guide everyday work tasks.

STANDING PLANS.   Of course, not all plans are one-of-a-kind. For example, a manager may have specific plans to launch a particular product, but will have a standing plan for how to perform ongoing work. **Standing plans** provide guidance for activities that are performed repeatedly. For organizations, standing plans help members to meet ongoing goals. For example, a university may have the ongoing goal of keeping student records up-to-date. The plan for meeting this goal may include collecting and inputting information from new students, maintaining a system that backs up computer files every hour, and following a list of instructions for filling transcript requests.

There are three basic types of standing plans:

- Standard operating procedures
- Policies
- Rules and regulations

Standard operating procedures outline specific steps that must be taken when performing certain tasks. For example, Microsoft has standard operating procedures on how to package its software (e.g., which sorts of cables, earphones, and paperwork go into each box), and McDonald's has standard operating procedures

DIGGING DEEPER

Contingency Planning

Sometimes managers develop operational goals and plans that they hope will never need to be implemented. **Contingency plans** (sometimes called *scenarios*) lay out in advance how managers will respond to possible future events that could disrupt existing plans, such as a natural disaster or an economic recession. For example, managers might determine what the effect of a sudden 10 percent decrease (or increase) in sales would be and then develop plans to handle this situation. Similarly, organizations in areas such as New Orleans would be wise to develop contingency plans in case they are struck by another hurricane.[29]

An important part of contingency planning is to monitor the potential sources of crises. **Crises**—events that have a major effect on the ability of an organization's members to carry on their daily tasks—are the most intense type of contingency (e.g., earthquake, flood, computer virus, strikes). Managers can take three steps to limit the impact of such a crisis.

First, managers can perform *preventive* work to avoid or minimize the effects of a crisis. Most important here is developing healthy and trusting relationships with key stakeholders. For example, a labor strike is less likely if workers enjoy a good working relationship with management.

Second, managers can *prepare* for a crisis by assembling information and defining responsibilities and procedures that will be helpful in a time of crisis. For example, they can designate a "spokesperson" to represent the public face of the organization during the crisis and predetermine the location from which the crisis will be managed. This location may be a specific room where the relevant information is stored and where access to communication systems is assured.

Third, managers can contain the crisis by making a *timely response* to it. A speedy reaction can help to minimize the damage, get the truth out, and meet the safety and emotional needs of stakeholders. For example, if a fire occurs in a factory, managers should call the fire department, inform neighbors of any potential dangers, contact family members of factory workers, provide access to counseling services as needed, and phone key customers and suppliers to explain the implications of the fire. The importance of a timely response was illustrated after Hurricane Katrina caused serious damage and halted production in Procter & Gamble's largest Folgers coffee roasting plant. To maintain business continuity, managers provided a "hotline" to locate displaced employees, hosted press conferences to explain the damage and reason for lack of product on store shelves, and helped to rebuild the devastated area by coordinating donations with the American Red Cross for relief work. Thanks to actions like these, within three months of the disaster Folgers' market share had rebounded to its pre-Katrina level.[30]

---

on how to assemble a Big Mac (which ingredients are used, and in what order they are assembled).

Policies provide guidelines for making decisions and taking action in various situations. For example, retail stores have return policies that describe the conditions under which a customer can receive a full refund for a purchase, and universities have policies that describe the conditions when it may be possible to waive the prerequisites to register for specific courses or programs.

Rules and regulations are prescribed patterns of behavior that guide everyday work tasks. They tell people what can and cannot be done. For example, food preparation workers may be required to wear hairnets and wash their hands regularly, and grocery store clerks may be required to wear a name tag at all times.

Ideas such as goals, performance standards, and standard operating procedures—all of which are part of the *planning* function—overlap with the other three management functions. For example, they are closely linked with standardization,

Preparing contingency plans beforehand can help managers respond to crises like Hurricane Katrina in New Orleans.

Standardization is the process of developing uniform practices for organizational members to follow in doing their jobs.

which is a central feature of the *organizing* function. **Standardization** refers to the process of developing uniform practices for organizational members to follow in doing their jobs. Without standard operating procedures or standardization, it would be difficult to conceive of an organization or of organizing. Likewise, performance standards, standing plans, and standardization are an integral part of the *controlling* function. Indeed, the first step in the Mainstream control process is establishing performance standards. Finally, goal setting and standards are important components of the *leading* function, where leaders set the goals that maximize member performance.

Step 4: Implement and Monitor Goals and Plans

As plans are implemented, managers monitor for either of two possible outcomes:

1. The goals are met.
2. The goals are not met and there is a need to develop new plans or goals.

The first outcome is typically associated with some sort of recognition, particularly if the goals were very difficult. For example, each year FedEx provides 150 members with "Five Star Awards" for achieving their goals, and as many as 50,000 "Bravo Zulu" (a naval term meaning "well done") cash awards up to $100 that managers can hand out on the spot immediately after members have accomplished something significant.[31]

Of course, there are many occasions when plans do not result in the achievement of goals, leading to the second outcome. One important reason is unexpected changes in other parts of the organization or in the larger environment, such as those faced by managers of the Folgers coffee plant when Hurricane Katrina damaged their factory. This possibility points to the importance of managers providing opportunities to make appropriate changes to goals and plans on an ongoing basis.

Failure to meet goals can also occur when some stakeholders are not convinced of the legitimacy of a goal. This skepticism might arise when a goal is imposed on members without their buy-in or when customers question the legitimacy of a goal. For example, Wal-Mart has encountered some resistance from customers, employees, and suppliers who argue that the company's single-minded focus on lower prices has gotten in the way of Wal-Mart treating its people with dignity.

Another problem may emerge when managers place too much emphasis on members' change-oriented goals rather than on their ongoing goals. Something like this happened to Jean Stelmach, an accounting services manager at York Investments. She expressed extreme dissatisfaction with her subordinate, Romain Grodecki, after he completed his first year with the firm as its payroll supervisor. Grodecki had failed to make much progress on four SMART goals that had been assigned to him at the beginning of the year. Unfortunately, Stelmach was so concerned with these four change-oriented goals—none of which was essential for the ongoing operation of the payroll department—that she failed to see that Grodecki had performed admirably during the year by meeting his ongoing responsibilities despite all sorts of mini-crises facing his department. Grodecki could easily have met the four change-oriented goals had he been willing to compromise the smooth operation of his department.[32]

Sometimes implementing and monitoring goals and plans will prompt managers to reconsider the mission or vision statement of their organization. Perhaps a vision will be found to be unattainable, or perhaps it has already been attained. For

MANAGEMENT IN PRACTICE

Four Steps to Reduce Global Inequity[33]

Bill Gates, who has been called "Harvard's most successful dropout," describes his time as a student at Harvard University as a wonderful experience and privilege. However, in retrospect, he does have a "big regret:"

> "I left Harvard with no real awareness of the awful inequities in the world—the appalling disparities of health, and wealth, and opportunity that condemn millions of people to lives of despair. . . . It took me decades to find out."

Gates describes how he and his wife Melinda were shocked at how many millions of children were dying of diseases solely because of a lack of medication, deaths that could easily be prevented for less than one dollar per person. They asked themselves how the world could let these children die.

> "The answer is simple, and harsh. The market did not reward saving the lives of these children, and governments did not subsidize it. So the children died because their mothers and their fathers had no power in the market and voice in the system."

Who will help those stakeholders who have little economic or political clout in the current system? Gates notes that many good people care about these problems, but don't know what to do because of the overwhelming complexity. In response, he describes an ongoing four-step cycle that can be used to cut through the complexity to find solutions.

The four steps are similar to the four steps described in this chapter:

1. Identify your goal (e.g., identify a problem and make it your mission to solve it).

2. Find out what approach has the highest leverage to meet your goal (e.g., identify which combination of resources will be the most strategic to meet your goal).

3. Determine the best technology for that strategy (e.g., identify the best techniques and operational plans to implement your strategy).

4. Apply the technology you have in the smartest way possible (e.g., implement your plans).[34]

Gates remains optimistic. Present-day technology, coupled with the increased awareness of global problems that today's university students have, bodes well for a future where people with many opportunities will help those who have few resources. He quotes a letter from his mother: "From those to whom much is given, much is expected."

Is Gates right to be optimistic? Are today's university students more inclined to work on behalf of people who have little economic and political clout? Will technology be used to improve equity, or will it broaden the gap between the rich and the poor? Can you think of a way to apply Gate's four-step cycle to an important problem in the world today?

example, once Wal-Mart became the biggest retailer in the United States and the world, what should its next vision be? Although Wal-Mart still has plans to open new stores in the United States, it simply is not able to sustain the growth rate of earlier decades. This slower growth rate, in turn, has an effect on the goals and plans within the organization. For example, potential employees may not be as willing to accept low-paying entry-level jobs if they can no longer expect to be promoted as quickly because fewer higher-level positions are opening up in new stores.[35]

THE MULTISTREAM APPROACH TO GOALS AND PLANS

Multistream managers generally follow the same four-step process in setting goals and plans as do Mainstream managers, albeit with two differences. First, the Mainstream process emphasizes how *managers* carry out the four steps, whereas the Multistream approach emphasizes how managers *and other stakeholders* carry out the steps.[36] Second, the Mainstream approach focuses on the mission, vision, goals, and plans that serve the *acquisitive economic* interests of owners, whereas the Multistream approach is concerned with larger issues of *sustenance economics* and the well-being of a large variety of stakeholders. Rather than focus on goals and plans to maximize productivity, the Multistream approach considers aspects of life that may be difficult to measure, such as ecological well-being or social justice.

? WHAT DO YOU THINK?

What Is the Meaning of Life?

From a Multistream perspective, an organization's goals and plans include financial and economic issues, but also go well beyond those concerns. In this way, the Multistream perspective is more consistent with historical meanings of the words "mission" and "vision." A couple of centuries ago, both of these terms were used to refer to spiritual and meaning-of-life matters. To think about one's mission in life was to think about one's calling and purpose.[37] Similarly, "vision statements" related more to visions of *prophets* before they eventually became associated with Mainstream visions of *profits*. Over time, we have largely forgotten these deeper "What is the meaning of life?" aspects of mission and vision statements, so that today these terms are often used to express an organization's pursuit of materialist–individualist purposes. As a result, people may start to believe that materialist–individualist concerns are what life is all about.

Obviously, we cannot provide a deep answer to the question "What is the meaning of life?" in a management book like this one. Nevertheless, we do believe that the question is important and that merely asking it helps people to think about their goals and plans. For example, consider that a majority of the 6 billion people in the world are religious but that spiritual goals, by their nature, often defy numerical measurement. Inherently difficult-to-measure goals such as "glorifying the Creator" or "drawing nearer to one's spiritual center" are difficult to address within a Mainstream materialist perspective. The same holds true for noble goals such as "making the world a better place" or "living in peace." Many secular and religious philosophies teach that the true meaning of life comes from sharing rather than accumulating,

Make a list of what you find to be the most important things in life. Are these things easily measured? How much overlap do you think there is between the items on your list and the items on the lists of your classmates? Should the items on your list be important in the workplace or just in your private life? How important do you think material well-being is to most people?

"Not everything that counts can be counted, and not everything that can be counted counts." This quote, attributed to Albert Einstein, hung on the wall of his office at Princeton University.[38]

Step 1: Develop the Organization's Mission and Vision

The first step in the Multistream approach is to involve a variety of stakeholders in the development of an organization's mission and vision statements. Stakeholders can include owners, employees, suppliers, customers, and community members. The benefits of such an approach are twofold:

- It permits the development of stronger mission and vision statements.
- It increases support for the work of the organization.

First, the input and knowledge that are acquired from the different stakeholders allow for the development of more compelling mission and vision statements. Recall from the opening case how Dan Wiens deliberately invited people from different walks of life to give shape to the mission and vision of Wiens Family Farm. Indeed, the mission and vision of Shared Farming could not have been conceived without the input of external stakeholders.

A similar approach was evident in Eliza Jennings Group, a long-term healthcare provider with five facilities ranging from independent living housing to Alzheimer's care units. At one time in its history, Eliza Jennings managers followed a top-down approach of having a consultant interview top executives to develop a mission statement. Under the leadership of CEO Deborah Hiller, however, the mission statement at Eliza Jennings was revised through a process of visioning sessions that included a cross section of many stakeholders—employees at multiple levels and from all facilities, patients, children of patients, and managers. The revised mission statement, though similar in many ways to the old version, was enthusiastically embraced as a result of the participative process.[39]

Second, when a variety of key stakeholders become aware of an organization's mission and vision, everyone has a greater appreciation of the work of the organization. It is valuable for all organizational members—both managers and non-managers—to understand how their daily work fits with that of others in their organization *and beyond*. For example, it is important for frontline workers to see how they contribute to their organization's mission and vision, just as it is valuable for top managers to see how their work contributes to the experience of frontline members.[40] Furthermore, when organizational plans are sensitive to the needs of the larger socioeconomic and ecological environment, members may experience their work as more meaningful and motivating.

Although such mutual understanding may be easier to develop in smaller organizations, managers can promote such cross-level understanding even in large organizations. For example, managers have done so at AES, which has 40,000 employees in 30 countries and nearly $10 billion in annual revenues (see the opening case in Chapter 15). Reducing the number of hierarchical levels and emphasizing transparent information sharing will foster feelings of teamwork and a sense of shared mission, as members build understanding and trusting relationships with others in the organization.

This sense of teamwork can also extend beyond the boundaries of the organization. Research points out the merits of developing long-term trusting relationships with key suppliers (and customers) to gain the advantage of their expertise and knowledge in making organizational decisions.[41] For example, managers at the First Fruits Orchard (refer to the opening case in Chapter 3) note how members of the local banking community have gone beyond their standard operating procedures to support First Fruits initiatives that are designed to improve the standard of living for orchard workers.

The mission and vision statements of some organizations signal that the organizations are being managed from a Multistream perspective. For example, Gaiam is a retailer with the mission "to provide choices that foster a sense of belonging to a healthy and conscious community that can make a difference in the world." They coined the term LOHAS (Lifestyles of Health and Sustainability), which is now the title of a magazine, is quoted in leading media, and is the name of an annual four-day business conference.[42]

Two organizations may have similar mission and vision statements, yet those statements may be implemented differently because of differences in the organizations' underlying values and priorities. Consider the similarity between the mission

Delegates register at the annual LOHAS conference.

statements of Wal-Mart and Costco. With more than $50 billion in annual sales, Costco is number one in the warehouse retail marketplace, followed by Wal-Mart's subsidiary Sam's Club. The mission of Costco is "to continually provide our members with quality goods and services at the lowest possible prices." This is not unlike Wal-Mart's catchphrase, "Always low prices. *Always*." However, Costco has a markedly different management philosophy than Wal-Mart. For managers at Costco, keeping prices low and rewarding shareholders do not come at the "cost" of maintaining their commitment to first take care of the firm's customers and employees, and to respect its suppliers.[43]

Of course, an organization's underlying values and goals are not always written down. Unspoken or tacit goals are the ongoing, well-accepted organizational goals that "go without saying." For example, a goal such as "do whatever it takes to get the product out the door fast" may not be made explicit. Nevertheless, through observation and experience this *unstated* goal may be accepted by organizational members as a higher priority than a *stated* goal of quality. The importance of unstated values is also illustrated in international organizations where, for example, separate factories operating in different countries are often managed differently even though both operations have identical explicit goals. Chapter 4 discussed how people in individualistic countries often assume that everyone wants to "get ahead" of their coworkers, whereas in collectivistic countries the assumption is that coworkers will help one another. Managers need to attend to both the tacit goals and the explicit goals of the organization, and to consistently communicate (in word and in deed) the priorities among goals in pursuit of the mission and vision.

Step 2: Develop Strategic Goals and Plans

The second step in the planning process is to develop strategic goals and plans that will help to achieve the mission and vision. Like their Mainstream counterparts, Multistream managers develop strategic goals and plans based on an analysis of the organization's strengths and weaknesses as well as the opportunities and threats evident in the external environment. However, because Multistream managers have a broader range of mission and vision, and because their philosophy and values are more likely to go beyond a sole concern for acquisitive economics, Multistream managers think differently about an organization's strengths, weaknesses, opportunities, and threats. For example, rather than focus primarily on economic opportunities, these managers are just as interested in opportunities to improve the natural environment. Multistream managers are also more likely to be sensitive to strategies that emerge from practice instead of just those strategies that derive from formal planning. These ideas will be presented more fully in Chapter 9, but for now it is sufficient to note that Multistream managers pay more attention than Mainstream managers to issues such as sustenance economics and stakeholder participation in developing and implementing strategic goals and plans.

Consider the ongoing process of strategic learning at Wiens Family Farm, which is consistent with Dan and Wilma Wiens' understanding of their farm as an "experiment" and their eagerness to listen to the ideas of others. Of course, not all possible strategic goals should or can be implemented. For example, early in the process, one committee member wanted to create a "Land Trust" to ensure that the land being farmed was not owned by any one person but rather by the larger community in perpetuity. Members saw the merit of this idea and its underlying philosophy and values, but practical-mindedness suggested that pursuing this strategic goal could take up a lot of time and distract from the overall project.

Step 3: Develop Operational Goals and Plans

OPERATIONAL GOALS.   We have already seen how SMART goals are characteristic of a Mainstream management approach, and how they can be used to increase productivity. A parallel process—which we call SMART2 goals—is evident in the Multistream approach (see Figure 8.4). Some of the characteristics of SMART2 goals are consistent with SMART goals, including the merit seen in setting achievable yet challenging goals. However, Multistream managers do not fully embrace some of the other SMART criteria. Most notably, they remain concerned that a single-minded focus on measurable goals might cause managers to ignore important goals that are more difficult to measure. For example, research shows that while a focus on measurable goals does, in fact, increase productivity, at the same time it decreases "organizational citizenship behavior," which includes positive activities such as helping coworkers.[44] This is an example of **goal displacement,** which happens when people become so focused on specific goals that they lose sight of more important overarching goals.

Let's explore the SMART2 goal characteristics in more depth. First, SMART2 goals are *significant*, both in terms of being challenging and in terms of being motivating to members. The idea of goals that are challenging is consistent with the Mainstream model of SMART goals that are challenging yet attainable. The idea of stretch goals is also significant. However, the Multistream approach to stretch goals differs from the Mainstream approach practiced by managers such as Jack Welch. Welch used stretch goals to improve operations (e.g., productivity) but seldom referred to their personal costs and benefits (e.g., stress, morale, development). At Goldman Sachs, in contrast, rather than using *instrumental* stretch goals (e.g., to increase annual sales by 100 percent instead of the regular 15 percent), stretch goals are used to meet *developmental* goals (e.g., a sales manager might be asked to lead a temporary team that is responsible for coming up with a new process for developing products). In essence, Multistream managers use stretch goals to invite members to think about both their work and themselves in a broader way.[45]

Second, SMART2 goals are *meaningful* because they relate to the mission and vision of members as well as the mission and vision of the organization as a whole. Recall Gary Latham's description of how setting high goals for loggers caused their productivity to soar and "instilled purpose, challenge, and meaning" into workers' tasks. From

Goal displacement occurs when people get so focused on specific goals that they lose sight of more important overarching goals.

Figure 8.4   The five characteristics of Multistream goals

Significant	The goal is challenging and engaging.
Meaningful	The goal has meaning beyond simply maximizing productivity.
Agreed-upon	The goal is developed participatively.
Relevant	The goal is linked to important issues for a variety of stakeholders.
Timely	The goal is appropriate for the times and situation.

Mahatma Gandhi identified *seven blunders of the world:* (1) wealth without work, (2) pleasure without conscience, (3) commerce without morality, (4) science without humanity, (5) knowledge without character, (6) worship without sacrifice, and (7) politics without principles. His grandson Arun notes that *seven noble goals* are created when we replace the word "without" with the word "with" for each blunder, and he challenges people to live accordingly.[48]

a Multistream perspective, an even deeper sense of meaning might emerge if the goals were linked to a larger vision or mission, such as taking pride in eco-friendly logging practices. For example, First Fruits employees work hard to enhance the productivity of the cherry orchard, because they know that all profits go to charity (see the opening case in Chapter 3).

Third, SMART2 goals are *agreed upon* by the people who are expected to implement them. The Mainstream approach tends to focus on the top-down assignment of goals, whereas the Multistream approach is much more open to bottom-up involvement. The Mainstream approach advocates participation in goal setting in some limited circumstances (such as when there are multiple goals and participation helps to avoid goal conflict[46]), whereas the Multistream approach welcomes participation even if it does not provide cost savings to the organization. When members understand how their department contributes to other departments and to the larger organization, they are prepared to participate in setting (and fulfilling) the goals and plans for *their* part in this process. This participation can take place via an interaction between a member and a manager, or it can occur in larger meetings where members can develop group goals and plans for one another. Group participation will make members even more highly aware of the resources and responsibilities of each member, and because the goals and plans are connected, members will be more sensitive to the need for changing or fine-tuning goals and plans. For example, because managers at Eliza Jennings Group involve stakeholders to develop and agree upon goals, each stakeholder has a greater ownership of the final goals and an improved appreciation for the contributions made by other stakeholders.[47]

Fourth, SMART2 goals are *relevant*, both for the organization's mission and vision and for the aspirations of members and other stakeholders. Because Multistream managers are concerned about a variety of forms of well-being and stakeholders, they may have goals that are not relevant for Mainstream managers. In the case of Wiens Family Farm, it is striking how the relevance of the goals for the farm has contributed to the ongoing engagement of stakeholders. Sharers join the Wiens Family Farm because they appreciate its goal of providing locally grown, fairly priced organic vegetables. Certainly, the Wiens family and others who work on the farm could earn considerably more money elsewhere, and the "sharers" could likewise find vegetables at a lower price. For them, however, involvement is clearly not just about money or about vegetables; it is about relevance and having found an organization in which to live out their Multistream values.

Finally, SMART2 goals are *timely*. Managers could set many different goals in an effort to improve the various forms of well-being, but they always must be attuned to which goals are right for the times. For example, Dan Wiens talks about keeping in step with "the spirit of the times," and believes that he would not have been able to start Shared Farming in his community five years earlier than he did, simply because people were not yet ready for such an organization. Similarly, other management professors have told the authors of this book—which contrasts and compares Mainstream and Multistream management—that it would not have been successful five years earlier, because people were just not ready for this perspective. Multistream managers must know when others are ready for specific ecological, social justice, or economic goals.

Note that the timely goals of the Multistream approach differ from the time-specific goals of the Mainstream approach. Multistream managers realize that a singular focus on materialist short-term goals, such as quarterly financial reports, often results in other kinds of goals being overlooked. Moreover, the Mainstream view that a five-year time horizon represents long-range planning suggests to Multistream managers that people have lost the proper perspective of their place on this planet. Consider the tradition of some Native Americans, who think about how current actions will affect their descendants seven generations later (see Figure 8.5).[49] While this very-long-term view may seem extreme, it does point to the possibility of thinking beyond a five-year time horizon. What if managers placed as much emphasis on the implications of their actions for their children as they do for the next quarterly report? No doubt material riches would be cut drastically for some, but perhaps everyone would enjoy a more sustainable lifestyle.

OPERATIONAL PLANS. Once agreement is reached on goals, the next step in the Multistream goal-setting and planning process is to develop and agree on the "action plans" that will be used to achieve those goals. Both the Mainstream and Multistream approaches concur that two pieces of information are critical when making plans: (1) what activities need to be performed and (2) what constraints and contingencies apply.

First, when it comes to identifying activities, Multistream managers are more likely to seek the advice and participation of other people. They are also more likely to consider a wider range of nonfinancial issues. For example, the person who is developing a new ice cream flavor may plan to develop the recipe using local, organic, or healthy ingredients rather than focusing only on tasty and low-cost ingredients.

Second, when it comes to identifying constraints and contingencies, Multistream managers are more likely to consider the effects of their actions on the ecological environment and on other stakeholders. For example, the person developing the new ice cream flavor may wish to offer maximal nutritional content and minimal calories, rather than merely optimal taste. This perspective is consistent with the move by companies such as Frito Lay that have eliminated unhealthy trans fats from their products.

As we shall see in Step 4, when it comes to putting the information together to make the final plans, Multistream managers are more likely than Mainstream managers to emphasize flexibility and to consider the roles of other stakeholders. For the person developing ice cream, this flexibility may mean listening to feedback from customers and suppliers and, in response, introducing a new frozen yogurt product that has nutritional, ecological, taste, and cost benefits.

Step 4: Implement and Monitor Goals and Plans

The operational goals and plans developed in the third step of the goal-setting and planning process are "living documents," which means that they are open to being revised when they are revisited at regular intervals (e.g., every three months or less). This review usually takes place within the work group, but it can also include stakeholders outside the work group. Multistream managers are likely to ask questions

Figure 8.5 Circle of life
The First Nations peoples of North America often use a "circle of life" or a "medicine wheel" that depicts the interconnectedness and sacredness of everything, which helps them to think about how their goals and responsibilities fit into the larger picture. In the wheel pictured here, yellow depicts the sunrise, springtime, and new beginnings; red depicts midday, summer, and maturation; blue depicts evening, autumn, and a time of gathering; and green depicts nighttime, winter, and a time to rest and dream. The wheels used by different tribes may use different colors and emphasize different symbolism. The description here is based on "The Medicine Wheel—Circle of Life" (http://www.spiritualnetwork.net/native/medicine_wheel.html).

Figure 8.6   The "Toyota way"
The hardest thing for Toyota's new U.S. employees to accept is the bar charts on the bulletin boards that show everyone how well each employee is doing in meeting his or her goals. The charts are not meant to humiliate workers, but rather to alert and enlist the help from coworkers to find solutions. Rather than hide problems from managers, this is part of the "Toyota way" to get everyone working together to improve operations. *Source:* Fackler, M. (2007, February 15). The "Toyota way" is translated for a new generation of foreign managers. *New York Times.*

such as these: Do plans need to be revised in the face of contingencies? Have unexpected events occurred in organizational subunits that need to be considered? Is there a danger of goal displacement, such as happens when ongoing maintenance activities are compromised due to certain plans? In sum, goals and action plans are revised as appropriate, and members are reinforced for their efforts as appropriate.

At the Wiens Family Farm, this feedback and monitoring process is seamlessly integrated into the fabric of the organization. For example, each year managers focus on improving a different part of the organization's operations. In early years, the change needed was a matter of finding a good system to distribute vegetables to sharers in an environmentally friendly manner. In subsequent years, it was learning how to use the greenhouse and staggering planting times. In other years, it was fine-tuning growing practices in an effort to solve irrigation problems during drought or heavy rains and to minimize weeding. When these goals are met, the lessons learned become part of the ongoing operations at the farm. Ongoing feedback is also received at harvest festivals, neighborhood drop-off depots, and sharer questionnaires, and from volunteers who work on the farm. Another example of ongoing feedback being built into an organizational system is evident in the "Toyota way" described in Figure 8.6.

Managing a City[50]

An increasing number of people around the world are moving into cities. For the first time in the history of the world, the number of people living in cities exceeds the number living in rural settings. This trend is worrisome for many observers because although cities occupy only 2 percent of the planet's surface, their residents consume at least 75 percent of the resources used by the world's population. Others, like James Lerner who has been mayor of Curitiba, Brazil, for many years, argue that "Cities are not the problem, they are the solution." It depends, in part, on how cities are managed.

When Lerner first became Curitiba's mayor in 1971,[51] its population was about half a million people, and it was experiencing many of the same problems faced by other rapidly growing cities: traffic congestion, pollution, growing unemployment, and so on. Today, Curitiba has a population of approximately 2 million people, but fewer problems.

Lerner's vision and master plan, and his management style, helped Curitiba to become an exemplary world-class city. For example, even though its GDP per capita is relatively low by Western standards,[52] Curitiba is thought to have the best public bus system in the world: self-financing, inexpensive, comfortable, and efficient. Curitiba's buses carry approximately 75 percent of the city's commuters (more than 2 million passengers per day), with 89 percent user satisfaction. And because so many people prefer taking the bus to driving a car, the city experiences less traffic congestion. Its population uses 23 percent less fuel per capita than Brazil's national average.

How did Lerner do it? First, he started with a "master plan" that had several important characteristics. Its central and most explicit component was the plan to improve the city's public transportation system. Lerner knew that how people move around has a great effect on a city's level of overall well-being, including where people choose to live and work. Two other key characteristics were more implicit:

- Lerner followed an experimental management approach—with challenging yet attainable goals—that allowed plans to be implemented quickly. In particular, he looked for ideas that were "simple, fast, fun, and cheap" (such as converting retired buses into classrooms and libraries).[53]

- Lerner was a participative manager who welcomed ideas and treated stakeholders with respect. Lerner had a vision of a city where getting around was easy and environmentally friendly, where people treated one another and the environment with dignity, and where many stakeholders participated in and contributed to its ongoing improvement.

Lerner's basic vision has served Curitiba well for a generation. In this city, the mayor is seen as a servant of the citizens—that is, as someone who facilitates participative problem solving and nurtures creative entrepreneurial partnerships among private firms, NGOs, municipal agencies, and community groups.

How did Lerner manage to implement this vision? An important step was to change the transportation system by making bus travel more rider-friendly. Think of the center of Curitiba as the "hub" of a wheel, and then imagine a series of roads that are "spokes" going out from the hub into the different neighborhoods. Basically, five of these streets were designated for use by express buses and local traffic only. The streets on each side of these five spokes were made into one-way streets: one for automobile traffic going into the city, and the other for traffic going out from the city. The genius of this plan was that it was inexpensive: It used the existing road system (no leveling of buildings to make multiple-lane highways, as is the case in many

other cities), and it was aboveground (much cheaper than subways).

The redesign of the transportation system was not left to traffic engineers. Instead, Lerner relied on professionals from a wide variety of disciplines—including those who studied land use, jobs and income, politics and culture, health and education, and flows of nutrients and wastes—to look at the issue in terms of an integrated design problem. Curitiba's primary goal-setting and planning mechanism is what architects call an interdisciplinary charrette—"a brief but intense design workshop in which stakeholders and interested citizens are invited to contribute to the work of an interdisciplinary team of urbanists during the earliest stages of design and planning."[54] Thanks to the decisions made by the interdisciplinary teams, for example, the only new buildings permitted near major bus lines are high-rise apartments (to improve access and convenience) with stores on the bottom two floors (to reduce the need to travel for shopping). Passengers insert their tokens in the stations prior to boarding buses to improve efficiency (similar to the system used in many subways).

One of Lerner's earliest successes—and one that shows how the transportation system is linked to the revitalization of the city's core—was the transformation of a central historical boulevard into one of the world's first pedestrian shopping malls. After agreement that the vision called for more people and fewer cars in the downtown area, a meticulous plan was developed to convert the area. It took only one weekend (starting Friday evening) to jackhammer the pavement and to install cobblestones, kiosks, streetlights, and tens of thousands of flowers. By midday on Monday the pedestrian mall was so thronged with shoppers that shop owners, who initially had fears that this radical experiment might hamper their business, were petitioning to have the pedestrian mall expanded. Today Curitiba has more than 20 blocks of pedestrian malls.

Over time the success in applying the vision to the transportation system spilled into the goals and plans evident in other aspects of the city's management. For example, over a period of 25 years, as Curitiba's population more than doubled in size, its green space grew from 5 square feet to 581 square feet per person (about four times the amount recommended by the United Nations or enjoyed by New Yorkers). It is now illegal to cut down a tree without permission, and two trees must be planted for every one that is cut down.

Curitibans were also world leaders in recycling household "garbage." In addition, the city operates a food-for-trash program in its poorest neighborhoods, where it would be difficult for garbage trucks to go. When garbage trucks arrive at designated areas, the drivers ring a bell and then provide one "ticket" for each kilogram of garbage collected by residents. Sixty tickets yields enough food to feed a family for a month (or to provide bus tokens or school notebooks).

Programs like these have been warmly embraced and consistently supported by the people of Curitiba. One survey reported that 99 percent of Curitibans wouldn't want to live anywhere else (by contrast, 70 percent of Sao Paulo residents thought life would be better in Curitiba, and 60 percent of New Yorkers wanted to leave their city). Curitiba's literacy rate is 95 percent, 99.5 percent of households have electricity and drinking water, and the poverty rate is one-third the national average.[55] Curitiba's community spirit is reflected on the cover of the ticket booklet for the food-for-trash program: "You are responsible for this program. Keep on cooperating and we will get a cleaner Curitiba, cleaner and more human. You are an example to Brazil and even to the rest of the world."[56] Curitibans are rightly proud of their city, and happy to participate in its innovative programs.

QUESTIONS FOR DISCUSSION

1. Would you want your future mayor to be a graduate from your current program of study? Why or why not? What are some of the differences in managing a city versus managing a for-profit business or a nonprofit organization? What are some of the similarities?

2. What are the most important lessons for managers to learn from Mayor Lerner?

3. Describe how the four steps of the goal-setting and planning model described in this chapter are evident in the Curitiba case. Which step do you think Lerner would point to as the most important?

4. Is the Mainstream model or the Multistream model more helpful for understanding Curitiba's success? Explain your answer.

5. How does the approach to goal setting and planning practiced in Curitiba compare to that taken by the Wiens family's Shared Farm (see the chapter-opening case)?

SUMMARY

Mainstream and Multistream managers follow similar four-step processes to set goals and make plans, but proceed through each step a little differently.

Mainstream managers follow this process:

1. Identify a mission and vision for the organization that maximizes the financial return for the organization's owners.

2. Set strategic goals and plans with an eye toward optimizing the organization's competitive advantage.

3. Implement operational goals that are SMART (specific, measurable, achievable, results-based, and time-specific) and plans that cover both new and ongoing goals.

4. Check that goals are properly implemented and that members who meet goals are rewarded.

Multistream managers work together with members and other stakeholders to follow this process:

1. Identify a mission and vision for the organization that contribute to a variety of forms of well-being and stakeholders.

2. Set strategic goals and plans with an eye toward optimizing the benefits for many different stakeholders, including shareholders.

3. Implement operational goals that are SMART2 (significant, meaningful, agreed upon, relevant, and timely) and plans that cover both new and ongoing goals.

4. Continually learn from and improve upon goals and plans as they are being implemented.

1. Identify the four steps in the process of setting goals and plans. What are key differences in the content of the steps from a Mainstream perspective versus a Multistream perspective?

2. Choose any one of the four steps in the goal-setting and planning process, and describe how the four-step decision-making process described in Chapter 7 can be used to explain how that step is accomplished.

3. Which management approach for setting goals and plans—Mainstream or Multistream—do you think would be the most effective? Explain your answer. Be explicit in how you define "effective."

4. Which of the four steps in the goal-setting and planning process do you think is perceived as the most challenging to do properly from the Mainstream perspective? From the Multistream perspective?

5. What are the similarities and differences between SMART goals and SMART2 goals?

6. What are the most important components to include in a mission statement? Which of the mission statements in the text includes the most of these components? Which include the fewest of these components? Why might these differences arise?

7. Choose an organization with which you are familiar (e.g., your current employer or an organization where you would like to work in the future) and analyze its mission and vision statements in light of the material covered in this chapter. Based on the material in this chapter, identify the strengths and weaknesses of these vision and mission statements.

HANDS-ON ACTIVITIES

Where Does Your Management Style Fall Along the Mainstream–Multistream Continuum?

For each pair of statements below, circle the number on the continuum that reflects your view.

TO BE AN EFFECTIVE MANAGER, I SHOULD . . .

Set an organization's mission and vision based on an underpinning philosophy that seeks to *maximize the financial return for owners.* — 1 2 3 4 5 6 7 — Set an organization's mission and vision based on an underpinning philosophy that seeks to *contribute to a variety of forms of well-being and stakeholders.*

Set organizational strategic goals and plans to *optimize the organization's competitive advantage.* — 1 2 3 4 5 6 7 — Set organizational strategic goals and plans to *optimize the benefits to many different stakeholders, including shareholders.*

Implement operational goals that are SMART (*specific, measurable, achievable, results-based, and time-specific*). — 1 2 3 4 5 6 7 — Implement operational goals that are SMART2 (*significant, meaningful, agreed upon, relevant, and timely*).

Check that goals are properly implemented and that members who meet goals are rewarded. — 1 2 3 4 5 6 7 — Continually learn from and improve upon goals and plans as they are being implemented.

For each statement below, circle the number that reflects your view.

TO BE AN EFFECTIVE MANAGER, I SHOULD . . .	Strongly Disagree	Disagree	Neutral	Agree	Strongly Agree
Set organizational goals to maximize the financial return for owners/shareholders.	1	2	3	4	5
Set organizational goals to reflect a variety of stakeholders.	1	2	3	4	5
Set organizational goals to reflect a variety of forms of well-being (e.g., environmental, social, financial, intellectual well-being).	1	2	3	4	5
Set organizational goals that focus on owners/shareholders above all other stakeholders.	1	2	3	4	5

ENDNOTES

1. This case is based on personal interviews with Dan Wiens (most recently in June 2007) and is reprinted with his permission; Dyck, B. (1994a). From airy-fairy ideals to concrete realities: The case of Shared Farming. *Leadership Quarterly*, 5, 227–246; and Dyck, B. (1994b). Build in sustainable development, and they will come: A vegetable field of dreams. *Journal of Organizational Change Management*, 7(4), 47–63.

2. Miner, J. B. (2003). The rated importance, scientific validity, and practical usefulness of organizational behavior theories. *Academy of Management Learning and Education*, 2, 250–268. Cited in Locke, E. A. (2004). Guest editor's introduction: Goal-setting theory and its applications to the world of business. *Academy of Management Executive*, 18(4), 124–125.

3. The basic four-step process we describe in this chapter adapts and builds on the work of Peter Drucker and his management-by-objectives (MBO) process: Drucker, P. F. (1954). *The practice of management*. New York: Harper; and Drucker, P. F. (1974). *Management tasks, responsibilities, practices*. New York: Harper.

4. Cited in Peyrefitte, J., & David, F. R. (2006). A content analysis of the mission statements of United States firms in four industries. *International Journal of Management*, 23(2), 296–310.

5. Accessed October 16, 2006, at http://www.uca.edu/uca/mission.php. Reprinted by permission of the University of Central Arkansas.

6. Accessed October 3, 2006, at http://www.icrc.org/Web/Eng/siteeng0.nsf/htmlall/68EE39?OpenDocument&style=custo_print. International Committee of the Red Cross (ICRC) Mission Statement. © International Committee of the Red Cross. Reprinted with permission.

7. Accessed February 21, 2008, at http://www.dell.com/content/topics/global.aspx/corp/investor/en/faqs?c=us&l=en&s=gen#faq8.

8. Peyrefitte & David, 2006.

9. Accessed November 12, 2007, at http://www.southwest.com. Reprinted by permission of Southwest Airlines.

10. Bart, C. (2006, March). Hands on: Words to grow by. *Profit*. Accessed October 3, 2006, at http://www.canadianbusiness.com/entrepreneur/managing/article.jsp;jsessionid=JLPCAKLDOCBL?content=20060210_130330_4684.

11. Baum, J. R., Locke, E. A., & Kirkpatrick, S. A. (1998). A longitudinal study of the relation of vision and vision communication to venture growth in entrepreneurial firms. *Journal of Applied Psychology*, 83, 43–54. Cited in Kirkpatrick, S. A., Wofford, J. C., & Baum, J. R. (2002). Measuring motive imagery contained in the vision statement. *Leadership Quarterly*, 13, 139–150.

12. Kirkpatrick et al., 2002.

13. Collins, J. C., & Porras, J. (1991). Organizational vision and visionary organizations. *California Management Review*, 34, 30–52. Cited in Kirkpatrick et al., 2002.

14. Accessed October 16, 2006, at http://www.birnbaumassociates.com/mission-vision-values.htm.

15. Similarly, the arrow built into the "Ex" part of FedEx draws attention to how the organization offers speed and precision as part of its services (http://www.funonthenet.in/content/view/344/31/).

16. Page 7 in Fishman, C. (2006). The Wal-Mart effect and a decent society: Who knew shopping was so important? *Academy of Management Perspective*, 20(3), 6–25.

17. Wal-Mart stores are especially likely to be located in lower-income neighborhoods, where the consumer benefits of its low prices are the most significant.

18. This impressive dedication to its mission has contributed to Wal-Mart's success in the marketplace, but it has also left some of its shoppers feeling conflicted. One study (cited in Fishman, 2006, p. 18) showed that Wal-Mart has four "types" of shoppers. The most frequent shoppers—called "missionaries"—go to a Wal-Mart store about 95 times each year, spend about $50 per trip, account for 29 percent of Wal-Mart shoppers, and love the store and presumably the mission statement on its bags. "Conflicted" shoppers are the second most frequent shoppers; they shop at Wal-Mart about 67 times each year, spend about $50 per trip, account for 15 percent of Wal-Mart shoppers, and "actively dislike Wal-Mart because of its impact on communities, wages, and jobs." "Enthusiasts" shop fewer than 15 times per year but spend closer to $100 per trip. "Rejecters" go about 9 times per year and spend $50 per trip.

19. Locke, 2004, p. 132.

20. Shaw, K. N. (2004). Changing the goal-setting process at Microsoft. *Academy of Management Executive*, 18(4), 139–142.

21. Latham, G. P. (2004). The motivational benefits of goal-setting. *Academy of Management Executive*, 18(4), 126–129.

22. Shaw, 2004.

23. Latham, 2004.

24. Kerr, S., & Landauer, S. (2004). Using stretch goals to promote organizational effectiveness: General Electric and Goldman Sachs. *Academy of Management Executive, 18*(4), 134–138.

25. Locke, E. A. (2004). Linking goals to monetary incentives. *Academy of Management Executive, 18*(4), 130–133.

26. Latham, 2004.

27. Adams, S. (1996). *Dogbert's top secret management handbook.* New York: HarperCollins.

28. Shaw, 2004.

29. Piotrowski, C. (2006). Hurricane Katrina and organization development: Part 1. Implications of chaos theory. *Organization Development Journal, 24*(3), 10–19.

30. Crisis management. (2006, October 16). *PR News, 63*(1).

31. Tom Mosely explains what makes Federal Express so good (no date). Accessed June 21, 2007, at http://www.ecustomerservice world.com/earticlesstore_articles.asp?type=article&id=343.

32. Drawn from a case found in Starke, F. A., & Sexty, R. W. (1995). *Contemporary management in Canada* (2nd ed., pp. 114–115). Scarborough, ON: Prentice-Hall Canada.

33. Gates, B. (2007, June 7). Remarks of Bill Gates: Harvard commencement (text as prepared for delivery). *Gazette Online.* Accessed September 24, 2007, at http://www.news.harvard.edu/ gazette/2007/06.14/99-gates.html.

34. Gates also points out the importance of measuring the impact of your work, and sharing with others your successes and failures so that they can learn from your efforts.

35. Serpkenci, R. R., & Tigert, D. J. (2006). Wal-Mart's new normal is here: Is everyone ready to accept the future? *International Journal of Retail and Distribution Management, 34*(1), 85–100.

36. While there is a philosophical basis to support this participative approach (e.g., it is inherently "good" when people can make decisions as to the nature of their everyday work lives), research suggests that worker involvement can also help to increase productivity [e.g., Cooper, C., Dyck, B., & Frohlich, N. (1992). Improving the effectiveness of gainsharing: The role of participation and fairness. *Administrative Science Quarterly, 37,* 471–490.]

37. See discussion in Chapter 2 of how Max Weber pointed to the importance of "calling" for understanding contemporary management.

38. See Cunningham, H., & Scott, D. (2004). Software architecture for language engineering. *Natural Language Engineering, 10*(3/4), 205–209.

39. Wong-Ming Ji, D. J., & Neubert, M. J. (2001). *Voices in visioning: Multiple stakeholder participation in strategic visioning.* Washington, DC: Academy of Management Meetings.

40. For example, as we will see in Chapter 9, this understanding facilitates the emphasis on emergent strategic learning, which further differentiates the Multistream approach from the Mainstream approach.

41. Minato, T. (1994). *Strategic alliances between small and large businesses.* Paper presented at the International Federation of Scholarly Associations of Management (IFSAM) conference, Tokyo, Japan, September 8, 1994.

42. http://corporate.gaiam.com/crp_aboutmission.asp?Type=about. For more information about the annual LOHAS conference highlighted in the photo on page 246, see press release at LOHAS website, accessed April 26, 2008, at http://www.lohas .com/forum/press.html.

43. Accessed October 3, 2006, at http://www.google.com/search?hl= en&lr=&client=safari&rls=en&q=costco+mission+statement &btnG=Search.

44. Wright, P. M., George, J. M., Farnsworth, S. R., & McMahan, G. C. (1993). Productivity and extra-role behavior: The effects of goals and incentives on spontaneous helping. *Journal of Applied Psychology, 78*(3), 374–381.

45. Kerr & Landauer, 2004.

46. Latham, 2004, p. 129. Of course, this rule of thumb—to permit participation when there are multiple goals—applies all the time to Multistream management, because Multistream management has as its premise the existence of multiple goals and multiple forms of well-being.

47. Wong-Ming Ji & Neubert, 2001.

48. See Gandhi, A. (2003). Foreword: My grandfather's footsteps. In C. Ingram, *In the footsteps of Gandhi: Conversations with spiritual social activists* (revised edition, pp. 9–12). Berkeley, CA: Parallax Press.

49. Coates, J., Gray, M., & Hetherington, T. (2006). An "ecospiritual" perspective: Finally, a place of indigenous approaches. *British Journal of Social Work, 36,* 381–399.

50. Rizvi, H. (2007, May 3). Cities are not the problem, but the solution in the battle for biodiversity. *City mayors: Environment.* Accessed February 21, 2008, at http://www.citymayors.com/ environment/biodiversity.html; Basagio, A. D. (1999). Economic, social, and environmental sustainability in development theory and urban planning practice. *The Environmentalist, 19,* 145–161; McManus, R. (2006, January/February). Interview: "Imagine a city with 30 percent fewer cars." *Sierra Magazine,* Accessed February 21, 2008, at http://www.sierraclub.org/sierra/200601/inter-view.asp; Hawken, P., Lovins, A., & Lovins, L. H. (1999). *Natural capitalism: Creating the next Industrial Revolution.* Boston: Little, Brown; Brazil: Curitiba's urban experiment. (December 2003). *FRONTLINE/World.* Accessed October 4, 2006, at http://www .pbs.org/frontlineworld/fellows/brazil1203/architects.html.

51. Lerner is not a typical politician. He is an architect, engineer, urban planner, and humanist. His first term as mayor was not by election, but rather by the appointment of the governor (Brazil was under a military dictatorship at the time), who chose Lerner for his knowledge and his supposed lack of political talent. He has since been reelected numerous times.

52. The GDP per capita in Curitiba in 1996 was approximately $10,000, which is about twice the average for Brazil as a whole and about one-fourth of the U.S. GDP per capita (*Integration of land use and bus systems in Curitiba, Brazil.* Asia-Pacific Environmental Innovation Strategies (APEIS) Research on Innovative and Strategic Policy Options (RISPO). Accessed September 24, 2007, at www.iges.or.jp/APEIS/RISPO/inventory/db/pdf/0001.pdf).

53. Page 298 in Hawken, P., Lovins, A., & Lovins, L. H. (1999). *Natural capitalism: Creating the next Industrial Revolution.* Boston: Little, Brown.

54. The process can be seen to have three phases. First, the design team listens to and gathers information for stakeholders. Next, it begins to design a response by taking into consideration the larger vision and becoming ever more focused on the issue at hand (repeatedly inviting stakeholder review and participation as the process unfolds). Finally, it develops a report that restates the goals and offers recommendations and guidance for implementation. This definition and description of three stages of charrettes is taken from the following source: Musty, P. J. (no date). *A charrette is an urban design and planning process.* Accessed October 4, 2006, at http://www.charrettecenter.com/ newlongview/newlongview.asp?a=spf&pfk=1&gk=7.

55. Hawken et al., 1999, p. 307.

56. Hawken et al., 1999, p. 302.

CHAPTER 9

This chapter provides an overview of some basic concepts and models for understanding strategic management. These theories and ideas can serve as a foundation as you sharpen your skills in strategic management in later courses and real-world experiences. It can be challenging to think strategically, because such thinking encompasses so many different aspects of management. It requires the manager to analyze opportunities and strengths in the external environment in light of an organization's internal strengths and weaknesses. Moreover, these wide-ranging concerns must be integrated and communicated as a coherent strategy that can be understood and embraced by key stakeholders. Oh, and then the strategy must be implemented!

ROAD MAP

FOUR STEPS OF STRATEGIC MANAGEMENT

Step 1. Review mission and vision
Maximize
Emphasis on

Step 2. Analyze external and internal factors (SWOT)
External factors (opportunities and threats)
- Key stakeholder relationships
- Supplier power
- Buyer power
- Threat of substitutes
- Threat of new entrants
- Intensity of rivalry

Internal factors (strengths and weaknesses)
Key organizational resources are:
- Valuable
- Rare
- Inimitable
- Nonsubstitutable

Step 3. Formulate a strategy
Which strategy an organization should pursue *within* an industry:
- Typology
Which industries a diversified organization should operate in:
- Key dimensions/criteria ...

- Typology ...

Step 4. Implement the strategy
- Managers' preferred approach
- Secondary/backup approach

Strategic Management

MAINSTREAM APPROACH	⟷	MULTISTREAM APPROACH

Shareholder wealth
Achieving competitive advantage

Stakeholder well-being
Nurturing community and ecological sustainability

Minimize stakeholders' power:
- Increase the number of suppliers
- Increase the number of buyers

- Minimize possible substitutes
- Erect entry barriers
- Accentuate uniqueness

Establish mutually beneficial relationships with stakeholders:
- Use previously wasted resources
- Help buyers meet community needs

- Find positive substitutes
- Remove barriers to cooperation
- Find healthy interdependencies

Manage key resources:
- Enhance financial well-being
- Increase profits
- Exclude others (monopolize)
- Increase owners' financial wealth

Manage key resources:
- Serve humankind
- Act responsibly
- Teach others
- Improve stakeholder well-being

Cost leader versus differentiator

Minimizer versus Transformer

- Use BCG portfolio matrix: market growth rate and market share
- Star; cash cow; question mark; dog

- Use a Multistream portfolio matrix: sustainability and restorativeness
- Sustainability hero; fragile player; innocent bystander; lavish actor

---

- Deliberate, top-down mode
- Emergent, bottom-up mode

- Emergent, bottom-up mode
- Deliberate, top-down mode

Attempting to Climb Higher Than Mount Everest[1]

Ray C. Anderson (shown in the photo) is the founding CEO of Interface, a company with more than $1 billion in annual sales and the largest supplier of modular carpeting in the world. Anderson has lived three different lives as a professional. He spent his first "life" preparing himself to become the entrepreneur who founded Interface. During those years he learned important lessons about competitiveness and the importance of hard work in family, in school, and in the workplace.

Anderson's second professional life, which lasted about 20 years, began when he was 38 years old and started Interface. By then he had accumulated enough knowledge of the carpet industry to recognize a golden opportunity when he saw it. It was 1969 when Anderson was introduced to the idea of "carpet tiles," which are 18-inch squares of carpet that can be installed without being glued to the floor and can be easily changed and rearranged. He immediately recognized that such a product would find a growing market in the "office of the future," which required easy access to under-floor wiring for computers, and flexibility to accommodate open floor plans. Thanks to its differentiated product for this new and growing market—and thanks to a "Compete, compete, compete!" approach—by the end of the millennium Interface had become a global giant, with 29 factories in six countries, selling about 40 percent of the world's carpet tiles, and enjoying the largest market share in almost all of the 110 countries in which it competed.

Of course, not everything was smooth sailing, and Interface frequently needed to fine-tune its strategy during those years. For example, in 1984, when its primary market—new office buildings in the United States—went into a depression, the company reinvented itself. Interface expanded into different markets. It began to target the flooring needs specifically for building renovations, it entered foreign markets, and it developed businesses in the textile and chemical industries. Anderson was pleased that in many people's eyes he was like a modern-day hero, an entrepreneur with a company that employed 7000 people who supported their own spouses and children—more than 25,000 people worldwide.

Anderson's third life began when he was 59 years old and had hired a senior management team to run the company. He began to think about his vision for the future of Interface—his then 21-year-old "child"—after customers prompted a group of international employees to ask him what Interface was doing for the ecological environment. Until that moment, Anderson had little special concern for the natural environment, except that Interface was trying to "make a buck"[2] developing products for the "indoor air quality" market. When Anderson was asked to give a speech about Interface's "environmental vision," he realized that he did not have such a vision, and that he had not given much thought to what Interface was "taking from the earth or doing to the earth."[3] This situation changed when he started to read *The Ecology of Commerce* by Paul Hawken. Anderson was embarrassed to find out that in the previous year Interface had used 1.2 trillion pounds of the Earth's stored natural capital, and that more than 5 billion pounds of carpet in landfills has "Interface" on the label. "I was running a company that was plundering the earth . . . someday people like me will be put in jail!"[4] For Anderson, these issues are "personally, as well as to Interface—in the highest sense of the word, strategic. I'm talking about *ultimate purpose*. There is no more strategic issue than that."[5] He talks about the planet Earth being perhaps the most rare resource in the universe, and notes that we had better be good stewards of it.

Anderson's *vision* is for Interface to be a world leader in the next industrial revolution by becoming the first sustainable corporation, and then becoming a restorative organization (putting back *more* than it takes from the Earth by helping suppliers and customers to do the same).

For him, achieving this goal is like climbing higher than Mount Everest. Interface has quite a vision statement:

> To be the first company that, by its deeds, shows the entire industrial world what sustainability is in all its dimensions: people, process, product, place, and profits—by 2020—and in doing so we will become restorative through the power of influence.[6]

Anderson's initial strategy for this new vision followed the mantra of the day: reduce, reuse, reclaim, recycle, and redesign—and then adopt, improve, and share the best practices. He is pioneering what he calls a new business model for success: "doing well [financially] by doing good [ecologically friendly]."[7] It is a strategy designed to achieve both acquisitive and sustenance economic success. Anderson also says it is both a smart strategy and the right strategy: "I believe that in the 21st century, the most resource-efficient companies will win!"[8] Anderson believes that it is inevitable that the market for environmentally friendly products and organizations will grow. And just as his company struck gold in a changing marketplace by introducing carpet tiles, so Anderson believes that Interface will enjoy continued success by becoming a world leader in ecological concerns.

Within four years after introducing its new strategy, Interface was listed on the *Fortune* 100 list of "Best Companies to Work For," had doubled its employment, and tripled its profits. In 2007—at the halfway point between Anderson's 1994 "conversion experience" and the 2020 sustainability goal—Interface was about halfway to its ultimate goal. The company's use of fossil fuels was down 45 percent, its net greenhouse gas production was down 60 percent, its contribution to landfills was down 80 percent, and its carpet-manufacturing operations used approximately 33 percent as much water as they once did. Meanwhile, Interface's profit margins are up. A winning strategy indeed![9]

THE IMPORTANCE OF STRATEGIC MANAGEMENT

Of all the topics in management textbooks, none gets more coverage or mention than competitive strategies. In fact, the single most-cited scholar in these texts is Michael Porter, who has written a series of influential books on competitive strategy. Similarly, it is no coincidence that the most-cited business practitioner has been Jack Welch, the former CEO of General Electric (GE). Welch is widely admired for the strategies he developed toward helping GE become one of the top two competitors in each industry where it chose to compete.

Strategic management refers to the analysis and decisions that are necessary to formulate and implement strategy. **Strategy** refers to the combination of goals, plans, and actions designed to accomplish an organization's mission. The importance of strategic management is illustrated by the difference between Wal-Mart and Kmart. Both companies were founded in 1962, and both chains have other striking similarities: names, store atmosphere, markets served, and organizational purpose. Yet Wal-Mart's financial performance has far surpassed that of Kmart. Why? Because managers vary in how well they formulate and implement strategies, and this difference affects their organization's competitiveness. Wal-Mart is very good at Mainstream strategic management, whereas Kmart continues to struggle to find the right blend of strategic direction and appropriate implementation.[10]

The basic idea of strategic management has a long history. The word "strategy" comes from the Greek word *strategos*, which was used about 2500 years ago to refer to a military commander. One of the most famous historical writings on strategy— *The Art of War*, written by Sun-tzu around that time—is still being read by contemporary managers today.[11] Strategic management is used in all sorts of organizations because it provides a way to answer questions about the direction an organization should take and the ways it should move toward its objectives. It is a tool that can be used by both Mainstream and Multistream managers, albeit usually with different results.

Strategic management is the analysis and decisions necessary to formulate and implement strategy.

Strategy is the combination of goals, plans, and actions designed to accomplish an organization's mission.

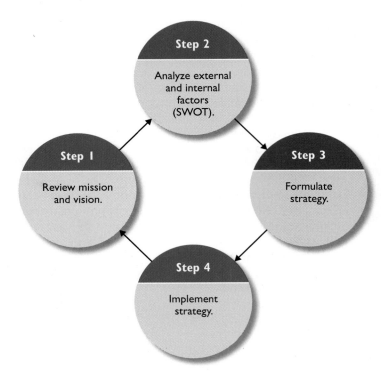

Figure 9.1 Overview of the strategic management process

Strategic management can be described as a four-step process:

1. Review the mission and vision of the organization.
2. Analyze the organization's external environments and internal resources.
3. Choose and develop the strategy to be followed.
4. Implement the chosen strategy.

Successful implementation then feeds back to the beginning of the process as managers ensure that the strategy remains relevant. Each of these four steps in the strategic management process will be discussed in this chapter, first from a Mainstream perspective, and then from a Multistream perspective.

Although the four-step process as depicted in Figure 9.1 is a useful way to think about strategic management, the four steps are rarely as neatly laid out in real life, and each step in the model can be seen as related to the others. The Mainstream approach tends to emphasize how managers develop the *content* of strategy before it is implemented, whereas the Multistream approach tends to emphasize how managers oversee the ongoing *process*.

MAINSTREAM STRATEGIC MANAGEMENT

In this section, we review the four steps in the Mainstream strategic management process. Given that Chapter 8 provided well-developed descriptions of mission and vision, our focus here will be on the final three steps, which lie at the core of strategic management.

Step 1: Review the Organization's Mission and Vision

The first step in the strategic management process is to review and refine the mission and vision of the organization. Strategic management models typically assume that an organization's mission needs to be revisited on a regular basis to ensure that it continues to reflect the organization's strengths and weaknesses in light of its current opportunities and strengths. This process is both shaped by and shapes the values and identity of an organization. In general terms, a Mainstream approach to mission and vision can be characterized by its emphasis on maximizing *organizational competitiveness*.

Step 2: Analyze External and Internal Factors (SWOT)

SWOT analysis examines an organization's internal strengths and weaknesses in light of external opportunities and threats.

The second step in the strategic management process is to perform a SWOT analysis. SWOT is an acronym for Strengths, Weaknesses, Opportunities, and Threats. A **SWOT analysis** examines an organization's *internal* strengths and weaknesses in light of *external* opportunities and threats.

Strengths refer to valuable or unique resources that an organization has or any activities that it does particularly well. A strength is a positive internal characteristic that can help managers to achieve their strategic objectives. For example, one strength of Interface, the company described in the opening case, is its mastery of carpet-tile technology.

Weaknesses refer to a lack of specific resources or abilities that an organization needs for it to do well. A weakness is a characteristic that hinders the achievement of the strategic objectives of an organization. When Interface CEO Ray Anderson first developed his vision of the company becoming ecologically sustainable, for example, a weakness was that the firm lacked the technology to do so.

Opportunities are conditions in the external environments that have the potential to help managers meet or exceed organizational goals. Sometimes recognition of these opportunities will prompt managers to revise goals. Anderson, for example, has recognized the opportunity in being a world leader in selling ecologically friendly flooring; he is a well-known speaker who encourages managers in other organizations around the world to follow the path trod by Interface.

Threats are conditions in the external environments that have the potential to prevent managers from meeting organizational goals. For example, new legislation that requires additional pollution control measures may threaten the profitability of a factory. An analysis of the external environment is key to uncovering which current and future opportunities and threats might exist.

We will now provide a more in-depth discussion of SWOT analysis, including an introduction of analytical tools and techniques that help managers perform such analyses. We start with the external factors (opportunities and threats) that provide the context for identifying an organization's internal factors (strengths and weaknesses).

EXTERNAL FACTORS (OPPORTUNITIES AND THREATS).   As described in Chapters 2 and 3, managers try to monitor many aspects of an organization's external environment. These aspects include key stakeholders and different dimensions in their local and global environments. In particular, managers must pay attention to the environment and stakeholders in their organization's industry. The term **industry** refers to a subset of organizations that can be grouped together because they are all active in the same branch of the economy (e.g., the automobile industry, the fast-food industry). Because strategic management is also important for managers in nonbusiness organizations, we will use the term "industry" to refer to subsets of both business and nonbusiness organizations that can be grouped together. Examples of nonbusiness organizations can be found in the education sector and the social services sector.

Industry is a subset of organizations that can be grouped together because they are all active in the same branch of the economy or society (e.g., the automobile industry, the fast-food industry, the education sector, the social services sector).

Fortunately, many helpful tools and resources are available to assist in the complex process of analyzing an industry. When it comes to strategic management in particular, Michael Porter's "Five Forces Model" is the best-known Mainstream tool to help managers think about key external opportunities and threats.[12] Porter's model focuses on five "competitive forces" to which strategic managers should pay special attention:

- Supplier bargaining power
- Customer bargaining power
- The threat of substitutes

TABLE 9.1

Overview of Porter's Five Competitive Forces and Strategic Management

Five Competitive Forces	Attractive to Strategic Managers When . . .	The Force Is Lower When . . .
Supplier power	Low	There are numerous suppliers.
Buyer power	Low	There are numerous customers.
Threat of substitutes	Low	There are few substitutes, or when the use of substitutes requires extra resources.
Threat of entrants	Low	There is a high capital requirement to start a new organization in the industry.
Intensity of rivalry	Low	There is a lot of differentiation among organizations, so that managers face little direct competition from other organizations.

Sources: Adapted from Porter, M. E. (1980). *Competitive strategy: Techniques for analyzing industries and competitors.* New York: Free Press; and Porter, M. E. (1985). *Competitive advantage: Creating and sustaining superior performance.* New York: Free Press.

- The threat from new competitors entering the industry
- The intensity of rivalry among competitors

Together these five forces determine the level of competition (and thus the profit potential) in an industry. Some industries have relatively high competition and low profits (e.g., the steel industry), whereas other industries have relatively low competition and high profits (e.g., the pharmaceutical industry). As summarized in Table 9.1, strategic managers strive to maximize their organization's competitiveness by keeping each of these five competitive forces low or locating in industries where these competitive forces are low.

Suppliers' bargaining power describes how much influence suppliers have over organizations in an industry. When managers don't have many choices regarding where to purchase inputs, the power of suppliers is high. For example, oil cartels such as OPEC (Organization of the Petroleum Exporting Countries) have a lot of power because there are relatively few places where companies like Exxon and Mobil can purchase oil. Conversely, when managers have many choices regarding where to purchase inputs, then the power of suppliers is low, and the suppliers' ability to control prices or the terms of any deal is limited. For example, managers may be able to negotiate low prices for basic office supplies because there are many different suppliers of commodities like paper and pens.

Customers' bargaining power is the mirror image of supplier power; it describes how much influence customers have on organizations in an industry. Customers typically want to minimize the price they pay for the level of quality that they desire. It is important to consider exactly who the organization's customers are. For many organizations, the customers are the end users of the product or service. This is the case with McDonald's and Kinko's, for example. For other companies, such as large manufacturers like toy maker Mattel, retailers are the main customers. Merchandisers such as Wal-Mart and Toys-R-Us hold great bargaining power over Mattel, as they are the main contact points between Mattel's products and the end user. A customer's bargaining power over an organization increases if the customer represents a significant percentage of sales or is seen as a trendsetter in the industry.

Substitutes refer to products or services that are similar or that meet the same needs of a customer, but come from a different industry. For example, when managers of airlines try to attract customers who are traveling from one city to another, those customers may also find substitute travel opportunities in the form of trains or buses. Similarly, managers at newspapers are currently facing pressure from substitutes such as Internet news providers, which make news accessible on a computer or cell phone.

The threat of entrants, which is closely related to the idea of substitutes, refers to conditions that make it difficult for other organizations to enter or compete in a particular industry. The lower the barriers to entry, the higher the threat of new entrants. The barriers to entry can come in many forms, such as government regulations. For example, licenses are required to start a new television station. Brand identity serves as another example of a barrier to entry. Because of its brand identity, many people would likely continue to purchase Tylenol even if its price was twice as high as that of an unfamiliar brand of painkiller. Other barriers to entry may come from access to capital or from **economies of scale,** where managers of large organizations enjoy lower costs owing to their size advantage. For example, because the cost to open an income tax service is much lower than the cost to open an oil refinery, we would expect more new competitors to enter the income tax service industry than oil refining. But, as discussed in Chapter 4, barriers to entry for some global industries are being lowered as the technology of a "wired world" and the development of standardized software permit organizations from around the world to attract professional and white-collar work.[13]

Economies of scale are evident when increases in volume are associated with lower organizational costs for providing a specific product or service.

Intensity of rivalry refers to the intensity of competition among existing organizations in an industry. Rivalry intensity will increase in the following situations:

- An organization has many competitors seeking similar customers. (**Competitors** are other organizations that offer similar products or services, or offer products or services that meet the same customer need.)
- The industry growth rate slows down or declines (which means that there are more competitors for every remaining customer).
- The industry has intermittent overcapacity (e.g., post-Christmas sales of wrapping paper, or sale of farm produce during harvest of a bumper crop).
- Brand identity and switching costs are low. (Customers can shop based only on price because long-term relationships with a buyer is not an issue.)
- An organization's fixed costs are high and cannot be easily converted to a new industry or product.
- There is little ability to differentiate the product or service being offered. (For example, rivalry in the airline industry is intense because it is difficult to differentiate service and to convert airplanes and staff to purposes other than flying passengers.)

Competitors are other organizations that offer similar products or services, or offer products and services that meet the same customer need.

All organizations face varying levels of the five competitive forces in their external environments. There are also other characteristics that are important for managers to consider. For example, is their industry *emergent* (e.g., new products or services such as fitness training facilities targeting preteens) or *mature* (e.g., long-standing products or services such as beer, cement, oil, and banking)? Is it *fragmented* (e.g., farmers' markets) or *global* (e.g., automobiles, soft drinks)? An analysis of all of the relevant external factors allows managers to understand the attractiveness of their industry. In Porter's model, an industry is deemed attractive to managers when the combined weight of the five forces is low. For example, such an analysis reveals that the pharmaceutical industry is more attractive than the airline industry. Mainstream managers try to use Porter's model to maneuver their organizations into positions where they enjoy more power, which they can then use to increase profitability.

INTERNAL FACTORS (STRENGTHS AND WEAKNESSES). Once managers have a sense of the larger industry in which their organization operates, they are better able to understand their own organization's strengths and weaknesses. Recognizing these aspects of the organization requires that managers become familiar with their organization's basic resources, including its capabilities. From a Mainstream perspective, **resources** are organizational assets that represent a possible source of competitive advantage that can be sustained over time.[14] It is helpful for managers to look at three types of internal resources:

- Physical
- Human
- Infrastructural[15]

Physical resources—which refer to material assets an organization owns or has access to—include its factories and equipment, its financial assets (e.g., cash, stocks, and bonds), its real estate, and its inventory. Some physical resources represent tremendous strengths that other organizations may not have, such as "deep pockets" (i.e., financial resources). Other assets are strategically less important, including assets that are necessary simply to "play in the game," such as buildings, office furniture, organizational websites, or vehicles. As the leading carpet-tile manufacturer in its industry, Interface owns important physical resources in many countries.

Human resources refer to specific competencies held by an organization's members. It includes things such as formal training (e.g., some members have valuable education or highly valued professional designations) and informal experience (e.g., tacit knowledge, networks, and "street smarts" that come from many years of experience). Organizations have strengths if they have particularly gifted or experienced members, and weaknesses if their members lack required experience or training. Examples of strengths include a sports team that has an outstanding athlete, a law firm with a retired judge, and a university that employs a Nobel Prize winner. Examples of weaknesses include a sports team that lacks adequately skilled players in some positions, a law firm whose members lack training in important legal areas, and a university with poor teachers.

Infrastructural resources refer to an organization's structures and systems. Included

Resources are organizational assets that can represent a possible source of competitive advantage that can be sustained over time.

In light of growing obesity concerns among children—30 percent of children in the United States are now overweight—a new industry is emerging for fitness clubs for children, where stationary bikes are hooked up to video games, and electronic dance pads hooked up to big-screen televisions.[16]

in this category are things such as the organization's formal and informal planning processes and control systems, the nature of informal relationships among group members, the level of trust and teamwork, and other aspects of the organizational culture. An organization may be designed to work efficiently, with a well-developed bureaucracy, or perhaps it is suited to quickly respond to change and bring new products and services to market before its rivals can do so. A key infrastructural resource that has helped Wal-Mart is its advanced logistics system, which allows the firm to distribute goods to its stores much more efficiently than its rivals.

Managers assess their organization's physical, human, and infrastructural resources to identify the organization's strengths and weaknesses. They then use this information to develop strategies to take advantage of strengths and minimize the impact of weaknesses as they seize opportunities and neutralize threats in the external environment. Sometimes managers will identify key weaknesses that need to be overcome, and even unnecessary strengths that can be sold off. This practice is evident when, for example, sports teams trade players with one another. Michael Lewis describes how baseball teams with lower salary scales have competed successfully against high-payroll teams by not pursuing overvalued baseball skills (e.g., batting averages, runs batted in, and number of bases stolen) and focusing on less-recognized lower-priced skills (e.g., on-base percentages, including walks and total bases) that are better indicators of a team's success.[17]

Not all strengths and weaknesses are equally important. For example, a flower shop may own a powerful computer, but this technology is of little importance if managers do not take advantage of its power—for example, to develop an information system about the shop's customer base. A strength is a **core competency** when it is *central* for the achievement of organizational goals, such as when the flower shop has human resources that are knowledgeable about floral arranging. A **distinctive competency** is a core competency that an organization has that is superior compared to its competitors. For example, a flower shop may have a prize-winning member who arranges the flowers, or perhaps the flower shop's location is close to a hospital, wedding chapel, or funeral home. These characteristics represent distinct advantages compared to competitors that have less accomplished staff or less favorable locations.

Managers use information about their organization's strengths and weaknesses, and its core and distinctive competencies, to develop the organization's strategy. A **competitive strategy** is one that seeks to create value for customers by providing low prices or unique features that are not offered by rival organizations. Managers achieve competitive advantage over similar organizations to the extent that their prices or features are better than those of rivals. **Sustained competitive advantage** refers to a competitive strategy that other organizations are unable to duplicate.

The key to developing sustained competitive advantage is to identify resources that, either on their own or bundled together in a group, have four characteristics: They are valuable, they are relatively rare, they are inimitable, and they lack substitutes (see Table 9.2).[18]

Core competency is a strength that is central for achieving an organization's goals.

Distinctive competency is a core competency that an organization has that is superior relative to its competitors'.

Competitive strategy is a strategy designed to create value for customers by providing lower prices or unique features not offered by rival organizations.

Sustained competitive advantage is a competitive strategy that other organizations are unable to duplicate.

- A resource is *valuable* if it can be used by managers to neutralize threats or exploit opportunities. Resources that help managers to maximize the financial interests of owners are particularly valuable.

- A resource is *rare* when no (or few) other organizations have the same resource. For example, pharmaceutical firms may hold patent rights to drugs for which people are willing to pay a lot of money. Examples of rare and valuable human resources might include highly skilled sports stars and CEOs with an excellent track record.

TABLE 9.2

Four Characteristics of Resources That Help to Achieve Sustained Competitive Advantage

Valuable	The resource can serve as the basis of a competitive advantage.
Rare	The resource is held by no (or very few) other organizations.
Inimitable	The resource cannot easily be copied or developed in another organization.
Nonsubstitutable	The resource cannot be easily replaced by other resources.

- A resource is *inimitable* when it cannot be copied or developed by other organizations, or when it is costly or difficult to do so. This characteristic increases the likelihood that the resource will remain rare, thereby ensuring a sort of monopoly for it. For example, Toyota's highly efficient production system is a resource that competitors have found difficult to imitate.

- A resource is *nonsubstitutable* when it cannot be easily substituted by other resources. Substitutes are different resources (or bundles of resources) that can be used to achieve an equivalent strategic outcome, even though the substitutes may not be rare or inimitable. Nonsubstitutable resources permit managers to guard the owners' financial interests from threats by other organizations with different resources.

Sometimes managers will engage in "espionage" to acquire or copy valuable, rare, inimitable, and nonsubstitutable resources from their competitors. For example, prior to the success of mass-production techniques to manufacture Mars candy bars, the lion's share of the chocolate confection industry was held by Cadbury's, which used a labor-intensive process to produce many of its chocolates. Eager to find out how the Mars bar technology worked, Cadbury's approached people in companies that supplied machinery to Mars; it also hired managers who had worked inside the Mars factory (they were dubbed "the men from Mars").[19]

Managers in organizations that have resources with these four characteristics can expect to enjoy a sustained competitive advantage. These four characteristics are evident at Microsoft, one of the most successful competitive businesses in the world over the past three decades. Microsoft's key resource is its patents and proprietary technology related to its computer operating system, which is valuable because it is sold on most personal computers (PCs) in the world, and is required to run other software on PCs. Its operating system is rare and difficult to imitate because Microsoft retains proprietary ownership over it. It is nonsubstitutable because most software will not run on any other PC operating system.

Because SWOT analyses take place in a dynamic environment, a particular bundle of strengths that leads to success at one point may be a recipe for failure at a different point. The key skill needed by managers is the ability to anticipate which bundles of resources will help to seize the opportunities and overcome threats in the future. For example, IBM has remained successful over a long period of time, but not because of any ongoing set of strengths or resources that are valuable, inimitable, rare, and nonsubstitutable. In the early 1900s, the firm's resources and strengths changed from being a computer punch-card manufacturer to becoming the world's largest producer of typewriters; in the 1950s, IBM evolved into the largest producer of mainframe computers; and in the 1980s, it transformed itself into the world's largest producer of PCs. More recently, IBM has become a leading developer of computer software, plus a hardware and service provider.[20] In short, SWOT analysis is an ongoing activity needed to formulate the appropriate strategy for the current situation.

Step 3: Formulate a Strategy

The information and insights generated during the SWOT analysis help strategic managers to formulate or refine their organization's strategy. In this section, we first describe some key tools managers use to formulate strategy for a single organization competing within a specific industry—this is probably the most familiar understanding of strategy. We then describe some tools strategic managers use for diversified organizations that conduct business in a variety of industries.

DILBERT: © Scott Adams/Dist. by United Feature Syndicate, Inc.

COMPETING WITHIN A SPECIFIC INDUSTRY. The strategy that is followed by an organization in its particular industry is called its **business-level strategy** (or competitive strategy). For example, Kia Motors follows a business-level strategy to compete in the automobile industry. Business-level strategies are also used by managers of nonbusiness organizations (e.g., a charitable thrift store).

Michael Porter has developed a framework for understanding three basic types of business-level strategies:

- Cost leadership
- Differentiation
- Focus[21]

The key to success for managers pursuing a **cost leadership** strategy is to increase their profit margin by keeping their costs lower than the costs of their competitors, while still maintaining their price and quality at roughly the same level as their competitors. Cost leaders can offer to pass a portion of their cost savings to buyers, thereby increasing their market share and enabling even greater cost savings from increased economies of scale. Choosing this strategy requires managers to pay attention to efficiencies in production and distribution systems through tight controls. Wal-Mart is the classic example of a company that uses a cost leader strategy. Internally, the firm has a world-class inventory management system that it uses to lower costs. Externally, Wal-Mart's volume provides it with massive buyer power that enables it to purchase products from suppliers at lower prices than can its competitors. As a result, Wal-Mart can price its products lower than its competitors' products and still generate the higher revenues needed to finance its growth.[22]

The key for managers pursuing a **differentiation** strategy is to offer a product or service for which buyers are willing to pay a higher price than they would for a competitor's product or service. There are several ways an organization might differentiate its product or service from that of its rivals: exceptionally high quality, extraordinary service, creative design, unique technical ability, and so on. Of course, the differentiation must be significant enough that customers are willing to pay a higher price. The watches marketed by Patek Philippe—the only manufacturer that crafts all of its mechanical movements according to the strict specifications of the

Business-level strategy is a strategy followed by an organization within its industry.

Cost leadership refers to increasing profit margins by keeping financial costs lower than competitors', while still maintaining price and quality at roughly the same level as competitors'.

Differentiation refers to offering a unique product or service for which buyers are willing to pay a premium price.

◎ MANAGEMENT IN PRACTICE

Choosing the Right Strategic Window of Opportunity for the Time

The inevitability of a dynamic and changing environment means that an organization's strategy should be expected to change over time. For example, by the early 1990s, Loewen Windows had become very successful as the leading window manufacturer on the Canadian prairies. The firm essentially had a cost leader strategy that allowed it to provide good-quality windows appropriate for most of the homes in that market. That's when CEO Charles Loewen decided that the company needed to adopt a differentiation strategy, focusing on the market outside of Canada.

Why change what clearly was a successful strategy? Loewen saw that trade agreements such as NAFTA would open up the Canadian market to much larger competitors from the United States, whose size advantage would allow them to take over as cost leaders in the Canadian market. Loewen also knew that an important strength of his company was the craftsmanship ability of his employees. By coupling this craftsmanship with a new focus on elegant, energy-efficient, and environmentally friendly design and manufacturing, Loewen was confident the company could compete in the upscale market. Today, Loewen Windows is a leader in the luxury window market (homes that cost $1 million or more), with 75 percent of its sales coming in the United States—and Charles Loewen is already rethinking the strategy the firm will use in the future.[23]

Geneva Seal—are a good example of differentiation. The firm's reputation enables it to charge tens of thousands of dollars for its watches.[24]

Whereas differentiation and cost leadership are broad-market strategies, managers might alternatively choose a narrow-market strategy called focus. A **focus** strategy means targeting a small niche in the overall market, such as a specific geographic area or a small product segment. For example, managers of a local pizza restaurant must decide whether to distribute flyers throughout the city or only in their local neighborhood, whether to create an ambiance that appeals to a broad cross-section of customers or to a particular subgroup (e.g., families versus college students), which items to offer on the menu (e.g., pizza made from organic-only products), and so on. Similarly, managers of a car manufacturer must decide whether their distribution network will be worldwide or focus on particular regions, whether their product line will span from entry-level to luxury vehicles, and so on. It is possible to combine the focus strategy with either differentiation or cost leadership.[25]

COMPETING IN MULTIPLE INDUSTRIES.   Corporate-level strategy helps managers in diversified organizations decide which industries to compete in. A **diversified organization** competes in more than one industry or sector, or serves customers in several different product, service, or geographic sectors. General Electric is an example of a diversified organization: It sells aircraft engines, appliances, capital services, lighting, medical systems, broadcasting services, plastics, and power systems. Often each separate division in a diversified company is treated as a strategic business unit (SBU). Each SBU has its own mission statement, business-level strategy, products or services, markets, and competitors, and each is evaluated based on its own financial statements.

While large corporations often diversify their operations to compete in a number of different industries, smaller organizations may face similar issues, albeit on a smaller scale. For example, a small vegetable farm may sell fresh produce at a farmers' market, provide specialty produce to local grocery stores, sell farm-fresh salsa via the Internet, provide a consulting service to other farmers or consumers, and rent out equipment and services to neighboring farms. The farmer might decide to compete in industries that offer year-round income and offset the seasonality of fresh produce.

Focus refers to choosing a small niche in the overall market.

Corporate-level strategy is the strategy followed by an organization to determine in which industries it will compete.

Diversified organizations compete in more than one industry, or serve customers in several product, service, or geographic markets.

In deciding how much diversification they want, managers can choose between two basic types of diversification strategies: related and unrelated.

Related diversification expands an organization's activity in industries related to its current activities; it includes both horizontal integration and vertical integration. **Horizontal integration** is evident when an organization's services or product line are expanded or offered in new markets. Managers choose to enter new industries based on how they can use existing strengths to their advantage. For example, PepsiCo has transferred its advertising expertise to benefit businesses in a variety of markets where it competes—snack food, soft drinks, Gatorade, orange juice, and so on. Related diversification can also generate synergies. **Synergy** occurs when the performance gain that results from two or more units working together—such as two or more organizations, departments, or people—is greater than the simple sum of their individual contributions. For example, corporations such as Canwest Global Communication are looking for synergies when they acquire and operate television and radio stations, newspapers publishers, and Internet providers in an attempt to build a seamless multimedia news and advertising organization.

Related diversification can also take the form of **vertical integration**, which occurs when an organization produces its own inputs (backward integration) or sells its own outputs (forward integration). Managers facing strong supplier power may purchase a supplier (backward integration), whereas managers facing a strong buyer power may purchase the buyer (forward integration). Major oil companies, for example, have grown through backward integration by getting involved in oil exploration, extraction, transportation, and refining operations. They have also grown through forward integration by operating retail gas stations and convenience stores. An example of forward integration on a smaller scale occurred when Wiens Family Farm opened a vegetable stand at a local farmers' market rather than sell its produce through grocery stores.

In **unrelated diversification,** an organization grows by acquiring or entering new industries unrelated to its current activities, as General Electric did. Sometimes an unrelated diversification strategy is chosen to reduce a threat identified by a SWOT analysis. For example, managers may diversify if they believe that their current industry is in danger of declining, or if they believe such diversification to be critical to sustain growth. The Chinese company Haier, which was originally a small appliance company, has diversified into the unrelated industries of catering, financial services, and pharmaceuticals (although many of these ventures ended in failure or only modest success).[26] Recently, there has been a trend away from unrelated diversification, in recognition of the fact that unrelated business units can be difficult to synchronize with an organization's established core competencies.

A variety of portfolio management tools have been developed to help managers of conglomerates (organizations with unrelated diversification strategies)

Related diversification expands an organization's activity in industries related to its current activities.

Horizontal integration is a type of diversification that is evident when an organization's services or product line are expanded or offered in new markets.

Synergy occurs when the performance gain that results from two or more units working together—such as two or more organizations, departments, or people—is greater than the simple sum of their individual contributions.

Vertical integration is a type of diversification that occurs when an organization produces its own inputs (backward integration) or sells its own outputs (forward integration).

Unrelated diversification refers to growing an organization by entering new industries or by acquiring other organizations unrelated to the organization's current activities.

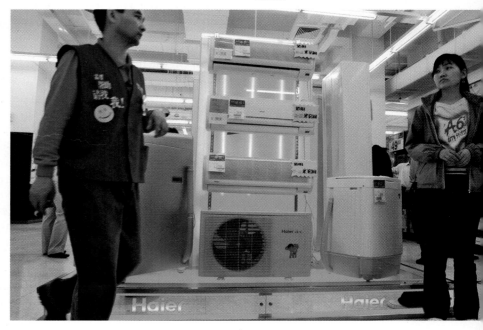

Some Haier products available at the first Wal-Mart Supercenter in Beijing, China.

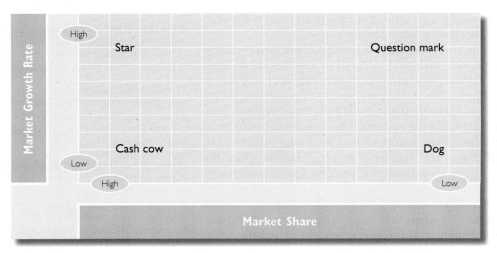

Figure 9.2   BCG portfolio matrix for managing diversified organizations

BCG matrix is a tool that, by classifying organizations according to (a) their market share in an industry and (b) the rate of growth of the industry they are operating, helps managers make decisions about unrelated diversification strategy portfolios.

Product life cycle consists of four phases in the life of a product—introduction, growth, maturity, and decline.

decide which particular industries to remain active in and which to divest from. These managers may treat their various lines of business much like financial investments. Similar to individual investors who seek to diversify their personal investments, managers in conglomerates look for an optimal mix of types of businesses and industries in which to operate.

Perhaps the most well-known tool for business portfolio planning is the **BCG matrix,** which was developed by the Boston Consulting Group (see Figure 9.2).[27] Using the BCG matrix, each business is classified according to (a) its market share and (b) the rate at which the industry is growing. This tool is intended to help managers decide how to allocate scarce resources to businesses among the industries where they have operations.

In a BCG matrix, *market share* is measured relative to its competitors. For example, a division that enjoys a 10 percent share of the market in its industry may be rated as *high* if its nearest competitor has only 1 percent of the market, whereas it could be rated as *low* if its three competitors each have 30 percent of the market. Microsoft currently has a very high share of the overall market for operating systems on personal computers, but that share may be lower in developing countries, where Microsoft's product is often unaffordable.

The *market growth rate* is an indicator of an industry's strength and future potential. The idea of a product life cycle is helpful to understand this dimension of the BCG matrix. The **product life cycle** consists of four phases in the life of a product—introduction, growth, maturity, and decline (see Figure 9.3).[28]

- Introduction phase: There is not yet widespread demand for the product. It is new on the market, and demand for it is not yet proven. Not all products leave this phase and enter the second phase of the product life cycle.

- Growth phase: In this phase the demand for the product increases significantly. However, the costs of building the organizational capacity to meet customer demand may cause cash-flow problems. Nevertheless, organizations that invest in the production capabilities will gain significant market share in a growing market.

- Maturity phase: The demand for the product levels off, some competitors consolidate efforts or are forced to drop out of the industry, and efforts are made to differentiate products and services from those of the competition.

- Decline phase: Demand drops, profitability drops, and the advantage goes to the most efficient competitors and to those that have managed to diversify into new products and service.

Similar to products, industries can be characterized as experiencing early growth, accelerated growth, slowing growth, and declining growth. Industries with increasing or high growth rates are more attractive.

Taken together, the two dimensions of the BCG matrix tell managers of diversified corporations that there are four basic types of organizations in their portfolios: stars, cash cows, question marks, and dogs.

In a rapidly growing industry, an organization that has a relatively high market share is called a *star*. For example, a star in Apple's portfolio is iPod, with its commanding share of the personal music and video player market. Like movie stars, such lines of business generate a lot of cash, but they also need a lot of cash to keep going. A star has a high profile and promises to generate profits and positive cash flows even after the growth of the industry stabilizes.

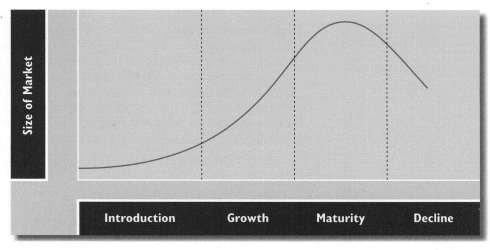

Figure 9.3   The product life cycle

A *cash cow*, by contrast, enjoys a high market share in a low-growth or mature industry. Cash cows should be "milked" and the profits invested in other organizations that are "stars" or "question marks." For example, a cash cow in Gillette's portfolio has been shaving cream, which accounts for the majority of the company's profits.[29]

A *question mark* has a low market share, but operates in a rapidly growing industry. A question mark presents a difficult decision for managers, as the risk of no return on the investment is very real. In the end, only those question marks with the most likely chance of success warrant investment. For example, at one time it was uncertain which of the numerous companies competing in the video game console industry would survive.

Finally, a *dog* has both low market share and low growth potential. Dogs typically do not produce much (if any) profit and have little potential to improve in the future. They should be divested (sold off) if a turnaround is not possible, unless the dog offers synergies to related products. For example, a vegetable farmer may have only a small share of revenue from a declining farmers' market, but may continue to participate in this "dog" if it provides an important source of information about trends in consumer tastes.

The BCG matrix helps managers make strategic decisions by focusing on two important and practical dimensions. Unfortunately, this tool is also known to have shortcomings, such as the limitations of focusing exclusively on market share and market growth as indicators of success and industry attractiveness, and the failure to account for possible operating synergies among an organization's different divisions.[30]

Step 4: Implement the Strategy

Once the overall vision for the organization has been set (Step 1), SWOT analyses completed (Step 2), and an appropriate strategy selected and developed (Step 3), it is time to implement the chosen strategy. While the strategic process can fail at any stage, failure in this stage is not uncommon. Members of an organization are generally receptive to implementing changes that *fine-tune* an organization's strategy, but it is much more challenging for managers to implement *major* changes in strategic direction. Some research suggests that as few as 15 percent of intended major strategic changes are implemented successfully.[31]

Lessons for how to go through the four-step strategic management process can be drawn from reflecting on the successful entry of Honda motorcycles into the U.S. market.[32] Honda was able to gain the largest share of the U.S. motorcycle marketplace within four years of entering it. During that same period, Harley-Davidson fell from being number one in the market to number four. This story suggests that implementation is relatively straightforward if the first three steps of the strategic management process are carried out properly.

Step 1 (Vision): Honda's vision was to successfully establish a competitive presence in the U.S. market.

Step 2 (SWOT): In terms of opportunities and threats in the external environment, Honda's managers recognized that other competitors focused on the black-leather-jacket crowd, which left Honda with an opportunity to target "everyday Americans." Managers also decided to limit the buyer power held by motorcycle shop owners across the United States who sold their bikes only on consignment (meaning that Honda would get paid only after the bikes were actually sold off the retail floor). After becoming number one in the marketplace, Honda managers refused to sell on consignment. In terms of identifying its own internal strengths and weaknesses, managers realized that Honda had developed a superior technology in a two-stroke, lightweight, quiet motor. Moreover, because of the popularity of this product in Japan, Honda enjoyed economies of scale in producing this bike. The company recognized that its technology was valuable, rare, inimitable, and difficult to substitute.

Step 3 (Formulation): Honda managers adopted a cost leader strategy, taking advantage of the firm's expertise and economies of scale in making smaller bikes. They also decided to focus their strategy on the untapped market of everyday Americans.

Step 4 (Implementation): With a well-designed strategy and plan in place, Honda was able to become the industry leader within four years of entering the U.S. market.

As presented from a Mainstream perspective, the lesson from Honda's story is clear: Strategy makers who have a compelling vision, perform a careful SWOT analysis, and choose an appropriate generic strategy that uses the five competitive forces to their advantage will outsmart their competitors and prosper.

Both this version of Honda's story (which draws from a Harvard Business School case) and our description of the first three steps of the strategy management process are consistent with what has been called the **content school** approach to strategy. The content school emphasizes the rational–analytic, top-down, and linear aspects of strategy formulation.

However, a description of the implementation of strategy would not be complete without reference to what has been called the "process school" approach to strategy.[33] The **process school** of strategic management is more of a bottom-up, emergent (unplanned), and egalitarian approach that emphasizes strategic learning. The process school says that, yes, strategic managers perform rational analyses in the first three steps, but the key skill for managers is not SWOT or portfolio analysis, but rather **strategic learning.** Strategic learning demands that managers find out what works and does not work once strategy implementation is under way.

Content school refers to a linear, rational–analytic, top-down, and linear approach to strategic management.

Process school is a bottom-up, emergent, and egalitarian approach to strategic management that emphasizes strategic learning.

Strategic learning is using insights from an organization's actual strategy to improve its intended strategy.

The process school emphasizes that strategy formulation and implementation are ongoing and iterative, where one aspect influences the other. This view is more closely aligned with the Multistream approach to strategic management, whereas the content school is more aligned with the Mainstream approach. Even so, the process school is relevant for the Mainstream approach, just as the content school is relevant for the Multistream approach. Figure 9.4 illustrates how the process school approach fits into the four-step strategic management model.

As indicated in Figure 9.4, from a process school perspective, it is important to recognize the difference between an organization's *intended* strategy (what managers want to do) and its *actual* strategy (what is implemented). The first three steps of the strategic process help managers to formulate the intended strategy that they

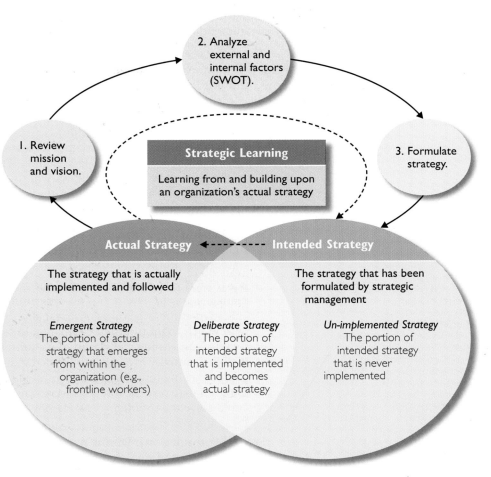

want to implement in their organization. However, some aspects of this intended strategy never get put into practice; these portions are called the *unimplemented strategy*. The parts of the intended strategy that are implemented are called the *deliberate strategy*. The deliberate strategy is only one part of an organization's actual strategy—the other part is called the *emergent strategy*. The emergent strategy includes actions taken by organizational members that were not anticipated by strategic managers. The emergent strategy captures the idea that an organization's actual strategy depends, in part, on the bottom-up actions of frontline organizational members.

From a process school perspective, formulating an intended strategy based on the content school approach is important, but it is not the most important work involved in strategic management. Rather, the most important component of strategic management is strategic learning, which involves examining an organization's actual strategy and using it to inform subsequent intended strategy. Strategic learning demands focusing on three things:

1. Managers try to understand why some of their original intended strategy was not implemented.

2. Managers identify elements of the (unintended) emergent strategy that were implemented with positive outcomes for the organization.

Figure 9.4   A process school overview of strategic management

Source: Adapted from Mintzberg, H., & Waters, J. A. (1985). Of strategies, deliberate, and emergent. *Strategic Management Journal, 6,* 257–272.

3. Managers determine the implications of this analysis for the organization's next intended strategy.

The process school is messier than the content school, but research suggests that it may be a more accurate description of what actually happens inside organizations. And if it is more accurate, then managers would do well to master the art of strategic learning. This means paying close attention to and learning from others in the organization.

To illustrate the workings of the process school, and to contrast and compare it with the content school, let's take another look at the story about how Honda motorcycles became number one in the U.S. market. This time, rather than draw lessons from analyzing the story in hindsight, we will try to capture the story as it unfolds as told by the Honda managers involved in the process. From a process school perspective, Honda's success can be attributed to using the four steps as follows.

Step 1 (Vision): The managers who oversaw the process said that Honda's strategic intended strategy had been based on the goal of wanting to "sell something" in the U.S. market.

Step 2 (SWOT): Honda had enjoyed success in winning motorcycle races, and managers thought there was an opportunity for them to compete in the U.S. market for large bikes. A threat was that they did not have a big budget with which to mount their campaign. In terms of its internal strengths and weaknesses, Honda was proud of its ability to engineer products. When its big bikes initially broke down in the United States (e.g., from blown head gaskets) owing to the fact that they were being driven much longer distances than in Japan, the motorcycles were flown to Japan so that the engineers could solve the problems. Honda saw its ability to adapt and to learn on the fly as a key strength.

Step 3 (Formulation): During personal interviews, Honda's managers were very clear in stating that when they first entered the U.S. market, it was with every intention of competing head-to-head with Harley-Davidson by selling large bikes to "black leather jacket" customers. Indeed, when representatives from a U.S. Sears department store initially expressed interest in selling the smaller bikes that Honda employees had brought along for themselves to use for running errands, Honda was very clear in *not* wanting to tarnish its reputation among the black-leather-jacket riders by placing such a small bike on the market. Honda tried hard to find space on the shop floor of the regular motorcycle retailers, and it was quite willing to follow the practice of selling on consignment to share the floor with its competitors.

Step 4 (Implementation): Honda's original intended strategy—to compete head-to-head with Harley-Davidson—failed miserably. The firm's big bikes broke down, retail outlets did not embrace the Honda product, and U.S. black-leather-jacket bikers were not interested. Out of desperation and in attempt to generate sales and cash flow, Honda's salespeople in the United States began to sell the lightweight bikes that they had initially brought along for running errands. Seeing the potential in this emergent strategy, Honda adopted the "You meet the nicest people on a Honda" slogan[34] on the advice of its team in the United States (even though the president of Honda was personally against the idea). It was only after—and perhaps because of—the failure of Honda's original intended strategy that managers were able to engage in the strategic learning that helped them develop their winning strategy.

The lesson of the process school version of this story is this: Success awaits managers who are able to learn from mistakes and from unplanned ideas that emerge in the everyday operations of an organization.

MULTISTREAM STRATEGIC MANAGEMENT

The Multistream approach follows the same basic four-step strategic management process as the Mainstream approach, albeit with two important differences. First, Mainstream management is based on acquisitive economics and maximizing the owners' financial wealth, whereas the Multistream perspective is more focused on sustenance economics and balancing the material well-being of owners with the overall well-being of all stakeholders. Second, whereas the Mainstream four-step model emphasizes how *managers* develop the *content* of strategy by analyzing stakeholders, the Multistream approach pays greater attention to how *stakeholders* contribute to the overall *process* by which strategy is developed.

Step 1: Review the Organization's Mission and Vision

Whereas maximizing competitiveness and shareholder well-being are important considerations from a Mainstream approach to mission and vision, the Multistream approach includes concern for mutually beneficial cooperation and the well-being of multiple stakeholders. For example, when then CEO Dennis Bakke set up the mission statement for AES, one of the world's largest energy providers, he included creating "the world's most fun place to work" and serving "society in an economically sustainable manner with *safe*, clean, reliable electricity."[35]

 WHAT DO YOU THINK?

What Are the Pros and Cons of Competitiveness?

Some people argue that competitiveness is good for society because it motivates people and organizations to do their best. It encourages organizations to continuously improve, promotes efficiency, and reduces opportunities to gouge the consumer. Besides, it seems so natural for people to compete against others and themselves.

But even proponents of competitiveness would admit that competition can go awry, such as when people cheat to win (think of Enron or WorldCom). A "win at all costs" mentality can bring out the worst in people, such as when athletes take illegal performance-enhancing drugs that offer a short-term performance boost at the expense of long-term health costs, when politicians resort to "mud-slinging" during election campaigns, or when managers engage in illegal or unethical behavior to maximize profits. Competitiveness can bring out the worst in humankind when we seek to injure our competitors in an effort to improve our own chances of winning.

Other people argue that even at its best, competitiveness simply is not good enough to warrant its central role in management theory. Why do we assume that the desire to compete brings out the best in humankind? Would not the desire to share, or to eradicate poverty, or to live sustainably on the planet, or to ensure that everyone is treated with dignity be much more likely to truly bring out the best in us? What if our organizational structures and systems were designed toward these ends, instead of being designed simply to out-compete the "opposition"?

Richard Chewning and his colleagues[36] tell the story of what happened when one of two poultry-processing organizations in a Virginia community burned down. Had the managers in the undamaged firm followed Mainstream theory, they could easily have improved their own competitive position by offering to purchase poultry from their competitor's suppliers at reduced rates and by selling the processed poultry at increased prices to their competitor's buyers. Instead, the managers invited their competitor to utilize their operational facilities for a second shift until the competitor's facilities could be rebuilt. These Multistream managers were more interested in nurturing community than in improving their short-term financial return.

How might you react if you were a shareholder in the undamaged poultry-processing company where managers opted to help their stricken competitor? What if managers of the burned-out firm rebuilt with state-of-the-art facilities, thereby developing a significant strategic advantage that made your company less able to compete? What are the short- and long-term implications of competitiveness? Of cooperation? Explain your reasoning. Is competitiveness a good way to bring out the best in humankind and in organizations? Are there better ways?

Step 2: Analyze External and Internal Factors (SWOT)

In terms of SWOT analysis, the Multistream approach considers a broader range of issues than does the Mainstream approach. Perhaps the most striking difference is the emphasis on the ecological environment.[37] As discussed in Chapter 3, from a Multistream perspective an important part of the external environment is the effect an organization has on the larger ecosystem. Which ecological threats does the organization pose, and which opportunities does it have to transform existing "waste" into useful inputs (for itself or for others)? Multistream managers are also more likely to consider issues such as the impact that choosing overseas suppliers has on the communities where the workers live,[38] the effect of strategic decisions on employees' work–life balance, and the nonfinancial goals of shareholders. Moreover, because they do their SWOT analyses in a spirit of strategic learning associated with the process school, Multistream managers are more likely to be attuned to the emergent strategies of a larger variety of stakeholders than are their Mainstream counterparts. Mainstream managers also seek to keep in tune with the views of their stakeholders, but with an agenda that is focused more narrowly on improving financial sustainability.

EXTERNAL FACTORS (OPPORTUNITIES AND THREATS). As we have seen, a Mainstream approach focuses attention on how managers can use Porter's five competitive forces to maximize financial well-being. The Multistream approach draws attention to five parallel factors that managers can use to serve the overall well-being of the community (see Table 9.3). As discussed in earlier chapters, managers are increasingly paying attention to issues related to the community as a whole. This trend is reflected in the growing interest in corporate social responsibility and stakeholder theory, and it is evident in the specific practices of organizations such as Green Mountain Coffee Roasters, H-P Intel, and Timberland.

An example of the five Multistream factors in practice can be found in a community of organizations in Kalundborg, Denmark, where managers take the "waste" produced by one organization and turn it into valuable inputs for another organization (see Figure 9.5). This synergetic cooperation started when the coal-fired Aesnes Power Plant stopped pouring its "waste" heat as condensed water into a nearby fjord. Instead, managers at Aesnes began to sell the heat directly to the Statoil refinery and the Novo Nordisk pharmaceutical firm. Shortly thereafter, the Statoil refinery installed a process to remove sulfur from its "wasted" gas. It then sold the extracted sulfur to the Kemira

TABLE 9.3

Mainstream Versus Multistream Approaches to External Relationships

Mainstream Approach	Multistream Approach
Enhance power by minimizing:	Nurture community by increasing:
• Supplier power	• Usage of previously wasted resources
• Buyer power	• Capacity for customers to meet community needs
• Substitutes	• Substitutes that enhance overall well-being
• Threat of entry	• Bridge-building among organizations
• Rivalry intensity	• Mutually beneficial interdependence

chemical company and the cleaner-burning gas to both the Gyproc sheetrock factory and Aesnes (thereby saving 30,000 tons of coal). When Aesnes began to remove the sulfur from its smokestacks, it produced calcium sulfate, which it sold to Gyproc where it was used in place of mined gypsum. "Waste" fly ash from Aesnes coal generation is also used for road construction and concrete production. In time, Aesnes began to provide surplus heat to residents of the town (who were then able to shut off 3500 oil-burning heating systems), to greenhouses, and to a fish farm. Soon "waste" heat from Statoil also went to the fish farm, which produces about 200 tons of turbot and trout sold in the French market. Sludge from the fish farm is used as fertilizer by farmers, who also receive sludge from the Novo Nordisk pharmaceutical firm.

All of these relationships happened spontaneously without direct government regulation. Initially the relationships were often motivated primarily by acquisitive economics, but over time initiatives have been made for largely ecological reasons, and these have also yielded financial benefits.[39] This example nicely illustrates differences between a Mainstream approach and a Multistream approach to managing an organization's external relationships (summarized in Table 9.3):

Figure 9.5 Transfer of previous "waste" within a community of organizations

- The Mainstream approach is concerned with minimizing the organization's dependence on *suppliers.* In contrast, the Multistream approach welcomes becoming dependent on new (trustworthy) suppliers who transform their underutilized resource outputs ("waste") into materials for inputs. For example, nearby greenhouses were happy to depend on "waste" heat supplied by the Aesnes Power Plant.

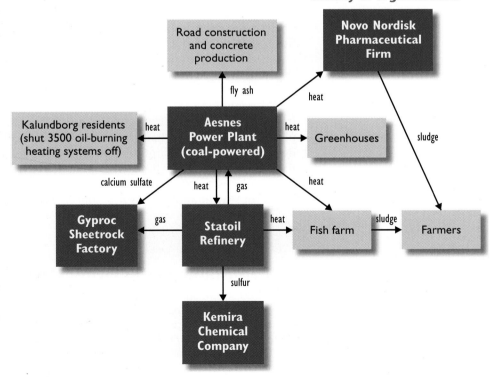

- The Mainstream approach is concerned with minimizing the power that *buyers* have over an oganization. In contrast, the Multistream approach welcomes becoming dependent on specific buyers to nurture community or transform waste. For example, the Kemira chemical company's primary motive in transforming the waste "sludge" was not to increase its power over the farmers who were the buyers of the sludge, but rather to help farmers meet their needs for fertilizer and simultaneously foster environmental sustainability.

- The Mainstream approach is concerned with minimizing competition from *substitutes*. In contrast, the Multistream approach embraces substitutes that enhance overall community well-being. For example, Statoil welcomed the "substitute" heat that Aesnes provided for what had been 3500 oil-burning customers. Similarly, community well-being was enhanced when Statoil's waste gas served as a "substitute" for burning 30,000 tons of coal at Aesnes.

- The Mainstream approach is concerned with erecting *entry barriers* that make it difficult for others to compete. In contrast, the Multistream approach is more concerned with removing barriers that prevent firms from cooperating with one another. Barriers to cooperation were removed when technology permitted Statoil's "waste" sulfur gas to serve as new sources of sulfur for Kemira and cleaner-burning gas for Gyproc.

- The Mainstream approach is concerned with decreasing *rivalry intensity* by a company differentiating itself from other organizations. In contrast, the Multistream approach focuses on increasing mutually beneficial interdependence across organizations. For example, Statoil and Aesnes cooperate to use their "waste" heat for a fish farm, which in turn willingly provides fertilizer for farmers. Recall also the earlier example of the two poultry-processing "rivals" in Virginia.

The Mainstream analysis of the external environment emphasizes external relationships that achieve sustainable *competitive* advantage, whereas the Multistream analysis focuses on achieving sustainable *mutually* advantageous relationships. The five forces are similar, but the agenda toward which they are applied is quite different in each case. Although the Kalundborg example emphasized ecological goals, the same five forces can be used to think about other goals, such as achieving sustainable social justice. For example, to improve social justice, managers might use a SWOT analysis to see how they could work together to minimize oppressive working conditions for poorly paid workers. Starbucks and Pura Vida Coffee are examples of organizations that promote Fair Trade coffee to help coffee growers earn a living wage. Ten Thousand Villages is an example of a Multistream organization that links with craftspeople in low-income countries and imports their products at a price that ensures that the craftspeople earn an adequate livelihood. A keyword in this Multistream approach is *trust* among managers of different organizations.

 WHAT DO YOU THINK?

Can Managers in Other Organizations Be Trusted?[40]

A Mainstream approach suggests that organizations should try to gain influence over and be wary of suppliers and buyers, whereas a Multistream approach puts emphasis on nurturing trust and community among suppliers and buyers. Can managers who practice Multistream principles survive in the marketplace, or will they be taken advantage of by their Mainstream-minded counterparts? Can managers really employ Multistream strategies that are designed to achieve mutual and interdependent benefits?

In his study of the fashion industry in New York, Brian Uzzi found that many external relationships were characterized by managers who looked out for the concerns of their suppliers and customers, rather than simply maximizing their short-term or narrow economic gain. In other words, it seems that managerial relationships across organizations emphasized sustenance economics, neighborliness, and trust. For example, because negotiating contracts and specifying their content took time away from a quick response to the marketplace and the ability to make changes on the fly, Uzzi found that many orders were placed and delivered before any prices had been set. Both the supplier and the buyer trusted that at the end of the day, they would agree upon a mutually satisfactory price. They also tried to accommodate each other in other ways. For example, during slow times one partner in the relationship might place orders sooner than usual so as to create work for the other. There is a sense of satisfaction that comes from working in such a climate of neighborliness and trust, where people respect one another's knowledge and needs (which often cannot be codified ahead of time in a contract). On the rare occasions where a firm's manager tried to take unneighborly advantage of this trusting community—such as when the manager refused to pay a fair higher price for above-contract services—then that manager was unlikely to be included in the community for long.

Uzzi also described what happened after the leading fashion retail outlets were purchased by large corporations whose managers had a more Mainstream approach that emphasized, for example, negotiating contracts up front. An unintended consequence of this trend was that fashion became more of a commodity, with less time and emphasis being placed on ensuring its aesthetic beauty. For example, a supplier was less likely to make the costly changes required for unexpected characteristics of fabrics and to ensure that the cloth would "hang" the right way. The price of the clothes was lower, but to the trained eye the quality and artistic quality had been compromised. Also, the sense of interorganizational neighborliness and trust had been lost.

Consider what sorts of external and internal conditions support the neighborliness and trust that Uzzi had initially found in the New York fashion industry. What conditions stifle it? Do you think that the Mainstream approach is at odds with fostering trust and neighborliness in an industry? Is it at odds with enhancing aesthetic well-being? Alternatively, would you have concerns about a Multistream approach that emphasizes trust and community? Explain your answers.

INTERNAL FACTORS (STRENGTHS AND WEAKNESSES).   Like their Mainstream colleagues, Multistream managers examine the relative strengths and weaknesses of their organization's physical, human, and infrastructural resources. However, Multistream managers are more likely to be sensitive to the ecological strengths and weaknesses of their physical resources, more aware of the need for a work–life balance among their human resources, and more inclined to develop infrastructural resources that nurture meaningful work, even if these initiatives do not contribute to their financial bottom line.

Multistream managers can use the same four criteria as their Mainstream colleagues to identify which internal resources represent particularly strategic strengths and weaknesses. Recall that a resource-based view suggests that resources are the most useful for strategic management if they have four characteristics: They are valuable, rare, inimitable, and nonsubstitutable. However, as highlighted in Table 9.4, there is a significant difference in the *meaning* Multistream management assigns to these four characteristics compared to Mainstream management.

First, whereas Mainstream managers equate the *value* of a resource to its eventual contribution to the financial bottom line of the organization, Multistream

TABLE 9.4

Mainstream and Multistream Criteria for Strengths

Characteristic	Mainstream Emphasis	Multistream Emphasis
Valuable	Enhance profitability	Enhance the well-being of humankind
Rare	Increase revenues	Increase need for responsibility
Inimitable	Enhance monopoly	Teach others
Nonsubstitutable	Protect financial interests	Protect stakeholder overall well-being

managers are more likely to find resources valuable if they satisfy genuine human needs. For example, there is little incentive for a Mainstream organization to invent, patent, produce, and market a portable radio that is powered by winding it up—after all, there is not much demand for such a radio in affluent markets that have easy access to batteries. However, a wind-up radio may be of great value in many parts of the world where people do not have ready access to electricity or batteries. In many low-income countries, an entire village may own just one wind-up radio, which permits its residents to keep in touch with the outside world and to listen to news and weather reports.[41]

Second, *rare* resources are valuable to Mainstream managers because they can bring in higher revenues. In sharp contrast, Multistream managers see rarity as increasing the need to act responsibly. For example, as Ray Anderson of Interface notes, the Earth may be the rarest thing in the universe.[42] We know of only one planet that can sustain human life, so we must manage this rare resource responsibly. Similarly, Multistream principles are evident when pharmaceutical companies permit generic versions of their patented antiretroviral drugs to be made available in Africa for a fraction of the price at which they are sold in higher-income countries.[43] Multistream managers recognize that rare resources that are valuable to humankind should not be seen merely as an opportunity to maximize financial gain.

Third, Mainstream managers value resources that are *inimitable* because this characteristic enhances their ability to enjoy a kind of monopoly in the marketplace. Multistream managers, in contrast, will often volunteer "secrets" of their resources. For example, when Dan and Wilma Wiens started their Shared Farm, they had a waiting list of hundreds of "sharers" who wanted to join (see the opening case in Chapter 8). Dan Wiens recognized that few potential competitors would have the know-how to grow vegetables in an environmentally friendly manner, so he invited interested farmers to his farm and even hosted a series of information sessions

The Lifeline wind-up radio, designed specifically for humanitarian purposes, is an essential source of information in low-income countries where the majority of the population cannot read, where radio is the primary medium of communication, and where up to 95 percent of the population does not have access to electricity. The value of this resource was recognized when it won a Tech Museum Award for technological innovation that improves the condition of humankind.

to teach others the farming techniques that he had learned. Soon Wiens was happy to have numerous competitors in his region. His vision, after all, was to create rural–urban relationships and foster environmental sustainability—not to maximize his own financial wealth. Similarly, managers of organizations that were pioneers in the microfinancing movement (as described in Chapter 6) are also eager to share their best practices with other banks and nonprofit organizations that wish to provide credit to micro-entrepreneurs.

Finally, for Mainstream managers, the fact that no other organization can offer *substitutes* for their valuable, rare, and inimitable resources gives managers more opportunities to maximize their own shareholders' financial interests. This is similar to a monopoly, in that customers cannot find equivalent resources elsewhere. Multistream managers also want to ensure that their organization remains financially viable, but they are likely to encourage the development of substitutes that enhance overall community well-being. For example, when Dan Wiens was told that his Shared Farm might inspire sharers to start their own backyard vegetable gardens, he was happy even though this form of substitution meant that he would lose some "customers." His response came from knowing that other people would join as sharers and, even if they did not, that he had helped people to get more in tune with nature and to eat healthy vegetables (which was his overarching purpose).

Earlier in the chapter, we described Microsoft as a prototypical example of how Mainstream managers use valuable, rare, inimitable, and nonsubstitutable resources to attain sustainable competitive advantage. In contrast, perhaps the Linux operating system provides an appropriate Multistream counterpoint. Linux is thriving precisely because its inventor did not see it simply as a valuable resource to maximize his own financial interests. Instead, Linus Torvalds allows others to freely copy the Linux operating system, welcomes others to improve on it, and is building a community of computer users and programmers who share their work with one another. (More details about Linux are presented in the closing case.)

Step 3: Formulate a Strategy

Both Mainstream and Multistream approaches look at which industry a company wants to inhabit and which strategy to pursue within that industry. A Mainstream approach tends to focus on acquisitive economics and formulating strategy in a rational–analytic, top-down, linear manner. In contrast, the Multistream formulation of strategy focuses on sustenance economics and is more sensitive to emergent strategies from a larger variety of stakeholders. As a consequence, it is more likely to take issues such as ecological sustainability and social justice into consideration. We will contrast and compare differences between a Mainstream approach and a Multistream approach to developing a strategy for an organization to pursue within an industry, and highlight Multistream tools that strategic managers use to make choices about which industries to set up operations in.

COMPETING WITHIN A SPECIFIC INDUSTRY. Mainstream strategies such as "differentiation" and "cost leader" are helpful for managing an organization in the acquisitive economy, but Multistream managers are also interested in strategies based on a broader range of issues. For example, it might be more accurate to call the Mainstream "cost leader" strategy a *"financial* cost leader" strategy because, from a Mainstream perspective, financial costs are the most important. A Multistream approach, in contrast, is sensitive to a wider variety of costs, including social costs and ecological costs. Minimizing the financial cost (Mainstream) an organization pays for its inputs can be very different from minimizing overall cost (Multistream).

For example, one of the goals at Interface is to use environmentally friendly transportation and to use only renewable energy (e.g., solar power rather than oil). This preference reflects Interface's goal to redesign commerce so that it is based on the overall costs of natural resources, not merely financial costs. Ray Anderson notes that Interface pays the market price for oil, but it does not pay for cleanup or health costs that are related to toxic emissions. Similarly, managers may be able to lower the financial cost of production by reducing members' pay or insurance benefits, but such a move may entail higher overall social costs (e.g., the stress placed on families who are unable to pay for their medical needs).

Two basic types of Multistream strategies can be identified:

- Minimizer strategy
- Transformer strategy

Minimizer strategy provides desired goods and services in a way that limits different kinds of costs (e.g., financial, social, ecological).

Transformer strategy provides desired goods and services in a way that redeems what were previously discarded or underappreciated resources (e.g., waste, pollution).

A **minimizer strategy** seeks to provide desired goods and services in a way that limits various costs (e.g., financial, social, ecological). For example, because it is aware that many coffee farmers do not earn a living wage, Pura Vida Coffee uses a minimizer strategy that reduces social injustice when it sells Fair Trade coffee over the Internet to consumers who are willing to pay extra because they know that the farmers growing their coffee beans can then earn a living wage. [44] A minimizer strategy that relates to the natural environment is evident in Mountain Equipment Co-op's approach to reduce its waste through recycling water and using environmentally friendly geothermal heating and cooling systems in its retail stores.

A **transformer strategy** seeks to provide desired goods and services in a way that redeems what were previously discarded or underappreciated resources (e.g., pollution). For example, a transformer strategy is evident in organizations that recycle tires and use them to make floor mats, garden hoses, office supplies, and road surfacing. [45] The same strategy is evident in volunteer agencies that encourage seniors to participate in after-school programs that help children with reading difficulties.

Some managers may try to combine aspects of both a minimizer strategy and a transformer strategy. This is evident when organizations such as Staples promote the use of recycled paper as well as accept computers and monitors for recycling, instead of sending this waste overseas where it becomes an environmental problem. [46]

COMPETING IN MULTIPLE INDUSTRIES. Just as the BCG matrix in Figure 9.2 may help Mainstream managers make decisions, so too similar matrices can help Multistream managers make decisions about which industries to enter or exit. For example, rather than choose industries using only criteria like market share or market growth, Multistream managers may seek to operate in industries that are characterized by a high degree of social justice, or perhaps in industries that are characterized by low social justice and, therefore, have a high need for an exemplary organization to model

Toxic and obsolete computer equipment from high-income countries often finds its way to junkyards in China, India, and Pakistan. Here a man looks for parts to recycle from a pile of old computers dumped at a market in Lahore, Pakistan.

social justice. Similarly, Multi-stream managers may choose which industry to operate in based on the technological needs of humankind. For example, the Swiss pharmaceutical company Novartis devotes part of its product mix to develop and distribute drugs at cost or for free to people in developing countries who suffer from malaria, leprosy, or tuberculosis.

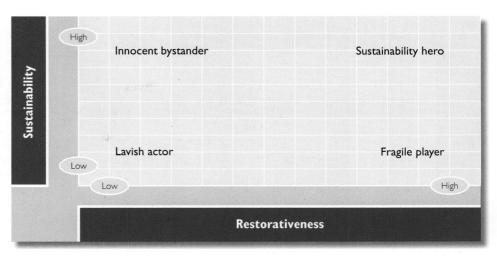

Figure 9.6   A Multistream portfolio matrix

Figure 9.6 illustrates what a Multistream portfolio matrix might look like if the focus was on the natural environment. The first dimension, *sustainability*, focuses on the eco-friendliness of an industry. Unlike the Mainstream usage of the term, which focuses on the long-term financial success of an organization, from a Multistream perspective sustainability has to do with concerns such as minimizing one's ecological footprint and reducing pollution. In this way, for example, the automobile industry may be less sustainable than the bicycle industry. Sometimes debates arise over sustainability considerations, such as whether coal power or nuclear power is more sustainable in the long term. At other times there is general agreement, such as that wind power is more sustainable than either coal or nuclear power (although wind power is not without problems, such as birds being killed by the fast-moving blades).

Recall from the opening case how Ray Anderson initially was alarmed to learn that the carpet industry had very low sustainability because both manufacturing and disposal were hard on the environment. Rather than exit the industry, Anderson invested his efforts to *minimize* Interface's ecological footprint and lead the way for decreased wastefulness in the industry. Toward this end, he "de-materialized" Interface by minimizing its inputs and waste. Part of the company's success comes from designing new products that use less material without compromising quality. Also, using a program called QUEST (Quality Utilizing Employees' Suggestions and Teamwork), Interface was able to reduce the total waste in its global business by 40 percent in the first three years of this initiative. That saved the company $67 million—money that has helped pay for other parts of the change at Interface. New technologies that are being developed by and for Interface are making key contributions to the sustainability of the carpet industry as a whole.

Wind turbines near Copenhagen, Denmark.

Re-TRAC™ - A Recycling and Solid Waste Data Management Tool

Home | Surveys | My Account | Manage Users | Admin | Help | Logout

You are logged in as: User #034

Edit data for year 2007:
- DEMOGRAPHIC
- RESIDENTIAL
  - Recycling
    - Materials
  - Special Waste
  - Solid Waste
  - Yard Waste
- COMMERCIAL
- INSTITUTIONAL
- INDUSTRIAL

Export data

Create reports

Jackson Town

Unity County

Residential Recycling - Add New Material Transaction
Remember to click the **Submit** button after entering data or your changes will be lost.

Search Transactions

Sector:	Residential
Module:	Recycling
Community:	Jackson (Township)
Transaction Date:	March 14 2007

Paper	Collected (in Pounds)
NEWSPAPERS (ONP)	22.350
MAGAZINES (OMG)	
MIXED PAPER GRADES	
OFFICE PAPER	
#8 NEWSPAPER	

Emerge Knowledge Design, Inc. develops and sells web-based applications that help communities manage and reduce waste through better data collection, analysis, and program decision-making to increase recycling.[47]

Restorativeness, the second dimension of the Multistream portfolio matrix in Figure 9.6, refers to how well organizations in an industry help to reduce waste produced by others. A high level of restorativeness helps to *transform* the way stakeholders think about and treat the ecological environment, enabling them to better reduce their own ecological footprints. The restorative side of Anderson's strategy seeks to offer products and services that help Interface's stakeholders to become more sustainable, and to provide education on the process of reducing one's ecological footprint. For example, the company has a special department where managers from other organizations can come to learn about how Interface is becoming more sustainable. In 2007, some 80,000 Ford cars had 100 percent recycled fabric in their seating, supplied by Interface Fabrics. Interface is also helping to reduce customers' waste by having used carpets returned to Interface, where they are recycled rather than being thrown in a landfill. This "cradle-to-cradle" thinking also helps Interface to reduce its own inputs. Along these lines, the company acted as a pioneer in developing its "Evergreen Lease"; with this initiative, instead of buying carpets, customers perpetually lease the service of carpeting and Interface is responsible for cleaning and replacing carpet tiles as necessary.

An organization that is both eco-friendly and good at transforming others' existing waste is called a *sustainability hero.* Managers should devote as many resources as possible to sustainability heroes, because they provide the best assurance of long-term viability. Sustainability heroes, such as the trash recycling program in Curitiba described in the closing case in Chapter 8, are attractive because they reduce the total amount of waste in the world.[48] Another example is an organization that takes sawdust from wood furniture manufacturers and transforms it into particle board using environmentally friendly chemicals and glues.

Managers may also wish to diversify by investing in an *innocent bystander.* Such an organization does not add much pollution to the environment. Moreover, research and development (R&D) initiatives may help to turn an innocent bystander into a sustainability hero—perhaps by finding ways that take existing "wastes" in the environment and transforming them into non-waste-producing outputs. For example, a tree nursery might be an innocent bystander because it produces little waste but also does little to transform others' existing waste. However, if an infrastructure were developed so that the nursery would receive material for composting that might otherwise end up in a landfill (e.g., "wastes" from restaurants), then it could move toward becoming a sustainability hero.

A *fragile player* represents a somewhat less attractive organization, because it creates significant waste itself. Its redeeming feature is that it decreases the waste created by others. For example, managers at Allegiant Air have found a niche in the airline industry by using a fleet of used and heavily discounted airplanes that other airlines do not want because they are noisier and less fuel efficient than recently built aircraft. Allegiant is a fragile player because it takes these planes that are avoided by other airlines and "transforms" them to carry passengers; at the same time, however, it lowers the eco-friendliness of its industry because of its use of old technology.[49]

Lavish actors are the least attractive quadrant in this matrix because they create new ecological problems without doing much in the way of solving existing problems. The only time lavish actors may be desirable is if they transform a little bit of particularly toxic waste, and the waste that they produce is relatively easy to transform. In other cases, a lavish actor can make changes that move it toward being a sustainability hero. For example, the Statoil oil refinery in Kalundborg, Denmark, was at one time more of a lavish actor that created ecological waste while doing little to transform others' waste. More recently, managers at the refinery have begun to utilize "waste" steam from the coal plant, have improved the refinery's own filtering process so that it emits less wasteful sulfur gas, and now provide sulfur inputs that are valued by neighboring companies.

Although this specific portfolio matrix and discussion have focused on *ecological* waste, it is possible to develop similar analyses with broader conceptions of "waste." For example, some industries may be associated with *socially* undesirable side effects of "waste." This might be evident in industries that provide jobs with poor working conditions that threaten people's physical health. Other industries may provide socially desirable side effects, such as when participating in the arts or recreational activities rejuvenates the human spirit. From this perspective, we might see industries characterized by highly repetitive assembly-line work as stifling to the human spirit, and industries such as recreational snowboarding and Big Brothers/Big Sisters organizations as redeeming the human spirit. Along similar lines, other Multistream portfolio matrices could be developed to rate organizations based on how well they provide a safety net for people who are facing temporary distress or other disadvantages, how well they promote a more just distribution of benefits or burdens, or how well they defend human rights when those rights are threatened.[50]

Step 4: Implement the Strategy

From a Multistream perspective, the most important work of strategic management is not using analytical tools to formulate a strategy, but rather engaging in the strategic *learning* that occurs while implementing strategy. The key to strategic management is learning from other stakeholders and identifying the emerging patterns in the "stream of actions" that make up organizational life. This approach places much more emphasis on the "art" or "craft" of management, rather than on the "analytical science" of management.[51]

If a strategy is not working as intended, then it is important to reconsider the information and assumptions underlying the SWOT analysis. This revisiting of the analysis may prove difficult if it involves challenging assumptions and worldviews in an industry. For example, when the idea of leasing floor covering was first considered, it seemed very strange because this notion went against the way people normally thought about carpeting. Now, however, it is becoming more common. Managers would do well to uncover the problems embedded in taken-for-granted assumptions. This contrasts with a top-down approach, which is more likely to avoid reexamining assumptions and instead focus on redoubling efforts and pressure to implement the plan.

A second key element of the Multistream approach is its focus on emergent strategies. Sometimes these strategies are very visible and hard to miss. Often, however, emergent strategies are difficult to see simply because they are not expected. For example, Ricardo Semler describes how an emergent strategy led to the creation of Semco's fast-growing division that provides consulting for environmental sustainability. The ball was started rolling when a customer wanted to purchase pumps from Semco, and Semco's engineers discovered an environmentally friendlier solution to the customer's needs that did not require the pumps. Semco lost a sale, but gained what has become an important business opportunity in environmental consulting.

In a Multistream approach, strategies are more likely to emerge and be based on consultation with members and other stakeholders. Indeed, as illustrated by Honda's "You meet the nicest people on a Honda" slogan, often the strategy will be formulated by frontline members of the organization and then subsequently be "blessed" by top managers. After all, workers farther down the hierarchy have a more direct knowledge about the issues at hand.

From a Multistream perspective, strategic management is not like a "brain" that performs rational scientific analysis and then *tells* the rest of the members in the organizational body what to do. Instead, strategic management is more like a brain that is the focal point of the central nervous system and that *listens to and learns from* the unexpected signals it receives from its members. Thus strategic managers are not "smarter" than other members of the organization. Rather, thanks to their unique position overseeing the whole organization, strategic managers have access to a unique bundle of information that they must use responsibly.[52]

CLOSING CASE

The Strategy of Microsoft Versus Linux[53]

Microsoft has long been the leading organization in its industry, but the open-source Linux computer operating system may pose a considerable threat to Microsoft's position. The Multistream strategy advocated by proponents of Linux is radically different from the Mainstream strategy used by Microsoft. At stake is the dominance of Microsoft's most valuable organizational resource—namely, its operating system.

Microsoft's operating systems have been the industry standard for decades. Recognizing the valuable financial opportunity that comes from having this resource, Microsoft uses its patent rights and proprietary knowledge to "lock in" users to its products. Proprietary knowledge of software such as the Windows operating system is licensed—not sold—and severe restrictions are placed on copying and modification of the software. By virtue of

its control of the operating system that runs on so many computers, Microsoft can in turn exert control over other software manufacturers. For example, the operating system determines which word processing software can be used on a computer. As an indicator of its acquisitive economics success, Microsoft has 57,000 employees and is said to have created about 10,000 millionaires through employment stock options.[54]

The Linux strategy is very different. Linus Torvalds wrote the original Linux operating system "kernel" in 1991, when he was 21 years old. Rather than follow Microsoft's strategic approach, Torvalds opted for an "open-source model" invented by Richard Stallman, an MIT scientist who was not impressed with corporate maneuvering to maximize profits. Basically, the open-source approach permits anyone who wants it to copy Torvalds's code, and it invites others to modify and improve the code as long as they in turn are completely transparent about any changes they have added and make those changes freely available to the public.[55] This General Public License (GPL) approach is designed to encourage collaboration and to restrict the emergence of monopoly. It values knowledge sharing and wide engagement, and it seeks to protect the interests of the public and consumers.[56] Compared to proprietary approaches, the open-source model has little need for management hierarchy, patenting, branding, and so on. Worldwide, the Linux workforce is about 10,000 people, with about 10 percent working at Red Hat Software, the leading commercial vendor of Linux. Customers are willing to pay Red Hat Software for the Linux operating system because the organization provides 24/7 telephone support, guarantees service for seven years, certifies applications, and provides and tests device drivers.

Linux has benefited from two external factors. First, the Internet makes it easy for electronic software distribution and allows for decentralized collaboration among many programmers working independently. Second, there is growing frustration with proprietary software vendors, especially Microsoft and Sun Microsystems. Several years ago, IBM began to contribute money and programmers to open-source software development, and it joined Intel and Dell in investing in Red Hat Software. Today Linux is becoming increasingly popular on desktop computers (estimated to be installed on about 6 percent of machines in 2008, and growing at a rate of nearly 25 percent per year). Linux runs on Web servers, routers, cell phones, and IBM mainframes. Linux-run computers can be purchased from many computer retailers, including Wal-Mart.

Despite its growth into a major force in the software industry, the Linux movement still prides itself on following an emergent strategy. For example, when asked about his long-term vision for Linux, Torvalds replied that he was an "anti-visionary," suggesting that when people look too far into the future they miss and stumble on what is in front of them. Linux's strengths and opportunities exist because the operating system is smaller than Windows, runs on many more devices, can run on inexpensive hardware, and is an attractive option for "students, poor people, educational institutions, and the majority of the developing world."[57]

This latter point may prove particularly important in the future. Bill Gates sees China, with its 1.2 billion people, as eventually becoming the second or third largest PC market in the world. Proprietary software products such as Microsoft Windows have prices that are affordable only in high-income countries. In China, the cost of a copy of Linux is about 5 percent of the cost of Microsoft's operating system. Moreover, heavyweight companies such as Hewlett-Packard are promoting open-source software in China. Open-source software is also poised to make great inroads in India, which has similar needs for low-cost software and is the world's second most populous country.

QUESTIONS FOR DISCUSSION

1. Go through each of the four steps of the strategic management process, and contrast and compare the strategies at Microsoft and Linux.

2. If you were a manager at Microsoft, would you identify Linux as a threat in the external environment? What might Microsoft do to minimize this threat?

3. Which strategic approach do you think will be most viable in the future?

SUMMARY

Strategic management is a four-step process that describes the analysis and decisions that are involved in the formulation and implementation of strategy. A Mainstream approach to strategic management tends to be top-down, emphasize the content of strategy, and be designed to achieve acquisitive economic goals. A Multistream approach is more bottom-up, emphasizes the process of strategy making, and is designed to achieve sustenance economic goals.

For Mainstream strategic management, the four steps proceed as follows:

1. Review the organization's overarching mission and vision.

- The underlying goal is to maximize competitiveness and owner wealth.

2. Analyze strengths, weaknesses, opportunities, and threats (SWOT).

- Minimize supplier power, buyer power, threat of substitutes, threat of entrants, and intensity of rivalry.
- Identify internal resources that are valuable, rare, inimitable, and nonsubstitutable.

3. Formulate a strategy.

- Choose one of two basic generic types of strategies: (a) a cost leader strategy, which focuses on reducing costs, or (b) a differentiation strategy, which focuses on innovative products or services for which customers are willing to pay extra.
- Choose industries that are growing and where the organization has a large market share.

4. Implement the strategy.

- Preferred mode: Pursue a top-down approach (content school)—explain the intended strategy to other members, and expect them to comply and put it into practice.
- Secondary mode: If necessary, resort to a bottom-up approach (process school)—observe what is actually working, and tell people to do more of it.

For Multistream strategic management, the four steps proceed as follows:

1. Review the organization's overarching mission and vision.

- The underlying goal is to serve the well-being of many different stakeholders.

2. Analyze strengths, weaknesses, opportunities, and threats (SWOT).

- Seek to use previously wasted resources, serve community needs, develop interrelationships across organizations and industries, and establish mutually beneficial interdependence with stakeholders.
- Identify internal resources that are valuable, rare, inimitable, and nonsubstitutable.

3. Formulate a strategy.

- Choose between two basic generic strategies: (a) a minimizer strategy, which seeks to limit the organization's negative impact on the environment, or (b) a transformer strategy, which seeks to maximize the organization's positive impact on the environment.
- Enter industries where the organization is minimizing or solving problems.

4. Implement the strategy.

- Preferred mode: Use a bottom-up approach (process school)—observe what is actually working, and encourage people to do more of it.
- Secondary mode: When necessary, use a top-down approach (content school)—explain the intended strategy to other members, and expect them to comply and put it into practice.

QUESTIONS FOR REFLECTION AND DISCUSSION

1. Describe the four steps of the strategic management process. Which one of the four steps is the most important? Defend your answer.

2. Do you think that strategic management plays a more central role in Mainstream management or in Multistream management? Which approach is more difficult to put into practice? Explain your answers.

3. Which approach to strategic management is most likely to maximize long-term financial return? Which is most likely to enhance overall social well-being? Which is most likely to be put into practice? Explain your answers.

4. Develop a portfolio matrix that has two dimensions that you personally feel are important. Try to find examples of organizations in each quadrant.

5. Briefly describe the differences between the content and process school analyses of how Honda motorcycles became number one in the U.S. market. The process school description, which is based on interviews with the managers involved, may be the more accurate portrayal of what *actually* happened.

But is the content school description more valuable for teaching purposes? Put differently, if Honda had completed a SWOT analysis and had chosen the correct strategy *prior* to entering the United States (as consistent with the content school approach), then it could have saved a lot of time and money and avoided floundering around after it arrived. However, perhaps doing the rational analysis up front would not have resulted in the successful strategy the company eventually developed; perhaps the real key to Honda's success was that its managers engaged in strategic learning during times of floundering. Which approach should be taught in business schools? Defend your answer.

6. Why was Honda successful? Should Honda's approach be copied?

7. Now that you have read the chapter, use the concepts you have learned to analyze the opening case. How are the four steps of the strategic management evident at Interface? Where would you place Interface along a Mainstream–Multistream continuum? Explain your answer.

HANDS-ON ACTIVITIES

Where Are You Along the Mainstream–Multistream Continuum?

Circle the number that best corresponds to your views.

TO BE AN EFFECTIVE MANAGER, I SHOULD . . .	Strongly Disagree	Disagree	Neutral	Agree	Strongly Agree
Focus organizational strategies on maximizing owner/shareholder wealth	1	2	3	4	5
Implement a top-down organizational strategy	1	2	3	4	5
Implement a strategy to achieve a competitive advantage over competitors	1	2	3	4	5
Implement a strategy focused on profit maximization, because all stakeholders benefit from this strategy	1	2	3	4	5

E N D N O T E S

1. Dean, C. (2007, May 22). Executive on a mission: Saving the planet. *New York Times*. Accessed February 22, 2008, at http://www.nytimes.com/2007/05/22/science/earth/22ander.html?_r=1&scp=1&sq=&st=nyt&oref=slogin; Anderson, R. C. (1998). *Mid-course correction: Toward a sustainable enterprise: The Interface model*. Atlanta, GA: Peregrinzilla Press; company website: http://www.interfaceinc.com; Nature and the industrial enterprise: Mid-course correction. (2004, Spring). *Engineering Enterprise*, 6–12; and Hawken, P., Lovins A., & Lovins, L. H. (1999). *Natural capitalism: Creating the next Industrial Revolution*. Boston: Little, Brown.

2. Page 51 in Anderson, R. C. (1998). *Mid-course correction: Toward a sustainable enterprise: The Interface model*. Atlanta, GA: Peregrinzilla Press.

3. Anderson, 1998, p. 38.

4. Dean, C. (2007, May 22). Executive on a mission: Saving the planet. *New York Times*. Accessed February 22, 2008, at http://www.nytimes.com/2007/05/22/science/earth/22ander.html?_r=1&scp=1&sq=&st=nyt&oref=slogin.

5. Anderson, 1998, p. 40.

6. Interface's mission statement spells out some of the day-to-day details in how to achieve this vision: "Interface will become the first name in commercial and institutional interiors worldwide through its commitment to people, process, product, place, and profits. We will strive to create an organization wherein all people are accorded unconditional respect and dignity; one that allows each person to continuously learn and develop. We will focus on product (which includes service) through constant emphasis on process quality and engineering, which we will combine with careful attention to our customers' needs so as always to deliver superior value to our customers, thereby maximizing all stakeholders' satisfaction. We will honor the places where we do business by endeavoring to become the first name in industrial ecology, a corporation that cherishes nature and restores the environment. Interface will lead by example and validate by results, including profits, leaving the world a better place than when we began, and we will be restorative through the power of our influence in the world."

7. Anderson, 1998, p. 71.

8. Anderson, 1998, p. 73.

9. Of course, such growth is difficult to sustain. Like all organizations, Interface has had its ups and downs since then.

10. Robbins, S. P., & Coulter, M. (2003). *Management* (7th ed., p. 198). Upper Saddle River, NJ: Prentice-Hall.

11. Sun, T. (1963). *The art of war* (S. B. Griffith, Trans.). Oxford, UK: Oxford University Press.

12. Porter, M. E. (1980). *Competitive strategy: Techniques for analyzing industries and competitors*. New York: Free Press; and Porter, M. E. (1985). *Competitive advantage: Creating and sustaining superior performance*. New York: Free Press.

13. See Zakaria, F. (2005, May 1). Book review: *The World Is Flat: The wealth of yet more nations*. *New York Times*. Accessed February 22, 2008, at http://www.nytimes.com/2005/05/01/books/review/01ZAKARIA.html?scp=1&sq=&st=nyt; Gerth, A. B., & Rothman, S. (2007). The future IS organization in a flat world. *Information Systems Management*, 24(2), 103–111; and Friedman, T. L. (2005). *The world is flat: A brief history of the twenty-first century*. New York: Farrar, Strauss & Giroux.

14. See Barney, 1991, p. 106. The definition of resources from a resource-based view is simultaneously very broad and yet narrowly related to the idea of acquisitive economics: Resources include "all assets, capabilities, organizational processes, firm attributes, information, knowledge, etc. controlled by a firm that enable the firm to conceive of and implement strategies that improve its efficiency and effectiveness" (Barney, 1991, p. 101).

15. We have decided to use the term "infrastructural" resources to refer to Barney's (1991) third category, which he calls "organizational resources"; we found it awkward to talk about an organization's organizational resources.

16. Gulli, C. (2006, April 10). Junior gyms: How do you get kids to exercise? Give them some laughs. *Maclean's*, p. 41.

17. See Ackman, D. (2003, May 28). *Moneyball: The art of winning an unfair game*. Forbes.com. Accessed June 1, 2007, at http://www.forbes.com/2003/05/28/cx_da_0528bookreview.html; and Lewis, M. (2003). *Moneyball*. New York: W. W. Norton.

18. Barney, J. (1991). Firm resources and sustained competitive advantage. *Journal of Management*, 17, 99–119; Wernerfelt, B. (1984). A resource based view of the firm. *Strategic Management Journal*, 5, 171–180; and Dierickx, I., & Cool, K. (1989). Asset stock accumulation and sustainability of competitive advantage. *Management Science*, 35(12), 1504–1511.

19. Smith, C., & Child, J. (1990). *Reshaping work: The Cadbury experience*. New York: Cambridge University Press.

20. Levitas, E., & Ndofor, H. A. (2006). What to do with the resource-based view: A few suggestions for what ails the RBV that supporters and opponents might accept. *Journal of Management Inquiry*, 15(2), 135–144.

21. Porter, 1980, 1985.

22. Schermerhorn, J. R. (2000). *Management* (7th ed., p. 216). New York: John Wiley & Sons.

23. Based on in-class presentation by Charles Loewen, March 8, 2007, I. H. Asper School of Business, University of Manitoba, Winnipeg, Manitoba, Canada.

24. Accessed September 26, 2007, at http://www.patekphilippe.com/patek-philippe.html.

25. Although Michael Porter himself argues against simultaneously pursuing both low-cost and differentiation strategies because it is a recipe for getting stuck in the middle, others have argued that an integrated low-cost/differentiation strategy may well work [e.g., Murray, A. I. (1988). A contingency view of Porter's "generic strategies." *Academy of Management Review*, 13(3), 390–400]. Indeed, even one of the examples Porter himself uses as a low-cost exemplar (Ivory soap) could be argued to have a differentiation strategy (99 44/100 percent pure).

26. Fan, Y. (2006). The globalisation of Chinese brands. *Marketing Intelligence & Planning*, 24(4), 365–379.

27. Henderson, B. D. (1979). *Henderson on corporate strategy*. Cambridge, MA: Abt Books. Cited in Hambrick, D. C., MacMillan, I. C., & Day, D. L. (1982). Strategic attributes and performance in the BCG matrix: A PIMS-based analysis of industrial product businesses. *Academy of Management Journal*, 25(3), 510–531.

28. Anderson, C. R., & Zeithaml, C. P. (1984). Stage of the product life cycle, business strategy, and business performance. *Academy of Management Journal*, 27(1), 5–24.

29. Daft, R. L. (2003). *Management* (6th ed.). Mason, OH: Thomson South-Western.

30. Armstrong, J. S. (1996). Management folklore and management science: On portfolio planning, escalation bias, and such. *Interfaces, 26,* 25–55.

31. Dyck, B. (1997). Understanding configuration and transformation through a multiple rationalities approach. *Journal of Management Studies, 34,* 793–823.

32. Adapted from Pascale, R. T. (1984). Perspectives on strategy: The real story behind Honda's success. *California Management Review, 26,* 47–72. A series of articles characterizing the debate between the process school and the design school was published in *California Management Review,* under the title "The 'Honda Effect' Revisited": Mintzberg, H. (1996). Introduction. *California Management Review, 38*(4), 78–79; Mintzberg, H. (1996). Learning 1, planning 0. *California Management Review, 38*(4), 92–93; Goold, M. (1996). Design, learning and planning: A further observation on the design school debate. *California Management Review, 38*(4), 94–95; Mintzberg, H. (1996). Reply to Michael Goold. *California Management Review, 38*(4), 96–99; Goold, M. (1996). Learning, planning, and strategy: Extra time. *California Management Review, 38*(4), 100–102; Rumelt, R. P. (1996). The many faces of Honda. *California Management Review, 38*(4), 103–111; and Pascale, R. T. (1996). Reflection on Honda. *California Management Review, 38*(4), 112–117.

33. There are more than these two schools of thought within the strategy literature—Henry Mintzberg provides an analysis of ten different types. We have chosen to focus on the content and process schools because (1) to look at more schools added more complexity than we thought was appropriate for an introductory chapter on strategy and (2) these two schools are perhaps the most well-known approaches and can be seen as opposite ends of the same continuum. For an overview, see Mintzberg, H., & Lampel, J. (1999, Spring). Reflecting on the strategy process. *Sloan Management Review,* 21–30.

34. Pascale, 1984.

35. Bakke, D. W. (2005). *Joy at work: A revolutionary approach to fun on the job* (pp. 31, 162). Seattle, WA: PVG.

36. Chewning, R. C., Eby, J. W., & Roels, S. J. (1990). *Business Through the Eyes of Faith.* San Francisco: Harper (in conjunction with Christian College Coalition),

37. The ecological environment receives little coverage in most management textbooks.

38. Some of these sorts of issues are explored in greater depth in Chapter 4.

39. This example is taken from Hawken, 1993; Hawken, P. (1993). *The Ecology of Commerce: A Declaration of Sustainability,* New York: HarperBusiness; see especially pages 62–63.

40. Uzzi, B. (1997). Social structure and competition in interfirm networks. *Administrative Science Quarterly, 42*(1), 35–68.

41. Such a radio was invented by Trevor Baylis, who heard of the need for something like it in Africa and had it assembled in South Africa by people with disabilities (information found June 5, 2007, at http://www.windupradio.com/trevor.htm). For more information on this and similar new technologies, such as the radio highlighted in the photo or a portable energy source for use in low-income countries, go to www.freeplayfoundation.org.

42. Ray C. Anderson attributes this observation to David Brower, former Executive Director of the Sierra Club, who quotes his son Ken Brower.

43. Riviere, P. (2003, December). A historic agreement: At last, generic anti-AIDS medicine for sub-Saharan Africa. *Le Monde Diplomatique.* Accessed November 14, 2007, at http://mondediplo.com/2003/12/19aids.

44. For an example of a living wage study, see the following source: *Living wage study for Brevard County.* (2005, June). Accessed May 31, 2007, at http://www.bwdb.org/Download Documents/Misc20%Documents/BWDB%20Living%20Wage%20Study.doc.

45. For a list of such organizations, see http://www.ciwmb.ca.gov/Tires/Products/ (accessed October 31, 2006).

46. Jewell, M. (2007). Staples starts computer recycle program. Associated Press, *Physorg.com.* Accessed June 4, 2007, at http://www.physorg.com/news98937884.html.

47. Kirbyson, G. (2005, August 15). City firm makes treasure from trash. *Winnipeg Free Press,* p. B3.

48. As discussed in Chapter 3, it would be better yet if there was less waste to put into blue boxes in the first place.

49. Bailey, J. (2006, September 21). Flying where big airlines aren't. *New York Times.* Accessed February 22, 2008, at http://travel.nytimes.com/2006/09/21/business/21air.html?scp=1&sq=&st=nyt.

50. These examples build on ideas by Dees, J. G. (1994). Social enterprise: Private initiatives for the common good. *Harvard Business School Teaching Note* 9-395-116.

51. Mintzberg, H. (1987, July–August). Crafting strategy. *Harvard Business Review,* 66–75.

52. This is the kind of "brain" described by Durkheim, É. (1958). *Professional ethics and civic morals* (C. Brookfield, Trans.). Glencoe, IL: Free Press. Extending this metaphor even further, a Mainstream approach is akin to the brain deciding that the body should run a marathon and then being surprised when the body is unable to do so. A Multistream approach is more sensitive to the needs and capacity of the body, and seeks to develop them appropriately, before running any marathon.

53. Ferguson, C. (2005). How Linux could overthrow Microsoft. *Technology Review, 108*(6), 64–69; Shen, X. (2005). Developing country perspectives on software: Intellectual property and open source—a case study of Microsoft and Linux in China. *International Journal of IT Standards and Standardization Research, 3*(1), 21–43; and Economides, N., & Katsamakas, E. (2006). Two-sided competition of proprietary vs. open source technology platforms and the implications for the software industry. *Management Science, 52*(7), 1057–1062. The last article suggests that the Linux approach maximizes social welfare, whereas the Microsoft approach maximizes total industry profit.

54. Page 68 in Ferguson, C. (2005). How Linux could overthrow Microsoft. *Technology Review, 108*(6/June), 64–69.

55. Another open-source software product, OpenOffice, competes with Microsoft Office.

56. Page 27 in Shen, X. (2005). Developing country perspectives on software: Intellectual property and open source—a case study of Microsoft and Linux in China. *International Journal of IT Standards and Standardization Research, 3*(1), 21–43.

57. Ferguson, 2005, p. 67.

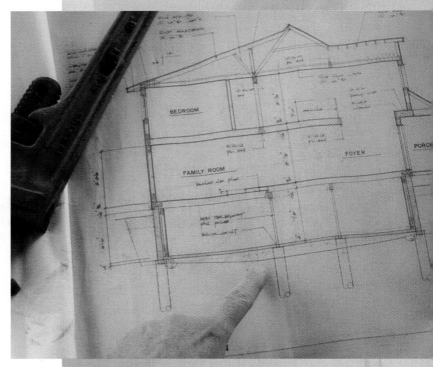

In the previous three chapters, we looked at the planning function, including making decisions (Chapter 7), setting goals and making plans (Chapter 8), and designing strategies (Chapter 9). In the next four chapters, we will explore the organizing function, which describes how resources should be arranged to make the plans work as intended. In this chapter, we first describe the four Mainstream fundamentals of organizing, and then contrast and compare them with the four Multistream fundamentals of organizing. Chapter 11 examines organization design, with an emphasis on how the four different fundamentals of organizing fit together with other factors (environment, strategy, and technology) to form different organizational types. The organizing function in human resources management is so important that we devote an entire chapter to it (Chapter 12). The final chapter in this organizing section (Chapter 13) deals with managing the process of organizational change, an ongoing theme in this book.

ROAD MAP

FOUR FUNDAMENTAL ISSUES IN ORGANIZING

1. **How to ensure that work activities are being completed in the best way**

2. **How to ensure that members' subtasks contribute to the whole**

3. **How to ensure orderly deference**

4. **How to ensure that members work together harmoniously**

Fundamentals of Organizing

MAINSTREAM APPROACH ⟷	MULTISTREAM APPROACH
Standardization Specify desired behaviors	**Experimentation** Encourage constant improvement
Specialization Provide job descriptions	**Sensitization** Seek and respond to needs and opportunities
Centralization Create authority structures	**Dignification** Respect everyone
Departmentalization Create formal job groupings	**Participation** Encourage mutuality

The Fundamentals of Organizing at Semco[1]

When 21-year-old Ricardo Semler took over his father's company, Semco, the firm employed about 100 people and generated $4 million in annual revenues. Semco produced marine pumps for Brazil's shipping industry. The company was managed in a traditional manner. Specifically, it had well-developed operating standards, formal rules, and detailed job descriptions that indicated the training and experience required for each position. It also had a fairly centralized authority structure and an established departmental structure. In short, Semco's structures and systems were developed enough for the father to hand over the reins of power to his 21-year-old son.

Ricardo Semler, however, was not fond of the way things were organized at Semco. He had previously worked for a summer in Semco's purchasing department, and asked himself: "How can I spend the rest of my life doing this? How can I stomach years of babysitting people to make sure they clock in on time? Why is this worth doing?" So, when he took the reins at Semco, Semler threw out all of those books of rules and regulations that had been the result of years of standardization and formalization.

Although Semco has since grown to employ more than 3000 employees and generate $200 million in annual revenues, its employee manual has been reduced to 20 pages, complete with cartoons. The company doesn't even have a written mission statement, preferring instead to foster *experimentation*. Workers seldom take minutes at meetings in Semco, because once things get written down, they can constrain future experimentation. Semler wants the standards that guide activity at Semco to be fluid and constantly (re)constructed by its members.

Specialization is also downplayed at Semco: There are no job descriptions. It even has a "Lost in Space" program that assumes young recruits often don't know what they want to do with their lives. The program allows them to roam through the company for a year, doing what they want to do, moving to a different unit

Ricardo Semler, chosen "Business Leader of the Year" on several occasions.

whenever they want to. Semler himself spends little time at work (he doesn't even have his own office), preferring instead to expose himself to a wide variety of inputs and stimuli. This approach creates opportunities for everyone to be *sensitized* to needs and opportunities that might otherwise be overlooked.

Semler is also not too keen on the centralization of authority. Even though Semco has diversified and grown, it still has only three levels of hierarchy. Semler himself is one of six "Counselors" (top management), who take turns leading the company for six months at a time. Workers at Semco choose their own work hours, set their own salaries, and decide who will be their managers. Managers trust workers and treat them with *dignity*. As Semler notes, "Most of our programs are based on the notion of giving employees control over their own lives. In a word, we hire adults, and then we treat them like adults."[2]

Finally, regarding departmentalization, Semler dismantled Semco's large departments. He prefers smaller, more autonomous units with 150 or fewer members, where each person knows that his or her *participation* truly matters. The heavy emphasis on participation is consistent with Semler's commitment to democracy, a watchword at Semco.

Ricardo Semler revels in the fact that he is not a Mainstream manager, and he wants to keep it that way. Even though Semco has enjoyed an outstanding growth rate, Semler is very clear that growth and profits are not his primary goals. He says, "I can honestly say that our growth, profit, and the number of people we employ are secondary concerns. Outsiders clamor to know these things because they want to quantify our business. These are the yardsticks they turn to first. That's one reason we're still privately held. I don't want Semco to be burdened with the ninety-day mindset of most stock market analysts. It would undermine our solidity and force us to dance to the tune we don't really want to hear—a Wall Street waltz that starts each day with an opening bell and ends with the thump of the closing gavel."[3]

Semler goes on to say, "Profit beyond the minimum is not essential for survival. In any event, an organization doesn't really need profit beyond what is vital for working capital and the small growth that is essential for keeping up with the customers and competition. Excess profit only creates another imbalance. To be sure, it enables the owner or CEO to commission a yacht. But then employees will wonder why they should work so the owner can buy a boat."[4]

Semler is enjoying his opportunity to demonstrate that organizations can thrive when you treat people with dignity, foster trust and participation, value experimentation and learning, and remain sensitive to the larger needs and opportunities around you. For him, these are the genuine fundamentals of organizing. His approach seems to have attracted admiration among his peers, because a poll of 52,000 Brazilian executives has chosen him as "Business Leader of the Year" on several occasions.

INTRODUCTION TO ORGANIZING

As we learned in Chapter 1, the management function of organizing refers to ensuring that tasks have been assigned and a structure of relationships created that facilitates meeting organizational goals. Although humankind has a long history of organizing, modern-day organizations as we know them really came into existence only during the last few hundred years. Many of the basic ideas of organizational structure that we take for granted today were management innovations developed by people such as Josiah Wedgwood (see the opening case in Chapter 2). We live in a time when ideas such as division of labor are taken for granted, and we no longer marvel at the productivity and wealth that they help to create.

When we take Mainstream ideas of organizational structure for granted, we forget how they influence us, just as we forget how we are influenced by the physical structures in which we live and work. For example, the floor plan of your home and your office shapes whom you interact with and how you interact with them (Is the setting formal or informal?). Frank Lloyd Wright, the famous architect, reportedly said that he could design a home that would cause newlyweds to get divorced within a few months. Along the same lines, Winston Churchill observed that "we shape our buildings, and hereafter our buildings shape us."[5] Today we take basic features such as indoor plumbing, hallways, and door locks for granted, and it is difficult to imagine what life would be like without them. Similarly, many managers take ideas such as standardization, specialization, and centralization for granted, and they find it difficult to think of organizing without reference to these concepts. Nevertheless, just as issues of ecological sustainability and aesthetic appeal are prompting people to rethink the *physical* structures in which we live and work, so too Multistream managers such as Ricardo Semler can help us to rethink the basic building blocks of *organizational* structure.

According to Max Weber—one of the most influential thinkers in management and organization theory—the essence of organizing involves managing four fundamental issues, which are listed below and highlighted in Figure 10.1:

1. *Ensuring that work activities are completed in the best way.* This involves breaking down the overall work of the organization into individual subtasks and identifying the optimal way to perform each subtask.

2. *Ensuring that each member's subtasks contribute to the whole.* It is important that each member understands which specific organizational subtasks he or she is responsible for performing.

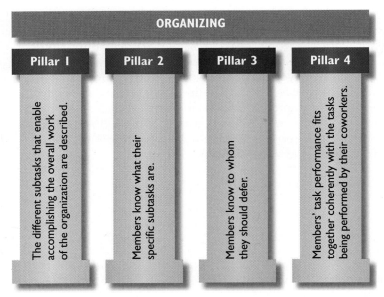

ORGANIZING

| Pillar 1 | Pillar 2 | Pillar 3 | Pillar 4 |

The different subtasks that enable accomplishing the overall work of the organization are described.

Members know what their specific subtasks are.

Members know to whom they should defer.

Members' task performance fits together coherently with the tasks being performed by their coworkers.

Figure 10.1 The four fundamental pillars of organizing

3. *Ensuring that there is orderly deference among organizational members.* This helps members know from whom to take their cues in the everyday operation of the organization.

4. *Ensuring that members work together harmoniously.* Accomplishing the overall work of the organization may be enhanced by specifying whether members work alongside people who have similar jobs or complementary jobs. This coherence among the tasks performed by immediate coworkers determines what sources of mutual help and learning members have easy access to.[6]

These four issues are managed differently by Mainstream and Multistream managers. We will first describe how Mainstream managers deal with these four fundamentals of organizing, and then contrast and compare their approach with the Multistream approach.

THE FOUR MAINSTREAM FUNDAMENTALS OF ORGANIZING

Mainstream managers emphasize four basic elements of organizational structure, each of which corresponds to one of the fundamental elements identified by Weber:

Standardization: The emphasis is on developing uniform practices for organizational members to follow in doing their jobs; this ensures that work activities are being completed in the best way to accomplish the overall work of the organization.

Specialization: The emphasis is on grouping standardized organizational tasks into separate jobs; this ensures that members know which subtasks they should perform.

Centralization: The emphasis is on having decision-making authority rest with managers at the top of an organization's hierarchy; this ensures orderly deference among members.

Departmentalization: The emphasis is on grouping members and resources together to achieve the work of the larger organization; this ensures that members work together harmoniously.

Fundamental 1: Standardization

Standardization is the Mainstream response to Weber's first fundamental of organization. It is a way for managers to design basic work activities so that members perform tasks in the best way to accomplish the overall work of the organization, and don't use suboptimal methods or spend time doing unrelated tasks. By standardizing tasks, Mainstream managers try to ensure that members perform the

Standardization is the development of uniform practices for organizational members to follow in doing their jobs.

Specialization refers to grouping standardized organizational tasks into separate jobs.

Centralization is having the decision-making authority rest with managers at the top of an organization's hierarchy.

Departmentalization refers to grouping organizational members and resources together to achieve the work of the larger organization.

activities that are most appropriate for achieving overarching organizational goals. For example, in order to facilitate the overall goal of providing post-secondary education, most universities offer "standard" timetables that describe how long classes are and at what times of day they start and stop. This makes it easier for students to enroll in courses in more than one academic department. Similarly, the beginning and end of terms are often standardized across schools. Finally, if you complete a Principles of Management course in one university, you can usually transfer the credit to another university, because standardized curricula ensure that the same basic material will be covered in any location.

In the business world, McDonald's hamburgers and french fries provide perhaps the most well-known examples of standardization. McDonald's has invested a lot of resources and developed thick manuals to ensure that the quality and taste of its food remain consistent over time and across locations. For example, when McDonald's opened its first restaurant in Moscow, it discovered that local farmers could not provide the high-quality potatoes needed to meet the company's standards. So, McDonald's flew in experts, imported the appropriate seeds and harvesting machinery, and trained Russian farmers how to grow and harvest the potatoes it needed. The Russians who were hired to manage the Moscow branches were trained in Canada and at "Hamburger University" in Chicago.

McDonald's managers from around the world learn about McDonald's standards at Hamburger University in Chicago.

Usually when we think of standards, we think of formal standards. The more *written* documentation there is, the higher the degree of *formalization*. This relationship is particularly evident in very bureaucratic organizations. Although the tendency is to look at formalized standards, *informal* standards that govern and give meaning to members' behavior are also important. For example, informal standards are evident in the classroom when students arrive on time and stay until the end of class, turn off their cell phones, ask questions by raising their hands, and so on. These standards are not usually formally written into course outlines because they are part of the "culture" or informal expectations of university students and professors. In this way, part of the role of organizational culture is to provide standards for members' behavior. Research suggests that a link exists between formalization and organizational values, showing that an increase in formalization is a barrier to trust (in individualistic countries).[7]

The challenge for Mainstream managers is to design standards that maximize productivity. As depicted in Figure 10.2, placing too little or too much emphasis on standards can cause undesired outcomes. With an optimal level of standardization, members know which tasks need to be performed and how to perform them to reach organizational goals. Standards serve as guidelines for decision making, and they provide an overarching framework that give members confidence and ensures coordinated

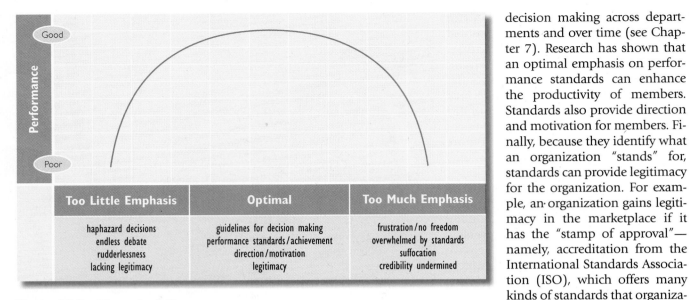

Too Little Emphasis	Optimal	Too Much Emphasis
haphazard decisions endless debate rudderlessness lacking legitimacy	guidelines for decision making performance standards/achievement direction/motivation legitimacy	frustration/no freedom overwhelmed by standards suffocation credibility undermined

Figure 10.2 Characteristics of optimal and suboptimal standardization

Recent WTO regulations have empowered food retailers from high-income countries to introduce agriculture standards that allow them to increase food imports from Africa, thereby helping the private agrifood sector to quickly become more global and oligopolistic, and providing welcome foreign currency and export markets for countries like Kenya and Zimbabwe. Source: Busch, L. and C. Bain (2004). New! Improved? The transformation of the global agrifood system. *Rural Sociology*, 69(3): 321–346.

decision making across departments and over time (see Chapter 7). Research has shown that an optimal emphasis on performance standards can enhance the productivity of members. Standards also provide direction and motivation for members. Finally, because they identify what an organization "stands" for, standards can provide legitimacy for the organization. For example, an organization gains legitimacy in the marketplace if it has the "stamp of approval"—namely, accreditation from the International Standards Association (ISO), which offers many kinds of standards that organizations can adopt, including the popular ISO 9000 series that represents international consensus on quality management practices.

In contrast, having too few standards may result in haphazard decision making, and their absence may lead to endless debate among members about precisely which goals should be pursued, and how tasks should be performed. Members who are unsure of which tasks need to be accomplished, or how to perform them, are more likely to spend less time actually working and more time trying to find out what to do. Inadequate standards may also result in a perception of the organization as rudderless, where managers do not know where the organization is going. This would stifle members' sense of direction and motivation. Finally, too little emphasis on standardization may undermine the legitimacy of an organization and lead to inconsistent quality of the organization's outputs.

At the other extreme, placing too much emphasis on standardization and having too many standards may cause members to become frustrated because they have little opportunity to express their creativity. Members may also feel overwhelmed by the sheer number of standards they must meet. Having too many standards may also leave members feeling suffocated and squelch initiative and organizational learning. Finally, having too many standards may undermine the organization's credibility and legitimacy, especially if the standards are competing or are perceived to be mutually exclusive or unrealistic. For example, a political party that runs on a platform of reducing taxes for everyone, increasing social services for everyone, and keeping a balanced budget may have less legitimacy than a party that chooses only one or two of these standards.

Is the Level of Standardization in Schools Appropriate?

There is an ongoing debate about the role of standards in the U.S. school system. On one side of the debate are people who argue that there is *too little* emphasis on standards. They think that students from different schools should all be required to take the same standardized tests, thereby permitting officials to measure which schools and which teachers do the best job of teaching subjects such as mathematics or science. For them, it is reasonable to use standardized tests to monitor whether graduating students have learned what they are supposed to.

On the other side of the debate are people who argue that we have placed *too much* emphasis on standards, and that this overarching concern gets in the way of managing what actually goes on in the classroom. They point out that the educational sector is rife with standards that focus on providing external legitimacy, such as specific credentials for teachers and legislated course content. Such standards may have little direct effect on day-to-day instruction. Even elite schools are recognized for how well they meet external legitimacy standards, rather than what actually goes on inside a classroom. For example, elite programs have a lower student-to-teacher ratio, the latest computer technology, and excellent facilities for sports and music programs.

Why might standards be beneficial for students, parents, or communities? Are there too many or too few standards in schools? Which kinds of standards are overemphasized, and which kind of standards are underemphasized? Is teaching an art, or can it be formalized?

Fundamental 2: Specialization

The second fundamental of organizing involves ensuring that all organizational members know the specific subtasks they are required to perform. If everyone performed identical tasks, then there would be little value added in having an organization. This is reflected in the concept of division of labor, as famously illustrated by Adam Smith's pin factory, where productivity improved one thousandfold when workers performed specialized tasks rather than working independently and doing all the tasks (see Chapter 2). The challenge for managers is to ensure that the activities performed by each member are designed to enhance the productivity of the whole group.

Specialization entails taking standardized organizational tasks and allocating them into separate jobs. Job specialization can be "narrow" (which means that the tasks a member performs are fairly limited and focused) or "broad" (which means that the member performs a wide range of tasks). For example, Henry Ford revolutionized productivity in the automobile industry when he pioneered the assembly line, where members work on one subcomponent of building a car, rather than having one worker assemble an entire car.

Typically, the specialized knowledge, skills, abilities and other characteristics required to perform each job are written out in job descriptions, which also may describe the formal qualifications required for jobholders. For example, an accounting firm might require a staff accountant to pass the CPA exam before being promoted to senior accountant. Similarly, universities require qualifications to take courses, such as having a high school diploma and having completed any prerequisites for a course.

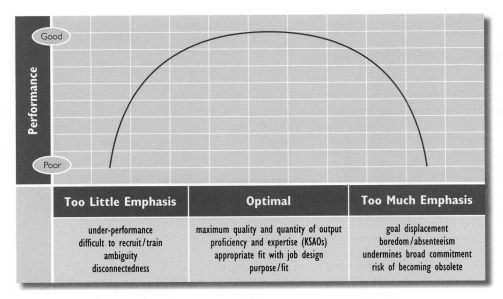

Too Little Emphasis	Optimal	Too Much Emphasis
under-performance difficult to recruit/train ambiguity disconnectedness	maximum quality and quantity of output proficiency and expertise (KSAOs) appropriate fit with job design purpose/fit	goal displacement boredom/absenteeism undermines broad commitment risk of becoming obsolete

Figure 10.3 Characteristics of optimal and suboptimal specialization

Managers must set an optimal level of specialization (see Figure 10.3) because there are disadvantages in having too little or too much specialization. From the Mainstream perspective, optimal levels of specialization are evident when each member's specific tasks are clear and help to maximize productivity. Optimal specialization will ensure that job descriptions identify the knowledge, skills, abilities, and other characteristics (KSAOs) required by members to perform their jobs well. Having clear and well-defined job descriptions makes it easier to recruit, select, and train people for jobs. Finally, specialization at its best provides members with a sense of purpose and understanding of how their work contributes to the overall organization, and it allows members to obtain a high degree of proficiency and expertise in their particular tasks. Such members will take pride in their work and, therefore, will be motivated and enabled to help maximize the productivity of the organization.

Too little specialization means that tasks are not being performed as efficiently as possible, which results in underperformance. This extreme may also create difficulties in recruitment and training members, because it is unclear which sorts of skills members need to perform. In addition, too little specialization may lead to ambiguity in terms of decision making, as no one is quite sure who has the responsibility for and/ or information needed to make different decisions. This lack of focus can destroy members' motivation and leave them feeling unsure of exactly what is expected of them and disconnected from how their work fits into the overall organization.

Conversely, too much specialization can lead to situations where specialized tasks displace the overarching work of the organization. This is a variation of goal displacement.[8] As discussed in Chapter 8, *goal displacement* occurs when people get so focused on specific goals that they lose sight of more important overarching goals. Too much emphasis on specialized tools and skills can also cause a gradual shift in the overall goals of the organization. For example, think about an organization that hires many efficiency specialists: Over time, the goal of the organization will evolve into being the industry leader in efficiency, and less emphasis may be placed on other important goals, such as providing innovative or high-quality services and products. The result may be a watch company offering the least expensive product in the industry, but with low sales because its product is cheap and of poor quality.

Too much specialization can also result in jobs that are very repetitive and boring, which in turn leads to increased turnover and absenteeism. This is illustrated by highly specialized assembly-line jobs, where workers perform the same task hundreds of times each hour or day. To counteract the ill effects of overspecialization, managers at automobile manufacturers such as Volvo became industry leaders in replacing traditional assembly lines with a more cellular or team-based approach, which allows members to perform a greater variety of tasks and to experience the sense of accomplishment that comes from knowing which particular cars their team built.

In addition, too much specialization can cause members of an organization to focus only on completing their narrow tasks without developing any sense of how their work contributes to the larger processes. This will undermine group ownership and commitment. Finally, too much specialization may create a sense of job insecurity among members, because they know that their jobs are vulnerable to obsolescence (especially in this era of rapid technological change and globalization).

WHAT DO YOU THINK?

How Much Emphasis Should Universities Place on Specialization?[9]

There is an ongoing tension regarding how much emphasis should be placed on specialization in universities. On the one hand, some argue that educational programs at universities should become increasingly specialized. In particular, this specialization is thought to increase graduates' abilities to get jobs and make specific contributions to society as a whole. From this perspective, students majoring in, say, accounting should be permitted to take most of their courses in accounting. This will help them to become better accountants and get better jobs.

On the other hand, some argue that universities should live up to their name by exposing students to a wide range of knowledge, as they offer a universe of academic disciplines on one campus.[10] They point out that if management students learn only about Mainstream business, with its emphasis on material and individual well-being, then they will lack a balanced understanding of other forms of well-being (e.g., ecological or aesthetic well-being). Moreover, this lack of exposure to a variety of forms of well-being will make it more difficult to integrate them into their everyday professional lives.[11]

From your perspective as a student, what are the arguments for and against offering more specialized courses in your major versus offering a wider array of general courses? Should university programs of study become increasingly specialized, or should they become more generalist to ensure that graduates gain a well-rounded education? Which level of specialization will serve society better in the long term?

Specialized skills can become obsolete quickly with a change in technology or politics, as was discovered by economists who specialized in analyzing the fortunes of West and East Germany until the Berlin Wall was torn down.

Fundamental 3: Centralization

The third fundamental of organizing draws attention to the need for members to know who has authority over whom and for which issues. From the Mainstream approach, the extent to which decision-making authority resides with top managers in one central location refers to the degree of centralization. **Authority** refers to the formal power given to specific members—usually managers—to arrange resources, assign tasks, and direct the activities of other members so as to achieve organizational goals. Organizational members are expected to defer to the people who have authority over them. Managers can use their authority to reward behavior that is consistent with organizational goals and plans, and punish behavior that is inconsistent.

Authority may be dispersed in organizations, with different members having different rights to make decisions about specific kinds of resources and activities. For example, a marketing manager has authority to make decisions within the

Authority is the formal power given to managers to arrange resources and to assign tasks and direct the activities of other members in ways that help to achieve organizational goals.

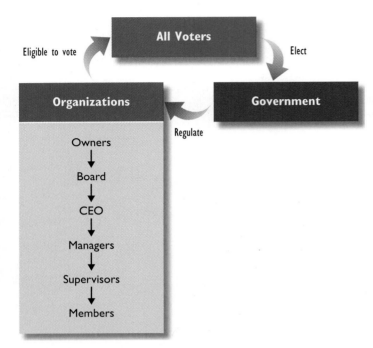

Figure 10.4 How authority is delegated

Line authority refers to the formal power that a member is given to manage and make decisions about other people and resources lower down the chain of command.

Staff authority refers to the formal power a member is given to provide advice and offer specific technical expertise to other members.

Delegation is the process of giving authority to a person or group to make decisions in a specified sphere of activity.

Span of control is the number of members a given manager has authority over.

Responsibility is the obligation or duty of members to perform assigned tasks.

marketing department, but lacks authority in the finance department. It is also helpful to distinguish between managers' line authority and staff authority. Managers with **line authority** have formal power to direct and control their immediate subordinates, whereas managers with **staff authority** have formal power to advise and provide technical support for others, but not to tell them what to do. For example, a human resources manager has line authority over other members in her department, and has staff authority to provide her expert advice to managers of other departments. Staff managers provide advice, and line managers make decisions.

So where does the authority of managers come from? As shown in Figure 10.4, in the end managers' authority derives from everyday people in society. The authority of managers is given by the chief executive officer (CEO), whose authority to manage the whole organization comes from board members, who in turn get their authority from the owners of the organization, who in turn get their authority to own the organization from the government, which has been given its authority by the electorate (in a democracy).

Delegation refers to the process of giving authority to a person or group to make decisions in a specified sphere of activity. The more authority managers delegate to others, the more decentralized an organization is said to be, and vice versa. In a centralized organization, the authority to make decisions tends to rest with managers at the top of an organization's hierarchy. In contrast, the authority to make decisions is dispersed more widely throughout a decentralized organization. Note that an overall organization may be very centralized (e.g., authority for most decisions is retained in the CEO's office), while any particular subunit within that organization may be relatively decentralized (e.g., what little decision-making authority resides in the finance department is dispersed widely throughout that department). Of course, the reverse is also true: A relatively decentralized organization may have centralized departments if the department head insists on making all the major and minor decisions for the department. Finally, the organization and its subunits can both be centralized, or both can be decentralized.

It is helpful to think of centralization in terms of a continuum, with high levels of centralization at one end and low levels (i.e., decentralization) at the other end. All organizational units find themselves somewhere along this continuum. In recent years, there has been a trend toward greater delegation and decentralization by adopting wider spans of control. **Span of control** refers to the number of members over whom a given manager has authority. Managers with wide spans have many subordinates reporting to them, whereas managers with narrow spans have few subordinates reporting to them. A wide span reduces the number of hierarchical layers in an organization, such that the organization is said to have a "flat" or "short" structure.

When members accept authority to make decisions in a certain domain of organizational operations, they also accept responsibility for the decisions that they make (or fail to make) and accept accountability for their actions. **Responsibility** refers to the obligation or duty of members to perform assigned tasks. Problems arise when someone is given responsibility without also being given the authority needed to meet that responsibility. For example, suppose a new marketing manager has the responsibility of increasing sales by 10 percent. That manager will be very frustrated if she is not also given the authority to do the things that are necessary to reach the goal (e.g., to hire competent salespeople and retrain or remove incompetent salespeople).

Of course, not all the decisions that a member makes will have the desired outcome. **Accountability** refers to expectation that a member is able to provide compelling reasons for the decisions that he or she makes. If a member is unable to explain those actions, then he or she may be given professional training and development, have authority taken away, or be removed from his or her current position.

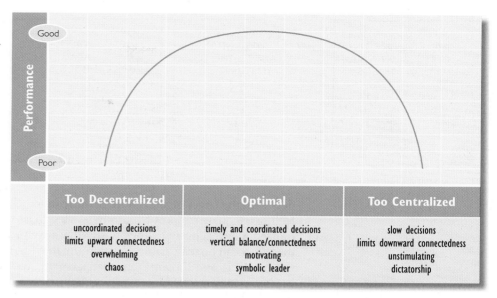

Too Decentralized	Optimal	Too Centralized
uncoordinated decisions limits upward connectedness overwhelming chaos	timely and coordinated decisions vertical balance/connectedness motivating symbolic leader	slow decisions limits downward connectedness unstimulating dictatorship

Figure 10.5   Characteristics of optimal and suboptimal centralization

As shown in Figure 10.5, optimal centralization is characterized by timely and coordinated decision making. An optimal level of centralization frees up enough time for top management to develop overarching plans and strategies, and it allows lower-level managers and frontline workers to handle the routine, everyday matters. Optimal centralization is evident when there is a proper balance between providing appropriate levels and types of authority to lower-level members (who have firsthand frontline knowledge and can make timely decisions) and upper-level managers (who have more access to systemic knowledge and can facilitate coordinated decisions). Providing an appropriate balance of responsibilities and authority helps to motivate members of the organization and enhances their personal and professional development. It also facilitates interpersonal working relationships among members at various levels, and fosters a sense of shared belonging to a larger team where each member—from the leader on down—is seen as having something valuable to contribute.

Finally, the optimal level of centralization will ensure that an organization has meaningful "symbolic leaders." Research suggests that we have been socialized to have high expectations of our leaders: We give too much credit to leaders when things go well, and we are too eager to blame leaders when things go badly.[12] Some scholars have suggested that the most important thing that leaders do is to provide "symbolic leadership." Leaders do very little of the actual work of the organization (i.e., the CEO of Ford does not build cars, the director of a library does not place books in the stacks), but they play important symbolic roles.[13] For example, when the St. Paul, Minnesota, public school system announced that Dr. Patricia Harvey, a national expert on urban education, had been hired as its new superintendent, the division was excited and provided celebrity treatment for Harvey. People voiced great hope in her ability to single-handedly transform a chaotic and complex system. Although Harvey was hired for her skills, there was also widespread recognition that she needed to fulfill the role of symbolic leader required by the organization.[14]

Too much decentralization is evident when each member of the organization has the right to make decisions on the spot, but members lack the larger perspective

Accountability is the expectation that members of an organization, if called upon, will be able to provide compelling reasons for the decisions that they make.

DILBERT: © Scott Adams/Dist. by United Feature Syndicate, Inc.

needed to ensure that their decisions are coordinated as a whole. For example, customers will be disappointed when a quick delivery is promised by a salesperson who is unaware that the supply of that product is limited because of similar promises being made by other salespeople. Too much decentralization also erodes a sense of belonging and connectedness with the larger organization, because members are left struggling to cope without feeling adequate support from others. Members of organizations that are too decentralized may feel overwhelmed when they are given more authority and responsibility than they can be reasonably held accountable for. Overdelegation will be perceived as irresponsible and incompetent management. Too much decentralization may result in chaos, characterized by a lack of identifiable symbolic leaders to rally around and to hold the organization together.

Conversely, organizations that are too centralized will be plagued by slow decision making, because decisions have to work their way up and down the hierarchy. Similarly, not giving members enough responsibility and authority will erode their sense of belonging, their connectedness with the larger organization, and their commitment. Finally, organizations that are too centralized may become dictatorships from which members will try to exit as quickly as they are able.

Fundamental 4: Departmentalization

After identifying all the tasks needed to meet organizational goals (standardization), assigning different tasks to each member (specialization), and determining who has the authority to arrange resources and assign tasks (centralization), we come to the final fundamental of organizing, which looks at how members work together. This fundamental focuses on ensuring that all the tasks performed by organizational members fit together harmoniously and contribute to a larger whole. As organizations grow in size, this will mean deciding where and with whom members perform their tasks. From a Mainstream perspective, this effort is facilitated by departmentalization—that is, how members and resources are grouped together to achieve the work of the larger organization.

As depicted in Figure 10.6, departmentalization has two key dimensions. Along the horizontal dimension is departmental *focus*, which looks at the rela-

Figure 10.6 Different types of departmentalization, based on membership and focus

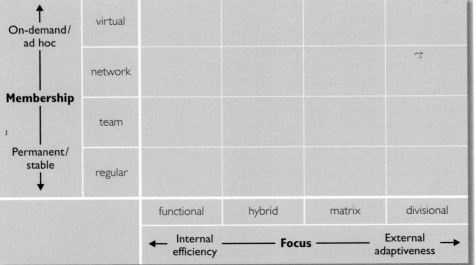

tive emphasis on internal efficiency versus external adaptiveness. The second dimension looks at whether departmental *membership* is permanent or short term. Focus is concerned with the content of what each department is assigned to do, whereas membership looks at whether members of the department are permanent and whether they come from within the organization.

DEPARTMENTAL FOCUS. The "focus" dimension describes the basis upon which an organization is divided into smaller, more manageable subgroups. There are four basic structures:

- Functional
- Hybrid
- Matrix
- Divisional

At one end of this dimension are organizations with a **functional** structure. Here members are placed into the same department because they have similar technical skills and use similar resources to perform their tasks. For example, as illustrated in Figure 10.7(a), a computer manufacturing firm might have a Purchasing

Functional departmentalization occurs when members of an organization are placed into the same department based on having similar technical skills and using similar resources to perform their tasks.

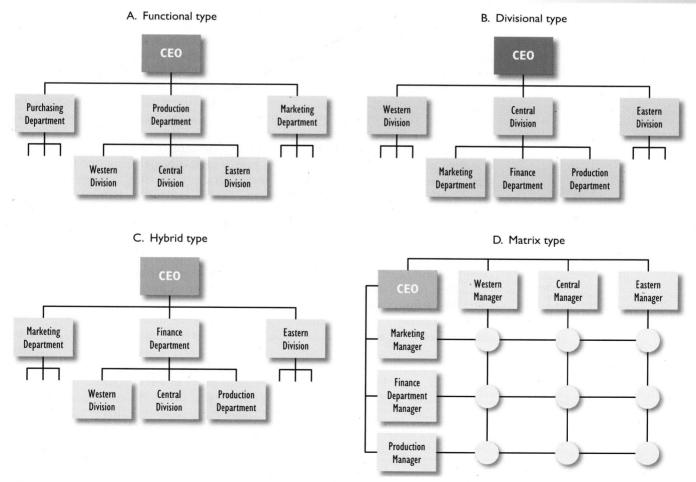

Figure 10.7   Four types of departmentalization

Department, a Production Department, and a Marketing Department. Within each of these three basic functions, there might be subdepartments. For example, the Production Department may have separate subdepartments for each factory where each type of product is manufactured (product departmentalization), or it may have separate subdepartments for each major region that it serves (geographic departmentalization). The top management team coordinates the work of these functional departments, and each department makes its own unique contribution to the organization.

At the other end of the horizontal dimension are organizations with a **divisional** structure. Here members are placed together based on their working as a subunit that provides specific kinds of products or services, serves similar customers, or works in the same geographic region. Figure 10.7(b) shows a regionally based departmental structure with a Western Division, a Central Division, and an Eastern Division. An example of a product-based divisional structure for a computer manufacturer might have a Desktop Division, a Laptop Division, and a Handheld Division. A customer-based divisional structure for a computer manufacturer might have a Consumer Division, a Business Division, and an Educational Institutions Division.

Of course, a divisional structure will often have functional subdepartments, just as a functional structure will often have divisional subdepartments. Thus, in the end, the same people might work in each organization, but how they are grouped together depends on the departmentalization of the organization. However, this similarity across different kinds of departmentalization is not meant to suggest that departmentalization is unimportant. Quite the contrary: The structures that we inhabit have a great deal of influence over how we see the world and the work that we do (recall the discussion on the social construction of reality in Chapter 2). The difference is not unlike the difference between taking a university course with students from a wide variety of academic disciplines versus taking the same course with students who are all in the same discipline.

The relative strengths and weaknesses of a divisional approach versus a functional approach to departmentalization mirror each other. On the one hand, consider the advantages for an automobile manufacturer to have functional departments rather than ten separate divisions. First, the functional approach offers economies of scale. For example, the per-unit cost to produce 10,000 cars on one assembly line is less than it would be to produce 1000 cars each on ten assembly lines scattered around the globe. Another advantage of the functional approach is that it offers opportunities for in-depth skill development in each specialization. For example, one Legal Department with ten lawyers may have specialists in commercial, labor, patent, and international trade law, whereas having one lawyer in each of ten divisions means that the lawyers must necessarily be more generalists. Finally, functional departmentalization permits increased spans of control and lower management costs, because it is easier to manage people with similar training and backgrounds under this scheme than it would be in a divisional approach, which demands managing people in a variety of functional areas.

On the other hand, a divisional approach offers different strengths relative to the functional approach. In a divisional approach, decision-making authority resides more closely with the organization's customers. As a result, managers are more likely to be attuned to and have the ability to readily adapt to changing preferences in their divisions' regions or customer groups. Also, whereas the reason for profits may be somewhat unclear in a functional approach (e.g., there may be debate as to whether success was due to excellent engineering work by the Research and Development Department, high-quality work in the Production Department, or a bril-

---

Divisional departmentalization occurs when members of an organization are grouped so that they canwork together as a subunit in order to provide specific products or services, serve similar customers, or work in the same geographic region.

liant campaign designed by the Marketing Department), in a divisional approach each of an organization's divisions is accountable for making a profit, so that it becomes easier to recognize the performance of managers in specific divisions. In this way, the divisional approach also helps to develop more well-rounded managers, as they coordinate the work of members from different functional areas.

These two basic kinds of departmentalization, with their differing built-in strengths and weaknesses, influence how members view their organization, just as eyeglass lenses shape our vision. Some lenses are designed to help us see in the distance, whereas other lenses help us see close-up. So it is with different approaches to departmentalization. Functional departments help us to see close-up: They help to maximize efficiency and encourage members to develop fine-tuned skills and expertise in functional areas. However, when a great deal of change is occurring outside the organization and warrants a quick response, then divisional departments are preferred. Divisional departments are better for seeing in the distance, beyond the borders of the organization. They help members of the organization to focus on shifts in customer preferences, in emerging technologies, in changing government legislation, and so on. Unfortunately, divisional structures are not as good at paying attention to and optimizing internal efficiencies.

Hybrid organizations are like bifocals. A **hybrid** structure tries to realize simultaneously the advantages of the functional structure (by achieving internal efficiencies and developing internal expertise in some areas) and the advantages of the divisional structure (by being able to adapt to changes in a dynamic external environment). There are two basic "types" of hybrid structures.

> **Hybrid** departmentalization occurs when an organization has both functional departments and divisional departments.

The first hybrid approach is simply a situation where an organization has both functional and divisional departments simultaneously. Figure 10.7(c) provides an example of a hybrid organization that has a Marketing Department, a Finance Department, and an Eastern Division.

A second hybrid approach, called a **matrix** structure, is evident when an organization has both divisional and functional departments, and members are simultaneously assigned to both. Rather than being like bifocals, the matrix structure is more like having a lens for seeing close for one eye, and a lens for seeing far with the other eye. Just as such glasses would take some practice to use, and probably cause some headaches as users try to close one eye or the other as needed, so too matrix structures can be quite challenging to manage and work in. As depicted in Figure 10.7(d), a matrix structure breaks the "unity of command" rule. In a matrix structure, members (represented by the "circles" in Figure 10.7) are responsible to two managers. As a result, these structures demand that more time is spent in

> **Matrix** departmentalization is a type of hybrid structure in which members are simltaneously assigned to both functional and divisional departments.

MANAGEMENT IN PRACTICE

Managing a Matrix Organization

Perhaps the largest and most well-documented example of a matrix organization is ABB, which was created by the merger of the Swedish firm Asea and the Swiss firm Brown Boveri, and managed by Percy Barnevik for its first decade after the merger. Barnevik's challenge was to create a streamlined entrepreneurial organization with as few hierarchical layers as possible, starting with what was essentially a group of 1300 companies with more than 200,000 employees in 150 countries. To do so, he introduced what came to be a highly regarded and very complex matrix structure, which divided ABB into 35 business areas, more than 100 country organizations, and 5000 profit centers (i.e., managers of each of these 5000 divisions were expected to show a profit). The manager of a profit center would report to both a country manager and business area managers.[15]

meetings to ensure that the amount of work being assigned to members is reasonable. A matrix structure is not unlike the situation where university students are simultaneously enrolled in different courses with different professors. It would be stressful, indeed, if each instructor chose to coincidentally schedule an exam or report due on the same day.

DEPARTMENTAL MEMBERSHIP.   The second dimension of departmentalization—membership—has emerged as an increasingly important concern in the past few decades. Until recently, it was simply assumed that an organization's departments consisted of organizational members who had fairly permanent and well-defined individual jobs. Today, however, it is not uncommon for organizations to be structured according to "teams" whose membership may be fluid. Teams may disband when their work has been completed, or members may "float" from one team to the next as the need arises. This increased fluidity has allowed organizations to be more flexible and adaptable.

A second change related to membership has been the trend of having members who are outside the traditional boundaries of the organization. Organizations have always had to rely on suppliers for their inputs, but recently the relationship with suppliers has changed owing to the growing emphasis on outsourcing, network structures, and virtual organizations. As described in Chapter 6, outsourcing refers to the practice of using contracts to transfer some of an organization's recurring internal activities and decision-making rights to outsiders. Many U.S. companies outsource their payroll functions, for example. Likewise, duplicating, catering, and informational technology functions are being increasingly outsourced.[16]

A **network structure** is evident when an organization enters into fairly stable and complex relationships with a variety of other organizations that provide essential services, including manufacturing and distribution. For example, Nike employs only some 1500 people in its Beaverton, Oregon, headquarters. This core staff designs the prototypes of Nike's products, and then outsources the production overseas to factories where labor costs are low. Nike then distributes the finished products to retailers through its large distribution warehouse in Memphis, Tennessee, home of FedEx, which Nike uses to distribute its goods.[17] Thus this network has a functional structure, but most of the members of Nike's functional "departments" are actually located outside the organization's boundaries.

An example of network structure that has more of a divisional focus is evident in the three-way alliance network across Coca-Cola, Disney, and McDonald's. Coca-Cola is an exclusive supplier to Disney's theme parks and to McDonald's, which is a marketing channel for both Disney and Coca-Cola. McDonald's and Coca-Cola use

Network structure occurs when an organization enters fairly stable, complex relationships with a variety of other organizations that provide essential services, like manufacturing and distribution.

Outsourcing is occurring in an increasing number of areas, such as when a technician in India reads the X-ray for a patient with a broken arm in the United States.

MANAGEMENT IN PRACTICE

Ethical Issues in Virtual Network Organizations

Thanks to cyberspace, networked virtual organizations such as Nike are becoming increasingly commonplace. Managers of virtually networked organizations manage the four fundamentals of organizing somewhat differently than do their traditional counterparts, and in doing so, they encounter an array of new challenges as well. In virtually networked organizations, members enter and exit on an as-needed basis, depending on the needs of the organization or changes in the marketplace. For example, Nike may keep some suppliers for a long time but replace others for a variety of reasons. **Switching** refers to the extent to which the membership in a virtual organization changes over time.[18]

When switching is high, managers face the sometimes daunting challenge of managing new partners. In the past, Nike has been the target of criticism for its use of manufacturers in low-income countries that paid substandard wages, employed underage workers, or provided poor working conditions. In failing to disclose its supplier network, critics claimed that Nike was hiding its unethical conduct. In 2005, Nike earned praise by becoming more transparent and revealing its list of 7000 suppliers.[19] Moreover, the company has increased its charitable contributions to low-income countries, focusing on improving the lives of children and women.[20]

Some network organizations that partner with suppliers or distributors that engage in unethical practices may try to distance themselves from these disreputable actions, but increasingly investors and activists are holding organizations accountable for the actions of their partners. This movement, which focuses on network organizations in a variety of industries, is helping to promote higher wages and better working conditions in low-income countries.

Disney characters in their marketing, and new Disney movies are often promoted by McDonald's. All three companies share a mutual focus on families, and the heightened exposure when all three combine forces increases sales and revenue for each organization.[21]

A **virtual organization** is characterized by having members who come and go on an "as-needed" basis and who are networked together with an information technology architecture that enables them to synchronize their activities. For example, some computer software allows people in different parts of the world to work simultaneously on the same document. Virtual organizations allow for people to be hired for short (or long) periods of time from anywhere around the world. Members may never see one another, and they may not have any ongoing commitment to the organization. They are hired to do a specific job, and when the job is finished, their membership may be over. For example, this textbook can be seen as the product of a virtual organization, including the authors, the professional editors and staff at Houghton Mifflin Company, the different firms that it hires on an outsourcing basis to produce its products, the various professors from around the world who serve on the advisory board, and so on. When the book is completed, some elements of that virtual organization will remain, and others will not.

Switching is the extent to which the membership in a virtual organization changes over time.

Virtual organization is one where members come and go on an "as-needed" basis and are networked together with an information technology architecture that enables them to synchronize their activities.

THE FOUR MULTISTREAM FUNDAMENTALS OF ORGANIZING

Research indicates that both Mainstream and Multistream managers address the same four fundamentals of organizing, but that each does so differently.[22] A Multistream approach to the four fundamentals places more emphasis on aspects of organizing that go beyond material productivity concerns, and on including a variety of stakeholders in the ongoing process of organizing.

Experimentation is the emphasis placed on an ongoing voluntary implementation of new ways of performing tasks on a trial basis.

Sensitization is the emphasis on searching for and responding to needs and opportunities in order to improve the status quo.

Dignification is the emphasis on treating everyone with dignity and respect in community.

Participation is the emphasis on mutuality and giving stakeholders a voice in how the organization is managed and how jobs are performed.

Experimentation: The emphasis is on an ongoing voluntary implementation of new ways of performing tasks on a trial basis; this ensures that work activities are completed in the best way to accomplish the overall work of the organization.

Sensitization: The emphasis is on searching for and responding to needs and opportunities to improve the status quo; this ensures that members know which subtasks they should perform.

Dignification: The emphasis is on treating *everyone* with dignity and respect in community; this ensures orderly deference among members.

Participation: The emphasis is on mutuality and giving stakeholders a voice in how the organization is managed and how jobs are performed; this ensures that members work together harmoniously.

Taken together, Mainstream managers focus more on the *content* of organizing, whereas Multistream managers tend to place greater emphasis on the *process* of organizing. In addition, the Mainstream approach emphasizes *rational* competence, whereas the Multistream approach emphasizes *relational* competence.[23] This is not to say that the content of formal structures is unimportant for Multistream managers. Indeed, Multistream managers, such as Ricardo Semler in the chapter-opening case, are very aware of how socially constructed reality is determined by the content of structures and systems. They have chosen to design structures that promote experimentation, sensitization, dignification, and participation.

Multistream managers are also aware of structures and systems beyond the boundaries of their organization in a way that further differentiates them from Mainstream managers. For example, Multistream managers are conscious of how an organization's structures and systems affect suppliers, buyers, neighborhoods, and, of course, the natural environment.

Fundamental 1: Experimentation (versus Standardization)

From a Multistream perspective, the merits of standardization and the fears attached to too little standardization are both overrated. If there is a standard that Multistream managers emphasize, it is the standard of "experimentation." Rather than spending a lot of effort trying to ensure that organizational members conform to a host of specific standards, a hallmark of a Multistream approach is to facilitate members constantly trying new ways of doing things. The focus here is on the dynamic process of organizing (experimenting), rather than on the static outcome of organizing (standards). From a Multistream perspective, members should be encouraged to learn and constantly improve how tasks are completed. This is the best way to accomplish the overall work of the organization.

Multistream managers are more likely to think in terms of team and group standards—that is, they go beyond the individual level of analysis. Multistream management includes a concern for groups outside the organization and for the nonmaterialist concerns of people within the organization. For example, when managers at First Fruits Orchards decided to offer evening tutoring programs for their employees' schoolchildren, the goal was not to improve profits, but rather to provide more opportunities for the children. Eventually they considered dropping or revising the program—not to save money, but rather because they discovered that an unintended consequence of the program was to make parents less involved with their children's lives.

DIGGING DEEPER

The Effect of Organizational Structure on Behavior[24]

Life in prisons can be brutal and dehumanizing. There is some debate over whether this outcome is attributable to the innate psychological characteristics of the inmates or to the organizational structural characteristics of prisons. A famous experiment was carried out with students at Stanford University to shed light on this debate. The experiment involved 24 male participants, chosen from a group of 75 volunteers based on tests that showed they were the most psychologically stable. The experiment, which was intended to last two weeks, took place in the basement of the building housing Stanford's Psychology Department.

Half the participants were assigned to be Prisoners. Prisoners were intentionally not told what to expect or how to act, but they were assured that they would receive adequate food, clothing, and medical care. On the first day of the experiment, they were "arrested" by the local police department, blindfolded, taken to prison, and dressed in simple gowns and mandatory nylon caps.

The other half of the participants were assigned to be Guards, whose assignment was also left deliberately vague: "to maintain a reasonable degree of order within the prison necessary for its effective functioning." They were given khaki uniforms and given symbols of authority, such as silvered sunglasses.

The outcome of the experiment was dramatic and unexpected. Within 36 hours, the first of five prisoners who would show signs of severe psychosomatic disturbance was released. Guards were aggressive and, on at least one occasion, abusive.

At the end of only six days we had to close down our mock prison because what we saw was frightening. It was no longer apparent to most of the subjects (or to us) where reality ended and their roles began. The majority had indeed become prisoners or guards, no longer able to clearly differentiate between role playing and self. There were dramatic changes in virtually every aspect of their behavior, thinking and feeling. In less than a week the experience of imprisonment undid (temporarily) a lifetime of learning; human values were suspended, self-concepts were challenged, and the ugliest, most base, pathological side of human nature surfaced.[25]

In short, the results of the Stanford experiment suggested that the organizational structural characteristics of a prison have a great influence on the people inside. It can bring out the worst even in psychologically well-adjusted people. The influence of organizational structure may be less dramatic in everyday organizations, but it may be every bit as real.[26]

Experimentation involves the ongoing voluntary implementation of new ways of performing tasks on a trial basis, in contrast with simply following "tried and true" standards. Usually experimentation involves ideas that have been discussed in a group setting because individuals generally don't start doing experiments without benefiting from the input and refinement available from others. Many experiments may fail, in which case reverting to the "old" way is fine, because the organization has still gained new knowledge from the experiment. In other cases, the experiments may be a rousing success, and other members of the organization can benefit from and adapt to the lessons learned. Experimentation was evident when businesses began to experiment with on-site daycare centers, which were fine-tuned and are now available at an increasing number of employers. It was also evident when members of The Body Shop experimented with recycling and reusing different containers for their products, which became a model for other organizations.

Both Mainstream and Multistream approaches agree that proper management of this first fundamental issue of organizing can foster direction, motivation, guidelines for decision making, performance, and legitimacy. Nevertheless, the ways in which these qualities are fostered are different. For example, whereas the Mainstream approach fosters direction and motivation by providing each member with specific standards to follow, the Multistream approach fosters direction and motivation by inviting each member to experiment and improve the way that tasks are done. Similarly, Multistream decision making is enhanced because people consult and receive information from one another rather than relying only on managerially developed guidelines. This interaction enhances group ownership, mutual learning, and achievement. It also fosters legitimacy because internal and external stakeholders are informed about what is going on and provide input to experiments.

Too little experimentation may result in organizational rigidity, where people feel stifled and complacent, and where there is a failure to take advantage of the most up-to-date knowledge of members. A lack of experimentation can also perpetuate systemic shortcomings and injustices in the status quo. Of course, too much experimentation could lead to chaos, especially if organizational members are not accountable to others and if there is no coordination of how the different pieces fit together to form a whole. This is especially the case if experimentation is not linked with participation—it is participation that lends coordination to experimentation.

Experimentation is quite visible in organizations such as 3M and Google, which are well known for their leadership in areas such as pollution prevention and encouraging employees to spend 20 percent of their time developing ideas of their own choosing.

Fundamental 2: Sensitization (versus Specialization)

From a Multistream management perspective, the merits of specialization and the fears of underspecialization are both overemphasized. If there is a specialized task that all members should have, it is the task of "sensitization." Rather than ensure that organizational members conform to specific job descriptions, a hallmark of the Multistream approach is to encourage members to continuously adapt and improve how they do their jobs in harmony with others around them. Again, the focus is on the *dynamic process* of organizing (being sensitive to new needs and opportunities), rather than on the *static outcome* of organizing (having the skills to perform tasks listed in a job description).

Moreover, when Multistream managers do divide tasks into separate jobs, this activity is often undertaken at a group level. Whereas the Mainstream emphasis on specialization tends to be at the level of the individual jobholder, Multistream management tends to focus on the group, team, or departmental level of analysis. As a consequence, job descriptions and designs focus on the interrelationships among members, rather than on the specific tasks of each member. Multistream managers value the complementary skills of a team as a unit more than the individual skills of particular team members, and they recognize that some members may have valuable experience or knowledge that goes beyond the materialist needs of the organization. Multistream management values and nurtures such skills.

In short, sensitization refers to how predisposed managers are to recognizing opportunities and needs that go beyond the current "specialized" way of doing things. It describes an openness to look for new ways of doing things. Sensitization helps find new opportunities to meet productivity needs, and it includes being sensitive to stakeholders' physical, social, and spiritual needs. In many ways, sensitization is similar to the idea of Multistream intrapreneurship described in Chapter 6. For example, because they are becoming more sensitive to the lack of economic opportunities for inner-city kids, an increasing number of universities are following an innovative entrepreneurship "summer camp" program developed at the I. H. Asper School of Business at the University of Manitoba, which seeks to develop campers' entrepreneurial skills. At a societal level, more people are becoming sensitized to improve global justice, as is evident in the introduction of ethical mutual funds and an increased emphasis on corporate social responsibility.

Because it enables the input and insight from a variety of organizational stakeholders, an optimal emphasis on sensitization helps to improve an organization's performance, not only in terms of productivity, but also in terms of social and ecological and other measures of performance. An optimal emphasis on sensitization enhances members' proficiency and expertise, not by spelling out beforehand exactly what they are to do, but rather by allowing and encouraging them to develop their existing skills and abilities. This phenomenon is illustrated by Semco's "Lost in Space" program, which might be better

Photos like these are increasing the sensitivity to ecological concerns for an increasing number of people.

named "Exploring Space" because it gives new members and managers the opportunity to sensitively match skills with jobs. By welcoming members and encouraging them to take the initiative in areas where they think improvement is possible, members experience a greater feeling of purpose, meaningful work, and loyalty.[27]

Along the same lines, whereas goal displacement is seen as a bad thing when it results from an overemphasis on specialization, it can have positive aspects when it reflects an appropriate emphasis on Multistream sensitization. It is desirable when organizational members, regardless of their place in the hierarchy, can work together to improve and gradually shift the overall goals of the organization and the means by which they are met. The distinguishing feature, of course, is that a Multistream approach starts with the expectation that the multiple goals will and should change as its members grow and learn from one another and from other stakeholders.

To consider a situation where goal displacement had positive results, consider what happened at the historical Mission Church located in a city in the American Southwest. A series of unintended changes occurred at this church after some young people, sensitive to the needs of homeless people in the neighborhood of their downtown church, began an experiment by providing them with a hot breakfast on Sunday mornings. They wanted to serve the homeless people with dignity and respect, and even considered providing round tables and waiting on them. Soon volunteers were providing over 200 meals each Sunday morning. Six months later, a medical doctor who had been serving breakfast brought along his stethoscope and a medical bag, and began to examine people who wanted to discuss medical problems. Soon thereafter, full-scale medical, dental, and eye clinics emerged as part of the Church's Sunday morning offerings. Within a few years, the Church had opened a Day Center, was serving over 20,000 meals a year, and had hundreds of homeless people participating in worship services, singing in choirs, serving as ushers, and so on. The identity of the Church changed, which prompted some long-standing members to leave it. Even though the leaders of the Church were not at the forefront of this transformation, their sensitivity was evident in how they interpreted and helped to make sense of the changes that were occurring.[28]

When there is too little sensitization in organization, members are not encouraged and permitted to act on things to improve the organization. This inertia may hamper organizational productivity, social justice, or environmental friendliness.[29] In the extreme, it makes people simply go through the motions at work and makes them become callous toward their fellow humans. This is evident, for example, when we allow pollution to spew into the air and water without regard to future generations and when we produce and market products or services of dubious value.

Too much sensitization, by contrast, can lead to inaction from being overwhelmed! Knowing that there are millions of people with AIDS in Africa whose lives could be made more bearable with available medicines, knowing that 30,000 children die of starvation every day, knowing that an increasing number of people rely on soup kitchens for their meals, and so on can be overwhelming. Trying to respond to too many of these crises at the same time can result in an inability to help anyone. Therefore, managers who are sensitized to the needs of the communities they work in should consider needs that can be addressed with the unique capabilities and resources of their organization. For example, pharmaceutical companies, such as Novartis, are well suited to dealing with needs for vaccines or medicines and devoting some of their resources to treat diseases like malaria at little or no cost to the poor.

Inspired by a vision to be sensitive to the needs of the poor and treat them with dignity, in 1950 Mother Teresa established an organization called "The Missionaries of Charity." She received the Nobel Peace Prize in 1979, and today the Mission has more than 4500 nuns and is active in more than 130 countries.[30]

Fundamental 3: Dignification (versus Centralization)

From a Multistream management perspective, the merits of centralization and the fears of decentralization are both overrated. Multistream management is less concerned about how much authority each member should have, and more likely to promote the idea that everyone is better served if *all* stakeholders are treated with dignity. Efforts spent on properly distributing *authority* through the structure would be better invested in creating ways of organizing that distributed *dignity* throughout the organization. And unlike authority, which is usually seen as a limited resource that must be parceled out sparingly, dignity is an unlimited resource that can be distributed generously; everyone has inherent worth that should be recognized.

Dignification entails treating people with dignity and respect in community. In the workplace, it is evident when people are provided with appropriate choices and freedom. Dignity may be present when members are allowed to decorate their offices with personal touches and are given some discretion in setting their own work hours to permit them to attend, for example, special programs at their children's schools. This contrasts with an inflexible emphasis on "company regulations" or, even less personal, monitoring by time clocks and electronic surveillance. In our technologically oriented, globalized world, there is a tendency to treat people as numbers rather than as people. As Martin Buber put it, rather than treat people as faceless "its," we must learn to treat one another more like "thous."[31]

Multistream management tends to favor decentralization and to have authority reside in groups rather than in individuals. Decision making is pushed down to the front lines and beyond the organization's boundaries, wherever appropriate. As one Multistream CEO notes about having employees make decisions, "Sometimes it's been shown that their way is better than mine would've been. And even when it isn't, just allowing them the freedom to do that [make decisions], I think, is worthwhile."[32]

Consider the dignity evident when Ricardo Semler gives Semco employees the authority to set their own salaries. According to Semler, "Arguably, Semco's most controversial initiative is to let employees set their own salaries. Pundits are quick to bring up their dim view of human nature, on the assumption that people will obviously set their salaries much higher than feasible. It's the same argument we hear about people setting their own work schedules in a seven-day weekend mode. The first thing that leaps to mind is that people will come as late or little as possible—this has never been our experience."[33]

Treating people with dignity also means providing them with the information they require to use their decision-making authority responsibly. Semler describes five pieces of information that help employees determine what an appropriate salary is. The first three are provided by managers, and the last two are pieces of information that employees know but managers may not:

1. Managers give employees market surveys about what people earn who do similar work at competing organizations.

2. Employees are told what everyone else in the company earns (all the way from Semler to the janitors).

3. Managers openly discuss the company's profits and future prospects to provide employees with a sense of whether the current market conditions allow above- or below-average salaries.

4. Employees themselves decide how much they would like to be earning at this point in their career, keeping in mind how happy they are with their job and work–life balance.

5. Employees themselves know how much their spouses, neighbors, former schoolmates, and other significant "comparison others" are earning.

Very seldom has this system been abused, perhaps because employees know that if they request too large a salary, they run the risk of annoying their colleagues and suffering the stress that comes from making a decision that they know to be unjust and undignified.

An optimal emphasis on dignification will enhance decision making because, by its very nature, it allows decisions to be made at the appropriate level of analysis in the organization. If a member at the front lines of an organization is capable of making a decision (e.g., if the member has enough knowledge to make an informed and appropriate decision), then there is no reason for the decision to be pushed higher up the hierarchy.[34] This practice also encourages connectedness between and across organizational levels because lower-level members rather than fearing managers with more authority will treat those managers with dignity and try to understand their needs and strengths. Being treated with dignity is expected to be motivating for all members of the organization, as everyone gets satisfaction from respecting and seeking the positive worth in their coworkers and other stakeholders. In such

Dignification Promotes Better Mental Health

Treating people with dignity in the workplace may improve the overall mental well-being among members and external stakeholders. Dr. Harvey Chochinov has studied a process he calls "dignity therapy" for dying cancer patients. The process involves having healthcare professionals tape-record patients' most important memories and insights from their lives, and then edit the transcripts with the help of the patients. Most patients believe that their written life stories will help surviving family members, and this opportunity to continue to serve others in turn helps the patients. Patients who received this therapy reported decreased suffering and depression, and those patients who were the most distressed received the greatest benefits from it. The financial cost of "dignity ther-apy" is much lower than the cost of many drugs used in palliative care.[35]

Semler would argue that similar emotional benefits occur when employees are treated with dignity: "Workers who control their working conditions are going to be happier than workers who don't."[36] He adds that similar benefits go to the manager who is treating others with dignity: "I admit that the lack of control is often hard to live with. . . . Does it make me feel that I have given up power and governance? You bet it does. But do I have more sleepless nights than the manu-facturer who runs his business with an iron hand and whose employees leave their troubles in his lap every night? I think I probably sleep better. I know I sleep well."[37]

cases, the symbolic leadership role that is most valued is that of the servant leader, who seeks to bring out the best in others (see Chapter 15).

By contrast, too little dignity results in treating people as objects, as "cogs" in the organizational machinery. According to Art DeFehr, CEO of one of the largest furniture manufacturers in Canada, globalization has robbed us of the opportunity to put a face on the people who produce our goods. And, because their faces are so far away, we often make our decisions based on dollars and cents, regardless of the effect those choices have on working conditions or lives. Too little dignification not only makes people feel less worthy, but can also act as a self-fulfilling prophecy when people begin to act consistently with how they have been treated. Such members find little intrinsic meaning in their work.

Managers should take care not to provide so much concern for specific individuals that they neglect other important stakeholders. A form of counterfeit dignification is evident when individuals feel that they have all sorts of rights and forget about the rights of, say, future generations. A common example is the "spoiled child" syndrome, where children learn to expect others to serve them without recognizing their own equal responsibility to treat others with dignity. Of course, spoiling children is really not treating them with dignity.

WHAT DO YOU THINK?

Is It Risky to Put the Multistream Fundamentals into Practice?

Many people are attracted to the four Multistream fundamentals of organizing, but those concepts are often curiously difficult to put into practice. Perhaps these ideas simply fly too much in the face of the Mainstream emphasis on maximizing short-term efficiency and productivity. For example, from a Mainstream perspective, it may seem risky for managers to devote one day each week to experimenting with new ideas for the long term, especially knowing that competitors who do not conduct this sort of experimentation will be significantly more productive in the short term. Moreover, because it might be considered a distraction from maximizing productivity, it can seem risky to invest the time and energy required to be sensitive to the people around you, to treat them with dignity, and to invite them to participate in making decisions. We are often so caught up in the tyranny of the urgent, and so obsessed with the immediate pressures that we face on a day-to-day basis, that we fail to consider stakeholders across the street or around the world.

What advice do you have for people who want to put the Multistream fundamentals into practice as part of their everyday lives? Which kinds of support might help them to accomplish this goal? What has helped you to become more sensitive to the needs of others, and to treat others with dignity? Do you know people in organizations that practice these Multistream fundamentals? What helps them to do so?

Fundamental 4: Participation (versus Departmentalization)

From a Multistream management perspective, the merits of departmentalization and the fears of too little departmentalization are both overestimated. This is not to say that Multistream managers do not value the importance of bundling tasks and assigning them to identifiable organizational units. Certainly, this activity is important. Nevertheless, Multistream managers have a "lighter hand," giving more freedom to members to collectively decide how specific tasks should be carried out.

With regard to the *focus* of departments, Multistream managers generally prefer a divisional structure over a functional structure. They prefer divisions that essentially operate as autonomous subunits, where each member has a sense of the overall goals of the unit and understands how his or her efforts work together with others' efforts to meet those goals. As illustrated at Semco, the ideal size for a division is about 120 to 150 members. Once a division grows much beyond this size, it should subdivided into two divisions.[38]

With regard to *membership*, Multistream managers are more likely to include and invite the participation of external stakeholders. Inviting, listening to, and responding to a variety of stakeholders allows members to be sensitized to new opportunities. In addition, it enhances goodwill when inevitably mistakes are made. For example, managers at Shell require every business unit to create and implement a stakeholder engagement plan. This plan identifies the specific external stakeholders with which the unit will work; those stakeholders may include suppliers, environmental groups, labor organizations, local community, and nonprofit energy organizations. The plan describes the precise role that each stakeholder should play in helping monitor and improve Shell's programs and enhancing its sustainability. These stakeholders are even offered uncensored space in Shell's annual sustainability report to comment on Shell's efforts. When Shell mistakenly overstated its oil reserves in 2004, the financial community was highly critical. However, perhaps because of the goodwill established by Shell's stakeholder engagement work, environmental and social activists' public criticism was short-lived and muted. Managers who set up structures to work with key external stakeholders certainly seem to enjoy advantages that come from the good ideas, goodwill, and other forms of capital that are seen as increasingly valuable in our interdependent world.[39]

Participation refers to the emphasis on mutual discernment and the process of giving stakeholders a voice in how the organization is managed and how jobs are performed. It means that members and other stakeholders join together in running the organization. It means that managers value stakeholders' input both in making decisions and in setting the agenda as to which issues require decisions. Participation also has to do with how approachable managers are. Participative managers

Figure 10.8   Organizational chart for Caja Navarra

Source: The information and figure for Caja Navarra were drawn from Ayuso, S., Rodriguez, M. A., & Ricart, J. E. (2006). Responsible competitiveness at the "micro" firm level: Using stakeholder dialogue as a source for new ideas: A dynamic capability underlying sustainable Innovation. *Corporate Governance,* 6(4), 475–490. Copyright 2006 by Corporate Governance. Reproduced with permission in the format Textbook via Copyright Clearance Center and Emerald Group Publishing Limited.

will facilitate discussion of an issue and then, as appropriate, invite people to participate in its implementation. Participation nurtures mutuality, which occurs when a variety of members assume joint responsibility for the organization's operations and share its goals.[40]

Multistream managers have an aversion to traditional pyramid-shaped organizational charts. Specifically, the image of managers at the top with subordinates underneath goes against the organizational identity Multstream managers wish to nurture. Sometimes Multistream managers invert the organizational chart, placing customers and other stakeholders at the top, and managers closer to the bottom. Other Multistream managers use circles to draw organizational charts. For example, Semco can be envisioned as three concentric circles, with the top managers in the innermost circle, middle managers in the next circle, and the remainder of the organization in the outer circle. In other cases, the organizational chart might look more like a flower, with the top management team in the inner circle, which is surrounded by a series of "petals" representing various organizational subunits and other stakeholders.

Caja Navarra, an organization known for its sustainable innovations, is a savings bank that has about 250 branches. Most of these branches are located in the Navarre region of Spain, where it is the leading financial institution, accounting for more than half of deposits and more than one third of loans.[41] In 2000, Caja Navarra moved from a pyramidal structure to the circular structure depicted in Figure 10.8. Managers at Caja Navarra banks are now known for bending over backward to solicit and act on advice from clients on how to improve their service. The bank invests at least 25 percent of its profits into social issues, and it is known for a "You choose: You decide" program, in which customers decide where investments should go: assistance for disabled people, heritage conservation, employment and entrepreneurs, development cooperation, environment, culture, sports and leisure, and an option that includes all of the above.

Participation in virtual departments may also be difficult to depict in a normal organizational chart. For example, managers at PepsiCo have set up a virtual "sustainability department" consisting of an electronic bulletin board and e-room devoted to corporate social responsibility. This measure facilitates communication among members and supports sustainability education and the involvement of key managers. To supplement virtual communication, managers can hold face-to-face meetings every three to six months, perhaps for a half- or full-day session in an off-site location, where issues can be discussed in greater depth than is practical with electronic communication.[42]

Ricardo Semler believes participation is the key to having the kind of organization he wants. Creating an entirely new kind of organization involves "a deceptively simple principle—relinquishing control in order to institute true democracy at Semco."[43] Semler even trusts employees to choose their own managers. This is clearly a foreign concept to Mainstream management, as Semler attests:

At workshops outside Semco, participants tell me that they'd expect workers to choose leaders who are nice to them, even if those managers are ineffective. They also assume that employees favor bosses who are politically able but technically weak. But Semco's history proves that's not what happens. People will not follow someone they don't respect. Our employees know that their livelihood depends on the company doing well, and they won't support an ineffective leader.[44]

Too little participation will result in a dictatorship, where managers impose decisions in a top-down fashion onto subordinates, which has negative effects in the workplace. This is true even in the case of a "benevolent" dictator who imposes "good" decisions. For example, in a series of laboratory experiments, where participants mutually agreed upon a decision rule for a fair distribution of their earnings, their productivity increased while working under the distribution rule they developed themselves. In subsequent experiments, when the identical decision rule was "imposed" by the experimenter, productivity did not increase in the same way.[45] This result suggests that there is a difference depending on whether a good decision rule has been developed participatively or has been imposed by a benevolent dictator.

Too much participation may result in death-by-meetings. If input is sought for every little decision, and if consensus is always required, then activity can be stifled. Participation may be dysfunctional if stakeholders have little desire to participate or if meetings are intended only as a "show" of activity to serve as an excuse to delay action.

CLOSING CASE

Lessons for Tomorrow's Managers from *Tamara*[46]

While no one would deny that an organization's structure can have an enormous influence on the behavior of its members, we seldom give much thought to the role of structure. We become much more aware of structure when we learn about structures that are quite different from what we are familiar with, such as those employed by Semco and ABB. An instructive example that illustrates the importance of structure, and the way in which it affects an organization's members and stakeholders, comes from an experimental theatrical play called *Tamara*, created by director Richard Rose and playwright John Krizanc. *Tamara* has been performed in Toronto and New York, and it broke the record for the longest-running play in Los Angeles (ten years).

The structure of this play, which has been called the first fully interactive drama ever produced, is unique. The play has a dozen characters (including a Commandante who owns the opulent villa where the play takes place, a glamorous Art Deco painter named Tamara for whom the play is named, a light-fingered maid, a dilettante

composer, a mysterious chauffeur, a butler, and a ballerina), and about 100 people in the audience. Instead of taking place in a large theater in front of a seated audience, the play takes place in a mansion where the audience follows the characters of their choosing through 13 rooms and hallways, across three floors, with more than 100 episodes.[47] Here each actor is the star of his or her own story. David Boje, an organizational scholar, describes his visit:

> For example, when attending the play I followed the chauffeur from the kitchen to the maid's bedroom; there she met the butler, who had just entered the drawing room. As they completed their scene, they each wandered off into different rooms, leaving the audience, myself included, to choose whom to follow. As I decided which characters to follow, I experienced a very different set of stories than someone following another sequence of characters. No audience member gets to follow all the stories since the action is simultaneous, involving different characters in different rooms and on different floors. At the

play, each audience member receives a "passport" to return again and again to try to figure out more of the many intertwined networks of stories. Tamara cannot be understood in one visit, even if an audience member and a group of friends go in six different directions and share their story data. Two people can even be in the same room and—if they came there by way of different rooms and character-sequences—each can walk away from the same conversation with entirely different stories.

Compared to other theater productions, *Tamara* is clearly more experimental than it is standard, and it places more emphasis on sensitization than on specialization. For example, to be sensitive to the different buildings in which *Tamara* has been performed, and to refine the content, 40 percent of the play was different in Los Angeles from the version that initially opened in Toronto, and 30 percent of the play was different in New York than it had been in Los Angeles. There is an energy that goes with this willingness to experiment.

In terms of its emphasis on dignification versus centralization, *Tamara* reminds us that each organizational member can be seen as the "star" of the show. It is not just managers who matter, with a supporting cast that helps them star in the organization. As Krizanc notes, in *Tamara* "[Y]ou can follow anyone and have a sense of a complete story. On a proscenium stage [as used in standard plays], you can explore your protagonist in depth, but there will always have to be secondary characters. Here, each actor is the star of his [or her] own story." It does not matter whom the audience members follow: They always see the star of the play.

In terms of its emphasis on participation versus departmentalization, *Tamara* encourages the audience itself to participate in the play, choosing which character to follow after each episode. The audience members are not passive external stakeholders, but rather active participants. The play reminds us that because we don't know what has happened in other rooms, we never quite know what is happening in the room that we are in. Others will always have valuable knowledge that we do not have, just as we have unique knowledge that they do not have. This perspective points to the importance of participation that draws on information from many different stakeholders.

QUESTIONS FOR DISCUSSION

1. The director of *Tamara* says his play has an orderly structure, but that it is a very different kind of order than most plays. Do you agree that it is just as orderly? Why are there not more plays like *Tamara*? What are its challenges, its strengths, and its weaknesses?

2. Do you think that there is a link between people's management style and their interest in a play like *Tamara*? Of managers you have had or know about, which ones do you think would enjoy *Tamara* and which ones would feel frustrated with it? Why? Do you think you would enjoy going to the play?

3. It's been estimated that about 20 percent of people at *Tamara* have seen it before, but have returned presumably to understand the play from the perspective of different characters. Do you think you would want to see the play more than once?

SUMMARY

There are four fundamental issues in organizing, and they are managed differently from a Mainstream versus Multistream approach.

From a Mainstream approach, the four fundamental issues of organizing are managed via:

- *Standardization:* The emphasis is on developing uniform practices for organizational members to follow in doing their jobs; this ensures that work activities are being completed in the best way.

- *Specialization:* The emphasis is on grouping standardized organizational tasks into separate jobs; this ensures that members know which subtasks to perform.

- *Centralization:* The emphasis is on having decision-making authority rest with managers at the top of an organization's hierarchy; this ensures orderly deference.

- *Departmentalization:* The emphasis is on grouping members and resources together to achieve the work of the larger organization; this ensures members are working together harmoniously.

From a Mainstream approach, the four fundamental issues of organizing are managed via:

- *Experimentation:* The emphasis is on an ongoing voluntary implementation of new ways of performing tasks on a trial basis; this ensures that work activities are being completed in the best way.
- *Sensitization:* The emphasis is on being aware of and responsive to needs and opportunities; this ensures that members know which subtasks to perform.
- *Dignification:* The emphasis is on treating everyone with dignity and respect in community; this ensures orderly deference.
- *Participation:* The emphasis is on mutual discernment and guidance; this ensures that members work together harmoniously.

QUESTIONS FOR REFLECTION AND DISCUSSION

1. Describe the four fundamental issues of organizing. Describe how each of the four operate in practice in Mainstream and Multistream organizations.

2. Define, contrast, and compare standardization and experimentation. Is one merely the opposite of the other? Or are they qualitatively different, and not even on the same continuum? That is, could you have a high (or low) emphasis on both at the same time?

3. What are the similarities and differences between the idea of sensitization and the idea of intrapreneurship (described in Chapter 6)? To which step of the intrapreneurial process is sensitization most closely related? Explain.

4. What are the two dimensions of departmentalization?

5. Do you think virtual organizations will become more prevalent during your career? Why or why not?

6. If you treat others with dignity, will that practice change the amount of power that you have? Will it increase or decrease your overall power? Is this the same for all people? Explain.

7. Consider Semco, the company described in the opening case. Should employees be trusted to set their own salaries, choose their own hours, and hire their own managers? Should university students be trusted to assign their own grades? In your view, what sort of information should instructors provide, and what sort of information should students provide, to set up a fair way to assign marks?

8. Ricardo Semler writes: "I'm not preaching anti-materialism. We do, however, desperately need a better understanding of the purpose of work, and to organize the workplace and the workweek accordingly. Without it, the purpose of work degenerates to empty materialism on one side and knee-jerk profiteering on the other."[48] Do you agree with Semler's observations? Explain what you understand to be the purpose of work. How might you as a manager best organize the workplace based on your understanding?

HANDS-ON ACTIVITY

Where Are You Along the Mainstream–Multistream Continuum?

Circle the number that best corresponds to your views.

Managers should develop standards to ensure that members complete their work activities in the best way.	1 2 3 4 5 6 7	Managers should encourage members to develop and experiment with new ways of performing tasks.
Managers should use specialized job descriptions to ensure that staff members do their specific jobs.	1 2 3 4 5 6 7	Managers should encourage members to be sensitive to and address the opportunities and needs around them.

Continued

A centralized hierarchy of authority is the best way to achieve orderly deference.

1 2 3 4 5 6 7

Everyone should be treated with dignity and respect.

Members should be grouped into departments to ensure that everyone works together harmoniously.

1 2 3 4 5 6 7

Members should be welcome to participate and practice mutual discernment and guidance.

ENDNOTES

1. Semler, R. (2004). *The seven-day weekend.* New York:Portfolio/ Penguin Group; Semler, R. (1989, September/October). Managing without managers. *Harvard Business Review,* 76–84; and Vogl, A. J. (2004, May/June). The anti-CEO. *Across the Board,* 30–36.

2. Page 77 in Semler, R. (1989, September/October). Managing without managers. *Harvard Business Review,* 76–84.

3. Page 12 in Semler, R. (2004). *The seven-day weekend.* New York: Portfolio/Penguin Group.

4. Semler, 2004, p. 92.

5. This quote, and the reference to Frank Lloyd Wright, are taken from Orr, D. (2006). Design: Part I. *Geez,* 3, 8.

6. This is an adapted and somewhat simplified interpretation of Weber's ideas. A more detailed description of these four fundamentals, as well as theoretical and empirical support for the Mainstream versus Multistream approaches to the four fundamentals, can be found in Dyck, B., & Schroeder, D. (2005). Management, theology and moral points of view: Towards an alternative to the conventional materialist-individualist ideal-type of management. *Journal of Management Studies,* 42(4), 705–735; and Dyck, B., & Weber, M. (2006). Conventional and radical moral agents: An exploratory look at Weber's moral-points-of-view and virtues. *Organization Studies,* 27(3), 429–450. See also Weber, M. (1958). *The Protestant ethic and the spirit of capitalism* (trans. T. Parsons). New York: Scribner's.

7. Huang, X., & Van de Vliert, E. (2006). Job formalization and cultural individualism as barriers to trust in management. *International Journal of Cross Cultural Management,* 6(2), 221–242.

8. We recognize that Selznick's idea of goal displacement goes beyond our definition. For example, see Raab, J. (2004). Selznick revisited: Goal displacement as an unavoidable consequence of cooptation? Working paper, Department of Organization Studies, Tilburg University, Netherlands.

9. Meyer, J. W., & Rowan, B. (1977). Institutionalized organizations: Formal structure as myth and ceremony. *American Journal of Sociology,* 83(2), 340–363. See also Meyer. J. W., & Rowan, B. (1978). The structure of educational organizations. In M. W. Meyer and Associates (Eds.), *Environment and organizations* (pp. 78–109). San Francisco: Jossey-Bass.

10. Consistent with this generalist approach, for example, it was not so long ago that many universities required students to know at least two different languages. Of course, the idea of a university was established at a time when there was much less knowledge written down. For example, it is estimated that 1800 was the last year when a person in his or her lifetime could have read all the books that had ever been written.

11. See some of the literature reviewed in Ferraro, F., Pfeffer, J., & Sutton, R. I. (2005). Economic language and assumptions: How theories can become self-fulfilling. *Academy of Management Review,* 30(1), 8–24. Giacalone, R. A. (2004). A transcendent business education for the 21st century. *Academy of Management Learning & Education,* 3(4), 415–420.

12. Meindl, J. R., Ehrlich, S. B., & Dukerich, J. M. (1985). The romance of leadership. *Administrative Science Quarterly,* 30, 78–102.

13. Schein, E. H. (1985). *Organizational culture and leadership.* San Francisco: Jossey-Bass.

14. Heuerman, T. (with D. Olson). (no date). *Heroic leadership.* Accessed December 26, 2006, at http://www.selfhelpmagazine .com/articles/wf/heroic.html.

15. In January 2001, under the leadership of CEO Joergen Centerman and facilitated by advances in information technology, ABB began to transform its matrix into a "customer-centric" model, becoming one of the first organizations in its industry to align its structure with the structures of its customers and channels to the market. The new model had four divisions based on customers, supported by two generic product divisions. This description of ABB's structure is taken from Fitzgerald, S. P. (2002). *Organizational models.* Oxford, UK: Capstone.

16. Fitzgerald, 2002.

17. Hellriegel, D., Jackson, S. E., & Slocum, J. W. (2002). *Management: A competency-based approach* (9th ed., p. 307). Cincinnati, OH: Thomson South-Western.

18. See Travica, B. (2005). Virtual organizations and electronic commerce. *DATA BASE for Advances in Information Systems,* 36(3), 45–68.

19. Brearton et al. (2005, February 25). Corporate social responsibility: 2nd annual ranking. *Globe and Mail.* Accessed December 26, 2006, at http://www.globeinvestor.com/servlet/ArticleNews/ story/GAM/20050225/RO3PG65.

20. Similarly, Adidas-Salomon and Reebok are known to promote environmental initiatives, and require suppliers to comply with a set of work standards. These practices have helped both companies earn accreditation from the Fair Labor Association (FLA) in 2005 (Brearton et al., 2005).

21. Hellriegel et al., 2002, p. 307.

22. Dyck and Weber (2006) explicitly examined the relative emphasis that managers place on materialism and individualism. They found that managers who placed more emphasis on materialism and individualism placed more emphasis on standardization, specialization, centralization, and formalization, and less emphasis on experimentation, sensitization, dignification, and participation. In addition, they found that managers who placed less emphasis on materialism and individualism placed less emphasis on standardization, specialization, centralization, and formalization, and more emphasis on experimentation, sensitization, dignification, and participation.

23. This Multistream emphasis on process and relational competence is consistent with Mintzberg's notion of "strategic learning" discussed in Chapter 9. The Multistream approach does not see a lack of formal structure as a weakness to be overcome, but rather embraces it as a hallmark of an appropriate way to manage the organizing function process.

24. Brady, F. N., & Logsdon, J. M. (1988). Zimbardo's "Stanford Prison Experiment" and the relevance of social psychology for teaching business ethics. *Journal of Business Ethics, 7*(9), 703–710.

25. Zimbardo, P. (1982). Pathology of imprisonment. In D. Krebs (Ed.), *Readings in social psychology: Contemporary perspectives* (2nd ed., p. 249). New York: Harper & Row. Cited in Brady, F. N., & Logsdon, J. M. (1988). Zimbardo's "Stanford Prison Experiment" and the relevance of social psychology for teaching business ethics. *Journal of Business Ethics, 7*(9), 703–710.

26. "The individual comes to the job in a state of what we have previously defined as role-readiness, a state that includes the acceptance of legitimate authority and compliance with its requests, a compliance that for many people extends to acts that they do not understand and that may violate many of their own values." [Katz, D., & Kahn, R. (1978). *The social psychology of organizations* (2nd ed., p. 194). New York: John Wiley & Sons. Cited in Brady & Logsdon, 1988)].

27. See also Baddaracco & Webb, 1995.

28. The name of the church is disguised. Plowman, D. A., Baker, L. T., Beck, T. E., Kulkarni, M., Solansky, S. T., & Travis, D. V. (2007). Radical change accidentally: The emergence and amplification of small change. *Academy of Management Journal, 50*(3), 515–543.

29. Sensitized managers who are unable to have their concerns addressed in-house may also resort to whistleblowing or join or start more Multistream organizations. See Badaracco, J. L., Jr., & Webb, A. (1995). Business ethics: A view from the trenches. *California Management Review, 37*, 2, 8–28.

30. http://en.wikipedia.org/wiki/Missionaries_of_Charity.

31. Buber, M. (1958). *I and thou.* New York: Scribner.

32. Dyck, B. (2002). A grounded, faith-based moral point of view of management. In T. Rose (Ed.), *Proceedings of Organizational Theory Division* (Vol. 23, pp. 12–23). Winnipeg, MB: Administrative Sciences Association of Canada.

33. Semler, 2004, p. 179. Semler talks about trusting employees to choose their own hours: "People from CNN were at my company last week to do a special. They spent five days going through the whole company. We told them, Interview anybody you want—nobody will chaperone you. The CNN people showed up on the first working day after Carnival, and went through entire floors without seeing a single person. 'Where were all the people?' they asked. But later, after interviewing, they calculated that our employees worked more hours than their counterparts at other companies. Which goes to say that when people are given freedom, they'll do whatever it takes to get the job done" [quoted on page 34 of Vogl, A. J. (2004, May/June). The anti-CEO. *Across the Board*, 30–36].

34. This is consistent with Baake's principle of allowing everyone in the organization to make important decisions, to "shoot the game-winning basket." See Chapter 15 in Baake, D. (2005). *Joy at work: A revolutionary approach to fun on the job.* Seattle, WA: PVG.

35. Researchers are now looking at the benefits of having family members prepare a life story. Based on Fallding, H. (2005, August 20). "Dignity therapy" helps cancer care. *Winnipeg Free Press,* p. B2. See also Chochinov, H. M. (2004). Dignity and the eye of the beholder. *Journal of Clinical Oncology, 22*(7), 1336–1340.

36. Semler, 1989, p. 77.

37. See page 72 in Semler, R. (1994, January/February). Why my former employees still work for me. *Harvard Business Review,* 64–74.

38. The advantages of relatively small organizational subunits and organizations are also described in Dyck & Schroeder, 2005.

39. Savitz, A. W., & Weber, K. (2006). *The triple bottom line: How today's best-run companies are achieving economic, social, and environmental success—and how you can too.* San Francisco: Jossey-Bass.

40. Amason, A. C., & Sapienza, H. J. (1997). The effects of top management size and interaction norms on cognitive and affective conflict. *Journal of Management, 23*(4), 495–516.

41. The information and figure for Caja Navarra were drawn from Ayuso, S., Rodriguez, M. A., & Ricart, J. E. (2006). Responsible competitiveness at the "micro" firm level: Using stakeholder dialogue as a source for new ideas: A dynamic capability underlying sustainable innovation. *Corporate Governance, 6*(4), 475–490.

42. Savitz & Weber, 2006.

43. Semler, 2004, pp. 10–11.

44. Semler, 2004, p. 185.

45. Cooper, C., Dyck, B., & Frohlich, N. (1992). Improving the effectiveness of gainsharing: The role of fairness and participation. *Administrative Science Quarterly, 37*, 471–490.

46. Blumenthal, E. (1987, November 29). "Tamara" from the ground floor up. *New York Times.* Accessed on February 23, 2008, at http://query.nytimes.com/gst/fullpage.html?res=9B0DEFDE133CF93AA15752C1A961948260&scp=1&sq=&st=nyt; Rinaldi, W. (2003, April 2). Toronto revives *Tamara. The Arts Report,* CBC Radio Two. Accessed on February 23, 2008, at http://origin.www.cbc.ca/arts/story/2003/04/02/tam020403.html; Boje, D. (1995). Stories of the storytelling organization: A postmodern analysis of Disney as "Tamara-Land." *Academy of Management Journal, 38*(4), 997–1035; and Weinrib, D., & Stewart, A. (2003). *Tamara:* Groundbreaking, international sensation returns! News release from D. W. Communications.

47. The number of characters and rooms changes depending on the physical location of the production, demonstrating again how action is determined by structure—in this case, the physical structure of the theater.

48. Semler, 2004, p. 25.

CHAPTER 11

Now that we've covered the four fundamental elements of organizing, we are ready to see how they fit together to form coherent types of organization structures and how these structures, in turn, fit with an organization's environment, strategy, and technology. Together, these components describe what we will call the *organizational type*. In short, in this chapter we introduce the idea of managing organization design—a challenging and vital part of the organizing function.

ROAD MAP

FOUR ASPECTS OF ORGANIZATION DESIGN

Organization structure

Three key factors
Environment
Strategy
Technology

Four organizational types
Simple organization
Internally focused organization
Externally focused organization
Dual-focused organization:
    partly inside-looking and partly outside-looking

Staying fit

Organization Design

MAINSTREAM APPROACH	⟷	MULTISTREAM APPROACH
Mechanistic versus organic		Inward versus outward
Stable versus changing		Narrow versus broad interest
Cost leader versus differentiation		Minimizer versus transformer
Analyzable versus unanalyzable		Intra-organizational versus extra-organizational
Simple type: entrepreneurial start-up		*Voluntary Simplicity type:* alternative to status quo
Defender type: internal efficiency		*MultiDefender type:* internal well-being
Prospector type: external adaptability		*MultiProspector type:* external well-being
Analyzer type: internal efficiency and external adaptability		*MultiAnalyzer type:* internal well-being and external well-being
Organizational life cycle		Responding to adversity

Managing a Smile Factory[1]

Managers at Disney theme parks have a big challenge: to design an organization structure that makes the parks the "Happiest Place on Earth." As Walt Disney noted, "You can dream, create and design the most wonderful place in the world . . . but it takes people to make the dream a reality." Which approach to organizing do Disney managers choose? And how are the four fundamental elements of organizing designed to work together to accomplish their goal? According to people who have worked there in the past, Disney managers place a great deal of emphasis on standardization, specialization, centralization, and rigid departmentalization.

In terms of standardization, each new hire at Disney attends the much-renowned University of Disneyland, a 40-hour program of studies established in 1955. There employees learn, for example, that the standard term for customers is "guests," rides are called "attractions," uniforms are "costumes," and accidents are "incidents." Employees also learn standard answers to typical questions asked by customers. For example, when asked whether Disneyland gives rain checks, the correct answer is this: "We don't offer rain checks at Disneyland because (1) the main attractions are all indoors; (2) we would go broke if we offered passes; and (3) sunny days would be too crowded if we gave passes."[2] Employees are also given elaborate checklists of appearance standards, including standards such as the need to practice friendly smiles and use only friendly and courteous phrases. For example, Jon Storbeck, director of park operation, noted 50 years after the University started, "The Disney grooming guidelines take constant upkeep on behalf of cast members, and one unshaven employee can ruin everything." Others note that this can turn into a process of standardizing and making into "objects" employees' physical selves, where managers ensure that each part of peoples' bodies and social lives are "polished, groomed, and controlled."[3]

In terms of specialization, once employees are assigned to a particular position, there may be little room for change, even from one year to the next: "Once a sweeper, always a sweeper." Job applicants are assigned to their positions based on specialized skills, as is evident in the five basic "classes" of jobs. The most skilled employees are the bilingual Ambassadors and Tour Guides, the second most skilled employees operate tricky rides or rides that require live narration, the third level are employees who operate regular rides, then come sweepers, and finally the food and concession workers.

In terms of centralization, Disney has been described as having rather intense top-down management monitoring, where supervisors hide in observation posts to try to catch employees who break the rules (e.g., taking too long on a break, not wearing the correct shoes or belt). Employees have complained about "being watched," but most get used to the feeling. This approach is consistent with the management style of the founder, Walt Disney, who is said to have "ruled by fear."[4] It also creates tension between hierarchical levels. For example, a former Jungle Cruise operator describes how supervisors "are regarded by ride operators as sneaks and tricksters out to get them and representative of the dark side of park life. It also draws operators together as cohesive little units who must look out for one another while they work (and shirk)." This leads to the final fundamental element of organizing.

In terms of departmentalization, employees' social status is greatly influenced by where they work in the park. Managers do not encourage movement across jobs, and when it does happen it is usually within an area and job category. There is also little fraternization across the different types of jobs.[5]

In sum, it is quite an impressive feat of organization design and "social engineering" that Disney's frontline workers play their kindly and smiling roles so effectively in light of the fact that Disney does not pay particularly well, offers fairly mindless jobs with a repetitive technology, and has strict supervisors. Disney creates its smile factory by means of clear standards, specialized jobs, tight supervision, and rigid job groupings—a formula that has worked for decades to help it develop its reputation as a leading vacation destination.

INTRODUCTION TO ORGANIZATION DESIGN

This chapter starts with a description of organization structures. **Organization structure** refers to the combination of the four fundamental elements of organizing:

- Ensuring that the optimal way to perform different subtasks is identified
- Ensuring that each member knows what his or her specific subtasks are
- Ensuring that members know to whom they should defer
- Ensuring that members' task performance fits coherently with the task performance of their coworkers

After describing basic organization structures, we will focus on several basic organizational types. An **organizational type** is a specific, coherent way that the four elements of an organization's structure fit with each other *and* the way that the organization structure as a whole "fits" or is consistent with the organization's environment, strategy, and technologies.

Organization design refers to the process of developing an organizational type by ensuring that there is a fit between and among an organization's structural characteristics and its environment, strategy, and technology. As depicted in Figure 11.1, when working on organization design, managers must pay attention to "fit" at three levels:

1. Managers must ensure that the four fundamental elements of organizing "fit" together with each other in a way that makes sense (top-right box in Figure 11.1).

2. Managers must ensure that the organization's environment, strategy, and technology fit together in a way that makes sense (top-left box in Figure 11.1).

3. Managers must ensure that the triad of environment–strategy–technology "fits" with the fourfold organization structure in a way that makes sense (lower-center box in Figure 11.1).

How does the material in Chapter 10, which introduced the four fundamental elements

Organization structure is the combination of the four fundamental elements of organizing, which describe how managers ensure that (1) work activities are being completed in the best way, (2) members know which subtasks they should perform, (3) there is orderly deference among members, and (4) members work together harmoniously.

Organizational type refers to a specific, coherent way that the four fundamental elements of an organization's structure fit with one another, and how the organization's structure as a whole fits with the organization's environment, strategy, and technology.

Figure 11.1 An overview of the organization design process

Environment, Strategy, and Technology

How an organization's environment, strategy, and technology influence, and coherently "fit" with, its structure

Organization Structure

How the four fundamental elements of organizing "fit" together to form a coherent whole

Organizational Types

How the four elements of an organization's structure fit with each other, *and* how the organization's structure as a whole fits with the organization's environment, strategy, and technology

Organization design is the process of developing an organizational type by ensuring that there is a fit between and among an organization's structural characteristics and its environment, strategy, and technology.

Mechanistic structure is an organization structure characterized by relatively high levels of standardization, specialization, and centralization, and by a functional departmentalization.

Organic structure is an organization structure characterized by relatively low levels of standardization, specialization, and centralization, and by a divisional departmentalization.

Just like a few twists can transform a toy robot into the shape of a car, so also can a manager have a huge influence on the basic design of an organization by changing some of its key elements.

of organization, relate to the material in this chapter? Consider this metaphor: Chapter 10 was like saying that the structures of all motorized vehicles have four basic parts: an engine, tires, seats, and a chassis. In this chapter, we are saying that these four parts can be combined in different ways, depending on whether you wish to design a motorcycle, a sports car, a van, or a bus. It would be rare to find the same engine or chassis used on a motorcycle, a sports car, and a bus, but sometimes identical tires may be used for sports cars and motorcycles, and identical seats may be used in cars and vans. The kind of vehicle you produce should be consistent with, and appropriate for, the conditions and purposes for which it will be used. You would not try to haul refrigerators on a motorcycle or go on a family camping vacation in a two-door sports car. So it is with organization structures: The different components of structure should be selected and combined in a way that is appropriate for the task to be achieved.

MAINSTREAM ORGANIZATION DESIGN

As suggested by Figure 11.1, our presentation of the Mainstream organization design process focuses on three things. We begin by describing the two basic types of Mainstream organization structure: organic and mechanistic. We then describe how an organization's structure is influenced by, and fits with, its larger environment, strategy, and technology. Finally, we describe four basic Mainstream organizational types that help managers when they are thinking about the kind of organization they wish to design.

Organization Structure

Mainstream managers and scholars have found it helpful to talk in terms of two basic kinds of organization structures: mechanistic and organic[6] (see Figure 11.2). A **mechanistic structure** is characterized by relatively high levels of standardization, specialization, and centralization, and by a functional departmentalization. The U.S. Postal Service is a mechanistic organization. In contrast, an **organic structure** is characterized by relatively low levels of standardization, specialization, and centralization, and by a divisional departmentalization. A neighborhood "ultimate Frisbee" league—where people show up on an "as available" basis once a week and are divided into different teams—is an example of an organic structure.

The logic behind the continuum is that interrelationships exist among each of the four Mainstream fundamental elements of organizing. For example, a mechanistic structure is evident when managers place a high emphasis on each of the four

Mainstream fundamental elements of organizing. Thus managers who place a high emphasis on standardization (by developing manuals filled with policies and rules) also tend to place a high emphasis on specialization (by developing detailed job descriptions). They emphasize centralization (with a clear hierarchy of authority and carefully laid-out reporting and decision-making procedures), and tend to favor functional departmentalization (because it is easier to manage groups of people with similar functional skills than it is to manage groups of people with diverse backgrounds). In sum, in a mechanistic structure, the four fundamentals of organizing fit together to form a coherent whole that operates like a well-oiled machine.

To see how the four Mainstream fundamentals fit together for an organic structure, let's look at them in reverse order. Recall that members of divisional departments come from a variety of functional backgrounds (e.g., marketing, finance, and production people all work in the same department). Because it is unlikely that a division's manager will have full expertise in all of these areas, it is appropriate for the manager to decentralize decision making, thereby giving authority to members who do have the relevant expertise in each functional area. This decentralization will facilitate the kind of collaboration required for people from different functional areas to work together. As they work together, their specialization will broaden as they understand how the different functions fit together in the work of the division. Finally, because of this decentralization and collaborative specialization, it will be relatively difficult to have very detailed procedures and standards for the overall work of members. Thus, in an organic structure, the four fundamentals also fit together to form a coherent whole, but the resulting organization operates in a less machinelike fashion and is more like a highly adaptive organism.[7]

Figure 11.2 A continuum showing the two basic varieties of Mainstream organization structure

Mechanistic Structure		Organic Structure
Highly formalized	Standardization	Low
High/narrow	Specialization	Low/broad
Centralized	Centralization	Decentralized
Functional	Departmentalization	Divisional

Environment, Strategy, and Technology

Organizational scholars have long sought to discover the "one best way" to structure an organization. But there is no *one* best way! Rather, the best way to design an organization depends on recognizing that its structure should fit with a number of external and internal factors. Three of those factors are highlighted in Figure 11.3.[8]

ENVIRONMENT. An organization's structure is influenced by events and resources in its environment. Just as wildlife must "fit" with its environment (e.g., the number of deer or

Figure 11.3 Effect of environment, strategy, and technology on Mainstream organization structure

Mechanistic Structure		Organic Structure
	External Environment	
Stable/certain	In general	Changing/uncertain
Rigid	Norms and practices	Flexible
	Strategy	
Cost leader	Generic strategy	Differentiation
	Technology	
Easy to divide into substeps	Divisibility	Difficult to divide into substeps
High	Task analyzability	Low
Low (mass production)	Task variety	High (custom, batch production)
Low	Interdependence	High

How the Environment Influences Which Organizations Survive[9]

The importance of managers staying in touch with their environment is highlighted by research in an area called population ecology. Just as the sizes of duck, fish, and deer populations are determined by those animals' access to resources in their natural habitat, and not by how smart the ducks or fish or deer are, so too the kind of organizations that thrive or die are determined by the resources in their environment.

An excellent example of this relationship comes from a study of the different kinds of gas stations in the city of Edmonton, Alberta. In the early 1960s, as in most cities at that time, almost all of the 300 gas stations in Edmonton were service stations, where customers could buy gasoline, have their

oil changed, and have repair work done on their cars. By the mid-1980s, however, things had changed considerably. There were still about 300 gas stations, but only 75 also had service bays. Another 75 had car washes, another 75 included convenience stores, and another 75 just sold gasoline.

What had happened? The environment for gas stations had changed because cars had become more difficult to service and required greater expertise to repair. In addition, customers began to want convenient access to car washes and food when they purchased gas. This example points to the importance of managers paying attention to changes in their environment and being willing to change their organizations accordingly.

Change in Diversity and Distribution of Population Forms in Gasoline Retail, Edmonton, 1958–1988

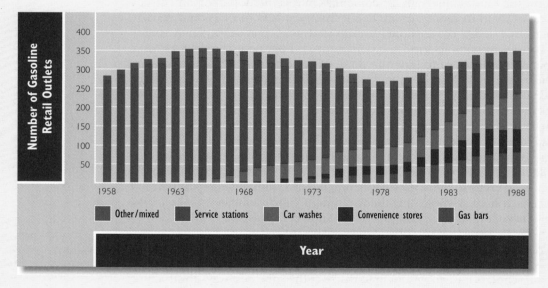

eagles that a geographic region can support is determined by the weather and the supply of food), so too organizations must fit with their environment (e.g., the number of restaurants and gas stations a geographic region can support is determined by the number of people and cars).[10] In much the same way as the natural environment determines which sorts of living organisms can survive and flourish, the larger environment determines which sorts of organization structures can survive and flourish.

Mainstream organization designers are particularly interested in the *stability* of the larger environment. If the environment is very unstable, then managers should design an adaptable structure where members are able to monitor and adapt to the environment on an ongoing basis. In these situations, an organic organization structure is preferred, because it is more flexible and allows members to continually realign the organization's products and services with changes in the environment. For example, given the pace of change in software design and development, it is not surprising that many firms in this sector have a relatively organic organization structure. Consistent with this philosophy, recall that 20 percent of Google employees' time is unstructured, where they are encouraged to develop new products and services of their own choosing.

If the environment is very stable and predictable, then Mainstream managers will want to design a rigid organization structure that is highly efficient. This more mechanized organization structure will enhance uniform quality and reduce downtime. In such organizations, the costs of permitting members to spend 20 percent of their time experimenting with new ideas far outweigh the financial benefits. Thus, for the mass production of "commodity" items such as T-shirts and soda, managers will set up very mechanistic organization structures like those found at many companies in the garment and beverage industries.

Managers must also pay attention to both social and industry norms and values when they design an organization's structure. For example, high levels of centralization and hierarchy are expected in some countries, whereas decentralization is expected in others (see Chapter 4).[11] This preference provides some direction for how organization structures should be designed, and it explains why the same structure will operate and be interpreted differently by members in a variety of countries. For example, in Mexico, people tend to have a high deference to authority; as a consequence, managers who try to empower subordinates and promote participative decision making may be perceived to be shirking their responsibilities. By contrast, in Israel, people tend to have a low deference to authority; thus managers who try to use a centralized decision-making approach may foster resentment among subordinates.

Managers must also recognize that an organization's structure must fit with the norms and practices in its industry. For example, Silicon Valley has many programmers and engineers who work on the cutting edge of computer software and hardware development. The norm in this industry is for employees to complete a project at one company, and then move to whichever firm has a new project that interests them.

The need to adapt to industry practices is especially evident among organizations that are dependent on a particular customer or supplier, or that have strong ties to multiple-firm networks. For example, firms may change their structures to fit more easily with the firms that they deal with the most often. Managers of suppliers that are particularly dependent on Wal-Mart's orders, for example, may design their firm's information systems to fit neatly with the mechanistic system used at Wal-Mart.

STRATEGY. The link between strategy and organization structure is widely acknowledged, well developed, and straightforward. Recall that in Chapter 9 we identified two basic Mainstream strategies: cost leadership and differentiation, each of which may have a broad or narrow focus. A cost leadership strategy is typically best supported by a mechanistic organization structure. The mechanistic structure is designed to improve internal efficiency and reduce costs, which is entirely consistent with the goal of a cost leader strategy—that is, to increase profit margins by keeping costs lower than competitors' costs. In contrast, the differentiation strategy is often best supported by an organic organization structure. The organic structure is designed to develop innovative products and services, which is consistent with the goal of the differentiation strategy—that is, to offer products or services for which consumers are willing to pay a premium.[12]

TECHNOLOGY. *Task technology* refers to the combination of equipment (e.g., computers, machinery, tools) and skills (e.g., techniques, knowledge, processes)

Although solving the Rubik's cube is very complex, it is a task that can be analyzed and broken into steps. The world record for solving the cube is less than ten seconds. The world record for solving a cube blindfolded (including the time spent looking at it before you put on the blindfold) is less than one minute.[13]

Task analyzability refers to the ability to reduce tasks down to mechanical steps and to create objective, computational procedures for problem solving.

Task variety refers to the frequency of unexpected, novel, or exceptional events that occur during work.

that are used to acquire, design, produce, and distribute goods and services. Some kinds of task technologies are more likely to be associated with an organic structure, whereas others fit more neatly with a mechanistic organization structure. Repetitive work and work that can be practically subdivided into its separate steps—even something as complex as building a car—tend to be mechanistically structured. By contrast, tasks that are difficult to subdivide into separate tasks tend to be associated with an organic organization structure. This includes tasks where it is difficult to create objective and computational procedures for problem solving. For example, works of art are not created in an assembly line.

It is rare to find an example of pure mechanistic or pure organic organization structures. Instead, most organizations fall somewhere in the middle between these two extremes. For example, before cell phones became widely available, telephone companies relied on land-line technologies that were stable and could be managed with a mechanistic organization structure. When the new cellular technology was introduced, it was changing relatively quickly, which called for a more organic organization structure. To keep these two services separate, managers at telephone companies such as MTS deliberately placed staff in two different buildings. Employees working with the more predictable and more monopolistic land-line technology in one office building operated under a tried-and-true mechanistic organization structure. Employees working with the emerging and more competitive cellular technology worked in a different building and managed with a more organic organization structure.[14]

Variety and Analyzability.   Research suggests that a mechanistic structure is more appropriate for task technologies that have high degrees of analyzability and low variety. **Task analyzability** refers to the ability to reduce work to mechanical steps and create objective, computational procedures for problem solving. **Task variety** refers to the frequency of unexpected, novel, or exceptional events that occur during work. Combining these two dimensions results in a 2 × 2 framework, as shown in Figure 11.4.

Routine technology is characterized by work that has high analyzability and low variety. Work in such organizations can be broken down into separate steps, and there are few exceptions to standard ways of operating. A common example is traditional assembly-line technology. Jobs like those of bank tellers, data entry workers, or toll booth operators are also highly routine. A classic study by Joan Woodward found that when manufacturers relied on assembly-line technology, then a mechanistic organization structure was associated with increased financial performance.[15] In general, organizations that mass-produce items are more profitable when their managers emphasize standardization, specialization, centralization, and functional departmentalization.

Engineering technology is characterized by work that is very analyzable and has many exceptions. Examples include the work performed by lawyers, engineers, and tax accountants. The best structure for this technology is moderately mechanistic, but not as mechanistic as routine technology.

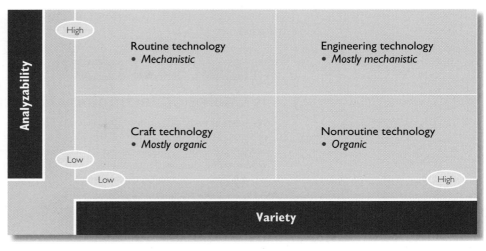

High	Routine technology • *Mechanistic*	Engineering technology • *Mostly mechanistic*
Low	Craft technology • *Mostly organic*	Nonroutine technology • *Organic*
	Low	**High**

Analyzability (vertical axis) · **Variety** (horizontal axis)

Figure 11.4 Task analyzability and variety versus organization structure

Source: Adapted from Daft, R. L. (2001). *Organization theory and design* (7th ed.). Cincinnati, OH: South-Western College, which in turn adapted it from Daft, R., & Macintosh, N. (1978). A new approach to design and use of management information. *California Management Review*, 21, 82–92.

Nonroutine technology is characterized by work that has low analyzability and has many unexpected or novel events. Work in such organizations cannot easily be broken down into separate steps, and many one-of-a-kind activities are necessary. An example is custom-built products and services, and jobs like researchers and strategists who do nonroutine work. Woodward found that when manufacturers relied on "small-batch" technologies to do custom work (e.g., unique short-run or one-of-a-kind products), then an organic organization structure was associated with increased financial performance. In general, organizations that offer tailor-made products and services are more profitable when managers adopt an organic organization structure.

Finally, *craft technology* is characterized by work that is difficult to analyze, but does not have many exceptions. Work in such an organization is based on a lot of tacit knowledge that is applied in predictable settings. Work with these character-

The process of creating a custom-made motorcycle is featured on the popular television show *American Chopper.*

istics might include the performing arts, teaching, and general management. Craft technology may also be evident in some "continuous process" organizations where much of the work is done by machines, but people's tacit knowledge is required to oversee the machines and ensure that they are operating properly. Examples include the work of a master brewer in a brewery and chocolate taste-testers at Hershey. Just like teachers and artists, they work as "troubleshooters" in areas where the nature of problems is often difficult to predict. Woodward found that "continuous process" manufacturers

achieved higher financial performance if they had a more organic organization structure.

WHAT DO YOU THINK?

Is Choice of Technology Objective or Subjective?

We have already noted how norms and values can influence the organization design process. The determination of the analyzability and variety of a task is also socially constructed, often being based on people's values. This is illustrated in situations where some debate arises about how to classify the nature of a task. In such cases what is considered to be the meaning of a technology can depend more on people's subjective beliefs than on objective data. For example, recall from Chapter 2 how new technology—a CT scanner—helped to improve the collegiality in one hospital, but reinforced hierarchical differences in another hospital.[16]

Consider the task of helping youths who have committed crimes. For some people, helping young people escape a life of crime is a very analyzable task that has low variety. From such a perspective, reform is best accomplished by a mechanistic structure: Such youth need to be disciplined, and the best way to do so is with clear rules and structures. This result might be achieved, for example, through a mechanistic "boot camp" setting where such youth face regimented hours and learn to appreciate hard work.

Other people may think that it is difficult to analyze the best way to help youth in trouble with the law because each person has a unique personal history. From this perspective, the best organization structure to achieve reform would be more organic in nature, with specialists who work one-on-one with such youth, providing personalized and appropriate counseling and support.

How do your own beliefs influence your views on the best way to help young people in trouble with the law? Describe an organization structure that is consistent with your views. What are the implications of your view for how governments should create and design organizations that deal with such youth?

Task Interdependence. Another technology factor that has an effect on structure is the interdependence among different work units in an organization. Generally speaking, the greater the interdependence, the more difficult it is to design a mechanistic structure that anticipates and prepares for all the exceptions. James D. Thompson identified three kinds of task interdependence:[17]

- Pooled
- Sequential
- Reciprocal

Pooled interdependence—where each part of the organization works separately to contribute to the common good of the organization—is the most agreeable to a mechanistic structure. For example, think of organizations like Burger King, where managers at each separate location do not need to coordinate their activities with managers at other restaurants, but rather the coordination and standardization across all locations is achieved by managers at a centralized head office.

Sequential interdependence occurs when the output of one individual or work group becomes the input for another individual or work group. If the output does not arrive in a timely fashion or is not of appropriate quality, then the downstream members are unable to do their work. Thus there is a need for close coordination between the two groups. This coordination may be achieved in part with mechanis-

Other Factors That Influence Organization Structure

In addition to environment, strategy, and technology, several other factors influence organization structure. Examples include organization size, managers' personal preferences, human resources management practices, and information technology.

The simplest of these is *organization size,* where bigger generally means more standardization, formalization, and specialization. This makes intuitive sense: You might be able to manage 5 or even 50 people with minimal formal rules and standards, but to manage 5000 or 50,000 people requires a more mechanistic structure.

Managers' *personal preference* also influences organization structure. Some managers value stability, predictability, and order, whereas others value flexibility, adaptability, and spontaneity.[18] The former are more likely to create mechanistic structures, whereas the latter are more likely to promote organic structures. The manager who prefers a mechanistic structure would like knowing that there is a department meeting every Monday morning from 9 to 12, and that every Friday afternoon he or she will receive a copy of the productivity reports for that week.

Human resources management (HRM) is another important factor related to how managers perform the organizing function. Mechanistic organization structures tend to be associated with external motivators such as financial pay. Such structures will attract people who choose jobs based primarily on paychecks or status symbols such as having a corner office. Organic organization structures, in contrast, are more likely to emphasize intrinsic and expressive motivators, which appeal to members' desires to express their creativity and passion at work. Organic organization structures are also more closely associated with subjective rewards, such as the feeling of satisfaction that comes from belonging to a certain type of organizational culture.

Finally, with the growing importance of *information technology,* there is increasing interest in understanding its influence on organization structure. Some argue that because "information is power," the more information that is available to more people, the more power and freedom that everyone will have. For example, the increasing importance of virtual organizations, which are enabled by information technology, will free people from needing to commute to the office and instead allow them to work wherever they please (e.g., at a beach or in their office at home). Proponents of this view believe that information technology can liberate people from ignorance and empower people. In contrast, others argue that because information is power, managers can use this additional information to enhance their own power, resulting in less overall freedom for most employees. For example, thanks to cell phones, personal digital assistants, and computer-top cameras, employees may never be free from the gaze of managers, either at home or at the beach. Proponents of this view believe that information technology oppresses people and makes the world a less humane place. As it turns out, research seems to offer some support for both views.[19]

---

tic rules and procedures, but there will be times when a more organic face-to-face coordination is called for. Many organizations that manufacture products or assemble parts into products work in this manner. A computer assembler such as Gateway Computers relies on suppliers to provide the necessary parts on time and in sufficient quantity and quality. In addition, during the actual assembly process, the core computer hardware needs to be installed in the appropriate configuration so that subsequently installed hardware and software will operate properly.

Reciprocal interdependence refers to the situation where the output of one work unit becomes the input for one or more other work units, which in turn provide outputs that serve as the original unit's inputs. This type of interdependence is most likely to be associated with an organic structure. For example, a hospital patient may move back and forth between surgery, physical therapy, and X-ray departments. Specialists from each area must coordinate their information and treatments.[20]

Mainstream Organizational Types

Just as it is helpful to think about two basic kinds of structure (mechanistic and organic) and two basic kinds of strategy (cost leadership and differentiation), there is some consensus among scholars and practitioners that it is helpful to think about four basic organizational types, listed at the top of the next page.

- Simple
- Defender
- Prospector
- Analyzer[21]

Of course, there is considerable variation among organizations *within* each type. Drawing on the analogy that we introduced earlier, there may be four types of motorized vehicles (e.g., motorcycles, cars, vans, and trucks), but there can still be a lot of variation within any one of those types. For example, there are many different kinds of motorcycles.

Table 11.1 provides an overview of the four organizational types. Note how each type can be characterized by its organization design elements:

- Its organization structure
- Its environment, strategy, and technology

The organization design process suggests that the most appropriate organizational type is influenced by the fit between and among the various parts of an organization's structure, environment, strategy, and technology.

The **Simple type** refers to small organizations that

- Have an organic structure,
- Operate in a narrow segment of a changing environment,
- Have a focus strategy, and
- Rely on technology with high task variety, often with high interdependence.

The Simple type organization structure may be organic simply because managers do not have the need or ability to create a well-developed mechanistic structure. Think of an entrepreneur who starts up a new organization in a garage or home office. This organization starts with one person, so there is little need for developing written guidelines or job descriptions. The job description of the lone entrepreneur is to do everything, and to work as a one-person profit center. Entrepreneurs who manage such Simple organizations have identified what they believe is an opportunity in a changing environment, and they are eager to demonstrate the viability of their new venture to make a profit and to attract investors. Their strategy is to focus on a particular segment of the market, where they tout their differentiated new-and-improved product or service (e.g., "a better mousetrap") or offer low-cost products or services (e.g., thanks to their lower overhead and operating costs). Managers often rely on their tacit knowledge to invent and fine-tune the unique technology required for producing and delivering their product or service.

> **Simple type** organizations have an organic structure, operate in a narrow segment of a changing environment, have a focus strategy, and tend to rely on technology with high task variety and high interdependence.

TABLE 11.1

Organization Design of the Four Basic Mainstream Organizational Types

	Simple Type	Defender Type	Prospector Type	Analyzer Type
Organization Structure	Organic	Mechanistic	Organic	Mechanistic/organic
Environment	Changing	Stable	Changing	Split
Strategy	Focus	Cost leader	Differentiation	Dual
Technology	High interdependence	Single core technology	Reciprocal interdependence	Some interdependence

For example, Ken Reimer started Kendall's Automotive in a small shop in his back-yard. He may be a mechanic, but his organization structure started off being organic, relying on his expertise and that of his suppliers to service customers' automobiles.

The **Defender type** refers to organizations that

- Have a mechanistic structure,
- Operate in a well-defined segment of a stable environment,
- Have a cost leader strategy, and
- Often rely on a single core technology.

Defender organizations have a well-developed mechanistic structure, with high levels of standardization that spell out policies and guidelines, detailed job descriptions that characterize specialization, and a clear hierarchy where decision-making authority is centralized in top managers. Defenders are typically functionally departmentalized, which further enhances specialization in the functional areas of expertise. The most powerful departments within this type of organization are the production and finance departments, which reflects the organization's focus on maximizing efficiency and productivity. This is consistent with pursuing a cost leader strategy in a stable and well-defined environment. Defenders typically have a single core technology, which they have mastered in terms of analyzability and variety, and they constantly fine-tune that core technology to maximize efficiencies. Technology is characterized by an emphasis on explicit knowledge, and on pooled interdependence within departments, or sequential interdependence between departments.

A well-known example of a Defender type is American Brands, the tobacco company where managers took a retrenchment response to the Surgeon General's announcement that smoking was associated with lung cancer (described in Chapter 7). Another example of a Defender strategy is Lincoln Electric,[22] which started in 1895 and has become one of the most successful manufacturing companies in the world thanks to an organization design that helps it achieve significantly lower production costs than its competitors. At the heart of its success are two policies built into its organization structure: One policy guarantees employment for Lincoln Electric's workers even in downtimes, and the other policy guarantees that the standard rates for piecework will not be changed simply because employee earnings are deemed to be too high. The resulting structure provides workers with plenty of incentives to increase efficiency (piece rates will not be changed due to their improvements) and no disincentives (jobs will not be lost due to increased efficiency). Average wages are about twice the going rate for similar work in other firms.

The fact that this organization design provides a sustainable competitive advantage is illustrated by an event during World War II, when the U.S. government asked all welding equipment manufacturers to add capacity. At that point the president of Lincoln Electric went to Washington, D.C., to explain that the nation's existing capacity would be sufficient if it were used as efficiently as at Lincoln Electric, and proceeded to provide proprietary knowledge about techniques that soon improved industry-wide production sufficiently. For a while, competitors had costs close to those at Lincoln Electric, but over time the implementation of the Defender type at Lincoln allowed it to outperform its competitors just as it had before.

The **Prospector type** refers to organizations that

- Have an organic structure,
- Operate in a broad market of a changing environment,
- Have a differentiation strategy, and

Defender type organizations have a mechanistic structure, operate in a narrow segment of a stable environment, have a cost leader strategy, and often rely on a single core technology.

Prospector type organizations have an organic structure, operate in a broad market of a changing environment, have a differentiation strategy, and rely on technology that is difficult to analyze.

- Rely on technology that is difficult to analyze, often with reciprocal interdependence.

Prospector organizations are characterized by their focus on constant innovation, which means that they are always searching for new market opportunities and remaining flexible and entrepreneurial. Prospectors have an organic structure, characterized by departmentalization that has many different relatively independent divisions acting as profit centers. In Prospector organizations, decision-making authority is decentralized down to the level of the profit center or lower, the level of standardization is low to permit flexibility, and specialization is low to permit people to adapt to change and do what is needed. Managers in Prospector organizations see their environment as changing, and because of their desire to develop new products and new markets, top managers often have a background in marketing and research and development. Prospectors pursue a differentiation strategy, and they rely on multiple technologies and reciprocal interdependence, which underscore the merits of the adaptable organic structure.

Philip Morris is a well-known example of a Prospector type, as demonstrated by the way it developed new products and markets in response to the Surgeon General's announcement that smoking was associated with lung cancer (described in Chapter 7). The success of Philip Morris has allowed it to purchase other companies where managers have implemented a Prospector strategy (e.g., Kraft Foods, Miller Brewing, and General Foods). Apple and 3M are other companies with a Prospector strategy, and both are well known for being innovation leaders in their industries.[23]

The **Analyzer type** refers to organizations that

Analyzer type organizations essentially have two spheres of operations, with some parts of the organization operating like a Defender, and other parts operating like a Prospector.

- Have two spheres of operations, with parts of the organization operating like a Defender type and other parts operating like a Prospector type, and
- Have a combination of mechanistic and organic organization structures, using both a cost leader strategy and a differentiation strategy.

Analyzers often develop hybrid structures to accommodate their two spheres of operations. The resulting structure may include both functional departments (with high levels of standardization, specialization, and centralization) and divisional profit centers (e.g., product or regional departments that act as self-contained profit centers and have relatively low levels of standardization, specialization, and centralization). Analyzer organizations use a cost leader strategy and predictable technologies in stable sectors of the environment, and a differentiation strategy and evolving technology in changing parts of the environment.

A classic example of an Analyzer type is the tobacco company R. J. Reynolds (RJR). After the Surgeon General announced that smoking was associated with lung cancer, RJR managers retrenched some parts of their business and copied new innovations in other parts (described in Chapter 7). A more recent example is Tech Data, a *Fortune* 100 company that distributes computer software, hardware, and networking products throughout the world. Its main customers are "resellers," which refers to organizations that purchase computer components, package them, and then resell the bundled components to end-user companies that lack a network infrastructure. The key to Tech Data's success has been its ability to operate like a Defender in its distribution and to operate like a Prospector in offering new products and entering new markets. The structure for distribution is highly mechanistic, with functionally organized distribution centers that have high levels of standardization and routines designed to maximize efficiency. The structure for the Prospector side relies on monitoring and adapting to changes in the environment, using face-to-face technology such as customer "summit meetings" that are held four times each year to aid in identifying viable new products.[24]

Staying Fit

Figure 11.5 presents a visual overview of our discussion so far, by depicting the essential components of the Mainstream organization design process. As indicated in the figure, the four Mainstream organizational types are influenced by the fit between key aspects of the organization:

- The fit between the Mainstream environment, strategy, and technology
- The fit between the four Mainstream dimensions of organization structure

It is one thing to *describe* how the pieces of the organization design puzzle fit together to form one of the successful organizational types as described above; it is quite another to maintain such fitness in *practice* over time. The **Misfit** organizational type refers to organizations that have misalignments among their internal organization structures and/or their environments, strategy, and technology.[25] A classic example of a Misfit is the Ligget & Myers tobacco company, where managers, after the Surgeon General announced that smoking was associated with lung cancer, failed to achieve efficiencies in stable operations and failed to copy new innovations in the industry (described in Chapter 7). Of course, there are many reasons that a Misfit type can emerge, providing plenty of incentives for managers to remain vigilant in regard to organization design.

Research suggests that organization design usually involves fine-tuning an existing organizational type. This means that Defender organizations must become even more cost-efficient, and that Prospector organizations must become even more innovative. Lincoln Electric (a Defender) was able to sustain its competitive cost advantage even after sharing its secrets during World War II, and 3M (a Prospector) encourages its members to spend 20 percent of their time pursuing the products and services that will be the company's mainstay market offerings five years into the future.

While most managers may spend the majority of their time fine-tuning their existing organizational type, some organizations will become Misfits unless they change from one

Misfit type organizations have misalignments among their internal organization structures and/or environments, strategy, and technology.

Figure 11.5   Overview of the Mainstream organization design process

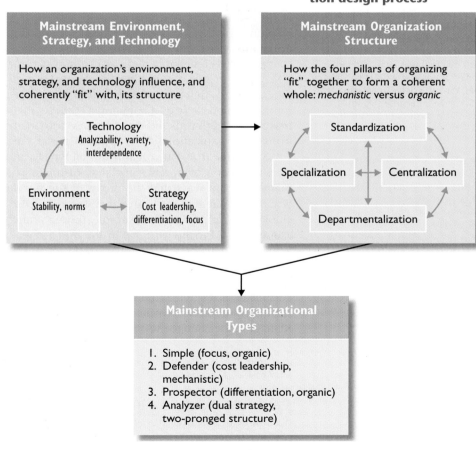

Mainstream Environment, Strategy, and Technology

How an organization's environment, strategy, and technology influence, and coherently "fit" with, its structure

- Technology
  Analyzability, variety, interdependence
- Environment
  Stability, norms
- Strategy
  Cost leadership, differentiation, focus

Mainstream Organization Structure

How the four pillars of organizing "fit" together to form a coherent whole: *mechanistic* versus *organic*

- Standardization
- Specialization
- Centralization
- Departmentalization

Mainstream Organizational Types

1. Simple (focus, organic)
2. Defender (cost leadership, mechanistic)
3. Prospector (differentiation, organic)
4. Analyzer (dual strategy, two-pronged structure)

The Honda Fit was the top-selling car in Japan in 2002, and was one of Honda's top-selling cars in Japan and Europe for more than five years (where it was sold under the name Jazz) before it was launched in the United States in the 2007 model year. Why the delay in entering the U.S. market? Because this small, fuel-efficient car did not "fit" the American market until then.

organizational type to another. Such change may be necessary for at least two reasons. First, it may be demanded because of changes that are occurring in the environment, including competitive pressures and new technologies. For example, a major shift occurred in the airplane manufacturing industry with the change from propeller technology to jet engine technology, and many propeller plane manufacturers were unable to maintain an appropriate fit between the environment–strategy–technology triad and their organization structure.

Second, managers may need to develop new organizational types because the very factors that explain why a particular type is successful will, over time, cause it to fail. Danny Miller calls this phenomenon the *Icarus paradox*, referring to the Greek myth where Icarus achieved great success thanks to his ability to fly using feathers attached to his arms with wax. However, when this key to his success resulted in his climbing to new heights, Icarus got too close to the sun; the wax melted, and he plunged to his death in the Aegean Sea.[26] A similar argument is found in organizational life-cycle theory, which suggests that mastering any one of the successful organizational types inevitably requires changing to a new type in order to avoid becoming a Misfit.[27] Organizational life-cycle theory suggests that just as people must abandon the basic skills that served them well in one phase of their life and embrace new skills for the next phase (e.g., a baby must learn to abandon the safety of crawling and embrace learning to walk like a toddler), so too organizations must be managed to move from one organizational type to another over time.[28]

Switching from one organizational type to another can be extremely challenging, as it requires a comprehensive view of organization design that takes into account many different ways that the pieces of the puzzle fit together. It often takes several years to implement such a change because it is seldom sufficient to make a small change here and there. For example, through much of its history Sony was a textbook example of a Prospector type. In the mid-1980s, its CEO, Noria Ohga, attempted to achieve efficiencies by installing centralized and relatively rigid control standards and budgeting requirements. In short, he tried to add some characteristics of a Defender organization, but the end result did not provide a coherent fit. Observers both outside and inside Sony agree that this lack of coherence in Sony's organization design is at least partly to blame for its subsequent problems in adapting to the environment.[29] Managing the change process will be described more fully in Chapter 13.

MULTISTREAM ORGANIZATION DESIGN

Multistream organization design shares a similar format to Mainstream organization design, but has different content. The four fundamental issues of organization structure are the same, but they are viewed differently from a Multistream perspective, as are the key aspects of the Multistream environment, strategy, and technology triad. Taken together, these differences yield variations on the organizational types.

Organization Structure

Recall that the Mainstream approach has two basic kinds of organization structures: mechanistic and organic. The Multistream approach also identifies two basic kinds of organization structures: **inward structure** (where the four Multistream fundamental elements of organizing are emphasized among stakeholders *within* an organization) and **outward structure** (where the four Multistream fundamentals are emphasized among stakeholders *outside* the organization). Figure 11.6 presents a graphic depiction of the inward–outward continuum.[30]

As with the Mainstream mechanistic–organic continuum, the logic behind the Multistream inward–outward continuum is that the four Multistream fundamentals of organizing are interrelated. Thus, in an inward organization structure, when members treat one another with respect (i.e., high dignification), there is also likely to be an emphasis on mutual decision making among members (high participation), members are likely to look for new opportunities to improve the tasks they perform (high sensitization), and they will likely seek new ways to improve internal operations (high experimentation). In this way, the four Multistream fundamentals form a self-reinforcing system, where emphasis on any one fundamental is expected to be associated with a similar emphasis on the others. This interplay between the four fundamentals is evident in the inward organization structure at Semco (see the opening case in Chapter 10). Under the management of Ricardo Semler, members of this organization choose their own hours, experiment with different jobs, and call meetings to initiate change whenever they find worthwhile opportunities to do so.

Similarly, for an outward organization structure, when managers place a great deal of emphasis on treating external stakeholders—especially stakeholders who are not well served by the status quo—with respect (that is, high dignification), then it follows that the advice of these stakeholders will be sought (high participation), that stakeholders will look for ways to improve overall well-being (high experimentation), and that members will seek new ways to improve the effect of the organization's activities on external stakeholders (high sensitization). Mohammad Yunus and the Grameen Bank (described in the opening case in Chapter 6) provide an example of an outward organization structure in action: Poor people are treated with dignity and invited to participate as members of the Grameen Bank, and members are especially sensitive to the needs of the marginalized (women and children) and are willing to experiment with new products (e.g., a program that provides loans to beggars).

As with the mechanistic–organic continuum, the inward–outward continuum does not describe perfectly what goes on in all Multistream organizations. Nevertheless, it does provide a

> **Inward structure** is an organization structure where managers emphasize experimentation, sensitization, dignification, and participation among an organization's internal stakeholders and operations.
>
> **Outward structure** is an organization structure where managers emphasize experimentation, sensitization, dignification, and participation among an organization's external stakeholders and operations.

Figure 11.6   A continuum showing the two basic varieties of Multistream organization structure

Inward Structure		Outward Structure
(focus on stakeholders *within* organizational boundaries)		(focus on stakeholders *beyond* organizational boundaries)
Improve operations with and for stakeholders inside the organization	Experimentation	Improve relationships and links with stakeholders outside the organization
Focus on opportunities with and for stakeholders inside the organization	Sensitization	Focus on opportunities with and for stakeholders outside the organization
Respect coworkers	Dignification	Respect external stakeholders
Include all members	Participation	Include external stakeholders

helpful conceptual framework to think about organization structure and, in particular, about how to develop a Multistream organization structure and how changes in one of the Multistream fundamentals of organizing can affect the other three fundamentals. Managers must ensure that the various fundamental elements are managed in a consistent fashion. For example, it is inconsistent to put up posters proclaiming that "We respect our employees" and at the same time require employees to "punch in" at a time clock every day.

Environment, Strategy, and Technology

Just as is the case for their Mainstream counterparts, managers must be aware of various factors that influence the design of Multistream organization structures. Some important aspects from the environment, strategy, and technology triad are highlighted in Figure 11.7.

ENVIRONMENT. Recall that the Multistream approach emphasizes a wide range of forms of well-being, from spiritual to aesthetic to physical to ecological to social. The broader the interest in the larger environment in these multiple forms of well-being that are offered by an organization, the greater the likelihood that an outward organization structure will be developed. For example, when a broad cross section of motorists begin to desire environmentally friendlier forms of transportation, then it is possible to provide integrated solutions such as hydrogen fuel cells, improved public transportation, and bicycle paths. The expensive infrastructure that must be developed to serve these purposes requires a broad base of interested drivers. However, when only a small portion of society is seeking such services, then managers must rely on smaller specialty or niche markets and be characterized by an inward organization structure. This is illustrated by bicycle shops that recondition old bikes, and organizations such as CarShare and ZipCar, which enable their members to share cars because they do not need the cars on a 24-hours-a-day/7-days-a-week basis.

Whether a Multistream organization structure is inward or outward also depends on its specific impetus. Sometimes managers will implement Multistream structures primarily to improve working conditions and provide meaningful jobs (inward); at other times, such structures are adopted because managers wish to change the way the larger industry operates (outward). Managers may be motivated to implement Multistream fundamental elements *within* the boundaries of the organization when they find it difficult to retain qualified workers. This is the case in the Silicon Valley, where many organizations offer on-site child care, physical fitness activities, flextime, and other benefits that are consistent with inward organization structures. Managers may want to implement Multistream fundamental elements *beyond* the boundaries of the organization due to external environmental factors, such as opportunities or pressure from

Figure 11.7 Effect of environment, strategy, and technology on Multistream organization structure

Inward Structure		Outward Structure
	External Environment	
Narrow/segmented	Breadth of interest	Broad/general
Satisfy members	Impetus	Satisfy customers/suppliers/regulators
	Strategy	
Minimizer	Type	Transformer
	Technology	
Intra-organizational waste	Emphasis	Inter-organizational waste
Low	Available knowledge/capacity	High

external organizations such as suppliers, customers, or regulators. For example, when customers actively seek out Fair Trade goods or locally grown vegetables, it may encourage managers to adopt more outward structures. Once managers in Mainstream organizations see Multistream structures in action, they are more likely to implement such structures themselves. This is especially true if the Multistream organization is an industry leader, and if it offers valuable resources for other organizations.[31] For example, when Costco performs social audits on its suppliers, it signals to the industry that it prefers suppliers with Multistream structures.

STRATEGY.   Recall from Chapter 9 that the two basic Multistream strategies were labeled as minimizer and transformer, and that each could operate in a broad or a narrow niche. An inward organization structure provides a good fit with a minimizer strategy, because both tend to focus on what happens inside an organization and the balance between multiple forms of intra-organizational well-being. This structure/strategy combination is apparent at AES, where managers seek to minimize the firm's ecological footprint while improving the quality of work life for its employees (see the opening case in Chapter 15). An outward organization structure provides a good fit with a transformer strategy, as both tend to focus on what happens outside an organization and seek to transform underutilized external resources into valuable inputs and outputs. An excellent example of this structure/strategy combined was described in Chapter 9 in the community of organizations in Kalundborg, Denmark, where the waste by-products of some organizations serve as valuable inputs for other organizations.

TECHNOLOGY.   Another difference between inward and outward structures is related to technology. Managers who develop inward organization structures focus on improving internal technologies. For them, this means becoming more environmentally friendly by reducing waste, minimizing energy use, and reducing physical fatigue by redesigning jobs. It also means becoming more socially responsible by listening to all employees and promoting meaningful work. Managers who develop outward structures seek to improve extra-organizational technologies. For them, this may mean educating consumers on how to consume *fewer* resources, taking "waste" from one industry and transforming it into valuable inputs for another industry, or hiring marginalized people and providing them with valuable job training.

Which Multistream organization structure is implemented is also influenced by the technology and the amount of available knowledge for Multistream structures. Managers and organizations that lack experience with Multistream organization structures often start with inward—rather than outward—structures. The inward structure allows them to become familiar with and gain confidence in using Multistream structures. Developing the capacity to work in a Multistream structure takes time, especially when people have little experience working in such a structure. Recall from the opening case in Chapter 2 that it took a long time for people to get used to working in Mainstream structures when they were first being introduced and fine-tuned by managers like Josiah Wedgwood. Similarly, it took some time and shared experience for the Multistream structure at Semco to be developed to the point where employees could choose their own salaries, set their own hours, and select their own managers. Part of this learning process can be enhanced by hiring practices, as is evident in Semco members' choosing their coworkers. It can also be managed by the approach used at Southwest Airlines, where managers increase employees' capacity to work in a Multistream structure by providing training programs in which members acquire the skills to exhibit and practice dignification, experimentation, sensitization, and participation.[32]

WHAT DO YOU THINK?

Can You Introduce Multistream Structures in the Classroom?

When it comes to designing courses and assigning grades, most students have grown accustomed to and have developed a preference for a mechanistic structure. For example, students want to know ahead of time what percentage mark they need to earn on exams and assignments in order to earn a particular letter grade, how much weight is given to each test and assignment, and which pages in the textbook they are responsible for, and they typically prefer "objective" multiple-choice questions to "subjective" essay questions.

What would happen if an instructor wanted to introduce a more Multistream approach and invited students to choose which chapters of the textbook they wanted to focus on, to write their own exam questions, and to assign their own grades? Would this experiment facilitate learning in the classroom, or would students be inclined to minimize their efforts and maximize their grades? If you could design a Multistream structure for your course, what would it look like? How do you think professors and other students would respond?

Multistream Organizational Types

We can identify four basic Multistream organizational types, as shown in Table 11.2. Like the Mainstream types, each Multistream organizational type is characterized by its combination of organization design elements:

- Its organization structure
- Its environment, strategy, and technology

The names of the four Multistream types—Voluntary Simplicity, MultiDefender, MultiProspector, and MultiAnalyzer—point out their similarities to their Mainstream counterparts. Nevertheless, these Multistream types are also qualitatively different from the Mainstream types.

Voluntary Simplicity type organizations have an outward structure, operate in a narrow segment of the environment, have a narrow minimizer or transformer strategy, and focus on enhancing well-being within and/or beyond the organization.

The **Voluntary Simplicity type** refers to small organizations that usually

- Have an outward structure (but also strong inward dimensions),
- Operate in a very narrow sector of the environment,
- Have a niche (minimizer or transformer) strategy, and
- Seek well-being within and/or beyond the organization.

TABLE 11.2

Organization Design of the Four Basic Multistream Organizational Types

	Voluntary Simplicity Type	MultiDefender Type	MultiProspector Type	MultiAnalyzer Type
Organization Structure	Outward	Inward	Outward	In/outward
Environment	Very narrow	Narrow	Broad	Broad
Strategy	Niche	Minimizer	Transformer	Dual
Technology	Intra/extra-organizational	Intra-organizational	Extra-organizational	Intra/extra-organizational

Often this organizational type is managed by people who are disillusioned with the Mainstream approach. This group includes "downwardly mobile" managers who are willing to take a pay cut in order to work in organizations where they are allowed to pursue multiple forms of well-being and are treated with dignity. Surveys suggest that the larger Voluntary Simplicity movement includes at least 25 percent of Americans,[33] and it is not unusual to hear sentiments such as "I quit my 40-hour-a-week slavery and got a 20-hour-a-week job that I love."[34] When people in this larger movement do not find working in Mainstream organizations satisfying, some start or join Voluntary Simplicity organizations such as organic grocery stores, restaurants, bakeries, used-clothing stores, bookstores, bicycle repair shops, childcare centers, various craft shops, alternative healthcare centers, alternative schools, and so on.[35] At the start-up of these operations, managers of Voluntary Simplicity organizations invite external stakeholders to help them to find a viable vision for the organizations, and they are sensitive to different niches in the environment where their alternative organization is needed (as an example, recall the early start-up phase of the Grameen Bank described in the opening case in Chapter 6).[36]

The **MultiDefender type** refers to organizations that

- Have an inward structure,
- Operate in a stable environment,
- Have a minimizer strategy, and
- Focus on maximizing well-being within the organization.

These kinds of organizations might appear on "Best Green Companies" or "Best Employers of the Year" lists because of their highly satisfying jobs and corporate social responsibility records. They include organizations such as Recreational Equipment, Wegman's Food Markets, HomeBanc Mortgage, and Standard Pacific.[37] These organizations are known for their participative management practices, which experiment with new ways to treat employees with dignity and sensitivity. They often have a specific niche in the marketplace, and they strive to continuously make their internal operations more socially just and environmentally friendly. An excellent example of a MultiDefender organization is Semco, which was described in the opening case of Chapter 10.

The **MultiProspector type** refers to organizations that

- Have an outward structure,
- Operate in an area of the environment where there is broad interest in their product or service,
- Have a transformer strategy, and
- Focus on maximizing well-being beyond the organization.

These organizations promote environmentally friendly products and technology, such as The Body Shop, Eat-it (a virtual organic grocery store), and manufacturers of composting boxes made from recycled materials. Managers in these organizations work closely with suppliers and customers—often because of their high interorganizational interdependence—to educate them about the benefits of their products and services. Sandra Rothenberg presents case studies of three MultiProspector organizations where managers—aware that to become a truly sustainable society, everyone ultimately needs to consume less—encourage customers to purchase *fewer* of their products.[38] For example, Gage Chemical is helping Chrysler to become increasingly environmentally friendly in its paint operations by providing better ways to clean

MultiDefender type organizations have an inward structure, operate in a segmented environment, use a minimizer strategy, and focus on enhancing well-being within the organization.

MultiProspector type organizations have an outward structure, operate in an area of the environment where there is broad receptivity, have a transformer strategy, and focus on enhancing well-being beyond the organization.

paint circulation systems and use less product. Chrysler's paint plant environmental manager has said, "We couldn't do it without [Gage]. [Their representative] has the specialized knowledge. What shows his commitment is that when he wants to cut the usage, he cuts into his own pockets. He puts the plant's goals ahead of money for his company. That is real teamwork."

Finally, the **MultiAnalyzer type** refers to organizations that essentially have

- Two spheres of operations, with parts of the organization operating like a MultiDefender and other parts operating like a MultiProspector, and
- A combination of inward and outward organization structures, utilizing both a minimizer strategy and a transformer strategy.

Managers of this organizational type strive to achieve the best of both worlds, providing excellent workplaces and helping external stakeholders to have structures and practices that meet multiple forms of well-being. The MultiAnalyzer type is illustrated by the Interface carpet company, which was described in the opening case in Chapter 9. Recall CEO Ray Anderson's twofold vision for Interface: (1) to be a world-leading sustainable organization in its internal operations (MultiDefender) and (2) to become a restorative organization that helps suppliers and customers put back more than they take from the Earth (MultiProspector). Interface's vision statement recognizes that all components of its organization design must work together to achieve this twofold goal. The dematerialization of internal operations, and the collaboration and capacity sharing that characterize its relationships with external stakeholders, requires a Multistream structure where both internal and external stakeholders are treated with dignity.[39]

Staying Fit

Figure 11.8 presents a visual overview of our discussion so far, by depicting the essential components of the Multistream organization design process. As indicated in the figure, the four Multistream organizational types are influenced by the fit between key aspects of the organization:

- The fit between the Multistream environment, strategy, and technology
- The fit between the four Multistream dimensions of organization structure

Just as for Mainstream managers, the organization design challenge for Multistream managers is to develop and maintain a successful organizational type and avoid becoming a Misfit. As with Mainstream types, the need to change a Multistream organizational type may be triggered by events in the larger environment (such as the emergence of new technology) or changes that are built into the type itself (such as described by the Icarus paradox and organizational life-cycle theory).

And just as some social trends and ecological concerns are increasing the pressure on Mainstream managers to implement a Multistream organizational type, so too Multistream managers may face other pressure to implement a Mainstream organizational type. Anecdotal evidence suggests that this is especially the case when a publicly owned Multistream business faces some sort of disaster, such as is eventually confronted by all organizations, no matter how well managed.

This was the challenge that faced Dennis Bakke when he was CEO of AES. Bakke tried to design an organization where work was fun—a smile factory of a different sort than that operated by Disney. AES is a global energy giant, with 40,000 employees in 31 countries and annual revenues of more than $8 billion.[40] Because Bakke believes that Mainstream organization design stifles joy at work, AES avoided written job descriptions, official organizational charts, and tall hierarchies (three layers were enough).

Bakke also refused to place primary emphasis on quantifiable financial goals. Instead, he argues, joy at work can be found when the four fundamental elements of Multistream organizing are evident. For example, *sensitization* was facilitated at AES in that performance was explicitly evaluated based on AES principles that transcend economic goals, and on effects on the larger environment. *Dignification* was evident because leaders saw their role as serving other employees, rather than as ruling over people and resources. *Participation* was evident in the many ad hoc task forces that ensured smooth relationships across organizational subunits. AES decisions were made in community by nonleaders at the lowest practicable organizational level. All of this fostered *experimentation*, which was evident when members and external stakeholders were invited to participate in AES's decision-making process, when annual reports acknowledged the contributions of ordinary employees, and when people were not fired for making mistakes.

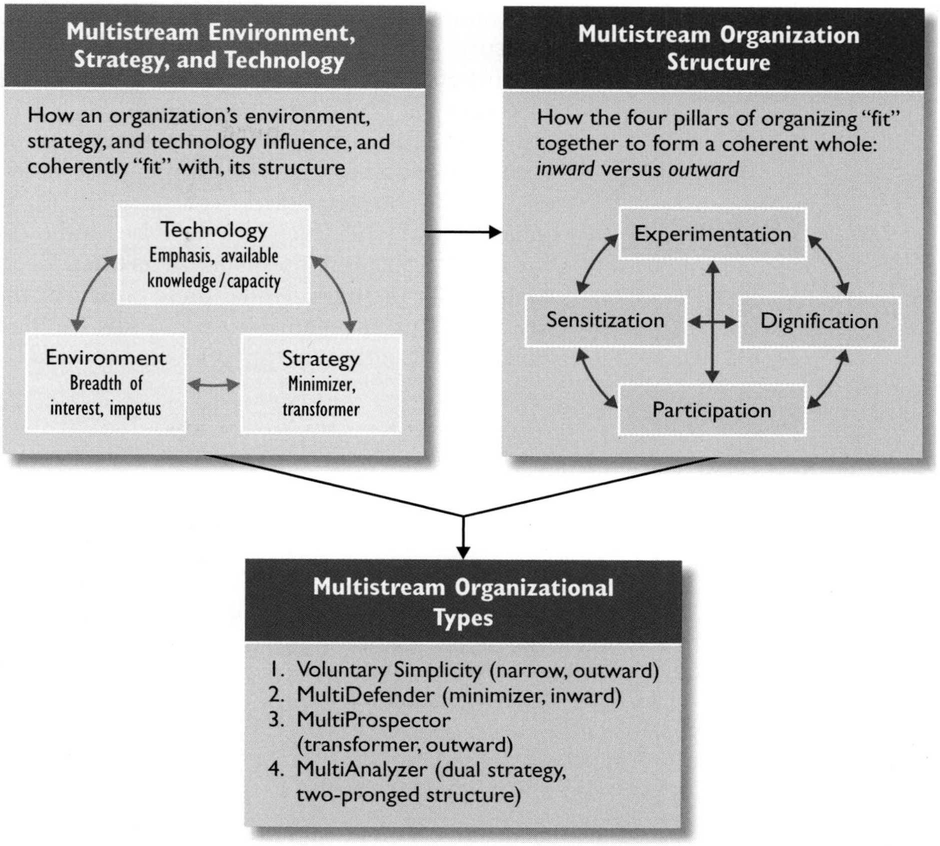

Figure 11.8 Overview of the Multistream organization design process

Perhaps the most important part of Bakke's story is how Bakke responded to difficult times. On one occasion, AES employees had falsified the results of water testing at an AES plant in Oklahoma. Even though no ecological damage resulted from this deception, the price of AES stock dropped 40 percent on the day it released a letter that both acknowledged the falsification and recommitted itself to being an organization based on integrity. Soon Bakke's job was on the line:

> Several of our most senior people and board members raised the possibility that our approach to operations was a major part of the problem. It was as if the entire company were on the verge of ruin. They jumped to the conclusion that our radical decentralization, lack of organizational layers, and unorthodox operating style had caused "economic" collapse. There was, of course, no *real* economic collapse. Only the stock price declined. . . .
>
> All of this put an enormous strain on the relationship between Roger [Sant, AES cofounder] and me. The board had lost confidence in me and my leadership approach. (I believe Roger had, too.) Should we split the company? Should one of us quit? He wasn't having fun, and neither was I. I told him I wanted to stay and make the company work. . . .
>
> The breach by our Oklahoma group was minor relative to similar missteps by dozens of large, conventionally managed organizations. There was nothing to suggest that the company operating in a more conventional manner would have protected AES from such mistakes.[41]

The important part of this story is that Bakke remained committed to his Multistream management approach to organization design, even though he faced enormous pressure to adopt a more Mainstream approach. Bakke faced similar pressure, somewhat ironically, when the price of AES stock plunged in the Enron downdraft. When sailing had been smooth, everyone had been congratulating Bakke for his Multistream approach. Bakke believed that there was nothing inherent in his approach that would make AES more vulnerable to missteps than if the company followed a Mainstream approach.

Many managers have been admired for adopting Multistream management practices, but when they face the crises and economic downturns that are inevitable for *any* organization, these managers often face pressure to revert to "tried-and-true" Mainstream methods. Under these pressures, many managers do adopt Mainstream fundamentals of organizing, even if the Multistream initiatives may have been part of a solution rather than part of the problem.[42]

CLOSING CASE

Design for a Soup Kitchen[43]

You are both troubled and intrigued by a challenge you received at a chance meeting on the bus with your older sister's former classmate, whom you hadn't seen for years. Even though Nancy is five years older than you, she always seemed to be interested in talking with you, and once she even helped you solve a knotty physics problem in high school. Nancy did not seem to be her usual cheerful self (perhaps because it was too early in the morning to be cheerful). You were surprised at how her eyes lit up when you told her that you were taking business courses at college.

Nancy asked if you had learned anything about organization design. You mumbled something about a course in management you were struggling through. Excited, she asked if you knew anything about the way in which values influence how organizations are designed. Puzzled, you said that your professor actually talked about that sort of stuff a lot. After she had told you her story, you understood why Nancy was so interested in your course.

> After high school, I decided that I would try to make this world a better place. I didn't want to go to college just for the sake of enhancing my own career; I wanted some hands-on experience in helping people. It didn't take long before I was doing volunteer work in a soup kitchen.

You were surprised to hear how many people depend on food banks and soup kitchens. Your city's food bank is one of its fastest-growing corporations in town, providing food for more than 5 percent of its population. You learn that a typical soup kitchen in your city feeds about 250 people per day.

Nancy told you about three basic types of soup kitchens. The first model she called the "carrot and stick" soup kitchens. She mentioned several examples of this organizational type where to get the food, you needed to pass through a church. Quite literally, the building was designed so that the only way to the soup kitchen was to go through the chapel. You could only get your reward (carrot) after hearing a sermon (stick).

The second model Nancy called the "self-serving" model (incorrectly, visions of a buffet-style brunch filled your thoughts). These soup kitchens, which are the ones you read about in the newspapers occasionally, have a large staff and are able to raise hundreds of thousands of dollars, but only 2 percent of the money raised actually goes to purchase food for hungry people. At worst, staff in such soup kitchens work there for *their* self-serving reasons: Feeding hungry people provides a means for the staff to raise funds for their own livelihood.

The third model Nancy called the "charity" model. She had worked for an organization of this type for five years. In this model, well-meaning people donate money and manage a soup kitchen to feed people who are less fortunate than themselves. This model relies on volunteer help and charity; anyone who wants soup does not have to do anything except walk through the door and eat.

At first, Nancy said, she thought the charity model was the best way to organize. She worked hard and successfully in that setting, and after a few years became the paid manager of one such soup kitchen. The organization also had two part-time staff members and an abundance of volunteers who would come in to serve the 200 or so simple hot lunches prepared each day in a church basement. Most of the food served was donated through a local food bank. The organization was governed by a board of individuals who wanted to help people less fortunate than themselves.

After a while, however, Nancy began to have doubts about how the charity model worked. Her misgivings were triggered by the things she heard people say who came there to eat: "I never thought I'd drop so low as to become a charity case." "It is humiliating for me to be here." "I feel that I have no more dignity." Nancy described how this affected her:

> I started to think about those comments, and I talked about the comments with my friends and associates. Were we robbing people of their dignity? Was our organization designed in such a way that we could not help but rob people of dignity? It bothered me to see how the attitude of our "regulars" seemed to change. At first, they felt badly because they felt that they did not have anything to contribute back. Then, after a while, they started to think that they should not contribute anything.
>
> I listened some more, and asked probing questions. I tried to put myself in the shoes of the people who came to eat our soup. Would I like to be treated as a charity case? What would it do to me, to my sense of self-worth, to depend on handouts?
>
> I started talking about my concerns with my board members. I thought that they would provide a receptive ear for my concerns. And at first they did, but any suggestion I made about transforming our organization into a "dignity" model was resisted.
>
> I became almost obsessed by my frustration with the charity model. Finally, the board gave me an ultimatum: "Focus your efforts on our charity-type organization, or take a bus ride."

Nancy asks if you would be willing to give her some advice on designing a "dignity" model organization. She has already made some progress in identifying sources where she thinks she could get food donations to start up such a soup kitchen, and she has some friends and acquaintances who could provide start-up money. She also says she has a site she could use. Nancy just needs help in envisioning this new organization. How should it be managed? Who is welcome to join? How to start?

QUESTIONS FOR DISCUSSION

1. Draw on concepts from this and earlier chapters to describe each of the three types of soup kitchens discussed in the case—carrot and stick, self-serving, and charity. Describe the organization structure you think characterizes each type. Are there differences in how their managers might view the environment, strategy, and technology? Do they represent three different organizational types, or are they variations of one (or two) particular types?

2. Develop an organization design for Nancy's dignity-model soup kitchen. Describe each of the four fundamentals of organizing as well as relevant factors pertaining to the environment, strategy, and technology.

3. Which ideas from the chapter were most useful in your analysis? Which ones would you like to learn more about?

4. Think about an organization with which you are familiar (it could be your school), and describe the intended and unintended outcomes associated with its organization design.

SUMMARY

Organization design is the process of developing an organizational type by ensuring that there is a fit between and among an organization's fundamental structural elements and its environment, strategy, and technology.

Mainstream organization design considers how (1) two basic kinds of organization structure (mechanistic versus organic) and (2) factors in an organization's environment (stability and norms), strategy (cost leader versus differentiation), and technology (analyzability, variety, and interdependence) fit together to (3) form one of four organizational types:

- The *Simple* type refers to small organizations and new ventures that have an organic structure, operate in a narrow segment of a changing environment, have a focus strategy, and rely on technology characterized by high task variety and interdependence.

- The *Defender* type refers to organizations that have a mechanistic structure, operate in a narrow segment of a stable environment, have a cost leader strategy, and have a single core technology.

- The *Prospector* type refers to organizations that have an organic structure, operate in a broad market of a changing environment, have a differentiation strategy, and rely on technology that is difficult to analyze.
- The *Analyzer* type refers to organizations that essentially have two spheres of operations, with some parts of the organization design operating like a Defender and other parts operating like a Prospector.

Multistream organization design considers how (1) two basic kinds of organization structure (inward versus outward) and (b) factors in an organization's environment (general interest and impetus), strategy (minimizer versus transformer), and technology (waste reduction, capacity) fit together to (3) form one of four organizational types:

- The *Voluntary Simplicity* type refers to small organizations that have an outward structure, have found a niche in the environment, have a narrow minimizer or transformer strategy, and focus on enhancing well-being within and/or beyond the organization.
- The *MultiDefender* type refers to organizations that have an inward structure, have found a niche in the environment, have a minimizer strategy, and focus on enhancing overall well-being within the organization.
- The *MultiProspector* type refers to organizations that have an outward structure, operate in an area of the environment where there is broad receptivity, have a transformer strategy, and focus on enhancing overall well-being beyond the organization.
- The *MultiAnalyzer* type refers to organizations that essentially have two spheres of operations, with some parts of the organization operating like a MultiDefender and other parts operating like a MultiProspector.

QUESTIONS FOR REFLECTION AND DISCUSSION

1. What are the generic elements in organization design that are important from both a Mainstream approach and a Multistream approach?

2. How are the four fundamentals of organizing related to one another? Why do you think that it is difficult to change one fundamental without also changing the others?

3. How is the Mainstream mechanistic–organic continuum similar to the Multistream inward–outward continuum? What are key differences between the two? Can you think of organizations that might represent each quadrant if the two models are crossed, as indicated below?

		Mainstream Approach	
		Mechanistic	*Organic*
Multistream	*Inward*	Quadrant 1	Quadrant 2
Approach	*Outward*	Quadrant 4	Quadrant 3

4. Describe the four Mainstream organizational types. What are their key features? How might they be related to one another over time?

5. Describe the four Multistream organizational types. What are their key features? How might they be related to one another over time?

6. If one of the factors that influences the "fitness" of an organization design is the environment, then how is it possible that the Defender, Prospector, and Analyzer organizational types are all present in the same environment? (Recall from Chapter 9 that American Brands, Philip Morris, and R. J. Reynolds were competitors in the cigarette industry.)

7. What sort of organizational type best describes the management of Disney theme parks as described in the opening case? Do you think there is a better way to manage a "smile factory"?

8. Visit an organization with which you are familiar (perhaps a local soup kitchen) and interview the manager to determine how it operates and what kind of organization structure it has. Describe its environment, strategy, and technology. Where would you place it along the Mainstream–Multistream continuum? Why? Which organizational type is it most like? What advice would you give to its managers to help the organization develop a better fit? Do you think that the organization will have to change to a different organizational type in the future to maintain its fitness?

HANDS-ON ACTIVITIES

Where Are You Along the Mainstream–Multistream Continuum?

Circle the number that best corresponds to your views.

EFFECTIVE MANAGERS WOULD MORE LIKELY BE FOUND IN. . .

Small organizations that have an organic structure, operate in a narrow segment of a changing environment, have a focus strategy, and rely on technology with high task variety and interdependence.	1 2 3 4 5 6 7	Small organizations that have an outward structure, have found a niche in the environment, have a narrow minimizer or transformer strategy, and focus on enhancing well-being within and/or beyond the organization.
Organizations that have a mechanistic structure, operate in a narrow segment of a stable environment, have a cost leader strategy, and have a single core technology.	1 2 3 4 5 6 7	Organizations that have an inward structure, have found a niche in the environment, have a minimizer strategy, and focus on enhancing overall well-being within the organization.
Organizations that have an organic structure, operate in a broad market of a changing environment, have a differentiation strategy, and rely on technology that is difficult to analyze.	1 2 3 4 5 6 7	Organizations that have an outward structure, operate in an area of the environment where there is broad receptivity, have a transformer strategy, and focus on enhancing overall well-being beyond the organization.
Organizations that essentially have two spheres of operations, with some parts of the organization design operating like a Defender and other parts operating like a Prospector.	1 2 3 4 5 6 7	Organizations that essentially have two spheres of operations, with some parts of the organization operating like a MultiDefender and other parts operating like a MultiProspector.

ENDNOTES

1. Van Maanen, J. (1991). The smile factory: Work at Disneyland. In P. J. Frost, L. Moore, M. Louis, C. Lundberg, & J. Martin (Eds.), *Reframing organizational culture* (pp. 58–76). Newbury Park, CA: Sage. Some facts were drawn from Boje, D. M. (1995). Stories of the storytelling organization: A postmodern analysis of Disney as *"Tamara*-land." *Academy of Management Journal,* 38(4), 997–1035; MacDonald, C. (2005). The quest for perfect customer service never stops. *Amusement Business,* 17(5), 18–19; and Brannan, M. Y. (2004). When Mickey loses face: Recontextualization, semantic fit, and the semiotics of foreignness. *Academy of Management Review,* 29(4), 593–616.

2. Of course, some of the exact wording and specific practices described here may have changed since the research was conducted upon which this case is based.

3. Page 305 of Fjellman, S. M. (1992). *Vinyl leaves: Walt Disney World and America.* Boulder, CO: Westview Press; cited in Boje, D. M. (1995). Stories of the storytelling organization: A postmodern analysis of Disney as *"Tamara*-land." *Academy of Management Journal,* 38(4), 997–1035. See also Brannan, M. Y. (2004). When Mickey loses face: Recontextualization, semantic fit, and the semiotics of foreignness. *Academy of Management Review,* 29(4), 593–616.

4. Boje, 1995, p. 1027. For example, Disney's management of the studio was authoritarian, micromanaged, and surveillance oriented.

5. For example, the fact that the reigning Alice in Wonderland would move in with a lowly sweeper was a source of some bewilderment, even though people knew that she was a local junior college student and he was in pre-med studies at the University of Southern California.

6. Our discussion of Mainstream organization structure builds on the work of Burns, T., & Stalker, G. M. (1966). *The management of innovation* (2nd ed.). London: Tavistock.

7. Note two caveats of this continuum. First, in actual practice there will be exceptions to the tendency for the four fundamentals to appear exactly in the way that they are shown on the continuum. New ventures, for example, may have a high degree of centralization (e.g., the entrepreneur makes all the decisions) and low levels of standardization and specialization (e.g., the entrepreneur does everything "on the fly" and develops policies only on an as-needed basis). Also, some start-up organizations may require a high level of standardization because they are operating in highly regulated industries or because of demands of key customers. Other exceptions to the continuum may occur

in departmentalization, where large mechanistic organizations may have divisional departmentalization and smaller organic organizations may adopt functional departments. Second, although thinking about the mechanistic–organic structure along a continuum has proven to be both elegant and useful, scholars have noted that some of its dimensions may be oversimplified. For example, rather than place centralization and decentralization on opposite ends of a *single* continuum, it may be more accurate to have two separate scales, where an organization could conceivably be seen to be becoming simultaneously more centralized and decentralized. This might occur if decision-making authority was removed from middle management, with some of that authority going to lower-level managers (decentralization) and some of it going to top managers (centralization). For more on this debate, see Cullen, J. B., & Perrewe, P. L. (1981). Decision making configurations: An alternative to the centralization/decentralization conceptualization. *Journal of Management*, 7(2), 89–103.

8. Mainstream management theory adopts a contingency theory approach to organization design. For example, see Child, J. (1972). Organizational structure, environment, and performance: The role of strategic choice. *Sociology*, 6, 1–22.

9. The example in this box is taken from Usher, J. M., & Evans, M. G. (1996). Life and death along gasoline alley: Darwinian and Lamarckian processes in a differentiating population. *Academy of Management Journal*, 39(5), 1428–1466. Bar graph: *Academy of Management Journal* by Usher/Evans. Copyright 1996 by Academy of Management (NY). Reproduced with permission of Academy of Management (NY) in the format Textbook via Copyright Clearance Center.

10. Usher, J. M., & Evans, M. G. (1996). Life and death along gasoline alley: Darwinian and Lamarckian processes in a differentiating population. *Academy of Management Journal*, 39(5), 1428–1466.

11. For a description of four organizational models that arise from using Hofstede's data to develop clusters of national cultures, see Fitzgerald, S. P. (2002). *Organizational models*. Oxford, UK: Capstone.

12. Although the organization design process usually highlights how strategy influences organization structure (indicated by the direction of the arrow in Figure 11.2), it is worth remembering that structure also influences strategy. For example, recall from Chapter 9 that an organization's structure can sometimes serve as a key resource to achieve sustained competitive advantage.

13. http://www.worldcubeassociation.org/results/regions.php.

14. Separating the operations in this way also allowed MTS to fulfill its mandate to keep the two spheres of operations operating at arm's length from each other, with no cross-subsidization between the two operations.

15. Woodward, J. (1965). *Industrial organizations: Theory and practice*. London: Oxford University Press; and Woodward, J. (1958). *Management and technology*. London: Her Majesty's Stationery Service.

16. Barley, R. S. (1986). Technology as an occasion for structuring evidence from observations of CT scanners and the social order of radiology departments. *Administrative Science Quarterly*, 31, 78–108.

17. Thompson, J. D. (1967). *Organizations in action*. New York: McGraw-Hill.

18. Quinn, R. E. (1988). *Beyond rational management*. San Francisco: Jossey-Bass; and Kabanoff, B., Waldersee, R., & Cohen, M. (1995). Espoused values and organizational change themes. *Academy of Management Journal*, 38(4), 1075–1104.

19. Travica, B. (1998). Information aspects of new organizational designs: Exploring the non-traditional organization. *Journal of the American Society for Information Science*, 49(13), 1224–1244; and Wang, E. T. G. (2001). Linking organizational context with structure: A preliminary investigation of the information processing view. *Omega*, 29, 429–443. Both Travica and Wang measured two aspects of a mechanistic structure—centralization and formalization.

20. This example is adapted from page 298 in Hellriegel, D., Jackson, S. E., & Slocum, J. W. (2002). *Management: A competency-based approach* (9th ed.). Cincinnati, OH: Thomson South-Western.

21. Much of this discussion draws from and builds on the typology developed by Miles and Snow (1978), which has been the most enduring, scrutinized, and used of numerous strategy classification systems introduced over the past three decades (Hambrick, 2003). Their typology is sometimes used to describe different *strategic* organizational types—and its overlap with Porter's strategic types is well accepted—but the deeper merit of their typology is its *comprehensive* nature, spanning organization structure, strategy, environment, and technology (Ghoshal, 2003; Ketchen, 2003). [*Sources*: Ghoshal, S. (2003). Miles and Snow: Enduring insights for managers. *Academy of Management Executive*, 17(4), 109–114; Hambrick, D. C. (2003). On the staying power of defenders, analyzers and prospectors. *Academy of Management Executive*, 17(4), 115–118; Ketchen, D. J. (2003). An interview with Raymond E. Miles and Charles C. Snow. *Academy of Management Executive*, 17(4), 97–104; Miles, R. E., & Snow, C. C. (1978). *Organizational strategy, structure, and process*. New York: McGraw-Hill.]

22. Charles Snow is confident that Lincoln Electric is an example of a Defender type (Ketchen, 2003). The details of Lincoln Electric in this paragraph were drawn from Carmichael, H. L., & MacLeod, W. B. (2000). Worker cooperation and the ratchet effect. *Journal of Labor Economics*, 18(1), 1–19.

23. Menguc, B., Auh, S., & Shih, E. (2007). Transformational leadership and market orientation: Implications for the implementation of competitive strategies and business unit performance. *Journal of Business Research*, 60, 314–321.

24. Brunk, 2003.

25. The "Misfit type" corresponds to what Miles and Snow (1978) called the "Reactor" organization, referring to organizations that lack consistency in their organization design.

26. Miller, D. (1992). *The Icarus paradox*. New York: HarperCollins. The idea of "path dependence" describes a similar idea—that every organizational type has a specific trajectory built within it. Research consistent with what has been called a "punctuated equilibrium" view suggests that organizations are usually in a period of equilibrium (incrementally fine-tuning an existing organizational type, which may last five or more years) but must occasionally experience a period of punctuation (a transformational change from one organizational type to another). Organizations that fail to make qualitative changes to their organization design risk becoming Misfits and failing. For more studies in this area, consult the following sources: Dyck, B. (1997). Understanding configuration and transformation through a multiple rationalities approach. *Journal of Management Studies*, 34, 793–823; Greenwood, R., & Hinings, C. R. (1993). Understanding strategic change: The contribution of types. *Academy of Management Journal*, 36, 1052–1081; Hinings, C. R., & Greenwood, R. (1988). *The dynamics of strategic change*. Oxford, UK: Basil Blackwell; and Romanelli, E., & Tush-

man, M. L. (1994). Organizational transformation as punctuated equilibrium: An empirical test. *Academy of Management Journal,* 37(5), 1141–1163.

27. Although much has been written about organizational life-cycle theory, the classic article still is Greiner, L. E. (1972). Evolution and revolution as organizations grow. *Harvard Business Review, 50,* 37–46. While organizational life-cycle theory is too prescriptive, it does have an underlying truth that continues to make it attractive to both practitioners and students. Also, some research supports the basic contention that managers change their organizations from one type to another over time. The research suggests that organizations may spend from 5 to 13 years in any one type (with some exceptions, such as Lincoln Electric), but that as they outgrow this type, managers feel compelled to change it (e.g., Dyck, 1997). For example, although life-cycle theorists might argue that an organization that has grown out of the Simple type must enter the Defender type (no skipping of types is permitted in the Simple → Defender → Prospector → Analyzer pathway outlined in endnote 28), subsequent scholarship suggests that this dictum is too rigid, so we expect that managers will be able to choose to change into any one of the remaining types. We will describe the change process more fully in Chapter 13.

28. Just as the changes to be managed in the human life cycle are predictable, so too it is helpful to think of the sequence of organizational types to proceeds as follows: Simple → Defender → Prospector → Analyzer. Organizations are often born as a Simple type that offers new products and services. As that Simple organization grows in size, its managers must develop the mechanistic administrative structures to accommodate its growth. Failure to do so creates a danger that the Simple organization will become an "Administrationless Misfit." Organizational life-cycle theory suggests that changing to become a Defender is the best way for managers of a Simple type to avoid becoming an Administrationless Misfit. A Defender organization may enjoy success for many years, but it may become a "Stifled Misfit" over time. A Stifled Misfit is one where decision making is so centralized, specialization so narrow, and standardization so rigid that members' creativity is stifled and the organization fails to respond to the changing needs of its customers. Organizational life-cycle theory suggests that the way to avoid becoming a Stifled Misfit is to change into a Prospector. Similarly, Prospector organizations are vulnerable to becoming "Scattered Misfits," where decentralization and the lack of standards across departments lead to failure. From an organizational life-cycle perspective, a Prospector can avoid failure by becoming an Analyzer. Finally, over time the Analyzer is in danger of becoming a "Stressed-Out Misfit" because the ambiguity created by this type leads to psychological stress and a difficulty in coping among members. Note that these general arguments are consistent with life-cycle theory, but that the particular names we give to the various types of organization differ from the names and build on the description used by life-cycle theorists (Greiner, 1972).

29. Ghoshal, 2003.

30. The Multistream continuum is similar to, but also different from, the Mainstream mechanistic–organic continuum, where the mechanistic structure tends to focus on internal concerns and the organic structure deals with external issues. Also, the same caveats apply here that apply to the mechanistic–organic continuum. First, there will be exceptions to the tendency for managers to place their emphasis across each of the four Multistream fundamentals of organizing either internally or externally. For example, a manager may be very sensitive to *external* stakeholders, but emphasize *internal* experimentation, dignification, and experimentation. Second, rather than use a continuum, it may be more accurate to offer two separate scales for each of the four dimensions so that, for example, dignification could be high (or low) *both* internally and externally. However, as with the mechanistic–organic structures, we will see that the elegance and parsimony of the inward–outward distinction are useful for understanding Multistream organization design and organizational types.

31. Pfeffer, J., & Salancik, G. (1978). *The external control of organizations: A resource dependence perspective.* New York: Harper & Row.

32. Benefiel, M. (2005). *Soul at work.* New York: Seabury Books.

33. Etzioni, A. (2001). *The monochrome society.* Princeton, NJ: Princeton University Press.

34. There is also strong interest in Multistream organizations among retired people. A survey of Americans aged 50 to 70 years found that more than half wanted to dedicate their time to community or national service after their primary career ended. This finding has prompted faculty at the Harvard Business School to create a new multidisciplinary leadership studies program to help these people design multidimensional solutions to pressing external problems [described in Dearlove, D., & Crainer, S. (2006). Recent research: AARP University. *Strategy + Business, 43,* 1–4. Accessed December 12, 2006, at www.strategy-business.com/recent_research.xml].

35. Elgin, D. (1993). *Voluntary simplicity: Toward a way of life that is outwardly simple, inwardly rich* (rev. ed.). New York: Quill.

36. See Chapter 6 on entrepreneurship.

37. 100 best companies to work for. (2006). *Fortune.* Accessed December 12, 2006, at http://money.cnn.com/magazines/fortune/bestcompanies/best_benefits/work-life.html.

38. Rothenberg, S. (2004). Selling small and smart: The future of sustainable enterprise. *Research Monograph.* Rochester, NY: Printing Center of Rochester Institute of Technology.

39. Anderson, R. C. (1998). *Mid-course correction: Toward a sustainable enterprise: The Interface model.* Atlanta, GA: Peregrinzilla Press.

40. Bakke, D. W. (2005). *Joy at work: A revolutionary approach to fun on the job.* Seattle, WA: PVG.

41. Bakke, 2005, pp. 68, 70, 71.

42. This is a point made by Benefiel, 2005.

43. *2007 Honda Fit Sells 2 Million Review.* Accessed July 24, 2007, at http://digiads.com.au/car-news/latest-HONDA-news/2007_Honda_Fit_Sells_2_Million_200707.html.

CHAPTER 12

In your journey through this chapter, you will be exposed to human resource management ideas and practices that are used by human resource professionals and managers. We'll travel down two paths, with the Mainstream path being more detailed and well traveled, and the Multistream path, perhaps, being more provocative and less traveled. Regardless of the path, we'll walk through the same steps described in the road map.

ROAD MAP

FOUR STEPS OR PRACTICES OF HUMAN RESOURCE MANAGEMENT

1. Job analysis and planning:
   Identify what people need to do

2. Staffing: Get the right people onboard

3. Performance management: Provide sufficient feedback and rewards for people

4. Training and development:
   Prepare and develop the people

Human Resource Management

MAINSTREAM APPROACH ⟷	MULTISTREAM APPROACH
Focus on the individual job	Focus on context or team
Use input primarily from jobholders	Use input from multiple stakeholders
Emphasize efficiency	Emphasize meaning
Recruit from traditional applicant pools	Recruit from marginalized or minority applicant pools
Select members based on their individual performance potential	Select members based on their growth potential or fit
Use the input of managers	Use the input of coworkers
Use appraisals to reward members	Use appraisals to develop members
Recognize individual performance	Recognize collective performance
Reinforce independence through individual incentives and rewards	Reinforce community through group-based incentives
Focus on financial rewards	Balance financial and nonfinancial rewards
Provide training in exchange for short-term production	Provide training as a long-term investment in people
Favor organizational needs over personal development	Favor personal development over organizational needs

High-Tech Loyalty at SAS Institute[1]

"I'm never gonna leave SAS, just bury me here. I'm just gonna stay here forever," said one SAS employee. SAS Institute, a software pioneer, has an impressive record of more than 30 years of consecutive increases in revenue growth and profitability. It is the largest privately held software company, with 400 offices across the world and more than 11,000 employees. At the heart of its success is a simple employee-focused philosophy: "Satisfied employees create satisfied customers." In an industry characterized by hyper-competition, where employees tend to act like free agents signing with the highest bidder, SAS has maintained a high level of loyalty and a low level of turnover (historically, less than 5 percent).

When they established SAS, James Goodnight, John Sall, Anthony Barr, and Jane Helwig set out to create a workplace that was as fun for employees to work in as it was for top managers. Their two guiding principles were to treat people fairly and to treat them with dignity. In a business that depends on its intellectual capital for success, SAS's cofounders believe these guiding principles, coupled with interesting work and interesting people to work with, are critical for attracting and retaining people. Their strategy has certainly worked: One estimate from a Stanford University professor is that SAS saves more than $75 million per year thanks to its high morale and low turnover.

The management at SAS "put their money where their mouth is" in creating their famous work environment and family-friendly benefits. The grounds of their Cary, North Carolina, headquarters are aesthetically pleasing, with picnic areas and hiking trails winding through the property. On-site are an expansive fitness facility with basketball courts and a pool, a subsidized Montessori daycare center, and a 7500-square-foot medical facility offering free care to employees. Inside, the atriums and artwork contribute to an engaging setting where all employees, including assistants, have private offices with up-to-date computer systems, access to a subsidized cafeteria, and enough free M&M candy to compel a person to use the fitness facilities. The attractive setting might be perceived as an attempt to lure people to spend all their waking hours at SAS, but the opposite is actually true:

Company policy is for employees and managers to work only 35 hours per week.

The human resource practices at SAS also demonstrate the firm's commitment to its employees. In addition to generous healthcare benefits and facility perks, SAS provides advice for managing elder-care, financial assistance for adoptions, competitive scholarships for children of employees, and laundry services for exercise clothes. These attractive benefits have lured a steady stream of job applicants who are interested in working at SAS. In deciding who to hire, fit is a paramount concern for SAS. SAS wants team players, not those who are concerned about individual recognition and "star treatment."

SAS follows a simple formula for performance management: provide people with the necessary resources for the job, empower them to do their work, and hold employees accountable. Managers set high expectations, but formal appraisals are nonexistent because of perceptions that employees hate them and such evaluations are a waste of time. Instead of appraisals, managers are expected to regularly provide feedback to their employees and be available to support them. Pay practices at SAS also are different from other companies in the same industry. Instead of using stock options to entice employees to work harder, the company pays a competitive market wage, contributes the allowed maximum (15 percent) to employees' profit-sharing retirement plans, and gives small annual bonuses based on company performance (typically ranging from 5 to 8 percent of the employee's base salary). SAS de-emphasizes individual pay for performance, believing that it is not an effective motivator compared to meaningful work and a long-term loyal employment relationship.

SAS managers hope that their company's culture of loyalty will translate into employees spending a majority of their working lives with SAS. Although employees may have several careers, SAS makes room for those careers within its organization. If an employee has the skill set to contribute in another role in the organization, the firm's structure makes it easy to move laterally across the organization. Training for new positions as well as orientation for new hires is handled almost entirely by long-term employees who enjoy training others—keeping it within the family, so to speak. In sum, SAS supports its employees in the process of discovering what they like to do and what they are good at doing, then allows them a great deal of freedom to do what they like to do and do it well.

Introduction to Human Resource Management

Human resource management (HRM) involves developing, organizing, and administering the people systems of an organization. Even though HRM has a short history as a formal subdiscipline of management, basic HRM practices have existed as long as humans have organized themselves to promote survival and prosperity. For example, forms of human resource practices such as employee *selection* processes have been traced back to Chinese practices prior to 1115 B.C.[2] Furthermore, modern *training and development* was birthed in the apprenticeships of Greek and Babylonian civilizations.[3] Even ancient philosophers such as Socrates noted that success for a society (or an organization) required two things: (1) identifying the roles or jobs that needed to be performed as well as the personal aptitudes required for people to perform the jobs (*job analysis and design*), and (2) filling those positions with individuals who have the relevant aptitudes to perform those roles (*staffing*).[4]

As a result of the Industrial Revolution (late 1700s) in Europe and eventually the New World (early 1800s), potential immigrants were *recruited* to meet increasing demands for agricultural and manufacturing operations.[5] At the same time, the pioneering management practices of Wedgwood (described in the opening case in Chapter 2) provided early evidence of other steps in the modern HRM process, such as *rewarding* and *training* workers. These early techniques became more formalized in the early 1900s, when "personnel departments" were established by organizations such as B. F Goodrich, National Cash Register, and Ford. These personnel departments began actively experimenting with HRM practices in an attempt to reduce problems such as excessive turnover. For example, some estimates put the turnover rate in the automotive industry in 1914 at 370 percent.[6]

Today's HRM is concerned with an organization's people practices, policies, and systems. Nevertheless, employees and managers have at times disliked or disparaged HRM practices due to perceptions that these practices have limited value and place too much emphasis on compliance and cost reduction.[7] More recently, Stanford University professor Jeffrey Pfeffer argues that research shows the enormous economic benefit of putting people first.[8] HRM practices are gaining prominence as a potential source of competitive advantage. In this age of hyper-competition, products and services—and even many technologies—are easily copied. As a consequence, they quickly become obsolete as sources of competitive advantage. In contrast, how the managers of a company organize, train, develop, and reward their employees is more difficult to copy. Perhaps in an attempt to refashion the image of HRM and emphasize its positive contributions, some organizations now speak about the process of pursuing competitive advantage through HRM practices as "talent management."

Human resource management (HRM) is management of the people in an organization, including development, organization, and administration of the organization's "people systems."

The rest of this chapter describes the main "people" management practices that make up HRM. Typically, HRM focuses on four steps:

1. Identify what people need to do (job analysis and planning).
2. Get the right people onboard (staffing).
3. Provide sufficient feedback and rewards for people (performance management).
4. Prepare and develop the people (training and development).

Mainstream Human Resource Management

From a Mainstream perspective, materialist–individualist values guide HRM practices. As a consequence, HRM tends to emphasize individual capability and performance, and it highlights employees' objective contributions to productivity, profitability, and competitiveness. There is also a tendency to reward individual performance.

The Mainstream perspective focuses on immediate and narrow exchanges between the employee and the organization. Managing headcount is the prevailing emphasis when HRM departments are pressured to cut costs and "right-size" operations. This approach has been referred to as the "new employment contract" where—instead of offering the old model of a secure career and consistent raises—employers offer challenging jobs, pay-for-performance compensation packages, and opportunities to learn skills that will increase employee marketability.[9] In this economic exchange relationship, the employer asks for immediate and well-defined contributions from employees and, in return, delivers short-term financial benefits to those employees.

The assumptions of the Mainstream employment relationship influence all four steps of HRM practice, as depicted in Figure 12.1.

Step 1: Job Analysis and Planning

At the individual level, job analysis involves identifying the knowledge, skills, abilities, and other characteristics **(KSAOs)** that are necessary for a specific job. At the organizational level, HRM planning involves determining the KSAOs needed for all jobs in the organization.

JOB ANALYSIS. **Job analysis,** which is the foundation for much of HRM, is an investigative process of gathering and interpreting information about a job and its required KSAOs. This information, in turn, feeds into the job design process, which seeks to craft a job description that summarizes the specific duties, tasks, and responsibilities of a particular position. The job description specifies the duties associated with the position as well as the knowledge, skills, education and training, credentials, prior experience, physical abilities, and other characteristics that are required to fulfill those duties. A good job description that clarifies tasks and roles can improve employee satisfaction and performance.[10]

A Mainstream approach to job analysis and design tends to be mechanistic, strongly rooted in scientific management, and oriented toward maximizing efficiency through individual task specialization and task simplification. The main objective is to create defensible,

KSAOs are the knowledge, skills, abilities, and other characteristics associated with specific positions.

Job analysis is an investigative process of gathering and interpreting information about a job and its required KSAOs.

Figure 12.1 The four steps of HRM practice

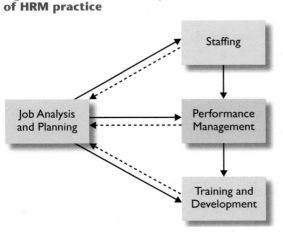

verifiable specifications and descriptions that are independent of any particular person. The McDonald's restaurant chain is a master of this mechanistic approach; jobs are highly specified and people are plugged in as needed to efficiently run the system. Under this approach, a job at a McDonald's restaurant in Minneapolis should essentially be the same as a job at a McDonald's restaurant in Dallas, Beijing, or Moscow.

Several methods of collecting information are used in job analysis. For example, a formal job analyst or manager might collect data by observing a job being performed by another employee or even by performing the actual job. More often, job analysts interview or survey **subject matter experts (SMEs),** who either hold the job or observe the job regularly, to generate a list of job tasks or KSAOs. One popular way to survey SMEs is the Position Analysis Questionnaire (PAQ), a standardized questionnaire that asks respondents to rate the extent to which a job reflects a very detailed (approximately 200 questions) set of tasks and processes.[11] Other approaches ask jobholders to fill out job diaries (lists of daily activities) or analysts to use external resources such as job descriptions and specifications in the Occupational Information Network (O*Net).[12]

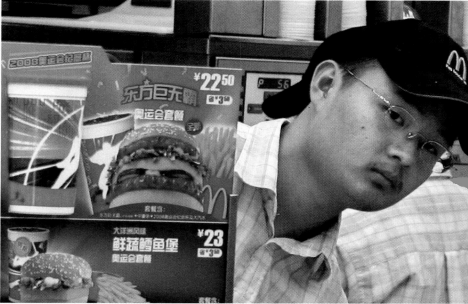

A Chinese worker in Beijing serves customers from behind the counter at a branch of U.S. fastfood giant, McDonald's.

Subject matter expert (SME) is an expert in a specific occupation or specific task.

❓ WHAT DO YOU THINK?

Analyzing the Past or Predicting the Future?

The approaches to job analysis described here rely on information about the KSAOs that are currently necessary for job performance. This information is based mostly on the experience of the people who have held this job and are looking back into the past. Why might that be a problem in this age of dynamic change? What might a future-oriented job analysis look like?

Human resource management (HRM) planning is the process of using job analysis and design information to develop a human resource requirements forecast that identifies the "people needs" of the organization in various departments and positions.

HRM PLANNING. The **HRM planning** process draws on job analysis and design information to develop a human resource requirements forecast, which summarizes the future "people needs" of the organization in various departments and positions. This "labor demand" plan is then compared to the external supply of KSAOs among people in local and sometimes global labor markets. Well-developed HRM planning systems often rely on **human resource information systems (HRIS)** to track demand—based on jobs or specific skills—against a database of the current supply of talent within the organization. The output of the HRIS identifies the gaps between the forecasted needs and the available supply and provides a basis for planning.

One way to address the gap between needs and available resources is by using **contingent workers.** A worker who is contracted for a specific project or fixed time period, but not considered an employee of the host organization, is considered to

Human resource information system (HRIS) is a system that tracks demand for human resources based on jobs or specific skills by comparing those needs with a database of the current supply of talent within the organization.

Contingent workers are those who are contracted to work for a host organization on a specific project or for a fixed time period, but who are not considered to be employees of the organization.

be a contingent or temporary worker. The largest employer in the United States today is not General Motors, McDonald's, or even Wal-Mart, with its more than 1 million employees. Rather, the largest U.S. employer is Manpower, Inc., a temporary-employment agency (see http://www.manpower.com). In the past most temporary workers filled clerical and manufacturing positions, but today a growing number of these workers are professionals. Contingent workers, who constitute an increasing percentage of the workforce, constitute a diverse group of skilled people who work for an organization on a nonpermanent, non-full-time basis.[13] They help to reduce payroll and benefit costs (e.g., health insurance, pension obligations) and increase flexibility for employers. For example, IBM employs more than 40,000 temporary employees per year, and Microsoft uses 5000 contingent employees to carry out special projects.

A strategic approach to HRM planning emphasizes the organization's overall strategy in determining job tasks and the priorities for filling positions. If the organization's strategy is one of differentiation, for example, then tasks or positions that are oriented toward innovation will receive more attention. By contrast, if cost leadership is the driving strategy, then tasks and positions that are oriented toward reducing time and promoting efficiency may be given more prominence. David Ulrich, an HRM scholar and consultant, argues that HRM professionals should be involved in making strategic decisions and play significant roles in implementing strategic change.[14] By emphasizing strategy, a job can be designed to have the greatest impact on profitability through alignment and efficiency, and positions can be easily prioritized.

Step 2: Staffing

Once jobs have been analyzed and job descriptions have been developed that fit with the overall organizational strategy, the next step is to recruit and select people for the jobs. **Staffing** is the HRM process of identifying, attracting, hiring, and retaining people with the necessary KSAOs to fulfill the responsibilities of current and future jobs in the organization.

Staffing has two main components: recruitment and selection. The process of identifying and attracting the people with the essential KSAOs is **recruitment;** the process of choosing who to hire among job applicants or recruits is **selection.** In a sense, staffing can be considered to be like two parts in a mining operation. Recruiting is similar to the process of locating and digging out the raw materials, and selection is similar to the process of sifting through the raw materials to determine what is of specific interest and what is not. Both components of this operation share a joint objective, however: to find the jewels with value to the organization. Of course, if you are the one trying to find a job, the staffing process is your opportunity to shine.

RECRUITMENT. The recruiting process involves establishing and building **recruitment channels** to funnel potential members into the selection process. A steady flow of applicants is necessary to ensure that jobs and roles are filled efficiently. Traditional recruitment channels include relationships with universities or employment agencies, newspaper or industry employment ads, and internal job postings. Notably, organizations are increasingly turning to Internet channels such as the organization's website or external websites such as www.Monster.com in an effort to locate and attract talented employees. Some organizations, such as the huge accounting firm Ernst and Young, are turning to social networking websites such as

Staffing is the human resource management (HRM) process of identifying, attracting, hiring, and retaining people with the necessary KSAOs to fulfill the responsibilities of current and future jobs in the organization.

Recruitment is the staffing process of identifying and attracting the people with the essential KSAOs.

Selection is the staffing process of choosing which people to hire from all the job applicants or recruits.

Recruitment channels are the means by which organizations funnel potential members into the selection process (e.g., relationships with universities or employment agencies, newspaper ads, postings on internal or external websites).

Facebook and blogs to promote their organization, solicit feedback, and build relationships with potential employees.[15] Of course, organizations also can use the Internet to search for information about potential employees such as embarrassing pictures or associations posted on social networking sites. In addition, the use of the Internet as a recruitment tool can backfire when bitter former employees add their comments to open blogs or chats.

Employees can be an effective channel for recruitment, in terms of either referring candidates to the organization or filling positions themselves. Employees know the organization and its culture, and they can sense whether a friend or a relative would fit in well with the organization. Some organizations use referral bonuses to encourage employees to do recruiting. In other cases, the best recruits for a position

Facebook is a useful tool for businesses to share information with and gain feedback from customers regarding current and future products and services. *Source:* Image provided by Facebook. Reprinted by permission.

may already work for the organization in another job. Some organizations have a policy that gives preference to in-house applicants when recruiting for a position. Internal recruiting is less costly, and it may help to improve members' commitment, development, and satisfaction.[16] On the downside, internal recruiting as a channel may not supply the necessary quantity or even quality of applicants.

Recruiting channels can be evaluated in terms of their speed and cost to deliver "qualified" applicants—that is, people who have the specified KSAOs—to an HRM professional or hiring manager. For example, Web-based and newspaper postings typically deliver a high quantity of applicants, but they may not necessarily be qualified applicants. To address this shortcoming, some sophisticated websites can screen applicants for the appropriate qualifications. Without such screening, the existence of a large quantity of applicants requires extensive work on the behalf of human resource professionals or managers to sift through numerous applicant résumés. In the end, the costs of the posting as well as the time needed to identify viable candidates may make this channel slower and less cost-efficient than other recruitment channels. In contrast, employee referrals or relationships with universities and employment agencies may provide qualified applicants in a shorter time and perhaps at a lower cost because these channels may screen applicants before recommending them to the organization.

Effective recruiting not only expands the pool of applicants from which to choose at a reasonable cost, but also improves the chances of retaining those individuals once they become members of the organization. An important part of some recruitment processes is to communicate to applicants what it will be like to actually perform the job. Although it may not be cost-efficient to do so for all potential employees, as much as possible applicants should be given a **realistic job preview (RJP)**. An RJP provides information about a job's challenges and joys, including both its positive and its negative aspects. Such information helps to match members with positions, improves

Realistic job preview (RJP) provides information about a job's challenges and joys, including both its positive and its negative aspects.

job satisfaction, and reduces turnover. This information may be provided in the job listing, but sometimes it can only be experienced firsthand.

Instead of simply "selling" the job, RJPs try to provide balanced information before the applicant accepts a job. For example, one of the authors of this book consulted with a beef processing plant in Iowa that had enormous problems with turnover of employees within the first week of employment. Unfortunately, a person who quits at the end of the week has already cost the company a lot of time and money by going through days of orientation and training. The primary recommendation was to institute, as part of the interview process, walking the potential employee through the slaughterhouse. Although this tour added time to the initial interviewing process, the time and money saved by having many people decline the job (perhaps because they felt queasy in the slaughterhouse) more than made up for the costs of the RJP, and turnover after the first week was considerably reduced.

SELECTION.   Jim Collins argues in his best-selling book, *Good to Great*, that a critical process for every organization is selection—"getting the right people on the bus."[17] It may appear that once managers have a pool of candidates from which to choose, the selection process gets under way. In reality, however, selection begins when the relevant KSAOs for the position are identified as the criteria for whom to select. Without justified criteria for selection, a manager or organization can get in legal trouble if he or she is accused of selecting candidates based on criteria that have no relevance to the job, such as gender, race, or physical appearance (see the "Digging Deeper" feature on HRM and the law). Having identified the job-relevant KSAOs from the job analysis and planning process, the next step is to choose the selection methods and tools that best assess these desired characteristics.

Selection methods and tools should be evaluated in terms of the extent to which they are valid and reliable assessments of the job-relevant criteria. **Selection validity** refers to the relationship between the scores that applicants receive during assessment and their subsequent job performance. There are two ways to demonstrate validation:

- *Predictive validation* ensures that applicant scores correlate with actual job performance ratings.
- *Content validation* ensures that the content of the method or tool actually assesses the actual KSAOs performed on the job.

You cannot have validity unless you have reliability. **Selection reliability** refers to the ability of a selection method or tool to consistently provide accurate assessments. For example, if a characteristic such as personality is assessed with only one question, this approach is likely to have low reliability given the possibility of some applicants misinterpreting the item. This is the reason why selection tests can be so frustrating: It can seem like the tests ask the same questions over and over again in different ways! Could the tests be shorter? Yes, but not without sacrificing reliability—averaging several similar items that measure a single characteristic is a more reliable assessment of that characteristic than simply scoring a single item.

The most common selection tool is the *application form* that candidates complete to indicate their interest in a position or organization. This form collects information about the applicant's educational background, previous job experience, and other job-related information. When weighting is applied to questions on an application form, this tool is called a *weighted application blank* (WAB), where the weighting is based on an empirical measurement of the predictive validity of each question. In some cases, the application also asks for references; human resource personnel may then check

Selection validity is a measure of the relationship between the scores that applicants receive during assessment as part of the recruiting process and their subsequent job performance.

Selection reliability is a measure of the ability of a selection method or tool to consistently provide accurate assessments.

these references by contacting the individuals to confirm that the information on the application is true. Why follow up on references? The Society for Human Resource Management (SHRM) estimates that 25 percent of job applications and résumés contain errors, including many errors that are intentional.[18] The application form information also can be used as a screening device to see which applicants should be invited to complete one or more written *tests*.

Selection tests can take various forms, as shown in Figure 12.2. One form that has been used occasionally in Europe is graphology, or handwriting analysis. In this method, psychologists analyze a writing sample to determine applicant characteristics and performance ability. This may be an interesting method, but it lacks validity.[19]

On the other end of the predictive validity continuum illustrated in Figure 12.2 are cognitive ability tests and work sample tests. A *cognitive ability test* includes questions designed to assess general mental ability and/or verbal and numerical reasoning. The results of such a test are more valid for complex jobs that require critical thinking, such as higher levels of management.[20] An example of a cognitive ability test is the Wonderlic Personnel Test, which is designed to assess general mental ability in the short span of 12 minutes.[21] You may have heard of this test if you follow the National Football League. The draft positions of athletes, and particularly quarterbacks, can either rise or fall depending on their predraft scores on the Wonderlic test. A *work sample test* has the applicant simulate actual job tasks. For example, such a test might have an applicant work on an assembly line if applying for a job in an auto plant, write computer code if applying for a computer programmer position, or take a typing test for a clerical position.

Another selection tool that has moderate validity is personality tests, where sought-after traits include conscientiousness, and—for people-oriented jobs—extraversion or possibly agreeableness (Chapter 14 provides a deeper discussion of these personality traits).[22] Integrity (honesty) tests, despite concerns about faking, are more valid than standard personality tests in predicting job performance; they are also valid for predicting counterproductive behaviors such as stealing and absenteeism.[23] Some integrity tests ask direct questions about whether an applicant has taken home office supplies, lied about being sick, given away merchandise, or even stolen money from a past organization.

Like the application form, the personal interview is almost universally used as part of the selection process. Some organizations conduct a preliminary phone interview to gather more

Embellishing or lying about facts on resumes is a common problem, even among managers. Admissions Dean for the Massachusetts Institute of Technology (MIT), Marilee Jones, resigned after it was revealed that she had lied about having a degree herself. David Edmonson, former CEO of RadioShack, resigned after news surfaced of his claiming degrees he did not complete. Jeffrey Papows, former president of IBM's Lotus unit, claimed degrees he had not completed, embellished his titles and experiences as a Marine, and described himself as an orphan despite his parents being alive and well in Massachusetts. (See Endnote 18.)

Figure 12.2 Validity of selection methods or tools

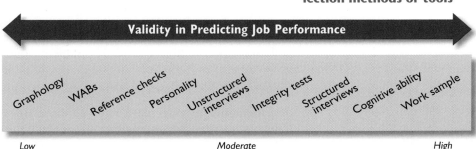

Validity in Predicting Job Performance

Graphology · WABs · Reference checks · Personality · Unstructured interviews · Integrity tests · Structured interviews · Cognitive ability · Work sample

Low   *Moderate*   *High*

information or to screen out people who are not a good fit with the company's culture before they schedule face-to-face interviews. Some interviews are one-on-one, others are conducted by a panel, and some involve several stages conducted by different interviewers. Having more interviews, or having more than one person conduct an interview, increases the likelihood that the resulting judgment will be more reliable and makes it less subject to the biases of individual interviewers.

Interviews may be either structured or unstructured. In structured interviews, questions are decided upon in advance and related to specific job-relevant KSAOs, such as resolving conflict or problems. Each interviewee is asked the same questions to ensure content validity and enhance the reliability of the interviewing process. By comparison, unstructured interviews are more like conversations, where the direction of the interview may change based on the interests and background of each applicant. Although the distinction may seem minor, the differences in validity are not. Structured interviews are considerably more valid than unstructured interviews.

Interview questions can take different forms. Situational interview questions, for example, ask applicants to respond to a specific scenario that is likely to arise on the job in the future. By contrast, behavioral interview questions ask applicants to draw from their past experience to share an example of their behavior related to teamwork or dealing with a difficult customer. Situational questions have the advantage of being more standardized and, therefore, more reliable; they also make it possible to question interviewees who lack experience in the specified area. Behavioral questions have the advantage of being based on past experience (which is a strong predictor of future performance) and, therefore, are a bit more valid.[24]

In any case, managers should be encouraged to take notes during interviews to minimize memory effects.[25] Often, managers will need to make judgments after interviewing several candidates, possibly over several days. Notetaking helps them avoid problems related to recalling information such as the "recency effect," which is the tendency to remember more about the last person interviewed.

In sum, a well-developed selection system typically involves multiple assessments, which in turn increase the validity and reliability of selection judgments. This thinking serves as the foundation of "assessment centers." Initially developed by psychologists at AT&T, assessment centers are most commonly used to select people for management. Testing often takes place over a period of two or three days, as potential managers participate in a series of tests and simulation exercises while trained judges evaluate their scores, behaviors, and decisions.

As you might expect, applicants react differently to different selection methods or tools.[26] Applicants tend to respond more favorably to selection tools that seem to be job related and valid. Interviews receive the highest favorability ratings by applicants, followed closely by work samples and résumés (application forms). Cognitive ability and personality tests are viewed less favorably by jobseekers, while graphology tests receive the lowest ratings—for good reason! As a manager, you need to consider the potential reactions of applicants in choosing your selection tools. For example, having applicants for an executive position take a cognitive ability test may be a valid approach, but it also may discourage qualified applicants from seeking the position: Many successful executives would be offended by someone questioning their intelligence.

Step 3: Performance Management

Performance management is the use of human resource management processes to ensure that each employee's activities and outputs are aligned with the organization's goals.

Performance management refers to those HRM processes used to ensure that employees' activities and outputs are aligned with the organization's goals.[27] Performance management has two components: performance appraisal and compensation.

DIGGING DEEPER

Legal Issues in Staffing

Many of the fundamental practices in the HRM process are governed by law. This is especially true in the recruitment and selection process, where a variety of laws have been passed to minimize discrimination. Discrimination occurs in staffing when some applicants are not recruited or hired for reasons that are not related to the specific job—and it can have serious consequences for both the employer and potential or existing employees. In 2005, for example, Abercrombie & Fitch settled a class-action suit for $50 million related to its recruiting and hiring practices, which discriminated against minorities and women.[28]

The protection against discrimination afforded employees in the United States and Canada is greater than that offered in many countries. For example, the United Kingdom protects against discrimination based on gender, but surprisingly not discrimination based on age, national origin, race, religion, or marital status. Germany, France, and Japan offer protection against gender, national origin, race, or religion discrimination, but not necessarily against discrimination related to age or marital status. Venezuela, Hong Kong, Indonesia, and Singapore offer few, if any, protections from any of these types of discrimination.[29]

In the United States, the Civil Rights Act Title VII (passed in 1964) prohibits discrimination in employment on the basis of race, religion, color, sex, or national origin. This law was amended by the Equal Employment Opportunity Act in 1972 and again in 1991. Compliance issues related to these and other laws are monitored by the Equal Employment Opportunity Commission. Affirmative action programs in the workplace attempt to balance out past discrimination through policies and actions that promote equal opportunity. In the United States, government contractors that have more than 50 employees and receive more than $50,000 in government contracts are required to file a written statement of affirmative action policies.[30]

Antidiscrimination laws do not prohibit making decisions based on bona fide occupational qualifications (BFOQs), such as the ability to lift a certain amount of weight or the possession of a specific certification (e.g., Certified Public Accountant). In this sense, it is legal to "discriminate" or chose one person over another based on BFOQs that are reasonably necessary to fulfill job requirements. The justification for BFOQs usually comes from the job analysis process; without this evidence, an employer runs the risk of a lawsuit that questions the "truth" of its claims about what is "job related."

Other important employment laws in the United States include the Age Discrimination in Employment Act (1967), which prohibits age discrimination; the Vocational Rehabilitation Act (1973), which prohibits discrimination based on physical or mental disability; and the Americans with Disabilities Act (1990), which prohibits discrimination based on disabilities.

A common situation where managers inadvertently violate employment law is in the interview process. Here are a few examples of illegal[31] and legal questions that might be asked during an employment interview:

ISSUE	ILLEGAL QUESTION	LEGAL QUESTION
Origin	Are you a U.S. citizen?	Are you authorized to work in the United States?[32]
Family/travel	Are you married?	Are you willing to travel?
Age	How old are you?	Are you older than age 18?
Disability	Do you have any disabilities?	Can you perform [a specific task]?
Background	What is your religion?	What is your past work experience?

Although many legal problems for managers relate to intentional behavior on behalf of organizational members, managers also can find themselves in trouble even for unintentional actions. For example, using a selection method that results in a disproportionately negative effect on a protected group is called *disparate impact*. Whether these actions are intentional or unintentional, organizations are held accountable for their HRM practices. As such, managers should be familiar with HRM-related legislation.

PERFORMANCE APPRAISAL. The foundation of an effective performance management system is the **performance appraisal** process, which specifies what level of performance is expected for an employee and then provides feedback on the employee's performance. If you are like most managers, then you know that talk of appraising performance can cause grown men and women to tremble. Rewarding employees for a job well done is one thing, but providing constructive feedback and having to make distinctions among employees to hand out raises is quite another. Being on the receiving end of an appraisal is not much better; employees often

Performance appraisal is the process of specifying what performance is expected of a member of the organization and then providing feedback on the member's performance.

complain that perceptions and politics influence their ratings more than their actual performance. Quality guru W. Edwards Deming even suggested that performance appraisals should be abolished due to their limitations and inaccuracies (see Chapter 18 for more on Deming and quality management).

Performance appraisals do not need to be an exercise in futility that both parties disdain. If performed well, they can be valuable in conveying important information and aligning employees with organizational goals. The key is to follow these steps:

1. Design a system with a clear purpose, defined roles, and agreed-upon criteria.
2. Equip managers with the skills and tools they need to be successful.
3. Reinforce and review the appraisal process.[33]

Administrative appraisals are performance appraisals that are used to justify pay and promotion decisions

Developmental appraisals are performance appraisals that are used to provide feedback on progress toward expectations and to identify areas for improvement.

Design a System.   The first step in designing an appraisal system is to decide why performance appraisal will occur and to what outcomes it will be linked. Two broad types of appraisals are **administrative appraisals,** which are used to justify pay and promotion decisions, and **developmental appraisals,** which are used to provide feedback on progress toward expectations and identify areas for improvement. In practice, most organizations use administrative appraisals on an annual or semiannual basis, whereas fewer organizations use formal developmental appraisals. Nonetheless, it is important to communicate to both managers and employees what the appraisal information will be used for. Beyond links to pay and promotion, some organizations, such as General Electric, use performance appraisal information to comparatively rate or rank employees, with the bottom 10 percent being fired—a "rank and yank" approach.

It also is important to specify who will be appraising whom and at what times. Clarifying these roles is important to ensure perceptions of fairness; no one wants to be surprised by who is providing input into decisions about their performance. An increasingly popular appraisal method, called 360-degree feedback, relies on self-report ratings and input from a full circle of people who work directly with the member whose performance is being appraised. Members of the appraisal group can include supervisors, coworkers, subordinates, and internal and external customers (see Figure 12.3). The advantage of this approach is that it increases the quantity and variety of information while reducing the bias that might come from using a single rating source. Dangers associated with this system include subordinates who use an anonymous program to "get back" at a boss and managers who coerce their subordinates to give them good evaluations. For example, IBM abandoned its 360-degree feedback process in part because employees and managers manipulated the ratings for political purposes. Finally, the design of a performance appraisal system should involve input from both managers and employees as to what should be assessed. Drawing from the job description and the organization's goals, performance appraisal criteria must be developed and agreed upon. In other words, the system must spell out clearly what performance is expected from the employee.

Figure 12.3   360-degree feedback appraisal method

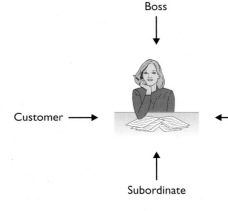

Equip Managers.   The second step in the performance appraisal process is to equip raters—who are typically managers—with the knowledge and tools that will help them make accurate ratings. Concerns about inaccurate and lenient ratings are said to be the motive

behind the employee-ranking systems used by General Electric and others.[34] Rater training (sometimes called *frame-of-reference training*) is meant to increase the accuracy and reliability of ratings by making raters aware of the following biases:

- Leniency: giving higher-than-deserved ratings
- Halo/horn effects: using one piece of known information—good or bad—to influence ratings of unknown information
- Representativeness: allowing one prominent trait or impression to stereotype the employee
- Availability: relying on memorable information—dramatic or recent—to make judgments
- Attribution errors: attributing poor performance to the person without giving adequate regard for situational factors
- Anchoring and adjustment effects: failing to sufficiently adjust a judgment from an initial impression (i.e., an anchor), even in the face of contrary evidence

The verdict is still out on the effectiveness of rater training in eliminating bias, with some researchers and practitioners indicating it is beneficial and others questioning its impact. Perhaps the main advantage of rater training is its ability to improve the attitudes of raters: The more confident a person feels in understanding how to use the system and the forms, the better he or she feels toward the process.

The primary tool for raters is the performance appraisal form. Typically, a rating form has one or more of the following elements:

- Questions rating specific characteristics or KSAOs
- Assessments of progress toward goals
- A summary judgment or rating

Graphic rating scales are one of the oldest and most popular methods to appraise KSAOs. This method often uses a five-point scale, where raters are asked to assess the degree to which they agree a characteristic is true of a person. A more advanced type of graphic rating scale called the "behaviorally anchored ranking scale" (BARS) focuses on specific behaviors of members. Figure 12.4 illustrates both types of rating scales. Because BARS items and their rating scales are more closely related to specific descriptions of work behavior, they are more valid and reliable than a simple graphic rating scale. Some rating forms go one step further by asking raters to provide a graphic rating as well as specific examples of performance to justify the rating.

Rating forms also may contain—or in some cases exclusively focus on—goals and progress toward goals. This approach is commonly found in

Figure 12.4 Two ways to rate a manager's legal knowledge of HRM

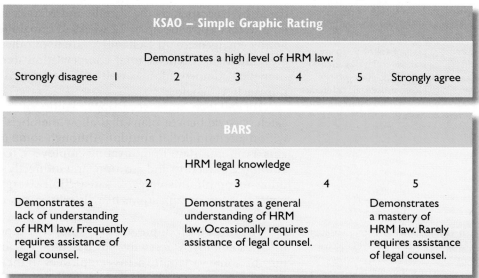

KSAO – Simple Graphic Rating						
Demonstrates a high level of HRM law:						
Strongly disagree	1	2	3	4	5	Strongly agree

BARS				
HRM legal knowledge				
1	2	3	4	5
Demonstrates a lack of understanding of HRM law. Frequently requires assistance of legal counsel.		Demonstrates a general understanding of HRM law. Occasionally requires assistance of legal counsel.		Demonstrates a mastery of HRM law. Rarely requires assistance of legal counsel.

organizations that systematically use a management-by-objectives approach for planning and goal setting. In such cases, the focus is on outcomes such as volume of sales, with less attention being paid to the means by which the outcomes were achieved.

Regardless of the types of ratings that are provided, an appraisal typically ends with a summary rating. This rating can be subjective, with the rater being asked to give an overall judgment of the employee's performance, or it can be "objective," with the individual item ratings being combined mathematically to yield an overall score. For example, a manager may score low (perhaps a 2) on legal knowledge of HRM yet score high on other items, giving her an overall average rating score of 4.2.

Reinforce and Review the Process. The third step in a performance appraisal system is reinforcing the importance of the appraisal process. To begin, top managers must model a thoughtful, thorough, and timely approach to appraising their subordinates. This behavior sends the message "Do what I do" rather than just "Do what I say." In addition to reinforcing the importance of performance appraisal through example, some organizations hold managers accountable for the quality and timeliness of their appraisals of employees.

Another clear way to communicate the importance of the appraisal process is to subject the whole process to regular review. Putting the appraisal process under the microscope of review requires making it measurable—and what gets measured usually gets done. Potential measures could include timeliness of the review, thoroughness, perceptions of fairness and accuracy, and the average, range, and variance of the rating scores. A review process that invites input from all participants can have a positive impact on employees' acceptance of the process.

COMPENSATION. Monetary payments such as wages, salaries, and bonuses as well as other goods or commodities used to reward organizational members are collectively referred to as **compensation. Benefits** refers to a subset of the compensation that is typically not directly contingent on performance. Benefits may include things such as retirement plans; health, disability, and life insurance; and possibly perks such as access to workout facilities, on-site daycare services, subsidized cafeteria food, education reimbursement, and laundry services. Some benefits are mandated by laws such as the Family and Medical Leave Act (1993), which requires employers to provide up to 12 weeks of unpaid leave for childbirth, adoption, and family emergencies. At Dell and a variety of other organizations, employees receive an annual statement of total compensation that details the value of their direct monetary compensation as well as the estimated value of their indirect compensation such as benefits.

To enhance employees' appreciation of benefits, some organizations offer cafeteria-style benefit plans that allow members to pick and choose their benefits within a certain dollar amount. Although some motivational theories dismiss benefits as unimportant in motivating employees, research suggests that they influence employee attraction and attrition, and indirectly influence performance by contributing to or diminishing job satisfaction. Despite these potential advantages of benefits, most organizations heavily rely on pay or incentive compensation to motivate performance.

The most basic approach to employee compensation is **job-based pay,** which involves employees receiving pay based on the jobs that they hold. Although there may be some variability across employees in the same job owing to individual differences in experience or job tenure, the pay is "banded" (that is, bounded by a

Compensation refers to all monetary payments such as wages, salaries, and bonuses as well as other goods or commodities that are used to reward organizational members.

Benefits are a subset of compensation that is not typically contingent on performance—for example, retirement plans; health, disability, and life insurance; and perks such as access to workout facilities, on-site daycare services, subsidized cafeteria food, education reimbursement, and laundry services.

Job-based pay is a compensation system in which employees receive pay based on the jobs that they hold.

predetermined minimum and maximum). The pay range for a job can be determined internally through a *comparable worth* analysis of a job's value in relation to other jobs in the organization. It can also be determined by the job market through using industry wage surveys. In the absence of a justified pay range or evidence of market influences, employers have been sued for discrimination by women who argue that the pay of certain female-dominated jobs is the result of discrimination rather than a reflection of the jobs' actual value to the organization. In the United States, the basis for these lawsuits is the Equal Pay Act (1963), which prohibits differences in pay based on gender.

In job-based pay systems, increases in pay may be either uniform—such as for cost of living—or merit based. In **merit-based pay** systems, employees essentially earn a permanent increase in compensation based on past performance that is captured in the performance appraisal. For example, Symantec Corporation, a California-based software company, used a merit-based pay system to reward top performers with "a bigger slice" of the annual raise "pie." Employees whose performance was appraised as "exceeding expectations" received 3 percent or more than average performers, whose performance was appraised as "meeting expectations."[35] Despite being intended as an incentive to increase performance, merit-based pay has a weak effect on improving performance because of the distant "line of sight." In other words, employees typically find it difficult to see how their behavior is linked to rewards because of the distance or time between their behavior and their receipt of the reward. Because of this weakness and the permanent nature of merit raises, many organizations are moving away from relying primarily on merit pay.

Although a job-based pay system is relatively simple to administer, it is falling into disfavor because it does not reward members who develop their skills. To encourage members to advance their competencies, some organizations use a **skill-based pay** system (e.g., Quaker Oats, Sherwin-Williams, and Au Bon Pain). In this approach, members are paid a base hourly wage rate for doing their jobs, and then get additional increments of pay for acquiring other skills valuable to the organization. For example, machine operators at Polaroid Company can increase their hourly pay by as much as 10 percent by acquiring skills in materials accounting, equipment maintenance, and quality inspection.[36]

> **Merit-based pay** is a compensation scheme in which employees earn a permanent increase in compensation based on past performance that is captured in the performance appraisal; it is used in job-based pay systems.

> **Skill-based pay** is a compensation system in which members are paid a base hourly wage rate for doing their jobs and then receive additional increments for acquiring other skills perceived as being valuable to the organization.

WHAT DO YOU THINK?

Are Executives Worth Their Wages?

Forbes magazine recently reported that executives from the top 500 U.S. companies earned on average $10.9 million.[37] In one year, the CEO of Capital One Financial, Richard D. Fairbank, took home $249.3 million in total pay, almost entirely from exercised stock options.[38]

Huge payouts to CEOs occur in other countries, but there is a much higher wage differential between those at the top and bottom of the pay scale in the United States. In the United States, one report asserts that CEOs of large corporations are paid $364 for every $1 paid to the average worker (a ratio of 364:1). By comparison, the ratio in the United States is approximately 15 times the same ratio in European firms, where the ratio averages close to 25:1.[39]

Theorists have attempted to explain the substantial pay disparity in the United States by arguing that it is the product of excessive management power in setting compensation, whereas others argue that the disparity is explained by free-market forces and the unique competitive environment of the United States. Some supporters of executive pay even argue that the pay is based on performance, but research evidence indicates otherwise.[40]

Do executives deserve their pay? Why do you think there are differences between the pay of U.S. and European executives? (You may wish to refer to Table 4.1 in Chapter 4 when considering these questions.)

Pay-for-performance (PFP) is a compensation scheme in which each member's pay is linked directly to individual, group, or organizational performance. The direct relationship is expected to raise productivity.

An increasing number of organizations today are moving to a **pay-for-performance (PFP)** system in an effort to raise productivity. This compensation scheme is among a select set of HRM practices that Jeff Pfeffer and others call "high-performance work practices."[41] In PFP (which is also sometimes called incentive pay), a member's pay is linked directly to individual, group, or organizational performance. Most companies now offer some form of incentive pay; this includes individually oriented piece-rate systems such as those made famous by Lincoln Electric, where employees receive a fixed amount for every unit of output. Salespeople often work on an individual commission basis, where their compensation is tied to sales as well as additional rewards for meeting specified goals. PFP also can include gain-sharing plans (where a group of employees are rewarded for reaching agreed-upon productivity improvements), goal-sharing plans (where a group of employees receive bonuses for reaching strategically important goals), profit-sharing plans (where a portion of an organization's profits are paid to employees), and stock options plans (where employees earn the right to purchase shares of their organization's stock at a potentially reduced cost). These types of PFP plans are particularly helpful in aligning employee goals with organizational performance goals.

Step 4: Training and Development

Thus far we have looked at determining the human resources an organization needs (job analysis and planning), recruiting and selecting the best people for the organization (staffing), and then appraising and rewarding performance (performance management). We now turn to the final step in the HRM process, that of training and developing employees. The American Society for Training & Development estimates that organizations spent more than $129 billion on employee training and development in 2006.[42] The terms "training" and "development" are sometimes used interchangeably. For the purposes of our discussion, **training** refers to learning activities that improve skills or performance in a specific area or current position, whereas **development** comprises learning activities that result in broad growth and development, usually beyond the scope of the current job, which prepares a person for future positions. As such, development activity is often referred to as career development.

Training refers to learning activities that improve an individual's skills or performance in a specific area or current position.

Development refers to learning activities that result in broad growth for a person, including growth in terms of a larger career or beyond the scope of the person's current job.

TRAINING.   The first exposure most employees receive to training is new-member "orientation training" programs that may run for a few hours or a couple of weeks. During work-unit orientation, new members become familiar with the people in their work unit, are exposed to its goals, and learn how their jobs fit with their co-workers' jobs. Organization orientations provide an introduction to the organization's history, its mission statement, its facilities, its key leaders, and its human resource policies and information (e.g., work hours, overtime policy, benefits). Orientations may range from very formal (e.g., a one-week course off-site) or informal ("Here's Sally—she'll take you around and introduce you to some of the people you'll be working with"). This early training is an important form of socialization that helps new employees navigate the new work environment.

DIGGING DEEPER

Unions and HRM

A labor union is an organization that represents workers and deals with employers—and, in some countries, with government—on the workers' behalf. In the United States, approximately 13 percent of the labor force is unionized, whereas in Western Europe unionization rates for workers range from 28.6 percent in the United Kingdom to close to 40 percent in Northern Ireland.[43] Unions seek to protect their members' interests through collective bargaining. In unionized organizations, the collective bargaining agreement (i.e., union contract) usually influences all four steps of the HRM process. It can cover agreements specifying the criteria and processes to be used in managing job requirements, recruitment, hiring, promotions, wage rates, discipline, grievances, layoffs, and even training eligibility.

A union may reinforce its bargaining position by threatening to strike (i.e., members of the union may refuse to come to work); in response, management may threaten to implement a "lockout" (i.e., refuse to let employees come to work) or to hire "strike-breakers" or "scabs" (i.e., non-union members hired to replace striking union workers). Despite their noble intentions, union activities have occasionally contributed to violent and destructive encounters between employers, union employees, and replacement workers. For example, a kindly grandmother and leader of union activism, Mother Jones, once challenged union miners to "take your high-power rifles and blow the . . . scabs out of the mines."[44] Although not always the case, in the United States labor–management relations typically have an adversarial (win-lose) tone.

Although union participation is on the decline in both the United States and Europe, some HRM professionals and managers spend a substantial amount of time responding to union demands, engaging in collective bargaining, and attempting to minimize the antagonistic relationship between employers and employees. Other HRM professionals and managers spend their time creating and sustaining favorable employment conditions that discourage union organization.

For example, Whole Foods Markets prides itself on its stores being nonunionized in the heavily unionized grocery industry. However, a lack of attention to growing dissatisfaction with the responsiveness of store leadership, combined with problems communicating with its predominantly Generation Y employees, recently created an opening for union organization at one store.[45] The response of top management was to redouble its efforts to be an employee-friendly environment that is better attuned to its workforce.

Perhaps this approach will continue to reduce the need for unions at Whole Foods Markets, but when organizations abuse their power, unions can serve as a counterbalance to the power of employers. This role is evident in union involvement in lobbying for government oversight of private equity firms that have been accused of buying up companies and laying off workers or cutting back on worker benefits.[46]

The most common method of training is **on-the-job training (OJT)**. OJT typically involves having a more experienced member "show the ropes" to a newer member. This type of training has a long history, going back centuries to the days when "apprentices" used to work with "master" craftspeople so as to become journeymen and then masters themselves. When it works, OJT is considered to be the fastest and most effective form of training. Some organizations engage in cross-training or job rotation, where people receive OJT in a variety of positions in the organization, thus permitting them to better understand how their jobs fit into the overall organization, and providing flexibility for the organization if another member is unable to come to work for an extended period of time. IBM chief learning officer Ted Hoff asserts that as much as 80 percent of the skills employees learn come from OJT.[47]

OJT is not appropriate for every training need. When this type of training causes too much disruption in normal operations, for example, it is not effective. Likewise, when tasks are too complex to learn by OJT, organizations use off-the-job training methods such as formal education, classroom lectures, films and videos, and simulation exercises. At Vanguard Investments Group, classroom instruction is utilized as part of the firm's extensive diversity training; its diversity program involves six courses for employees, with two additional courses for managers.[48] Of course, many

On-the-job training (OJT) is a type of training in which a more experienced member of the organization teaches a specific job or task to a newer member.

organizations offer training in other areas such as technology, customer service, safety, and specific product or service offerings.

In these off-the-job training environments, the successful transfer of the training to the work environment depends on several factors:[49]

- Training should be offered to those who have an interest in and aptitude for the training. In other words, trainees must be willing and able to be trained.

- The training content itself must be relevant and the instruction designed so that trainees are given multiple opportunities to practice using each component of the target skill or knowledge domain. The objectives of the training should be reinforced before, during, and after the training experience.

- There must be support for applying the training in the work environment. Many employees have returned from training eager to apply what they have learned, only to find no opportunities for, or interest in, using the training on the job. A supportive work environment can be created by a manager who is committed to encouraging investments in training, finding opportunities to apply training, and recognizing improvements gained through training.

Tad Waddington, director of performance measurement for Accenture People Enablement, a division of the Accenture consulting company, asserts that organizations spend billions on training annually, but most managers have no idea of the bottom-line impact of that expenditure.[50] From a Mainstream perspective, managers who take training seriously also take the time to measure training effectiveness. For example, 92 percent of the organizations listed in *Training* magazine's list of top 100 organizations claimed to evaluate their training activities at some level.[51] Although in most organizations trainees are asked to provide their reactions immediately after training, and in some cases organizations attempt to assess learning through pre- and post-training tests, very few organizations actually take the time to link training to behavioral change or business results. A comprehensive HRM system allows for such measurement. For example, if specific KSAOs are identified in the job analysis (or perhaps via a training needs analysis) and are measured in the performance appraisal, training that specifically addresses one or more KSAOs can be evaluated by tracking progress in performance appraisal ratings. In some cases, training can be directly tied to business results, such as when training in quality improvement leads to decreases in defects or reductions in waste that improve the performance of an manufacturing line or plant. In many other cases, however, it is difficult to prove the direct business benefits of training. Nonetheless, HRM professionals are under increasing pressure to demonstrate the "return on investment" of training expenditures.

CAREER DEVELOPMENT.   Approaches to career development are based on assumptions about the employment relationship. As mentioned at the beginning of this chapter, the Mainstream approach to the employment relationship is moving toward one of focusing on immediate and specific exchanges between the employee and the organization. As a consequence, a common development activity is assigning difficult or challenging tasks that extend the scope and complexity of a member's job. Such tasks might include leading a cross-functional problem-solving team or researching possible process improvements. Career development not tied directly to one's current job is typically perceived as being the responsibility of the employee, unless the employee has been identified in a talent management process as a high-potential employee who should be included in a succession plan. A **succession plan** is the management process of identifying talented employees who have the

Succession plan is the management process of identifying talented employees who have the potential to succeed in jobs of increased responsibility within the organization.

potential to succeed in jobs of increased responsibility within the organization. Organizations implement succession plans for a variety of reasons—ranging from ensuring that enough talent is in the pipeline to ensuring that a sufficient number of underrepresented people (often women or minorities) are advancing through the promotion system. Unfortunately, many organizations have either a limited succession plan or no succession plan at all.[52]

Given that more employees are being asked to take responsibility for their own development, it would be helpful to consider which development practices are viewed by practicing managers as important for their improvement and development. In research addressing this question, the practices listed in Table 12.1 were indicated as the top ten development practices for improving performance.[53]

It makes sense that many of the HRM practices already mentioned in this chapter—such as clear goals and performance expectations, effective performance appraisals, and 360-degree evaluations—made the "top ten" list. Likewise, it is not surprising to find on this list challenging job assignments and purposeful cross-training. Two areas on the list that we have yet to touch on and deserve attention are mentoring (number three) and formal career planning discussions (number six).

Most managers and other employees recognize the value of learning from others, particularly those who are more seasoned or experienced. Most junior managers are eager to receive **mentoring,** which entails the delivery of clear directions, accurate feedback, expert advice, and support from senior managers within the same organization. Deloitte and Touche is an example of an organization that has addressed the desire for mentoring with formal in-house resources and programs. For example, this company offers a Web interface that provides resources for mentors and a mechanism to help match mentors with mentees.[54] Not all organizations find it easy to satisfy requests for mentors. Many top managers today are overburdened with the challenges of their own responsibilities, and in flatter corporate structures these managers are finding it increasingly difficult to meet with their own direct reports, let alone mentor others.[55] If limited opportunities for mentorship exist within their own organization, junior managers and others may need to seek mentors outside of the organization.

> **Mentoring** is a means of coaching junior managers in which a senior manager within the organization gives a specific junior manager clear directions, accurate feedback, expert advice, and support.

TABLE 12.1

Managers' Beliefs About the Most Important Development Practices

Development Practice	Percentage of Managers Who Indicated It Was Important
1. Clarifying roles, goals, and performance expectations	86%
2. Ongoing performance measurement, feedback, and coaching	78%
3. Being mentored by senior managers	72%
4. Effective performance appraisals and reviews	62%
5. Challenging/difficult job assignments	61%
6. Formal career planning discussions	60%
7. Increased contact with external/internal customers	59%
8. Purposeful cross-training experiences	58%
9. Visiting other departments/organizations/facilities	51%
10. 360-degree feedback systems	48%

Source: Longenecker, C. & Neubert, M. J. (2003). The management development needs of frontline managers: voices from the field. *Career Development International,* 8(4), 210-218. Reproduced with permission of *Career Development Journal* in the format Textbook via Copyright Clearance Center and Emerald Group Publishing Limited.

Managers are also interested in receiving formal career development planning assistance. A few organizations offer this service as a separate benefit for employees, whereas others integrate career planning into the developmental component of performance appraisal. Outside vendors that offer career planning services often provide an extensive assessment process that helps identify participants' strengths, weaknesses, and interests. Of course, any employee can engage in career planning by doing an annual personal career SWOT analysis. In addition to identifying strengths and weaknesses, a personal career SWOT analysis involves considering how your strengths and weaknesses fit with opportunities and threats in your industry, your profession, or the broader job market (see the end-of-chapter Hands-On Activity, "Personal Career SWOT Analysis").

MULTISTREAM HUMAN RESOURCE MANAGEMENT

A Multistream approach to HRM emphasizes empowerment and dignity for all members in an organization's HRM processes. This approach is particularly sensitive to how employees are labeled and treated in organizations. Instead of managers considering employees to be resources, commodities, or expenses (which is where employment costs show up on the income statement), a Multistream approach suggests that managers might be better served by considering employees to be partners and that HRM professionals should serve as "people champions."[56]

Multistream HRM is consistent with several of the assumptions in the "old" employment contract, where the employer asks for both immediate and long-term contributions from the employee—including loyalty—and in exchange offers more security and benefits as well as broad development opportunities for the employee. A Multistream approach considers these HRM practices to be virtuous ends in themselves. Nonetheless, research comparing the "old" long-term mutual investment relationship to the "new" short-term economic exchange relationship (which is more typical of the Mainstream approach) has concluded that the "old" approach results in organizational members being more committed to the organization as well as performing better, helping more, and being absent less often.[57] Moreover, some evidence suggests that the whole organization performs better under the "old" approach.[58] In addition to emphasizing a long-term relationship, the Multistream approach tends to emphasize community by involving employees in a wide range of activities, emphasizing group goals, and sharing rewards with employees through group-oriented compensation.

Step 1: Job Analysis and Planning

JOB ANALYSIS.   The Multistream approach to job analysis focuses on the role of a job in the greater system or work flow of the department or business unit. The Multistream approach to gathering information for a job analysis involves consulting a wider array of stakeholders in comparison to the Mainstream approach, which is dominated by getting input from the jobholder. When Darrin Hartley was an HRM professional for Dell, he utilized a process he called "Job Analysis at the Speed of Reality," where a group of jobholders were brought together with an HRM professional to negotiate job expectations and tasks.[59] Although this approach is inclusive, Multistream managers are likely to go even further by inviting stakeholders from other departments and even from outside the organization, such as customers, to participate in job analysis and design.

Given the increased use of self-managed teams and project teams in organizations, a Multistream alternative to focusing on *individual* jobs may be to analyze and design *team* jobs. That is, the tasks and KSAOs of the team are designated in the job description and specifications. Researchers have already identified KSAOs that can be applied to teams.[60] A Multistream approach would involve team members in creating a team "job description" that includes not only team-oriented KSAOs, but also a description of who the team interacts with and influences through its work.

HRM PLANNING.   Both Mainstream and Multistream approaches to HRM planning include assessing and forecasting the demand for and supply of workers to ensure that the organization has the people it needs to fulfill its obligations and objectives. However, Multistream planning processes are typically more transparent and inclusive. Rather than tightly holding information related to needs and opportunities, a Multistream approach is more likely to make this information broadly available to organizational members at all levels. This greater access allows members to be aware of opportunities for development or advancement within the organization as well as keeps members informed of and included in solving potential problems. For example, if a shortage of people is evident, members on their own initiative may recruit others to join the organization. Conversely, if there is an excess of a set of skills within the organization, some members with those skills may retool their skills to fit with emerging needs.

Multistream managers also are less likely to use contingent workers, because their emphasis is on providing full and stable employment for all of the organization's members. In part reflecting its Multistream HRM planning practices and philosophy, Southwest Airlines was the only airline to not lay off employees during the industry downturn that followed the September 11, 2001, terrorist attacks. Instead, the airline redeployed members or cut back hours that members worked to respond to the difficult economic conditions.[61]

A Multistream perspective also emphasizes how job analysis and planning align with the organization's mission—its enduring purpose or reason for existence. This approach asks how a job, or a team, contributes to fulfilling the mission of the organization. For example, the mission at Men's Wearhouse includes maximizing sales, providing service and value to customers, and enhancing employee growth and sense of community. According to company founder George Zimmer, service and growth are not mere window dressings: He puts employees, customers, and the community ahead of shareholders in his ranking of stakeholder groups.[62]

Step 2: Staffing

RECRUITING.   Both Mainstream and Multistream managers recognize the importance of relationships in developing recruiting channels, but a Multistream approach is likely to differ somewhat in terms of the relationships managers form to aid recruiting. In particular, some Multistream managers may be more inclined to develop relationships with the outcasts or marginalized people in their communities.

For example, Julius Walls, Jr., runs a high-end bakery business, Greyston Bakery, guided by the belief that everyone has a right to a job, regardless of background or prior mistakes. As such, Greyston hires people off the street, many of whom are former substance abusers or convicted criminals. Although everyone is given an

Greyston Bakery is located in urban Yonkers, New York, in an area that other companies have abandoned. This location provides jobs in the inner city and stimulates economic development.

opportunity and provided support to cope with personal challenges, employees are held responsible for their actions and must prove themselves over a 12- to 16-week tryout period.[63]

A few organizations have recognized that nontraditional applicant pools may yield qualified applicants who stay longer and work harder. Such is the case with hiring people with physical or mental disabilities, who tend to have greater commitment to the organizations that hire them.[64]

Today many organizations use recruiting strategies that enhance diversity within the organization. American Airlines and Dell are among companies that encourage employee affinity groups or networking groups for minorities. In some cases, these groups provide input into recruiting and hiring practices as well as serve as a source of referrals for recruiting diverse applicants. Using referrals is consistent with a Multistream perspective in that it empowers employees and helps promote a sense of community within the organization. Additionally, referrals are beneficial in that these applicants are identified and prescreened by employees who are familiar with the organization's expectations and culture. Of course, this approach has some drawbacks—in particular, it could lead to an increasingly politicized workplace, where friends begin recruiting and promoting friends without regard to qualifications or fit.

SELECTION. A Multistream approach to selection includes selection methods and tools that reinforce and predict collective criteria such as team performance, contributions to organizational learning, and commitment to the organization's values and culture. For example, whereas the trait of agreeableness (i.e., being considerate, kind) does not predict performance in individual jobs, in the context of a team, the agreeableness of the team members predicts team performance and other important team dynamics such as social cohesion and interpersonal conflict.[65]

When selection is based on individual jobs, as is typically done in the Mainstream approach, it is sometimes easy to overlook organization-wide considerations. As a result, important factors such as contributions to organizational learning or maintaining an organizational culture are not considered. Robert Sutton, in his *Harvard Business Review* article entitled "The Weird Rules of Creativity," proposes that managers should hire people who make other members uncomfortable—that is, people who are not like other members and whose skills do not fit into any specific job.[66] The organization benefits from this approach by increasing the diversity of perspectives that are brought to bear on workplace challenges and included in decision making. A Multistream manager is more likely to heed this advice and select individuals who will contribute to organizational learning. This is not to say that a Multistream approach suggests randomly hiring anyone; rather, who is hired is sometimes based on different criteria.

A Multistream approach to selection also is more likely to emphasize fit with the organization, rather than short-term skill sets. Perhaps a person who has a breadth of experiences and is agreeable may not have a strong fit with an individual job, but nevertheless fits quite well with an innovative and collaborative culture. It is not as though Mainstream selection processes such as interviews do not consider fit (because increasingly they do), but the Multistream approach emphasizes team and organizational fit over job fit. Research suggests that basing hiring decisions on fit between the applicant and the organization can yield higher levels of commitment to the organization and lower turnover than a staffing approach that selects employees based on the fit between the applicant and the job.[67] Further, whereas job fit predicts job performance slightly better than organizational fit, the latter is a better predictor of whether an employee will step out of his or her job role to voluntarily do things that help the organization.[68] In other words, a person who fits with the values of an organization may not measure as high on individual productivity as someone who is chosen to fit a specific job, but the former types of employees are more likely to go beyond their individual responsibilities to help others (e.g., coworkers, customers).

Although fit may be assessed by an HRM professional or hiring manager, a more Multistream approach would be to include other organizational members in the hiring process. To some extent, team members and peers are included in panel interviews in many organizations, but Multistream organizations are more likely to give hiring authority to team members. Thus, a Multistream approach is consistent with relying on self-managed teams to do recruiting and hiring for their teams.

Step 3: Performance Management

PERFORMANCE APPRAISAL. A Multistream manager values feedback as a means to stimulate growth and development. Nonetheless, a major challenge in the performance appraisal process is how to deliver accurate feedback in such a way that it is accepted as helpful for development and improvement. When organizational members believe that feedback is related to an administrative decision, such as a raise or promotion, the developmental value of the feedback is often lost or at least diminished as the recipient focuses on what is necessary to get these "carrots." Further complicating the appraisal process is the reality that many managers provide ratings that are lenient or exclude negative feedback to avoid the negative reactions of employees who would otherwise miss out on a raise or promotion.[69]

A Multistream manager is more likely to deliver feedback more frequently and informally, rather than waiting for formal reviews. At minimum, a Multistream approach follows the practice of separating (in time) developmental appraisals from the administrative appraisals that determine raises and promotions. Such a separation can increase the receptivity of organizational members to feedback offered during developmental appraisals. Some Multistream managers, like those at SAS Institute, have gone one step further by abolishing administrative appraisals altogether.

COMPENSATION. A traditional feature of a Mainstream approach to performance management has been the focus on measuring and rewarding individual performance. The increased use of teams and

To avoid being like Dilbert's Pointy-Haired Boss, managers need to make a reasonable effort to understand the jobs of the people that they appraise or include input from team members who have a better understanding of the contributions of other team members. DILBERT: © Scott Adams/Dist. by United Feature Syndicate, Inc.

participative work environments has, however, increased the use of team- or group-level rewards in an effort to increase collaboration. Furthermore, team members and peers are increasingly likely to provide performance feedback and ratings. Unfortunately, many of the rating forms still focus on individual behavior, making the group's involvement an indirect—and possibly more coercive—means of policing and monitoring individual performance.

Two Multistream alternatives are (1) to emphasize team-oriented KSAOs in rating individual performance[70] or (2) to forgo rating individual performance altogether and rate the team, not its members. Rating the team suggests that rewards also would be targeted at the team. In essence, this Multistream approach to performance management focuses on group- or team-based HRM systems. These systems encourage cooperation and flexibility in accommodating the interests of other group members. When all team members share in the success of the team, its members are more likely to share tactical or technical information broadly and to help solve problems that benefit the whole group. Furthermore, team-oriented reward and feedback systems are often a practical necessity, as it is often impossible to separate out the contributions of individuals when the work is completed interdependently.

It may not be surprising, but research on employee attitudes suggests that compensation can be an important motivator for many people.[71] Whereas some Multistream managers attempt to de-emphasize money (see the chapter-opening case), others use money to communicate values by paying above-market wages for front-line employees and limiting the pay of executives. The Men's Wearhouse, for example, competes in a market environment that typically employs low-skilled labor at low wages. Bucking the industry norms, The Men's Wearhouse pays its salespeople (who are called wardrobe consultants) above-market wages as well as commissions. Furthermore, almost 100 percent of the firm's employees and managers own stock in the company. Although executives benefit from shared or group incentives, the top managers at The Men's Wearhouse are paid less than executives from similarly-performing organizations.[72] This practice is consistent with Multistream managers' concerns about justice and fairness, which make them less likely to accept compensation that is perceived to be excessive. For example, as noted in Chapter 1, at Reell Precision Manufacturing, executive pay is limited to roughly seven to ten times that of the lowest-paid employee.[73]

Multistream managers also are more likely to use nonfinancial rewards to motivate employees. From a simple "thank you" note to special work assignments, nonfinancial rewards send a message of recognition and appreciation without making money the primary focus of the exchange. Bob Nelson, in his book *1001 Ways to Reward Employees*,[74] provides numerous examples of how managers can use their imagination and appeal to nonfinancial forms of well-being to deliver creative rewards to employees. After a team reaches a goal or stays late to meet a deadline, a manager might bake a loaf of banana bread or a batch of cookies to serve to employees the next morning. Of course, not every manager has a "special" recipe or baking skills, but almost every manager can send employees home early on Friday or acknowledge the team's work in the company newsletter. For more notable contributions, managers might want to dig a bit deeper into their pockets to find an appropriate reward, such as a gift certificate for a local restaurant, lunch together as a team, or difficult-to-find tickets for a concert or ballgame. It sends a powerful message to employees when managers demonstrate creativity, self-sacrifice, and thoughtfulness in their rewards.

Step 4: Training and Development

TRAINING. From a Mainstream perspective, training is typically instrumental or linked to immediate returns in performance. In contrast, from a Multistream perspective, education and training are worth doing whether or not the organization will reap the benefits of that investment. For example, Shaw Industries, a flooring manufacturer, invests in training by paying for schooling, whether the training is geared toward enhancing a specific capability or toward earning a General Educational Development diploma (GED; the equivalent of a secondary education). In the latter case, Shaw even foots the bill for the cap and gown fees for its GED graduates.[75] Of course, supporting a person in completing a GED program may have value in the workplace, but it also enhances the dignity of the person who earns it.

A Multistream approach to training also relies less on structured or controlled environments such as classrooms. For example, IBM has a well-developed on-demand, organization-wide e-learning system where employees can access options to try a simulation, read about best practices, or even chat with a colleague about a specific work challenge or learning need.[76] In other words, a Multistream approach to training emphasizes creating an environment for learning in which members are encouraged to explore areas of interest and learn from others.

It is never too late to get more education. For people who have limited their education due to health crises, family obligations, financial limitations, or other personal reasons, an investment in more education can improve self-esteem and earning power.

CAREER DEVELOPMENT. As a result of the "new" employment contract, Mainstream managers are not likely to take responsibility for members' long-term development, and they are increasingly less likely to pay for activities that members engage in for their own development. In contrast, Multistream managers are more likely to invest in and support long-term development, even if the payoff to the organization is unclear. In one year, the consulting firm Booz Allen Hamilton paid out more than $10 million in tuition reimbursements for 21 percent of its employees.[77] Booz Allen Hamilton may benefit from its investment in education, or the company may not if employees leave to pursue other opportunities. Nonetheless, the firm's culture emphasizes development even when it is not clear how those development activities might address immediate needs within the organization.

Multistream managers also are more likely to support development activities that involve other stakeholders. These experiences can be especially enlightening to both managers and employees, who can sometimes get bogged down by the concerns and challenges of their own job or organization. Interacting with people in other organizations can stimulate creativity and enhance awareness of the needs, challenges, and concerns of others.

Taken as a whole, the Multistream approach to training and development is rooted in the virtue of promoting human growth and development. As such, Multistream managers are more likely to provide and pay for more training and development activity than are typical Mainstream managers, who often expect a direct and immediate payoff from these investments. A Multistream approach also tends to focus on creating and stimulating learning within the organization and in conjunction with its external stakeholders. In turn, managers taking this approach are more likely to seek out and provide opportunities for organizational resources or expertise to be used to train or develop members of their community.

CLOSING CASE

Starting from the Ground Up at Amica Wireless

Question: What happens when a start-up management team consisting of an engineer, an accountant, and marketing manager takes time over coffee to dream of a telecommunications company that defies the traditional "dog eat dog" industry norms of customer churning, and seeks to create an organization with a strong team spirit that will encourage employees to work collaboratively to satisfy customers? Answer: Amica Wireless.

It is one thing to talk about being a "team" and quite another to create a culture that actually reinforces team- or group-oriented behavior. The design of a distinctive HRM system was necessary to launch the unique organizational culture that these start-up managers envisioned. Drawing from their experiences, with a bit of research thrown in, the founders of Amica Wireless developed an integrated system of goals, feedback, and rewards that was linked to three principles:

1. Ensure fair and equitable distribution of profits.
2. Reinforce teamwork and cooperation.
3. Stimulate performance.

Most organizations in the telecommunications industry use primarily individually oriented compensation systems that vary significantly across departments, with members of the sales force being rewarded on a commission basis and engineers and customer service representatives receiving annual merit rewards. Some organizations also use group- or organizational-level bonuses, but they represent a small portion of each person's overall compensation. Although one initial proposal for Amica involved using *only* group- or organizational-level rewards, this departure from industry norms was too dramatic for the managers to adopt. Even after arriving at a balanced approach that included both individual and group incentives, the increased focus on group rewards made a clear impression on potential employees who interviewed with Amica. Some salespeople with a successful background in individual-based commission compensation found such a system to be appealing, whereas others were clearly "turned off." By comparison, the group reward structure received a decidedly positive response from experienced customer service and technical people who had grown disenchanted with the perceived inequities in rewards between sales and support personnel.

After selecting their employees and implementing the balanced reward system, the Amica managers drew several conclusions from their initial experience:

- Organization-wide group incentives had the effect of reinforcing the idea that all employees were on the same team.
- Group incentive systems at the regional level, where customer service representatives and salespeople shared the rewards of success for sales and customer retention, seemed to facilitate more cooperation in selling services and activating customers than is typically experienced in the industry.
- Bugs in the system led to some salespeople leaving the organization owing to dissatisfaction with pay. For those who left, it appeared that the benefits of a more collaborative work environment were not perceived to be worth the costs of reduced short-term financial rewards.

Using human resource systems to create a team-oriented culture turned out to be an adaptive process in which managers made adjustments to the balance of group and individual systems several times early in the implementation of the compensation systems. For managers at Amica, striking a balance between individual and group incentives was a difficult yet worthwhile challenge.[78]

QUESTIONS FOR DISCUSSION

1. How would you react to working under the Amica system?

2. What problems and potential do you see in such a system?

3. How might implementing these changes to an existing organization differ from including them as part of a new organization such as Amica?

SUMMARY

Four steps or practices are part of Mainstream human resource management:

1. *Job analysis and planning:* Identify what people need to do.

- Look at individual positions and use job analysis techniques such as observation, interviews, and surveys.
- Integrate job analysis information into an HRM planning process that includes both labor demands and available supply.

2. *Staffing:* Get the right people onboard.

- Recruit using traditional channels.
- Select employees based on their individual performance potential.

3. *Performance management:* Provide sufficient feedback and rewards for people.

- Use appraisals to assess and reward performance.
- Align compensation with individual performance; focus on financial rewards.

4. *Training and development:* Prepare and develop the people.

- Provide training to improve short-term production.
- Target employee development toward the needs of the organization.

Four steps or practices are also part of Multistream human resource management:

1. *Job analysis and planning:* Identify what people need to do.

- Use team-oriented job analysis techniques such as observation, interviews, and surveys.
- Integrate job analysis information into an HRM planning process that is consistent with the organization's mission.

2. *Staffing:* Get the right people onboard.

- Recruit using nontraditional channels.
- Select employees based on team or cultural fit.

3. *Performance management:* Provide sufficient feedback and rewards for people.

- Use appraisals to enhance development.
- Align compensation with team performance; balance financial and nonfinancial rewards.

4. *Training and development:* Prepare and develop the people.

- Provide training to improve short-term and long-term production.
- Recognize that employee development is an end in itself.

QUESTIONS FOR REFLECTION AND DISCUSSION

1. What would you like about working at SAS? What would cause you concern? If you did work there, what would it take for you to leave? Do you think SAS's approach is reasonable for other organizations?

2. It has been argued that managers should differentiate between "A" positions and other, less important jobs in an organization.[79] If a position makes an important contribution to achieving strategic objectives and the people in that position vary greatly in how well they perform, the position should be the focus of HRM initiatives from development to succession planning. Other positions are less important and deserve less attention in the HRM planning process. What are the potential benefits and drawbacks of rating the importance of jobs in this way?

3. Keeping job analysis and planning information up-to-date can be a time-consuming and laborious task. If you are asked by someone you are managing to explain why job analysis and HRM planning are worth the time, what would you say?

4. Reports from the National Football League scouting workouts had quarterback Vince Young scoring low on the Wonderlic test. Given that he led his college team, the University of Texas Longhorns, to a national championship and now is experiencing success in the NFL, what thoughts do you have about the validity of the Wonderlic?

5. Have the selection processes you've experienced seemed fair? Why or why not?

6. If you have been interviewed, to what extent did the process follow the suggestions from either Mainstream or Multistream HRM?

7. Which type of employment contract is more attractive to you: the "new" (Mainstream) contract, which is based on short-term exchanges, or the "old" (Multistream) contract, which featured general long-term commitments? Why?

HANDS-ON ACTIVITIES

The Occupational Information Network

Go to the O*Net website at http://online.onetcenter .org/. First, fill out an honest assessment of your skills. Second, pick out a job you aspire to do either now or in the not-too-distant future. Finally, compare your assessment to the job description and KSAO specifics. How do they match up? Are there areas you need to develop to be prepared for this job?

Personal Career SWOT Analysis

The objective of this exercise is to think reflectively and proactively about your career.

The first step is to look at yourself. Take a piece of paper and label one side as "Strengths," and label the other side of the same page as "Weaknesses." Under "Strengths," write down areas where you have excelled and what others say you do well (you might even ask a friend, coworker, or boss). Under "Weaknesses," list areas of struggle or failure, and areas that others say are "not your strength."

The second step is to look outside yourself. Flip the paper over, and label one side as "Opportunities." In this area, list promising opportunities in the job market or trends for certain careers and the availability of those jobs or careers. In the same area, list a few development activities that you could pursue, such as internships or leadership in student organizations. Label the other side of the paper as "Threats." List some factors such as competition or a lack of experience that might prevent you from getting the job or pursuing the careers that interest you. You might also consider factors such as bad habits, relationships, and other personal factors that could threaten your aspirations.

The final step is to take an honest look at your strengths, weaknesses, opportunities, and threats, and make specific action plans to enhance your strengths, develop your weaknesses, increase your opportunities, and minimize your threats. On a separate sheet of paper, make specific plans with clear deadlines.

ENDNOTES

1. http://www.cbsnews.com/stories/2001/02/08/eveningnews/ main270458.shtml; O'Reilly, C. III, & Pfeffer, J. (2000). *Hidden value:How great companies achieve extraordinary results with ordinary people.* Boston, MA: Harvard Business School Press; http://www.sas.com/corporate/overview/index.html; London, S. (September 26, 2003). Profit machines that put the people first. *Financial Times.* Accessed at http://search.ft.com/ftArticle?query Text=SAS+Institute+talent+&y=7&aje=false&x=14&id=0309 26000481&ct=0.

2. Mote, D, *Encyclopedia of business* (2nd ed.). Accessed March 3, 2008, at: http://www.referenceforbusiness.com/encyclopedia/ Gov-Inc/Human-Resource-Management-HRM.html.

3. Losey, M. (1998, March 15). HR comes of age: History of human resource management. *HR Magazine,* pp. 40–53.

4. Primoff, E., & Fine, S. (1988). A history of job analysis. In S. Gael (Ed.), *The job analysis handbook for business, industry, and government* (pp. 14–29). New York: Wiley.

5. Katz, H. C., & Kochan, T. A. (2004). *An introduction to collective bargaining and industrial relations.* New York: McGraw-Hill.

6. Katz & Kochan, 2004.

7. Hammonds, K. (2005, August). Why we hate HR. *Fast Company,* pp. 41–47.

8. Pfeffer, J., & Veiga, J. (1999). Putting people first for organizational success. *Academy of Management Executive,* 13(2), 37–48; and Pfeffer, J. (2005). Producing sustainable competitive advantage through the effective management of people. *Academy of Management Review,* 19(4), 95–106.

9. Tsui, A., & Wu, J. (2005). The new employment relationship versus the mutual investment approach: Implications for human resource management. *Human Resource Management,* 44(2), 115–121.

10. Neubert, M., & Longenecker, C. (2003). Creating job clarity: HR's role in improving organizational focus and performance. *HR Advisor,* 9(4), 17–21.

11. McCormick, E., & Jeannerette, R. (1988). The Position Analysis Questionnaire. In S. Gael (Ed.), *The job analysis handbook for business, industry, and government* (pp. 825–842). New York: Wiley.

12. http://online.onetcenter.org/.

13. http://www.contingentworkforce.org/.

14. Ulrich, D. (1997). *Human resource champions: The next agenda for adding value and delivering results.* Boston, MA: Harvard Business School Press.

15. White, E. (2007, January 11). Employers reach out to recruits with Facebook. *Wall Street Journal Online.* Accessed January 11, 2007, at: http://executiverecruitment.com/columnists/ theorypractice/20070111-theorypractice.html.

16. Pfeffer, 2005.

17. Collins, J. (2001). *Good to great: Why some companies make the leap . . . and others don't.* New York: HarperCollins.

18. SHRM resources are available for members at http://www .shrm.org; Winstein, K. J., & Golden, D. (2007, April 27). MIT Admissions Dean Lied On Resume in 1979, Quits. *Wall Street Journal,* p. B1; Bulkeley, W. M. (2000, January 7). Jeffrey Papows Says He Plans to Resign As Lotus President—Questions Arising From Claims About Background Marred Tenure at the IBM Unit. *Wall Street Journal,* p. B6.

19. Neter, E., & Ben-Shakhar, H. (1989). The predictive validity of graphology inferences: A meta-analytic study. *Personality and Individual Differences,* 10, 737–745.

20. Menkes, J. (2005). Hiring for smarts. *Harvard Business Review,* 83(11), 100–109.

21. Wonderlic, E. L., & Associates. (1992). *Wonderlic personnel test and scholastic level exam.* Libertyville, IL: Wonderlic Personnel Test, Inc.

22. Mount, M. K. & Barrick, M. R. (1995). The Big Five personality dimensions: Implications for research and practice in human resource management. *Research in Personnel and Human Resource Management,* 13, 153–220; Hough, L. M., & Furnham, A. (2003). Use of personality variables in work settings. In Weiner, I. B. (Ed.), *Handbook of psychology* (Vol. 12, pp. 131–170). New York: John Wiley & Sons.

23. Ones, D. S., & Viswesvaran, C. (2001). Integrity tests and other criterion-focused occupational personality scales (COPS) used in personnel selection. *International Journal of Selection and Assessment,* 9(1–2), 31–39.

24. Taylor, P., & Small, B. (2002). Asking applicants what they would do versus what they did do: A meta-analytic comparison of situational and past behaviour employment interview questions. *Journal of Occupational and Organizational Psychology,* 75, 277–294.

25. Taylor & Small, 2002.

26. Hausknecht, J. P., Day, D. V., & Thomas, S. C. (2004). Applicant reactions to selection procedures: An updated model and meta-analysis. *Personnel Psychology,* 57(3), 639–683.

27. Noe, R., Hollenbeck, J., Gerhart, B., & Wright, P. (2006). *Human resource management: Gaining a competitive advantage.* New York: McGraw-Hill.

28. http://www.eeoc.gov/press/11-18-04.html.

29. Adapted from Schermerhorn, J. R. (2002). *Management* (7th ed.). New York: John Wiley & Sons.

30. http://www.dol.gov/dol/topic/hiring/affirmativeact .htm#lawregs.

31. The questions themselves are not illegal, but instead are likely to provide prima fascia evidence of illegal discrimination.

32. Laws also govern the employment of undocumented workers or illegal immigrants. Although penalties for organizations employing undocumented workers are meant to restrict demand for such workers, they could inadvertently contribute to organizations attempting to minimize this risk by recruiting fewer legal immigrants (http://www.usatoday.com/money/economy/ employment/2006-05-04-immigration-usat_x.htm).

33. Longenecker, C., & Fink, L. (1999). Creating effective performance appraisals. *Industrial Management,* 41(5), 18–23.

34. Rynes, S., Brown, K., & Colbert, A. (2002). Seven common misconceptions about human resource practices: Research findings versus practitioner beliefs. *Academy of Management Executive,* 16(3), 92–103.

35. White, E. (2006, January 30). The best vs. the rest: Companies eschew across-the-board increases to give top performers a bigger slice of the raise pie. *Wall Street Journal,* p. B1.

36. Citation from Robbins, S. P., & Coulter, M. (2003). *Management* (7th ed., P. 323). Upper Saddle River, NJ: Prentice-Hall.

37. DeCarlo, S. (2006, April 20). What the boss makes. *Forbes.* http://www.forbes.com/2006/04/20/ceo-pay-options-cz_sw_ 0420ceopay.html.

38. DeCarlo, 2006.

39. Sahadi, J. (2007, August 29). *CEO pay: 364 times more than workers.* CNNmoney.com; http://money.cnn.com/2007/08/28/news/

economy/ceo_pay_workers/index.htm; Bruce, A., Buck, T., & Main, B. G. M. (2005). Top executive remuneration: A view from Europe. *Journal of Management Studies, 42*(7), 1493–1506.

40. Bebchuk, L., & Grinstein, Y. (2005). The growth of executive pay. *Oxford Review of Economic Policy, 21*(2), 283–303; Bebchuk, L. A., & Fried, J. M. (2004). *Pay without performance: The unfulfilled promise of executive compensation.* Cambridge, MA: Harvard University Press.
41. Pfeffer & Veiga, 1999.
42. *Training* magazine's annual industry report and ASTD annual survey. http://www.astd.org/.
43. http://www.statistics.gov.uk/cci/nugget.asp?id=4.
44. Stevenson, G. (1977). *That's no lady, that's Mother Jones: 200 Years of American worklife* (pp. 104–108). Washington, DC: U.S. Department of Labor.
45. Tejada, C. (2002, August 21). Pay and piercings: A union victory hints at how to organize the young. *Wall Street Journal*, p. B2.
46. Bartiromo, M. (2007, July 2). Bashing private equity. *Business-Week*, pp. 110–111.
47. Weinstein, M. (2006). Suite success: On demand delivers for IBM. *Training, 43*(3), 18–20.
48. *Training* best practices (2006). *Training, 43*(3), 60–63.
49. Baldwin, T. T., & Ford, J. K. (1988). Transfer of training: A review and directions for future research. *Personnel Psychology, 41*, 63–105; Colquitt, J. A., LePine, J. A., & Noe, R. A. (2000). Toward an integrative theory of training motivation: A meta-analytic path analysis of 20 years of research. *Journal of Applied Psychology, 85*(5), 678–707.
50. Lester, M. (2003, September 8). The ROI of training. http://www.larta.org/lavox/ArticleLinks/2003/030908_roi.asp.
51. Galvin, T., Johnson, G., & Barbian, J. (2003). The 2003 *Training* top 100. *Training, 40*(3), 18–38.
52. Rothwell, W. (2002, May/June). Putting success into your succession plan. *Journal of Business Strategy*, 32–37.
53. Longenecker, C., & Neubert, M. J. (2003). The management development needs of front-line managers: Voices from the field. *Career Development International, 8*(4), 210–218.
54. *Training* best practices, 2006.
55. Hymowitz, C. (2006, March 13). Today's bosses find mentoring isn't worth the time and risks. *Wall Street Journal*, p. B1.
56. Ulrich, 1997.
57. Tsui, A., Pearce, J., Porter, L., & Tripoli, A. (1997). Alternative approaches to the employee–organization relationship: Does investment in employees pay off? *Academy of Management Journal, 40*, 1089–1121.
58. Wang, D., Tsui, A., Zhang, Y., & Ma, L. (2003). Employment relationships and firm performance: Evidence from an emerging economy. *Journal of Organizational Behavior, 24*, 511–535.

59. Hartley, D. (2004, September). Job analysis at the speed of reality. *Training and Development*, 20–24.
60. Stevens, M. J., & Campion, M. A. (1994). The knowledge skill and ability requirements for teamwork: Implications for human resource management. *Journal of Management, 20*, 503–530.
61. Berdardin, 2003.
62. O'Reilly, C. III, & Pfeffer, J. (2000). *Hidden value: How great companies achieve extraordinary results with ordinary people.* Boston: Harvard Business School Press.
63. Gunther, M. (2001). God and business. *Fortune, 144*(1), 58–80.
64. Presentation at the Colorado Teaching Ethics Conference (2006).
65. Barrick, M., Stewart, G., Neubert, M. J., & Mount, M. (1998). Relating member ability and personality to work-team processes and team effectiveness. *Journal of Applied Psychology, 83*, 377–319.
66. Sutton, R. I. (2001). The weird rules of creativity. *Harvard Business Review, 79*, 94–103.
67. Kristof-Brown, A. L., Zimmerman, R. D., & Johnson, E. C. (2005). Consequences of individual's fit at work: A meta-analysis of person–job, person–organization, person–group, and person–supervisor fit. *Personnel Psychology, 58*(2), 281–342.
68. Kristof-Brown et al., 2005.
69. Murphy, K. R., & Cleveland, J. N. (1995). *Understanding performance appraisal: Social, organizational, and goal-based perspectives.* Thousand Oaks, CA: Sage.
70. Stevens, M. J., & Campion, M. A. (1994). The knowledge skill and ability requirements for teamwork: Implications for human resource management. *Journal of Management, 20*, 503–530.
71. Rynes et al., 2002.
72. O'Reilly & Pfeffer, 2000.
73. Benefiel, M. (2005). *Soul at work* (p. 21). New York: Seabury Books.
74. Nelson, B. (2005). *1001 ways to reward employees* (2nd ed.). New York: Workman.
75. *Training* best practices, 2006.
76. Weinstein, 2006.
77. Kronick, J. (2006). Booz Allen Hamilton puts people first: One firm, one goal. *Training, 43*(3), 11–16.
78. Ultimately, as was the intention of the venture capitalist who funded the formation of Amica Wireless, the company was sold to Leap Wireless: /PRNewswire/—Leap Wireless International, Inc. (Nasdaq: LWIN), an innovator of wireless communications services, today announced that it has completed two previously announced acquisitions, one of which was Amica Wireless Phone Service, a BRK Wireless Company, covering approximately 466,000 potential customers (1998 POPs). (2001, May 30).
79. Huselid, M., Beatty, R., & Becker, B. (2005). A positions or A players? The strategic logic of workforce management. *Harvard Business Review, 83*(12), 110–117.

CHAPTER 13

O n a long journey a traveler might arrive at a special place where he or she acquires a deeper understanding of the previous stops. Pausing to look back after reaching a crest on a ridge, an opening in a clearing on a hill, or even the top of the mountain sometimes offers a deeper understanding of the steps along the way. The current chapter may be one such place, because it helps the reader to see how the four-step processes that are described in other chapters can be seen as variations of a more general four-step change process. Thus, in a way, this entire book is about managing change in organizations. It is in times of change that the role of manager is most visible. The Mainstream view is characterized by a top-down approach, where change is managed by top managers. The emphasis is on managers deciding the *content* of change and ensuring that it is properly implemented. In contrast, the Multistream approach has a more bottom-up approach, emphasizes the process of change, and looks at a broader range of change issues.

ROAD MAP

FOUR STEPS OF ORGANIZATIONAL CHANGE

Step 1. Recognize the need for change

Step 2. Unfreeze

Step 3. Change

Step 4. Refreeze

Organizational Change

MAINSTREAM APPROACH ⟷	MULTISTREAM APPROACH
Based on managerial insight and sense of urgency	Based on organization-wide sensitization and openness
Overcome members' resistance and sell new vision of change	Involve members and treat them with consideration and dignity
Exert top-down authority and use persuasion to gain commitment	Employ participation to gain commitment
Implement structures and systems that reinforce and reward members who implement change	Support structures and systems that facilitate continuous learning and celebrate improvement

Whole-Systems Change at Brio Technology[1]

Brio Technology was in free fall when Craig Brennan took on the role of CEO. Brennan quickly realized that the crisis at the database software company required an altogether different response than the "command and control" approach that he had experienced in other technology companies.

Brennan put in a call to Kathy Dannemiller to help him take a whole-systems view in approaching the problem. Dannemiller's approach to change was formed in the trenches at Ford Motor Company in the early 1980s, when the company sought to transform its culture from a "command and control" model to a more participative style. Brennan and Dannemiller partnered to implement a change initiative at Brio that would bring about "one brain and one heart" among all its employees. Brennan was convinced that the only way Brio could be turned around was through a collective vision of the future that was understood and accepted throughout the whole system. Leaders, including Brennan himself, would need to throw out old leadership rules and adopt a new set of rules.

Old rule: Leaders know all and act as the final authority in important decisions.

New rule: Leaders call people together to uncover and connect the wisdom of the people.

Old rule: Leaders control information, people, . . . everything.

New rule: Leaders ask questions and encourage conversations across the system.

Old rule: Leaders drive performance and punish failure.

New rule: Leaders inspire performance and celebrate success.

A critical component of leading in this new way is to engage the whole system in addressing problems and creating solutions. The "whole-scale change" approach created by Dannemiller is a large-group intervention intended to get the organizational members representing the whole system into one room to discuss common dissatisfactions, a vision of what is possible based on common yearnings, and a set of action steps to move toward the future. Typically, the large-group event lasts three days.

The first step was to get widespread recognition of the need for change. This occurred during the first day at Brio's three-day event, when 400 employees across different levels were brought together and placed in mixed groups to share their stories of what was working, what was not working, and what each person wanted to see change in the future. This activity was supplemented by brief presentations from other stakeholders such as Brio partners and customers.

Once the need for change was evident, the next step was to get members talking about what the change might look like and to overcome their desire to hold on to the status quo. To stimulate thinking about the future, Brennan presented a draft strategic plan and asked the members who were seated randomly at different tables to discuss and react to the proposal. The first day concluded with a revised draft of a picture of the future built upon the suggestions of those in attendance.

On the second day, the focus was to get people involved in thinking about and designing specific changes. It started with a presentation of results from day 1, which was handled by a cross-sectional group of employees who served as the event planning team. The Brio event team members sorted through reams of flipchart paper and notes to summarize the firm's current state and strategic vision.

Members were then given time to work together to put flesh on the bare bones of the strategic vision by proposing and discussing potential action steps for specific goals. This creative process was summarized and presented during the morning of the third day, where for the first time participants were organized by functional areas. That final morning was used to translate ideas into concrete action steps that the group committed to implementing in the next few weeks and months.

Feedback from this event indicated that the participants—many of whom had entered the event with skepticism from a previous change that was poorly implemented—had committed to the new collective vision for Brio. The action steps from this initial planning event and the subsequent changes in the structure and focus of Brio's operations resulted in a substantial reduction of costs and the introduction of several products that helped begin a reversal of fortune at Brio. The changes at Brio, although formulated and implemented in a distinct whole-systems approach, did not easily translate into tangible results. A competitive environment marked by a reduction in IT spending on products at the heart of Brio's business slowed the transformation, but the process resulted in Brio approaching profitability for the first time in years.

Ultimately, after much positive change, Brio was acquired by its competitor Hyperion. Was the change a success? Perhaps not, if the goal of the change was to return to profitability and rebuff buyout offers. Nevertheless, the positive changes at Brio enabled it to stay in business and increased the company's value as an acquisition target. Alternatively, consider what might have happened if the organization's free fall had not been reversed. In the end, positive change within an organization contributes to—but does not guarantee—growth or survival in complex and dynamic competitive markets where innovations, customer preferences, and competitive forces change on a day-to-day basis.

INTRODUCTION TO ORGANIZATIONAL CHANGE

Organizational change is any substantive modification to some aspect of an organization. It may consist of a change in technology (e.g., the process used to transform inputs into outputs), structures (e.g., where the organization falls on the mechanistic–organic or closed–open continuum), people (e.g., training and skills), or mission or values (e.g., philosophy and culture). Change is an organizational reality, and managing change is an integral part of every manager's job. "The handwriting on the wall is clear: The world is changing, and those companies that fail to change . . . find themselves out of business."[2] Managers must understand when change is needed and be able to guide their organization through it.

The change process can be described as following four steps:[3]

1. Recognize the need for change
2. Unfreeze
3. Change
4. Refreeze

Although the basic four-step change process can be seen in all types of change, the way these steps unfold and need to be managed may be influenced by the type of change. As shown in Figure 13.1, there are at least three ways to differentiate between types of change:

- Scope
- Intentionality
- Source

First, the scope of the change can be either transformational or incremental.[4] **Transformational change** occurs when an organization changes its strategic direction or reengineers its culture or operations in response to dramatic changes such as a technological

> **Organizational change** is any substantive modification to some aspect of an organization.
>
> **Transformational change** occurs when an organization changes its strategic direction.

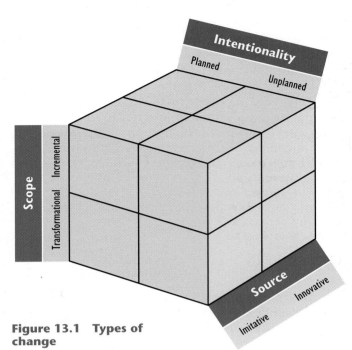

Figure 13.1   Types of change

Incremental change occurs when an organization makes improvements in moving in its current strategic direction.

Planned change is designed and implemented in an orderly and timely fashion; it is generally a direct response to the recognition of a performance gap—that is, a discrepancy between the desired and actual state of affairs.

Unplanned change involves making ad hoc or piecemeal responses to unanticipated events or crises as they occur.

Innovations involve the development and implementation of new ideas and practices.

Imitation involves the replication of existing ideas, which may come from other units within the organization or from outside the organization.

breakthrough or a merger.[5] **Incremental change** occurs when an organization makes improvements in moving toward its strategic direction, perhaps by restructuring to be more efficient or expanding its line of products or services to promote more growth. Transformational changes often are a reaction to a major problem or challenge in the competitive environment. For example, the music sales industry underwent a transformational change in response to losing revenue to Napster and other Internet companies that made downloads of songs easily accessible. Put in the terms used in Chapter 11, transformational changes occur when managers move a firm from one organizational type to another, whereas incremental changes occur when managers fine-tune or expand on a firm's existing organizational type. Research suggests that usually organizations are in periods of "equilibrium" where managers focus on fine-tuning an existing organizational type, and that these periods of equilibrium are occasionally interrupted or "punctuated" by bursts of transformational change where the organizational type is replaced with a new one.[6]

Second, change can vary in the intentionality of management actions.[7] A common problem faced by organizations is the failure of managers to anticipate or respond to changing competitive conditions; in such circumstances, instead of planned change, they must resort to reactive or unplanned change. **Planned change** is designed and implemented in an orderly and timely fashion. It is generally a direct response to the recognition of a performance gap—that is, a discrepancy between the desired and actual state of affairs. Often planned changes are prompted by an opportunity facing the organization. When members perceive opportunities for change, they increase their support for change and decrease their support for the status quo.[8] **Unplanned change** involves making ad hoc or piecemeal responses to unanticipated events or crises as they occur. Unexpected strategic moves by competitors are a common reason for unplanned change. These reactive changes usually need to be implemented quickly to minimize negative consequences and maximize possible benefits.

Third, types of changes may be differentiated by whether they arise from innovation or from imitation. **Innovations** involve the development and implementation of *new* ideas and practices. For example, organizational innovation has taken place when a kitchen cabinet manufacturer in southern Manitoba, Canada, develops and implements sophisticated software to manage materials purchase and assembly lines. **Imitation** involves the application of *existing* ideas, which may come from other units within the organization or from outside the organization. It occurs, for example, when a cabinet shop in British Columbia licenses use of the Manitoba firm's software. Innovation is considered to be more difficult to manage than imitation.

? WHAT DO YOU THINK?

How Would You React to These Types of Changes?[9]

Grand Canyon University (GCU) experienced a change that was transformational and unplanned. After funding for the historically nonprofit school evaporated, GCU faced likely closure. Its board of trustees agreed to sell the university to a group of investors, who then changed the university into a for-profit organization. The changes involved lowering tuition, raising faculty salaries, enhancing the facilities and grounds, increasing access for minorities, and expanding enrollments both on-campus and online. The tenure system that guaranteed lifetime employment also was replaced by a merit-based system of three- or five-year contracts. The changes at GCU continue, but in two short years, enrollments had doubled and more than $35 million had been invested to reduce debt and improve programs and facilities. Although other universities such as the University of Phoenix and DeVry University are also for-profit organizations, this transition from nonprofit organization to for-profit business is relatively new in the educational setting.

If you were a student at GCU, how would you react to the news that GCU managers did not renew contracts for 17 professors, 5 of whom were tenured under the old system? What if one of the professors had been a favorite among students? How would you react? What if the decisions were made based on student evaluations? Do you think this would affect the quality of instruction in the classroom? In what way? How do you think professors would react to these changes in deciding what sorts of activities to spend their time on?

In addition to classifying changes according to these three dimensions, we can think about organizational change in three different content areas, all of which are often interrelated:

- Technology
- Structures and systems
- People

Changes in technology affect the conversion process by which organizational members transform inputs into outputs. Technology-based changes generally focus on work flows, production methods, equipment, and information systems. They are designed to make products or services more efficient. Because of the rapid rate at which technological advancements are emerging, technological changes occur frequently and are important to organizations. For example, Grand Canyon University (GCU) experienced changes in technology as it expanded its online class offerings. In response to increased demand, faculty who had previously not used this technology had to learn how to use it to deliver online classes. Today many organizations are using information technology to achieve equally dramatic changes. For example, companies such as Marathon Oil use information technology in their purchasing or supply chain functions to reduce inefficiencies in tracking purchases, increase the speed of the bidding process, and save time and money by having online auctions.

Changes to an organization's structure may affect its levels of centralization, standardization, specialization, and departmentalization. For instance, when automotive giants Chrysler and Daimler Benz merged, one of the structures had to change. Chrysler's more decentralized, team-based structure had to change to a centralized hierarchy in response to demands by the leaders of Daimler. Other changes were required in Chrysler's human resource and information systems to support the new structure. In the end, the stress of adjusting to these changes and other challenges in the automotive industry contributed to their eventual breakup.

Finally, changes often affect people. These effects may stem from something as simple as changes in the everyday jobs that members perform or changes that affect members' self-identity or employment. For example, not only did many GCU professors have to adjust to teaching online classes, but some faculty also lost their jobs.

Sometimes changes in technology or structure can have a profound effect on people, and vice versa.

In the remainder of this chapter, we will describe the four-step change process from a Mainstream perspective, and then contrast and compare it with a Multistream approach. From a Mainstream perspective, change and learning are essentially managed with a top-down process, where managers work to ensure that their changes are implemented in the organization. In Multistream management, the process is much more bottom-up in nature, so that everyone participates in developing and implementing the change. These two perspectives represent ends of a continuum of approaches to managing the change process.

The sign on this Chrysler PT Cruiser, "Verkauft," is the German word for "sold." Although initially sold on its merger with Chrysler, Daimler later ended the relationship.

MAINSTREAM FOUR-STEP CHANGE PROCESS

Change can be seen to unfold in a four-step change process, as illustrated in Figure 13.2, which is based on the work of Kurt Lewin.[10] This process can be helpful for understanding all types of change, but its full implications are probably most evident when we consider transformational changes.[11] As such, our examples will be drawn from a variety of types of change, but we will focus mostly on the transformational types, which are the most challenging.

Step 1: Recognize the Need or Opportunity for Change

Everything and anything could be changed in an organization, including its name, its human resource policies, the way it processes its payroll, its dress code, its location, its structure, its products, and so on. However, Mainstream management concentrates on looking for and recognizing the need for changes that will help to maximize profits, efficiency, productivity, and competitiveness. These Mainstream criteria determine which change opportunities are urgent and which can be overlooked (at least for the moment). To identify opportunities for changes, managers rely on a variety of sources, ranging from formal information systems to the "intuition" that comes from having a deep understanding of existing operations. The recognition of the need for organizational change can be triggered by internal or external factors.

On an internal level, in response to recognizing that decisions are being made too slowly, the organization may move to a decentralized structure. For example, Dana Corporation, a parts supplier to the automotive industry, moved from a centralized organizational structure, with lengthy manuals outlining policies and procedures, to a decentralized structure based on a small set of values and guiding principles.

Managers also may recognize the need to change due to issues that arise in their external environment, such as a shift in consumer buying habits. For example, in the

Step 1: Recognize Need for Change
• Managers monitor opportunities and threats in order to maximize productivity and financial benefits.
• Managers recognize need for change.

Step 2: Unfreeze
• Managers use influence tactics to establish a sense of urgency and reduce resistance among members.
• Managers develop new vision and communicate it to other members.

Step 4: Refreeze
• Managers make adjustments to systems and structures to reinforce the changes.

Step 3: Change
• Managers act as change agents to model changes in behavior.
• Managers gain members' commitment to the vision by promoting positive attitudes and confidence in abilities.

Figure 13.2   A Mainstream approach to managing the four-step change process

home improvement sector, members of the "non-handy" baby-boom generation re-placed their "do-it-yourself" parents as the dominant consumer group. As a result, home improvement stores today are more successful if they offer simple training seminars and easy-to-install décor elements such as stylish plumbing fixtures to home-owners, as well as hard-core products such as nuts and bolts to tradespeople. As an-other example, change may be triggered by managers' recognition of the increasing costs of natural raw materials the company relies upon as inputs (e.g., coal and oil for energy companies) or a lack of employees with specific skills (e.g., nurses). An organi-zation may also need to respond to new government regulations (e.g., affirmative ac-tion programs, pollution regulations) or new directives from shareholders (e.g., greater transparency related to compensation packages of senior managers). Finally, organiza-tions may need to respond to technological innovations by competitors or suppliers.

Note that the same trigger may prompt different changes among organizations. For example, as described in Chapter 7, when the U.S. Surgeon General announced the link between cigarette smoking and cancer, American Brands perceived the an-nouncement as a threat and fine-tuned its existing strategy in response. In contrast, Philip Morris saw the announcement as an opportunity to try innovative packaging and to target female smokers with low-tar cigarettes.

Recognizing the need for change is not always easy. Managers who keep their proverbial nose to the grindstone and push out products and profits can miss or dismiss internal or external triggers that suggest the need for change. (Recall the decision-making pitfalls such as selective perception and escalation of commitment, described in Chapter 7.) In particular, success has a way of blinding managers to internal and external signals pointing to the need for change. Consider IBM manag-ers, who, given the success of IBM's large mainframe computers, for many years dismissed the potential customer appetite for personal computers.

Step 2: Unfreeze: Prepare Members for Change

The primary objectives in this stage are to ensure that organizational members un-derstand the need for change, to reduce possible resistance to change, and to create a sense of openness and willingness to change. Once managers have established that

The failure of managers to notice changes in their environment can be illustrated by a frog placed in a kettle. When it is placed in a kettle of hot water, the frog will immediately jump to safety. A frog placed in a kettle of cool water that is gradually heated, however, will tend to remain in the water even as it reaches the point of boiling. Like the frog, managers can "get cooked" by their failure to recognize gradual changes in the environment.

Burning platform is an approach to unfreezing organizational members that may be painful; it may involve using rational persuasion or pressure to expose members to alarming information or potential negative consequences.

there is a need for change, one might expect that it should be easy to persuade others in the organization to hop onboard. While this may often be true for incremental changes, it is often not true for transformational change.

In this step, managers explain or "interpret" the need and ideas for change to others, and they try to convince others of the merit of the manager's insight. The emphasis in this step is on getting other members to "buy into" the ideas that the manager is promoting. An idea or vision without a critical mass of support among members will not get to the next stage. Managers draw on a range of influence tactics in formulating a message to unfreeze employees, some of which are listed in Table 13.1.

Commonly recommended influence tactics typically draw attention to either the *crisis* that demands change or the *opportunity* that a change offers. The first approach can create an almost painful sense of discomfort or dissonance among members, whereas the second approach tries to capture their imagination of what could be. The first approach often involves drawing members' attention to alarming information or potential negative consequences by using rational persuasion or pressure. In John Kotter's words, this approach focuses on creating a **burning platform**—a metaphor based on the real-life experiences of some oil platform workers in the Gulf of Mexico.[12] Oil rigs in the deep water are built to a height that assures that the machinery and its operators remain above the swells of the ocean. Of course, this design also means that in case of a fire, which is not uncommon in this environment, workers are on an actual burning platform. Given the likelihood of being burned by the fire if they stay put, workers are more likely to dive into the water below, despite the uncertainty of this outcome (i.e., will they survive the fall and

TABLE 13.1

Tactics to Prepare Members for Change

Rational persuasion	Use logical arguments and factual evidence
Inspirational appeal	Arouse enthusiasm by appealing to values, ideals, and aspirations
Consultation	Involve others in planning or formulating an idea or strategy
Ingratiation	Use praise, flattery, or friendly behavior before making a request
Personal appeal	Appeal to feelings of loyalty or friendship
Exchange	Indicate willingness to reciprocate or share benefits
Coalition tactics	Appeal to the buy-in of others in attempting to persuade
Legitimizing tactic	Appeal to an agreed-upon authority such as a vision, mission, or goal
Pressure	Introduce or suggest threats or negative consequences

Source: Yukl, G. (1998). *Leadership in organizations.* Upper Saddle River, NJ: Prentice Hall.

possibly the sharks). A burning platform in organizations is a clear recognition that the organization needs to change, that members may even need to jump into the uncertainty of something new, to avoid potential dangers such as a loss of market share or organizational extinction.

The second possible approach, which is much less harrowing and more pleasurable, is to show organizational members that they will be better off if they change. Another way to describe the difference between this opportunity-based approach to change and the crisis-based approach is to say that painful approaches *push* change whereas pleasurable approaches *pull* change. This pull approach, which is characterized by inspirational appeal or exchange tactics, has proven to be more effective in gaining the commitment of organizational members. Of these two influence tactics, inspirational appeal is more likely to contribute to commitment, as it involves painting an attractive and compelling picture of the future. Although both painful and pleasurable approaches to unfreezing are based on creating dissonance, the painful approach is likely to result in only short-term compliance, not the long-term commitment that is more likely by using the pleasurable approach.

 WHAT DO YOU THINK?

How Does Change Make You Feel?

Change is inevitable, but is it necessarily good? Change evokes a range of emotions from those who are facing or experiencing change. In the workplace, unsuccessful or difficult changes often leave employees stressed, disengaged, and cynical.[13] The very nature of planned organizational change, whether successful or not, can expose employees to increased uncertainty, disrupt informal networks of support, and entrench the purposes and powerful position of management.[14] Employees under such conditions experience a loss of control and become dependent on managers to provide direction, stability, and, possibly, self-assurance. Even if the change seems to be in the best interests of all organizational stakeholders, there is little doubt that change exerts a heavy toll on employees.

According to research by Lynn Isabella, people experience change in a four-stage process that mirrors the four-step change process.[15] Metaphorically speaking, change is experienced as a puzzle. First, organizational members *anticipate* a change as they see pieces of a puzzle emerge in the form of rumors and scattered information from managers (recognize need). Second, members receive *confirmation* that these pieces are part of a picture of change that will be occurring, but they don't have the box cover to see quite what the final picture will look like (unfreezing). Third, in the *culmination* stage, the pieces of the puzzle come together in actual changes that begin to form the picture (change). Finally, during the *aftermath* stage, the new overall picture comes into focus and members reflect on which groups in the organization may have lost or gained as a consequence of the change, and which behavior is being rewarded or punished (refreezing).

Consider a change you have experienced (at work, in school, or in your family). Did it feel like a puzzle? How did it make you feel when you first heard about it and then later as you began adjusting to the change? Were you angry or enthused, frustrated or encouraged, numb or invigorated, sad or happy? What can you do as a manager to minimize the negative emotions associated with change and promote positive emotions? What would make you feel better or worse?

The unfreezing step is easier if managers can explain their ideas using words and actions in a way that will provide members with information to lessen the

DIGGING DEEPER

Managing the Morning After the Merger

A transformational change of dramatic proportions is the "big" merger or acquisition deal. For example, Internet star America Online (AOL) acquired media powerhouse Time Warner. Automotive titans Chrysler and Daimler Benz merged, only to separate later. These bold mergers and acquisitions are undertaken with the hope of achieving efficiency gains or synergies.[16] Unfortunately, the majority of these kinds of partnerships fail to realize their potential.[17] Somewhat like marriages based on a superficial or idealistic view of one's partner, the morning (or months) after the merger these corporate relationships often experience difficulties caused by a lack of full disclosure and the daily effort required to become one entity.

The failure of such mergers and acquisitions is not necessarily due to financial or structural irreconcilable differences. Instead, it is often attributed to a weak understanding of important human and cultural factors, and a lack of alignment or adjustment to the systems that affect these factors.[18] In the wake of these poorly implemented partnerships, traumatized employees often exhibit attitudinal and performance problems that ultimately may result in a "breakup," with the employees leaving the organization.[19]

One way to address the "human" side of change is for managers to provide clear and consistent communication about what direction the new-look company will take and how and when changes will occur.[20] In one study comparing two plants operated by the same company that was involved in a merger, one plant experienced increased employee stress and turnover and decreased satisfaction and commitment in the months following the announcement. By contrast, communication at the other plant, which included a "hotline," a merger newsletter, and frequent updates in departmental meetings, dramatically minimized these negative effects.[21]

Another common problem in mergers and acquisitions is clashes in the merging organizations' cultures. One may be very formal, whereas the other may be laid-back and informal. The differences in the feel, practices, and expectations in the work environment can contribute to employees developing negative attitudes and even leaving the new organization.[22] Even more pressing is the need to align systems across the two organizations. In one merger between automotive parts suppliers, employees who performed the same job but came from different organizations received different salaries for months after the merger, even though news of this discrepancy spread quickly through the organization's "grapevine."

Similar to a marriage, a merger or acquisition has a honeymoon period where the excitement of the potential of the union masks any potential problems. Managers need to take advantage of this initial goodwill by communicating the successes and challenges of the change and working to unite members around shared goals and expectations, best practices, and a common identity. When it comes to businesses, marriages are not made in heaven—they are made through hard work.

---

uncertainty that comes with change. Nonetheless, there are several reasons why members might resist change.

First, given the presumption that a change initiative is likely designed to increase organizational profits, members may be suspicious that the change will require them to work harder or for less money. In this sense, they feel a sense of inequity or a violation of their psychological contract. A **psychological contract** can take various forms, but essentially is an unwritten expectation related to the exchanges between an employee and the organization.[23] That is, an employee might feel the contract has been violated when more hours of work are expected but nothing is offered in exchange, raising the violation of "I wasn't hired for this."

Second, members may resist change because their personal identity is closely tied to their job and the organization's identity. For example, one of the first questions we ask new people we meet is "What do you do?" which is often translated as "Where do you work?" Consider for a moment what people ask once they know you are a student: They likely ask where you go to school. People's self-understanding also is shaped by their position within a social structure and the power they hold in the system, whether it is an educational institution, a company, a government agency, or a nonprofit organization. That's why some resistance

Psychological contract is an unwritten expectation about the exchanges that will take place between an employee and the organization.

comes from the sense of loss that is associated with change. In fact, some research-ers have suggested that organizational members may respond to organizational change in the same way that people grieve when they respond to the death of someone they know.

Third, change brings with it uncertainty and ambiguity. Many people prefer a stable but mediocre status quo to a promising but ambiguous change. The biggest cause of employee resistance to change is lack of information about future events. In the face of impending change, employees may become anxious and nervous. Uncertainty is especially threatening for employees who have a low tolerance for change and fear the new and unusual. Consider again the changes at Grand Canyon University: Faculty with careers primarily in academia may be more resistant to change than faculty with extensive experience in industries that have experienced more change.

Step 3: Change

In this stage, the change ideas are put into practice, and the change becomes a real-ity in how work is completed. This may be the stage where the role of managers is the most visible. Although change agents are important throughout all four stages of change, during this stage it is critical that change agents model appropriate be-havior and provide visible support for the initiative. A **change agent** is someone who acts as a catalyst and takes leadership and responsibility for managing part of the change process. Change agents are most often managers or human resource specialists from within the organization, although they may sometimes be outside consultants. Change agents make things happen, and a part of every manager's job is to act as a change agent in the work setting.

Change agents sometimes work in conjunction with idea champions. An **idea champion** is a person who actively and enthusiastically supports new ideas. To-gether, change agents and idea champions promote productive change within the organization by building support, overcoming resistance, and ensuring that innova-tions are implemented. For example, as a middle manager in a multinational auto parts supplier, Mike McDaniel took it upon himself to promote his organization's continuous improvement initiatives by being one of the first managers to imple-ment participative methods of problem solving in his department.[24] His early adop-tion served as an example for others to follow.

A manager's goal in this stage is to ensure that organizational members are com-mitted to the change. Commitment of organizational members is important be-cause it influences individual behavior and the performance of tasks that are critical to implementing the change.[25] Figure 13.3 presents a simplified model that de-scribes how managers contribute to members' commitment to an organizational change. As this model shows, members' commitment to a change is influenced by the following factors:

- Their confidence in the competence of their manager who is promoting the change
- Their confidence in their own ability to put the change into practice
- Their attitude toward the change

Figure 13.3 also suggests that the confidence members have in managers also influ-ences members' confidence in their own abilities and their attitudes toward change.

Change agent is someone who acts as a catalyst and takes leader-ship and responsibility for managing part of the change process.

Idea champion is a person who actively and enthusiastically supports new ideas.

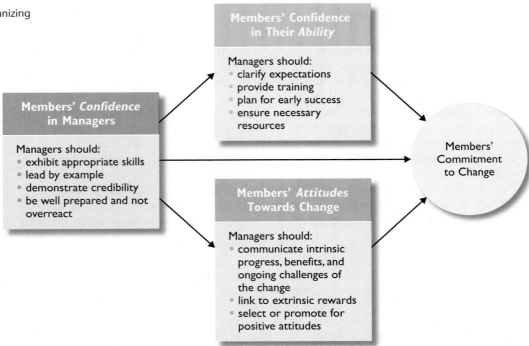

Figure 13.3   How managers can increase members' commitment to change

MEMBERS' CONFIDENCE IN MANAGERS.   Members will be more committed to change if they have confidence in the competence of their managers.[26] Research suggests that managers can build this confidence in at least four ways:

- Develop and display the skills set required to manage a change. On occasions where changes do not achieve the desired results, seven out of ten times members will attribute it to a manager having the wrong skills set or person–job fit.
- Model the desired behavior, and not fall back into the previous pattern of behavior.
- Demonstrate integrity and be consistent in their actions to gain members' commitment to change.
- Utilize good planning skills, and take care not to create crises by exhibiting reactionary behavior.

MEMBERS' CONFIDENCE IN THEIR OWN ABILITY.   Members will be more committed to a change if they have confidence in their own ability to put the change into practice.[27] Research suggests that managers can facilitate this confidence in at least four ways:

- Demonstrate good communication skills and practices, and provide enough information so that members have clear expectations regarding how to perform in the new work environment.
- Provide training to enhance the skills and behaviors that are needed for change.[28]
- Plan for early successes or small wins to build confidence.[29]
- Provide the appropriate resources and time for members to adapt to their new responsibilities.

MANAGEMENT IN PRACTICE

Why Managers Fail to Get Results[30]

The growing pressure on managers to successfully implement change has been documented in a number of research studies. In two studies, one involving more than 2000 U.S. managers and another including more than 5000 managers, "getting results" was cited as the single most important factor for keeping one's job and career on track. Recent research in which more than 1000 managers participated in 160 focus groups helps explain the causes and consequences of managers failing to get results in the midst of organizational change.

Why Managers Fail to Get Results During Change: The Top 10 Causes

Causes	Percentage	Consequences
1. Ineffective communication skills/practices	80%	Leaves employees uncertain and stressed, making it difficult to make informed business decisions
2. Poor work relationships and interpersonal skills	79%	Isolates managers from the informal network of knowledge that is necessary to cope with change
3. Person–job mismatch/skills gap	69%	Puts managers in positions in which they are ill equipped to deliver results
4. Failing to set clear direction/clarify performance expectations	61%	Hinders planning, saps motivation, and, ultimately, immobilizes staff
5. Delegation and empowerment breakdowns	56%	Contributes to confusion and frustration.
6. Failing to break old habits and adapt	54%	Perpetuates behaviors and actions that no longer add value in the new work environment
7. Inability to develop cooperation/teamwork	51%	Destroys collective performance
8. Lack of personal integrity and trustworthiness	49%	Destroys a manager's credibility with the people who are essential to getting results
9. Inability to lead/motivate others	45%	Leads to minimal performance at a time when change requires extra effort
10. Poor planning practices/reactionary behavior	44%	Creates disruptive crises that damage performance and morale

MEMBERS' ATTITUDES TOWARD THE CHANGE.   Members will be more committed to a change if they can see the personal benefits they will gain from the change. Research suggests that managers can promote positive attitudes toward change in at least three ways:

- Persuade members that the change is good for them; beyond pure facts, people respond best to emotional appeals that target the heart.[31] If members fail to see the benefits of the change, particularly as those benefits relate to their own jobs, their motivation will decrease and their efforts will be directed elsewhere.

- Provide extrinsic incentives such as bonuses, pay raises, or potential promotions.

- Select or promote those members who have a disposition or personality that facilitates coping with change and having a positive attitude toward change.[32]

DIGGING DEEPER

Diverging Thoughts at Harvard

One way to characterize a change process is by describing who is prominently featured, who is guiding the process, and who is in control. In other words, is the process top-down and management focused, or is it bottom-up and member focused?

Mainstream change models tend to emphasize a top-down approach. This approach is evident in the work of Harvard professor and management consultant John Kotter. In his model, top managers are seen as the ones who recognize the need for change and direct the change process. These managers unfreeze employees by establishing urgency and pulling together a guiding coalition of other powerful managers who develop the change vision and strategies and communicate the vision. Communication continues into the changing stage (step 3), where empowerment is encouraged in the implementation, short-term wins (i.e., early successes) are planned

to occur, and management consolidates gains and encourages more change. Finally, refreezing occurs as managers anchor the changes in the culture and systems of the organization through reinforcement and management example.[33]

The approach of Harvard professor Michael Beer (and colleagues) is more Multistream in being bottom-up.[34] In contrast to the top-down process described by Kotter, Beer's model is distinctly more participative and open to influence than Kotter's model, particularly as it relates to how organizational members become unfrozen during the change process. The bottom-up approach is represented by an upside-down triangle, where the hierarchy of who is featured, who guides the process, and who is in control shows that power has shifted to organizational members. As such, Beer's approach is more consistent with the Multistream stages of change.

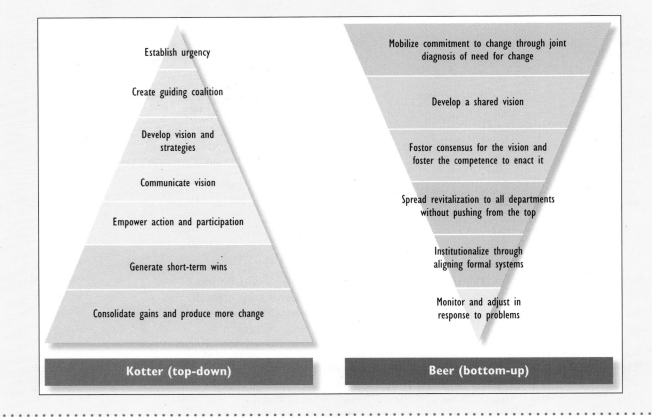

Kotter (top-down)
- Establish urgency
- Create guiding coalition
- Develop vision and strategies
- Communicate vision
- Empower action and participation
- Generate short-term wins
- Consolidate gains and produce more change

Beer (bottom-up)
- Mobilize commitment to change through joint diagnosis of need for change
- Develop a shared vision
- Foster consensus for the vision and foster the competence to enact it
- Spread revitalization to all departments without pushing from the top
- Institutionalize through aligning formal systems
- Monitor and adjust in response to problems

Step 4: Refreeze

Once the change has been implemented, it needs to be reinforced and become institutionalized. Ideally, the change will become second nature to members, embedded in their everyday actions and thoughts. Achieving this goal requires creating structures that reinforce the change, and dismantling structures and systems that undermine it.

In the refreezing stage, managers make adjustments to the design of the organization and human resource management systems. This may involve making structural changes in the fundamentals of how work is organized (more or less standardization, specialization, centralization) and in who reports to whom (departmentalization). It also requires revising job descriptions, aligning the performance appraisal and reward systems with the new expectations, and adapting recruitment and promotion practices to reinforce the new culture. Ideally, by this stage, everyone involved in the change will have acquired new attitudes and competencies, so that the final step of refreezing is merely reinforcing the change structurally and systematically so that the new way of doing things is repeated and rewarded.

MULTISTREAM FOUR-STEP CHANGE PROCESS

As shown in the road map at the beginning of the chapter, the Multistream four-step change process builds on the four fundamentals of organizing that were introduced in Chapter 10: sensitization, dignification, participation, and experimentation. In Chapter 11, we described how these four fundamentals can be placed along a continuum depending on how "inward" or "outward" the organization's structure is. In Chapter 12, we discussed how human resource practices also can be dignifying and participative. In this chapter, we examine how these principles of Multistream organizing from the previous three chapters can be integrated into a four-step Multistream change process:

1. Change starts with sensitization to the need or opportunity for change.
2. Change proceeds when other members are invited to help understand the underlying issues and articulate the need or opportunity for change.
3. Change continues when members participatively develop and design a change initiative that takes into account other aspects of the organization.
4. Change concludes when members are invited to experiment with implementing changes and celebrating any successes associated with the changes.

This four-step model is consistent with, and builds on, a number of other models described in the literature,[35] particularly those that consider change from the perspective of organizational members.[36] Research indicates that Multistream processes that empower employees and increase their job satisfaction are also linked to improved individual performance.[37]

The Multistream four-step model depicted in Figure 13.4 is consistent with a servant leadership orientation and reflects many of the core values of the organizational development (OD) approach to change management. Both OD and servant leadership affirm that organizational members are inherently valuable and should be treated as such by encouraging their involvement in shaping changes. Moreover, changes should help enhance meaningful interpersonal relationships in organizations, and organizational structures and systems should be set up to encourage personal development and support teams and collaboration. Servant leadership

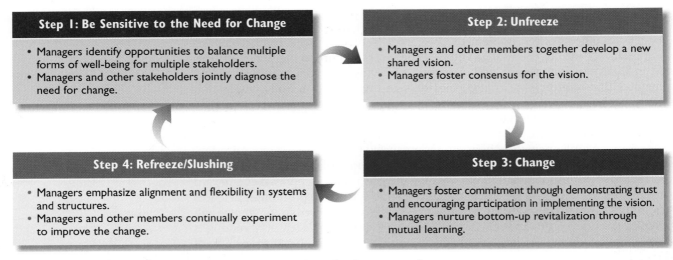

Figure 13.4   A Multistream approach to managing the four-step change process

also adds an emphasis on having a positive effect on—or at least not harming—those stakeholders who are the least privileged in society.

Step 1: Be Sensitive to the Need for Change

Similar to Mainstream managers, Multistream managers do not have the time or interest to change everything, or just to change for the sake of change. In contrast to Mainstream managers, who focus primarily on identifying change opportunities that will improve an organization's productivity or enhance its competitive position, Multistream managers are more likely to also watch for opportunities to improve members' on-the-job experience, to foster social justice for people who are marginalized, and to act responsibly with respect to the natural environment. Multistream managers are also predisposed to being in tune with the needs of the least privileged in society. This might be the poor people of Bangladesh (see the chapter-opening case on the Grameen Bank in Chapter 6) or the underemployed people of Philadelphia. Thus, unlike with the Mainstream approach, the *primary* motivator is not to improve organizational productivity or competitiveness.

Like Mainstream managers, Multistream managers draw on their experience and unique organizational vantage point to identify areas that could be changed. But unlike Mainstream managers, for whom identifying areas for change is a top-down process, Multistream managers involve organizational members in a *joint diagnosis* process that exposes both managers and members to information and ideas that might lead to a recognition that change is necessary. As such, Multistream management involves openness, which invites more members to become sensitized to the broader issues of concern for the company and its stakeholders. This approach requires that managers use their expertise to educate organizational members—for example, in how to read financial statements and link their own actions to the organization's health and well-being.

Open book management is an approach to management whereby managers share detailed information concerning the financial and operational condition of the organization.

An example of this approach is sometimes referred to as **open book management.** Jack Stack was an early pioneer in this approach to sharing information with employees: "It's amazing what you can come up with when you have no money, zero outside resources, and 119 people all depending on you for their jobs, their homes, even their prospects for dinner in the foreseeable future."[38] Stack and a handful of managers purchased their small manufacturing company from International Harvester when given the choice of either ownership or a shutdown. The company was in a dire situation that could be reversed only by taking a radical approach that required employees to understand the business in a new way so that everyone could make decisions to keep the company afloat. Taking advantage of the combined wisdom of the whole company, they changed their company for the better. Open book management is an ongoing approach to managing change whose core belief is that significant change occurs when people at the bottom are meaningfully engaged and allowed to have a voice.

Step 2: Unfreeze

The second step is to unfreeze the business-as-usual assumption. Unlike in the Mainstream approach, where managers use their power of influence to overcome resistance by getting other members to "buy into" their vision and the need for change, Multistream managers disarm resistance by approaching others with dignity and consideration.

If the Multistream manager has helped create a workplace where members have access to information and are conscious of organizational issues, then, as Harvard's Michael Beer suggests, this involvement from the bottom up is likely to naturally lead to a *shared vision*. Instead of using influence tactics of rational persuasion or even inspirational appeal, the use of a participative approach (consultative) creates a powerful sense of ownership. As management guru Tom Peters says, when you allow people to share in the process of gathering information, it becomes theirs.[39]

The Multistream manager operates with the assumption that all organizational members have a desire to grow and develop, and a desire to make a meaningful difference. Tapping into this desire will ultimately facilitate changes that are widely embraced. Put differently, members should not be treated as "pieces" of a puzzle or as "parts" of a problem, but rather as human beings who desire to help their organization become a better place. In return, members have less reason to fear that management will take advantage of them. Rather, when a crisis or an opportunity is recognized, members have a standing invitation to help develop a win-win solution. By being informed and involved in the process, members are more likely to accept even changes that are not in their own material self-interests. For example, 36 percent of employees at database management company Acxiom agreed to take pay cuts in exchange for stock.[40] Essentially, employees agreed to the cut to reduce the potential for layoffs, but by assuming some of the risk they also stood to gain if the company rebounded from its financial struggles. It turned out that subsequent performance was rewarding for both employees and stockholders.[41]

Step 3: Change

Unlike Mainstream managers, who often rely on their hierarchical position and use their authority to implement their desired changes, Multistream managers continue to foster participation in implementing the change (Figure 13.5). Beer asserts that managers play a critical role by providing forums for open discussion as well as resources and recognition for change agents and idea champions. For example, at Eliza Jennings, a multistage retirement and nursing home services organization, managers worked in partnership with a broad cross section of organizational stakeholders to revisit and revise the company's mission and vision statement. In addition to developing a draft of a potentially new shared mission and vision in a

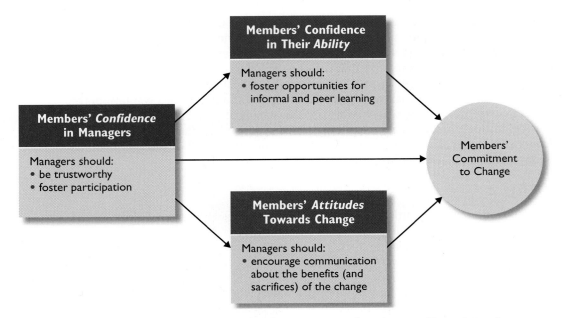

Figure 13.5   How managers can increase members' commitment to change

participative manner, Eliza Jennings managers arranged to meet in small forums with all employees to hear their responses to the proposed changes. These meetings not only served to increase commitment to the mission and vision, but also resulted in a few additional changes to the statement before it was adopted throughout the facilities. From the Multistream perspective, commitment to change is not a particular focus as much as it is a natural result of treating others with dignity and consideration.

MEMBERS' CONFIDENCE IN MANAGERS.   Members' confidence in their managers has two bases: trust and participation. Members will have confidence in managers whom they can trust, and who dignify the contributions and skills of others through participation and teamwork. Managers who are capable and demonstrate integrity earn the trust of others. In addition, managers who show a willingness to put themselves at risk to defend the interests of their team or department members gain the trust of others.[42] This self-sacrificing behavior is likely to be more typical of a Multistream manager who places a high value on treating everyone with dignity and protecting those who are less powerful. Multistream managers nurture empowered or team-based work environments, where members have a greater voice and autonomy in decision making. When managers are humble and share power, members are more likely to commit to change because they have greater confidence that the manager is doing what is best for the organization.[43] Furthermore, enhancing teamwork contributes to personal satisfaction as well as improvments in productivity and performance.[44]

MEMBERS' CONFIDENCE IN THEIR OWN ABILITY.   Multistream managers recognize the benefit of training and clear expectations in building members' self-confidence. However, compared to Mainstream managers, Multistream managers are more likely to create spaces or opportunities for informal or peer learning to enhance the skills of employees and to provide relevant information. Instead of tightly controlling and delivering training and information, Multistream managers nurture an environment where people learn from one another. Multistream managers may also involve other stakeholders in the learning process. Sometimes the participation of a variety of stakeholders, some of whom may even be outside the organization, will lead in unexpected directions or even yield counterintuitive corporate decisions. Yet, participation has several benefits. First, it builds confidence by enhancing participants' understanding of stakeholder relationships and the complexity of the system. Second, confidence is built as broad participation brings to bear more resources and perspectives in meeting the challenge of designing and implementing changes. For example, in the Brio change process described at the beginning of this chapter, members of Brio interacted with customers and suppliers before making action plans on how to best implement changes. This is not to say that managers leave communication up to others; rather, they are aware of their critical role in helping others make sense of what is happening in the organization as change brings about intended and unintended outcomes.[45] That is, managers must be able to pick up on issues that have the potential to discourage members or create dissension within the organization, and explicitly communicate their confidence in members' abilities to overcome the challenges.

Al Caperna, the founder and owner of CMC Group companies in rural Ohio, delegates management of his companies to others and instead spends much of his time working with employees to find better ways to produce products or serve customers. In doing so, he gains the confidence of his employees by working alongside them and getting his hands dirty serving.[46]

MEMBERS' ATTITUDES TOWARD CHANGE. Like Mainstream managers, Multistream managers can affect the attitudes of members by communicating the benefits of the change. This trust is further enhanced by practices that help to build trust among all team members. Sometimes members' attitudes are influenced by informal channels or by those without a formal position. Following the suggestion of Beer to *spread revitalization* throughout the organization, the Eliza Jennings managers invited members from throughout the organization to forums where the benefits and challenges of the change could be discussed openly. Other means to facilitate information sharing might include intra-organizational chatrooms, testimonials in newsletters, or loaning out members to other departments as internal trainers. Multistream managers spread revitalization throughout the organization not by issuing management directives, but rather by providing a learning infrastructure where those who are "getting" the change or even those who are coming up with new means to implement the change can connect with like-minded members.

Step 4: Refreeze (Slushing)

As in the Mainstream approach, Multistream management seeks to ensure that positive changes are implemented throughout the organization. Unlike Mainstream managers, who seek to "*refreeze*" the changed organization by mandating extensive formal changes in systems, Multistream managers are more likely to want to "*reslush*" the organization because they expect ongoing experimentation to generate more changes. That is, Multistream managers may make some changes to the structures and systems (such as adjusting misaligned reward systems), but they place greater emphasis on changes that facilitate learning and flexibility. Change is viewed as an ongoing process, not an event that happens once every few years. Thus Multistream management encourages flexible structures that can support continuous change.

Flexible structures involve agreeing on the end, yet allowing latitude in the specific means used to achieve the end. For example, Mike McDaniel, the manager from the automotive supplier who was mentioned earlier as a change champion, realized that job roles were outdated after a restructuring in his division. A more formalized approach would have been to ask the firm's human resource personnel to do a formal assessment and revision of all jobs in his new department. Although this approach would have improved the clarity in roles McDaniel was seeking, instead he brought the department members together for an afternoon to participatively revise the job descriptions. As employees arrived, they noticed the existing job descriptions blown up and taped to the walls. Over the course of the next few hours, employees used Post-it notes and markers to add or subtract responsibilities and negotiate new agreed-upon job descriptions. This approach may not be sufficient to make formal changes in the human resource system, but it did provide ownership and role clarity for a fraction of the time and money that a formal process typically requires, and it set an example of working and learning collaboratively.

"Slushing" assumes that a change may not work uniformly well throughout the organization. It acknowledges that making whole-scale changes to systems can cause unintended consequences when the changes do not fit perfectly with particular contexts. As such, Multistream managers encourage experimentation and celebrate the learning associated with both successful and unsuccessful attempts to implement change. Consistent with Beer's recommendation of *monitoring and adjusting* the change process, Multistream managers are diligent in staying informed as to what is working and what is not, and they encourage organizational members to make adjustments that best suit their work environment. Multistream managers monitor the outcomes of experimental changes and provide opportunities to share these success stories with others to promote further learning. When new changes are seen to have the desired effects, others are given an opportunity to implement them. Positive change is celebrated and disseminated not as a mandate but instead as a possible example for others to follow. Ultimately, changes that begin and grow informally may be institutionalized, but the process is bottom-up—not top-down, where management decides what is best.

 WHAT DO YOU THINK?

Should You Follow the Kotter Model, the Beer Model, or Both?

The Mainstream approach to managing change was described as being consistent with John Kotter's top-down approach, whereas the Multistream approach was described as being consistent with Michael Beer's bottom-up approach. An article in *Harvard Business Review* shows how two similar approaches can have different goals. The top-down approach focuses on creating short-term economic value for shareholders, and the bottom-up approach focuses on creating long-term organizational capability.[47] The article discusses whether one approach is better than the other, or whether both can be used in sequence to implement a change. One might argue that some situations require a directive top-down approach, such as when time is a critical issue or when the decision is likely to encounter stiff resistance due to conflicting goals between management and employees. In other situations, management may be better off being more participative due to a lack of information or the necessity of strong buy-in to implement the decision. Another approach would be to integrate the approaches by having one manager who is more directive working alongside another manager who is more participative. Or maybe one manager might incorporate both approaches but in a sequence—that is, first being directive and then attempting to be more participative after difficult decisions are made.

Do you think that one approach is uniformly better than the other? As an employee, which would you prefer and why? Can the approaches be integrated together, perhaps in a sequence starting with one approach and moving to the other?[48]

CLOSING CASE

Engineering Change[49]

Until the 1970s, agricultural practices in Bangladesh were hampered by a lack of irrigation. Most villagers drank water from hand-dug wells or ponds that were shared with bathing cows and water buffaloes. Cholera and diarrhea flourished, and each year hundreds of thousands of deaths resulted from drinking contaminated water. The need for change was clearly evident.

This distressing situation prompted various organizations to import and subsidize diesel and cast-iron pumps that they believed, based on their experience in other contexts, would solve the problem. Unfortunately, these imported technologies did not seem to be appropriate for that setting. They cost too much money to purchase, required expensive fuel to operate, and could not be easily repaired locally when they broke down. Little wonder that farmers resisted these imposed change attempts.

To understand the change that eventually did help to revolutionize irrigation in Bangladesh, one needs to start with one particular North American engineer, George Klassen, working for Mennonite Central Committee (MCC) alongside Bangladeshi farmers in the fields for several years contributing to community building and earning their trust. Despite his emphasis on building relationships and mutual understanding, he had little "explicit" success to show for his efforts in terms of quantifiable performance measures like the number of mouths fed, students taught, hospital beds served, and so on. However, it was this "struggling" engineer who eventually had the insight to develop what is called a "rower pump" (so named because operating it requires a motion that looked similar to rowing). By

experiencing the rhythms of the rural life and being attuned to the needs of the farmers, he had learned that they required a pump that could be operated by one person, could be manufactured and serviced locally, and was an affordable "low-tech" option.

Moreover, Klassen's good working relationship with farmers had two positive benefits. First, the farmers had learned to trust the engineer, and they were motivated and willing to work alongside him in refining the idea of a rower pump. Second, Klassen benefited greatly from the knowledge that farmers shared with him as together they developed and tested many different prototypes. The rower pump could not have been fine-tuned without the expertise and knowledge of both the engineer and the farmers. They experimented with different designs, talked about how to deliver the product, learned from one another, and worked together.

After the prototype had been developed, the step of implementing the change began in earnest. Other staff at MCC developed relationships with local businesses to build, sell, and service the pumps. This effort led to the development of a local infrastructure of expertise in installation, repair, and inventory of parts. MCC workers also did field tests and trained people how to use the pump. In the early years, MCC workers also provided subsidies for the pump, but with clear plans to phase out the organization's involvement to ensure that the pump would be self-financing. Furthermore, the MCC workers planned to completely phase out their own involvement after several years.

Five years after the change was started, there was a critical mass of farmers using the rower-pump technology

(1000 units sold) and the infrastructure had been developed to enable the further production, sale, and service of rower pumps. This provided the foundation for other entrepreneurs to get in on the action, and soon, with the addition of "copy-cat" and "clone" rower pumps in the market, sales reached 50,000 pumps. Today the rower pump has become second nature to Bangladeshi farmers, engrained as a central element of agricultural practice.

QUESTIONS FOR DISCUSSION

1. Identify each of the four steps in the change process for the introduction of the rower pump to Bangladeshi agriculture. Which steps do you think were the most challenging to manage?

2. Why did attempts to introduce cast-iron pumps and diesel-powered pumps fail? Which step of the process did managers fail to negotiate properly?

SUMMARY

Organizational change is complex and varies in its scope (transformational versus incremental change), intentionality (planned versus unplanned change), and source (innovative versus imitative change).

The Mainstream approach to the four-step change model is typically a top-down, content-driven approach:

1. Managers conceive of the need for change.
2. Managers use influence tactics to overcome resistance and get others to buy into the change.
3. Managers use top-down authority to implement the change, and persuasion to gain commitment.
4. Managers set up structures and systems to ensure the change remains entrenched.

The Multistream approach to the four-step change model is typically an inclusive, bottom-up, process-driven approach:

1. Managers and members are sensitized to a wider scope of areas where change may be appropriate (i.e., not just changes that enhance materialism and individualism).
2. Managers invite members to consider how to define the need for change.
3. Managers employ participative approaches to implement change and gain commitment.
4. Managers encourage others to learn from one another and through experimentation.

QUESTIONS FOR REFLECTION AND DISCUSSION

1. Identify the four steps in the process of change. What do you believe are the main differences between the Mainstream and Multistream approaches in each step?

2. Which management perspective for change—Mainstream or Multistream—do you think would be the most effective in the organizations where you have worked? Why?

3. How do you generally react to change? Why do you think people resist change? What can be done to minimize resistance and increase commitment?

4. What are the benefits and drawbacks to including more stakeholders in shaping and implementing the change process?

5. Consider for a moment how you might respond to changes within your class. How would you respond to a professor who started out very directive and demanding, but later loosened up? Alternatively, how would you respond to a professor who was initially very inclusive and encouraging, but later tightened up the class and became more demanding?

6. Many organizations talk of the need to be collaborative and work as a team. What changes might be necessary in an organization's human resource systems to reinforce teamwork?

7. Robert Greenleaf provided an example at AT&T of working alongside other managers to encourage them to *experimentally* implement new ideas or procedures that might help overcome shortcomings in current work practices. How might viewing change as an "experiment" encourage or hinder commitment to changes?

HANDS-ON ACTIVITIES

How Do You Cope with Change?[50]

Using a scale of 1 to 5 (where 1 = strongly disagree, 3 = uncertain, and 5 = strongly agree), indicate your agreement with the following questions given your opinions of and experiences with change.

_____ When dramatic changes happen, I feel I handle them with ease.

_____ I have been a leader of transformation efforts within an organization.

_____ When changes happen, I react by trying to manage the change rather than complain about it.

_____ When changes occur in organizations of which I am a member, it causes me stress.

_____ I see the rapid changes that occur as opening up new opportunities for me.

_____ When changes are announced, I try to react in a problem-solving mode, rather than an emotional mode.

_____ I often find myself leading change efforts in organizations.

_____ I think I cope with change better than most of those with whom I work.

Sum your scores. A score of 33–40 indicates strong proactive change coping skills; a score of 25–32 indicates some hesitation and concerns about change; and a score of 24 or less indicates resistance to change or a passive approach to coping with change.

Where Are You Along the Mainstream–Multistream Continuum?

Circle the number that best corresponds to your views.

Change should be based on managerial insight.	1 2 3 4 5 6 7	Change should be based on organization-wide sensitization, openness, and discernment.
The best way to increase members' receptivity to change is to get them to buy into the vision that underpins the change.	1 2 3 4 5 6 7	Members should be involved in the change process and should be treated with consideration and dignity.
Managers should use their influence to overcome resistance and get others to buy into an organizational change.	1 2 3 4 5 6 7	Managers should employ participative approaches to implement change and gain commitment for a change.
Managers should set up structures and systems that reward members who implement the change consistently.	1 2 3 4 5 6 7	Managers should set up structures and systems that facilitate continuous improvement and celebrate improvement.

ENDNOTES

1. Dannemiller, K. D., & Fitzpatrick, T. (2002). A vision without action is a daydream. Action without collective vision is a nightmare. *Organizational Development Journal, 20*(2), 104–109; Dannemiller, K. D. (2001). Unleashing magic. *Executive Excellence,* 18(9), 20; Badore, N. L. (1999). Preface. In K. D. Dannemiller, *Whole-scale change toolkit.* San Francisco: Berrett-Koehler Publishing; http://www.dannemillertyson.com/new_rules.php.

2. Haveman, H. (1992). Between a rock and a hard place: Organizational change and performance under conditions of fundamental environmental transformation. *Administrative Science Quarterly,* 37, 48–75.

3. Based on Lewin, K. (1951). *Field theory in social science: Selected theoretical papers.* New York: Harper.

4. Van de Ven, A. H., & Poole, M. S. (1995). Explaining development and change in organizations. *Academy of Management Review, 20*(3), 510–540.

5. Kavanagh, M. H., & Ashkanasy, N. M. (2006). The impact of leadership and change management strategy on organizational culture and individual acceptance of change during a merger. *British Journal of Management,* 17, 81–103.

6. Greiner, L. E. (1998). Evolution and revolution as organizations grow. *Harvard Business Review, 76*(3), 55–68; Haveman, H. A., Russo, M. V., & Meyer, A. D. (2001). Organizational environments in flux: The impact of regulatory punctuations on organizational domains, CEO succession, and performance. *Organization Science, 12*(3), 253–273.

7. Nadler, D. A., & Tushman, M. L. (1990). Beyond the charismatic leader and organizational change. *California Management Review, 32*(2), 77.

8. Dyck, B. (1996). The role of crises and opportunities in organizational change. *Non-profit and Voluntary Sector Quarterly,* 25, 321–346.

9. Bollag, B. (2004). For the love of God (and money). *Chronicle of Higher Education, 51*(2), A29; http://chronicle.com/free/v51/i02/02a02901.htm; http://www.christianitytoday.com/ct/2005/mayweb-only/24.0c.html; http://www.insidehighered.com/news/2005/05/18/canyon.

10. Although the four-step description provided here is based on Lewin's (1951) basic change model, it draws from and builds on a variety of studies, including the four-phase learning model in Crossan, M., Lane, H. W., & White, R. E. (1999). An Organizational learning framework: From intuition to institution. *Academy of Management Review, 24*(3), 522–537.

11. Dyck, B., & Schroeder, D. (2005). Management, theology, and moral points of view: Towards an alternative to the conventional materialist-individualist ideal-type of management. *Journal of Management Studies, 42*(4), 705–735.

12. Kotter, J. (1996). *Leading change.* Boston: Harvard University Press.

13. Armenakis, A. A., & Bedeian, A. G. (1999). Organizational change: A review of theory and research in the 1990s. *Journal of Management, 25*(3), 293–315.

14. McKendall, M. (1993). The tyranny of change: Organizational development revisited. *Journal of Business Ethics,* 12, 93–104.

15. Isabella, L. A. (1990). Evolving interpretations as a change unfolds: How managers construe key organizational events. *Academy of Management Journal, 33*(1), 7–41.

16. Capron, L., Dussauge, P., & Mitchell, W. (1998). Resource deployment following horizontal acquisitions in Europe and North America. *Strategic Management Journal,* 19, 631–661.

17. Light, D. A. (1999). Acquisitions: Can you learn from experience? *Harvard Business Review, 77*(2), 18–21.

18. Mirvis, P. H. (1995). Negotiations after the sale: The roots and ramifications of conflict in an acquisition. *Journal of Occupational Behavior,* 6, 65–84; Fulmer, R. M., & Gilkey, R. (1988). Blending corporate families: Management and organizational development in a post-merger environment. *Academy of Management Executive, 2*(4), 275–283.

19. Cartwright, S., & Cooper, C. (1993). The psychological impact of mergers and acquisitions. *Human Relations, 46*(3), 327–348.

20. Covin, T. J., Sightler, K. W., Kolenko, T. A., & Tudor, R. K. (1996). An investigation of post-acquisition satisfaction with the merger. *Journal of Applied Behavioral Science, 32*(2), 125–142.

21. Schweiger, D. M., & DeNisi, A. S. (1991). Communication with employees following a merger: A longitudinal field experiment. *Academy of Management Journal, 34*(1), 110–135.

22. Chatterjee, S., Lubatin, M. H., Schweiger, D. M., & Weber, Y. (1992). Cultural differences and shareholder value in related mergers: Linking equity and human capital. *Strategic Management Journal, 13*(5), 319–334.

23. Rousseau, D. M. (1995). *Psychological contracts in organizations: Understanding written and unwritten agreement.* Thousand Oaks, CA: Sage.

24. Mike McDaniel shared this example with one of the authors.

25. Neubert, M. J., & Cady, S. H. (2001). Program commitment: A multi-study longitudinal field investigation of its impact and antecedents. *Personnel Psychology,* 54, 421–448; Herscovitch, L., & Meyer, J. P. (2002). Commitment to organizational change: Extension of a three-component model. *Journal of Applied Psychology, 87*(3), 474–487; Robertson, P. J., Roberts, D. R., & Porras, J. I. (1993). Dynamics of planned organizational change assessing empirical support for a theoretical model. *Academy of Management Journal,* 36, 619–634.

26. Reichers, A. E., Wanous, J. P., & Austin, J. T. (1997). Understanding and managing cynicism about organizational change. *Academy of Management Executive, 11*(1), 48–59; Kotter, 1996.

27. Neubert & Cady, 2001.

28. Bandura, A. (1986). *Social foundations of thought and action: A social cognitive theory.* Englewood Cliffs, NJ: Prentice-Hall; Gist, M. (1989). The influence of training method on self-efficacy and idea generation among managers. *Personnel Psychology,* 42, 787–805.

29. Kotter, 1996.

30. Longenecker, C., Neubert, M. J., & Fink, L. (2007). Causes and consequences of managerial failure in rapidly changing organizations. *Business Horizons, 50*(2), 145–155.

31. Fox, S., & Amichai-Hamburger, Y. (2001). The power of emotional appeals in promoting organizational change. *Academy of Management Executive,* 15, 84–94.

32. Judge, T. A., Thoresen, C. J., Pucik, V., & Welbourne, T. M. (1999). Managerial coping with organizational change: A dispositional perspective. *Journal of Applied Psychology, 84*(1), 107–122.

33. Kotter, 1996. See also Kotter, J. (2005). *The heart of change.* Boston: Harvard University Press.

34. Kotter, J. (1995). Leading change: Why transformation efforts fail. *Harvard Business Review, 73*(2), 59–67; Beer, M., Eisenstat, R., & Spector, B. (1990). Why change programs don't produce change. *Harvard Business Review, 68*(6), 158–166.

35. This discussion modifies and builds on work on the four-step friendly disentangling process used by Greenleaf as described by Nielson, R. (1998). Quaker foundations for Greenleaf's servant leadership and 'friendly disentangling' method. In Spears, L. C. (Ed.), Insights on leadership: Service, stewardship, spirit, and servant-leadership (pp. 126–144). New York: John Wiley & Sons.

36. Beer, Eisenstat, & Spector, 1990.

37. For research on the empowerment–performance relationship, see Spreitzer, G. M., & Quinn, R. E. (2001). *A company of leaders: Five disciplines for unleashing the power in your workforce.* San Francisco: Jossey-Bass. For research on the job satisfaction-performance relationship, see Judge, T. A., Thoresen, C. J., Bono, J. E., & Patton, G. K. (2001). The job satisfaction-job performance relationship: A qualitative and quantitative review. *Psychological Bulletin,* 127(3), 376–407.

38. Stack, J., & Burlingham, B. (1992). *The great game of business.* New York: Doubleday.

39. Peters, T., & Waterman, R. H. (2004). *In search of excellence.* New York: HarperCollins.

40. Armour, S. (2001, April 13). Workers take pay cuts over pink slips. *USA Today,* p. B01.

41. http://www.acxiom.com/default.aspx?ID=2002.

42. Hurley, R. F. (2006). The decision to trust. *Harvard Business Review,* 84(9), 55–62.

43. Hurley, 2006.

44. Salas, E., Rozell, D., Mullen, B., & Driskell, J. E. (1999). The effect of team building on performance. *Small Group Research,* 30(3), 309–329.

45. Balogun, J. (2005). Managing change: Steering a course of between intended strategies and unanticipated outcomes. *Long Range Planning,* 39(1), 29–49.

46. http://www.cmcgp.com/index.html; and Mangelsdorf, M. (1995). *The class of 1985.* http://www.inc.com/magazine/19951015/2681.html.

47. Beer, M., & Nohria, N. (2000). Cracking the code of change. *Harvard Business Review,* 78(3), 133–141.

48. Negotiations research suggests that starting firm and softening your approach results in more positive reactions than the alternative. See Hilty, J., & Carnevale, P. J. (1993). Black hat/white hat strategy in bilateral negotiation. *Organizational Behavior and Human Decision Processes,* 55(3), 444–469.

49. This case is based on personal correspondence with Harold Harder (most recently March 13, 2008) and on information found in Dyck, B., Buckland, J., Harder, H., & Wiens, D. (2000). Community development as organizational learning: The importance of agent-participant reciprocity. *Canadian Journal of Development Studies,* 21, 605–620.

50. Adapted from Judge, T. A., Thoresen, C. J., Pucik, V., & Welbourne, T. M. (1999). Management coping with organizational change: A dispositional perspective. *Journal of Applied Psychology,* 84(1), 107–122.

CHAPTER 14

Just as different people have different outdoor travel destinations that they like to visit—some want to climb mountains, others prefer to hike through rainforests, and others want to walk along beaches—so there are also different ways that people are motivated in organizations. These differences among people may be due to the personalities and innate needs people were born with, or they may reflect things that individuals have experienced and learned in life. In this chapter, we explore the various things that motivate people in organizations.

ROAD MAP

A. Natural Bases of Motivation

1. *"Big Five" personality traits*
   Manage by using extraversion, agreeableness, conscientiousness, openness to experience, and emotional stability to . .

2. *Innate needs*

   Manage by emphasizing . . .

   Manage by focusing on . . .

B. Nurtured Bases of Motivation

1. *Desire for accomplishment*
   Manage by setting goals that are . . .
   Manage by increasing
   - Expectancy
   - Instrumentality
   - Valence
   Manage by providing appropriate reinforcements

2. *Desire for fairness*
   Manage by treating . . .

3. *Desire for relationships*
   Manage by ensuring opportunities to . . .

4. *Desire for power*
   Manage by providing opportunities to . . .

Motivation

MAINSTREAM APPROACH ⟷	MULTISTREAM APPROACH
Increase members' productivity	Foster organizational community
Self-actualization/personal growth	Community-happiness/balance
Motivator factors more so than hygiene factors	Hygiene factors balanced with motivator factors
Achievement Specific and measurable; difficult; time-specific	*Significance* Difficult to measure; challenging; timeless
"I can do it."	"We can do it."
"There's something in it for me."	"There's something in it for others."
"I value my desired outcomes."	"We value balanced outcomes."
Positive reinforcement; punishment; negative reinforcement; extinction	Overall societal well-being
Equity Members equitably	*Justice* Stakeholders justly
Affiliation Receive affirmation from others and network with others	*Community* Develop trusting and caring relationships
Individual power Acquire legitimate, reward, coercive, referent, or expert power	*Shared power* Trust others and share power with others

A Cup Full of Motivation: Starbucks[1]

Starbucks seems to have cracked the code explaining how to unleash employee enthusiasm. There is plenty of energy at Starbucks, and it's not due to too much caffeine. From healthcare benefits for part-time employees to intense training, Starbucks understands what it takes to ensure its "partners" (as employees are called at the company) are happy and motivated. Sure, partners appreciate receiving the occasional MUG (Moves of Uncommon Greatness) and Spirit of Starbucks awards for their passionate service, but Starbucks has realized that the keys to motivating its partners are ensuring competence, promoting social responsibility, and encouraging ownership. If these conditions are in place, partners will work harder and stick around longer.

Customers can expect competent partners at Starbucks. Managers receive eight to ten weeks of training prior to stepping into managerial roles, including "Coffee Knowledge 101." In turn, managers ensure that all employees are fully trained. Every Starbucks employee completes 24 hours of training at one of the company's regional training centers prior to serving up his or her first cup of coffee. Partners also learn by observing their managers who model positive attitudes and supreme customer service.

Coffee immersion students from Honolulu, Beijing, and Kuwait City go through the basics of tasting coffee at a Starbucks immersion training class for international employees.

Partners and customers alike find motivation in the corporate social responsibility emphasis of Starbucks. In 2005, almost 30 percent of the company's coffee was purchased from growers who either were Fair Trade Certified or adhered to Coffee and Farmer Equity Practices. This is nearly double the percentage in 2004, and it is expected to grow even higher in the future. Starbucks managers also encourage community volunteerism. In a five-year span, Starbucks' partners across the United States and Canada volunteered more than 790,000 hours of service to the community, and Starbucks matched those efforts by contributing to these community-based nonprofit organizations $10 for every hour served by its partners and even by some of its customers.

Partners who work at least 20 hours per week and have been employed for more than six months receive full benefits, including shares of stock that are referred to as "Bean Stock." This stock plan—the first of its kind among private companies—provides partners with an ownership stake in the success of the organization. Ownership enhances the desire of partners to have input into, and promote the mission of, establishing Starbucks as "the premier purveyor of the finest coffee in the world while maintaining our uncompromising principles while we grow." Those principles include, but are not limited to, treating one another with respect and dignity, embracing diversity, enthusiastically satisfying customers, and contributing positively to the community and the environment. If partners sense that the company is drifting away from this mission, Starbucks' Mission Review program allows them to raise questions, express concerns, and receive answers from managers.

Although a culture of enthusiasm pervades most stores, not everyone is all smiles at Starbucks. The work demands at some stores meant that many managers worked long hours without receiving overtime pay, an issue that resulted in Starbucks moving its store managers from salary to hourly pay plans. Furthermore, partners in some locations such as New York and Chicago complained that starting wages were below a living wage in their areas and joined forces with unions to press the issue with both local and corporate managers. Even with these concerns about pay, Starbucks is reaping the benefits of motivated partners. Like many organizations, Starbucks relies heavily on repeat customers to drive its business. In fact, some of the company's customers return as often as 20 times per month. Customers often comment that the partners at Starbucks are always happy and having fun. Regular customers also appreciate that in comparison to other organizations in this industry, there is relatively low turnover among the partners (most retailers and fast-food chains have more than 300 percent turnover annually, whereas Starbucks' turnover rate is a relatively low 60 percent).

INTRODUCTION TO MOTIVATION

Motivation is a psychological force that helps to explain what arouses, directs, and maintains human behavior. People who are highly motivated will persist in behaving a certain way. The study of motivation helps managers to better understand what prompts people to initiate action, how much effort they exert, and why their effort persists over time.

Understanding and managing motivation can be quite challenging because it has two broad bases: those we bring into the world and those that are shaped by our experiences in this world. Using the computer as a metaphor, each person has unique hardware (i.e., natural personality and innate needs that he or she was born with) and each person has developed unique software (i.e., nurtured needs and values from childhood experiences, the country lived in, television shows watched, and so on). In this chapter, we consider how people's hardware and software can influence their motivation, first from a Mainstream approach and then from a Multistream approach.

 WHAT DO YOU THINK?

How Are You Motivated?

Think about a time when you were highly motivated in an organization. Why were you so motivated? Do you think most other people would be motivated in the same circumstance? Compare your motivational moments with those of your classmates. How are they similar, and how are they different? What can you learn from this experience that might help you motivate others?

MAINSTREAM NATURAL BASES OF MOTIVATION

Personality

A person's personality or disposition shapes what the person is motivated to do.[2] **Personality** is the unique and relatively stable pattern of behaviors, thoughts, and emotions shown by individuals. Individuals' personalities are rooted in their biological make-up much more than in their background or upbringing. This relationship is illustrated by considering how members from one family can be very different—one sibling being organized and the other messy, one being talkative while the other is shy.

In the last few decades, researchers have described personality traits as falling into broad categories called the "Big Five."[3]

- **Extraversion:** sociable, talkative, assertive, adventurous
- **Agreeableness:** good-natured, cooperative, trustful, not jealous
- **Conscientiousness:** achievement oriented, responsible, persevering, dependable
- **Openness to experience:** intellectual, original, imaginative, cultured
- **Emotional stability:** calm, placid, poised, not neurotic

Mainstream management is especially interested in research based on the Big Five that shows how personality influences individual behavior and performance.[4] For example, the personality trait of conscientiousness has been shown to be a good

Motivation is a psychological force that helps to explain what arouses, directs, and maintains human behavior.

Personality is the unique and relatively stable pattern of behaviors, thoughts, and emotions shown by individuals.

Extraversion is a personality trait associated with being sociable, talkative, assertive, and adventurous.

Agreeableness is a personality trait associated with being good-natured, cooperative, trustful, and not jealous.

Conscientiousness is a personality trait associated with being achievement oriented, responsible, persevering, and dependable.

Openness to experience is a personality trait associated with being intellectual, original, imaginative, and cultured.

Emotional stability is a personality trait associated with being calm, placid, poised, and not neurotic.

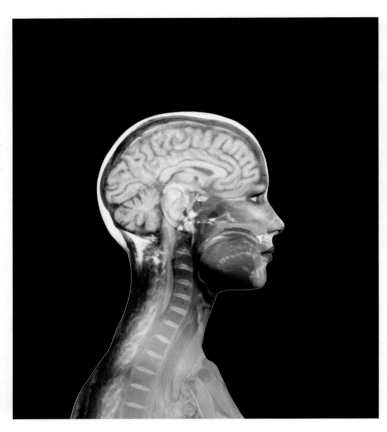

Research suggests that personality has its basis in the makeup of the brain.

Myers–Briggs Type Indicator (MBTI) is a personality inventory based on Carl Jung's work on psychological types.

predictor of performance in most jobs, and extraversion is particularly helpful for predicting success in jobs with a great deal of social interaction. In a team or group context, conscientiousness and extraversion contribute to team performance, but agreeableness becomes even more important in helping the team bond, reduce conflict, and perform.[5] Research into the Big Five can help managers explain behavior and identify people who will be motivated to be productive in a variety of situations.

Although the Big Five are helpful for research and selection, often managers find other personality categories more useful for thinking about personality differences among the people at work. One popular and user-friendly personality inventory is the **Myers–Briggs Type Indicator (MBTI),** which is based on Carl Jung's work on psychological types. The MBTI was developed by Isabel Briggs Myers and her mother, Katharine Briggs, to make the insights of type theory broadly accessible. It is less evaluative in terms of "good" and "bad" and more focused on description and understanding. Nonetheless, Table 14.1 illustrates that the MBTI includes four psychological types that are roughly similar to four of the Big Five personality types. Missing from the MBTI is a set of types corresponding to emotional stability; not surprisingly, this attribute is missing because it's hard to put a positive spin on labeling someone as emotionally unstable. To learn more about the MBTI and discover your unique personality type, see the end-of-chapter Hands-On Activity on assessing your personality with the MBTI.

As an example of how this works, consider Shaffer Title and Escrow, Inc. of Chesapeake, Virginia. Jarett and Susan Shaffer set out to build a different kind of title company, one that preserved and promoted the "old-fashioned" values of manners, dependability, and professionalism. As their new company grew, they recognized that communication was a critical means of maintaining these values. The Shaffers decided to use the MBTI to improve communication between their growing

TABLE 14.1

Comparing the Big Five and the MBTI

Big Five Trait	Myers–Briggs Types
Extraversion	Introversion–*extraversion*
Agreeableness	Thinking–*feeling*
Conscientiousness	*Judging*–perceiving
Openness to experience	Sensing–*intuitive*
Emotional stability	Not applicable

Source: Furnham, A. (1996). The Big Five versus the Big Four: The relationship between the Myers–Briggs Type Indicator (MBTI) and NEO-PI five factor model of personality. *Personality and Individual Differences,* 21(2), 303–307.

DIGGING DEEPER

Beliefs About Human Nature

Renowned management theorist Douglas McGregor argued that "every managerial act rests on assumptions, generalizations, and hypotheses—that is to say theory . . . and theory and practice are inseparable."[6] These theories tend to grow out of our experiences and observations, as well as our upbringing and education. As part of his work, McGregor identified what he called Theory X and Theory Y assumptions that managers have about the human nature of workers.[7]

Theory X states that managers assume that people are inherently lazy, dislike work, will avoid working hard unless forced to do so, and prefer to be directed rather than accepting responsibility for getting their work done. As a consequence, Theory X managers design structures and systems that will ensure that people will work hard. These measures usually take the form of control systems that set specific and narrow rules for behavior, monitor employee behavior, reward compliance, and punish those who "break the rules" or fail to work hard enough.

McGregor argued that Theory X assumptions reflected the "classical" approach to management. He proposed that managers adopt **Theory Y** assumptions because they are a more humanistic (and realistic) approach to management practice. Theory Y states that managers assume that work is as natural as play, that people are inherently motivated to work, and that people will feel unfulfilled if they do not have the opportunity to work and thereby make a contribution to society. Under Theory Y, workers are not seen as merely sets of hired "hands" and managers the "brains" of an organization. Instead, managers design systems and structures that encourage creativity and discretion by employees and allow them to use their full selves in doing their work.

The discussion of human nature has not faded into the background of management thought. For example, William Ouchi introduced Theory Z as an alternative theory on managing people.[8] One of its key assumptions is that people like to be members of a group and will work most productively in stable groups. More recently, the discussion of human nature has resurfaced in the work of evolutionary psychology, where some scholars have made claims regarding the nature of people by ascribing to humans the characteristics of evolved mammals with purely selfish instincts.[9] Appealing to science, proponents of this theory argue that selfishness explains it all, which is consistent with classic Theory X thinking. Others offer alternatives to a simply selfish interpretation of human nature by giving examples of altruistic acts that range from aiding Jewish people during the Holocaust to helping coworkers in organizations.[10]

And so, the debate continues among scholars. You may find as a manager that these issues are unresolved in your mind as well. Nonetheless, assumptions about human nature help to predict how managers will approach the task of motivating organizational members.

---

staff and their diverse customers. After overcoming some initial resistance from employees who were concerned they would be "pigeonholed" by personality labels, experience with the MBTI convinced employees of how its use improves daily interactions and reduces conflicts.[11]

In addition to the preferences they are born with that are rooted in their personality, people are born with basic needs. Undoubtedly, people need to eat and sleep. In addition, to varying degrees, people by nature have innate desires to relate to others and make contributions or to create. These desires or basic human needs are described in the following section.

Innate Needs

One of the best-known theories of motivation is **Maslow's hierarchy of needs.** Abraham Maslow argued that people are motivated to satisfy five levels of needs: physiological needs, safety needs, belongingness needs, esteem needs, and self-actualization needs. He suggested that these needs constitute a hierarchy, as illustrated in Figure 14.1. The most basic or compelling needs—physical and safety needs—are at the bottom of this hierarchy, and esteem and self-actualization needs are at the top. Although it is no longer highly regarded in academic circles because research has offered little support for it,[12] Maslow's work bears review as a foundational theory of motivation.

Theory X states that managers assume people are inherently lazy, dislike work, will avoid working hard unless forced to do so, and prefer to be directed rather than accepting responsibility.

Theory Y states that managers assume people are inherently motivated to work and will feel unfulfilled if they do not have the opportunity to work and make a contribution to society.

Maslow's hierarchy of needs is the theory that people are motivated to satisfy five need levels: physiological, safety, love, esteem, and self-actualization.

SELF-ACTUALIZATION needs reflect the desire to realize one's full potential.

Esteem needs reflect the desire for recognition and respect from others.

Love needs reflect the desire to be accepted by peers, or to be part of a group.

Safety needs reflect the desire for security, stability, and protection from physical and emotional harm.

Physiological needs reflect the desire for food, clothing, drink, shelter, and other physical requirements that people try to satisfy.

Figure 14.1   Maslow's hierarchy of needs

Maslow believed that people are motivated by unmet needs that are activated in a particular order. His theory stated that low-order needs always take priority: They must be substantially satisfied before higher-order needs are activated. According to Maslow, if managers want to motivate an individual, they need to understand which level that person is focused on in the needs hierarchy and direct attention to satisfying needs at that level. Later research challenged the assumption that needs are satisfied in sequence, with physiological needs having to be satisfied before safety needs become dominant, safety needs coming before social needs, and so on. An additional problem with Maslow's hierarchy is that people from different cultures are likely to have different need categories and hierarchies.[13] Although researchers have questioned the details of Maslow's theory, it provided an initial framework for the types of innate needs that might motivate people.

Clayton Alderfer built on Maslow's work to construct his **ERG theory,** which collapsed the five categories into three universal categories:

- Existence
- Relatedness
- Growth[14]

Existence corresponds to physiological and safety needs. *Relatedness* needs focus on how people relate to their social environment; in Maslow's hierarchy, they would encompass both the need to belong and the need to earn others' esteem. *Growth* needs—the highest level in the ERG system—are desires for continued psychological growth and development, including the needs for esteem and self-actualization.

Alderfer's ERG theory also differs from Maslow's theory in that it does not assume that lower-level needs must be satisfied before higher-level needs become activated. According to ERG theory, any or all of these types of needs can influence individual behavior at any given time. Alderfer also introduced the **frustration–regression principle,** which suggests that people who are unable to satisfy higher-order needs at a basic level will compensate by focusing on oversatisfying lower-order needs. For example, a worker who cannot fulfill a need for relatedness may direct his or her efforts toward making a lot of money.

Fredrick Herzberg developed his theory of motivation by interviewing employees and asking them to recall occasions on the job when they had been satisfied and motivated and occasions when they had been dissatisfied and unmotivated. Herzberg's findings suggested that the work characteristics associated with dissatisfaction

ERG theory describes three universal categories of needs: existence, relatedness, and growth.

Frustration–regression principle suggests that people who are unable to satisfy higher-order needs at a basic level will compensate by focusing on oversatisfying lower-order needs.

were quite different from those pertaining to satisfaction. That is, his research promoted the notion that two factors influence work attitudes and motivation:

- Hygiene factors
- Motivator factors

Hygiene factors refer to the presence or absence of sources of job dissatisfaction, such as working conditions, pay, company policies, and interpersonal relationships. When hygiene factors are unfavorable, work is dissatisfying. However, favorable hygiene factors simply remove the dissatisfaction, they do not in themselves cause

Before taking over as Chairman and CEO of Sara Lee, Brenda C. Barnes left a promising career as an executive at PepsiCo for a six-year leave to raise her three young children. Relationship needs may have been a more critical motivator than achievement needs in her decision.

people to become highly satisfied and motivated in their work. **Motivator factors** refer to the presence or absence of sources of job satisfaction, such as interesting work, autonomy, responsibility, being able to grow and develop on the job, and a sense of accomplishment and achievement.

Although many factors influence both dissatisfaction and satisfaction to some degree, Herzberg's most prominent contribution to management theory was his challenging of the prevailing assumption that pay is the most important motivator. In his research, satisfying needs associated with growth and autonomy prevailed as more important motivating factors than pay.[15] Herzberg's theory and findings continue to be contested, but managers can draw on his work to consider the influence of a variety of factors in motivating workers.

One practical example of theory building on Herzberg's research is the **job characteristics model,** which specifies how to increase the motivational potential of a job by improving the meaningfulness, autonomy, and feedback associated with the job.[16] *Meaningfulness* is increased by using a variety of skills to complete the work (skill variety), having responsibility for completing more or all of a project or product (task identity), and understanding how the work affects the lives of other people (task significance). *Autonomy* is increased by providing more freedom and responsibility for deciding how the work is done. *Feedback* is increased by providing information related to the quality or quantity of the work. Redesigning one or all of these aspects of a person's job is likely to increase his or her motivation.

Despite concerns about the lack of research support for specific needs-based theories, managers can benefit by applying a few general conclusions from these theories:

- People have needs and seek to meet those needs, in part, in the context of organizations. Managers should consider how to create a work environment that reasonably accommodates these needs.
- Low-level needs are important to people, but higher-level needs are powerful sources of internal motivation. As such, managers should not only consider how to create a work environment that provides sufficient pay, safety, and respect, but also focus on appealing to workers' needs to grow and contribute.

Hygiene factors refer to the presence or absence of sources of job dissatisfaction.

Motivator factors refer to the presence or absence of sources of job satisfaction.

Job characteristics model specifies how to increase the motivational potential of a job by improving the meaningfulness, autonomy, and feedback associated with the job.

MAINSTREAM NURTURED BASES OF MOTIVATION

McClelland's acquired needs theory states that certain types of needs or desires are acquired during an individual's lifetime.

A well-known conceptual framework for managing motivation, and the one that we will use as a basis to organize the remainder of our chapter, comes from **McClelland's acquired needs theory.** According to David McClelland, certain types of needs or desires are acquired during an individual's lifetime. In other words, people may be born with needs, but McClelland's focus was on how certain needs are developed or learned through life experiences and interactions with the surrounding environment. The names for three needs are attributed to McClelland's work—the needs for achievement, affiliation, and power; another need we include in our discussion, the need for fairness, also is generally considered to be an important source of motivation at work.

- The *need for achievement* is the extent to which an individual has a strong desire to perform challenging tasks well and to meet personal standards for accomplishment.
- The *need for fairness* is the desire to be treated fairly and equitably compared to others.
- The *need for affiliation* is the desire to form close meaningful relationships, avoid conflict, and establish warm friendships.
- The *need for power* is the desire to control other people, to influence their behavior, or to be responsible for them.

Because each of these needs is thought to be present within every person to varying degrees, each is important for managers to understand and nurture. From a Mainstream perspective, this is critical because nurtured motivation combines with natural motivation and abilities to affect productivity.

As indicated in the road map at the beginning of this chapter, we will describe the four Mainstream acquired needs or desires that influence the motivation of people, and then draw upon **process theories of motivation** to describe how managers can ensure that people are motivated by these desires. Process theories of motivation describe *how* people can be motivated. For example, managers can use goals and reinforcements, treat people equitably, and build others' self-confidence.

Process theories of motivation describe how people can be motivated.

Desires for Achievement

Most people have a desire or need to accomplish something at work. Of the four main "needs," the need for achievement has received the most research attention, presumably because it has a direct impact on productivity. Research suggests that, from a Mainstream approach, "ideally motivated employees" are characterized by a high sense of achievement coupled with a low sense of anxiety.[17] According to McClelland, the need for achievement is satisfied by being productive and accomplishing goals. Further, those individuals with a high need for achievement will pursue *goals* that they can reasonably *expect* to achieve and that will be rewarded or recognized as important (*reinforced*). This relationship sets the stage for three types of theories related to the desire for achievement:

- Goal-setting theory
- Expectancy theory
- Reinforcement theory

GOAL-SETTING THEORY. One of the most studied of all management theories, with perhaps some of the strongest research support, is goal-setting theory. The appropriate use of goals can increase performance. Recall from Chapter 8 that this is most likely to happen when the goals are SMART—that is, specific, measurable, achievable, results oriented, and time specific. Yet, the single most important lesson is this: The more committed employees are to reaching a goal, the more motivated they will be to reach it.

A great deal of research indicates that goals must be both difficult and specific if they are to motivate high levels of productivity.[18] Specific and difficult goals produce higher levels of output than do either easy goals or the general goal of "Do your best." Specific goals involve clarity and precision and help focus attention on a well-defined task. Specific and difficult goals are effective only if people have the capability and commitment to achieve the goals and if they receive feedback about their progress toward achieving those goals.

Consider for a moment how goals and feedback were utilized by Clyde Hart, the track coach of Olympic 400-meter gold-medalist Jeremy Wariner. On the one hand, the goal of winning the gold medal was specific and difficult, but it was achievable given Jeremy's training and past performance. On the other hand, setting a goal for Jeremy to also win the 5000-meter race would not be achievable because he lacked the ability and training to compete in a longer race. As for feedback, how would Jeremy feel if after each practice run Coach Hart simply said, "Nice job—you are getting closer." If you were Jeremy (or an employee), wouldn't you want to know how close you are to reaching the goal? Feedback helps people learn and regulate their behavior. It is not surprising, then, to learn that adding feedback to goals dramatically improves performance.[19]

Research also shows that the greater the confidence employees have that their efforts will produce desired outcomes, the greater will be their motivation. Confidence is a critical component for a number of theories of motivation. Admittedly, some of this confidence may be a function of innate ability, but much of it can also be tied to factors managers can influence. **Self-efficacy** refers to a person's belief that he or she will be able to complete a task successfully.[20] In particular, research suggests that people's self-efficacy can be increased by coaching, training, ample resources, clear expectations, and other influences under the control of managers. One interesting example (discussed in Chapter 2) relates to research supporting the **self-fulfilling prophecy effect,** which shows that subordinates often live up (or down) to the expectations of their managers.[21] In other words, a simple word of encouragement—for example, saying, "I believe you can do it"—can go a long way toward building someone's confidence to achieve a goal.

Self-efficacy refers to a person's belief that he or she will be able to complete a task successfully.

Self-fulfilling prophecy effect is the idea that subordinates often live up (or down) to the expectations of their managers.

Expectancy theory states that motivation depends on an individual's learned expectations about his or her ability to perform certain tasks and receive desired rewards.

EXPECTANCY THEORY. Another motivational theory that recognizes the importance of a person's confidence is **expectancy theory,** which was originally proposed by Victor Vroom. According to this theory, motivation depends on individuals' learned expectations about their ability to perform certain tasks and receive desired rewards. In particular, motivation is seen as a function of thought calculations related to three separate issues (Figure 14.2):

- Expectancy
- Instrumentality
- Valence

Figure 14.2 Expectancy theory

Can I achieve the goal?

Will I get something for achieving the goal?

Do I value what I get?

Expectancy **x** Instrumentality **x** Valence = Motivation

Expectancy refers to the probability perceived by an individual that exerting a given amount of effort will lead to a certain level of performance.

Instrumentality refers to the perceived probability that successfully performing at a certain level will result in attaining a specific outcome.

Valence is the value an individual attaches to an outcome.

If you are motivated to earn an all-expenses-paid ski trip because you want to try skiing or snowboarding, and you end up earning the trip, be careful. First-day skiers are more likely to get injured, particularly if you try to snowboard on your first day out.[23]

Expectancy refers to the probability perceived by an individual that exerting a given amount of effort will lead to a certain level of performance (i.e., "Can I achieve the goal?"). You might recognize this characteristic as being similar to self-efficacy, in that it reflects confidence.[22] High expectancy contributes to high levels of effort and persistence. High levels of expectancy are likely if the individual has the appropriate capability, experience, and resources (e.g., time, machinery, tools). For example, a student may be motivated to earn an "A" in a class if he or she believes that with hard work getting this grade is possible. However, if the student believes earning an "A" is not possible given his or her limited capability or available time to study, then the student is likely to have low expectancy.

Instrumentality refers to the perceived probability that successfully performing at a certain level will result in attaining a specific outcome (i.e., "Will I get something for achieving the goal?"). Employees will be motivated to perform at high levels only if they think that their high performance will serve as "means" to certain "ends" or outcomes such as pay, job security, interesting job assignments, bonuses, or feelings of accomplishment. For example, a student may be motivated to earn an "A" in a class if he or she believes that this grade will be instrumental in gaining entrance into a professional program or securing a job. If an "A" grade is not perceived to be linked to any foreseeable outcome, then the student's motivation is likely to be low.

Valence is the value an individual attaches to an outcome. To motivate organizational members, a manager needs to determine which outcomes have high valence (are highly valued) for each member and make sure that those outcomes are provided when each member performs at high levels. Simply put, the higher the value of the outcome to the employee, the greater the motivation. Returning to the student example, the more the student values the outcome of entrance into a professional program (i.e., "I've always wanted to be a lawyer"), the more motivated he or she might be. Conversely, if being a lawyer was Mom's or Dad's dream for the student and not his or her own dream, then this outcome is not likely to be as highly motivating.

An example from the Greg May Honda automobile dealership can help explain how all three elements work together. If a salesperson has learned from watching other salespeople that increased time and effort devoted to selling will lead to reaching a sales goal, expectancy is high. Additionally, if the salesperson has been told that reaching the goal will lead to an all-expenses-paid ski trip to Colorado, instrumentality is high. Lastly, if the salesperson places a high value on skiing in Colorado, valence is high. Such a salesperson would be highly motivated. However, if the salesperson believes any one of these components to be low, such as if the salesperson has no interest in skiing (low valence), motivation to reach that goal is limited.

The bottom line for managers is that expectancy theory is very practical: Managers can take action to make sure that employees believe they can achieve goals, that goals are linked to clear outcomes, and that the outcomes are valued by employees. Research supports the idea that expectancy, instrumentality, and valence each has an effect on motivation, though there is less support for the assertion that motivation is the multiplicative effect of all three thought processes.

WHAT DO YOU THINK?

Is Your Motivation Intrinsic or Extrinsic?

Motivation can come from intrinsic or extrinsic sources. **Intrinsic motivation** comes from doing the activity or work itself—for example, from feelings of increased competency, the satisfaction of achievement, and the enjoyment of learning and growing while doing the work. **Extrinsic motivation** comes from factors outside the task itself—that is, behavior is performed to receive outcomes given by another person, typically a supervisor or higher-level manager. Extrinsic motivation comes from seeking or receiving promotions, pay increases, time off, special assignments, awards, and verbal praise. Research suggests that if both extrinsic and intrinsic sources of motivation are present in a job or task, extrinsic motivators that are linked to the work can dominate the intrinsic motivators to the point that intrinsic motivation disappears.[24]

Think about your current or most recent job. What were the sources of motivation? Can you think of something you used to do for the sheer fun of it (intrinsic motivator) and then you started to get paid for doing the same thing (extrinsic motivator)? How did the addition of pay affect your motivation? What would happen to your motivation if you were no longer paid for that behavior?

As a student, is your motivation more intrinsic or extrinsic? Can your motivation on the job or in the classroom be explained by an overemphasis on extrinsic motivators such as pay or grades? What are the implications for management practice?

Intrinsic motivation is a source of motivation that comes from doing the activity or work itself.

Extrinsic motivation is a source of motivation that comes from factors outside the task itself.

REINFORCEMENT THEORY.   Reinforcement theories draw attention to the use of outcomes or consequences to promote learning and achievement. **Reinforcement** is a response or consequence linked to a behavior. Specifically, this perspective focuses on motivating employees to change their on-the-job behavior through the appropriate use of immediate rewards and punishments. According to reinforcement theories, human motivation and behavior are determined by the external environment and the consequences it holds for the individual.

The psychologist B. F. Skinner described this process of motivating behavior by manipulating its consequences with the term **operant conditioning** (also called learning by reinforcement). Another way of describing this process is *behavior modification*—that is, a set of techniques by which reinforcement theory is used to modify human motivation and behavior. The goal of behavior modification is to use reinforcement principles to systematically reinforce desirable work behavior and discourage undesirable work behavior. Four basic kinds of behavior are associated with reinforcement theory:

Reinforcement is a response or consequence linked to a behavior.

Operant conditioning is the use of reinforcement principles to systematically reinforce desirable work behavior and discourage undesirable work behavior; also called *behavior modification*.

- Positive reinforcement
- Punishment
- Negative reinforcement (or avoidance)
- Extinction

Positive reinforcement is the administration of a pleasant and rewarding consequence following a desired behavior. When a manager observes an employee doing an especially good job and offers praise, that praise serves as a positive way to reinforce the

Positive reinforcement is the administration of a pleasant and rewarding consequence following a desired behavior.

The business office comic classic, *Office Space,* offers several examples of motivational techniques gone wrong. Whether it be the example of Peter's boss berating him for not filing a TPS report on time or other examples, the response of Peter and many others to misused motivational tools is that they "just don't care."

Punishment decreases the frequency of or eliminates an undesirable behavior by making an unpleasant consequence contingent on that behavior's occurrence.

Negative reinforcement is the removal of an unpleasant consequence following a desired behavior; also called *avoidance learning.*

Extinction is the absence of any reinforcement—either positive or negative—following the occurrence of a behavior.

behavior of good work. Other positive reinforcers include pay raises, promotions, and almost anything that people regard as a desirable consequence. For managers, positive reinforcement is the preferred approach for increasing desirable behavior and increasing learning. Of course, a reinforcer is positive only if it is something that is valued by the person who receives the reinforcement. For example, tickets to an NBA basketball game might be a positive outcome for some people, but not for others.

Punishment seeks to decrease the frequency of or eliminate an undesirable behavior by making an unpleasant consequence contingent on its occurrence. For example, a supervisor might berate an employee for performing a task incorrectly or a professor might deduct points for a late assignment. The supervisor and the professor expect that the negative outcome will serve as a punishment and reduce the likelihood of the unwanted behavior recurring.

Negative reinforcement (sometimes called *avoidance learning*) is the removal of an unpleasant consequence following a desired behavior. Many of us have learned that if we fasten our seatbelt shortly after we get in our car, we can avoid the annoying warning bell. People learn to do certain things to avoid unpleasant consequences. This is evident, for example, when employees learn to complete work before a deadline to avoid the stress of working up to the last minute or having to explain a missed deadline to the boss. Note the key difference between negative reinforcement and punishment: While punishment causes unwanted behavior to occur less frequently, negative reinforcement causes desired behavior to be repeated.

Extinction is the absence of any reinforcement—either positive or negative—following the occurrence of a behavior. It can be used to weaken an unwanted behavior, especially one that has previously been rewarded. Extinction can involve the withholding of pay raises, praise, and other positive outcomes. The idea is that a behavior that is not positively reinforced will be less likely to occur in the future. For example, a manager who observes an employee disrupting meetings with crude jokes could refrain from smiling and laughing at the jokes. Removing the positive reinforcement (smiling and laughing) makes the employee more likely to stop the disruptive behavior.

Research strongly suggests that not only is the kind of reinforcement important, but so is the pattern of when it occurs. Schedules of reinforcement describe the frequency and regularity of reinforcement:

- *Fixed-interval schedules* reward employees with reinforcement at fixed intervals of time, such as regular pay checks or annual appraisals.
- *Fixed-ratio schedules* reward employees after a specific number of desired responses or behaviors have occurred. For example, a piece-rate system that pays a field hand $1.50 for picking 10 pounds of peppers is a fixed-ratio schedule.

DIGGING DEEPER

Hot Stove Principles for Punishment

Punishment has been proven to reduce certain types of behavior, and it can send a signal to others that people are held accountable for their behavior.[25] Punishment should be used for the right reasons, however—not to satisfy the need for attention or to demonstrate power. Ken Blanchard, in his popular book *The One-Minute Manager*, describes one-minute (i.e., short, specific, immediate) reprimands as an effective means to correct behavior and get employees back on track.[26] Even so, punishment should be used sparingly because it can have some undesirable side effects, including resentment, loss of self-respect, and desire for retaliation.

To avoid the unintended side effects, managers can appropriately use punishment by adhering to the example of the response of a hot stove to curious hands. The response is as follows:

- Punishment is immediate (e.g., "It is hot to the touch"); this increases the likelihood of a connection between behaviors and consequences.

- Punishment provides specific information (e.g., "This is hot and this is not"); this strengthens connection between behaviors and consequences.

- Punishment should be consistent across time and people (e.g., "Everyone gets burned"); this shows no favoritism.

- Punishment is directed toward the person's actions, rather than the person's personality (e.g., "The hand is burned, not the heart"); this demonstrates that the appropriate use of punishment is impersonal.

- *Variable-interval schedules* provide reinforcement at varying intervals of time, such as occasional visits by the supervisor.

- *Variable-ratio schedules* provide reinforcement at variable amounts of output, such as having sales bonuses tied to a certain number of sales calls one month and a different number another month.

Desires for Equity

People want to be treated fairly. In particular, from a Mainstream perspective, people typically want to get what they think that they deserve. We all have an inherent sense of fairness that influences our thinking about interactions with others, particularly in regard to the outcomes we receive for our performance compared to others in the workplace. For example, workers who feel underpaid compared to their coworkers are likely to be demotivated due to a perceived lack of fairness.

Equity theory developed from J. Stacy Adams's work on people's responses to inequity.[27] This theory, which is based on the logic of social comparisons, assumes that people are motivated to seek and preserve social equity in the rewards they expect for performance. In particular, perceived inequity has been shown to relate to decreased performance and increased turnover and absenteeism.[28] People evaluate equity by calculating a ratio of inputs to outcomes. Inputs to a job include education, experience, effort, and ability; outcomes from a job include pay, recognition, benefits, and promotions. The input–outcome ratio may be compared to the ratio of another person in the work group or to a perceived group average. If an employee perceives his or her ratio to be equal to those of relevant others, then a state of equity exists, as shown in Figure 14.3. In other words, the employee perceives that the situation is fair.

Equity theory is based on the logic of social comparisons and assumes that people are motivated to seek and preserve social equity in the rewards they expect for performance.

Figure 14.3 The process of comparison

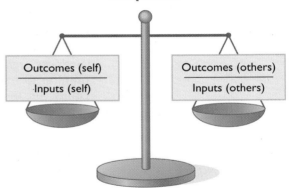

Both the formulation of the ratios and the comparisons between them can be very subjective and are based on individual perceptions. As a result of the comparison, one of three conditions may result:

- The individual may feel equitably rewarded.
- The individual may feel underrewarded.
- The individual may feel overrewarded.

The equity question is this: "In comparison with others, how fairly am I being compensated for the work that I do?" Individuals may feel *equitably rewarded* if, for example, they feel that they are being paid fairly compared to their coworkers. This situation may occur even though another person's outcomes are greater than an individual's own outcomes—provided that the other person's inputs are also proportionately higher. Suppose one employee has a high school education and earns $30,000. He may still feel equitably treated relative to another employee, who earns $45,000 because she has a college degree.

Workers may feel *underrewarded* when, for example, they have a high level of education or experience but receive the same salary as a new, less educated employee. Equity theory predicts that when individuals perceive that they are being treated unfairly in comparison to others, they will be motivated to act in ways that reduce the perceived inequity. For example, employees may try to deal with this type of inequality in the following ways:

- Putting less effort into the job and thereby lowering inputs (self)
- Asking for a pay raise or some other higher outcomes (self)
- Pressuring others to provide more inputs (others)
- Attempting to limit or reduce others' outcomes (others)
- Rationalizing the differences as explainable by some other means (both)
- Changing the situation by leaving the job (self)

Dana Corporation, a large parts supplier to the automotive industry in Detroit, regularly lost engineers to rival parts manufacturers because of its practice of paying a salary near the market average. Professional recruiters (also known as "head hunters") hired by other organizations would prey on the fairness needs of Dana engineers by telling them about higher salaries available in other companies. In response to the perceived inequity, some Dana engineers would then leave for new jobs that offered higher pay. In many cases, these engineers were asked by their new employers to "input" many more hours to receive the higher salary. In retrospect, the outcomes that many of these other organizations provided, such as limited decision-making authority and fewer benefits, were less attractive than what Dana offered as part of its organizational culture and total compensation package. It was not uncommon to have a former Dana engineer come back to work at Dana after the "equity" picture became clearer.

Lastly, an individual may feel *overrewarded* relative to another person. This situation is not likely to be terribly disturbing to most people, but equity theory suggests that some people who experience inequity under these conditions are somewhat motivated to reduce it. In these situations people might (1) increase their inputs by exerting more effort, (2) reduce their outcomes (e.g., take a voluntary pay cut), or (3) rationalize the situation as somehow appropriate (perhaps the most likely response from a materialist–individualist perspective).

Desires for Affiliation

Relationships are not only a source of social comparisons; people also tend to look to relationships for affirmation. That is, people seek to identify or affiliate with those who make them feel good about themselves. Similar to the need for love and relationship noted in our discussion of motivation at the beginning of the chapter, the need for affiliation implies that people are motivated by receiving affirmation from others, especially if they think highly of those others. Almost everyone likes to be part of a winning team that accepts and values them. For some people, this need for affiliation can be a strong motivational driver.

People may seek to affiliate with people, groups, or even organizations. **Organizational commitment** is a motivational force that binds a person to a particular organization.[29] Mainstream managers promote organizational commitment so as to lower turnover costs or to increase group productivity. Although this sense of attachment can stem from affection, obligation, or limited options, research suggests that employees who are emotionally attached to the organization (affective commitment) are motivated to contribute positively to the organization by willingly exerting effort, helping others, and making creative contributions.[30] Some organizations try to encourage affiliation among their members and with the organization by hosting picnics, sponsoring softball teams, and providing a fun environment in which to work. Others, such as Badger Mining Company (BMC), which manufactures silica sand and limestone aggregates, build commitment to the organization by supporting an extensive wellness program, sharing 20 percent of profits with its associates, and allowing associates to take as much time off as needed for personal reasons.[31]

Finally, the principle of exchange is central to the Mainstream perspective on affiliation. People will be especially motivated by affiliations if they receive benefits that are in their self-interests. For example, "knowing the right people" can pay off in gaining promotions or prized assignments. Managers who spend a great deal of time networking or building relationships with powerful people in their organization typically receive more promotions. In this sense, the need for affiliation is not an end in itself so much as it is a means to get something of value.

> **Organizational commitment** is a motivational force that binds a person to a particular organization.

Desires for Individual Power

People can desire power for a variety of reasons. Mainstream theories of power have tended to focus on the desire of an individual to gain and exercise control over organizational resources and members, or over his or her own job. Not surprisingly, a high need for power is often associated with successful attainment of top levels in the organizational hierarchy. Sources of individual power have been described as being based on either position or personal factors. French and Raven identified at least five sources of power.[32]

Three sources of power relate most closely with positions within an organization:

- Legitimate power
- Reward power
- Coercive power

The other two sources or power relate more to personal factors:

- Expert power
- Referent power

Power is important for motivation in two ways. First, people will be motivated to work hard to acquire power and thereby fulfill their need for power. Second, once they have power, people can use it to help motivate others.

Legitimate power is the capacity of a manager to influence other people owing to his or her position in an organization's hierarchy. This type of power gives managers the authority to set the agenda for their organization, to make decisions, and to develop and implement strategies. Legitimate power and authority are basically the same. In other words, a person with legitimate power has the ability to say, "Because I am the boss, you must do as I ask." Most employees comply with the requests of those with legitimate power. When one has legitimate power, it is common to also have coercive and reward power. Nevertheless, a person may sometimes have reward or coercive power without legitimate power.

Reward power is the ability to give or withhold positive benefits or rewards. These can be tangible rewards, such as pay raises, bonuses, or choice job assignments, or they can be intangible rewards, such as verbal praise, a pat on the back, or respect. In short, rewards can be anything that one person has access to and can give that is valued by another person. A person who uses reward power says, in effect, "If you do what I ask, I'll give you a reward."

The opposite side of the coin to reward power is **coercive power,** which refers to someone's ability to motivate others through the threat of punishment. This type of power can force compliance by psychological, emotional, or physical threat. Today, for the most part, coercive actions are limited to verbal and written reprimands, disciplinary layoffs, fines, demotion, and termination.

Legitimate, reward, and coercive powers are likely to motivate others' compliance, but they do not necessarily result in lasting motivation.[33] In such cases, workers may obey orders and carry out instructions, even though they may personally disagree with those orders and instructions and may not be enthusiastic about their work. There is a greater chance of resistance developing in members if these types of power are overemphasized. In contrast, expert and referent power are more likely to motivate employees to a high level of commitment.

Expert power is based on the special knowledge, skills, and expertise that someone possesses. People who have a desire for power will find it motivating to have their expert power recognized by their coworkers. Moreover, they can use their expert power to motivate others. When a person has a great deal of technical know-how or information pertinent to the task at hand, others will be motivated to go along with that individual's recommendations because of his or her superior knowledge. To develop expert power, one must acquire the competencies, knowledge, or experiences that others value in the organization.

Referent power is the ability to motivate through identification with or association with others; in this sense, it has some overlap with affiliation. Referent power is more informal and abstract than the other kinds of power and comes from an individual's personality characteristics that command others' respect, admiration, and loyalty, or that contribute to a sense of likeability that draws others to the individual. This source of power transcends a formal title or position and is associated with charismatic leadership (described in detail in Chapter 15). Someone with referent power often has a strong network of relationships within the workplace. Not unlike expert power, referent power is based on the ways someone is viewed by others.

Legitimate power is the capacity that someone has, owing to his or her position in an organization's hierarchy, to influence other people.

Reward power is the ability to give or withhold positive benefits or rewards.

Coercive power is the power that rests on a person's ability to motivate others' behavior through threat of punishment.

Expert power is based on the special knowledge, skills, and expertise that someone possesses.

Referent power is the ability to motivate through identification with or association with others.

MULTISTREAM NATURAL BASES OF MOTIVATION

Personality

Mainstream managers are especially interested in understanding how the Big Five personality traits can be used to help manage individuals' behavior and to enhance members' productivity—for example, by selecting people for specific jobs based on their level of conscientiousness or extraversion. Multistream managers are interested in this possibility as well, but are just as interested in how personality traits can nurture a sense of collaboration and community.[34] Personality is also interesting to Multistream managers because it offers insight into the tasks and activities that are intrinsically motivating for various members of the organization. For example, Multistream managers would be interested in how personality helps explain who engages in volunteer behavior and how much effort they exert.[35]

Multistream managers are interested in MBTI not so that they can determine "which buttons to press" to maximize the productivity of members, but rather because they are likely to use the MBTI to promote self-understanding and workplace harmony. The emphasis for such managers is on *harmony*, where members embrace interpersonal differences and diversity, instead of *unity*, where all members march to the beat of a single drum.

Multistream managers are also much more likely to make assumptions about human nature and take action based on McGregor's Theory Y than on Theory X. Moreover, Multistream managers would assume that other members are motivated to work so as to make a contribution not only to the material output of the organization, but also to other aspects, such as the organization's social and spiritual nature. This brings us to the idea of innate needs.

Innate Needs

From a Multistream perspective, it comes as no surprise that empirical research provides little support for motivation theories such as Maslow's hierarchy of needs. Perhaps the ongoing popularity of this theory within the Mainstream approach arises partly because the very idea of a hierarchy of needs is consistent with materialist–individualist assumptions that some needs are more important than others and that the ultimate goal of individuals is "self-actualization." This view stands in contrast to the Multistream perspective, which argues for an equal balance among a variety of needs and where the ultimate goal might better be called "community actualization."

Recall from Chapter 1 that from Aristotle's perspective, true happiness cannot be achieved at the individual level of analysis (e.g., self-actualization), but rather comes from practicing the four cardinal virtues in community. Put in terms of motivation, Aristotle's theory essentially argues that people will be motivated when they participate in an organization where members practice and experience the four virtues. Extending the argument a bit further, from a Multistream perspective everyone has an innate need to practice and to experience the following virtues:

- *Practical wisdom*—evident in foresight and acting to serve the overall well-being of the community

- *Justice*—evident when all stakeholders connected with an organization get their due

- *Courage*—evident when actions improve overall happiness, even at a threat to self
- *Self-control*—evident when members overcome impulsive actions and the self-serving use of power

This is quite different from Maslow's idea of satisfying one need before other needs are activated; likewise, it is very different from Alderfer's frustration–regression principle, which suggests that people who are unable to satisfy higher-order needs at a basic level will compensate by oversatisfying lower-order needs. A Multistream approach also favors a balance of hygiene factors and motivators, recognizing that hygiene factors make contributions toward building community and dignifying those members who may not have direct links to the organization's performance. Multistream management emphasizes job characteristics that enhance meaningful work, responsibility, and feedback because these are dignifying practices in themselves even if they are associated with enhanced motivation and performance. In particular, Multistream management focuses on meaningful work that allows members to develop and use a variety of skills, experience a sense of completion, and make significant contributions to benefit others.

In sum, the Multistream approach concurs with the Mainstream approach that people have innate needs. However, a Multistream perspective differs from a Mainstream perspective in the following ways:

- A Multistream perspective places a greater emphasis on the need to *balance* various innate needs (rather than differentiating between lower- and higher-order needs that are met in a specific sequence).
- A Multistream perspective emphasizes *community* well-being (versus self-actualization or individual growth).
- A Multistream perspective is more likely to value meeting needs that enhance the dignity of members even if they do not maximize productivity (a greater interest in virtue, "hygiene" factors, and meaningful work).[36]

MULTISTREAM NURTURED BASES OF MOTIVATION

Research has shown that there is a strong link between Mainstream motivation theory and workers' productivity and on-the-job performance. Although Mainstream motivation research also extends beyond the productivity of individual workers, its focus on individuals' efforts and their productivity is entirely consistent with the materialist–individualist Mainstream perspective. In this section, we briefly introduce and develop Multistream motivation theories that are less materialist–individualist. Our descriptions focus on modifying the basic process theories we have previously associated with accomplishment, fairness, relationships, and power. From a Multistream perspective, there are four motivating needs or desires:

- Significance
- Justice
- Community
- Shared power

Desires for Significance

According to Mainstream management, a need for achievement drives goal-setting theory, expectancy theory, and reinforcement theory. A parallel idea from Multistream management is related to peoples' need for significance—namely, the desire to live a life worth living and to make an enduring contribution to others.

MULTISTREAM GOAL-SETTING THEORY.   The benefits of Mainstream goal setting are noteworthy. However, focusing on achievement-oriented goals, such as individual productivity and the immediate bottom line, can encourage counterproductive behaviors such as failure to maintain machinery, deficiencies in developing employees, and even ethical violations.[37] Consider the story of Walt Pavlo, a former employee at MCI.[38] When asked to assume responsibility for managing a profitable portfolio of high-risk account receivables, he encountered increasingly difficult performance expectations. To meet goals, he began to manipulate the accounts of the worst-performing customers. Eventually, he began defrauding MCI and its customers. The causes of Pavlo's actions may be numerous, but the specific and difficult goals that he was expected to meet as an individual seem to be one factor contributing to his crimes.

As discussed in Chapter 8, paying attention to easy-to-measure and time-specific goals distracts us from pursuing difficult-to-measure and timeless goals. Robert Giacalone refers to the latter as "transcendent" goals, and he points to the growing interest and need for goals that relate to people's need or desire to do something significant in their work lives. Put differently, Multistream managers do not want to focus *all* of their energy on achieving easily measured financial or sales goals; rather, they are also motivated to work toward timeless and possibly difficult-to-measure goals that are significant. Indeed, such goals should be more intrinsically motivating than Mainstream goals. Also, even though Multistream goals may have relatively lower levels of material output and financial wealth, they facilitate relatively high amounts of spiritual, social, ecological, aesthetic, and intellectual "well*th.*"

For example, consider the noble goal of promoting peace. PeaceWorks, a for-profit organization in the specialty foods industry, is devoted to creating relationships between suppliers and customers of countries or ethnicities historically at odds with one another.[39] No doubt, the members of PeaceWorks find great motivation and satisfaction in serving the cause of promoting peace, but even members of homebuilders such as David Weekly Homes can be inspired by the purpose of the company to "enhance people's lives: our team, our clients, and our community.[40]

Motivating with an authentic sense of significance does not mean expectations are lower. Transcendent goals that are difficult to measure and hard to force into firm deadlines can be very

Walt Pavlo is a former MCI employee and a convicted felon. He now tours the country warning others to avoid the snare of unethical behavior. His account of his experiences at MCI is detailed in his book, *Stolen Without a Gun,* co-authored with Neil Weinberg.

challenging to accomplish. They are more ambiguous and often require novel and complex approaches to achieve. Take the goal of promoting peace at PeaceWorks or the goals at the Mayo Clinic of developing new treatments and cures for cancer—these are quite challenging goals.

 WHAT DO YOU THINK?

When Is the Best Time to Develop Your Game Plan?

Bob Buford, drawing on his experience and the experience of others in business, proposed the idea that many people spend a majority of their work years pursuing *success* or achievement goals, only to find that much of this activity lacked *significance*.[41] Using a football analogy, he argues that people often make a change in their "game plan" at half-time in their work lives.

Extending Buford's analogy, we suggest that there are three times when people might adopt a Multistream "game plan" for their careers:

- They can do so before the game even starts (when planning and practicing for the game).
- They can make changes to their game plan at half-time (after personal firsthand experience with their pregame plan).
- They can make changes at the end of the game (when they realize they are running out of time and need a new plan).

Applying this analogy to organizations, managers typically develop their basic career game plan during their formal education and early on-the-job experience, often change their game plan at a mid-life crisis (usually around 40 years of age), and not infrequently adopt a new game plan toward the end of their career (perhaps with an urgency driven by regret).[42]

Think of managers you know and admire. Have they made changes to their game plans? What is your current game plan? Which goal dominates your thinking more—achieving personal material success or achieving significance? Explain why.

MULTISTREAM EXPECTANCY THEORY. Relative to the Mainstream approach, the Multistream approach also takes a different perspective on the three hallmarks of expectancy theory: expectancy, instrumentality, and valence.

Rather than an "I can do it" view of *expectancy*, the Multistream approach is more likely to take a "We can do it" view. Whereas the difference may appear subtle, the implications for managing motivation can be profound. Instead of primarily focusing on and building self-efficacy, a Multistream approach tends to focus on pursuing goals in the context of community and building **group efficacy,** which is the collective belief (i.e., expectancy) about the group's performance capability. Not only do groups with high levels of efficacy perform well over time, but members are also likely to be motivated to engage in participative decision making, cooperative problem solving, and workload sharing.[43]

The Walt Pavlo story described earlier in this section is one where goals were pursued by an individual in isolation. Pavlo grew tired of juggling payment dates and flying all over the country listening to promises of payment that rarely materialized. When he approached his boss with a recommendation to write off $88 million in receivables, he was told he could write off only $15 million, "no matter what."[44] Rather than expect Pavlo to be able to do it on his own, a Multistream manager might have said, "Let's see what we can do together to meet organizational goals." Moreover, perhaps Pavlo and his manager might have in-

Group efficacy is the collective belief about the group's performance capability.

volved other stakeholders, and even customers, in the discussion of potential solutions.

In terms of *instrumentality*, rather than the Mainstream approach of answering the question of "What's in it for me?" with individual extrinsic motivators such as money, a Multistream approach is more likely to answer the question of "What are the effects on others, especially those at the margins of society?" In this sense, Multistream management broadens the outcomes that are linked to performance from typical individual extrinsic motivators such as a pay increase to group outcomes such as a group bonus, the group's learning, or community well-being. Research shows that the more people are given individual goals and incentives, the less effort or attention is directed toward **organizational citizenship behavior (OCB)**.[45] OCBs include behaviors such as helping others even if it is not your job, and going above and beyond normal practices to serve organizational stakeholders. By raising the question of "What's in it for others?" and encouraging more collective thinking, a Multistream approach encourages OCBs.[46]

Finally, in terms of *valence*, the Multistream approach takes a less materialist–individualist approach in determining what is valuable. A Multistream approach may emphasize outcomes that relate to increased employee development, decreased ecological impact, or fewer work–family conflicts. For example, allowing for flexibility in work schedules is likely to be particularly valued by people who balance both family and work roles.[47] In other words, a Multistream approach to motivation is more likely to provide a balance of financial and nonfinancial outcomes, acknowledging that people can be motivated by more than money.[48] For example, Barbara Barnard and other managers at ORC Industries sometimes put in 12- to 14-hour days—not because it means more money for them, but because they are motivated by the value of their organization in providing jobs for mentally and physically disabled workers.[49]

At the organizational level, a management tool called the **Balanced Scorecard** can provide a Multistream counterweight to the Mainstream emphasis on financial outcomes. The Balanced Scorecard is used to balance the use of financial goals with the use of other valuable goals that are important to overall organizational well-being (Figure 14.4). Robert Kaplan and David Norton developed this tool to help managers recognize the importance of measuring nonfinancial elements of their organizations, such as customers' perceptions, innovation and learning, and work processes.[50] They argue that managers can better manage their organizations by maintaining a balanced organization that is aligned with the significance aspects of its mission and vision. A balanced set of goals encourages excelling at activities such as developing employees, satisfying stakeholders, maintaining equipment or reducing emissions, and pursuing other activities that would be likely to receive less recognition if financial performance was the sole focus of measurement. A Multistream approach would heighten the valence of goals that are considered

Organizational citizenship behavior (OCB) is a behavior that goes above and beyond normal role expectations to help others or benefit the organization.

Balanced Scorecard is a management tool used to balance the use of financial goals with the use of other valuable goals that are important to overall organizational well-being.

Figure 14.4   A Balanced Scorecard of performance measures

worthwhile to pursue, even if it is not clear that accomplishing these goals will contribute to financial performance.

MULTISTREAM REINFORCEMENT THEORY.   Recall that Mainstream reinforcement theory tends to focus on managing motivation through material rewards directed at the individual level. In contrast, Multistream reinforcement theory tends to focus on managing motivation using nonmaterial rewards directed toward the group or the community. Simply recognizing the group's contributions toward significant goals and providing feedback at the group level can be motivational.[51] Just as people's behavior can be reinforced with money, so it can be reinforced with the satisfaction that comes from working in a participative workplace or by recognition that, for example, the organization is a leader in employing people who have disabilities or respecting the ecological environment. Furthermore, a Multistream approach is less likely to engage in punishment or the use of coercive power. It is much more invitational by nature: People are welcomed—not forced—to participate in Multistream practices.

Desires for Justice

The Mainstream approach to fairness focuses on the motivation that comes when someone is treated equitably compared to others in similar jobs. In contrast, the Multistream approach to fairness focuses on the motivation that can result when people enable others on the margins of society to be treated more justly. The question is not so much "Am I getting my fair share?" as it is "What can I do to help others who are not getting their fair share?"

Distributive justice is concerned with comparing one's inputs and outcomes to others' inputs and outcomes.

Procedural justice is concerned with the extent to which policies and rules are participatively developed, transparent, and fairly administered.

The Mainstream concern for fairness focuses on **distributive justice.** Similar to equity theory, distributive justice is concerned with comparing the individual's inputs and outcomes to other members' inputs and outcomes. A Multistream perspective on distributive justice goes beyond the concerns of personal equity and is concerned with ensuring that there is procedural justice in developing and administering rules for distributing outcomes. **Procedural justice** is a specific aspect of justice that is concerned with the extent to which policies and rules are participatively developed, transparent, and fairly administered without bias or favoritism. Research suggests that procedural justice has a stronger positive influence than distributive justice on organizational commitment, job satisfaction, and positive organizational citizenship behavior.[52] When people participatively develop "fair" distribution rules, research shows that the rules tend to take into account *both* the needs of members (e.g., the poorest-paid members should not be in poverty) and their performance (e.g., highly productive people should be paid more). Research also suggests that those who experience receiving rewards based on both needs *and* contributions within the group tend to be more motivated than those who receive rewards based on only need *or* contributions.[53]

From a Multistream perspective, people may be motivated to distribute resources more justly, especially if managers provide opportunities and examples of doing so. In equity theory terms, most people recognize when they are being overcompensated (monetarily or otherwise), but given the opportunity to rationalize the inequity (e.g., "That's what the market says I'm worth") are not likely to take any action unless a compelling option is available. Some Multistream managers set an example by insisting on reasonable salaries, removing unnecessary perks such as executive dining areas and parking spots, and focusing some of the organization's resources (time or money) on addressing community needs. Genentech managers, for example, defy traditional logic by devoting resources to the development of drugs that meet human and community needs.[54] It's not that Genentech, a biotech firm, is not making money: Quite the contrary—the firm has turned a profit during every year of its 29 years in existence. It's just that at Genentech it is taboo to make decisions primarily by appealing to return-on-investment analysis or market projections.

Whereas from a Mainstream perspective it is natural to emphasize the need for individuals to ensure that *they* are being treated fairly from their own self-interested perspective, from a Multistream perspective it can be motivating to look for justice *beyond* oneself and one's own material concerns. For example, many people are motivated to forgo large salaries, extensive benefits, and luxurious accommodations to serve the needs of others. Consider people who devote themselves to work at Doctors without Borders or the Peace Corps. Even for-profit organizations such as Starbucks can enhance the motivation of employees by aligning some of their practices and finances—for example, promoting Fair Trade coffee—to serve causes that go beyond ensuring individual equity.

Desires for Community

Relationships are the source of considerable motivation. Mainstream theories of affiliation are primarily influenced by the principle of exchange or utility. That is, affiliation is especially motivating when people get something from a relationship with a person or organization. In this sense, affiliation is a means to a materialist–individualist end. A Multistream approach to affiliation extends beyond simple exchanges, however, and includes a sense of community and service to others. Relationships with other people are motivating not only because *we* need love and affirmation, but also because we need *to* love, affirm, and make sacrifices for others. It is inherently motivating to belong to a community and to use your gifts, time, and resources to serve others.

The Multistream approach is based on the belief that given a chance, many people can be motivated to behave in ways that benefit others outside the organization, even in communities far away. Managers at Green Mountain Coffee have found that trips to Mexico serve to connect employees with the community of people who grow coffee. After experiencing firsthand the difficult working conditions of those who hand-pick the beans, U.S. employees say they "will never spill a bean again."[55] In an attempt to get more money back to the coffee growers, Green Mountain has become a leader in Fair Trade practices that buy coffee directly from the growers and guarantee purchases at prices that contribute to improved wages for workers. As a company, Green Mountain also donates money to programs that seek to improve the quality of life of these low-wage international workers by providing either education, food, or sanitation assistance.[56]

Managers do not need to look far to help create a sense of community. For example, footwear manufacturer Timberland introduced a program that pays its employees for up to 40 hours per year of service to the community. Although there may be some positive public relations effects for organizations that engage in community service, the financial payoff is not the motivating reason for serving; rather, the motivation is the desire for affiliation with the community. To date, projects undertaken by Timberland employees include improving the drinking water in the Dominican Republic and reducing soil erosion in New York's Bronx River by planting native plants on the shore.[57] Timberland's motto of "Doing well and doing good" is lived out not only by helping others, but also by using environmentally friendly materials for the company's shoes and even its buildings.[58]

The Multistream focus on community, regardless of the instrumental value received in return, runs against the current of Mainstream management thought that is dominated by a materialist–individualist exchange perspective of affiliating with those who offer you benefits. A Multistream approach to management begins with a profound respect for all people within and outside the organization. John Beckett, president of R. W. Beckett Corporation, a leader in the residential heating industry, concluded, "I must place a high value on each person and never look down on another, regardless of their station and situation in life . . . there is something sacred about every individual."[59]

Desires for Shared Power

Whereas a Mainstream perspective focuses on gaining more power for oneself, a Multistream perspective focuses on sharing power with others. It is clear from research on goals that when employees have meaningful participation in goal setting, they are more committed to those goals.[60] Similarly, influence tactics research shows that consulting with employees and seeking their input increase their motivation.[61] Employees who have autonomy, responsibility, and opportunities to participate, with appropriate levels of authority and resources, are generally more motivated because they feel more ownership.

Multistream managers share power and trust employees to do the right thing. Multistream managers tend to believe that collectively members have the expert power needed to manage their own jobs. In environments characterized by high levels of shared power, people are motivated to spot problems, solve problems, engage customers, and satisfy customers because they own the work. Organizational members who see themselves as empowered are generally more innovative, less resistant to change, more satisfied, less stressed, and judged as more effective by others.[62] Research indicates that empowered people also have a stronger bond with the organization, greater confidence in their abilities, and a clear sense of being able to make a difference.[63]

In contrast, managers who seek to gain and hold power in organizations may create a sense of powerlessness and helplessness that demoralizes employees. Consider how frustrating it is to know how to solve a problem, but not being given the opportunity to do it. In contrast, organizations such as Griffin Hospital bring out the best in their people while providing exceptional service. From using therapy dogs to providing roaming musicians and well-stocked kitchens, Griffin is at the forefront of a patient-centered environment that is not possible without employees who have a sense of ownership.[64] Griffin was not always so successful in attracting patients or retaining employees. Indeed, in the early 1980s, the company had serious patient and employee problems. It reversed its fortunes by becoming a radically patient-focused hospital. Not only are the employees empowered at Griffin, but so are the patients. Managers at Griffin encourage patient participation in treatment planning and even allow patients and their families to examine medical records. Similarly, Multistream managers share power, and in the end they often receive a great deal of measurable and immeasurable rewards in return.

The Motivational Monk[65]

Kenny Moore was a Catholic monk for 15 years and is now a businessperson and author. His transition from the cloister to the boardroom was a difficult one; more so in dealing with leaving the priesthood than in entering the business world. Although Kenny may have had reservations regarding his transition, someone at Brooklyn Union Gas, one of the largest energy companies in the Northeastern United States, saw promise in how Kenny's experience as a priest could benefit the company as a human resource management professional. One of Kenny's first tasks was to help implement a performance appraisal process. "I knew nothing about business, but I realized I could help people. We were training them in a system that required having difficult conversations. Priests know how to do that."

Kenny adjusted well and was promoted but left Brooklyn Union Gas for a time due to a life-threatening health condition. After fighting back from death's doorstep, Kenny had a new perspective. He did not care about climbing the corporate ladder; he simply wanted to make a difference. It turns out that his employer had also gone through a major change, as Brooklyn Union Gas had now merged with Long Island Lighting Company to become KeySpan. CEO Bob Catell recognized that Moore's ability to connect with people and his understanding of interpersonal politics made him a perfect fit for ombudsman—a position within the human resources department that mediates complaints or conflicts between organizational members.

Kenny's skills and unique perspective were in high demand as the organization underwent the challenging transition from Brooklyn Gas to KeySpan. Believing the change was about endings as well as beginnings, one of the first suggestions Kenny had in his new role was to hold a "funeral" for the "old" company. Catell agreed, and most of Keyspan's executives participated in a funeral service with mock tombstones in one corner of the room as Moore presided in priestly attire over a process of grieving the past and envisioning the future. He provided managers with slips of paper and asked each attendee to write down things that were ending, such as a monopoly position in the industry, and then place their slips in an urn. Moore blessed these "endings" and bid them farewell. He also asked attendees to write down

what they wanted to take with them into the new organization, such as dedication to the local community. He even encouraged them to draw pictures of what the company might look like in the future. Why did Moore take the chance of hosting such a strange event? Kenny remarked, "People are dying to be connected, invited, involved. They don't like having things shoved down their throats in a formulaic way."

The funeral wasn't Kenny's only novel idea. In the wake of the merger, Moore was asked to help bring together the two companies' information technology (IT) departments. He suggested that the new KeySpan Chief Information Officer (CIO) try an "Open Space" meeting, an idea that Moore had read about but did not fully understand. Moore simply knew it had something to do with self-organizing systems that involved "large numbers of people sitting in a circle with no set agenda except a pressing problem." It seemed to Kenny that Open Space was based on a few key principles: "Singularly we're stupid, but collectively we're smart," and "One person with passion is worth more than 99 with good ideas."

The CIO, who was faced with few options and the need for dramatic results, agreed to host a full-day Open Space meeting on the theme: "How do we in IT use our expertise to meet business needs?" The day would begin with all 400 IT staff members sitting in a circle with a single microphone in the center where participants could voice a topic they would like to discuss in "breakout sessions" that would take place during the remainder of the day. As the event neared, however, the CIO began to panic. "What happens if nobody comes to the microphone?" he asked. "Maybe we should plant some topics with the directors, in advance, to ensure that at least a few people come forward?" Kenny reminded him that there are few secrets in organizations. If word leaked out that senior management "programmed" the participation, the event would be a farce. Kenny responded by saying that he and the CIO would need to trust the process and be vulnerable. "We can't ask our employees to take risks if we're unwilling to do it as well."

The big day arrived. After a few awkward comments from the CIO, Moore introduced the concept of the Open Space, explained how the group would self-manage the process, and asked them to join in. After a few anxious moments of silence, one person finally stepped to the microphone to suggest a topic. After a minute another person came forward. Soon over 50 topics for breakout sessions had been suggested and the event was on its way. According to Moore, the resulting discussion was "something that could never have been managerially orchestrated. It all seemed to get energy from the freedom inherent in a business 'invitation.' Employees sensed that they were in charge. And indeed, they truly were."

At the end of that day, there was time for only a few employees to share the results of their breakout sessions, but the comments were enthusiastic and full of energy. The direction and agenda for implementing a successful merger had been set, and the event was deemed a rousing success. Moore explained the key to its success: "Ownership for a successful merger had migrated from the hallowed halls of senior management into the cubicles of the ordinary worker. This could never have been mandated,

only invited. Fortunately, there is a vast expanse within the human soul longing to respond to such invitations."

QUESTIONS FOR DISCUSSION

1. The careful reader will note that the word "motivation" is not used once in this case, and yet the case clearly has a lot to say about motivation and how it is managed in the workplace. Use the previously discussed theories to explain why people were motivated.

2. Identify parts of the case where Mainstream motivation theory seems particularly helpful to understand what is going on, and parts where Multistream motivation seems more helpful.

3. Would you be motivated by participation in an "Open Space" meeting? Why or Why not?

SUMMARY

Managing motivation can be tricky, because people are born with different personalities and traits and then acquire different values and needs over time. Whereas there are many ways to manage motivation, much of the literature can be summarized to show how managers make use of four basic human needs or desires—the need for accomplishment, fairness, relationship, and power—to manage motivation.

From a Mainstream perspective, the management of motivation involves appealing to people's need for:

- *Achievement* by providing goals that are measurable, time specific, challenging, and accompanied by feedback; appropriate individual reinforcement; and increasing expectancy, instrumentality, and valence
- *Fairness* by treating people equitably compared to others working in similar positions
- *Affiliation* by providing people with affirmation and opportunities to build productive networks
- *Individual power* by seeking to gain legitimate, reward, coercive, expert, and referent power

From a Multistream perspective, the management of motivation involves appealing to people's need for:

- *Significance* by allowing goals that are transcendent, timeless, challenging, and accompanied by feedback; providing appropriate collective reinforcement; and facilitating cooperative expectancy, citizenship instrumentality, and balanced valences
- *Justice* by providing opportunities to treat stakeholders justly, especially people who are on the margins
- *Community* by modeling and providing opportunities for trust and caring relationships
- *Shared power* by developing a sense of ownership

QUESTIONS FOR REFLECTION AND DISCUSSION

1. How does your personality affect your motivation? List some things you naturally like to do. Is there an underlying pattern in these activities that hints at your personality?

2. Maslow's hierarchy of needs theory is a well-known theory. What about it do you think fits with your motivational experiences? What does not?

3. Goal setting is a well-established means to improve performance. What is your experience with goal setting? When did it work or not work well?

4. Discuss why two people with similar abilities might have very different expectancies for performing at a high level. What can you do as a manager to increase workers' expectancies?

5. You may have heard a few teachers complain that their pay is poor, yet they continue to teach. How can this discrepancy be explained by motivational theory?

6. What do you think of the distinction between success (achievement) and significance?

7. Compare and contrast Multistream and Mainstream views on the need for fairness. How is equity different from justice?

8. Explain how Mainstream and Multistream perspectives on affiliation differ. Is one necessarily better than the other?

9. Many managers have been accused of abusing power in organizations. How can you make use of power without abusing it?

HANDS-ON ACTIVITIES

Assessing Your Personality with the Myers–Briggs Type Indicator

Several MBTI questionnaires are available, including some that are administered and interpreted by certified MBTI consultants. To get a relatively short but reasonably accurate assessment using the web, visit http://www.humanmetrics.com/. How well does your type, as described in the table below, fit your view of yourself?

ISTJ
Process ideas through reflection; concerned with the present and ensure that details and facts are considered; value objectivity and analysis; prefer specific procedures and formal methods.

ISFJ
Process ideas through reflection; concerned with the present time and ensure facts and details are measured; value relationships and promote agreement within groups.

INFJ
Process ideas through reflection; concerned with broad perspective of key issues; open to change and enjoy challenges; look for recognition; bring teams to a decision.

INTJ
Process ideas through reflection; concerned with broad perspective of key issues; open to change and enjoy challenges; confront the status quo; ensure high quality in all outputs.

ISTP
Process ideas through reflection; make decisions based on logical and objective thought; use analytical thought to solve complex problems; use realistic approach to problem solving.

ISFP
Process ideas through reflection; concerned with personal values and appreciate others; solve problems immediately; concerned with the people side of problem solving.

INFP
Process ideas through reflection; concerned with personal values; appreciate company; give insight and want acceptance in group activities; focus on team agreement and listening.

INTP
Process ideas through reflection; concerned with logic and objectivity; provide rational insight and center effort on the central issue of an argument or problem.

ESTP

Process ideas through interaction; concerned with the present time, facts, and details; take action and ensure tasks are completed in time; easily take lead during emergencies while organizing assets.

ESFP

Process ideas through interaction; concerned with present time, details, and facts; ensure that everyone is included in group discussions; enjoy humor and apply a realistic approach to problem solving.

ENFP

Process ideas through interaction; concerned with the future; ensure that a broad or novel perspective is considered; value relationships and consensus; prefer flexibility and remain open to change.

ENTP

Process ideas through interaction; concerned with the global viewpoint; embrace change and new challenges; overachieve and lead others to better comprehension of theories; overcome challenges.

ESTJ

Process ideas through interaction; concerned with truth, logic, and justice; identify errors in situations; ensure tasks are completed on time; ensure the message is straightforward.

ESFJ

Process ideas through interaction; concerned with values-based foundation; look for unity in relationships; ensure deadlines are met; respect the chain of command; want others happy with output.

ENFJ

Process ideas through interaction; make decisions on a values-based foundation; look for unity in relationships; comfortable leading discussions; look for understanding within the team; high energy.

ENTJ

Process ideas through interaction; concerned with truth, logic, and justice; concerned with staying on task; provide a high-quality product on time; thrive when having to sort out confusing and difficult tasks.

E = extraverted, I = introverted, S = sensing, N = intuitive, F = feeling, T = thinking, P = perceiving, J = judging.

ENDNOTES

1. Weiss, N. (1998). How Starbucks impassions workers to drive growth. *Workforce, 77*(8), 60–64; http://www.bizjournals.com/bizwomen/consultants/return_on_people/2000/03/13/column72.html; Starbucks 2005 corporate social responsibility report; http://www.starbucks.com/aboutus/csrannualreport.asp; Great Place to Work award for credibility. (2003). http://www.greatplacetowork.com.

2. See Barrick, M. R., Stewart, G. L., & Piotrowski, M. (2002). Personality and job performance: Test of the mediating effects of motivation among sales representatives. *Journal of Applied Psychology, 87,* 1–9; Judge, T. A., & Ilies, R. (2002). Relationship of personality to performance motivation: A meta-analytic review. *Journal of Applied Psychology, 87,* 797–807.

3. Digman, J. M. (1990). Personality structure: Emergence of the five-factor model. In M. R. Rosenzweig & L. W. Porter (Eds.), *Annual review of psychology* (Vol. 41, pp. 417–440). Palo Alto, CA: Annual Reviews.

4. Barrick, M. R., & Mount, M. K. (1991). The Big Five personality dimensions and job performance: A meta-analysis. *Personnel Psychology, 44,* 1–26; Tett, R. P., Jackson, D. N., & Rothstein, M. (1991). Personality measures as predictors of job performance: A meta-analytic review. *Personnel Psychology, 44,* 703–742.

5. Barrick, M. R., Stewart, G. L., Neubert, M. J., & Mount, M. K. (1998). Relating member ability and personality to work-team processes and team effectiveness. *Journal of Applied Psychology, 83,* 377–391.

6. McGregor, D. (1960). *The human side of enterprise.* New York: McGraw-Hill.

7. McGregor, 1960. See also Heil, G., Bennis, W., & Stephens, D., et al. (2000). *Douglas McGregor revisited: Managing the human side of the enterprise.* New York: John Wiley & Sons.

8. Ouchi, W. G. (1981). *Theory Z.* Reading, MA: Addison-Wesley.

9. Nicholson, N. (2000). *Executive instinct: Managing the human animal in the Information Age.* New York: Crown; Pierce, B. D., & White, R. (1999). The evolution of social structure: Why biology matters. *Academy of Management Review, 24*(4), 843–853.

10. Oliner, S. P. M., & Oliner, P. M. (1988). *The altruistic personality: Rescuers of Jews in Nazi Europe.* New York: Free Press; Schloss, J. P. (1998). Evolutionary accounts of altruism and the problem of goodness by design. In Dembski, W. (Ed.), *Mere creation: Science, faith, and intelligent design* (pp. 237–263). Downer's Grove, IL: InterVarsity Press.

11. For more information about how Shaffer Title uses the MBTI see www.shaffertitle.com/Shaffer_CaseStudy.pdf.

12. Mitchell, T. R., & Daniels, D. (2003). Motivation. In W. C. Borman, D. R. Ilgen, & R. J. Klimoski (Eds.), *Handbook of psychology: Industrial and organizational psychology* (Vol. 12, pp. 225–254). Hoboken, NJ: John Wiley & Sons.

13. Mitchell, T. R., & Daniels, D. (2003). Observations and commentary on recent research in work motivation. In L. Porter, G. Bigley, & R. Steers (Eds.), *Motivation and work behavior* (7th ed.). New York: McGraw-Hill.

14. Alderfer, C. P. (1969). An empirical test of a new theory of human needs. *Organizational Behavior and Human Performance, 4,* 142–175.

15. Bassett-Jones, N., & Lloyd, G. C. (2005). Does Herzberg's motivation theory have staying power? *Journal of Management Development, 24*(10), 929–943.

16. Hackman, R., & Oldham, G. (1980). *Work redesign.* Boston: Addison-Wesley.

17. Mitchell & Daniels, 2003, p. 33.

18. Locke, E. A., & Latham, G. P. (1990). *A theory of goal setting and task performance.* Englewood Cliffs, NJ: Prentice Hall.

19. Neubert, M. J. (1998). The value of feedback and goal setting over goal setting alone and potential moderators of this effect: A meta-analysis. *Human Performance, 11,* 321–335.

20. Bandura, A. (1986). *Social foundations of thought and action: A social cognitive theory.* Englewood Cliffs, NJ: Prentice-Hall.

21. Eden, D. (2003). Self-fulfilling prophecies in organizations. In J. Greenberg (Ed.), *Organizational behavior: The state of the science* (2nd ed., pp. 91–122). Mahwah, NJ: Lawrence Erlbaum Associates.

22. Cady, S. H., Grey-Boyd, D., & Neubert, M. J. (2001). Multilevel performance probability: A meta-analytic integration of expectancy and self-efficacy. *Psychological Reports, 88,* 1077–1090.

23. http://www.ski-injury.com/stats1.htm.

24. Deci, E. L., Koestner, R., & Ryan, R. M. (1999). A meta-analytic review of experiments examining the effects of extrinsic rewards on intrinsic motivation. *Psychological Bulletin, 125,* 627–668; Deci, E. L., & Ryan, R. M. (1985). *Intrinsic motivation and self-determination in human behavior.* New York: Plenum.

25. Butterfield, K. D., Trevino, L. K., & Ball, G. A. (1996). Punishment from the manager's perspective: A grounded investigation and inductive model. *Academy of Management Journal, 39*(6), 1479–1512.

26. Blanchard, K., & Spencer, J. (2003). *The one-minute manager.* New York: HarperCollins.

27. Adams, J. S. (1965). Inequity in social exchange. In L. Berkowitz (Ed.), *Advances in experimental social psychology* (Vol. 2, pp. 267–299). New York: Academic Press.

28. Mitchell & Daniels, 2003. See also Greenberg, J. (1988). Equity and workplace status: A field experiment. *Journal of Applied Psychology, 73,* 606–613.

29. Meyer, J. P., & Herscovitch, L. (2001). Commitment in the workplace: Toward a general model. *Human Resource Management Review, 11,* 299–326.

30. Cohen, A. (2003). *Multiple commitments in the workplace: An integrative approach.* Mahwah, NJ: Lawrence Erlbaum Associates.

31. *Building the best on a solid foundation.* http://www.greatplacetowork.com/best/best-small-and-medium-2007.php (accessed March 8, 2008).

32. French, J. R. P., & Raven, B. (1959). The bases of social power. In D. Cartwright & A. Zander (Eds.), *Studies in social power* (pp. 150–167). Ann Arbor, MI: University of Michigan, Institute for Social Research.

33. Yukl, G. (1998). *Leadership in organizations.* Upper Saddle River, NJ: Prentice Hall.

34. Organ, D. W. (1994). Personality and organizational citizenship behavior. *Journal of Management, 20*(2), 465–478.

35. Neubert, M. J., Taggar, S., & Cady, S. H. (2006). The role of conscientiousness and extraversion in affecting the relationship between perceptions of group potency and volunteer group member selling behavior: An interactionist perspective. *Human Relations, 59*(9), 1235–1260.

36. Luthans, F., & Youssef, C. M. (2007). Emerging positive organizational behavior. *Journal of Management, 33*(3), 321–349.

37. Schweitzer, M., Ordonez, L., & Douma, B. (2004). Goal setting as a motivator of unethical behavior. *Academy of Management Journal, 47*(3), 422–432.

38. Weinberg, N. (2002). Ring of thieves. *Forbes.com;* http://www.forbes.com/business/forbes/2002/0610/064.html; Bashir, M. (2006, January 30). Walt Pavlo: *The visiting fellow of fraud.* ABC News. http://abcnews.go.com/Nightline/Business/story?id=1557957.

39. http://www.peaceworks.com/aboutUs/index.html.

40. http://money.cnn.com/magazines/fortune/bestcompanies/2007/snapshots/12.html; http://www.davidweekleyhomes.com/Site/SubPage.aspx?UID=3bc2e249-2b54-42af-ab52-3c36e41c3bba (accessed March 8, 2008).

41. Buford, B. (1994). *Half-time: Changing your game plan from success to significance.* Grand Rapids, MI: Zondervan.

42. For research that is consistent with managers being especially open to change at the beginning, middle, and end of their careers, see Dyck, B. (1995). Transformational change and organizational half-lives. In W. A. Pasmore & R. W. Woodman (Eds.), *Research in organizational change and development* (Vol. 8, pp. 145–180). Greenwich, CT: JAI Press.

43. Campion, M. A., Medsker, G. J., & Higgs, A. C. (1993). Relations between work group characteristics and effectiveness: Implications for designing effective work groups. *Personnel Psychology, 46,* 823–850; Jung, D. I., Sosik, J. J., & Baik, K. B. (2002). Investigating work group characteristics and performance over time: A replication and cross-cultural extension. *Group Dynamics: Theory, Research, & Practice, 6,* 153–171.

44. Bashir, 2006.

45. Wright, P. M., George, J. M., Farnsworth, S. R., & McMahan, G. C. (1993). Productivity and extra-role behavior: The effects of goals and incentives on spontaneous helping. *Journal of Applied Psychology, 78*(3), 374–381.

46. Paine, J. B., & Organ, D. W. (2000). The cultural matrix of organizational citizenship behavior: Some preliminary conceptual and empirical observations. *Human Resource Management Review, 10*(1), 45–59.

47. Carlson, D. S., & Kacmar, K. M. (2000). Work–family conflict in the organization: Do life role values make a difference? *Journal of Management, 26*(5), 1031–1054.

48. Etzioni, A. (1988). *The moral dimension: Toward a new economics.* New York: Free Press.

49. For more information about ORC Industries, see www.orcind.com.

50. Kaplan, R. S., & Norton, D. P. (1996). *The Balanced Scorecard: Translating strategy into action.* Boston: Harvard University Press.

51. For an example, see Matsui, T., Kakuyama, T., & Onglatoco, M. L. U. (1987). Effects of goals and feedback on performance in groups. *Journal of Applied Psychology, 3,* 407–415.

52. Viswesvaran, C., & Ones, D. S. (2002). *Journal of Business Ethics, 38*(3), 193–203.

53. See Cooper, C., Dyck, B., & Frohlich, N. (1992). Improving the effectiveness of gainsharing: The role of participation and fairness. *Administrative Science Quarterly, 37,* 471–490.

54. http://money.cnn.com/2006/01/06/news/companies/bestcos_genentech/index.htm.

55. Raths, D. (2006). 100 best corporate citizens for 2006. *Business Ethics Magazine, 20.* http://www.business-ethics.com/BE100_2006.

56. Raths, 2006.

57. http://www.timberland.com/corp/index.jsp?clickid=topnav_corp_txt.

58. http://www.timberland.com/corp/index.jsp?clickid=topnav_corp_txt.

59. Beckett, J. (1998). *Loving Monday: Succeeding in business without selling your soul.* Downers Grove, IL: Intervarsity Press.

60. Locke & Latham, 1990.

61. Yukl, 1998.

62. Spreitzer, G. M., & Quinn, R. E. (2001). *A company of leaders: Five disciplines for unleashing power in your workforce.* University of Michigan Business School Management Series. San Francisco: Jossey-Bass.

63. Spreitzer & Quinn, 2001.

64. http://www.greatplacetowork.com/best/list-bestusa-2005.htm; http://www.griffinhealth.org/ (accessed August 8, 2007).

65. Some of the quotes form this case were shared as part of the Association for Spirit at Work's "A First Authors Teleconference Series" (http://www.spiritatwork.org/index.shtml). It was entitled, "We Are Prophets of a Future Not Our Own." Quotes and information were also found in Tischler, L. (2007, December). Kenny Moore Held a Funeral and Everyone Came. *http://www.fastcompany.com/magazine/79/firstperson.html,* and in Monk Works in Good Company. *http://www.cbsnews.com/stories/2007/04/09/sunday/main611253.shtml.* Moore is also coauthor of a wonderful book, *The CEO and the Monk: One Company's Journey to Profit and Purpose* (Hoboken, NJ: John Wiley & Sons, 2004).

CHAPTER 15

Leadership is an important but complicated topic. In fact, it may be the most researched topic in all of the social sciences—but there is still much to learn. In this chapter, we begin by briefly describing different ways to think about leadership in comparison to management. We then consider how studies of leadership have grown from looking at leaders' traits, to looking at leaders' behaviors, to looking at the influence of situations. We will examine these issues first from a Mainstream perspective, and then from a Multistream point of view.

ROAD MAP

THREE WAYS TO UNDERSTAND LEADING

1. Five key leadership traits
- *Desire to lead*
- *Drive*
- *Self-confidence*
- *Honesty and integrity*
- *Intelligence and knowledge*

2. Two key leadership behaviors
- *Support (relationship-oriented)*
- *Direction (task-oriented)*

3. Situational leadership

Need for Support	*Need for Direction*
Low	High
High	High
High	Low
Low	Low

Photo: The leader of a flock of geese flying in a V-formation is easy to spot—it's the one at the front, doing the hard work of creating wind currents that make flying easier for the others. Geese also take turns flying in the lead position, sharing the workload and maintaining the course, resulting in many geese serving as leaders over their thousand-mile migrations.

Leadership

MAINSTREAM APPROACH	⟷	MULTISTREAM APPROACH

For personal gain	For others' gain
To get ahead	To make a difference
"I can do it"	"We can do it"
As an effective *means* to an *end*	As an *end* in and of itself
Narrow focus	Broad holistic focus

Consideration/employee-centered	Socioemotional
Initiate structure/job-centered	Structural

Four styles of leading	**Four styles of leading**
Directing Improve immediate productivity	*Enabling* Improve learning capability
Coaching Address weaknesses/develop capability	*Equipping* Develop strengths and creativity
Supporting Sustain high productivity	*Engaging* Enhance meaning
Delegating Facilitate efficient division of labor	*Empowering* Facilitate ownership and responsiveness

The Power of Joy at Work: "Bakke Ball" at AES[1]

AES is one of the largest energy companies in the world, but few people know about the powerful leadership vision that has guided it since its start-up. Former CEO Dennis Bakke is a driven, determined, self-confident leader who doesn't play by the rules. That isn't to say that he lacks honesty and integrity; in fact, Bakke has those virtues in spades. Rather, it means that he marches to the beat of a different drum. He and cofounder Roger Sant started AES with a simple leadership philosophy: (1) People should be trusted and (2) businesses exist to serve, not to make money. Do not call employees "human resources" in front of Bakke: He values the dignity and uniqueness of people far too much to lump them in with other resources such as fuel or capital, or to consider them as mere means to an end. Moreover, in Bakke's view, work should be fun for all employees, and leaders should focus on ensuring that together they live up to shared values that are worth pursuing. This outcome is far more important to Bakke than merely making money.

It is not that AES doesn't make money. In fact, the company is the largest provider of electricity in the world. Revenues and profits have been impressive since the inception of AES in 1981. Within two decades after its launch, it had grown to 40,000 employees in more than 100 plants in 31 countries with revenues of $8.6 billion annually. Nonetheless, profits are not the ultimate measure of success at AES.

Bakke likes to tell the story of how "the U.S. government thought it was very risky to attempt to operate a business with integrity, fairness, social responsibility, and a sense of fun." Bakke was describing the 1990 review of documentation that AES had submitted to the Securities and Exchange Commission when AES sought to become a publicly traded company. That documentation made it clear that AES was not a typical profit-maximizing corporation:

> An important element of AES is its commitment to four major "shared" values: to act with integrity, to be fair, to have fun, and to be socially responsible. AES believes that

earning a fair profit is an important result of providing a quality product for its customers. However, if the Company perceives a conflict between these values and profits, the Company will try to adhere to its values—even though doing so might result in diminished profits or forgone opportunities. Moreover, the Company seeks to adhere to these values not as a means to achieve economic success, but because adherence is a worthwhile goal in and of itself. The Company intends to continue these policies after this offering.

Bakke, who has since retired from his position, led an organization that embodied the principles of empowerment. During his tenure as CEO, the AES hierarchy was limited to no more than two levels between the frontline employees and top management. In this structure, employees were required to make important decisions about their work and the organization, but could do so only after seeking the advice of others throughout the organization. In one example of empowerment in action, Bakke advised a team leader to bid $170 million for two coal plants; ultimately, after seeking advice from other team members across the world, the team leader bid $143 million and won the bid. That is not to say that every decision at AES resulted in a happy ending; yet, employees were not fired for bad outcomes, though some were fired if they did not live up to the expected process of seeking advice from others. This level of empowerment may seem extreme to some, but it is part of what might be called "Bakke ball"—a work environment where almost anyone might be counted on to figuratively take the winning shot at the end of a basketball game. This process of fully engaging your reason and values to make decisions is Bakke's idea of fun. Others within AES must have agreed, given the very low turnover rate during his time as their leader.

It might appear to a distant observer that laying someone off is inconsistent with values that emphasize employee empowerment, social responsibility, and fun. Bakke thinks otherwise: "One of the least socially re-

Bakke believes that a rubber band ball is a picture of AES: A group of diverse people from around the globe who are stretched and bound together to serve the world.

sponsible things in the world is to have one extra person working when they're not needed. In other words, an unproductive person." He believes that laying someone off, or even firing a person, may be necessary to value fairness, but notes that it can be done compassionately to ensure that the employee can take care of personal or family needs while searching for a productive role in society. For example, team members offered a severance package of five years to a displaced employee in India, which was at least 20 times the normal length of typical severance plans in that country. Supporting decisions such as this can be costly, but it is consistent with Bakke's view that the principal concern of leaders should be affirming and perpetuating the organization's values.

LEADERSHIP AND MANAGEMENT

Perhaps no topic in management has been studied as much as leadership, and possibly no other area of management evokes such strong and diverse opinions. Leadership is clearly a complex concept with great importance for organizations. Recall that for scholars such as Henri Fayol, "leading" is one of the four functions of management (alongside planning, organizing, and controlling). From this point of view, leading is a subset of a manager's activities.

A competing view suggests that *leading* and *managing* are distinctly different functions, sometimes performed by different organizational members. Sometimes this idea is stated directly; at other times this distinction is cloaked in leadership language. For example, leaders have been classified as either transactional or transformational.[2]

Transactional leaders, sometimes equated with managers, focus on fair exchanges with organizational members to motivate achieving established goals. They clarify role or task requirements, set up structures, provide appropriate rewards, and try to be considerate to the needs of subordinates. They take pride in keeping things running smoothly and efficiently, have a sense of commitment to the organization, and encourage conformity to organizational norms and values.

> **Transactional leaders** focus on fair exchanges with organizational members to motivate them to achieve established goals.

Transformational leaders, sometimes differentiated from mere managers, focus on inspiring change in members and the organization. They inspire and arouse others to unite in seeking extraordinary performance accomplishments. These leaders take pride in challenging the status quo and stimulating change in their organization's mission, strategy, structure, and culture.

> **Transformational leaders** focus on inspiring change in members and the organization.

There are four major ways that transformational leaders go about making change in subordinates and the organization:[3]

- Transformational leaders identify with followers, creating personal loyalty.
- They motivate employees to transcend individual goals for the sake of a team or organization by articulating a clear vision.
- They pay personal attention to followers' needs by supporting and encouraging followers in their attempts to work toward the vision.
- Transformational leaders challenge followers to be innovative, model new behaviors, and exhibit a high moral standard in their actions.

Ken Chenault, CEO of American Express since 2001, is a transformational leader. In the post–September 11 turbulence of the travel industry, Chenault was able to draw upon his reputation as a gentleman, innovator, and problem solver to communicate a credible message to his employees. He talked about how the company had reinvented itself and emerged from past crises stronger, and he assured members of his organization that this crisis also would make them better. Chenault delivered this message in person to employees in New York one week after the attack. He presented a realistic road map that acknowledged current challenges and difficult decisions (e.g., reductions in staff), but offered hope for the future. Chenault's transformational leadership galvanized members of the organization and prepared them for the subsequent three years of solid growth.[4]

Distinctions between management and leadership have some merit, but taking this approach tends to make management the punching bag for criticism: "We need more leaders, not more managers." We might need more managers who are better leaders, but it is doubtful that organizations don't need managers! For the purposes of this textbook, leading will be seen as a subset of management. **Leadership** is the process of influencing others so that their work efforts lead to the achievement of organizational goals. As with all of the functions of management, sometimes it is not the formal "manager" who does all of the leading within a work unit. There are likely many informal leaders and, as we shall discuss, different "substitutes" that can lower the need or opportunity for a manager to perform the leading function. In the following sections, we explore the traits, behaviors, and situational characteristics related to leadership, first from a Mainstream approach and then from a Multistream approach.

MAINSTREAM LEADERSHIP

Leadership Traits

Traits are personal characteristics that are relatively stable. The study of leader traits was the initial focus of early leadership research, in which scholars sought to identify characteristics that differentiate leaders from nonleaders. The goal was to analyze great leaders, find out what made them great, and then use those traits that they held in common to identify future leaders. Unfortunately, early research generally found a weak relationship between personal traits and leader success. That is, for every set of leaders who possessed a common trait, a long list of exceptions was also found.

Over the years, instead of finding traits that were *always* present within a leader, many traits were found that were *likely, but not certain, to be associated with* leadership. The traits most commonly associated with effective leadership include these:

- The desire to lead
- Drive
- Self-confidence
- Honesty and integrity
- Intelligence and job-relevant knowledge[5]

For example, Mainstream leaders are likely to enjoy having influence over others (desire to lead), demonstrate a strong ambition to get ahead (drive), believe in their abilities to achieve organizational goals (self-confidence), recognize the value of being truthful and keeping their word (honesty and integrity), and have excellent conceptual skills for understanding how the organizational structures and systems work together to achieve overall goals (intelligence and knowledge). Recently, the general personality traits of extraversion, conscientiousness, and openness to experience also were found to be related to who becomes the leader within a group and the performance ratings of leaders.[6]

Leadership is the process managers use to influence others so that their work efforts lead to the achievement of organizational goals.

Traits are personal characteristics that remain relatively stable.

Are Leaders Born or Made?

S. Truett Cathy, CEO of Chick-fil-A restaurants, has led the company he founded to an impressive position as the second largest quick-service chicken restaurant chain in the United States. Under his leadership, Chick-fil-A introduced the first boneless chicken sandwich and pioneered restaurants in shopping malls.[7]

At an early age, Cathy demonstrated a clear drive to succeed. At age eight, he began selling Cokes and magazine subscriptions door-to-door despite a speech impediment so severe he often could not pronounce his own name. Cathy's story might be used to support the argument that leaders are born, not made, because of his initiative in business at the early age of eight. Alternatively, Cathy's story might be used to support the argument that leaders are made, not born, because he worked hard from an early age to overcome communication difficulties that he was born with.

Consider leaders whom you know or are familiar with. Are they born leaders, or were they made leaders through learning and life experience?

Charisma is one trait commonly thought to make great leaders. **Charisma** refers to a special trait or "gift" that some leaders have to attract and inspire others. Charismatic leaders exude enthusiasm and self-confidence that influence people and establish an interpersonal connection. A charismatic leader has the ability to motivate people to do more than they normally do, especially in the face of obstacles and personal sacrifice. Typically, these leaders are visionaries who persuasively communicate their vision, demonstrate a willingness to take risks to achieve their vision, are sensitive to how their vision meets follower needs, and display extraordinary behavior in pursuit of their vision. In many ways, this behavior is similar to what was described earlier as the behavior of transformational leaders. If there is a difference between the two, it may be that a charismatic leader's influence tends to be tied to the strength or force of his or her personality or traits. Richard Branson, the founder of Virgin Records, is one example of a charismatic leader who—through the power of his personality and his ability to communicate a compelling vision—has led others to take risks to achieve great successes in the airline and wireless industries (Virgin Airlines and Virgin Mobile, respectively).

Despite the popularity of charismatic leadership ideas, there are lingering ethical issues regarding this form of leadership.[9] Notorious leaders such as Hitler have used their personal charisma to encourage followers to engage in behavior that the followers might otherwise have rejected. In business, former CEOs Bernie Ebbers of WorldCom and Jeffrey Skilling of Enron also have been described as charismatic personalities. Under Ebbers's leadership, WorldCom was forced into bankruptcy after it defrauded investors. Under Skilling's leadership, Enron collapsed under the weight of its culture of greed and fraud. Both Ebbers and Skilling were sentenced to prison for the broad-based unethical behavior that occurred within their organizations during their reigns as CEO.

Charisma is a personal trait or "gift" related to attracting and inspiring followers.

Richard Branson has turned his charismatic personality toward selling trips into space. Inspiring employees and customers to go where no man—or at least few people—have gone before, Branson launched Virgin Galactic with the dream of bringing space travel to the public.[8]

Whereas possessing certain traits makes it more likely that an individual will emerge as a leader and be successful in accomplishing organizational goals, this outcome is not guaranteed. Some effective leaders do not possess all of these traits, and some leaders who do possess them are not effective in their leadership roles. Clearly, traits alone are not sufficient for explaining the emergence of and influence exerted by leaders. Nonetheless, traits that are more stable, such as intelligence, can be used as a source of information in decisions regarding who to hire or promote into leadership positions. Traits are not appropriate as targets that "need improvement," however. Conversely, characteristics that can be learned or developed, such as behaviors, are more appropriate as targets for development than traits. Reflecting this perception, in the middle part of the twentieth century, researchers shifted their focus to behavioral styles and examined whether there is something unique about what the best leaders *do*.

Leadership Behavior

Behaviors are the ways or manner in which people act.

The move from trait theory to behavioral theory shifts the attention from who leaders *are* to what leaders *do*. **Behaviors** are the ways or manner in which people act. If some leader behaviors are associated with highly productive workers, then any leader could potentially maximize worker productivity simply by adopting the correct behavior through appropriate training.

Consideration is a category of behaviors that are supportive, relational, and/or employee oriented.

DIMENSIONS OF LEADERSHIP BEHAVIOR.   Important research studies on leadership behavior were conducted at Ohio State University and the University of Michigan in the 1940s and 1950s. It was hoped that the focus on behavior would provide better answers about the nature of leadership.

The initial findings from the Ohio State studies identified two general dimensions of leadership behavior: consideration and initiating structure.[10] In these studies, the two dimensions were found to be separate (that is, independent) of each other. This contrasted with earlier conceptions of leadership, where relationship-oriented and task-oriented behaviors were seen as being opposite ends of the same continuum.

Consideration is a category of behaviors that are supportive, relational, and/or employee oriented. Mainstream leaders engage in consideration behavior when they show concern for subordinates and attempt to establish a friendly and supportive climate where job relationships are defined by mutual trust and respect for group members' ideas and feelings. Examples of consideration behavior are listening, showing support, expressing appreciation, and asking for input. Other terms used to describe consideration include "employee centered," "concern for people," and "relationship oriented."

Initiating structure is a category of behaviors that are directive, structural, and/or task oriented.

Initiating structure is a category of behaviors that are directive, structural, and/or task oriented. Mainstream leaders engage in initiating structure when they take steps to make sure that work gets done, subordinates perform their jobs in an acceptable fashion, and the organization is efficient. Examples of structuring behavior are clarifying roles, explaining tasks, providing direction, and communicating procedures. Other terms used to describe initiating structure include "job centered" and "concern for production."

Teri Robertson, a senior business controller at Nokia, Inc., engages in initiating structure when she assigns and establishes timelines for projects.[11] She also initiates structure when she orients new employees, explains the latest compliance challenges for existing staff, and generates career development plans for employee annual reviews. Robertson demonstrates consideration when she shows an interest in employees' well-being, expresses confidence in their abilities to solve challenging problems, involves them in decision making, and celebrates team achievements.

Consideration and initiating structure are independent leader behaviors. Leaders can rate

- High on both behaviors
- Low on both behaviors
- High on one behavior and low on the other behavior

Research shows that in some cases productivity is enhanced when leaders rate high in both relationship behavior (consideration) and task behavior (initiating structure). In general, however, initiating structure is more strongly related to productivity, whereas consideration is more strongly related to employee satisfaction.[12] Both dimensions have been incorporated into leadership training, including the popular training program known as the Leadership Grid.

LEADERSHIP GRID.   Robert Blake and Jane Mouton developed the **Leadership Grid** (initially known as the Managerial Grid) as a two-dimensional management development framework. The Leadership Grid identifies five leadership styles that combine different degrees of concern for production (initiating structure) and concern for people (consideration). These behaviors are ranked on a scale of 1 (low) to 9 (high). As shown in Figure 15.1, a leader's behavioral style can potentially fall into 81 categories. Among these possibilities, five basic types are emphasized:

- **Impoverished style** (1, 1): characterized by low concern for both people and production. Managers who use this style tend to avoid engagement in the work environment, in hopes of avoiding trouble by "going with the flow." This lack of engagement tends to promote neither a trusting work environment nor high productivity.
- **Country club style** (1, 9): characterized by a high concern for people and a low concern for production. Managers who use this style try to create a secure, comfortable atmosphere of trust with their subordinates based on friendship. This style will generally lead to a very friendly work environment, but not necessarily high productivity.
- **Task management style** (9, 1): characterized by a high concern for production and a low concern for people. Managers who use this style are very directive, tend to emphasize organizational productivity and compliance, and show little regard for employees' personal needs. This style tends to promote performance, but not a trusting work environment.

Leadership Grid identifies different leadership styles based on combinations of consideration and initiating structure.

Impoverished style is characterized by low concern for both people and production; it is a Leadership Grid style.

Country club style is characterized by a high concern for people and a low concern for production; it is a Leadership Grid style.

Task management style is characterized by a high concern for production and a low concern for people; it is a Leadership Grid style.

Figure 15.1   The Leadership Grid

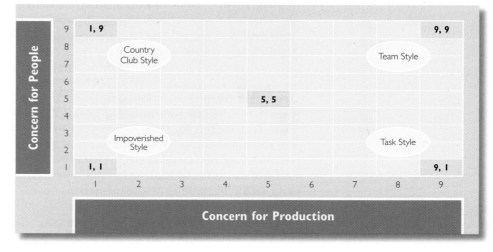

DIGGING DEEPER

Gender and Leadership Behavior

Does gender influence leadership style? This is an important question because although an increasing number of women are becoming managers, women remain underrepresented in management. Male and female managers share many similarities. Nevertheless, research indicates that women managers tend to be significantly more participative and more considerate and nurturing, whereas male managers tend to make decisions more independently and be more assertive in leading.[13] Some research even points to behavioral differences in how men and women communicate. In *The Power of Talk*, linguist Debora Tannen argues that women use language that is more inclusive and participative, going so far as to frame opinions as questions and assertions as suggestions.[14] Whereas in the past this tendency may have been perceived as a weakness, a leadership style that places a greater emphasis on shared power, communication, cooperation, and participation seems to be an excellent fit with the demands of a diverse workforce and team-oriented environments.

In addition, some research points to men as generally leading others in a more compartmentalized and job-oriented manner that is less holistic than the leadership style demonstrated by women. Whereas this approach may aid men in focusing on the task at hand, women may be more aware of the personal concerns of employees and customers that may affect long-term performance or satisfaction. For example, given the personal challenges she faces in balancing her work and family responsibilities, Lynn Palmer, CEO of MedTrials, looks at employee and customer issues holistically, recognizing the interaction of work and family pressures.[15]

Of course, no one style of leadership is best for all situations. The most appropriate leadership style depends on the situation. Just because men and women may have somewhat different leadership styles, it should not be assumed that one gender is preferable to the other or that men and women should be held to different standards to receive leadership positions. Both male and female managers can be equally effective as leaders. Gender differences simply point to behavioral tendencies that may influence their approach to leadership.

Middle-of-the-road management style is characterized by both relational and task behaviors in an insufficient or underdeveloped manner; it is a Leadership Grid style.

Team style is characterized by both high levels of concern for people and production; it is a Leadership Grid style.

- **Middle-of-the-road management style** (5, 5): characterized by both relational and task behaviors in either an insufficient or underdeveloped manner. This style tends to result in adequate organizational performance, but falls short of producing high levels of commitment or achievement.

- **Team style** (9, 9): characterized by high levels of concern for both people and production. Managers who use this style emphasize common productivity goals and use participative or team-oriented processes that value individuals' opinions and concerns. This style tends to yield both high levels of productivity and feelings of commitment and trust.

Training associated with the Leadership Grid typically involves having managers participate in a series of leaderless group activities and stressful interactions. Over the course of several interactions, it is believed that a manager's "real" leadership style will become evident. After a manager's style has been identified, behavioral training is provided to move the manager toward the optimal *team* style.

According to Blake and Mouton, managers are thought to perform best when using the team management style (9, 9). However, most researchers and managers agree that leading is more complex than suggested by this relatively simple approach. An unlimited number of personal and situational factors interact to determine why leaders lead the way they do and why followers respond in the ways they do. One interesting issue is that of how gender influences leadership behavior, as discussed in the "Digging Deeper" feature.

Just as studies of leadership *traits* were incomplete in their explanation of leadership, so too did studies of leadership *behaviors* fall short of providing a full explanation of this process. These studies were not sufficient to answer the question of what constitutes effective leadership. Taking up where they left off, the next stream of leadership research examined the impact of different leadership styles in different situations.

Situational Leadership

According to contingency models of leadership, the *situation* determines which leadership style is most effective at maximizing productivity. Given the wide variety of situations in which leadership occurs, an effective leadership style in one situation will not necessarily work in another situation. For example, a directive style is well suited to the demands of an army general, but it is not likely to fit well with the demands of a university president. However, it is possible for a person to perform well as a general and then as a university president; such was the case with Dwight Eisenhower before he was elected president of the United States. A task-oriented style of leading new hospital nurses might be ineffective in leading seasoned financial planners. The goal of contingency theories is to identify key situational factors that help to determine which leader behavior best meets organizational goals.

Several contingency models explaining the relationship between leadership styles and specific situations have been developed. Among the most influential are these three models:

- Fiedler's contingency theory
- House's path–goal theory
- Hersey and Blanchard's situational leadership theory

FIEDLER'S CONTINGENCY THEORY.   Fred Fiedler's theory of leadership was based on the premise that effective leadership depends on a match between leadership style and situational demands. At the heart of his theory is the assumption that a leader's style is predominantly either *relationship oriented* or *task oriented* and that this style is *fixed*. This idea suggests that a leader will need to seek out or be assigned positions that fit his or her style.

Fiedler examined three basic situational "contingencies" that he thought would help determine the best type of leader for a given situation:[16]

- *Leader–member relations:* the nature of the relationship between the leader and the work group. In other words, do followers have trust or respect for their leader?
- *Task structure:* the degree to which tasks performed by subordinates are well defined, formalized, and standardized. In other words, do followers know what needs to be accomplished and how to go about doing it?
- *Position power:* the degree of legitimate and reward power vested in the leader's position. In other words, does a leader have the power to assign work and to reward and punish employees?

Figure 15.2   Summary of Fiedler's situational contingencies

As indicated in Figure 15.2, the three situational contingencies can be used to measure how "favorable" a specific situation is for leaders. In general, Fiedler's theory suggests the following:

- When situational contingencies are either very favorable or very unfavorable, a task-oriented leader will be most successful.
- When situational contingencies are moderately favorable, a relationship-oriented leader will be most successful.

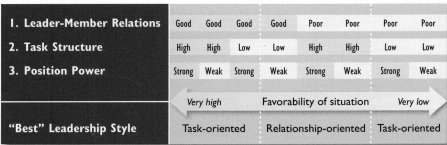

1. Leader-Member Relations	Good	Good	Good	Good	Poor	Poor	Poor	Poor
2. Task Structure	High	High	Low	Low	High	High	Low	Low
3. Position Power	Strong	Weak	Strong	Weak	Strong	Weak	Strong	Weak
	Very high		Favorability of situation				Very low	
"Best" Leadership Style	Task-oriented			Relationship-oriented			Task-oriented	

First Break All the Rules; Now, Discover Your Strengths; The One Thing You Need to Know . . . About Great Managing, Great Leading, and Sustained Individual Success; and other books promote the important idea of knowing your personal strengths and working in areas where they will help you succeed.

Fiedler's results were important because they highlighted the impact of situational factors on leadership effectiveness. Later, his specific model came under criticism from other researchers, and it has since failed to receive adequate research support. Fiedler's assumption of fixed management styles also has been rejected by many researchers. Nonetheless, the idea of identifying and working in your areas of strength has considerable merit. In their popular book *First Break All the Rules*, Buckingham and Coffman offer convincing evidence based on extensive data collected by the Gallup Organization that working in your areas of strength has many benefits.[17] This finding has implications for which type of leader should be assigned to manage specific work groups to optimize goal attainment. For example, if an organizational change requires a manager to cut costs and change well-liked structures or systems, a task-oriented leader may be best suited for this job. Conversely, if organizational change requires a manager to get input from workers, a relationship-oriented leader may be best suited to the task.

HOUSE'S PATH–GOAL THEORY.   One of the most-respected leadership theories among researchers is path–goal theory. Developed by Robert House, it focuses on what leaders can do to motivate and align their subordinates' or followers' behavior to achieve organizational goals.[18] The leader's behavior is motivational to the extent that he or she is successful in clarifying the *path* to subordinates' payoffs, making the path easier to travel by providing support and reducing roadblocks, and ensuring that subordinates are rewarded for performance that results in *goal* attainment.

In path–goal theory, a leader's behavior is considered *acceptable* to a follower to the degree that it satisfies a follower's needs. What a follower needs depends on two factors: characteristics of the follower and characteristics of the workplace. House identifies four leadership styles that may be used in this path–goal sense:

- *Directive leadership* occurs when the leader tells subordinates exactly what is expected of them. This includes giving guidance, setting goals, and scheduling work. This kind of behavior is similar to the initiating structure leadership style. *Directive behaviors* are advisable when job assignments are unclear and followers need to know how the reward structures work.

- *Supportive leadership* involves leader behavior that shows concern for subordinates' well-being and personal needs. It means treating subordinates as equals and being friendly and approachable. This kind of behavior is similar to consideration leadership behavior. *Supportive behaviors* are advisable when followers are experiencing a high level of stress or anxiety, or when their jobs are boring or tedious.

- *Participative leadership* means that leaders consult with their subordinates about decisions. Leaders meet with subordinates in their workplace setting to encourage group discussion and hear suggestions. *Participative behaviors* may increase motivation when subordinates' support of a decision is required or when their self-confidence needs a boost.

- *Achievement-oriented leadership* occurs when leaders set clear and challenging goals for subordinates. Leaders show confidence in subordinates' abilities and expect them to perform at high levels. *Achievement-oriented behaviors* can motivate highly capable employees who are bored from having too few challenges and who would thrive if given new responsibilities and decision-making authority.

Although path–goal theory focuses on only a few prominent situational factors, it acknowledges that a vast number of situational factors influence whether a particular leadership behavior is appropriate. In one example of related research that was more narrowly focused on participative decision making, Vroom and colleagues described 12 situational factors—ranging from decision importance to time constraints—that a leader should consider in determining the appropriate level of follower participation in a particular decision.[19]

According to path–goal theory, managers should use leadership styles that complement the situational needs. In other words, the leader adds value by contributing things that are missing from the situation or need strengthening. In contrast to Fiedler's view that leaders cannot change their behavior, path–goal theory assumes that leaders are flexible and can display any or all of these leadership styles as needed. Most research evidence supports the logic underlying this theory—namely, that employee performance and satisfaction are likely to be positively influenced when the leader adjusts to situational factors related to the employee and the work setting.[20] Because personal and environmental characteristics are always changing, House's intention was to develop a contingency theory of leadership that is dynamic and responds to ongoing research and practice.

HERSEY–BLANCHARD SITUATIONAL LEADERSHIP THEORY. Paul Hersey and Ken Blanchard developed a leadership theory that continues to receive strong support from practitioners. More so than previous theories, their approach focuses a great deal of attention on the characteristics of followers in determining appropriate leadership behavior. In fact, according to an article in *Harvard Business Review*, "What Great Managers Do" is understand and adapt to the uniqueness of individual followers.[21]

In their original model, Hersey and Blanchard argued that leaders can and should adjust their style of leadership depending on the maturity or "readiness" of the follower to perform in a given situation. "Readiness" was based on how (1) able and (2) willing or confident followers are to perform required tasks. Organizational members have varying degrees of readiness, depending on their maturity, expertise, and experience in relation to the specific tasks that they undertake.

After extensive experience using Situational Leadership with business leaders, Blanchard modified the original model. His **Situational Leadership II** model describes four leadership situations and the appropriate leadership styles based on the "developmental level" of employees or followers (instead of "readiness"). Development level includes two components:

- Competence (instead of "ability")
- Commitment (instead of "willingness")[22]

Situational Leadership II
describes four leadership situations and the appropriate leadership styles based on the "developmental level" of followers.

As depicted in Figure 15.3, the Situational Leadership II model serves as a framework to combine aspects of other contingency and behavioral theories. The arrows represent the idea that in the workplace as employees develop, their needs change. As these needs change, the most appropriate leadership style to manage employees also changes.

Directing involves instructing a follower on how to do a task or job; it is a Situational Leadership II style.

- A **directing** style is appropriate when organizational members lack technical knowledge, yet are enthusiastically committed to learning the new task or position. This might be the case, for example, when a new, enthusiastic, but untrained employee joins a department. In response, the leader defines roles and tells the new employee what, how, when, and where to do various tasks. Specific task directions are given in this high-direction, low-support style.

Coaching involves providing training and specific feedback for a task or job; it is a Situational Leadership II style.

- A **coaching** style is appropriate when organizational members lack technical knowledge, but their motivation or commitment is waning. For example, consider the new employee, faced with a long training period or adjustment to an organizational change, who begins to lose heart. In response, the leader uses a high-direction, high-support style that could be described as a hands-on approach to providing task directions and feedback in a supportive and convincing way.

Supporting involves expressing confidence in the follower's abilities and sharing decision-making authority; it is a Situational Leadership II style.

- A **supporting** style is appropriate when organizational members have the competence necessary to perform the job, but are uncertain or lack confidence in their ability to perform. For example, an employee who has been micro-managed or led by a dictatorial leader may have the skills but not the confidence to take on more responsibilities and act independently. In response, the leader encourages this person through expressing confidence in the employee's abilities, offering praise or recognition, and sharing decision-making authority in this low-direction, high-support style.

Delegating involves assigning tasks and responsibilities; it is a Situational Leadership II style.

- A **delegating** style is appropriate when organizational members have the appropriate job-related competence and are highly committed to perform independently. For example, this style might be appropriate for an employee with a lot of experience, skills, and loyalty. In response, the leader provides little direction or support, allowing this person to make and take responsibility for task decisions in this low-direction, low-support style.

Figure 15.3   Four basic Mainstream leadership styles

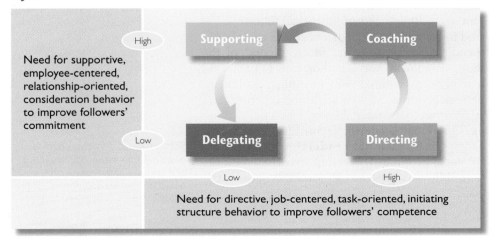

Need for supportive, employee-centered, relationship-oriented, consideration behavior to improve followers' commitment

Need for directive, job-centered, task-oriented, initiating structure behavior to improve followers' competence

Managers using a Situational Leadership II model must be able to implement the alternative leadership styles as needed on a case-by-case basis. As a leader helps followers to become more independent, leadership style also needs to adapt. During times of organizational change, leaders may need to revert back to earlier styles with some employees or followers.

For example, Brian Wharton, a UPS Store operator in Dallas, uses different styles with his employees depending on their developmental level. When interacting with new employees, he tells them the exact steps involved in the process of accepting a package and sending it out the door (*directing*). Later, as employees struggle through the learning process, Wharton continues to provide specific and detailed *coaching* to ensure that employees understand the nuances of packaging and labeling according to the UPS system but does so in a highly encouraging manner. As employees grow in competence and yet still lack confidence, he shifts to a *supporting* style that affirms their competence and encourages more independence. Ultimately, Wharton hopes to move each employee to a level of competence and commitment that will allow each employee to accept his *delegation* of most tasks and responsibilities.

An important strength of Situational Leadership II is that it builds upon previous leadership theories. It can be used to summarize behavioral and contingency theories and to build an integrated model of Mainstream theory:

- From a behavioral perspective, a leader's style can be described as a combination of supportive (relational) and directive (task-oriented) behaviors.
- The appropriate or best-fitting leadership style depends on contingencies, particularly a member's or follower's competence and commitment.

Despite its popularity and intuitive appeal, research on Situational Leadership models has not been as supportive as expected; in part this is due to the complexity of testing the models as well as failures to account for other factors that affect the situation.[23] Additional factors that may be considered in deciding the appropriate set of leadership behaviors include task structure, goal clarity, alignment of rewards, quality of relationships, cultural context, and time. Some of these factors can be considered substitutes for leadership and are discussed in the "Digging Deeper" feature.

The integrated model of Mainstream theory (combining behavior and contingencies) has theoretical value in explaining how leadership should work given certain assumptions and conditions. Even so, it is often difficult for managers to apply what they have learned and to use the appropriate style for the situation. Perhaps this challenge arises because managers can be so preoccupied with their own agenda and organizational goals that they become insensitive to the full range of needs important to their followers. For example, Ken Blanchard notes that a vast majority of managers respond enthusiastically when they learn about his techniques and tools, but a much smaller number of managers actually apply them appropriately over time. Why do leaders fail to adopt the style appropriate to the situation? Blanchard believes the determining factor is whether the leader is truly committed to serving others. This difference lies at the heart of Multistream leadership.

MULTISTREAM LEADERSHIP

Similar to the Mainstream perspective, a Multistream approach to leadership can be explained by discussing traits, behaviors, and contingencies. As illustrated in the opening case, Multistream leaders do not place their primary focus on *maximizing* productivity, profitability, or material success. Instead, the Multistream approach elevates other success criteria, such as employee well-being and social responsibility, to equal or higher status. This does not mean that a Multistream approach is not concerned with financial viability—just that financial concerns are not the *primary* focus. S. Truett Cathy, the founder of Chick-fil-A, has insisted since the inception of his restaurants that they remain closed on Sunday. Despite the advice of industry experts, he has remained true to this priority of enhancing his employees' well-being rather than pursuing more

DIGGING DEEPER

Do We Really Need Leaders?

Does a leader always need to be the source of all task direction and relational support? Not necessarily. Substitutes-for-leadership theory argues that characteristics of the task and work environment may

- Substitute for the influence of leaders,
- Neutralize the influence of leaders, or
- Enhance the influence of leaders.[24]

Specifically, when a task is highly structured or highly formalized according to specific policies and procedural rules, the leader does not need to provide as much direction. Similarly, in highly cohesive teams or when followers perform work that they find intrinsically interesting, the leader does not need to provide as much socioemotional support. For example, Teri Robertson, from Nokia, may not need to provide specific task direction about new compliance rules when the procedures are spelled out clearly in legal documents. Likewise, Brian Wharton, from the UPS Store, may not need to be as attentive to the relational needs of his staff if they are a close-knit work group. This is not to suggest that leaders are not necessary, but rather that the need for specific leadership behaviors may be reduced in certain situations.[25]

Sometimes leadership behavior becomes irrelevant or is hindered because the task or the work environment neutralizes the influence of a leader. Examples of "neutralizers" include a chronic indifference on the part of the follower, a low position power for the leader, and a dispersed work environment. This suggests that project managers in matrix organizations, where employees have multiple bosses, may find that their normal leadership behavior is ineffective. In other situations, the impact of certain behaviors may be increased by situational factors. For example, a leader's team-oriented behavior is particularly likely to enhance productivity in collectivistic or group-oriented cultures.[26]

Substitutes-for-leadership theory provides a helpful reminder that the effectiveness of leadership is often influenced by factors beyond follower characteristics and behaviors of the leader. Managers must find the right mix of behaviors—in some cases refraining from behaviors that might be counterproductive or a waste of effort—to focus leadership energy in other places. For example, if directions for a specific task (such as how to work a cash register) are clearly spelled out in documents, then task-oriented leadership behavior can be concentrated on areas (such as how to respond to angry customers) where the ideal behavior is not as straightforward. In practice, an awareness of possible leadership substitutes can help managers diagnose followers' needs and adapt their leadership behavior to help followers perform well in a variety of work settings.

---

profits. Nonetheless, in many markets his restaurants outsell its competitors that are open seven days a week, and Chick-fil-A has grown into a billion-dollar business.

Servant Leadership

Servant leadership is an active approach to leadership that promotes the interests of others over the leader's own interests.

The idea of servant leadership lies at the center of what distinguishes Multistream leaders from their Mainstream counterparts. **Servant leadership** is an active approach to leadership that promotes the interests of others. According to Robert Greenleaf,[27] the essence of servant leadership involves three interrelated components:

- Servant leaders help others to "grow as persons." This focus on *persons* refers to people in relation to others—rather than on *individuals* apart or separated from others—and thus fosters community.

- Servant leaders want others to become "healthier, wiser, freer, more autonomous, [and] more likely to themselves become servants." Multistream leaders model service, treat employees and others with dignity, and encourage them to do likewise.[28]

- Servant leaders have a positive effect on—and certainly not a negative effect on—the stakeholders who are "the least privileged in society." Servant leaders have a special concern for changes that improve the situation for people who are particularly disadvantaged by the status quo, whether those people are within or outside the organization's boundaries.

Although servant leadership is evident in many religious traditions (i.e., Jesus Christ, Confucius, and Gandhi are examples of leaders who emphasized putting the needs of the larger community ahead of their own interests), Greenleaf's concept of a servant leader builds on an example of leadership that he read in Hermann Hesse's novel *Journey to the East*. In this story, a group of travelers enjoy success and good cheer along their journey without taking much notice of a faithful servant, Leo, who does the menial but necessary tasks and encourages the others with his positive spirit and song. Leo is, to a large degree, invisible to the traveling party. After he leaves the party, however, his leadership role becomes obvious to everyone when the group falls into disarray and the journey is forsaken. One of the travelers, after years of wandering aimlessly, meets up with Leo again, only to find out that although Leo had taken on the role of a servant to the travelers, among his own people Leo is recognized as a great and noble leader.

S. Truett Cathy has stayed true to his family values while growing Chick-fil-A into the second largest quick-service chicken restaurant in the United States. Under his leadership, Chick-fil-A introduced the first boneless chicken sandwich, pioneered restaurants in shopping malls, and launched the popular "cows" ads.[30]

As discussed in Chapter 1, Greenleaf practiced servant leadership while a manager at AT&T, where he experimented with Multistream practices that contrasted with the prevailing Mainstream managerial practices. Other managers also have practiced servant leadership in their workplaces. William Pollard, former CEO and chairman of ServiceMaster, is one such leader. Pollard recounts that he learned about servant leadership through the "school of hard knocks."[29] He was recruited to head legal and financial affairs at ServiceMaster, but he almost lost the job in his final interview by pressing for information regarding the possibility of becoming the CEO in the future. Ken Hansen, who was at that time the chairman of ServiceMaster, explained that if Pollard wanted the job because of its prospects for delivering impressive titles and power, then he would be disappointed because at ServiceMaster, leaders have to learn how to put the concerns of others ahead of their own interests. To reinforce this principle, upon accepting the position, Pollard was assigned six weeks of cleaning floors and doing the custodial work that is the core business of ServiceMaster. Pollard believes these early lessons about service to others were critical to shaping his leadership style.

Pollard, perhaps shaped by his experience in the trenches as much as by his own spiritual values, believes that it is immoral to take away an employee's right to make decisions and take action, and that leaders have a moral responsibility to help employees grow and develop their full potential. This use of spiritual language and convictions as a basis for servant leadership is characteristic of some, but not all, Multistream leaders.

Traits of Multistream Leaders

In many ways, the traits that characterize a Multistream leader are similar to those that distinguish a Mainstream leader. However, as summarized in Figure 15.4, these traits are put into practice in Multistream management in a very different way.

Spiritual Leadership[31]

Laura Nash of Harvard University declares that spirituality in the workplace is exploding. **Spirituality** is a state or quality of a heightened sensitivity to one's human or transcendent spirit. At the beginning of the twenty-first century, Gallup pollsters found that 78 percent of surveyed employees felt a need for spiritual growth, which is triple the percentage who voiced this sentiment in the mid-1990s. In their roles as leaders, managers are increasingly faced with a growing sentiment among their employees that it is appropriate, and maybe even necessary, for work to be a place for spiritual growth and expression. Even so, managers who promote the idea of spirituality at work sometimes meet with resistance because they go against some long-standing views about keeping private spiritual beliefs separate from the public workplace. Nonetheless, Jose Zeilstra, a vice-president at Chase Manhattan, argues that "leaders who are guided by spiritual principles should thrive in the new economy" where they no longer need to "flex muscles, drive loyalty, and institutionalize hierarchy," but instead must be able to communicate vision and meaning and be "attuned to people and ideas."

Dick Green, president of the lip-care products manufacturer Blistex, has been wrestling—along with other business leaders in the Chicago area—with the question of how their theology influences their leadership. Among other things, he has arrived at the belief that although his products could be made for lower costs in other locations, he has an obligation to his community to retain local jobs for those who have faithfully worked for the company. Although Green is still learning what it means to integrate spirituality into his leadership, he is convinced that he cannot avoid it. He says, "I don't think I can make business decisions and ignore who I am." David Miller, the Director for the Center of Faith and Culture at Yale University, agrees, "This is about who you are, your being, your character within the organization."

Although promoting spirituality in the workplace may have benefits, a manager should be careful not to inadvertently isolate or suppress the opinions of those who do not share similar views. This may mean accommodating various expressions of faith at work. Of course, spirituality in the workplace is not always related to a specific faith or religious lifestyle. Spirituality at work can be a discussion of what it means to be fully human and alive. For example, in his model of spiritual leadership, scholar Louis Fry uses nonreligious descriptions of vision, faith, hope, and love as means to align values and build commitment.

In the end, encouraging more spiritual expression in organizations, despite its challenges, means acknowledging that the work of people is more than the sum of contributions from their hands, heads, and hearts; it is recognizing that spiritual motivations and values are critical to the overall well-being of the organization and its members.

Spirituality is a state or quality of a heightened sensitivity to one's human or transcendent spirit.

Undoubtedly, Multistream leaders such as Bakke and Cathy have self-confidence, drive, the desire to lead, honesty and integrity, and intelligence and job-relevant knowledge. Yet, their values and motivations compel them to apply these traits to less materialist–individualist causes such as employee well-being and social responsibility.

Greenleaf contends that the greatest leader is a servant first, who aspires to lead for others' sake. This view stands in sharp contrast to the idea of a leader as someone who seeks to maximize his or her own power or to acquire material possessions. For example, when Jimmy Dorrell of Mission Waco champions the cause of the unemployed and initiates projects to encourage economic development in the inner city, he demonstrates a *desire to lead* based on his motivation to serve others. In scholarly terms, this motivation to lead for the sake of serving others is called a "socialized power motive" and contrasts with a "personalized power motive"—that of being driven and desiring to lead for personal gain. Although few people know the academic terms, employees can easily recognize the difference in underlying motives when they see it in their workplaces. Whereas managers with a personalized power motive may get promoted and gain status, often their career stalls or derails as other people resist their self-centered motives and insensitivity toward others.[32]

Multistream leaders also have a sense of *drive*, but it is different than the drive demonstrated by Mainstream leaders. Whereas Mainstream leaders are often propelled by a sense of competitiveness and getting ahead financially, Multistream leaders are driven by a desire to nurture community and foster a variety of forms of well-being. In other words, their drive is not to get ahead, but rather to make a positive difference. For example, Cathy's drive to promote character and education in the community is apparent in Chick-fil-A's sponsorship of educational scholarships for both community members and employees. Even the toys for the kids' meals sold at the restaurants are typically drawn from virtue-based children's stories. Evidence is mounting that a self-centered drive can have short-term benefits, but ultimately destroys the collective capability and morale of a department or organization.[33] In contrast, the research of Jim Collins contrasting good- and great-performing companies indicates that leaders who combine humility with a strong will to succeed—who he calls Level 5 leaders—are critical to the long-term profitability and success of great companies.[34]

Jimmy Dorrell leads Mission Waco in service of three goals: (1) developing relationship-based, holistic programs; (2) providing middle-class volunteers with "hands-on" involvement; and (3) addressing systemic issues that disempower the poor.[35]

The humility and strong will of Multistream leaders also affect their expressions of *self-confidence.* Collins describes the Level 5 leaders from his research as attributing their success to others, rather than to their own abilities or decisions. Their confidence does not come from the attitude that they are somehow better or smarter than others; rather, it is rooted in beliefs about the capability of the members of their organization. Colman Mockler, CEO of Gillette, against the wishes of some investors, resisted the takeover attempts of Revlon and an investment group because he had confidence in the employees of Gillette and believed that their innovative capability was undervalued by prospective buyers.[36] This confidence in the people and collective potential of Gillette led Mockler and his executive team to take their message out to individual investors to block these takeovers. Subsequent innovations by the employees of Gillette resulted in more than a decade of sustained growth and financial success. Of course, not all Multistream managers experience the success that Mockler achieved, but they do exhibit confidence that comes from believing "we can do it." These leaders believe in the potential of collaboration and draw confidence from the power of people working together to solve problems.

For both Mainstream and Multistream leaders, "honesty is the best policy." Nonetheless, managers from the two perspectives may disagree about *why* it is the best policy. Mainstream management can make a strong argument for valuing *honesty and integrity* because they keep the organization out of trouble and enhance the organization's reputation. In Multistream management, honesty and integrity are not merely a means to an end. Leaders are honest and demonstrate integrity not because it is good for business, but because they believe these

Figure 15.4 Personality traits from Mainstream and Multistream perspectives

Trait	Mainstream	Multistream
• Desire to lead	for personal gain	for others' gain
• Drive	to get ahead	to make a difference
• Self-confidence	"I can do it"	"We can do it"
• Honesty and integrity	as an effective *means* to an *end*	as an *end* in and of itself
• Intelligence and knowledge	narrow instrumental focus	broad holistic focus

traits to be good or right regardless of the circumstances. When AES employees falsified reports to the Environmental Protection Agency, Dennis Bakke wrote an open letter to everyone in the company acknowledging the misdeed and committing to redouble efforts to teach company values. He did not try to hide the problems, nor did he take the company lawyer's advice to fire the employees to solve the problem. When the letter became public, AES's share price plummeted, but Bakke had no regrets.

Finally, Multistream leaders score high in terms of *intelligence and job-relevant knowledge*, but their intelligence and knowledge extends beyond the traditional bounds of the organization. Compared to Mainstream leaders, Multistream leaders are more likely to apply their intellect to acquiring knowledge about how their organization affects a wider variety of stakeholders along a wider array of dimensions. They educate themselves broadly regarding the opinions and interests of their stakeholders. For example, at Whole Foods, managers are expected to build connections with and promote the practices of local organic farmers. According to Ram Charan, author of the book *Know How*, this application of intellect to understanding the broader organizational context helps managers avoid emerging threats and seize upon opportunities for growth or innovation.[37]

EMOTIONAL INTELLIGENCE. Everyone seems to know a person who is "book smart" but totally clueless when it comes to emotional and interpersonal skills. **Emotional intelligence (EI)** is the innate or developed ability to recognize, manage, and exercise emotions in relationships. Although EI, as a leadership trait, may lie anywhere along the continuum between Mainstream and Multistream management, it is discussed here due to its other-centered focus and sensitivity to issues other than productivity. EI is generally described as having five components:

- Self-awareness
- Self-management
- Empathy
- Internal motivation
- Social skills

> **Emotional intelligence (EI)** is the innate or developed ability to recognize, manage, and exercise emotions in relationships.

Emotional *self-awareness* is the ability to recognize when emotional responses are triggered and by what. Leaders with self-awareness are in tune with their own emotions and know when to expect them. *Self-management* of emotions is the skill of being able to harness emotions to positively influence interactions with others. In some cases, a leader may need to maintain his or her cool in a conflict, whereas in another situation revealing a certain level of frustration may be useful in emphasizing an idea or point of view. A leader with *empathy* can read nonverbal messages and understand the emotional content of others' communications. As such, he or she has a strong sense of what others are feeling or experiencing. Altogether, a leader with EI is willing (*internal motivation*) and able to translate this knowledge of self and others into behavior (*social skills*) that facilitates commitment and enhances collaborative action.

Sometimes people who lack EI have risen to management positions thanks to their technical expertise or short-term accomplishments. Even so, Daniel Goleman, in his research on leadership, has determined that more than anything else, EI helps explain the success of leaders. In his review of 188 leadership competency models—used by such organizations as British Airlines and Lucent technologies—he found EI to be at least twice as important as intellectual or technical skills in predicting leadership performance.[38] Follow-up research suggests that as much as 79 percent of leadership success in the United States is attributable to EI.[39] In the context of motivating change, the rational approach of stating facts and figures can be ineffective, whereas an emotional appeal can resound deeply and compel action.[40] In addition, EI is suggested to be critical for effective team leadership.[41] Finally, when coupled with cultural awareness, EI is argued to be a crucial factor in determining leadership success working in other cultures.[42]

Of course, intellectual and technical knowledge and skills are necessary for leadership, but those who perform best as leaders excel in demonstrating EI. Even though EI has some basis in personality traits, leaders can improve their emotional intelligence with coaching, feedback, and consistent practice.

Leadership Behavior

Earlier in this chapter, we described Mainstream behavior as being either supportive or directive. Building on this initial distinction, we can describe Multistream behaviors as being either socioemotional or structural. **Socioemotional behaviors** include, but go beyond, supportive behavior to address interpersonal and emotional needs.[43] **Structural behaviors** include, but go beyond, directive behavior to address the structure of the task and work context. From a Mainstream perspective, managers may give either high or low levels of support or direction, depending on their leadership style or the situation. From a Multistream perspective, it is rarely appropriate for managers to provide low levels of socioemotional or structural behavior. The socioemotional and structural behaviors that leaders demonstrate vary not by how often they occur, but by their *transparency* (how visible the behavior is to the person being led). By using "transparency"—instead of the "frequency" of behaviors, as in Mainstream theory—a Multistream approach affirms that leaders' socioemotional behavior varies along a continuum between "visible" and "invisible." and structural behavior varies along a separate continuum between "visible" and "invisible." Socioemotional behavior is visible when the leader offers words of encouragement and empathy, and invisible when without the follower knowing, a leader gives credit for and supports the follower's idea in an upper-management meeting. Similarly, structural behavior is visible when the manager organizes and leads a training session, and invisible when the manager works behind the scenes to provide the resources required for employees to experiment with new ideas.

The examples of the invisibility, yet constancy, of leadership behavior bring to mind the image of Hesse's servant leader Leo. He deliberately chose to work "invisibly" behind the scenes. It was only after Leo had left the group that the importance of his leadership became obvious to others. Of course, Mainstream managers may behave similarly, but there is an underlying difference: Mainstream management implements such initiatives to increase productivity, whereas Multistream management does so to stimulate personal and collective growth and well-being.

Situational Leadership

As shown in Figure 15.5, the four types of Multistream leadership styles are arranged along two dimensions that are similar to the Mainstream dimensions depicted in Figure 15.3. The idea of "appropriate socioemotional behavior" along the vertical dimension refers to both (1) the type of socioemotional behavior that a leader shows to others (behavioral theory) and (2) the type of socioemotional that is

Socioemotional behaviors address interpersonal and emotional needs.

Structural behaviors address the structure of the task and work context.

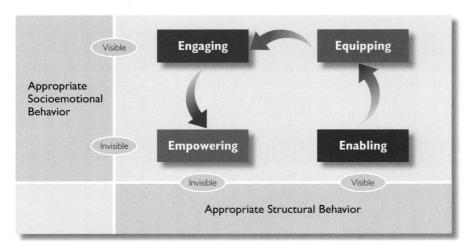

Figure 15.5   Four basic Multistream leadership styles

required by others or appropriate for the situation (contingency theory). Similarly, the idea of "appropriate structural behavior" along the horizontal dimension refers to both (1) the type of structural behavior that a leader initiates (behavioral theory) and (2) the type of structural behavior that is appropriate for the situation (contingency theory).

As summarized in Table 15.1, the four Multistream styles of enabling, equipping, engaging, and empowering run parallel to the four Mainstream styles of directing, coaching, supporting, and delegating, respectively, but differ in their practices and purposes. In addition to being less materialist–individualist than Mainstream management, the Multistream approach is oriented toward growth, mutual gain, and pursuing ideals. Recent theory and research support the assertion that leaders with this emphasis stimulate in followers an eagerness to learn, take risks, and be creative.[44] Furthermore, the servant leader approach of a Multistream manager not only encourages creativity, but also promotes helping behavior—where organizational members go beyond their specific job expectations to listen to others and assist them with their work.[45] These differences are evident in the following descriptions of Multistream leadership styles.

TABLE 15.1

Contrasting and Comparing Mainstream and Multistream Leadership Styles

Need for Support	Need for Direction	Four Styles of Mainstream Leading	Four Styles of Multistream Leading
Low	High	**Directing** Telling followers what their job is and describing how the job or a task is to be completed most efficiently Used when followers lack capability *Goal:* improve immediate productive capability	**Enabling** Emphasizing learning, providing general information, and allowing experimentation without performance pressure Used when followers lack capability *Goal:* improve learning capability
High	High	**Coaching** Providing training and specific feedback Used when followers lack both capability and commitment *Goal:* address weaknesses and develop capability	**Equipping** Creating an environment for continuous learning Used when followers lack both capability and commitment *Goal:* develop strengths and group capability
High	Low	**Supporting** Motivating through praising and extrinsic motivators Used when followers are capable but lack commitment or confidence *Goal:* enhance productivity	**Engaging** Appealing to intrinsic motivators and a sense of community Used when followers are capable but lack commitment or confidence *Goal:* enhance meaning and affiliation
Low	Low	**Delegating** Assigning tasks and responsibilities Used when followers are capable and committed *Goal:* facilitate efficient division of labor	**Empowering** Honoring and freeing others to be responsible Used when followers are capable and committed *Goal:* facilitate ownership and responsiveness

ENABLING.   The focus of Mainstream directing is primarily concerned with immediate improvements in productivity. In contrast, Multistream enabling is primarily concerned with having others learn the necessary skills for long-term performance. **Enabling** is the process of sharing or explaining information related to a job and its context. Multistream managers are *visibly* involved in providing information, guidelines, and structures to facilitate learning but are less apt to emphasize immediate productivity. This approach of emphasizing learning over immediate productivity also is an *invisible* source of socioemotional support, in that it is patient and accepting of the time that learning requires. What leaders emphasize in their words and actions greatly influences whether followers focus on learning or productivity.[46] Although a Multistream approach may take longer for followers to produce output, the focus on learning ultimately contributes to greater adaptability by helping workers to perform well on tasks of increasing complexity and variety.[47]

Darren Avrea and Dave Foster, cofounders of AvreaFoster Marketing, enable new employees by explaining broad expectations for projects or tasks, providing the relevant information regarding available resources and time constraints, and encouraging a variety of approaches to completing the project. This mastery orientation improves in-depth understanding, minimizes productivity-related stress, and fosters long-term performance.[48] In contrast, emphasizing short-term task performance tends to evoke a performance orientation that can lead to superficial learning or learning just enough to reach productivity goals.

EQUIPPING.   The Mainstream coaching style focuses on responding to followers' needs for both direction and support. This coaching approach can have an implicit top-down bias, where the coach acts as the "brains" of the organization, develops the strategies and game plans, and provides the necessary instruction and training. In contrast, Multistream equipping responds to similar needs but with an emphasis on recognizing progress, building on strengths, and learning from one another. **Equipping** involves creating an environment for continuous learning on the job. Typically, in a coaching session progress is acknowledged, but the focus is on providing feedback to address shortcomings or weaknesses in current performance. In contrast, in Multistream equipping, the focus is on what a follower has done well, not on where he or she has struggled. For example, whereas a coaching approach may point out that two of ten skills need improvement, an equipping approach celebrates the eight of ten skills that have been learned.[49] In short, equipping involves offering praise for progress and encouraging continued experimentation and creativity.[50]

A Multistream approach may also include providing specific training and instruction, but equipping places much greater emphasis on an environment of organizational learning rather than top-down coaching. Shortly after assuming his position, Donny Sequin, the chief operating officer (COO) of Scott and White Hospitals, enhanced the organization's training and development offerings and encouraged employees to meet in informal groups to discuss the nuts and bolts of implementing what they were learning. Sequin also sponsored a daylong off-site training session on servant leadership involving community members and Scott and White employees. Ultimately, he partnered with business and community leaders in the surrounding area of central Texas to form an institute that equips others by sharing ideas about servant leadership throughout the community.

As this example demonstrates, Multistream managers are sensitive to creating an environment where opportunities for learning are frequent, even if the learning has little relevance for the specific task that an employee is doing and even if the

Enabling involves sharing or explaining information related to a job and its context.

Equipping involves creating an environment for continuous learning on the job.

source of learning is a not a manager. Whereas the goal of Mainstream coaching is to ensure that followers address areas of weakness or shortcomings in specific areas, the goal of Multistream equipping is to ensure that others are encouraged to build on their successes, try new approaches, and learn transferable and adaptable skills for a range of work challenges.

ENGAGING.   The Mainstream supporting style responds to followers' need for support by offering praise or extrinsic motivators to improve the commitment of followers. In contrast, Multistream engaging focuses on intrinsic motivators that increase employees' self-respect and joy in coming to work because they perceive themselves to be fulfilling a meaningful role as part of a team or group. **Engaging** is the process of encouraging affiliation and enhancing the intrinsic meaningfulness of work.

For example, Ken Melrose,[51] CEO of Minnesota-based Toro, the maker of lawnmowers and snowblowers, used this approach to reverse the decline of Toro in the early 1980s. As part of his remake of the company, he emphasized the values of trust and respect for others, teamwork, and win-win partnerships. Melrose nurtured an organization that encouraged broad participation—something easier said than done given the historical us-versus-them relationship between management and employees in manufacturing. Some Toro employees hesitated to accept the idea that managers truly welcomed their input into decisions. Eventually, consistent efforts to include employees in decisions, to encourage their development, and to share success as a community (e.g., including an employee stock ownership program) yielded the collaborative organization that Melrose envisioned.

Although the Mainstream approach of supporting involves participation, engaging is more than asking for input from others or sharing decision making. Engaging involves addressing the intrinsic motivations of meaning, purpose, and community. It *visibly* affirms employees' worth to the organization by giving them voice and *invisibly* sets up systems and structures that create a sense of shared purpose and community. Melrose, for example, is motivated by his belief that his leadership approach at Toro influences organizational performance as well as the personal lives of his employees by enhancing their self-esteem. In sum, the goal of Mainstream supporting is to enhance productivity, whereas the goal of Multistream engaging is to enhance employees' sense of self-worth and meaningful contribution.

EMPOWERING.   The Mainstream delegating style is similar to the Multistream empowering style in that it acknowledges that followers' needs for support and direction are low. However, Mainstream delegating often has an implicit connotation of managerial control, with specific tasks with specific expectations being assigned with the intention of increasing efficiency through the division of labor. In contrast, Multistream empowering trusts others to make informed decisions and to be wise in carrying out their tasks as they see fit.[52] **Empowering** involves honoring the inherent power and potential in others and freeing them to be responsible. Multistream empowering expects followers to do things differently—and possibly better—than the leader might suggest. A Multistream leader believes that many tasks and roles should be performed by the members who are most knowledgeable about the issues—and that means the frontline employees performing the hands-on work at the lowest organizational levels. This approach requires the Multistream manager to work behind the scenes to champion followers' independence, and to provide resources and decision-making freedom for the empowered employees within the scope of the organization's mission.

Engaging involves encouraging affiliation and enhancing intrinsic motivators.

Empowering involves honoring the inherent power and potential in others and freeing them to be responsible.

Gary Keller, of Keller–Williams Realty—the fastest-growing realty business and one of the largest consumer realtors in the world—believes that he made a profound discovery in his own life when he recognized that agents did not work for him, but rather that *he* worked for *them*. At Keller–Williams, this leadership approach means that employees bear some of the risks and expenses of operating independently, but they also reap a larger portion of the rewards of profit and personal satisfaction. Beyond providing increased autonomy for local agents, Keller has continuously worked to make organizational systems more democratic. For example, the wildly popular employee profit-sharing program was adopted after bringing the issue to a vote among the agents. Although Keller–Williams is privately owned, Keller's empowering style has created an organization in which agents have a significant say in decision making at all levels.[53]

In sum, the goal of Mainstream delegating is to assign tasks and responsibilities to employees to enhance efficiency, whereas the goal of Multistream empowering is to give people decision-making freedom and responsibility to enhance ownership and responsiveness.

C L O S I N G   C A S E

Multistream Leadership at Work in Hawaii

Situated on the North Shore of Oahu, Hawaii, in the Turtle Bay Resort, is a small but popular bar and grill called Lei Lei's. The proprietors and managers, Mike Neubert and Ian Buscher, are examples of Multistream leaders. Although Neubert and Buscher prefer to be *empowering* in their behavior—by freeing experienced employees to decide how to best do their jobs—their approach is also at times enabling, equipping, or engaging. For example, each new employee, regardless of his or her prior experi-

Mike Neubert, center, is pictured with guests who experienced firsthand the "aloha spirit of joyful service" during their visit to Lei Lei's.

ence in the industry, is not given a defined role, but instead begins by doing the "dirty work" of cleaning the Tiki torches. New hires also pitch in to do whatever else needs doing to create an inviting and pleasing customer experi-

ence. During these several weeks or even months of orientation, employees learn through experience the many ways to live out the "aloha spirit of joyful service" that defines the Lei Lei's way of doing business (*enabling*). Gradually, the employee's responsibilities evolve to include more complex tasks that fit his or her strengths—such as cooking or waiting tables—but this on-the-job training occurs in partnership with experienced cooks and wait staff (*equipping*).

Neubert and Buscher use *engaging* behavior when creating a sense of belonging by frequently inviting all employees—cooks, bus persons, hosts, waiters and waitresses—to join in a shared meal after closing most nights. Neubert and Buscher also affirm the worth of their employees by rejecting the typical practice of keeping many of their workers' hours under the legal threshold above which requires benefits such as insurance. Instead, they offer benefits to all employees. Moreover, they pay wages and offer enough hours so that employees at Lei Lei's earn a livable wage that does not require them to take second jobs to make ends meet. Despite their success as owners, Neubert and Buscher maintain a servant leadership approach by working extra hours as cooks or waiters to minimize the burnout of staff who, for example, may have personal issues to manage or a particularly heavy workload on any one day.

Neubert and Buscher take a Multistream approach to leading based on their values, but they also believe that in the long term this approach benefits the business as well. For example, treating their employees with respect and paying them well tend to increase commitment to the organization and reduce turnover. As such, Lei Lei's employees are highly skilled, are highly motivated, and have long-term relationships with customers—all of which contribute to creating a service-oriented restaurant with excellent food that attracts loyal customers. At Lei Lei's, a Multistream approach is good for all the stakeholders.

QUESTIONS FOR DISCUSSION

1. Neubert and Buscher have been offered several opportunities to expand their management responsibilities to other restaurants on the North Shore of Oahu. How might that expansion influence their ability to be servant leaders?

2. Can the management practices at Lei Lei's be easily transferred to other existing restaurants or even other businesses? Explain your answer.

SUMMARY

Management and leading can be seen as mutually exclusive roles, but in this chapter we treat leading as one of the four main functions of management.

Mainstream leadership is characterized by the following traits:

- Enjoying having influence over others (desire to lead)
- Wanting to get ahead (drive)
- Believing in one's ability to achieve organizational goals (self-confidence)
- Recognizing that following the law enhances financial well-being in the long term (honesty and integrity)
- Having expertise and excellent conceptual skills for understanding how an organization's structures and systems work together to achieve its overall goals (intelligence and knowledge)

Mainstream leadership varies according to how frequently leaders exhibit the following two basic kinds of behavior:

- Providing support (i.e., consideration, concern for people)
- Providing direction (i.e., initiating structure and showing concern for the task)

Finally, Mainstream leadership also involves one of four types of leadership style, depending on the situation:

- *Directing* for a member who lacks capability but has commitment
- *Coaching* for a member who lacks capability and lacks commitment
- *Supporting* for a member who has capability but lacks commitment
- *Delegating* for a member who has capability and commitment

Multistream leadership is characterized by the following traits:

- Serving others (desire to lead)
- Making a difference (drive)
- Believing in the noble goals that the leader is pursuing (self-confidence)
- Striving to have virtuous character (honesty and integrity)

- Having a well-developed understanding of how organizational processes and goals interrelate with multiple stakeholders (intelligence and knowledge)

Multistream leadership varies according to how visibly leaders exhibit the following two basic kinds of behavior:

- Providing socioemotional support (i.e., addressing interpersonal and emotional needs)
- Providing structure (i.e., addressing structural needs in the work context)

Finally, Multistream leadership also involves one of four types of leadership style, depending on the situation:

- *Enabling* for a member who lacks capability but has commitment
- *Equipping* for a member who lacks capability and lacks commitment
- *Engaging* for a member who has capability but lacks commitment
- *Empowering* for a member who has capability and commitment

QUESTIONS FOR REFLECTION AND DISCUSSION

1. Do you think that most managers have basically a fixed "one size fits all" leadership style, or are they quite flexible as appropriate to the situation? Give examples to support your view.

2. Consider the best boss for whom you have worked. Which characteristics define his or her leadership? Are these characteristics predominantly traits or behaviors?

3. Identify a strength of a leader whom you know. Is it possible that this strength could also be a weakness? Explain.

4. Is it possible for a leader to be a servant in a for-profit organization? Why or why not?

5. Which problems and potential opportunities might arise from integrating leadership and spirituality?

6. What do you see as the main differences between the four Mainstream leadership styles (directing, coaching, supporting, delegating) and the four Multistream leadership styles (enabling, equipping, engaging, empowering)? As a follower or organizational member, how would you respond to each style?

HANDS-ON ACTIVITIES

Self-Assessment Exercise: What Type of Leader Are You?

Circle a number on the continuum that best represents your leadership style.

PART A.[54] AS A LEADER, I . . .

Like to call the shots and make the decisions.	1 2 3 4 5	Want input from followers to influence decisions.
Focus on my followers' at-work responsibilities.	1 2 3 4 5	Am sensitive to followers' outside-work responsibilities.
Believe that my employees work for me.	1 2 3 4 5	Believe that I work for my employees.
Emphasize the importance of seizing opportunities in the environment.	1 2 3 4 5	Emphasize the importance of giving back to the community.

PART B. I AM GOOD AT . . .

Telling followers what to do to enhance production.	1 2 3 4 5	Explaining to followers how their jobs contribute to the big picture.
Thinking up a strategy and training followers how to implement it.	1 2 3 4 5	Creating a workplace where everyone learns together to develop and implement strategy.
Motivating people by providing praise and giving out rewards.	1 2 3 4 5	Helping people to find meaning in their work and fun in their work group.
Knowing how much work I can delegate to followers.	1 2 3 4 5	"Letting go" and providing behind-the-scenes support for followers to take charge.

PART C

I want to become a leader to influence others.	1 2 3 4 5	I want to become a leader to serve others.
I want to get ahead.	1 2 3 4 5	I want to make a difference.
I have confidence in my abilities.	1 2 3 4 5	I have confidence in my goals.
Honesty and integrity are good for business.	1 2 3 4 5	Honesty and integrity are always good.
I value the "know-how" that enhances our organization's interests.	1 2 3 4 5	I value the "know-how" that enhances all our stakeholders' interests.

ENDNOTES

1. Bakke, D. (2005). *Joy at work: A revolutionary approach to fun on the job.* Seattle, WA: PVG; Wetluafer, S. (1999). Organizing for empowerment: An interview with Roger Sant and Dennis Bakke. *Harvard Business Review, 77*(1), 110–123; and Sinatra, M. (2005, March 28). Dennis Bakke and the general management club. *Wharton Journal News.* http://media.www.whartonjournal.com/media/storage/paper201/news/2005/03/28/News/Dennis.Bakke.And.The.General.Management.Club-904163.shtml.
2. Bass, B. M. (1985). *Leadership and performance beyond expectations.* New York: Free Press; Burns, J. M. (1978). *Leadership.* New York: Harper & Row.
3. Judge, T. A., & Piccolo, R. F. (2004). Transformational and transactional leadership: A meta-analytic test of their relative validity. *Journal of Applied Psychology, 89*(5), 755–768; Pawar, B. S., & Eastman, K. K. (1997). The nature and implications of contextual influences on transformational leadership: A conceptual examination. *Academy of Management Review, 22*(1), 80–109.
4. Farrell, G. (2005, April 25). A CEO and a gentleman. *USA Today,* B.1.
5. Yukl, G. (1998). *Leadership in organizations* (4th ed.). Upper Saddle River, NJ: Prentice Hall; Kirkpatrick, S. A., & Locke, E. A. (1991). Leadership: Do traits matter? *Academy of Management Executive, 5*(2), 48–60.
6. Judge, T., Ilies, R., Bono, J., & Gerhardt, M. (2002). Personality and leadership: A qualitative and quantitative review. *Journal of Applied Psychology, 87*(4), 765–780.
7. http://www.chick-fil-a.com/#story.
8. http://www.virgingalactic.com/flash.html.
9. DeCelles, K., & Pfarrer, M. (2004). Heroes or villains? Corruption and the charismatic leader. *Journal of Leadership and Organizational Studies, 11*(1), 67–77.
10. Stogdill, R. M. (1950). Leadership, membership and organization. *Psychological Bulletin, 47,* 1–14.
11. http://www.baylor.edu/business/mba/index.php?id=33316.
12. Judge, T. A., Piccolo, R. F., & Ilies, R. (2004). The forgotten ones? The validity of consideration and initiating structure in leadership research. *Journal of Applied Psychology, 89*(1), 36–51.
13. Eagly, A. H., & Johnson, B. T. (1990). Gender and leadership style: A meta-analysis. *Psychological Bulletin, 108*(2), 233–256. Lyness, K. S., & Heilman, M. E. (2006). When fit is fundamental: Performance evaluations and promotions of upper-level female and male managers. *Journal of Applied Psychology, 91*(4), 777–785. For a discussion of gender leadership in teams, see Neubert, M. J., & Taggar, S. (2004). Pathways to informal leadership: The moderating role of gender on the relationship of individual differences and team member network centrality to informal leadership emergence. *Leadership Quarterly, 15,* 175–194.
14. Tannen, D. (1995). The power of talk: Who gets heard and why. *Harvard Business Review, 73*(5), 138–148.
15. Neubert, M. J., & Palmer, L. D. (2004). The emergence of women in healthcare leadership: Transforming the impact of gender differences. *Journal of Men's Health and Gender, 1*(4), 383–387.
16. Fiedler, F.E. (1972). The effects of leadership training and experience: A contingency model interpretation. *Administrative Science Quarterly, 17*(4), 453–470.

17. Buckingham, M., & Coffman, C. (1999). *First break all the rules: What the world's greatest managers do differently.* New York: Simon and Schuster.

18. House, R. J. (1971). A path-goal theory of leadership effectiveness. *Administrative Science Quarterly, 16,* 321–339.

19. Vroom, V. H., & Jago, A. G. (2007). The role of the situation in leadership. *American Psychologist, 62(1),* 17–24.

20. Yukl, 1998.

21. Buckingham, M. (2005). What great managers do. *Harvard Business Review, 83(3),* 70–79.

22. Blanchard, K., Zigarmi, P., & Zigarmi, D. (1985). *Leadership and the one-minute manager: Increasing effectiveness through situational leadership.* New York: William Morrow.

23. Norrise, W. R., & Vecchio, R. P. (1992). Situational leadership theory: A replication. *Group and Organization Management, 17(3),* 331–342.

24. Kerr, S., & Jermier, J. M. (1978). Substitutes for leadership: Their meaning and measurement. *Organizational Behavior & Human Performance, 22(3),* 375–403.

25. Podsakoff, P. M., & MacKenzie, S. B. (1997). Kerr and Jermier's substitutes for leadership model: Background, empirical assessment, and suggestions for future research. *Leadership Quarterly, 8(2),* 117–132.

26. Wu, C., & Neubert, M. J. (2005). *Transformational leadership, organizational justice, and employee cynicism about organizational change.* Academy of Management Meetings, Honolulu, Hawaii. August 7–10.

27. Greenleaf, R. (1977/2002). *Servant leadership.* New York: Paulist Press.

28. Ehrhart, M. G. (2004). Leadership and procedural justice climate as antecedents of unit-level organizational citizenship behavior. *Personnel Psychology, 57,* 61–94; Graham, J. W. (1991). Servant-leadership in organizations: Inspirational and moral. *Leadership Quarterly, 2(2),* 105–119.

29. Pollard, W. (2003, Spring). Leading in turbulent times. *Baylor Business Review, 20(1),* 22.

30. http://www.chick-fil-a.com/#thecows.

31. Gunther, M. (2001). God and business. *Fortune, 144(1),* 58–80; Nash, L., & McLenna, S. (2001). *Church on Sunday, work on Monday: The challenge of fusing Christian values with business life.* San Francisco: Jossey-Bass; Tischler, L. (2005, May). God and Mammon at Harvard. *Fast Company,* 80–83; Fry, L. W. (2003). Toward a theory of spiritual leadership. *Leadership Quarterly, 14(6),* 693–727.

32. McCall, M., & Lombardo, M. (1983). *Off the track: Why and how successful executives get derailed* (Technical Report No. 21). Greensboro, NC: Center for Creative Leadership.

33. Spreier, S., Fontaine, M., & Malloy, R. (2006, June). Leadership run amok: The destructive potential of overachievers. *Harvard Business Review, 84(6),* 72–82.

34. Collins, J. (2001). *Good to great: Why some companies make the leap . . . and others don't.* New York: HarperCollins.

35. http://www.missionwaco.org.

36. Collins, 2001.

37. Charan, R. (2007). *Know how: The 8 skills that separate people who perform from those who don't.* New York: Crown.

38. Goleman, D. (1998, January). What makes a leader. *Harvard Business Review, 82(1),* 93–102.

39. Goleman, D., Boyatzis, D., & McKee, A. (2002). *Primal leadership: Realizing the power of emotional intelligence.* Cambridge, MA: HBR Press.

40. Fox, S., & Amichai-Hamburger, Y. (2001). The power of emotional appeals in promoting organizational change. *Academy of Management Executive, 15,* 84–94.

41. Druskat, V., & Wolff, S. (2001). Building the emotional intelligence of groups. *Harvard Business Review, 79,* 80–91.

42. Alon, I., & Higgins, J. (2005). Global leadership success through emotional intelligence and cultural intelligence. *Business Horizons, 48,* 501–512.

43. For a list of socioemotional behaviors in the context of teams, see Barry, B., & Stewart, G. L. (1997). Composition, process, and performance in self-managed groups: The role of personality. *Journal of Applied Psychology, 82(1),* 62–78.

44. Brockner, J., & Higgins, E. T. (2001). Regulatory focus theory: Implications for the study of emotions at work. *Organizational Behavior & Human Decision Processes, 86(1),* 35–66; Kark, R., & Van Dijk, D. (2007). Motivation to lead, motivation to follow: The role of the self-regulatory focus in leadership processes. *Academy of Management Review, 32(2),* 500–528.

45. Neubert, M., Kacmar, M., Carlson, D., Roberts, J., & Chonko, L. (2007). *Regulatory focus as a mediator of leadership influence on employee behavior.* Academy of Management Meetings, Philadelphia, PA. August 12–15.

46. Vandewalle, D. (2001). Why wanting to look successful doesn't always lead to success. *Organizational Dynamics, 30(2),* 162–171; Yperen, N. W. V. (2003). The perceived profile of goal orientation within firms: Differences between employees working for successful and unsuccessful firms employing either performance-based pay or job-based pay. *European Journal of Work & Organizational Psychology, 12(3),* 229–244.

47. Kozlowski, S. W. J., Gully, S. M., Brown, K. G., Salas, E., Smith, E. M., & Nason, E. H. (2001). Effects of training goals and goal orientation traits on multidimensional training outcomes and performance adaptability. *Organizational Behavior & Human Decision Processes, 85(1),* 1–31.

48. Vansteenkiste, M., Simons, J., Lens, W., Soenens, B., Matos, L., & Lacante, M. (2004). Less is sometimes more: Goal content matters. *Journal of Educational Psychology, 96(4),* 755–764.

49. Lee, A. Y., Aaker, J. L., & Gardner, W. L. (2000). The pleasures and pains of distinct self-construals: The role of interdependence in regulatory focus. *Journal of Personality and Social Psychology, 78(6),* 1122–1134.

50. Higgins, E. T. (1997). Beyond pleasure and pain. *American Psychologist, 52(12),* 1280–1300.

51. Melrose, K. (1995). *Making the grass greener on your side: A CEO's journey to leading by serving.* San Francisco: Berrett-Koehler.

52. Spreitzer, G. M., & Quinn, R. E. (2001). *A company of leaders: Five disciplines for unleashing the power in your workforce.* San Francisco: Jossey-Bass.

53. Comments taken from speech at Baylor University. September 28, 2005.

54. A few items were adapted from Ehrhart, M. (2004). Leadership and procedural justice climate as antecedents of unit-level organizational citizenship behavior. *Personnel Psychology, 57(1),* 61–94.

CHAPTER 16

This chapter marks the end of our journey through the leadership functions of a manager. This is familiar territory for many managers, given that their work takes place in the context of groups—a work group, the organization, and the community. This chapter discusses the differences between groups and teams, and then focuses more directly on teams and their development. Mainstream and Multistream perspectives are offered for each stage of team development, with a discussion of the differences highlighted in the road map.

ROAD MAP

FOUR STAGES OF TEAM DEVELOPMENT

Stage 1: Team is created
Recommended actions:

Stage 2: Obstacles emerge
Recommended actions:

Stage 3: Habits are established
Recommended actions:

Stage 4: Team excels
Recommended actions:

Groups and Teams

MAINSTREAM APPROACH	⟵⟶	MULTISTREAM APPROACH
Forming Set direction, create cohesion		*Originating* Foster sense of purpose/identity
Storming Resolve conflict, stay on task		*Elaborating* Transform conflict, refine roles
Norming Affirm performance norms		*Collaborating* Emphasize interdependencies
Performing Provide feedback, recognition		*Disseminating* Diffuse learning

Teamwork at Gore[1]

When Diane Davidson started at W. L. Gore, she kept asking, "Who is my boss?" But there are no bosses at Gore—or at least very few to speak of. There are no titles either, other than "associate"—which is the title for everyone from the janitor to the top managers. There must be secret bosses, Davidson thought, but eventually she came to understand that your team is your boss. That is, as you work in teams, your commitment to your team and the desire to not let team members down become your boss.

No titles and teams without bosses: Gore might sound like a start-up in someone's garage, but it is not. Actually, Gore started in the basement of the Gore family, but it won't fit in a basement or garage any longer. Today the company has more than $1.5 billion in annual revenues and more than 6000 employees. Gore has created products as varied as guitar strings and dental floss. Perhaps its most well-known products are the GORE-TEX® fabrics and linings used for outdoor clothing. Most of the firm's products are based on the use of innovative plastic coatings, but its competitive advantage may be Gore's team culture.

Teams are the dominant organizational structure and most, if not all, work is done in teams. Even the personnel in each manufacturing facility are considered to be on the same team and, as such, are not allowed to grow in number much beyond 200 associates to maintain the sense of team spirit. Smaller teams of less than a dozen associates operate like task forces, emerging as needed to pursue opportunities as well as to handle such critical administrative functions as deciding the compensation of associates. Associates emerge as leaders only if they have something that others believe is worth following. If your ideas are not compelling or you are not providing a service that others consider valuable, there is no chain of command to ensure followers.

Assigned and well-defined roles also are difficult to find at Gore. If a team forms around an idea or task, those who choose to participate in the team look for a fit between what the team needs and individual skills, filling those roles that they are best suited to perform.

Teams typically end up having a diverse set of skills—something that is more likely at Gore than at other organizations, because associates are not segmented by functions such as sales, engineering, or production. New associates often feel out of place and confused about what they should be contributing in such an environment, but longtime associates insist the process works if new associates invest the time—sometimes as much as six months—necessary to get to know other associates.

Associates at Gore value the collaborative style that allows all team members to speak up on behalf of what they think is the best course of action for everyone. Although this style can be confusing to outsiders, who typically want to know who makes the decisions, decisions are made by the team, and any one team member can overrule another. In one instance, when one team member verbally agreed to a price increase with the vice-president of a computer supplier, he was overruled by a fellow team member in the same meeting. Communicating with customers, suppliers, or other teams is a responsibility for all team members. Whereas Gore associates may be described as impatient with those who want to take charge and decide things for others, they are incredibly patient when it comes to putting in the time and resources needed to develop and perfect new ideas before bringing them to market. Associates are encouraged to devote at least 10 percent of their week's activities to pursuing new ideas. Innovation takes patience and time.

The compensation of team members at Gore is based on their perceived contributions and takes into account work on long-term projects that have yet to make a dime, work on others' projects, and even failed projects. But failure is not punished: On the contrary, it is even celebrated with ceremonies and dinner parties when the failure represents a good-faith effort to innovate. At Gore, failed-project team members disperse throughout the organization, applying the lessons learned from the abandoned project to other projects. You fail at Gore only when you fail to learn.

INTRODUCTION TO GROUPS AND TEAMS

Organizations have many different groups and teams. Teams, in particular, have great potential. They can improve the quality of decision making, enhance creativity, increase motivation, and help facilitate organizational change. Implementing teams also can allow managers to decrease their direct supervision of employees, and then reassign some job duties from supervisors to team members.[2] Managers create teams for a variety of reasons. Teams are a good way for managers to respond to the movement toward high-involvement work cultures, flatter and more flexible organizational structures, changes in technology, and the goal of getting more work out of fewer employees.[3]

This chapter differentiates between groups and teams, describes different types of teams, and explores how groups and teams develop over time. As with other chapters, we review theory and practice first from a Mainstream approach and then from a Multistream approach.

Often the terms "group" and "team" are used interchangeably, which, in many cases, may be appropriate. Both terms refer to the interplay between two or more members within an organization. However, there are significant differences between them, as shown in Table 16.1. Whereas a **group** is a collection of two or more people who share a common interest or association, a **team** is a collection of people who work interdependently as a unit. Teams are task oriented, and their members share common goals, work toward those goals interdependently, and are accountable to one another to achieve those goals.

Whereas the notion of teams focuses on how members achieve tasks, the notion of groups focuses more on affiliation or the nature of the interpersonal relationships among members. Not all groups are teams. For example, members of the same department may be formally designated as a group, but they may not work together as a team. Also, organizational members who eat lunch together regularly can be seen as an informal group. Sometimes referred to as "interest groups," these kinds of informal groups are typically not created with organizational goals in mind, but rather to help individuals achieve personal goals and meet their mutual needs. For example, a number of organizations such as Dell support affinity groups based on race or religion by offering the use of facilities for meetings and allowing publicity of group events using the organization's communication infrastructure.

Groups are typically more concerned with a common interest and the benefits of the interpersonal relationships of their members, whereas teams are generally more concerned with task and goal achievement. That is not to say that groups don't work together to accomplish things; nevertheless, group members typically carry out their tasks without having to rely on the work of other members. In teams, members rely on other members' work or contributions to successfully complete tasks.

Group is a collection of two or more people who share a common interest or association.

Team is a task-oriented collection of people who work interdependently as a unit to achieve common goals, and are accountable to one another to achieve those goals.

TABLE 16.1

Typical Characteristics of Groups and Teams

Group	Team
Informal or formal	Formal
Share common goals	Work interdependently toward common goals
Affiliation oriented	Achievement oriented
Small or large in size	Generally, small in size

Groups may range in size from a few people to a thousand or more. Generally, teams are smaller in size owing to limitations on how many people can work together interdependently. However, a large team may be possible if work is divided among subteams.[4]

Although the differences between groups and teams are important, some of what is discussed here when we describe teams applies to groups, and vice versa. Unless otherwise noted, we will focus primarily on teams in the rest of this chapter, in part because managers are more likely to be interested in teams due to their task and goal orientation.

 WHAT DO YOU THINK?

What Makes an Effective Student Team?

As a student, you no doubt have worked in a number of "teams" to complete work for class projects. From your experiences as a team member, respond to the following questions:

1. In what ways were your "teams" really teams, and how were they more like groups?
2. What were the characteristics of your "effective" team experiences?
3. What were the characteristics of your "ineffective" team experiences?
4. In future teams, which characteristics or behaviors could you model or promote to improve your chances of having an effective team experience?

TYPES OF TEAMS

Teams may be configured in many different ways:

- Permanent or project
- Hierarchical or self-managed
- Functional or cross-functional
- On-site or virtual

Permanent Teams and Project Teams

Teams can be relatively stable and ongoing (permanent), or their existence may be relatively fleeting and intended to meet short-term needs (project).

A project team is set up to accomplish specific goals or to solve a particular problem. Members typically are chosen for their expertise and may include both managers and nonmanagers who represent various departments.[5] Project teams differ from permanent teams in that project teams have a predefined, limited life and role to serve in the organization.

The importance of having healthy interpersonal relationships is more important for permanent teams, as their members will have to work with one another on an ongoing basis. Social relationships, while helpful, are not as crucial in short-term task forces because members know that they will not need to work with annoying members for a long time. At a company such as Gore, social relationships cannot be ignored because most of one's work life is spent in teams, even if a person might work in a series of different teams over time.

Hierarchical Teams and Self-Managed Teams

Usually hierarchical structures in organizations are quite clear, with one person being given the responsibility and legitimate authority to manage each department. In such situations, the primary responsibility of managers is to coordinate the task activities of members, with a secondary emphasis on developing the team.

As is illustrated by this *Dilbert* comic, sometimes teams are launched that are teams in name only. They neither work as teams nor are given the authority to make decisions on their own without management oversight. DILBERT: © Scott Adams/Dist. by United Feature Syndicate, Inc.

In recent years, however, there has been a steady increase in the use of self-managed work teams. A self-managed work team typically consists of a small number of employees who are given primary responsibility to manage themselves on a daily basis.[6] Their responsibilities may include scheduling, defining work tasks, rotating jobs, and deciding on leadership. Members in self-managed teams tend to find satisfaction from the perception of having more decision-making responsibility and job security, whereas immediate supervisors often experience just the opposite reaction.[7] Self-managed teams tend to be very cost-effective and reduce the need for various levels of management, which explains the feelings of insecurity that lower-level supervisors and managers may experience.

With the use of self-managed teams, the role of management is reduced but not eliminated, as teams may run into problems that they are unable to resolve. Thus, in this type of structure, managers become coaches and liaisons to other teams or organizational members.

Functional Teams and Cross-Functional Teams

A functional team consists of a manager and a team of employees in a particular area within the organization. Examples include a marketing department, a finance department, and a research department. Because members do not come from a variety of areas, there is greater homogeneity among members and greater likelihood that they will get along socially as a group. Functional teams are formed with a specific functional goal in mind, such as improving a work activity or solving a specific problem.

In contrast, cross-functional teams bring together people with a variety of expertise and knowledge from different organizational levels. They are assembled to achieve specific organizational-level goals or goals that require cooperation across functions.

On-Site Teams and Virtual Teams

Most team members work alongside one another in the same building or factory. On-site members see each other regularly, often many times a day. They may share the same office space or work on the same assembly line. There is plentiful opportunity—and need—for team members to develop relationships that allow them to become a group.

More recently, technological advances have made virtual teams more feasible. A virtual team is composed of members who live in geographically diverse settings. A virtual team may also involve members of other organizations. Members rarely, if ever, meet face-to-face; instead, they interact by computer, video, and/or voice mail.

MANAGEMENT IN PRACTICE

Avoiding Team Dysfunctions

The ability of a manager to create, maintain, and lead teams is essential to maximizing the performance of an organization in the rapidly changing environment faced by most modern-day organizations.[8] According to Patrick M. Lencioni, author of *The Five Dysfunctions of a Team,* effective teams within an organization represent a competitive advantage because they are so powerful and yet so rare.[9] He argues that effective teams are rare because of the following dysfunctions:

- *Absence of trust*. Team members who are not genuinely open with one another about their mistakes and weaknesses make it impossible to build a foundation for trust.

- *Fear of conflict*. Team members who lack trust are incapable of engaging in unfiltered and passionate debate of ideas.

- *Lack of commitment*. Team members who have not participated in open discussion and debate are not likely to buy in and commit to decisions, though they may feign agreement during meetings.

- *Avoidance of accountability*. Team members who lack commitment and are uncertain about goals often hesitate to confront their peers on actions and behaviors that are detrimental to the good of the team.

- *Inattention to team results*. Team members who lack commitment put their individual needs, or even the needs of their divisions, above the collective goals of the team.

Management consultants and authors Jon Katzenbach and Douglas Smith recommend that leaders of teams establish a sense of urgency and heighten members' commitment by clearly explaining the purpose of the team and establishing specific goals.[10] Moreover, they recommend that leaders pay particular attention to actively reinforcing the importance of the team by making time with the team a priority and publicly recognizing the accomplishments of the team.

Virtual teams have grown in popularity as organizations become increasingly global in nature. In addition, the need for highly specialized workers and the flexible nature of virtual teams has increased their use. Perhaps the most obvious example is telecommuters, who work from their homes and rarely go to their offices. In such a case, it is the manager's job to pay attention to the interdependent task relationships among team members who rarely see one another or have the opportunity to bond as a group.

Consider the example of international design teams. Designers in California might work an eight-hour shift designing an automobile and then pass the design electronically to team members in India; the Indian team members might work on it for another eight-hour shift and then forward the design to team members in the United Kingdom; the U.K. designers might work for another eight hours before sending the design back to California for the next shift.

Virtual teams, like those at American Express Technologies (AET), often interact using groupware software and technology.[11] Members of AET's virtual teams believe that technology makes teaming easier by increasing accessibility and facilitating tracking and documentation of work. But technology also has its downsides. There is a learning curve, and at times maintaining and updating the features of the software can increase the workload of team members. In addition, viruses, power outages, and other issues can turn a virtual conversation into dead air.

The potential benefits of teamwork can be enticing to managers, but they may potentially be a "fatal attraction" if teams are not managed to draw out the benefits and minimize the drawbacks of teaming. Managers need to be adept at knowing how to manage groups and teams to avoid the problems described in the "Management in Practice" feature.

THE FOUR STAGES OF MAINSTREAM TEAM DEVELOPMENT

While no two teams are the same, group development research suggests that most teams will go through a series of predictable developmental stages:[12]

1. *Forming:* Team is created
2. *Storming:* Obstacles emerge
3. *Norming:* Habits are established
4. *Performing:* Team excels
5. *Adjourning (a final step for some teams):* Team disbands

Taken together, these stages include important team processes that are common to many teams—processes that research suggests may be influenced by time pressures that the teams experience.[13] Regardless of the time spent in each of the stages, progress through the stages has been shown to be important for team success.[14]

Although the stages may be thought of as one following the other, team development is also an iterative process. Thus, while "forming" may be especially important in the early stages of a team's life cycle, team members must also engage in "re-forming" as new members join or when the teams' responsibilities change.

The first four stages are common to all teams, while the fifth is evident only when a team disbands. Adjourning is, in many ways, really the opposite of forming. As a team disbands, members are likely to have some form of emotional response. They may bask in the glow of their individual and team achievements and may be saddened by the loss of friendship and camaraderie. In this stage, it is important that managers ensure that team members are recognized and that a "closure" event clearly marks the end of the team's activities together.

But we are getting ahead of ourselves: A happy ending can result only from a team passing through the prior stages of development. In the rest of this section, we discuss these steps in sequence, noting specific managerial challenges that can arise during each stage.

To navigate the stages of team development we use the acronym FIT—that is, Feelings, Issues, Techniques. Table 16.2 shows the FIT typical for each stage of team development. Although the feelings, issues, and managerial techniques that we discuss can apply to more than one stage, our exploration here is intended to help managers "fit" specific techniques with specific stages of team development. This is similar to the Situational Leadership process discussed in Chapter 15. The development process for teams in some ways mirrors the development process for individuals, suggesting that at each stage of development a different set of supportive and directive behaviors is critical to manage the team. The manager may provide those behaviors directly if he or she is a member of the team. If the manager is not a member of the team, then he or she must find ways to support the team leader in providing what is necessary for the team's development.

Stage 1: Forming

The first stage of team development is forming. Members may volunteer to join a team or they may be selected for their task-specific experience or perspectives. If a manager has the opportunity to select team members, one common view suggests

TABLE 16.2

FIT for Each Stage of Team Development

Brief Description of Stage	*Feelings* Members Are Experiencing	*Issues* Members Are Dealing With	*Techniques* Managers Can Use to Help
Stage 1: Team is created	Excitement of new Uncertainty of new	What will team do? Why is it important?	Ensure expectations are clarified
Stage 2: Obstacles emerge	Frustration Discouragement	Can we do it? What about barriers and conflict?	Remove barriers
Stage 3: Habits are established	Optimism about ability Acceptance of team members	Are we able to deliver? Will barriers reemerge?	Share information Ensure accountability
Stage 4: Team excels	Pride in accomplishment Confidence	Will we be recognized? What is next challenge?	Provide feedback and rewards

In its choice of successor to Steve Reinemund, PepsiCo demonstrated its commitment to diversity by appointing Indra Nooyi as Chairman and CEO.

that selection should maximize diversity of function, tenure, age, ethnicity, and even personality to ensure that the team has a variety of perspectives and experiences to draw on. Research indicates that this type of diversity has the potential to benefit the group through enhancing the quantity of information brought into the team. However, research also shows that diversity can cause significant problems in the quality of interactions, leading to lower team performance, less communication, more conflict, and the withdrawal of team members from the group.[15]

With many organizations having global operations and its members working virtually, the issue of ethnic or cultural diversity is becoming more important. Here, too, diversity of cultural backgrounds may create problems early in the team's formation as members tend to be less satisfied and feel less connected in culturally diverse teams than in teams where members share similar cultural backgrounds.[16] This can be an even bigger problem if only one or two members are from a different culture than the majority of team members. The minority members are bound to feel out of place and marginalized, or the team may divide into subgroups. If a team will be culturally diverse, it is probably better that the manager make every effort to have it be multicultural, with members representing a number of cultures.[17] This increase in diversity will minimize the tendency of subgroups to form and avoid having any one culture be positioned as the minority. In other words, having "everyone in the same boat" forces every member to reach out to others and do his or her share to improve communication. Even this effort may not help, however, if team members are pressured by management to act the same. Steve Reinemund, former CEO of PepsiCo, believes that cultural and ethnic diversity works only if "employees feel free to express their views, even if those are sometimes negative."[18]

During the forming stage, members typically have *feelings* of anticipation and apprehension. There is excitement about being part of something new and potentially important, but there is also uncertainty regarding how the team members will work together and whether the team will be successful. The main *issues* in members' minds tend to be questions about what the team will be doing and why it is important. Because these feelings and issues reflect generally high levels of commitment but low levels of competency, the team may require more directive behavior from the manager. During this period, the team's goals are set and members begin to get to know one another while starting to see themselves as part of the team. Team members also begin to test each other for relationship potential and to determine what sorts of behaviors are acceptable.

During the forming stage, the manager's *techniques* should focus on the following tasks:

- Providing direction regarding the goals of the team
- Clarifying expectations regarding the roles of the team members
- Establishing the ground rules for interaction

At this stage, the manager helps the team members to understand the meaning and importance of the team's goals in meeting larger organizational objectives. During forming, a team may benefit from bringing into its meetings a sponsoring manager—that is, someone who supports the team's goal and is willing to publicly affirm it. Moreover, some organizations create an informal or formal contract that states the goal of the project; this document is then signed by the manager and the team members.

Roles may relate to team facilitation such as note taker, scribe, and timekeeper. Alternatively, roles may relate to team task function, such as project manager, department liaison, analyst, and team spokesperson. Of the many team-building activities available, role clarification has possibly the greatest impact on team performance.[20]

Ground rules are explicit agreements among team members regarding how to behave, such as timely arrival, forms of communication, and tactics for resolving conflict. In Honeywell's manufacturing environment, an explicit ground rule always relates to sharing safety information, such as where to exit in case of fire, at the beginning of every meeting. Ground rules may be instituted by the manager or agreed upon as a group.

Leadership techniques for goals, roles, and ground rules contribute to task cohesion within the team. **Task cohesion** is the shared commitment among members to achieving a goal. It can be fostered by ensuring that team members have a "voice" in decision making. Cohesiveness will increase when managers use their legitimate authority to invite members to participate in establishing the group's goals and ground rules. Moreover, task cohesion will be high when the rewards

Task cohesion refers to the shared commitment among members to achieving a goal.

Those who team to attempt to climb Mount Everest are bound together by a dream to ascend the world's highest peak, a voyage that requires a substantial investment of time and training, and may cost some team members their lives.[19]

for team success are clear and compelling. For example, an elite team of clinicians and scientists at the Campbell Family Institute for Breast Cancer Research at Princess Margaret Hospital are dedicated to goals related to cures for breast cancer.[21]

Although task cohesion is more important than social cohesion in contributing to team performance, social cohesion is also important to the team to "grease the wheels"—that is, to decrease friction and help the team run smoothly.[22] **Social cohesion** is the attachment and attraction of team members to one another. Typically, this type of cohesion is related to similarities within the group, time spent together, shared positive experiences, and shared goals. Managers can increase social cohesion by encouraging a healthy amount of competition with other groups. Groups will be more cohesive if members believe that they must unite to do well compared to a different group. For example, when a sales force in one region competes against a sales force in another region, it creates an "us versus them" mindset that increases cohesion within the team.

Social cohesiveness is also fostered when members learn to trust one another. This mutual trust takes time to develop. Managers can hasten trust building by modeling trustworthiness in their relationships and encouraging open communication among members. For example, a manager might start meetings with "warm-up" questions such as "If you had the day off, what would you do?" Learning about the interests of other team members personalizes team members and enhances relationships. Managers also can encourage interaction outside of formal meeting times by hosting meals or organizing a fun night out. In addition, they might consider investing in team-building experiences such as solving a mystery, navigating a ropes course, or making decisions to survive a simulated plane crash in the wilderness. Such exercises or outdoor activities simulate important team dynamics in a fun and memorable environment.

Finally, social cohesiveness can be facilitated by something as mundane as managing the team's size. Teams that are smaller tend to be more cohesive. If a department or team has many members, then the manager may be wise to subdivide it.

 WHAT DO YOU THINK?

Is Cohesion a Good Thing?

Social cohesiveness is the degree to which members are committed to the team. It is the measure of how members feel toward one another and toward the team as a whole. It is possible to have a team whose members like one another, but are not committed to the team's task. Consider a team in a manufacturing environment. Perhaps due to working together for a long period of time, ongoing past success together in accomplishing goals, and sharing similarities in their background and interests outside of work, they are very close. Yet, they may be currently experiencing frustration with management over recent changes in work rules. In an act of rebellious solidarity, such a team might decide among themselves that they will do just enough work to keep from getting in trouble for poor performance.

In contrast, an international work group collaborating on software design may have minimal social cohesion owing to differences in backgrounds, language barriers, remote physical locations, and different functional affiliations. Nonetheless, the group may enjoy a high level of task cohesion because its members recognize the importance of the task to the organization and, as a result, might accomplish a great deal.

Consider a class of management majors in a business school. Within the class, students are divided up into teams to complete a variety of assignments. What might

Social cohesion is the attachment and attraction of team members to one another.

contribute to the teams being more or less socially cohesive? What might contribute to more or less task cohesion within the team? What might you recommend that a professor do to increase social or task cohesion? Have the student teams you have worked in had social or task cohesion? Why or why not? How did it contribute to your performance as a team?

Stage 2: Storming

In the second stage of team development, obstacles emerge from working on the task and interacting with team members. The hallmarks of this stage—storming— are conflict and disagreement. **Conflict** refers to a real or perceived difference in interests between two or more individuals, groups, or organizations. It can cause one or more members of the team to attempt to thwart or block other members from reaching their goals or satisfying their interests.

In some cases, it may appear as though the team is "going in circles," making little or no progress during this stage. *Feelings* tend to be those of discouragement and frustration, opening up the possibility of withdrawal or even angry outbursts. The central underlying *issues* for team members are the questions of whether the team will get through this time of conflict and whether the team goals can be achieved. A manager can address these feelings and issues through *techniques* such as acting to resolve conflict among team members, developing commitment to shared goals, and promoting a shared belief that progress is possible.

Applying proper techniques for managing conflict requires a deeper understanding of the source of conflict. Sometimes conflict may be healthy, such as when it motivates members to rally around their "cause" and work harder, or when the discussion of diverse opinions and perspectives increases the quality of the discussion and resulting decisions. At other times, conflict can be dysfunctional, such as when members' work efforts are undermined by others, communication becomes defensive and accusatory, or the most productive members leave the organization to find more harmonious environments in which to work. In one study, conflict was found to be dysfunctional in that it decreased individual performance, but functional in that it increased group performance.[23]

Moderate amounts of conflict within a team may result in optimal team performance. When there is too little conflict, performance suffers because members become complacent and fail to respond to new ideas, and groupthink sets in. **Groupthink** is the tendency of cohesive group members to strive for and maintain unanimity on a decision rather than thoroughly considering all alternatives.[24] When there is too much conflict, performance suffers because members are uncooperative and chaos erupts. When there are moderate amounts of conflict, performance is optimized because members constantly question and improve work practices, members push one another to innovate, and there is a healthy tension in the organization. Research is unclear as to whether an optimal middle ground exists in every team, but clearly extreme conflict is stressful and often counterproductive, and little or no conflict can be a sign of complacency or a sign of groupthink (see the "Digging Deeper" feature).

Conflict can occur for a variety of reasons, as shown in Figure 16.1. First, conflict may arise when members must compete against one another for key scarce resources. A scarce resource may include money, information, or supplies. This competition among group members undermines any attempts to develop a positive

Conflict refers to a real or perceived difference in interests between two or more individuals, groups, or organizations.

Groupthink is the tendency of cohesive group members to strive for and maintain unanimity on a decision rather than thoroughly considering all possible alternatives.

Groupthink: A Case of Too Much Agreement[25]

The phenomenon of groupthink has been argued to contribute to a number of tragedies throughout history, from the failure of the United States to defend itself from attack at Pearl Harbor to the space shuttle disasters at the National Aeronautics and Space Administration (NASA). Problems in team decision processes were cited as contributing factors in the destruction of the *Challenger* shuttle shortly after lift-off and in the disintegration of the *Columbia* shuttle at reentry to the Earth's atmosphere. Irving Janis, the originator of the term "groupthink," regards it as a disease that can afflict previously healthy teams. Symptoms of this disease include censoring of dissent within the group, suppression or discrediting of information from other sources, overconfidence, and an aversion to questioning the ethics of the group's decision.

The causes of groupthink are overblown social cohesion, pressures for team members to conform to the majority, rationalization that highlights the positive aspects and discounts the negative aspects of an issue, isolation or an insular group that has minimal contact with outsiders, stressful working conditions that promote quick decisions, and leaders who are controlling and dominating, intentionally or otherwise.

To prevent groupthink, team members must thoroughly examine a wide range of issues and alternatives. To ensure that this happens, a leader must refrain from stating personal opinions at the outset of the discussion, require a full analysis of each issue regardless of presumed consensus, invite criticism of ideas and suggestions, and use information-sharing and decision-making techniques that maximize input and minimize concerns about retribution.

One simple technique that can help with these processes is to assign someone within the team, perhaps on a rotating basis, to play the role of the "critic" or "devil's advocate." This role should be publicly assigned to ensure that the role player does not suffer being considered a jerk. This person is required to raise issues, call into question premature decisions, and demand justification.

Another provocative technique, **dialectical inquiry,** is a staged debate between a dominant perspective or opinion and a counterargument that represents an opposing point of view.[26] A variation of this approach is to assign roles in the debate that are contrary to the expressed opinion of the participants. In other words, for the sake of discussion a set of team members is required to defend a point of view whether or not they initially supported it.

In sum, the strengths of teams—the ability to provide an attractive social environment and the potential for improving decision-making quality—if not managed correctly can leave a team open to the dangerous disease of groupthink. When this occurs, dissention is suppressed and the team becomes overconfident to the point of not thoroughly examining its alternatives and weighing the potential weaknesses of its decisions. Given the consequences, this is, indeed, a dangerous disease.

Dialectical inquiry is a staged debate between two dominant perspectives.

Task interdependence is the interconnection of tasks, such that all members must do their part to complete the team task.

group identity, because members have to worry that a colleague will "steal" some of the scarce resources.

Conflict is also likely when the ability to achieve goals or objectives is connected to—and hampered by—the actions of another team member. **Task interdependence** is the interconnection of tasks, such that all members must do their part to complete the team task.[27] For example, in student team projects, each member of the team is typically expected to complete a different part of the team's assignment. Conflict is likely to arise if one member fails to complete his or her part of the assignment in an adequate manner, which would frustrate other members' ability to compete their parts of the project.

In addition, the goals of one organizational department may conflict with the goals of other departments. For example, production managers usually concentrate on efficiency and cost cutting; they focus on producing quality goods or services in a timely and efficient manner. In contrast, marketing managers focus on sales and responsiveness to customers. When a team consists of members from different departments, this diversity increases the potential for conflict within the team as individual members promote agendas that put the interests of their department above the interests of the team.

Conflict also may arise when individual group members do not get along with one another. In such a case, the problem may be as simple as having personality traits that irk coworkers. While some level of personality differences is almost inevitable, it can be disruptive if it gets in the way of the everyday functioning of members. In most cases personal conflict can be managed, particularly if the problem is a matter of personal style (see the next "Digging Deeper" feature).

Techniques to resolve conflict from a Mainstream perspective typically involve one of four approaches, as shown in Table 16.3.

First, eliminating the competition for resources may reduce conflict. An obvious way to resolve conflicts where there are not enough resources to permit members to do their work properly is to increase the number of resources available. This may be accomplished by redefining the boundaries of the team, lobbying other departments and upper management, or rearranging resources within the department itself. For example, if conflict is occurring in a marketing department because there is not enough time to adequately track the progress of customer orders, perhaps some of those responsibilities could be moved to the information systems department.

Second, sometimes conflict can be resolved by redesigning and improving the underlying structures and systems that caused the problem in the first place. This may include, for example, working out inconsistencies in the incentives systems of various departments or reengineering the production process so that team members are less reliant on others to complete their jobs.

A third approach to resolving conflict involves appealing to a **superordinate goal**—that is, a higher-level goal—that may be jeopardized if the issue remains unresolved. An appeal to a superordinate goal is evident when a labor union decides to make wage concessions to ensure survival of an airline. The union's immediate goal may be higher wages for its members, but the union members may realize that without concessions to achieve the superordinate goal of earning enough profit to survive as an airline, they might not even have jobs. For a team, a superordinate goal may be completing work by a certain deadline or delivering a certain level of performance improvement. For example, a running back or receiver on a football team may argue about who should get the ball, but a wise quarterback will focus his attention on the superordinate goal of winning the game.

Finally, managers with strong interpersonal and behavioral skills may be able to help members work out interpersonal issues with their colleagues. This may involve

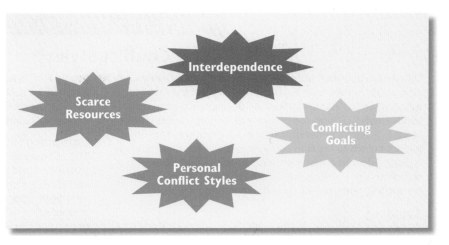

Figure 16.1 Causes of conflict
Source: Dyck, B., Bruning, S. and Driedger, L. (1996). Potential conflict, conflict stimulus, and organizational performance: An empirical test. *The International Journal of Conflict Management,* 7, 295–313. Reproduced with permission of The International Journal of Conflict Management in the format Textbook via Copyright Clearance Center and Emerald Group Publishing Limited.

Superordinate goal is a higher-level goal.

TABLE 16.3

Causes of and Cures for Conflict

Causes	Cures (Techniques)
Scarce resources	Increase resources
Task interdependence	Redesign structures and systems
Conflicting goals	Appeal to superordinate goal
Personal conflict styles	Help members work out issues

DIGGING DEEPER

Conflict Styles[28]

Different people deal with conflict differently, based on the relative concern they have for their interests and the interests of others. (See the Hands-On Activity dealing with interpersonal conflict styles.) A high concern for one's own interests tends to result in assertive behavior, whereas a high concern for others' interests tends to result in cooperative behavior. Five styles are typically identified that represent unique combinations of assertive and cooperative behavior: avoiding, accommodating, competing, compromising, and integrating.

Avoiding

The avoiding style is a passive response to conflicts that is both uncooperative and unassertive. Avoidance is marked by withdrawal from conflict or suppression of the reasons why the conflict has occurred. It may be useful in situations where conflict may be too costly to resolve or where the issue is trivial. Drawbacks include avoiders missing out on opportunities to provide input and leaving both parties frustrated.

Accommodating

The accommodating style—sometimes referred to as obliging—has a high level of cooperativeness and a low level of assertiveness. It is concerned with satisfying others' interests. It may be useful when harmony is desired, for building a relationship, or if the issue is more important to the other party. Drawbacks include accommodators leaving legitimate interests unresolved and feeling used or taken advantage of over time.

Competing

The competing style—sometimes referred to as dominating—reflects a high level of assertiveness and a low level of cooperation. It is characterized by a strong desire to satisfy one's own needs. This style, which is concerned with "winning" the conflict, may be useful if a quick decision is needed or when facing another competitor. Drawbacks include competitors burning bridges or harming relationships.

Compromising

The compromising style has moderate levels of both cooperativeness and assertiveness. It requires each side to give up and receive something of importance. This style may be useful if both sides are equally powerful, if a temporary solution is needed, or when all options for a win-win solution have not resulted in agreement. Drawbacks include compromisers short-circuiting creativity and both parties feeling unsatisfied.

Integrating

The integrating style—sometimes referred to as collaborating—reflects a high level of cooperation and a high level of assertiveness. With this style, there is a focus on creating a win-win situation. Integration seeks to find the advantageous solution for all parties. It may useful if all interests in the conflict are too important to compromise and when consensus is needed. Drawbacks include integrators potentially making a simple decision very complex by taking too much time to talk through every issue.

Research indicates that a person's natural conflict style, which is rooted in his or her personality or shaped by his or her culture, will dominate as the conflict endures. For example, people with collectivistic orientations are more likely to prefer the integrating and compromising styles than people with individualistic orientations. Even so, a leader of a team should generally favor using an integrative style. If the leader finds this difficult, an outside facilitator or mediator may be helpful.

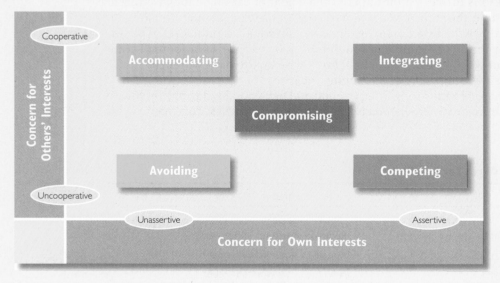

sitting down with them, modeling and practicing active interpersonal listening skills, providing training in diversity awareness that may serve to reduce conflict by making individuals more sensitive to cultural and gender differences, and so on. In some situations, it may be appropriate for a manager to transfer members to another group, or it may even be necessary to dismiss a member altogether.

Stage 3: Norming

The third stage of team development is norming—that is, the step in which members develop shared norms for their roles and behaviors. **Norms** are shared beliefs about social and task behavior in a group.[29] After members resolve points of conflict and confusion, they develop shared mental models of the best ways to complete tasks and the appropriate ways to interact with one another.[30] These norms can promote group performance because they indicate common expectations, provide regularity, help the group avoid interpersonal problems, and define the group's identity.[31] In one sense, norming is "getting on track."

Team members during this stage tend to experience *feelings* of optimism and acceptance of one another and the task. In other words, if the team emerges from the storming, its progress contributes to the formation of a positive attitude toward the team and its goals. The main *issues* in the minds of team members relate to questions of whether the team will now work together effectively or whether the team will spiral back into conflict.

Team norms can be informal (e.g., dress code, whether members work overtime to help one another meet deadlines) or formal, such as standardized operating procedures (e.g., frequency of group meetings, process for sharing information). Leaders play a critical role in establishing and promoting team norms that help improve team performance.[32] *Techniques* for leading the team through the norming stage include making functional norms explicit by "driving a stake in the ground." This can be as simple as saying to the team, "We're really making progress because everyone is going the extra mile to get tasks done on time." Or this can occur during a time outside the team meetings where positive contributions are celebrated. Other examples include providing tangible yet symbolic rewards such as giving a smoothie to someone who helped defuse tensions in the team or providing lunch for the whole team when they have worked overtime.

Two team norms that are critical to team performance relate to the following issues:

- Workload sharing
- Information sharing

A typical dysfunctional norm relating to workload sharing is evident when one or more team members engage in free-riding. Simply put, **free-riding** is not doing your best or contributing your fair share to reach the team's goal. Free-riders can be team members who, due to a lack of commitment to the team's goals, don't perform their fair share of the work. Free-riders also can be team members who are

Symbolic gestures within teams can be effective in reinforcing a message because they are memorable. Why not give a smoothie to someone who smoothed over conflict?

Norms are shared beliefs about social and task behaviors in a group.

Free-riding is not doing your best or contributing your fair share to reach the team's goal.

committed to the goal, but reduce their contributions to the team because they believe the team can achieve the goal and receive the benefits without their full contribution.[33] Free-riding is most common when individual contributions are difficult to monitor or measure, when the team is perceived to be highly capable, and when team members are low in conscientiousness.[34]

When a team member is perceived to be not doing his or her fair share, managerial intervention may be necessary. One free-rider can create a downward spiral of reduced effort that infects the entire team. To avoid the "sucker effect"—which is evident when other team members reduce their effort to avoid being the sucker who does more than his or her fair share of the work—a leader needs to be aware of and address issues of motivation within the team.[35] Techniques to reduce free-riding include making contributions explicit, monitoring team member contributions, and providing accountability for individual contributions.

How people respond to inequities resulting from poor performance can be explained in part by attribution theory. **Attributions** are people's explanations of the causes of behaviors or circumstances. Research on attributions suggests that most people, including other team members, make attributions regarding the cause of a team member's poor performance. The first attribution, or judgment, a person makes is whether the poor performance is the fault of the team member or is due to an external factor (e.g., the actions of a supplier or a customer, faulty equipment). If the person attributes the poor performance to the team member, further thought is given to whether the source is a lack of ability or a lack of motivation. Generally, when motivation is considered the source of the poor performance, team members get angry, and they either withhold effort themselves or punish the team member who performs poorly. In contrast, if the problem stems from a lack of ability, team members are more willing to help the poor performer.[36] The differences in behavior are related to beliefs about whether the cause of poor performance is controllable (e.g., motivation) or not controllable (e.g., ability).[37] Most people seem to give others the benefit of the doubt if they are trying hard, but just do not have high ability. Nonetheless, even team members with the best intentions can get tired of doing others' work. This suggests that leaders should select competent team members or develop the competence of team members when needed.

Another norm that requires the attention of managers and leaders of teams is information sharing. Team members can withhold information for a variety of conscious and unconscious reasons. First, a dominant team member could discourage input from other team members. Team members may hold back information in deference to the passion or expertise of the dominant member or to avoid the stress of conflict. Team members also can withhold input because they have an introverted personality or a lack of confidence in their ideas. Further, team members can intentionally withhold information to speed up the decision-making process once a satisfactory option is presented. *Satisficing* describes a decision process in which an adequate option—one that meets the minimum criteria for a solution—is chosen instead of the best possible option (see Chapter 7).[38] Satisficing may result in suboptimal team decisions, unless the decision is relatively unimportant and the cost of more time and energy is greater than the benefits of finding a better option. Team members also can unconsciously withhold information that is easy to forget because it represents a unique perspective not generally held within the team and, therefore, is not brought up in team discussions. Withholding information, whether intentionally or not, is a dysfunctional norm that should be addressed by the leader of the team.

Attributions are people's explanations of the causes of behaviors or circumstances.

Several techniques for improving information sharing are available to the leader, including these:

- Brainstorming
- Nominal Group Technique
- Delphi Technique

Brainstorming typically involves an unstructured process of group members providing spontaneous ideas—sort of a "thought shower"—while at the same time not criticizing others' ideas so as to encourage free thinking and creative, even wild suggestions.[39] In this technique, the focus is on the quantity and novelty of ideas. Ideas may be captured on a flipchart, computer, or whiteboard by someone who serves as a scribe. After the shower of ideas, the group can evaluate the quality of the ideas in relation to the issue at hand.

Brainstorming solves some of the issues related to a lack of information sharing, but not others, such as the fear of conflicting with a dominant or powerful team member. One alternative that addresses this shortcoming is the **Nominal Group Technique,** a simple information-sharing technique that typically proceeds in the following steps:

Post-its have helped the sharing of information whether while brainstorming in groups or throughout the office. Some have even turned Post-it notes into art. David Alvarez created a portrait of Ray Charles with more than 2000 colored Post-it notes.[41]

1. The leader asks participants to silently and individually write down on a Post-it or piece of paper all their ideas or suggestions related to a specific question, problem, or possibility.[40] This minimizes the impact of dominant team members or prevailing opinions on reducing input.

2. The leader or a facilitator asks for one idea at a time from group members in a round-robin format until all ideas have been shared. By capturing all team members' information and then sharing it in a systematic fashion, more information is made available for the team's task.

3. Group members are allowed to ask clarifying questions about ideas but are not allowed to criticize an idea or champion it.

4. Group members individually rank the ideas, the leader or facilitator compiles the rankings, and the group discusses and confirms a final group ranking.

The Nominal Group Technique also can be done using technology, with members sending in or posting ideas anonymously.[42]

A similar technique is the **Delphi Technique.** In this case, questions are posed to team members remotely and responses are returned to the leader. The leader then compiles all of the ideas without attaching names to them, and sends the list back out to team members for further consideration and response.[43] This process typically involves several rounds of soliciting ideas, and individual members are generally asked to individually rank or vote on the ideas. The anonymity of this technique encourages information sharing from less assertive or powerful people. Moreover, this process helps introverted team members who may be more comfortable taking time to contemplate their responses before submitting ideas.

Brainstorming is an unstructured process of sharing ideas.

Nominal Group Technique is an information-sharing technique in which the leader asks participants to silently and individually write down all their ideas related to a specific question.

Delphi Technique is a technique where questions are posed to team members remotely and responses are returned to the leader; the leader then compiles the ideas without attaching names to them and sends the list back to team members for further consideration and response.

The norming stage is complete when the team members have developed a shared set of expectations for workload, information sharing, and other norms for guiding team member behavior.

Stage 4: Performing

The fourth stage of team development is performing. By this stage, members have had experience working alongside one another. During the preceding stages, they have improved and fine-tuned their social as well as task-oriented interrelationships. As a result, teams are often more mature, are more organized, and function better by the time they reach the performing stage. Members are likely to have a clearer understanding of team goals and, consequently, are more likely to be motivated to achieve them.

During the performing stage, the team members tend to experience *feelings* of pride and confidence in their ability to reach the goals of the team. The main *issues* in the minds of team members relate to how the team is doing in the minds of others and what might be the next challenge for the team to conquer. The team seeks recognition of its performance and feedback to meet the challenges of improved performance and new goals. In addition, the team is usually willing to assume more responsibility for team management. If the manager or leader is not already doing so, this stage presents the opportunity to delegate leadership responsibility to another team member or the team as a whole.

Techniques for leaders to employ during this stage include maintaining and improving team performance by managing the motivation of team members through providing rewards and feedback. In moving from norming to performing, the leader's task changes from affirming progress to addressing deficiencies, and from recognizing behaviors to rewarding results. Two approaches to rewarding and providing feedback to the team may be used:

- Focusing on team contributions and achievement
- Focusing on individual contributions and achievement

Focusing on team goals, feedback, and rewards will unite individuals in pursuit of a common goal, encourage cooperative behavior, and increase collective effort and performance. Focusing on the team draws upon the motivational power of outcome interdependence—the situation where "team members share a common fate."[44] Feedback alone may be sufficient to motivate employees in the short run, but the addition of financial incentives may be necessary to sustain motivation.[45] Another advantage of group systems of feedback and rewards is that group performance measurements may be more readily available and easier to use than individual performance measurements because, from a practical standpoint, it is often impossible to separate out the contributions of each individual when members work interdependently.

Concerns about free-riders in teams can lead managers to provide feedback and rewards to individual team members. Managers need to approach this delicate situation carefully. Most team members acknowledge that managers have a legitimate right to provide individual ratings and believe managers to be less biased than fellow team members. However, when managers are outside the team or don't spend much time with the team, they are viewed as having less information with which to rate individuals accurately.[46]

Concerns about the weaknesses of both approaches (individual focus and team focus) have led some organizations to attempt to provide rewards and feed-

MANAGEMENT IN PRACTICE

Middle Management Teams

Some middle- to lower-level managers can talk a good game about the importance of teamwork, but then fail miserably when they become members of a team with other managers. Such managers frequently do not demonstrate even rudimentary levels of cooperation with one another. The resulting problems are alarming: Communication breaks down, productivity plummets, time and resources are wasted, morale takes a nosedive, customers and profits evaporate, and political activity escalates.[47]

In a study that investigated the issue, more than 200 practicing managers shared their thoughts about teamwork among frontline managers. *Frontline managers* are those who are closely involved with workers on the production line, in the office, on the sales floor, and so on. The managers discussed barriers that prevent teamwork among frontline managers and identified the gateways to improve frontline management cooperation and teamwork. The barriers and gateways as suggested by managers are listed below (with the percentage of respondents who mentioned the barrier or gateway).

Stage	Reasons for Poor Frontline Management Teamwork	Ways to Improve Frontline Management Teamwork
Forming	• Lack of unifying vision (35%) • Conflicting goals (37%)	• Develop a common vision and superordinate goals (36%)
Storming	• Personality conflicts (42%) • Poor teamwork skills (30%)	• Promote team skills development at all levels (28%)
Norming	• Deficient top management modeling and low emphasis on the importance of teamwork (33%) • Personal agendas and organizational politics (24%)	• Ensure top management communicates the importance of teamwork in word and deed (31%) • Involve frontline managers in decision making (21%)
Performing	• Rewards based on individual performance (36%) • System and structural barriers to cooperation (29%)	• Implement team-based performance feedback and reward systems (33%)

back at both levels. This was the decision of the managers at Amica Wireless, which we discussed in Chapter 12 during our exploration of human resource management practices. Problems attributed to using only team incentives led this company to adopt a compensation plan that included both individual- and team-level incentives.

THE FOUR STAGES OF MULTISTREAM TEAM DEVELOPMENT

Mainstream managers are likely to use teams if they believe that teams help to improve productivity and efficiency. In contrast, the Multistream perspective has a bias toward working in groups rather than as individuals, because being in groups and teams is believed to be inherently good. It is good to build a sense of community, to embrace diversity, to foster interpersonal relationships, and to create healthy interdependencies. Certainly, from this perspective, teams also are desirable because they have the potential to improve productivity and performance, but this is not the defining motive for teamwork. The Multistream perspective is oriented toward the belief that team-based work environments dignify organizational members, contribute to meaningful work and creative expression, and promote individual and collective well-being. In such a context, members can rely on one another to work toward the common good, rather than to advance their narrowly defined self-interests. Also, team members are likely to be motivated to sacrifice for others, rather than look for opportunities to shirk (free-ride) or to undermine colleagues' efforts. When team members treat one another fairly and with respect, absenteeism decreases and team performance is likely to increase.[48]

A Multistream perspective on team development addresses the *feelings* and *issues* of team members with *techniques* that emphasize community and nonmaterial criteria. The four Multistream stages of team development are as follows:

1. Originating
2. Elaborating
3. Collaborating
4. Disseminating

At each stage, the general behaviors of managers also can be argued to follow the Multistream leadership framework discussed in Chapter 15 and illustrated in Figure 16.2. Specifically, the Multistream manager attends to both the socioemotional and structural needs of the team. For example, as this relates to structural behavior, in the initial stages of development the Multistream manager is visibly active in helping to arrive at a mutually acceptable direction for the team and in reframing conflicts as opportunities for deeper understanding. As the team matures, the manager acts in less visible ways—"behind the scenes"—to establish connections between the team and its stakeholders, which ensures the flow of adequate resources and information. This invisible behavior of managers is boundary-spanning behavior in which the manager serves as an ambassador for the team outside the boundaries of the team.[49]

The Multistream perspective on leadership in teams differs from the Mainstream perspective in a number of additional ways. First, leadership is considered to be critical from a Multistream perspective, but it does not necessarily have to come from a formal role or a narrowly defined position. Leaders can emerge from within teams, and members may share leadership responsibilities. Indeed, shared leadership in new businesses has been demonstrated to have a significant impact on the success of start-ups.[50] In manufacturing teams, more shared leadership within teams has been shown to contribute to team cohesion.[51] From a Multistream perspective, shared leadership may be beneficial from a productivity standpoint, but more importantly it minimizes power differences and respects the leadership potential and contributions of all team members.

Second, from a Multistream perspective, what is valued as leadership behavior is defined more broadly than what is valued as leadership behavior from a Mainstream perspective. In particular, a Multistream approach may welcome a wider variety of people as leaders than the Mainstream approach. For example, in Mainstream organizations, where leadership is closely related to task behavior, men still emerge more often as leaders than do women.[52] Although women make substantial contributions to the team's task, they

Figure 16.2 Four basic Multistream stages of team development and suggestions for manager behavior

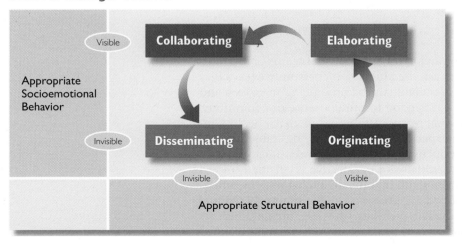

tend to be more willing than men to be inclusive and focus on nurturing behavior. In a Mainstream environment, women do not tend to get the credit they deserve for these leadership behaviors.[53] In contrast, Multistream managers recognize that leadership takes many forms and are more likely to acknowledge the contributions of members who work behind the scenes to build relationships and help others. In particular, Multistream managers recognize and promote the contributions women make as leaders within teams. Interestingly, some research in manufacturing teams suggests that as more women participate as informal leaders within a team, the team performs better.[54]

Third, the issue of control is different across the Mainstream and Multistream perspectives, as will be discussed in depth in Chapter 18. In the context of teams, increasing participation, autonomy, and self-management result in a reduction in bureaucratic top-down controls. This leads to **concertive control,** which occurs when the control moves from residing with management to residing with the workers or team members.[55] In other words, people keep each other accountable or, as Diane found out in the opening case, "your boss is your team." Concertive control, which stems from peer expectations and shared outcomes, is characteristic of the Multistream approach. With concertive control, team members set standards and expectations, keep one another in line, and make sure members are aware of shortcomings or deficiencies. Control is exercised for the sake of the team and its members and their common goals and aspirations. Although it can be liberating for team members to be free from management control, team members also can exert considerable pressure on one another to meet team expectations,[56] even if those expectations reinforce materialist–individualist values within the team.

> **Concertive control** is when control moves from residing with management to residing with workers or team members.

Stage 1: Originating

The first stage of team development from a Multistream perspective involves developing a shared understanding of the team's sense of place and purpose in the organization. The emphasis is on a shared team identity that is grounded in its organizational context. The heart of a team's identity comes not from its goals (Mainstream), nor even from how it fits with improving organizational performance, but rather from how it relates to other groups and the mission of the organization. Put differently, the emphasis is on connecting with others (individuals and teams) and with the overarching purpose of the organization.

The manager may be the one to identify and originate the team in a Multistream organizational culture. However, teams may also be self-originating in that members of the organization realize the need to act collectively and self-organize to meet identified needs. Consistent with the example of the Open Space technique described in the closing case in Chapter 14, teams may emerge when an organizational member identifies a need or hot button and proposes it as a possible team focus. Recall from the opening case that most of the teams at Gore originate from the ideas of team members, and members join based on their interest or their ability to add value, not as a result of "orders" from management.

As with the Mainstream teams, during the originating stage members of Multistream teams typically have some *feelings* of anticipation and apprehension. The main *issues* in members' minds tend to be questions regarding what the team will do and why it is important. Although the answers to these questions may be self-evident if the team members themselves have originated the team, the purpose of the team should be commonly understood. Here the team can benefit when the manager helps provide an explicit understanding of the purpose of the team and its role in the organization and, in conjunction with team members, generates a basic set of agreements about how to work together.

As should be clear at this point in the book, the *techniques* associated with the Multistream approach are much more participative, even in the development of team goals and structures. The role of a leader in the team is to ask the right questions. For example, a leader might ask, "Given the mission of the organization and our understanding of our current needs, what should be the purpose and goals of this team?" Upon mutually agreeing on the goals, a leader might then ask the team to suggest ground rules for working together toward those goals.

Another question to ask is who should be welcome to join the team. From a Mainstream perspective, the answer may relate to who has the expertise to help the team achieve its goals; in contrast, from a Multistream perspective, the answer is more an issue of who might offer a unique perspective through their participation or find it meaningful to be a part of the team. Teams from a Multistream perspective are more inclusive of organizational members as well as suppliers, customers, and possibly even community members. Membership also is more transient during this stage, as members move in and out of the meetings to explore the team's purpose and to provide input. As with the teams at Gore, the emphasis for team members during the originating stage is exploring potential roles instead of defining specific roles. Eventually, a core of committed team members emerges and this stage draws to a close.

Stage 2: Elaborating

In the second stage, the team moves toward elaborating, a group process of exploring and enhancing awareness of the tasks and roles that may be necessary to fulfill the shared goals of the team. Here there is greater emphasis on internal group dynamics, while maintaining openness that ensures connectivity with other stakeholders. During this stage, the manager maintains an active role in structuring participative discussions about the tasks necessary to fulfill the goals of the team, but also visibly engages in socioemotional behavior that builds relationships and trust.

In the elaborating stage, even for those who are comfortable with participative processes and evolving structures, *feelings* can include discouragement and frustration. The central underlying *issues* for team members are the questions of whether the team will get going and fulfill its purpose. As with Mainstream team development, a central issue can be conflict, particularly given that the Multistream perspective encourages input and participation from a diverse set of stakeholders. Whereas the Mainstream approach views multiple opinions as a source of conflict to be resolved, the Multistream approach welcomes multiple views as an opportunity for members to broaden their own understanding and build relationships. It is the ability to hold multiple views simultaneously that transforms these views from a source of conflict into a source of deeper understanding and greater appreciation of diverse perspectives. Instead of debating positions or issues, the Multistream approach is similar to transformational conflict resolution in that it emphasizes dialogue or conversation to help each person to understand the other's perspective and be mindful of the person behind the position. By reframing the conflict from a dispute to a search for deeper understanding, participants become more self-aware, empathetic, and open to mutually beneficial alternative solutions.[57]

The *techniques* used during the elaboration stage involve facilitating and reframing conflict from something negative to something positive, thereby minimizing discouragement and frustration. Encouraging a diversity of opinion is important because having more team members who have different perspectives than those in the majority increases the creativity of teams.[58] Using a transformative approach, the Multistream manager addresses conflicts by asking questions and offering suggestions that prompt team members to look at conflicts from a higher level of abstraction. The perspective changes from specific positions to more general goals, from parts of an issue to a broader view, and from individual concerns to system concerns.[59] For example, a team might be at odds about how much the development of video game software emphasizes the specific dimensions of speed or dexterity, but at a higher level of abstraction speed and dexterity are both related to motion. Thus a manager can direct the team conversation toward how motion is captured in the video game and, in turn, how motion fits with the gaming hardware to shape the overall gaming experience. The focus on more abstract ideas helps dissenting members concentrate on common interests and challenges that can stimulate creative or transformative solutions, such as innovations to gaming hardware, which were not under consideration prior to the discussion.

During this stage of team development, the manager also focuses on socioemotional behavior that further develops a sense of shared identity and trust among members. A leader can provide team-building activities that build trust and allow team members to test out and refine various roles. Furthermore, the inclination of Multistream managers to affirm team members is evident in everyday behavior such as drawing attention to strengths of members and reminding members of past behaviors that have served to benefit others. This active role modeling of socioemotional behavior helps build interpersonal relationships where the focus is on positive aspects of members' characteristics. Deliberately promoting the good in others becomes a virtuous cycle in which this affirming behavior is embraced by others.[60] This other-centered attitude makes it easier for members to exhibit self-control over their own narrowly defined self-interests and better serve the interests of the team.

During this stage, it is critical for a manager to affirm evolving roles, to intentionally nurture trust within the group, and to communicate that holding divergent goals can contribute to high-quality decisions and results. The manager needs to be sensitive to the possibility that team members will tire of working through these differences, and should look for opportunities to celebrate progress and refresh relationships—perhaps by scheduling a dinner out together. If team-building activities and the manager's facilitative behavior fall short of alleviating the concerns of team members, the manager or its members may need to originate another team to satisfy the interests of the broad set of participants. A team is not likely to move into the next stage of collaboration without committing to a shared purpose, building trust between team members, and developing team plans and member agreements that are mutually satisfying.

Stage 3: Collaborating

In the collaborating stage of team development, the manager pulls back from visible involvement in structuring team interactions while continuing to visibly support team members socioemotionally. During this stage, team members tend to experience *feelings* of optimism and a sense of community. The main *issues* in the minds of team members are related to working together effectively and maintaining the priority of shared interests over any conflicts due to personal interests. The manager during this stage affirms collaborative norms and downplays competitive norms.

Whereas the elaboration stage of encouraging diversity of ideas and input could isolate members, this stage involves managers using *techniques* that emphasize interdependency, common ground, and collaborative links throughout the organization and beyond. Multistream managers encourage collaboration by working behind the scenes to promote meetings and relationships with other stakeholders. For example, at Gore, team members communicate directly with customers, suppliers, or even other teams. This approach might seem strange or even offensive to other companies that are not accustomed to having a low-level team member become involved in negotiations or decision making. In these cases, the Multistream manager serves as an ambassador to the other organization, explaining the Gore culture and how teams typically operate.

During this stage of team development, the Multistream manager can promote collaboration by helping team members understand others' contributions and by communicating how he or she sees members working together toward mutually beneficial ends. In this sense, the manager provides a bird's-eye view of the forest (i.e., a system view) that can be lost by team members who are engaged in the detailed work of planting or cultivating one tree at a time. In turn, this promotes a similar broad perspective among the team members. The manager's focus is encouraging but not dictating linkages both inside and outside the team, and empowering members to participate in the fine-tuning of collaborative behavior. With the trust built in previous stages of team development, increasing levels of empowerment dignify the team and its members and contribute to high performance.[61]

The collaborative norm of workload sharing may still be an issue here, but the approach to dealing with it is different from a Multistream perspective than from a Mainstream perspective. Whereas Mainstream theory focuses on limiting the negative effects of free-riders through monitoring and accountability, a Multistream approach tries to promote the positive effects of **consistent contributors.**[62] According to the Multistream view, there are three kinds of team members:

- Free-riders (those who do as little as possible)
- Conditional contributors (those whose contribution depends on the situation)
- Consistent contributors (those who contribute regardless of how little their teammates contribute and, therefore, are sometimes considered to be "suckers" from a Mainstream perspective)

Research shows that over the long term, on average, teams with consistent contributors outperform teams that do not have consistent contributors. It also reveals that the consistent contributor effect holds for both high- and low-status team members, although the influence of the high-status members is more likely to be recognized by others. Part of the reason for this outcome is that the behavior of consistent contributors influences the norms of the group through modeling service to the team. When the source of consistent contribution is an agreeable or cooperative personality, having more consistent contributors on a team can increase performance, cohesion, and workload sharing while reducing conflict.[63]

Unfortunately, the servant orientation of consistent contributors can make them vulnerable to being exploited by other members of the team. Furthermore, to get more competitive team members to become aware of and be influenced by persistent cooperation, a consistent contributor may need to relentlessly cooperate (and suffer, in relative terms) for a long time. Even then cooperation is not guaranteed. Indeed, it is this fear of exploitation and the potential for being a sucker that makes being a consistent contributor seem irrational from a Mainstream point of view. In the face of this vulnerability, Multistream managers provide socioemotional support by recognizing, encouraging, and drawing attention to the behavior of consistent contributors.

Consistent contributor is someone who contributes regardless of how little his or her teammates contribute.

During the collaborating stage, the manager increases his or her boundary-spanning activities, directing more energy outside the team to engage the system to ensure that resources and information are available, and using the manager's legitimate authority to minimize system performance barriers or roadblocks. In other words, the manager works as a servant outside the team to smooth the road the team is traveling. In this stage, most, if not all, of the explicit task leadership within the team is carried out by team members with little or no direction from the manager. Nonetheless, the manager demonstrates socioemotional support by visibly maintaining contact with the team through attending meetings, listening to concerns, and recognizing milestones and achievements related to material (i.e., task or goal) and nonmaterial (i.e., social or virtuous) progress.

Stage 4: Disseminating

In the disseminating stage, information related to what the team has accomplished and learned diffuses throughout the organization and beyond to benefit others. The manager serves the team in primarily invisible ways, looking for opportunities to recognize the team and promote learning. At this stage, team members tend to experience *feelings* of pride and confidence in their ability to reach the goals of the team. The main *issues* in the minds of the team members relate to how the team is doing in the view of others and what might be the next challenge for the team to conquer. The manager works to stimulate a balance of appreciation for past performance and passion for new challenges.

Again, although the feelings and issues are similar to what was discussed under Mainstream team development, the *techniques* used by managers during this stage are quite different from a Multistream perspective. The main difference lies in how the issues and needs are addressed and what the source of control within the team is. A Mainstream perspective emphasizes the role of the leader in providing extrinsic reinforcement, establishing formal feedback systems, and sustaining team processes. By contrast, although a Multistream manager may informally offer ideas and feedback, the emphasis is on the team as the source of intrinsic motivation, learning, and concertive control. That is, the manager relies on and empowers team members to identify motivating activities, assess progress, and hold one another accountable.

During the disseminating stage, the manager maintains an invisible attention to the tasks and socioemotional processes of the team. When a team keeps its members accountable, this process has the potential to promote blaming and individual defensiveness. Instead, if a manager can subtly reframe failures or shortcomings as problem-solving opportunities, even negative feedback has the potential to stimulate cooperative behavior within the team.[64] The manager is not likely to directly deliver the feedback or prescribe solutions to issues during this stage. Instead, the manager seeks out and provides sources of information that team members may use to enhance team learning. Furthermore, a Multistream manager would naturally focus on team-level rewards to reinforce a sense of community. That being said, there are related reasons for using team-level rewards—for example, to promote cooperation, reinforce interdependency, and increase collective motivation. If individual recognition or rewards are deemed necessary, a Multistream manager would be inclined to have teams decide how these rewards should be awarded. This is illustrated by how Gore used compensation teams to decide how individuals would be rewarded for work within their teams as well as work that spanned several teams or, in the case of coaching and mentoring, helped others to succeed.[65]

Boundary spanning becomes the primary activity of the manager during the disseminating stage of team development. Yet, even in this role the manager should not step away from the team entirely. In a study of nuclear plants, managers who remained as members of teams were better able to help the teams disseminate their learning throughout the organization.[66] A Multistream manager would encourage a team that has developed collaborative skills to spread its learning beyond its boundaries to tackle new challenges inside and outside the organization. For example, at one time in its history, team members at Saturn used their experiences and successes working collaboratively to train others within General Motors and also consulted with other organizations—both for-profit and nonprofit. No doubt these opportunities were intrinsically satisfying and provided more extensive learning experiences than simply hearing feedback from their managers.

From a Mainstream perspective, this activity can be threatening given that the team may seem out of control and unfocused. From a Multistream perspective, however, the work of these teams outside of traditional or Mainstream boundaries is an important part of the organizational learning process. The team's engagement with other teams or organizations benefits others, but also accelerates the learning within the team itself. The process of serving others—who may be very different in their goals, work demands, and culture—enhances flexibility and exposes the team to others' best practices, which can in turn further their own well-being.

CLOSING CASE

LEGO Mindstorms[67]

The LEGO company, established in 1932, for a long time had been one of the most successful and well-known toy companies in the world. It functioned in a traditional hierarchical fashion that focused on efficiency, encouraged incremental improvement, and counted on predictable product life cycles. In the mid-1990s, LEGO began experiencing struggles as increased competition, Internet-based games, and a changing customer led to reduced profits and concerns about long-term viability. In response, LEGO launched the Mindstorms product development team consisting of Ben Smith, a recent addition to the company with experience managing an information technology company, and Thomas Atkinson, a long-time product manager. Essentially, they were to create a robotic LEGO toy. Working with a limited budget, they had the following charge:

> Take some partially developed programmable LEGO brick technology, develop an original product based on this technology, and bring it to market.

The team was placed in the low-profile educational division and allowed to create a novel product development process that was described as follows:

The Mindstorms team could experiment more freely with unorthodox operating procedures, which it set out to do. "We threw away most of the rulebook, and operated like a small, entrepreneurial business," said Atkinson . . . what Smith described as "an entirely new business system, emphasizing speed to market, alliances with carefully selected partners, high annual novelty share, a close relationship and interaction with the consumer, and lean, globally centralized operations."

Given that it had only limited funding, the Mindstorms team had to borrow people from within the existing system, which contributed to a great deal of conflict for these folks as they were expected to maintain their current jobs while contributing to the Mindstorms project. Originating with only two members, facing a challenging charge, and getting help on borrowed time, the Mindstorms team was intentionally more inclusive of customers and embarked on cultivating an Internet community who would help shape the product's design and features. The team developed a large network of partnerships and alliances—a computer manufacturer, a museum, a software company, a children's learning organization. In contrast to the typical LEGO way, they set out to work with these partners as equals. Such an approach carried with it a set of challenges not present when one partner has power over others. Atkinson noted, "It is not like we can just say, 'This is the way it is going to work, this is the way to do it' . . . [the partner] would just say, 'stop.'"

In the elaboration stage, the new way of working and the extended partnerships led to conflict, or in some cases a lack of conflict. Smith said, "People weren't confronting each other with their differences of opinion. We had to make people talk directly to each other about this." Team members seemed to be looking for more clarity about working relationships, so Smith devised an organizational chart and talked to a few people about it. Ultimately, however, he ended up throwing the chart out. He realized that the Mindstorms process would suffer if it was formalized. Instead, he increased his communication, making it a point to chat with team members and ask questions—sometimes about work, many times not. He also encouraged the same behavior from other team members. He explained his reason for investing in relationships by saying, "Employees are like bank accounts: If you just deposit money regularly, they grow like crazy!"

Collaboration occurred as the team adopted a form of parallel processing where development and implementation of ideas occurred concurrently. Often implementation issues surfaced that resulted in real-time adjustments in the design, thus saving time and resources. The benefits were numerous, but so were the challenges. It was an exhausting, fast-paced environment where feedback was almost immediate. At one point a marketing consultant concluded that the Mindstorms product was too complex for kids and would not sell. Smith called a two-week "timeout" that excluded partners and even people from the parent company from discussions with the core team. Instead of making knee-jerk adjustments during this time, the team reaffirmed a vision for itself to "establish the LEGO company as the leading supplier of child centered robotics in the . . . mass consumer market," and redoubled its efforts to position its emerging product as unique and distinct from existing LEGO products.

As word of the progress and potential of the Mindstorms team spread throughout the LEGO organization, top managers within LEGO decided to put resources behind another product, TechToy, which was based on the same underlying technology. TechToy received a commitment from top management of four times the resources that Mindstorms received. The TechToy team operated like traditional product teams at LEGO—more hierarchical, slower, more sequential. Although the hard technology was the same, the soft technology of how the team operated was not. The differences also were obvious to outsiders:

> The guy from Mindstorms [Product Development Engineer B] did all he could for that product, his heart was in it. The engineer working on TechToy took a holiday right in the middle of a very critical phase!

In the final analysis, the Mindstorms team's efforts paid off. Despite enduring a dual launch with TechToy (a decision imposed by top management), the Mindstorms team received most of the publicity from the launch, in part due to support from its extensive network of partners. In fact, the Mindstorms launch was considered the most successful LEGO new-product launch in years. Moreover, the LEGO Mindstorms robot kits were wildly popular beyond its target audience of children and educational markets. They began showing up in computer labs and among other techies. LEGO Mindstorms has become the best-selling product in LEGO history, and without any advertising. Sticking with its partnership approach to development, LEGO Mindstorms NXT was recently released to rave reviews.

QUESTIONS FOR DISCUSSION

1. If you were asked to be one of the original members of the Mindstorms team, what would excite you? What would keep you up at night in the initial stage of the team's development?

2. What were the benefits and the drawbacks to including a variety of stakeholders in the team discussions?

3. Why do you think LEGO managers supported the TechToy team more than the Mindstorms team?

SUMMARY

Organizations include both groups and teams. A group is a collection of two or more people who share a common interest or association. A team is a collection of people with shared goals, who work interdependently as a unit and are accountable to one another to achieve those goals. Teams, and most groups, progress through a series of relatively predictable developmental stages. The stages include important processes common to teams and critical for team success.

From a Mainstream perspective, teams are a means to the ends of optimized productivity and efficiency. As such, progress through the four Mainstream stages of team development requires managers to exhibit the following behaviors to reap the material benefits of teams:

- Forming: set direction, create cohesion
- Storming: resolve conflict, stay on task
- Norming: affirm performance norms
- Performing: provide feedback, recognition

From a Multistream perspective, teams are a worthwhile end in that they foster community. As such, progress through the four Multistream stages of team development requires managers to exhibit the following behaviors to benefit the organization and community:

- Originating: foster sense of purpose/identity
- Elaborating: transform conflict, refine roles
- Collaborating: emphasize interdependencies
- Disseminating: diffuse learning throughout the organization

QUESTIONS FOR REFLECTION AND DISCUSSION

1. What is a group? What is a team? Provide an example of each.

2. Reflect back on your experiences on a school team. In what ways did your team experience the stages of development described in this chapter? In what ways did your experience differ?

3. As manager, what would be your approaches to improving team task cohesion and social cohesion?

4. List and briefly describe the benefits and drawbacks of your conflict style. When will it work best? When might you need to use another style?

5. Suppose you are asked to head up a problem-solving team. Identify and explain information-sharing techniques that will reduce the likelihood of groupthink and improve the team's decision making.

6. How do you typically respond to free-riders in teams? Do the perceived causes of free-riding influence how you respond?

7. Have you ever been on a team with a consistent contributor? What effect did the consistent contributor have on the rest of the members? Was he or she treated like a "sucker"?

8. Explain your experience of having team members evaluate your performance. If you have no experience in this area, how do you think you would respond to team members giving and receiving feedback that influences grades?

9. List some of the differences in Mainstream and Multistream management techniques that are used during each stage of team development.

HANDS-ON ACTIVITIES

Interpersonal Conflict Styles[68]

Please indicate the extent to which each sentence typically describes your behavior in conflict situations, with a 1 indicating "rarely" or "never," and a 5 indicating "almost always."

		Rarely				Always
1.	I argue my case with others to show the merits of my position.	1	2	3	4	5
2.	I negotiate with others so that a compromise can be reached.	1	2	3	4	5
3.	I try to satisfy the expectations of others.	1	2	3	4	5
4.	I try to investigate an issue with others to find a solution acceptable to both of us.	1	2	3	4	5
5.	I am firm in pursuing my side of the issue.	1	2	3	4	5
6.	I attempt to avoid being "put on the spot" and try to keep my conflict with others to myself.	1	2	3	4	5
7.	I hold on to my solution to a problem.	1	2	3	4	5
8.	I use "give and take" so that a compromise can be made.	1	2	3	4	5
9.	I exchange accurate information with others to solve a problem together.	1	2	3	4	5
10.	I avoid open discussion of my differences with others.	1	2	3	4	5
11.	I accommodate the wishes of others.	1	2	3	4	5
12.	I try to bring all our concerns out in the open so that the issues can be resolved in the best possible way.	1	2	3	4	5
13.	I propose a middle ground for breaking deadlocks.	1	2	3	4	5
14.	I go along with the suggestions of others.	1	2	3	4	5
15.	I try to keep my disagreements with others to myself to avoid hard feelings.	1	2	3	4	5

Scoring Key: To determine your score for each conflict style, sum the response values from the questions associated with each category. The highest score is your dominant style.

Questions representing category	Category score
Avoiding (6, 10, 15)	_____
Accommodating (3, 11, 14)	_____
Competing (1, 5, 7)	_____
Compromising (2, 8, 13)	_____
Collaborating (4, 9, 12)	_____

ENDNOTES

1. Deutschman, A. (2004, December). The fabric of creativity. *Fast Company*, pp. 54–59; Weinreb, M. (2003). Power to the people. *Sales and Marketing Management*, 155(4), 30–36; Corporate culture, www.gore.com.

2. Hunter, L. W., MacDuffie, J. P., & Doucet, L. (2002). What makes teams take? Employee reactions to work reforms. *Industrial and Labor Relations Review*, 55(3), 448–472.

3. Glassop, L. I. (2002). The organizational benefits of teams. *Human Relations*, 55(2), 225–249.

4. Cohen S. G., & Bailey, D. E. (1997). What makes teams work: Group effectiveness research from the shop floor to the executive suite. *Journal of Management*, 23, 239–290.

5. Cohen & Bailey, 1997.

6. Cohen, S., Ledford, G., & Spreitzer, G. (1996). A predictive model of self-managing work team effectiveness. *Human Relations*, 49(5), 643–676.

7. Batt, R. (2004). Who benefits from teams? Comparing workers, supervisors, and managers. *Industrial Relations*, 43(1), 183–212.

8. Longenecker, C., Neubert, M. J., & Fink, L. (2007). Causes and consequences of managerial failure in rapidly changing organizations. *Business Horizons*, 50(2), 145–155.

9. Lencioni, P. M. (2002). *The five dysfunctions of a team*. San Francisco: Jossey-Bass.

10. Katzenbach, J. R., & Smith, D. K. (2005). The discipline of teams. *Harvard Business Review*, 83(7/8), 162–171.

11. Katzenbach, J. R., & Smith, D. K. (2001). The discipline of virtual teams. *Leader to Leader*, 22, 16–25.

12. Tuckman, B. W. (1965). Developmental sequence for small groups. *Psychological Bulletin*, 63, 384–399.

13. Gersick, C. J. G. (1988). Time and transition in work teams: Toward a new model of group development. *Academy of Management Journal*, 31(1), 9–41.

14. Subramony, M., Beehr, T. A., & Johnson, C. M. (2004). Employee and customer perceptions of service quality in an Indian firm. *Applied Psychology: An International Review*, 53(2), 311–327.

15. Milliken, F. J., & Martins, L. L. (1996). Searching for common threads: Understanding the multiple effects of diversity in organizational groups. *Academy of Management Review*, 21(2), 402–433; Barrick, M. R., Stewart, G. L., Neubert, M. J., & Mount, M. K. (1998). Relating member ability and personality to work-team processes and team effectiveness. *Journal of Applied Psychology*, 83(3), 377–391.

16. Staples, D., & Zhao, L. (2007). The effects of cultural diversity in virtual teams versus face-to-face teams. *Group Decision & Negotiation*, 15(4), 389–406.

17. Hopkins, W. E., Hopkins, S. A., & Gross, M. A. (2005). Cultural diversity recomposition and effectiveness in monoculture work groups. *Journal of Organizational Behavior*, 26(8), 949–964.

18. Hymowitz, C. (2006). Turning diversity into dollars: How some companies are reaping the benefits of a mixed work force. *Wall Street Journal: Classroom Edition*. http://wsjclassroomedition.com/archive/06feb/bigb1_diversity.htm.

19. For more on this topic, see Kayes, D. C. (2004). The 1996 Mount Everest climbing disaster: The breakdown of learning in teams. *Human Relations*, 57(10), 1263–1284.

20. Salas, E., Rozell, D., Mullen, B., & Driskell, J. E. (1999). The effect of team building on performance and integration. *Small Group Research*, 30(3), 309–329.

21. http://www.campbellfamilyinstitute.com/Pages/research/team.aspx.

22. Mullen, B., & Copper, C. (1994). The relation between group cohesiveness and performance: An integration. *Psychological Bulletin*, 115(2), 210–227; Jordan, M. H., Feild, H. S., & Armenakis, A. A. (2002). The relationship of group process variables and team performance: A team-level analysis in a field setting. *Small Group Research*, 33(1), 121–150.

23. Dyck, B., Bruning, S., & Driedger, L. (1996). Potential conflict, conflict stimulus, and organizational performance: An empirical test. *International Journal of Conflict Management*, 7, 295–313.

24. Janis, I. L. (1972). *Victims of groupthink*. Boston: Houghton Mifflin.

25. Forsyth, D. (1990). *Group dynamics*. Pacific Grove, CA: Brooks/Cole; Janis, I. L. (1972). *Victims of groupthink*. Boston: Houghton Mifflin; Kaplan, M. F., & Miller, C. E. (1983). Group discussion and judgment. In P. B. Paulus (Ed.), *Basic group processes* (pp. 65–94). New York: Springer-Verlag.

26. Katzenstein, G. (1996). The debate on structured debate: Toward a unified theory. *Organizational Behavior and Human Decision Processes*, 66(3), 316–332.

27. Wageman R. (1995). Interdependence and group effectiveness. *Administrative Science Quarterly*, 40(1), 145–180.

28. Cai, D. A., & Fink, E. L. (2002). Conflict style differences between individualists and collectivists. *Communication Monographs*, 69(1), 67–87; Volkema, R. J., & Bergmann, T. J. (1995). Conflict styles as indicators of behavioral patterns in interpersonal conflicts. *Journal of Social Psychology*, 135(1), 5–15; Rahim, M. A. (1983). A measure of styles of handling interpersonal conflict. *Academy of Management Journal*, 26(2), 368–376; Antonioni, D. (1999). Relationship between the Big Five personality factors and conflict management styles. *Journal of Conflict Management*, 9(4), 336–355. Gundlach, M., Zivnuska, S., & Stoner, J. (2006). Understanding the relationship between individualism–collectivism and team performance through an integration of social identity theory and the social relations model. *Human Relations*, 59(12), 1603–1632.

29. Taggar, S., & Ellis, R. (2007). The role of leaders in shaping formal team norms. *Leadership Quarterly*, 18, 105–120.

30. Lim, B., & Klein, K. J. (2006). Team mental models and team performance: A field study of the effects of team mental model similarity and accuracy. *Journal of Organizational Behavior*, 27(4), 403–418; Edwards, B. D., Day, E. A., Arthur, W., & Bell, S. T. (2006). Relationships among team ability composition, team mental models, and team performance. *Journal of Applied Psychology*, 91(3), 727–736.

31. Feldman, D. C. (1984). The development and enforcement of group norms. *Academy of Management Review*, 9, 47–53.

32. Taggar & Ellis, 2007.

33. Olson, M. (1965). *The logic of collective action: Public goods and the theory of groups*. Cambridge, MA: Harvard University Press; Kidwell, R. E., & Bennett, N. (1993). Employee propensity to withhold effort: A conceptual model to intersect three avenues of research. *Academy of Management Review*, 18, 429–456.

34. Neubert, M. J., Taggar, S., & Cady, S. H. (2006). The role of conscientiousness and extraversion in affecting the relationship between perceptions of group potency and volunteer group member selling behavior: An interactionist perspective. *Human Relations*, 59(9), 1235–1260.

35. Kerr, N. L. (1983). Motivation losses in small groups: A social dilemma analysis. *Journal of Personality and Social Psychology, 45,* 819–828.

36. Taggar, S., & Neubert, M. J. (2004). The impact of poor performers on team outcomes: An empirical examination of attribution theory. *Personnel Psychology, 57,* 935–968.

37. Weiner, B. (1986). *An attributional theory of motivation and emotion.* New York: Springer-Verlag; LePine, J. A., & Van Dyne, L. (2001). Peer responses to low performers: An attributional model of helping in the context of groups. *Academy of Management Review, 26,* 67–84.

38. March, J. G., & Simon, H. A. (1958). *Organizations.* New York: Wiley.

39. Garrett, A. G. (2006, October). Crash course . . . in brainstorming. *Management Today,* 16.

40. Delbecq, A. L., Van de Ven, A. H., & Gustafson, D. H. (1975). *Group techniques for program planning: A guide to Nominal Group Technique and Delphi Processes.* Glenview, IL: Scott-Foresman; Lago, P. P., Beruvides, M. G., Jian, J., Canto, A., Sandoval, A., & Taraban, R. (2007). Structuring group decision making in a web-based environment by using the nominal group technique. *Computers & Industrial Engineering, 52(2),* 277–295.

41. http://www.artnewsblog.com/2007/08/post-it-notes-and-marketing-art.htm.

42. Lago et al., 2007.

43. Rowe, G., & Wright, G. (1999). The Delphi Technique as a forecasting tool: Issues and analysis. *International Journal of Forecasting, 15(4),* 353–375.

44. Guzzo, R. A., & Shea, G. P. (1992). Group performance and intergroup relations in organizations. In M. D. Dunnette & L. M. Hough (Eds.), *Handbook of industrial and organizational psychology* (2nd ed., Vol. 1, pp. 269–313). Palo Alto, CA: Consulting Psychologists Press.

45. Campion, M. A., Medsker, G. J., & Higgs, A. C. (1993). Relations between work group characteristics and effectiveness: Implications for designing effective work groups. *Personnel Psychology, 46,* 823–847; Pritchard, R. D., Jones, S. D., Roth, P. L., Stuebing, K. K., & Ekeberg, S. E. (1988). Effects of group feedback, goal setting, and incentives on organizational productivity. *Journal of Applied Psychology, 73,* 337–358.

46. Neubert, M. J., & Scullen, S. (2004). *The potential and volitional accuracy of supervisors and team members as ratings sources of individual team members.* Working paper.

47. Longenecker, C., & Neubert, M. J. (2000). Barriers and gateways to management cooperation and teamwork. *Business Horizons, 43,* 37–44.

48. Colquitt, J. A., Noe, R. A., & Jackson, C. L. (2002). Justice in teams: Antecedents and consequences of procedural justice climate. *Personnel Psychology, 55(1),* 83–109.

49. Druskat, V. U., & Wheeler, J. V. (2003). Managing from the boundary: The effective leadership of self-managing teams. *Academy of Management Journal, 46(4),* 435–457.

50. Ensley, M. D., Hmieleski, K. M., & Pearce, C. (2006). The importance of vertical and shared leadership within new venture top management teams: Implications for the performance of startups. *Leadership Quarterly, 17(3),* 217–231.

51. Neubert, M. J. (1999). Too much of a good thing or the more the merrier? Exploring the dispersion and gender composition of informal leadership in intact manufacturing teams. *Small Group Research, 30(5),* 635–646.

52. Karau, S. J., & Eagly, A. H. (1999). Invited reaction: Gender, social roles, and the emergence of leaders. *Human Resource Development Quarterly, 10(4),* 321–327.

53. Neubert, M. J., & Taggar, S. (2004). Pathways to informal leadership: The moderating role of gender on the relationship of individual differences and team member network centrality to informal leadership emergence. *Leadership Quarterly, 15,* 175–194.

54. Neubert, 1999.

55. Barker, J. R. (1993). Tightening the iron cage: Concertive control in self-managing teams. *Administrative Science Quarterly, 38,* 408–437.

56. Barker, 1993.

57. Gaynier, L. P. (2005). Transformative mediation: In search of a theory of practice. *Conflict Resolution Quarterly, 22(3),* 397–408; Putnam, L. L (2004). Transformations and critical moments in negotiations. *Negotiation Journal, 20(2),* 275–295.

58. De Dreu, C. K. W., & West, M. (2001). Minority dissent and team innovation: The importance of participation in decision making. *Journal of Applied Psychology, 86(6),* 1191–1202.

59. Putnam, 2004.

60. Cameron, K. S., Dutton, J. E., & Quinn, R. E. (2003). *Positive organizational scholarship: Foundations of a new discipline* (pp. 48–65). San Francisco: Berrett-Koehler.

61. Chen, G., Kirkman, B. L., Kanfer, R., Allen, D., & Rosen, B. (2007). A multilevel study of leadership, empowerment, and performance in teams. *Journal of Applied Psychology, 92(2),* 331–346.

62. This section draws heavily from Weber, J. M. (2004). *Catalysts for cooperation: Consistent contributors in public good dilemmas.* Doctoral dissertation, Management and Organizations, Northwestern University, Evanston, IL.

63. Barrick, M., Stewart, G., Neubert, M. J., & Mount, M. (1998). Relating member ability and personality to work-team processes and team effectiveness. *Journal of Applied Psychology, 83,* 377–319.

64. Tjosvold, D., Yu, Z., & Hui, C. (2004). Team learning from mistakes: The contribution of cooperative goals and problem-solving. *Journal of Management Studies, 41(7),* 1223–1245.

65. Weinreb, M. (2003). Power to the people. *Sales and Marketing Management, 155(4),* 30–36.

66. Carroll, J. S., Hatakenaka, S., & Rudolph, J. W. (2006). Naturalistic decision making and organizational learning in nuclear power plants: Negotiating meaning between managers and problem investigation teams. *Organization Studies, 27(7),* 1037–1057.

67. Kesler, K. (2006). Robots are child's play. *Portable Design, 12(12),* 7–8; Oliver, D., & Roos, J. (2003). Dealing with the unexpected: Critical incidents in the LEGO Mindstorms team. *Human Relations, 56(9),* 1057–1082; http://www.wired.com/wired/archive/14.02/lego_pr.html.

68. Adapted from Rahim's original measure: Rahim, M. A. (1983). A measure of styles of handling interpersonal conflict. *Academy of Management Journal, 26(2),* 368–376. Copyright 1983 by Academy of Management (NY). Reproduced with permission of Academy of Management (NY) in the format Textbook via Copyright Clearance Center.

CHAPTER 17

Communication is a critical part of all four management functions. Managers communicate when they design and implement strategies and plans, when they arrange resources, when they motivate others, and when they design and use information systems. In this chapter, we provide an overview of communication within organizations and describe the basic four steps of the communication process from both a Mainstream and a Multistream perspective.

ROAD MAP

FOUR STEPS OF THE COMMUNICATION PROCESS

1. Identify your message

- Perspective
- Intent
- Content

2. Encode and transmit the message
- Potential barriers
- Media and channels

3. Receive and decode the message
- Perception bias
- Listen

4. Information flow from receiver to sender

Communication

MAINSTREAM APPROACH ⟷	MULTISTREAM APPROACH
Manager focuses on ideas that will enhance productivity • Management • "Sell" ideas to receivers • Task-based knowledge transfer	Participants focus on ideas serving overall well-being • Multiple stakeholders • "Acquire" divergent ideas from receivers • Relational, identity formation
Analyze barriers, available media, and channels • Reduce noise • Prefer large-scale and written	Analyze diversity, available media, and channels • Embrace diversity • Prefer small-scale and face-to-face
Overcome barriers and limitations of media and channels • "Tune out" noninstrumental ideas • As individuals	Emphasis on managers listening to subordinates • "Tune in" diversity • As a collective
Feedback: Confirm whether message has been understood as intended	Feedforward: Seek divergent and reflective feedback

Change Takes Flight at an Airport[1]

Sandra Montclair, CEO of one of the largest airports in the country, had a message to communicate to others in her organization. Montclair wanted to improve members' quality of work life, and she thought the best way to do so would be by replacing the airport's top-down management style with an approach that emphasized teamwork and participative management. She recognized that this transformation might be challenging for an organization operating in such a regulated environment. Montclair believed the changes she desired would help to improve the airport's productivity and efficiency, but that was not the ultimate issue for her: "I believed in it in terms of this issue of human dignity."

Based on a similar change she had implemented at a previous organization, Montclair knew that getting her message across to the several thousand employees at the airport would require a huge communication effort. She decided that the communication process would start with her top management team of eight, and then eventually include all the different hierarchical levels in the organization. Montclair had eight managers reporting to her (e.g., terminal manager, cargo manager, commissary manager), who in turn had duty managers reporting to them, who in turn had a host of supervisors reporting to them. For example, the Terminal Manager had 3 duty managers, 22 supervisors, and another 400 or 500 people below that level in the hierarchy.

In terms of how she delivered her message, Montclair knew that she would have a better chance of convincing senior managers of the merits of her message if she exposed them to a whole range of experts from other organizations who had implemented similar changes and could talk to them about it. She pulled in a person from the human resource department and invited her senior management team to join her on a journey of learning: "I wanted us all to learn the stuff together." Of course, the senior managers did not have much of a chance to opt out of the journey, but Montclair was trying to make it easier for them to opt in and accept her message. She wanted to transmit her message in a participative way, and she wanted to have some fun doing it. So the team did a lot of things together, such as go on retreats and conferences and learning experiences: "We used the company expense account quite liberally to go out and have meals together . . . which was a way of kind of breaking down some barriers."

In terms of how the message was received, this participative process helped senior managers to understand and agree to the message. They learned from the various speakers and from one another. Moreover, the very process that had been put in place to communicate the message was also an example of the new management style, where team members work together participatively and develop mutual understanding.

Even so, feedback showed that further work was required. For example, special training was provided to at least one senior manager who did not recognize his autocratic management style.

After this communication cycle with the senior managers had been completed, a similar process took place at the other hierarchical levels within the organization. For example, the Terminal Manager went on retreats and learning events with his immediate subordinates. Once the message had been successfully communicated to the members of this group, they would develop the plans and procedures for how to implement changes in their area, figure out how to communicate with the staff, and so on. The Terminal Manager would then host information events for the rest of his department. This might require three or more sessions to accommodate the 500 members in his unit who were all doing shift work.

At those information sessions we would say, "Hey folks, we want to run this place differently in the future. This is what the implications we think are for you. This is what we need from you in order to work in this new way. This is what the advantage to you could be." So we would've done that three different times for each of the different departments. So this was a huge communications effort.

These events were often planned alongside daylong sports or barbecue events with a dunk tank and so on, and then there would be an opportunity to make speeches, and I would be there to do that. And I would also take my turn in the dunk tank.

The investment in the communication process was worthwhile. Members' quality of work life improved, as demonstrated by in-house surveys of jobs, as did more conventional measures of success: "[W]e had unprecedented performance, in terms of productivity, in terms of on-time departures, reduced line-ups at checkout counters, reduced damaged baggage claims, improved safety . . . we just had incredible performance."

INTRODUCTION TO COMMUNICATION

Communication is the process of transferring information by using meaningful symbols so that a message is understood by others. In this chapter, we focus on the management of communication among organizational members.[2]

Managers spend about 75 percent of their time communicating with others.[3] This includes communicating about all sorts of topics, from announcing a major organizational change to asking what time a meeting is scheduled to start. Communication can be downward, upward, or horizontal. Perhaps the most common image is that of a manager communicating with subordinates—downward communication—which may include motivating members, assigning responsibilities, giving direction, and providing performance feedback. Of course, managers also communicate with their own bosses—upward communication—which includes pointing out exceptions and problems, making suggestions or complaints, providing performance reports, and conveying financial information. Finally, managers communicate with their peers—horizontal communication—to build networks and coordinate problem solving.

The communication process has four basic steps, as shown in Figure 17.1. In the first step, the sender identifies an idea or a message that is to be communicated. In the second step, the sender selects the medium and encodes and transmits the message. In the third step, the receiver hears and decodes the message. In the fourth step, information travels from the receiver to the sender, completing the communication cycle and ensuring that the message has been understood (or indicating that more clarification is needed).

Communication is challenging because moving from one step to the next in the communication process can be hampered by two basic factors:

- The overall context in which the communication takes place (e.g., a noisy room)
- The media used to transmit the message (e.g., an e-mail message that does not convey as much information as a face-to-face conversation)

MAINSTREAM COMMUNICATION

The Mainstream approach focuses on how managers' messages are crafted, transmitted, and understood by others, and how managers use communication to motivate others. The intent is to ensure that ideas and information travel efficiently from the

Communication is the process of transferring information by using meaningful symbols so that a message is understood by others.

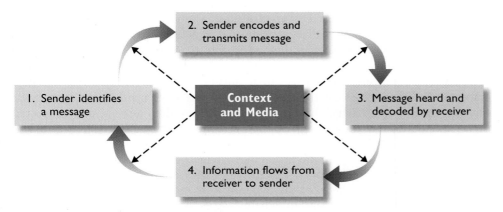

Figure 17.1   The four-step communication process

sender to the receiver. From this perspective, communication is seen as effective if others understand and do what the manager wants them to do.

Step 1: Identify the Main Idea or Message to Be Transmitted

Message is a specific idea or general information that one person wants to convey to others.

The Mainstream communication process typically begins when a manager has a **message**—a specific idea or general information—that he or she wants to communicate to others. Mainstream managers typically focus on messages that they think will help the organization's efficiency and profitability. Managers must be selective in the information they communicate because time is a limited resource for both the manager and the target of his or her communication. Put differently, managers must decide which messages are worth communicating and which messages are not.[4]

Filtering occurs when information is withheld or not communicated to others.

Filtering occurs when information is withheld or not communicated to others. It can have either positive or negative outcomes. Filtering is positive if managers withhold information that is not relevant to the other person. For example, a manager is filtering in a positive way when he does not tell his boss exactly which brand of coffee spilled and ruined his laptop computer. Filtering may also be negative if managers withhold information that could help the organization, but may harm the manager's self-interest. For example, the manager whose computer was ruined by coffee is withholding information if he fails to mention that he spilled the coffee on purpose, hoping to get a new and improved computer.

Several factors in the filtering process help to determine which messages are transmitted. Research suggests that different types of managers will manage ideas differently.[5] Managers tend to focus on messages that are consistent with their view of how to enhance organizational productivity, and they then try to get receivers to adopt these ideas. Although Mainstream managers make a point of personally "owning" the ideas that they communicate—even if these ideas were developed by others—they work hard at communicating and *selling* these ideas to others. As one manager put it: "That's what management is: It's moving other people, getting them to think your idea was theirs."[6] Mainstream managers who work in more organic organization structures[7] are more likely to welcome the input and participation of others: "I look to others to see what works and what doesn't." They also use communication to ensure that their message has the support of other members: "I make sure we all agree on goals and objectives."

The Mainstream approach emphasizes communication as a means to improve organizational productivity and competitiveness. Mainstream managers—especially those who work in mechanistic organizational structures—tend to use a relatively narrow, predetermined agenda in their approach to acquiring and communicating information and ideas. They are especially likely to look for ideas that will improve the current operations, and to use their authority to direct others toward goal achievement. To ensure that their messages are not haphazard or random, these managers think about what their organization's overall strategy is, and then craft their messages so that the strategy will be implemented by others.

This approach was evident in one organization where employees were constantly complaining. To solve the problem, managers created and distributed a diagram to members that described exactly what they should and should not talk about. In a circle at the center of the diagram were the things that *should* be talked about: sharing of new information, solving legitimate problems, discussing violations of processes, clarifying organizational values, and refining mutual expecta-

DIGGING DEEPER

Five Different Ways to Filter Communication

Phillip Clampitt and his colleagues suggest that managers tend to use one of five approaches to filtering communication.[8] We present them here in order from least to most filtering. In the first style (spray and pray), managers filter the least and thus provide the greatest volume of information; in the fifth style (withhold and uphold), managers filter the most and thus provide the least amount of information.

Spray and Pray. In this approach, managers shower members with a lot of data, and hope that the members will be able to sort out the important information. This tactic can overwhelm others with information and is not useful when members lack the ability to identify which parts of the messages are valuable.

Tell and Sell. Managers using this approach tell others what the main issues are, and then sell their preferred solution. Tell-and-sell managers generally aren't interested in getting feedback and input from others.

Underscore and Explore. This approach is similar to "tell and sell," except that these managers explicitly listen to feedback from other members so that they can be aware of potential misunderstandings and unrecognized obstacles to their solutions. Of the five approaches, Clampitt and his colleagues argue, the "underscore and explore" approach is clearly the best communication approach.

Identify and Reply. In this approach, it is the employees who identify concerns and issues. Managers adopt a defensive posture to reply to those issues. In short, employees set the agenda and managers respond to rumors, innuendo, and leaks.

Withhold and Uphold. In this approach, managers provide very little information to others, and when they are confronted with rumors, they uphold the party line. Such managers believe that they have all the answers, and that others are not able to understand the big picture.

The type of filtering strategy used affects people deeply. Filtering can influence the perceived quality of the communication and determine whether organizational members feel included in decision making. These perceptions, in turn, influence organizational members' feelings of uncertainty and strain—feelings that accompany typical organizational changes.[9]

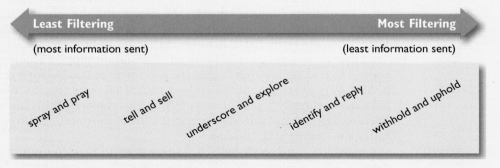

Least Filtering → Most Filtering

(most information sent)   (least information sent)

spray and pray   tell and sell   underscore and explore   identify and reply   withhold and uphold

---

tions. Outside the circles were things that should *not* be talked about: self-induced problems, gossip, problems without solutions, issues out of the control of organizational members, and complaints about problems that were currently being addressed.[10]

More generally, such examples illustrate how messages play an important role in the social construction of reality (see Chapter 2) and in processes such as framing (see Chapter 7). Thoughtful managers pay close attention to the language that they use in everyday discourse. For example, managers at Xerox call the organization "a document company," which is significantly different from being "a photocopy company."[11] Similarly, managers who want to foster innovation can learn from the example of managers at 3M, who routinely record and tell stories about breakthrough ideas, processes, and products.[12] Managers must also be aware of unintended

FOXTROT © 1998 Bill Amend. Reprinted with permission of UNIVERSAL PRESS SYNDICATE. All rights reserved.

messages, such as a manager's message that "mistakes will not be tolerated," which tend to stifle innovation.[13]

Step 2: Encode and Transmit the Message

After determining which message they want to communicate, managers must determine *how* to communicate that message. Managers **encode** their message when they use symbols and media to transmit it. When encoding, managers must perform two tasks:

1. Identify any communication barriers that must be overcome.
2. Choose the medium and channel that will be used to transmit the message.

Encoding is putting a message in understandable terms by using symbols and media.

IDENTIFY AND OVERCOME COMMUNICATION BARRIERS. When choosing how to encode a message, managers must be aware of potential barriers—sometimes called **noise**—that may impede communication at all four steps of the process. Sometimes noise can be literal, such as when workers are trying to talk over the noise of machinery, or when you have a poor cell phone connection. At other times, noise is more figurative, such as when a manager sends an e-mail to someone who is already overwhelmed with e-mails. Noise may also occur when there are personality differences or ongoing conflicts between the sender and the receiver, or when there is a history of mistrust among members of the organization. Communication is made easier when the relationship between the sender and the receiver is cordial.[14]

Noise refers to potential barriers that may impede communication at all four steps of the communication process.

Time is another general barrier to communication, including both the time needed to craft and encode a message and the time needed for a receiver to decode it. Managers often underestimate how long it takes to fully communicate a major message—generally a year or more.[15] We saw evidence of this phenomenon in the opening case, where Montclair invested a lot of time and resources into communicating the change at the airport.

Managers must work hard at finding ways to take complex ideas and present them as succinct messages. This insight is captured by Charles Loewen, CEO of Loewen Windows, who recounts the story of someone who had written a long letter and at the end apologized, saying, "If I had had more time, I would've written a shorter letter."[16] Managers must describe their plans for change in the fewest words possible.[17]

Ambiguous words and symbols can also be a barrier to communication. Consider the mixed message sent when the body language of a person does not fit the words the person is speaking (e.g., if a manager is smiling while announcing the number of people to be laid off). As we saw in Chapter 4, these problems become magnified when communicating across cultures, as similar gestures or actions may be interpreted very differently in different cultures. For example, an American manager working in Mexico may intend to send a message of empowering subordinates by asking them to participate in making important decisions, but workers may interpret the manager's actions as laziness and the shirking of the manager's responsibilities.

Even people who speak the same language may not understand one another. **Semantic problems** arise when words have different meanings for different people.

Semantic problems arise when words have different meanings for different people.

Part of this misunderstanding may be related to the demographic group one belongs to. For example, use of the slang expression "phat" as to signal approval first occurred among hip-hop fans on the U.S. East Coast.[18] Jargon and technical language used in one profession may not be relevant in another. For example, after reading this book you will be able to talk with your classmates about the differences between Mainstream and Multistream management, but it may not be reasonable to expect your coworkers to know what you mean by these terms when you refer to your boss's management style. How often have you intended to send a specific message, only to be misperceived by a receiver? It can be difficult to convey messages in language that is clear, unambiguous, and easy to understand.

CHOOSE COMMUNICATION MEDIA AND CHANNELS.   The communication **medium** refers to the method used to carry a message from the sender to the receiver. For example, should an employee who has accomplished a noteworthy achievement be sent a letter of congratulations from the CEO, be presented with a plaque at a departmental meeting, be featured in an organizational newsletter, or be praised in an organization-wide e-mail? Or should several of these media be used? What sorts of media should managers invest in—should they provide personal digital assistants to all employees, or should they design workspaces to increase opportunities for informal face-to-face chats around the "water cooler"? Should they encourage members to travel and meet clients in person, or should they invest in videoconferencing technology? These are important decisions to make because the medium that is chosen becomes part of the message.

A helpful concept in choosing a communication medium is **media richness,** which refers to a medium's ability to resolve ambiguity. Media richness is determined by the speed of feedback, the number of cues and number of channels employed, the "personalness" of the source, and the richness of the language used.[20]

As shown in Figure 17.2, face-to-face is the richest communication medium because it allows participants not only to hear the content of each other's messages and their tone of voice, but also to see subtle body language. Face-to-face communication can take place one-on-one or within a group, where it can serve to facilitate formation of a group identity. Because this medium also allows for instant feedback—such as a puzzled expression—it provides much more information than, say, memos. Research suggests that in a face-to-face exchange, the actual words spoken may account for less than 20 percent of the information that is communicated.[21] Another 30 percent is accounted for by the vocal characteristics of the message, and approximately 50 percent by the facial and body language.

Eighty-five percent of supervisors prefer one-on-one,

Medium is the method that is used to carry a message from the sender to the receiver.

Media richness refers to a communication medium's ability to resolve ambiguity.

Marshall McLuhan's famous phrase "The medium is the message" suggests that a communications technology must be understood in its context. For example, rather than think about media such as cell phones or the Internet in terms of how many kilobytes of information per second they could transmit, McLuhan would note that such media contribute to the creation of a "global village" thanks to their ability to shrink the distances between people and to increase opportunities for cross-cultural sharing. In this photo, Kenyan environmental activist Wangari Maathai takes a call congratulating her for winning the Nobel Peace Prize. Similarly, for McLuhan, the "message" of the "car" is not found in its features such as its color or size, but rather in the growth of suburbs, freeways, and the ways we think about geography, energy, and time.[19]

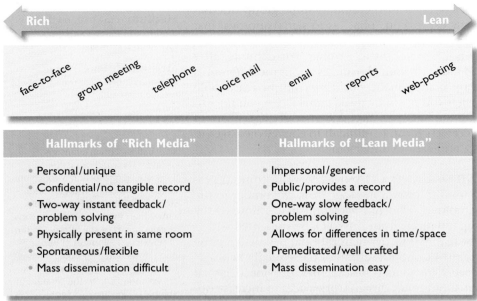

Figure 17.2   Richness of communication media

face-to-face communication versus meetings.[22] Even so, research generally shows that Mainstream managers have a preference for what may be perceived to be more efficient media, such as written messages that can be transmitted to many people.[23]

Telephone calls are still quite rich, because the participants receive many cues. They do not, however, receive visual cues. A voice mail, in turn, is leaner than a telephone conversation because it offers fewer cues and no possibility of immediate feedback.

Media that emphasize the written word—such as e-mails, intranets, and regular memos and letters—are leaner because they offer neither verbal nor visual cues, and they do not allow for immediate feedback. Some people try to add richness to e-mail messages by using emoticons. An emoticon is a combination of punctuation symbols. For example, the emoticon ;-) represents a wink. Written communication is useful when managers need to transmit a lot of detailed information, especially if it is information that the receiver will need to reference in the future. E-mails are also effective when they are used by members who enjoy a strong working relationship.[24] The amount of information that is sent by e-mail in today's environment may be up to 15 times greater than the amount that was sent before e-mail became common, but there has been a related decrease in richness and personalized messages.[25] This growth in the amount of information transmitted has contributed to the phenomenon known as "information overload." As one manager who is overwhelmed by e-mail put it: "Previously I did not know what I was missing, and I was really happy in that ignorance. Now I get information, and I think 'I really should read this,' and I can't, I really don't have the time, and I feel really inadequate."[26]

Impersonal formal written documents—including unaddressed bulletins, mass e-mails, and numeric reports—may offer detailed data but are considered lean communication media because they do not build on known interpersonal relationships and understandings.

Different managers will have different skills and comfort levels with various media. Some will be gifted at writing reports, others at telling stories that capture the essence of their message, others at presenting engaging figures and charts, and so on. Similarly, receivers will prefer certain types of media to others. Some prefer e-mails, others prefer the telephone, and others prefer face-to-face meetings. Communication works best when there is a match between the preferred media of the manager and members. Often it is a good idea for a message to be sent using various media, and carried by various messengers, to cover all the bases.

The importance of media richness can be seen in the following example: Managers in one organization relied almost exclusively on written communication, and had developed excellent skills and extensively used their e-mail system. However, they were frustrated because their messages and ideas lacked "buy-in" from members. This

Proxemics is the study of how physical space conveys messages.

Ergonomics is the science of designing work spaces and tools in an effort to improve working conditions without compromising productivity.

situation changed only when new managers recognized the limitations of relying exclusively on written communication.[27]

The importance of some communication media is not always obvious. An organization's processes, culture, structures, and systems are all communication media, for example. A message is "sent" just by the way an organization is designed. **Proxemics** is the study of how physical space conveys messages. The physical layout in an organization represents an important form of nonverbal communication. **Ergonomics** is the science of designing work spaces and tools to improve working conditions without compromising productivity. Research suggests that training people in ergonomics can facilitate on-the-job communication and collaboration with coworkers.[28]

This Honda manager tore down his walls and put in glass so he was visible and accessible to employees and customers.

Channel is the pathway along which a message travels through a medium.

As an example, Figure 17.3 shows how seating arrangements around a table influence the nature of the communication that takes place between participants. Sitting next to a person signals collaboration, sitting at a corner with someone is associated with conversation, sitting directly across from someone can be perceived as either conversational or confrontational, and sitting diagonally across a table is the preferred position if two people need to share the same space but do not wish to interact.[29]

Once the appropriate communication media have been selected, managers complete the encoding process by choosing a **channel**—the path that a message travels through a medium—to communicate the message. The "Digging Deeper" feature describes five basic channels managers can choose from. For example, a CEO might send a message about an impending organizational change directly to frontline workers (using the "wheel" channel), or she might send the message to supervisors, who in turn tell the frontline workers about it (using the "Y" channel). Research suggests that employees typically prefer receiving information from their immediate supervisor rather than from senior managers.

For an example of the importance of choosing the "right" communication channel, consider the case of Max, a supervisor at an integrated steel mill. Max's department has the best safety record, least amount of downtime, and lowest absenteeism rate in the organization. Max knows his stuff and is revered by his crew. However, senior management plans to abolish all the supervisor positions and instead train existing supervisors to become "team facilitators." The idea is to empower frontline employees. In this case, senior managers may be wise to use the Y channel, and let the supervisors know about the change several weeks prior to telling frontline workers. This advance warning will

Figure 17.3 Effect of seating on communication

Source: Wickhorst, V., & Geroy, G. (2006). Physical communication and organization development. *Organization Development Journal, 24*(3), 58, Figure 1.

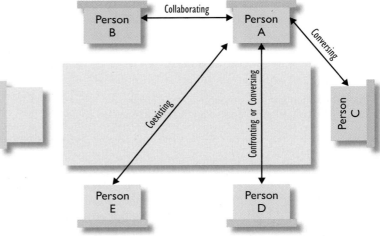

DIGGING DEEPER

Tuning In to the Right Channel[30]

Five general types of communication channels have been identified. These channels can be either formal or informal. Which channel is used is important because as much as 25 percent of information may be lost each time it is passed from one person to the next.[31]

The Wheel

In this arrangement, all information flows through one person (who acts as the "hub" of the wheel), and this person communicates with each group member. It is especially appropriate when group members do not need to coordinate their activities. For example, a central dispatcher for a taxi or trucking firm may communicate with 200 drivers, but the drivers need not communicate with one another.

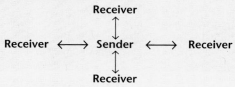

The Y

In this arrangement, the sender tells an inner circle of three people, who in turn relay the information to other members of the organization. The resulting arrangement is similar to the wheel, but with extended "spokes." The potential problem here is that members beyond the inner circle will probably receive less than 100 percent of the message. Another problem is that this strategy can become divisive if it creates an exclusive "inner circle" around a manager and an "outgroup" further from the center.

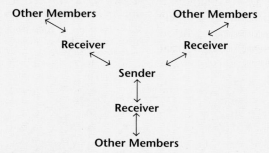

The Chain

In this arrangement, the sender tells one person, who tells another, who tells another, and so on. A "chain" may go up and down an organization's hierarchy, or it may run across organizational work flows. An assembly line is a good example of a chain structure.

Sender → Receiver → Receiver → Receiver → Receiver

The Circle

This arrangement is similar to the chain, except that the last person reports to the original sender to confirm that the message was received in full and correctly. In the circle, members talk only to those who are "next" to them. For example, the manager of a produce department in a grocery store may ask an assistant to have more watermelons ordered. The assistant will put in an order, which will go to the distribution office, which will send a memo to the produce manager to confirm the request.

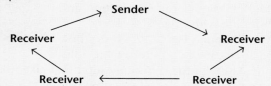

All-Channel Communication

In this arrangement, everyone communicates with everyone else. Examples are top management teams, cross-functional teams, and self-managed teams. Sometimes team members have virtual communication (by computer).

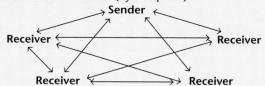

Some channels are more appropriate for certain messages than are other channels. For example, if building a sense of camaraderie is important for a group, all-channel communication is more suitable than the chain. Research suggests that for simple tasks and problems, centralized channels (wheel, Y) are faster and more accurate. For complex tasks and problems, the more decentralized information channels are recommended (circle, all-channel).

give supervisors like Max time to better understand and accept the changes, so that they will be more likely to provide the crucial "thumbs up" when frontline employees ask them about the change. If senior managers use a wheel channel and tell everyone in the company the message at the same time, the likelihood of getting support from supervisors—and thus from frontline workers—decreases.[32]

Managers can choose from both formal and informal channels. An organization's **formal communication channels** follow the lines of authority that are shown on an organizational chart. For example, a new employee in the produce department of a grocery store should ask questions to and receive job assignments from a manager in the produce department, not from the store manager or the regional manager. In contrast, **informal communication channels** may skip hierarchical levels and cut across vertical chains of command into different departments. For example, informal communication occurs when people meet in the company cafeteria, at baseball games, or at the bus stop.

Some MBA programs recommend that their students take up golf in recognition of the important role this game plays in the informal networks of some industries.

The **grapevine** is the information network along which unofficial information flows. The grapevine can carry both organizational information (e.g., rumors about an impending merger) and personal information (e.g., who gets along with whom). It provides a valuable window into what is important to organizational members. The grapevine helps employees meet their needs for social interaction, and it is a fast and efficient channel of communication. Sometimes the grapevine passes inaccurate information, but generally it is 75 to 95 percent accurate.[33] Managers should be quick to correct misinformation, but they should not try to suppress the grapevine. Rather, when planning their own communication efforts, they should assume that the grapevine will be very active.

Step 3: Receive and Decode the Message

In this step, the receiver attributes meaning to the message through a process called **decoding.** The decoding process mirrors the encoding process and, therefore, has two components. First, like senders, receivers must be aware of potential for noise and barriers to communication to impede their understanding of the message. For example, if a receiver does not trust a sender, then the receiver will tend to have a skeptical interpretation of the message. Second, the communication medium and the channel chosen can affect the richness and meaning of a message. For example, a personalized "thank you" for a job well done from a CEO is decoded quite differently than a "form letter" sent from an unknown staff person in the human resource department.

Perception refers to the meaning given to a message by either the sender or the receiver. Researchers have identified two kinds of perception biases that can act as barriers to communication:

- Stereotyping
- Selective perception

Formal communication channels follow the lines of authority that are shown on an organizational chart.

Informal communication channels may skip hierarchical levels and cut across vertical chains of command into different departments.

Grapevine is the informal information network in an organization.

Decoding is the process by which the receiver attributes meaning to a message.

Perception refers to the meaning given to a message by either the sender or the receiver.

Is there a stereotypical manager in the movies or on television, e.g., Michael (center) from *The Office*? Managers at Procter and Gamble had rules against placing ads on shows that promoted negative stereotypes of managers: "There will be no material on any of our programs which could in any way further the concept of business as cold, ruthless, and lacking all sentiment and spiritual motivation." If managers are cast in the role of villains, "it must be made clear" that this is not typical and is despised by other managers as much as by society in general.[35]

Stereotyping involves making assumptions about other people based on the categories to which we assign them due to their gender, race, age, or some other characteristic. These categories allow us to sort and remember information, make decisions, and simplify communications. For example, we rely on cultural categories such as those in Hofstede's classification to point out general differences across countries (see Chapter 4), we use personality categories to help us understand differences between our introverted and extraverted friends, and so on. Using these categories of information can facilitate our interactions and communication with others as long as *we remain open-minded and sensitive to the unexpected.*[34] For example, some people from individualist cultures value community, and some extraverts may be very shy in certain social settings. Stereotyping distorts reality when all people in a particular category are always treated as though they share the same characteristics. Communication is hampered when we treat people according to stereotypes that are negative or inaccurate. For example, communication can come to a standstill if a union leader perceives all managers as being concerned only with making more money and not caring about the welfare of workers, and if managers perceive all union members as being lazy and not caring about company profitability.

Selective perception occurs when people screen out information that they want to avoid. This is evident, for example, when people "tune out" television commercials or banner ads on the Internet. On the upside, selective perception helps us focus on our areas of expertise and avoid distraction. On the downside, we may tune out things that are important. In organizations, people often tune out bad news or negative feedback. Managers, therefore, need to be creative in finding ways to convey the message so that selective perception does not occur. For example, if a manager feels as if people are tuning out important information that appears in the weekly newsletter, then she may want to use a different approach—such as face-to-face meetings—to convey a message.

 WHAT DO YOU THINK?

Stereotyping makes assumptions about other people based on their gender, race, age, or some other characteristic.

Selective perception occurs when people screen out information that they want to avoid.

How Does Context Influence the Perceived Meaning of Messages? (Part 1)[36]

The following story, which is based on a true event, illustrates how context and noise influence what we perceive the meaning of a message to be. In this example, think about how the meaning of the cellist's message depends on what you know about the context.

Imagine that Vedran Smailovic, the lead cellist from the national orchestra, is serenading you as you sip mocha in a coffee shop. Imagine that it is lunchtime, and that the coffee shop is in the middle of Sarajevo, with its open doors facing a famous public plaza where Smailovic is performing.

Now imagine that yesterday Smailovic's opera house had been destroyed and 22 people were killed in the "Bread Queue Massacre" in that same public plaza, and that Smailovic had committed himself to giving a free concert in their honor by the coffee shop for 22 consecutive days. On the first day, when he donned his formal attire and sat on his folding chair in the plaza playing his cello, he was briefly interviewed by a radio reporter who asked: "Why are you sitting here while people are shooting at you . . . are you crazy?" Smailovic's reply was equally brief: "I'm playing my cello; that's not crazy. Why don't you go up the mountain and ask the people shooting down here why they're doing what they're doing, because *that* is crazy." Smailovic's actions served as an inspiration for civil resistance in Bosnia.

As you read the first paragraph of the story, what message did you think Smailovic was sending? What message did the reporter hear amidst the snipers? Now that you have finished the story, what message do you think Smailovic was trying to send? Think about an organizational setting where similar multiple interpretations are possible for a single message.

Decoding a message can be challenging. The more we understand about the context and the history of a situation, the more deeply we understand the message. The various people who heard Smailovic play his cello might all decode a different message, depending on their assumptions, and none of the interpretations may have been consistent with the message Smailovic was trying to send! While most messages in organizations may be less ambiguous and the history between senders and receivers may be longer, the way in which the same message is decoded may nevertheless be quite different from one person to the next. This is why feedback (Step 4) is so important.

The most important decoding skill is being a good listener. This means being attuned to the words being communicated and any other signals, including the sender's tone, body language, and word choice, as well as what is *not* said. Nonverbal communication is especially important in the decoding process. Research reveals that when someone is trying to be deceptive in the message he or she is sending, some nonverbal indicators increase in frequency and others decrease. There is, for example, a decrease in the frequency of simple hand gestures, but an increase in a "hand shrug" that disclaims responsibility for the statements just made. There is also an increase in hand-to-face contact such as touching the hair or covering the mouth, and an increase in shifting the body (which may explain why we call some people "shifty").[37]

Being a good listener is hard work, and it is much more difficult than speaking. We often confuse simply "hearing" a message with truly "receiving" a message. Good listeners are able to focus and absorb what another person is trying to communicate.[38] Table 17.1 describes the characteristics of good and poor listeners.

While listening is recognized as a central part of the communication process, most studies have focused on how subordinates listen to managers; very little research has looked at how managers listen to their employees.[39] This is unfortunate, because it is important for managers to be good listeners. Listening provides inexpensive positive reinforcement and helps to create general positive feelings that may increase workers' support for a manager.[40] These benefits don't appear if managers fail to *show* that they are listening. One manager said:

I know that some of my associates don't think that I listen to them, but they're wrong. I do listen. I just don't show them how well I listen. Besides, in some positions, managers have to pay attention to the people who report to them, and hold their hands. But my

TABLE 17.1

Hallmarks of Active and Poor Listening

Active Listening	Poor Listening
Concentration on verbal and nonverbal messages	Mind wanders, thinking of what to say next
Eye contact, nodding, mirroring body language	Being easily distracted (e.g., multitasking)
Open mind, assimilating information	Anticipating and prejudging what the person will say, impatience
Providing feedback, paraphrasing, clarifying	Assuming the message was understood as intended

job isn't like that, and my people don't need it. I listen to others the same way my boss listens to me.[41]

There are multiple messages in this quote. Like many of us, the manager may be guilty of fooling herself when she says that she is listening. And, unfortunately, the manager is probably accurate when she says that she listens in the same way as her boss listens to her.

Step 4: Information Flows from Receiver to Sender (Feedback)

Feedback lets the sender know whether the message has been received as intended.

The final step—**feedback**—focuses on how the receiver lets the sender know whether the message has been received as intended. This step is essentially a repeat of the first three steps, except that the roles of the original sender and receiver are reversed. Sometimes feedback is as simple as clicking a "reply" button to confirm that an e-mail message was received and that a request has been fulfilled as instructed. At other times feedback is much more complicated, especially when the receiver does not fully understand what the message means or how to respond to it. In such cases, it is often helpful to choose a richer medium to provide feedback than the medium that was used to transmit the message originally. For example, if an organizational member is unclear about how to interpret a written policy regarding sick days, the member would be well advised to talk to the manager or, if appropriate, call someone from the human resource department. Table 17.2 describes characteristics of helpful and unhelpful feedback.

Feedback has several benefits. First, it allows checking to make sure that the original message was received as intended. Sometimes feedback is evident in the nonverbal communication of a subordinate. A puzzled look, for example, implies that additional information is needed. Similarly, noncompliance to a request may mean that the request has not been understood. Face-to-face communication is an excellent choice for providing immediate feedback, and it also facilitates the process of paraphrasing messages and asking questions of clarification. In this sense feedback is similar to active listening, where the receiver paraphrases the message and provides nonverbal cues of attention.

Second, feedback provides an opportunity for the original *sender* to learn something new that will help create a new and improved message to be sent. For example, feedback received during a performance review can enable members to learn how to change their behavior to make a more valuable contribution to the organization. Alternatively, the feedback may help members decide to join a different organization that is better aligned with their personal aspirations.

TABLE 17.2

Hallmarks of Helpful and Unhelpful Feedback

Helpful Feedback	Unhelpful Feedback
Seeks to help person who is receiving feedback	Seeks to promote relative status of the person sending the feedback
Is presented in a way that the receiver can understand	Is presented with jargon/professional terms
Is seen as valid and plausible by the receiver	Is seen as invalid and implausible
Is descriptive and specific	Is evaluative and general
Deals with issues the receiver can change	Focuses on issues that the receiver cannot change
Is given in manageable doses	Is given in overwhelming amounts

Perhaps the most important aspect of feedback is the constructive criticism that managers can receive about how to improve the way that the organization is managed. **Constructive criticism** refers to a serious examination or judgment of something delivered in a way that is intended to help the listener to improve.[42] Unfortunately, managers are not very eager to receive constructive criticism from their subordinates. In one study, receptivity to upward feedback was identified as a strength for only 16 percent of managers, and was rated as the lowest of 49 measures of managerial effectiveness.[43] This finding is problematic given the fact that decision making improves when upward feedback systems are functioning well.[44]

Most organizational members are hesitant to provide critical upward communication. In one survey, 85 percent of respondents indicated that they had been unable to raise an issue or concern with their manager even though they thought the issue was important.[45] This is consistent with the finding that managers tend not only to fail to accept criticism, but also often denounce those who provide such criticism.[46] This outcome is sometimes called the "shoot the messenger" effect. When subordinates challenge their manager, they fear that they will become less respected and less likely to be promoted. As a consequence, managers receive mostly positive news about a new plan that they have championed, and are not likely to hear about the plan's negative aspects. Of course, if they are not aware of these negative aspects, then they are not likely to correct them.

This failure in communication has serious consequences. When managers are unable to listen and receive feedback from others, they are prone to holding unrealistic ideas about their organization. For example, senior managers of failing organizations often have a much rosier picture of their organization than the view held by outsiders. Likewise, senior managers often recognize fewer organizational problems than do their junior colleagues.[47]

A positive example of how to receive negative feedback is illustrated by Bill Gates of Microsoft. After his sales managers had received feedback from the market that the events associated with new-product launches were too technical and boring, they decided to stage a Broadway-style musical in a New York City theater. But this idea didn't work well either, and very little product information got through, which resulted in even more negative feedback. Gates sent out an e-mail that basically said, "Better to have tried to do something interesting and failed than to do the same old event still one more time. It was a fiasco, sure. Now, learn from the mistakes we made and move on."[48]

Constructive criticism refers to providing a serious examination or judgment of something in a way that is intended to help the listener to improve.

Here's a tip on communicating while serving others: Research suggests that restaurant customers give larger tips when food servers compliment them on their menu choice (15 percent increase in tip size), and when the food server lightly touches the shoulder of a customer while returning the change (50 percent increase in tip size).[52]

Management-by-wandering-around (MBWA) allows managers to communicate face-to-face with members in their workplace and to take the pulse of everyday organizational life.

In addition to direct feedback, managers sometimes get indirect feedback on how things are going by practicing **management-by-wandering-around (MBWA)**.[49] MBWA allows managers to communicate face-to-face with members in their workplace, keeping a finger on the pulse of the organization's everyday work as well as organizational structures and systems. MBWA was developed at Hewlett-Packard,[50] where William Hewlett and David Packard used it to communicate with employees. Since then, it has been applied by many other managers in different contexts. For example, one factor in Phil Staley's success in turning around an old Ford plant in Edison, New Jersey, was the fact that he walked around the shop floor every day.

The benefits of MBWA have also been linked to getting feedback from customers. For example, John Couch, an engineer at Apple Inc. who has a Ph.D. in computer science, is credited with playing an important role in developing the user-friendly computer software for which Apple is famous. The source of his ideas? Couch worked anonymously at a local computer retail outlet on weekends while designing the software: "I learned about the fears and frustrations of the average first-time user and the more sophisticated user firsthand. I believe it was the single most significant source of what we came up with."[51]

MULTISTREAM COMMUNICATION

The Mainstream approach focuses on communication as a way to enhance productivity. By contrast, the Multistream approach, while recognizing the importance of productivity, also focuses on broader issues such as celebrating diversity, nurturing interpersonal relationships, and building community.[53] The emphasis on building community is important because organizations are increasingly replacing the neighborhood as the primary place where social connections occur.[54] This transition has far-reaching implications, because community is an essential contributor to overall well-being. An emphasis on Multistream *communication* in organizations can reinvigorate the power of *community* in contemporary life. According to James Autry, a well-known author and former *Fortune* 500 executive:

> By invoking the metaphor of community, we imply that we in business are bound by a fellowship of endeavor in which we commit to mutual goals, in which we contribute to the best of our abilities, in which there is a forum for all voices to be heard, in which our success contributes to the success of others, in which we can disagree and hold different viewpoints without withdrawing from community, in which we are free to express what we feel as well as what we think, in which our value to society is directly related to the quality of commitment and effort, and in which we all take care of one another.[55]

Step 1: Identify the Main Idea or Message to Be Transmitted

In the messages they transmit, Multistream managers consciously try to do three things.

First, they try to reflect the perspective of multiple stakeholders. A hallmark of Multistream communication is its emphasis on involving others in developing the content of messages. The people who choose the topics and messages and who set the language and symbols, in effect, control the organization.[56] While Mainstream managers are expected to exercise such control, Multistream managers deliberately share this control with other stakeholders.

Second, Multistream managers focus less on "selling" preferred ideas to others, and more on *seeking* and welcoming *divergent* ideas and views. This openness to diversity is consistent with the argument that fostering a healthy and peaceful community requires an ongoing sense of curiosity, trust, and openness to change. Once you develop a singular message where you "think you have it," then you sacrifice the deeper understanding that comes from incorporating aspects of the truth held by others.[57] This view reflects a paradox: What might seem to be conflicting ideas are enhanced "if they are held together, like two sides of a coin."[58]

Along these same lines, Multistream managers are more likely to pursue several divergent ideas *at the same time,* and are less limited in the ideas or messages that they personally endorse. As one manager put it, "I've always liked to push the envelope a little bit. When I push my people, it is more to push them to think and to ask a series of questions to make sure they thought about it thoroughly than it is to tell them my opinion."[59] Noted another manager, "I don't feel there is anything wrong with changing your mind."[60] For Multistream managers, organizational communication is based on deliberate dialogue, which creates a space where multiple stakeholders can learn from one another what is best for the overall community.[61]

Their emphasis on "trust" provides one example of the difference between Mainstream and Multistream communication. Mainstream communication is premised on trusting others to act in accordance with their own self-interests and acquisitive economic principles. By contrast, in their communication, Multistream managers are more likely to trust that others will act in the best interests of the community. James Despain, manager of Caterpillar Inc.'s 3000-member Track-Type Tractors division, describes how this kind of trust helped him to move from a Mainstream approach to a more Multistream approach:

> The road to change for me began with the value of Trust. My epiphany was the realization that for my entire life I had trusted no one. I had been taught not to—not purposely, but in subtle ways. Over many years, I was encouraged to write things down for the purpose of "proving" my innocence later if conflict or failure should occur. I had learned to not discuss certain things with certain people, to "spin" information to make things seem better, and to never fully admit being responsible for mistakes or failure. And I was a very good student. After struggling most of one night with what I should do, I decided to trust everyone—everyone. I decided to share what I knew without thinking of any particular motive for sharing. If I were going to get hurt from this, then hurt I would get. This decision at this moment liberated me! From then on, I saw people differently. I began to care for them and was willing to listen to them without judgment. Later I would see how feelings of trust would permeate our organization and would witness the power of it.[62]

Third, Multistream managers do not focus solely on communication dealing with task-related topics, but also try to build relationships and community.[63] The following quote describes how one manager, who had been trained in a Mainstream approach, chose to change from communicating with her employees only about task-related matters to talking with them so as to build relationships:

> I knew that I needed to become more interested in people. I remember, early on in our business, when I had arrogantly said to someone: "Well, our employees, they are people who come in and get the job done and then go home, and that's it." And even though [initially] I personally wasn't very interested in the people, I committed myself to try, every day, to say "Hi" and set aside a few minutes with each person. Even if I didn't feel like it, I could force myself to do it. It was like [it was] on my "to do" list. And first thing in the morning I would go to so-and-so, who was a morning person, and say, "So, how is it going? What did you do last night?" and just talk with them. "Okay, great, thanks." And then I'd move on, and through the day I would see everybody in that way. And after a while it changed from something that I had to do, to something that I was actually interested in.[64]

Multistream managers recognize their influence in modeling communication practices, and in creating a setting that encourages members to express divergent points of view as they work toward building a sense of harmony. The quality of their interpersonal relationships with their managers is especially important to workers.[65]

We noted earlier that "explore and underscore" messages are thought to be the best Mainstream way to communicate. The corresponding Multistream nickname might be "trust and adjust." That is, managers trust others with information, and this vulnerability in turn fosters mutual trust among members. Everyone is encouraged to express his or her view and to learn from others, thereby creating a flexible community where people are constantly adjusting to one another.[66]

Step 2: Encode and Transmit the Message

Multistream encoding and Mainstream encoding parallel each other, but with two important differences.

First, many of the barriers to communication that Mainstream managers identify as "noise" are seen by Multistream managers as "opportunities" for improvement. Multistream managers accept that differences and diversity can never be overcome—people are simply different and diverse—and they recognize that this multiplicity of views can be a source of strength and insight. Thus any effort to create a communication system that tries to circumvent or suppress these differences misses out on a chance to enrich community in the organization.

For example, Charles Loewen, CEO of Loewen Windows, chooses people for his top management team who have different strengths from his own. Rather than stifle or push away views that differ from his own views, Loewen welcomes them and believes that this embracing of diversity has been a key to the company's success. This ability to transform "noise" into a message that celebrates the differences among people is a key component to what James Autry calls "caring leadership." He describes situations where members were facing changes in their personal lives and made requests for special consideration, such as flexible work hours, that went outside of company policy. Rather than dismiss these applications as noise that stood in the way of sending a clear message on policy issues, Autry accommodated the requests—sometimes with poor outcomes and at other times with great outcomes. In any case, the overall message transmitted was that *all* people are treated as special, in contrast with the conventional mantra: "Nobody gets special treatment around here."[67]

Second, although Mainstream and Multistream managers may use the same media or channels to communicate messages, they do so with different intentions and outcomes. For example, in some organizations the use of e-mail and other technology has resulted in a greater concentration of power and control in the hands of managers who use them, for example, to micromanage employees. In other organizations, the same media and channels are used to enhance participative management, such as when decision-making opportunities for frontline employees increase thanks to the additional information they can easily access.[68] In short, although Mainstream and Multistream managers may use the same media, how those media are used and what the nature of the communication is may be very different under each approach.

Some research suggests that there may be differences in the media preferred by Mainstream and Multistream management. For example, Mainstream managers may be more inclined to prefer e-mail, while Multistream managers may prefer face-to-face communication.[69] Compared to face-to-face relationships, e-mail places greater emphasis on the importance of individuals versus groups, is associated with individualist rather than consensual decision-making processes, and is more inclined to look for a single solution rather than achieving an awareness of different views.[70] The increase in Internet usage has coincided with a shift away from relating in groups and toward networked individualism: The more time people spend on the Internet, the less time they spend with family, friends, and colleagues.[71] One study of friendships among young people suggests that the choice of medium may determine the quality of interpersonal relationships. Compared to offline relationships, online friendships seem to be weaker, have a narrower range of topics shared, and are less personal.[72]

In terms of channels, Multistream managers prefer smaller groups where they can practice face-to-face communication. Recall from Chapter 10 that many Multistream managers prefer departments that have fewer than 150 people. Once departments grow larger than that size, communication dynamics change and it is time to subdivide the department. One communication model that has been found to work particularly well is one in which organizational members find opportunities for meaningful communication in smaller groups of 10 to 15 members, and where these groups are linked together by members who relate to and thereby connect several groups.[73]

Step 3: Receive and Decode the Message

There are two key differences between Mainstream and Multistream decoding.

First, Mainstream decoding focuses on task-related issues such as productivity and efficiency, whereas Multistream decoding is receptive to ideas that go beyond productivity. Multistream managers want to improve productivity, but they also recognize that an obsessive focus solely on task-related issues—where everything else is considered "noise"— often leads to situations where we miss out on the truly important and beautiful things in life.

"Social butterflies" facilitate organizational communication when they act as go-betweens among different subgroups within an organization.

WHAT DO YOU THINK?

How Does Context Influence the Perceived Meaning of Messages? (Part 2)

Sometimes we are so focused on the task at hand that we miss out on the true beauty around us. The following story, by *Washington Post* columnist Gene Weingarten, prompted a greater response than he has ever received for anything else he has published.

> Imagine that you are in Washington D.C., in an acoustically vibrant hall, listening to violinist Joshua Bell, winner of the Avery Fisher Prize as the best classical musician in the United States, as he plays some of the most beautiful music ever composed. Says Bell, "When you play a violin piece, you are a story teller, and you're telling a story."
>
> Although he has a truly magnificent message to convey, Bell has accepted an invitation from *The Washington Post* to encode it in an unusual context. Bell is dressed like a common street entertainer, and is playing his $3.5 million Stradivarius violin during rush hour in a metro station. In this context, not many people seem to notice or even try to decode the message. Indeed, of the 1097 people who pass by him during his 43-minute concert, only 7 stop to listen for more than a minute, and his busker's haul is $32.17.[74]
>
> When watching the video of his performance afterward, the feedback Bell finds particularly painful was what happens right after each musical piece ends—*nothing* happened, no applause, no acknowledgment. "I'm surprised at the number of people who don't pay attention at all, as if I'm invisible. Because, you know what? I'm makin' a lot of noise!"
>
> Noise indeed!

What are your thoughts on this comment by Gene Weingarten: "If we can't take the time out of our lives to stay a moment and listen to one of the best musicians on Earth play some of the best music ever written; if the surge of modern life so overpowers us that we are deaf and blind to something like that—then what else are we missing?"[75]

Can you think of other times when people mistake something beautiful or important for "noise"?

We often admire people who focus so well on a task that they can tune out distractions. Joshua Bell was able to tune out the distractions of playing in a busy metro station (which is good), but the unreceptive commuters were also able to tune out Bell's beautiful music (which may not be so good). Of course, this example draws attention to the huge role of "context" in receiving and decoding messages. What people think of as the most beautiful music ever composed in one context is considered "noise" in another. Context is equally important in organizations, and managers must take care to ensure that the context promotes the message that they send. They must also be aware of the context they are in when they receive and decode messages from others. For Mainstream managers, the context or "frame" of organizational communication is focused on achieving results and competing with others.[76] In contrast, Multistream managers have a larger frame or context: They deliberately focus their attention on multiple forms of well-being.

The second difference between Mainstream and Multistream decoding arises in the area of individual versus collective listening. Mainstream decoding tends to be at the individual level, whereas Multistream decoding occurs more at the group level.[77] The Multistream tendency to embrace diverse voices and multiple forms of well-being also influences the very nature of listening. Whereas the Mainstream approach emphasizes listening as being about knowledge acquisition, Multistream decoding highlights how listening contributes to the formation of a group's identity. Multistream listening is not about filling our minds with thoughts about what to do; rather, it is about who we are and what we do in relation to others. Decoding is, therefore, oriented toward achieving mutual understanding, which is more than simply the linear transfer of knowledge from one person to the next.[78]

Consider what happened when Larry Mauws, CEO of Westward Industries, announced to his employees that they were going to completely redesign their main product, a three-wheeled car used by park-

DILBERT: © Scott Adams/Dist. by United Feature Syndicate, Inc.

ing patrol officers throughout the United States. This major change, based largely on customer feedback, created a time of collective decoding. **Collective decoding** occurs when a message is interpreted by a group of two or more people, with the result being that each member learns more than any one person could alone (and typically more than the sender could have put into the original message). At a basic level, everyone in the organization understood the message: They needed to redesign the car so it had specific additional features. At a deeper level, however, the decoding took weeks and months of work because it required members to reconsider their overall work and the identity of the organization. At this deeper level, the message could not be fully decoded by any one person, including Mauws himself. Rather, to understand what it meant to make a new car required members to relearn their own tasks *in the context of their interrelationships with the work of the people around them.*[79]

The notion of collective decoding is important for the organizational learning process, because developing a shared language is a prerequisite for shared understanding.[80] Organizational members have many good ideas, but most of them are never implemented because they have not been collectively decoded. If the implications of new ideas are not understood by the group, then the group cannot implement the ideas.[81]

When collective decoding occurs, members understand ideas more fully and are less likely to resist them. If all members have their voices heard, they are more likely to accept decisions even when they are not in their own self-interest, because they understand how the change benefits the whole. This kind of decoding involves not only hearing the words and content of the message being sent, but also a deeper relational acknowledgment of the sender as a person. Collective decoding recognizes and respects the unique knowledge that each member brings to the organization, thereby providing the opportunity to create new meanings that are richer than either the sender or the receiver could come up with on his or her own.[82]

> **Collective decoding** occurs when a message is interpreted by a group of two or more people with the result that each member learns more than any one person could alone (and typically more than the sender could have put into the original message).

Step 4: Information Flows from Receiver to Sender (Feedforward)

This step may represent the most important difference between Mainstream and Multistream communication. Both approaches try to ensure that the original message was received accurately. However, Mainstream managers are often reluctant to accept critical upward communication, while Multistream managers welcome it. Research shows that managers who welcome feedback also tend to exhibit other skills and characteristics that are consistent with a Multistream approach.[83] For example, managers who seek feedback tend to be perceived as more interested in nurturing community, in developing positive working relationships with others, and in demonstrating consideration and concern for others. Likewise, they are perceived as being more friendly, approachable, and empathetic. Such managers tend to value differences, work well with people who hold different points of view, find ways to enhance multiple views, are open to new ideas and ways of doing things, and have excellent listening skills. Such managers are also known for giving honest and direct feedback.

Rather than naming this step "feedback communication" and placing it at the end of the communication cycle, it might be more accurate to call it "feedforward communication" and place it at the beginning of the Multistream four-phase cycle. For Multistream managers, identifying the message to be sent is influenced by the feedforward information the sender has previously received from others.[84] **Feedforward communication** refers to the relationships and prior communication that influence subsequent messages.[85]

Feedforward communication can help to perpetuate a vicious cycle, or it can reinforce a virtuous cycle. For an example of how feedforward communication can contribute to a vicious cycle, consider the example of mid-level managers at Omega, a 400-employee organization that provides residential care in Ireland.[86] In this organization, mid-level managers felt ignored by senior managers, who seemed oblivious to feedback from below. After one frustrating encounter with the head office, a mid-level manager lamented, "I miss conversation. Why should I bother next time?" Another mid-level manager described whose voices are heard at meetings:

> There had been maybe 20 people at the previous meeting. But the only people that had [been recorded in the] minutes or made points were the head office staff. In eight pages there was nothing that I would have said, that anyone [other than top management] would have said. It was as if we weren't there.

Top managers' feedforward communication sets the stage for subsequent messages that local managers will (and will not) send. If senior managers have clearly—even if unintentionally—communicated that they have no interest in building community with mid-level managers (as was the case at Omega), then mid-level managers will limit the sorts of messages they communicate to the head office. This may have certain short-term efficiencies, but it will minimize long-term organizational learning.

For an example of how Multistream managers use feedforward communication, consider again James Despain, the manager of Caterpillar Inc.'s 3000-person Track-Type Tractors Division. As described earlier, Despain decided to make himself vulnerable by trusting everyone in the organization. This vulnerability and trust, in turn, created the context for employees to engage in critical upward communication, consistent with their motto: "Share information in all directions, both good news and bad news."

> Instead of being forceful or loud in an effort to get our individual ways, we started to listen, really listen, to what others were trying to say. Instead of hurting feelings as sensitive issues surfaced, we began to practice real respect. We lost our need for ownership of ideas and began giving meaningful recognition to others. Our collective ideas were more innovative and powerful.[87]

Eventually antagonistic union–management relations improved, and hourly and salaried members began to treat one another with respect and dignity. Everyone at Caterpillar changed, from top managers to hourly workers, thanks to the growing influence of its virtuous cycle of communication. Soon employees' approval of management rose by more than 30 percent; there was a 25 percent increase in employee participation, satisfaction, and accountability; and workers' identification with the organization's goals jumped by 40 percent. Before long the division, which had been losing tens of millions of dollars a year, was again profitable.[88]

Feedforward communication refers to the relationships and prior communication that influence subsequent messages.

Communication in a Hostile Context[89]

Some managers and some organizations thrive on open communication. In other cases, people who want to enjoy open communication must leave their existing jobs or must establish social support groups or new organizations to create opportunities to communicate freely. Such was the case when 20 peasant leaders formed the Association of Peasant Workers in Carare (APWC). These peasants lived along the Carare River in the jungles of Magdalena Medio in Colombia, which has been one of the world's most violent countries.[90]

This region has experienced ongoing violence since at least the 1960s, when a growing military, paramilitary, and guerrilla movement prompted people in the region to create their own self-defense groups of armed vigilantes. The issues driving the conflict are very complex, but include the quest for political power and profits from Colombia's lucrative drug trade. However, the consequences for regular citizens are clear. If a citizen is known to have helped one of the armed groups (even by providing its members with food at gunpoint), he or she is in danger of being killed by a competing group. As a result, people are always on the run, and there are now more displaced persons in Colombia than almost anywhere else in the world.

Needless to say, the ongoing violence has created havoc with communication patterns. Peasants refer to "the code of silence," which is enforced by the armed groups competing for power in the region: "It is prohibited to talk about the death of any friend or family member, about those who killed them or the reasons they were killed. If you open your mouth, the rest of your family will be killed."

After a period of especially intense fighting and large-scale massacres, a particularly violent captain of the Colombian army gathered and met with a group of 2000 peasants from the region. He told them that if they would accept his weapons and join his militia in the fight against the guerrillas, then he would provide them amnesty and "forgiveness" for their "support" of the guerrillas in the past. The crowd was stunned—they had not provided support for *any* of the groups. Then a peasant named Josué spoke up and stated that he was fed up with this continuing cycle of violence. Today you will still find

peasants in the area, some of whom weren't even at the meeting, who can recite his speech, word for word:

> We have arrived at the conclusion that weapons have not solved a thing and that there is not one reason to arm ourselves. . . . Look at all these people you brought here. We all know each other. And who are you? We know that some years ago you yourself were with [the] guerrilla[s] and now you are the head of the paramilitaries. You brought people into our houses to accuse us, you lied, and you switched sides. And now you, a side switcher, you want us to follow your violent example. Captain, with all due respect, we do not plan to join your side, their side, or any side. And we are not leaving this place. We are going to find our own solution.[91]

Within a week, the APWC was formed: "[W]e decided that day to speak for ourselves." This movement started when members broke the code of silence, and replaced it with a new code of communication that had four guiding principles.

First, the members' **message** was to work together in solidarity when they were faced with threats of violence or intimidation. They would not succumb to divide-and-conquer tactics. They were committed to treating others with dignity and respect, just as they expected to be treated with dignity and respect. They sought to communicate with and build an overarching sense of community with everyone. Their deep commitment to this message is expressed in their pledge: "We shall die before we kill." In the months and years that followed, members of the APWC stayed true to their radical principles of communication.

Second, they would **encode** their message in a very transparent and open way. Instead of following laws of silence and secrecy, they work to do everything publicly: "Speak loud and never hide anything." For example, much in the same way that managers create posters of their organization's mission statement, the peasants posted handmade signs outside their villages proclaiming, "What the people from here say," which declared that no weapons would be allowed in their villages and that their lands were a territory for peace.

Third, they worked very hard at **decoding** the messages of others, especially those who had differing views and those who believed that violence could solve their problems: "We shall understand those who do not understand us." They sincerely and diligently sought to establish true dialogue. They sent delegations to meet with different armed groups, and they sought to approach each such meeting seeking to connect with the real person, the human being, with whom they spoke.

Finally, even when faced with violent **feedback,** they were committed to talk and negotiate with everyone: "We have no enemies." Members held to their promise of never giving in to weapons and never giving up on dialogue. Transparency was carried out to its fullest extent: Everyone—friends and foes alike—were welcome in public debriefings of meetings.

Was this new approach to communications effective? During subsequent years, violence was greatly reduced, though Magdalena Medio remained a hotbed of armed conflict. Josué and several other leaders were assassinated by unknown hired guns. But their legacy lives on, and to-day many people believe that organizations like the APWC hold the key to bringing about peace in Colombia.

QUESTIONS FOR DISCUSSION

1. Where would you place the communication pattern being modeled by the APWC along the Mainstream–Multistream continuum? Identify the criteria you used in your analysis.

2. Most readers have not faced the consequence of death for breaking a "code of silence." Yet there are taboos in every society and organization that influence what can, and cannot, be openly discussed. In many organizations, it is taboo to question the decisions of top managers, and whistleblowers often lose their jobs and find it difficult to resume their careers. What sorts of things can managers and other organizational members do to ensure open and free communications in organizations?

SUMMARY

Managers spend three-fourths of their time communicating with others.

From a Mainstream perspective, the four-step communication process proceeds as follows:

1. Managers craft messages that are consistent with improving task-related organizational performance.
2. Managers encode and transmit messages based on an attempt to reduce noise, with a bias toward choosing large-scale and written communication media and channels.
3. Receivers decode messages individually, tuning out distraction so as to maximize the amount of task-related knowledge being acquired.
4. Receivers provide feedback to the sender to confirm that the message was understand as intended.

From a Multistream perspective, the four-step communication process proceeds as follows:

1. Members craft messages that are consistent with a wide variety of perspectives about how to enhance collective well-being.
2. Members encode and transmit messages based on an attempt to embrace diversity, with a bias toward choosing small-scale, face-to-face communication media and channels.
3. Receivers decode messages collectively, paying attention to the meaning of messages for their coworkers so as to enhance relational understanding in the organization.
4. Members seek feedback, and use feedforward information previously received from others, to identify messages to be sent.

QUESTIONS FOR REFLECTION AND DISCUSSION

1. Identify and briefly describe the four steps of the communication process. What are the key differences between a Mainstream approach and a Multistream approach to the communication process? Are there any similarities? Explain.

2. Explain why feedback is such a challenge in the Mainstream approach.

3. Why is context important in decoding a message? Give an example.

4. What is the difference between treating contextual features as "noise" that *hampers* the communication process and treating them as "diversity" that *enhances* the communication process?

5. Think of a time when you experienced "collective decoding"—that is, when your own understanding of a message was enhanced because you were interpreting it with others. Was the sender of the message part of the process of decoding it? Do you think the message that you understood after this process was clearer and more complete than the original message sent? Explain your answer.

6. Explain the difference between rich and lean communication media. Which criteria should managers use to select a medium for their message?

7. Consider the following statement:

   In this era of globalization and intense competition, managers really don't have any alternative except to communicate in a Mainstream way. If they don't continually focus on the importance of productivity and profitability in their communications, their subordinates will not get the message and their company's profitability and productivity will suffer because other companies are relentlessly pursuing these goals. The Multistream approach to communication sounds good, but it simply will not work.

   Do you agree or disagree with the statement? Explain your reasoning.

HANDS-ON ACTIVITIES

Where Are You Along the Mainstream–Multistream Continuum?

Circle the number that best corresponds to your views.

TO COMMUNICATE EFFECTIVELY AS A MANAGER, I SHOULD . . .

Focus on messages that will enhance productivity.	1 2 3 4 5 6 7	Welcome messages on all facets of organizational well-being.
Focus on messages that are consistent with my own view.	1 2 3 4 5 6 7	Welcome messages that represent diverging views.
Choose media and channels that reduce noise and expense.	1 2 3 4 5 6 7	Choose media and channels that embrace diversity and richness.
Decode messages in a way that tunes out non-instrumental distractions.	1 2 3 4 5 6 7	Decode messages in a way that looks for hidden differences and opportunities.
Focus on the content of messages.	1 2 3 4 5 6 7	Focus on the relational implications of messages.
Seek confirmation that messages were received as intended.	1 2 3 4 5 6 7	Decode messages collectively.
Expect critical upward communication to be poorly received.	1 2 3 4 5 6 7	Expect critical upward communication to be well received.

ENDNOTES

1. This case is based on a personal interview with one of the authors (March 27, 2001). Some of the details have been changed for reasons of confidentiality and pedagogy.

2. This chapter will not focus on other important kinds of communication, such as communication between organizations (e.g., supply chain management) or communication between organizations and customers (e.g., marketing).

3. Mintzberg, H. (1973). *The nature of managerial work.* New York: Harper & Row.

4. Clampitt, P. G., DeKoch, R. J., & Cashman, T. (2000). A strategy for communicating about uncertainty. *Academy of Management Executive,* 14(4), 41–57.

5. Our discussion in this paragraph builds on ideas found in Vandenbosch, B., Saatcioglu, A., & Fay, S. (2006). Idea management: A systemic view. *Journal of Management Studies,* 43(3), 259–288. Their study describes four types of managers. Mainstream managers correspond roughly to what they call Incrementalists, and Multistream managers correspond roughly to what they call Searchers. Their remaining two types account for less than 20 percent of their sample.

6. Vandenbosch et al., 2006.

7. "Consensus-builders" in Vandenbosch et al., 2006.

8. Clampitt et al., 2000.

9. Bordia, P., Hobman, E., Jones, E., Gallois, C., & Callan, V. J. (2004). Uncertainty during organizational change: Types, consequences, and management strategies. *Journal of Business & Psychology,* 18(4), 507–532.

10. Clampitt et al., 2000.

11. Clampitt et al., 2000.

12. Clampitt et al., 2000.

13. Clampitt et al., 2000.

14. Cross, R., & Sproull, L. (2004). More than an answer: Information relationships for actionable knowledge. *Organization Science,* 15(4), 446–462.

15. Clampitt et al., 2000.

16. This may be based on a comment made by Blaise Pascal, who wrote to a friend: "I have made this letter longer than usual because I lack the time to make it shorter." Cited in Kroeker, W. (2007, August 20). Dear editor. *Canadian Mennonite,* 11(16), 11.

17. Larkin, T. J., & Larkin, S. (1996, May–June). Reaching and changing front-line employees. *Harvard Business Review,* 95–104.

18. Accessed November 27, 2007, at http://www.websters-online-dictionary.com/definition/PHAT.

19. For more, see the following source: Old messengers, new media: The legacy of Innis and McLuhan (n.d.). *Library and Archives Canada.* Accessed November 28, 2007, at http://www.collectionscanada.gc.ca/innis-mcluhan/index-e.html.

20. Daft, R. L., & Lengel, R. H. (1986). Organizational information requirements, media richness and structural design. *Management Science,* 32(5), 554–571; Daft, R. L., Lengel, R. H., & Trevino, L. K. (1987). Message equivocality, media selection, and manager performance: Implications for information systems. *MIS Quarterly,* 11, 335–366; Neufeld, D. J., Brotheridge, C. M., & Dyck, B. (2001). *Electronic mail as a rich communication medium in global virtual organizations.* HICSS 34, Minitrack Information Systems in Global Business, Hawaii, January 3–6, 2001. Richness also includes the ability to express language variety.

21. Martin, S. (1995). The role of nonverbal communications in quality improvement. National Productivity Review, 15(1), 27–40; Fatt, J. P. T. (1998). Nonverbal communication and business success. Management Research News, 21(4/5), 1–10.

22. Larkin & Larkin, 1996.

23. This discussion builds on Peters, L. D. (2006). Conceptualising computer-mediated communication technology and its use in organizations. *International Journal of Information Management,* 26, 142–152.

24. Hart, R. K. B. (2002). *The conversation of relationships: The communication content and quality of strong and weak relationships in geographically dispersed teams.* Ph.D. dissertation, Department of Organizational Behavior, Case Western Reserve University, Cleveland, OH.

25. Neufeld et al., 2001.

26. Peters, 2006, p. 145.

27. Clampitt et al., 2000.

28. Huang, Y. H., Robertson, M. M., & Chang, K.-I. (2004). The role of environmental control on environmental satisfaction, communication, and psychological stress: Effect of office ergonomics training. *Environment and Behavior,* 36(5), 617–637.

29. Wickhorst, V., & Geroy, G. (2006). Physical communication and organization development. *Organization Development Journal,* 24(3), 54–63.

30. Bavelas, A., & Barrett, D. (1951). An experimental approach to organization communication. *Personnel,* 27, 366–371; Bavelas, A. (1950). Communication patterns in task-oriented groups. *Journal of the Acoustical Society of America,* 22, 725–730; Guetzkow, H., & Simon, H. A. (1955). The impact of certain communication nets upon organization and performance in task-oriented groups. *Management Science,* 1(3–4), 233–250.

31. See page 591 in Daft, R. L. (2003). *Management* (6th ed.). Mason, OH: Thomson South-Western.

32. Larkin & Larkin, 1996.

33. Spread the word: Gossip is good. (1988, October 4). *Wall Street Journal,* p. B1. Cited on p. 569 in Griffin, R. W. (2002). *Management* (7th ed.). Boston: Houghton Mifflin.

34. Flynn, F. (2005). Having an open mind: The impact of openness to experience on interracial attitudes and impression formation. *Journal of Personality & Social Psychology,* 88(5), 816–826.

35. The photo is from the television comedy series *The Office,* which depicts less than fully competent managers at work. The content and quotes for the caption were drawn from material cited on page 85 in Dispensa, J. M., & Brulle, R. J. (2003). Media's social construction of environmental issues: Focus on global warming—a comparative study. *International Journal of Sociology and Social Policy,* 23(10), 74–105.

36. Becker, E., & Becker, L. (2003, August/September). Interview with Peter Seeger. *New York Spirit.* Accessed May 8, 2007, at http://www.nyspirit.com/issue121/article2.html; Portilla, J. (2004). Interview with John Paul Lederach. BeyondIntractability.org; Vedran Smailovic. Accessed August 23, 2007, at http://www.appleseedrec.com/sarajevo/vedran/.

37. Fatt, 1998.

38. Szulanski, G. (1996). Exploring internal stickiness: Impediments to the transfer of best practice within the firm. *Strategic Management Journal,* 17, 27–43.

39. Tourish, D., & Robson, P. (2006). Sensemaking and the distortion of critical upward communication in organizations. *Journal of Management Studies*, 43(4), 711–730.

40. Fox, S., & Amichai-Hamburger, P. (2001). The power of emotional appeals in promoting organizational change programs. *Academy of Management Executive*, 15(4), 84–94.

41. Page 7 in Folkman, J. R. (2006). *The power of feedback*. Hoboken, NJ: John Wiley & Sons.

42. This definition builds on the definition of criticism as "a serious examination and judgment of something; 'constructive criticism is always appreciated.'" Accessed August 23, 2007, at wordnet .princeton.edu/perl/webwn.

43. Folkman, 2006.

44. Tourish & Robson, 2006.

45. Tourish & Robson, 2006.

46. Folkman, 2006.

47. Moreover, cognitive biases serve to filter any feedback that they do receive (Tourish & Robson, 2006).

48. Page 70 in Baker, D., Greenberg, C., & Hemingway, C. (2006). *What happy companies know*. Upper Saddle River, NJ: Pearson Prentice-Hall.

49. Peters, T. J., & Waterman, R. H., Jr. (1982). *In search of excellence*. New York: Harper & Row.

50. Morden, T. (1997). Leadership as competence. *Management Decision*, 35(7), 519–526.

51. Page 14 in Peters, T., & Austin, N. (1985). MBWA (Managing by Walking Around). *California Management Review*, 28(1), 10–34.

52. Seiter, John S. (2007). Ingratiation and gratuity: The effect of complimenting customers on tipping behavior in restaurants. *Journal of Applied Social Psychology*, 37(3), 478–485; Ebesu Hubbard, Amy S., Tsuji, A. Allen, Williams, C., & Seatriz, V., Jr. (2003). Effects of touch on gratuities received in same-gender and cross-gender dyads. *Journal of Applied Social Psychology*, 33(11), 2427–2438. (Note that there was an increase regardless of the gender to the food server or client but the greatest increase was when female servers touched the shoulder of male clients.)

53. Putnam, L. L., Phillips, N., & Chapman, P. (1996). Metaphors of communication and organization. In S. R. Clegg, C. Hardy, & W. R. Nord (Eds.), *Managing organizations: Current issues* (pp. 125–158). London: Sage.

54. Boyes-Watson, C. (2006). Community is not a place but a relationship: Lessons for organizational development. *Public Organization Review: A Global Journal*, 5, 359–374.

55. Page 74 in Autry, J. A. (1991). *Love and profit: The art of caring leadership*. New York: William Morrow.

56. Putnam et al., 1996; Despain, J. M., & Brulle, R. J. (2003). Media's social construction of environmental issues: Focus on global warming—a comparative study. *International Journal of Sociology and Social Policy*, 23(10), 74–105.

57. Portilla, J. (2004). Interview with John Paul Lederach. Accessed April 2007 at BeyondIntractability.org. See also Huebner, C. K. (2006). *A precarious peace*. Waterloo, ON: Herald Press.

58. Lederach, J. P. (1995). *Preparing for peace: Conflict transformation across cultures*. Syracuse, NY: Syracuse University Press.

59. Vandenbosch et al., 2006.

60. Vandenbosch et al., 2006.

61. Buchanen, A., & O'Neill, M. (2001). *Inclusion and diversity: Finding common ground for organizational action: A deliberative dialogue guide*. Ottawa: Canadian Council for International Co-operation.

62. Page 143 in Despain, J., & Converse, J. B. (2003). *And dignity for all: Unlocking the greatness of value-based leadership*. Upper Saddle River, NJ: Prentice-Hall/Financial Times.

63. These three differences build on Vandenbosch et al., 2006.

64. Dyck, B. (2002). A grounded, faith-based moral point of view of management. In T. Rose (Ed.), *Proceedings of organizational theory division*, 23, 12–23. Winnipeg, MB: Administrative Sciences Association of Canada. The names of people drawn from this article have been disguised, but the situations are accurate.

65. Mai, R., & Akerson, A. (2003). *The leader as communicator*. New York: Amacon American Management Association.

66. Such an approach also promises to "add" more "just" practices to everyday communication and decisions in the workplace.

67. Autry, 1991, p. 23.

68. Barley, S. R. (1986). Technology as an occasion for structuring: Evidence from observations of CT scanners and the social order of radiology departments. *Administrative Science Quarterly*, 31, 78–108; Brotheridge, C. (2003). *Structuring deference and solidarity in a manager–expatriate employee dyad in the context of changing communications media within the Mennonite Central Committee*. Ph.D. dissertation, University of Manitoba.

69. Peters, 2006.

70. Peters, 2006.

71. Taher, M. (2006). Book review: *The Internet in Everyday Life*. *Information Resources Management Journal*, 19(1), 98–100.

72. Mesch, G., & Talmud, I. (2006). The quality of online and offline relationships: The role of multiplexity and duration of social relationships. *Information Society*, 22, 137–148. Another study looked at whether the choice of media, and the content of messages sent, was influenced by the strength of interpersonal relationships (Hart, 2002). This study looked at members of geographically dispersed teams. When interpersonal relationships were weak, the preferred medium was group meetings. Messages downplayed task-related information and emphasized expression of personal opinions and feelings. In contrast, when relationships were strong, the preferred medium was e-mail, the emphasis was on providing task-related information that the receiver would find helpful, there were fewer expressions of personal opinions and feelings, and more issues were left open-ended. This offers some support for the idea given in Chapter 16 that investing in developing interpersonal relationships early in a team's development is critical. This investment builds trust that allows for less personal and more task-oriented communication later in the team's development. In addition, Multistream managers should try to regularly bring the team members together to reconnect and deepen interpersonal relationships through face-to-face communication.

73. Nelson, R. E., & Mathews, K. M. (1991). Network characteristics of high-performing organizations. *Journal of Business Communication*, 28, 367–386.

74. This figure does not take into account $20 given to Bell by someone who recognized who he was. A video of his performance and this little social experiment can be viewed online. Weingarten, G. (2007, April 8). Pearls before breakfast: Can one of the nation's great musicians cut through the fog of a D.C. rush hour? Let's find out. *Washington Post*, p. W10.

75. About 10 percent of readers responding to this story said it made them cry: *Post Magazine: Too busy to stop and hear the music*. Accessed May 6, 2007, at WashingtonPost.com.

76. Ucok, O. (2006). Transparency, communication and mindfulness. *Journal of Management Development*, 25(10), 1024–1028.

77. In one sense, everyone receives and decodes messages from others in terms of their own context, agenda, fear, and filters (Ucok, 2006). Multistream managers try to be aware of their own voice and their own agenda, and they try to hear the voices of others without judging or criticizing.

78. This discussion builds on Jacobs, C., & Coghlan, D. (2005). Sound from silence: On listening in organizational learning. *Human Relationships*, 58(1), 115–138. See also Nonaka, I. (1994). A dynamic theory of organizational knowledge creation. *Organization Science*, 5(1), 14–37.

79. This description builds on case material found in Dyck, B., Starke, F. A., & Mauws, M. K. (2008). Teaching versus learning: An exploratory longitudinal case study. *Journal of Small Business and Entrepreneurship*, 21(1), 37–58.

80. Jacobs & Coghlan, 2005.

81. Lawrence, T., Dyck, B., Maitlis, S., & Mauws, M. (2006). The underlying structure of continuous change. *MIT Sloan Management Review*, 47(4), 59–66.

82. Crossan, M., Lane, H., & White, R. (1999). An organizational learning framework: From intuition to institution. *Academy of Management Review*, 24, 522–537. See also Nonaka, 1994.

83. Folkman, 2006.

84. Of course, this may also be true for the Mainstream approach (i.e., the sender's message is influenced by previous experiences), but it is qualitatively different from a Multistream approach.

85. Put in more scholarly terms, feedforward communication prepares the ground for intersubjective meaning generation (Jacobs & Coghlan, 2005).

86. Jacobs & Coghlan, 2005.

87. Despain, 2003, pp. 142–143.

88. Despain, 2003, p. 169.

89. Adapted from a keynote speech given by John Paul Lederach at the Association for Conflict Resolution's Annual Conference, Sacramento, CA, September 30, 2004. Accessed April 27, 2007, at http://www.acrnet.org/conferences/ac04/lederachspeech .htm. The story also appears in Lederach, J. P. (2005). *The moral imagination: The art and soul of building peace*. Oxford, UK: Oxford University Press. Lederach draws on the work of historian Garcia, A. (1996). *Hijos de la Violencia*. Barcelona, Spain: La Catarata. (See p. 189.)

90. Country profile: Colombia. *BBC News*. Accessed April 27, 2007, at http://news.bbc.co.uk/2/hi/americas/country_ profiles/1212798.stm.

91. Garcia, 1996, p. 189. *Hijos de la Violencia*. Barcelona, Spain: La Catarata.

CHAPTER 18

The final stop on our journey—the topic of control—is an appropriate place to conclude this book, because control encourages us to think back about many of the places that we have visited. Controlling involves designing and implementing systems to ensure that actions of organizational members are consistent with organizational goals, standards, and values. It requires managers to keep an eye on the important points at which an organization is linked to the environment—in terms of both the organization's inputs and its outputs—and to understand how tasks within different departments are carried out. Managers oversee the entire range of activities that are important for an organization, and they use controlling to ensure that all the pieces of the puzzle work together to meet organizational goals.

ROAD MAP

FOUR-STEP CONTROL PROCESS

1. Establish performance standards

2. Monitor performance

3. Evaluate performance

4. Respond accordingly

Control

MAINSTREAM APPROACH ⟷	MULTISTREAM APPROACH
Value chains help identify key control points and standards • Targets (e.g., Six Sigma)	Value loops help identify key performance standards • Process standards
Information systems help monitor outcome measures	Information systems help enhance processes, share, self-monitor
Use top-down approach • Rational	Include multiple stakeholders • Relational
Managers take action	Managers expect help from others

Like Father, Unlike Son[1]

Michael Mauws was completing a graduate degree in business when his father, Larry, asked him to manage his small car company, Westward Industries. The company designed and manufactured three-wheeled cars used by police forces throughout the United States for traffic control parking enforcement. Its three-wheeled "Go-4" vehicle had taken the market by storm and become a leader in its market segment.

Larry wanted Michael to take over the firm so that Larry could devote his attention to his favorite part of the business, which was redesigning the car and inventing new products. Michael agreed to help out his father, and had visions of making the company a "self-managed organization" where workers have as much control as possible.

Michael knew that he and his father had different visions for how Westward should be managed. Larry was an entrepreneur who liked to invent things but did not like paperwork. He was always tinkering with the car, improving it because he enjoyed responding to customer feedback. For him, the best way to grow Westward was by improving the design of its product. It was his company, and his car, and he called the shots. Westward had few policies and a very short paper trail. Managing the firm's inventory and ensuring timely delivery of parts were especially problematic, so that often the assembly line had to wait for a rush order of missing parts.

Workers were happy that Westward was going to be managed by someone with Michael's administrative and organizational skills, and they were glad that Larry would stay on as vice-president of research and design. Michael's management style was the opposite of his father's. Rather than top-down control, Michael wanted the firm to have bottom-up control; that is, he wanted members to have control over their work. He wanted to be treated like a member of the "team"—a team where everyone in the organization did their part and respected one another. Michael wanted everyone to have ownership of their jobs and to enjoy their work. He also wanted everyone to be empowered to make deci-

The largest customer for Westward's Go-4 vehicles is the New York Police Department, which purchased hundreds of Go-4s. You may have seen them on the television show *NYPD Blue*.

sions about their jobs, including what time they arrived in the morning and left in the afternoon. After all, they were the experts in the work that they did.

As part of his efforts to change the organization, Michael created a "What's Happening" binder that he left on the staffroom table, which contained letters to suppliers, customers, and financial reports. He wanted everyone to know what was going on. He also developed a profit-sharing plan, where some of the profits were to be spent in ways that benefited everyone in the firm as a group (e.g., a staff benefits program) and another portion were to benefit the outside community (e.g., a play structure for a nearby playground). Michael started to hold weekly staff meetings, where problems were discussed and decisions made.

Perhaps Michael's most important contribution was to overhaul the management information systems at Westward. He knew that getting the right information into the hands of employees was key to his vision of a self-managing organization. His new system provided basic information that had never been available at Westward before—such as how many parts were available in inventory—and it was welcomed by everyone. At first Larry despised the system, because it demanded that everyone—even him—account for each part and piece of material being used. Michael also overhauled the accounting system, which made it easier to find out which custom orders were more profitable, which costs were associated with adding special features to the vehicle, and which components should be produced in-house versus being obtained from outside suppliers.

Clearly, compared to his entrepreneurial father, Michael had a different set of values and ideas about control, and a different way of relating to others and of making decisions. This perspective, in turn, resulted in his developing different structures and information systems. However, even six months after his arrival and the introduction of all these changes, most employees at

Westward had not embraced Michael's management approach. They had spent years working under Larry's approach, and most did not buy into his son's vision for a "self-managed" organization.

Then, due to external reasons, Michael left Westward and Larry was reinstated as manager/owner. Although Larry appreciated the systems improvements that Michael had made, he was quick to revert to his "old school" approach to managing the company. Likewise, employees, who were very familiar with Larry's management style, were ready to embrace it. Michael's vision for a self-managed firm and his changes seemed destined to fail.

But the story does not end there. One year *after* his departure, Michael's idea of a "self-managed organization" finally started to take root at Westward. This change was in large part due to the way that he had designed Westward's management information systems, which Larry had not changed after Michael's departure. By working in accordance with these information systems—which Michael had designed to support his vision of a self-managed organization—workers at Westward began to realize what Michael had been trying to accomplish. They grew to enjoy the empowerment that the information systems provided. Gradually, employees began to challenge Larry, primarily because Michael's systems provided them with information to make better decisions than Larry could make. For example, when Larry wanted to tinker with vehicles on the production line, his workers reminded him that those changes needed to be documented in the records that were being created for each vehicle. Similarly, ordering supplies and parts was no longer based on "guesstimates," but rather on the more accurate information provided by Michael's information systems.

In sum, the information systems that Michael had developed and implemented were shaping a self-managed organization, where control formerly held by the manager was now held by workers. The control systems were influencing the other three functions of management: planning, organizing, and leading.

INTRODUCTION TO CONTROL

The opening case illustrates two things. First, it shows that a manager's understanding of what it means to be "effective" will influence how the manager performs the controlling function. This is consistent with what we have seen in previous chapters, where managers' values have been shown to influence how they perceive the environment and how they perform the planning, organizing, and leading functions.

Second, the opening case shows the importance of controlling compared to the other three functions. Long after Michael had left Westward and had been replaced by a manager with a different approach, it was Michael's relatively invisible information systems that enabled the changes that he had tried to implement to finally take hold. This outcome suggests that even though charismatic leadership and strategic decision making are important, the kinds of control systems that managers set up may have even greater influence in the long term.

Controlling means ensuring that actions of members are consistent with an organization's underpinning values and standards. At its best, controlling is the most thoughtful, reflective, and forward-looking of the four functions of management. It demands reinforcing organizational priorities, and understanding how operations are going, to determine where room for improvement exists. It involves reflecting on the values evident in organizational relationships, decisions, structures, and systems.

This chapter is organized around the four-step control process:

1. Establish key organizational performance standards.
2. Monitor performance.

3. Evaluate performance.

4. Respond accordingly.

The first two steps provide the foundation for the control process. As in previous chapters, we will first describe the Mainstream approach to control, and then we contrast and compare it to the Multistream approach.

MAINSTREAM APPROACH TO THE FOUR-STEP CONTROL PROCESS

From a Mainstream perspective, managerial effectiveness focuses on maximizing productivity, efficiency, profitability, and owner wealth. The challenge for Mainstream managers is to design control systems that are consistent with, and will help achieve, these goals.

Step 1: Establish Performance Standards

It is impossible for managers to control everything that happens in an organization. As a result, managers must be selective when they design control systems. In this step, managers identify the most important activities that need to be controlled and determine how these activities fit together. By doing so, managers can identify and establish *key* performance standards that need to be met.

For example, imagine that you manage an organization that builds medical devices. Your control system needs to ensure that the devices meet technical, operational, and safety performance standards. This requires establishing performance standards to ensure that the following criteria, among others, are met:[2]

- Suppliers follow stringent quality controls.
- All raw materials are traceable and a recall system is in place to identify which products would need to be removed from the market in case of a problem.
- Chemicals used in your device are stored safely and with proper documentation.
- Adequate measures are in place for cleaning the equipment.
- Staff have proper training in safety standards.
- Pest control is in place.
- Packaging materials are not contaminated.
- Shipping occurs under proper environmental conditions, including temperature and humidity.

A **value chain**—the sequence of activities needed to convert an organization's inputs (e.g., raw materials, new employees) into outputs (e.g., products and services)—is a crucial tool for helping managers identify and establish key performance standards (see Figure 18.1). Value chains include many different aspects of an organization's activities, including inbound logistics, operations, outbound logistics, marketing and sales,

Value chain refers to the sequence of activities needed to convert an organization's inputs (e.g., raw materials, new employees) into outputs (e.g., products and services).

Figure 18.1   The three basic parts of a value chain

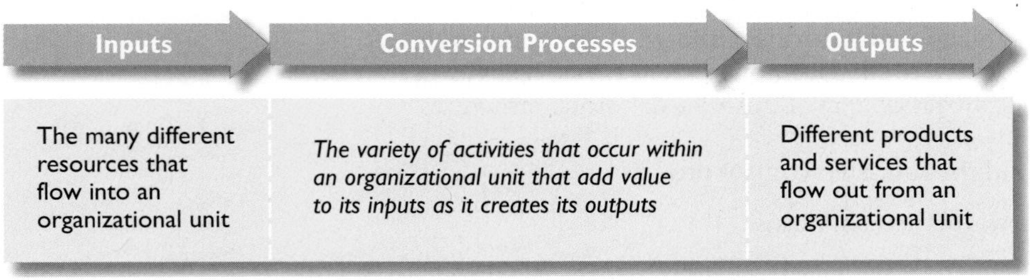

Inputs	Conversion Processes	Outputs
The many different resources that flow into an organizational unit	*The variety of activities that occur within an organizational unit that add value to its inputs as it creates its outputs*	Different products and services that flow out from an organizational unit

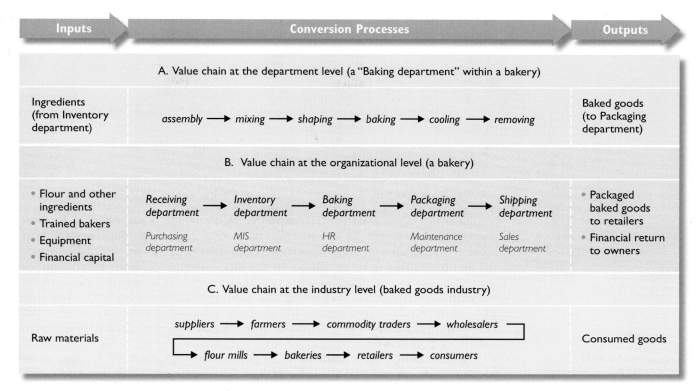

Figure 18.2   Examples of value chains

service, and various other support functions. Expertise in production and operations and **logistics** helps to manage these complex links in the value chain. Understanding the key elements of the value chain in their organization enables managers to design systems that monitor and ensure that each "link" in the chain adds financial value to an organization's products or services as its inputs are converted into outputs. Value chains can also help managers design control systems that minimize costs associated with waste,[3] overproduction, waiting, transportation, inventory, and defects.[4]

Figure 18.2 provides simple examples to show how value chains can be applied at various levels of analysis. The value chain for a manager of a baking department within a bakery is different than the value chain for the CEO of the bakery, which in turn is different than the value chain for a manager interested in the overall industry. As highlighted in the Figure 18.2(a), the manager of a baking department can use a value chain to examine how the steps at each station in the department add value as members of the department transform inputs (e.g., ingredients from the inventory department) into outputs (e.g., baked goods sent to the packaging department). As shown in Figure 18.2(b), the manager of the bakery company can use a value chain to examine how each department contributes to transforming inputs (e.g., ingredients, trained employees, equipment, financial capital) into outputs (e.g., packaged baked goods, financial return to owners). Finally, as shown in Figure 18.2(c), a value chain can help managers understand the sequence of activities within an industry or sector. This may provide valuable information suggesting whether to pursue a forward or backward integration strategy, for example. It may

Logistics refers to the structures and systems required to physically move resources into, within, and out from an organization.

also help policy makers use hazard analysis and critical control points to ensure farm-to-table food safety.[5] For example, in 2007 the global value chain for pet food came under scrutiny after 60 million packages of dog and cat food were recalled because the industrial chemical melamine—a banned ingredient—was discovered in food coming from China.[6]

A control system helps managers to identify and monitor the *key* steps in the entire value chain. Managers use three general types of controls, which correspond to the three basic parts of the value chain:

- Feedforward controls
- Concurrent controls
- Feedback controls

First, managers need to determine the nature of the *inputs* required for their organization to create the goods and services that it provides. **Feedforward controls** are designed to reduce organizational problems *before they occur* by anticipating and preventing those problems. In this step, managers identify meaningful information needed about inputs and then set up systems to acquire this information. For example, managers may check out the viability of another firm before they enter into contracts with it as a client. They may also administer drug tests before hiring new employees, inspect raw materials from suppliers, or hire only staff who have specific college degrees.

Second, **concurrent controls** identify the most important information about an organization's conversion processes, and help managers to identify and correct problems *as they occur*. Managers use concurrent controls in operations management. The focus here is on all of the direct and indirect *processes* that convert an organization's inputs into its outputs. These items include things such as developing standard operating procedures and detailed job descriptions. Managers often implement quality control checks at the specific steps in the conversion process that are most important. For example, managers in the beef industry spend about $350 million per year to ensure that meat sold to the public does not contain harmful pathogens. Companies such as Tyson Fresh Meats use complex technologies to test hundreds of meat samples each day, and they have added huge chambers to their slaughterhouses where carcasses are scalded and washed in acid, and where steam vacuums suck away microbes.[7]

Feedback controls are designed to identify and correct problems *after they occur* so as to avoid future problems. In particular, managers work hard to ensure that the organization's *outputs* are valued by the marketplace. For example, an organization may produce unique iPod cases at a very low price, but still go bankrupt if there is insufficient demand for its product. However, if managers correctly identify a segment of the market that values their product (e.g., music-loving students), and if they market the product in a way that is valued by this market segment (e.g., Internet ads on MySpace), then they may achieve financial viability. Using feedback controls, managers monitor the external marketplace to keep track of changes in which products and services are valued. They also look at measure of output values such as sales per square foot, number of product defects, or actual expenses incurred versus income generated. Shifts in these kinds of measures provide feedback that signals to managers that changes may be needed.

Zara, a fashion business owned by the Spanish Inditex Group, has become one of the most successful organizations in the international fashion industry, with

Feedforward controls are designed to reduce organizational problems by anticipating problems *before they occur* and preventing them.

Concurrent controls are designed to identify and correct problems *as they occur*.

Feedback controls are designed to identify and correct problems *after they occur* so as to avoid future problems.

more than 1000 retail stores in approximately 30 countries. Zara is well known for how effectively it has managed its value chain and, in particular, how sensitive it is to feedback controls from customers. In this integrated organization, managers are able to control products from the design decision to the point of sale. Unlike most of the fashion industry, where goods sold in one season have been designed in the previous season (i.e., a three-month turnaround time), 85 percent of Zara's goods are manufactured in the season they are sold (Zara has a two-week design-to-delivery cycle). As a result, customers know that they can come back in two weeks and see a new product on Zara's shelf; they also recognize that they may not be able to purchase the product they had liked two weeks earlier.[8]

Once managers understand the key points in the value chain, they can identify the key performance standards that need to be met. Mainstream management is likely to emphasize controls that can be quantified and written down. These standards may be expressed in terms of standard operating procedures, specifications for input components, piece-rate pay systems, and constraints and targets built into departmental budgets. For example, managers at an automobile manufacturer may specify exactly which sort of steering wheel they want from suppliers and then open the process up for bidding. Managers in a human resource department may specify which type of educational training and experience is required for each job and then recruit accordingly. Similarly, department managers are given financial goals and target ratios to meet.

Women shopping in a Zara store in Madrid, Spain.

Perhaps the best-known example of Mainstream control standards comes courtesy of Jack Welch. During his tenure as CEO of General Electric, he established a policy that employees in the lowest-performing 10 percent of the workforce would lose their jobs. Welch is also credited with popularizing control systems based on Six Sigma performance standards, which require managers to work toward developing processes that allow outputs to be defect-free 99.9997 percent of the time. Welch attributed billions of dollars in GE savings to the efficiency and productivity gains associated with the Six Sigma approach.

The Six Sigma quality standard can be applied to each point in the value chain—inputs, conversion processes, and outputs. For example, managers may use statistical quality control techniques to test the quality of incoming components, for "in-process sampling," and for final output "acceptance sampling." Over time, the Six Sigma approach has been broadened to include the idea of "disciplined and relentless pursuit of higher quality and lower costs."[9] It can be implemented in a wide variety of settings, from industry giants such as GE to agribusinesses such as dairy farms, where tools have been applied to help managers draw flowcharts intended to maintain milk productivity while minimizing financial costs and ecological pollution.[10]

Popular Performance Standards

Five types of performance standards are especially popular in Mainstream management across a wide variety of organizations.

Liquidity Ratios. Is the organization able to quickly convert assets into cash if needed to meet short-term obligations? If for some reason the organization doesn't sell its inventory, will it still be able to meet its short-term obligations?

$$\text{Current ratio} = \text{current assets} \div \text{current liabilities}$$
$$\text{Quick ratio} = (\text{current assets} - \text{inventory}) \div \text{current liabilities}$$

Leverage Ratios. Is the organization's financing mainly from borrowed money or from owners' investments? Is the organization technically insolvent (that is, are its debts greater than its assets)?

$$\text{Debt-to-assets ratio} = \text{total debt} \div \text{total assets}$$
$$\text{Times-interest-earned ratio} = \text{profits before interest and taxes} \div \text{total charges for interest}$$

Activity Measurements. Is the organization carrying more inventory than it needs? How well does the organization convert potential customers into actual customers?

$$\text{Inventory turnover} = \text{cost of goods sold} \div \text{average inventory}$$
$$\text{Conversion ratio} = \text{purchase orders} \div \text{customer inquiries}$$

Profitability Ratios. How well is the organization using its resources to generate profits? How much profit does it make on each dollar of sales?

$$\text{Return on investment (ROI)} = \text{net profit after taxes} \div \text{total assets}$$
$$\text{Profit margin} = \text{net income} \div \text{sales}$$

Factor Productivity. How well is the organization performing, all things considered? How well does the organization perform with regard to specific inputs (such as labor)?

$$\text{Total factor productivity} = \text{value of outputs} \div (\text{value of labor} + \text{capital} + \text{materials} + \text{energy})$$
$$\text{Labor productivity} = \text{value of outputs} \div \text{value of direct labor}$$

Step 2: Monitor Performance

Information systems help to identify, collect, organize, and disseminate information.

Once managers understand the critical steps in the value chain and identify the key performance standards to be met, they must develop appropriate information systems that allow them to monitor performance. An organization's **information systems** help managers to identify, collect, organize, and disseminate information. Information systems are important for each of the four functions of management: planning, organizing, leading, and controlling. Information is especially important for decision making. Spending on information technology accounts for more than half of all capital spending annually (more than $1 trillion).[11] Information systems are important in each phase of the control process, but are perhaps most readily evident when they are used by managers to monitor performance.

Data are facts and figures, some of which may provide valuable information.

Conceptually, perhaps the most important thing an information system does is to allow managers to control what are considered *data* and what is treated as *information*. **Data** are facts and figures, some of which managers deem to be useful; the majority are not. Organizations generate almost infinite amounts of data, including which clothes people are wearing on a particular day, what they are eating for lunch, which color the walls are painted, where offices are located, how many clocks are present, which sorts of paper are used in the photocopier, what is being placed in wastebaskets, how many words are used in e-mail messages, what the tone of someone's voice is, and so on. Most data are ignored because they have not been deemed meaningful enough to warrant further attention.

Information refers to data that have been given meaning and are deemed to have value.

Information refers to data that have been given *meaning* and are deemed to have value. Managers design control and information systems to monitor meaningful data. For a Mainstream manager, meaningful data are those that help to maximize productivity and, therefore, are considered information. Data that do not help to achieve Mainstream goals are not considered information. For example, for many years managers at fast-food restaurants found that data about the *price* of the paper used to wrap their burgers provided useful information (the data allowed managers to reduce costs and, therefore, increase profits), but these managers did not have any interest in whether the paper was recycled. Today, given changes in consumer demand, paper recycling facts are recognized as important information, as is the price of the paper.

It is precisely this process of giving data meaning that makes management information systems an essential part of the management function of controlling. When managers ignore some data but pay attention to other data, they transform data into information. By creating an organization's information systems, managers signal what is meaningful and valued in the organization (and what is not). For example, Mainstream managers may design information systems that monitor and collect financial data and pay attention to market analyses. They may also be inclined to focus on the performance of *individual* employees rather than on *group* performance. However, Mainstream managers may not be interested in data describing the effect the organization is having on the ecological environment or in the local neighborhood where it operates, unless these data are linked to profitability. As our opening case shows, information systems can complement—or challenge—how the other three management functions are performed.

Basketball players may be among the most carefully monitored employees in the world. A company called Synergy Sports Technology sells fine-grained statistics and video clips to help coaches and players analyze the opposition. For example, Synergy has a record of every step Dirk Nowitzki has made since he joined the NBA in 1998, including, for example, whether he is more successful driving right or left, and how his performance differs in home versus away games. Synergy can also provide video clips of the last 10, 100, or 1000 times Nowitzki makes a particular move.[12]

? WHAT DO YOU THINK?

What Values Are Built into the Information That We Consume?

We live in an "information age" where many new organizations seek to capitalize on our growing capacity and thirst for information (e.g., see the closing case in Chapter 6 on Google). When we consume information, we often forget that, by definition, the information has a hidden "meaning." The process of transforming data into information, although it may appear to be objective and scientific, actually reflects underlying values.

Consider how media influence what we focus on and define as meaningful. When managers of a television news program decide to provide daily reports of companies that meet or beat profit projections, they are deeming these data to be important information that viewers should find meaningful. If the news reports gave daily reports on jobs created by organizations, dollars invested in the community, or improvements in ecological footprints, however, this information would likely influence viewers in a different way. Perhaps instead of making investment decisions based primarily or solely on expected financial returns, investors might place equal weighting on concerns of social responsibility.

In organizations, financial and accounting information is especially important to Mainstream managers, and it has become important information for many other people as well. If managers keep hearing that quarterly financial reports or daily stock prices are key to defining success, then they will be encouraged to act in ways that focus on short-term performance. This behavior is consistent with acquisitive economics and documentational capitalism (see Chapter 3). In contrast, if managers are provided with information about the maintenance of equipment, the development of employees, the organization's environmental impact, or the progress of research projects, then they will likely be more inclined to focus on longer-term performance and sustainability. This orientation is consistent with sustenance economics and relational capitalism.

We are bombarded with media messages declaring that financial security and early retirement are keys to happiness. What if we kept hearing that reducing poverty, wiping out AIDS, increasing the quality of parent–child relationships, or finding truly meaningful work were the keys to happiness? Would that message change the way we manage our organizations and our lives?

In organizations where you have worked, what was measured and communicated as important information? How did that information influence how you or your managers acted on a daily basis? What was communicated in your organization that defined "success"?

DESIGNING AN INFORMATION SYSTEM. Regardless of the content of a management information system, managers should keep in mind these rules of thumb when designing information systems:

- Managers should ensure that information is based on accurate data.

- Managers should try to have information about all the aspects of their organization that they deem meaningful, but should be aware that sometimes the costliness of information will dictate that it remain incomplete.

- Information should be timely, so as to provide the necessary feedback to allow people to make better decisions and perform their jobs better.

- Information should be user-friendly and understandable.

A basic decision in monitoring performance is whether to create systems that monitor *behaviors* or ones that monitor *outcomes*. For example, a professor might monitor how well students are learning course material by keeping track of how many hours they invest in reading the textbook and reviewing lecture notes (behavior) or by measuring how many multiple-choice questions are answered correctly on a quiz (outcomes). Measuring outcomes is often less costly than measuring behavior, but it may result in problems being detected too late to be corrected.

Another basic decision is whether to use single measures or multiple measures to monitor key activities. Single measures may be less costly. Even so, it may be advisable to use multiple measures and frequent monitoring for particularly uncertain or complex tasks. For example, should the course instructor have one final exam at the end of the course, or should he or she give multiple tests and assignments throughout the term so that students and the instructor can monitor performance on an ongoing basis? The latter approach may be costlier to implement, but it may provide helpful information for the complex process of teaching and learning.

The use of computers has had an enormous effect on *how* managers monitor performance and also *what* kinds of performance are monitored. In terms of *how* control is carried out, prior to the proliferation of computers, a manager's control and information systems were very closely tied to an organization's hierarchical structure. Regular daily and weekly reports were fed up the management hierarchy so that top managers could make decisions; those decisions were then relayed back down the hierarchy where they were carried out. This basic model began to change in the 1960s, when new information technologies emerged and computers became more affordable and information more accessible for everyone in the organization.

In terms of *what* is being controlled, new information technology often enables—and thus encourages—monitoring performance using quantifiable information rather than face-to-face information. Technological advances make it increasingly easy for managers to *count* (numerically) the things that *count* (i.e., matter).[13]

For example, **transaction-processing systems** are used to record customer orders, track purchases from suppliers, and so on. Grocery stores use scanners to record the sale of items and track inventory levels. Bank tellers are being replaced by automated teller machines, which are in turn being replaced by online banking. Most managers use transaction-processing systems to handle tasks such as customer billing, payment of suppliers, and payroll preparation and payment.[14] The data collected through these systems are often used in **operations information systems,** where software helps managers to monitor and coordinate the flow of work between various organizational subunits and their suppliers. The information collected in this way helps to identify and overcome potential bottlenecks, shortages in inventory, and overproduction. This information also provides helpful input for **decision support systems,** which allow managers to gather and manipulate data from a variety of sources to help evaluate performance. For example, managers might want to examine past sales figures in light of seasonality and the timing of new-product introductions by competitors. Such information will let them know how important it is to consider factors such as seasonality or competitors' advertising campaigns.

An excellent example of how new technologies and information systems have helped managers to reduce costs is found in managers' increased ability over the past few decades to gain control over inventory at all levels in the value chain. Improved control over inventory has helped managers to reduce inventory holding costs, which include financial costs (i.e., financial capital tied up in the inventory) and other costs associated with carrying inventory (e.g., warehousing, security, spoilage, obsolescence). Three "types" of inventory need to be managed:

- "Raw materials inventory" refers to the basic inputs used in the organization's production process.
- "Work-in-process inventory" refers to the materials that are moving through the stages of the production process.
- "Finished-goods inventory" refers to the items that have passed through the production process but have not yet been sold to customers.

Managers can manage all three types of inventory using tools such as **just-in-time** inventory management, which brings all the needed materials for production together literally just in time for them to be combined into the finished product. For

Expert systems and artificial intelligence allow managers to program computers to perform operating procedures that had previously been dependent on tacit knowledge and prone to human error and costs. For example, expert systems were developed to capture the knowledge of a key quality control expert at Campbell's Soup and General Electric's top locomotive troubleshooter.[15]

Transaction-processing systems record and process recurring and routine activities that take place in an organization.

Operations information systems help managers to monitor and coordinate the flow of work between various organizational subunits and their suppliers, and in particular help to identify and overcome potential bottlenecks, shortages in inventory, and overproduction.

Decision support systems allow managers to gather and manipulate data from a variety of sources to help evaluate performance.

Just-in-time inventory management systems bring all the needed materials for production together literally just in time for them to be combined into the finished product.

example, a Dell computer factory in Austin, Texas, uses the Internet to communicate with its suppliers so effectively that the factory keeps just two hours of inventory on hand, thereby minimizing raw materials inventory. The finished computer is loaded onto a truck less than 15 hours after a customer submits an order. These controls help to lower the costs associated with the high rate of obsolescence in high-tech industries. (On average, the value of a personal computer decreases by about 1 percent every week.[16])

 WHAT DO YOU THINK?

Computer-Based Control Systems: Friend or Foe?

Computer-monitoring software is commonplace in today's companies. Approximately three-fourths of U.S. employers monitor their employees' e-mail, and more than half monitor their Internet connections. Thirty-nine percent of employers track telephone calls (number of calls and time spent on those calls), and 11 percent record and review telephone conversations.[17]

Critics argue that because managers have relatively easy access to computer-based data, these data are increasingly likely to be given the status of meaningful information for measuring performance. As a result, performance is increasingly being defined by quantifiable measures such as the number of customer orders entered, the average length of time taken to fulfill a customer's order, the number of banking transactions handled, and the frequency of errors in payroll delivery.

An unintended effect of computerized information systems is that they may downplay interpersonal relationships. For example, it is more difficult to set up computerized information systems that measure whether customers or suppliers are treated with dignity. Even so, as we saw in the opening case, computer-based information systems can be designed to empower organizational members to make decisions and decrease their dependence on managers.

Does the growing use of technology as a means of organizational control "dehumanize" the workplace? Is there a difference in the "meaning" of getting paid if your salary is deposited directly into your bank account versus your employer physically handing you cash (or a check)? Technology certainly allows us to get increasingly better at counting things and decreases the need for face-to-face relationships. In this way—reflecting Marshall McLuhan's famous maxim that "The medium is the message"—technology affects the meaning of relationships in the workplace.

Not so long ago, intra-organizational interactions and relationships were mostly of the face-to-face variety (supplemented with written reports). This changed with the advent of telephone, voice mail, e-mail, and other transaction-processing systems. Today's managers can interact with other organizational members solely by electronic means, whether they are around the world or in the office next door.

Do virtual offices provide welcome freedom for workers, or does technology such as cell phones and personal digital assistants ensure that workers are always "on call" and under stress? How is technology putting more distance between people instead of meeting its promise of "bringing people closer"? Does technology help us, or does it distract us from counting the things that truly count?

Step 3: Evaluate Performance

During this step, Mainstream managers compare the information collected in the second step to the goals or standards established in the first step. Have Six Sigma quality standards been met? Is the liquidity ratio within the desired range? Are inventory levels acceptable? Has a salesperson's performance improved as planned?

In addition, managers must consider extenuating circumstances to help to explain factors that affect performance. For example, did a competitor introduce a new product? Did a competitor go bankrupt? Were there other unforeseen shifts in the industry or in the overall economic picture? Did an employee experience health problems that affected his or her performance?

Consistent with their materialist–individualist emphasis, it may seem natural for Mainstream managers to focus on evaluating the performance of individual workers. This practice is clearly still the norm in many organizations and among many managers. However, theory and practice in popular control techniques—such as Six Sigma, just-in-time manufacturing, and statistical process control—are increasingly pointing out the merit of evaluating the performance of *systems* rather than the performance of *individuals*. Even when such a shift is designed to improve productivity, it can be seen to represent a step toward a Multistream approach because it places less emphasis on individuals.

Perhaps the best example of this movement away from evaluating individual performance, and toward managing organizational systems, comes from **Total Quality Management (TQM).** TQM emphasizes how managers can continuously improve organizational work systems so that the organization's products or services better meet the quality desired by its customers. Indeed, W. Edwards Deming,[18] a founding father of the quality movement, considers an organization to have a "deadly disease" when managers evaluate individual workers based on their numerical output or quantified standards. For Deming, variability in quality of output is largely attributable to *organizational* systems and processes, rather than the efforts of *individual workers*.

Deming is well known for the "Red Bead Experiment" that he often used at his four-day seminars. In this experiment, ten volunteers are recruited to work in an "organization": six willing workers, two inspectors, an inspector of the inspectors, and one recorder. Deming pours 3000 white beads and 750 red beads into a box, where they are mixed together. Each worker scoops beads out of the box with a scoop that holds 50 beads. Each full scoop is considered a day's production: White beads are acceptable; red beads are defects. Workers are asked to scoop out only white beads and no red beds. Of course, due to the laws of statistical variability, each worker scoops out some red beads, regardless of how motivated the worker is to get only white beads, how much the "manager" (Deming) exhorts them not to, or how much he praises workers who have fewer-than-average red beads.

Deming's message is simple: From a statistical point of view, it is foolish for a manager to use *data* about the number of red beads any particular worker produces as *information* for promoting or demoting workers. Rather, statistically speaking, (1) there

Total Quality Management (TQM) emphasizes how managers can continuously improve an organization's work systems so that its products or services better deliver the quality desired by customers.

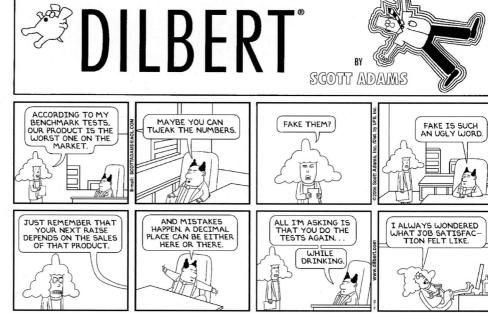

DILBERT: © Scott Adams/Dist. by United Feature Syndicate, Inc.

will always be variation in any process or system, so (2) there will always be variation in the performance of workers, with some performing well and others performing not so well (i.e., there will be differences in individual workers' performance because performance is often more determined by systemic factors beyond their own control than by their individual efforts); and (3) it is up to management to improve the systems (not to reward and control the individuals within the system).[19]

Many organizations have enjoyed improved performance when implementing the sorts of control systems consistent with Deming's principles. For example, Ford Motor Company found that transmissions manufactured according to these principles resulted in warranty repairs decreasing tenfold, and that "things gone wrong" customer reports dropped by 50 percent over a period of five years. Other research claimed a fourfold increase in productivity when systems such as TQM are introduced.[20]

Step 4: Respond Accordingly

Responding accordingly is an ongoing activity, and one that can involve any or all steps or stakeholders in the value chain. Mainstream managers are especially interested in taking corrective actions that serve to get performance up to standards. For example, if input standards are not met, then it may be necessary to reconsider suppliers. If conversion process or output standards are not met, then managers will correct the behavior of those individuals who are responsible for not meeting standards. This may mean providing employees with further training or professional development, transferring staff to other jobs that they are more capable of handling, or dismissing employees outright.

Sometimes "responding accordingly" may prompt managers to reconsider an organization's entire value chain. This rethinking may require drawing on members from the entire organization. In one method, managers who wish to better understand the value chain in their organization, or who wish to improve it, start by creating a cross-functional team consisting of seven to ten managers drawn from a variety of departments throughout the organization. These managers are then invited to a three-day "change-for-the-better" (*kaizen* in Japanese) event: They spend the first day learning about the basic ideas of value chains, the second day describing the value chain in their organization, and the third day identifying how the value chain could be improved.[21]

As is evident in the opening case, it may take a long time before comprehensive changes in an organization's information or control systems result in noticeable changes in members' views or productivity. Unfortunately, it is not unusual for managers to become disappointed when their changes do not immediately generate the hoped-for productivity improvements. Research suggests that expected productivity improvements may take three or more years to materialize, and that it is important that changes not be implemented on a piecemeal basis. In such cases, "responding accordingly" means that managers must be patient and ensure that their approach to control is implemented consistently throughout the organization and in all four steps of the control process.[22]

MULTISTREAM APPROACH TO THE FOUR-STEP CONTROL PROCESS

Unlike the Mainstream approach, where the emphasis is on designing control systems that maximize productivity and profitability, the Multistream approach also shows concern for issues such as work–life balance and the natural environment, among others. The Multistream focus is not so much on systems that control employee behavior, but on systems that help stakeholders to participate in the control process.

Step 1: Establish Key Performance Standards

Value chains help managers to identify and establish key performance standards. However, from a Multistream perspective, the idea of value chains has two key drawbacks:

- The two ends of a value chain remain unconnected, so that managers fail to recognize how their organization's outputs are linked to inputs, and vice versa.

- The various components of value chains tend to be treated as sequential and linear in nature, so that managers often fail to recognize the interplay and the processes that connect the various "links" in the chain.[23]

For these reasons, Multistream managers are more likely to think in terms of a "value loop," which essentially adds links that connect the two ends of a value chain. A **value loop** describes the activities whereby an organization's inputs are converted into outputs, which in turn are linked to the organization's future inputs. Like a value chain, a value loop includes many different aspects of an organization's activities, such as inbound logistics, operations, outbound logistics, marketing and sales, service, and various other support functions. However, as shown in Figure 18.3, there are some key differences between value chains and value loops.

First, a value loop adds a new node—"Environmental resources and processes"—that describes both where the organization's inputs are drawn from and what the organization's outputs contribute to. This additional node helps managers to understand how organizational activities contribute to, and resolve, larger system (e.g., societal and ecological) problems.

Second, value loops *explicitly* recognize that the flow of resources travels in both directions between the links. The fatter arrows in Figure 18.3 indicate the direction in which managers usually see the resources flowing, while the thinner arrows indicate that managers must also be sensitive to how resources and information can be seen to flow in the opposite direction. An example of the counterclockwise flow occurred when managers in fast-food restaurants began to receive requests for food prepared in a healthier fashion (i.e., grilled, not fried; no bun versus with bun; fruit instead of fries) that influenced conversion processes, and when customer inquiries regarding the environmental impact of fast-food packaging began to influence input decisions such as looking for suppliers that used recycled paper. Managers can gain valuable information by developing control systems that adapt to changes in customer preferences or trends in the larger environment.

The New England grocer Hannaford Brothers has developed a system called Guiding Stars that it uses to rate the nutritional value of 27,000 different food products on its shelves. Seventy percent of products receive no star, including foods that are advertised as healthy (e.g., V8 juice contains too much sodium to warrant a star). The Guiding Stars serve as performance standards that the grocer provides for its customers.[24]

Value loop describes the activities whereby an organization's inputs are converted into outputs, which in turn are linked to the organization's future inputs.

Figure 18.4 shows a variation of the value loop that has been developed by managers at Interface, Inc., one of the world's largest interior furnishing companies (see the opening case in Chapter 9).[25] Interface managers work hard at improving the systemic conversion processes *within* the company (e.g., the interplay between processes, people, capital, and values). They also strive to improve *outward* operations, thereby ensuring that Interface's activities fit into the natural cycle and Earth's biosphere. Interface managers are mindful of technical cycles and sustainability links, and they keep tabs on what the organization contributes to and receives from the larger community. For example, managers have established performance standards and try to control how much pollution Interface emits; they also monitor how much the company helps other firms to reduce their pollution.

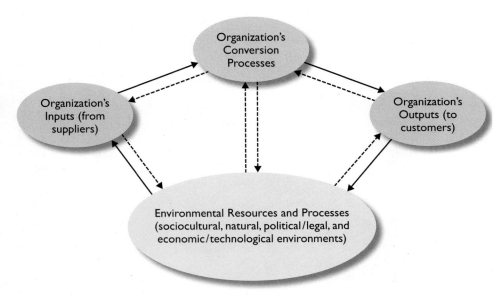

Figure 18.3   A general Multistream value loop

Figure 18.4 identifies separate value loops related to each of the four dimensions of the environment discussed in Chapters 3 and 4. In terms of the *sociocultural environment*, managers at Interface recognize that societal values shape their employees and provide the legitimacy that allows the company to do its work. At the same time, Interface contributes to the sociocultural environment by creating jobs and products that provide symbolic and social meaning. In terms of the *natural environment*, Interface requires raw materials as inputs, and its managers strive to minimize the amount of pollution or waste that the company creates (unsaleables) and to maximize the biodegradability of its outputs. In terms of the *political–legal environment*, managers at Interface depend on the legal institutions and regulations that allow it to exist as a corporation, and it in turn pays taxes to support the infrastructure created and maintained by government. Finally, in terms of the *financial–technological environment*, Interface requires invest-

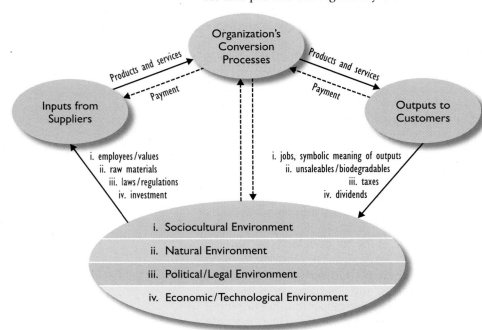

Figure 18.4   A specific Multistream value loop at Interface, Inc.

The Challenge of Thinking in Terms of Feedback Loops

Even though many people are able to understand the concept of feedback loops, research suggests that they often do not take them into consideration in their decision making. This is true even of policy makers, senior managers, and other professionals who are paid to think about the far-reaching implications of strategic decisions. Research suggests that people are likely to act based on the simplest or shortest cause-and-effect chain that they think makes sense. For example, consider the simple cause-and-effect loops associated with one member-owned sports club:[26] Managers responded to downturns in the financial viability of the club by increasing the price for an annual membership. They increased annual membership fees because they believed that this action would increase revenues from annual membership fees.

This simple decision-making formula helped to keep the club financially viable for a number of years, but it eventually led to the club's closing. Managers failed to recognize the negative feedback loop: Increasing the price for annual memberships decreased the number of members (due to difficulties in attracting and retaining new and existing members). This decrease in number of members led, in turn, to a decrease in revenues from annual membership fees and thus a decrease in the club's financial viability. Moreover, as a result of their simplistic focus on increasing annual membership fees as a means to increase revenues, managers overlooked other possible positive feedback loops that could have helped the club to generate the necessary funds to stay viable. For example, hiring staff to improve the quality of the restaurant/bar might have increased the number of members (by helping to attract and retain new and existing members), which could in turn have increased the revenues both from annual membership fees and from food sales, both of which could in turn have increased the financial viability of the sports club.

In sum, because it is much easier to understand and manage according to simple, linear cause-and-effect relationships, many managers fail to pay attention to the somewhat more complex feedback loops that provide a richer explanation of what is truly going on. This tendency to focus on simple cause-and-effect relationships is also apparent in everyday life. For example, as suggested in the closing case in Chapter 3, people are glad when energy policies (e.g., focusing on oil) lead to low-priced gasoline, but they seldom think of the negative feedback loops that result. For example, lower gas prices lead to greater gas consumption, which leads to greater dependence on suppliers and greater pollution, which leads to greater cleanup costs, which lead to higher net energy costs.

ment capital and existing technology, and it pays out dividends and develops more sustainable technologies that create benefits for others.

The concept of a value loop helps Multistream managers to establish different performance standards in each of the traditional three control areas: inputs, conversion, and outputs.

In terms of *inputs*, both Multistream and Mainstream managers are likely to weigh considerations such as price, reliability, technical expertise, proximity, and willingness to form partnerships. Nevertheless, Multistream managers are more likely to also take into account the working conditions or ecological record of potential suppliers, or the needs of potential employees who live at the margins of society.

In terms of *conversion processes*, Mainstream managers are more likely to be attuned to the *acquisitive economic* pros and cons of initiatives such as telecommuting or flexible work hours, whereas Multistream managers will be more sensitive to the *sustenance economic* pros and cons. For example, managers at First Fruits Orchards built a new packaging plant rather than pursue the financially less expensive option of running double shifts in its existing facility, noting that double shifts would have had a detrimental effect on employees' family life (see Chapter 3).

Finally, in terms of *outputs*, Multistream managers are more likely than Mainstream managers to consider the effect of their activities on the physical and social environment (e.g., pollution and the effects of layoffs).

Multistream managers also differ from their Mainstream counterparts in terms of the content and nature of performance standards being established in this step of

the control process. In terms of content, the popular generic Mainstream measures focus on output measures (e.g., 99 percent defect-free) and accounting measures (e.g., profitability ratios). Multistream managers might also employ the same productivity measures and accounting ratios, but they would supplement them with standards that measure a much wider variety of well-being and that are relevant for a broader spectrum of stakeholders. One way managers can keep diverse information in the forefront, including information relating to inputs and processes, is through the use of the Balanced Scorecard tool.[27] As discussed in Chapter 14, this tool balances the use of financial goals with other valuable goals that are important to overall organizational well-being.

Goldman Sachs, the Wall Street investment bank, has a four-person research team that evaluates the social, environmental, and management performance of companies in the same way as other colleagues assess financial performance.[29] In this photo, Laura Liswood, Senior Advisor at Goldman Sachs and Secretary General of the Council of Women World Leaders (seated at far right), participates in a plenary session entitled "Women's responsibility in improving society: A new dimension" at the Women's Forum for the Economy and Society (Deauville, France).

Using a Balanced Scorecard may create a host of positive feedback loops, including having a positive effect on profits.[28] For example, when IBM and Nokia invest substantial resources in community educational initiatives, this move may also enhance their corporate reputation and aid in recruiting employees or developing future employees. When DuPont reduces energy consumption and McDonald's alters its food packaging to reduce waste, these decisions score well in community and environmental assessments as well as pay off by reducing the companies' costs.[30] In any case, from a Multistream perspective, the effects of these positive feedback loops on profitability are no more important than their positive effects in serving a broad range of stakeholders.

Jack Welch and his ideas about Six Sigma and low defect rates are well-known examples of Mainstream control. Ricardo Semler provides a well-known example of Multistream control (see Opening Case, Chapter 10). Semler is the "anti-CEO" of Semco—a definitely-not-Mainstream company in Brazil—who describes Welch's policy of firing the lowest-performing 10 percent of the workforce as "microterrorism."[31] Whereas Mainstream managers place primary emphasis on productivity and competitiveness, the key values and standards for managers like Semler are interpersonal trust, democracy, and the flow of empowering information. If he can manage Semco toward these ends, then Semler is confident that other goals—such as financial profitability, meaningful work, motivated employees, and work–life balance—will follow. Even though Semco has few written regulations and standards, and does not have a written mission statement, Semler does have a mission: "to find a gratifying way of spending your life doing something you like that is useful and fills a need."[32] For Semler, productivity and the financial bottom line are a *means*—obviously a very important means—to this larger *end*.[33] One reason that Semler does not have a formal mission statement is because he wants the organization's mission, and the key values, to be constantly socially created by the workers and other stakeholders. A desire to allow a variety of stakeholders (owners, members, customers, suppliers, and neighbors) to shape an organization's "barometers of success" is a hallmark of Multistream management.[34] "Redesigning the workplace for the twenty-first century means letting in fresh air and giving up control."[35]

In time, Multistream managers may develop generally accepted ways, such as the Balanced Scorecard approach, to evaluate performance using factors that currently seem to defy measurement. For example, a Multistream approach to control might focus on measuring things like meaningful work, work–life balance, happiness, and social justice. Some existing societal measures for alternative performance include the Genuine Progress Index (see Figure 18.5) and the Gross National Happiness Index.[36]

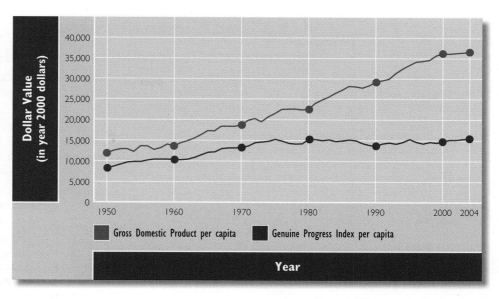

Figure 18.5   U.S. "genuine progress"
In the United States, "genuine progress" (which is based on items that measure things like leisure time, income distribution, and pollution) has remained unchanged since the late 1970s, even though the GDP per capita has almost doubled over the same span.

Source: Accessed August 24, 2007, at http://www.rprogress.org/sustainability_indicators/genuine_progress_indicator.htm. © Redefining Progress, www.rprogress.org. Reprinted with permission.

Step 2: Monitor Performance

In order to monitor performance—the second step of the control process—both Mainstream and Multistream approaches rely on information systems. However, there are three important differences in the two approaches:

- Whereas Mainstream information systems are built around value chains, Multistream information systems are built on value loops.
- Whereas Mainstream information systems are designed to help managers monitor performance, Multistream information systems are designed to help stakeholders monitor performance.
- Whereas Mainstream control systems are designed to help managers maximize financial well-being, Multistream information systems are designed to help all stakeholders improve a variety of forms of well-being.

We will look at each of these three themes in turn.

As we have seen, Mainstream information systems are designed to enable managers to achieve better control over all three aspects of the value chain: inputs (suppliers), conversion process, and outputs (customers). However, because they are intended to look at the different parts of the value chain sequentially, there is often a disconnect between the subcomponents of such information systems. Even world-class information systems like those at Wal-Mart or Volvo sometimes result in mistakes because of such disconnects. For example, when Wal-Mart managers in Mexico had a tough time selling ice-hockey skates in that market, they reduced the prices to get the skates off their shelves. However, Wal-Mart's information system automatically reordered more skates to be shipped to Mexico. Similarly, when U.S. Volvo dealers had a tough time selling green cars, they got rid of their inventory by selling such cars at discount prices—only to have the information system order more green cars to be shipped to the United States.[37]

By contrast, Multistream managers prefer information systems that go beyond value chains operating as a simple sequential process. One such technology, called **electronic hubs (eHubs),** allows information to be transmitted in real time to all stakeholders, thereby enabling coordination and mutual adjustment by stakeholders

Electronic hubs (eHubs) are computer-based information systems that have the ability to transmit information in real time, thereby enabling coordination and mutual adjustment by stakeholders from a variety of organizations.

Multistream Performance Standards

Whereas Mainstream performance measures are typically based on managers counting and adding up the dollar value of different aspects of the organization, Multistream management is more likely to establish performance standards that are based on input from a variety of stakeholders and include nonmonetary measures. As Semler notes, the key is to involve other stakeholders in developing the appropriate measures: "By evaluating success from everyone's point of view, we believe we'll land on the new list of companies that unite sustainability with all-around satisfaction. Let's call this list the Fortunate 500."[38]

Here are some possibilities of what Multistream performance measures might look like.

Participation/Inclusion: How involved are stakeholders in making decisions?

Project group diversity = number of external stakeholders in the group ÷ total number of group members
Shareholder input = number of shareholder proposals accepted ÷ number of proposals submitted

Financial/Ecological: How efficient is the organization at transforming ecological resources into economic value?

FinEco ratio = financial value of outputs ÷ ecological footprint
Waste ratio = financial value of outputs ÷ costs to clean up waste

Ecological Transformation: Is the organization creating more waste than it is reducing?

Ecological efficiency = outputs that are perceived to be pollution ÷ inputs that had been perceived to be pollution
Indirect ecological efficiency = amount of waste the organization has helped other organizations to reduce ÷ amount of waste created to achieve the reduction

Social Justice: What effect has the organization had on the marginalized social communities?

Workforce composition = number of employees hired from specified marginalized groups ÷ total number of employees hired
Social investment = donations and volunteer hours to address social concerns of marginalized communities ÷ donations and volunteer hours for all charities

Long-Term Perspective: What percentage of our time and resources is devoted to long-term concerns?

Time balance = number of employee hours spent on long-term projects ÷ total number of employee hours
Resource balance = dollars spent on research, maintenance, and employee development ÷ total expenditures

---

from a variety of organizations. For example, managers at Cisco installed an eHub system after they had to write off $2.2 billion worth of computer components that had been ordered because of inflated consumer demand information provided by salespeople. Had there been a well-functioning eHub in place, all the stakeholders would have recognized that the demand figures were inflated because many customers placed multiple orders at different companies, but intended to make their final purchase at the first company that could supply what they were purchasing.

In an eHub, control does not reside with managers, who serve as the linchpins in traditional information systems. Rather, the electronic hub essentially takes control away from managers by providing other stakeholders with the information that they need to exhibit self-control. As a result, managers become "advocates" who work on behalf of others—for example, customers and suppliers—responding to changes as they occur. Put differently, Multistream managers do not try to control the various stakeholders in the system. Instead, they prefer systems that enable stakeholders to practice informed self-control that improves the flow of resources throughout the system.

While eHub information systems are in many ways far superior to traditional systems, they demand that participants in the system trust one another. Can your suppliers be trusted to deliver on time and give good prices if they know who your customers are and how much they're willing to pay? Will your customers still make purchases if they know exactly what your costs have been to secure and develop their product or service? Will your employees be tempted to use the information from the system to start their own competing organization? Or, more optimistically, will all the stakeholders appreciate the strengths of such a transparent information system and do their part to support it?

Because Multistream information systems are prone to abuse if participants are driven primarily by acquisitive economic principles, it is important that participants establish and share performance standards consistent with sustenance economic principles. For example, rather than basing their decisions solely on financial criteria such as short-term prices, customers and suppliers must factor in the merits of belonging to such a transparent information system, including the sense of community it nurtures and its long-term positive feedback loops. Such relationships are evident *within* organizations such as Semco, and *across* organizations such as the New York fashion industry prior to its being taken over by large Mainstream companies (see Chapter 9).

Other differences distinguish the Mainstream and Multistream approaches to performance monitoring. In the Mainstream approach, managers are primarily interested in financial *outcomes* of organizational behavior, so they set up structures and systems to monitor whether these desired outcomes are achieved. For example, have productivity targets been met? Multistream managers, by contrast, are interested in the *process* of organizational behaviors, so they set up structures and systems to monitor whether the process is achieved. For example, have people been treated with dignity and respect?

In the case of Semco, where a primary emphasis is on nurturing trust, dignity, and sharing of information, this result is achieved precisely because of the firm's *lack* of conventional structures and systems to monitor behavior. Research suggests that members treat one another more respectfully when there are no monitoring systems.[39] Managers at Semco do not set up structures and systems, such as internal audits or inspections, to monitor whether workers are complying with regulations. To monitor in a conventional way sends the message that workers cannot be trusted. Instead, as described in Chapter 11, Semco favors an organizational structure that is designed to foster trust and demonstrate democracy. For example, workers at Semco decide which coworkers to hire, set their own working hours, determine their own salaries, and decide which manager they will work for. There are no job descriptions, no dress codes, and no monitoring of expense accounts. Attendance at company meetings is voluntary and open to everyone, and meetings are chaired by the person most knowledgeable about the subject matter on the agenda.

Semler believes that information is power, and he does not want to use that power as a form of hierarchical control. For this reason, he has implemented a transparent information system. For example, everyone at Semco has access to its financial statements (including everyone's salaries). For Multistream managers, there is power in sharing this type of information. Semco's books are open for inspection by employees and for audit by their unions. Great effort and care are invested to ensure that the information in these reports is timely, and Semco invites the union to train its members on how to read the financial statements. This willingness to share information also spills outside Semco's boundaries. For example, Semler sometimes offers detailed financial information to a potential customer that shows exactly how much profit Semco will make from a given order.

Although Multistream managers limit traditional top-down monitoring of performance, they do use bottom-up performance-monitoring systems. For example, each year Semco employees fill out—anonymously—a survey about the company, its future, and its managers. The survey includes questions about whether workers feel like coming to work on Monday mornings, whether they believe the company's internal and external communications, and whether they trust their leaders. Since 1996, between 85 percent and 96 percent of responses have been in the top brackets (good and great), and those percentages have risen every year. Every six months workers fill out a "Seen from Below" questionnaire that asks 36 questions, such as whether a manager treats subordinates and peers in the same way. Other numerical measures are also available. For example, observations that only 3 of its 3000 members left Semco on their own over a two-year period, and that 1400 engineers applied for a job advertisement, suggest that Semco is seen as a good place to work.

Step 3: Evaluate Performance

Recently, popular techniques such as TQM have encouraged managers to shift their attention away from only individuals and to look at organizational systems. The Multistream approach extends the TQM approach in three ways:

- By focusing on even larger systemic feedback loops
- By going beyond performance criteria that focus on maximizing productivity and profitability
- By involving numerous stakeholders in evaluating performance

First, the Multistream approach evaluates how the organization affects the larger sociocultural, ecological, political–legal, and economic–technological environments. This broader range of concern is consistent with, for example, the "intelligent product system" described in Chapter 3. As part of this approach, organizational performance is evaluated more positively if it adopts "cradle-to-cradle" systems that minimize waste (i.e., unsaleables). The emphasis is on keeping "used-up" products out of landfills and designing them to become valued inputs for future products.

Second, and related to the first point, the Multistream approach uses a wider variety of criteria to evaluate performance. Because of their emphasis on multiple forms of well-being, Multistream managers expect stakeholders to have a variety of sometimes competing goals. However, rather than treat this diversity as a threat to evaluating performance, it becomes a welcome challenge that sensitizes all stakeholders to the need to balance their personal goals with the larger goals of the community. This is evident when workers and managers at Reell Precision Manufacturing treat the concerns of others (coworkers, customers, and suppliers) as equal to their own, and when they handle periodic economic downturns by mutually agreeing to take temporary pay cuts until the financial picture improves (see Chapter 7).

Third, and following from the first two points, the Multistream approach encourages a wide variety of stakeholders to participate in evaluating the organization's performance. This is evident when systems are developed to allow members to evaluate the performance of their managers, when organizations' annual reports include social audits prepared by external evaluators (see Chapter 5), and when managers invite external stakeholders to participate in the decision-making process (see Chapter 7).

As a result of these three characteristics, the Multistream process generally places greater emphasis on relational and qualitative measures of performance than on the rational and quantifiable measures associated with the Mainstream approach. One reason that Mainstream management is so popular is because it emphasizes "rational" and "objective" measurable goals—such as increasing productivity and profits—which seem to be comparatively easy to measure in terms of dollars and cents. It *appears* to be more difficult to monitor or evaluate goals such as increasing trust, democracy, ecological sustainability, and social justice.

However, upon closer inspection, the so-called rational financial measures that characterize Mainstream management may be less objective than people's own personal experiences. An annual report has the appearance of objectivity and reality, but numbers and reports are poor representations of the human, intellectual, social, and spiritual capital that makes up an organization. In contrast, our actual relationships with others have a grounded-in-experience quality, and they provide a fundamental contribution to the essence of our personal identities. Although we may lack well-developed, explicit tools to measure important aspects of personal relationships, they are still very real to us, and we can easily point to people who bring out the best in others, who nurture community, who foster trust, and whose company makes us happy. Likewise, we also know of some people who seem to bring out the worst in others, and who foster mistrust and distress.[40]

Step 4: Respond Accordingly

When Mainstream managers encounter inadequate performance, they often respond by unilaterally taking action to resolve the problem. Such responses may include firing low-performing workers or redesigning organizational systems. In contrast, when Multistream managers encounter inadequate performance, they often seek help from others to understand why it occurred and to develop a way to resolve the problem. Rather than assume that problems must be solved from the top down, Multistream managers are more likely to assume that problems are best solved from the bottom up.[41] Because it is a characteristic of Multistream management to treat stakeholders with respect and foster community, stakeholders often have a genuine interest in helping to solve organizational problems.[42] Ricardo Semler is often asked, "How do you control a system like the one at Semco?" He answers, "I don't. I let the system work for itself."[43]

For example, trust was threatened at Semco when equipment theft started to be a problem in the workplace. Adding to the concern was that people agreed that the thief must be a coworker. Managers deliberately waited for a grass-roots solution to develop. Some employees suggested installing surveillance cameras, while others noted that this would undermine the trust that was valued so highly at Semco. Over time, the problem was resolved without direct managerial action—managers just let the system work the problem out itself. (In this case, Semco managers never did find out exactly how this particular problem was solved; it just stopped.)

Members are less likely to resist the Multistream control process. They have a voice in developing and enforcing the control, and they understand the trade-offs of different stakeholders' various forms of well-being. Because of this understanding, stakeholders are more likely to seek opportunities to improve the control process, rather than to exclusively defend their positions in the status quo.[44]

Of course, there are times when "responding appropriately" will require Multistream managers to take decisions into their own hands. However, this is not the default mode—the Multistream default is to trust and welcome the input of others. From a Mainstream perspective, such an approach might seem as if managers are avoiding responsibility. From a Multistream perspective, however, it is merely part of treating others with dignity and respect. This respect is evident and built into each of the four parts of the Multistream control process.

Control at a Business and Technology Solutions Organization[45]

Protegra—professionals with integrity—is an award-winning firm that was started in 1998 in a basement by three experienced software developers who wanted to solve a common problem in the industry—namely, clients would receive the information technology that they had ordered, but it would not solve the problems that it had been purchased to resolve. The founders of Protegra knew how to design and develop software, and they wanted to partner with customers to provide the technology that would solve their problems.

Protegra emphasizes teamwork and delivering products on time. Within a decade after its founding, it had grown from 3 to 75 members, and from a 600-square-foot basement to a 24,000-square-foot Global Solutions Center. The company now has clients around the world.

As an employee-owned firm, Protegra uses a Balanced Scorecard approach where all employees can participate in *establishing performance standards.* Members set financial goals for the firm as well as aspire to provide interesting work and excellent working conditions. For example, employees enjoy flexible work hours, free soda in the company cafeteria, and a Stress Relief Lab with exercise equipment and a table-tennis table. According to CEO Wadood Ibrahim, the most important feedforward control may be in hiring the right people: "It's about the people . . . it always has been." Having the "right people" is particularly important because everyone has a voice in the firm's strategy and operations, and because—reflecting the company's flexible structure—employees are not hired to fill specific positions. Employees are encouraged to "think like owners." "Protegra believes that if a company takes care of the people, they will take care of the business."

> The company realizes that true wealth begins with creating a rewarding experience for people. Protegra's corporate philosophy is to hire the right people, take into account their passions and skills, and give them the freedom, flexibility, and environment to perform well. Corporate values of quality, integrity, innovation, and teamwork, imparted to employees and passed on to clients, create powerful opportunities imbued with loyalty and trust.[46]

In terms of *monitoring performance*, on a weekly basis employees submit reports indicating the time they have invested in each project they are working on. On a monthly basis the Operations Team (senior managers) monitors how each project is doing. In terms of bottom-up feedback and monitoring, the firm supports a Protegra Employee Committee, which is a group of employees to whom others can anonymously raise concerns about issues to bring to the Operations Team.

In terms of *evaluating performance*, the monthly reports provide an opportunity for members to evaluate whether projects are on schedule. The scorecard for the various goals is also evaluated at monthly company meetings, which are attended by all employees of the company. Information sharing assures that all members know what is happening and are able to ask any questions they like. Evaluation also takes place at annual meetings. Because of Protegra's emphasis on "lean" principles and elimination of waste, great emphasis is placed on ensuring that the reports provide information that is useful for managing the Balanced Scorecard tool.

Responding accordingly is an ongoing process. Adjustments are made on a daily, weekly, and monthly basis as information and reports become available for all to see and respond to. The annual general meeting, Protegra Advantage Conference, provides another opportunity for establishing the performance standards for the upcoming year.

In some ways, the control system at Protegra seems straightforward. It is simply based on treating clients and employees with integrity and respect. And yet, in an industry where many businesses have fizzled out, its innovative approach may be a key to Protegra's success. It is clearly well received in the marketplace. Clients value how Protegra partners with them to design solutions, employees enjoy thinking like owners and participating in establishing a Balanced Scorecard, and the emphasis on being lean reduces waste. As one customer put it, "What [Protegra] achieved [for us] within three months is nothing short of exceptional."[47]

QUESTIONS FOR DISCUSSION

1. Wadood Ibrahim has worked hard to develop information systems at Protegra that reflect the Company's values. What do you think are the keys to Protegra's success? Which changes would you advise in the future?

2. How much difference does it make to most employees if they are also part owners of the firm where they work? Why aren't there more employee-owned firms? What general effect would being employee-owned have on an organization's information and control system?

SUMMARY

The four-step control process helps to ensure that the actions of organizational members are consistent with the organization's underpinning values and standards.

From a Mainstream perspective, during the control process managers should take these four steps:

1. Establish key organizational performance standards by understanding the overall value chain, and identifying the key activities and outcomes that need to be monitored.
2. Monitor performance by developing information systems and appropriate technology that allow managers to measure the key performance standards.
3. Evaluate the performance of members, using a top-down rational process.
4. Respond accordingly by rewarding, punishing, and training members as appropriate, and by fine-tuning and improving each step in the control system.

From a Multistream perspective, during the control process managers should work with stakeholders to take these four steps:

1. Establish key organizational performance standards by understanding the overall value loop and identifying the key activities and processes that need to be monitored.
2. Monitor performance by developing information systems and appropriate technology that facilitate mutual coordination and performance measurement among stakeholders.
3. Evaluate performance of the organization with the help of various stakeholders.
4. Respond accordingly, often by allowing stakeholders to help fine-tune the control system.

QUESTIONS FOR REFLECTION AND DISCUSSION

1. Describe the four steps of the control process. Compare and contrast the managerial actions and assumptions that are evident in the Mainstream approach and the Multistream approach for each of the four steps in the process.

2. Describe the difference between data and information. Describe a situation at an organization you are aware of where what were formerly data are now treated as valuable pieces of information. Can you think of the reverse situation—that is, where information has become data? Explain your answer.

3. Describe the difference between feedforward, concurrent, and feedback controls. What are the management challenges associated with each type of control?

4. Explain why you agree or disagree with the following statement: "Because value chains are simpler, and because managers opt for the simplest cause-and-effect relationships that are relevant, learning about value loops is of little value to most managers."

5. Draw a value loop that includes a key economic transaction in your personal life (e.g., purchasing food, transportation, clothing).

6. Explain why you agree or disagree with the following statement:

   Thanks to computer-based technology, there is a de-emphasis on things that are difficult to measure quantifiably, such as compassion, empathy, meaningful work, aesthetic beauty, and neighborliness. As a result, what has happened to higher-order virtues and noble goals such as peace, love, joy, prudence, and wisdom? Because these are difficult to measure with the computer-based software that has been developed so far, they are left outside of the information deemed meaningful in organizations. When we do not look into the eyes of workers on the shop floor in low-income countries, we miss out on a whole lot of meaning, and our information systems have failed us.

HANDS-ON ACTIVITIES

Where Are You Along the Mainstream–Multistream Continuum?

Circle the number that best corresponds to your views.

Managers should use value chains to identify which activities and outcomes should be monitored.	1 2 3 4 5 6 7	Managers should use value loops to identify which activities and outcomes should be monitored.
The best way to monitor performance is by developing information systems that allow managers to measure the key performance standards.	1 2 3 4 5 6 7	Information systems should facilitate mutual coordination and performance measurement among stakeholders.
Managers should evaluate the performance of workers by using a top-down, rational process.	1 2 3 4 5 6 7	The best way to evaluate organizational performance is with the help of a variety of stakeholders.
Managers should use control systems to reward/punish/retrain workers as appropriate.	1 2 3 4 5 6 7	Stakeholders should be welcome to fine-tune/develop control systems as appropriate.

Have Your Views on Effective Management Changed Since Chapter 1?

Rate your response to the following statements on the five-point scale provided. Your instructor will have information on how other students have responded to these statements, and how their responses changed from the beginning of the term to the end.

TO BE AN EFFECTIVE MANAGER, I SHOULD. . .	Strongly Agree	Agree	Neutral	Disagree	Strongly Disagree
1. Maximize organizational efficiency (e.g., minimize inputs while maximizing output).	1	2	3	4	5
2. Maximize organizational profitability.	1	2	3	4	5
3. Focus on maximizing productivity, efficiency, and profitability.	1	2	3	4	5
4. Maximize organizational productivity.	1	2	3	4	5
5. Genuinely care for the people around me.	1	2	3	4	5
6. Be a kind-hearted person.	1	2	3	4	5
7. Be a loyal and faithful person.	1	2	3	4	5

	Strongly Agree	Agree	Neutral	Disagree	Strongly Disagree
8. Be someone who generously "goes the extra mile" for those around me.	1	2	3	4	5
9. Look after my own self-interests first.	1	2	3	4	5
10. Expect the people around me to be looking after their self-interests first.	1	2	3	4	5
11. Look after the self-interests of shareholders.	1	2	3	4	5
12. Recognize that everyone is motivated to maximize their own self-interests.	1	2	3	4	5

Questions About Mainstream Versus Multistream Management Style

Rate your responses to the following statements on the five-point scale provided. Your instructor has information about how other students have responded to these statements.

	Very Mainstream	Somewhat Mainstream	In the Middle	Somewhat Multistream	Very Multistream
I consider my management style to be	1	2	3	4	5
In the future I would like my management style to be	1	2	3	4	5
I would like to work in an organization that is	1	2	3	4	5
I currently work in an organization that is	1	2	3	4	5

ENDNOTES

1. This case is based on one of the authors' observations and research. Some of the details have been altered, and it is offered for pedagogical purposes only. See Dyck, B., Starke, F., & Mauws, M. (2008). Teaching versus learning: An exploratory longitudinal case study. *Journal of Small Business & Entrepreneurship*, 21(1), 37–58; Mischke, G. A., Mauws, M. K., Starke, F., & Dyck, B. (2001). Westward Industries Ltd. *Case Research Journal*, 21(1), 15–42; Starke, F., Sharma, G., Mauws, M., Dyck, B., & Dass, P. (2008). *A multi-level longitudinal exploration of the dynamics of an attempted archetypal change: The role of strategic leadership and its substitutes*. Working paper, University of Manitoba.

2. This example taken from Rooney, J. J. (2001). 7 steps to improved safety for medical devices. *Quality Progress*, 34(9), 33–41.

3. Manos, T. (2006). Value stream mapping: An introduction. *Quality Progress*, 39(6), 64–69.

4. Bhasin, S., & Burcher, P. (2006). Lean viewed as a philosophy. *Journal of Manufacturing Technology Management*, 17, 56–72.

5. Rooney, J. J., & Kilkelly, J. (2002). On today's menu: Quality. *Quality Progress*, 35(2), 25–32. Sometimes it is helpful to think about how pressures for change can move "up" or "down" the value chain. As an example of moving downstream, consider what happened with the introduction of genetically modified seeds by suppliers, which had an effect on farming practices (e.g., use of pesticides, inability to use seeds from the previous year's crop), which eventually worked its way down the value chain to consumers (perhaps a lower cost). As an example of movement upstream, consider what happened when consumers began to rebel against the genetically modified seeds and demanded clear labeling of genetically modified foods on their packaging. Another example of upstream movement is what happened when consumers began to demand low-carbohydrate diets, which caused retailers to ask bakeries for low-carbohydrate breads, so that bakers requested different types of flour from mills, and so on up the value chain. All of these examples demonstrate how managers can use the value chain not only to ensure that each link in the chain is adding value, but also to identify how making a change in one part of the link can have significant implications both upstream and downstream.

6. Barbosa, D. (2007, April 24). China yields to inquiry on pet food. *New York Times*. Accessed May 11, 2007, at http://www.nytimes.com/2007/04/24/business/worldbusiness/24pets.html?ex=1179028800&en=077cd3a2fdc0a55b&ei=5070.

7. Martin, A. (2007, December 6). Meat processors look for ways to keep ground beef safe. *New York Times*. Found March 17, 2008, at http://www.nytimes.com/2007/12/06/business/06meat.html?scp=1&sq=&st=nyt.

8. Zara creates a ready to wear business. (2003). *Strategic Direction*, 19(11), 24–26.

9. Page 669 in Daft, R. L. (2003). *Management* (6th ed.). Mason, OH: Thomson South-Western. A number of techniques other than Six Sigma also relentlessly pursue continuous improvement and cost reduction (e.g., lean production, Kaizen techniques, statistical process control). As is explained more fully

later in the chapter in the discussion of Deming's work, these approaches are associated with control systems that focus less on the performance of individual employees and more on how to improve organization-wide systems.

10. Tylutki, T. P., & Fox, D. G. (2002). Mooooving toward Six Sigma. *Quality Progress, 35*(2), 34–41.

11. Greenwald, C. (2004). *WITSA study: World IT spending rebounds thanks largely to developing world.* Arlington, VA: World Information Technology and Services Alliance.

12. Stross, R. (2007, April 29). Technology to dissect every dunk and drive. *New York Times.* Accessed March 17, 2008, at http://www.nytimes.com/2007/04/29/business/yourmoney/29digi.html?scp=1&sq=&st=nyt.

13. This also makes it more likely for managers to say that the things that matter (count) are the things that can be counted numerically. A counterbalance to the disappearance of "face-to-face" monitoring is evident in technologies such as videoconferencing and webcams.

14. Page 594 in Jones, G. R., & George, J. M. (2003). *Contemporary management* (3rd ed.). Boston: McGraw-Hill Irwin.

15. For more on how systems can help to minimize dependence on particular employees, see Starke, F., Dyck, B., & Mauws, M. (2003). Coping with the sudden loss of an indispensable employee: An exploratory case study. *Journal of Applied Behavioral Science, 39*(2), 208–228; and page 597 in Jones, G. R., & George, J. M. (2003). *Contemporary management* (3rd ed.). Boston: McGraw-Hill.

16. Daft, 2003, pp. 726, 730.

17. Wen, H., & Gershuny, P. (2005). Computer-based monitoring in the American workplace: Surveillance technologies and legal challenges. *Human Systems Management, 24,* 165–173; page 513 in Robbins, S. P., & Coulter, M. (2003). *Management* (7th ed.). Upper Saddle River, NJ: Prentice-Hall.

18. Gartner, W. B., & Naughton, M. J. (2000). Out of crisis. In J. L. Pierce & J. W. Newstrom (Eds.), *The manager's bookshelf: A mosaic of contemporary views* (5th ed., pp. 53–58). Upper Saddle River, NJ: Prentice-Hall. The description of the Red Bead Game and the Mazda/Ford case are drawn from this article.

19. Deming originally had greater influence in Japan than in Western countries, perhaps because Western countries place a higher emphasis on individualism. Japanese managers initially thought Deming was showing them how it was already being done in America.

20. For other examples, see Bhashin, S., & Burcher, P. (2006). Lean viewed as a philosophy. *Journal of Manufacturing Technology Management, 17*(1), 56–72.

21. Manos, 2006.

22. Bhashin & Burcher, 2006. Deming suggests that the process of transforming an entire organization to adopt his approach can take a minimum of ten years (Gartner & Naughton, 2000).

23. For an interesting history of how and why things unfolded this way within management theory and practice, see Sheer, S. A. (2005). From supply-chain management to value network advocacy: Implications for e-supply chains. *Supply Chain Management, 10*(2), 77–83.

24. Martin, A. (2006, November 6). The package may say healthy, but this grocer begs to differ. Accessed March 17, 2008, at http://www.nytimes.com/2006/11/06/business/06grocery.html?scp=1&sq=&st=nyt *New York Times.*

25. This figure simplifies and expands on ideas presented in Anderson, p. 129. Anderson, Ray C. (1998). *Mid-course correction: toward a sustainable enterprise: The interface model.* Atlanta, GA: Peregrinzilla Press.

26. The description and this example are adapted from Hall, R. I. (2002). Gaining understanding in a complex cause–effect policy domain. In A. Huff & M. Jenkins (Eds.), *Mapping strategic knowledge* (pp. 89–111). London: Sage. See also Axelrod, R. M. (Ed.). (1976). *The structure of decision: Cognitive maps of policy elites.* Princeton, NJ: Princeton University Press; Hall, R. I., & Menzies, W. B. (1983). A corporate system model of a sports club: Using simulation as an aid to policy making in crisis. *Management Science, 29,* 2–64. In Hall's study, the sports club happened to be a curling club in Canada, but his analysis could be and has been applied to a wide variety of organizations.

27. Kaplan, R., & Norton, D. (1996). *The Balanced Scorecard.* Boston: Harvard Business School Press; Kaplan, R., & Norton, D. (2006, March). How to implement a new strategy without disrupting your organization. *Harvard Business Review, 84*(3), 100–109.

28. Porter, M. E., & Kramer, M. R. (2006, December). Strategy and society: The link between competitive advantage and corporate social responsibility. *Harvard Business Review,* 78–92; Kaplan, R., & Norton, D. P. (2004). Keeping score on community investment. *Leader to Leader, 33,* 13–19.

29. Strom, S. (2007, May 6). Businesses try to make money and save the world. *New York Times.* Accessed March 17, 2008, at http://www.nytimes.com/2007/05/06/business/yourmoney/06fourth.html?scp=1&sq=&st=nyt.]

30. Porter & Kramer, 2006; Kaplan & Norton, 2004.

31. Page 35 in Vogl, A. J. (2004, May/June). The anti-CEO. *Across the Board,* 30–36.

32. Vogl, 2004.

33. Lloyd, B. (1994). Maverick! An alternative approach to leadership, company organization and management. *Leadership & Organization Development Journal, 15*(2), 8–12.

34. Semler, R. (2004). *The seven-day weekend* (p. 98). New York: Portfolio/Penguin Group.

35. Semler, 2004, p. 234.

36. A number of these measures can be found online, such as at http://www.redefiningprogress.org/ (accessed December 7, 2007).

37. Sherer, S. A. (2005). From supply-chain management to value network advocacy: Implications for e-supply chains. *Supply Chain Management: An International Journal, 10*(2), 77–83.

38. Semler, 2004, p. 98.

39. Even weak monitoring systems undermine interpersonal respect. Note also that introducing sanctions tends to make members see decisions more in business terms than in ethical terms. Tenbrunsel, A. E., & Messick, D. M. (1999). Sanctioning systems, decision frames, and cooperation. *Administrative Science Quarterly, 44*(4), 684–707.

40. For a description of the special managerial skills required to handle "toxic" personalities in the workplace, see Frost, P., & Robinson, S. (1999, July–August). The toxic handler: Organizational hero—and casualty. *Harvard Business Review,* 97–106.

41. Recall the four-step servant leadership model of Robert Greenleaf described in Chapter 1.

42. For example, the suppliers and key customers of Malden Mills were very gracious in allowing delays and extending credit when the firm's factory burned down, thanks in large part to

Multistream management at the firm. Malden Mills employees received pay even though they could not work during the time when the factory was not operating (see the opening case in Chapter 5).

43. Semler, 2004, p. 122.
44. These ideas were discussed in Chapter 7.

45. Based on a presentation by Cari Hunter, April 5, 2007; also company website accessed May 10, 2007, at http://www.protegra .com/About/TheProtegraStory.aspx.
46. From company website, accessed May 10, 2007. http://www .protegra.com/.
47. David Primmer, Chief Information Officer, Manitoba Government.

Photo Credits

FRONT MATTER   p. xvii: *Top:* Courtesy of the Asper School of Business; *Bottom:* Courtesy Mitch Neubert.

CHAPTER 1   p. 2: © Maxine Cass 2005. All rights, including moral rights, reserved; p. 4: Michael Buckner/Getty Images; p. 7: Ron Chapple/Taxi/Getty Images; p. 9 *(cartoon)*: DILBERT: © Scott Adams/Dist. by United Feature Syndicate, Inc.; p. 13: Ben Stechschulte/Redux.

CHAPTER 2   p. 30: © The Print Collector/Alamy; p. 32: © Andreas von Einsiedel/NTPL/The Image Works; p. 34: AFP/Getty Images; p. 36: © Tom Pantages; p. 41: *The New York Times*/Redux; p. 42: Lillian Gilbreth Stamp Design © 1984 United States Postal Service. All Rights Reserved. Used with Permission; p. 43: Western Electric Company Hawthorne Studies Collection. Baker Library Historical Collections. Harvard Business School.

CHAPTER 3   p. 62: *Left:* Barrie Rokeach/Jupiter Images; *Right:* © Mike Dobel/Alamy; p. 64: Jon Warren/World Vision 2003; p. 73: © Paul Slaughter/omniphoto.com; p. 87: © Wilfried Krecichwost/zefa/CORBIS; p. 90: Flevobike Technology.

CHAPTER 4   p. 98: Map courtesy of The Seeger Map Co., Inc.; p. 100: 20th Century Fox/ Photofest; p. 103: © Manfred Habel/Agefotostock; p. 114; © Grove Pashley/CORBIS; p. 116: © *The New York Times*/Redux; p. 117: Courtesy Bruno Dyck; p.123 *(two maps)*: © Copyright 2006 SASI Group (University of Sheffield) and Mark Newman (University of Michigan). www.worldmapper.org; p. 124: Courtesy Global Water, www.globalwater.org.

CHAPTER 5   p. 136: Radius Images/Jupiter Images; p. 138: © Rick Friedman/CORBIS; p. 142: Universal/Photofest; p. 147 *(cartoon)*: © *The New Yorker* Collection 2007 Leo Cullum from cartoonbank.com. All Rights Reserved; p. 150: Scott J. Ferrell/*Congressional Quarterly*/Getty Images; p. 154: Scala/Art Resource, NY; p. 156 *(two photos)*: Courtesy Mitch Neubert.

CHAPTER 6   p. 172: Rafiqur Rahman/Reuters/Landov; p. 174: DIGGER D-2 at work in Sudan © Digger Foundation; p. 176: C.J. Gunther/*The New York Times*; p. 181: Philippe Wojazer/Reuters/Landov; p. 185: Namas Bhojani/*International Herald Tribune*/Redux; p. 187: Courtesy of GiveMeaning. www.givemeaning.com; p. 188: Stock4B/JupiterImages; p. 191: Newscom; p. 192: Newscom.

CHAPTER 7   p. 200: © AAA, used by permission; p. 202: © Bettmann/CORBIS; p. 204: WireImage/Getty; p. 212: © Connie Toops; p. 216: © A. H. C.; p. 217: © Reuters/CORBIS; p. 220: © Ray Dirks; p. 224: Courtesy Rhino Party.

CHAPTER 8   p. 230: © Lawrence Manning/CORBIS; p. 232: Courtesy Dan Wiens; p. 236: Newscom; p. 238 *(cartoon)*: DILBERT: © Scott Adams/Dist. by United Feature Syndicate, Inc.; p. 240: © Tony Savino/The Image Works; p. 241: Chang W. Lee/*The New York Times*/Redux; p. 244: Newscom; p. 246: Courtesy LOHAS Forum; p. 248: © Bettmann/CORBIS.

CHAPTER 9   p. 256: © Paul Souders/CORBIS; p. 258: Newscom; p. 264: Armando Arorizo/ Bloomberg News/Landov; p. 267 *(cartoon)*: DILBERT: © Scott Adams/Dist. by United Feature Syndicate, Inc.; p. 269: © Lou Linwei/Alamy; p. 280: Freeplay Foundation; p. 282: Arif Ali/AFP/ Getty Images; p. 283: Paul Langrock/LAIF/REA/Redux; p. 284: Courtesy Emerge Knowledge Design Inc.

CHAPTER 10   p. 292: Courtesy Bruno Dyck; p. 294: © James Leynse/CORBIS; p. 297: Tannen Maury/Bloomberg News/Landov; p. 298: Christopher Pillitz/Getty Images; p. 301: © Reuters/ CORBIS; p. 304 *(cartoon)*: DILBERT: © Scott Adams/Dist. by United Feature Syndicate, Inc.; p. 308: © Dinodia/The Image Works; p. 313: © Julio Etchart/The Image Works; p. 314: Time & Life Pictures/Getty Images.

Glossary/Index